Management

PEOPLE / PERFORMANCE / CHANGE

Management

PEOPLE / PERFORMANCE / CHANGE

Luis R. Gomez-Mejia
Arizona State University

David B. Balkin
University of Colorado

PRENTICE HALL

Boston Columbus Indianapolis New York San Francisco Upper Saddle River
Amsterdam Cape Town Dubai London Madrid Milan Munich Paris
Montréal Toronto Delhi Mexico City São Paulo Sydney Hong Kong
Seoul Singapore Taipei Tokyo

Editorial Director: Sally Yagan
Editor in Chief: Eric Svendsen
Acquisitions Editor: Kim Norbuta
Editorial Project Manager: Claudia Fernandes
Editorial Assistant: Carter Anderson
Director of Marketing: Patrice Lumumba Jones
Marketing Manager: Nikki Ayana Jones
Marketing Assistant: Ian Gold
Senior Managing Editor: Judy Leale
Senior Production Project Manager/Supervisor:
   Lynn Savino Wendel
Senior Operations Supervisor: Arnold Vila

Operations Specialist: Cathleen Peterson
Senior Art Director/Design Supervisor: Janet Slowik
Senior Art Director: Kenny Beck
Text and Cover Designer: Laura C. Ierardi
Cover Art: xc/Shutterstock
Editorial Media Project Manager: Denise Vaughn
Media Project Manager: Lisa Rinaldi
Full-Service Project Management and Composition:
   Integra Software Services, Inc.
Printer/Binder: Courier/Kendallville
Cover Printer: Lehigh-Phoenix Color /Hagerstown
Text Font: 10/12 Times

Library of Congress Cataloging-in-Publication Data
Gomez-Mejia, Luis R.
   Management/Luis R. Gomez-Mejia, David B. Balkin.
      p.   cm.
   ISBN 13: 978-0-13-217640-8
   ISBN 10: 0-13-217640-8
   1. Management. I. Balkin, David B., 1948- II. Title.
HD31.G58955 2012
658—dc22   2010042395

Prentice Hall
is an imprint of

www.pearsonhighered.com

10 9 8 7 6 5 4 3 2 1
ISBN 10: 0-13-217640-8
ISBN 13: 978-0-13-217640-8

to my sons, Vince and Alex, my daughter,
Dulce Maria, and my wife, Ana—LG-M

to my parents, Daniel and Jeanne—DBB

Brief Contents

Contents

Preface

Ask your incoming students what "management" is and they'll talk about the kind of management they know from their own (limited) work experience. Managers assign people their hours, give raises or promotions, tell people what job to do—the manager, in other words, is "the boss."

In most other work settings, however, management means something far more important and complex. In addition to people, managers also manage performance, processes, relationships, and more increasingly in today's world, they deal with the pressure and flux of constant change. This, coupled with the fact that workplaces have steadily become less hierarchical and more team- and group-driven, means that the traditional responsibilities of the manager have gradually been dispersed throughout the organization. Students preparing to work in today's business environment may not start in a corner office with an assistant, but they still need *to think like* managers and understand the strategic goals of the organization.

Management prepares your students to join a new kind of workplace, one where management is *everyone's* business.

In order to prepare your students for a rapidly changing workplace, *Management* seeks to go beyond the scope of other management textbooks in our approach and our content. It does this in three key aspects:

Beyond the Ordinary

Your students start the course thinking of managers as little more than traditional "bosses." *Management* helps your students to move beyond this perception by offering coverage and exercises that emphasize the multifaceted nature of modern management. In particular, the "Management Close-Up" boxed feature offers unique perspectives. Each close-up has a theme of **Ethics, Customer Focus**, or **Dealing With Change**, which illustrates contemporary issues that managers and organizations confront that go beyond merely "being the boss."

Beyond Theory

Nothing as complex as management can be understood by merely reading about theory. While *Management* is careful to ground students in the relevant theories, it also gives your students numerous opportunities to apply their learning to real-world management situations. Strategically placed throughout the chapter, the **L**earning **O**bjective **C**heck-Ins, or **LOC-Ins**, help students apply information they have just read by asking scenario-based multiple choice questions based on a Learning Objective at the beginning of the chapter.

Beyond Your Expectations

We've worked hard to make this *Management* textbook more comprehensive, more useful, and more flexible than any other on the market. It opens whole new avenues of teaching for you while at the same time being easy to read. Hundreds of contemporary examples are provided throughout the text to illustrate key points.

Text Features

Management is full of innovative chapter features to make studying productive and hassle-free. The following are examples of the kind of engaging, helpful pedagogical features that make up *Management's* powerful approach.

Learning Objective Check-Ins or LOC-Ins

In response to the need for better assessment of learning objective goals, these scenario-based multiple choice questions occur within each chapter and directly correspond to a Learning Objective specified at the beginning of the chapter. Each question is designed to assess the application of the Learning Objective, with answers found in the Instructor's Manual. Professors can choose to share the answers with their students by either posting to an online course-delivery site or by printing and distributing them.

Manager's Notebook

These features supplement chapter content with a practicing manager's perspective. Manager's Notebooks provide valuable insider tips for dealing with common situations, and they are ideal jumping-off points for classroom discussion.

Management Close-Ups

To help students get an up-close look at the issues real managers deal with, *Management* includes "Management Close-Up" boxes. The Ethics, Customer Focus, and Dealing With Change subtitles in these boxes highlight aspects of management that are particularly important today.

ETHICS Ethical conduct in business has become an increasingly public issue. Whether the issue lies in recognizing the importance of stakeholders, a regulatory matter, or concerns with employees, ethical behavior and policies cut across all areas of management. Nearly every chapter of *Management* includes these special illustrations of how ethics and trust play an important role in all aspects of business.

CUSTOMER FOCUS In today's hyper-competitive world, relationships and trust are increasingly important. For the manager, everyone is a customer, whether *internal* or *external.* Within their organizations, managers rely on maintaining good relationships with managers and employees in other departments to get things done. Just as important are relationships with external customers, potential partnerships, and alliances. The Customer Focus boxes offer real-world examples of how relationships play crucial roles in the success of organizations.

DEALING WITH CHANGE New technology or new CEOs, globalization and the information economy, regulatory changes: all of these factors constantly conspire to reshape the contemporary business workplace or a particular organization. The successful manager needs to be able to anticipate and adapt to change, and these boxes illustrate how a particular change can impact the successful functioning of a firm.

Focusing on the Future

Appearing before the Summary, "Focusing on the Future" boxes give students a glimpse of how they will use the skills they are acquiring from the text in their future careers. "Day in the life" snapshots from five types of managers—accounting/finance, operations/general, human resources, marketing/communications, and entrepreneurs—show students how working managers use the theories discussed in the text to solve real-world problems. The author of the feature, Carol Moore, California State University–Hayward, interviewed real-life managers, including: Roxana Carbajal—HR Director, Embassy Suites; "Barbara DeLong"—HR Director, telecommunications industry; Mary Kelley—CEO, Sleep Garden; Mark Hasting—Group Vice President, Target Corporation; Brendan Geary—Director of Human Resources, Panalpinia Corporation; David Moore—Pastor, New Summit Presbyterian Church.

End-of-Chapter Exercises and Applications

The end-of-chapter material provides a variety of exercises, including skill-building exercises, individual/collaborative learning cases and exercises, management mini-cases, and Internet exercises to further facilitate student assimilation of the concepts.

Skill-Building Exercises

Most chapters include skill-building exercises that summarize management skills crucial to workplace effectiveness. "Manager's Check-Up" exercises provide students fun and interesting ways to practice and refine those skills.

Individual/Collaborative Learning Cases and Exercises

Each chapter includes a case accompanied by critical thinking questions that can be answered individually, in-class, or as an assignment. It also has a collaborative learning exercise designed to be completed in teams. Teams read the case and then recommend a course of action for resolving the issue or problem presented in the exercise.

Management Mini-Cases

Each chapter has two Management Mini-Cases that provide excellent, real-life examples to stimulate class discussion.

Internet Exercises

Each chapter has at least one Internet exercise relevant to the chapter material. Internet exercises demonstrate how to find specific information online and offer additional current resources.

Supplements

At the Instructor Resource Center, www.pearsonhighered.com/irc, instructors can access a variety of print, digital, and presentation resources to accompany this text in downloadable format. Registration is simple and gives you immediate access to new titles and new editions. As a registered faculty member, you can download resource files and receive immediate access to and instructions for installing course management content on your campus server. In case you ever need assistance, a dedicated technical support team is ready to help with media supplements that accompany this text. Visit http://247.pearsoned.com for answers to frequently asked questions and toll-free user support phone numbers.

The following supplements are available for download to adopting instructors:

- Instructor's Manual
- Test Item File
- TestGen (test-generating program)
- PowerPoint Slides

Videos on DVD

Video segments illustrate the most pertinent topics in management today and highlight relevant issues that demonstrate how people lead, manage, and work effectively. Contact your Pearson representative for the DVD.

CourseSmart eTextbook

CourseSmart is an exciting new choice for students looking to save money. As an alternative to purchasing the print textbook, students can purchase an electronic version of the same content. With a CourseSmart etextbook, students can search the text, make notes online, print out reading assignments that incorporate lecture notes, and bookmark important passages for later review. For more information, or to purchase access to the CourseSmart eTextbook, visit www.coursesmart.com.

About the Authors

Luis R. Gomez-Mejia holds the Benton Cocanougher Chair in Business at the Mays Business School, Texas A&M University. Before joining Texas A&M, he taught at Arizona State University, the University of Colorado, and the University of Florida. He has also been on the faculty at University Carlos III de Madrid and Instituto de Empresas and has offered seminars in both Spanish and English in many countries and universities around the world.

He received his Ph.D. and M.A. in industrial relations from the College of Business at the University of Minnesota and a B.A. (summa cum laude) in economics from the University of Minnesota. Prior to entering academia, Professor Gomez-Mejia worked in human resources for the City of Minneapolis and Control Data Corporation and served as consultant to numerous organizations.

He has served three terms on the editorial board of the *Academy of Management Journal* and is editor and cofounder of two journals: *Journal of High Technology Management Research and Management Research* and *Management Research*. Dr. Gomez-Mejia has published more than 150 articles in the most prestigious management journals including the *Academy of Management Journal, Academy of Management Review, Administrative Science Quarterly, Strategic Management Journal, Industrial Relations*, and *Personnel Psychology*. He has also written and edited a dozen management books. His research has been cited approximately 8,000 times (as per Google scholar, 2011), making him one of the most highly cited members in the field of Management.

Dr. Gomez-Mejia has received numerous awards including "best article" in the *Academy of Management Journal* and the Outstanding Alumni Award at University of Minnesota. He has been named a Dean's Council of 100 Distinguished Scholar at Arizona State University every year since 1994, holds the Horace Steel Chair at Arizona State University, was a member of the *Academy of Management Journal's* Hall of Fame, and is a Fellow of the Academy of Management.

He was also president and founder of the Iberoamerican Academy of Management (an affiliate of the Academy of Management), which covers Spain and Portugal, all of Latin America, and Hispanic faculty in U.S. universities.

David B. Balkin is Professor of Management at the Leeds School of Business at the University of Colorado at Boulder. He received his Ph.D. in industrial relations from the University of Minnesota. Prior to joining the faculty of the University of Colorado, he served on the faculties of Louisiana State University and Northeastern University. He has published over 60 articles appearing in such journals as the *Academy of Management Journal, Strategic Management Journal, Personnel Psychology, Journal of Organizational Behavior, Journal of Business Venturing*, and *Journal of Management Studies*. One of his publications (coauthored with Luis R. Gomez-Mejia) was selected as the best article published in 1992 in the *Academy of Management Journal*. Professor Balkin has written or edited several books on human resources, the management of innovation, compensation, and other topics. He has served as Chair of the Management Department at University of Colorado and also served on advisory boards of non-profit organizations. Professor Balkin is currently the associate editor for *Human Resource Management Review* and has previously served on the editorial boards of the *Academy of Management Journal* and the *Journal of Management*. As an expert witness, he has provided testimony in civil cases dealing with employment and pay discrimination. Professor Balkin has extensive international experience as a scholar and teacher and was a visiting professor at University of Toulouse (France), Copenhagen Business School (Denmark), Helsinki University of Technology (Finland), University of Regensburg (Germany), National University of Singapore, Hong Kong University of Science and Technology, HEC Montreal (Canada), and Indian School of Business (India).

1

Learning Objectives

1 Understand the challenges organizations face in the new millennium.

2 Specify the functions and roles of successful managers.

3 Explain the origins of management as an academic discipline.

4 Describe the bureaucratic and administrative approaches to the study of management.

5 Explain the behavioral perspective in analyzing management issues.

6 Interpret recent approaches to the study of management.

Gaining and Losing a Competitive Edge: The Case of the Automobile Companies

By the end of 2009 the bad news for American automobile manufacturers kept on mounting: 60,000 U.S. and Canadian jobs gone, 24 factories closed, GM and Chrysler declaring bankruptcy, and the federal government bailing out GM and acquiring 61 percent of its stock. The majority of these troubles were attributed to a combination of bloated bureaucracy, poor management, a disconnect with customers, overly generous labor contracts, and high production costs with poor attention to quality.

Around the same time Toyota had become the indisputable winner in the automobile industry, with a reputation for high innovation, low manufacturing cost, strong cooperation with suppliers, high employee engagement, excellent customer service, and near perfect quality. Then disaster struck Toyota in 2010 after wide negative media exposure, the filing of hundreds of legal suits against the company, congressional hearings, and the recall of more than 8 million Toyota cars. Faulty brakes and other mechanical troubles in some of Toyota's models allegedly had caused a number of serious highway accidents, some involving deaths. The reputation that took decades to build was seriously damaged in just a few months and may

Management and Its Evolution

Sources: Based on D. Welch, "The man with the toughest job at GM," *BusinessWeek*, March 1, 2010; D. Welch, "Why VW is the car giant to watch." *BusinessWeek*, January 25, 2010, 16–18; A. Ohnsman, J. Green, and K. Inoue, "The humbling of Toyota," *BusinessWeek*, March 22, 2010, 17–19; D. Welch, N. Naughton, and B. Helm, "Detroit's big chance," *BusinessWeek*, February 22, 2010, 22–23; B. Saporito, "Toyota got tangled" *BusinessWeek*, February 22, 2010, 29–32; L. Denning, "Detroit's life after death is no paradise," *BusinessWeek*, January 11, 2010, 39–40; M. Dolan, "Ford to begin hiring at new lower wages," *Wall Street Journal*, January 26, 2010; B. Saporito, "Toyota's recall," *BusinessWeek*, February 25, 2010, 32–24; K. Linebaugh, "Toyota heir faces crisis at the wheel," *Wall Street Journal*, January 28, 2010; K. Linebaugh and N. Shirouzu, "Toyota's U.S. chief is on the hot seat," *Wall Journal Street*, February 8, 2010, C-1.

take a long time to repair. As noted by *BusinessWeek*, "Toyota got carried away with high-speed growth, market share, and productivity gains year in and year out. All that slowly dulled the commitment to quality embedded in Toyota's corporate culture. Then the tent came crushing down in a hurry."

In the meantime VW sees Toyota's troubles as a historic opportunity and is bent on displacing Toyota as the world's biggest car company by the year 2018.

CRITICAL THINKING QUESTIONS

1. *Why did the U.S. automobile manufacturers allow their financial situation to deteriorate while Toyota was prospering?*

2. *Why was Toyota (a foreign company) so successful in entering the U.S. market, beating the largest domestic automobile manufacturers on their own turf?*

3. *Even though some of the brake allegations against Toyota were later shown to be exaggerated, why did Toyota seem to fall off its pedestal so quickly at the beginning of this decade?*

We'll revisit these questions again in our Concluding Thoughts on page 25, after you have had the opportunity to read the discussion in this chapter.

This chapter provides the "big picture," or an overview, of the field of management. First, we explain what management is. We discuss the different types of managers, the functions that managers perform, and the skills needed to successfully carry out managerial activities. Next, we describe the history and evolution of the field, along with ideas that have affected the practice of management. Some ideas, such as bureaucratic management, were in vogue and then fell out of favor, while other ideas have withstood the test of time and continue to be used by managers today.

■ Management in the New Millennium

Organizational performance depends, to a large extent, on how resources are allocated and management's ability to adapt to changing conditions. In successful organizations, people are managed wisely and resources are used efficiently and effectively. This helps managers reach key organizational goals, such as keeping the company functioning in a changing external environment in which technology, governmental activities, and competition create constant challenges.

To be successful, a company must be both efficient and effective. A firm is *efficient* when it makes the best possible use of people, money, the physical plant, and technology. It is *effective* when goals are met which sustain a company's competitive advantage. A firm with excellent goals could still fail miserably by being *inefficient,* meaning that the company hired the wrong people, lost key contributors, relied on outdated technology, and made poor investment decisions. A firm is *ineffective* when it fails to reach goals that sustain a company's competitive advantage. High quality companies do things right (they are efficient) and do the right things (they are effective).

The 21st century world of business is strongly influenced by three issues. The first is the *management of change.* Organizational leaders must cope with and adapt to rapid change on a daily basis. Change creates uncertainty and risk. The number of competitors and product offerings are greater than ever before. Globalization means that most firms are exposed to competitive challenges both domestically and internationally. Many products (such as software) become obsolete in a matter of a few years or even months, forcing the firm to continuously innovate or die. Today's managers must effectively deal with a host of technological, legal, cultural, and organizational changes, such as downsizing, restructuring, and mergers.

Skills for Managing 1.1 on page 5 provides an exercise to help you and your classmates think about your future career in light of these changes.

The second major new issue is an increasing emphasis on *customer service.* The company must satisfy the needs of customers in ways that contribute to long-term loyalty. The term *customer* is now used in a broader sense. It refers to anyone who receives a service from an employee. Customers are both external (current or prospective consumers of the firm's products or service) and internal (other managers or employees who depend on the manager's performance or inputs in some capacity). For most successful operations, the customer represents the starting point and an ending point for almost every activity.

Globalization is playing an increasingly important role in the process of serving both internal and external customers as many companies are outsourcing entire functions overseas (see Management Close-Up 1.1, "How Outsourcing Is Transforming Whole Industries and Changing the Way We Work" on page 6).

The third critical issue affecting the management profession in the 21st century is the need for higher *business ethics.* Ethics are the standards and values which are considered necessary for the collective interests of employees, shareholders, and society. Several well-publicized examples of cheating, dishonesty, and use of the firm's resources for personal gain have emerged in firms such as WorldCom, Tyco, General Dynamics, Enron, Arthur Andersen, and Radio Shack. In the long run, these violations will have a negative impact on

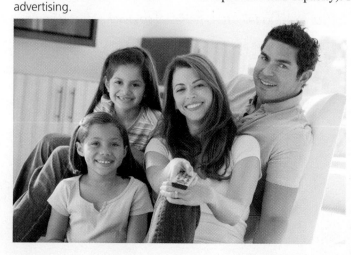

Among the many cultural changes facing business managers today is the rising number of Hispanic consumers in the United States, which advertisers see as akin to the baby boom, and the increasing assimilation of Latino culture into the mainstream. Companies' desire to reach this fast-growing market with its divergent tastes and preferences is spurring a creative revolution in Spanish-language television advertising.

SKILLS FOR MANAGING 1.1

What the Future Will Bring

You might think that 21st century college students aren't looking much farther into the future than next week's exam or Friday's beer bash. During this second decade, college students are contemplating something quite different, say campus recruiters and researchers: their future security.

As companies begin their next round of campus visits to recruit the undergraduate class, recruiters say it's clear that the bad news of the past few years has shaken this new crop of grads. More than any recruits in memory, they're asking employers for assurance of security, so they don't wind up on the unemployment line or flipping hamburgers for minimum wage.

Students have learned from watching the financial crash a few years back that corporate fortunes can turn—and campus job offers can be rescinded—on a dime. Grads are showing a preference for stable, diversified companies, helping propel such giants as Lockheed Martin and Johnson & Johnson sharply higher in Universum's rating of grads' "ideal employers" among big corporations in all fields, from consulting and finance to manufacturing and retailing. Martin Slevin, manager, retail recruitment, for Walgreen Co., says today's campus recruits are far more interested in his company's 110-year history and 36 straight years of record profits than grads have been in the past.

Before the financial crash at the end of the first decade business school seniors were graduating with two or three job offers and starting salaries that often exceeded $50,000 with big signing offers. Then came what is now known as the great recession and only a small percentage of graduates were lucky enough to land a position with any promising future.

Gender seems to make a big difference in how business graduates see their career prospects. While women now exceed men in most business schools, less than half as many women as men believe that future opportunities to move into middle management or executive ranks are equal for men and women.

Skill Building Exercise

Make a list of five things that are highest in priority for you when considering alternative employment opportunities. Submit your list to your instructor, who will merge the lists provided by you and the rest of your class members and distribute it to the entire class (with names removed). As a class, discuss what it is that new employees expect from their organizations, whether or not those expectations are realistic, and what factors are likely to impinge upon companies' success or failure in meeting those expectations.

Sources: S. Needleman, "Study asks: Who has easy path to top?" *Wall Street Journal*, January 28, 2010, A-1; G. Gloeckler, "With jobs scarce, Business Schools get creative," *BusinessWeek*, March 15, 2010, 18–19; L. Gerdes, "The best places to launch a career," *BusinessWeek*, September 15, 2010, 22–23; S. Shellenberger, "Avoiding the next Enron: Today's crop of soon to be grads seeks' job security," *Wall Street Journal*, February 16, 2010, C-1.

those who are influenced by such managers' bad decisions, including employees, other managers, and customers.

Globalization also complicates ethical decision making as companies may feel that they have to compromise ethical standards to do business in certain countries. For instance, during 2006–2007 Yahoo!, Google, Microsoft, and Cisco came under criticism after revelations that they have cooperated with the Chinese government to censor online searches and even to turn in dissidents to the government.[1]

Many organizations are appointing ethics officers to advise top executives, enforce ethical standards, and monitor potential misconduct at any level within the firm (see Management Close-Up 1.2, "Enforcing Ethics at Work" on page 7).

In this book, we will deal with managing change and improving customer service, along with various ethical concerns as various topics are discussed. We will provide examples of what we consider to be both good and bad management practices.

Traditionally, the term *manager* referred only to individuals responsible for making resource allocation decisions and with the formal authority to direct others. There are three levels of management: **strategic managers**, the senior executives with overall responsibility for the firm; **tactical managers** responsible for implementing the directives of strategic managers; and **operational managers** responsible for day-to-day supervision.

In varying degrees successful managers at any level have certain things in common. Each chapter of this book has a feature called "Management Is Everyone's Business" that summarizes how successful *managers* apply sound principles derived from that particular chapter. A broad set of managerial implications of the contents discussed in this introductory chapter, several of which will be explored in greater detail in subsequent chapters, appears in Management Is Everyone's Business 1.1 on page 7.

Managers still have authority over people and financial resources, but today's organizations are more decentralized than ever before, and employees have more autonomy to define their

strategic managers
The firm's senior executives who are responsible for overall management.

tactical managers
The firm's management staff who are responsible for translating the general goals and plan developed by strategic managers into specific objectives and activities.

operational managers
The firm's lower-level managers who supervise the operations of the organization.

How Outsourcing Is Transforming Whole Industries and Changing the Way We Work

In theory, it is becoming possible to buy, off the shelf, practically any function you need to run a company. Some examples follow below:

- Want to start a budget airline but don't want to invest in a huge back office? Accenture's Navitaire unit can manage reservations, plan routes, assign crew, and calculate optimal prices for each seat.
- Have a cool new telecom or medical device but lack market researchers? For about $5,000, analytics outfits such as New Delhi-based Evalueserve Inc. will, within a day, assemble a team of Indian patent attorneys, engineers, and business analysts, start mining global databases, and call dozens of U.S. experts and wholesalers to provide an independent appraisal.
- Want to quickly market a new mutual fund or insurance policy? IT services providers such as India's Tata Consultancy Services Ltd. are building software platforms that furnish every business process needed and secure all regulatory approvals.
- The $57 billion consumer-products company Procter and Gamble has outsourced everything from IT infrastructure and human resources to management of its offices from Cincinnati to Moscow.
- If a Penske truck is held up at a weigh station because it lacks a certain permit, the driver calls an 800 number. Genpact staff in India obtains the document over the Web. The weigh station is notified electronically, and the truck is back on the road within 30 minutes.
- Outsourcing figures heavily in pharmaceutical company Lilly's strategy to lower costs. The drugmaker maker now does 20 percent of its chemistry work in China for one-quarter the U.S. cost and helped fund a start-up lab, Shanghai's Chem-Explorer Co., with 230 chemists. Lilly now is trying to slash the costs of clinical trials on human patients, which range from $50 million to $300 million per drug, and is expanding such efforts in Brazil, Russia, China, and India.
- More and more American hospitals are using radiologists in India who work around the clock virtually interpreting CT scans and x-rays and then send their reports back to the hospitals. This is all done at a fraction of the expense it would take in the United States where radiologists typically earn over $300,000 a year.
- OnStor Inc., a Los Gatos, California, developer of storage systems, says its tie-up with the Bangalore engineering-services outfit HCL Technologies Ltd. enables it to get customized products to clients twice as fast as its major rivals. "If we want to recruit a great engineer in Silicon Valley, our lead time is three months," says CEO Bob Miller. "With HCL, pick up the phone and get somebody in two or three days."

Based on M. Ihiwan "While Sony bets on outsourcing TV's, the Korean giant is building an edge by making its own," *BusinessWeek,* January 18, 2010, 11–12; P. Conlin, M. Conlin, and M. Herbst, "The disposable worker," *BusinessWeek*, January 18, 2010, 19–21; B. Steverman, "The action stays offshore," *BusinessWeek*, January 4, 2010, 34–36; S. Federico, "Outsourcing versus integration at home or abroad and firm heterogeneity," *Empirica*, 37(1), February, 2010, 15–28; "Can't afford employees? Then outsource/subcontract," www.prlog.org., 2011.

Penske Truck Leasing and India's Genpact collaborate closely on the documentation required when Penske buys a truck and leases it to a U.S. customer. Genpact's Indian staff works remotely to secure titles, registrations, and permits online. When the truck comes back, the driver's log and other documentation for fuel and taxes are forwarded to Genpact's Mexican office for entry to Penske's computer system. Genpact in Hyderabad, India, processes the data for tax filings and accounting.

Enforcing Ethics at Work

Patrick J. Gnazzo is among the more visible examples of a new species of executive: high-profile former government lawyers and judges who have been tapped, usually by scandal-tainted companies, to police employees. Others in this group include former Securities and Exchange Commission Chairman Richard C. Breeden, who was named outside monitor of KPMG in 2006 and is now taking a similar role at Hollinger International Inc. Eric R. Dinallo and Beth L. Golden, alumni of New York Attorney General Eliot Spitzer's office, have taken jobs at Morgan Stanley and Bear, Stearns & Co., respectively. Old-style ethics officers reported to managers far down the ladder. But now they can report directly to the board, bypassing even the CEO. For instance, Gnazzo has the power to go right to independent directors with problems. Whenever needed, he can quiz CEO John Swainson, the former IBM vice president who joined CA to clean it up. He also confers regularly with the CEO and five other top officers on a new disclosure committee that meets to talk about SEC filings and news releases. In the words of Gnazzo, "You did the right thing. You created an ethics program for your organization built around a workable and enforceable code of behavior for employees. You appointed compliance or ethics officers to administer the program, and you built a structure to receive employee allegations and feedback.

Have you done enough? No.

Here's a simple truth: A certain number of your employees will not raise issues to management unless they are promised confidentiality throughout the process, including in any potential litigation. Under current law, your ethics program cannot guarantee that protection. Consequently, you will not hear some things that you should."

Sources: Based on G. R. Wratney "Are you serious about ethics: For companies that can't guarantee confidentiality the answer is no," *The Conference Board*, www.conference-board.org., 2011; M. O'Connor, "Federal Procurement Ethics: The complete legal guide," http://books.google.com, 2010; A. Onifade, " The indispensable secretary," *Journal of Social Science*, 2010, 22(1); 47–51; J. Goldberg, "Compliance officers take their own path," *New York Law Journal*, 2007, April 19, 15–25; J. Weber, "The New Ethics Enforcers, *BusinessWeek*, February 13, 2006, pp. 75–77.

jobs, prioritize tasks, allocate time, monitor their own work, and set their own objectives. By being *empowered* to make these important choices, employees are less dependent on superiors to tell them what to do and are encouraged to use their own expertise and ideas. In a very real sense, employees are increasingly being asked to manage themselves.

Each chapter of this book has a "Management Is Everyone's Business" feature that emphasizes working as an individual and that summarizes the practical implications of the material being discussed for your *individual* success in organizations, whether or not you have or will have supervisory responsibilities. The first such Management Is Everyone's Business feature reflects much of what we discuss in this introductory chapter, although these issues will be revisited in greater depth in future chapters. See Management Is Everyone's Business 1.2 on page 8.

Barriers between departments are also breaking down. Functional areas, rivalries, and divisions cause people to develop narrow, parochial views of their jobs and this discourages innovation. Departmentalization prevents employees from understanding corporatewide objectives and

MANAGEMENT IS EVERYONE'S BUSINESS   1.1

WORKING AS A MANAGER   To become a successful manager requires that you learn how to be flexible and adaptable to be able to do a variety of things:

- Develop an appreciation for the big picture as well as how the details fit into the big picture.
- Be in touch with what is happening inside and outside your unit, as well as externally, with an eye toward setting goals that capitalize on opportunities and deal with potential threats.
- Plan activities to meet personal and organizational goals making best use of resources available to you.
- Treat your peers and those below and above you with respect.
- Energize subordinates to fully use their talents and provide them with an example to imitate of highly ethical behaviors.
- Be fair, honest, and consistent in your dealing with subordinates, but build on their unique strengths.
- Communicate clearly and persuasively, making effective and accurate use of all information available to you.
- Do not be afraid to make bold decisions, but be sure that these are made after careful consideration of all available data and the inputs of various parties who have a stake in these decisions.

MANAGEMENT IS EVERYONE'S BUSINESS 1.2

WORKING AS AN INDIVIDUAL To succeed in most modern organizations you will be asked as an individual to meet multiple expectations:

- *Show initiative.* Most successful firms value individuals capable of acting autonomously without close supervision. Some people refer to it as "self-leadership."
- *Show a capacity to become a leader.* This means that you should be able to influence others and not simply follow directions.
- *Learn to appreciate the organization's culture* and how you can work within that culture.
- *Be trusted.* This means that you are reliable, honest, loyal, and keep your word.
- *Show a capacity to keep on learning.* Challenging assignments most likely will go to individuals who can stretch their knowledge and skills and strive for personal growth.
- *Be willing to change your approach as situations change.* Inflexible people are unlikely to succeed in a rapidly changing environment.

---

promotes interunit conflict rather than cooperation, so the organization loses flexibility and is unable to respond to competitive challenges in a more integrated, cohesive fashion. For this reason, firms are increasingly relying on employee *teams* that form to work on common projects. When these teams are composed of individuals from different parts of the organization, they are referred to as *cross-functional teams;* when team members have diverse backgrounds, the teams are *cross-disciplinary.* Teams are asked to perform many of the managerial roles of traditional managers. That is, rather than relying on a superior for direction, a team often defines the problem, sets objectives, establishes priorities, proposes new ways of doing things, and assigns members to different tasks. Teams fulfill important managerial roles by linking various parts of the organization to focus on common problems, issues, and complex tasks that require integration and concerted actions by dissimilar individuals.

Each chapter has a "Management Is Everyone's Business" feature that centers on working as a team and that points out how the materials discussed in the chapter help *teams* operate more effectively. The first such feature is Management Is Everyone's Business 1.3, summarizing the practical implications for teams of the concepts presented in this introductory chapter. As was the case for managers and individuals (Management Is Everyone's Business 1.1 and 1.2), these implications for teams will be discussed in greater depth in future chapters.

The next sections of the chapter describe the critical aspects of most management jobs. Figure 1.1 summarizes these aspects, namely, the ability to perform basic managerial functions (planning and strategizing, organizing, leading, and controlling) and the ability to perform major managerial roles (interpersonal, informational, and decisional). While the relative importance of each aspect may vary (for instance, strategic managers may be more involved in planning and strategizing than are operational managers), those capable of doing well on each of these job aspects are more likely to have a successful managerial career and be promoted to more responsible positions over time.

MANAGEMENT IS EVERYONE'S BUSINESS 1.3

WORKING AS A TEAM Most successful organizations nowadays strongly support the team concept, believing that employees with diverse skills working together on common problems are more likely to be innovative and that employees working as part of a team are more committed to doing a good job. This means that organizations that truly believe in the team concept should:

- Evaluate and reward team performance, not just the contribution of individual employees.
- Give sufficient autonomy for teams to make their own decisions.
- Select team members who are different yet complement each other.
- Form teams to deal with identifiable problems or issues, but also support teams whose task is to be creative and "think outside the box."
- Select and train managers capable of coordinating or linking the activities of various teams.

LOC-In 1 Learning Objective Check-In

Gen-Art is a custom framing and art service boutique that is considering expansion into the surrounding regional market. The 20-person company has highly decentralized job authority and decision making. Instead of strict functional areas, the firm uses a team-based approach to satisfying client needs. Gen-Art avoids many levels of management in favor of a barebones approach to structure, with executives, project managers, and teams of technical staff. Ginny and Mercedes are two managers at Gen-Art.

1. Ginny is the Vice President of Operations at Gen-Art. She helps make decisions regarding growth, goals, and longer-term issues. Ginny is a _____.
   a. strategic manager
   b. operational manager
   c. front-line manager
   d. tactical manager

2. As one of the project managers for Gen-Art, Mercedes operates at the _____ level. She is the direct link between the executive level of the firm and the technical staff she oversees.
   a. strategic
   b. controlling management
   c. tactical
   d. bureaucratic management

The Four Management Functions

More than once the question has been posed, "What do managers do?" Or perhaps more precisely, "What *should* they do?" Whether at the managerial, individual, or team level, the management process should include planning and strategizing, organizing, leading, and controlling. Some of these activities are typically performed at particular organizational levels; for example, planning and strategy making are core activities for senior executives. However, in most contemporary

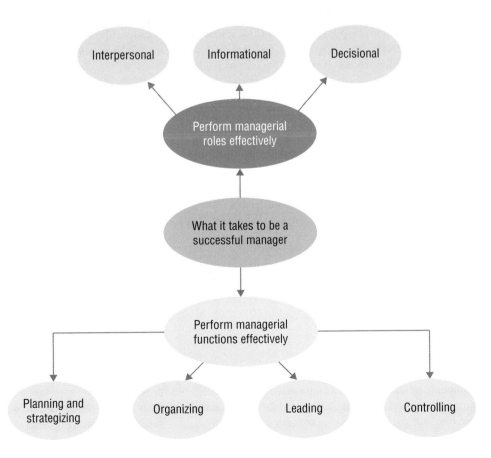

FIGURE 1.1

Key Aspects of Managerial Success

organizations, all employees are responsible for at least some aspects of the various management functions.

The four management functions are closely linked. For instance, the control system warns the organization when plans and strategies are not working and should be reconsidered. Inspiring leadership would quickly lead to frustration if people did not know what their roles were or if there were no procedures to guide their actions. Grouping employees into teams may lead to much wasted time and confusion unless there is an overarching plan for unifying their efforts.

PLANNING AND STRATEGIZING   Planning and strategizing are designed to lead the company to fulfill its mission. **Planning** includes setting future objectives and mapping out the activities necessary to achieve those objectives. To be effective, the objectives of individuals, teams, and management should be carefully coordinated.

Because no firm operates in a vacuum, reaching the firm's mission in spite of changes in the environment and competitive landscape is difficult. It involves a continuing assessment of the firm's strengths, weaknesses, opportunities, and threats (referred to as SWOT, to be discussed in detail in Chapter 7), so that appropriate strategies may be taken. Chapter 2, Managing in a Global Environment; Chapter 5, Managing the Planning Process; and Chapter 7, Strategic Management; and Chapter 8, Entrepreneurship and Innovation, focus on issues related to planning and strategizing.

ORGANIZING   Specifying how the firm's human, financial, physical, informational, and technical resources are to be arranged and coordinated is the process of **organizing**. This includes defining roles for all players, delegating tasks, marshalling and allocating resources, clarifying procedures, and determining priorities. Chapter 4, Managing Organizational Culture and Change; Chapter 9, Managing the Structure and Design of Organizations; Chapter 10, Human Resource Management; and Chapter 13, Managing Teams, describe various aspects of organizing.

LEADING   Energizing people to contribute their best individually and in cooperation with other people is the **leading** function. This involves clearly communicating organizational goals, inspiring and motivating employees, providing an example for others to follow, guiding people, and creating conditions that encourage people from diverse backgrounds to work well together. Chapter 3, Managing Social Responsibility and Ethics; Chapter 6, Decision Making; Chapter 11, Managing Employee Diversity; Chapter 12, Leading and Motivating Others; and Chapter 14, Managing Communication, focus on various aspects of leadership.

CONTROLLING   Measuring performance, comparing it to objectives, implementing necessary changes, and monitoring progress are the functions of **control**. Collecting quality feedback, identifying potential problems, and taking corrective action are crucial to long-term success. Organizations should use many approaches to detect and correct significant variations or discrepancies in the results of planned activities designed to meet the specific challenge of those activities.

As can be seen in Management Close-Up 1.3 ("Key Performance Indicators"), technology is playing a key role in control systems that would have seemed impossible just a few years ago.

Chapter 15, Operations Management and Management Control, deals with specialized issues related to control.

Managerial Roles

The traditional management functions described above may give the false impression that day-to-day management activities are routine, orderly, and rational. A researcher named Henry Mintzberg studied a group of managers and came to the conclusion that the typical manager is not a systematic person who carefully decides how to plan, organize, lead, and control. Rather, managers face constant interruptions, make decisions based on limited data, change tasks frequently depending on shifting priorities, spend most of their time in meetings and informal discussions, and experience a hectic work pace that leaves little room for reflection. Using a method called "structured observation" that involved keeping track of the activities of top-level executives, Mintzberg summarized what managers do on a day-to-day basis by identifying a set of

---

planning
The management function that assesses the management environment to set future objectives and map out activities necessary to achieve those objectives.

organizing
The management function that determines how the firm's human, financial, physical, informational, and technical resources are arranged and coordinated to perform tasks to achieve desired goals; the deployment of resources to achieve strategic goals.

leading
The management function that energizes people to contribute their best individually and in cooperation with other people.

controlling
The management function that measures performance, compares it to objectives, implements necessary changes, and monitors progress.

Key Performance Indicators

The dashboard is computer software that makes the gritty details of a business, which are often buried deep within a large organization, accessible at a glance to senior executives. So powerful are the programs that they're beginning to change the nature of management from an intuitive art into more of a science. Managers can see key changes in their businesses almost instantaneously—when salespeople falter or quality slides—and take quick, corrective action. At Verizon, executives can choose from among 300 metrics to put on their dashboards, from broadband sales to wireless subscriber defections. At General Electric Co., James P. Campbell, chief of the Consumer & Industrial Division, which makes appliances and lighting products, tracks the number of orders coming in from each customer every day and compares that with targets. "I look at the digital dashboard the first thing in the morning so I have a quick global view of sales and service levels across the organization," says Campbell. "It's a key operational tool in our business." At Oracle managers track on a continuous basis how many hours technicians spend solving problems for customers and the ratio of sales-to-service requests. The dashboard relies on "key performance indicators" (KPI). Key performance indicators are quantifiable measurements, agreed to beforehand, that reflect the critical success factors of an organization. They will differ depending on the organization. A business may have as one of its KPI the percentage of its income that comes from return customers. A school may focus its KPI on graduation rates of its students. A customer service department may have as one of its KPI in line with overall company KPI, percentage of customer calls answered in the first minute. A key Performance Indicator for a social organization might be number of clients assisted during the year.

Whatever KPI are selected, they must reflect the organization's goals, they must be key to its success, and they must be quantifiable (measurable). Key performance indicators usually are long-term considerations. The definition of what they are and how they are measured do not change often. The goals for a particular KPI may change as the organization's goals change, or as it gets closer to achieving a goal.

Sources: Based on Reh, J., "Key Performance Indicators," About.com Management, 2011, http://management.about.com; "Management dashboards," www.LogiXML.com, 2011; "Visual calc-management dashboards and online calculators," www.visualcalc.com, 2011; Business Performance Management software dashboard web," www.business.com, 2011; Ante, S.E., "Giving the boss the big picture," *BusinessWeek*, February 13, 2006, pp. 48–50.

specific roles. A role consists of the behaviors expected of people who hold certain positions. These roles have been grouped by Mintzberg into three major categories, although managers often perform several of them simultaneously.

INTERPERSONAL ROLES Managers engage in a great deal of interaction, continually communicating with superiors, peers, subordinates and people from outside the organization. In doing so, a manager serves as *a figurehead,* or the visible personality representing an organization, department or work unit; a *leader* who energizes others to get the job done properly; and a *liaison* who links together the activities of people from both inside and outside the organization. Various chapters deal with the interpersonal role of managers, in particular Chapter 4 (Managing Organizational Culture and Change), Chapter 10 (Human Resource Management), Chapter 11 (Managing Employee Diversity), Chapter 12 (Leading and Motivating Others), Chapter 13 (Managing Teams), and Chapter 14 (Managing Communication).

INFORMATION ROLES Managers obtain, interpret, and give out a great deal of information. These roles include being a *monitor* and *disseminator,* as well as the organization's spokesperson. While effective communication underlies almost everything discussed in this book, Chapter 14 specifically focuses on communication issues at work.

DECISIONAL ROLES Managers are also asked to choose among competing alternatives. This includes balancing the interests of the various parties who have a stake in a decision. Four decisional roles include that of *entrepreneur,* who introduces changes into the organization; *disturbance handler,* who takes corrective action, provides damage control, and responds to unexpected situations or crises; *resource allocator,* responsible for assigning people and other resources to best meet organizational needs; and *negotiator,* reaching agreements and making compromises. These activities occur within and outside the firm when working with parties who control valuable resources, such as other organizational managers, suppliers, and members of various financial institutions. Four chapters are particularly relevant to the decisional roles of managers, namely Chapter 5 (Managing the Planning Process), Chapter 6 (Decision Making), Chapter 7 (Strategic Management), and Chapter 8 (Entrepreneurship and Innovation).

The Evolution of Management Thought

Many of the key management ideas that blossomed in the 19th and 20th centuries are practiced by managers to this day. This section examines these early management ideas, from the operational perspective, the bureaucratic management approach, the administrative management approach, and the behavioral perspective, and contemporary management approaches. Systems theory, contingency theory, and the learning organization are part of the contemporary management perspective. These contemporary ideas represent recent thinking on sound management practices in the 21st century. We also present what we believe are emergent ideas in the management field during the latter part of this decade which are likely to influence management practices in the future, namely the modular organization and the intangible organization.

The following section is a rough chronology of the time period in which each particular management perspective originated. It is important to keep in mind that some of the "old" views are still being applied in varying degrees today. For instance, the operational approach with an emphasis on scientific management is still alive and well at Lincoln Electric in Cleveland, Ohio, and faithfully applied in countries that are industrializing rapidly such as China and India. Many of the principles of bureaucratic management, with its emphasis on rules and procedures, still ring true in the U.S. Postal Service and most government agencies. The military is still largely organized following the prescriptions of the administrative management school. You may find many of the ideas of the behavioral perspective, with its emphasis on human relations, present in "high-tech" firms such as Google and Intel. And you may even think of some modern organizations that follow a Machiavellian leadership style, in which tight control through fear and punishment is the norm.

In other words, classical management insights are still valuable today even though the complexity and diversity of organizations have increased dramatically since most of these ideas were created (see Figure 1.2 "Origin of Key Management Perspectives over Time").

Early Management Thought

The art and practice of management have been present for many centuries. Designing and building such huge public works projects as the Great Wall of China, the pyramids of Egypt, and the aqueducts that provided water to cities in the Roman Empire required an understanding of management. For many years management was viewed as an art and was verbally passed on without documenting theoretical principles that could be used by future generations of managers. However, a few early thinkers laid the foundation for the classical and behavioral schools of management thought that arose during the last century. These thinkers include Sun Tzu in China, Niccolò Machiavelli in Italy, and Adam Smith in Great Britain.

EARLY IDEAS ABOUT MANAGEMENT STRATEGY Some of our earliest management concepts are found in *The Art of War,* written about 2,500 years ago by Sun Tzu, a Chinese general. Sun Tzu's ideas focus on developing military strategies that can lead to victory in battle. For example, he recognized that it is better to use intelligence and cunning to subdue an enemy than to rely on

FIGURE 1.2

Origin of Key Management Perspectives over Time

500 BC	1500s	1700s	Late 1800s Early 1990s	1930s–1960s	1960s–1990s	2000–2020s
Sun Tzu *Art of War*	Machiavelli's *The Prince*	A. Smith's *Wealth of Nations*	Operational Perspective	Behavioral Perspective	Systems Approach	Emergent Perspectives
			• Scientific management	• M.Parker Follett	Contingency Theory	• Modular organization
			• Quantitative Management	• Hawthorne Studies	Learning Organizations	• Intangible organization
			• Quality management	• Human relations		
			Bureaucractic Management			
			Administrative Management			

violence and destruction. Alliances and negotiated settlements allow a military leader to expand his empire without sacrificing soldiers or resources or destroying cities. Sun Tzu recognized that strategy involved a long-term perspective. He recommended attacking the enemy's weak points and taking advantage of one's own army's strengths. Sun Tzu's insights about dispassionately taking stock of strengths and weaknesses are still prominent features of strategic management.

EARLY IDEAS ABOUT LEADERSHIP Niccolò Machiavelli wrote *The Prince* during the Renaissance in 16th-century Florence, Italy. It was one of the first books that described leadership. Machiavelli was a government official during a period of warfare and political intrigue between city-states vying for control of the region, and he had a cynical view of human nature, believing that people were motivated by very narrow self-interests.

Machiavelli advised the leader or prince that it was better to be feared than to be loved. Love is a fickle emotion, whereas fear is constant. In other words, survival is a basic human instinct that dominates other emotions. Machiavelli also suggested that a leader may engage in lies or deceptions for the good of society, as long as he appears to be virtuous to the people. The leader should be fair yet tough, harshly punishing disloyal subjects to discourage others from engaging in treason. Machiavelli believed that the aristocrats close in stature to the prince posed the greatest threat to his welfare and that the prince had to use cunning and intrigue to keep them off balance. Thus, he warned the leader not to trust his peers. He believed that an effective leader forms alliances of convenience with some enemies to keep the more powerful ones off balance.

Machiavelli's leadership philosophy was that "the end justified the means." Contemporary leaders are called Machiavellian if they engage in manipulative and self-serving tactics. Although many contemporary executives and leaders might judge Machiavelli's advice to be extreme and unrealistic, even today rivals fight behind the scenes in highly politicized corporations, and sibling rivalry runs rampant in some family businesses.

EARLY IDEAS ABOUT THE DESIGN AND ORGANIZATION OF WORK The efficient organization of work has its roots in the classic 18th-century book *The Wealth of Nations*, written in 1776 by Adam Smith. As a professor of logic and moral philosophy at Glasgow University in Scotland, Smith was the first to recognize the principle of the **division of labor** in a manufacturing process. Division of labor converted production by craftsmen or artisans who were generalists into simple steps. Each worker became a specialist who repeated one step over and over, thereby achieving greater efficiencies in the use of time and knowledge. Smith showed how the manufacture of pins could be reduced to 18 steps done by 10 specialists who each performed one or two steps. Organizing the 10 laborers in a small factory made it possible to produce 48,000 pins in one day. When the pin makers operated independently as generalists, the total daily output was 200 pins.

division of labor
The production process in which each worker repeats one step over and over, achieving greater efficiencies in the use of time and knowledge.

Smith observed that the division of labor was responsible for revolutionary gains in factory output. His work laid the theoretical groundwork for scientific management.

The Operational Perspective

operational perspective
The management perspective formed during the 19th and early 20th centuries when the factory system and modern corporations evolved to meet the challenges of managing large, complex organizations.

The **operational perspective** on management thought originated in the 19th and early 20th centuries. It coincided with the rise of the factory system and the formation of modern corporations, both of which provided challenges in efficiently operating and coordinating large, complex organizations. The operational perspective attempted to apply logic and the scientific method to management so as to discover and practice the one best way of doing a job.

Some of the legacy of the operational perspective is found today in a sub-field called "productions and operations management" (see Chapter 17), although most contemporary management thinkers note the crucial role played by the human element of an organization. Three approaches fall into the operational perspective: scientific management, quantitative management, and quality management.

SCIENTIFIC MANAGEMENT In the last half of the 19th century, organizations were unable to obtain increased productivity from employees despite making large investments in new technologies. Frederick Winslow Taylor (1856–1915) believed his life's calling was to change this situation. Born to a Philadelphia lawyer in 1856, Taylor learned the trades of common laborer and machinist in a small Philadelphia machine shop where he worked for four years. He was then hired by the Midvale Steel Company in Pennsylvania, where he moved quickly through the ranks while studying for a mechanical engineering degree at night. At Midvale, Taylor carefully documented the large amount of time that was wasted by workers who were ill equipped and poorly trained to perform the simplest tasks. Even shoveling coal was inefficient, because workers brought their own shovels with differing weights, sizes, and sharpness. No one had any idea which type of shovel worked best.

Taylor discovered that workers sometimes avoided doing their best work, a practice called *soldiering,* because they feared that management might raise quotas without increasing pay or that some employees would lose their jobs. Complicating the situation, there were no systematic rules to serve as guidelines for doing the jobs most efficiently. Workers learned their jobs by the use of rules of thumb and trial-and-error processes.

scientific management
A management method that applies the principles of the scientific method to the management process: determining the one best way to do a job and sharing the rewards with the workers.

In response to the inefficiencies he observed in the steel industry, Taylor developed **scientific management**, which is summarized in Table 1.1. The scientific method should be applied to determining the one best way to do a particular job. This optimal approach to work spares the worker from management criticism and provides managers and owners with the most output from each worker. Taylor encouraged management to share productivity gains with employees by using a piecework production system in which each worker's output would be measured against standardized productivity quotas. When workers reached or exceeded the quota, the financial gains would be shared. The result would be that workers could earn more by cooperating with management.

Next, Taylor supported the use of scientific selection methods to make the best matches between workers and jobs. At the time, seniority or the boss's preference was used to match workers with jobs. Taylor found this approach inefficient, and he suggested using measures of worker aptitudes, traits, and performance to scientifically determine the fit between person and job.

TABLE 1.1 Taylor's Four Principles of Scientific Management

1. Scientifically study each part of a task and develop the best method of performing the task.
2. Carefully select workers and train them to perform the task by using the scientifically developed method.
3. Cooperate fully with workers to ensure that they use the proper method.
4. Divide work and responsibility so that management is responsible for planning work methods using scientific principles and workers are responsible for executing the work accordingly.

Source: F. W. Taylor, *The Principles of Scientific Management.* New York: Harper, 1911.

Finally, Taylor perceived a clear separation between the work of employees and managers. In Taylor's view, employees did the physical work, and managers planned, directed, and coordinated employees' efforts so that the goals would be reached. He believed that managers and employees should be dependent on each other to achieve desired output, which would encourage cooperation and result in fewer conflicts or strikes. Taylor also believed that the job of management was to inspire and motivate workers to fully cooperate and learn the scientific management principles applied to their job. Until his death in 1915, Taylor committed himself to what he termed a "mental revolution" in the practice of industrial management.

Following Taylor's footsteps Frank Gilbreth and Lillian Gilbreth introduced the idea of time and motion studies using the stopwatch and motion picture camera to improve workplace efficiencies. The Gilbreths analyzed each movement a worker performed during a particular task by filming the task actions and observing the film frame by frame. They then looked for better ways to perform each step to ensure that all the steps could be performed more efficiently with less time and effort.

Henry Gantt was a school teacher who felt that Taylor's piece rate incentive system placed employees under a great deal of stress. He introduced the notion of a "guaranteed day rate," in which employees knew the minimum income they would receive. When employees exceeded certain standards they were paid bonuses. Gantt also developed work scheduling charts which are still used today.

Scientific management had a profound effect on the captains of U.S. industry. In one of the most famous applications, Henry Ford utilized scientific management in the production process of the factory that manufactured the Model-T Ford. The lasting contribution of scientific management was to transform management into a more objective, systematic body of knowledge in which best practices can be discovered for different jobs. It also gave managers and supervisors more active and clearly defined roles.

Despite these noteworthy contributions, scientific management had shortcomings. It did not appreciate the social context of work and the needs (beyond pay) of workers. It often led to dehumanizing working conditions in which every aspect of a worker's effort was measured, prohibiting employee initiative. Scientific management also assumed that workers had no useful ideas, and that only managers and experts were capable of coming up with good ideas or innovations.

A major problem that Taylor, the Gilbreths, and Gantt did not anticipate was that many firms would "pick and choose" what they wanted from scientific management while ignoring worker interests. For example, "some managers using scientific management obtained increases in performance, but rather than sharing performance gains with workers through bonuses as Taylor had advocated, they simply increased the amount of work that each worker was expected to do. Many workers experiencing the reorganized work system found that as their performance increased, managers required them to do more work for the same pay. Workers also learned that increases in performance often meant fewer jobs and a greater threat of layoffs, because fewer workers were needed."[2]

These problems have given scientific management a "bad name" in some circles, which continues to this day. They were at least in part responsible for the rapid rise in legislation designed to protect labor unions in the 1930s. They still provide some of the rationale for unions' existence in the 21st century. Workers continue to join together to defend their interests collectively as well as to prevent employers' abuses. Employment in manufacturing, where scientific management is most appropriate, as a percentage of the labor force has declined steadily over the years. The percentage of unionized workers has also been dropping, from about 35 percent of the workforce in the mid-1940s to less than 10 percent in 2012.[3] In general, unions have not been able to repeat their success in organizing "blue collar" workers when they have tried to organize "white collar" workers in the service sector, that is, retail stores, banks, schools, and governmental agencies, which is where most new jobs are located.

QUANTITATIVE MANAGEMENT The scientific management perspective later became known as the "quantitative management" school. The focus is on the development of various statistical tools and techniques to improve efficiency and allow management to make informed decisions regarding the costs and benefits of alternative courses of action. Four of these quantitative methods, which are still widely used today, include: (1) break-even analysis, (2) basic economic order quantity (EOQ) model, (3) material requirements planning (MRP), and (4) quality management. These are briefly described below and will be revisited in greater detail in Chapter 15, Operations Management and Management Control.

Break-even analysis provides formulas which assess the total fixed costs associated with producing a product, the variable costs for each unit, and the contribution made by the sale of each unit to recovering both fixed and variable costs. The break-even point is the number of units which must be sold at a given price to recover all fixed and variable costs. At that point there is neither a profit nor a loss, but rather the company "breaks even." Additional sales result in profits and fewer sales result in losses.

The *economic order quantity (EOQ) model* dates back to 1915. The formula is generally credited to Ford W. Harris, who argued in his book *Operations and Cost* that effective management of inventories is critical to sustained profitability.[4] EOQ's objective is to minimize the total costs of inventory. The inventory holding costs include housing costs (building rent, taxes, and insurance), investment costs (interest payments), material handling costs (equipment and labor costs) and other miscellaneous expenses (pilferage, scrap, and obsolescence). The holding cost increases as the order quantity increases, because larger average inventories need to be maintained. On the other hand, as the quantity ordered increases, the annual setup or ordering cost per unit decreases (for instance, material handling and tooling may be made more efficient as the quantity purchased increases). Mathematically, the EOQ model demonstrates that the optimal reorder point occurs when the total setup cost is equal to the total holding cost.

Material requirements planning (MRP) is a set of tools designed to manage components where the demand for the items is linked to another demand. For example, the demand for TV antennas is linked to the demand for TVs. To determine the number of antennas needed, a TV manufacturer starts by determining the number of TVs that will be built and when. Once management forecasts the demand for TVs, quantities required for all other components such as antennas, knobs, and screens can be computed, because all components are dependent items. MRP helps a company reduce inventory costs and ensures that all items will be available when needed. Consider the following example: "Nancy Mueller turns quiche into cash. Her firm, Nancy's Specialty Foods, is designed for today's busy lifestyle, producing 750,000 prepackaged, frozen quiche hors d'ouvres each month. MRP software has been key to her growing success. MRP is the primary management tool that keeps the ingredients and labor coming at the proper times and the schedule firm. Once Nancy's Specialty Foods knows the demand for her crabmeat quiche, she knows the demand for all of the ingredients from dough, to cheese, to crab meat, because all of the ingredients are dependent."[5]

QUALITY MANAGEMENT The need for improved product quality emerged in the 1980s, when it became apparent that the United States was lagging behind some industrialized countries, most notably Japan, in the area of product quality. Many of the tools and techniques that were used to identify quality problems and take corrective action date back decades earlier. For instance, Walter A. Shewhart, a Bell Labs statistician, developed a set of methods in the 1920s that were designed to ensure standardization and reduce quality defects. His book *Economic Control of Quality,* published in 1931, is still considered a classic. Joseph M. Juran was a statistician who in the 1940s introduced the concept of "pareto analysis," which argues that 80 percent of all quality problems may be traced to a relatively small number of causes. Phillip Crosby spent his entire career at International Telephone and Telegraph. While there, Crosby documented the enormous costs of having to fix something that was not done right the first time. His ideas were later published in the 1970s in the business best seller *Quality Is Free*. Arnand V. Feigenbaum developed the concept of *total quality control* in the 1940s, which argued for an integrated quality improvement effort across all functional areas (e.g., purchasing, finance, marketing) and not only in production and manufacturing. These ideas were later published in his 1951 book, *Total Quality Control.*

By now, most people are familiar with the concept "total quality management" popularized by W. Edwards Deming. Deming was an American statistician who advanced the use of statistics for constant quality improvement. Deming assisted many Japanese business leaders after World War II. His approach was to put quality first. Ironically he was largely ignored in the United States for most of his professional life. Deming finally achieved recognition as a quality guru in the United States when he was well into his eighties, following the publication of his book *Out of the Crisis* in 1986.

LOC-In 3 Learning Objective Check-In

Karen is a new production supervisor pondering her role as a part of management. She knows from her studies that it is important to take a long-term perspective toward strategy. She also knows that managers have to be crafty in order to survive against competition in the form of other companies. She was also thinking of how important the division of labor has been to productivity, and she could see the effects of this idea in her own work situation. Karen could not remember who, specifically, introduced these management ideas.

1. Who recognized that management strategy meant taking a long-term perspective?
   a. Adam Smith
   b. John Maynard Keynes
   c. Niccolò Machiavelli
   d. Sun Tzu

2. _____ advised leaders to be cunning and crafty in order to survive against competitive rivals.
   a. Niccolò Machiavelli
   b. Adam Smith
   c. Sun Tzu
   d. John Maynard Keynes

3. _____ recognized the powerful effect that the division of labor could have on productivity.
   a. Winslow Taylor
   b. Adam Smith
   c. Sun Tzu
   d. Abraham Maslow

Total quality management (TQM) is an organizationwide approach that focuses on quality as an overarching goal. The basis of this approach is the understanding that all employees and organizational units should be working harmoniously to satisfy the customer. Since the customer's needs are in constant flux, the organization must strive to continuously improve its systems and practices. The TQM perspective views quality as the central purpose of the organization, in contrast to the focus on efficiency advocated by the operational perspective. In TQM, quality is viewed as everybody's job, not just the role of quality control specialists, as in bureaucratic management (to be discussed below).

TQM reflects the thinking and practice of management in many of the world's most admired companies, including Toyota, Motorola, Xerox, and Ford. The key elements of the TQM approach are

- *Focus on the customer.* It is important to identify the organization's customers. External customers consume the organization's product or service. Internal customers are employees who receive the output of other employees.
- *Employee involvement.* Since quality is considered the job of all employees, employees should be involved in quality initiatives. Front-line employees are likely to have the closest contact with external customers and thus can make the most valuable contributions to quality. Therefore, employees must have the authority to innovate and improve quality. In TQM workers are often organized into empowered teams that have the authority to make quality improvements.
- *Continuous improvement.* The quest for quality is a never-ending process in which people are continuously working to improve the performance, speed, and number of features of the product or service. Continuous improvement means that small, incremental improvements that occur on a regular basis will eventually add up to vast improvements in quality.

W. Edwards Deming, considered the father of TQM, developed a set of quality principles. A summary of these principles are:

- Build quality into the product rather than rely on quality inspections after the product has already been made.
- Develop long-term relationships with suppliers, building loyalty and trust.
- Engage in continuous quality improvement.

total quality management (TQM)
An organization-wide approach that focuses on quality as an overarching goal. The basis of this approach is the understanding that all employees and organizational units should be working harmoniously to satisfy the customer.

- Supervisors should see themselves as helping employees do their job better rather than serve as monitors watching over their shoulders.
- Get employees to be more productive by using their talents rather than through fear.
- Break down departmental silos. Different units (research, design, sales, production) should work in teams.
- Do not blame employees for quality problems that usually are the result of faulty systems.
- Deemphasize quantitative goals and objectives as quality tends to suffer.
- Do not discourage employees through annual reviews and merit pay raises based on assessed individual performance as these often create defensiveness and diminish teamwork.

Bureaucratic Management

bureaucratic management
The management approach that examines the entire organization as a rational entity, using impersonal rules and procedures for decision making.

Another traditional perspective is **bureaucratic management**, which examines the entire organization as a rational entity. Max Weber (1864–1920), a German sociologist, introduced the concept of bureaucratic management as an "ideal" model that managers should try to emulate in order to operate an organization on a fair, rational, and efficient basis. According to Weber, the ideal bureaucracy should use impersonal rules and procedures for decision making rather than custom, family connections, or social class. Bureaucratic management challenged the aristocratic notion that authority should be based on birth and divine right. Instead, competence should be the criterion. For example, in the Germany of Weber's day only men of aristocratic birth could become officers in the Prussian army.

Table 1.2 summarizes the important principles of Weber's bureaucratic management. Building on Adam Smith's early work on the division of labor, the ideal bureaucracy uses the principle of *specialization of labor* to break jobs down into well-defined tasks at which a person can become very competent. Formal rules and procedures are applied consistently and uniformly so that employees and customers can count on a rational and predictable environment. Weber opposed the idiosyncratic management style of bosses who lorded it over underlings in an unpredictable and arbitrary manner. He suggested that a well-defined hierarchy with clearly delineated reporting relationships was an effective way to maintain accountability. Thus the most appropriate organizational form was a pyramid structure with many reporting levels and a vertical downward chain of command. Finally, Weber strongly believed in career advancement based on merit, which stressed competency over nepotism and family connections.

Today bureaucracy is often associated with meaningless rules and red tape, but in fact Weber's bureaucratic management made positive contributions to management thought. The use of impersonal rules and procedures provides a fair and consistent way to deal with employee relations; for example, an employee handbook spells out the rules for employee discipline, performance appraisal, and work schedules rather than allowing management to handle

TABLE 1.2 Key Characteristics of Weber's Ideal Bureaucracy

1. *Specialization of labor*	Jobs are broken down into routine, well-defined tasks so that members know what is expected of them and can become extremely competent at their particular subset of tasks.
2. *Formal rules and procedures*	Written rules and procedures specifying the behaviors desired from members facilitate coordination and ensure uniformity.
3. *Impersonality*	Rules, procedures, and sanctions are applied uniformly regardless of individual personalities and personal considerations.
4. *Well-defined hierarchy*	Multiple levels of positions, with carefully determined reporting relationships among levels, provide supervision of lower offices by higher ones, a means of handling exceptions, and the ability to establish accountability of actions.
5. *Career advancement based on merit*	Selection and promotion are based on the qualifications and performance of members.

Source: M. Weber, *The Theory of Social and Economic Organizations,* ed. and trans. A. M. Henderson and T. Parsons. New York: Free Press, 1947, pp. 328–337.

employment policies in an arbitrary manner. Similarly, Weber's emphasis on merit as the basis of career advancement is now deeply embedded into the business culture of the United States and many other countries.

Other aspects of bureaucratic management are open to criticism. In particular, the need for a well-defined hierarchy has been challenged by the quality management viewpoint, which argues that hierarchies form barriers between employees and customers and result in reductions in quality and customer satisfaction. Current practice suggests that for firms facing rapid change and competing in markets that require constant innovation (for instance, the software industry) hierarchies should be minimized, moving away from a pyramid structure toward one that is flatter, with less direct supervision and more cooperation between workers and managers. On the other hand, the bureaucratic model developed by Weber still applies to organizations seeking to minimize deviations from standard procedures and norms. In other words, the bureaucratic approach to organizing is still advisable when reliability and efficiency are paramount.

Administrative Management

The **administrative management** approach examines an organization from the perspective of the managers and executives responsible for coordinating the activities of diverse groups and units across the entire organization. It views management as a profession that can be learned by understanding basic principles. The key advocate was Henri Fayol (1841–1925), a French mining engineer and industrialist. In 1916, he wrote a book titled *Administration Industrialle et Generalle* featuring what he considered to be practical guidelines for effective management based on his administrative experiences. Even though the book was not translated into English until almost four decades later, it had a significant impact on management thought and teaching.

> **administrative management**
> The management approach that examines an organization from the perspective of the managers and executives responsible for coordinating the activities of diverse groups and units across the entire organization.

Fayol identified five functions generic to all management activities: planning, organizing, commanding, coordinating, and controlling. He codified general principles of management that he thought could be applied to the management of any organization. Conceiving of management as being made up of diverse functions is known as the *functional approach* to management.

Today, most organizations try to incorporate the following principles into policies and procedures:

- *Unity of command.* Each employee should be assigned to only one supervisor.
- *Unity of direction.* The employees' efforts should be focused on achieving organizational objectives.
- *Equity.* Employees should be treated with justice and respect.

Some other principles advocated by Fayol have not held up as well over time. For example, his principle that the *scalar, chain of command* should define the path of communication in a top-down direction has been challenged. Both upward and horizontal communication can be equally important ways of communicating in organizations. In some situations, poor communication flows through the ranks have led to major mistakes, as documented by the investigations into what went wrong at the FBI and other government agencies before the September 11 terrorist attacks. Fayol could not have foreseen the revolution that has made the knowledge worker, who may be located at the base of the organization, a source of critical information and competitive advantage for organizational decision makers.

LOC-In 4   Learning Objective Check-In

1. Nathaniel is trying to solve some management issues at his firm ABC International. He thinks that management can be learned by understanding some basic principles and functions. He believes that everyone should approach his or her role from the perspective of the managers and executives responsible for coordinating the activities of the organization. Nathaniel's approach has its roots in _____.
   a. bureaucratic management
   b. the behavioral perspective
   c. administrative management
   d. total quality management

Still, as was the case for Weber's bureaucratic model, there may be some situations (such as the military) in which Fayol's administrative principles are still applicable. In general Fayol's main contribution to management was to specify the "best universal" way to organize by separating managerial tasks into interdependent areas of responsibilities or functions. Fayol's contention that these functions should flow in a logical manner from planning to controlling is still reflected in many modern management texts, even though they are often criticized for being too orderly and rigid to help the company adapt to a changing environment.

Behavioral Perspective

behavioral perspective
The management view that knowledge of the psychological and social processes of human behavior can result in improvements in productivity and work satisfaction.

The **behavioral perspective** incorporates psychological and social processes of human behavior to improve productivity and work satisfaction. Operational theorists view management as a mechanical process in which employees would fit into any job or organization designed for optimum efficiency if given monetary incentives to do so. The behavioral perspective argues that human factors alone may affect workplace efficiency. The behavioral perspective traces its roots to the work of Mary Parker Follett and the Hawthorne studies, a series of long-term behavioral research experiments performed in an industrial setting. These works led to the human relations approach to management, which stresses the need for managers to understand the dynamics of the work group so as to positively influence employee motivation and satisfaction.

MARY PARKER FOLLETT Questioning much of the wisdom of scientific management, because it ignored the many ways in which employees could contribute ideas and exercise initiative, was Follett's primary contribution. She advocated increased employee participation, greater employee autonomy, and organizing the enterprise into "cross-functional" teams, composed of members of different departments working together on common projects. This would, in turn, foster upward and downward communication across various units. She also proposed that authority should rest with knowledge and expertise rather than with one's position in the hierarchy. "In other words, if workers have the relevant knowledge, then workers, rather than managers, should be in control of the work process itself, and managers should behave as coaches and facilitators—not as monitors and supervisors."[6]

Hawthorne effect
The finding that paying special attention to employees motivates them to put greater effort into their jobs (from the Hawthorne management studies, performed from 1924 through 1932 at Western Electric Company's plant near Chicago).

THE HAWTHORNE STUDIES The Hawthorne studies were performed at the Western Electric Company's Hawthorne plant near Chicago from 1924 to 1932 under the direction of Harvard University researchers Elton Mayo and Fritz Roethlisberger. Their original purpose was to study the effects of physical working conditions on employee productivity and fatigue.

In the first set of studies, light was steadily decreased for an experimental group of employees, while illumination remained constant for the control group of employees working in a different area. Despite the different levels of illumination, the performance of both groups of employees rose consistently. This result surprised the researchers, who expected the control group to outperform its experimental counterpart. They concluded that the special attention paid to the employees in the studies motivated them to put greater effort into their jobs. They labelled the phenomenon the **Hawthorne effect**, and suggested that when a manager or leader shows concern for employees, their motivation and productivity levels are likely to improve.

Although individual workers perform specialized tasks on an assembly line, they work as a group rather than as individuals.

Later studies at Hawthorne revealed that the informal organization had a profound effect on group productivity. Mayo and Roethlisberger discovered that a work group would establish its own informal group performance norm, which represented what it considered to be a fair level of performance. Individuals who exceeded the group performance norm were considered "rate-busters," and those who performed below the norm were viewed as "chiselers." The work group disciplined both types of norm violations because ratebusters could speed up the pace of work beyond what was considered fair, while chiselers avoided doing their fair share of the work. The work group was likely to convince rate-busters to slow down and chiselers to work faster. These findings suggest that the influence of the work group may be as significant as the influence of the supervisor. Thus supervisors need the support of group members in establishing performance norms that converge with the work expectations of management.

The Hawthorne studies provided evidence that employee attitudes significantly affect performance in a manner which differs from the financial incentives championed by advocates of scientific management. Understanding the informal work organization made it possible to create cooperation between employees and management that resulted in a more productive organization.

HUMAN RELATIONS   The Hawthorne studies generated intense interest in the human side of various companies. Managers who previously concentrated on job design, work methods, or applications of technology to the task environment turned their attention to group behaviors, leadership, and employee attitudes. The **human relations approach** to management made relationships between employees and supervisors a vital aspect of management. Its advocates were people trained in the behavioral sciences, such as clinical and social psychologists, who emphasized building collaborative and cooperative relationships between supervisors and workers. Two key aspects of the human relations approach are focused on employee motivation and leadership style.

human relations approach
A management approach that views the relationships between employees and supervisors as the most salient aspect of management.

Employee Motivation   Abraham Maslow (1908–1970), a clinical psychologist who developed a theory of motivation based on a *hierarchy of needs,* assumed that unsatisfied human needs motivate behavior. The underlying assumption in Maslow's work was *humanism,* or the belief that the basic inner natures of people are good. This represented a stark contrast to Freudian psychology, which assumed the inner nature of personality was destructive, violent, and evil. This new, more positive view of human nature had a substantial impact on the fields of both psychology and management.

The hierarchy of needs model, explained in greater detail in Chapter 12, suggests that managers can motivate employees by providing an environment in which the employees can satisfy their most pressing needs. From a human relations perspective, this suggests that managers must develop positive relationships with subordinates in order to discover what their motivational needs are. For example, a manager who knows that employees are motivated by social relationships may be able to facilitate good coworker relations that will be nurturing to work group

LOC-In 5   Learning Objective Check-In

Iris from finance, Sampson from marketing, and Josephine from operations are on a cross-functional team of managers with the purpose of developing an approach by which to manage all three departments, which will be working together much more on client projects in the near future. In their first meeting, each manager offered his or her individual perspective on management. Iris said, "Employees are motivated by more than just pay. I find that when I praise my workers and tailor the job characteristics to their abilities, they work much harder." Sampson quickly pointed out that if he simply pays special attention to his employees, it motivates them to put greater effort into their jobs. Josephine recognized Sampson's point, and then offered her advice based on her own assumptions about employees. She said, "Employees are inherently lazy and lack ambition. We have to make sure we supervise them closely, or they will not work hard."

1. Which management perspective best reflects what Iris initially proposed?
    a. Bureaucratic management
    b. Administrative management
    c. Behavioral perspective
    d. Human relations approach

2. Which management phenomenon was Sampson talking about?
    a. The Hawthorne effect
    b. Behavioral perspective
    c. Theory Y assumptions
    d. Total quality management

3. Josephine thought that employees are lazy and lack ambition. Which perspective was she demonstrating?
    a. Human relations approach
    b. Contingency theory
    c. Theory X assumptions
    d. Theory Y assumptions

TABLE 1.3 McGregor's Theory X and Theory Y Assumptions

Assumptions of Theory X

1. The average human being has an inherent dislike of work and will avoid it if he or she can.
2. People need to be coerced, controlled, directed, and threatened with punishment to get them to put forward adequate effort toward the organization's ends.
3. The average person prefers to be directed, wants to avoid responsibility, has relatively little ambition, and wants security above all.

Assumptions of Theory Y

1. The expenditure of physical and mental effort in work is as natural as in play or rest—the typical human being does not inherently dislike work.
2. External control and threat of punishment are not the only means for bringing about effort toward a company's goals. A person will exercise self-direction and self-control in the pursuit of the objective to which he is committed.
3. The average person learns, under the right conditions, not only to accept but to seek responsibility.
4. The capacity to exercise a relatively high degree of imagination, ingenuity, and creativity in the solution of organizational problems is widely, not narrowly, distributed in the population.
5. The intellectual potential of most people is only partially utilized in most organizations.

Source: Adapted from D. McGregor, *The Human Side of Enterprise.* New York: McGraw-Hill, 1960, pp. 33–48.

productivity. Maslow's ideas suggest that employee motivation is more complex than was assumed by the scientific management approach, which focused strictly on pay. Maslow assumed that pay can motivate only lower-level needs, and once those are satisfied it loses its power to shape employee behavior. Instead, nonmonetary factors such as praise, recognition, and job characteristics motivate human behavior.

Leadership Style Douglas McGregor (1908–1964), a professor at MIT, used a human relations perspective to compare the assumptions leaders make about employees. He called them Theory X and Theory Y (see Table 1.3).

Leaders and managers who operate under Theory X assumptions believe that employees are inherently lazy and lack ambition, and these managers use the external controls of punishments and rewards to drive employees to achieve organizational goals. They tend to supervise subordinates closely and deprive them of opportunities to show individual initiative and creativity. McGregor believed that highly controlling and autocratic supervisory styles based on Theory X assumptions would most likely be inefficient because they waste the human potential that could make substantial contributions to the organization.

According to McGregor, leaders who hold Theory Y assumptions believe that most employees enjoy work and seek to make useful contributions to the organization. Employees are looking for ways to exercise creativity and initiative, and will most likely perform up to or even exceed job expectations when given responsibility. McGregor believed that managing on the basis of Theory Y assumptions allows the organization to utilize the human potential of all employees and become more productive. Sharing power and responsibilities with employees will make them more committed to organizational goals. McGregor's Theory Y assumptions fit with contemporary leadership styles that stress employee participation and empowerment, and they are often used in knowledge-based organizations where employee knowledge is a source of competitive advantage.

Contemporary Management Perspectives

Contemporary management perspectives include systems theory, contingency theory, and the learning organization perspective. Each of these contemporary viewpoints builds on the work of earlier management thinkers.

THE SYSTEMS APPROACH The operational, bureaucratic, administrative, and behavioral approaches studied management by dividing it into elements or components such as work scheduling, motions, and functions, or employee needs and attitudes. While taking things apart is useful for analytical purposes, in reality all relevant parts of organizational activity interact with each other. System theorists warn us that "reductionism" in management thought may lead to simplistic prescriptions and may not help us understand why some firms perform at higher levels than others. In other words, system theorists believe that the whole is greater than the sum of the parts.

Chester I. Barnard's Early Systems Perspective   Barnard was a former president of New Jersey Bell Telephone Company. Based on his experience as a practicing executive, he believed that isolating specific management functions and principles may lead to the proverbial failing to see the forest for the trees. In his classic book, *The Functions of the Executive* (1938), Barnard depicted organizations as cooperative systems: "A cooperative system is a complex of physical, biological, personal, and social components which are in a specific systematic relationship by reason of the cooperation of two or more persons for at least one definite end."[7] He viewed organizations as complex, dynamic wholes where willingness to serve, common purpose, and communication are critical.

General Systems Theory   From the perspective of **systems theory** an organization is a *system* consisting of interrelated parts that function in a holistic way to achieve a common purpose. The system takes *inputs* (resources) from the external environment and puts them through a *transformation process* (a technology) that converts them to *outputs* (finished products and services). The outputs are then put into the external environment.

> **systems theory**
> A modern management theory that views the organization as a system of interrelated parts that function in a holistic way to achieve a common purpose.

The *environment* is the market, technological, social, and political conditions and forces that surround the system, critical factors that managers must consider as they seek to achieve organizational goals and objectives. The manner in which the outputs are received in the environment determines organization survival. If the environment rejects the outputs because quality is too low, the organization is likely to perish. The system receives **feedback**, information about how well the outputs were received, and uses the feedback to adjust the selection of inputs and the transformation process.

> **feedback**
> Information received back from the receiver, which allows the sender to clarify the message if its true meaning is not received.

Systems theory has contributed some important concepts that affect management thinking. These include open and closed systems, subsystems, synergy, and equifinality.

Open and Closed Systems   Open systems interact with the environment in order to survive. Closed systems do not need to interact with the environment. In reality, all organizations depend on the environment for inputs and for the purchase of outputs. The operational and bureaucratic perspectives on management treated the organization as if it were a closed system by overlooking the effect of the environment on management practice. Systems theory argues that the environment must always be taken into consideration in management decision making.

Subsystems   Subsystems are interdependent parts of a system. A change in one subsystem affects the other subsystems. For example, when a company changes its reward system for sales representatives from salary to commission, the volume of sales revenues is likely to increase, which in turn, increases the level of output required from the manufacturing system. If the manufacturing system is operating at full capacity, an improved manufacturing process may be needed in order to satisfy the increased demand.

Synergy   When the whole is greater than the sum of its parts, *synergy* exists. Management of organizational subsystems can result in synergies. For example, Microsoft sells more business applications software because all its applications software products are compatible with the Windows operating system. In other words, Microsoft's Windows operating system unit provides synergy for its business applications unit because the compatible products create value for the customer. Without the operating system unit, Microsoft would sell less business applications software.

Equifinality   In an open system, equifinality means that an organization can reach the same goal through a number of different routes. Also, not every organization must begin from the same place or use the same tactics to achieve success. Advocates of scientific management believed that management could be reduced to "one best way." By contrast, systems theory suggests that different inputs, subsystems, and transformation processes can lead to similar outcomes.

contingency theory
The management theory that there is no "one best way" to manage and organize an organization because situational characteristics, called contingencies, differ; also, the view that no HR strategy is "good" or "bad" in and of itself but rather depends on the situation or context in which it is used.

CONTINGENCY THEORY   According to **contingency theory**, what works for one organization may not work for another, because situational characteristics differ. The situational characteristics are called *contingencies*. Managers need to understand the key contingencies that determine the most effective management practices in a given situation. Thus, whether application of a management principle or rule (such as division of work and a well-defined hierarchy) leads to positive results depends on the particular conditions. Each situation has its own nuances and presents to the manager a unique set of problems. Lack of "fit," or a mismatch between management practice and what the situation calls for, leads to poor performance. Alternatively, high performance results when management practice is attuned to or congruent with the demands of the particular context being faced. Contingency theory strongly warns that managers must be flexible in order to apply those practices and techniques that are most appropriate to specific situations.

An example of an important contingency is the degree of change in the environment. Change can include the development of new technologies or the entry of new competitors to the market. When the environment is turbulent, managers are likely to select a *decentralized organization structure* in which authority is pushed to lower levels so that decisions can be made rapidly and flexibly. When the environment is stable and predictable, managers select a *centralized organization structure* in which decisions are made on a top-down basis to exercise more efficient control over resources. Contingency theory suggests that a manager should first identify and understand the contingency, then select the management practice that best fits the situation. Other contingencies include organization cultures, industry structures, and products and process or manufacturing technologies.

LOC-In 6   Learning Objective Check-In

1. Leon and jerry, both managers at the same firm, were having a conversation on the management approaches they take. Leon finished telling Jerry how he successfully motivated one employee by offering him tangible rewards for higher output. Jerry quickly pointed out that what works for Leon's department might not work for his because of different situational characteristics. "What's more," he said, "if I don't fit my management style to the situation at hand, I can always predict poor performance." Which management perspective best reflects what Jerry is explaining?
   a. Contingency theory
   b. Behavioral perspective
   c. Administrative management
   d. Total quality management

---

learning organization
The management approach based on an organization anticipating change faster than its counterparts to have an advantage in the market over its competitors.

THE LEARNING ORGANIZATION   The **learning organization** approach suggests that organizations that can "learn" faster than their counterparts have an advantage over competitors in the marketplace. Rather than *reacting* to change, which is a normal part of the business landscape, organizations need to *anticipate* change so they are well positioned to satisfy their customers' future needs with the most appropriate products and services. Therefore, a learning organization attempts to institutionalize continuous learning. This means that knowledge and information will be shared between employees and teams rather than controlled by an elite group of technocrats. Organizational structures should facilitate the sharing and transfer of information as broadly and quickly as possible. Flat structures with few management layers and cross-functional teams that bring together people from different business or scientific disciplines are examples of ways to break down barriers that keep people from sharing information and learning from each other.

■ Emerging Perspectives and Issues

There are two trends that are likely to influence management practice and theory in the foreseeable future, reflecting fundamental changes in how organizations create and deliver products and services: the modular organization and the intangible organization.

The Modular Organization

The classical organizational form with employees who work in departments that are housed within functional units (such as production, sales, human resource management, and so on), which are in turn housed within business units or divisions (corresponding, for instance, to product lines), which in turn report directly to corporate top executives, is being replaced in varying degrees by the so-called *modular corporation,* or what some people refer to as "disaggregated corporation." What this means is that every function not regarded as crucial is outsourced to an independent organization, often on a global basis (see Management Close-Up 1.1 on page 6). Hence, internal organizational forms are simplified since managers contract with and coordinate the activities of outsourcing partners rather than supervise long-term company employees who used to perform these tasks. This evolving organizational form is likely to have a major impact on most of the management issues discussed in this text (such as organizational culture, leadership, and motivation) but the effects are as yet not well understood.

The Intangible Organization

Technology is playing a dramatic role in how organizations function. The emphasis on innovation and creativity means that businesses are shifting their resources from tangible (such as plant and equipment) to intangible (such as know-how and product design) investments. For instance, according to *BusinessWeek's* calculations, the top 10 biggest U.S. corporations have increased R&D spending by 42 percent since 2000 but they have increased capital spending on tangible goods by only 2 percent.[8] The modular corporation discussed above probably has something to do with this trend since factories and production facilities of outsourcing partners, mostly overseas, are replacing such investments in the United States. This is likely to have huge implications for the practice of management as we know it. In the words of one management expert, "ideas, information, and relationships are becoming more important than production machinery, physical products, and structured jobs. Many employees perform much of their work on computers and may work in virtual teams, connected electronically to colleagues around the world. Even in factories that produce physical goods, machines have taken over much of the routine and uniform work, freeing workers to use more of their minds and abilities. Managers and employees in today's companies focus on opportunities rather than efficiencies, which requires that they be flexible, creative, and unconstrained by rigid rules and structured tasks."[9]

CONCLUDING THOUGHTS

In the chapter's introductory vignette, we posed some, critical thinking questions regarding Toyota's success up to 2010 compared with the well-publicized recent problems of General Motors. Now that you have had the opportunity to learn about different management perspectives, let's look again at the questions.

First, General Motors was a pioneer in the use of scientific management techniques, it lost much of its edge in efficiency and has suffered from a reputation for spotty quality. Toyota was able to produce cars at lower costs and of better quality. Second, General Motors was not able to adapt to change as well as Toyota. International competition eroded much of the domestic market share General Motors used to enjoy, and its company was not able to make the necessary adjustments early on to prevent the slide.

Third, General Motors seem to have put in place strategies that have not led to a sustainable competitive advantage. These strategies appear to have missed the target in terms of what customers want. Toyota's strategy, on the other hand, has been customer driven during the past 30 years or so. Fourth, while

starting from a position of overwhelming advantage 40 or so years ago (when they dominated the automobile market), General Motors and Ford appear to have made poor use of human, financial, and physical resources. Toyota, on the other hand, became an exemplar of successful delegation of tasks, hiring and retaining highly committed workers, and marshalling and allocating resources in a timely and cost-effective manner. Toyota beat General Motors with low engineering costs, low manufacturing costs, and near-perfect quality. Toyota was able to accomplish this with less hierarchy, which saves on middle-management costs and spurs greater worker initiative, since workers are expected to act on their own rather than follow orders under close supervision.

Fifth, Toyota was able to manage environmental forces successfully by globalizing its operations, and it became very flexible in its ability to respond to local conditions. Sixth, Toyota was able to achieve its success while creating a lot of goodwill and cultivating a positive image as a great place to work, hiring hundreds of thousands of American workers and making billions of dollars of purchases from domestic suppliers. This means that Toyota amassed a lot of political capital, making it difficult for General Motors to secure government protection on nationalistic "Buy American" grounds. Lastly, General Motors was not able to break away from their confrontational bargaining relationships with labor unions, and their inability to meet prior commitments (for high wages, health care, retirement, and the like) is fueling an already negative labor relations climate.

Paradoxically it became obvious at the beginning of this decade that Toyota had become complacent and a victim of its own success. An intense emphasis on cost-cutting and rapid expansion resulted in quality problems, poor customer relations, and a public perception that the company was trying to hide its mistakes. Many feel that "managing by the numbers" led to a culture where what really mattered was meeting financial targets and softer performance criteria, such as customer satisfaction, employee commitment, innovation and reputation, were neglected. As noted in the introductory vignette, the situation imploded in 2010 when Toyota was forced to admit its mistakes, faced trial in 51 deaths, and had to spend billions of dollars in rebates to attract weary customers who had been bombarded in the press with news of Toyota's troubles. Some politicians made Toyota's situation even worse by blowing out of proportion Toyota's quality problems and publicly accusing the company of ethical lapses by not recognizing the mechanical problems early on.

FOCUSING ON THE FUTURE: Using Management Theory in Daily Life

Your Management Career

Welcome to management! A degree in management offers you many career options. Five of the most common career tracks are described below. As you read this text and think about your skills, abilities, and interests, you may decide that one of these is right for you.

General or Operations Manager

If organization is your strong suit, and you can move easily between the "big picture" and the smallest details, you may want to consider a career in operations. Students with an operations emphasis may end up in positions such as COO (Chief Operating Officer) or General Manager. These managers are responsible for improving the flow of the work process throughout the organization, and they need to be knowledgeable about everything "P"— production, pricing, people, profit, policy, and products. General or Operations Managers place a heavy emphasis on efficiency and effectiveness. Like most managers, Operations Managers spend a lot of their time in meetings—reviewing tasks and supplies for the day, checking on general project status, assigning and reassigning resources based on market projections, performance data, work flow, and personnel, coordinating with other departments to ensure that employees get the right resources at the right time and that schedules are coordinated, and handling administrative issues such as performance reviews, inventory, quality assessments, and changes to policies and procedures.

Accounting or Financial Manager

If numbers are your playthings, and money matters most to you, you may want to consider a career in either accounting or finance. Accountants are the "detail people"—they handle the books for an organization, and they create and manage accounting records that conform to reporting regulations. They also prepare tax returns and reports, and ensure that taxes are paid in a timely fashion. Financial Managers look at "big picture" money issues—analyzing the financial status of the organization, preparing financial forecasts and budgets, assessing the risks of potential investments, and controlling risk and loss through insurance and other programs. Accounting and Financial Managers often work for consulting companies, and when they do, they must have sales and relationship management skills in addition to their mathematical and analytical abilities.

Human Resources Manager

If problem solving is your gift, and people come to you for advice about everything from how to handle their personal relationships to what to do with their investments, HR may be for you. HR managers are responsible for the flow of people through the organization—everything from planning what types of people and skills will be needed, to recruiting and hiring, to training and development, to compensation and benefits, to retirement and/or termination. They spend a lot of their time resolving conflicts between employees, between employees and managers, and between the company and various outside vendors such as insurance agents and other benefits providers. Many students who "like people" think that they may want a career in HR, but be careful. The most successful HR managers have a firm grasp of finance and accounting principles, can think strategically in the interests of the organization, and have the ability to sell their programs and policies at all levels of the organization.

Marketing or Communications Manager

If you are a "creative type" and you are particularly good with either visual images or words, marketing may be the career for you. Marketing is all about getting an organization's products to the customer at a price that works for both buyer and seller, and encouraging people to buy using words and images. During this process you may have to develop pricing strategies, analyze market trends, work closely with product designers and distributors to match market trends with products or services, and create marketing campaigns with advertising and promotions managers. The other side of marketing is the Communication Manager, who presents the face of the company to the public. Communication Managers must be politically savvy—they know how to use words and the media to the best advantage of the company. They are responsible for writing press releases, drafting speeches for company executives, developing and maintaining the company's image through logos and signs, and managing special events to promote the company name, products, or services. The best Marketing and Communication managers are highly skilled interpersonally. They truly care about customer satisfaction and understand how others will interpret their words.

Entrepreneur

As a child, did you ever charge your friends to play your video games? Start your own Web site with an eye toward making a profit? Entrepreneurs often start creating businesses at a very early age. If you have a passion for hard work, a tolerance for taking risks, and a focus on the bottom line, you may want to consider becoming an entrepreneur. Successful entrepreneurs have skills in all aspects of management, and they know how to cover the skills they don't have by hiring the right people for their organization. They must be able to organize their business, plan tasks for themselves and others, handle the company's books and finances, sell their ideas to others, manage the people working for them, evaluate risks, take initiative, and develop new products, services, and processes for the business. Entrepreneurship is often lonely and undercompensated work, but it offers freedom and unlimited potential to those who are willing to risk everything.

A Note on Management Careers

Remember that all of the preceding are *managers* and as such, their jobs share certain similarities. For example, all managers have to get work done through others and that means that they have to know how to motivate and inspire their employees, which is different from doing the work yourself. In addition, managers have to be aware of more big picture issues—their job is to plan and organize the work for others, then to make sure that the work gets done, not necessarily to do the work themselves. In addition, most people find that as they move higher on their chosen career ladders, their jobs become more heavily focused on sales. A manager who cannot sell his or her ideas to others in the organization, or a manager who cannot bring new clients into the organization, is not likely to be successful. Finally, all managers are concerned about money—they create and approve budgets, and then must manage resources to fit within those budgets.

If you want to learn more about any of the jobs listed above, the best place to start is on the Internet. 0*NET (http://online.onetcenter.org) is published by the U.S. government, and it contains a wealth of information on occupations, including tasks, abilities, work activities, knowledge, skills, work context, job zones, work styles and wages and employment trends. The Small Business Administration Web site (http://www.sba.gov) is a key resource for entrepreneurs—their "Starting Business" page (http://www.sba.gov/starting_business/index.html) covers start-up basics, planning, financing, marketing, employees, tax topics, legal aspects, and special interest topics for people considering starting their own business. Vault (http://www.vault.com) is a Web site devoted to providing career information—their "Day in the Life" reports can give you new insights on what life in various industries is really like (http://www.vault.com/nr/ht_list.jsp?ht_type=1.)

Now that you know a little about the different kinds of management jobs, you will probably want to know how these managers use the information you are learning in this class. Each of the managers described above uses the concepts and theories described in this text on a daily basis. Look for boxes like this one at the end of each chapter called "Focusing on the Future: Using Management Theory in Daily Life" to find out more.

Summary of Learning Objectives

This chapter has provided an overview of the field of management and how it has evolved over time. The following are summaries of the chapter discussions for each of the learning objectives that we stated at the outset of this chapter.

1 Understand the challenges organizations face in the new millennium.

- *Be both efficient and effective.* This requires making the best use of resources and achieving goals that provide the firm with a sustainable competitive advantage.
- *Deal with key contemporary management issues.* Three key issues have been identified in this chapter: coping with and adapting to rapid change on a daily basis, satisfying the needs of demanding customers who have more choices than ever before, and making ethical decisions.
- *Be capable of managing new forms of organizations.* This requires coordination of different levels of managers (strategic, tactical, operational), employees who are expected to show initiative and enjoy high autonomy (empowerment), and teams composed of employees who cut across functional and disciplinary lines.

2 Specify the functions and roles of successful managers.

- *Managerial functions.* These are **planning** and strategizing (to assist the firm in meeting its mission), **organizing** (allocating of resources to meet the firm's mission), **leading** (energizing organizational members to contribute their most, both as individuals and as members of a team), and **controlling** (monitoring results and processes on an ongoing basis to detect deviations from the preferred state).
- *Managerial roles.* There are three major roles or behaviors expected of managers, namely an *interpersonal role* (engage in active communication with relevant parties), an *informational role* (obtain, interpret, and provide information to others), and a *decision-making role* (make choices and take responsibility for them).

3 Explain the origins of management as an academic discipline.

The earliest management thinkers include Sun Tzu, an ancient Chinese general who recognized that management strategy meant taking a long-term perspective; Niccolò Machiavelli, a Renaissance Italian who advised leaders to be cunning and crafty in order to survive against ambitious rivals; and Adam Smith, an 18th-century philosopher who recognized that the division of labor could have a powerful effect on an organization's productivity.

- **Scientific management**, represented by the ideas of Frederick Winslow Taylor, focuses on using experts to teach workers the best methods and techniques to do their jobs. Employees do the physical labor and managers provide the planning and organizing. It was assumed that employees would be willing to cooperate with managers, since employees were to be paid according to their level of output, and they could earn more pay this way.
- **Quantitative management** emphasizes the development of statistical tools and techniques to improve efficiency.
- **Quality management** focuses on approaches that may be used to improve quality and reduce the time and effort devoted to replacing what was done wrong in the first place. While originally concerned with manufacturing, many quality-management concepts have since been applied to the service sector as well.

4 Describe the bureaucratic and administrative approaches to the study of management.

These perspectives emerged during the early 20th century and were primarily concerned with the efficient use of organizational structures and processes. Many of the following ideas are still used today when deciding how to set up organizational hierarchies, reporting relationships, and policies and procedures.

- The idea of **bureaucratic management** was developed by Max Weber, a German sociologist. Bureaucratic management is governed by a set of impersonal rules and policies, including merit as a basis for career advancement. Weber believed that bureaucratic management was the most efficient way to organize and govern an enterprise.
- The **administrative management perspective,** advocated by Henri Fayol, assumes that general principles of management can be applied to any situation or circumstance. Fayol divided the activities of management into five functions that are still used today: planning, organizing, commanding, coordinating, and controlling.

5 Explain the behavioral perspective in analyzing management issues.

The **behavioral perspective** in management thought focuses on understanding how to manage human factors to improve workplace productivity. It traces its roots to the works of Mary Parker Follett and the Hawthorne studies performed at the Western Electric Company during the 1920s and 1930s. These studies suggested that leaders are able to positively influence employee motivation and productivity by showing concern for employee relationships.

Inspired by the works of Follett and the Hawthorne studies, the *human relations* approach to management emphasized work relationships as the key to a productive workplace. Abraham Maslow developed a theory of employee motivation based on a hierarchy of human needs. Maslow believed that managers need to view employees from a humanistic perspective, identify unfulfilled employee needs, and then show employees how these needs may be satisfied in the context of the workplace. The result should be a higher level of employee motivation and productivity. Douglas McGregor, another advocate of the human relations approach, examined the assumptions made by leaders. Theory X leaders assume that subordinates avoid work, whereas Theory Y leaders assume that subordinates want to do good work and are interested in taking on more desirable tasks, and they encourage employees to utilize more of their human potential for the good of the organization. While difficult to test empirically, with mostly conflicting results in academic studies, these human relations concepts are still very influential among management practitioners.

6 Interpret recent approaches to the study of management.

- Contemporary management perspectives that came to light in the mid-to-late 20th century include **systems theory, contingency theory,** and the **learning organization.** According to these perspectives, it is futile to search for "one best way" to manage a firm because organizations are in constant interaction with the external environment. Instead, managers must take the external environment into account so as to match the appropriate management practices to the surrounding circumstances for an effective outcome. The so-called learning organization is more concerned with problem solving than efficiency (which was the primary focus of the bureaucratic and administrative management perspectives).
- Some emerging management perspectives include the "modular organization" (where the firm becomes a shell, outsourcing many of its activities to separate independent organizations) and the "intangible organization" (where ideas, information, and relationships are critical to success).

Discussion Questions

1. Going back to the chapter's introductory vignette, do you think Toyota and General Motors can reverse their fortunes in the foreseeable future? Why or why not? What should they do in order to improve their situation? Explain your answer.
2. Explain Machiavelli's advice to leaders that "it is better to be feared than loved." In the context of contemporary management, consider this modification of Machiavelli's advice: "It is better for a leader to be *respected* than loved." Would you agree or disagree with this statement? Discuss its implications.
3. What were the important contributions of scientific management? What were its limitations?

4. Examine the list of Fayol's 14 principles of management. Which principles are still useful today? Which principles appear to be obsolete, according to contemporary management thinking?

5. According to the human relations perspective, leaders can influence certain factors within work groups that can result in improved performance and satisfaction. Describe how a leader would be likely to put knowledge of this perspective into practice and obtain increased performance from his or her subordinates.

6. Think of an example that illustrates an application of the following contemporary theories:
   a. Systems theory.
   b. Contingency theory.

7. How do the management perspectives discussed in this chapter relate to each of the chapter's Management Close-Ups ("How Outsourcing Is Transforming Whole Industries and Changing the Way We Work," "Enforcing Ethics at Work ," and "Key Performance Indicators")? Explain your answer.

Management Minicase 1.1
Biz Majors Get an F for Honesty

Research by the Center for Academic Integrity (RCAI), a think tank affiliated with the Kenan Institute for Ethics at Duke University, shows that undergraduate business students do more cheating than just about anyone else. The survey of nearly 50,000 students at 69 schools found that 26 percent of business majors admitted to serious cheating on exams, and 54 percent admitted to cheating on written assignments, including plagiarism and poaching a friend's homework. Another survey shows that only 40 percent of the top 50 U.S. business schools have a stand-alone ethics course. The U.S. Ethics Institute recommends that all business students have concrete knowledge of ethical issues in business; develop concrete ethics skills, such as learning when to speak up; and be engaged in a process where they can develop greater understanding of their own ethical views and the views of others.

DISCUSSION QUESTIONS

1. What do you think the survey results imply for people who are likely to become managers?
2. Do you think that the ethical climate is getting better or worse? Explain.
3. What can business schools do to promote ethical thinking among students? Are they doing enough?

Based on: "Business Schools receive only a C+ in ethics," *Ethics World*, March 30, 2010, http://www.ethicsworld.org, "Ethics education at top 50 business schools," *Ethics World*, March 30, 2010, http://www.ethicsworld.org; A. Oh, "Upfront," *BusinessWeek*, February 6, 2006, p. 14.

Management Minicase 1.2
Google: Using a Company's Culture to Conquer the World

Google is a company that is quirky and practically shouts about it. The lava lamps and electric scooters that replaced the original Segways at the "Googleplex" headquarters in Mountain View have become iconic. There is also a sand-volleyball court, a pair of heated lap pools, and, for some reason, a ball pit with dozens of brightly colored plastic balls, like the one you throw the kids into at Ikea. The dress code? "You have to wear something," says CEO Schmidt. And even he can't explain the (phoneless) London-style phone booth that stands in one hallway—"Who bought that?!" he wonders aloud, sounding like the sole sane person in a loony bin. Above all, there is Google's fetishistic devotion to food; the company serves three excellent meals a day, free, to its staff, at several cafes. One of their chefs, Charlie Ayers, once cooked for members of the Grateful Dead. At Google, we are not talking meat loaf and bug juice. For example, the executive chef from an acclaimed area restaurant recently prepared sugar-pie pumpkin lasagna and cedar spring lamb chops for Google employees.

What's intriguing is that this slightly goofy, self-indulgent culture has proved so adept at nuts-and bolts business. Schmidt says he intentionally propagated the perception of Google as a wacky place to allow the company to build up its business under the radar. "With the lava lamps and scooters, everybody thought we were idiots, the last vestiges of the dot-coms," he says. "It worked until it leaked out how well we were doing." Many details didn't become known until Google had to file its financials just before going public in 2004.

Every Google employee is meant to divide his or her time in to three parts; 70 percent devoted to Google's core businesses, search and advertising; 20 percent on pursuits related to the core; and 10 percent on far-out ideas.

Google's Motto is "Don't be evil." Google was accused of being hypocritical after purportedly collaborating with the Chinese government in censoring the Internet (what was called "neutered Google") and helping the Chinese government crack down on dissidents. In 2010 Google decided that it will take a bold step on the right side by refusing to censor even if this means pulling out of the potentially lucrative Chinese market (more on this in the introductory vignette of Chapter 6, Decision Making).

DISCUSSION QUESTIONS

1. What management aspects are unique to Google as described in this case? How and why have these aspects contributed to Google's success? Explain.
2. Do you see any downside to how Google is managed? Do you think Google can maintain its unique management approach well into the future?
3. To what extent do you think Google's management style may be effectively used by other organizations? Explain.
4. Do you think Google had more to gain or to lose by refusing to collaborate with the Chinese government?

Sources: Based on R. McKinnon, "Google gets on the right side of history," *Wall Street Journal*, January 14, 2010, c-1; J. Vascellaro, "Google warns of China exit over hacking," *Wall Street Journal*, January 13, 2010, A-1; L. Crovitz, "China's web crackdown continues," *Wall Street Journal*, January 11, 2010. A-17; J. Vascellaro and A. Back, "Google prepares for its next step in China," *Wall Street Journal*, January 20, 2010, B-5; B. Einhorn, "Google and China; A Win for Liberty and Strategy," *BusinessWeek*, January 25, 2010, p. 35; A. Back and L. Chao, "Google's Tangled Chinese Web," *Wall Street Journal*, March 26, 2010, B-2; L. Chao, "Google braces for fallout in China," *Wall Street Journal*, March 24, 2010, p. A-1; J. Vascellaro, "Brin drove Google's pullback," *Wall Street Journal*, March 25, 2010, B-1, D. MacMillan, "Google's new billion dollar baby," *BusinessWeek*, February 22, 2010, p. 22.

Individual/Collaborative Learning Case 1.1
Is the United States Falling Behind in Global Brain Race?

Science and technology are fundamental to a sustainable competitive advantage for companies across a wide range of industries. There is a growing controversy between those who believe the United States is about to be deposed as the world's leader in science and technology (which will undermine the competitiveness of U.S firms) and those who believe that the doomsayers are focusing on the wrong indicators. A summary of each perspective follows.

We Are Falling Behind!

While the 20th century had the arms race, the competition in this century will be a brain race, says science policy analyst Michael Lubell of the American Physical Society. "Today's Sputnik? It's a little bigger. It's called China," he says. "The projected growth in high-technology products from there is staggering." The stakes are high. The United States now leads the world in spending on research and development—estimated to reach $328.9 billion this year—from both government and private sources. Innovation driven by such spending creates as much as 85 percent of the growth in economic productivity, according to a National Academy of Sciences report, "Rising above the Gathering Storm." And productivity growth determines who is the leader and who is a follower in the global economy. A 15 percent shortfall in British productivity by 1990 transformed "the once proud empire to a second-rate economy in little more than a lifetime," in the words of economic writer Sylvia Nasar.

According to the National Academy report, "Although the United States continues to possess the world's stronger science and engineering enterprise, its position is jeopardized both by evolving weakness at home and by growing strength abroad." The report notes some "alarming" concerns:

- One U.S. chemist's or engineer's salary is enough to hire five Chinese chemists or 11 Indian engineers. Last year, China graduated 500,000 engineers; India, 200,000; and North America, 70,000. The training quality of a high proportion of Chinese and Indian engineers matches and in some cases surpasses that of U.S. engineers.
- The U.S. trade balance in high-technology goods fell from $33 billion in the black in 1990 to $24 billion in the red a few years later.
- U.S. funding of "research in most physical sciences, mathematics, and engineering has declined or remained flat—in real purchasing power—for several decades."
- Leadership in high-energy physics, a U.S. franchise since the Manhattan Project built the atomic bomb, is shifting overseas. The most powerful particle accelerator on Earth is now outside the United States for the first time in decades. The atom smasher was successfully tested in 2010 at Europe's CERN lab in Switzerland. Similarly, U.S. scientists complain that fusion reactor tests and underground physics labs needed to stay ahead in the most cutting-edge areas are all overseas.
- According to a *BusinessWeek* survey 71 percent of senior executives believe that poor math and science education in the United States will lead to higher unemployment. Another *BusinessWeek* survey indicates that at the beginning of this decade U.S. employment of scientists and engineers—the inventors who create the next generation of products—has fallen by 6.3 percent, much faster than that of other occupations, reducing the incentive for young people to follow this career path.

Our Culture Makes Us Number 1

You can pick your statistics. The U.S. leads the world by an immense margin in just about every measure of intellectual and technological achievement: Ph.D.s, patents, peer-reviewed articles, Nobel Prizes. But in the end, it's the culture. The economy follows culture, and U.S. culture is today, as ever, uniquely suited for growth, innovation, and advancement. The most obvious bedrock of success is entrepreneurial spirit. The United States has the most risk-taking, most laissez-faire, least regulated economy in the advanced Western world. The United States is heartily disdained by its coddled and controlled European cousins for its cowboy capitalism. But it is precisely American's tolerance for creative destruction—industries failing, others rising, workers changing jobs and cities and skills with an alacrity and insouciance that Europeans find astonishing—that keeps its economy churning and advancing.

The United States is uniquely socially mobile, ethnically mixed and racially tolerant. The United States is, in Ben Wattenberg's phrase, the first universal nation, indeed the only universal nation. Every street corner in New York City is a rainbow of humanity. The resulting interaction and fusion of cultures produce not just great cuisine and music and art but also great science and technology. Intel was co-founded by a Hungarian, Google by a Russian, Yahoo! by a Taiwanese. We are the world's masters of assimilation. A recent study shows that foreigners account for about 40 percent of all science and engineering Ph.D. holders working in the United States and a larger fraction of those in the engineering, math, and computer fields. Sixty percent of foreigners who earned science and engineering degrees remain in the United States, including 92 percent of those from China, 81 percent of those from India and more than half of those from Canada and Germany. Where else do you see cultures and races so at home with one another? In China?

CRITICAL THINKING QUESTIONS

1. Which of the two positions presented do you agree with the most? Explain your answer.
2. If you were the manager of a high technology organization, what would you see as the main consequences or implications to your firm of the contrasting points of view discussed? Explain your answer.
3. Do you think the government should be the primary actor to spur technological achievement or should this responsibility fall on private firms? Defend your answer.

COLLABORATIVE LEARNING EXERCISE

Class is divided into groups of five. Half of the groups are asked to defend the first position described above ("We are falling behind!"). The other half of the groups are asked to defend the opposite position ("Don't believe the hype"). Groups can prepare their arguments outside class or during class, depending on time constraints and instructor's preference. Both "pro and "con" teams are asked to present their arguments in class, with the instructor acting as moderator.

Sources: Based on M. Mandel, "By overlooking cuts in research and development, product design, and worker training, GDP is greatly overstating the economy's strength," *BusinessWeek*, November 9, 2009, p. 35; *Bloomberg BusinessWeek Research Service* "Poor Math and Science education in the U.S. will lead to higher unemployment," March 29, 2010, p. 15; D. Wessel, "U.S. Keeps foreign Ph.D's," *Wall Street Journal*, January 27, 2010, A-3, D. Vergano, "U.S. could fall behind in global brain race," *USA Today*, February 9, 2006, D-1; C. Kranthammer, "Don't believe the Hype: we are still no. 1," *BusinessWeek*, February 13, 2006, p. 41.

Internet Exercise 1.1

Lincoln Electric

www.lincolnelectric.com

Explore the Web site of Lincoln Electric (www.lincolnelectric.com), a leading producer of arc-welding products. Lincoln has dominated its markets by utilizing a management philosophy that is similar to the early 20th-century ideas of Frederick Winslow Taylor, the father of scientific management. Use the site's map feature to locate and read about the' history of Lincoln Electric ("our history") and also learn what it is like to work at Lincoln Electric ("career opportunities"). Then answer the following questions:

1. What are the important features of the Lincoln Electric Perforrnance System?
2. What do you think it would be like to work at Lincoln Electric? Would you enjoy working there? Why or why not?
3. What are Lincoln Electric's mission and vision? How does its Incentive Performance System support them?
4. Do you think Lincoln Electric is a well-managed company based on what you have read about it? On what information do you base your conclusion? Explain.

Manager's Checkup 1.1

Self-assessment of Your Own Theory X or Theory Y Orientation

Instructions: Rate how you feel about each of the following ten points.

1 = This is almost always true
2 = This is generally true
3 = This is true sometimes
4 = This is seldom true
5 = This is almost always false

1. It is important for employees to know that the supervisor is in charge.   1   2   3   4   5
2. Few employees are willing to work harder when needed.   1   2   3   4   5
3. Most employees need close direction and supervision in order to give their best.   1   2   3   4   5
4. For most people work is not enjoyable and see it as something to be avoided.   1   2   3   4   5
5. A manager needs to make it clear that he or she is tough and decisive.   1   2   3   4   5
6. A good manager should not waste time getting employees involved in major decisions, even if these concerns them.   1   2   3   4   5
7. A manager needs to inspire fear if necessary so that employees do not take advantage of him or her.   1   2   3   4   5

8. Often a manager needs to "divide and conquer" among employees to ensure that he or she retains control of the group.	1	2	3	4	5
9. Punishment, at least by example, can make a unit become more productive.	1	2	3	4	5
10. Most employees need to be told what to do, giving them little freedom to innovate.	1	2	3	4	5

Note: Add your scores (maximum is 50). Instructor may calculate the mean for entire class and show the distribution of scores. This can serve to stimulate class discussion as to why some people are closer to the "Theory X" extreme (those who are 35 or higher), some are closer to the "Theory Y" extreme (those who are 15 or lower), and those who are somewhere in the middle (those who are between 16 and 34).

Source: Based on McGregor, D. (1960). *The Human Side of Enterprise*. New York: McGraw-Hill. 33–48.

Endnotes

1. M. V. Copeland, "The ultimate personal technology," *Fortune*, May 3, 2910, 161 (6), 55–58; T. Zeller, "Microsoft Amends Its Policy for Shutting Down Blogs," *New York Times*, February 1, 2006; T. Zeller, "Internet Firms Face Questioning about Censoring Online Searches in China," *New York Times*, February 15, 2006, p. C-3; T. Zeller, "Web Firms Are Grilled on Dealings in China," *New York Times*, February 16, 2006, p. C-1; L. Grossman and H. Beech, "Google under the Gun," *Time*, February 13, 2006, pp. 53–54; and B. Elgin, "Outrunning China's Web Cops," *Business Week*, February 20, 2006, pp. 38–40
2. G. R. Jones, J. M. George, and C. W. Hill, *Contemporary Management*. New York: McGraw-Hill/Irwin, 2011.
3. L. R. Gomez-Mejia, D. B. Balkin, and R. Cardy, *Managing Human Resources*. Englewood Cliffs, NJ: Prentice Hall, 2012.
4. Harris, 1915.
5. J. Heizer and B. Render, *Production and Operations Management*. Englewood Cliffs, NJ: Prentice Hall, 1996, p. 650.
6. Jones, George, and Hill, *Contemporary Management*, p. 64
7. C. I. Barnard, *The Functions of the Executive*. Cambridge, MA: Harvard University Press, 1938, p. 65.
8. M. Mandel, S. Hamm, and C. Farrell, "Why the Economy Is a Lot Stronger Than You Think," *Business Week*, February 13, 2006, pp. 20–32; D. Burke, "By the numbers," *Fortune*, May 3, 2010, 161 (6), 27–30; J. Fortt & M. V. Copeland, "Which Fortune 500 tech giants will climb the rankings-and which ones will stumble, in the next five years"; *Fortune*, May 3, 2010, 161 (6), 27–30.
9. R. L. Daft, *Management*: Thompson: Southwestern Press, 2011, p. 72. Chouharaki & Morsing (2010), (see ref. list).

2

Learning Objectives

1 Describe the changing pattern of international business.

2 Identify major factors affecting international business.

3 Determine key decisions firms face when contemplating foreign expansion.

4 Differentiate the various ways firms can enter foreign markets.

5 Identify alternative ways of managing a foreign operation.

6 Recognize the key human resource policies that firms can develop to help expatriates succeed.

7 Understand the ethical and social responsibility implications of doing business in different countries.

Toys That Travel the World

Playmobil's sturdy little toys are popular in many countries around the world. In fact, they may now be more popular in other countries than they are in their native Germany.

The problem is not that German children do not enjoy the figures of farmers, policemen, knights, pirates, and soccer players, or the finely detailed ships, planes, castles, and other environments the toys inhabit. The award-winning play sets are designed to spark imaginative and independent make-believe play and are manufactured to last for generations. They appeal strongly to their primary audience: boys and, to a lesser degree, girls between 3 and 9. The problem is, German couples aren't having enough children to bring the toy business out of the four-year stump plaguing the German economy as a whole. Families are small, and spending on all sort of consumer goods is down, including cars, refrigerators, electronics—and toys.

Playmobil's manufacturer, the family-owned company Geobra Brandstätter, did not wait for the bad news to arrive before it turned to overseas sales. Playmobil toys have already been popular abroad for many years and sell well in France, Italy, and Canada, in particular. The company earns nearly two-thirds of its $448 million in sales every year from countries other than Germany. CEO Andrea Schauer would like to expand sales in the

Managing in a Global Environment

United States, Latin America, and Asia, too. In fact, her strategy is one that many German companies are falling back on, sending German exports skyrocketing even as the unemployment rate, hammered by big layoffs at companies like Volkswagen, hovers around 12 percent. "You don't need a strong home base for sales anymore," says a Goldman Sachs economist in Frankfurt, Germany. "You just need Germany to be a good base for manufacturing."

For Playmobil, Germany remains a good manufacturing base despite high labor costs. With pay-per-hour rates quite a few times higher in Germany than in, say, China, where nearly three-quarters of the world's toys are now made, Playmobil still prefers to make most of its products in a factory a few miles away from headquarters. The reason is quality. "You can get any level of quality in China," says Schauer. "The question is, at what cost?" Changes in that policy may come, but Schauer doesn't see it happening for several years. A 50-strong development team frequently introduces new toys specifically aimed at children ages 6 to 12.

Another advantage of the decision to keep manufacturing at home is flexibility to adjust production quickly to meet demand. Still, Playmobil does outsource some of its manufacturing to Malta and some assembly work to the Czech Republic. And Germany remains important as a testing ground for new toy ideas, like World Cup soccer figures with moveable limbs and a Soccer Shoot-Out play set. Schauer plans still more new figures, including classic fairy-tale characters, and hopes the new products will appeal to more girls as well as to older boys. "It would be difficult if we had to learn that [Germany] is a market where we can't grow any longer," she says. "But we would find strategies to overcome that." Look for new toys coming soon to a store near you.

Sources: www.playmobil.com, accessed April 2010; www.collectorbil.com, 2011; www.millionaireplay.com, 2011; www. best-german-gifts.com/playmobil-toys.html, 2011; www.markosweb. com, 2011; http://en.wikipedia.org/wiki/playmobil, 2011. Mark Landler, "Selling Well Everywhere but Home," *The New York Times,* February 3, 2006, pp. C_1 and C_4; Natascha Gewaltig. "Can Germany Escape the Doldrums?" *BusinessWeek Online,* February 13, 2006, www.businessweek.com.

CRITICAL THINKING QUESTIONS

1. *What international trends are exemplified by Playmobil's increasing dependence on foreign markets?*

2. *What social and economic trends within Germany have influenced Playmobil's corporate strategies?*

3. *What factors would influence Playmobil to change its strategy and decide to manufacture Playmobil toys abroad, say, in China?*

We'll revisit these questions in our Concluding Thoughts at the end of the chapter after you have had an opportunity to read the chapter material, which should give you a better understanding of the issues raised.

■ The Environment of International Business

global shift
A term used to characterize the effects of changes in the competitive landscape prompted by worldwide competition.

The world of international competition is one which eliminates companies that fail to adapt. The term **global shift** characterizes the effects of changes in the competitive landscape prompted by worldwide competition. Global shift means the international business environment is changing faster than ever. In industries ranging from automobiles to steel, banking to financial services, airlines to shipping, and low-technology manufacturing to R&D-intensive firms, each individual company faces a growing number of competitors for whom national barriers are almost irrelevant. In other words, the international business environment is forcing many firms to see the entire world as the stage for manufacturing, production,[1] and marketing. Old animosities must be replaced by a new, more global view, as described in the opening vignette about Playmobil. According to one observer, "We are moving away from an economic system in which national markets are distinct entities, isolated from each other by trade barriers and barriers of distance, time and culture, and toward a system in which national markets are merging into one huge global marketplace. . . . In many industries it is no longer meaningful to talk about the 'German market,' the 'American market,' or the 'Japanese market'; there is only the 'global market.'"[2]

The Changing Pattern of International Business

International competition is fierce in this new millennium. Successful firms survive by creating high-quality, competitively priced products and services. These goods must be well received both locally and globally. Some of the major developments in the global business community are changing world output and the world trade picture; lower trade barriers; integrated economic markets; global consumer preferences; technological innovation; globalized production; and management across cultures. See Figure 2.1 on page 37.

CHANGING WORLD OUTPUT AND WORLD TRADE PICTURE Four major changes in the world output and world trade picture occurred during the last few decades. This period corresponds to the time when most of the senior executives now in charge of major corporations were in low- to mid-level management positions.

Perhaps the single most important innovation affecting globalization has been the development of the microprocessor. Not only has it enabled the explosive growth of high-power, low-cost computing, but it has vastly increased the amount of information that can be processed by individuals and firms.

First, the United States no longer dominates the world economy. World output attributed to the United States was almost 40 percent lower at the start of the new century than in the 1960s. Similarly, the percentage of world exports of manufactured goods represented by goods from the United States in the 1990s was about half what it had been in the 1960s.[3] In the second decade of this century, this trend seems to be accelerating. Since the U.S. economy grew at an average of approximately 3 percent annually during this period, this decline means that other economies, such as Germany's and those in Asia, grew even faster. While powerhouses such as Japan and Germany have not done as well in the 2000s, China has been making enormous strides and is quickly becoming a major economic world player (see Figure 2.2 "China's Bewildering Numbers" on page 39).[4] Currently none of the top 30 most rapidly growing countries are in the west (www.cia.gov). This group includes such places as Macau, Azerbaijan, Qatar, Republic of Congo, Laos, and Vietnam.

Second, large U.S. multinationals no longer dominate international business. In the mid-1970s, U.S. firms made up almost half of the largest multinationals, while Japanese firms accounted for only 3.5 percent of them.

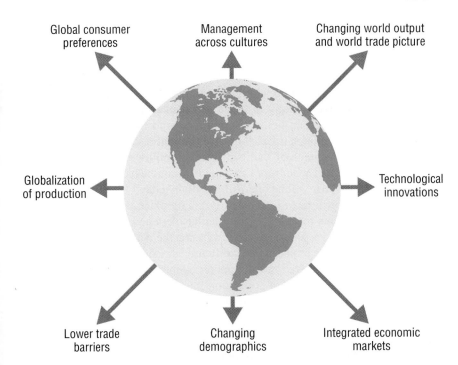

FIGURE 2.1

Major Global Business Developments

Global consumer preferences

Management across cultures

Changing world output and world trade picture

Globalization of production

Technological innovations

Lower trade barriers

Changing demographics

Integrated economic markets

By the mid-1990s, Japan and the United States were nearly even, with Japanese firms accounting for 29.8 percent and U.S. firms for 30.2 percent.[5] Small and medium-sized businesses, many of them in rapidly industrializing Asian countries, are becoming "mini-multinationals" in the late-2000s. In the Americas, Brazil, with a population rapidly approaching 200 million people, is now poised to become a major global player. This trend is opening the door to greater participation in the world economy for countries that traditionally remained on the sidelines. For instance, Sainco is a relatively small high-technology firm focusing on electronic control devices. Located in Seville, Spain, Sainco was started from scratch about 30 years ago. Today, the company has facilities in more than 10 developing countries and does close to 70 percent of its business internationally.

Third, the centrally planned communist economies that made up roughly half the world suddenly became accessible to Western businesses during the late 1980s. Before that, their international dealings were often guided by political rather than economic considerations. Although the economies of formerly communist nations and the few remaining communist enclaves are not robust, most of these countries are committed to free market economics. Over time, they are likely to have a major effect on international trade. For instance, Shanghai and other Chinese provinces and cities have the fastest growing economies in the world and, if current trends continue, China's per capita income could approach that of southern European countries by the year 2025. China has almost a third of the world's population, so the global economic consequences would be enormous. In Europe, 10 of the 12 new members that entered the European Union since 2004 (discussed in some detail below) are formerly communist countries that used to have tightly controlled economies (Romania, Bulgaria/Latvia, Estonia, Lithuania, Poland, Hungary, Czech Republic, Slovakia, and Slovenia). Most Europeans that form part of the 27-nation bloc of 500 million people also expect to expand the European Union in the future to possibly include Russia and Turkey.[6]

Finally, the global economy has become more knowledge-intensive and national barriers to labor markets are falling. This means that a growing number of firms consider the entire world their labor market, and companies now hire talent wherever it may be found. For instance, Delphi Automotive Systems (which filed for bankruptcy in the United States in 2005) had 66,000 employees in 51 plants around Mexico in 2006. India, which graduates more than 200,000 lawyers a year, now provides litigation support for many law firms in the United States.[7] Foreign recruitment is no longer exclusively the province of companies in more developed nations. China's new companies are wooing away executives from such well-known multinationals as Microsoft, Morgan Stanley, Nokia, Procter & Gamble, and Motorola.[8] Japan, India, and to a lesser extent Brazil and Mexico are also attracting European and U.S. talent to some of their firms.[9]

CHANGING DEMOGRAPHICS In general, the population is getting older in the industrialized countries. Western Europe would have actually dropped in population during the past two decades had it not received several dozen millions of immigrants, mostly from prior colonies (it is estimated that approximately 200 million people now live in countries other than their place of birth). Estonia's president sounded an unusual warning to his 1.4 million countrymen: "Let us remember," said Arnold Ruutel in a live TV address, "that in just a couple of decades [2023] the number of Estonians seeing the New Year will be one-fifth less than today."[10]

That same downward trend in birth rates is apparently taking place in other parts of the world, although it is not as severe. This means that both the business and government sectors must be more attuned to the needs of older people. It also means that the management of diversity (see Chapter 6) is likely to become more important in the future as richer countries experience rising levels of both legal and illegal immigration from poorer countries. As can be seen in the Table 2.1 only four out of the top 20 countries in population (the United States, Russia, Japan, and Germany) are generally considered as developed, industrialized nations, although China,

TABLE 2.1 Population Distribution of Countries with More than 65 Million in Population (2011 Est.)

Rank	Country	Population	Rank	Country	Population
1	China	1,338,612,968	11	Mexico	111,211,789
2	India	1,156,897,766	12	Philippines	97,976,603
3	United States	307,212,123	13	Vietnam	88,576,758
4	Indonesia	240,271,522	14	Ethiopia	85,237,338
5	Brazil	198,739,269	15	Germany	82,329,758
6	Pakistan	174,578,558	16	Egypt	78,866,635
7	Bangladesh	156,050,883	17	Turkey	76,805,524
8	Nigeria	149,229,090	18	Congo, Democratic Republic of the	68,692,542
9	Russia	140,041,247	19	Iran	66,429,284
10	Japan	127,078,679	20	Thailand	65,998,436

Distribution by gender and age: The Case of China

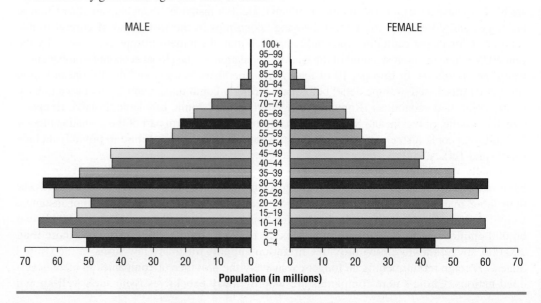

India, and Brazil are quickly catching up. Each of these countries differ in their population demographics. In general, less developed countries have younger populations. The gender distribution is also unequal in some countries, most notably in China. Cultural traditions in China tend to cause parents to see a male child as more beneficial to the family than a female child; therefore, a striking imbalance has resulted between the number of males and females (see bottom half of Table 2.1). For the entire world it is estimated that 245 births occur each minute, while fewer than 102 die each minute, meaning that the world population keeps rising very rapidly.

LOWER TRADE BARRIERS   For many years, most industrialized countries placed high tariffs on foreign goods in order to protect domestic producers. Countries such as West Germany, Italy, and Great Britain imposed tariffs that averaged about 25 percent of the value of the goods in the 1950s. Developing countries followed a policy of "import substitution" designed to stimulate domestic industry by establishing artificially high prices for foreign producers. These tariffs often exceeded 100 percent of the value of the product.

Most countries now realize that nationalistic trade policies do not work. Consumers pay higher prices for lower-quality goods when competition is curtailed. Also, countries are tempted to progressively raise trade barriers against each other, depressing world demand. This was a major factor behind the worldwide depression of the 1930s. As firms disperse production around the globe in search of cost efficiencies, identifying a product with a particular country has become increasingly difficult. A tariff on "foreign" products harms domestic firms and the citizens of the country that imposes the tariff because companies within that country miss out on global business opportunities. A University of Kentucky study credits Toyota's Georgetown presence with creating 22,000 jobs in the state, of which 6,500 were in the plant itself, and adding $1.5 billion to Kentucky's economy during its first eight years in operation.[11] Lower trade restrictions led to this economic windfall for the state.

Although protectionism is still popular in some quarters—including some U.S. politicians, industry associations, and union leaders who advocate "buy American" legislation—trade barriers continue their downward trend.[12] In the 2010s, tariff rates imposed by various countries are generally three to five times lower than in the 1950s. Even during the severe recession of 2008–2011 most countries resisted the temptation to raise tariffs in order to artificially protect domestic employment (by keeping foreign products out and thus promote employment by local industry). The goal of removing tariffs is embodied in the comprehensive **General Agreement on Tariffs and Trade (GATT)** treaty signed by 120 nations. Under GATT there have been eight rounds of negotiations, resulting in a lowering of trade barriers for manufactured goods and services. In 1993, the GATT negotiations in Uruguay, known as the Uruguay Round, created a **World Trade Organization (WTO)** to ensure compliance by member nations.

General Agreement on Tariffs and Trade (GATT)
A treaty signed by 120 nations to lower trade barriers for manufactured goods and services.

World Trade Organization (WTO)
Organization created in 1993 to ensure compliance with GATT.

Population: 1.4 billion
Greatest population concentration: Chongqing (30,596,900 million)
GDP Growth rate: 8.7%
Per capita income $6,500 ($10,000 plus in main cities)
Mobile phone test messages: 250 billion
Communist party officials disciplined for corruption per year: 171,000
World ranking in automobile deaths: 1
Engineer graduates per year: 500,000 plus
Total exports per year in billions: $600 plus
Retail sales per year in billions: $700 plus
Second largest economy in the world after the United States (per 2011 data)

China's Bewildering Numbers
Sources: Based on the world fact book, https://www.cia.gov, 2011; All China Data Center, China Date Online, http://chinadataonline.org, 2011; www.Geohive.com, 2011; B. Hannah, E. Chaim, F. Matthew, J. Susan Shannon, and E. Shannon, "Small World, Big Stakes," *Time*, June 27, 2005, pp. 30-44.

INTEGRATED ECONOMIC MARKETS   Economic integration between groups of countries in a particular geographical area is gaining momentum, and today there are 35 such agreements, compared to 11 in the 1980s. The objective of economic integration is to reduce or eliminate barriers to the free flow of goods, services, labor, capital, and other inputs of production between member nations. The 27-member European Union (EU) has achieved the highest level of political and economic integration, allowing unrestricted movement of merchandise, people, and capital among member countries (see Figure 2.3). The EU has also established a uniform set of product standards and financial regulations, a common central bank, and monetary union, although some management issues still remain unresolved. During the past decade the EU expanded by incorporating eastern European countries that were once behind the "iron curtain" (such as the Czech Republic and Romania) as well as such "fringe" countries as Malta and Cyprus. Turkey is currently negotiating with the EU for future membership. One of the challenges facing the EU in the future is how to manage an increasingly diverse group of countries, some whose economies (such as Poland and Lithuania) are far behind those 15 EU members that formed the union up to 2004.

Attempts to pass a so-called European constitution have failed, and glitches remain in the European Union that require companies to adapt their products to individual countries.[13] For instance, Kellogg, of Battle Creek, Michigan, has to manufacture four different varieties of corn flakes and other cereals at its plants in Manchester, England, and Bremen, Germany, to satisfy different vitamin and folic acid requirements set by countries such as Denmark, the Netherlands, and Finland.[14] Caterpillar Inc., which sells tractors throughout Europe, faces a similar situation. In Germany it must install a louder backup horn and locate lights in different places. The yield signs and license-plate holders on the backs of vehicles must be different, sometimes by just centimeters, from country to country. All this means that companies must still be flexible to respond to these political realities, even in one of the most economically integrated regions of the world. In addition there are economic strains as in many ways each country can still act independently yet its actions affect all others. This became evident this decade when Greece incurred a huge deficit and had to be bailed out by other members of the European Union in order to protect the value of the Euro.

In the Americas, the major economic alliance, the **North American Free Trade Act (NAFTA)**, is now more than 17 years old, and despite its controversial beginning (many feared it would lead to massive job losses), it is now viewed positively by most politicians and business leaders on both the U.S. and Mexican sides of the border.

Ratified in 1994 by the United States, Mexico, and Canada, NAFTA eliminated tariff and most nontariff barriers among member nations in 2004. It also allows for the free flow of agricultural products between the United States and Mexico. Most experts agree that NAFTA has

NAFTA
The major economic alliance in the Americas.

FIGURE 2.2

The 27-Member European Union: An Economic Partnership Working to Improve the Economic Conditions of Citizens

confounded many predictions by increasing U.S. employment rather than moving U.S. jobs to Mexico.

Similar to NAFTA, the Central American-Dominican Republic Free Trade Agreement was ratified in 2005 between the United States and five Central American Countries (Costa Rica, El Salvador, Guatemala, Honduras, Nicaragua) and the Dominican Republic. The six are home to 44 million people. The treaty (known as CAFTA) makes more than 80 percent of U.S. exports duty free immediately, with remaining tariffs phased out over 10 years. Other economic unions in the Americas, namely Mercosur (composed of Brazil, Uruguay, Paraguay, and Chile) and the Andean Pact (Boliva, Peru, Colombia, Ecuador, and Venezuela) do not involve the United States directly. Political winds at the time of this writing (2011) do not seem highly supportive of an expanded free-trade zone between the United States and these South American countries, but this could well change in the next few years. A major issue of contention appears to be agricultural subsidies in the United States (which is also an issue with European Union) to protect domestic farmers; South American countries see this as a problem since most of their exports are related to agriculture.

Two major regional economic groups are present in Asia. The oldest is the Association of Southeast Asian Nations, or ASEAN, formed in 1967. It includes Brunei, Indonesia, Laos, Malaysia, Myanmar, Philippines, Singapore, Thailand, and Vietnam. While its intent is to foster trade among its members and achieve greater economic cooperation, progress has been slow.

The second is the Asia Pacific Economic Cooperation (APEC) group, founded in 1990. This group of countries has the potential to become highly influential if it were to turn itself into a free trade area. Doing so would make it the world's largest trade bloc, because the 18 member states account for more than half of the world's GNP. The APEC group consists of countries such as China, Japan, and the United States. Several well-publicized meetings have been held among the heads of state with the intent of removing their trade and investment barriers first for the richest members and subsequently for the poorest members. However, some members complain that the plan is vague and commits APEC members to doing little more than holding additional meetings.[15]

GLOBAL CONSUMER PREFERENCES Consumer tastes and preferences are converging, even though some national differences persist. The success of such firms as Coca-Cola, Levi Strauss, Taco Bell, Sony, and McDonald's illustrates this trend. Thus, for example, Taco Bell is now a market leader in Mexico even though the chain started in the United States and its offerings bear little resemblance to native Mexican food. Part of the reason for the development of worldwide tastes and preferences is the presence of the mass media, exposure to goods from various countries, and marketing strategies of multinational firms that tend to offer standardized products worldwide, because doing so costs less than customizing goods to local conditions.

GLOBALIZED PRODUCTION To be cost efficient, firms are increasingly splitting up production around the world to take advantage of other countries' ability to perform parts of the process better for less money. By establishing a global web of production activities, firms hope to achieve the highest quality standards at the lowest possible cost. For instance, of the $20,000 sticker price of a General Motors Chevrolet LeMans,

- $6,000 goes to South Korea, where the car is assembled.
- $3,000 goes to Japan for sophisticated high-tech parts, including engines, transaxles, and electronics.
- $800 goes to Taiwan, Singapore, and Japan for small parts.
- $500 goes to Great Britain to cover advertising and marketing services.
- $1,000 goes to Ireland for data processing.
- About $7,600 goes to GM and to the lawyers, bankers, insurance agents, and consultants that GM uses in the United States.[16]

TECHNOLOGICAL INNOVATIONS Technology has made what was once impossible possible. In 1990, it would have been a logistical

The French automaker Renault discovered how much consumer tastes are converging when demand for its new midsize sedan, the Logan, spilled over into other Western European countries such as Germany and Spain and generated a months-long waiting list. Renault had planned to produce a low-cost car for emerging markets like Poland and Romania and designed the stripped-down Logan to sell there for as little as $6,000.

Global Is Local in a New World Order of Business

Communications technology has transformed the world into a single work place. Workers collaborate in different locations using a computer network in ways they never could before. Caterpillar's global engineers in different countries simultaneously collaborate on tractor designs with a 3-D model over a computer network. ParaGraph International, a software company started by a Russian, Stepan Pachikov, links product development in Moscow and Campbell, California. The 50,000 employees at Schlumberger, a technology services company, work around the world but stay connected through the Schlumberger Information Network.

IBM has a system called "Java around the clock" whereby the company has computer programmers at Tsinghua University in China, IBM programmers in Seattle, scientists at the Institute for Computer Science in Belarus Software House Group in Latvia, and R & D teams within the Tata Group in India work on projects simultaneously. The company

Oracle developed a system whereby sports fans around the world could keep track of the Winter Olympics in Vancouver with a highly graphical user interface (the official Web site for the 2010 winter games attracted more than 1.5 billion hits from almost every cover of the globe).

The cost of doing business globally has also diminished thanks to technology. Eastman Chemical found the cost of three or four managers in the United States is the same as the cost of stationing one U.S. manager abroad; its U.S.-based managers can now use communication technology to manage by long distances. Of the company's 1,500 employees who work outside the United States, only 130 are Americans.

Sources: http://Java.sys-con.com, 2011; http://www.IBM.com/developerworks/Java, 2011; http://Java.sun.com/features/, 2011; special issue of *BusinessWeek* on globalization, February 2, 2003.

nightmare to build the Boeing *777* by outsourcing 132,500 parts to suppliers around the world. Now, Boeing outsources most of the components for the Boeing *777* commercial jet aircraft to 545 of the best suppliers around the world, and these companies produce the 132,500 engineered parts.[17]

Advances in communications, information processing, and transportation technology have made today's large international business feasible. Fiber optics, wireless technology, and the Internet and World Wide Web make it possible to process a vast amount of information at very low cost. For example, the cost of a three-minute phone call from London to New York fell from $13.73 in 1973 to about $4.30 by the late 1990s. By 2006 the cost had fallen to pennies and now it is free when connected through the Internet (for instance, by using Skype).

Many firms depend on satellite technology to link worldwide operations and integrate plants and activities. Texas Instruments uses satellite technology to link 50 plants in 19 countries and to coordinate production planning, cost accounting, financial planning, marketing, customer service, and the personnel function.[18] Management Close-Up 2.1, "Global Is Local in a New World Order of Business," provides other examples of how technology is diminishing both time and distance challenges.

MANAGEMENT ACROSS CULTURES Culture still plays a major role in shaping consumer preferences and tastes. For instance, "Mattel's Barbie doll was a faltering product in Japan until marketing research determined that few Japanese identified with the Americanized doll. For the Japanese, Barbie was too tall, too long legged, and her blue eyes were the wrong color. Mattel produced a Japanized Barbie—shorter, with brown eyes, and a more Asian figure. Not surprisingly, 2 million Barbies were sold in two years."[19] When Arab satellite TV network MBC decided to introduce "The Simpsons" to the Middle East, Homer was called "Omar" and drank Coke, not beer.[20]

International firms often respond to local needs by customizing products and the marketing strategies that are designed to meet different consumer tastes. At the same time, successful firms try to create a need for their products without costly adaptations (even though management needs to be flexible to respond to customer desires). One good example is Ikea, the Swedish retailer, which in relatively few years has been able to establish a global cult brand around the world while remaining highly sensitive to local needs (see Management Close-Up 2.2, "Ikea Is Conquering the Global Furniture and Accessories Retail Market" above).

LOC-In 1 Learning Objective Check-In

1. Trevon is a manager at a health services firm. Which of the following represents a current global trend that will directly impact the way Trevon should help develop strategy at his firm?

   a. The management of diversity will become less important in the future as richer countries experience falling levels of immigration.

   b. An upward trend in birth rates is taking place now in almost every region of the world.

   c. An aging world population means needing to be more attuned to the needs of older people.

   d. Firms are establishing a global web of production activities to achieve high quality despite high costs.

MANAGEMENT CLOSE-UP 2.2 — THEME: **CUSTOMER FOCUS**

Ikea Is Conquering the Global Furniture and Accessories Retail Market

Ikea, the Swedish retailer, has become a global cult brand around the world, with more than 250 stores in Europe, Asia, Australia, North America, and South America welcoming 450 million shoppers a year. What enthralls shoppers is the store visit—a similar experience the world over. The blue and yellow buildings average 300,000 square feet in size, about equal to five football fields. The sheer number of items—7,000 products from kitchen cabinets to candlesticks—is a decisive advantage. "Others offer affordable furniture," says Bryan Roberts, research manager at Planet Retail, a consultancy in London. "But there's no one else who offers the whole concept in the big shed." The global middle class that Ikea targets shares buying habits. The $120 Billy bookcase, $13 Lack side table, and $190 Ivar storage system are best-sellers worldwide. (U.S. prices are used throughout this Close-Up.) Spending per customer is similar across different countries. According to Ikea, the figure in Russia is $85 per store visit— exactly the same as in affluent Sweden. To keep customers coming back, Ikea replaces a third of its product line each year.

Ikea works very hard at maintaining a positive image as a good corporate citizen around the world, forcing its suppliers to agree to a code of conduct that outline accepted procedures. Ikea has a book called *IKEA's Way on Purchasing* used to monitor all of its suppliers across geographically, economically, and culturally diverse areas of the world. It covers more than 90 issues on which the furniture company expects compliance. To make sure these expectations are met, all suppliers receive periodic audits by Ikea inspectors. A supplier anywhere in the world found in violation has 24 months to take corrective action; otherwise it is terminated by Ikea's headquarters.

Sources: www.Ikea.com, 2011; S. Ganesan, M. George, S. Jap, R. W. Palmatier, and B. Weitz, (2009). "Supply Chain Manager and Retailer Performance," *Journal of Retailing*, 85(1), pp. 84–94; S. Burt (2010). *Retailing in Europe: The International Review of Retail Distribution and Consumer Research*, 20(1), 9–27; A. Sains, A. J. Palmer, J. Bush, D. Roberts, and K. Hall, "Ikea: How the Swedish Retailer Became a Global Cult Brand," *BusinessWeek*, November 14, 2005, pp. 95–106.

IKEA PS - dal 1995, la galleria del Design IKEA

As Ikea has expanded its warehouse-style furniture and accessories stores worldwide, it has attracted millions of devoted consumers striving to enter the middle class. With over 225 stores in Europe, Asia, Australia, and the United States, the store has hit on the right combination of mass-market products, like its best-selling Billy bookcases, and products customized for specific markets, like rooster placemats for China in the year of the rooster and more boldly colored showrooms for Hispanic neighborhoods in the United States.

Lastly, firms establishing ventures overseas may need to adapt business strategies, structures, operational policies, and human resource programs to the culture. For instance, nepotism, or the hiring of relatives, is discouraged in Anglo-Saxon countries, but it is a common practice in many southern European, South American, and Asian countries.

■ Major Factors Affecting International Business

As firms internationalize to take advantage of global opportunities and to meet the competition, they need to consider factors that vary across countries and that are often very different from the familiar domestic setting. These factors include the general business environment, the legal system, economic conditions, and cultural norms.

GENERAL BUSINESS ENVIRONMENT   The general business environment of a country consists of all the factors that combine to affect the benefits, costs, and risks of conducting business in that country. Benefits are affected by the size of the market, the purchasing power of the population, and most important, the likely future wealth of consumers. Sometimes these factors can change unexpectedly. For example, Argentina was one of the eight wealthiest countries in the world until the 1940s, but fell below the top 50 by 2011 in part due to political instability, mismanagement of the economy, and widespread corruption. South Korea, on the other hand, was a very poor third-world nation in 1960. It is currently one of the 10 largest economies in the world and the fourth largest trading nation after Japan, the United States, and Germany.

The cost of doing business varies greatly from country to country. It may be necessary to make payments to the government or the political elite, or there may not be an appropriate infrastructure, or adherence to regulations may involve a major financial commitment. In some European countries, for example, it is necessary to give employees a month's paid vacation, numerous government-mandated holidays, and double pay for Christmas. McDonald's discovered that it had to develop dairy and vegetable farms, cattle ranches, and food-processing plants in Russia in order to serve food that met its quality standards in its Moscow outlet.

Operating in a foreign country also involves risk. Risks come in three forms and vary dramatically from nation to nation. *Political risk*, which is common in developing countries, may involve government changes (often by force), social unrest, strikes, terrorism, and violent conflict. Political risk may also come in more subtle forms, particularly in richer countries. For instance, both President Jacques Chirac and Prime Minister Dominique Villepin of France reacted to Hewlett-Packard Co.'s announcement in 2005 that it would lay off 1,200 workers in France by proposing that "companies might be required to sign a code of conduct limiting their ability to lay off workers if, as in HP's case, the government financed road works and other improvements benefitting their factories."[21] There are several well-known consulting and publishing firms that provide up-to-date information on political risks country by country. These include:[22]

- Bank of America World Information Services
- Business Environment Risk Intelligence (BERI) S.A.
- Control Risks Information Services
- Economist Intelligence Unit (EIU)
- Euromoney
- Institutional Investor
- Standard and Poor's Rating Group
- Moody's Investor Services

A firm may also be exposed to *economic risk*. Some countries, such as Bolivia, have experienced annual inflation rates exceeding 26,000 percent, while others, such as Russia, make it difficult for foreign firms to get paid in hard currency (such as U.S. dollars) that can be repatriated to corporate headquarters, or may be riddled with corruption. Finally, firms may incur *legal risks*. For instance, some governments insist on local or government ownership of a percentage of equity of foreign firms. In other countries, intellectual property rights are not adequately protected. The illegal reproduction of CDs and software is a booming business in some Asian countries, and estimated annual losses exceed $2.2 billion.[23] And practices that are perfectly legal in the United States may be illegal overseas. For example, the European Union banned Coca-Cola Co. from offering volume-linked rebates as well as from signing exclusivity deals with retailers (which is not uncommon in the United States). Coca-Cola now has to hand over as much as 20 percent of the room in its European coolers and vending machines to rivals such as Pepsi-Co Inc. to stock their own brands. If Coke is found in violation of this European Union order, "it faces the possibility of massive penalties of 10 percent of its worldwide revenue, the equivalent of 2.2 billion dollars."[24] This decade, Toyota executives felt that the company became an easy target of some American politicians pursuing their own political ambitions by "over blowing" Toyota's safety problems.

LEGAL SYSTEMS   The legal system of a nation consists of the rules defining what is permissible or illegal, the process for enforcing the laws, and the procedures available to redress grievances. A country's legal system reflects its culture, religion, and traditions. A firm must comply with the host country's legal system.

In general, there are three major types of legal systems. Countries with an Anglo-Saxon background or influence rely on **common law**, in which precedents based on past court decisions play a key role in interpreting the meaning and intent of legal statutes. This legal system is used in the United States and 26 other countries. **Civil law** relies on a comprehensive set of rules that form part of a highly structured code, and enforcement and interpretation of laws are made in reference to this code. About 70 countries, including most European nations and Japan, use a civil law system. **Muslim law**, based on religious beliefs, regulates behavior in approximately 27 Islamic countries, although interpretations and levels of enforcement vary significantly from country to country.

ECONOMIC ENVIRONMENT   Firms entering international markets are subject to unpredictable economic shifts that may have major effects on earnings. High inflation is one example, as in the Bolivian case noted above. The *exchange rate*, or the rate at which the market converts one currency into another, may also fluctuate. A devaluation occurs when more local currency is necessary to obtain a given amount of foreign currency, in effect making the local currency worth less outside the country. Companies are normally paid in local currency and later convert it into the currencies of their home countries. If the local currency is devalued relative to the company's domestic currency, the firm may receive less value for its products or services than was expected. To maintain profit levels, the firm must raise its prices, which may lead to fewer sales in the future.

Between late December 1994 and mid-January 1995, the value of the Mexican peso dropped 40 percent relative to the dollar, and U.S. firms in Mexico experienced an abrupt decline in revenues. Wal-Mart's Mexican stores were selling merchandise purchased with U.S. dollars prior to the devaluation. Chrysler, Ford, and General Motors had imported parts from the United States and Canada to use in Mexican plants, and this caused the price of their automobiles to increase by 40 percent in early 1995, causing demand to drop between 30 percent and 50 percent below the levels attained in 1994.[25] Although the peso continued to fluctuate, by 2000 Mexico's car prices had recovered and demand had risen to almost their precrisis levels. As another example of the effect of devaluation, the French tourism industry suffered a 30 percent decrease in profits as the value of the dollar dropped up to 40 percent relative to the euro during the prior decade (which kept many American tourists home). After the riots that exploded in several French cities at the end of 2005, most severely in Paris, the euro dropped by approximately 10 percent almost overnight, negatively affecting U.S. firms that were repatriating European earnings back into the United States.[26] More recently, the Obama administration has vociferously complained to China about its policy of maintaining the value of its currency low relative to the dollar in order to make Chinese goods cheaper overseas (and thus promote Chinese exports at the expense of other exporting countries that do not "undervalue" their currency).

Taxation represents another economic factor. Variations in tax policies are a major challenge to firms trying to minimize global tax liabilities. In Europe, the top corporate income tax rate ranges from 25 percent in Finland to 60 percent in Germany. A U.S. manager sent to a subsidiary in Norway is exempted from domestic taxes for two years, but one sent to Spain must pay domestic taxes, which are far higher than in the United States, after a six-month stay. *Forbes* conducts an annual analysis of the tax burden in 47 countries (including corporate income tax,

common law
The legal system in which precedents based on past court decisions play a key role in interpreting the meaning and intent of legal statutes.

civil law
The legal system that relies on a comprehensive set of rules that form part of a highly structured code; enforcement and interpretation of laws are made in reference to this code.

Muslim law
The legal system based on religious Muslim beliefs that regulates behavior; strict interpretation and enforcement varies significantly from country to country.

personal income tax, wealth tax, social security, and sales tax); this annual report can be found on the Web at www. forbes.com/misery.

Also, firms that rely on technological innovations as a source of competitive advantage may have to deal with complicated licensing agreements and royalties. In Germany, royalties on patents are limited to 10 percent of sales, with the duration of patents and trademarks set at 20 years and 10 years, respectively. Egypt, on the other hand, places no limits on royalties, but only production processes may be patented and only for a maximum of 15 years.

More than 80 countries adhere to the International Convention for the Protection of Industrial Property (often referred to as the Paris Union), but the rules may be interpreted differently. What constitutes industrial espionage may also differ among countries, and firms face major risks in protecting their technology. A firm may find that its proprietary technology is copied by joint-venture partners, franchisees, licensees, and former employees who are hired by other firms, encouraged in part by lax enforcement of so-called intellectual property laws.

CULTURAL ENVIRONMENTS According to Hofstede, *culture* is the "collective programming of the mind which distinguishes the members of one group from another. . . . Culture, in this sense, includes systems of values; and values are among the building blocks of culture."[27] Culture reflects differences in the social structures, religions, languages, and historical backgrounds of various countries. **Culture shock** occurs when a person is exposed to a new culture with different norms, customs, and expectations and has difficulty adjusting.

To succeed internationally, businesses need to understand and be willing to make accommodations for cultural differences. Hofstede uses five dimensions to summarize different cultures:

1. **Power distance** is the extent to which individuals expect a hierarchical structure that emphasizes status differences between subordinates and superiors. For example, in countries that are high in power distance, such as the Philippines, Mexico, and most Arab nations, employees expect visible rewards that project power for people higher up in the organizational pyramid, such as a large office or an elegant company car.
2. **Individualism** is the degree to which a society values personal goals, autonomy, and privacy over group loyalty, commitment to group norms, involvement in collective activities, social cohesiveness, and intense socialization. In countries that are high in individualism, such as the United States, Great Britain, and New Zealand, employees believe they should look after their own interests.
3. **Uncertainty avoidance** is the extent to which a society places a high value on reducing risk and instability. Greece, Portugal, Italy, and other countries with high uncertainty avoidance have organizations with extensive rules and procedures and careful delineation of the work each individual is supposed to do.
4. **Masculinity/femininity** is the degree to which a society views assertive or "masculine" behavior as important to success and encourages rigidly stereotyped gender roles. Countries that are high in masculinity, such as Austria, Mexico, and the United States, value stereotypically male traits such as aggressiveness, initiative, and leadership.
5. **Long-term/short-term orientation** is the extent to which values are oriented toward the future (saving, persistence) as opposed to the past or present (respect for tradition, fulfilling social obligations). Japan and China value employee seniority and believe that wisdom increases with age, which reflects a longer-term orientation.[28]

Figure 2.3 on page 47 shows the alignment of countries in terms of power distance and uncertainty avoidance. Latin, Mediterranean, and Far Eastern countries with relatively high masculinity and strong uncertainty avoidance make up the largest cluster, in the bottom right corner. The other clear cluster, in the top left corner, groups countries with low masculinity and weak uncertainty avoidance and includes mostly Anglo countries.

As a general principle, management practices that conform to prevailing societal norms are more likely to succeed, and those that do not are more likely to fail. A firm with operations in two or more countries should carefully consider how management practices are likely to mesh with the other countries' cultural values. Table 2.2 on page 48 summarizes the organizational features and human resource management policies that work best in countries with high and low individualism.

culture shock
The reaction when exposed to other cultures with different norms, customs, and expectations.

power distance
The extent to which individuals expect a hierarchical structure that emphasizes status differences between subordinates and superiors.

individualism
The degree to which a society values personal goals, autonomy, and privacy over group loyalty, group norms, collective activities, social cohesiveness, and intense socialization.

uncertainty avoidance
The extent to which a society places a high value on reducing risk and instability.

masculinity/femininity
The degree to which a society views assertive or "masculine" behavior as important to success and encourages rigidly stereotyped gender roles.

long-term/short-term orientation
The extent to which values are oriented toward the future as opposed to the past or present.

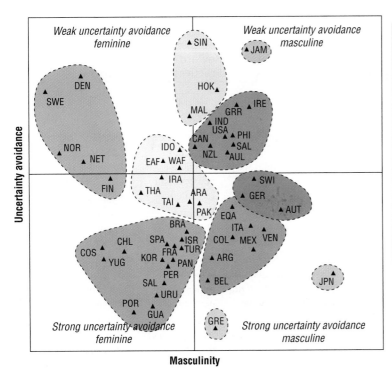

Abbreviations for Countries and Regions

ARA	Arab countries (Egypt, Lebanon, Libya, Kuwait, Iraq, Saudi Arabia, U.A.E.)	JAM	Jamaica
		JPN	Japan
ARG	Argentina	KOR	South Korea
AUL	Australia	MAL	Malaysia
AUT	Austria	MEX	Mexico
BRA	Brazil	NET	Netherlands
CAN	Canada	NZL	New Zealand
CHL	Chile	PAK	Pakistan
COL	Colombia	PAN	Panama
COS	Costa Rica	PER	Peru
DEN	Denmark	PHI	Philippines
EAF	East Africa (Kenya, Ethiopia, Zambia)	POR	Portugal
		SAF	South Africa
EQA	Equador	SAL	El Salvador
FIN	Finland	SIN	Singapore
FRA	France	SPA	Spain
GBR	Great Britain	SWE	Sweden
GER	Germany	SWI	Switzerland
GRE	Greece	TAI	Taiwan
GUA	Guatemala	THA	Thailand
HOK	Hong Kong	TUR	Turkey
IDO	Indonesia	URU	Uruguay
IND	India	USA	United States
IRA	Iran	VEN	Venezuela
IRE	Ireland	WAF	West Africa (Nigeria, Ghana, Sierra Leone)
ISR	Israel		
ITA	Italy	YUG	Yugoslavia

FIGURE 2.3

Alignment of Countries in Terms of Power Distance and Masculinity

Source: From Geert Hofstede, Gert Jan Hofstede, Michael Minkov, *Cultures and Organizations, Software of the Mind*, Third Revised Edition, McGraw-Hill 2010, ISBN 0-07-166418-1. Quoted with permission.

LOC-In 2 Learning Objective Check-In

Smythwick Direct Essentials is global in the sense that it has global customers and a global supply chain. The strategic managers at Smythwick, however, want to increase proportion of workers who come directly from other countries in order to improve its global reach and customer service. This would involve farming talent from other countries and would require the new employees to relocate to the firm's headquarters in Indianapolis:

1. Daniel, from France, has had trouble coping with new expectations and demands on his time since joining Smythwick. He has been exposed to a very new culture in the Midwest, and has experienced _____ as a result of his difficulty adjusting.
   a. individualism
   b. power distance
   c. culture shock
   d. homesickness

2. Jerry, from New Zealand, has strong goals and values personal autonomy. He is also eager to bring his ideas to the collective activities of his work team. He has had little trouble adjusting since he relocated to Indianapolis and joined the team at Smythwick. Jerry's direct supervisor attributes his quick success to the shared high degree of _____ in both the United States and New Zealand.
   a. individualism
   b. power distance
   c. masculinity
   d. uncertainty avoidance

3. Smythwick recently hired Ilya as a senior-level manager responsible for finance. She was pleased to find that the individuals at Smythwick did not seem to expect a hierarchical structure that emphasized status differences. Given her choice of offices, she chose one in the center of the department, rather than the largest corner office, because she wanted to remain in close proximity to the daily operations of her department. Ilya's attitude reflects _____ .
   a. high individualism
   b. high power distance
   c. high masculinity
   d. low power distance

TABLE 2.2 **Cultural Characteristics and Dominant Values (Individualism, Organizational Characteristics, and Selected HR Practices)**

Dominant Values	Sample Countries	Organizational Features	Reward Practices	Staffing/Appraisal Practices
High Individualism				
Personal accomplishment Selfishness Independence Belief in individual control and responsibility Belief in creating one's own destiny Business relationship between employer and employee	United States Great Britain Canada New Zealand	Organizations not compelled to care for employees' total well-being Employees look after their own individual interests Explicit systems of control necessary to ensure compliance and prevent wide deviation from organizational norms	Performance-based pay Individual achievement rewarded External equity emphasized Extrinsic rewards are important indicators of personal success Attempts made to isolate individual contributions (i.e., who did what) Emphasis on short-term objectives	Emphasis on credentials and visible performance outcomes attributed to individual High turnover; commitment to organization for career reasons Performance rather than seniority as criterion for advancement "Fitting in" deemphasized; belief in performance as independent of personal likes and dislikes Attempts at ascertaining individual strengths and weaknesses and providing frequent feedback to employee
Low Individualism				
Team accomplishment Sacrifice for others Dependence on social unit Belief in group control and responsibility Belief in the hand of fate Moral relationship between employer and employee	Singapore South Korea Indonesia Japan Taiwan	Organizations committed to high-level involvement in workers' personal lives Loyalty to the firm is critical Normative, rather than formal, systems of control to ensure compliance	Group-based performance is important criterion for rewards Seniority-based pay utilized Intrinsic rewards essential Internal equity guides pay policies Personal needs (such as number of children) affect pay received	Value of credentials and visible performance outcomes depends on perceived contributions to team efforts Low turnover; commitment to organization as "family" Seniority plays an important role in personnel decisions "Fitting in" with work group crucial; belief that interpersonal relations are important performance dimension Limited or no performance feedback to individual to prevent conflict and defensive reactions

Source: From *Managing Human Resources* by Gomez-Mejia, et al. Copyright © 2012. Reprinted by permission of Pearson Education, Inc., Upper Saddle River, NJ.

MANAGEMENT IS EVERYONE'S BUSINESS   2.1

WORKING AS A TEAM   Many firms are entering joint ventures with companies in other countries. Joint ventures usually require that employees from different nations work in teams. Their success largely depends on the ability of international teams to work together in a climate of mutual respect. This requires not only a great deal of cultural sensitivity but also an understanding of the international context in which the firm operates. As a team member in a globalized economy you should:

- Be prepared to work closely, either physically or virtually, with employees who may be very dissimilar to you in terms of language, ethnic background, past experiences, and the like.
- Keep in mind that most other countries are far less individualistic than the United States and that the boundaries between "what I am supposed to do" and "what other specific members of the team are supposed to do" may not be as clear. In other words, as an American you might need to share more responsibilities with others than you may want to.
- Try to be humble and avoid an "ugly American" image of superiority. People in most foreign countries are very sensitive to that, and cross-national teams are quick to react to what they perceive as U.S. arrogance (even if they are all working for the same U.S. multinational).
- Be aware that social interaction, trust, and personal bonds that go beyond the particular technical issue or task at hand are important for effective teams, particularly in cross-national operations. You need to be patient and give sufficient time for those social ties to grow and strengthen, even if at first it seems like you are wasting too much time talking about nonwork related things.
- Be careful to avoid displays of wealth or discussions that might reflect your economic status (for instance, boasting about great fishing at your summer cottage or the SUV you drive). You are probably earning substantially more than locals that are part of the team, and this is likely to engender resentment.
- The team should develop procedures to ensure that everyone's ideas are considered, particularly when English proficiency may vary greatly from person to person (the individual with the best ideas may have the weakest English!).

There has been a noticeable trend for multinational organizations to hire executives from foreign countries, in the belief that they "can better affect change than a homegrown executive."[29] These organizations include, for instance, Sony, Nissan Motor, Renault, and Sanyo.[30]

Management Is Everyone's Business 2.1 offers a set of recommendations for those who are now part of a cross-cultural team or might be in the future.

■ Entry Strategy

A firm contemplating foreign expansion faces three key entry decisions: (1) which countries to enter, (2) when to enter, and (3) scale of involvement. Each of these decisions is described in turn.

Choosing Foreign Countries

There are more than 180 countries in the world. Not all of them are equally attractive. Ultimately, the decision to sell products in a new country should be based on long-term profit potential considerations. While profit potential depends on the type of firm and what it looks for (for instance, a mining company may be most interested in the existence of certain minerals while a high technology firm may be more interested in the availability of scientific talent), in general there are some factors that most companies would consider. Other things being equal, the appeal of a particular country is likely to be greater when:

1. The size of the domestic market is large. For instance, Starbuck's has chosen China as a foreign location, even though the president of Starbuck's admits that "per capita consumption of coffee in China is very small." He quickly adds, however, that "what you have is a tremendous amount of people, so the market will grow."[31]
2. The present wealth (purchasing power) of consumers in the market is high and projected to grow in the future. For instance, only about 40,000 people in the world can afford to buy a

$300,000 Rolls Royce. Almost all of them are found in about 12 countries.[32] Wal-Mart doubled its investments in Japan during 2007–2011. After years of being in the doldrums, the Japanese economy is starting to grow again. Its $1.2 trillion retail market is the world's largest after the United States.[33]

3. The needed resources are readily available. "British entrepreneur Richard Branson opened several of his Virgin Megastores in Japan despite its reputation as a tough market to crack. One reason for Branson's initial attraction to Japan was a cost of capital of only 2.5 percent—roughly one-third its cost in Britain."[34] For many firms, a key factor is the availability of qualified labor at a cost that is lower than the firm would pay in the domestic labor market.

4. The firm's product offerings are suitable to a particular market. For instance, a sports firm specializing in baseball paraphernalia is likely to face an uphill battle in countries such as France and Italy, where baseball is practically unknown.

5. A positive business climate exists. Political risks, laws, business practices, and cultural norms all have a profound effect on the appeal of a particular location. A sudden change in a government may mean that contracts signed under a prior government may no longer be enforceable. Government regulations can restrict international firms from withdrawing profits. Cultural norms may influence the kinds of products that are sold and the extent to which they need to be adapted to suit local preferences. An accurate assessment of a nation's business climate is crucial when considering an international opportunity. While in the end there is some subjectivity involved in assessing the degree to which a business climate is favorable or not, firms have access to a great deal of information that can help them make this judgment. For instance, worldatlas.com (www.worldatlas.com) and the *World Factbook* (published by the CIA) provide detailed data on the sociopolitical and economic situations of most countries around the world, which is continually updated. Table 2.3 on page 51 shows a recent summary profile obtained from these sources of Mexico, China, and Japan, countries that are important to keep an eye on for many American firms competing in international markets.

When to Enter Foreign Countries

The timing of entry into a foreign market is a key consideration. Being the first to enter a market offers *a first-mover advantage* by preempting rivals, capturing demand by establishing a strong brand name, and in general making it difficult for later entrants to win business. For example, Gillette controls a large market segment in Latin America for razor blades, in part because it was the first international shaving company to move aggressively into that market. On the other hand, these advantages also have a downside. First movers face higher *pioneering costs,* such as the effort, time, and expense of entering a national market and educating consumers (particularly when the product or service is unfamiliar to local consumers). Late entrants may also learn from the experience of the first movers and perform better as a result. Kentucky Fried Chicken is generally credited with creating a market in China for U.S.-style fast food, yet it was latecomer

FIGURE 2.4
Key Entry Decisions

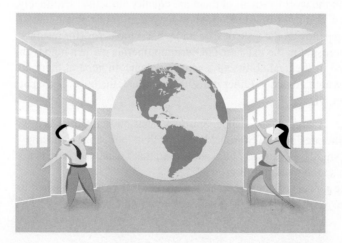

Which country should we enter?

When should we enter?

How much should we commit?

What mode of entry should we use?

TABLE 2.3 Select Country Profiles: The Cases of Mexico, China, and Japan

Mexico

Mexico has a population of approximately 112 million. A third of the population is under the age of 14. Almost 90 percent of Mexico's exports go to the United States, and 75 percent of its imports come from the United States. Mexico is the largest U.S. trading partner. Gross domestic product per capita is $13,500 a year. Spanish is the official language but various Mayan, Nahuatl, and other indigenous languages are also spoken. Approximately 60 percent of the population is mestizo (Native American-Spanish), 30 percent Native American, 9 percent of European origin, and 1 percent from other ethnic groups.

The site of advanced Amerindian civilizations, Mexico was under Spanish rule for three centuries before achieving independence early in the 19th century. Ongoing economic and social concerns include low real wages, underemployment for a large segment of the population, inequitable income distribution, and few advancement opportunities for the largely Amerindian population in the impoverished southern states.

Mexico has a free market economy that recently entered the trillion-dollar class. It contains a mixture of modern and outmoded industry and agriculture, increasingly dominated by the private sector. Recent administrations have expanded competition in seaports, railroads, telecommunications, electricity generation, natural gas distribution, and airports. Per capita income is one-fourth that of the United States; income distribution remains highly unequal. Trade with the United States and Canada has tripled since the implementation of NAFTA in 1994. Mexico has 12 free-trade agreements with over 40 countries, including Guatemala, Honduras, El Salvador, the European Union, and Japan, putting more than 90 percent of its trade under free-trade agreements. The government is cognizant of the need to upgrade infrastructure, modernize the system and labor laws, and provide incentives to invest in the energy sector, but progress is slow.

China

China's population is almost five times greater than that of the United States even though its territory is slightly smaller (over 1.3 billion inhabitants). Mandarin is the official language of business, though there are many dialects. Twenty-one percent of China's exports are to the United States, while 10 percent of its imports come from the United States.

In late 1978, the Chinese leadership began moving the economy from a sluggish Soviet-style centrally planned economy to a more market-oriented system. The system operates within a political framework of strict communist control; however, the economic influence of nonstate managers and enterprises has been steadily increasing. China's authorities have switched to a system of household responsibility in agriculture in place of the old collectivization. The government has increased the authority of local officials and plant managers in industry, permitted a wide variety of small-scale enterprise in services and light manufacturing, and opened the economy to increased foreign trade and investment. The result has been a quadrupling of GDP since 1978. With its 1.3 billion people but a GDP of just $6,500 per capita, China stands as the second largest economy in the world after the United States. Agricultural output doubled in the 1980s, and industry also posted major gains, especially in coastal areas near Hong Kong and opposite Taiwan, where foreign investment helped spur output of both domestic and export goods. On the darker side, the leadership has often experienced in its hybrid system the worst results of socialism (bureaucracy and lassitude) and of capitalism (windfall gains and stepped-up inflation). Beijing thus has periodically backtracked, retightening central controls at intervals.

Access to the World Trade Organization helps strengthen China's ability to maintain high growing rates, but at the same time it puts additional pressure on the hybrid system of strong political controls and growing market influences. China has benefited from a huge expansion in Internet use, with an estimated 105 million people online in 2011. Foreign investment remains a strong element in China's remarkable economic growth. As an indicator of this growth, Shanghai already has 4,000 skyscrapers, almost double the number in New York. And there are designs to build 1,000 more by the end of this decade. Shortages of electric power and raw materials may affect industrial output during 2012–2020. In its rivalry with India as an economic power, China has a lead in absorption of technology, rising prominence in world trade, and alleviation of poverty; India has one important advantage in its relative mastery of the English language, but the number of competent Chinese English-speakers is growing rapidly.

Japan

Japan's population consists of approximately 127 million inhabitants living in an area slightly smaller than California. Japan is a homogeneous country, with 99.4 percent of the population speaking Japanese, and little ethnic diversity. A third of Japan's exports are to the United States while 19 percent of its imports come from the United States. Gross domestic product per capita is $32,600 a year.

(Continued)

TABLE 2.3 (Continued)

Government-industry cooperation, a strong work ethic, mastery of high technology, and a comparatively small defense allocation (1 percent of GDP) have helped Japan expand economically. Japan holds the rank of the second most technologically powerful economy in the world after the United States and has the third largest economy in the world after the United States and China. One notable characteristic of the economy is the cooperation between manufacturers, suppliers, and distributors in closely-knit groups called Keiretsu. A second feature has been the guarantee of lifetime employment for a substantial portion of the urban labor force. Both of these features are now eroding.

Japanese industry, the most important sector of the economy, is heavily dependent on imported raw materials and fuels. The much smaller agricultural sector is highly subsidized and protected. Crop yields in Japan are among the highest in the world. Usually self-sufficient in rice, Japan imports about 50 percent of its requirements of other grain and fodder crops. Japan maintains one of the world's largest fishing fleets and accounts for nearly 15 percent of the global catch.

For three decades, overall real economic growth had been spectacular: a 10 percent average in the 1960s, a 5 percent average in the 1970s, and a 4 percent average in the 1980s. Growth slowed markedly in the 1990s largely due to the aftereffects of overinvestment during the late 1980s along with contractionary domestic policies designed to wring speculative excesses from the stock and real estate markets. During 2001–2010 Japan is the only industrialized nation since the Great Depression that has experienced a sustained period of declining prices, or deflation. The crowding of habitable land area and the aging of the population are two major long-run problems. Robotics constitutes a key long-term economic strength, with Japan possessing 410,000 of the world's 720,000 "working robots." Recently the Japanese economy has been improving. At the same time, many Japanese firms have taken drastic measures to reduce labor costs, cut back on employment security guarantees, and increase productivity through managerial practices borrowed from the United States (such as widespread use of incentive systems and the hiring of employees at any level, not just at entry level). This is requiring a major adaptation for much of the Japanese workforce and managers who had become accustomed to permanent employment, strict promotion-from-within policies, pay pegged to seniority, egalitarian distribution of rewards, and weak ties between compensation received and individual contributions or performance.

Source: Adapted from www.CIA.gov, 2011, with further statistical updates by the authors obtained from various sources.

McDonald's which became most profitable in that market.[35] And many Western firms are learning that, in some markets, local companies can "learn the ropes" quickly from the foreign firm and become major competitors. For instance, India (which graduates more than 300,000 qualified engineers a year, and whose universities award 2.5 million more degrees) is quickly catching up with the likes of IBM and Microsoft, which have large investments there. India's annual software exports have gone from nonexistent to $42 billion in barely a decade and now exceeds more than $90 billion.[36]

Scale of Involvement

The firm must consider not only where and when to enter but also the magnitude of its commitment to the foreign location. For instance, Motorola invested more than $30 billion in China during the past decade.[37] The decision to enter a foreign market on such a large scale is a major strategic commitment with long-term consequences for the corporation. It is also difficult to reverse. The scale of involvement decision is closely tied to mode of entry, to be discussed next. In general, scale of involvement is lowest if the firm simply decides to export its products to the foreign location and highest if the firm decides to have a wholly owned subsidiary in the foreign country.

■ Mode of Entry

The seven ways to enter foreign markets are exporting, turnkey projects, licensing, franchising, joint ventures, wholly owned subsidiaries, and strategic alliances. The advantages and disadvantages associated with each entry mode are discussed on the next page.

Exporting

Manufacturing firms typically begin globalization by **exporting** products to other countries and retaining production facilities within domestic borders. Exporting has two advantages. First, the firm may realize substantial savings through economies of scale. In other words, expanding the market creates greater demand, which requires increasing production, which results in fuller use of plant and equipment and improved learning as a result of practice, so unit costs tend to go down. Second, the firm avoids the expenses of establishing, controlling, and coordinating manufacturing operations on foreign soil. Japanese firms that have used this entry mode successfully, particularly in U.S. markets, include Sony, Matsushita, Honda, and Toyota.

The vast Chinese market is hungry for goods of every kind, both imports and home-grown products. The country struggles with enormous contrasts, such as that between the growing wealth of its cities, like Shenzhen pictured here, and the continued poverty of its rural areas. Some observers say that technological innovation will be the key to continuing the increase in income for many of the country's 1.3 billion people, though with patent protection often tenuous, some multinationals are cautious about expanding their research and development efforts there.

exporting
A means of entering new markets by sending products to other countries and retaining production facilities within domestic borders.

LOC-In 3 Learning Objective Check-In

Film Café is a growing, national restaurant chain that features a dining experience where photographers circulate and take candid pictures, and then send them to an e-mail address provided by the patron after the dinner is over. Customers can order prints, share with friends online, etc. Film Café is considering foreign expansion.

1. Which of the following represents the first key entry decision facing Film Café?
   a. When should we enter the foreign market?
   b. Which countries should we enter?
   c. What should our scale of involvement be?
   d. Should we consider licensing?

2. Because this service idea is unusual in other markets right now, Film Café could experience higher pioneering costs. Pioneering costs are associated with _____.
   a. timing of entry into foreign markets
   b. the present wealth of consumers in the foreign markets
   c. the firm's suitability of products to a particular market
   d. late entrance to the market

The most obvious limitation of exporting is that foreign competitors may enjoy a cost advantage that far exceeds the economies of scale the company realizes. For instance, unskilled and semiskilled labor in most less-developed countries may be hired at a fraction of the cost of comparable labor in the domestic market. This is one reason why established and relatively simple products like bicycles, irons, and small domestic appliances are no longer manufactured in the United States. Moreover, bulk products, such as chemicals, may be expensive to transport from the home country to distant locations. Finally, imports are a politically sensitive issue in many countries, including the United States, and tariffs may be imposed on imported goods.

Turnkey Projects

Turnkey projects are a specialized type of exporting. The selling firm handles the design, construction, start-up operations, and workforce training of a foreign plant, and a local client is handed the key to a plant that is fully operational. Turnkey projects are most often used in newly developed and less-developed countries. Limited access to complex, expensive production process technologies such as chemical production, pharmaceutical production, petroleum refining, and metal refining makes them more viable. A turnkey project allows a company to use its know-how to earn a profit in a foreign country without making a major, long-term investment. Some host countries, including many oil-rich nations, prohibit foreign ownership of an asset such as a petroleum refinery. In such cases, a turnkey deal may be the most attractive business option available.

Turnkey projects also have potential disadvantages. For one, the selling firm may be creating a competitor by giving away its technological superiority. For example, Saudi Arabia, Kuwait, and other Persian Gulf nations are using turnkey-built petroleum plants to directly compete with the Western firms that built those facilities. Also, the selling firm may lose a source of competitive advantage by transferring complex knowhow to actual or potential competitors.

turnkey projects
A specialized type of exporting in which the firm handles the design, construction, start-up operations, and workforce training of a foreign plant, and a local client is handed the key to a plant that is fully operational.

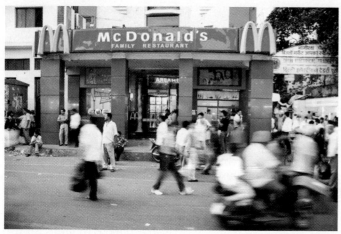

McDonald's restaurants serve a varied, yet limited, value-priced menu in 120 countries around the world. Franchisees are independent entrepreneurs, typically local businesspeople.

licensing
A means of entering new markets, primarily used by manufacturing firms, by transferring the rights to produce and sell products overseas to a foreign firm. In return, the licensing company receives a negotiated fee, normally in the form of a royalty.

franchising
A means of entering new markets similar to licensing, mainly used by service companies, in which the franchisee pays a fee for using the brand name and agrees to strictly follow the standards and abide by the rules set by the franchise.

joint venture
A means of entering new markets where two or more independent firms agree to establish a separate firm; the firms normally own equivalent shares of the joint venture and contribute a corresponding proportion of the management team.

Licensing

In **licensing**, a company transfers the rights to produce and sell its products overseas to a foreign firm. In return, the licensing company receives a negotiated fee, normally in the form of a royalty. The typical licensing arrangement involves intangible property, such as patents, inventions, formulas, trademarks, designs, and copyrights. For instance, Xerox receives 5 percent of net revenues from Fuji-Xerox for allowing Fuji-Xerox to sell Xerox's photocopying technology in the Asian Pacific region.

An advantage of licensing is that the firm does not have to incur the expense and risk of opening a facility overseas. Instead, the licensee puts up most of or all of the capital necessary to start production. When a local government will not allow a firm to set up a wholly owned subsidiary, licensing may be the best alternative. This was why Xerox set up a joint venture with Fuji and licensed its technology to Fuji-Xerox. Also, a firm may own intangible property that has commercial value but may not wish to engage in manufacturing activities. For example, Bell Laboratories at AT&T invented the transistor in the 1950s but licensed the technology to other firms for manufacture.

A disadvantage of licensing is that the foreign firm may build on the technology and use an enhanced version to compete in global markets against the licensing firm that invented it. This happened to RCA when it licensed its color television technology to several Japanese firms, including Matsushita and Sony. Licensing also imposes constraints on the firm, limiting strategic flexibility on a global scale. Because each licensee establishes its own manufacturing operations, costs will go up, and increased prices will reduce demand for products using that technology (which would have an adverse effect on royalties). Licensing also greatly limits a firm's ability to use profits earned in one country to make bold competitive moves in other countries.

Franchising

Franchising is similar to licensing, except that it is mainly used by service companies, whereas licensing is primarily used by manufacturing firms. The franchisee pays a fee for using the brand name and agrees to strictly follow the standards and abide by the rules set by the franchise. McDonald's, for example, has over 4,000 locally owned franchises around the world. The menu, cooking methods, ingredients, and physical appearance of these restaurants must comply with McDonald's standards. McDonald's helps the stores obtain supplies and is closely involved in training managers to ensure that uniform quality standards are met.

Like licensing, franchising allows a firm to expand rapidly with relatively small capital investment and little risk exposure. The main drawback of franchising is that the firm depends on franchisees for quality control, and there is a risk that standards followed by the different stores may not be uniformly met by all the stores. Since the franchise name is intended to guarantee consistent product quality, a lack of uniformity hurts the reputation of the franchise. Franchise owners also complain about decisions made from corporate headquarters that are onerous to them, such as recent pressures from McDonalds and Burger King on their franchise restaurants to offer one-dollar menus (which many owners claim is a money loser for them).

Joint Ventures and Strategic Alliances

In a **joint venture**, two or more independent firms agree to establish a separate firm that is owned by the participating companies. The firms normally own equivalent shares of the joint venture and contribute a corresponding proportion of the management team.

Joint ventures are increasing in popularity. One major advantage is that foreign firms benefit by establishing a working relationship with a domestic firm that is familiar with the local labor market, political environment, competitive landscape, tastes and preferences, cultural norms, language, and legal systems. In return, the local partner receives access to the know-how, technology, and capital of the foreign firm. Further, the two firms gain by sharing development costs and risks, reducing the potential of unacceptably large losses in the case of poor results or business failure. Also, local equity partners may discourage a government from interfering with a

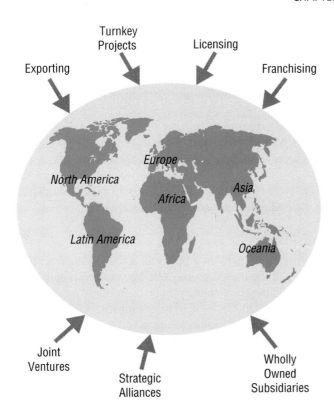

FIGURE 2.5

Different Ways to Enter Foreign Markets

multinational. Joint ventures are another way for companies to do business in countries that do not allow foreign firms to maintain fully owned subsidiaries.

Joint ventures have two serious drawbacks. First, the goals, strategies, culture, and personalities of the firms may conflict. Unless it is successfully resolved, conflict may lead to a dissolution of the union, with considerable cost to all involved. Second, the local partner may use the foreign firm's technology for its own competitive advantage.

International **strategic alliances** are cooperative arrangements between competitors or potential competitors from different countries. They may involve establishment of a formal joint venture as discussed above, such as the case of Fuji-Xerox, or collaboration between firms on specific projects. Strategic alliances have become extremely popular in recent years. Among the firms involved in these arrangements are

strategic alliances
Cooperative arrangements between competitors or potential competitors from different countries, possibly to establish a formal joint venture or collaboration between firms on specific projects.

- *General Electric Snecma of France.* Joint venture to develop and manufacture a variety of low-thrust commercial aircraft engines.
- *Toshiba-IBM.* Sharing the $1 billion cost of developing a 64-megabyte and 256-megabyte memory chip facility, technology that will be transferred to a new IBM plant in Virginia.
- *Mitsui-General Electric.* GE's power-systems unit has picked up Asian contracts with Mitsui's well-connected bank. GE has the technology; Mitsui has the contacts and deep pockets.
- *GM–Daewoo.* To build 160,000 Buick Excells in Shanghai with the key parts for the car shipped from Korea.[38]
- *Texas Instruments–Compel Communications.* To build ultra-cheap cell phones to sell to people in developing nations.[39]
- *Canon–Hewlett Packard.* The two share laser printer technology. Hewlett-Packard buys engines from Canon, but they compete with end products around the world.
- *Mitsubishi-Caterpillar.* A long-time joint venture has become Cat's primary Asian manufacturing source. American and Japanese staff jointly designed a successful excavator line made in Japan, the United States, Indonesia, and China.[40]

Several advantages account for the recent growth of strategic alliances. First, "keeping pace with technological change and competing globally have stretched the resources of even the richest companies."[41] Pooling resources enables firms to accomplish tasks that neither can afford to do alone. Strategic alliances also allow firms to enter relatively closed foreign markets.

A strategic alliance means that firms can utilize complementary skills and assets. This was the case, for instance, in the alliance between Mitsui and GE noted above. Sharing core competencies can create synergies that enhance the competitive positions of both companies. Strategic alliances may result in the creation of technological standards for the industry, which would simplify the manufacturing process for the firms involved and also benefit the end user.

Strategic alliances have drawbacks similar to those of joint ventures. Most notably, the firm runs the risk of losing its competitive advantage by "giving away" proprietary know-how to the partner. The firm may also misjudge the partner's capabilities. The success of any strategic alliance depends on the interpersonal relationship between the managers of the firms. Lack of trust, misunderstandings, and opportunistic behaviors may cause the alliance to dissolve, which may result in writing off millions of investment dollars.

Wholly Owned Subsidiaries

wholly owned subsidiary
A means of entering new markets in which a firm fully owns its subsidiary in foreign countries.

When a multinational firm fully owns a company in a foreign country, the local company is a **wholly owned subsidiary** of the multinational. Wal-Mart owns all of its stores worldwide. This arrangement has several advantages. A wholly owned subsidiary offers a firm maximum control over proprietary knowledge and technology, so that competitors cannot gain access. In addition, the foreign company retains full discretion to move resources to other countries and thereby enjoys greater strategic flexibility. For instance, it may use profits from one country to move aggressively into other countries. A global production system may provide efficiencies because "the various operations must be prepared to accept centrally determined decisions as to how they will produce, how much they will produce, and how output will be priced for transfer to the next operation."[42]

On the other hand, wholly owned subsidiaries require large capital outlays, and ownership is thus the most expensive method of operating in foreign markets. The firm bears the full brunt of business risks, since these are not shared with a local partner. Corporate managers of a wholly owned subsidiary may not sufficiently understand local conditions. A firm that exclusively relies on wholly owned subsidiaries may be unable to operate in markets where legal or political imperatives require foreign firms to establish joint ventures with local partners.

LOC-In 4   **Learning Objective Check-In**

1. Sim Squad, a successful business simulation company, is a service firm that has built a strong brand name in the United States. The company is considering entrance to new markets in foreign countries. Sim Squad's strategic managers plan to use _____ because they want to allow for rapid expansion in the foreign markets with relatively small capital investment and little risk exposure. The one drawback they face is concern over quality control in the various stores.
   a. licensing
   b. wholly owned subsidiaries
   c. joint ventures
   d. franchising

■ Managing the Global Firm

ethnocentric approach
An approach to managing an international subsidiary that involves filling top management and other key positions with people from the home country (expatriates).

polycentric approach
An approach to managing an international subsidiary in which subsidiaries are managed and staffed by personnel from the host country (local nationals).

The success of a foreign venture depends on who is in charge. If a manager does not perform up to par in a domestic unit, others can fill in. This is not the case in an overseas operation. The importance of choosing the right managers was underlined by CEOs of U.S. companies with revenues in the $300 million to $1 billion range who identified the choice of management for overseas units as one of their most crucial business decisions.[43]

There are three basic approaches to managing an international subsidiary: the ethnocentric, polycentric, and geocentric approaches. The **ethnocentric approach** involves filling top management and other key positions with people from the home country. These managers are known as *expatriates*. In the **polycentric approach**, international subsidiaries are managed and staffed by personnel from the host country, or local nationals. Nationality is deliberately downplayed in

SKILLS FOR MANAGING 2.1

Opening a Facility Abroad

AACC is a U.S. manufacturer of prosthetic devices, including canes, crutches, walkers, and other devices that help partially disabled people maintain some independence. All of AACC's management functions are located in the United States. Domestic sales account for 85 percent of its revenues, with the remaining 15 percent originating mostly in Canada and Mexico. AACC has decided to expand its international operations in order to remain competitive and increase its market share. CEO Ralph Solomon met with the firm's top executives and set up a committee within AACC to develop concrete proposals for internationalizing the company. Solomon has prepared the following memo that lists four areas that should be covered as part of the committee's recommendations.

TO: Members of AACC International Task Force
FROM: Mr. Ralph Solomon
SUBJECT: International Task Force

If we are to remain a strong and competitive firm, AACC must begin to exploit opportunities abroad. Several task forces will study alternative means of internationalizing AACC, including opening a manufacturing site abroad and moving aggressively into international markets.

I have appointed you to a task force to provide recommendations to guide future actions. Your analysis and recommendations must be clearly supported by facts. Any reasonable assumptions you make as part of your analysis should be justified in a clear and logical manner.

I am counting on you to develop a high-quality proposal, covering the following areas:

1. If AACC should be involved in overseas production, indicate where plants should be located and why.
2. AACC will entertain any of the following alternatives:
   - *Licensing of AACC Technology and Patents:* In this option, AACC would license its technology and patents to a foreign producer who would then produce products for AACC at a contracted price. AACC could purchase all or part of this producer's total output under this arrangement.
   - *Joint Venture: AACC* could invest funds in a new or existing company within a country with a partner in that country.
   - *Wholly Owned Facility:* Instead of having a host country partner, AACC could build or buy a production facility on a wholly owned basis.
   - *Strategic Alliance:* In this option AACC may develop a partnership with a foreign firm to conduct R&D on prosthetic devices and manufacture a variety of such products without formally setting up a joint venture.

   Analyze the pros and cons of each option. What alternative should be used for foreign manufacturing in the country you have selected? Justify your choice.
3. Develop a plan outlining how the foreign venture will be managed and the steps that should be taken to minimize potential problems that may emerge.

Exercise

Form committees, each consisting of four students, with the following roles assigned:

Chairperson

- Coordinates team members' activities.
- Monitors team members' progress.
- Acts as a clearinghouse for information from various functional areas so that it can be easily understood and used by the entire team.
- Develops, proposes, and evaluates various scenarios, in close collaboration with other team members.
- Establishes agendas and protocol for team meetings, and controls any dysfunctional behavior, such as long monologues, personality clashes, and unfocused argumentation.
- Develops implementation and corporate strategy plans that integrate the team's functional areas.

Political/Legal Adviser

- Conducts political risk analysis for various countries under consideration.
- Provides legal support to the team including judicial interpretation of issues being discussed.
- Makes recommendations regarding the legal and political ramifications of various manufacturing arrangements overseas, such as joint venture versus wholly owned subsidiary.
- Analyzes government policies that may have an effect on AACC's operation, such as laws controlling profit repatriation to the United States.

Financial/Economic Adviser

- Provides the team with relevant data and recommendations concerning the general economic conditions of countries under consideration.
- Conducts research on the tax advantages and disadvantages in various countries.
- Analyzes business factors that may affect AACC's operations, such as inflation, devaluation, and convertibility of local currency into dollars.

Human Resources Adviser

- Analyzes human resources of those countries under consideration
- Works with the political/legal adviser in evaluating legal restrictions concerning expatriates.
- Estimates labor costs for AACC's foreign operation.
- Develops a resource plan for managing AACC's international venture.

Each committee will prepare a written report and make an oral presentation of an independent proposal covering the areas noted in the memo. The instructor will play the role of CEO and may ask questions of committee members to assess the soundness of the recommendations being offered.

TABLE 2.4 Advantages and Disadvantages of Using Local and Expatriate Employees to Staff International Subsidiaries

Advantages	Disadvantages
Locals	
• Lowers labor costs • Demonstrates trust in local citizenry • Increases acceptance of the company by the local community • Maximizes the number of options available in the local environment • Leads to recognition of the company as a legitimate participant in the local economy • Effectively represents local considerations and constraints in the decision-making process	• Makes it difficult to balance local demand and global priorities • Leads to postponement of difficult local decisions (such as layoffs) until they are unavoidable, when they are more difficult, costly, and painful than they would have been if implemented earlier • May make it difficult to recruit qualified personnel • May reduce the amount of control exercised by headquarters
Expatriates	
• Cultural similarity with parent company ensures transfer of business/management practices • Permits closer control and coordination of international subsidiaries • Gives employees a multinational orientation through experience at parent company • Establishes a pool of internationally experienced executives • Local talent may not yet be able to deliver as much value as expatriates can	• Creates problems of adaptability to foreign environment and culture • Increases the "foreignness" of the subsidiary • May involve high transfer, salary, and other costs • May result in personal and family problems • Has disincentive effect on local-management morale and motivation • May be subject to local government restrictions

Source: From *Managing Human Resources* by Gomez-Mejia, et al., Copyright © 2012. Reprinted by permission of Pearson Education, Inc., Upper Saddle River, NJ.

geocentric approach

An approach to managing an international subsidiary in which nationality is deliberately downplayed, and the firm actively searches on a worldwide or regional basis for the best people to fill key positions.

third-country nationals

Citizens of countries other than the host nation or the firm's home country.

the **geocentric approach** as the firm actively searches on a worldwide or regional basis for the best people to fill key positions. Many of these individuals are likely to be **third-country nationals**—citizens of countries other than the host nation or the firm's home country.

Table 2.4 summarizes the pros and cons of using local nationals and expatriates in foreign operations. It costs firms more than a third of a million dollars annually to transfer and compensate expatriates. Consequently, firms use them only for key positions, such as senior managers, high-level professionals, and technical specialists.

Twenty percent to 40 percent of expatriates return before completing their assignments, compared with fewer than 5 percent of Japanese expatriates.[44] Premature returnees cost $85,000 to $260,000 each, and the costs of business disruptions, lost opportunities, a leadership vacuum, and family hardships are probably many times greater. Six factors, which are summarized in Table 2.5 on page 59, account for most failures, although their relative importance varies by firm. Selection, training, career development, and compensation practices can deal with the factors that lead to failure.

Management Is Everyone's Business 2.2 on page 59 offers a set of recommendations that those who are now in or plan to be in management positions should consider in light of our discussion so far.

Selection

Choosing expatriate managers with the best odds of success means utilizing an effective selection process. Selection criteria should include cultural sensitivity. The selection board should have some expatriates. The company should require previous international experience and verify that the candidate's spouse and family are flexible, patient, and adaptable.

TABLE 2.5 Why International Assignments End in Failure

Career blockage	Initially, many employees see the opportunity to work and travel abroad as exciting. But once the initial rush wears off, many feel that the home office has forgotten them and that their career has been sidetracked while their counterparts at home are climbing the corporate ladder.
Culture shock	Many people who take international assignments cannot adjust to a different cultural environment, a phenomenon called culture shock. Instead of learning to work within the new culture, the expatriate tries to impose the home office's or home country's values on the host country's employees, tending to internal conflict.
Lack of predeparture cross-cultural training	Surprisingly, only about one-third of multinationals provide any cross-cultural training to expatriates, and those that do tend to offer rather cursory programs.
Overemphasis on technical qualifications	The person chosen to go abroad may have impressive credentials and an excellent reputation in the home office for getting things done. Yet this person may lack cultural adaptability as an important trait to be effective overseas.
Getting rid of a troublesome employee	International assignments may seem to be a convenient way of dealing with managers who are having problems in the home office. By sending these managers abroad, the organization is able to resolve difficult interpersonal situations or political conflicts at the home office, but at a significant cost to its international operations.
Family problems	The inability or unwillingness of the expatriate's spouse and children to adapt to life in another country is one of the most important reasons for failure. In fact, more than half of all early returns can be attributed to family problems.

Source: From *Managing Human Resources* by Gomez-Mejia, et al. Copyright © 2012. Reprinted by permission of Pearson Education, Inc., Upper Saddle River, NJ.

MANAGEMENT IS EVERYONE'S BUSINESS   2.2

WORKING AS A MANAGER Two major barriers preventing firms from capitalizing on business opportunities overseas are a lack of awareness about (1) how to enter foreign markets and (2) how to operate in diverse national settings. Managers can learn how to function well in foreign lands by developing a better appreciation of the unique challenges that may confront them. Few firms today have the luxury of avoiding globalization. New managers should be groomed to play a key role in internationalization.

As a manager you should:

- Be on the lookout for emerging business opportunities overseas, not only in your own backyard.
- Keep attuned to trends in international business that may have an effect on your company. These may involve changes in the law, exchange rates, trade pacts, political risks, and the like. Much of this information is readily available in business periodicals (such as *The Wall Street Journal*, *BusinessWeek*, and *The Economist*), on the Internet, and from trade, industry, and regional associations.
- Be sensitive to cultural differences among employees and customers but do not stereotype people.
- Try to attract and retain employees from various ethnic and cultural backgrounds, as this might help the company target its products and services to diverse foreign markets.
- Encourage subordinates to be involved in international efforts, and if appropriate, include this as part of the performance appraisal and merit pay/promotion review process.
- Actively develop external networks with influential people inside and outside the industry (for instance, by attending important international conferences), as this might help you establish personal contacts that could evolve into common projects, joint ventures, or strategic alliances with foreign firms. In most non-Anglo-Saxon countries business transactions tend to be very personal. Thus cultivating networks is critical for success.
- Make sure you do everything within your power to give the impression that as a manager you are fair, ethical, and socially responsible. A bad reputation, whether it is deserved or not, is almost certain to increase political risks for your company.

LOC-In 5 Learning Objective Check-In

1. DigiShot is in the process of choosing managers to head its overseas operations. The firm plans to deliberately downplay nationality in the managers it selects. Instead, DigiShot is actively searching on a worldwide basis for the best people to fill the key positions. The company believes that this _____ approach to managing the subsidiary will determine its success.
   a. bureaucratic
   b. geocentric
   c. ethnocentric
   d. polycentric

Training

Cross-cultural training sensitizes candidates to the local culture, customs, language, and government. Table 2.6 provides an example of how an American expatriate being sent to Greece for an assignment might learn to appreciate differences in communication between the American and

TABLE 2.6 Learning to Appreciate Cultural Noise in International Communications: The Case of Greece versus the United States

Behavior		Attribution	
American:	"How long will it take you to finish this report?"	*American*:	I asked him to participate.
		Greek:	His behavior makes no sense. He is the boss. Why doesn't he tell me?
Greek:	"I don't know. How long should it take?"	*American*:	He refuses to take responsibility.
		Greek:	I asked him for an order.
American:	"You are in the best position to analyze time requirements."	*American*:	I press him to take responsibility for his actions.
		Greek:	What nonsense: I'd better give him an answer.
Greek:	"10 days."	*American*:	He lacks the ability to estimate time; this time estimate is totally inadequate.
American:	"Take 15. Is it agreed? You will do it in 15 days?"	*American*:	I offer a contract.
		Greek:	These are my orders: 15 days.

In fact, the report needed 30 days of regular work. So the Greek worked day and night, but at the end of the 15th day, he still needed to do one more day's work.

American:	"Where is the report?"	*American*:	I am making sure he fulfills his contract.
		Greek:	He is asking for the report.
Greek:	"It will be ready tomorrow."	(Both attribute that it is not ready.)	
American:	"But we agreed it would be ready today."	*American*:	I must teach him to fulfill a contract.
		Greek:	The stupid, incompetent boss! Not only did he give me the wrong orders, but he doesn't even appreciate that I did a 30-day job in 16 days.
The Greek hands in his resignation.			The American is surprised.
		Greek:	I can't work for such a man.

Source: Reprinted with permission from Deresky, H. (2011), *International Management*, Pearson Prentice Hall, p. 118.

SKILLS FOR MANAGING 2.2

How Would You Train Expatriates to Go Overseas?

Assume that you are a human resource manager for a large energy firm with facilities in Colombia, Norway, Nigeria, and Saudi Arabia. In five months or so the company intends to send approximately 10 American expatriate managers to each of those locations. They are expected to stay at least a year.

You have been asked to develop a training program to help those expatriates and their families to adjust. Provide an outline of a training program, with key features that may be more appropriate for each of these countries such as security concerns and language training. (The instructor may decide to make this a team project by dividing the class into teams of five.)

Greek cultures. More rigorous and lengthy training is generally reserved for key executives and those expected to be overseas for an extended period of time. Skills for Managing 2.2, "How Would You Train Expatriates to Go Overseas?" asks you to develop such a program.

Career Development

Expatriates are more likely to complete foreign assignments and to be highly motivated to succeed when they believe that the assignments are instrumental to their future career opportunities. Unfortunately, this has not always been the case. Only 15 percent of the top 50 executives in U.S. corporations have worked abroad as compared with 35 percent of European executives and 27 percent of Japanese executives.[45] About 80 percent of executives posted abroad feel that employers do not value their international experience. Although 75 percent expect the move to benefit their careers, only 10 percent receive promotions when they return to the home office.[46] Female executives have less access to opportunities overseas than male executives, and the perceived value of international experience in their careers is also lower.[47]

At a minimum, successful career planning for expatriates requires firms to position international assignments as a step toward advancement within the firm. In addition, the home office should provide continued support to expatriates, such as by appointing a senior executive as a mentor, offering short sabbaticals in the home office, and bringing expatriates back to the home office occasionally.

One trend in the latter half of this decade is short-term expatriate assignments. Instead of relocating employees and their families for two years or more (a three-year assignment can easily cost $1 million) the stint overseas would last from several weeks to 12 months and leave the family behind.[48] There are several reasons for this trend, including cost savings, the high rate of expatriates who decide to renege on their contract and come home early if given a lengthy assignment, a belief that short-term assignments are less traumatic for the family, and the prevalence of dual careers (the spouse may continue to work at home when the expatriate is gone for a shorter time period).

On the other hand, there are also some problems to consider with short-term foreign assignments. One is that it takes time to learn about a foreign culture, and the expatriate may have to leave just when he or she feels comfortable with local conditions. Often the "short-term" assignment needs to be extended to 18 months or more, which can be an unpleasant shock for families. And families may not be as happy with this approach as some companies seen to assume. The spouse left at home must do "your job plus 100 percent of the chores, plus filling in for your partner with the kids. The days are extremely long, tiring and mentally exhausting," writes one wife in a study of families involved in short-term assignments by Anne Copeland, director of the Interchange Institute, a Brookline, Massachusetts, nonprofit research concern.[49]

Management Is Everyone's Business 2.3 on page 62 offers a set of career recommendations that you might wish to follow in order to enhance your personal success in a globalized economy.

Compensation

In the international management setting, money makes the world go around. When salaries are inappropriately low, misgivings that the expatriate manager and spouse may have about foreign assignment rise. The cost of housing, food, and other consumer goods is far higher in many foreign locations than in the United States. For example, it is almost impossible to find decent accommodations in a 1,000 square foot apartment in a city like London, Paris, or Tokyo for less than $4,000 a month. Ninety-eight percent of companies offer some type of additional financial incentive and housing allowance for expatriates, but often this may not be enough to compensate for the cost disparity.[50]

MANAGEMENT IS EVERYONE'S BUSINESS 2.3

WORKING AS AN INDIVIDUAL The career mobility of an employee is likely to be enhanced if the individual has international skills. International savvy is increasingly valued, particularly by medium-sized to large firms that are expanding their foreign operations or that face foreign competition. Many firms require employees to have international experience before they can move into the upper management ranks. Your ability to function well internationally should improve your chances of assuming an important managerial role. Although some firms have not valued international experience in the past, its importance is rapidly increasing. For you as an individual this means that to further your career, you should:

- Try to acquire foreign experience through internships, study-abroad programs, voluntary work overseas, and the like.
- Learn a foreign language. Even though English has become the "common language" of business around the world, people will feel more at ease with you if you can speak their language.
- Demonstrate cultural sensitivity in dealing with recruiters, peers, managers, customers, and other employees. A reputation for being culturally biased or insensitive to the feelings of those who are different from you (for instance, through ethnic or gender-based jokes) is likely to hinder your career opportunities both inside and outside the firm.
- Make your superiors aware that you are willing and capable of handling overseas assignments. Don't assume that they will approach you first; you are more likely to get the opportunity if you express an interest.

Planning expatriate compensation should follow two guidelines. First, the firm should provide the expatriate with a disposable income that is equivalent to what he or she would earn in the home office. This may require special allowances for housing, children's education, medical care, and so on. Second, the firm should provide an explicit "add-on" incentive, such as a sign-on bonus and a bonus at the end of the assignment for going overseas, and the bonus should be larger for less desirable locations.

LOC-In 6   Learning Objective Check-In

1. Jared is going to become an expatriate manager at his company. He will be in the other country for about 12 months. Jared is in the middle of his 4-week cross-cultural training sessions. He is learning the other language, studying cases, learning about stress-reduction techniques, and doing some role-playing to deal with critical incidents that may arise while he is in that country. Jared's cross-cultural training program is taking the _____ approach.
   a. information-giving
   b. affective
   c. impression
   d. experiential

■ Ethics and Social Responsibility

Globalization greatly increases the possibility that a manager will face an ethical dilemma. Different cultures have different notions of right and wrong. For instance, as noted in Management Close-Up 2.3, "Blow the Whistle—No, Wait: Ethics Hotlines May Be Illegal in Europe" on page 63, reliance on anonymous tips to identify unethical employee behavior is becoming common in the United States, but Europeans (who still have memories of authoritarian regimes in places like Spain, Italy, Germany, and much of Eastern Europe) find this practice appalling.

Another dilemma may be that a firm may lose business if it applies a stricter code of ethics than foreign competitors follow. A transaction that an American might perceive as bribery could be construed by others as a commission or as an incentive necessary to conduct business in a foreign country. While many Americans were disgusted by news reports that Salt Lake City officials had bribed the Olympic Commission to select Salt Lake City as a future Olympic site, several of the officials defended the practice on the grounds that gifts were expected in that situation.

MANAGEMENT CLOSE-UP 2.3

Blow the Whistle—No, Wait: Ethics Hotlines May Be Illegal in Europe

Hotlines are phone numbers employees can use to anonymously report to the company what they believe to be unethical behavior or practices (e.g., "cooking up" sales numbers, sexual harassment, overcharging the government and other clients). It is estimated that more than half of Fortune 500 firms in the United States have hotlines in place. But when trying to use hotlines in their international operations they are encountering a lot of unexpected opposition. For instance, France has blocked McDonalds and Exide Technologies from using hotlines because the accuser can remain anonymous. Wal-Mart faced a similar problem in Germany. Because of historical reasons (European countries in the mainland still have bitter memories of totalitarian regimes) they are reluctant to allow American firms to collect anonymous data about individuals who may not have a chance to prove their innocence.

Sources: "Blow the Whistle—No, Wait: Ethics Hotlines May Be Illegal in Europe," *Business Ethics,* Fall 2005, p. 10. See also D. Reilly, "France Ends Impasse with SEC," *The Wall Street Journal,* November 21, 2005, p. A-8. Based on M. Castells, M., (2010), *End of Millennium: The information age: Economy, society, and culture.* New York, NY: Wiley-Blackwell; K. H. Brunk (2010), "Exploring origins of ethical company/brand perceptions—A Consumer perspective of corporate ethics," *Journal of Business Research,* 63(3), 255–62; J. Hardwig (2010), "The stockholders—A lesson for business ethics from bioethics," *Journal of Business Ethics,* 91(3), 329–41.

The U.S. Foreign Corrupt Practices Act of 1977 is a tough anticorruption law governing international business. The Act was passed as a result of United Brands's $2.5 million bribe to Honduran government officials to reduce the banana tax. The law expressly forbids substantial payments by American firms to foreign officials to influence decisions. Many businesspeople believed that the act would put U.S. firms at a disadvantage overseas, but there is little evidence that this has occurred. It is possible that the legislation created a better image for American firms internationally counterbalancing any losses.

LOC-In 7 Learning Objective Check-In

1. In theory, _____ means poor countries reduce unemployment, wealthy countries get cheaper labor, and workers earn far more aboard than they could at home. In practice, the brokers who make the labor deals have incentives and opportunities to gouge the workers they control. This is one element of globalization that demonstrates the need for firms to develop their own codes of ethical conduct for foreign operations.
   a. debt bondage
   b. foreign contract work
   c. uncertainty avoidance
   d. the U.S. Foreign Corrupt Practices Act of 1977

Many firms and industry groups have developed their own code of conduct for foreign operations. For example, the American Apparel Manufacturers Association (AAMA), whose members include Sara Lee, Jockey International, and VF, requires members to pay the existing minimum wage, maintain certain minimum safety standards, and avoid the use of child labor. Companies such as Nike, GAP, and Adidas have formed the Joint Initiative on Corporate Accountability and Worker Rights, or JOIN, to monitor their foreign suppliers for abuses.[51] Some companies, such as Ikea (see Management Close-Up 2.2), have their own internal monitoring process to ensure that suppliers across the globe comply with the firm's ethical standards. Nevertheless, firms continue to face many ethical issues when they go overseas in search of cheaper labor. These include child labor issues, gender discrimination issues, unsafe working conditions, and environmental contamination, among others.[52] At the same time that globalization continues to increase dramatically, abuses by some multinational firms and governments have given globalization a bad name for many, even though it has improved the economic conditions of many countries around the world.

CONCLUDING THOUGHTS

At the beginning of the chapter we posed some questions pertaining to Playmobil's operations in Germany. Now that you have had the opportunity to read the chapter, it's time to revisit those questions. Playmobil's example shows the reliance on foreign markets is becoming increasingly necessary, and possible, as firms capitalize on opportunities beyond their borders. Firms without a global vision are more likely to experience a major competitive disadvantage. To earn profits, Playmobil has chosen to expand its markets beyond Germany and even Europe, and strengthen its sales presence in the United States, Latin America, and Asia as well. This globalization of business is fueling unprecedented economic growth in many parts of the world.

The competitive landscape is more complex than ever, and globalization presents many additional challenges. This chapter has dealt with the unique issues and problems firms face in the global environment, but the roots of many decisions that multinational firms make still lie at home. A stagnant or declining birth rate and a slowing economy in Germany have cut into the markets for many consumer products, forcing many German companies like Playmobil to look elsewhere for customers. Together, their decisions have helped make Germany the biggest merchandise exporter in the world, boosting corporate profits and the German stock market to new highs.

For Playmobil to consider making a deeper investment abroad, such as a licensing agreement or joint venture to move manufacturing to China, for example, the firm would want to be assured of quality control and the kind of logistical flexibility that management now wields over its domestic manufacturing operations. The cost of obtaining these safeguards would have to be outweighed by labor cost savings.

FOCUSING ON THE FUTURE: Using Management Theory in Daily Life

Managing in a Global Environment

Bruce Humphrys serves in a general manager capacity for a nonprofit technical organization. As the Executive Director of Compatible Technology International (CTI), he must encourage his employees—a group of volunteer engineers, food scientists, and technicians—to create food processing tools that can be used in underdeveloped nations all over the world. To create products that will be used, rather than abandoned, Bruce has to take into consideration the general business environment, legal systems, the country's economic environment, and cultural environments. Take the case of the breadfruit dryer, for instance.

One of Bruce's senior food scientists, George Ewing, saw a need to give people in Haiti a way to dry breadfruit. Fresh breadfruit is a vegetable similar to squash. It has a very short shelf-life; fruit lasts only a day or so after being harvested. But when breadfruit is dried, it can be turned into a flour which keeps well and enriches both the islanders' diet and their economy. Fortunately, Ewing met Camille George, a professor at the University of St. Thomas in St. Paul, Minnesota, at a political lunch. She had the expertise in heat transfer technology to help him create a simple breadfruit drying machine.

If Professor George and her students had been tasked with creating a food dryer for use in Minneapolis, their job might have been simple. But obviously, this was not the case. How could these engineers determine if their invention was meeting the needs of clients a half a world away? They knew that they would have to test their product extensively, and take the general business environment, the legal systems, the economic environment, and the cultural environment of their clients into account when doing so.

General Business Environment

Because Haiti is a country in turmoil, the general business environment was less favorable than it is in other parts of the world. The former President, Jean-Bertrand Aristide, resigned from office in 2004, which opened the door for the interim government to take steps to encourage foreign investments. But there is still a great deal of political turmoil in the area, and the Haitian government continues to be unstable. In fact, although a trip to Haiti was scheduled to test an initial food dryer design, it had to be cancelled. Instead, Professor George and her students traveled to the island of St. Vincent, where climate conditions were similar but the general business environment was much more stable.

Legal Environment

Like the general business environment, the legal environment in Haiti is difficult and complex. While on the surface, Haiti is a democracy, with a civil law system based on the Napoleonic Code, in practice, the Haitian legal environment is often chaotic. There is widespread corruption, and disputes are often resolved through bribery and favoritism. Steps are being taken to modernize the legal system and make Haiti more open to foreign investors, but at this time, changes are not fully in place. Fortunately for Bruce Humphrys, CTI is a nonprofit organization, and therefore not bound by as many legal restrictions as a for-profit organization would be.

Economic Environment

Haiti is a developing country, with high levels of poverty and a poor infrastructure. The 2010 earthquake that killed almost 200,000 people in the Haitian capital, Port-au-Prince, has only made a dire situation even more extreme. Jobs are scarce, and the average Haitian worker supports up to six other people at any one time. If an invention is to benefit the Haitian people, it is imperative that it be simple, useful, and use few natural resources (such as fuel). For example, CTI developed a food grinder that is nothing more than a metal cylinder with a blade at the bottom and a crankshaft. Setting up the grinder is simple, and powering it requires nothing more than the ability to turn the crankshaft. The breadfruit dryer developed by CTI was solar powered and consisted of little more than wood and plastic sheeting, so it would be easy to build and transport.

Cultural Environment

Culture, is the final, key ingredient in determining whether or not a CTI project will work. Humphrys tells the following story about how culture impacted a CTI project in Guatemala: "Our guys visited a group of Guatemalan women hand-shelling corn. They saw the hard time they were having, how labor-intensive the shelling was, and on the spot they developed a sheller. The sheller consisted of a piece of wood with a hole in the middle. The women pushed the ear of corn through the hole, shaving the kernels from the cob. When the engineers passed out their device, the women said thanks and put the sheller to work. But when the volunteers returned to that village several months later, they found the group still hand-cutting kernels from corn. The women told them, 'Thanks for your invention, it's much easier. But this is the time we use to talk about men, school, and kids, and your device makes our work too fast for that.'" Extensive conversations and tests with the women of St. Vincent showed that there were no obvious cultural problems with the breadfruit dryer, but interestingly enough, a different problem emerged.

George and her group of engineering students found that the dryer was not going to work in Haiti—it dried the outside of the breadfruit without drying the inside, causing the fruit to spoil. It turned out that breadfruit dried better when placed directly in the sun, where the island breezes provided continuous airflow. The good news was that during the testing process, the women of St. Vincent suggested another way to put the dryers to work making money for the islanders. It seems that Italian restaurants in the United States demand red pepper flakes that are just one color—a dark red. The dryers allowed flakes to uniformly dry to exactly that color, and the islanders in St. Vincent are now using them to improve their economy.

Sources: G. Smith "Cereal socialism in Venezuela," *BusinessWeek*, 2010, March 29, 46–51; B. Steverman, "The action stays offshore," *BusinessWeek*, 2010, January 4, 60–64; C. Forelle, "Haitian resource stymied amid chaos," *Wall Street Journal*, 2010, February 1, A-2; Jean Thilmany, "Managing across Cultures," *Mechanical Engineering*, February 2005, http://www.memaga2ine.org/backissues/feb05/features/mngcult/mngcult.html; U.S. Department of State, 2005 *Investment Climate Statement—Haiti*, March 2006, http://www.state.gov/e/eb/ifd/2005/42043.htm.

Summary of Learning Objectives

Firms increasingly compete in a global market characterized by high uncertainty, many players, and great complexity. This chapter's discussion will help you in your future career as a manager, as a member of a work team, or as an individual to succeed in this new global environment. The material presented to meet each of the chapter's learning objectives stated at the outset of the chapter is summarized below.

1 Describe the changing pattern of international business.

- *Changing world output and world trade picture.* The United States no longer dominates the world economy. Large U.S. multinationals no longer dominate international business. Centrally planned economies are opening to Western businesses, and national barriers to labor markets are folding (particularly in knowledge intensive industries).
- *Changing demographics.* The population in industrialized countries is getting older, and immigration is growing worldwide.
- *Lower trade barriers.* While some protectionism is still present and perhaps receiving growing political support in some areas, lower trade restrictions are now the norm.

- *Greater market integration.* Economic integration between groups of countries is growing, and today there are 37 such agreements, compared to 11 in the 1980s. Of these, the greatest level of integration has been achieved by the European Union composed of 27 countries.
- *Converging global consumer preferences.* Consumer tastes and preferences are becoming more similar around the world.
- *More globalization of production.* A growing number of firms spread their production around the world in order to realize savings, particularly in labor costs.
- *Rapid technological innovations.* Advances in communications, information processing, and transportation are making it much easier to conduct business across geographical boundaries.
- *Greater cultural diversity.* To be effective, firms need to learn to adapt to an increasingly diverse set of customers, employees, and ways of doing business.

2 Identify major factors affecting international business.

- *General business environment.* You must consider all factors that might influence the costs, benefits, and risks of operating in particular world areas or countries.
- *Legal systems.* The firm must be able to comply with vastly different rules and regulations around the world.
- *Economic environment.* The firm must consider a host of economic factors that can vary from one time period to another and across countries. These include differences in per capita income, inflation, exchange rates, taxation, licensing agreements, and royalties.
- *Cultural environment.* To succeed internationally, firms and their members must be sensitive to cultural differences and be willing to adapt products, services, and management practices to those differences. Some well-known cultural aspects that might influence management practices and that vary across countries include prevalent ideas about appropriate **power distance** between superiors and subordinates, degree of **individualism, uncertainty avoidance,** and **masculinity–femininity** in a culture, and whether a culture has a **long- versus short-term orientation**.

3 Determine key decisions firms face when contemplating foreign expansion.

- *Which countries to enter.* In general, countries are more attractive from a business perspective when the size of the domestic market is large, purchasing power is high or likely to increase in the future, the firm's products are appropriate for a particular country market, and there is a positive business climate.
- *When to enter particular countries.* There are both advantages and disadvantages to being one of the first ones in a particular market. Being first can help a firm solidify its position in that market. However, this also involves greater investment in opening a new market and there is greater uncertainty since the firm cannot benefit from the experience of other firms that were there first.
- *What the scale of involvement should be.* The magnitude of the commitment to a foreign country increases as the investment in that country rises. In general, the scale of involvement is lowest if the firm is only exporting products and services into a country and highest if the firm owns and operates a plant in that country.

4 Differentiate the various ways firms can enter foreign markets.

- **Exporting.** Used primarily by firms entering international markets for the first time. In this mode, all manufacturing takes place within the domestic borders, which may result in foreign competitors enjoying significant cost advantages.
- **Turnkey.** Used by firms that prefer to receive payment for designing and building a plant that is then handed over to locals.
- **Licensing.** The firm generates profits in the form of a fee or royalty by granting rights to manufacture and sell a product in another country.
- **Franchising.** Similar to licensing, except franchising is used primarily for services.
- **Joint ventures and strategic alliances.** This approach allows quick access to international markets by establishing new entities in conjunction with local firms.
- **Wholly owned subsidiaries.** The deepest level of foreign involvement, whereby the multinational finances and manages the foreign facility, gives the firm maximum control over the foreign facility, but also incurs all the costs and risks of the foreign venture.

5 Identify alternative ways of managing a foreign operation.

- **Ethnocentric approach.** Foreign subsidiary is managed by personnel sent from the home office or by expatriates.

- **Polycentric approach.** Foreign subsidiary is managed by hiring individuals from each country in which subsidiaries are located.
- **Geocentric approach.** Multinational recruits personnel regardless of nationality. Many of these individuals are likely to be **third country nationals**—employees who are not citizens of the multinational's home country nor the country where the foreign subsidiary is located.

6 Recognize the key human resource policies that firms can develop to help expatriates succeed.

- *Selection.* Choose expatriates who are sensitive to cross-cultural differences, including a consideration of how the candidate's spouse and family might respond to the foreign assignment.
- *Training.* Provide cross-cultural training that sensitizes candidates to what they may confront in the foreign assignments.
- *Career development.* Ensure that the expatriate perceives the foreign assignment as part of a long-term career path within the company.
- *Compensation.* Maintain parity with the standard of living at home and provide additional incentives if expatriate successfully accomplish the foreign assignment.

7 Understand the ethical and social responsibility implications of doing business in different countries.

- Norms vary by country and a major concern for firms operating internationally is defining ethical behavior.
- Although competitors may abide by a different set of rules, U.S. firms must comply with regulations that prohibit the payment of bribes.
- Firms develop their own codes of conduct or may follow codes drawn up by international organizations.

Discussion Questions

1. If you were CEO of a medium-sized U.S. manufacturing firm, which of the changing patterns of international business identified in this chapter would concern you most? Explain.
2. Do you think there should be a large common market from Alaska to Tierra del Fuego, similar to the European Union? Why or why not?
3. What do you think accounts for the success of Ikea (see Management Close-Up 2.2) around the world? Can other struggling U.S. retailers such as K-Mart and Sears imitate Ikea's success? Explain your answer.
4. Which of the two perspectives concerning the use of ethics hotlines described in Management Close-Up 2.3

seem more reasonable to you (i.e., the European versus the American perspectives)? Explain your answer.
5. If you were the owner of a small but rapidly growing high-tech firm making sophisticated computer chips for medical equipment, which mode of entry would you prefer for entering foreign markets? Explain.
6. Do you think an international firm should have local managers in all important posts? Why or why not?
7. Is a firm justified in paying a bribe if it believes a competitor will do so to win an important contract? Explain.

Management Minicase 2.1
Sweatshop Swipe

United Students Against Sweatshops (USAS) have mounted demonstrations on 40 campuses demanding that universities force companies that license and make their sports clothes and other apparel to use only suppliers that pay a living wage and respect unions. USAS wants clothing companies to agree to pay higher prices to overseas factories that make college goods, which have annual sales of about $3 billion. Factories would have to boost wages, now about $97 a month in China. Jim Wilkerson, Duke University's director of trademark licensing and stores, calls the idea "workable," adding: "It would raise prices, but only by about 25 cents on a $30 garment." As outsourcing increases companies keep looking for suppliers that will provide what they need at the lowest possible cost. This might help the company's

shareholders and suppliers but make the living wage objective discussed above much harder to achieve.

DISCUSSION QUESTIONS

1. Do you think U.S. companies have the moral responsibility to offer a so-called living wage and to fight exploitative practices in foreign countries, even if doing so means putting the company at a competitive disadvantage? Explain your answer.
2. Do you think most consumers care about potential abuses of overseas contractors? Would most consumers be willing to pay slightly higher prices to improve the standard of living of foreign workers? Explain your answer.

3. Some believe that a company might actually increase business by convincing customers that it is socially responsible and that it values human dignity more than making an extra buck. Do you agree? Why or why not?

Sources: B. Steverman, "The action stays offshore," *BusinessWeek*, 10, January 4, 60–64; http://www.prlog.org, "Can't afford employees? Then outsource, subcontract," 2011; A. Berstein, "Sweatshop Swipe," *BusinessWeek*, October 10, 2005, p. 14.

Management Minicase 2.2
Drug Testing Goes Offshore

Patients can be recruited for clinical trials of drugs 10 times faster in Russia than in the United States, shaving precious time and millions of dollars off the drug-development cycle. From Azerbaijan to Nigeria, pharmaceutical companies are increasingly shifting clinical trials to emerging markets—as much as 40 percent of all drug trials. And they are doing it by outsourcing many of those trials to contract research organizations, which in turn subcontract the work of finding patients to local doctors. Merck's Vioxx and Zocor were tested in Russia and other developing countries, as were many of Pfizer's billion-dollar drugs, before gaining approval in the United States. While the vast majority of the trials are conducted without problems, there have been enough instances of ethical abuse and breakdowns in the scientific process to cause concern. A lawsuit still making its way through U.S. courts alleges that Pfizer tested a meningitis drug on Nigerian children without their consent, resulting in five deaths. And there have been charges over the years that other trials have endangered patients or have been conducted without proper ethical review.

The shift of drug testing to poorer countries is largely being driven by economics. Running a trial for a drug in the United States costs ten times more (about $30,000) than in Rumania (about $3,000). In less developed countries paperwork can be minimal and this means saving time and money. In the United States "there is a lot of useless bureaucracy and . . . too many middlemen" says Robert Califf, co-chair of the Clinical Trials Transformation Initiative and Duke's Vice Chancellor for clinical research. "Right now most of the money is going to the middle people," he says, referring to the monitors who are sent to trial sites in the United States to check on the experiments.

DISCUSSION QUESTIONS

1. Do you think it is appropriate for a pharmaceutical firm to conduct most of its clinical trials in less developed countries? Why or why not?

2. The Food and Drug Administration (FDA) in the United States requires that all trials submitted to it meet internationally accepted guidelines, known as Good Clinical Practice, that demand "the establishment of local review boards; ask government health ministries to approve all trials before they begin; warn against excessive payment to doctors; and outline how to obtain informed consent and avoid taking advantage of vulnerable patients." But as noted by Ward Cates, president of the research arm of nonprofit Family Health International. "How do you meet procedures required by the FDA in settings where electricity is going off two hours a day?" In your view, how can a pharmaceutical company ensure that clinical trials meet the FDA standards noted above? Is this realistic? Explain your answer.

3. Some companies argue that, cost savings aside, there are important benefits to more clinical trials overseas. From a mechanical standpoint, testing on ethnically diverse populations may offer more insight into the ways drugs can affect different people. And patients who would otherwise not receive any help get medication and treatment during the trials. Lastly, it helps drug companies penetrate new markets badly in need of new treatments. Russia's drug market is estimated at $5 billion this year, India's at $5.4 billion. Do you believe that these positive aspects outweigh potential problems with clinical trials overseas? Why or why not? Should the U.S. government become more involved in regulating these practices? Explain.

Source: Based on R. J. Trent (2010), "Pathology practice and pharmacogenomics," *Pharmacogenomics*, 11(1), 105–11; R. K. Belforti, M. S. Wall, P. Lindenauer, P. Pekow, M. Rothberg (2010), "International outsourcing of medical research by high income countries," *Journal of Investigative Medicine*, 58(2), 287–94; A. Lustgarten, "Drug Testing Goes Offshore," *Fortune,* August 8, 2005, pp. 67–72.

Individual/Collaborative Learning Case 2.1
Got 6,000 Euros? Need a New Car?

In 2005, Renault launched a new car called "The Logan," originally planned for poorer countries, but which has became enormously successful around the world, including the richest European countries. The Logan, which sells for as little as 6,000 euros, may soon be a major competitor in the U.S. market, putting additional pressure on struggling U.S. car companies such as GM and Ford.

No matter where the Logan sells, Renault has engineered a small miracle by making a car that is modern but stripped of costly design elements and superfluous technology. Its 1.4 liter, 75 horsepower engine and 1.6 liter 90 horsepower engine are very fuel efficient. Deutsche Bank pegs production costs for the Logan at $1,089 per car, less than half the $2,468 estimate for an equivalent Western auto. "The Logan is the McDonald's of cars," says Kenneth Melville, the Scot

who headed the Logan design team. "The concept was simple: Reliable engineering without a lot of electronics, cheap to build and easy to maintain and repair." The Logan has 50 percent fewer moving parts than a high-end Renault vehicle and offers a limited number of electronic devices. Some parts, which are simpler than those of the competition, include a symmetrical rear view mirror, a single-injection molded piece for the dashboard, and an engine prepared to handle lower quality fuel.

The Logan was first produced in Romania, where gross pay for a line worker is $324 per month, versus an average $4,723 a month for auto workers in Western Europe. Now, Renault is being produced in Brazil, Colombia, Russia, Morocco, India, Iran, and South Africa.

CRITICAL THINKING QUESTIONS

1. How does a multinational firm benefit from seeing the entire world as its labor pool? Do you see any potential problem with this vision? Why or why not?
2. How does this case illustrate the changing pattern of international business discussed in this chapter? Explain your answer.
3. What are the implications of this case for U.S. car manufacturers' shareholders, managers, employees, and labor unions? Explain your answer.

COLLABORATIVE LEARNING EXERCISE

You have been appointed to a task force that advises the Chief Executive Officer of General Motors (GM) of the competitive implications to GM of Renault's planned expansion of the Logan during the next several years. The task force (composed of three to five students) will provide its recommendations and reasoning to the CEO (played by instructor).

Sources: http://en.wikipedia.org/wiki/Dacia-Logan, 2011; http://www.renault-dacia-Logan.com, 2011; http://indiacar.com, 2011; G. Edmondson & C. Faivre de'Arcier, "Got 5,000 Euros? Need a New Car?" *BusinessWeek,* 2005, July 4, p. 49.

Internet Exercise 2.1

Colgate's Clean Sweep

www.colgate.com

Colgate was started in 1806 by an English immigrant who set up a starch, soap, and candle business on Dutch Street in New York. From these humble origins the company has become one of the largest multinational corporations with operations in almost all countries of the world, despite its "low-tech" product line of toothpaste, razor blades, soaps, and shaving creams. Visit Colgate's Web site as well as other related Internet sites to answer the following questions:

1. What accounts for Colgate's international success, despite the potential for intense competition in most markets?

2. Colgate boasts that its "Colgate Culture" has a worldwide basis. How can a company create such a culture despite operating in many different cultural milieus? What are the advantages and disadvantages of a company culture that transcends national culture?
3. Compare and contrast the structure of Colgate's executive team with another company's, which you can research on the Internet. Analyze the implications of your comparison from an international perspective.
4. After researching Colgate, would you advise the company to engage in licensing patents, joint ventures, or strategic alliances, or to establish wholly owned subsidiaries? Explain your answer.

Manager's Checkup 2.1

Careers in Global Management

Instructor divides up the class into groups of 4–6 students. Each group is asked to make a list of the pros and cons of accepting a foreign assignment that (a) is expected to last less than 6 months, (b) is expected to last at least a year but may require up to a 5-year commitment, (c) would take place outside of western European countries, and (d) would take place in a western European country. After listing the pros and cons under each scenario, the group is asked to report back to entire class, with the instructor serving as a moderator.

1. What are the main reasons that would lead you to accept an international assignment? List three.
2. What are the main reasons why you would turn down an international assignment? List three.
3. What, if any, are the major challenges for women successfully pursuing global careers that include international assignments (which do not exist for men)?

Manager's Checkup 2.2

Analyzing Your Own Values

Instructor divides class into teams of five students. Each team will meet for approximately 20 minutes. Each team is asked to make a list of 7–10 values that best describe the American culture. Each team must justify its choices, explaining how these values either singly or in combination impact organizational practices. Teams that include members with foreign experience may compare the set of American values with those of another culture. Each team will then report to entire class.

Endnotes

1. Deresky (2011). (see reference list); Osha & Kollarsky (2010) (see reference list); Zolmar & Tencati (2010). (see reference list). G. de Jonquieres, "Foreign Direct Investment Worldwide Figures to Reach $430 Billion," *Financial Times*, November 11, 1998, p. 6; D. I. Oyama, "World Watch," *The Wall Street Journal*, June 1, 1999 p. A16.
2. C. W. Hill, *International Business.* New York: McGraw-Hill/Irwin, 2011.
3. Hagherian (2010) (see reference list). World Trade Organization, *International Trade Trends and Statistics.* Geneva: WTO, 1998; see the special issue of *BusinessWeek* on globalization, February 3, 2003.
4. Hill, *International Business.*
5. "The 2010 Fortune 500," Special Issue, *Fortune*, May 3, 2010. "The Global 500," *Fortune*, August 7, 1995, pp. 130–131.
6. R. L. Hudson, "Europe's Great Expectations," *Wall Street Journal*, January 24, 2003, p. A-10.
7. E. Bellman and N. Koppel, "More U.S. Legal Work Moves to India's Low-Cost Lawyers," *The Wall Street Journal*, September 28, 2005, p. B-1.
8. F. Balfour and D. Roberts, "Stealing Managers from the Big Boys," *BusinessWeek*, September 26, 2005, p. 54.
9. Farndale, Pauwe, Morris & Stahl (2010) (see reference list) M. Kripalani, (2005, Oct. 10). "A Quiet Shopping Spree Overseas," *BusinessWeek*, October 10, 2005, p. 54.
10. G. V. Naik, J. Karp, J. Millman, F. Fassiti, and J. Slater, "Global Baby Bust," *Wall Street Journal*, January 24, 2003, p. B-1.
11. T. Raithel, "Panel to Look at Changes Brought by Toyota," *Evansville Courier and Press*, July 2, 1999, pp. 3–4.
12. L. Gomez-Mejia, et al., *Managing Human Resources.* Upper Saddle River, NJ: Pearson Education, Inc., 2012.
13. Ibid.
14. Steers et al. (2010) (see reference list) G. T. Sims, "Corn Flakes Clash Shows the Glitches in European Union," *The Wall Street Journal*, November 1, 2005, p. A-1.
15. Hill, *International Business.*
16. Ibid., p. 6.
17. Nankervis & Stanton (2010) (see reference list) S. N. Mehta, "Enterprise: Small Companies Look to Cultivate Foreign Business," *The Wall Street Journal*, July 7, 1994, p. B-2.
18. Hill, *International Business*, p. 11.
19. J. H. Donnelly, J. Gibson, and J. M. Ivancevich, *Fundamentals of Management.* Burr Ridge, IL: Irwin, 1995, p. 67.
20 Y. El-Rashidi, "D'oh! Arabized Simpsons Aren't Getting Many Laughs." *The Wall Street Journal*, December 2, 2005, p. A-1.
21. C. Matlack and P. Burrows, "HP's French Twist." *BusinessWeek*, October 10, 2005, p. 53.
22. D. A. Ball, W. H. McCulloch, P. L. Frantz, J. M. Geringer, & M. S. Minor, *International Business: The Challenge of Global Competition.* New York: McGraw-Hill, 2011.
23. R. S. Greenberger and C. S. Smith, "CD Piracy Flourishes in China," *The Wall Street Journal*, April 28, 1997, p. A1.
24. C. Balfour and D. Roberts, "Stealing Managers from the Big Boys," *BusinessWeek*, Septermber 26, 2005, p. 54.
25. J. Darling and D. Nauss, "Stall in the Fast Lane," *Los Angeles Times*, February 19, 1995, p. 1.
26. J. Graff, "Why France Is Burning," *Time*, November 14, 2005, p. 36.
27. G. Hofstede, *Culture's Consequences: International Differences in Work Related Values*, Beverly Hills, CA: Sage, 1984, p. 21.
28. Ibid.
29. Deresky (2011) Donkin (2010), Ambos et al. (2010) (see reference list for all three) C. Hymowitz, "More American Chiefs Are Taking Top Posts at Overseas Concerns," *The Wall Street Journal*, October 17, 2005, p. B-1.
30. Steers et al. (2010) (see reference) P. Dvorak, "Stringer Faces First Big Test as Sony's Chief," *The Wall Street Journal*, September 19, 2005, p. B-1; P. Dvorak, "Culture Clash Crimps Sony CEO," *The Wall Street Journal*, September 24, 2005, p. A-6; and J. Wrighton & J. Sapsford, "For Nissan's Rescuer, Ghosn, New Road Rules Await at Renault," *The Wall Street Journal*, April 26, 2005, p. A-1.
31. J. Wild, K. C. Wild, and J. C. Han, *International Business.* Englewood Cliffs, NJ: Prentice Hall, 2011.

32. A. Taylor, "Got 300,000?" *Fortune*, January 20, 2003, pp. 118–125.
33. M. Fackler, "Wal-Mart Doubles Down on Its Investment in Japan," *The New York Times*, October 29, 2005, p. B-4.
34. Wild et al., *International Business*, p. 376.
35. Hill, *International Business*.
36. C. Chandler, "India's Bumpy Ride," *Fortune*, October 31, 2005, p. 134.
37. C. Rhoads, "Motorola's Modernizer," *The Wall Street Journal*, June 23, 2005, p. B-1.
38. M. Ihlwan, & D. Roberts, "Made in Korea, Assembled in China," *BusinessWeek*, August 1, 2005, p. 48.
39. R. Buckman, "Cellphone Game Rings in New Niche: Ultracheap," *The Wall Street Journal*, August 18, 2005, p. B-4.
40. Buckman, "Cellphone Game"; Ihlwan & Roberts, Made in Korea.
41. B. Bremner, Z. Schiller, T. Smart, and W. Holstein, "Keiretsu Connections," *BusinessWeek*, July 22, 1996, p. 2.
42. Hill, *International Business*, p. 412.
43. R. Cohen, "For Coke, World Is Its Oyster," *The New York Times*, November 21, 1991, pp. DI, D5.
44. P. Oster, "Why Japan's Execs Travel Better," *BusinessWeek*, November 1993, p. 68.
45. Zgolnai & Tereati (2010) (see references) L. Grant, "That Overseas Job Could Derail Your Career," *Fortune*, April 14, 1997, p. 166.
46. Ibid.
47. Deresky (2011) (see references); Ferraro (2010) (see references) G. Koretz, "A Woman's Place Is . . .," *BusinessWeek*, September 13, 1999, p. 28; H. Lancaster, "To Get Shipped Abroad, Women Must Overcome Prejudice at Home," *The Wall Street Journal*, July 29, 1989, p. B1; M. L. Wilson, "She Got the Last Laugh When Colleagues Bet She Would Fail in Japan," *The Wall Street Journal*, July 16, 1999, p. B1.
48. S. Shellenberger, "Separation Anxiety: Short Job Transfers Create Problems for Families Left Behind," *The Wall Street Journal*, October 27, 2005, p. D-1.
49. Cited in ibid.
50. Farndale et al. (2010) (see references) G.W. Latta, "High Mobility International Employees," *WorldatWork*, 2005, p. 48; S. Trolman, "Rationalizing Global Incentive Pay Plans Look at the Big Picture," *Workspan*, August 5, 2005, p. 17; R. Rosenzwaig, "How Much Did We Spend This Year?" *Workspan*, July 5, 2005, p. 25; "Expatriate Programs," *Workspan*, July 5, 2005, p. 19; "Premiums and Allowances for Expatriates," *Workspan*, August 5, 2005, p. 13.
51. M. Gunther, "Can Factory Monitoring Ever Really Work?" *Fortune*, Fall 2005, p. 12.
52. Deresky (2011) (see references); M. Gunther, "Cops of the Global Village," *Fortune*, June 27, 2005, p. 158.

3

Learning Objectives

1 Apply the four key ethical criteria that managers and employees should use when making business decisions.

2 Explain why businesses establish codes of ethics as a method of guiding employee conduct.

3 Recognize ways to encourage ethical behavior in business.

4 Recognize morally challenging situations where ethical decisions should be made.

5 Identify important categories of stakeholders.

6 Recognize the influence of various stakeholders on a company's priorities, policies, plans, and goals.

Eating for Credit

What does a former schoolteacher see when she travels between her home and her job every day and passes a blighted schoolyard? If she is Alice Waters, she sees an opportunity for her company If to make a difference in kids' lives.

Waters, a former Montessori teacher, is the founder of Chez Panisse, a popular restaurant in Berkeley, California, that's been breaking new culinary ground for more than 35 years by serving local, seasonal, and sustainably grown foods. She has become a revolutionary force in the culinary world, championing organic food and helping popularize it from local farmers' markets all the way to the Clinton White House. The unused acre of the Martin Luther King Jr. Middle School's yard that lies between Waters's home and her restaurant had weeds poking through cracks in its cement several years ago when Waters was inspired to do something about it. With the school's approval, the help of some friends, and donated funds, Waters broke up and removed the cement, tilled and enriched the soil, and planted a bold swath of fruits, vegetables, herbs, and edible flowers. Students from the school worked with Waters and crew in planting, nurturing, and harvesting the organic garden. Then the idea really began to take off.

A kitchen was soon added, and the school's 1,000 students began to learn how to prepare the food they'd

Managing Social Responsibility and Ethics

agreement with the Berkeley Unified School District to create a new food curriculum for all the district's students in kindergarten through grade 12. The curriculum incorporates organic gardening, healthy cooking, and nutritious communal lunches for students and teachers alike. Lunch is an academic subject, and food-related activities permeate the curriculum, from math classes that measure garden beds to science classes that study drainage and erosion, while history classes look at the agricultural methods of pre-Columbian peoples. The program is beginning in five of the district's 16 schools with a $3.8 million grant from the foundation, and it has already become a model for other schools and organizations nationwide.

The foundation hopes its School Lunch Initiative will spearhead changes in the way patents, schools, and children everywhere think about growing and preparing food, beginning with "every public school child in Berkeley." Waters's concerns about rising rates of childhood obesity and diabetes are shared by many parents and educators, and she sees the Foundation's activities as a positive way to change consumers' dependence on the fast food industry, unhealthy foods valued for their convenience, and wasteful methods of producing food. "These values are changing us," she wrote recently in the *New York Times.* "As a nation, we need to take back responsibility for the health of not just our children, but also our culture."

grown. "Give me any kid," says Waters today, "In six weeks, they'll be eating chard." Her project, known as The Edible Schoolyard, is now fully supported by the Chez Panisse Foundation, which Waters founded with a commitment to "transforming public education by using food traditions to teach, nurture, and empower young people." A new cafeteria where students and teachers will eat lunch together is under construction at the school. And not long ago, the Chez Panisse Foundation signed an

Will the Edible Schoolyard catch on? Will the School Lunch Initiative grow into a nationwide curriculum movement? Waters and the Chez Panisse Foundation hope so. "This is not just changing the food in the cafeteria and making that an educational experience," says Waters. "This is for every single child."

Sources: "Chez Panisse Foundation," www.chezpanisse.com, accessed April 11, 2010; Alice Waters, "Eating for Credit," *The New York Times,* February 24, 2006, p. A23; Karola Saekel, "Culinary Pioneers: Pioneering Garden Marks a Decade," *San Francisco Chronicle,* September 7, 2005, p. F2; Kim Severson, "Food Joins Academic Menu in Berkeley School District," *San Francisco Chronicle,* August 29, 2004, p. A1.

CRITICAL THINKING QUESTIONS

1. *What benefits does Chez Panisse receive by focusing attention on corporate social responsibility through the actions of its foundation?*

2. *Organizational stakeholders are groups that have an interest in how a company performs or uses its resources. Who are Chez Panisse's organizational stakeholders?*

3. *Which organizational strategy most closely corresponds to how Chez Panisse manages relationships with its stakeholders? Is it a proactive approach or an accommodation approach?*

We'll revisit these critical thinking questions regarding Chez Panisse in our Concluding Thoughts at the end of the chapter.

It's a tricky world out there. Consequently, ethics and social responsibility should be a high priority for every member of an organization. This chapter examines the nature of business ethics and the basis of ethical decisions. It presents codes of ethics and provides examples of ethical challenges you are likely to encounter as an employee or a manager in a business setting. Skills for Managing 3.1 lists the management skills related to business ethics and social responsibility.

Next, the broader context of corporate social responsibility as well as the key stakeholders involved are examined. The goal is to help you gain a heightened awareness of the many ethical challenges that are present in the new millennium.

■ What Are Business Ethics?

ethics
Principles that explain what is good and right and what is bad and wrong and that prescribe a code of behavior based on these definitions.

business ethics
Standards or guidelines for the conduct and decision making of employees and managers.

Ethics are principles that explain what is right or wrong, good or bad, and what is appropriate or inappropriate in various settings. These ideas make it possible to prescribe a code of behavior for both work and one's personal life. **Business ethics** provide standards or guidelines for the conduct and decision making of employees and managers. Without a code of ethics, there is usually no consensus regarding ethical principles. Different people will use different ethical criteria in determining whether a practice or behavior is ethical or unethical. For example, it is not unusual in all good conscience for a manager to exaggerate the positive accomplishments of an employee in order to promote the employee or provide a salary increase. But another manager may consider inflating an employee's performance record a distortion of the truth, and thus unethical conduct.

Business ethics are not the same thing as laws. Law and ethics are in agreement in some situations but not in others. For example, it is both illegal and unethical to steal merchandise from an employer, but often it is not illegal to engage in conduct that is unethical. While it may not be illegal to take credit for the work of a colleague, it is highly unethical. Unfortunately, more than a few individuals have engaged in such tactics in order to advance their careers. When an organization does not condemn such behavior, others are encouraged to imitate it. Soon the organization develops a culture of political back-stabbing that drives away the most talented people and drains the energies of those who remain.

Nearly half the workers surveyed in a recent study admitted to engaging in at least one unethical act during the previous year. The most frequent unethical behaviors included cutting corners on quality, covering up potentially damaging incidents, lying about sick days, and deceiving customers. The workers blamed such daily pressures as trying to balance work and family, being forced to work longer hours due to layoffs, and poor manager-worker communications. They felt that ethical dilemmas could be reduced by better communication and a serious commitment by managers to establishing ethical standards of conduct.[1]

Table 3.1 lists some different categories of ethical issues in business. It suggests that many business relationships have the potential for unethical conduct, including those between employer and employee, company and customer, company and shareholder, and company and the community.

■ Ethics Approaches

Different people utilize different ethical value systems. These systems are based on personal experiences along with religious, educational, and family training. One manager might consider it beneficial to downsize a company's workforce because the surviving employees, who make up the majority, will be employed by a more effective and efficient firm. Another manager might view a downsizing decision as unethical because the employees who lose their jobs are deprived of economic opportunities simply because it is cost effective. The different ethical value systems of the two managers lead them to place different judgments on the attractiveness or repulsiveness of downsizing.

Managers typically use one of four key ethical approaches when making business decisions. They are utilitarianism, individualism, the rights approach, and the justice approach. Each takes a different view of what is most important to individuals and society.

Utilitarianism

Decisions should be made on the basis of what is good for the greatest number of people from a **utilitarian** perspective. To apply the utilitarian criterion, one would examine all the people affected by a decision and choose the solution that satisfies the most people. Utilitarianism is sometimes referred to as the "calculus of pain, because it tries to minimize pain and maximize pleasure for the greatest number of people." Although utilitarianism strives to attain the ideal of democracy by promoting good for the majority, it may overlook the rights or needs of a minority of individuals.

Individualism

People who base ethical decisions on **individualism** believe that personal self-interests should be promoted as long as they do not harm others. Individualism as a basis for making business decisions is derived from the principles of capitalism first expressed in the 18th century by Adam Smith. In *The Wealth of Nations,* Smith wrote that markets should be free, that they

utilitarianism
A means of making decisions based on what is good for the greatest number of people.

individualism
The degree to which a society values personal goals, autonomy, and privacy over group loyalty, commitment to group norms, involvement in collective activities, social cohesiveness, and intense socialization; ethical decisions based on individualism promote individual self-interest as long as it does not harm others.

TABLE 3.1 Selected Ethical Issues in Business

Employee–Employer Relations

- Taking credit for work done by other employees
- Spreading false rumors that can harm an employer's reputation
- Sharing sensitive company information with a competing firm
- Recording false performance information to qualify for undeserved rewards

Employer–Employee Relations

- Performance evaluations that display favoritism to friends of managers
- Hostile treatment of employees who report unethical conduct
- Expecting that employees work "off the clock" without compensation
- Being negligent at regularly maintaining the operation of machines and equipment that could break down and harm employees

Company–Customer Relations

- Withholding information on products that could be harmful to customers
- Making deceptive claims of a product's performance in advertising
- Selling products or services not needed by a customer by aggressive sales staff

Company–Shareholder Relations

- Having individuals serve on the board of directors with conflicts of interest with what is best for the shareholders
- Withholding financial information that would be of material interest to shareholders
- Taking excessive risks with shareholders' financial resources

Company–Local and Global Communities

- Engaging in manufacturing or extraction processes that result in long-term harm to the environment
- Breaking commitments made to improve the community after being granted privileges to take natural resources out of it
- Exploiting labor in developing countries with low wages and poor working conditions that do not meet minimum international standards of fairness

Source: Based on A. B. Carroll and A. K. Buchholtz, *Business and Society*, 7th ed., Cincinnati, OH, Southwestern, 2008.

should be the basis of all transactions, and that they should be subject to a minimum of interference by other forces such as governments. All available information is utilized when individuals make economic choices. Lying and other unethical behavior are penalized because it is in people's self-interest to do business with ethical firms and individuals rather than with liars and cheats.

At the same time, the costs of obtaining information about individuals' or firms' motives may be steep, and there are differences in power between individuals bargaining in the market. In such cases, some individuals can take advantage of their power or access to information to the detriment of others. For example, American consumers of health care have less power than insurance companies and have little access to specific information on the implications of choosing one policy or one doctor over another. Citizens of France, Germany, and Sweden believe individualism has resulted in the lack of a national health care plan for U.S. citizens. Consequently, they believe, the weakest members of society are the ones who suffer the most.

Rights Approach

rights approach
A means of making decisions based on the belief that each person has fundamental human rights that should be respected and protected.

The belief that each person has fundamental human rights that should be respected and protected is the **rights approach**. People have the rights of freedom of speech, privacy, and due process when charged with a crime or rule infraction. They also have the right to a safe and healthy environment. These rights make it possible for them to act in their own best interests, which in turn benefits society. According to the rights approach, a decision is unethical if it deprives an individual of fundamental human rights.

The rights approach provides specific criteria for judging the ethics of a decision; however, conflicting rights must often be sorted out when making business decisions. For example, a manager who shares negative information about personal problems experienced by a former employee with another employer who is considering hiring that individual exercises the right of free speech but may also have violated the employee's right to privacy. Whose rights should have priority?

Justice Approach

Treating all people fairly and consistently when making decisions is the basis of the **justice approach**. This includes considering both distributive and procedural justice. *Distributive justice* examines the fairness of rewards, punishments, and outcomes in an organization. It asks whether an employee received compensation equitable with performance or whether the employee was overpaid or underpaid. *Procedural justice* involves the fair and consistent application of rules and procedures. When an employee is disciplined for a safety rule infraction, the procedural justice standard would be violated if other employees who broke the rule were not similarly disciplined.

justice approach
An approach to decision making based on treating all people fairly and consistently when making business decisions.

The justice approach is more flexible than other ethical approaches, because it recognizes that standards of fairness vary depending on the individuals involved in the decision. For example, unionized auto workers see equal raises for all workers as the fair way to distribute salary increases. Equality raises union solidarity. Managers consider rewarding people on the basis of individual performance as fair, because they believe rewards should be based on the workers' contributions to profitability.

Applications of Ethics Approaches

To see how the four approaches to ethical decision making differ, consider the policy of random drug testing. A utilitarian sees random drug testing as ethical because more employees and customers are protected from accidents caused by drug-using employees than are angered by having to submit to random drug tests. Random drug testing would also be perceived as ethical when applying the criterion of individualism: owners are free to enact policies that make the company more efficient, and employees are free to exercise their disapproval by quitting and seeking employment at a firm that does not require random drug testing.

On the other hand, a manager who applies the rights approach may consider random drug testing unethical because it violates an employee's right to privacy and the right of protection from searches without probable cause to justify the test. Similarly, random drug testing would be seen as unethical in the justice approach because it presumes that an employee is guilty of using drugs and makes employees prove that they are innocent based on the chemical analysis of body fluids. In American justice, a person is innocent unless proven guilty.

In 2005 former WorldCom CEO Bernard Ebbers was sentenced to 25 years in prison, one of the longest sentences ever received by a former chief executive. The stiff sentence stemmed in large part from the estimated $2 billion investor losses prosecutors attributed to Ebbers' fraud at WorldCom. AP/Wide World Photos.

Comparison of Ethics Approaches

One way to compare the four approaches to ethical decision making is to view them on the basis of how well they satisfy two elements of a fair and just society: (1) the degree of economic freedom in society to earn and retain wealth compared to how wealth is redistributed and shared with the less fortunate; and (2) the degree of concern a society has for individuals compared to the degree of concern for the community. Notice that in some social systems concern for the community will take precedence over concern for individuals, while in other social systems concern for individuals will matter more. Similarly in some social systems economic freedom based on free enterprise takes precedence over having an equal distribution of the wealth in the society, while in other social systems a fair and equal distribution of the wealth produced in the society takes precedence over the freedom to accumulate individual wealth.

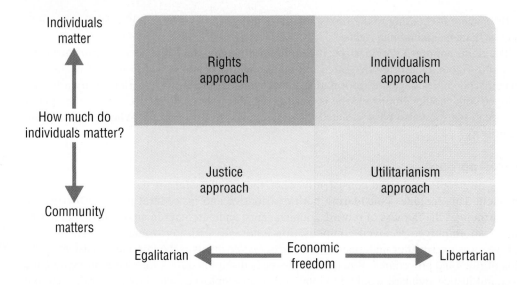

FIGURE 3.1

Comparison of Ethics Approaches

For example, we would not be surprised if employees at a Wall Street investment bank had strong preferences for economic freedom and concern for individuals, while employees who work for the Red Cross are likely to reflect strong preferences for equal distribution of wealth and concern for the community.

Figure 3.1 above compares the four approaches to ethical decision making by classifying them according to their degree of economic freedom and concern for individuals. The individualism approach to ethics reflects a high concern for individuals and high degree of economic freedom. The justice approach to ethics reflects a high concern for the community and for an egalitarian distribution of wealth. Similarly, the rights approach to ethics displays a high concern for individualism and for an egalitarian distribution of wealth. The utilitarianism approach to ethics reflects a high concern for the community and for economic freedom.

LOC-In 1 Learning Objective Check-In

Hillsdale Ceramics is reevaluating its approach to ethics. The firm has had problems in the past with inconsistent application of rules across different employees. Its managers also want to make sure that the decisions that are made affecting the entire company satisfy the greatest number of workers and cause "pain" to the fewest number. Lastly, the firm wants to make sure that the employees all enjoy a safe and healthy environment.

1. The decision to apply rules consistently across worker situations is demonstrative of _____.
   a. distributive justice
   b. procedural justice
   c. individualism
   d. the rights approach

2. The approach used in making business decisions that benefit the greatest number of workers is called _____.
   a. individualism
   b. distributive justice
   c. the rights approach
   d. utilitarianism

3. The approach of making sure no business decision deprives an individual of the right to a safe and healthy environment is called _____.
   a. utilitarianism
   b. the rights approach
   c. individualism
   d. procedural justice

MANAGEMENT IS EVERYONE'S BUSINESS 3.1

WORKING AS A MANAGER It is critical for a manager to protect his or her reputation as an ethical person. Managers are role models for other employees and consequently are held to a higher standard of personal conduct. A tarnished moral reputation interferes with a manager's ability to influence employees and makes it difficult to serve as a communication link between executives and front-line employees.

Managers are responsible for creating an environment that supports ethical behavior and discourages unethical conduct. A manager should set ethical conduct goals. For example, a financial securities manager may set a goal of zero tolerance for dishonesty among stockbrokers.

■ Codes of Ethics

When there is a void of ethical guidelines in a company, employees rely on personal value systems. Creating a more standardized approach can be accomplished by developing a code of ethics.

A **code of ethics** is a formal statement of ethics and values that is designed to guide employee conduct in a variety of business situations. It is particularly useful for giving employees ways to deal with conflicts of interest, gift giving and receiving, communicating with competitors, and making political contributions. More than 50 percent of large U.S. companies and almost half of smaller firms have established codes of ethics.[2] Codes are typically published as either corporate credos or ethical policy statements. Also, many professions, such as doctors, lawyers, engineers, literary agents, and college professors, have codes of ethics. Managers should also be concerned with their reputation for ethical conduct as explained in Management Is Everyone's Business 3.1.

code of ethics
A formal statement of ethics and values that is designed to guide employee conduct in a variety of business situations.

Corporate Credos

A **corporate credo** details a company's responsibility to its stakeholders. *Stakeholders* are groups or individuals with vested interests in the performance of the enterprise, including how managers distribute company resources. Stakeholders include employees, customers, and shareholders. The corporate credo focuses on principles and beliefs that can provide direction in a variety of ethically challenging situations.

corporate credo
A formal statement focusing on principles and beliefs, indicating the company's responsibility to its stakeholders.

The credo of Johnson & Johnson is reproduced in Figure 3.2. As shown, the company identifies its responsibilities to consumers, employees, communities, and stockholders. This led to an extraordinary response to a difficult situation in the 1980s. When a criminal put capsules laced with cyanide in Tylenol bottles and some customers died as a result of taking the tainted medicine, Johnson & Johnson immediately took Tylenol off the market until it could be reissued in tamper-proof packaging. The credo was one factor that helped Johnson & Johnson effectively handle the crisis.

Ethical Policy Statements

Sometimes a credo is not specific enough for a large company that faces complex ethical challenges in many different markets and cultures. In such situations, more concrete guidelines on ethical conduct are needed. **Ethical policy statements** provide specific formulas for employee conduct. They answer such questions as whether a salesperson may offer a gift to a good customer, how much technical information can be shared with a competitor, whether an executive may purchase company stock in advance of a proposed merger, and whether the company can award a franchise to a relative of an employee.

ethical policy statements
A firm's formal guidelines that provide specific formulas for employees' ethical conduct.

Numerous companies have adopted ethical policy statements that inform employees of acceptable standards of conduct. Examples of such employers include:

1. St. Paul Companies, which specializes in commercial and personal insurance, and states that employees may accept gifts of inexpensive pens or appointment diaries, but not liquor, lavish entertainment, travel, or clothing.[3]

FIGURE 3.2

Johnson & Johnson Corporate Credo

Source: Reprinted with permission of Johnson & Johnson, www.jnj.com.

Our Credo

We believe our first responsibility is to the doctors, nurses, and patients,
to mothers and fathers and all others who use our products and services.
In meeting their needs everything we do must be of high quality.
We must constantly strive to reduce our costs in order to maintain reasonable prices.
Customers' orders must be serviced promptly and accurately.
Our suppliers and distributors must have an opportunity to make a fair profit.

We are responsible to our employees,
the men and women who work with us throughout the world.
Everyone must be considered as an individual.
We must respect their dignity and recognize their merit.
They must have a sense of security in their jobs.
Compensation must be fair and adequate, and working conditions clean, orderly and safe.
We must be mindful of ways to help our employees fulfill their family responsibilites.
Employees must feel free to make suggestions and complaints.
There must be equal opportunity for employment, development
and advancement for those qualified.
We must provide competent management, and their actions must be just and ethical.

We are responsible to the communities in which we live and work
and to the world community as well.
We must be good citizens—support good works and charities and bear our fair share of taxes.
We must encourage civic improvements and better health and education.
We must maintain in good order the property we are privileged to use,
protecting the environment and natural resources.

Our final responsibility is to our stockholders.
Business must make a sound profit.
We must experiment with new ideas.
Research must be carried on, innovative programs developed and mistakes paid for.
New equipment must be purchased, new facilities provided and new products launched.
Reserves must be created to provide for adverse times.
When we operate according to these principles, the stockholders should realize a fair return.

Johnson & Johnson

2. Eli Lilly and Company, a pharmaceutical firm, in which employees may not conduct business with a company with which they or their relatives are associated, unless Eli Lilly has given specific approval and authorization.[4]

3. General Dynamics Corporation, a defense-industry contractor, where employees may not use or share inside information that is not available to the general public for personal gain.[5]

4. Google considered exiting the China market because of attempts by Chinese authorities to censor searches and hack Google's e-mail system, which violated Google's ethical values that promote the free exchange of information.[6]

LOC-In 2 Learning Objective Check-In

1. Markway is a high-end office supply company that often deals with upscale clients and establishes strong relationships with the communities it operates in. Sometimes, employees face conflicts of interest regarding gift giving and receiving, communicating with competitors, and making political contributions. The _____ at Markway is a formal statement of values that is designed to guide employee conduct at the company. It is especially useful in these conflicting situations.
   a. code of ethics
   b. vision statement
   c. mission statement
   d. ethical structure

■ Managing Ethics

Is it possible to actually change the ways in which employees behave? Many organizational leaders, who are interested in creating more ethical climates, believe the answer is "yes." To do so means establishing a corporate culture in which ethical behavior is the norm. Among the approaches that are available are ethics training, ethical structures, and whistleblower policies.

Ethics Training

Ethics training gives employees and managers the opportunity to actually practice handling the ethical dilemmas they are likely to experience. More than 40 percent of large U.S. companies provide **ethics training** to their employees. Most courses contain the following elements:

ethics training
A means of providing employees and managers practice in handling ethical dilemmas that they are likely to experience.

1. Messages from top executives emphasizing ethical business practices.
2. Discussion of codes of ethics.
3. Procedures for discussing or reporting unethical behavior.

Ethics training at aircraft manufacturer Boeing provides an excellent model for other firms. Led by the business ethics adviser of the division involved, it includes a customized videotape with an opening message by the division's general manager and the presentation of dramatic and routine situations.

At Matsushita, a large Japanese consumer electronics company, ethics training emphasizes treating customers with dignity and respect. Manager's Notebook 3.1 on business ethics in Japan provides examples of ethical values instilled in Japanese employees at Matsushita.

Management Is Everyone's Business 3.2 stresses that teams need to ensure that team members behave ethically, and one way to do this is to provide ethics training to team members.

MANAGER'S NOTEBOOK 3.1

Business Ethics in Japan: The Case of Matsushita

Business ethics have international dimensions. In large Japanese firms, business ethics blend Confucian philosophy—the basis of Asian values—with capitalist values. Here are some examples of ethical principles taught to employees at Matsushita, the world's largest consumer electronics company, with headquarters in Osaka, Japan.

- A corporation is a public entity and it can exist only if it receives the support of society and therefore must contribute to society.
- Treat people you do business with as if they were part of your family. Prosperity depends on how much understanding one receives from the people with whom one conducts business.
- After-sales service is more important than assistance before sales. It is through such service that one gets permanent customers.

- Do not sell customers goods that they are attracted to. Sell them goods that will benefit them.
- It is not enough to work conscientiously. No matter what kind of job, you should think of yourself as being completely in charge of and responsible for your own work.
- If we cannot make a profit, that means we are committing a sort of crime against society. We take society's capital, we take their people, we take their materials, yet without a good profit, we are using precious resources that could be better used elsewhere.

Source: Based on J. P. Kotter, "Matsushita: The World's Greatest Entrepreneur," *Fortune*, March 31, 1997. pp. 105–110; Corporate Citizenship at Matsushita, www.panasonic.net/citizenship/index.html, 2010.

MANAGEMENT IS EVERYONE'S BUSINESS   3.2

WORKING AS A TEAM It is a good idea to provide team members some ethics training as part of the team development process. If a team tolerates unethical conduct from one member, others may also be influenced by the conduct of this team member. Tolerance of such unethical activities as inflating an expense account can lead to more serious breaches of conduct that damage the reputation of the entire team. A team is only as ethical as its "weakest ethical link."

Ethical Structures

Ethical guidelines are one component of an **ethical structure**. The other is the division or department that is assigned the responsibility of overseeing those guidelines. These two elements must be carefully coordinated.

One type of ethical structure uses an *ethics officer* with a title like "director of ethics compliance." This individual deals with potential ethical violations and advises decision makers regarding ways to comply with the company's code of ethics. This is the case at General Dynamics Corporation, which established an ethical structure in the 1980s after being sanctioned for overcharging the military for defense contract work. Currently 40 divisional ethics program directors report to the corporate director of ethics, and they operate 30 hotlines over which employees can request information or counsel and report incidents of potential misconduct.

Another ethical structure approach is to have senior-level managers from different functions and units serve on an *ethics committee* that provides ethical oversight and policy guidance for management decisions. Dow Corning's business conduct committee conducts ethical audits of company plants on a worldwide basis. An auditor from the committee interviews managers and other employees to determine whether the ethical code is being followed and the kinds of violations that are occurring. The auditor of a sales unit, for example, looks for kickbacks or inappropriate gifts given or received, while the auditor of a manufacturing unit focuses on environmental pollution. Universities also use ethics committees, which focus on allegations of such unethical conduct as faking research data and situations in which a faculty member plagiarizes the work of students or colleagues.

Whistleblower Policies

Employees who are willing to disclose illegal, immoral, or illegitimate practices by their employer require the protection of a **whistleblower policy**.[7] Companies with whistleblower policies rely on individual employees to report unethical activities to the ethics officer or committee, which then gathers facts and investigates the situation in a fair and impartial manner. Whistleblower policies protect these individuals from retaliation by executives or coworkers whose practices have been exposed. In situations in which whistleblower policies are not present, employees face many obstacles. For example, the quality control officers for the Trans Alaska Pipeline were threatened with actual physical harm and demotion, and were victims of spying, as other employees attempted to keep them from reporting problems that might lead to oil spills.[8]

While the federal government and some states have enacted laws to protect whistleblowers from retaliation, there is scant protection for those who report unethical activities that are not specified in the laws. The Sarbanes-Oxley Act, a federal law enacted in 2002 after the financial scandals at Enron and WorldCom, provides protection to whistleblowers who disclose financial fraud in publicly traded corporations. The law protects whistleblowers from retaliation from the company or its employees and those who violate the law are liable for both civil and criminal penalties.[9] However, this federal law does not protect whistleblowers who report unethical conduct not related to financial fraud. A whistleblower policy provides a communication channel to report unethical activities. Whistleblower policies should include the following key features:

1. The policy encourages reporting unethical conduct and sets up meaningful procedures to deal fairly with reported violations.
2. Those who report violations are protected from retaliation. Even if an informant is incorrect about the alleged wrongdoing, the protection is extended as long as the informant acted in good faith in making the complaint.
3. Alternative reporting procedures are provided in cases where those to whom the report must be given are involved in the wrongdoing.
4. A provision is made for anonymous reporting to an ethics officer or committee.
5. Feedback on ethics violations is provided to employees so that they are aware that the policy is being taken seriously and that complaints are being investigated.
6. Top management supports and is involved in the whistleblower policy.[10]

The financial scandals at Enron and WorldCom have put the whistleblowers, who tried to report the misconduct of executives at these firms, in the limelight.[11] In 2001, Enron executive Sherron Watkins wrote a blunt memo to Enron CEO Kenneth Lay warning him that the company might "implode in a wave of accounting scandals." Instead of thanking her, management factions tried to squelch the bad news and intimidate her for not being a team player. After the financial scandal broke and became a media event, Watkins was congratulated for her courage in confronting a CEO about Enron's controversial off-the-books partnerships and shaky finances. She serves as a positive role model for whistleblowers.[12]

Personal Ethics

Ethical decisions are among the most difficult decisions you will ever have to make. When one presents itself, allow yourself plenty of time to consider the alternatives. Examine the consequences as well as the proposed procedures established to arrive at the outcome. Think about how the decision would look if it were made public in the company newsletter. Make sure you consider all the people who are directly or indirectly affected by the decision. It is a good idea to get feedback from a trusted friend or colleague before you act.

Manager's Notebook 3.2 provides some tips for making ethical business decisions.

The U.S. military has recognized the importance of having officers set examples for enlisted personnel and holds officers to a higher standard of conduct. Officers who disobey a command or act unethically face harsh sanctions. Managers set the tone for employees through their actions and by their examples. If a manager's behavior conflicts with the company's code of ethics, employees may decide to disregard the code of ethics.

Managers can influence the ethical behavior of those within their units in the following ways:

1. Take actions that develop trust, such as sharing useful information and making good on commitments.
2. Act consistently, so that employees are not surprised by unexpected management actions or decisions.
3. Be truthful and avoid white lies and other actions designed to manipulate people by giving a false impression.
4. Demonstrate integrity by keeping confidences and showing concern for others.
5. Meet with employees to discuss and define what is expected of them.
6. Ensure that employees are treated equitably, giving equivalent rewards for similar performance and avoiding actual or apparent special treatment of favorites.
7. Adhere to clear standards that are seen as just and reasonable—for example, neither praising accomplishments out of proportion nor imposing penalties disproportionate to offenses.
8. Respect employees, showing openly that you care about employees and recognize their strengths and contributions.[13]

In addition, Manager's Notebook 3.3 includes approaches for ensuring that a climate for ethical conduct is maintained on your team.

Next read the ethical dilemma in Management Is Everyone's Business 3.3, and apply the ethics tests given there to the situation that is described.

LOC-In 3 Learning Objective Check-In

Susan believes it is possible to change the ways employees at her firm behave. She is interested in making the climate at her firm more ethical, She understands that the corporate culture will have to value ethical behavior and cultivate it as a company norm. Susan is currently discussing several approaches with the other strategic decision makers at the company.

1. Susan's first idea is to give employees and managers the opportunity to actually practice handling ethical dilemmas that they are likely to encounter. This is part of the _____ approach.
   a. ethical code of conduct
   b. ethical structure
   c. ethics training
   d. whistleblower

2. Susan thinks it is crucial to specifically appoint an ethics officer to deal with potential ethics violations. The person would also help decision makers at the company with ways to comply with the code of ethics. This idea involves _____.
   a. ethical structure
   b. whistleblower policies
   c. ethics training
   d. personal ethics

3. Lastly, Susan wants to make sure that those who report violations are protected from retaliation as long as they act in good faith in issuing a complaint. She wants to make sure that _____ are protected at the firm.
   a. violators
   b. ethics officers
   c. administrators
   d. whistleblowers

MANAGER'S NOTEBOOK 3.2

Tips for Making Ethical Business Decisions

Here are some tips to consider when facing a business decision where ethics are an important part of the decision.

- *Take time to learn the facts.* It is important to take time to know the facts surrounding the situation at hand. Jumping to conclusions on incomplete evidence can lead to poor decisions. For example, a manager may lose his temper with a colleague who pesters him about an unfilled request. What may not be known without investigating further is that the angry manager had just learned minutes before about a tragic situation concerning his son's health. To conclude that this manager is rude and unprofessional due to losing control of his anger without knowing all the facts of the situation would result in an awkward confrontation with the manager.
- *Identify the ethical concerns.* What are the essential ethical values that are of concern in the situation? In the situation concerning the angry manager described previously, an ethical concern is that each employee deserves to be treated with dignity and respect and being the target of someone's anger is disrespectful. However, understanding the motivations of the party who loses his temper may provide some mitigating circumstances that sheds light on how to deal with it.
- *Identify the people impacted by the decision.* It is important to identify all the people who are both directly affected and the ones who are indirectly affected by the decision. In the preceding situation where an angry manager yells at a colleague, the primary parties are the angry manager and the target person. However, employees who witness this incident may feel sympathy for the person who was yelled at and this may lower the morale of the work group, which in turn could also result in a reduction in the quality of service that is given to customers. Many parties may be indirectly impacted by an angry verbal communication between two people. A good decision that improves the relationship between two people in conflict may benefit many others.
- *Consider the consequences.* Consider the consequences to each of the parties you have identified when you take action or even decide to do nothing. Identify any negative consequences that should be avoided by selecting a certain course of action. Also consider both the short-term and long-term consequences of the decision.

MANAGER'S NOTEBOOK 3.3

Tips for Managing the Ethical Climate of Teams

Here are some practical ways for improving the ethical climate governing the conduct of employees on your team:

1. Agree on a code of ethical conduct that the team expects from all members.
2. Require that all new team members learn the code of ethical conduct.
3. Integrate ethics into the team performance evaluations so that there is accountability for ethical conduct.
4. Recognize and reward ethical behavior in team members.
5. Ensure that unethical behavior is not tolerated by the team.
6. From time to time let team members explain how they handled an ethical dilemma so that others can benefit from this experience.
7. Use surveys to find out the ethical concerns of customers that the team serves.
8. Find the ethical concerns of other teams and units of your organization and share this information with your team members.

Source: Adapted From R. L. Daft, *The Leadership Experience*, 3rd ed., Mason, OH: Thomson, 2005, p. 576. © 2005 South-Western, a part of Cengage Learning, Inc. Reproduced by permission. www.cengage.com/permissions.

MANAGEMENT IS EVERYONE'S BUSINESS   3.3

WORKING AS AN INDIVIDUAL   Suppose you face an ethical dilemma that is putting your personal values to the test.

What would you do in the following situation?

The company where you are employed has a very clear procedure for a task but you know a "better" way to do the job. Your productivity results are a bit low this month. If you use your new approach and violate the "rules," you can raise your results to a higher level.

It can be useful to check your choices against some ethical tests:

- *Front-page test.* How would I feel if my decision became a headline in a local newspaper? Would I feel comfortable describing my actions or decision to a customer or stockholder?
- *Golden rule test.* Would I be willing to be treated in the same manner?
- *Personal gain test.* Is an opportunity for personal gain clouding my judgment? Would I make the same decision if the outcome did not benefit me in any way?

Source: © 2010, Ethics Resource Center. Used with permission of the Ethics Resource Center, 2345 Crystal Drive, Ste 201, Arlington, VA 22202, www.ethics.org.

■ Ethical Dilemmas in the Workplace

The workplace presents a variety of ethical challenges to managers, teams, and employees. Four examples of ethical dilemmas at work are: (1) performance appraisals, (2) employee discipline, (3) romantic relationships, and (4) gift giving.

Performance Appraisal

Performance appraisal is a formal evaluation of an employee's performance provided on a recurring basis. Typically, an employee receives feedback regarding his or her strengths and weaknesses in a document summarizing the employee's performance over the period of evaluation, which is usually one year. In most cases, the individual providing the performance appraisal is the supervisor. More specific information about performance appraisals is presented in Chapter 10 (Human Resource Management).

In order to do an effective job at evaluation, the supervisor should devote substantial time to collecting accurate performance information. This feedback will be used to let employees know which skills they have mastered and those which require improvement. Performance ratings are also used as the basis for pay increases, future work assignments, promotions, and sometimes layoffs. So it is crucial to collect accurate and fair information. Managers who deliberately provide false or misleading information for reasons of vengeance, dislike of a subordinate, or racial or sexual discrimination are violating ethical and legal standards.

Employee Discipline

One tool that managers use to change an employee's behavior when it does not meet expectations or when it is inappropriate is the discipline system. An example of a behavior that fails to meet expectations is when an employee arrives late to work without a reasonable excuse. An illustration of inappropriate employee conduct requiring immediate intervention would be when a server in a restaurant uses profanity or verbally attacks a customer.

Supervisors can misuse discipline by making it a way to intimidate employees they do not like or for retribution when an employee makes a mistake. When a supervisor uses employee discipline for purposes of revenge rather than to correct an inappropriate behavior, the abuse of power is of course unethical. The following are examples of unethical employee discipline.

- Closely monitoring the behavior of a disliked employee, looking for the opportunity to use discipline to punish the employee, while giving more slack to employees who are not on the supervisor's "hit list."
- Using rumors and unsubstantiated evidence as a basis to apply discipline to a targeted employee without giving the employee an opportunity to defend his or her conduct.

Such examples suggest that the application of employee discipline requires some basic guidelines to protect employees from being victimized by supervisors. Here are some basic guidelines for giving employee discipline in a fair and impartial way.

1. *Notify* employees in advance of a company's work rules and the consequences for violating them. An employee who violates a work rule should be given the opportunity to correct the behavior without being punished.
2. *Investigate* the facts of an employee's misconduct before applying discipline. Give an employee the opportunity to give his or her side of the story before a decision is made about whether the misconduct actually took place.
3. *Be consistent* in the response to rule violations. Discipline should be administered consistently without favoritism or discrimination.

Office Romance

Romance often blossoms in the workplace. People who spend time together are likely to develop romantic feelings. Unfortunately, when a romantic relationship ends, as many of them do, one partner may feel angry and abandoned. A broken relationship can be highly disruptive to people who are simply trying to focus on work. Co-workers may even be drawn into the conflict, which can strain working relations if the unit requires a high degree of collaboration between employees.

Further, when romantic partners are publicly affectionate in front of customers or other employees, it makes some people uncomfortable. Public displays of affection are almost always inappropriate. Jealousy or suspicion may result, if someone else has romantic intentions toward the co-worker involved, or if it is a boss involved in the romance. Subordinates may suspect that the boss is being manipulated by his or her romantic partner and showing favoritism as a result. The supervisor's credibility may be undermined in the eyes of subordinates.

Few companies actually ban romantic relationships in the workplace. However, many try to provide basic rules of conduct regarding office romances. Employees should be sensitive not only to the feelings of the partner in the relationship but also to co-workers and customers who may be affected by the couple's behavior. Here are two basic suggestions for ethical employee conduct in a romantic relationship at the workplace.

- Public displays of affection at the workplace should be discouraged.
- Employees should be prohibited from dating people they directly supervise. If a romance begins, one or the other partner should be transferred.

Giving Gifts in the Workplace

Gift giving routinely occurs in the workplace. Employees often exchange gifts with each other during the Christmas holidays, managers give flowers to their secretaries on special occasions, and vendors customarily give merchandise such as coffee mugs or pens to prospective customers. These situations represent constructive gift giving to build relationships between people by letting them know they are appreciated.

Sometimes, however, by accepting a gift from a vendor or employee a person faces an ethical dilemma. A test of the ethical appropriateness of accepting the gift would be to first think about how a manager or co-worker would perceive the gift and the person who gave it. If you would feel uncomfortable explaining the gift, the discomfort probably means it would be ethically problematic. Here are some examples of situations where it would be clearly unethical to give or accept gifts:

- A vendor seeking to develop a business relationship with a company may offer to provide lucrative financial opportunities to the executive in charge of purchasing, expecting to influence the executive to buy the vendor's product. The vendor is, in fact, using the gift as a bribe. The executive may be unduly influenced to purchase inferior goods. Closing deals with bribes probably means the products cannot compete in the marketplace. For example, several executives at Qwest, one of the major U.S. telecommunications companies, received valuable stock options from some smaller suppliers of Internet gear, and later steered large contracts to those companies. After the financial scandal was exposed, it became clear that Qwest executives made purchasing decisions based on who gave them stock options, not on the best equipment. One of the former members of Qwest's board of directors called the practice of suppliers giving stock options as an enticement an "ethical nightmare."[14]

■ In part of a larger investigation of employee misconduct at A. T. Kearney Inc., a management consulting firm, it was revealed that CEO Fred Steingraber used funds from his personal expense account to purchase gifts for family members. Steingraber used company funds to purchase a laptop computer for his son, and paid $37,000 for a lavish 50th birthday party for his wife, complete with a magician and surprise visits from her sisters, who were flown in from Germany. In defense of his spending for his wife's birthday, Steingraber stated that the party was also attended by executives from A. T. Kearney customers who would later purchase consulting services from the firm.[15] Inviting potential customers to a birthday party for the CEO's wife in order to influence their purchasing decisions is probably more than merely inappropriate. It may have been criminal.

LOC-In 4 Learning Objective Check-In

Marie has found that her job as a manager presents a variety of ethical challenges. She is often involved in determining whether employees should receive pay increases, certain future assignments, promotions, or even layoffs. While she does not particularly like one of her subordinates, she knows that she will have to collect accurate and fair information about him in order to help in the evaluation process. Another situation Marie has been dealing with involves two of her subordinates, one of whom is directly responsible for supervising the other as part of a work team. These two individuals have become romantically involved since Marie assumed her role in managing them, and she is debating whether or not to transfer one of them to another area of the company.

1. Which of the following is a true statement about an ethical way for Marie to deal with the subordinate she does not like?
   a. Marie should devote substantial time to collecting accurate performance information about him.
   b. Marie does not have to let her subordinate know what skills he has or has not mastered and which require improvement.
   c. Marie may deliberately provide misleading information because she dislikes the subordinate.
   d. Marie should incorporate her personal feelings toward the employee into the evaluation so that he knows why she does not like him.

2. Marie wants to ensure that her employees conduct themselves ethically. She does not mind the idea of an office romance, but her firm does require that relationships cannot exist between employees and their direct supervisors. For this reason, _____.
   a. Marie will likely require both employees to transfer to new positions.
   b. Marie will likely require that the two individuals limit public displays of affection, but they may continue the relationship in their current work roles.
   c. Marie will likely require the transfer of one or the other of the two employees involved with each other.
   d. Marie will likely initiate an investigation into employee misconduct regarding the romantic relationship.

A common approach companies use to avoid conflicts of interest in gift giving is to have a gift policy that limits the dollar value to a modest amount, such as $25. The policy may also require that each employee fully disclose each gift that is given and received along with its dollar value.

In cultures outside the United States, especially in developing economies, the laws and ethics related to giving gifts between parties as a business practice are highly diverse. In the African nation of Senegal, 40 percent of executives were reported to believe that bribery was necessary to obtain a public contract.[16] Managers seeking to do business within foreign cultures that are more tolerant of bribery and kickbacks may wish to avoid the temptation of using these practices, even if it means losing some business. Companies in countries with laws against giving bribes still face ethical challenges related to gift giving. For example, there is a tradition in the pharmaceutical industry of allowing sales representatives to give free samples of drugs to

TABLE 3.2 The Corruption Perceptions Index 2009

Least Corrupt Countries			Most Corrupt Countries		
Country	Score	Ranking	Country	Score	Ranking
New Zealand	9.4	1	Haiti	1.8	168
Denmark	9.3	2	Iran	1.8	168
Singapore	9.2	3	Turkmenistan	1.8	168
Sweden	9.2	3	Uzbekistan	1.7	174
Switzerland	9.0	5	Chad	1.6	175
Finland	8.9	6	Iraq	1.5	176
Netherlands	8.9	6	Sudan	1.5	176
Australia	8.7	8	Myanmar	1.4	178
Canada	8.7	8	Afghanistan	1.3	179
Iceland	8.7	8	Somalia	1.1	180
United States	7.5	19			

Source: Reprinted from "The Corruption Perception Index." Copyright © 2009 Transparency International: The global coalition against corruption. Reprinted with permission. For more information, visit http://www. transparency.org.

doctors. Police in Verona, Italy, opened an investigation of this practice by GlaxoSmithKline. They discovered a scheme that went beyond giving free samples to doctors. Company sales representatives gave gifts such as computers and lavish trips to doctors in exchange for writing of prescriptions for the company's drugs.[17] Such a "race to the bottom" of the ethical yardstick in order to win a foreign business contract is not worth the price, because public disclosure of this form of gift giving harms a company's reputation. A tarnished company reputation is nearly impossible to repair.

The Corruption Perceptions Index for 2009 displayed in Table 3.2 indicates the perceptions of corruption that occur in the 10 least corrupt (with high index numbers) and the 10 most corrupt countries (with low index numbers). It was based on a survey of international managers and academics. As shown, the United States is ranked as the 19th least corrupt country, behind countries with "cleaner" business practices such as Finland, Sweden, and New Zealand. There are a total of 180 countries ranked on corruption in the total survey. Countries ranked low on the Corruption Perceptions Index (most corrupt) are more likely to tolerate bribery as a business practice than countries with a high rank.

■ Social Responsibility

Do corporations have a responsibility to conduct their affairs ethically and to be judged by the same standards as individuals? Should a business be concerned with more than the pursuit of profits for its shareholders? **Social responsibility** is the duty a company has to conduct its affairs ethically in a manner that benefits both employees and the larger society. There are both benefits and costs associated with acting in a socially responsible manner.

The Benefits of Social Responsibility

Caring for the natural environment is one of several dimensions of social responsibility that must be considered in the allocation of a firm's resources. Companies that pollute the air, water, and land must consider the rights of people in the community to breathe clean air and drink clean water and must pay to help clean up the pollution or face government penalties. Companies spend billions of dollars each year in order to comply with laws that protect the environment.

Social responsibility ultimately leads to improved odds of long-term survival for the organization. A narrow focus on producing goods and services for profit only, without considering the ramifications of company activities, may impair company performance in the long run and result in a failure to survive. In fact, social responsibility can have a positive effect on company

social responsibility
The belief that corporations have a responsibility to conduct their affairs ethically to benefit both employees and the larger society.

performance. Research indicates that it is related to higher financial performance and the ability to recruit better quality job applicants.[18]

Some recent examples of the problems that corporations have faced as a result of failing to address social responsibility include the following:

1. In 1999 the courts determined that tobacco companies had purposefully withheld from the public knowledge that nicotine in tobacco is an addictive drug. Phillip Morris, R. J. Reynolds, and other large U.S. tobacco manufacturers agreed to pay $246 billion over a period of 25 years to compensate victims of lung cancer and other fatal illnesses related to cigarette smoking.[19]

The wing of an oil contaminated bird caused by the Exxon Valdez oil spill in Alaska. Chris Wilkins/ AFP/Getty Images.

2. Merck, a giant pharmaceutical firm, suddenly recalled its blockbuster arthritis drug Vioxx from the market in 2004, with the release of new evidence that the drug raises the risk of heart attacks and strokes. This news immediately cut Merck's share price in half, lopping $30 billion off the value of the world's fourth-largest drug company The lawsuits stemming from Vioxx users alleging harm from the product are estimated to range from a few billion dollars to as much as $20 billion.[20]

3. In 1989 the *Exxon Valdez* spilled 11 million gallons of oil and polluted 2,600 miles of shoreline along Alaska's Prince William Sound. Environmentalists, consumers, and local businesses mobilized and forced Exxon to pay $3 billion in damages and for the cleanup.[21]

4. In 2010 Toyota announced a massive recall of 8 million of its cars due to mechanical failures linked to 51 deaths in the United States, tarnishing its reputation for engineering excellence. Automotive experts believe that runaway acceleration was causing the crashes that might be linked to aggressive cost cutting pressures on the Toyota manufacturing process.[22]

5. Executives at Enron, a Houston-based energy company, approved risky financial investments with company resources in off-balance-sheet financial deals that lost billions of dollars. When these losses were disclosed in 2001, Enron stock suddenly collapsed. The stock lost 99 percent of its value within a few months, putting the company into bankruptcy, and forcing the layoff of thousands of employees as the company struggled to survive the scandal that followed. The lack of transparency of the financial dealings of Enron meant that the company did not give an important stakeholder group, shareholders, the opportunity to know about how funds were invested.[23]

As these examples indicate, actions by such stakeholder groups as environmentalists, consumers, and the government may threaten the stability and existence of a company. When the management team takes the interests of key stakeholders into consideration, the threat of dealing with hostile interest groups is reduced. When a company's executives adopt a socially responsible approach that is aligned with the goals of an important stakeholder group, the stakeholder may reciprocate and influence its members to patronize the products of the company. For example, Anheuser-Busch, the largest brewer of beer, has worked hard to cultivate positive labor relations with its unionized workforce, an important stakeholder group. In return, the unions have encouraged their membership to drink Budweiser and Busch brands of beer made by Anheuser-Busch, rather than consume the beer of companies that treat unions harshly.

The Costs of Social Responsibility

There are essentially two aspects of being socially responsible. The first is avoiding illegal and unethical activities, such as discrimination, sexual harassment, pollution, and tax evasion. These negative activities should be avoided as part of the ethical structure of a company. Other activities associated with social responsibility have costs, because the company spends money to support a social good, such as a neighborhood cleanup program, giving money to the United Way, and other beneficial activities.

Ethos Water, a bottled water company recently purchased by Starbucks, donates 5 cents for every $1.80 bottle purchased to fund sustainable clean-water projects in underdeveloped regions such as Ethiopia, Honduras, Kenya, and Bangladesh. In 2005, the company contributed $250,000 from its sales to such efforts; its five-year goal is to raise and donate $10 million. The Earth Policy Institute points out that U.S. consumers' fondness for bottled water leads to the manufacture of enough plastic bottles to use up 1.5 million barrels of oil a year. But Jonathan Greenblatt, one of Ethos's founders, says the company's pitch appeals to those with a social conscience who ask, "How do I do more?" Is selling bottled water for a worthy cause an efficient way to be socially responsible?

In these circumstances, social responsibility may be viewed by some as counter to the ethics of individualism, which suggest that individuals and companies should be able to pursue their own self-interests. Economist Milton Friedman argues that most managers do not own the businesses they operate and should act in the best interests of the stockholders, who are primarily interested in financial returns. Corporations should deploy resources to produce goods and services as efficiently as possible. Socially responsible firms that are less efficient may be driven out of business by more efficient competitors willing to singlemindedly pursue profits. These profit-maximizing firms are able to charge lower prices because social costs are not added to the cost of production.

Firms that give profits a low priority are more likely to fail and become a detriment to society because jobs and stockholders' investments are lost. In the late 1990s, when Levi Strauss lost market share to competitors Lee and Wrangler and profits decreased, some shareholders blamed the company's CEO, Robert Haas, for giving too high a priority to corporate social responsibility.[24]

A U.S. firm that has let social responsibility dominate its business strategy in a way that distracted management's attention from earning profits is Ben & Jerry's Ice Cream. Management Close-Up 3.1 discusses some of the factors that have resulted in reduced profits for this company.

Rather than making social responsibility the top priority or ignoring it altogether, management should give corporate social responsibility a high priority without neglecting other important priorities, such as competing successfully in its markets. A thriving organization will have resources to support its social responsibility goals, while a failing organization is too involved in trying to survive and meet its basic business obligations. The challenge for managers is to strike a balance that responds to the concerns of both stakeholders and the general society, bearing in mind that responsible behavior is linked to long-term survival.

The benefits and costs of corporate social responsibility are summarized in Table 3.3. As Table 3.3 suggests, in most cases the advantages of working toward the realization of corporate social responsibility goals outweigh the possible disadvantages.

TABLE 3.3 Benefits and Costs of Corporate Social Responsibility

Social Responsibility Benefits	Social Responsibility Costs
1. Socially responsible companies are good corporate citizens to the community and to the environment.	1. Socially responsible companies may lose focus on the business goals while focusing on goals related to good corporate citizenship.
2. Socially responsible company policies can enhance the image of a company as well as its product brands from the perspective of the consumers.	2. Socially responsible companies may divert needed resources for improving the business into social responsibility projects, which could put a company at a competitive disadvantage.
3. Socially responsible companies have fewer conflicts with stakeholder groups who disagree with the company over how it uses its resources.	
4. Socially responsible companies are more likely to influence stakeholders to become loyal customers and become advocates of the company's products.	
5. Research shows that corporate social responsibility is related to higher financial performance and the ability to recruit better quality job applicants.	

Ben & Jerry Did Good While Their Business Did Not

Ben & Jerry's Ice cream, founded in 1978 by two former Vermont hippies, Ben Cohen and Jerry Greenfield, had always given a high priority to integrating socially beneficial actions into the business. In 1993, it came out with a new flavor called Wavy Gravy, named after the musician who, according to Cohen, "symbolizes taking Sixties values, peace and love, and turning them into action in the Nineties." The company turned the proceeds from the flavor into action, too, by donating some of the proceeds to the musician's work with children.

The company gave away 7.5 percent of its pretax profits (three times the rate of the average U.S. corporation). For its brownie ice cream, it bought brownies that cost a little higher than average from a New York bakery that employed disadvantaged workers. The company had a pay policy that limited its CEO's salary to five times what the lowest-paid employee earned, a reflection of the founders' egalitarian philosophy. They stopped making Oreo Mint ice cream because the Oreo brand is part of tobacco giant RJR Nabisco. Ben & Jerry's paid Vermont dairy farmers extra for hormone-free milk, which cost the company $375,000 over other sources of milk.

The company profits declined and the stock price decreased, but the company continued its socially responsible style. In February 1995, the company moved from being founder-led to professional management when it hired Robert Holland as its CEO. Holland resigned less than two years later, following rumors that the co-founders opposed his support of the company's fat-free (and milk-free) sorbet products. Five years later the company became part of Unilever, a major multinational, which pledged to pursue and expand Ben & Jerry's social mission. Unilever paid $326 million and kept Cohen and Greenfield with the company, although they were not involved in the day-to-day operations.

In November 2000 Unilever ice cream veteran Yves Couette was appointed Ben & Jerry's CEO and vowed to build on Ben & Jerry's social mission. "Business has an important role to play in achieving social progress," said Couette, citing his earlier work for Unilever in Guadalajara, Mexico, where the company established an ice cream shop, run by a not-for-profit organization, to support disabled children. Perhaps more pragmatic than Cohen and Greenfield in viewing how a firm's social and economic missions need to work together, Couette said: "I firmly believe that the least socially responsible business is one that's out of business."

In 2004 Ben & Jerry's continued to put a high priority on being a socially responsible company. For example, it introduced a policy to purchase only "fair trade certified" coffee for its ice cream from coffee growers in developing countries who receive a fair price for their beans. However, four years of restructuring that followed the acquisition of Ben & Jerry's by Unilever, including hundreds of layoffs and the closing of two facilities, resulted in lowered employee morale for those who remained at the company, according to a 2004 company-wide employee survey.

Sources: Based on J. Tozzi, "The Ben & Jerry's Law: Principles before Profit," *Bloomberg Business Week*, April 26, 2010, 65–66; A. Taylor, "Yo, Ben! Yo, Jerry! It's Just Ice Cream!" *Fortune*, April 28,1997, p. 374; www.benjerry.com; "Consumer Group to Boycott Unilever Products," Reuters, December 6, 2000, available at http://dailynews.yahoo.com/h/nm/20001206/bs/unilever_benjerrys_dc_2.html; "Ben & Jerry's Social and Environmental Assessment," 2004, www.benjerry.com/our_company/about_us/

■ Organizational Stakeholders

Organizations are, in many ways, political arenas in which various forces and coalitions compete. Organizational **stakeholders** are individuals or groups that have an interest in or are affected by a company's performance and the way it uses its resources. Stakeholders may be part of either the internal or external environment of an organization. The female employees of a company are an internal stakeholder group, for example, and an organization of consumers is an external stakeholder group.

Stakeholder groups tend to have more specific interests that may not always be in agreement with the interests of management or of other stakeholder groups. For example, shareholders may want a poorly performing company to close inefficient manufacturing plants and focus on more profitable product lines, while the labor union wants to protect worker jobs in all manufacturing plants. The management team must balance the interests of clashing stakeholder groups with its own interests. Compromises are necessary when important stakeholders have legitimate concerns that should be addressed. Management may decide to close some inefficient plants to satisfy the shareholders and invest resources in retraining displaced workers to satisfy the labor union.

A large company will have dozens of stakeholder groups exerting pressure on management. Table 3.4 lists categories of stakeholders with whom a large firm is likely to deal. They are owners, employees, governments, customers, the community, competitors, and social activist groups.

stakeholders

The groups or individuals who have an interest in the performance of the enterprise and how it uses its resources, including employees, customers, and shareholders.

TABLE 3.4 Some Categories and Specific Stakeholders of a Large Firm

OWNERS	EMPLOYEES	GOVERNMENTS	CUSTOMERS
Trusts	New employees	Federal	Business purchasers
Foundations	Senior employees	EPA	Government purchasers
Board members	Retirees	FTC	Educational institutions
Management owners	Female employees	OSHA	Consumers
Mutual funds	Minority employees	State	
Employee pension funds	Labor unions	Local	
Individual owners		Foreign governments	

COMMUNITY	COMPETITORS	SOCIAL ACTIVIST GROUPS
United Way	Domestic competitor	Sierra Club
Public schools	International competitor	American Civil Liberties Union
Residents in community		NOW (National Organization of Women)
Local media		MADD (Mothers Against Drunk Driving)
		Consumers Union

Source: Adapted from A. B. Carroll and A. K. Buchholtz, *Business and Society,* 7th ed., Cincinnati, OH, Southwestern, 2008. © 2009 South-Western, a part of Cengage Learning, Inc. Reproduced by permission. www.cengage.com/permissions.

Owners

Owners who have invested a portion of their wealth in shares of company stock want a reasonable financial return on their investment. If small investors are not satisfied with the financial performance of the company, they are likely to sell their stock. Large individual investors, mutual funds, and pension funds are more likely to be actively involved in influencing management through the board of directors or by voicing their concerns at meetings of shareholders. The CEOs of WorldCom, Enron, General Motors, IBM, and American Express lost their jobs when activist investor groups put pressure on the boards of directors to dismiss them because of disappointing financial performance.

Employees

Employees are largely focused on their jobs. They want to be treated fairly and with respect by the company. New employees are likely to want challenging work assignments that will advance their careers, while senior employees may be more interested in job security and retirement benefits.

Firms that neglect employee stakeholders may have to deal with angry labor unions, which can disrupt output through work stoppages or loss of the most valuable and marketable employees to competitors. This can disrupt the firm's ability to compete in its markets. In 1997 the truck drivers represented by the Teamsters Union organized a strike against United Parcel Service (UPS) because management refused to create full-time jobs for the part-time truck drivers represented by the union. More than half of all truck drivers at UPS were part-time employees, and the wait to become a full-time driver was about 10 years. UPS settled the strike with the Teamsters after losing about $700 million in revenues and some of its market share to its competitors. UPS agreed to create 10,000 new full-time jobs over a five-year period.

Governments

The primary role played by the government is to make sure each company complies with regulations and laws. For example, automobiles must comply with Environmental Protection Agency (EPA) regulations that govern exhaust emissions. These regulations require auto manufacturers to invest in technologies such as catalytic converters to meet pollution regulations even though these investments add to the cost of manufacturing a car.

Companies' leaders will object when they believe that a proposed law will be detrimental. For example, McDonald's and other fast-food companies oppose hikes in the minimum wage because the cost structure of fast-food restaurants is highly sensitive to such increases. They may hire lobbyists to try to influence legislators to defeat proposed minimum wage increase legislation as a way of dealing with the threats in the political environment.

Customers

Many firms sell products to two types of customers: (1) individuals making purchases and (2) other businesses. Both types of customers are interested in purchasing quality products that are reasonably priced and safe to use. Customer groups sometimes organize to boycott companies that behave unethically or irresponsibly. Consumer pressure has protected old-growth forests from the timber industry's chainsaws, forced cigarette manufacturers to discontinue advertising on television, and generated international guidelines to reduce the production of ozone layer-depleting chlorofluorocarbons. On U.S. airlines, smoking is banned on domestic flights because of complaints from individual consumers and consumer groups. Consumer groups put market pressure on Volkswagen, the manufacturer of the Audi line of cars, to redesign the car's power train and transmission after a number of fatal accidents. Consumer opinion is influenced by periodicals such as *Consumer Reports* that judge the performance and reliability of consumer products and identify those that offer the best value and quality.

Community

There are local, national, and global communities. All types of communities expect corporations to be good citizens and to contribute to the quality of life. Firms that neglect or degrade their communities may be subject to pressure. When citizens in several communities in Maine opposed new Wal-Mart stores because of fears that they would hurt downtown businesses as they had done in other communities, Wal-Mart decided not to build the stores.

A business that operates in a local community pays taxes that support public services such as schools, police, and fire protection. It also creates jobs that may employ local people. Businesses can give the local community funds or equipment or can encourage employees to volunteer at community nonprofit organizations. IBM provides computer equipment to local colleges and encourages executives who qualify for sabbaticals (paid time off to pursue other interests) to teach in local public schools and to work with disadvantaged children. These investments in the community should pay off for IBM in the future because students trained on IBM equipment are more likely to purchase IBM products when they graduate from college.

Home Depot, the giant home improvement company, encourages its employees to build playgrounds for children in various local communities. It plans to build up to 1,000 playgrounds and has budgeted $25 million to do it. Nike has raised $20 million for cancer research through sales of its $1 yellow bracelets. Starbucks gives back to the community by sponsoring literacy programs as well as a holiday gift drive for seriously ill children.[25]

Patagonia, a manufacturer of outdoor recreation clothing, is a business that actively supports environmental causes, and has recently provided financial resources and employee volunteers to protect 1.5 million acres of wilderness in the Arctic Refuge coastal plain that supports a rich ecological oasis for bears, gray wolves, wolverines, musk ox, moose, and caribou. Patagonia's activities aim to protect the environment for the benefit of the global community.[26]

Competitors

Competitors expect a corporation to compete fairly in the market without engaging in such unethical business practices as industrial espionage, dumping products on the market at a below-cost price, and receiving unfair government subsidies. Competitor stakeholders can form economic coalitions to put pressure on any company that violates the principles of fair competition. They can also use the courts or the legislative branch of government to punish a corporate rule breaker. For example, competitors have charged Microsoft with unfair practices and have used the courts to break Microsoft into separate operating system and applications companies. Microsoft won its appeal of the court ruling to divide the company.

Globally, Airbus, the European manufacturer of commercial jets, threatened to lobby the European Union to boycott Boeing aircraft and successfully influenced Boeing to stop signing customers such as Delta, Continental, and American Airlines to 20-year exclusive contracts.[27]

Social Activist Groups

A business practice that runs counter to an important goal of a social activist group may result in negative media attention for the company or even a product boycott orchestrated by the social activist group. Although corporations cannot always satisfy such groups, it is often in their best interests to compromise with social activist groups to avoid being the focus of a campaign that can badly damage their reputation. Nestlé was the target of a national boycott led by the National Council of Churches because the infant baby formula it marketed to developing nations caused the sickness and death of thousands of babies. After seven years and millions of dollars unsuccessfully trying to resist the boycott, Nestlé altered some of its business practices.[28] People for the Ethical Treatment of Animals (PETA) organized a boycott against L'Oreal and other cosmetics companies that tested their products on animals. After four years of futile resistance, L'Oreal promised that it would no longer conduct animal testing. The Rainforest Action Network (RAN) pressures large multinational corporations to halt economic development in poor countries that could pollute the global environment. It uses pressure tactics such as Internet campaigns, street theater, and celebrity endorsements on firms that it targets for change. RAN demanded that Citigroup, the global financial services company, stop lending money for logging, mining, and oil-drilling projects that destroy rain forests, threaten indigenous people, and accelerate global warming. It persuaded 20,000 people to cut up their Citi credit cards. Eventually these tactics resulted in Citigroup's coming to a common understanding with RAN on key global sustainable development issues.[29]

This is not to say that social activist groups prevail in all situations. For example, when the Florida Citrus Commission hired conservative talk show host Rush Limbaugh as a spokesperson, the National Organization for Women (NOW) and the National Education Association (NEA) asked consumers to avoid purchasing Florida orange juice. The boycott had no effect.[30]

LOC-In 5 Learning Objective Check-In

1. Burton's is a textiles manufacturer that often gives money to support neighborhood programs for at-risk youth in the communities where it operates. While this does not contribute to the bottom line for Burton's, it is an important element of the company's value structure to give back to the communities which support it. The people who are affected by Burton's, including the local community, are collectively called its _____.
   a. business community
   b. stakeholders
   c. society
   d. ethics structure

■ Strategies for Managing Stakeholders

Balancing the interests of a variety of groups is the managerial form of a juggling act. Managers must consider various stakeholder groups while preparing an overall business strategy. The approaches stakeholders use to get their point across to management range from making suggestions at shareholder meetings to threatening to withhold resources from the firm. The latter approach was used by consumer groups that threatened a boycott of StarKist products unless the company stopped purchasing tuna from foreign fishing fleets that caught and killed thousands of dolphins in their tuna nets.

When a stakeholder group makes demands on a firm, management should first perform an analysis by answering the following questions:

1. Who are the stakeholders?
2. How are the stakeholders affected by the company policies?
3. What are the stakeholders' interests in the business?
4. How have the stakeholders behaved in the past, and what coalitions are they likely to form around their issue?
5. How effective have the company's strategies been in dealing with these and other stakeholders?
6. What new strategies and action plans need to be formulated to deal effectively with the stakeholders?[31]

Once an analysis of the stakeholders has been accomplished the management team can develop strategies for dealing with the stakeholders by selecting one of the following four general approaches: confrontation, damage control, accommodation, or being proactive.

Confrontation

Management may select a **confrontation strategy** to deal with a stakeholder group whose goals are perceived to threaten company performance. This includes using the courts, engaging in public relations, and lobbying against legislation. For many years, the tobacco companies used a confrontation strategy to deal with antismoking groups and individuals who sued them. For example, tobacco companies spent millions of dollars lobbying state legislatures to pass "smokers' rights" laws. United Parcel Service selected a confrontation strategy to deal with the Teamsters Union when contract negotiations failed, and the confrontation resulted in the costly labor strike mentioned earlier.

Management must be very careful when it chooses to use a confrontation strategy. Typically, the company spends considerable time and money fighting a stakeholder group rather than focusing on more positive outcomes. The long-term outcome may be a negative image for the company unless it is able to mend its relations with its stakeholders and with customers critical of the company's actions.

confrontation strategy
One means a firm may use to deal with a stakeholder group whose goals are perceived to threaten company performance; the firm may use the courts, engage in public relations, or lobby against legislation.

Damage Control

The **damage control strategy** is often used when a company decides that it may have made mistakes and wants to elevate its public image and improve its relationship with the stakeholder. In 1999, after years of confrontation, the tobacco companies admitted to having deceived the public and paid $246 billion to settle the claims of people who contracted fatal illnesses related to tobacco smoking. Similarly, when a leak of poisonous gas resulted in the death of more than 2,000 people and serious injuries to 200,000 in Bhopal, India, in 1984, Union Carbide used a damage control strategy and initiated a settlement with the Indian government for $470 million to be divided among victims and their families.

damage control strategy
A means a firm may use to deal with a stakeholder group when it decides that it may have made mistakes and wants to improve its relationship with the stakeholders and to elevate its public image.

Accommodation

The **accommodation strategy** is used when management decides to accept social responsibility for business decisions after pressure has been exerted by stakeholder groups. It may require changing business practices to better align with stakeholder goals. Long the target of environmental groups, McDonald's used the accommodation strategy when it changed its packaging from polystyrene foam to paper, which is less damaging to the environment. General Motors voluntarily recognized the United Auto Workers (UAW) union in the Spring Hill, Tennessee, Saturn manufacturing plant instead of forcing the union to undergo a formal election procedure. In return, General Motors obtained a labor agreement that allowed it to deploy its workforce more flexibly than is possible in other unionized auto plants.

accommodation strategy
A means of dealing with stakeholder groups when a firm decides to accept social responsibility for its business decisions after pressure has been exerted by stakeholder groups.

Proactive

A company chooses a **proactive strategy** when it determines that it wants to go beyond stakeholder expectations. Proactive companies form partnerships with stakeholders and cooperate with them. These partnerships increase management's ability to predict and control the stakeholder environment and fewer crises emerge. For example:

proactive strategy
A means of dealing with stakeholders when a firm determines that it wants to go beyond stakeholder expectations.

- The Colgate-Palmolive Company "adopted" a failing junior high school in Harlem that needed its buildings and curriculum modernized. Colgate-Palmolive contributed funds and personnel for the renovation and restructuring of the school. Company personnel worked with school staff on budgeting, strategic planning, and management. Student reading levels and math competencies improved dramatically in the renovated school.
- The Coca-Cola Company sets ambitious goals for purchasing goods and services from minority- and female-owned vendors and puts a high priority on recruiting and developing minority and female employees. One woman and two members of minorities sit on the 14-member board of directors, and there are seven women and six minority members among the top 57 corporate executives. Coca-Cola also encourages its employees to volunteer in community programs such as Adopt-a-School and provides assistance to the United Negro College Fund and the National Hispanic Scholarship Fund.

FIGURE 3.3

Approaches to Social Responsibility

Merck, the pharmaceutical company, formed a partnership with the Costa Rican National Institute of Biodiversity. The institute provides Merck with plant and insect samples that may become the basis for new medicines, and Merck shares its pharmaceutical product royalties with the Costa Rican institute. Merck also provides funds for conservation efforts to preserve the Costa Rican rain forest.[32]

Figure 3.3 shows how the different strategies for dealing with stakeholder concerns compare with respect to how they are related to an organization's commitment to social responsibility. The confrontation and damage control approaches reflect lower commitments to social responsibility and the accommodation and proactive approaches reflect higher commitments to social responsibility.

LOC-In 6   Learning Objective Check-In

1. Pine Crest Linens has been manufacturing a variety of linens in the mid-sized town of Oakdale, Wisconsin, for over 20 years. The founders of Pine Crest view the manufacturer as a waste stream and realize they use resources and emit waste depending on how their operations are run and what kind of efficiencies are achieved at every stage. Despite good intentions, the company has a mixed. political reception in the community—it provides above-average paying jobs, but also contributes to the local area's pollution problem. In order to limit its impact on the local environment, Pine Crest recently installed new technologies that allow it to recycle rinse water at least twice before drainage. This has lowered its water usage by almost 40 percent within the first two months of use. This represents a(n) _____.
   a. damage control strategy
   b. proactive strategy
   c. accommodation strategy
   d. confrontation strategy

CONCLUDING THOUGHTS

In the chapter's introductory vignette we presented some critical thinking questions about Chez Panisse and the Chez Panisse Foundation. Now that you've had the opportunity to study ethical and social responsibility issues, you can reexamine those questions. First, one benefit that Chez Panisse derives from the attention it gives to a socially responsible cause is increased visibility for its retail business, the Chez Panisse restaurant in Berkeley. This recognition could help the restaurant attract more customers, as well as employees who admire its values and want to help it succeed. The Foundation's transformation of a blighted schoolyard also has produced good will in the neighborhood that might encourage people to patronize the restaurant or inspire donors to contribute to the Foundation.

Chez Panisse's stakeholders include its customers; its employees; parents, teachers, and children in the Berkeley school district; neighbors in the local and national communities; other school districts; competitors; and activist groups that value and support organic farming and sustainable use of Earth's resources.

Chez Panisse's stakeholder strategy is the proactive approach. Before setting up the Foundation, Waters used her own initiative and gathered donations in support of a worthy social cause. The Foundation's creation of and support of the School Lunch Initiative signals its cooperative relationship with the district school board for the benefit of all its students.

FOCUSING ON THE FUTURE: Using Management Theory in Daily Life

Using Social Responsibility and Ethics in Daily Life

Barbara DeLong* was an HR Director at a medium-sized (900-person) telecommunications company when she used the "Eight Steps to Sound Ethical Decision Making in Business" to handle an ethics violation in her company.

The office manager came to Barbara one day and told her that she had noticed some irregular purchases on a bill from the company's office supply provider. Barbara handled the situation in the following way:

1. **Step 1.** *Gather the facts.* When Barbara asked to see the list, she was astonished to find items such as a vacuum cleaner, pocket thesaurus, lamps, cleaning supplies, and other items, which over the period of about one month totaled more than $1,000. However, she knew that she also needed to find out the other side of the issue, so she asked the employee why she needed these items, whose response was they were job-related and she used them to clean the booth at campus recruiting.

2. **Step 2.** *Define the ethical issues.* Barbara used the company's purchasing policy to define the ethical issues involved, and also looked at the situation from a broader perspective. According to the purchasing policy, all purchases required approval from the HR Director—obviously this "legality" had been overlooked. However, Barbara also considered whether or not different issues were at play—for example, did the employee have a legitimate need for the items, and was she aware of the policy?

3. **Step 3.** *Identify the affected parties.* In this case, it was apparent that Barbara, the employee, and the company as a whole were affected. However, when Barbara reviewed company policy with the employee, the employee claimed that she had received permission from another manager to make the purchases, thereby bringing another party into the picture.

4. **Step 4.** *Identify the consequences.* In one way, the consequences in this case were clear-cut—if the employee was purchasing things for her personal use, she would be fired. However, Barbara also had to think about the consequences of losing a fully trained employee over what might have been a misunderstanding.

5. **Step 5.** *Identify your obligations.* As HR Director, Barbara had several obligations—first and foremost to do what was right for the company, secondly, to abide by all written corporate policies, and finally to treat company employees with respect. As noted above, these obligations demanded that the situation be viewed in several different ways. As a result, Barbara pondered what she would do, taking all of her obligations into consideration.

6. **Step 6.** *Consider your character and integrity.* Barbara knew that if she let unauthorized expenses slip by, her own character and integrity could be called into question. She also knew that her decision would be scrutinized by other employees, company management, and her peers. More important, Barbara had firm convictions of her own about the importance of honesty in the workplace, and she was determined to live up to her beliefs.

7. **Step 7.** *Think creatively about your potential actions.* Barbara listened to the employee's side of the story, and took it seriously, but she also devised a plan for verifying that story. Since the employee claimed that another manager (the one she was recruiting for) had given her approval, Barbara offered to call that manager right then. At that point, the employee claimed that the manager would "probably forget that he gave me approval." Barbara balanced the company's need to retain the employee, her core values of honesty, and the importance she placed on respecting employees by allowing the employee to return the items purchased "for the campus recruiting booth" and letting the employee know that any similar behavior in the future would result in dismissal.

8. **Step 8.** *Check your gut feelings.* Barbara checked her gut feelings, which indicated that she should be somewhat lenient with the employee for a first offense, but to watch the employee carefully in the future. Sure enough, the employee was later terminated for a similar incident.

*Because of the nature of this incident, the manager involved has requested that her real name not be used.

Summary of Learning Objectives

Business ethics are principles prescribing a code of behavior that explains what is good and right, and what is bad and wrong. They provide standards for conduct and decision making by employees and managers. **Corporate social responsibility** means that a company has a duty to use some of its resources to promote the interests of various elements of society. This chapter's discussion will help future managers, work teams and employees better understand the importance of ethics and social responsibility. The ideas presented in this chapter that meet each of the learning objectives stated at the start of the chapter are summarized below.

1 Apply the four key ethical criteria that managers and employees should use when making business decisions.

- **Utilitarianism** looks at what is good for the greatest number of people.
- **Individualism** sees individual self-interest as the basis of the greatest good as long as it does not harm others.
- The **rights approach** represents and protects fundamental human rights.
- The **justice approach** emphasizes treating all people fairly and consistently.

2 Explain why businesses establish codes of ethics as a method of guiding employee conduct.

- A **code of ethics** is a formal statement of a company's ethics and values, which guides employee conduct in a number of business situations.
- The code can be a **corporate credo,** which focuses on general values and beliefs, or an **ethical policy statement,** which provides specific rules for employee conduct.

3 Recognize ways to encourage ethical behavior in business.

- A company provides **ethics training** to its employees to develop skills to deal with ethical challenges in business.
- An **ethical structure** can be developed to monitor and audit ethical behavior.
- A company can have a **whistleblower policy** that encourages employees to disclose illegal or unethical practices of co-workers without fearing retaliation.

4 Recognize morally challenging situations where ethical decisions should be made.

- Morally challenging situations where ethical decisions should be made include: (1) *performance appraisals;* (2) *employee discipline;* (3) *romantic relationships* in the workplace; and (4) *gift giving.*

5 Identify important categories of stakeholders.

- **Stakeholders** are individuals or groups with an interest in the performance of the business and the way it uses its resources; companies should respond to their concerns.
- Important categories of stakeholders are owners, employees, governments, customers, the community, competitors, and social activist groups.

6 Recognize the influence of various stakeholders on a company's priorities, policies, plans, and goals.

- Companies develop different strategies for managing stakeholder demands after analyzing the nature of the stakeholders' interests and the threats and opportunities that may result.
- The **confrontation strategy** challenges the stakeholder.
- The **damage control strategy** is used when management decides that it made a mistake in the way it treated a stakeholder and wants to minimize the damage to the company's reputation.
- The **accommodation strategy** is used when the company decides that it is in its best interest to accept the goals of a stakeholder.
- The **proactive strategy** is used by companies that want to go beyond meeting stakeholders' expectations in order to be a leader in social resonsibility.

Discussion Questions

1. Compare and contrast the four ethics approaches used for ethical decision making that are discussed in this chapter. Which criterion do you think is the best one? Which one would be the least useful? What is the basis for your selection? Now, suppose you were going to work at a business in China. Which of the four criteria would you be most likely to apply to an ethical business decision in China?

2. Why do you think companies invest resources in training their managers and employees in business ethics? Some people think that ethics should be learned within the family and by the time a person is a mature adult it is too late to learn about ethics. Do you agree or disagree with this statement? Explain.

3. Some sales organizations like to put their sales representatives on a straight commission pay plan, which means that they must successfully sell the product in order to receive any money at the end of the month. What type of ethical dilemmas or problems are likely to happen when the salespeople must operate under a straight commission plan? How might these ethical problems be managed?

4. Suppose you discover that your boss is embezzling funds from the company. Which of the policies described in this chapter would you use in deciding to disclose this situation to company officials who could take care of the problem before it becomes more serious? What kind of preparation should you make before you decide to disclose your boss's unethical conduct to the company authorities?

5. Is it possible for a business to do good for society and still make a reasonable profit? Explain.

6. In Germany, under the model of "stakeholder capitalism," employee representatives sit on company boards of directors. In the German model of business it is assumed that both labor (employee representatives) and capital (shareholder representatives) have important stakes in the enterprise and should work in harmony with each other. In the United States, the board of directors usually represents only the owners of the business. What advantages to employees as stakeholders are available in Germany that are not provided to employees in U.S. companies? In the United States, how do employees let management know their stakeholder concerns?

7. What does it mean to be a socially responsible employer? What are the benefits for a company that decides to give a high priority to its social responsibility?

8. Is it possible for a small business to take an active role in social responsibility? What are some ways that a small business (for example, a family business or a local business you are familiar with) can be socially responsible?

Management Minicase 3.1

Starbucks Gambles that Encouraging Its Coffee Suppliers to Act Socially Responsible Is Good for Business

Starbucks, the fast growing coffee retailer with over $4 billion in annual sales, places a high priority on corporate social responsibility. It gives all its employees who work over 20 hours per week health insurance benefits and stock options. It strives to give back to the communities that it does business in by supporting local schools, literacy programs, and environmental activities. One of its newest social resonsibility initiatives is to cultivate and reward environmentally and socially responsible coffee suppliers, a practice it calls sustainable sourcing. Company executives reason that making sustainable sourcing an important cornerstone of its global growth strategy will help build the Starbucks brand. The impetus for Starbucks to start a program of social responsibility with coffee growers originally had been a way to respond to critics from the "fair trade" movement—which advocates fair payments to farmers in developing nations—that had accused Starbucks of underpaying coffee growers, a claim Starbucks denied after it opened its books to them to prove that was not the case.

There were sound economic reasons for the initiative as well. With an annual growth rate of 20 percent Starbucks executives wanted to make sure that the future supply of coffee would be predictable and reliable for its customers. If the supply of the specialty coffee beans that Starbucks uses were disrupted, its growth plans and quality of its coffee would be at risk. To protect its coffee supply, Starbucks realized it had to identify and nurture partners that could meet its quality standards and keep up with increasing demand. At the same time, to protect its brand, the company needed to be certain that its suppliers shared its commitment to corporate citizenship. Therefore in 2001 the company launched its preferred supplier program to attract and reward farmers committed to socially and environmentally responsible farming. The company assumed that the growers that took the best care of their employees and land would also be the most effective, responsible and responsible suppliers—the kind of partners it wanted to fulfill its aggressive growth plan.

To become a preferred supplier to Starbucks, coffee growers must apply to the program. Reviewers evaluate the applicants on 20 measures to determine how well they adhere to sustainable environmental practices (procedures that protect the scarce land on which high-quality coffee can grow) and responsible social practices (methods, for example, that reduce the risk that deliveries will be compromised by labor unrest, corruption, or legal violations).

Suppliers accepted into the program are awarded points for meeting environmental, social, and economic criteria. The more points they earn, the more Starbucks pays them for their coffee. Preferred coffee growers will receive a 5 percent premium on each pound of beans they sell. They can also earn long-term contracts to reduce market risk and receive credit to fund improvements that promote sustainability. In 2009 Starbucks purchased 81 percent of its coffee from fair trade certified suppliers.

DISCUSSION QUESTIONS

1. How does Starbucks link its social responsibility goals of being a good corporate citizen with its business goals of aggressive growth?

2. What are the risks that Starbucks takes by attempting to influence how coffee growers treat their employees and use the land where they grow coffee?

3. Which strategy for managing stakeholders most closely corresponds to. the way Starbucks responded to the criticisms it received front the "fair trade" movement? Be able to justify your choice.

Sources: Based on "Starbucks Company Web site." (2010). www.starbucks.com/responsibility/.../coffee; E. Schrage, "Supply and Brand," *Harvard Business Review,* June, 2004, pp. 20–21; C. Hymowitz, "Asked to be Charitable, More CEOs Seek to Aid Their Business as Well," *The Wall Street Journal,* February 22, 2005, p. B1; A. Server "Hot Starbucks to Go," *Fortune,* January 26, 2004, pp. 60–74; P. Argenti, "Collaborating with Activists: How Starbucks Works with NGOs," *California Management Review,* Fall 2004, pp. 91–116.

Management Minicase 3.2

New Belgium Brewing Company Takes Environmental Responsibility Seriously

Founded by a social worker and an electrical engineer, New Belgium Brewing Company has always found ways to operate efficiently and in a socially responsible manner. Embracing new technologies, seeking out alternative forms of energy, and reducing its waste, New Belgium strives to make smart decisions that do well by the environment each and every day. New Belgium has shown that a company can be environmentally conscious and operate efficiently and effectively as a long-term, profit-seeking business.

The company makes environmental sustainability a big priority at the workplace. An on-site recycling center allows employees to recycle goods such as old car batteries and motor oil. The company also donates 1 percent of its profits to 1% for For The Planet, a global philanthropic network. New Belgium also has been using wind-power electricity, a clean energy, since 1999 for its brewing process when employees voted to use wind power instead of electricity from the local coal-based utility company. Employees voted to subsidize the higher cost of wind-powered electricity over cheaper coal-based alternatives from their profit-sharing bonuses.

New Belgium Brewing Company establishes environmental goals and reports on its progress on an annual Sustainability Report that it puts on its Web site. Here is a list of New Belgium's long-term environmental goals:

1. Lovingly care for the planet that sustains us.
2. Honor natural resources by closing the loops between waste and input.

3. Minimize the environmental impact of shipping our beer.
4. Reduce our dependence on coal-fired electricity.
5. Protect our precious Rocky Mountain water resources.
6. Focus our efforts on conservation and efficiency.
7. Support innovative technology.
8. Model joyful environmentalism through our commitment to relationships, continuous improvement, and the camaraderie and cheer of beer.

DISCUSSION QUESTIONS

1. How is New Belgium Brewing Company's approach to social responsibility different from that of other companies? What are the advantages and disadvantages of this approach? New Belgium is a small, regional brewer that serves a limited market. Do you think a large multinational corporation could adopt a similar approach to social responsibility?
2. Who are New Belgium's stakeholders? Which ones do you think have the most influence concerning the company's approach to social responsibility?

Sources: Based on "New Belgium Brewing Web site." (2010). www.newbelgium.com/sustainability; K. Spors, "Top Workplaces, 2008," *Wall Street Journal*, October 13, 2008, p. R8; "New Belgium Brewery: Four principles of sustainable business." (2008, June 7). www.triplepundit.com.

Individual/Collaborative Learning Case 3.1

Do Pay Incentives Cause Employees to Behave Unethically?

Pay incentives are used in diverse business applications to motivate employees to achieve high levels of performance linked to financial rewards when performance expectations are met or exceeded. Despite their popularity, the practice of using pay incentives as motivational tools has been heavily criticized in recent years for being closely associated with unethical employee conduct and unprofessional behavior, such as using deception to convince customers to buy products or services, gaming performance standards by faking performance or manipulating it, taking credit for the successful performance of other employees, and reporting false financial information to shareholders. Consider these examples:

- American International Insurance (AIG) decided to reward its executives with $165 million in retention bonuses in 2009 while the company was close to bankruptcy due to overly risky investment decisions having been made by its executives and concurrently receiving $180 billion from the U.S. government to a avoid financial disaster to the whole economy. An executive earns a retention bonus by simply staying employed at the company over a pre-arranged period of time.
- Sears auto mechanics were paid on a sales commission for auto repair work based on a quota of $147 per hour. This highly challenging performance goal prompted the auto mechanics to overcharge for work and to complete unnecessary repairs on a companywide basis. Customers who believed they were cheated on their repair work sued the company for millions of dollars and the bad publicity from the media damaged the reputation of the firm.

- Senior associates at Clifford Chance, one of the world's largest law firms, established a high performance goal based on the number of billable hours charged to clients that would be eventually rewarded with a partnership in the firm and a share in the profits. Some senior associates at the firm were alleged to pad their billable hour numbers with the work done by less expensive junior associates, which resulted in higher fees charged to some clients who eventually took legal action against the law firm for overpayment.

The poor experiences that companies have recently had with pay incentives, particularly in the financial services industry, has led some experts to conclude that pay incentives in some essential industries and high impact jobs, such as executives in large banks, should be regulated to prevent them from acting in ways that harm shareholders, customers and other stakeholders.

CRITICAL THINKING QUESTIONS

1. What role do high performance goals play in providing conditions for employees to engage in misconduct? For example, in the law firm example, what if the performance goal used was different than a high number of billable hours, do you think some of the lawyers would still try to falsely manipulate the number of hours to achieve the performance goal?
2. Is it possible to use pay incentives that encourage employees to behave in ethical ways? Can you think of an example of how this could be accomplished?

COLLABORATIVE LEARNING EXERCISE

With a partner or small group, assume you are management consultants brought into a law firm similar to the one in the above case that uses billable hours as a performance goal. As consultants you are asked to improve the performance goal setting and reward process for lawyers so that their interests in earning a partnership does not interfere with giving high quality service to clients of the firm. What is wrong with the use of billable hours as a performance goal? How would you improve the process of rewarding performance at the law firm?

Sources: Based on D. Slater, "At Law Firms, Reconsidering the Model for Associates' Pay," *The New York Times*, April 1, 2010, p. F10; B. Schwartz, "The Dark Side of Incentives," *Business Week*, November 23, 2009, p. 84; L. Ordonez, M. Schweitzer, A. Galinsky, and M. Bazerman, *Academy of Management Perspectives* 4(1) (2009), pp. 6–16; A. Likierman, "The Five Traps of Performance Measurement," *Harvard Business Review*, 87(10) (2009), pp. 96–101.

Internet Exercise 3.1

Social Responsibility at Levi Strauss

www.levistrauss.com

Visit the Web site of Levi Strauss, the clothing company, and find its "Corporate Citizenship" section. Answer the following questions:

1. How do the giving programs support the social responsibility goals of Levi Strauss?
2. Some of the Levi Strauss giving programs might be considered controversial by some people, such as providing resources to fight AIDS or to achieve social justice. Why would Levi Strauss support programs that some of its customers may not agree with?
3. How can Levi Strauss employees become involved with the giving programs? Provide an example. If you were an employee at Levi Strauss, which giving program would you like to become involved with? Why?

Manager's Checkup 3.1

What Are Your Beliefs about Business Ethics?

Instructions: Answer the following questions as honestly as you can. Circle the number between 1 and 5 that best represents your own beliefs about business.

	Strongly Disagree				Strongly Agree
1. The only important goal in business is the bottom line.	1	2	3	4	5
2. Business people usually have to compromise their ethical values.	1	2	3	4	5
3. Business people who make a lot of money tend to be the ones with the lowest ethical standards.	1	2	3	4	5
4. People who act on their moral values in business achieve limited success.	1	2	3	4	5
5. People should live by one set of moral rules in their personal life and a different set in business.	1	2	3	4	5
6. Business people are obsessed with making profits.	1	2	3	4	5
7. In the game of business, winning is everything.	1	2	3	4	5
8. In the business world people are totally driven by their self-interest.	1	2	3	4	5

9. In the dog-eat-dog world of business, managers are sometimes forced to do under-handed things to beat the competition.	1	2	3	4	5
10. People with high ethical standards will probably not fit in the world of business.	1	2	3	4	5

Scoring: Add the total number of points. The higher your score, the lower your expectations are that ethical business can be practiced. What are the reasons for the responses that you made? Be prepared to discuss them in class.

Source: Based on L. K. Trevino and K. A. Nelson, *Managing Business Ethics,* 3rd ed., New York: John Wiley & Sons, 2004, p. 19. Reprinted with permission of John Wiley & Sons, Inc.

Endnotes

1. M. Jackson, "50% of Workers Commit Unethical Acts, Survey Says," *Boulder Daily Camera*, May 12, 1997, p. 1B; "Business Ethics: Doing Well by Doing Good," *The Economist*, April 22, 2000, pp. 65–67.
2. C. Stohl and M. Stohl, "A New Generation of Corporate Codes of Ethics," *Journal of Business Ethics,* 90 (2009), 607–22; F. D. Sturdivant and H. Vernon Wortzel, *Business and Society*, 4th ed. Burr Rige, IL: Irwin, 1990.
3. P. E. Murphy, "Creating Ethical Corporate Structures," *Sloan Management Review* 30 (Winter 1989), 81–89.
4. Eli Lilly & Company, Guidelines of Company Policy, 1990.
5. General Dynamics, Standards of Business Ethics and Conduct, 1988.
6. M. Helft and D. Barboza, "Google Closes Search Service Based in China," *New York Times,* March 23, 2010, A1, A6.
7. M. Gundlach, S. Douglas, and M. Martinko, "The Decision to Blow the Whistle: A Social Information Processing Framework," *Academy of Management Review* 28 (2003), 107–123.
8. T. M. Dworkin and J. P. Near, "A Better Statutory Approach to Whistle Blowing," *Business Ethics Quarterly 7*, no. 1 (1997), 1–16.
9. M. Steinberg and S. Kaufman, "Minimizing Corporate Liability Exposure When the Whistle Blows in the Post-Sarbanes-Oxley Era," *Journal of Corporation Law*, August 2005, pp. 445–463.
10. Dworkin and Near, "A Better Statutory Approach to Whistle Blowing."
11. P. Dwyer and D. Carney, "Year of the Whistleblower," *BusinessWeek*, December 16, 2002, pp. 107–110.
12. W. Zellner, "The Whistleblower: A Hero—and a Smoking-Gun Letter," *BusinessWeek*, January 28, 2002, pp. 34–35.
13. M. Sashkin and K. J. Kiser, *Putting Total Quality Management to Work* (San Francisco: Berrett-Koehler, 1993).
14. I. Sager, "Tech's Kickback Culture," *BusinessWeek*, February 10, 2003, pp. 74–77.
15. A. Park, "Family Feuds Don't Get Nastier than This," *BusinessWeek*, February 10, 2003, pp. 62–63.
16. *Global Corruption Report 2003*, www.globalcorruptionreport.org.
17. "Pharmaceuticals: Pushing Pills," *The Economist*, February 15, 2003, p. 61.
18. D. B. Turban and D. W. Greening, "Corporate Social Performance and Organizational Attractiveness to Prospective Employees," *Academy of Management Journal* 40 (1997), 658–672; J. B. McGuire, A. Sundgren and T. Schneeweis, "Corporate Social Responsibility and Firm Financial Performance," *Academy of Management Journal* 27 (1988), 42–56; P. L. Cochran and R. A. Wood, "Corporate Social Responsibility and Financial Performance," *Academy of Management Journal* 31 (1984), 854–872.
19. S. V. Brull, "For All That Tobacco Money, Don't Stint on the Smoking War," *BusinessWeek*, May 10, 1999, p. 40; D. Noonan, "Lighting into Big Tobacco," *Newsweek*, July 24, 2000, pp. 30–31.
20. *The Economist*, "Big Trouble for Merck," November 6, 2004, pp. 61–62; A. Barrett, "Merck: How Much Misery After Vioxx?" *BusinessWeek*, November 22, 2004, pp. 48–50.

21. A. B. Carroll, *Business and Society*, 3rd ed. Cincinnati, OH: SouthWestern Publishing, 1996.
22. A. Ohnsman, J. Green, and K. Inoue, "The Humbling of Toyota," *Bloomberg BusinessWeek*, March 22 & 29, 2010, 33–36.
23. B. McLean, "Why Enron Went Bust," *Fortune*, December 24, 2001, pp. 58–68; and W. Zellner and S. Forest, "The Fall of Enron," *BusinessWeek*, December 17, 2001, pp. 30–36.
24. N. Munk, "How Levi's Trashed a Great American Brand," *Fortune*, April 12, 1999, pp. 82–90.
25. B. Grow, "The Debate over Doing Good," *BusinessWeek*, August 15, 2005 pp. 76–78; L. Gard, "We're Good Guys Buy from Us," *BusinessWeek*, November 22, 2004, pp. 72–74.
26. Patagonia Environmentalism Issues, April 30, 2010, www.patagonia.com
27. "Boeing v. Airbus," *Economist*, July 26, 1997, pp. 59–61.
28. A. B. Carroll, *Business and Society*, 3rd ed. Cincinnati, OH: SouthWestern Publishing, 1996.
29. M. Gunther, "A Pesky Environmental Group Called the Rainforest Action Network Is Getting under the Skin of Corporate America," *Fortune*, May 31 2004, pp. 158–164.
30. J. H. Jackson, R. L. Miller, and S. G. Miller, *Business and Society Today*. St. Paul, MN: West Publishing, 1997.
31. N. C. Roberts and P. J. King, "The Stakeholder Audit Goes Public," *Organizational Dynamics*, Winter 1989 pp. 63–79.
32. R. Will, "Corporations with a Conscience," *Business and Society Review* Spring 1995, pp. 17–20.

4

Learning Objectives

1. Identify the three major aspects of organizational culture.

2. Apply a simple assessment tool to quickly gain a sense of the culture of an organization.

3. Describe the importance of organizational culture.

4. Identify the processes through which organizational culture can be developed and sustained.

5. Use classification systems to identify various types of organizational culture.

6. Identify the sources of resistance to change.

7. Apply models to effectively manage change efforts.

Cisco's Collaborative Culture Enables It to Deal with Change

Cisco Systems is a technology company with $36 billion in sales in 2009 and is best known for producing routers and switches that handle traffic on the Internet. Cisco Systems has grown rapidly by making many acquisitions of smaller technology firms, having acquired 127 companies between 1993 and 2008. One of Cisco's core competencies is its ability to integrate the technology and people of the firms it acquires into its line of businesses, which is unusual in the technology industry where assets walk out the door at the end of the day.

In recent years, to sustain its growth Cisco has been expanding into businesses beyond its line of Internet hardware into video technologies by acquiring Scientific Atlanta, a maker of set-top boxes, for $6.9 billion and Pure Digital Technologies, a maker of handheld recorders for $590 million. The company has used its newly acquired technologies to create TelePresence, a life-size, high-definition video system that provides video conferences with the detail of each speaker's nonverbal gestures as if they were in the same room. In order to accommodate Cisco's greater complexity of businesses, CEO John Chambers has championed a move toward developing a culture of collaboration. In support of the collaborative culture at Cisco, CEO Chambers reorganized Cisco's lines

Managing Organizational Culture and Change

of businesses into an elaborate system of committees made up of managers from different functions. There are "councils" that are in charge of the largest markets up to $10 billion in revenues and "boards" in charge of smaller markets. Supporting both councils and boards are working groups that provide different operational activities within the councils and boards. This collaborative structure enables Cisco to increase the speed at which businesses share knowledge and lets Cisco improve its ease at entering new markets.

CEO Chambers sets the tone for the culture of collaboration by cultivating a cooperative management style and by encouraging other leaders to develop skills of empowering others. Some of the councils do without a formal leader at all and function more like a sports team. Many managers have leading roles both in a function such as engineering or manufacturing and also on a council or board that fosters cooperation. The effectiveness of how managers perform in teams determines 30 percent of their bonuses. Those managers who work well with others have been promoted, while those with deficient skills of collaboration have been pushed out.

Sources: Based on "Cisco Systems Web site." (2010). www.cisco.com/en/US/products/.../index.html; *The Economist*, "Briefing: Reshaping Cisco," August 29, 2009, pp. 59–62; M. Milo, "Not the Cisco You Think You Know," December 31, 2009. www.portfolio.com.

CRITICAL THINKING QUESTIONS

1. *In what ways does Cisco's collaborative culture enable it to better deal with changes brought about by acquisitions that add new people, technologies, and products to the company?*

2. *What role does the leader, CEO John Chambers, play in sustaining the culture and driving change at Cisco?*

We'll think again about these questions about Cisco System's culture in our Concluding Thoughts at the end of this chapter.

◼ Understanding the Nature of Culture and Change

The concept of company culture is complex. There are different levels of culture that influence employee behavior. First, the location of a company within a national culture can influence how employees act. In the United States, which is a highly individualistic culture, leaders may value risk taking and encourage employees to compete with each other: behaviors that are consistent with individualistic cultures. On the other hand, Japan is a highly collectivist culture, so leaders there may value risk avoidance and encourage employees to collaborate rather than compete. A second level of culture is the company level, which will be our focus in this chapter. The Walt Disney Company has a strong culture based on fun and creativity, with cultural values that support its mission of providing quality entertainment for the family. The Disney culture will be different from the culture of Wal-Mart, a giant retailer that offers low prices on merchandise to customers. Even within companies there can be differences in cultures. The well known Dilbert cartoons show the humorous side of differences in culture within a technology company, such as the contrast between the software engineers who dress casually, work in cubicles, and love the latest technology compared to the marketing staff members who wear formal business suits and care more about what the technology can do for the customer.

The chapter also examines organizational change. Change is presented from two perspectives: (1) when the change is planned, and (2) when the change is unplanned as a result from jolts from the external environment. Planned change can occur when a company changes its strategy, requiring that it redeploy its resources in a different way to compete in markets. It is the job of managers to prepare employees for the need for change so that employees and other stakeholders will be able to work collaboratively in the new strategic direction. When change comes about due to unexpected events, such as an economic downturn in demand for the company's product, managers develop approaches to deal with the change in a way that maintains organizational efficiency and effectiveness with a minimum of disruption. The culture often plays a role in the change process by giving direction to managers on how to prioritize various alternatives when changes are required.

◼ Section I: Organizational Culture

Organizational culture is a system of shared values, assumptions, beliefs, and norms that unite the members of an organization. Organizational culture reflects employees' views about "the way things are done around here." Culture gives meaning to actions and procedures within an organization[1] and may be considered to be the personality of the organization.[2] The culture specific to each firm affects how employees feel and act as well as the type of employee hired and retained by the company.

There are three aspects of an organization's culture, as shown in Figure 4.1. The most obvious is the **visible culture** that an observer can hear, feel, or see. Aspects of visible culture include

organizational culture
A system of shared values, assumptions, beliefs, and norms that unite the members of an organization.

visible culture
The aspects of culture that an observer can hear, feel, or see.

FIGURE 4.1
Levels of Corporate Culture

how people dress, how fast people walk and talk, whether there is an open floor plan without office doors or managers have private offices, and the extent to which status and power symbols are conspicuous. Assigned parking spots based on rank, differing cafeteria or eating arrangements based on organizational level, and the degree to which furnishings are plush and conservative versus simple and modern indicate the nature of power and status differentials.

The signs of a visible culture make it possible to study dominant cultural characteristics, such as whether the organization is competitive or easygoing, formal or informal, hierarchical or egalitarian, liberal or conservative. For instance, firms with *controlling* cultures often record and review their employees' communications, including telephone calls, e-mail, and Internet connections.

LOC-In 1 Learning Objective Check-In

ATC Macros is a marketing consulting firm that has no office doors. There are not even private offices except on one floor, for client meetings. There are no reserved parking spaces, and the furnishings inside the office are modern yet simple. ATC encourages its employees to take risks and managers are encouraged to accept and tolerate employee mistakes when taking risks. At ATC, employees are treated well and receive liberal fringe benefits. Employees enjoy an on-site fitness center, flexible work schedules, and other family-friendly policies.

1. The minimalist furnishings in the office, the lack of office doors, and the lack of private parking spaces all demonstrate part of ATC's _____.
   a. ethical code of conduct
   b. espoused values
   c. core values
   d. visible culture

2. ATC encourages employees to take risks. This is demontrated by accepting and tolerating employee mistakes when other firms may not do so. This reflects ATC's _____.
   a. core values
   b. visible culture
   c. espoused values
   d. stability

3. ATC considers employees central to the firm's success, and therefore takes care of them by being flexible with their schedules arid accommodating their family lives. Such policies at the center of ACT's organizational culture reflect its _____.
   a. core values
   b. espoused values
   c. visible culture
   d. ethical code of conduct

At a deeper level, **espoused values** are not readily observed but instead are the ways managers and employees explain and justify actions and decisions. For example, managers may justify layoffs primarily on the basis of a need to cut costs or to expedite decision making and improve response time by streamlining organizational levels. Other managers may say they tolerate mistakes because employees need to be encouraged to take risks or because it is better to treat workers with respect and provide them with second chances when necessary. Espoused values are those values that are expressed on behalf of an organization[3] or that are expressed as explanations for policies or actions.

espoused values
The aspects of corporate culture that are not readily observed, but instead can be perceived from the way managers and employees explain and justify their actions and decisions.

People may not always give the real reason behind their actions. Employees are quick to spot hypocrisy. Managers who are not honest about why actions were taken may create an organizational culture full of cynicism, dishonesty, lack of credibility and poor ethics, all of which eventually translate into poor firm performance.

Espoused values may vary substantially across organizations and this variability in expressed values can reflect real and important differences in these organizations. For organizations that have merged or been acquired it has been found that organizational performance after the merger is better for firms that had more closely matched espoused values to begin with.[4] This effect on postmerger financial performance illustrates the importance of espoused values.

core values
A firm's principles that are widely shared, that operate unconsciously, and that are considered nonnegotiable.

Espoused values are generally consciously and explicitly communicated. At the center of organizational culture are **core values** that are widely shared, operate unconsciously, and are considered nonnegotiable. In some organizations, a basic assumption may be that stability and commitment of the workforce are critical for success. Consequently, employees are well treated and receive liberal fringe benefits. At the other extreme, a basic assumption may be that employees are commodities and an expense that should be minimized in the business process, rather than an investment. Thus employees are tightly controlled, exceptions to established policy are kept to a minimum, there are detailed rules and procedures about what employees can and cannot do, and managers believe it is their duty to prevent deviations from the norms. Employees may be watching one another to ensure that no one breaks the rules, and people are trained to check with their superiors before making most decisions.

The basic underlying cultural assumptions create the lenses through which people perceive and interpret events. Someone sitting motionless may be seen as loafing in some firms, while at others, the employee would be perceived as pondering an important problem. When employees are absent from work, the organization's culture may lead managers to conclude they are shirking, and if an employee requests permission to perform some tasks at home, the request will probably be denied because the supervisor expects the employee will "goof off" rather than work.

LOC-In 2   **Learning Objective Check-In**

Raj Communications usually gives an award every quarter to the top performing teams in each of its three divisions. These awards are based on creativity and risk taking—not necessarily achievement of specific organizational objectives. In performance assessments, customer satisfaction is at the top of the evaluation list. Every division has customers, even if they are "internal"—meaning other divisions or departments.

1. Which of the quick culture test questions speaks to the way Raj Communications treats its most creative teams?
   a. What do we measure?
   b. What data is used to assess the effectiveness of the organization?
   c. What is celebrated, recognized, or rewarded?
   d. How do we evaluate individual performance?

■ The Importance of Culture

Organization culture can be a critical factor in determining the competitiveness of an organization. While culture may seem more of a concept than something that is physically real, the potential impact of culture can be very real and merits careful attention. Results from workplace studies indicate that organizational culture can be an even more important determinant of worker commitment and loyalty than pay.[5] Culture can also differentiate an organization in the labor market. For example, Cisco Systems has a culture that emphasizes teamwork and innovation that gives it a competitive advantage in the development of new products, which requires cross-functional collaboration between people with diverse backgrounds such as engineering, manufacturing, and marketing. Manager's Notebook 4.1 provides some tips on using organizational culture as a business tool.

Organizational culture can help managers achieve organizational objectives in several ways. As illustrated in Figure 4.2, key functions performed by culture include employee self-management, stability, employee socialization, and supporting a firm's strategies. We now turn to a description of each of these effects of organizational culture. Each of these aspects points out how organizational culture can help or hinder the achievement of organizational objectives.

Employee Self-Management

Organizations depend on a variety of rational means to coordinate and control employees. Defining jobs with job descriptions; creating vertical levels and reporting relationships; drawing organizational charts; establishing departments, business units, and divisions; and developing work schedules are examples of rational controls. Still, no firm can function effectively unless employees choose to behave in the way the firm desires.

MANAGER'S NOTEBOOK 4.1

Some Tips on Using Organizational Culture as a Business Tool

DETERMINE WHETHER THE CULTURE IN YOUR ORGANIZATION IS STRONG OR WEAK. Strong cultures give employees useful performance information. For example, innovative cultures encourage employees to take risks and experiment with new ideas and avoid punishing them when an experiment does not bear fruit. Often experimental ideas that fail lead to successful outcomes later.

LEADERS SHOULD ALIGN THEIR VISION TO THE ORGANIZATIONAL CULTURE. Leaders that link their vision to the organizational culture and its values are more likely to influence followers to be more committed to the vision rather than simply comply with it. Committed followers require less supervision so the leader has more time to focus on work that may have greater strategic significance.

IT IS VALUABLE TO PROVIDE AN ORIENTATION PROGRAM TO ALL NEW EMPLOYEES SO THAT THEY LEARN THE ORGANIZATIONAL CULTURE IN A CONSISTENT WAY. Orientation programs teach employees company history, the key products and services the company provides to the customer, and about company traditions. For example, the Walt Disney Company offers an orientation program to all new employees at a corporate training facility called Disney University.

Sources: Based on C. Lee, B. Tan and J. Chiu, "The Impact of Organizational Culture and Learning on Innovation Performance," *International Journal of Innovation and Learning,* 5 (2008), pp. 413–28; "Walt Disney Company Web site" (2010). www.corporate.disney.go.com/.../learning.html; M. A. Mitchell and D. Yates, "How to Use Your Organizational Culture as a Competitive Tool," *Nonprofit World* 20 (2002), pp. 33–34.

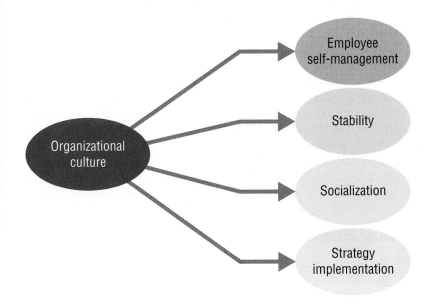

FIGURE 4.2

Key Effects of Organizational Culture

Organizational culture can induce employees to behave in a particular way without close supervision or formal control mechanisms. Most people like to feel that they belong; fitting into the culture and acting accordingly make it more likely that employees will be accepted by others. Conversely, failure to comply with cultural norms generates social pressures to conform; thus the individuals would either align with the cultural expectations or face ostracism and ridicule by their peers. Much of this process occurs informally and in an unspecified manner, filling in the gaps left by rational control systems. For example, companies with highly innovative cultures find it useful to empower employees with flexible work schedules and free time to devote to making improvements to products or work processes. Managers who attempt to closely supervise or tightly schedule the work of employees in a company with an innovative culture could be violating the cultural norms and would be likely to face resistance by the employees.

Stability

Culture provides a sense of continuity in the midst of rapid change and intense competitive pressure. In industries with "hyperturbulent environments" such as high technology, culture fulfills an important human need for predictability, security, and comfort. It can take the edge off the stress caused by projects that change overnight, products that become obsolete in a matter of months, changeable work teams and reporting relationships, and frequent shifts in work methods and operations. The continuity provided by organizational culture has become increasingly valuable, as most organizations are experiencing ever more rapid rates of change. Likewise, as virtual connections and temporary alliances become commonplace, organizational culture can be the common understanding that both binds people together and facilitates their operations as a cohesive unit.[6]

Socialization

socialization
The process of internalizing or taking organizational values as one's own.

prearrival
The first stage of socialization, consisting of the values, attitudes, biases, and expectations the employee brings to the organization when first hired.

encounter stage
The stage of socialization at which the individual begins to compare expectations about the firm's culture with reality.

metamorphosis stage
The stage of socialization at which the employee is induced to bring his or her values and ways of doing things closer to those of the organization.

One key hurdle new employees face is finding out how to "fit in." Organizational culture subtly teaches employees the values of the organization. The process of internalizing or taking organizational values as one's own is called **socialization.** For example, the Marine Corps uses boot camps to socialize new recruits in "the Marine way." Sanyo requires new employees to live and eat together for five months at a company-paid resort to learn "how to speak to superiors [and acquire] proper grooming and dress. The company considers this program essential for transforming young employees, fresh out of school, into dedicated Kaisha Senshi, or corporate warriors."[7] Once accomplished, socialization helps the new individual feel he or she is part of the organization.

Socialization is a three-stage process. The first stage, **prearrival,** consists of the values, attitudes, biases, and expectations the employee brings to the organization when first hired. These may have been learned in the family, at school, in other organizations, or as members of a profession or discipline. Most organizations, some more deliberately than others, attempt to select employees who are most likely to fit into the company's culture. Even if the firm succeeds in hiring "the right type," however, the employee still has to learn the culture.

As the employee moves into the organization, the individual reaches the **encounter stage.** At this point, the individual begins to compare expectations about the firm's culture with reality. To the extent that there are discrepancies between cultural expectations and reality, the employee is induced to bring his or her values and ways of doing things closer to those of the organization during the **metamorphosis stage.** Unfortunately, in their rush to fill positions, companies often do not pay enough attention to this stage.

Table 4.1 lists ways firms create a closer alignment between an employee's values and expectations and those of the firm. An organization can choose from among formal or informal, individual or collective, fixed or variable, serial or random, and investiture or divestiture socialization.

TABLE 4.1 Entry Socialization Options

Formal socialization occurs when an employee's newcomer status is made obvious, through separate training or orientation away from the job.	*Informal socialization* happens when the new employee receives little special attention and begins working right away.
Individual socialization occurs when the new employee is trained or receives orientation individually.	*Collective socialization* occurs when a group of new employees receive training or go through orientation together.
Fixed advancement socialization happens when new employees undergo the same time period for each stage of training and are expected to spend the same amount of time in the position before being considered for the next level.	*Variable advancement socialization* occurs when the next stage of training or career advancement within a company is flexible and based on the employee's development.
Serial socialization takes place in firms that assign new employees to other staff members for specific training and mentoring in different areas.	*Random socialization* occurs when new employees are not expected to resort to specific staff members but determine how to handle things themselves.
Divestiture socialization removes new employees' individual characteristics so that the employees will fit into their roles and the company as it exists.	*Investiture socialization* assumes the new employees' individual traits and characteristics are valuable to the employees' and the firm's success.

Sources: J. Van Maanen, "People Processing: Strategies of Organizational Socialization," *Organizational Dynamics,* summer 1978, pp. 19–36; E. H. Schein, "Organizational Culture," *American Psychologist,"* February 1990, p. 116.

Not all people are readily socialized. In extreme cases, an employee will feel disillusioned and decide that he or she is in the wrong place. Such an employee is likely to become disgruntled and/or leave the firm. Proper selection should reduce the probability of this happening.

Firms should also be wary of turning employees into conformists. A healthy organization tries to accommodate and take advantage of employee diversity, as discussed in Chapter 11, while maintaining cultural uniqueness.

Implementation of the Organization's Strategy

Organizational culture may contribute to firm performance by supporting implementation of the organization's strategy as well as desired changes in that strategy. In other words, if the firm's strategy and its culture reinforce each other, employees find it natural to be committed to the strategy. These shared values and norms make it easier for them to rally behind the chosen strategy.

LOC-In 3 Learning Objective Check-In

At SMECO, organizational culture performs several important roles. Matthew works at SMECO and appreciates the sense of continuity that the culture seems to provide. When he joined the company, his contract helped in defining his role at the firm, but he has learned much more from the way others interact in his department.

1. Providing a sense of continuity is one way that organizational cultures can _____.
    a. promote stability
    b. empower workers
    c. encourage self-management
    d. socialize workers

2. The most likely effect of the organizational culture defining Matthew's roles and expectations is _____.
    a. socializing workers
    b. creating cultural symbols
    c. self-management
    d. promoting stability

Beware the Dark Side

Very few things in management are absolute. While a company's culture can be a major advantage in the marketplace, there is also the potential for negative outcomes. For instance, a firmly entrenched set of cultural values and norms may cause employees to resist any change, even one that is vital for survival. Further, a strong culture may appear to some to be more like an exclusive club, causing valuable new employees or customers to feel like outsiders. Eventually these individuals may seek to work with other organizations. At the other end of the spectrum, there may be managers who neglect or fail to reinforce the key values present in a culture. This can lead to disregard for personal safety or little understanding and support for the firm's strategic efforts. Consequently, organizational leaders must continually assess the nature of an organization's culture, including what is valued and reinforced, or the problems associated with a culture that is too strong or too weak may emerge.

The Columbia Accident Investigation Board concluded that the 2003 loss of the shuttle Columbia and its crew was caused as much by a "broken safety culture" as by damage to the shuttle's wing during launch. The board's report warned that if culture did not change, mistakes would continue to occur.

■ Managing Cultural Processes

The culture of an organization evolves gradually over time. It is normally strongly influenced by the beliefs and philosophy of the organization's founder. A firm's founder transmits his or her beliefs to a small group of close associates, often family members who already share the same values or at least know each other well. As the firm grows, the founder's values determine who is hired and who is retained and promoted. Selection and socialization processes tend to reinforce the founder's values.

These values become firmly entrenched even after the founder is long gone. The Disney Company remains a close reflection of Walt Disney, even though he died four decades ago. Walt Disney strongly believed that every employee should present an ideal image to the public. This meant being impeccably groomed, cheerful, and friendly. Men were required to have no facial hair and to wear short hair.

Similarly, Jim Henson, creator of the Muppets, espoused beliefs that live on it his company. Henson "always wanted people to be creatively and emotionally invested in what they did.... He believed that projects worked best if they were a team effort.... He wanted people who were wildly and eccentrically different from himself at the company. He loved seeing what they could do and how they would surprise him."[8] "For many years, IBM was a reflection of J. Watson's personality. Southwest Airlines is made in Herb Kelleher's image. Mary Kay Cosmetics' culture reflects its founder's faith and beliefs. Microsoft's culture represents Bill Gates' intellectual, demanding, and perfectionist personality. Oprah Winfrey, the first African American and the third woman to own a TV and film production studio, runs an organization that reflects her high-energy, nurturing style."[9]

A variety of things maintain and reinforce culture over time. Some may be deliberately imposed by management, as in the case of cultural symbols, rituals and the choice of company heroes who best embody the firm's values. Others may be largely unconscious processes, such as the use of stories, language, and employee perceptions of the company's leadership style.

Cultural Symbols

People find it relatively easy to relate to or at least understand symbols or icons, such as flags, crosses, uniforms, or various logos (e.g., the three-pointed star on each Mercedes Benz car). **Cultural symbols** are the icons and objects that communicate organizational values. Management uses them to convey and sustain shared meaning among employees. For example,

- Tandem Computers' corporate headquarters in Cupertino, California, looks and feels more like a college campus than a business facility. Small buildings are separated by green space. Jogging trails, a basketball court, a large swimming pool, a dance hall, and other amenities are provided on site. These symbols reinforce a company culture characterized by openness, participation, informality, and equality.
- The president of Nashville's Centennial Medical Center dramatically conveyed an open-door policy by removing the door to his office and hanging it from the lobby ceiling.
- Best Buy, the electronics retail chain, allows employees at its Minneapolis headquarters the freedom to work from wherever they want as long as they accomplish the results they are responsible for on their job. Best Buy has a company culture that emphasizes work-life balance and its employees cherish having this opportunity to be able to work in the location of their choice.

Company Rituals and Ceremonies

Organizations plan activities and events that offer all employees an opportunity to share cultural meanings. One example of a dramatic ritual occurs when police departments conduct ceremonies to honor bravery, community dedication, or acts of heroism. Ceremonies convey organizational values and display examples of outstanding performance. Medtronic, a producer of high-tech implantable medical products, holds an annual service day during which the production facility is shut down.[10] The purpose of the ritual is to provide Medtronic employees with the opportunity to contribute time and effort to a charitable cause for one day. The ritual helps to make real to employees the community-based values that are part of the Medtronic culture. Another example of a company that uses an annual event to underscore their culture is Johnson Controls. The company holds an annual meeting, called Team Rally, in which employee teams present how they improved a work process.[11] The presentations use skits and teams include how the improvements are disseminated to the rest of the organization. From a cultural standpoint, the Team Rally is a vehicle for Johnson Controls to emphasize the values of teamwork, continuous improvement, and sharing knowledge throughout the organization. Mary Kay Cosmetics Company bestows awards to high-achieving sales consultants in an auditorium filled with sales agents and their families. Glamorously dressed, they cheer as their most successful peers receive gold and diamond pins, furs, and pink Cadillacs.

cultural symbols

The icons and objects that communicate organizational values, used by management to convey and sustain shared meaning among employees.

Company Heroes

Organizations effectively communicate values by identifying individuals whose deeds best reflect what the organization believes in, so that other people can emulate their behavior. Steve Jobs, the founder and CEO of Apple, is a company hero under whose leadership Apple brought to market highly successful new products such as the iPad, iPod, iTunes, iPhone, and the Macintosh computer.

Stories

Organizational culture is sustained by the narratives and legends that vividly capture the organization's values. At 3M, a commonly told story involves a worker who was fired for pursuing an idea that his boss asked him to drop. The former employee continued working on the idea without pay in an unused office. According to the legend, the product idea eventually became a big success, and the worker was rehired at the vice-president level. This story is used to communicate 3M's belief that perseverance is crucial to success.

Language

The language used by managerial employees may serve as a constant reminder of the organization's values. Language promotes both positive and negative values. For instance, the use of sexist language and ethnic jokes communicates to current and prospective workers that the company does not value diversity. Reliance on such euphemisms as "future enhancements" for "need to change a failing course of action," "reengineering efforts" instead of "layoffs," and "dehiring" for "termination" suggests the absence of an open, honest atmosphere in which issues can be discussed in a frank and candid fashion.

Firms often use slogans to succinctly express cultural values. For example, PepsiCo communicates the value of hiring the best people and teaching them to work together in its slogan, "We take eagles and teach them to fly in formation." Sequins International, a manufacturer of sequined fabrics and trimming, points out that "you don't have to please the boss; you have to please the customer."

Leadership

Employees infer a great deal about the organization from the leader styles they encounter. Effective leaders articulate a vision for the organization that employees find exciting and worth striving for. In addition, an effective leader provides a daily example of what the organization deems to be important. Employees make judgments about the underlying values of the organization not by what executives say, but by what they do. Many people attribute the survival of Chrysler in the early 1980s to its colorful CEO, Lee Iacocca. Iacocca negotiated a large loan from the federal government to save the company. He also served as an example by working for $1 a year plus Chrysler stock, which many analysts viewed as worthless. Within two years, Chrysler repaid the federal loan, and the value of its stock had skyrocketed. Iacocca showed Chrysler employees that perseverance, sacrifice, and commitment can overcome daunting challenges and can lead to personal success.

To reinforce an egalitarian and frugal image, Andrew Grove, CEO of Intel, the Silicon Valley manufacturer of computer chips, worked out of a cubicle similar in size to those of other engineers. Groves's cubicle was located on the main floor of the building for all to see. Grove insisted that all top managers fly coach class, rent subcompact cars, and avoid using company resources to bolster personal prestige. At Intel, offices were not to be elegantly furnished, and business meetings were not to take place at fancy restaurants.

Southwest Airlines has been profitable year after year, while most airlines struggle to survive and many have disappeared. Southwest's former CEO Herb Kelleher reinforced a culture of "be happy, enjoy your work, and make customers smile" through employee videos, "winning spirit" ceremonies, and speeches, and by serving as inspirational leader, kindly uncle, cheerleader, and clown.

Organizational Policies and Decision Making

Performance appraisals, budgets, new plans, and other policies and decisions clearly communicate company values, and therefore the company's culture. The criteria used for measuring success and the way they are used for control purposes tell employees what the organizational culture considers to be most important. For instance, some pharmaceutical firms measure innovation by the number of new patents, while others prefer to rely on the commercial value of existing or prospective patents. The former companies are signaling that they value many projects with small incremental changes to technology, risk aversion, a short-term orientation, and greater quantity. In the latter case, the signal is that focusing on fewer projects involving more radical technological changes and higher probability of large payoffs is preferred. This is more likely to lead to fewer patents, greater risk taking, a long-term orientation, and a search for one home run rather than four singles.

Employees learn what the company truly values by watching where scarce resources are spent. For instance, the word *innovation* may be used repeatedly in speeches, in company brochures, and on plaques positioned next to each elevator. But if research and development expenditures are the first thing to be cut during hard times, employees receive the opposite message.

Cultural values are also communicated by the ways people are rewarded. For instance, despite lip service to the value of effective teaching, many universities determine faculty salaries and promotions largely on research productivity. This sends a strong message to faculty that what the university values are publications, not student success stories.

LOC-In 4   Learning Objective Check-In

Mail One Corporation looks and feels like a college campus. There are jogging trails, open green spaces, small buildings, and recreation facilities. At Mail One, a common narrative told to new hires is about the founder's flying everyone at the firm to Dallas (from Idaho) at his own expense in order to give them a first-hand look at the shipping method the company was going to adopt. The trip proved more valuable to those employees than any on-site training in Idaho could have been. It reinforced the idea of personal sacrifice and the importance of sharing knowledge with employees.

1. The fact that the Mail One headquarters is more like a college campus than a traditional office building demonstrates the use of _____.
   a. leadership
   b. storytelling
   c. cultural symbols
   d. rituals and ceremonies

2. The narrative of the founder's flying everyone to Dallas for a first hand look at the new shipment method demonstrates _____.
   a. language
   b. storytelling
   c. rituals and ceremonies
   d. organizational policies

■ Characteristics and Types of Organizational Culture

The cultures of organizations can differ in a variety of ways. For example, cultural uniformity, the strength of a firm's culture, the degree of formalization, and the extent to which organizational culture differs from national culture vary from one firm to another and can determine the extent to which organizational culture influences employees. In addition to these various external characteristics, the nature or type of culture varies widely across organizations. There are numerous typologies of culture. It is useful to be familiar with the types in order to recognize the type of culture that is present. In this section some of the dimensions along which organizational cultures can differ as well as individual types of cultures are identified.

Cultural Uniformity versus Heterogeneity

Organizations vary in the extent to which a uniform culture permeates the entire organization. In some large corporations, different subcultures may be found in different parts of the firm. This is the case at Motorola, where the culture varies among divisions. Some divisions are conservative, bureaucratic, and risk-averse and value seniority, while others are entrepreneurial, freewheeling, innovative, and risk-seeking and place little value on seniority. At 3M, on the other hand, the dominant culture, which emphasizes innovation, a focus on related products, and tolerance for failure, is evident in all parts of the corporation.

Neither uniformity nor heterogeneity is right or wrong. When divisions are largely autonomous and each has a different strategy for its own unique products or services, it makes sense for each division to have a different culture. On the other hand, subcultures could be problematic for a firm where all units are interdependent and employees must work closely together to implement the overall corporate strategy.

Strong versus Weak Cultures

The more employees believe in the espoused values, the more they act in accordance with those values and the more the culture plays a boundary-defining role, creating a distinction between the organization and others. A strong culture pressures people to do what the organization wants with less reliance on formal control mechanisms such as close supervision, hierarchies, rules, and procedures. It may also increase the level of intrinsic motivation because employees work hard for the right thing. On the other hand, a strong culture may become a liability if it presents a barrier to adaptation in a rapidly changing environment, makes some groups of employees feel unwelcome, or makes it difficult for the firm to work cooperatively with other firms.

Culture versus Formalization

In varying degrees, organizational culture can substitute for such formal systems of control and decision making as organizational structures, rules, procedures, policies, and direct supervision. A common destiny and shared meanings make it less necessary to create mechanisms to ensure compliance, predictability, orderliness, and consistency. To the extent that organizational culture increases trust among employees, it reduces the need for written documentation and monitoring of organization members.

National versus Organizational Culture

The workplace behavior of individuals is a function of various levels of culture.[12] A national culture can guide behaviors, such as Americans tending to be more independent while citizens of other countries may more positively value collaboration. Of course, cultural influences can go beyond national levels and include regional influences and ethnic and religious identification. There are times when organizations use employee selection and socialization to develop cultures that mute these broad cultural influences and that might be significantly different from a specific regional or national culture. Some multinational firms, such as Colgate, deliberately attempt to create a "global company culture" to circumvent the barriers to communication and understanding present in many multinational operations.

In most countries, there is a great deal of diversity in the workforce, and most cultural traits overlap across countries. For instance, while the typical U.S. worker may be an individualistic risk seeker and the typical Japanese worker may be team and security oriented, numerous people in both countries are more like the typical person in the other country than the typical person in their own country. Thus, a firm is able to attract and retain the type of employee that fits into its culture regardless of where it is located.

Types

An increasing number of culture typologies are being used to identify various kinds of cultures. No one typology is better or more correct than the others. Regardless of which is utilized, classifying the type of culture in an organization can be useful for identifying the kind of employees and the management characteristics that are present in a culture. For example, knowing the type of culture indicates whether or not employees who are risk takers are hired. Further, the type of culture present has implications for how people should be managed. Some of the basic types of organizational culture along with implications for employees and management are described next.

One simple but powerful classification differentiates between two basic organization culture types: (1) traditional control or (2) employee involvement.[13] A traditional control culture emphasizes the chain of command and relies on top-down control and orders. Control systems are put

baseball team culture
The fast-paced, competitive, high-risk form of corporate culture typically found in organizations in rapidly changing environments, with short product life cycles, with high-risk decision making, and dependent on continuous innovation for survival.

club culture
A type of organizational culture that seeks people who are loyal, committed to one organization, and need to fit into a group, and rewards them with job security, promotion from within, and slow progress.

academy culture
A type of organization culture that seeks to hire people with specialties and technical mastery who will be confined to a set of jobs within a particular function and be rewarded by long-term association and a slow, steady climb up the organization ladder.

fortress culture
An organizational culture with the primary goal of surviving and reversing business problems, including economic decline and hostile competitors.

in place so that management can be assured that assigned projects and goals are being attained. In contrast, an employee involvement culture emphasizes participation and involvement. People work together to attain goals, not because they are externally coerced by rules and control systems, but because they are internally motivated.

A second approach identifies four types of cultures using terms with which you are familiar: teams, clubs, academies, and fortresses. Each type calls for a particular kind of employee. A quality match increases the odds that an employee will be successful. Having employees whose personalities match the organizational culture tends to enhance the overall performance of a firm by reducing disruptive internal friction and employee turnover.[14]

A **baseball team culture** is present in an organization facing a rapidly changing environment, with short product life cycles, high-risk decision making, and dependence on continuous innovation for survival. Organizations like this are typically in such fast-paced, competitive, high-risk industries as advertising, software development, movie production, and biotechnology. The employee who best fits this culture tends to be a risk-taker, enjoys being a "free agent," shows little commitment to one employer, and thrives on time pressure and stress.

The **club culture** seeks people who are loyal, committed to one organization, and need to fit into a group. Organization members prefer to spend their entire careers in one organization. The organization, in turn, rewards them with job security, promotes from within, and allows them to prove their competence at each level. Employees in firms with club cultures grant "bonus points" for age and experience. Club cultures are present in companies such as United Parcel Service, Delta Airlines, government agencies, and the military.

Like club cultures, an organization with **academy culture** prefers to hire individuals who are interested in a long-term association and a slow, steady climb up the organization ladder. Employees in academy cultures tend to be confined to a set of jobs within a particular function, so they should be people who enjoy becoming expert in one area. They should not expect broad individual development and intense networking with people from other areas. Specialization and technical mastery are the basis for rewards and advancement. Organizations that fit this mold include IBM, Coca-Cola, and Procter & Gamble.

Fortress cultures are obsessed with surviving and reversing sagging fortunes. These companies restructure and downsize to cope with the challenges of economic decline or a hostile competitive environment. Textile firms, savings and loans, large retailers, forest product companies, and natural gas exploration firms are found in this group. Fortress-type firms attract confident individuals who enjoy the excitement, challenge, and opportunities of a turnaround.

■ Managing Organizational Change

One of the more fixed aspects of a company is its culture. Employees tend to rely on the long-standing symbols, rituals, language, and values that provide a sense of continuity and stability. Unfortunately, the world surrounding the organization (and even the world inside the organization) is nowhere near as stable. In other words: Change happens! The second half of this chapter is devoted to the process of understanding and managing change. Only when managers effectively anticipate and execute change can the firm survive and succeed in the long term.

Types of Change

Change can be viewed as a planned event or as an unplanned and dynamic condition.[15] A planned change occurs when a change in an organization is anticipated and allows for advance preparation. In contrast, dynamic change refers to change that is ongoing or happens so quickly, such as with a crisis, that the impact on the organization cannot be anticipated and specific preparations cannot be made. For example, one organization may be in an industry in which government regulations will soon change. The change is known and can be anticipated and planned for. In contrast, a second organization may be in a field in which the market is volatile and fiercely competitive. Technological changes are the norm and difficult to anticipate. The change that this organization must contend with is dynamic and a continuous part of the organization's existence, rather than a discrete event, as with a planned change.

Whether facing a methodical shift required in a planned change or confronting a more dynamic change, many organizations have difficulty dealing with the need for change. General

Motors had a product mix for many years that was focused on selling light trucks and sports utility vehicles (SUVs), which were products that produced a large percentage of profits for the company. When the price of gasoline increased in 2008 due to increasing world demand for oil, General Motors found it had an over-supply of fuel guzzling trucks and SUVs that customers no longer wanted and not enough fuel-efficient smaller cars and hybrid cars that the customers craved in an environment of higher priced fuel. As a result General Motors experienced a financial crisis and bankruptcy in 2009 that required $30 billion in government assistance in order to survive.[16]

Forces for Change

Contrary to what many employees believe, companies simply do not make changes "just for the heck of it." Numerous internal and external forces can cause companies to make changes. In this section, an overview of the causes of change is provided.

ENVIRONMENTAL FORCES A great deal of pressure on a company can emerge from relationships with customers, suppliers, and employees. Environmental forces include these business relationships as well as changes in technology, market forces, political and regulatory agencies and laws, and social trends.

Both technology and market forces were pressuring Merrill Lynch, the financial brokerage firm, to make changes. The pressure resulted from the low-cost online trading that was pioneered by the discount broker Charles Schwab. Customers grew to prefer using the Internet to do their own research rather than paying brokers for advice about financial investments. Unfortunately, Merrill Lynch's commissioned brokers feared losing profitable commissions from clients. Consequently, the management team resisted offering online trading for several years, resulting in large losses of clients and market share to Charles Schwab. Finally, when it was evident that the market for financial services had permanently changed, Merrill Lynch management offered online trading service to customers for fees similar to those charged by Charles Schwab. Lynch was then able to curtail its loss of market share and maintain a client base.

Barnes & Noble, the large bookstore chain, faced a similar technological threat. The company was losing market share to Amazon.com, which offered books on the Internet rather than in brick-and-mortar stores. Barnes & Noble effectively responded by changing its market distribution policy to include a Web site to distribute books.

Political and regulatory forces for change include local, state, and national laws and court decisions that affect business relationships. For example, a change in the minimum wage translates into increased labor costs for firms paying the minimum wage. Low-wage employers, such as fast-food restaurants, may have to change both wage structures and use of labor to comply with the law.

Not all political forces that cause companies to change their work cultures are legally mandated. For example, after Supreme Court nominee Clarence Thomas was accused of sexual harassment, many companies added an explicit sexual harassment policy to employment policies to protect against allegations of harassment that could wind up in court. Similarly, as more women enter the workforce, companies have been changing rigid employment policies governing work schedules. More flexible work schedules enable employees who have dependent children at home to better juggle work and family responsibilities without neglecting either. The payoff is a more satisfied workforce with better morale, which translates into improved employee retention.

INTERNAL FORCES Internal forces for change arise from events within the company They may originate with top executives and managers and travel in a top-down direction or with front-line employees or labor unions and travel in a bottom-up direction.

In 1980, Jack Welch, CEO of General Electric (GE), decided to turn a mediocre collection of diverse and unrelated businesses into a world leader. He made each business-unit manager responsible for meeting high performance standards and reaching the ranking of first or second in market performance within the industry sector. Managers who failed to achieve this ambitious goal would lose their jobs, and their business units would be downsized or sold off. In the next

The Venezuelan government is offering cheap credit and debt reduction incentives to firms, like Alcasa, a state-owned aluminum plant in Venezuela, that adopt co-management policies allowing workers to make management decisions and even become owners. About 100 companies have so far accepted. David Rochkind/Polaris.

several years, 100,000 of 400,000 jobs were eliminated. GE had the highest market valuation in the world by the year 2000.[17]

Employees who demand amendment of policies that affect the way they are treated can also be internal forces for change. For example, physicians have recently begun forming labor unions. They want to protect the ability to practice medicine and treat patients as they see fit rather than as managed care organizations dictate. Doctors are counting on the new unions to provide them with bargaining power to regain decision-making authority in areas such as patient loads, prescription choices, and treatment options for their patients.

Resistance to Change

When change occurs, managers routinely encounter coalitions of employees or other managers who resist the proposed change. New work routines cause short-term anxiety as employees learn new ways of doing their jobs. Employees who thrived under one set of rules governing rewards have to adjust their efforts in order to meet a new set of performance expectations. Some of the reasons employees resist change include self-interest, lack of trust and understanding, uncertainty, different perspectives and goals, and cultures that value tradition.

Resistance to some changes is based on legitimate concerns. Consequently, these changes should be modified so that the concerns are dealt with.

Resistance to change can, in the extreme, involve acts of sabotage meant to undermine the change and to send a clear signal of firm resistance. For example, a large Massachusetts warehouse recently installed an automated conveyor system.[18] The project should have substantially improved company productivity. Instead, management encountered endless headaches and *reduced* productivity. Why? The workers feared that the change might cause them to lose their jobs. Various employees started jamming broomsticks into the conveyor system, an action that would shut the system down until a manager could track down the problem. If concern is great enough, resistance to a change can be fairly dramatic.

Some of the major reasons for resistance to change are described next. As illustrated in Figure 4.3, some of the major reasons for resistance to change include self-interest, lack of trust and understanding, uncertainty, different perspectives and goals, and cultures that value tradition. Understanding these causes can help you to manage resistance to change in others and even in yourself. We next turn to consideration of each of these reasons for resistance.

SELF-INTEREST Employees resist change when they fear losing something they value, such as economic benefits, status, or influence in the organization. Production employees may resist change in manufacturing technology because they fear having their jobs simplified and made more repetitive. A plant relocation from the city to the suburbs may mean that employees have a

FIGURE 4.3

Sources of Resistance to Change

longer commute. As mentioned earlier, commissioned financial brokers at Merrill Lynch resisted online trading services because they would lose lucrative commissions from clients who switched to online trading.

LACK OF TRUST AND UNDERSTANDING Employees may not trust the intentions behind a proposed change, or they may misunderstand its purpose. This type of resistance is most likely when previous changes were not well understood by employees or resulted in negative consequences. For example, some organizations launched Total Quality Management initiatives by telling employees that the objective of the quality initiative was to provide better service or product quality to the customer. The real goal was to use the quality gains to reduce the size of the workforce, but this was not disclosed to employees until later. Employees who embraced the initiative felt betrayed when the improved level of productivity was translated into layoffs. This deception has remained in the collective memory of the workforce, making it more difficult for management to obtain employee agreement to new changes.

A recent survey found that 77 percent of workers go in to work when they are ill. Often the result is actually lost productivity because, although they are present, employees are unable to accomplish very much. Organizational cultures that frown on calling in sick are largely to blame, according to one human resource consultant. Employees in such environments say they fear for their jobs if they take time off for illness, particularly if the boss always comes in when sick. How can companies successfully change this kind of culture?

UNCERTAINTY Uncertainty results from fear of the unknown and lack of information about the future. It can be particularly threatening when employees' fears are based on negative consequences of previous changes in the organization. Between 1991 and 1997, employees at Apple Computer experienced three major layoffs that reduced the size of the workforce by more than a third. Many amenities that made working at the company special, such as wine and cheese parties on Friday afternoons and free bagels and cream cheese in the mornings, were also discontinued. As a result, employees feared losing jobs when projects ended, and many people substantially slowed their progress in anticipation of being discharged. Key technical and marketing personnel left for greener pastures, preferring to be in charge of their own destinies rather than waiting for the ax to fall. The uncertainty of continuing layoffs at Apple, coupled with changes that reduced the pleasant working conditions at the company, made employees more likely to demonstrate their resistance to change by quitting rather than resolving to cope with the change and uncertainty.

DIFFERENT PERSPECTIVES AND GOALS A proposed change may be viewed through different lenses by employees with differing goals and perspectives. Even if a change is perceived as helping the organization, resistance may occur among employees who believe it will diminish the welfare of the unit to which they are attached. For example, the Saturn Division of General Motors in rural Tennessee represented a change from the way GM made automobiles in Detroit. Saturn was established to more closely follow the way the Japanese produced quality automobiles, and the improved manufacturing techniques perfected at Saturn were to be transferred to all other GM divisions to improve product quality and efficiency. Managers in the Chevrolet, Pontiac, and Oldsmobile divisions saw the Saturn Division as a rival that could threaten the flow of resources to their divisions. A coalition of division managers "ganged up" on the Saturn Division to ensure it would remain in the small-car niche, which began to shrink in the 1990s when customers switched their preferences to larger vehicles. Consequently, Saturn began to operate at a loss.

CULTURES THAT VALUE TRADITION Some organizational cultures are not supportive of change, valuing tradition and customary ways of doing things instead. Two organizations with strong cultures that resist change are the Catholic Church and the U.S. military. The Catholic Church continues to refuse to allow women to enter the priesthood despite the fact that there are not enough men entering seminaries to fill open positions. U.S. military leaders have resisted allowing openly gay and lesbian soldiers to serve in the military. Under the "don't ask, don't tell" policy, homosexual soldiers could serve only if they kept their orientation to themselves.

People are less likely to resist change if they do not see it as a threat to their interests. Management Is Everyone's Business 4.1 offers some suggestions for dealing with change by preparing for it at a personal level.

MANAGEMENT IS EVERYONE'S BUSINESS 4.1

WORKING AS AN INDIVIDUAL Change can be viewed as either a threat or an opportunity. It all depends how an individual chooses to perceive the change. People who are prepared for change feel less threatened by it when it occurs and are more likely to view it as an opportunity. Here are some useful ways employees can prepare for change at the workplace.

- *Make it a habit to update your résumé on a regular basis.* Having a résumé that is current with your most recent professional accomplishments, responsibilities, and skills facilitates marketing yourself and finding a new job if a change is not to your liking. Sharing your current résumé with people on a selective basis may present options that you might decide to act on in the future. Being in a situation where you always have alternative job options is empowering and avoids experiencing the feeling of being trapped in a job with nowhere to go.
- *Sustain your professional network of colleagues both inside and outside of the company where you are employed.* This requires devoting some attention to stay regularly in touch with friends or co-workers with whom you used to work or went to school, and who may have moved away for career or personal reasons. Take advantage of social networking tools to let colleagues know what you have been doing professionally. Go out of your way to share information with colleagues that might be helpful to their careers or interests. Investing in relationships and helping others achieve success will make it more likely that your colleagues will share some opportunities that will be helpful to you.
- *Keep your professional skills current so you are attractive not only to your current employer but to other employers.* To keep your professional skills current, it is important to take advantage of any training opportunities that are available in your company or other benefits that are available for furthering your professional education. Subscribe to industry trade magazines that report on the current trends within your industry. Take the initiative to improve your technical skills or management skills by assuming new job challenges, finding mentors, or learning new skills in your spare time that are relevant to your career goals. For example, it is possible to develop leadership skills by volunteering to coach Little League baseball or a youth soccer team.

■ Models of Organizational Change

Whatever the reason for change, an organization that effectively responds has a competitive advantage. The process begins when management recognizes and accepts the need for change. Once this is accomplished, other factors must be considered and possibly altered. There are two approaches that can help managers to effectively implement change and anticipate and deal with potential problems and resistance. These include Lewin's three-step model, and the force-field analysis model.

LOC-In 5 Learning Objective Check-In

Richard is one of the managers in charge of implementing change at his company. He often tries to overcome resistance by actually practicing the behaviors he has told his staff he will be expecting on a daily basis. One of his team members, Harry, has been resisting the changes Richard is trying to implement, claiming that the changes don't fit with the way the firm has always done things. Sarah, another team member, doesn't fully grasp the changes that are being implemented, and she is skeptical of the firm's and Richard's intentions in forcing change.

1. What source of resistance to change is affecting Harry?
   a. Uncertainty
   b. Lack of trust and understanding
   c. Different goals
   d. Cultures that value tradition

2. Why is Sarah resistant to the changes being implemented?
   a. Different goals
   b. Lack of trust and understanding
   c. Self-interest
   d. Cultures that value tradition

FIGURE 4.4

Lewin's Three-Step Model of Organizational Change

LEWIN'S THREE-STEP MODEL Kurt Lewin, a noted social psychologist, developed the **three-step model** of organizational change shown in Figure 4.4. The three steps are unfreezing, change (also called movement or transformation), and refreezing.

Unfreezing involves melting resistance to change by dealing with people's fears and anxieties so they can be more open to the change. People are given new information that makes them aware that the status quo is unacceptable and that some type of change is required.

The second step is the *change* itself, which is a departure from the status quo. Change can involve technology, people, products, services, or management policies and administration. It may be embodied in a new leader hired from outside the company to champion policies that were effective in another organization. Or, it may be represented by a new product that serves different customers and that requires new ways of selling and marketing.

The final step is *refreezing,* in which new management practices and employee behaviors become part of employees' routine activities. Coaching, training, and adopting appropriate reward systems facilitate the refreezing step.

For example, suppose management decides to change its corporate communication policy so that all company announcements are posted on a Web site instead of being distributed on paper. Step one would be to mobilize data to show employees that Internet communication is faster and more efficient than sending paper documents. Then the change would be made by setting up a Web site accessible to all employees (step two). In step three, employees who do not know how to read or post messages on the company Web site would receive training.

Lewin's three-step model of organizational change can be a useful framework when dealing with a planned event. As pointed out earlier in the discussion of types of change, not all change falls in the category of planned and discrete events. The three-step model would probably not be a useful framework when change is dynamic and ongoing. For example, some organizations, such as consulting firms, are organized around projects that constantly shift and confront workers with different challenges. This project framework can mean change that is ongoing and that doesn't provide much opportunity for unfreezing, change, and refreezing.

FORCE-FIELD ANALYSIS The **force-field analysis** model of change, also developed by Kurt Lewin, states that two sets of opposing forces are at equilibrium before a change takes place. The forces consist of *driving forces,* which are pushing for change, and *restraining forces,* which are opposed to change. When the two forces are evenly balanced, the organization is in a status quo state and does not change.[19] Figure 4.5 shows the restraining and driving forces when an organization is at status quo.

To implement change, the force-field model of change suggests that management can choose from one of three change strategies. Management can (1) *increase* the driving forces that

three-step model
A model of organizational change that features the three steps of unfreezing, change, and refreezing.

force-field analysis
A model of organizational change that states that two sets of opposing forces are at equilibrium before a change takes place and put at disequilibrium to make change come about: the driving forces, which are pushing for change, and the restraining forces, which are opposed to change.

FIGURE 4.5

Force Field Model of Change

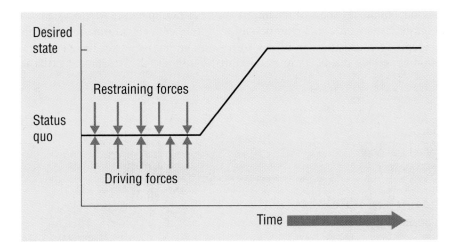

drive the change, relative to the restraining forces; (2) *reduce* the restraining forces that oppose the change, relative to the driving forces, or (3) do both.

Implementing Organizational Change

top-down change
Organizational change that is initiated by managers.

Practically every successful management activity requires someone to take charge. This is undoubtedly true when implementing change. In most cases, a change is led by the manager or executive who introduced it. Change that is initiated by executives is called **top-down change**. Top-down change can be implemented rapidly. It is often used to respond to a crisis. For example, when data were released in 2000 showing that the Bridgestone/Firestone tires used on Ford Explorers in the United States fell apart at freeway speeds, resulting in scores of fatal traffic accidents, Ford executives decided to absorb the cost of replacing the more than 6 million tires on vehicles that were still on the road. Some of the cost was to be reimbursed by Bridgestone/Firestone. Although they blamed Bridgestone/Firestone for supplying faulty tires, Ford executives acted proactively to manage the crisis. Unfortunately, later information indicated that Ford should have changed its dealings with the people to whom they sold Ford Explorers earlier; an investigation revealed that Ford executives were aware that design flaws in Bridgestone/Firestone tires had caused fatal accidents in Venezuela and Saudi Arabia, among other countries, prior to the publicity about accidents in the United States.

change agents
People who act as catalysts and assume responsibility for managing change.

People who act as catalysts and assume responsibility for managing change are called **change agents**. Change agents can be internal managers or outside consultants selected for their skill in dealing with resistance to change. Sometimes the change agents are the employees themselves.

bottom-up change
Organizational change that originates with employees.

A **bottom-up change** originates with employees. Bottom-up changes are put into effect more slowly than top-down changes. They generally begin with a series of meetings between employees and supervisors. Next, the change is discussed in meetings between supervisors and middle managers. Finally it is examined and approved or modified in meetings between managers and top executives. For example, an employee suggestion system may propose a change in a work practice that affects the whole company. After an employee-run suggestion committee approves the change, it is introduced to a policy committee composed of employees and managers for final approval and implementation.

Tactics for Introducing Change

When a major organizational change occurs, it is advisable to expect both skepticism and resistance. Advance preparation is often the key to successfully making a change. As presented in Figure 4.6, the choice of tactics for bringing about change in an organization include communication and education, employee involvement, negotiation, coercion, and top management support.

COMMUNICATION AND EDUCATION   One of the most effective ways to overcome resistance to change is to educate employees about why the change is needed. Information should flow in both directions. The individuals in charge should become aware of why people fear the change and provide information that eliminates some of the uncertainty. For example, Sun Microsystems, a California-based high-tech company, strives to be on the cutting edge of information systems technology by developing a steady stream of new software and hardware for its customers. Consequently, customer service managers must continually upgrade their technical skills in

FIGURE 4.6
Tactics for Introducing Change

Tactics
• Communication and education
• Employee involvement
• Negotiation
• Coercion
• Top management support

→ Successful change effort

order to understand clients' problems and educate them about the latest product and service technologies. The company provides excellent educational support, so Sun employees are less likely to resist the relentless change that accompanies being a cutting-edge technology company.

EMPLOYEE INVOLVEMENT Involving potential resisters in the design and implementation of change can often help diffuse resistance. Employees who are active in a change process become more committed to the change. A common approach is to organize employees into teams that focus on providing solutions to change issues. To deal with the need to improve service to customers, the GTE unit of Verizon, a large U.S. telecommunications company, organized its employees into quality-improvement teams that design and implement changes in work processes. Employees receive recognition and rewards for changes that are successfully implemented by the teams. In a recent year, 90 percent of GTE employees participated in at least one such team.[20]

NEGOTIATION Many times a manager is in a situation where bargaining is involved in implementing a change. Negotiation includes making concessions and giving resources or rewards to resisters in exchange for their cooperation. Individuals who have strong negative attitudes toward a change may be given the opportunity to take early retirement or to transfer elsewhere. In other cases, unions negotiate a labor contract to make trade-offs with management for their willingness to accept a proposed change. The negotiations could result in provisions that establish higher pay rates or more job security for union employees in exchange for their cooperation in plant closings, use of new technology, or mandatory overtime.

COERCION Confronting and forcing resisting employees to change is the use of coercion. Resisters may be threatened with loss of jobs or rewards if they continue to hinder the implementation of a change. Coercion may be necessary in a crisis, when speed is essential, or changes will not be popular. For example, any employee who resists efforts to improve diversity and cultural tolerance will probably face termination.

TOP MANAGEMENT SUPPORT The support of top management helps discourage resistance because it signals that the change is important. Change can require the collaboration of several organization units or departments, and some units may fare better than others, creating the potential for conflict over resources. In such cases, top management support can facilitate cooperation. For example, at Navistar International, a truck and heavy equipment manufacturer, top management supported the implementation of a new requisition process that affected maintenance, repair, and purchases of supplies and equipment. The goal was to reduce paperwork and increase the speed of purchasing of supplies while saving money by streamlining inventories. The change involved a redesigned requisition process, a computerized inventory control system, and a new procedure for analyzing vendor capability. An important reason for the success of the new requisition process was the support of top management.

Successfully introducing change is an important management skill. While resistance can be expected, successfully implementing change can be key to maintaining competitiveness or may even determine the survival of the organization. Management Is Everyone's Business 4.2 provides suggestions for successfully introducing change.

MANAGEMENT IS EVERYONE'S BUSINESS 4.2

WORKING AS A MANAGER An important responsibility of managers is to lead the process of change. Often this requires preparing employees for the changes that are about to occur so that they understand why the changes are necessary. Here are some ideas that should be helpful to managers when they lead change in their organizations.

- *Establish a sense of urgency for making a change.* A manager should become a strong advocate for change and point out that the status quo is no longer a viable option. This may involve sharing market and competitive business information with employees so they can understand the basis for the need for change. For example, CEO Lou Gerstner at IBM strongly advocated for change to employees by pointing out that the market for its core product, mainframe computers,

(Continued)

had collapsed and the company was seriously losing money and would go out of business if something was not done. He advocated to employees that IBM change the way it did business by marketing technical services and forming partnerships with competitors, something that it had avoided doing in the past.

- *Establish a compelling vision for change.* A manager needs to develop a compelling vision for change by crafting the change effort around core values that are shared by employees and other important stakeholders. The vision should be an all inclusive future state that energizes people and gets them excited about the change. The CEO at New Belgium Brewery proposed changing its source of electric power supply from traditional sources of energy at the company to sustainable wind power, which received overwhelming support and enthusiasm from the workforce that values protecting the environment.

- *Empower employees to act on the vision for change.* Once employees understand the need for change, find ways to eliminate obstacles to change that maintain the status quo. Systems or structures might need to be modified to align them with the change process. For example, jobs might need to be restructured, performance measures altered, and reward systems modified to be consistent with the change. At Cisco Systems the change toward having a culture of collaboration described at the start of this chapter resulted in managerial jobs being redesigned to have a strong emphasis on teamwork, with promotions and other rewards being based on how well a manager works with others as an important consideration.

CONCLUDING THOUGHTS

Some critical thinking questions about Cisco Systems were presented after the introductory vignette for this chapter. Now that you have read this chapter, you're ready to address the questions in more detail.

The first question asks: How does Cisco's collaborative culture enable it to better deal with changes brought about by acquisitions that add new people, technologies, and products to the company? A collaborative culture encourages employees in both the newly acquired and established units of Cisco to share knowledge and ideas for new products with each other. These collaborations should eventually bear fruit and result in new technologies that give Cisco's products improved features and capabilities that are attractive to customers. Without a collaborative culture, the newly acquired business units may have little impact on transferring technologies within Cisco because they assume they are competing with Cisco's core business units for resources. Cisco would not be obtaining the full value of the assets within the new businesses it acquired when internal competition is aroused.

The second question is: What role does the leader, CEO John Chambers, play at Cisco in sustaining the culture and driving change? The leader sets the tone by managing cultural processes. For example, CEO Chambers can establish new rituals and ceremonies at Cisco that reinforce a culture of collaboration. Cisco could start a new annual activity called the "Cisco Adventure Race" with teams of managers representing diverse business units that participate in an outdoor adventure activity that involves hiking and climbing in the wilderness of Alaska and that requires strong collaboration between the managers on each team in order to complete the adventure course. The outdoor adventure activity could strengthen the bonds of collaboration and positive attitudes between the managers who learned to depend on each other to survive the rigors of the outdoor adventure. In addition, as the leader of Cisco, CEO Chambers can lead by example and "walk the talk" by sharing credit for company successes with other managers and by telling stories about certain employees who become company heroes by being skillful role models for effective teamwork.

FOCUSING ON THE FUTURE: Using Management in Daily Life

Managing Organizational Culture and Change

Shelley Bird is the Chief Communications Officer at NCR. From 2003 through 2005, she and her staff faced a daunting task: handling communications for a major restructuring program while at the same time the company was cycling through two new CEOs and an interim CEO. How did they do it? In a recent article for *Strategic Communication Management*, Bird outlines the six key lessons they learned in the process.

1. *Communicate the vision.* Shelley found that when a new CEO starts working, everyone watches closely, not only to see what changes will be made, but to assure themselves that the new executive is not going to stray from the core values of the organization. For this reason, she recommends quickly

setting up meetings with influential groups so that the new CEO has an opportunity to make his position known. As she says, "If you can show that your new leader is creative and dynamic, yet embraces the company's core values, employees, customers, and other stakeholders will likely view any change objectively, rather than as an outright negative."

2. *Engage employees in the first 100 days.* Bird and her staff knew that it was imperative to communicate with employees frequently, especially in the early parts of a new CEO's tenure. Because any change of leadership is going to create concern and start rumors, Shelley publicized even small accomplishments and regularly communicated with employees "through a variety of channels— e-mail, frequent updates on our intranet, monthly breakfast meetings with small groups of employees, site visits and even broadcast voice messages." This empowered employees to act on the vision.

3. *Keep management in the loop.* In many organizations, the focus of communication is downward—the communication department is responsible for telling employees what managers want them to hear. But Shelley found that it was equally important to let managers know about problems, complaints and suggestions raised by employees. This enabled the managers to consolidate improvements and produce more change.

4. *Invite the community in.* Bird not only worked on communications within the company, but also outside the company. She worked hard to make sure community leaders were aware of planned changes, and that the effects those changes would make on the community were fully discussed. By doing so, she set up one branch of a powerful coalition of supporters of change.

5. In a similar fashion, Bird was also very *open with the press*—print, broadcast, and Internet. She knew that it was critically important to give the new CEOs time to delve into every aspect of the company they were managing, and that it wasn't possible for a brand-new CEO to have very specific plans from his or her first day on the job. So, to give the CEOs time to work, while at the same time giving the media something to work with, Shelley crafted messages "at the 30,000 foot-level." She also made sure that the media got the same stories employees got, to avoid surprises in both groups. Again, these actions helped to build a coalition for change.

6. Finally, Bird recommends *measuring results.* Once results are measured and reported, new approaches can be institutionalized in the organizational structure. She monitored company performance, a substitute for looking at such "small picture" issues as employee satisfaction, corporate focus, etc. She found that at NCR, employees produced stronger than expected third quarter earnings. She backed this information up with survey results which showed that "employees around the world are engaged and have accessed the channels they are most comfortable with through the CEO communications Web site."

Source: Shelley Bird, "Communicating through Changes in Leadership at NCR," *Strategic Communication Management, 10* (1) (December 2005/January 2006), pp. 30–34.

Summary of Learning Objectives

This chapter has addressed the topics of organizational culture and change. Organizational culture is a system of shared values, assumptions, beliefs, and norms that unite the members of an organization. Organizational culture reflects employee views about "the way things are done around here." Change is inevitable but can often meet resistance. Maintaining an effective culture yet implementing needed change is often a management balancing act in today's organizations. This chapter's discussion of its seven learning objectives to help you to effectively deal with culture and change issues as an individual worker, team member, and manager are summarized below.

1 Identify the three major aspects of organizational culture.

- **Visible culture**—things people can hear, see, or feel, such as formality or informality of employee dress.
- **Espoused values**—the expressed values of the organization.
- **Core values**—the fundamental values that drive what is important in an organization.

2 Describe the importance of organizational culture.

Organizational culture performs several important roles in organizations including:

- Encouraging employee self-management by defining roles and expectations.
- Promoting stability by providing a sense of continuity.
- Socializing workers by helping them fit in with the organization.
- Contributing to organizational performance by supporting the strategy of the organization.

3 Identify the processes through which organizational culture can be developed and sustained.

- Cultural symbols
- Rituals and ceremonies
- Stories
- Language
- Leadership
- Policies and decision making

All of the above can convey and sustain shared meaning and what is important in organizations.

4 Use classification systems to identify various types of organizational culture.

- *Control* versus *employee-involvement* culture.
- **Baseball team, club, academy,** or **fortress** cultures.

5 Identify the sources of resistance to change.

- Self-interest
- Lack of trust and understanding
- Uncertainty
- Different perspectives and goals
- Cultures that value tradition

6 Apply models to effectively manage change efforts

- Lewin's three-step model
- Force-field analysis

Discussion Questions

1. Think of a company you have worked at recently, either on a job or as an intern. What are the espoused values of this company? Did the managers or employees at this company behave consistently with those values? Give some examples if possible.

2. Pick one or more well-known companies that you are familiar with from media stories or firms that were discussed in some of your classes, such as Disney, General Motors, Microsoft, Apple Computer, Wal-Mart, Coca-Cola, or McDonald's. Give examples for each of the following approaches to sustain organizational culture for the company or companies that you have selected: *(a)* company rituals or ceremonies; *(b)* company heroes; *(c)* language; and *(d)* leadership. Does knowledge of these cultural activities reveal to you what it would be like to work at the company or companies you have selected? How might you use this information?

3. Compare and contrast strong and weak company cultures. What are the advantages of a strong company culture? What are the disadvantages of a strong company culture? In what circumstances is it preferable to have a weak culture?

4. Why do some people strongly resist change, a normal part of life in organizations?

5. What are the steps in Lewin's three-step model of organizational change? How can managers make use of this model? Are there situations in which the three-step model may not apply or be helpful? Describe.

6. Suppose you are a change agent and are planning to introduce a bottom-up change in an organization. Which

implementation tactics are likely to give you the most effective results, with less resistance and better commitment to change? Justify your choices. Answer the same question for a top-down change. Again, justify your choices.

7. Under what circumstances would a coercive tactic to manage change be the most effective? Give an example. Which circumstances are more likely to produce strong resistance to change when a coercive tactic to change is attempted? If you can, give an example.

Management Minicase 4.1
Domino's Delivers Change in Its Pizza Recipe

In a 2009 survey of consumer taste preferences among national pizza chains by research firm Brand Keys, Domino's was rated as last. In a follow up to this finding, company spokespersons humbly admitted that its product was "lacking" and the crust tasted like cardboard. While the company prided itself on providing fast home delivery service for its pizza, the negative reactions to the quality of the crust motivated CEO J. Patrick Doyle to change the pizza after its recipe had remained the same since the founding of the company 50 years ago.

Not only did CEO Doyle decide to substantially change the pizza but he took a calculated risk to advertise it this way and announced to the world that Domino's would change every part of its core pizza. The decision for change of this magnitude is a bold one because CEO Doyle had no backup plan if the taste of the new pizza did not catch on with Domino's customers. By refusing to consider going back to the old pizza formula, CEO Doyle indicated that the company would be committed to the changed pizza.

In its first quarterly earnings report since the change to the new pizza, Domino's reported profits more than doubled over those of the previous year, while an 8 percent growth in revenues was also reported. It remains to be seen whether the recent growth in pizza sales can be attributed to curious customers wanting to try Domino's new pizzas or whether the growth will be sustained in the long term.

DISCUSSION QUESTIONS

1. What are the sources of the forces for change at Domino's? What are some potential sources of resistance to change at Domino's?
2. Apply Lewin's three-step model of change (unfreezing, change, refreezing) to explain the process of change that occurred at Domino's.

Sources: Based on B. Watson, "Domino's Pizza Reborn? Risky Campaign, New Recipe Help Boost Sales," March 3, 2010. www.dailyfinance.com/story/ . . . / 19383979/; J.P. Doyle, "Hard Choices," *Bloomberg Businessweek*, May 3–9, 2010, p. 84; B. Horovitz, "Domino's Pizza Delivers Change in its Core Pizza Recipe," December 16, 2009. www.usatoday.com/. . ./2009-12-16-dominos1. . .

Management Minicase 4.2
How Jack Welch Changed Culture at General Electric

One way CEO Jack Welch reshaped and changed General Electric's (GE) culture was the Work Out program. Welch wanted to reach and motivate 300,000 employees and insisted that the people on the front lines, where change had to happen, should be empowered to create that change.

The Work Out began in large-scale offsite meetings. A combination of top leaders, outside consultants, and human resources specialists led them. Work Outs for each business unit followed the same basic pattern: hourly and salaried workers came together from many different parts of the organization in an informal three- to five-day meeting to discuss and solve problems. The events evolved to include suppliers and customers as well as employees. Work Out is no longer an event today but instead is the process by which work is done and problems are solved at GE.

The format for Work Out follows seven steps:

Choose a work process or problem for discussion.

Select an appropriate cross-functional team of 30 to 50 people, which may also include external stakeholders.

Assign a "champion" to follow through on recommendations.

Meet for several days and come up with recommendations to improve work processes and solve problems.

Meet with leaders, who are required to respond to recommendations on the spot.

Hold additional meetings as needed to implement the recommendations.

Start the process all over again with a new process or problem.

GE's Work Out process solves problems and improves productivity for the company, but the benefits go beyond these goals. Employees are able to openly and honestly interact with each other without regard to vertical or horizontal boundaries. Work Out is one of the foundations of what Welch called the "culture of boundarylessness" that is critical for continuous learning and improvement.

DISCUSSION QUESTIONS

1. Which types of change implementation tactics did Jack Welch apply to the Work Out program at General Electric? Do you think coercion would have been an effective tactic? Why or why not?
2. Describe what the "culture of boundarylessness" at General Electric might be like. What might company rituals and ceremonies look like? How do you envision a company hero behaving in this kind of a culture? What do you think are the key cultural values in this changed culture at GE?

Sources: Adapted from R. L. Daft, *Leadership*. Fort Worth: Dryden Press, 1999, pp. 444–445; J. Quinn, "What a Work-Out!" *Performance*, November 1994, pp. 58–63; www.ge.com/news/leadership.html, accessed July 25, 2001.

Individual/Collaborative Learning Case 4.1

A Culture of Empowerment Transforms Pike Place Fish Market

Work at a fish market is a dirty, smelly job where employees unload fish from the fishing boats onto trucks, unload the fish at the market, and then cut, slice, and gut the fish so they can be sold to customers in ready-to-purchase portions. When Pike Place Fish Market in Seattle was near bankruptcy, John Yokoyama, the owner, invited a consultant to help him save the business. The consultant, Jim Bergquist, recommended changing from a command-and-control culture to one of empowerment based on trust so that employees would be given more discretion to do their jobs without having a boss looking over their shoulders. The result was that Pike Place Fish Market became more successful and world famous for employees throwing fish from the truck to the market stalls, playing games with customers, and having fun at work. At the end of the day after the market is closed, all the employees frequently eat dinner together around a big table—family style.

What makes a local fish market world famous? At Pike Place Fish Market, the attitude of making a difference for every person the company interacts with is just one of the ways the organization has become famous. The company emphasizes trusting the workers and empowering them to make decisions on the company's behalf. Building this culture took the decision to commit to change and took lots of time working with the consultant before the employees accepted the idea that they could create their own futures. They use something called the power of personal responsibility—everyone has a choice and no one at Pike Place should be a victim of circumstance. This has led to employees who take responsibility for improving themselves, improving each other through coaching, and interacting well with the customers—or anyone. In hiring, Pike Place doesn't have "jobs available." Instead it has "positions open" if the potential employee makes the "team." The team concept is very important at Pike Place.

In order to have a dynamic company full of people who are energized about their work, it is important to open up their creativity. This is done by letting each employee express creativity in his or her own way. Each person at Pike Place has personal goals. The question is, "What is the next thing you want to master?" Everyone gives everyone else permission to coach each other. One person sees that he or she can possibly help another person based on personal experience. The key intention is empowerment—not making someone else see how they are wrong. The results are unlimited. The flip side of all this creativity and inspiration can lead to uncertainty, which can be uncomfortable. This risk taking, however, and willingness to deal with the sometimes uncomfortable aspects of change, has allowed Pike Place to improve drastically.

CRITICAL THINKING QUESTIONS

1. What are the benefits of the empowerment culture at Pike Place Fish Market?
2. When a new employee is being recruited to join a team at Pike Place, who should decide which employee to select for the position, the team or a manager? Explain the reasons for your choice.
3. What are some examples of company rituals and ceremonies that you noticed when you read the case about Pike Place Fish Market? What is the significance of each of these rituals and ceremonies?

COLLABORATIVE LEARNING EXERCISE

With a group of four of five students, discuss how the culture at Pike Place Fish Market affects the following functions of the business: employee-self management, stability, socialization, and strategy implementation. When you are finished, be prepared to share your explanations with the rest of the class.

Sources: Based on "Pike Place Fish Market Web site" (2010). www.pikeplace fish.com/philosophy.html; N. Lelyveld, "Pike Place Fishmongers Showing up as Examples of Fun at Work," *The Philadelphia Inquirer*, August 4, 2000. www.accessmylibarary.com/.../pike-place-fish...; J. Yokoyama and J. Michelli. *When Fish Fly: Lessons for Creating a Vital and Energized Workplace—From the World Famous Pike Place Fish Market*, New York: Hyperion, 2004.

Internet Exercise 4.1

Charles Schwab: Recommending Change as a Customer

www.schwab.com

Discount broker Charles Schwab provides online investing services and is an example of how the Internet has changed the way businesses provide services to their customers. Visit Charles Schwab's Web site and examines its features. Answer the following questions.

1. What features of Schwab's site do you like? Be specific.
2. Describe the advantages of making investments using the Web site of a company such as Schwab over the traditional method of working with a financial broker.
3. Describe the disadvantages of using the online investing services on the Schwab Web site. What improvements to its Web site would you recommend to Schwab for reducing them?

Manager's Checkup 4.1

How Comfortable Are You with Change?

Instructions

For each item, circle "T" if the statement is true or circle "F" if the statement is false. There are no right or wrong answers. Rather, the intent is to help you explore your attitudes about change.

Statement

T F   1. Among my friends, I am usually the first person to try out a new idea or method.

T F   2. When I take vacations, I prefer to return to a place I have been to already and know I will like.

T F   3. Compared to other people, I tend to change the way I look (hair, clothes) fairly often.

T F   4. I enjoy trying new foods, even if I am not sure about the ingredients.

T F   5. I would prefer to work for many different companies rather than just a few during the course of my career.

T F   6. I am happiest when I am working on problems that I am quite sure I can solve.

T F   7. At work I get annoyed by people who seem to always have suggestions for how to change the way things are done.

T F   8. I seldom follow rules that I think are silly or ineffective.

T F   9. I believe that taking needless risks is irresponsible.

T F   10. I would prefer a job that I can master and become a real expert at doing, rather than one where I am always doing something new.

T F   11. Most of my friends are pretty similar to me in their general interests and backgrounds.

T F   12. In five years, I am likely to be working at something that is so different I can't even imagine doing it today.

T F   13. If I am working on something new and run into a problem, I prefer to keep trying to solve the problem on my own rather than ask someone else for help.

Scoring

A. For the following items, circle those you answered "True." Then give yourself one point for each item you circled:

A	B
1	2
3	6
4	7
5	9
8	10
12	11
	13

B. For the following items, circle those you answered "False." Then give yourself one point for each item you circled:

Total points for Part A: _____   Total points for Part B: _____

C. Add your points for parts A and B to get your total score:

_____ + _____ = _____ (Total Points)

Interpretation

The higher your score, the more you enjoy change and the uncertainty associated with change. If you scored 10 or higher, you would enjoy working in an organization that offers highly innovative products or services. You are stimulated by change.

If you scored 4 through 9, you welcome incremental changes that do not disrupt your life. You would enjoy organizations that reward calculated risk taking and you prefer improving products rather than designing new ones.

If you scored 3 or less, you react to change as a burden and try to avoid changes that will cause you frustration. You would most enjoy working for organizations that provide clear performance measures and career guidelines.

Source: Adapted from D. Hellriegel, S. Jackson, and J. Slocum, *Management: A competency-based approach*, 10th ed., Mason, OH: Thompson, 2005, pp. 328–29. © 2005 South-Western, a part of Cengage Learning, Inc. Reproduced by permission. www.cengage.com/permissions.

Endnotes

1. J. C. Sarros, J. Gray, I. L. Demsten, and B. Cooper, "The Organizational Culture Profile Revisited and Revised: An Australian Perspective," *Australian Journal of Management* 30 (2005), 159–182.
2. L. Larson, "A New Attitude: Changing Organizational Culture," *Trustee* 55 (2002), 8–14.
3. J. P. Daly, R. W. Pouder, and B. Kabanoff, "The Effects of Initial Differences in Firms' Espoused Values on Their Post-merger Performance," *Journal of Applied Behavioral Science* 40 (2004), 323–343.
4. Ibid.
5. B. D. Gifford, R. F. Zammuto, E. A. Goodman, and K. Hill, "The Relationship between Hospital Unit Culture and Nurses' Quality of Work Life," *Journal of Healthcare Management* 47 (2002), 13–21.
6. R. L. Cardy, "HRM and the Virtual Workplace: Some Concluding Observations and Future Directions." In R. L. Heneman and D. B. Greenberger, eds., *Human Resource Management in Virtual Organizations* (Greenwich, CT: Information Age Publishing, 2002).
7. S. Robbins, *Organizational Behavior* (Englewood Cliffs, NJ: Prentice Hall, 2001), p. 693.
8. P. M. Wright and R. A. Noe, *Management of Organizations* (Burr Ridge, IL: Irwin, 1996), p. 185.
9. A. Nahavandi and A. R. Malekzadeh, *Organizational Behavior: The Person-Organization Fit* (Englewood Cliffs, NJ: Prentice Hall, 1999), p. 95.
10. R. Enderle, personal communication, November, 27, 2002.
11. D. Roznowski, "Johnson Control Employees Help to Reduce Cost, Waste, and Increase Safety Quality through Team Rally Event," *PR Newswire Association*, August 19, 1999.
12. E. Karachanns, J. R. Evaristo, and M. Srite, "Levels of Culture and Individual Behavior: An Integrated Perspective," *Journal of Global Information Management* 13 (2005), 1–20.
13. R. L. Heneman, M. M. Fisher, and K. E. Dixon, "Reward and Organizational Systems Alignment: An Expert System," *Compensation and Benefits Review* 33 (2001), 18–29.

14. C. Hymowitz, "Which Culture Fits You?" *The Wall Street Journal*, July 13, 1989, p. B1.
15. Cardy, "HRM."
16. C. Isadore. "GM bankruptcy: End of an Era," June 2, 2009. www.money.cnn.com/2009/06/01/news/companies/gm_bankrucptcy/index.htm.
17. P. Mornell, "Nothing Endures but Change," *Inc*, July 2000, pp. 131–132.
18. B. Trebilcock, "The Shadow Knows," *Logistics Management & Distribution Report* 41 (2002), 39.
19. K. Lewin, *Field Theory in Social Science: Selected Theoretical Papers* (New York: Harper & Brothers, 1951).
20. "Change Management: An Inside Job," *The Economist*, July 15, 2000, p. 61.

5

Learning Objectives

1 Identify the different elements of an effective plan.

2 Analyze the advantages and disadvantages of planning, and identify how planning pitfalls can be avoided.

3 Distinguish between formal and informal planning.

4 Recognize the features of well-designed objectives.

5 Identify the various types of action plans that managers can use to accomplish stated objectives.

Disney in Hong Kong: Bad Luck, or Bad Planning?

Although it is by far the smallest of the company's 11 theme parks at just 299 acres, the brand-new Hong Kong Disneyland was the object of lavish care in the months before it opened in September 2005. Disney wants to make a flawless entry into the potentially enormous Asian tourism market and has dreams of opening other Asian Disneylands, so the company invested a great deal of planning in making sure it avoided the mistakes of the past.

Disneyland Paris, for instance, opened several years ago under the burden of culturally insensitive rules that offended French vacationers and cost Disney years of profit from the park. Employees were told to speak English only, wine was prohibited, and ticket and merchandise prices were set too high. Attendance sagged until major changes were made.

So in creating Hong Kong Disneyland, the company's managers planned to make the park as accessible to Chinese tourists as possible. Auspicious dates were chosen for the groundbreaking and completion of each of its buildings. Lucky numbers figured prominently in the layout and architecture of the facilities (one of the hotels features a main ballroom of 888 square feet, 8 being a lucky number), and unlucky numbers, like 4, were omitted from the elevator panels.

Managing the Planning Process

Signs in the park and explanations of the rides appear in both Chinese and English. The Jungle Cruise boats have names like Lijiang Lady (Lijiang is a region of China famous for its beautiful rivers) and guides who speak Mandarin. Food and souvenirs are reasonably priced, and instead of cotton candy and hot dogs, hungry visitors can find drumsticks in soy sauce and black sesame ice cream. The park also participated in festivals and events offering a diverse assortment of unique traditional Chinese festivals such as events marking the birthdays of important deities like Tim Hau and Tam Kung, the fire dragon dances in the month of October, and the Chinese New Year celebration.

Few stones were left unturned in Disney's planning process. Even the main entrance to the park was carefully thought out. With the guidance of local masters of *feng shui* (the ancient Chinese practice of placement and arrangement of spate in pursuit of harmony with the environment), cash counters were set near corners or along walls to ensure prosperity. And Disney management shifted the entrance gate by 12 degrees to achieve the greatest possible harmony and success.

However, when success tried to come in the gate, harmony was in short supply, thanks to a last-minute slip-up in planning. Crowds of angry and dissappointed visitors were turned away from the park during the Chinese New Year holiday, because of a marketing promotion that mistakenly failed to prevent the use of discounted tickets during the week-long celebration. Thousands of people, far more than Disney anticipated, were drawn by the combination of cheap tickets and a long holiday break. They lined up in the early morning hours to wait for entry, and when Disney began to turn them away due to overcrowding, closing the gates and halting ticket sales, police and security guards had to be called in to control the situation. Disney issued refunds and apologies, but public feeling ran so high that even the government of Hong Kong asked the company to improve its admission policies.

According to a Chinese newspaper, since then the park has operated well below its daily capacity. Even so, by 2014 the park will grow by 23 percent with the addition of Toy Land and two areas for children that are unique to Hong Kong Disneyland.

Sources: Based on "Hong Kong Disneyland Expansion—2010–2014," http://www.youtube.com; http://www.discoverhongkong.com, "Festive Hong Kong 2010–2011," 2011; B. Denizer-Guillet and A. D. A. Tasci (2010) "An exploratory study of multicultural view on the Disney-McDonald's alliance," *Journal of Travel and Tourism Marketing*, 27(1), 82–95; A. Narpovich," (2010), "Theoretical approaches to film-motivated tourism," *Tourism and Hospitality planning and development*, 7(1), 7–20. Doris Ho, "Hong Kong Disneyland," *BusinessWeek Online*, www.businessweek.com, February 15, 2006; "Hong Kong's Tsang Hits Out at Disneyland Woes," *Forbes.com*, www.forbes.com, February 5, 2006;

Keith Brad-sher, "At Hong Kong Disneyland, the Year of the Dog Starts with a Growl," *New York Times*, February 4,2006, p. A5.

CRITICAL THINKING QUESTIONS

1. *What did Disney do right in planning its latest theme park? What did it do wrong? Could its mistakes have been prevented?*

2. *At how many different levels did the company plan Hong Kong Disneyland?*

3. *How far into the future of its Asian operations does Disney seem to be planning? How many years should a company's plan encompass? Three years? Five? Ten?*

4. *What are some of the advantages and disadvantages a company may face when establishing long-term plans?*

We will revisit these questions in our Concluding Thoughts at the end of the chapter after you have had an opportunity to read the materials in this chapter.

■ What Is Planning?

Does it make sense to plan in a world typified by rapid and dramatic change? The answer is a resounding "yes!" Planning programs identify what the organization wants to accomplish and how. **Planning** is a process that helps managers set objectives for the future and map out the activities and means that will make it possible to achieve those objectives.

There are both formal and informal planning processes. Most organizational leaders prefer to develop a formal written statement of future objectives and the approaches to reach them. The document can then be shared with those responsible for the execution of the plan, thereby reducing ambiguities and creating a common understanding. The written plan can be adjusted as necessary. As shown in Figure 5.1, there are four key elements to a plan: objectives, actions, resources, and implementation.

planning
The management function that assesses the management environment to set future objectives and map out the activities necessary to achieve those objectives.

FIGURE 5.1
Key Elements to a Plan

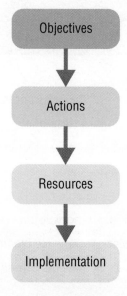

Objectives

Actions

Resources

Implementation

Objectives are goals or targets that the firm wishes to reach within a stated amount of time. One firm may wish to increase its return on investment from 8 to 14 percent in the next three years. Another may seek to increase market share from 5 to 10 percent over the course of five years. Setting objectives requires the firm to anticipate what is likely to happen in the future. A reasonable forecast allows a firm to set objectives that are both challenging and realistic. For instance, if a downturn is expected in the economy, ambitious profit objectives are less likely to be met. Likewise, if major players are entering the market, it will be more difficult to expand market share. A poor forecast may lead to objectives that are overly optimistic or that fall short of what the firm is capable of achieving.

Actions are the specific steps the firm intends to take to achieve the desired objectives. For instance, return on investment may be increased by downsizing, subcontracting some of the work, decreasing inventories, using technology to increase productivity, or developing new products. Company managers may also decide to increase advertising expenditures to expand its market share. Alternatively, it may be more efficient to undercut competitors by decreasing prices.

Planned actions cannot be carried out effectively without careful **resource allocation**. A quality plan states where resources will come from (for instance, borrowed versus internally generated funds) and how they will be deployed. The management team should be aware of the resource constraints the company faces so they can decide whether the company's goals can be realistically accomplished. As discussed later in this chapter, budgets are a way to allocate and control the resources committed to each step.

Finally, plans must be accompanied by **implementation guidelines** that show how the intended actions will be carried out. Implementation involves dividing tasks among the different actors, specifying reporting relationships, and establishing timelines.

For the sake of clarity, the four elements of planning are discussed individually in this chapter. In reality, they are closely intertwined. Objectives are not meaningful unless the firm can carry out the activities to achieve them and devote resources to support their implementation. An accurate assessment of the firm's resources provides an excellent starting point. Taking advantage of the firm's **core competencies** such as know-how, skills, brand recognition, and/or the company's reputation should clearly be considered in setting objectives and laying out action plans.

Planning occurs at every level within the organization. The plans made at higher levels direct and constrain the planning that takes place at lower levels. In general, planning at the top of the pyramid focuses on broad, long-term issues. For instance, a firm may decide to focus on a particular market segment, divesting itself of products or units that are unrelated to that market segment. Planning at lower levels tends to be primarily concerned with the operational details of the overall plan. Before going into details about the four elements of planning, it is important to keep in mind both the potential benefits and pitfalls of the planning process, to be discussed next.

objectives
The goals or targets that the firm wishes to accomplish within a stated amount of time.

actions
The specific steps the firm intends to take to achieve the desired objectives.

resource allocation
The planning step that determines where the resources will come from (for instance, borrowing versus internally generated funds) and how the resources will be deployed to achieve the agreed-on objectives.

implementation guidelines
The planning step that shows how the intended actions will be carried out.

core competencies
The unique skills and/or knowledge an organization possesses that give it an edge over competitors.

LOC-In 1 Learning Objective Check-In

1. Montclair Company wants to reemphasize planning throughout all levels of management. One way the company is doing this is by developing specific steps the firm intends to take to achieve its desired objectives. These _____ are a key element to planning.
   a. objectives
   b. actions
   c. resource allocations
   d. implementation guidelines

The Benefits of Planning

Several important benefits are associated with planning. To begin with, planning requires managers to assess the external forces that affect the company. This helps the company respond to challenges present in the environment. The goals that are established as part of the plan give company members a sense of direction and purpose in that environment. Further, when planning is properly conducted, it helps the management team to establish priorities, coordinate activities, develop standards, and clarify forces that will contribute to success. Effective planning processes result in increased participation by lower-level members. This, in turn, leads to improved managerial skills for all of the members of the company. Next, planning is the basis of control. A well-designed plan sets the standards that will be used to assess performance at every level in the organizational hierarchy, both in the short term and over time. And finally, planning may help a firm reduce future uncertainty by anticipating what may happen in the future, forcing managers to think long term. These advantages are described in greater detail below.

Assessment of External Forces

One of the key aspects of planning is examining various environmental factors. This helps the firm deal with environmental uncertainty and identify both opportunities and threats present in the environment. Then, the management team can mobilize resources to neutralize potential threats as well as take advantage of opportunities.

For example, video stores, such as Blockbuster, have been forced to adjust to the beta format, VHS format, the original DVD format, the Blu-ray format and now the threat from direct pay-per-view delivery systems. Each time, the company has responded, most recently by creating a cooperative agreement with Direct TV to provide pay-per-view movies. Even then the survival of "stand alone" movie rental stores may not be possible by 2020 as new technologies make them obsolete.

Developing a Sense of Direction and Purpose

A well-designed plan helps both managers and employees to understand what the organization is trying to achieve as well as the role that each plays in accomplishing those goals. Without a plan, managers and employees may not recognize how they share a common fate, even if they carry out the tasks they think are important. The lack of a clear sense of direction leads to multiple and often conflicting goals, and the ineffective use of resources.

Identifying the Factors that Affect the Organization

Properly conducted planning helps the organization focus on factors related to growth, renewal, and survival. Managers are able to reflect on issues that may not be obvious in the midst of day-to-day work pressures. For example, Pfizer is a leader in the development of new drugs, with some 60 drugs, for conditions ranging from diabetes to anxiety, in early stages of development. In its planning process Pfizer realized that it could take advantage of the opportunity to partner with the industry's smaller players to help them realize the potential of their own new medications. Consequently, Pfizer co-launched Lipitor, a cholesterol-lowering pill, in conjunction with Warner-Lambert. Pfizer's potent sales force, ranked no. 1 in physician surveys, helped the drug's sales smash an industry record.[1]

Encouraging Participation

When workers participate in managerial activities, they tend to "buy in" and work much harder to see an effort succeed. They also experience stronger feelings of commitment to the organization. The planning process is an excellent place to encourage managers and employees to share inputs about the goals of the organization, and to find the best ways to achieve those goals. Participation is likely to strengthen the efforts dedicated to attaining those goals and increase goodwill toward their immediate supervisors and the overall company.

Coordination of Efforts

Managers who operate independently may not be aware of what other managers are doing. The planning process may help them coordinate efforts more effectively. New technologies are constantly being introduced that facilitate the sharing of valuable expertise from one part of the organization to another or across organizational and international boundaries. (See Management Close-Up 5.2 "Technology Is Fostering Bottom-Up, Top Down, and Horizontal Planning from the Inside and the Outside" on page 142.)

In companies in which operations are decentralized, each unit may use different performance criteria and resource allocation priorities. This became a major problem at Motorola in the past, leading to a significant decline in overall firm performance. A centralized planning process can help managers understand how actions or decisions in one area have consequences for other units as well as for the entire firm.

Establishment of Priorities

Planning can help a firm prioritize its major problems or issues. Lack of priorities can dilute the organization's efforts or make it susceptible to managers who take advantage of the confusion to impose their own agendas. Also, the failure to define priorities causes the firm to drift and prevents it from developing a clear strategic focus. This was a primary reason why Pepsi lost the "war" against Coke in the not too distant past. Coke focused its energies on its core product, while Pepsi's efforts were dispersed across a variety of unrelated products such as restaurants, hotels, and retail outlets.

Focusing Attention on Different Time Horizons

Many business programs may take years to complete. Steps can be taken to achieve long-term objectives by balancing them with short-term goals. For instance, General Electric successfully competed against Rolls-Royce, Pratt & Whitney, and Snecma (a French government-owned engine shop) for a 3 billion contract offered by the Chinese government for plane engines to build a fleet of 500 regional jets for the Beijing Olympics. General Electric won in large measure because it began to plan for the design and production of regional jet engines almost 10 years earlier. GE has been chosen as a "Worldwide Olympic Sponsor" for several future Olympic games across various cities around the world, which is likely to drum up additional business in the long haul.[2]

Understanding Circumstances Contributing to Past Success or Failure

It is vital for managers to learn from past successes and failures. Planning can bring the reasons for poor and good performance into sharper view, enabling the firm to draw on experience. For example, in 1997 Kodak lost $100 million when it introduced an advanced-photo-system camera and film, only to find that it did not have enough stock on hand to meet the demand. The company could not process the new film at enough locations. It finally responded by spending another $100 million on the system in a more focused approach. The management team also learned that most customers preferred less expensive models. As a result, Kodak introduced a new camera for under $50 that was a hybrid between digital and analog cameras. The new camera was soon responsible for 20 percent of Kodak's camera sales.[3] Kodak ran into serious trouble again later in the decade after facing a 49 percent decline in photo-finishing revenue and a 28 percent drop in traditional and single-use camera sales.[4] This time Kodak is betting on digital technology, hoping that digital profits will grow faster than the drop in film profits. A key reason for the confidence, according to Kodak's CEO, is that "consumers are increasingly turning to retailers to make prints of their digital images, which is far more profitable than selling low-margin digital cameras."[5]

Ensuring the Availability of Adequate Resources

A well-designed plan leads to identifying the resources needed for the future., These resources may come from several sources. For example, the biotechnology firm Genentech reallocated 25 percent of its research staff to developing multiple products to achieve its new business objectives back in the early 2000s. Now Genentech is considered one of the top, if not the top, biotechnology innovator across a wide range of areas, including antibody engineering, bioinformatics, immunology, medicinal chemistry, molecular biology, pathology, biomedical imaging, and protein engineering.[6]

Establishing Performance Standards

The end result of any planning process is a series of statements regarding objectives to be met along with expected activities. These criteria define expected behaviors for organizational members and allow for the assessment of progress. As time passes, the relative contributions of individuals and groups can be assessed and rewarded.

Kodak's decision to revamp its original advanced film imaging camera, although costly, resulted in a much more profitable product.

A few years ago, General Electric (GE) established a tough quality standard called six sigma. Six sigma is equivalent to generating fewer than 3.4 defects per million manufacturing or service operations. To attain this goal, GE trained tens of thousands of employees in quality techniques. A reward system to support this quality initiative was also established. GE managers and employees who meet objectives may receive as much as a 25 percent increase in their annual base salaries without a promotion; cash bonuses can increase as much as 150 percent in a year to between 20 percent and 70 percent of base pay; and generous stock options are provided to 27,000 employees. As we enter the latter part of the 2010s, GE strongly believes that rewarding employees for achieving measurable quality objectives is fundamental to the continued success of its quality assurance plans.[7]

Supporting Organizational Control Systems

Organizations cannot be successful unless control systems are in place to ensure that objectives are being attained and that resources are being used appropriately. A *control* is "any process that helps align the actions of individuals with the interests of their employing firms."[8] A *control system* is "the knowledge that someone who knows and cares is paying attention to what we do and can tell us when deviations are occurring."[9]

Effective planning improves a company's control system by making it possible to compare target versus actual results. When a gap is detected between company goals and observed results, corrective actions are taken to modify activities for the future. In a few extreme cases, the existing plan may be completely abandoned. When company executives fail to abandon a plan after large resources have been spent on it even though all available evidence suggests that the plan is not working, the problem is called *escalation of commitment.* Some people believe, for instance, that the space shuttle disasters may be attributed to escalation of commitment to a space program that was doomed to failure from the beginning (see the Individual/Collaborative Learning Case at the end of this chapter titled "Why Did NASA Stick with the Space Shuttle So Long?").

Developing "What If" Scenarios

Long ago, Ben Franklin suggested that "the only sure things in life are death and taxes." Organizations, like individuals, face a great deal of uncertainty. Planning can help managers deal with uncertainty by anticipating what may happen in the future. No firm has a crystal ball to accurately forecast the future. Planning can help identify different future scenarios and spell out what to do in each scenario. This is known as *contingency or scenario planning.* Ben Franklin recognized that uncertainty is inevitable but is still manageable. Another of his famous proverbs states that "chance favors the prepared mind." Management Close-Up 5.1 offers some suggestions that companies should keep in mind to plan for unforeseeable circumstances such as 9/11, the Arab oil embargo, the outcomes of drug research and hurricane Katrina. Skills for Managing 5.1 is designed to help you develop a contingency plan.

Management Development

Individual managers should play a major role in focusing the organization on the future. Planning helps managers to be proactive and forward-thinking rather than being reactive and just letting things happen. By considering future possibilities and developing a long-term vision, managers can become more committed to the firm and learn to convert abstract ideas or objectives into concrete actions. Including managers from every level of the organization in company planning processes is an effective form of "on the job" training. These planning experiences "season" managers, so they are able to move into more responsible roles in the future.

Planning for What If

There are five lessons that every company could apply to plan for the worst, particularly in a volatile and fast-changing world.

1. *Be prepared for the unimaginable.* Few business people had envisioned the near collapse of the global financial system and the ensuing economic trauma during 2008–2011. The airline industry was taken completely by surprise in 2010 when a volcano in Iceland brought air travel to a halt in most of Europe for a week, costing the industry over 1.8 billion dollars. Another classical example of the unimaginable is 9/11, whereby a combination of large passenger planes with their tanks full of jetfuel brought down the World Trade Center. At the company level, who would have thought that Toyota's reputation for high quality would be smashed within a few weeks in 2010 as widespread news reports of brake problems and uncontrollable acceleration hit the mass media (eventhough many of these allegations were later found to be exaggerated; see introductory vignette in Chapter 1)? And then we have the recent case of British Petroleum, which had not conceived of the notion that an offshore rig could explode and create an environmental catastrophe. In their exploration plan "it was virtually impossible for an accident to occur that would lead to a giant crude oil spill and serious damage to beaches, fish and mammals." But this is exactly what happened when an explosion in 2010 killed 11 workers and billions of gallons of oil leaked from the well 5,000 feet below the surface into the Gulf of Mexico.

2. *Create alternative scenarios.* Being aware of different scenarios will help develop alternative responses "just in case." For example, Southwest Airlines has generally been successful in anticipating changes in fuel prices and has been able to forge favorable long-term contracts with fuel suppliers.

3. *Try to estimate probabilities.* Assigning probabilities to different events or scenarios will help you consider potential responses, particularly if these might involve major risk. Unfortunately, there is a human tendency to ignore the probabilities. Nassim Nicolas Taleb, in his book *Fooled by Randomness*, cites an example. Ask a sample of travelers at an airport how much they'd pay for an insurance policy that would give their beneficiary $1 million if they die from any cause on their trip. Then ask another sample how much they'd pay for a policy that would pay $1 million if they're killed by terrorists on their trip. People will pay more for the second policy, though that clearly makes no sense. We just do not think rationally about probabilities, a tendency every manager must fight.

4. *Use internal markets.* Using internal market is a forecasting technique in which employees bet small amounts of money furnished by the company to predict the likelihood of specific events. Hewlett-Packard has used internal markets to forecast sales more accurately than the marketing manager could; Eli Lilly has used them to predict the success of drug research with uncanny accuracy. Well-designed predictive markets can give managers new insight into specific risks and how they might affect the company.

Planning for the worst-case scenario is always easier in retrospect, but it is a process managers must train themselves to use. Understanding the effect of an airplane hitting the World Trade Center towers would have been a result of such planning. Another difficult planning task is accepting that the worst has happened and acting quickly in response, a flaw in many agencies' response to the flooding of New Orleans in the wake of Hurricane Katrina.

(Continued)

5. *Create a culture that insists on facing reality.* Prepare employees to respond quickly and effectively to the bolt from the blue, and the no. 1 impediment—incredible yet obvious—is failing to accept that the trouble has indeed happened. Even in New Orleans, immediately after Hurricane Katrina, TV showed images of people dancing in Bourbon Street; they thought everything would be okay.

Source: Based on P. B. Marren (2010), "Scenario planning for economic recovery," *Strategy & Leadership*, 38 (1), 15–26; J. Singer and J. Piluso (2010), "Five tools to prepare for future discontinuities," *Strategy & Leadership*, 38 (1) 27–39; S. Malakis, T. Kontogiannis, and B. Kirwan (2010), "Managing emergencies and abnormal situations in air traffic control," *Applied Ergonomics*, 41 (4); 620–27; J. Brinckmann, D. Grichnik, and D. Kapsa (2010), "Should entrepreneurs plan or just storm the castle? A meta analysis on contextual factors impacting the business planning—performance relationship in small firms," *Journal of Business Venturing*, 25 (1), 22–40; C. Burdeau and A. Mohr, "BP didn't plan for accident, data says," *The Eagle*, May 1, 2010, p. 1; G. Colvin,. "An Executive Risk Handbook," *Fortune*, October 3, 2005, pp.69–70.

SKILLS FOR MANAGING

Design Your Own Contingency Plan

You are part of a five-member group of students planning to study in France two years from now. The five of you are planning to travel together and to save on housing costs by renting a three-bedroom apartment. Your plans call for a six-month stay. Let's assume that the current exchange rate is 0.85 euro per dollar, so it will cost each of you approximately 10,000 euros (or $8,500). You plan to save this amount of money by working in the evenings and during summers, although it will require a great deal of sacrifice (skipping movies, eating at home, not buying new clothes, and so on). At a typical student wage rate of $6.00 per hour, this will require 2,125 hours of work (at $4 per hour after taxes and transportation costs) exclusively devoted to save the $8,500. Of course, you will need money in the meantime to cover your daily expenses in addition to the money you are saving for the trip.

Engage in a contingency planning exercise under the following assumptions:

1. Two years from now the euro will be .95 on the dollar, meaning the cost will be $9,500.
2. Two years from now the euro will be 1.05 on the dollar, so the cost will be $10,000.
3. Two years from now the euro will be 1.15 on the dollar, making the cost $11,500.
4. Two years from now, the euro will be 1.25 on the dollar, or a total cost of $12,500.

The team (appointed by instructor) will develop a contingency plan to deal with each of the possible scenarios above. Keep in mind that this is a problem similar to what firms face in international markets when they engage in contingency planning for the future based on the strength of the dollar (see Chapter 2, Managing in a Global Environment). Note: During the period 2002–2012, the exchange rate has oscillated between 0.80 euro per dollar and 1.46 euro per dollar.

■ The Pitfalls of Planning

Company leaders will not realize the benefits of planning if the planning process itself is flawed. Future conditions can be forecasted incorrectly, reporting relationships can become overly hierarchical, planning can become a self-contained activity, bureaucratization can become oppressive, and objectives and processes that are no longer optimal for the firm may be used. Each of these problems is described in greater detail in this section.

Poor Forecasts of Future Conditions

As you have seen, the business environment is changing faster than ever. Even the most sophisticated planning techniques may not predict accurately what is likely to happen in the future. The longer the time frame, the more likely that unforeseen circumstances will occur. This is one reason many firms became skeptical of the value of strategic planning in the 1980s. Major corporations such as the Adolph Coors Company, Campbell Soup, Exxon, General Motors, Oak Industries, Shaklee, Toro, and Wang Laboratories, among others, reported poor strategic decisions driven by inaccurate forecasts. Common problems included poor estimates of the demand for new products, miscalculation of

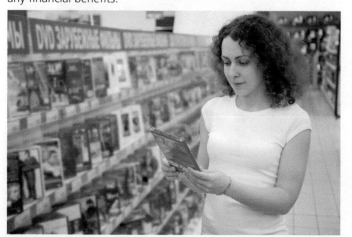

Poor forecasts can result in poor results, as Blockbuster discovered when it did away with late fees but failed to reap any financial benefits.

the effect of international competition on main product lines, the inability to predict technological innovations, and changes in the economic and legal systems.[10] More recently,

- Blockbuster introduced a "never a late fee" program in the mid-2000s thinking it would attract new customers, but additional revenues and profits never materialized. Most observers believe that Blockbuster has lost money in this deal.
- General Motors provided generous discounts to car buyers during the past decode, including a special "employee price" available to any customer, thinking it would take away market share from its rivals. This plan resulted in multibillion dollar losses for the car manufacturer without a corresponding increase in market share.
- Amway invested heavily in China between 1992 and 1998. In 1998, Beijing suddenly banned direct marketing, shutting down the $178 million-a-year China business of Amway Asia Pacific.
- Many construction firms went bust during 2008–2012 as housing prices collapsed, and the over supply of existing houses could not be absorbed by the market for years to come.

Plans Imposed from Above

The traditional approach to planning is from the top down, with the CEO and senior executives, and perhaps a planning department, establishing organizational objectives and laying out general business strategies. Managers at lower organizational levels then devise implementation methods and operational plans to support the objectives and strategies set at the top. Separating the plan generators from the plan implementers often leads to the development of plans that lower level managers begrudgingly try to put into practice. Such plans often do not benefit from the wisdom and experience of those at lower levels within the firm. Many "reengineering" plans have failed in part because they were imposed on the rest of the firm by the top of the hierarchy.

Planning as a Self-Contained Activity

There is a danger that the people engaged in planning will become so enamored of the process that they become a close-knit group divorced from the rest of the organization. Managers and employees may be cynical about objectives and suggestions for action emanating from specialized planning departments or units. Reflecting on this, one well-known consultant noted that "planning staff groups may gain much power and authority in organizations ... [where they are] thrust into the role of proponent and doer of plans—too often, the real doers are pushed aside."[11]

Extensive Bureaucratization

When planning is conducted by specialists without the participation of other managers, there may be a tendency to generate volumes of paperwork accompanied by fancy oral presentations. In other instances, planning becomes overly quantitative and formula driven. As a result, the logic behind the recommendations may be difficult to understand and may lack common sense. In addition, the predictions of elegant mathematical models succeed or fail on the data and assumptions employed. Formulas that work relatively well in stable conditions may totally miss the mark in turbulent times.

Inflexible Adherence to Objectives and Processes

A firm may become overly committed to an outdated plan, ignoring clues that it is time to change direction. People tend to justify "sunk costs" by continuing to defend objectives in spite of disappointing results. For instance, for years Apple was obstinate in producing its Macintosh computers for loyal users in spite of continuing drops in sales that occurred largely because its software was incompatible with IBM, the market leader.

In another case, Detroit's Big Three automobile firms in the early 2000s continued their investment in SUVs, which fueled much of their earning growth during the 1990s, even though the market had become saturated over the preceding years. To spur sales the auto firms had to offer incentives; after five years of steadily increasing SUV incentive packages profit margins had disappeared in 2006. The sudden jump in oil prices following hurricane Katrina in 2005 only made matters worse, even though prices began to recede later on. Nevertheless, the auto firms have continued pouring more resources into a dwindling market, ignoring the data showing that previously established objectives were no longer viable.[12] In the case of General Motors, the response to this crisis was to declare bankruptcy in 2009 and ask for government financial support. It remains unclear at this point if the company can break away from a business plan that has failed in the past.

LOC-In 2 Learning Objective Check-In

DB&H contractors have firsthand experience with many planning pitfalls. For instance, within their company, planning is conducted specialists without the participation of managers from the field. This tends to generate volumes of paperwork and fancy presentations, but can lack accurate recommendations. The planners are also a close-knit group who do not tend to associate with the rest of the organization's managers. This causes managers and employees elsewhere in the firm to look at "planning" with a cynical attitude and then dismiss the objectives. The senior executives at DB&H are always establishing organizational objectives and laying out general strategies, but the plan implementers are left to try to put those plans into practice without having had any input. The implementers' years of experience are repeatedly disregarded, and so many of the plans from the senior executives fail time and again for this reason.

1. The lack of accurate recommendations at DB&H illustrates _____.
   a. plans imposed from above
   b. planning as a self-contained activity
   c. extensive bureaucratization
   d. inflexible adherence to objectives and processes

2. The cynical attitude some employees and managers have toward planning stems from _____.
   a. planning as a self-contained activity
   b. extensive bureaucratization
   c. plans imposed from above
   d. inflexible adherence to objectives and processes

3. Plans from the senior executives fail because they reflect _____.
   a. poor forecasts of future conditions
   b. extensive bureaucratization
   c. planning as a self-contained activity
   d. plans imposed from above

MANAGEMENT CLOSE-UP 5.2

Technology Is Fostering Bottom-Up, Top Down, and Horizontal Planning from the Inside and the Outside

Corporate planners can now use technology so that different teams can work on the same problem, each proposing different solutions, even if they are in different parts of the world. Says Alpheus Bingham, vice president for Eli Lilly's e.lilly research unit. "If I can tap into a million minds simultaneously, I may run into one that is uniquely prepared." One example of this technology is called "GoToMeeting," which allows individuals to demonstrate, present, and collaborate right from their PC or Mac®.

How "GoToMeeting Works

1. **Create an Account** *Register online by creating a username and password for your account. Once registered, you'll be able to host an unlimited number of online meetings with anyone. Your meeting attendees don't have to be registered GoToMeeting users and can attend your meetings for free.*
2. **Set Up GoToMeeting on Your Computer** *The automatic setup takes seconds, and no configuration is required. GoToMeeting will download to your PC or Mac® and enable*

you to host and join online meetings with a few clicks. You'll have the option of scheduling meetings through the GoToMeeting Web site, via Microsoft® Outlook® and through instant-messaging applications.

3. **Organize a Meeting** *Even novices can begin organizing on-the-fly or scheduled meetings with absolutely no training. You can start a meeting immediately or schedule it for later. Begin presenting and sharing applications or documents with your business contacts across the country or with your colleagues down the hall.*

Source: http://www.GoToMeeting.com, 2011.

Proctor & Gamble's $1.7 billion-a-year R&D operation, for instance, is taking advantage of collective online brain trusts such as Lilly Company's InnoCentive Inc. in Andover, Masschusetts. It's a network of 80,000 independent, self-selected "solvers" in 173 countries who virtual-team-tackle research problems for the likes of Boeing Co., DuPont, and 30 other large companies. One solver, Drew Buschhorn, is a 21-year-old chemistry grad student at the University of Indiana at Bloomington. He came up with an art-restoration chemical for an unnamed company—a compound he identified while helping his mother dye cloth when he was a kid. Says InnoCentive CEO Darren J. Carroll, "We're trying for the democratization of science." Likewise, groups online are starting to turn marketing from megaphone to conversation. LEGO Group, for instance, brought adult LEGO train-set enthusiasts to its New York office to check out new designs. "We pooh-poohed them all," says Steve Barile, an Intel Corp. engineer and LEGO fan in Portland, Oregon, who attended. As a result, says Jake McKee,

LEGO's global community-development manager. "We literally produced what they told us to produce." The new locomotive, the "Santa Fe Super Chief" set, was shown to 250 enthusiasts, and their "word-of-mouse" helped the first 10,000 units sell out in less than two weeks with no other marketing.

Sources: Based on: http://www.gotomeeting.com, "Do More, Travel less, Enjoy the freedom of online meetings," accessed April, 2010; http://www.webex.com, "Cisco webex: Extend your reach with web collaboration from webex," accessed April, 2010; http://en.wikipedia.org, "Mass collaboration," 2011; R.D. Hof, "The Power of Us: Mass Collaboration on the Internet Is Shaking Up Business," *Businessweek*, July 20, 2005, pp. 78–81.

■ Keys to Successful Planning

The planning pitfalls described above can be avoided. Successful planning includes involving managers at different levels, using a combination of numerical and judgmental methods, viewing planning as a continuous activity capable of adapting to change, avoiding paralysis of the analysis, and concentrating planning efforts on a manageable set of issues.

Decentralizing the Planning Powers

To one degree or another, every level of management should be involved in planning. Planning cannot be viewed as the province of staff specialists or senior managers living in ivory towers. In general, both the quality of the plan and commitment to it are likely to increase when key managers and employees at various organizational levels contribute to its formulation and implementation.

One recent trend that seems to hold much promise is to secure the input of online groups to help develop, implement, and adjust business plans as necessary (see Management Close-Up 5.2, "Technology Is Fostering Bottom-Up, Top Down, and Horizontal Planning from the Inside and the Outside").

Using Both Numerical and Judgmental Methods

Planning is as much an art as a science. An effective planning process requires a thorough understanding of interrelated environmental and organizational factors. These factors provide clues about where the firm should be moving in the future, the resources it has at its disposal, and the constraints it faces. While numerical data can be helpful, the numbers need to be carefully interpreted. There are situations in which numerical approaches are not suitable. Systematically tapping the knowledge of employees at different levels in the organization allows the firm to benefit from their experiences and to profit from the collective judgment of company employees.

Viewing Planning as Continuous and Capable of Adapting to Change

Company leaders must be flexible enough to respond to changes in technology, competitors' reactions, international trends, and industry conditions if the planning process is to be successful. Almost any objective and the steps to accomplish it are likely to become obsolete relatively quickly unless there are built-in mechanisms to consider and respond to change. Results should be monitored continuously to detect major deviations from initial assumptions and expectations. Planning should question future directions, chosen alternatives, and priorities. In particular, the firm needs to guard against escalation of a failing course of action, as noted earlier. Past choices and sunk costs should not entice the firm to continue investing in a plan when there is sufficient evidence to question the wisdom of that plan.

Firms use a variety of approaches to keep objectives and action plans attuned to changes in internal and external environments. These include scheduled retreats of key managers and employees, workshops led by consultants, environmental scanning (see Chapter 7 on strategic management), the use of two-way feedback between managers and employees in the performance appraisal process (see Chapter 10 on human resource management), and the creation of standing cross-functional committees composed of executives and key employees to monitor progress, identify current or emerging problems, and recommend corrective actions.

In some cases the firm must react quickly to deal with unforeseen circumstances. Even with the best-made plans, managers of successful firms are often called to act by "the seat of their pants" to confront crisis situations that seem to come from nowhere. (See, for instance, at the end of the chapter, Management MiniCase 5.2, "Disaster Planning: How Wal-Mart Saved the Day.")

Avoiding Paralysis of the Analysis

An obsession with paperwork, technical reports, statistical tables, and other supporting documentation causes paralysis by analysis. Plans only succeed when those responsible accept the plan and become devoted to seeing it implemented effectively. The key to successful planning is action, not becoming bogged down in overanalyzing every detail.

Concentrating on a Manageable Set of Issues

It is important to limit planning to key priority areas. As discussed in Chapter 7, a good way to identify these key areas is to focus on the firm's core competence or the resources that enable it to do things better than competitors. This keeps planning from being a "pie in the sky" exercise and anchors it to the firm's strengths. Beside simplifying the planning task, it will make plans easier to explain, since managers and employees will be cognizant of the problems, challenges, alternatives, and priorities being addressed. Moreover, the levels of risk and uncertainty are lowered since the plan is confined to areas about which the firm has information and experience, reducing the probability of unpleasant surprises. For example, Apple computers has been extremely successful at introducing a steady stream of new products (most recently Aperture for professional photographers, powerbooks with high resolution displays, iPad, iPod, iChat RV, and iMac G5) by exploiting its core competence. Some of these products introduced in the 2010s were conceived as far back as 1987, when Apple decided that its future lay in merging the computing, communications, and entertainment industries.[13]

See Figure 5.2 for a summary of good planning techniques and bad planning techniques and bad planning pitfalls.

FIGURE 5.2

Summary of Good and Bad Planning

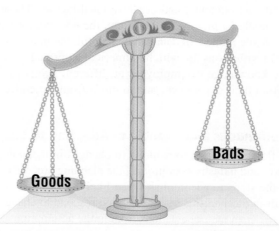

Goods	Bads
Decentralize planning process	Poor forecast of future conditions
Use numerical and judgmental methods	Plans imposed from above
Assess external forces	Planning as self-contained activity
Develop a sense of direction and purpose	Extensive bureaucratization
Identify factors that affect the organization	Inflexible adherence to objectives
Encourage participation	and processes
Coordinate efforts	
Establish priorities	

■ Formal Planning and Opportunistic Planning

A dynamic world requires dynamic planning programs. **Formal planning** systems are designed to identify objectives and to structure the major tasks of the organization to accomplish them. Formal planning is what has been described thus far in this chapter. No matter how careful the formal planning process is, however, unexpected events can derail the plan. A second type of planning, referred to as **opportunistic planning**, should coexist with formal planning and can help the formal plan function more smoothly.

As its name implies, opportunistic planning refers to programmatic actions triggered by unforeseen circumstances. Resources that are not totally committed as part of the formal planning process may be used at the discretion of managers to deal with unexpected events. For example, since its inception Federal Express has viewed the U.S. Postal Service (USPS) as a direct competitor, predicating its growth on stealing market share from USPS by sending materials faster with almost perfect reliability. FedEx marketing and delivery plans quickly changed when FedEx and the USPS became partners. The U.S. Postal Service now allows consumers to send FedEx packages directly from any U.S. Post Office using newly installed drop boxes, and FedEx now flies most of the Priority and Express packages for the Postal Service. This type of action as a result of "opportunistic planning" would have been unthinkable just a few years ago.[14]

> **formal planning**
> A system designed to identify objectives and to structure the major tasks of the organization to accomplish them.
>
> **opportunistic planning**
> A type of planning that involves programmatic actions triggered by unforeseen circumstances; it can coexist with formal planning and can help the formal plan function more smoothly.

LOC-In 3 Learning Objective Check-In

1. Kathryn, the CEO at WEBB Enterprises, always promotes opportunistic planning within a formal planning framework. She insists that it is important to identify objectives and structure the major tasks of the organization to accomplish them, which represents _____; and she also insists that unexpected events can derail any plan. Therefore, _____ should help the company with unforeseen circumstances.
   a. opportunistic planning; formal planning
   b. opportunistic planning; bureaucratization
   c. bureaucratization; opportunistic planning
   d. formal planning; opportunistic planning

It is important to strike the proper balance between these two types of planning. Organizations that rely exclusively on formal planning can become too rigid, whereas firms that use only opportunistic schemes will be constantly reacting to external forces and will have no clear sense of direction. Formal planning should provide a structured framework without binding every action of the enterprise, while opportunistic planning should allow for creative responses within that organized framework. GE has a formal planning process, and its longtime CEO, Jack Welch, strongly promoted opportunistic planning during his tenure:

> The story about GE that hasn't been told is the value of an informal place.... I don't think people have ever figured out that being informal is a big deal.... Making the company "informal" means violating the chain of command, communicating across layers, paying people as if they worked not for a big company but for a demanding entrepreneur where nearly everyone knows the boss.[15]

■ The Formal Planning Process

As indicated earlier, the four elements of the formal planning process involve setting objectives, charting a course of action to meet the objectives, allocating resources to carry out the planned activities, and implementing the activities (see again Figure 5.1). Each of these steps is discussed in turn.

Setting Objectives

Objectives are the performance targets set during the planning cycle. Objectives provide the answer to the question: What are we trying to accomplish? Inappropriate or poorly defined objectives invalidate the rest of the planning process since there is no clear guide for organizational efforts.

Objectives are set at every level in an organization. The goals established at higher levels direct and constrain the objectives set at lower levels. In general, objectives are more general at the top and become more specific at lower organizational levels. Some people refer to this as a *cascading of objectives.* DuPont stated an overall corporate objective in which one-third of sales would come from products introduced in the last five years (up from 24 percent during the past decade). To achieve this goal, DuPont's finance department set as its objective to increase the research and development (R&D) budget by 10 percent and to devote 65 percent of this budget to new product development (up from 33 percent in recent years). The objective of DuPont's 75 R&D centers distributed across 12 countries, was to identify 75 projects (an average of one per center) to launch new products that have the highest revenue potential. For one particular team, called the Suprel Group, the objective became much more specific: to develop a lightweight and puncture-resistant fabric to be used in gowns for surgeons and nurses.[16] In other words, DuPont's product introduction goal that began at the top of the organizational pyramid filtered down to lower echelons, where they became more specific. The goals at each level should support the goals established at the next higher level.

The overall objectives of the organization reflect its *mission,* which is a statement of the organization's reason to exist (more on this in Chapter 7 regarding strategic management). DuPont's objectives were consistent with the mission of being "a science company, delivering science-based solutions in markets such as food and nutrition, health care, apparel, home and construction, electronics, and transportation."[17]

Specific and measurable objectives motivate behavior more than general and ambiguous ones. It is important to give employees a clear sense of direction. Unambiguous objectives allow managers to determine whether key outcomes are being reached and to take corrective action if they are not. By knowing exactly where the firm is trying to go, managers and employees can focus on the most important activities, thereby concentrating on achieving the best results. Worthwhile objectives include:

- Profitability targets, such as return on investment, return on assets, and earnings per share.
- Quality goals such as percentage of rejects, customer complaints relative to number of orders, or quality certification standards.
- Marketing objectives, such as market growth, market share, and international sales.
- Innovation outcomes, such as number of patents, percentage of sales attributed to new products, and return on R&D investments.

Further, managers should make sure that objectives are *challenging* and will "stretch" employees to work harder to use their full potential. Difficult goals must be achievable; otherwise employees will not believe that their efforts will lead to success.

Objectives should specify a *timetable* or *deadline.* This can serve to motivate individuals. A timetable can cause individuals to organize tasks, prompting them to monitor work to ensure that completion is on time. It also helps management evaluate individuals or units on the extent to which work was done in a timely fashion.

Finally, managers and employees are more likely to devote time and effort to the accomplishment of objectives that they perceive as more critical and whose achievement is associated with greater prestige, rewards, and future career opportunities. Deciding which objectives should have highest *priority* is an integral part of the planning process.

When firms have multiple objectives, scarce resources preclude pursuing them all with the same zeal. Frequently, desired objectives may work at cross purposes. For example,

- Managers may increase short-term profits by cutting back on capital expenditures, reducing R&D investments, and laying off employees. This may decrease future profits because of lost technological superiority, the introduction of fewer products into the market, and less employee commitment.
- A firm may reduce its overall level of risk by diversifying into different market areas so that downturns in one market segment may be counterbalanced by upturns in other segments. However, the overall profitability of the firm is likely to be lower, because it loses the competitive advantage of applying a core set of knowledge and skills to a focused product niche. For example, in the mid-1990s, Altavista began as an Internet search engine. By the late 1990s the company had decided to diversify its scope and to explore new market

segments. Company executives invested $100 million to build the site into a multifaceted portal along the lines of Yahoo!. In the 2000s Altavista realized that expanding beyond its core knowledge had been a mistake and decided to return to its original mission.[18]

- A firm may pursue rapid growth to expand market share overseas, but company profits may suffer because it has to contend with diverse cultural milieus, is exposed to currency fluctuations, and is required to develop a management structure to deal with the complexities of a global operation (see Chapter 2).
- A firm may reduce costs by moving its manufacturing operations to a developing country where environmental regulations are lax. This would conflict with corporate social responsibility objectives.

As discussed in Chapter 3, a firm has many stakeholders, including employees, shareholders, consumers, and regulatory bodies. Each group may have different objectives. The planning process should identify the wishes of each of these groups and develop objectives that are clear, achievable, measurable, and prioritized so that they contribute to overall organizational performance.

One planning technique that is widely used in the United States and abroad is *Management by Objectives* (MBO). MBO is a program in which objectives are mutually set between the employee and supervisor. The employee is held accountable for the accomplishment of those objectives at various intervals which are normally part of an annual performance appraisal. MBO programs are popular because they combine planning (through participatively set objectives) and control (employees are responsible for the attainment of measurable goals).

Figure 5.3 shows the key steps of a typical annual MBO cycle. In step 1, objectives are agreed to between the superior and subordinate, and put in writing. Objectives such as company-wide profitability targets are first established at the top of the organizational pyramid. These more general objectives then filter down through successively lower layers. For instance, overall profitability targets are broken down into objectives for divisions and product lines. While normally these objectives are established annually, it is possible to use a longer or shorter time horizon. In step 2, managers at each level develop action plans to accomplish the objectives set for them by their immediate superiors in step 1. As the plans are implemented in step 3, there are frequent checkups to ensure that things are on track and make any necessary adjustments. In step 4 (which normally takes place a year after objectives were set in step 1), the pairs of superior and subordinate who established the mutually agreed-upon objectives in step 1 meet to discuss the extent to which objectives were met. This feedback is normally put in writing in a formal document called the *performance appraisal form*. In the words of a human resource planning consultant, "Many managers struggle with feedback precisely because of a lack of planning. Without front-end planning, feedback has no context...the outcome of effective feedback is clarity—clarity regarding the performer's recent performance against previously agreed-upon criteria".[19]

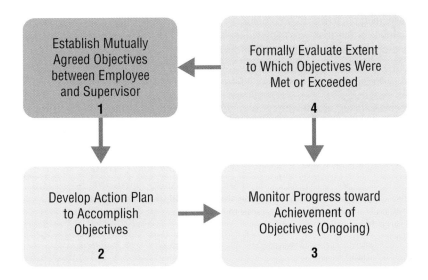

FIGURE 5.3

Key Steps of the Typical Management by Objectives Cycle

Establish Mutually Agreed Objectives between Employee and Supervisor
1

Formally Evaluate Extent to Which Objectives Were Met or Exceeded
4

Develop Action Plan to Accomplish Objectives
2

Monitor Progress toward Achievement of Objectives (Ongoing)
3

Employees are usually rewarded with cash bonuses, stocks, promotions, and other suitable benefits when they accomplish or exceed the performance targets set in step 1. This performance information is then used as part of goal-setting for the next review cycle. Targets may be revised downward if they were deemed to be unrealistic in the prior MBO cycle, or made more difficult if the employee is ready for greater challenges.

Unfortunately, the very strength of MBO—measurability—often becomes its major weakness. Managers can manipulate the system to choose easier-to-reach targets and ignore intangible things that may be more difficult to measure, such as customer goodwill. They may also become reluctant to change priorities for fear of not achieving the agreed-upon objectives when the situation demands it. Worse yet, the setting of numerical objectives may lead to gaming on the part of managers to reach or exceed the quantitative targets set in step 1 (see Figure 5.3), tempting them to engage in unethical behaviors. In fact, many of the well-documented ethical lapses during the past decade are attributed to top executives, managers, and even employees taking short cuts or manipulating numbers to reach challenging targets. In one of the most egregious cases, hospitals that were part of Tenet Health Care allegedly encouraged medical personnel to perform unnecessary medical procedures such as angioplasties, coronary bypasses, and heart catheterizations in order to meet or exceed profitability objectives.[20] Manager's Checkup 5.1 at the end of this chapter offers a set of ethical questions that all managers and employees should ask themselves from time to time to address ethical dilemmas that may arise at any phase of the planning process.

For an MBO system to be effective in the long run, the system must be flexible and allow for subjective judgments when assessing whether or not objectives are being achieved. The greater the volatility of conditions faced by the firm (rapid changes in technology, markets, competitors and the like) and the more its products and services change frequently, the greater the need for flexibility in the MBO system.

Management Is Everyone's Business 5.1 offers a set of recommendations that should help you develop personal plans to make you a more effective employee.

Charting a Course of Action

Once objectives have been established, the next step in the planning process (see again Figure 5.1) is to determine the actions necessary for producing orderly results. Three types of actions are normally planned: strategic, tactical, and operational. See Figure 5.4.

MANAGEMENT IS EVERYONE'S BUSINESS 5.1

WORKING AS AN INDIVIDUAL An old adage maintains that while we all have the same amount of time, successful people know how to allocate their time efficiently. Efficient time allocation requires setting personal objectives and determining the best way to accomplish them. It is also important to periodically reassess objectives, redefining or changing them as needed and adjusting implementation plans accordingly. This planning process can be learned with practice, greatly improving your use of time and talents. As an individual employee you are more likely to be successful if you:

- Establish specific, challenging objectives to accomplish.
- Stretch yourself to go a bit further than you think you can, but avoid unrealistic objectives that increase stress and end up discouraging rather then motivating you.
- Don't be afraid to show initiative, telling your boss the challenging objectives that you have set for yourself. Most managers react positively to employees who take charge of their jobs and careers.
- Ensure that your objectives are consistent with those of your superior or what the organization expects of you. If not, try to show your superior how your objectives are valuable in light of the operational plans for your unit (perhaps no one else thought of it and your boldness may be more than welcome!), but be willing to negotiate any necessary adjustments.
- Develop personal plans with different time horizons to accomplish your objectives (for in stance a daily "to do" list, an annual set of work plans, and "five years from now" career aspirations).
- Establish clear priorities for yourself so that you are not overwhelmed by details. Ineffective employees often complain that "I just don't know where my day goes" or "I just can't find sufficient time to do what I am supposed to do."
- Don't be afraid to seek feedback from peers and superiors; they might provide a "reality check" to see whether you are on the right track.

FIGURE 5.4

Charting a Course of Action

STRATEGIC ACTION PLANS Top executives are normally responsible for developing strategic action plans. At times divisional managers and the board of directors are also involved. **Strategic action plans** are based on overall organizational features, resources, and the environment. They establish long-term, corporatewide actions designed to accomplish the company's mission and major objectives. An important emphasis at this level is linking the action plans of different organizational functions and units so that they reinforce the strategies adopted by the entire organization.

To be effective, a strategic action plan should meet the following criteria:

1. *Proactivity,* which is the degree to which the strategic action plan takes a long-term view of the future and actively moves the company forward in the desired direction.
2. *Congruency,* or the extent to which the strategic action plan fits with organizational characteristics and the external environment (see Chapter 7).
3. *Synergy,* or the integration of the efforts of various organizational subunits to better accomplish corporatewide business objectives.

strategic action plans
Management plans based on macro approaches for analyzing organizational features, resources, and the environment and establishing long-term corporatewide action programs to accomplish the stated objectives in light of that analysis.

LOC-In 4 Learning Objective Check-In

Hickory, Norman & Schultz (HN&S) have various objectives that they want to pursue. For example, the firm wants to achieve a 15 percent increase in profitability on all new products in the next three years. This, in conjunction with rapid market share growth in China and parts of Africa, represents the most important objective for the firm. HN&S is concerned over the method it used to develop these objectives and which it plans to use to achieve them. Its concern is that 15 percent is too conservative a profitability increase and things like customer goodwill—intangibles—will be ignored throughout this process.

1. The 15 percent increase in profitability on all new products in the next three years represents _____ in the objectives.
   a. priority
   b. quality
   c. specificity and measurability
   d. challenge

2. The profitability increase and market share growth in China and Africa represent _____.
   a. quality
   b. priority
   c. challenge
   d. specificity and measurability

3. Based on what you know about the concerns the company has about the method it is using to develop and implement the achievement of these objectives, the company is likely using _____.
   a. Total Quality Management
   b. Management by Objectives
   c. the Balanced Scorecard Approach
   d. the Strategic Action Plan Approach

tactical action plans
Management action plans at the division or department level that indicate what activities must be performed, when they must be completed, and what resources will be needed at the division or departmental level to complete the portions of the strategic action plan that fall under the purview of that particular organizational subunit.

division of labor
The production process in which each worker repeats one step over and over, achieving greater efficiencies in the use of time and knowledge; also, the formal assignment of authority and responsibility to job holders.

budgeting
Controlling and allocating the firm's funds; *variable budgeting* allows for deviations between planned output and actual output by considering the fact that variable costs depend on the level of output, whereas fixed costs do not; *moving budgeting* creates a tentative budget for a fixed period of time and then revises and updates it on a periodic basis to take changes into account.

TACTICAL ACTION PLANS **Tactical action plans** are developed at the division or department level. They specify the activities that must be performed, when they must be completed, and the resources a division or department will need to complete the portions of the strategic action plan under its purview. The primary criterion of effectiveness for tactical action plans is the extent to which they contribute to the achievement of the company's strategic objectives. In general, tactical action plans cover a period of one to two years. Two important aspects of tactical action plans are division of labor and budgeting.

The formal assignment of authority and responsibility to job holders is referred to as **division of labor**. This helps ensure that tasks of job holders are appropriate for accomplishing the overall plan of the division or the department, which in turn should support the organization's strategic action plans. Common ways to change organizational design to achieve strategic action plans include:

- Assigning more job positions in the organization to work crucial to the attainment of strategic objectives.
- Creating specialized job positions that emphasize work crucial to the attainment of strategic objectives.
- Assigning work crucial to the attainment of strategic objectives to high-level job positions.[21]

By controlling and allocating funds, **budgeting** becomes an integral part of tactical action plans. Budgeting provides information about the strategic direction of the firm, makes clear the contribution to strategic objectives, forces budget committees to carefully ponder strategic perspectives to decide whether to accept or reject each proposal, and creates monitoring devices to examine the extent to which the projected contribution to strategic objectives is actually realized.

Managers and /or employees may also be asked to participate in the budget-setting process. Involving them promotes better understanding of the tactical action plan by those who will be carrying it out. It can also improve acceptance of decisions and commitment to them. Employee involvement may take a variety of forms, including:

- Creating budget forecasts.
- Preparing budget proposals.
- Allocating the overall budget to various activities.
- Developing significant rewards for reaching budgetary targets, such as bonuses, pay increases, and recognition at special events.
- Transferring resources from one activity to another in the event of unforeseen circumstances.

Budgets are based on forecasts, which in turn depend on assumptions about the future. For example, a production budget for a two-year period is projected by estimating the costs of materials, labor, and capital equipment required to produce an expected sales level. The assumptions made about both sales levels and the required resources could be wrong. The sales volume could be higher or lower than expected. Market demand, competitors' pricing, shifts in consumer tastes, and interest rates all affect sales. The resources needed depend on such factors as economies of scale, efficiency of production, introduction of new technology, and the cost of supplies. For instance, using copper instead of aluminum to make microchips cut IBM's and Intel's production costs of microchips almost in half in the late 1990s. On the other hand, the cost of wood and steel products almost doubled during 2007–2012, greatly increasing construction costs for home builders (and unfortunately, housing prices fell by as much as 50% in some areas after many of these homes sat empty for a long time).

Two budgeting techniques are designed to be more flexible: variable budgeting and moving budgeting. *Variable budgeting* accounts for deviations between planned output and actual output because variable costs depend on the level of output, whereas fixed costs do not. For instance, plant and equipment are fixed costs, because the firm pays principal, interest, and maintenance on those assets even when they are not being utilized at full capacity.

Variable budgets take into account the dependance of anticipated profits on the expected relationship between costs and output. A variable budget recognizes that planned profit and total costs do not vary proportionately with sales. The hypothetical variable budget in Table 5.1 shows how an increase in output of 30 percent, from 2,000 units to 2,600 units, can produce an increase

TABLE 5.1 An Example of a Variable Budget

Output (units)	2,000	2,200	2,400	2,600
Sales (at $10.00 per unit)	$20,000	$22,000	$24,000	$26,000
Variable costs (at $6.00 per unit)	12,000	13,200	14,400	15,600
Fixed costs	2,000	2,000	2,000	2,000
Total costs	14,000	15,200	16,400	17,600
Planned profit	$6,000	$6,800	$7,600	$8,400

in profits of 40 percent. To be accurate, variable budgeting also needs to consider how the cost of different inputs co-vary as a function of output level. For example, as output increases, administrative office support decreases as a percentage of total operating costs.

In contrast to variable budgeting, *moving budgeting* creates a tentative budget for a fixed period of time, normally a year. The budget is then revised and updated on a periodic basis to take changes into account. Reexamining the premises, assumptions, and estimates made when the tentative budget was initially created allows the budget to be a living, flexible document.

One downside of moving budgets is that they demand frequent revisions, requiring employees to spend additional time on the budgeting process. Also, some managers attempt to secure more resources by arguing that the financial resources originally received were inadequate.

Firms need to be careful that managers do not become obsessed with numbers and dollars, ignoring more "intangible" aspects of performance that in the long run are critical for financial success. For example, quality, customer service, employee commitment, innovation and creativity, reputation, consumer loyalty, and ability to attract and retain top talent may suffer if managers only receive pay raises and positive performance evaluations for strictly adhering to the budget.

OPERATIONAL ACTION PLANS Line managers and employees directly responsible for individual tasks or activities are the ones who create **operational action plans**. These plans tend to be narrowly focused on resources, methods, timelines, and quality control issues for a particular kind of operation. In general, the time frame for operational action plans is shorter than for tactical action plans.

Figure 5.5 illustrates a typical operation. Inputs (human, financial, raw materials, and other resources) are transformed (through assembly, chemical treatment, combination with other elements) into outcomes (products or services). The control component includes information about the required characteristics of inputs and outputs and how inputs must be modified to produce outputs. It ensures that the quantity and quality of inputs and outputs fall within certain parameters and that costs remain within a stipulated budget. Feedback is returned from output to transformation and input, so that continuing improvement may be achieved by using resources more efficiently. Any activity creating an output that affects tactical action plans and that uses significant resources can be analyzed using this general model.

operational action plan
A management plan normally created by line managers and employees directly responsible for carrying out certain tasks or activities.

FIGURE 5.5

A Typical Operating System

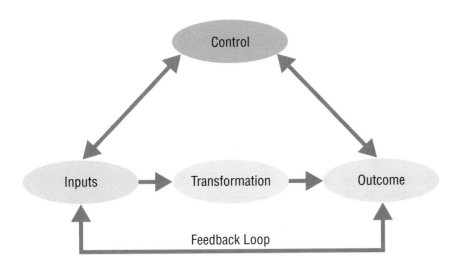

The main challenge of operational planning is using resources most efficiently. For instance, when the primary resource of an operation such as an R&D facility is people's know-how, operational plans may focus on how to transform employees' knowledge to produce an innovation (outcome). The goal should be to use these resources efficiently to generate innovations that add value to the company's overall operation.

When the relationship between resources and outcomes is uncertain, the control function must allow substantial latitude for failure. This is the case, for instance, in most pharmaceutical firms. There is typically less than a 10 percent chance of getting a therapeutic protein that works in the animal-disease model to market. The human testing required for approval takes at least six to eight years to complete. A particular drug may be dropped out during any of the three phases of clinical trials for reasons ranging from lack of efficacy to high toxicity.[22]

If properly conducted, operational planning offers several benefits to organizations, including:

- The opportunity to use feedback for continued incremental learning.
- The ability to visualize alternative types of operations—that is, alternative ways to use resources to create a product or service.
- The ability to predict the effects of modifications in operations on the efficiency of operations.
- The ability to evaluate the effectiveness of operations.

A more specific set of operational planning techniques have been developed in an area called *project management.* As the name implies, a project is a set of tasks designed to achieve certain objectives. In most cases, projects are completed by teams. Project management planning techniques allow one to identify specific tasks to be done, when they need to be completed, the resources required, and to document what has been accomplished so far. There are now many powerful Web-based programs that managers and team members cart use to schedule project tasks, monitor them from start to finish, and report variances from expected results. Figure 5.6 shows a description of one program, called Intuit QuickBase.

Implementation

Planning is meaningless unless it can be carried out successfully. The implementation phase is a critical part of the planning process. Implementation involves defining tasks to be accomplished, assigning individual responsibilities for those tasks, and managing individuals to ensure that the tasks are appropriately completed.

FIGURE 5.6
Intuit QuickBase

Source: Courtesy of
www.intuit.quickbase.com.

> *"With our company, 'QuickBase' has crossed over from a noun to a verb."*
> —Dr. Scott Friedman

Got a vital project? Now you can QuickBase it.

Project managers–those busy conductors of the office orchestra–now have a powerful Web-based solution that is simple enough for the whole team to use. QuickBase lets managers create a central online home for all their project data: project schedules, documents, issue lists, team rosters, information of all kinds. Everyone on the team can see and update current versions, so they're always on task and in sync.

Now you can manage your project to success with our dedicated <u>Project Manager</u>
application, which puts all the tools you need in one simple-to-use solution. Suddenly, life for the project manager just got easier.

With <u>Project Manager</u>, you get:

- **True accountability.** Everyone can see what's due and when. Updates and changes are available immediately. No more excuses.

- **Better collaboration.** Critical documents are never trapped on anyone's hard drive. Since QuickBase is Web-based, everyone on your team can use it anytime and anywhere they have Web access.

- **More time saved.** The familiar Web interface makes using QuickBase as easy as clicking a mouse. Your team spends less time e-mailing documents and more time on the job.

- **Immediate results.** Get your team up and running in minutes—no need to order, distribute and install new software. With QuickBase, everything you and your team need is instantly available on the Web.

One distinction that is often made is between *standing plans* and *single-use plans*. **Standing plans** regulate situations that occur repeatedly. That is, they are plans created to help the organization deal with issues that come up on a regular basis. Organizations implement standing plans using a programmed approach that includes policies, rules, and standard operating procedures. A **policy** is a general guide for managers and employees to follow. For instance, an organization with a flexible work hours policy provides employees with the opportunity to choose when to come to work and when to go home. A **rule** is a formal, written statement that states the general permissible bounds for the application of particular policies. For instance, a rule might be that employees need to arrive at work between the hours of 7 and 9 in the morning and work for nine consecutive hours, including a half-hour lunch and two 15-minute breaks. A standard operating procedure (SOP) describes in detail the precise steps to be followed in a specific situation. For instance, an SOP may specify that each employee must punch a time clock upon arriving at work, check with the supervisor, file a work plan for the day, and complete a computerized report at the end of the day that documents the percentage of time devoted to each major task and what he or she accomplished. In other words, employees are expected to show up for work regularly so standing plans may be developed to provide work scheduling flexibility and ensure that employees are there when they are supposed to be, do what they are supposed to do, and provide enough information to others so that supervisors and co-workers know the status of various tasks assigned to them.

Single-use plans are implemented for unusual or one-of-a-kind situations. For example, one of NASA's major goals was to reach the moon, which involved the design and construction of a lunar module to take astronauts to the moon and bring them back to earth safely.

Keep in mind that effective planning is not a lonely activity carried out by experts or by a few executives at the top of the organizational pyramid. Most successful business plans require a

standing plans
Plans created to help the organization deal with issues that come up on a regular basis.

policy
A general guide for managers and employees to follow.

rule
Written statement of the general permissible bounds for the application of particular policies.

single-use plans
Plans implemented for unusual or one-of-a kind situations.

LOC-In 5 Learning Objective Check-In

Nalgen, a chemical engineering firm, knows the value of developing action plans. It has several criteria for different levels of action plans at the firm. First, the top executives develop plans that are proactive, that fit with the external environment, and that actually integrate the efforts of various subunits. The action plans developed at the department level have to specify what activities are to be performed, when they are to be completed, and what specific resources will be required to complete the tasks involved. One very important facet of the departmental planning includes controlling and allocating the firm's variable costs,which depend on the level of output. The last areas where action plans are needed are mainly in product conversion.

1. At Nalgen, the top executives are designing _____ to fit with the external environment.
   a. operational action plans
   b. budgets
   c. strategic action plans
   d. tactical action plans

2. The departmental plans specifying resources required can also be referred to as _____.
   a. strategic action plans
   b. tactical action plans
   c. operational action plans
   d. unit action plans

3. Controlling and allocating variable costs is part of _____.
   a. operational action plans
   b. variable budgeting
   c. moving budgeting
   d. the division of labor

4. Which type of action plan is involved with product conversion?
   a. Operational action plans
   b. Tactical action plans
   c. Unit action plans
   d. Strategic action plans

MANAGEMENT IS EVERYONE'S BUSINESS 5.2

WORKING AS A TEAM Teams require a great deal of coordination and integration to function effectively. Otherwise, many hours may be lost in activities, meetings, and communication that lead nowhere. This not only wastes time, but it can also result in frustration, poor morale, lack of credibility, and high employee turnover. A sound planning process can help teams define what they are trying to accomplish and develop mechanisms to achieve objectives in a more efficient manner, keeping confusion to a minimum. As part of the planning process, teams should:

- Ensure that work done by the team fits with overall organizational objectives and those of other pertinent teams and units within the firm.
- Set up an effective communication system to keep others informed of what the team is trying to accomplish and any particular issues that are relevant to other teams and units within the firm (for instance, unexpected glitches that may make it difficult to meet deadlines and hence affect other teams whose work is interdependent). An inexpensive Web-based log can be very helpful in this regard and does not require a lot of time and paperwork.
- Allow for emergence of spontaneous teams that were not part of the original plan but which may offer innovative insights or come up with creative solutions to unexpected roadblocks found along the way.
- Establish a clear reason for the team's existence, including goals to be accomplished, timelines, means to evaluate attainment of team objectives, and "sunset" rules to determine when it might be a good time for the team to disband.
- When appropriate, create planning teams whereby planning experts (who might be planning specialists who report directly to top executives or hired outside consultants) work with groups of managers and key employees from major divisions or departments to come up with their own goals or plans. This tends to foster creativity yet helps ensure coordination of decentralized plans so the efforts of the entire organization move in the same direction.

team effort with a great deal of coordination and integration across departmental and organizational levels. Management Is Everyone's Business 5.2 provides a set of recommendations that teams should consider when involved in the planning process.

In the end, all plans must be implemented by people. Plan implementation requires thinking about four major issues: the means of implementation, a process for organizational problems solving, the linking of planning with organizational control systems, and mechanisms for dealing with organizational change.

MEANS OF IMPLEMENTATION Managers must find a way to induce people to take the necessary steps to accomplish the planned actions. Four major approaches may be used: authority, persuasion, policy, and feedback mechanism.

Authority Authority is formal power. It is accorded to the position rather than the person. As part of plan implementation, the employee at each position is vested with the authority to make certain decisions and is held accountable for those decisions. Subordinates are expected to comply with the requests of people in positions of authority unless they are asked to do something that is unethical or illegal.

Persuasion While most firms rely on some form of authority structure to ensure employee compliance with planned actions, a plan that is acceptable to employees increases commitment to that plan. Persuasion is an important aspect of effectively implementing plans. Employees who are convinced of the merits of a plan are more likely to respond enthusiastically to directives of managers who have formal authority and to "go beyond the call of duty" in finding better ways to effectively execute the plan.

Persuasion in most companies requires employee involvement rather than a manager simply making a speech extolling the virtues of a particular plan. For example, to become a change agent during Kellogg's conversion from cereal company to snack-foods company in the first decade of the century, CEO Carlos Gutierrez (who later became U.S. Commerce Secretary) encouraged communication instead of Kellogg's traditional top-down approach. Previously, new product ideas had been presented only at monthly meetings and only by the head of research and development. Gutierrez opened himself up to hearing from people, and now technicians from the company's three-year-old, $75 million W. K. Kellogg Institute for Food and Nutritional Research can bring their ideas directly to him.[23]

Policy   Both formal authority and persuasion must operate within a general institutional context that governs the relations and actions of individuals responsible for implementing the plan. To this end, organizations develop policies that define appropriate and inappropriate behavior. These guidelines usually appear in a formal document to ensure that relevant policy information is communicated to all individuals involved. Effective policies are flexible, comprehensive, coordinated with subunits whose actions are interrelated, ethical, and written clearly and logically.

Feedback Mechanism   Successful plan implementation requires a continuous flow of information that is used to determine to what extent the plan is being carried out as expected. It is also important to assess how and why individual activities are helping attain company objectives. If the information sought is threatening to people, then knowledge sharing, constructive analysis, and a spirit of open inquiry are inhibited. Active employee involvement includes initiative, honest discussion of ideas, and generation of inputs or suggestions from the "bottom up." The learning that occurs is a crucial part of problem solving during the plan implementation phase.

A PROCESS FOR ORGANIZATIONAL PROBLEM SOLVING   Plan implementation seldom, if ever, occurs smoothly. Many unknowns must be dealt with. Part of an effective implementation program is establishment of a system that allows for a careful diagnosis of problems so that individuals responsible for carrying out the plan can learn from their mistakes. A six-stage approach may be used to facilitate this problem-solving process:[24]

1. *Identify performance gaps.* A diagnosis begins with a manager and a team defining the difference or shortfall between objectives and achievements. This step must not become part of such personnel decisions as merit pay, performance appraisal, and promotion. Doing so dampens people's willingness to be self-critical and openly share information.

2. *Identify tasks and work processes necessary for accomplishing the plan.* This requires defining what each individual is expected to do, the sequence of tasks, and the degree of interdependence or integration among the critical tasks needed to ensure successful execution of the plan. For instance, some key managers faced the following tasks:

   At Medtek, Torrance realized that if he were to be successful at developing innovative new products, his laboratory would have to be world-class in chemical and hydraulic technologies and be able to link these technologies to manufacturing and marketing requirements. For Chow at BOC, a critical task identified for delivering customized service to global customers was close integration across geographically dispersed organizations. With the Grenzach team's goal of reducing costs, the critical tasks were to maintain the functional excellence within the plant as well as to increase integration across the functional areas.[25]

3. *Check for organizational congruence.* Once the tasks and work processes have been identified, it is necessary to determine the extent to which other organizational elements support or hinder their attainment. In other words, it is important to know if the planned activity is aligned or fits with organizational structure, culture, human resource policies, and individual competencies and motives. If these organizational building blocks are incongruent with task requirements, the planned activities are likely to fail.

SKILLS FOR MANAGING 5.2

Planning and Performance

Browse through several issues of major financial newspapers or business periodicals that provide in-depth coverage of firms, such as *The Wall Street Journal*, *BusinessWeek*, *Fortune*, or *Forbes*. Select five to ten firms that are in the news. Research these firms' recent activities and answer the following questions.

1. How did the planning process affect these companies' performance?
2. How could better planning have helped their performance?

4. *If any incongruencies or inconsistencies are found, intervene to create alignment in order to effectively implement the plan.* In general, incremental changes, such as modifying the incentive system, can be accomplished without actually reconsidering the feasibility of the plan itself. But if there is systemwide lack of congruence that requires extensive changes in formal organizational arrangements, culture, and people, it probably means that the plan is impractical. In such a case, the entire plan needs to be reconsidered and better adjusted to organizational realities.

5. *Execute the plan.* At this stage, managers and employees take actions targeted at achieving the key milestones of the plan, ideally reinforced by congruent organizational arrangements, culture, and people who facilitate the execution of those actions.

6. *Learn from the consequences.* This is an ongoing process during plan implementation. It is used to diagnose the causes of performance gaps, anticipate what may cause problems in the future, and reveal better ways of doing things. Skills for Managing 5.2 asks you to select five to ten firms that are in the news and analyze how the planning process may have affected their performance and how their planning process may have been improved.

LINKING OF PLANNING WITH ORGANIZATIONAL CONTROL SYSTEMS Planning and the organizational control system should go hand in hand. As noted above in the section regarding operational action plans, an effective control system alerts managers when something is going wrong and provides them the opportunity to respond. Once plans are formulated and carried out, an effective control system allows the organization to compare planned objectives with observed results. If there is a significant discrepancy between expected and actual results, then managers should take corrective action in order to improve future plans and make modifications to those plans being implemented. It is wise to leave open the possibility of abandoning existing plans and replacing them with new ones when the control system indicates that there is a high deviation of expected versus actual results.

MECHANISMS TO DEAL WITH ORGANIZATIONAL CHANGE Most plans require changes in the way things are currently done. This is particularly true if the firm is attempting to shift direction or is operating in a turbulent environment. There are three major challenges in trying to simultaneously implement a plan and manage change associated with its implementation: (1) dealing with power and politics, (2) reducing individual anxiety and resistance, and (3) maintaining control during the transition period. If managers can successfully handle these challenges, employees are likely to be eager to implement the plan and to make accommodations to ensure a smooth transition. If ignored, these three factors can stop the successful implementation of even the most carefully drawn plans.

Managing the Political Dynamics of Change   Practically every significant change results in politics and resistance. Managing politics can be accomplished in a number of ways, including enlisting the support of key players, being consistent, and ensuring stability.

It is important for managers to mobilize the support of key players. First, the manager must identify the people who have the power to make or break the change and who control critical resources or expertise. Once the pivotal individuals are identified, it is necessary to ascertain how the change will likely affect each of them, how each is likely to react to the change, and the methods available to influence them.

In managing the dynamics of change, managers must attempt to ensure consistency in words and actions. To prevent cynicism among those responsible for implementing the plan, what managers say is important must be congruent with the actions taken or being reinforced. If a plan calls for close cooperation among individuals and units, rewarding only individual actions would generate mixed messages, and employees might resist the change. Managers can use a number of symbolic activities and mechanisms to influence planned actions, including how they spend their time, the types of questions they ask, what they follow up on, what they discuss at meetings, the types of things they choose to summarize, how they use language, the type of special events they provide, and the new heroes and myths they create to illustrate the change in standards and direction.[26]

Finally, managers must build in stability. People can absorb only so much change at once, and it is necessary to create stability during the implementation. This requires sending consistent messages—signals—to lessen uncertainty:

Part of this signaling is to be clear about what is not changing—what people can hold onto in the future. If some aspects of culture, physical location, and staffing patterns will not change, these anchors to the past need to be communicated and reinforced early on. At Alcoa, even in the context of wholesale change, managers made it clear that the glorious Alcoa engineering heritage and its commitment to high-quality aluminum would not change. As Kodak [has refocused], George Fisher has reemphasized the firm's commitment to the photographic market and signaled an end to diversification. Clarity about what will not change helps moderate fears of the future.[27]

Managing Individual Resistance   Organizational change can generate individual anxiety and stress. Up to a point this energizes employees, and their attentiveness and motivation increase. Too much stress, however, causes individuals to oppose change, leading them to try to block the plan or to leave in search of better employment prospects elsewhere. Dysfunctional anxiety can be reduced by showing people why the change needs to occur, making them stakeholders in the change effort through active participation, recognizing and rewarding the new behaviors required by the plan, and providing opportunities to disengage from the past at public events such as lunches, ceremonies, and employee skits.

Maintaining Control during the Transition   The turbulence and uncertainty associated with the change should not be allowed to result in chaos. Both for operational and political reasons, it is important for managers to convey the idea that the situation is under control during the transition period. This can be done by communicating a clear idea of the future state, using multiple methods to promote change, designing transition management structures, setting transition milestones, and measuring progress on a continuing basis.[28]

To close this chapter, we'll note that while the planning process should not be a top-down exercise, managers still play a key role in mustering planning efforts so that these can be shepherded in an orderly fashion. Management Is Everyone's Business 5.3 offers a set of suggestions that managers should follow to help fulfill this role.

MANAGEMENT IS EVERYONE'S BUSINESS   5.3

WORKING AS A MANAGER   Managers are expected to collaborate with employees to define objectives for their units and to clearly communicate the relative importance of those objectives. Once the objectives are established, managers need to develop a plan to accomplish them and lay out the steps of implementation. This process provides a frame of reference that can facilitate orderly change and avoid unnecessary disruptions and turmoil when unexpected changes occur. In other words, a quality planning process is useful to the manager precisely because it smooths the way change is conducted and gives employees a sense of confidence and continuity even in the midst of rapid change. As a manager engaged in planning you should:

- Keep a pulse on what customers want and be on the lookout for changing consumer desires that might affect your company's business. The best of plans are useless if these are not designed to meet certain objectives that are important to those who are likely to invest in the company's products and services.
- Ensure that planning in your area of responsibility is closely linked with the rest of the organization.
    - If you are a top manager, planning emphasis should be on broad objectives to guide the entire organization and overall allocation of resources to support accomplishment of those objectives.
    - If you are a middle manager, emphasis should be on tactical plans that allow you to best utilize people and resources under your control to support the firm's general plan.
    - If you are a first-line supervisor or a lower-level manager, emphasis should be on drawing specific action steps to complete assigned objectives of your unit, including precise scheduling, concrete tasks to be accomplished, budgeting, assigning responsibilities to each subordinate and the like.
- Establish an effective goal-driven plan.
    - Goals should be specific and measurable so that people know what is expected and how success or failure will be evaluated.
    - Goals should be prioritized to ensure that most important ones are given greatest attention.
    - Goals should be challenging but attainable.
    - Goals should have a time horizon in order to facilitate scheduling and motivate individuals to have a sense of urgency.

(Continued)

- Goal achievement should be evaluated and rewarded, with appropriate feedback given to all employees who were involved in the process.
- Ensure that planning does not become a straightjacket.
  - Plans are seldom carried out as originally intended because of the unexpected. Hence, you need to think about "what if" and have backup plans just in case.
  - Be ready for a rapid response that may be needed under changing circumstances (for example, priorities may need to be readjusted quickly in response to a competitor's move).
- Engage others in plan design and implementation.
  - Plans are a poor motivational tool unless managers and employees truly believe that, such plans are a good idea and become committed to them. Unfortunately, many business plans end up collecting dust in drawers because plan designers never secured the necessary "buy in" from those supposed to carry them out.
  - Encourage spontaneous inputs from employees and outsiders that might help you develop a more realistic plan, and perhaps reconsider the wisdom of a particular plan.

CONCLUDING THOUGHTS

Now that you've had the opportunity to learn about the benefits and pitfalls of planning, as well as the elements that contribute to a successful plan, let's revisit the critical thinking questions raised at the beginning of this chapter. Disney could have prevented the fiasco of the New Year's holiday in Hong Kong by looking more carefully into the length of the holiday and making sure its discount tickets were void for the entire week. Nevertheless, the company got many things right in creating the park, including learning from the mistakes it made in Paris and giving cultural sensitivity a much higher priority when moving abroad. Local language, customs, food, and customer preferences for entertainment were studied and honored, with the help of input from local residents and experts.

The new park was planned on many levels. A strategic decision was made to enter the Asian market and Hong Kong was chosen as the first site. Tactical plans probably governed the design of the park, its size, features, and attractions. Finally, operational plans covered such individual issues as hiring policies and the issuing of discount tickets.

Disney is planning far into the future when it anticipates expanding its Asian operations. The longer the time period, the greater the uncertainty. Promising opportunities today may dry up in a few years. For instance, competitors characteristically move in quickly and the market for a new product or service can quickly become saturated. For this reason, company leaders must anticipate future opportunities so that the organization can take advantage of them when the time comes. If the company anticipates threats and opportunities, Disney's massive investment in the Chinese market may provide impressive payoffs in the years ahead.

The setting of long-term objectives, such as for continued growth in Asia, gives the firm concrete targets that outline the steps needed to accomplish them. Objectives also provide criteria against which to assess whether or not actual performance was satisfactory or unsatisfactory so that corrective steps (and perhaps a redefinition of objectives) may be undertaken. This is what Disney was forced to do in Paris. On the other hand, the setting of objectives can be dangerous if it robs the firm of flexibility to make necessary changes and if managers believe that they have to play a "numbers game" to meet numerical targets.

FOCUSING ON THE FUTURE: Using Management Theory in Daily Life

Managing the Planning Process

Mary Kelley thought that she was just going for an informational getaway when she attended an Esalen seminar on brainwave biofeedback in 2011. Instead, she met Robert deStefano, and Sleep Garden, Inc., was born. Today, Mary handles public relations, operations, accounting, fulfillment, and a multitude of other tasks in her role as entrepreneur. Robert acts as creative director, advertising manager, and chief salesperson for the company. Together, they produce noningestible sleep aids (typically CDs and DVDs) which are clinically proven to help people fall asleep and stay asleep without drugs.

When creating her company, Mary followed the four key elements of a plan: objectives, actions, resources, and implementation.

Objectives

In their early conversations, Mary and Robert spent a lot of time trying to decide exactly what the company was supposed to do. They developed three key objectives. Sleep Garden exists to: (1) Provide a natural alternative to drugs and ingestibles (herbs, melatonin, etc.) used in promoting sleep; (2) Make these alternatives available and accessible to a mass market; and (3) Deliver a high quality product. While their objectives have stayed the same over time, Mary and Robert must frequently reevaluate how to achieve those objectives. For example, they have changed their packaging and price structure to more effectively deliver products to consumers. Sometimes, however, they know that what they're doing is exactly right. One of the first 300 products they sold went to Beulah Mae, a lady in Louisiana who never would have had the opportunity to attend a seminar on California's central coast. Clearly, Sleep Garden products are now accessible to a mass market.

Actions

Mary and Robert based their actions on the results of an environmental scan (described in Chapter 7) to see if their venture might work. Once they had convinced themselves that Sleep Garden was a marketable idea, they set about enhancing their product for delivery to customers. The first step was to conduct clinical trials—could a CD with music designed to alter brainwaves actually help induce sleep? Tests showed that their product was viable, and the next step was packaging. Sleep Garden's first product was a 3 CD/book set that retailed for $59.95. While initial sales were good, they were not spectacular, and feedback from retailers gave the entrepreneurs important information. First, the product was 8 inches by 8 inches by 1.5 inches—too big for most retail shelves. Second, the box containing the product was not completely full, so it crushed in the warehouse. Finally, the $59.95 price was too high for consumers who might be interested in the idea, but not willing to invest over $60 for something they had never encountered before. Mary and Robert learned that they needed to talk with retailers in addition to end consumers when designing their product; and that was the action they took next.

Advertising the new products was another important action. Mary describes their different advertising strategies—everything from an Internet Web site to mass advertising in print, radio and catalogs. Some worked, and others were expensive failures, but each advertising campaign taught the duo important lessons. Each creative, packaging, production, distribution, and advertising decision required that Mary and Robert reassess and reallocate their resources—the third element of a successful plan.

Resource Allocation

Like most entrepreneurs, Mary and Robert were their own most important resources. Each of them brought different skills to the company. Robert, with his background in advertising, was a creative driving force whose contributions included everything from package design to video direction and postproduction. Mary, whose background was in areas as varied as ancient Mesopotamian art, business, and technology, brought funding and a willingness to tackle databases, scientific sleep research, public relations, operations, accounting, and order fulfillment. She even answered the Sleep Garden 800 number for a time. According to Mary, the most important resources the team brought to the project were their respective networks—the contacts each of them had built up over 20-year careers.

Despite their skills, Mary and Robert knew that they would have to outsource some work if their company was to be successful. They invested in artists (a composer and a yoga instructor), product development advisors, packaging printers, advertising placement, and CD/DVD manufacturers—all of whom had a role to play in getting their product to market.

Implementation

During the implementation process, Robert and Mary divided the tasks of running the business. Robert, with his strong graphic design and copywriting skills, worked on product development and copy for everything from packaging to advertising to Web site content. He also used his background in producing commercials to direct and do postproduction work on the yoga video that was to become one of Sleep Garden's biggest products. Mary did proofreading, because even the most creative artist needs a second pair of eyes. In addition, she created a direct marketing database and the Sleep Garden Web site, while at the same time handling accounting. Because of her previous experience in academic and marketing research, she was responsible for scouring the Web to find information on the latest sleep research and technologies. She also oversaw all of the clinical trials to determine whether or not Sleep Garden products actually worked.

Mary set up task lists for every phase of the business. Using project planning software, she created Gantt charts that let the partners know when they were dangerously overcommitted and helped them to see what could realistically be done in any given amount of time. Despite the charts, Mary and Robert soon learned the critical need for flexibility when implementing their plans. After the production of their first CD set, they parted ways with the person who had performed on those CDs—leaving them to find new artists who could help them to move their company forward.

Mary stresses that the implementation of their objectives has gone more smoothly because she and Robert have complementary, not similar, skills. While they don't always agree, the two partners know that their perspectives can be merged to give a more complete picture of any business issue. Together, they are turning Sleep Garden into a growing concern with good prospects for the future.

Summary of Learning Objectives

1 Identify the different elements of an effective plan.

- **Objectives.** Goals or targets to be accomplished.
- **Actions.** Specific steps needed to achieve the stated objectives.
- **Resource allocation.** Necessary financial and human resources to carry out the planned activities.
- **Implementation guidelines.** A description of how intended actions will be executed.

2 Analyze the advantages and disadvantages of planning, and identify how planning pitfalls can be avoided.

- *Benefits of planning.* These include assessing external forces, developing a sense of direction, identifying the factors that affect the organization, encouraging participation, coordinating efforts, establishing priorities, focusing attention on different time horizons, understanding circumstances contributing to past success or failure, ensuring the availability of adequate resources, establishing performance standards, supporting organizational control systems, developing "what if" scenarios, and management development.
- *Pitfalls of planning.* These include poor forecasts of future conditions, plans imposed from above, planning as a self-contained activity, extensive bureaucratization, and inflexible adherence to objectives and processes.
- *Avoiding planning pitfalls.* Managers can overcome disadvantages of planning by involving different organizational levels, using both numerical and judgmental methods, viewing planning as continuous and capable of adapting to change, avoiding paralysis of the analysis, and concentrating on a manageable set of issues.

3 Distinguish between formal and informal planning.

- **Formal planning.** A well-defined set of objectives, action plans, resource allocation procedures, and implementation guidelines, usually in a written document.
- **Opportunistic planning.** Programmatic actions to respond to unforeseen circumstances.

4 Recognize the features of well-designed objectives.

- *Cascading of objectives.* In general, objectives are broader at the top of the organization and become more specific at lower organization levels.
- *Specificity and measurability.* By knowing what is expected and how expectations will be measured, managers and employees can focus on the most important actions, thereby concentrating on achieving the best results.
- *Difficulty.* Challenging yet achievable objectives induce employees to work harder to use their full potential.
- *Milestones.* Timetables and deadlines serve to motivate individuals to try harder.
- *Priorities.* Ranking of objectives in order of importance.

5 Identify the various types of action plans that managers can use to accomplish stated objectives.

- **Strategic plans.** The primary purpose is to link the action plans of different organizational functions and units so that they can help support the business strategy adopted by the entire corporation.
- **Tactical plans.** Divisions or department leaders must decide what activities should be performed, when those activities should be completed, and what resources to allocate to accomplish them. This includes defining the responsibilities of jobholders and controlling and allocating resources through the budgeting process.
- **Operational plans.** Employees directly responsible for carrying out activities should develop systems to transform resources into products or services, including a control component to ensure that quantity and quality of inputs and outputs meet established criteria within budget constraints.

Discussion Questions

1. What types of firms are most likely to benefit from a formal planning process? What types are most likely to face the planning misfires discussed in this chapter?
2. Of all the planning benefits discussed in this chapter, which ones do you think are most important? Why?
3. How would you rank the relative difficulty of carrying out the five approaches to successful planning discussed in this chapter? Explain your choices.
4. Take a look at the list of ethics-related questions pertaining to planning in Manager's Checkup 5.1. Can you think of any specific situations (for instance, a plan that might involve extensive layoffs) where these issues become very important? Explain.

5. Based on Management Close-up 5.2, how do you think technology is likely to change strategic, tactical, and operational action plans in the future? Explain your answer.
6. Among the four means of implementation discussed in this chapter, which are easiest to use? Which are most difficult? Why?
7. Which of the six steps in the organizational problem-solving scheme presented in this chapter is most likely to fail? Why? What should a firm do to prevent this potential failure?
8. Some people argue that managing the political dynamics of change is likely to backfire, since employees may see it as an attempt to manipulate. Do you agree? Why or why not?

Management Minicase 5.1

Newspapers: A Plan that Seemed Like a Godsend Is Turning Sour

Weekday circulation of more than 700 newspapers nationwide (including such venerable names as *USA Today*, *Wall Street Journal*, *Los Angeles Times*, *Washington Post*, and *Houston Chronicle*) has showed almost a 20 percent drop during the past 10 years or so. Circulation figures are important because they are used to set advertising rates, a major revenue generator, apart from the actual income derived from sales of newspapers. For instance, Help-wanted and real estate advertising fell by more than 35 percent, while automobile classifieds dropped by 22 percent. Some newspapers thought they had an answer to this problem after developing and implementing what appeared to be an innovative business plan called "sponsored sales." These are newspapers sold in bulk to hotels, airlines, and other outlets. By getting a captive audience (for instance, airline passengers or hotel guests) and a guaranteed front-end contract from a buyer (such as a large hotel chain), circulation numbers increased significantly at much lower cost (in comparison, for example, to individual home delivery). Unfortunately, to the newspapers' dismay, most advertisers now consider such circulation less valuable and have lowered their fees to newspapers which invested heavily (and became successful) in sponsored sales plans. Newspapers are now required to show sponsored sales figures so that advertisers can adjust their payments accordingly.

DISCUSSION QUESTIONS

1. What do you think accounts for the trend of declining sales among newspapers? Could newspapers have planned for this? Explain your answer.
2. If you were responsible for corporate planning at one of the major newspapers, what process would you put in place to forecast what is likely to happen in the future? What types of plans would you put in place to ensure the newspaper remains profitable? How would you handle the unpredictable? Explain your answer.
3. What should firms do when they realize that their customer base, such as subscribers and advertisers in the case of newspapers, seem to be dwindling year after year? Can you think of another industry where a similar situation is occurring? Explain your answer.

Source: Based on http://newsosaur.blogspot.com, "Newspaper sales fall record $3B in 6 months," 2011; "Newspaper for sale?" http://www.forbes.com, 2011; Audit Bureau of circulations "Certified circulation figures," http://www.accessaba.com, 2011; J. Hagan, "Circulation Continues to Decline at Most Major Newspapers," *The Wall Street Journal*, November 8, 2005, pp. B7-B8.

Management Minicase 5.2

Disaster Planning: How Wal-Mart Saved the Day

Wal-Mart, America's biggest company, is many things to many people—discounter extraordinaire, union buster, guardian of small-town virtues, wrecker of small-town shops—but one thing most people agree on is how well it responded to Katrina. Wal-Mart's truckers hauled $3 million of supplies to the ravaged zone, arriving days before the Federal Emergency Management Agency in many cases. The company also contributed $17 million in cash to relief efforts. Wal-Mart

demonstrated how efficient it can be. As of September 16, 2005, all but 13 of the Wal-Mart facilities that Katrina had shut down were up and running again. The company had relocated 97 percent of the employees displaced by the storm and offered them jobs at any Wal-Mart operation in the country.

Wal-Mart began its response to Katrina on August 23—six days before the storm rampaged through New Orleans. That was the day

Jason Jackson, Wal-Mart's director of business continuity, noticed that a storm off the coast of Florida had become a tropical depression and was headed for the state's southern tip.

Jackson's drab title belies his importance. He oversees Wal-Mart's Emergency Operations Center (EOC) down the road from the home office in Bentonville. You'd expect the Emergency Operations Center at the nation's largest company to be a high-tech war room. In reality, it is just another chamber of blue cubicles at a company whose executives proudly disdain spending time or money on anything so frivolous as design. But what takes place in the EOC is truly artful.

Before Hurricane Katrina hit, Wal-Mart Stores, Inc. had learned some lessons from Hurricane Charlie, a year earlier. Alarmed by a lack of visibility into store conditions during that storm, Wal-Mart took a new approach to disasters that paid off during Katrina.

After Charlie, Wal-Mart built a dashboard to provide a single data source for store-by-store assessment of damage and to determine whether employees are at risk and communications and power are up. Wal-Mart also has an emergency operations center at its headquarters designed to get employees from different departments to work in close proximity during a disaster. Katrina put it to the test. By having people work in the operations center, employees from multiple parts of the company set priorities on which tasks and systems were most important.

DISCUSSION QUESTIONS

1. Based on what you have learned in this chapter, what did Wal-Mart do that many other firms and government officials did not do to deal effectively with the hurricane? Explain your answer.
2. How should corporate planners handle situations such as Katrina before they actually occur? Explain your answer.
3. Another company that was praised for its work in the aftermath of Katrina was Federal Express. It has a policy called "flexibility planning." Long before Katrina, FedEx conducted disaster drills several times a year—for everything from big earthquakes to bioterrorism to a monster typhoon hitting the company's hub in the Philippines. Do you think most companies should engage in this sort of planning exercise? Why or why not? Explain your answer.

Source: Based on L. Sullivan, "Wal-Mart: Lessons of the storm," *InformationWeek* Global CIO, http://www.informationweek.com, 2011; http://www.en.wikipedia.org," Wal-Mart stores Inc.," 2011; http://www.bitpipe.com, "Disaster planning reports," 2011. D. Leonard, "The Only Lifeline Was the Wal-Mart," *Fortune,* October 3, 2005 pp. 74–80; and, E. F. Xratz, "For FedEx, It Was Time to Deliver," *Fortune,* October 3, 2005, pp. 83–84.

Individual/Collaborative Learning Case 5.1
Why Did NASA Stick with the Space Shuttle So Long?

The core problem that lay at the heart of the Challenger tragedy in the mid-1980s applies to the Columbia tragedy in 2003 as well. That core problem may be the original plan for the space shuttle itself. For 20 years, the American space program has been wedded to a space-shuttle system that is expensive, risky, and too big for most of the ways it is used, with budgets that monopolize funds that could be invested in an alternative system that would make space flight cheaper and safer.

The space shuttle is four decades old, although first drawings preceded the Apollo programs of the 1960s. The shuttle's main engines, first tested in the late 1970s, use significantly more moving parts than do new rocket-motor designs. The fragile heat-dissipating tiles were designed before breakthroughs in materials science. Until recently, the flight-deck computers on the space shuttle used 8086 chips from the early 1980s, the sort of pre-Pentium electronics no self-respecting teenager would dream of using for a video game.

More important, the space shuttle was designed under the highly unrealistic assumption that the fleet would fly to space once a week and that each shuttle would need to be big enough to carry a 50,000-lb. payload. In actual use, the shuttle fleet has averaged five flights a year; in the year of the Columbia's disaster (2003), flights were to be cut back to four. The maximum payload is almost never carried. Yet to accommodate the highly unrealistic initial goals, engineers made the shuttle huge and expensive. The Soviet space program also built a shuttle, called Buran, with almost exactly the same dimensions and capacities as its American counterpart. Buran flew to orbit once and was canceled, as it was judged to be expensive and impractical. Originally projected to cost $5 million per flight in today's dollars, each shuttle launch instead runs to around $500 million.

In three decades of use, shuttles have experienced an array of problems—engine malfunctions, damage to the heat-shielding tiles, and other difficulties that have nearly produced other disasters.

Seeing this, some analysts proposed that the shuttle be phased out, that cargo launches be carried aboard by far cheaper, unmanned, throwaway rockets and that NASA build a small "space plane" solely for people, to be used on those occasions when men and women are truly needed in space. NASA, however, has remained faithful to the original plan of using the shuttle to send people into space even though in financial terms and safety terms the results have been disappointing, to say the least. The more money that has been invested in the shuttle, the harder it, has been for NASA to walk away from it. In fact, NASA renewed its shuttle program after the 2003 Columbia tragedy, and in 2006 the shuttle was grounded again after additional problems were discovered with the tiles, which almost caused another serious accident in 2005. While NASA had scheduled to retire the shuttle by 2010, future missions might be extended until 2015 (at the time of this writing, there are three more scheduled launches).

CRITICAL THINKING QUESTIONS

1. Why do you think NASA has been staunchly committed to the space shuttle program, more than three decades after the initial plans were drawn up, with a technology that had its origins in the 1960s? Was NASA justified in this long-term commitment to the space shuttle program, even after the Challenger disaster in the mid-1980s? Explain your answer.
2. Based on what you have learned in this chapter, what does the space shuttle program tell us about the pitfalls of planning? In retrospect, what should NASA have done differently in its planning process to prevent the problems discussed in this case? Explain.
3. Can planning help an organization better deal with uncertainty? What does the space shuttle case discussed above teach us about the difficulties of dealing with uncertainty? Explain.

COLLABORATIVE LEARNING EXERCISE

You have been appointed as part of a five-member independent panel to determine why the results of the space shuttle program differed from the objectives that were established in the original plans drawn up decades ago. Using the materials you have learned in this chapter, analyze whether the gap between objectives and results may be attributed to faulty objectives, or problems with the actions, resources, and implementation used to achieve the objectives. Based on this analysis, develop the outline of a plan to prevent past problems from happening again in the future. Carefully justify your recommendations.

Source: Based on http://nasa.gov, accessed April, 2011; http://en. wikipedia.org, "Nasa," 2011; J. O'Neill, "NASA is making preliminary plans to extend shuttle launches beyond 2010," http://www.universetoday.com, 2011; C. Easterbrook, "The Space Shuttle Must Be Stopped," *Time,* February 10, 2003, pp. 46–47; J. Kluger, "Why NASA Can't Get It Right," *Time,* August 8, 2005, p. 25.

Internet Exercise 5.1

E-Business Goes E-Bankrupt but Survivors Are Doing Well

The so called "dot-com" firms were supposed to be the wave of the future in the late 1990s until the bubble burst in early 2000. Hardly any dot-com firms made any money, meaning investors had received little, if any, returns. The Web site F**Kedcompany.com keeps track of the death struggles of troubled dot-com companies. Very few of them have survived. Surprisingly, four years later, most of those that survived are showing healthy profits. These include the an autoshopping Web site Autobytel Inc., financial news site Marketwatch.com, Web search site Ask Jeeves, online loan site Lendingtree, software management firm Digital River Inc., bookseller Amazon.com, jewelry retailer Blue Nile Inc., and e-Bay Inc. Research some of the dot-com firm successes and failures on the Internet and answer the following questions using the materials discussed in this chapter:

1. What reasons can you find for their success or failure? Is there a pattern? Explain.
2. Would better planning have averted the demise of those which failed? Why or why not?
3. Should the planning process be different for brick-and-mortal companies vis-à-vis dot-com firms?

Manager's Checkup 5.1

Ethical Checklist

Circle the appropriate answer on the scale:
"0" = not at all;
"6" = totally yes

1. **Relevant Information Test.** Have we obtained as much information as possible to make an informed decision and action-plan for this situation?

   0 1 2 3 4 5 6

2. **Involvement Test.** Have we involved as many as possible of those who have a right to have input to, or actual involvement in, making this decision and action-plan?

   0 1 2 3 4 5 6

3. **Consequential Test.** Have we attempted to accommodate for the consequences of this decision and action-plan on any who could be significantly affected by it?

   0 1 2 3 4 5 6

4. **Universal Ethical Principles Test.** Does this decision and action-plan uphold the ethical principles that we think are relevant to this situation?

   0 1 2 3 4 5 6

5. **Fairness Test.** If we were any one of the stakeholders in this situation, would we perceive this decision and action-plan to be fair, given all of the circumstances?

   0 1 2 3 4 5 6

6. **Universality Test.** Would we want this decision and action-plan to become "universally applicable" so it would apply to all in similar situations, including ourselves?

   0 1 2 3 4 5 6

7. **Preventative Test.** Does this decision and action-plan prevent or minimize similar situations from happening again?

0 1 2 3 4 5 6

8. **Light-of-day Test.** Can our decision and action-plan stand the test of broad-based public disclosure in which everyone knows everything about both what we decided and how we made the decision?

0 1 2 3 4 5 6

Total Ethical Analysis confidence Score.
Place the total of all circled numbers here.

___ ___ ___ ___ ___ ___ ___

Confidence Score of Planning Values

44–48 Extremely confident (definitely do not need to revise your decision)

39–43 Very confident (probably do not need to revise your decision)

33–38 Somewhat confident (should revise your decision)

24–32 Not very confident (definitely revise your decision)

0–23 Not at all confident (definitely redo your entire analysis)

Source: Copyright © Jon Pekel and Doug Wallace. Used with permission.

Endnotes

1. Hitt et al. (2011) (see references) Trigle & Sirmon (2010) (see references) D. Stipp, "Why Pfizer Is So Hot," *Fortune*, May 11, 1998, p. 88.
2. J. Muller, J. Green, and C. Tierney, "Chrysler's Rescue Team," *BusinessWeek*, January 15, 2001, pp. 48–50.
3. S. Holmes, "GE Little Engines That Could," *BusinessWeek*, January 20, 2003, pp. 62–64; www.ge.com, 2011.
4. www.kodak.com, 2011 L. Grant, "Why Kodak Still Isn't Fixed," *Fortune*, May 11, 1998, pp. 179–181.
5. W. M. Buckeley, "Kodak Swings to $1.03 Billion Loss," *The Wall Street Journal*, December 21, 2005, p. A-1.
6. Ibid.
7. www.gene.com, 2011.
8. www.ge.com, 2011.
9. S. A. Snell, "Control Theory in Strategic Human Resource Management: The Mediating Effect of Administrative Information," *Academy of Management Journal*, 35 (June 1992), 293.
10. Wowak & Hambrich (2010) C. O. O'Reilly "Corporations, Culture and Commitment: Motivation and Social Control in Organizations" *California Management Review*, Summer 1992.
11. *BusinessWeek*, September 17, 1985. Special feature issue on planning.
12. "The Year of the Dot.Bomb," *BusinessWeek*, January 15, 2001, p. 10; www.dotcomfailures.com, www.company.com.forrester research, *BusinessWeek*.
13. Valeen & McNamara (2010) (see references) E. H. Burack, *Creative Human Resource Planning and Applications* (Englewood Cliffs, NJ: Prentice Hall, 1988).
14. D. Welch, "Detroit's Big Steeds Are Losing Traction," *Time*, 2001, pp. 37–40.
15. www.apple.com, 2006.
16. "FedEx, Post Office Combine Deliveries," *The Arizona Republic*, January 12, 2001, p. D1.
17. J. A. Byrne, "How Jack Welch Runs GE," *BusinessWeek*, June 8, 1998 p. 95.
18. A. Barrett, "DuPont Tries to Unclog a Pipeline," *BusinessWeek*, 2003, January 27, pp. 103–104.
19. www.dupont.com, 2006.
20. "FedEx, Post Office Combine," p. D7; Altavista Co.
21. T. Satterfield, "From Performance Management to Performance Leadership," *Worldatwork* 2003, first quarter, *Journal*, pp. 15–20.
22. "Tenet's Bills to Calpers 50% More than Other Hospitals," *Sacramento BEE*, February 3, 2003.

CHAPTER 5 • MANAGING THE PLANNING PROCESS **165**

23. D. W. Jarrell, *Human Resource Planning* (Englewood Cliffs, NJ: Prentice Hall, 1993), p. 73.
24. P. Tsao, "Reports of Cancer's Imminent Death Were an Exaggeration," *BusinessWeek*, June 8, 1998, p. 13.
25. J. Muller, "Thinking out of the Cereal Box," January 15, 2001, pp. 54–55.
26. M. L. Tushman and C. A. O'Reilly III, *Winning through Innovation* (Boston: Harvard Business School Press, 1997).
27. Ibid.
28. Ibid.
29. Ibid.
30. Ibid.

6

Learning Objectives

1. Recognize the nature of management decisions: programmability, uncertainty, risk, conflict, decision scope, and crisis situations.

2. Utilize the six steps of decision making.

3. Apply the criteria of quality and acceptance to a decision.

4. Reap the benefits and avoid the problems of group decision making.

5. Develop time management skills to generate adequate time to make decisions.

6. Know when to delegate, and how to do so wisely.

Google Decides about China

Some management decisions are not only difficult, they are risky and even unpopular, as Yahoo! and Microsoft found when they entered the Internet market in China. To obtain licenses to conduct business there, both companies agreed to the many demands and restrictions placed on their operations by the Chinese government. They have withstood a storm of criticism from rights groups, the media, and a Congressional subcommittee, most of it springing from the results of their decisions. At the request of the Chinese government, Microsoft shut down the blog of a popular and outspoken writer in Beijing. The company also censors words the government considers sensitive, using its blog-hosting software. Yahoo! gave Chinese authorities information about a journalist who had sent outspoken e-mails to a U.S. human rights organization. He and two other dissidents have since been jailed based on the information.

In this uncertain environment, the belated decision by Google, the world's biggest search engine, to finally follow Yahoo! and Microsoft into the Chinese market was a difficult one that entailed a great deal of uncertainty, risk, and conflict. Wall Street analysts approved of the decision, given that with 130 million users, China is second only to the United States in its rate of Internet use and is expected soon to be first by a wide margin. To ignore such a huge market is, many feel, out of the question. Others argue that some

Decision Making

material restricted by Western companies slips by the censors and so does reach Chinese Internet users despite the government's efforts. The companies themselves say that they are less than enthusiastic about the restrictions placed on them, but that human rights conditions in China will not improve without widespread communication. But in spite of these defenses, and the argument that it is providing a service Chinese consumers would not otherwise have, Google has come in for its share of criticism for its decision as well.

Like Yahoo!'s and Microsoft's offerings, Google's Chinese search engine includes a build-in censor to prevent access to content that might be considered politically sensitive by the Chinese government, such as "Falun Gong" (the name of a spiritual movement banned in China) and "multiparty elections." Google also restricts certain news sites and information about democracy. Unlike its competitors, however, Google already hosts a Chinese-language site from a location outside China that it does not censor, though the Chinese government has tried to limit access to it from within the country. Google is also alone in notifying users

when search results have been filtered out, whether by censorship or for any other reason (such as copyright laws). Google has chosen not to introduce e-mail or blogging services, which the Chinese government insists must be heavily controlled when based in China. These products, says Google's senior policy counsel Andrew McLaughlin, "will be introduced only when we are comfortable that we can do so in a way that strikes a proper balance among our commitments to satisfy users' interests, expand access to information, and respond to local conditions."

After operating in China for several years, in 2010 Google considered closing down its operations within China due to several attempts by the Chinese government to hack into Google's email system and ever stronger government censorship of searches.

Sources: *The Economist*, "The Panda Has Two Faces," April 3, 2010, p. 70; Nicholas Kristoff, "China's Cyberdissidents and the Yahoos at Yahoo," *New York Times*, February 19, 2006, p. WK13; Tom Zeller, Jr., "Web Firms Questioned on Dealings in China," *New York Times*, www.nytimes.com, February 16, 2006; Steven Levy, "Google and the China Syndrome," *Newsweek*, February 13, 2006, accessed at http://msnbc.msn.com; and Ben Elgin, "Google's Dicey Dance in China," *BusinessWeek Online*, www.businessweek.com, January 25, 2006.

CRITICAL THINKING QUESTIONS

1. *How would you characterize the nature of Google's decision to enter China in terms of programmability, uncertainty, risk, conflict, and decision scope?*

2. *Did Google approach its decision differently from the way Yahoo! and Microsoft did? What might account for any differences?*

SKILLS FOR MANAGING 6.1

Decision Making

- *Time management skills.* To make good decisions, managers need time to understand the problem and develop creative solutions. They need to be proactive by planning activities and priorities so that enough time is budgeted for the important decisions to be made, and also to become aware of activities that waste time.

- *Delegation skills.* Managers who know how to delegate are able to accomplish more than those who feel the need to be involved in every decision, no matter how trivial. Many managers mistakenly believe that subordinates are not able to make effective decisions. Managers unable to delegate find themselves with too many tasks and decisions and too little time to do everything well.

At the end of the chapter in our Concluding Thoughts, we will revisit the critical thinking questions regarding the decisions made at Google, Yahoo!, and Microsoft.

The world of management in the new millennium is filled with risk and uncertainty. Most of the time, there is a lack of information and a limited amount of time available for managers to make decisions. In some cases, procrastinating and not making a decision (thus sustaining the status quo) takes on greater risk than a proactive change. Each management decision can contribute to or hinder the success of an enterprise. This chapter examines the characteristics of managerial decisions. It identifies the stages that decision makers move through from the beginning to the implementation of the decision. An explanation of group decision making is also provided. Finally, the chapter examines time management and delegation, two skills helpful in the decision-making process. Skills for Managing 6.1. lists the skills managers need to develop for the decision-making process.

■ Characteristics of Management Decision Making

decision making
The process of identifying problems and opportunities and resolving them.

Decision making is the process of identifying problems and opportunities and resolving them or taking advantage of them. Company decisions are made by managers, teams, and individual employees, depending on the scope of the decision and the design and structure of the organization. Organizations with decentralized structures delegate more decisions to teams and front-line employees.

This definition of decision making emphasizes *both* identifying *and* resolving a problem. At Intel, for example, CEO Andy Grove determined that the problem was that competing in the memory chip market was draining resources that could be better deployed in the microprocessor chip market. He made the decision to withdraw from the memory chip market, which entailed closing plants and selling off assets, and to concentrate on microprocessors, which involved investing in expanded facilities.

The characteristics of management decision making include programmability, uncertainty, risk, conflict, scope, and crisis.

Programmability

programmed decision
Identifying a problem and matching the problem with established routines and procedures for resolving it.

Many times, there are established routines and procedures for resolving company problems. These are **programmed decisions**. For example, the job of a retail sales clerk consists primarily of making programmed decisions about stocking shelves, taking sales orders, operating a cash register, and constructing sales displays that attract customers. Well-developed procedures are established for each of these tasks in sales policy and procedure manuals developed by the marketing unit.

nonprogrammed decision
The process of identifying and solving a problem when a situation is unique and there are not previously established routines or procedures that can be used as guides.

A **nonprogrammed decision** occurs when the situation is unique and there are no previously established routines or procedures that can be used. Situations that require nonprogrammed decisions are poorly defined and unstructured, yet they have important consequences for the organization. Managers and professionals who have more knowledge and experience make most nonprogrammed decisions. For example, an outside sales representative with a sales territory and the responsibility for calling on new and continuing customers has a job that requires nonprogrammed decision making. The sales representative must find and call on potential customers, develop rapport with them, determine whether they need the product, and close the sale. Since each customer's needs and financial situation are different, the sales representative must make a series of nonprogrammed decisions.

Nonprogrammed decisions tend to be more important than programmed ones because they are more complicated and difficult to make and are likely to have a greater effect on organization performance. Managers are likely to delegate programmed decisions to subordinates, which frees up more time to make the more difficult nonprogrammed decisions.

Uncertainty

If all the information needed is available, a decision may be made under a condition of **certainty**. An automobile manufacturer plans for annual employee labor costs because the company has a contract with a labor union and knows with complete certainty what employee wage rates will be. Of course, not all the factors affecting businesses can be controlled by a contract. And when contracts expire, there will be uncertainty until the terms of the new contract are finalized.

certainty
The condition when all the information needed to make a decision is available.

Most management decisions are made under varying levels of uncertainty. **Uncertainty** means that incomplete information is available to make a management decision. The decision maker does not know all the alternatives, the risks associated with each, or the outcomes associated with the alternatives. Many important management decisions must be made under high levels of uncertainty. When a company launches a new product, there is uncertainty about whether consumers will buy it. New Coke was rejected by consumers, even though market research gathered prior to the decision revealed that most consumers liked cola that tasted sweeter than traditional Coke.

uncertainty
The condition when the information available to make a management decision is incomplete.

In the network television industry, there is about a one in ten chance that a new prime-time television program will generate sufficient viewer ratings to make a profit. Sometimes television executives must rely on gut instincts because there is little information available. The situation comedy *Seinfeld* generated poor ratings in its first two seasons, but a few executives championed the show and ultimately it became one of NBC's profitable programs.

Risk

The degree of uncertainty about the outcome of a management decision is the degree of **risk**. Under a state of risk, the availability of each alternative and its outcome are associated with probability estimates. For example, medical research provides probability estimates for the risk of survival or mortality after five years of a medical diagnosis of a patient for lung cancer. Risk has both positive and negative aspects. When a manager of mutual funds tries to maximize the profit potential of the fund stock portfolio and minimize the loss potential when the market is falling, the manager copes with both aspects of risk. Many mutual fund managers select some stocks from countercyclical industries, which move in opposite directions in response to market fluctuations, in order to balance the risk by ensuring that all the fund's stocks do not lose value when the economy is declining.

risk
The level of uncertainty as to the outcome of a management decision.

Decision environments for risk vary depending on company culture and size. People who work in entrepreneurial firms must be more comfortable with making risky decisions than people who work in large corporations with established procedures. A high-technology company that must deliver cutting-edge products is likely to promote a culture of risk taking, while a U.S. government agency that can plan cash flow for 25 years into the future based on demographic forecasts, such as the Social Security Administration, is more likely to support a culture of risk avoidance. Companies with risk-taking cultures encourage decision makers to take moderate risks. Such companies even tolerate some failures as part of the learning process. Organizations with risk-avoidance cultures are less tolerant of decision outcomes that result in failure.

Management Is Everyone's Business 6.1 provides some examples of how individuals deal with decision-making risk in everyday life.

Conflict

It is always difficult to get everyone to agree about what to do. Management decision making is often characterized by conflict over opposing goals, utilization of scarce resources, and other priorities. To ensure that the implementation of the decision will go smoothly, effective

MANAGEMENT IS EVERYONE'S BUSINESS 6.1

WORKING AS AN INDIVIDUAL People deal with risk all the time in the decisions they make in everyday life. Here are some examples. When you are trying to decide what form of transportation to take in traveling to a destination, let's say between Chicago and St. Louis, there are risks associated with the choices of airline or automobile travel in regard to arriving safely at your destination. These risks are well known and collected by statisticians who publish rates of human mortality in accidents for insurance companies. If you choose to take a major airline, the chance of a fatal accident is approximately one in 1 million. However, if you choose to drive your car, the chance of a fatal accident goes up to about one in 300,000. Which form of transportation would you choose? What other factors would enter into your decision besides risk?

Another decision that people make all the time is what neighborhood to live in. Local police departments keep crime statistics that are available to residents to help them learn about the incidence of crime in each neighborhood. For example, in some large cities the incidence of crime (burglary, robbery, car theft, etc.) is about 30 percent per year, which means you have a three out of 10 chance of experiencing some form of crime each year. However, the rate of crime usually goes down dramatically for people who live in the outer suburbs of the same city. Suburban residents may have a 2 percent annual rate of crime in their neighborhood, which breaks down to a one in 50 chance of experiencing crime in a given year. Given these risks of experiencing crime where would you choose to live? What other factors would enter into your decision in addition to risk in selecting a neighborhood for your residence?

managers consider many different stakeholders. Otherwise, individuals or groups who are forced to accept a choice they oppose will not be committed to the decision and may even try to undermine it. An important criterion for choosing a decision alternative is its acceptance by key employee groups such as executives, managers, and front-line employees. This is discussed later in the chapter.

Conflict can enhance the quality of a decision by sharply focusing attention on diverse ways of thinking about the consequences of the decision from diverse agendas of the people involved. In other words, various people consider how the decision will affect them. Conflict is managed when individual perspectives are taken into consideration in fashioning the solution. Conflict is examined in greater detail in Chapter 13.

When a decision is being made about research and development funding, the chief financial officer may favor reducing funding because basic research is not expected to produce profits for the firm for six to eight years. At the same time, this executive may prefer to fund applied research that will pay off in two or three years. The chief technical officer in charge of research may strongly disagree with this "short-term" investment perspective and may seek to sustain funding for basic research so that the research pipeline for new products will not dry up. The conflict in this decision is over short-term versus long-term profits.

People who have different stakes and perspectives in a decision related to the expenditure of scarce resources should have a voice in the decision process. In most cases, involving them in the process and working through the differences makes it more likely that they will be committed to the decision outcome, even if it is not one they favored.

decision scope
The effect and time horizon of the decision.

strategic decision
Decisions that have long-term perspective of two to five years and affect the entire organization.

tactical decisions
Decisions that have a short-term perspective of one year or less and focus on subunits of the organization, such as departments or project teams.

Decision Scope

The effect and time horizon of the decision are what is meant by the **decision scope**. The effect of a decision includes who is involved in making the decision and who is affected by it. The time horizon of a decision may range from a single day to five years or more. **Strategic decisions** encompass a long-term perspective of two to five years and affect the entire organization. They include decisions about which product markets should be entered and left, as well as determinations of appropriate firm growth and profitability goals. Top executives are responsible for making strategic decisions.

Tactical decisions have a short-term perspective of one year or less and focus on subunits of the organization, such as departments or project teams. They include determining the distribution of departmental resources for various activities in the departmental budget. Middle managers are most likely to make tactical decisions. Tactical decisions should take into consideration the broader, strategic direction of the firm and be supportive of it.

Operational decisions cover the shortest time perspective, generally less than a year. They are often made on a daily or weekly basis and focus on the routine activities of the firm such as production, customer service, and handling parts and supplies. Supervisors, teams, and front-line employees are involved in operational decisions. Operational decisions must take into consideration both the long-term perspective of the strategic decisions and the shorter-term perspective of tactical decisions.

operational decisions
Decisions with a short time perspective, generally less than a year, and that often are measured on a daily or weekly basis.

Crisis Situations

Decision making during crisis is more challenging and difficult than under ordinary conditions. Crisis situations include: (1) highly ambiguous circumstances in which causes and effects are not known, (2) rare and extraordinary events that can threaten the survival of an organization, (3) an event in which there is a small amount of time to respond, (4) a surprise to organizational members that takes place, or (5) dilemmas in need of decisions that will result in change for better or worse.[1] A decision during crisis is likely to have the characteristics of risk, uncertainty, and non-programmability. Examples of crisis would include a hostile takeover of a company, a product defect discovered that is harmful to consumers, a work stoppage by organized labor, a natural disaster that disrupts the company's ability to provide service to customers, or a terrorist attack—such as what happened in New York City on September 11, 2001. See Management Close-Up 6.1 for a description of decisions made by UPS after 9/11.

After Hurricane Katrina struck the Gulf Coast in August 2005, there were shortages of food and fresh water and outages of power and telephone communication affecting millions of residents. Despite suffering shutdowns of 126 stores in the Gulf Coast region due to this disaster, Wal-Mart used its Emergency Operations Center at its Bentonville, Arkansas, headquarters to oversee the distribution by its company trucks of hundreds of thousands of cases of bottled water, food, and emergency generators into the stricken region to spearhead relief efforts. The Wal-Mart trucks arrived days ahead of the relief efforts of the Federal Emergency Management Agency (FEMA), which was criticized for its slow response to the crisis caused by Hurricane Katrina. The company donated $17 million in cash to support these efforts. Wal-Mart also offered jobs to 97 percent of the employees who were displaced and jobless due to the storm, and they were offered employment at any Wal-Mart store in the country.[2]

MANAGEMENT CLOSE-UP 6.1   THEME: **CUSTOMER FOCUS**

How UPS Managed to Deliver During the 9/11 Crisis

Many crisis decisions were made following the September 11, 2001, terrorist attacks at the World Trade Center in New York City and at the Pentagon in Arlington, VA. As the attacks took place, airborne aircraft were advised to land at the nearest airport, and subway trains that were headed toward the World Trade Center were halted, thereby saving thousands of lives. Thousands of people were evacuated from buildings close to ground zero. United Parcel Service (UPS), the package delivery service company, went into crisis management mode shortly after the attack. With all air traffic grounded, Joe Liana, UPS's Manhattan district manager, called in all employees to report to UPS's package sorting facility to identify high-priority packages such as medical supplies that were time sensitive. He ordered drivers to make 200 truck deliveries to hospitals, doctors, and pharmacies. Joe and other district managers had been given a great deal of autonomy to make decisions in their districts by UPS top management.

During the days immediately after the attacks UPS set up a crisis management plan to deliver more packages by truck because air travel was prohibited, and nobody knew when air transportation

would resume. UPS vice chairman Michael L. Eskew decided to transfer packages designated for aircraft to trucks when they met certain criteria. A package needed to be able to be delivered within three days by truck in order to avoid overwhelming the truck operations' ability to deliver. Eskew gambled that aircraft operations would be resumed within one week. This turned out to be a correct assumption. As a result of UPS's crisis-management decisions, the company was able to resume package delivery operations quickly, without losing market share.

The key decisions made at UPS were: (1) empowering local district managers to handle a crisis on their own, and (2) holding back from the ground delivery system any air packages that would have taken more than three days to deliver.

Sources: Based on C. Haddad, "How UPS Delivered through the Disaster," *BusinessWeek,* October 1, 2001, p. 66; J. Bram, J. Orr, and C. Rappaport, "Measuring the September 11 Attack on New York City," *Economic Policy Review,* November 2002, pp. 5–20.

LOC-In 1 · Learning Objective Check-In

1. Jack's work team recently made an important decision regarding the product line they are working on. The team had conducted several rounds of market research, including focus groups and other marketing techniques, to gauge if the product would be well received or not. The decision the team made was to launch the product in each key geographic region of the country within two months. However, because information available to make the decision to launch or not is still incomplete, there remains a moderate degree of _____.
   a. programmability
   b. uncertainty
   c. leadership
   d. crisis

2. The decision the work team made has a high degree of _____ for the company.
   a. programmed decision
   b. risk
   c. decision scale
   d. conflict

Making a decision in a crisis situation can make or break the career of a manager. When he became the CEO of IBM in 1993, Lou Gerstner decided to focus IBM on providing services to customers at a time of crisis when the survival of the company was at stake. The decision to change IBM's strategic focus by shifting its emphasis from making hardware to delivering services proved to be successful and a career-making move for Gerstner.[3]

◼ Stages of Decision Making

Decision making is a six-step process. The stages, which are summarized in Figure 6.1, are (1) identifying and diagnosing the problem; (2) generating alternative solutions; (3) evaluating alternatives; (4) choosing the best alternative; (5) implementing the decision; and (6) evaluating the results. The six-step decision-making process we present assumes a *rational process* with abundant information available to the decision makers. Later in the chapter we will add complexity to the decision-making process by relaxing the assumption of rationality.

Identifying and Diagnosing the Problem

The first stage of decision making is identifying and diagnosing a problem or opportunity. An *opportunity* is a special type of problem that requires committing resources in order to improve company performance. A *problem* occurs when performance is below expected or desired levels of performance. Typical problems include:

- A high level of employee turnover.
- A reduction in firm profits.
- Unacceptable levels of "shrinkage" in a store (employee theft).
- Low-quality finished goods.
- An increase in workplace injuries.
- The invention of a new technology that would increase the productivity of the workforce.

Once a problem has been recognized, the decision maker begins to look for the causes of the problem. This requires gathering information, exploring possible causes, eliminating as many causes as possible, and then focusing on the most probable causes. For example, a manager who observes a high level of employee turnover first gathers information to diagnose the problem and

FIGURE 6.1

The Stages of Decision Making

Identifying and diagnosing the problem → Generating alternative solutions → Evaluating alternatives → Choosing the best alternative → Implementing the decision → Evaluating the results then attempts to understand why the turnover is occurring. Some possible causes of turnover are job dissatisfaction with unchallenging and repetitive work, below-market pay rates, job stress, opportunities for better jobs in the labor market, and conflicts between work and family obligations. It is important to fully diagnose the problem before attempting to solve it. If the real cause of turnover is work and family conflicts due to inflexible work schedules and the manager assumes that it was caused by inadequate compensation and raised employee pay as a solution, the manager may not have solved the problem.

Generating Alternative Solutions

The second step is to generate possible solutions to the problem based on the perceived causes. Some problems can be solved using programmed solutions, when there are readymade answers. Novel situations require nonprogrammed decisions because there are no policies or procedures available to provide direction.

In the case of nonprogrammed decision making, it is important to come up with creative alternative solutions and to suspend judgment of their worth until all possible alternatives have been developed. If solutions are evaluated too soon during the second stage of decision making, creativity can be stifled, resulting in lower-quality solutions. Many companies use groups to generate solutions for nonprogrammed decisions because they provide a greater diversity of opinions and more innovative solutions than do people working individually. Consequently, group decision making is often used to develop continuous improvements in customer service to generate novel solutions to customer needs.

LOC-In   2   Learning Objective Check-In

1. Write Smart Co. has a very specific decision-making process that it follows for handling client problems that has been quite successful for the firm. The first stage, in which the team members at Write Smart help the client figure out exactly what the problem is that it faces, is _____.
   a. identifying and diagnosing the problem
   b. evaluating the results
   c. generating alternative solutions
   d. implementing the decision

2. Then, based on the perceived causes of the problem, the firm _____.
   a. chooses the best alternative
   b. evaluates the results of the decision
   c. generates alternative solutions
   d. identifies and diagnoses the problem

3. After making a decision, the final, and perhaps most important, step for Write Smart is to help clients recognize ways to _____. Based on this, the client may choose to pursue some modifications, which Write Smart can also help them do.
   a. choose the best alternative
   b. generate alternative solutions
   c. implement the decision
   d. evaluate the results of the decision

Evaluating Alternatives

The third stage requires the decision maker to examine the alternative solutions using a set of decision criteria. The decision criteria should be related to the performance goals of the organization and its subunits and can include costs, profits, timeliness, whether the decision will work, and fairness.

A practical way to apply decision criteria is to consider quality and acceptance. **Decision quality** is based on such facts as costs, revenues, and product design specifications. For example, a technical engineering problem can be solved by gathering data and using mathematical techniques. **Decision acceptance** is based on people's feelings. Decision acceptance happens when people who are affected by a decision agree with what is to be done.[4]

decision quality
The aspect of decision making that is based on such facts as costs, revenues, and product design specifications.

decision acceptance
The aspect of decision making that is based on people's feelings; decision acceptance happens when people who are affected by a decision agree with what is to be done.

Decisions can be classified by how important quality and acceptance are to their effectiveness. Some technical decisions require a high degree of quality but low acceptance, since people may be indifferent to the outcome. Buying raw materials at the best price is an example of a decision where quality is important but acceptance is not. An expert buyer of raw materials can make this decision. Other decisions place a high emphasis on acceptance, while quality is not important. High-acceptance, low quality decisions involve fairness issues, such as: Who will work the overtime hours? Who gets the office with the window? The important point in such decisions is not who gets to work overtime, but how people feel about the outcome and if they are willing to accept it.

The most difficult decisions require high quality and high acceptance. The decision to close an automobile assembly plant and lay off employees is an example. Decision quality requires a reduction of labor costs, but acceptance requires the support of the labor union so that it will not call a strike to protest the layoff, resulting in even greater losses to the firm. The decision maker must find ways to balance conflicting goals in this type of problem. Figure 6.2 presents a *decision tree,* a diagnostic tool that can be used to evaluate different decision alternatives. The figure shows a decision that is evaluated according to three decision criteria that must be satisfied: *feasibility,* quality, and acceptance. Decision feasibility seeks an answer to the question: Is it *practical* to make this decision? All decisions must first of all pass the test of *feasibility.* For example, a decision alternative in the example of the automotive plant that might meet all other criteria to fire the CEO and replace him with another person might not be feasible. In the decision tree presented in Figure 6.2, satisfactory levels of both quality and acceptance are needed once feasibility is determined. The decision to close an automobile plant and lay off the workforce could be evaluated with the help of the decision tree in Figure 6.2.

LOC-In 3 Learning Objective Check-In

Carrie wants to know whether or not the people who are affected by her recent decision to distribute overtime evenly across the work unit agree with her decision. She is not as concerned with the various costs associated with the decision, because all of the team members will receive very similar pay for the overtime hours worked.

1. Carrie's concern about the people who are affected reflects a question concerning _____.
   a. leadership
   b. decision quality
   c. decision control
   d. decision acceptance

2. The aspect of this decision making that focuses on the costs associated with evenly distributed overtime reflects _____.
   a. decision quality
   b. decision acceptance
   c. decision control
   d. decision measurement

FIGURE 6.2

Evaluating Alternatives in the Decision Making Process

Managers must thoroughly evaluate all the alternatives, which improves the probability that the alternative that is selected will be successful. Failure to evaluate an alternative according to all the decision criteria can result in a bad decision. The *decision tree* shown here is a diagnostic tool that aids the process of evaluating alternatives.

Choosing the Best Alternative

The next stage of decision making is the selection of the best alternative by either optimizing or satisficing. **Optimizing** involves selecting the best alternative from among multiple criteria. For example, assume the decision criteria used to select an individual to fill a vacancy consists of technical job knowledge, previous work experience, and leadership skills. Further, assume that it will take six months to be able to generate a large enough applicant pool to be able to find the best person to fill the job. The optimizing solution is available when the benefits of reaching the solution outweigh the costs. However, most of the time, the costs of keeping a job vacant for six months to find the optimizing solution are not worth the effort. Therefore, the optimizing approach would not be applied. Also, many important decisions must be made under conditions of risk, which constrain the ability of the decision maker to optimize.

Satisficing involves selecting the first alternative solution that meets a minimum criterion. Decision makers satisfice when complete information is not available or gathering it is too expensive. Satisficing means that the decision maker has found an acceptable if not optimal solution. For example, when selecting a new employee to fill a job vacancy, many organizations make a job offer to the first person who meets the basic selection criteria, rather than engaging in an extensive search for the best possible candidate, which takes more time and money.

Implementing the Decision

Putting the alternative solution into practice and making sure it works is the next step of decision making. Implementation requires the decision maker to put the solution into practice. Decision making without implementation is simply an intellectual exercise.

Implementation is a critical step because it requires the support and cooperation of executives, managers, and employees who may have different interests and goals. For example, a manager's decision to hire a minority group employee to fill a job vacancy under a corporate diversity plan may not be effectively implemented if other employees resent and avoid working with the employee. An important aspect of managing and implementing diversity is to train employees to value diversity so they are supportive of the plan's goals. The omission of training could lead to poor implementation. (See Chapter 11 for more information on implementing a corporate diversity plan.)

Several factors help make implementation successful. They include:

■ Providing resources, such as staff, budgets, and office space, that will be needed for successful implementation.
■ Exercising leadership to persuade others to move the implementation forward.
■ Developing communication and information systems that enable management to know if the decision alternative is meeting its planned objectives.
■ Considering ways to recognize and reward individuals and teams that successfully put the decision alternative into practice.[5]

Trader Joe's, the quirky and highly popular retailer of unusual foodstuffs like antioxidant trail mix, wild blueberry juice, and dark-chocolate covered espresso beans, extends its mystique by keeping many of its business practices under wraps. But a special tasting panel at the company's California headquarters meets regularly to evaluate new products, tasting several different varieties of each and offering frank opinions. Doug Rauch, company president, credits the process with helping Trader Joe's sell products that are "addictive" rather than just good.

optimizing
Selecting the best alternative from among multiple criteria.

satisficing
Selecting the first alternative solution that meets a minimum criterion.

Evaluating the Results

The final stage in the decision-making process is to evaluate the results. Decision makers gather information and try to learn if the implemented decision achieved its goals. The availability of accurate and timely information and feedback permits the decision maker to make a thorough evaluation and to determine whether modifications are needed.

Decision makers need to establish reasonable goals and benchmarks to make sound judgments about the effectiveness of the decision. It is also important to allow enough time for a decision to take effect. An executive collecting productivity data on a new manufacturing plant would be foolish to immediately judge its effectiveness without giving plant management time to eliminate the production bottlenecks that are typical in new manufacturing plants. It would be better to suspend

---

MANAGER'S NOTEBOOK 6.1

Pitfalls in the Decision-Making Process

Here are some pitfalls that decision makers need to know about. These pitfalls can result in low-quality decisions or poor implementation of the decision alternative. By following each stage of decision making in the correct sequence, managers can avoid many of them.

1. *Solution focus.* Time pressures often lead decision makers to shoot from the hip without taking enough time to thoroughly diagnose and understand the management problem in all its complexity. Unless all factors causing a system to be out of control are identified, proposed solutions to the problem are not likely to be responsive to the true problem.

2. *Premature evaluation.* The temptation is always present to evaluate and judge alternatives as they are being developed and expressed by peers, subordinates, or the decision maker. Idea generation is a creative process that can be stifled and frustrated by managers who pronounce early judgment when an alternative solution is suggested. A deeply flawed idea can inspire others to come up with novel solutions that may not be expressed unless people feel free to think creatively, without worrying about others judging them for their creative ideas.

3. *The "If it isn't broke, don't fix it" syndrome.* This bias favors programmed solutions based on what worked in the past, even though that may no longer be relevant to the present or future. In a business environment of changing customer needs, decisions that favor what satisfied customers in the past are not likely to meet current and future customer expectations.

4. *Bias toward objective data.* In environments of high uncertainty, decision makers may give a high priority to objective data. For example, data on viewer behavior is collected by market research analysts for a pilot television program. Such data, however, are not likely to be useful for making accurate predictions of program success when the new program is very different from others, such as *The Sopranos*.

5. *Overlooking important constituencies.* The decision maker should identify the diverse groups within (and sometimes outside) the organization that are likely to have strong feelings about the decision outcome and solicit their input.

---

judgment until plant personnel learn the best ways to operate the equipment and develop routines to work well together. The pitfalls associated with decision making are summarized in Manager's Notebook 6.1.

■ The Limits of Rational Decision Making

It is a major leap of faith to assume that all decision making is rational. It is not. This is because rational decision making is based on the following assumptions:

- The problem is clear and unambiguous.
- There is a single, well-defined goal that all parties agree to.
- Full information is available.
- All the alternatives and their consequences are known.
- The decision preferences are clear.
- The decision preferences are constant and stable over time.
- There are no time and cost constraints affecting the decision.
- The decision solution will maximize the economic payoff.[6]

Many decisions are complex and are made in situations where these assumptions do not apply. There are several factors that limit rational decision making. They include organization politics, emotions and personal preferences, the illusion of control, intuition, and escalation of commitment. By being aware of these biases, decision makers can improve the quality of their decisions.

Organization Politics

coalitions
Political alliances between managers who agree on goals and priorities.

organization politics
The exercise of power in an organization to control resources and influence policy.

Organizations are likely to have **coalitions**, which are political alliances between employees who agree on goals and priorities. Various coalitions may disagree about alternatives for a decision, and an executive or leader may need to exercise power and influence to build a consensus between diverse coalitions. **Organization politics** involves the exercise of power in an organization to

The Decision to Build the Sensor Razor at Gillette

Organization politics can influence key company decisions and affect a firm's welfare, for better or worse, as in Gillette's development of its Sensor razor. Although the Sensor was fabulously successful when it was released to the market, it came close to being a very different product due to a disagreement over its product design.

The Gillette Company's British research facility spent 13 years developing the idea behind the Sensor razor. The idea was to create a thinner razor blade that would make Gillette cartridges easier to clean. The cost for the product's research and development reached $200 million.

The technical demands of building a razor with thin blades and floating parts that could follow the contours of a man's face led researchers up several blind alleys. They tried established techniques, but none filled the bill. They tried innovative ideas, such as setting the blades on tiny rubber tubes, perhaps filled with fluid, but these ideas proved too costly and complicated to manufacture. Eventually Gillette came up with a prototype. The 500 men who tested it liked it, and the product was put into production.

The Sensor's next problems involved manufacturing and product placement. Because of the razor's innovative design, an entirely new manufacturing process was needed to laser-weld each blade to a support. Gillette management approved developing the new manufacturing equipment, but two groups of executives disagreed on the final product. One group wanted to produce and market a razor that was lightweight, expensive, and disposable; the other faction thought the product should be a heavier, more permanent razor with replaceable blades. When Gillette was threatened by an outside takeover, it reduced the resources allocated to the Sensor project. A new executive vice president made the decision to deemphasize razors that were disposable, so the Sensor's final form was determined.

The Sensor razor has been an unqualified success. It was quickly embraced by consumers, and Gillette recovered its huge investment in record time.

Gillette's decision process for the Sensor began because executives became aware of the potential for a new razor with floating, thin blades. Leaders proceeded with a trial-and-error custom design. When some alternatives were found unacceptable, Gillette returned to earlier steps until a workable product was created.

At Gillette, there is no such thing as getting ahead of oneself. New products go on the drawing board as much as a decade before they are introduced. Months before the Sensor was launched in 1994, the company already was working on its successor: the Mach 3 shaving system, a blend of leading-edge technology and relentless consumer testing, took seven years and $750 million to develop.

Sources: Based on R. L. Daft, *Leadership: Theory and Practice*, Fort Worth: Dryden Press, 1999, pp. 467–468; G. Rifkin, "Mach 3: Anatomy of Gillette's Latest Global Launch," *Journal of Strategy and Business*, 2nd quarter, 1999, www.strategy-business.com.

control resources and influence policy. Organization politics is more likely to be present in firms with democratic cultures where power is decentralized and decisions are made through consensus.

Decisions based on political coalitions do not always favor the most rational solution. Sometimes they favor the solution that sustains the power of the top executive or dominant individual or group. For example, an executive may provide resources to a coalition of managers to obtain their support on an important decision. Still, there are times in which organization politics can lead to a successful decision, as shown in Management Close-Up 6.2.

Emotions and Personal Preferences

Decision makers are not robots choosing alternatives without emotion or passion. Many times a poor decision is reached because the decision maker is having a bad day. The two emotions that are the most disruptive to quality decision making are anger and depression. An angry person is not going to look at an issue clearly, nor is someone who is depressed.

Personal preferences include a variety of individual quirks. For example, a manager who hates the idea of going into debt, both personally and in his or her company, will make decisions that may or may not benefit the company. Or the opposite may be true. The same is true for someone who enjoys taking risks as opposed to someone who is risk-averse. It is vital to make certain the person or group making a decision is not swayed by an individual agenda or pattern of decision making.

Greed is an emotion that drove bank executives to take risks that wreaked havoc on the financial services industry in 2008. Financial executives at the largest U.S. banks decided to buy securities that contained sub-prime mortgages, which turned out to be toxic investments that threatened the survival of the banks, which had made large bets on these securities. The bankers decided to buy these risky securities because other banks were making easy profits buying and selling them and the bankers did not want to miss out on earning generous bonuses from the expected profits. The emotion of greed blinded the bankers to the true risks of purchasing the sub-prime mortgages.[7]

Illusion of Control

illusion of control
The tendency for decision makers to be overconfident of their ability to control activities and events.

Another limitation of rational decision making results from the **illusion of control**, which is the tendency for a decision maker to be overconfident of his or her ability to control activities and events. Top executives are especially susceptible to this problem, because they can be isolated from the rank and file employees and may be surrounded with "yes men."

A good example of the illusion of control was the decision by President Richard Nixon to cover a break-in of Democratic party headquarters in the Watergate building by Republican party operatives during the 1972 presidential election. Nixon assumed he could control public perception of the incident because he was the president. The cover up turned out to be a disastrous error and ultimately led to talk of impeachment and Nixon's resignation from office in 1974.

Intuition and Escalation of Commitment

Intuition and escalation of commitment are two other factors that limit the rational decision-making process.

intuition
When a decision maker depends on gut feelings or innate beliefs as a basis for making a decision.

INTUITION When a decision maker depends on a gut feeling or innate belief about something and acts on it, then **intuition** is the basis for the decision. The feelings that lead to intuition are based on years of experience in making decisions in similar situations. These repeated occurences form patterns that are recognized by the decision maker when a new situation occurs that matches an earlier experience and is recognized to have similar properties. For example, a pilot of a commercial jet airplane who experiences a pocket of severe air turbulence may depend on intuition for his decision on how to maneuver the aircraft based on pattern recognition from previous experiences in dealing with turbulence.

In a recent book titled *Blink: The Power of Thinking without Thinking,* author Malcolm Gladwell explains that decision makers who must make quick decisions depend on their intuition by using a process called *thin slicing,* which focuses attention on a few factors to make a critical decision while filtering out a lot of other data that may be present.[8] A police officer who encounters a person in a dark alley that he suspects of committing a crime will depend on interpreting a few key factors such as body posture (is it aggressive or submissive?), facial expression (friendly or hostile?), position of hands (out in open or going for something in the pocket?) that influence how the officer responds to the situation. An officer's intuition based on previous experience related to how a threatening suspect would act affects whether an officer will draw a firearm and shoot the suspect or not. A mistake at reading the signals of the key variables could be tragic for the suspect and the officer. Sometimes useful data has been filtered out of the decision process when intuition is the basis for a decision resulting in a poor outcome. In the example of the police officer who encounters a suspect that matches the profile of a dangerous criminal, the officer may give a verbal command to the suspect to put his hands in the air, which the suspect may ignore, which may trigger an intuitive response from the officer to take out his gun and fire. The reason for the suspect's not responding to the officer's command might in fact be that he did not speak English and did not understand the police officer's order. If the officer does not somehow check out this fact, the officer's intuition may lead him to make a bad decision.

When a victim of a car crash is brought into the emergency room (ER), the doctor depends on intuition to quickly size up the patient's prognosis for survival by focusing on monitoring a few of the patient's vital signs such as blood pressure, temperature, or control of blood flowing from an open wound, and then must make a quick decision regarding which medical procedure to use to improve the patient's chance for survival. Medical training requires that a resident ER physician spend many hours at the hospital to build a reservoir of experience that can be used as basis for making intuitive medical decisions that require quick interventions.

Intuition depends heavily on there being a correspondence between a manager's past experiences and the current situations that require decision making. Intuition is less reliable for managers who lack experience or find themselves in a situation that is so unique that it cannot be compared to past experiences.

escalation of commitment
The refusal to abandon an earlier decision even when it is no longer appropriate, which happens because the decision maker is highly committed to a course of action and wants to stay the course.

ESCALATION OF COMMITMENT When a decision maker has made a past choice, and in hindsight it no longer appears to be valid, the decision maker may be in denial of new information that could lead to a different course of action. The refusal to abandon a choice from an earlier decision even when it is no longer appropriate from a rational decision-making perspective is called **escalation of commitment,** sometimes referred to as a *sunk-cost trap.*[9] This happens when a decision maker becomes so committed to a course of action that she or he decides to stay the course even when it appears to have been wrong. All this may do is make things worse when the decision maker allocates more resources to a goal that is not likely to pay off.

In banking, escalation of commitment shows up in decision making with disturbing regularity and can have dire consequences. A borrower's business can run into trouble, and the banker who made the loan will often advance additional funds in the hopes of providing the business with some extra time to recover and pay back the loan. If the business has a good probability of being turned around, this may be a sound decision. Otherwise, it is just throwing good money after bad.[10]

The harmful effects of escalation of commitment on decisions can be managed by having trusted advisors who were uninvolved with earlier decisions give honest views to the decision maker. Also cultivating a company culture that tolerates mistakes when it is possible to learn from them reduces the fear decision makers have of exposing their mistakes to the criticism of others.

Management Is Everyone's Business 6.2 explains how to avoid another barrier to the decision-making process, which is procrastination.

■ Nonrational Decision-Making Models

The actual conditions for most decisions tend to be complex and most decisions occur under conditions of uncertainty, often falling short of satisfying the assumptions of rational decision making. *Nonrational decision-making* models have been developed for these situations. Nonrational decision-making models assume that information-gathering and processing limitations make it difficult for managers to make optimal decisions. Two nonrational decision-making approaches are the administrative model and the garbage can model.

Administrative Model

Herbert Simon, a Nobel prize-winning economist, points out that even if all the necessary information is available to make a decision, many managers cannot completely absorb and evaluate the information appropriately.[11] The *administrative model* of decision making, developed by Herbert Simon, describes how decisions are actually made by managers and assumes the information available is incomplete and imperfect, a condition that most managers experience in reality. These insights led to his concept of *bounded rationality*. Bounded rationality means that the ability of a manager to be perfectly rational is limited by factors such as cognitive capacity and time constraints. A decision maker's perceptions about the relative importance of various aspects of data may cause him or her to overlook or ignore some important information.[12] Moreover, the human memory can retain and process only a limited amount of information at one time. Consequently, decision makers apply *heuristics,* or decision rules, that quickly eliminate alternatives. For example, when a manager says, "We can't afford to hire any more people," that manager has applied a decision rule that eliminates a variety of options.

As a result, managers do not assess every potential alternative. Instead, by using the heuristic known as *satisficing,* a manager seeks out the first decision alternative that appears to be

An agreement between Snapple and New York City to sell Snapple in city-owned buildings, including City Hall, pictured here, fell far short of its goal to generate $66 million in cash and $60 million worth of marketing and tourism promotion. In spite of the deficit, the city agreed to renegotiate the innovative but widely criticized agreement, lowering its sales goals and investing more funds in promoting the partnership.

MANAGEMENT IS EVERYONE'S BUSINESS 6.2

WORKING AS A MANAGER A major barrier to decision making is procrastination. Managers wait until the last minute to make decisions because of inertia, too many interruptions, improperly classifying a decision as simple and low priority, hoping that the need for the decision will go away, or having insufficient information and being afraid of deciding to do the wrong thing. As a manager you need to establish *clear priorities* and determine which of your activities produces the greatest value. Then you should set dates for the completion of these activities. Setting priorities forces you as a manager to make decisions and helps control procrastination.

satisfactory. Satisficing is an accurate representation of many management decisions. This is because the cost of delaying a decision or searching for a better solution is outweighed by the benefits of quickly finding a satisfactory solution. For example, a home owner is satisficing when she makes a decision to sign a contract with a company to paint her house after taking only three bids. The decision rule is to consider only the quality of materials, cost, and time needed to complete the job. Choosing a satisfactory bid to paint the house without seeking the optimal solution (the best of all possible painters) is satisficing.

Garbage Can Model

Managers often behave in a random pattern when making decisions. The *garbage can* model suggests that managers have a set of preestablished solutions to problems located in "garbage cans."[13] If such a solution to a problem appears to be satisfactory or appropriate, it is applied to the problem.[14] This means that managers have some preselected solutions or skills for which they are searching for problems to "fix."

The garbage can model is likely to be used when decision makers are undisciplined and have no clear immediate goals. As a result, the decision-making process lacks structure. While the garbage can model can sometimes result in a desirable outcome, it can also lead to serious difficulties. For example, for several generations the Bronfman family owned and managed Seagram's, a highly profitable manufacturer and distributor of whiskies and other alcoholic drinks. Edgar Bronfman, the son of Seagram's CEO, persuaded his father to buy Universal Pictures, a Hollywood movie studio, because Edgar had previously financed and produced a few independent movies and had friends in the entertainment industry. Bronfman assumed he possessed the skills to run a major studio. Ultimately, neither Edgar Bronfman nor Seagram's management displayed the ability needed to effectively operate a movie business. The company was forced to sell the studio while taking a huge loss that resulted in a dramatic reversal of fortune for the Bronfman family.

■ Personal Decision-Making Styles

Managers go about making decisions in different ways. The differences between how managers approach problems and make decisions are referred to as personal *decision styles.* There are four categories of decision styles: directive, analytical, conceptual, and behavioral.[15]

1. The *directive style* is used when a manager perceives a clear and simple solution to a problem. It is used when a manager prefers to avoid dealing with a lot of information and may consider only a few alternatives. The decision maker using this style tends to be efficient and rational and relies on existing rules and procedures for making decisions.
2. The *analytical style* is used by managers who prefer to gather as much data as possible before they make a decision. The decision maker considers more alternatives than a directive style and bases the decision on a rational and objective analysis of data gathered from different sources in order to make the best possible decision from the information that is available.
3. The *conceptual style* is used by managers who tend to be very broad in their outlook and examine many alternatives. Unlike the analytical style, the person who uses the conceptual style prefers to discuss the problem and alternatives with other people. Decision makers using this style rely on information from both people and systems and prefer to solve problems creatively.
4. The *behavioral style* is used by managers who place a high priority on other people's concerns and talk to them about how they feel about the problem and the effect of the decision on them. The decision maker is also concerned about the personal development of other people and how involvement in the decision process may help them achieve their goals.

Managers are most likely to choose among different decision styles depending on the type of decision that is being made. For example, with a programmed decision such as filling out a customer's product order, a manager is likely to select a directive style, and for a nonprogrammed decision a manager could choose from among the analytical, conceptual, and behavioral styles. However, most managers have a dominant decision style. For example, former U.S. President

Bill Clinton enjoyed sifting through a lot of data and considered many alternatives before making a decision, which suggests an analytical style, while former U.S. President Ronald Reagan liked to make decisions according to his values and intuition by considering fewer alternatives, which resembles the directive style of decision making.

■ Decision Making in Groups

When employee acceptance of a decision is important, it is usually necessary to involve a group of employees in the decision-making process. For example, the department chair organizes a recruitment committee to participate in the decision to hire a new professor in a university department. This is done because acceptance by colleagues is critical; all promotions and performance evaluations are performed by committees of peers in universities. Hiring decisions at law, accounting, and consulting firms also require input from groups of junior and senior colleagues. These professionals often work in cooperative teams to serve clients and expect to have a voice in selecting new organizational members. Committees, task forces, or teams can be the basis for a group decision.

The Benefits and Problems of Group Decision Making

Group decision making has several advantages as well as problems, which are displayed in Table 6.1. Group decisions can improve both the quality and the acceptance of a decision. By involving people in the process, management allows them to examine all the alternatives and criteria, opening the door for deeper understanding of the rationale for the alternative that was selected, and increasing the likelihood that they will accept and be committed to the decision. Groups tap a greater pool of knowledge and provide more diverse perspectives than any single individual could generate acting alone. Group decision making is also beneficial because it provides the opportunity for employees with less experience with group activities to learn how to cope with group dynamics by actually being involved.

The problems associated with group decision making arise from bringing people with different interests together. Dominant individuals or factions may intimidate others into agreeing with

TABLE 6.1 Benefits and Problems of Group Decision Making

Benefits	Problems
Increased acceptance. Those who play an active role in group decision making and problem solving tend to view the outcome as "ours" rather than "theirs"	*Social pressure.* Unwillingness to "rock the boat" and pressure to conform may combine to stifle the creativity of individual contributors.
Greater pool of knowledge. A group can bring much more information and experience to bear on a decision or problem than an individual acting alone.	*Minority domination.* Sometimes the quality of group action is reduced when the group gives in to those who talk the loudest and longest.
Different perspectives. Individuals with varied experience and interests help the group see decision situations and problems from different angles.	*Logrolling.* Political wheeling and dealing can displace sound thinking when an individual's pet project or vested interest is at stake.
Greater comprehension. Those who personally experience the give-and-take of group discussion about alternative courses of action tend to understand the rationale behind the final decision.	*Goal displacement.* Sometimes secondary considerations such as winning an argument, making a point, or getting back at a rival displace the primary task of making a sound decision or solving a problem.
Training ground. Less experienced participants in group action learn how to cope with group dynamics by actually being involved.	*"Groupthink."* Sometimes cohesive "in-groups" let the desire for unanimity override sound judgment when generating and evaluating alternative courses of action.

MANAGEMENT IS EVERYONE'S BUSINESS 6.3

WORKING AS A TEAM   Teams can rely too heavily on team meetings to make decisions, resulting in wasted time. Although meetings are important for building trust in the early stages of team formation, they can be an inefficient way to use time and frustrate people if they are used indiscriminately. By assigning tasks to subgroups or individual team members and giving them responsibility for decision making associated with these tasks, a team should be able to manage its workflow so that meetings are reserved for critical decisions or events that genuinely require the presence of all members.

---

groupthink
Valuing social harmony over doing a thorough job.

their goals. The group may be unwilling to deal with conflict and come to a quick settlement in order to keep the peace. Hidden agendas (such as a self-promoting individual's use of the group as a captive audience), political deal making, and **groupthink** (valuing social harmony over doing a thorough job) can all lead to low-quality decision outcomes unless the group decision process is managed by a leader who can protect the group from these problems.

One of the limiting factors in group decision making is time. The group requires sufficient time to go through all six stages of decision making in sequence. If time for decision making is limited, it may be better for a manager to make the decision alone and then attempt to persuade others to abide by it. Management Is Everyone's Business 6.3 suggests how teams can be more productive in their use of time devoted to team meetings.

Managing Group Decision Making

A leader must work to minimize the potential problems listed in Table 6.1. Some ways to ensure that quality decisions are made by groups include adapting leadership style, assuming the devil's advocate role, and using various decision-making techniques to stimulate creativity.

LEADERSHIP STYLE   A group leader can adapt his or her style to the requirements of the problem. Table 6.2 shows five different decision-making styles that leaders may select from, depending on the need for decision quality and acceptance, the time available, and leader and subordinate skills and competencies.

TABLE 6.2 Leader Decision-Making Styles

Decision-Making Style	Characteristics	Amount of Subordinate Participation
Decide and persuade	Leader solves the problem and makes decision with available information	None
Discover facts and decide	Leader gathers facts from subordinates and then makes the decision	Very little; indirect involvement
Consult and decide	Leader consults with individual subordinates, obtaining their ideas and opinions, and then makes the decision	Modest amount of participation through being presented with the problem by the leader
Consult with group and decide	Leader consults with group of subordinates, gathering their collective ideas, and then makes the decision	Substantial amount of participation by being engaged in the group discussion of the problem
Group decision	Leader shares problem with group and accepts the decision made by the group, acting as a coach to the group decision-making process	High involvement of subordinates in the decision-making process

Sources: Based on V. H. Vroom and A. G. Jago, *The New Leadership: Managing Participation in Organizations,* Englewood Cliffs, NJ: Prentice Hall, 1988; R. L. Daft, *Management,* 7th ed., Mason, OH: Thomson, 2005, p. 324; D. Goleman, R. Boyatzis, and A. McKee, *Primal Leadership,* Boston: Harvard Business School Press, 2002.

When a manager places a high priority on agreement among the group members about what is fair, the leader should focus on allowing each person to voice an opinion. The leader should try to involve all group members and discourage dominating individuals from monopolizing the discussion.

A manager who places a high priority on quality and acceptance must manage the decision process by carefully framing the problem and putting constraints on decision alternatives that are too risky or uncertain. In such cases, the leader may allow for some participation by group members but reserves the right to make the decision. A leader can frame the same problem as either a threat or an opportunity, which can influence how the group perceives the problem.

Research in the social sciences has shown that groups tend to take greater risks than individuals because responsibility for the outcome can be diffused over the entire group. The leader can remind the group to avoid considering decision alternatives that could lead to disastrous results. For example, the group responsible for deciding whether to go ahead with the launch of the *Challenger* space shuttle in 1986 would have made a different decision if NASA's leadership had examined the risk that a critical component would shrink when exposed to cold temperatures and cause the space shuttle to explode immediately after the launch.

Problems that involve technical or specialized knowledge are best solved alone by the decision maker. For example, if an important instrument malfunctions in the middle of an intercontinental flight, a commercial aircraft pilot may decide to land the plane at the nearest airport rather than continue to the original destination. Obviously, time is a critical factor in this situation, and the decision is best handled by the captain of the aircraft.

DEVIL'S ADVOCATE ROLE Social pressures to conform in groups can lead to the problem of groupthink, in which group members withhold critical comments or unpopular views in order to sustain social harmony in the group. If groupthink is not managed, it can reduce decision quality.

One way to reduce the threat of groupthink is to assign a group member the role of **devil's advocate**. The devil's advocate is expected to criticize and challenge decision alternatives that are agreed on by other members of the group. This person may (1) develop scenarios in which the majority-sponsored decision alternative could fail or (2) promote alternative solutions that challenge the one supported by the group. In this way, the devil's advocate introduces creative conflict and tension into the group decision-making process. This may ultimately lead to a better solution or one that is more deeply understood by members of the group. The payoff is likely to be stronger group commitment to the decision.

devil's advocate
The role of criticizing and challenging decision alternatives that are agreed on by other members of the group, to induce creative conflict and possible alternative better solutions.

DECISION-MAKING TECHNIQUES TO STIMULATE CREATIVITY Introducing criticism into the group decision-making process too early can stifle creativity. **Brainstorming** is a technique that is designed to generate creative decision alternatives verbally by interacting with members of a group. Critical and judgmental reactions to ideas from group members are not allowed during a brainstorming session. Instead, the group is encouraged to come up with the greatest number of ideas, and especially ideas that are wild and unusual. Group members are also asked to build on and extend earlier ideas, to increase the possibility of a truly innovative solution. The rules of brainstorming prohibit criticism of any ideas until all the ideas have been expressed. In the entertainment industry, teams of writers and other content creators make widespread use of brainstorming sessions. For example, brainstorming is used by the group of comedy writers who develop jokes for the "Tonight Show with Jay Leno."

For more complex problems, a variation of brainstorming called **storyboarding** is used. Storyboarding begins with group members jotting down ideas on index cards and posting them on a bulletin board or on conference room walls. Group members can shuffle, rewrite, or even eliminate cards. The technique is useful for examining complex processes involving technology in order to improve efficiency. At the Xerox corporate research laboratory in California's Silicon Valley, researchers sketch ideas onto a large white wall to begin discussions of ideas with other researchers.

The **nominal group technique (NGT)** helps a group generate and select solutions while letting group members think independently. NGT is a structured group meeting in which the following steps take place:

1. Group members meet and are presented with a problem. Prior to any discussion, each member independently writes down solutions to the problem.

brainstorming
A technique to generate creative ideas for solving problems by reducing critical and judgmental reactions to ideas from group members.

storyboarding
A variation of brainstorming in which group members jot down ideas on cards and then can shuffle, rewrite, or even eliminate cards to examine complex processes.

nominal group technique (NGT)
A decision-making technique that helps a group generate and select solutions while letting group members think independently; group members are given the problem and each presents one solution without discussion; then all solutions are discussed, evaluated, and ranked to determine the best alternative.

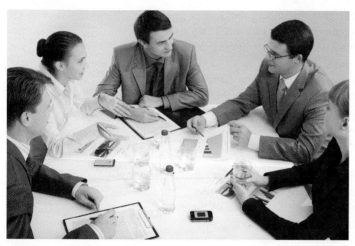

Creativity in solving problems often is fostered in a group situation, where members can build on each other's ideas and solutions by *brainstorming*.

Delphi technique

A decision-making technique in which group members are presented with a problem and complete an anonymous questionnaire soliciting solutions; the results are tabulated, summarized, and returned to the group members, and each is asked again for solutions; the process continues until a consensus decision is reached.

2. Next, each group member presents one of his or her ideas to the group. The idea is listened to and recorded on a flip chart or blackboard without any discussion or criticism.
3. After all the ideas have been presented and posted, discussion and evaluation begin.
4. At the conclusion of the evaluation, the group members anonymously vote and rank their top choices. The decision alternative that receives the highest ranking from the group is selected.[16]

NGT allows the group to discuss alternatives without inhibiting group members from engaging in independent critical thinking. NGT is often used in the strategic planning process, such as in the development of the corporate mission statement.

Another approach to group decision making is called the **Delphi technique**, which was originally developed by the RAND Corporation for technological forecasting. The Delphi technique is similar to NGT, but it does not involve face-to-face meetings of group members. Group members are presented with a problem and receive a questionnaire soliciting solutions. Each group member anonymously completes the questionnaire and sends it to a central location, where responses are tabulated and summarized. The results are then returned to the group members, and each is asked again for solutions. Having the input of all the other group members may inspire some group members to modify their positions or develop new ideas, while others may stick with their original ideas. Questionnaires are completed a second time and tabulated. The cycle of giving and receiving anonymous feedback continues until a consensus is reached on the best decision alternative.

The application of computer software provides for an electronic approach to the Delphi technique. The Leeds School of Business at the University of Colorado uses an electronic meeting room with 20 computer terminals with software that allows each person in a group to view his or her input to a decision posted anonymously on the computer screen along with all the other inputs from other group members. The software handles the complexity of bringing ideas together quickly, displaying them, and helping groups analyze them. The software lets the group go through several rounds of generating and evaluating decision alternatives until a consensus is reached. The electronic meeting room is useful for making controversial decisions when highly opinionated or high-status individuals should be kept from dominating the decision process, which means shy people are better able to participate in the process.

The Delphi technique is particularly useful when experts who are geographically separated need to make a decision. For example, a Wall Street investment bank may select a panel of 30 economists from different universities around the world to use the Delphi technique to forecast macroeconomic indicators such as interest rates, growth in the economy, and rate of inflation as a basis for thinking about future investment opportunities.[17]

LOC-In 4 | Learning Objective Check-In

1. Laura is in charge of facilitating group decision making regarding some proposed sales approaches within her company. The group members cannot gather together physically. Laura will have the group members complete a questionnaire, the results of which Laura will tabulate and return to the group. This cycle repeats with the group members modifying answers based on the feedback from the group as a whole. Laura is using _____.
   a. nominal group technique
   b. storyboarding method
   c. Delphi technique
   d. brainstorming

■ Decision-Making Skills

Effective managers know one of the most important things they will be asked to do is make quality decisions. Time management skills and delegation skills can improve the quality of those decisions. These skills are described next.

Time Management

A decision maker must have enough time to make effective decisions. Adequate time makes it possible to understand the problem, develop several suitable alternatives, evaluate the decision in light of goals and priorities, and establish a workable approach to implement the decision.

Not having enough time is stressful and puts the decision maker in a reactive mode. A **reactive manager** is always dealing with the most urgent problem and putting out fires. Decisions made this way are likely to be haphazard and to have major flaws in either quality or execution. For example, it may be necessary to have employees work overtime to satisfy an urgent customer demand. The reactive manager may feel pressured to randomly assign employees to work overtime, rather than involving the group in the decision. It is likely that working overtime will conflict with family or personal plans of at least some of the employees, which leads to resentment and resistance.

Reactive managers tend to lose control of their time and lose sight of the "big picture." Always dealing with crises means living on an emotional roller coaster. Those who skip planning their daily and weekly schedules because of looming crises have no time to think about goals and priorities.

Crises can be avoided by anticipating and dealing with problems when they are smaller and more manageable. A **proactive manager** anticipates problems before they become pervasive and "works smarter, not harder." Proactive people manage time. Time is set aside on both a daily and weekly basis to set goals and priorities. Proactive managers jealously protect this time from interruptions. This way, they can complete their work, deal with important decisions, and enjoy life outside of work with family and friends. They are able to lead more balanced and less stressful lives than reactive managers.[18]

One way to manage time is to eliminate or minimize "time wasters," activities that squander time. These include

- Television (the average American watches about four hours of television per day).
- Internet and e-mail messages.
- Lengthy telephone conversations.
- Random errands and waiting in lines.
- Interruptions by people who stop in to chat.
- Meetings (managers are often expected to attend many meetings to coordinate activities of their units).
- Cluttered workplace—includes your desk, work area, computer, and other organizing tools.

Manager's Notebook 6.2 lists helpful ways to avoid time wasters and practice effective time management.

Delegation

The transfer of decision-making authority from a manager to a subordinate or a team at a lower level in the organization is **delegation**. It should not be confused with participation, in which the group *shares* decision-making authority with management. When a manager delegates decision-making authority, the subordinate makes the decision.

Managers delegate decisions for several reasons. The most important is that delegation gives the manager more time to spend on the most important tasks and decisions. For example, the chief executive officer (CEO) of a large corporation can focus on the overall direction and coordination of the corporation and delegate operational responsibilities for profits and losses to the general managers who report to him or her. Another reason to delegate is that it teaches subordinates how to make their own decisions and to deal with the consequences of those

reactive management
The management style of responding to the most urgent problem first when not enough time is available.

proactive management
A management style in which problems are anticipated before they become pervasive and time is set aside on both a daily and weekly basis to plan goals and priorities.

delegation
The transfer of decision-making authority from a manager to a subordinate or a team at a lower level in the organization.

MANAGER'S NOTEBOOK 6.2

Effective Time Management Practices

The following practices help managers eliminate or reduce time-wasting behavior and allow them to be more proactive.

1. *Make a list of things that need to be done today.* Write your daily plan during quiet time the night before, rather than at the office in the morning when urgent matters may get in the way of writing your list.

2. *Plan weekly, monthly, and annual schedules of activities.* Weekly schedules allow you to organize work, school, personal, and family activities. Longer term schedules let you plan time for nonwork facets of your life. For example, monthly plans may include travel that requires advance purchase of tickets. Annual plans also give an opportunity to consider your values and long-term objectives.

3. *Schedule difficult and challenging activities when you are at your highest level of energy and alertness.* For example, if you are a "morning person," schedule demanding activities in the morning and reserve afternoons for less difficult things such as returning phone calls or doing routine record keeping.

4. *Set deadlines.* Deadlines improve your use of time. Work always expands to fill the time available—if you don't specify a termination time, tasks tend to continue longer than they need to.

5. *Answer phone messages and e-mail in batches during a lull in your work schedule.* Phone calls and e-mail can interrupt your train of thought on important projects. Returning them all at one time allows you to use your time more efficiently.

6. *Have a place to work uninterrupted.* When a deadline is near, you can concentrate on the task at hand. Trying to refocus on a task or project after interruptions wastes a lot of time.

7. *Do something productive during nonproductive activities.* Try to multitask (accomplish multiple tasks at the same time). Listen to educational or personal improvement tapes while driving to and from work or class. Read the newspaper or balance your checking account while you're waiting in line. When watching television, take care of household tasks such as cooking, cleaning, and doing laundry.

8. *Say no to nonessential tasks.* Consider your goals and schedule before agreeing to take on additional work.

Source: Based on D. A. Whetten and K. S. Cameron, *Developing Management Skills*, 8th ed., Upper Saddle River, NJ: Prentice Hall, 2010. Adapted by permission of Pearson Education, Inc; "Time Management: Tips to Reduce Stress and Improve Productivity," September 4, 2008. www.mayoclinic.com/health/.../w10004.

LOC-In 5 Learning Objective Check-In

1. Arthur works in the transportation industry, where technology is rapidly evolving and the work pace is very fast. Arthur anticipates problems before they become pervasive. He makes time on both a daily and weekly basis to set goals and priorities. Arthur is a _____.
   a. reactive manager
   b. consequential manager
   c. proactive manager
   d. behavioral manager

Delegating the responsibility for resolving customer complaints to the front-desk staff has resulted in satisfied customers and empowered employees for the Hampton Inn firm.

decisions. The subordinates receive feedback on the quality of their decision making and develop new skills that prepare them for future promotions. Finally, delegation may lead to higher quality decisions that result in greater customer satisfaction, because lower-level employees are closer to actual customers and therefore are more aware of their needs.

During the past decade, many corporations have relieved middle management of decision-making authority and have given it to teams of front-line employees, attempting to eliminate unnecessary layers of management in the process. Hampton Inn, a national hotel chain, has delegated authority to deal with customer complaints to desk clerks and housekeepers. Desk clerks can decide whether a complaint is justified and provide an immediate refund to a dissatisfied customer. This delegation of authority is part of Hampton Inn's "100% Satisfaction Guarantee," developed to gain a distinctive advantage in the highly competitive hotel industry, and it has resulted in higher levels of both customer and employee satisfaction, since Hampton employees feel more committed and motivated by being trusted to make important decisions involving guests.

Effective delegation involves the following steps:

1. Determine what you want done. Writing it down can be helpful.
2. Match the desired task with the most appropriate employee.
3. Be sure you communicate clearly when assigning the task. Follow up to make sure the task is fully understood. Set clear deadlines.
4. Keep communication channels open. Make it clear that you are available for consultation and discussion.
5. Allow employees to do the task the way they feel comfortable doing it.
6. Trust employees' capabilities. Do not hold such high expectations that they can only fail.
7. Check on the progress of the assignment, but do not rush to rescue the employee at the first sign of failure.
8. Hold the employee responsible for the work and any difficulties that may emerge, but do so as a teacher, not a police officer. Explore what is going wrong, and help employees develop their own solutions.
9. Recognize what the employee has done, and show appropriate appreciation.[19]

LOC-In 6 Learning Objective Check-In

1. Marco is a manager at a software engineering firm in Los Angeles. In the past, Marco has made all the decisions regarding his team and some of the more technical implementation decisions on a case-by-case basis. Because the group he oversees has more combined experience than he does in several matters relating to software development, he has recently transferred decision-making authority from himself to the entire team. Because of the effective team dynamics already in place and his confidence in the team's expertise, Marco believes this _____ will prove very successful.
   a. proactive management
   b. reactive management
   c. nominal group technique
   d. delegation

CONCLUDING THOUGHTS

At the end of the chapter's introductory vignette we presented some critical thinking questions about decisions made by top executives at Yahoo!, Microsoft, and, in particular, Google. Now that you've had the opportunity to learn about decision making in the chapter, consider those critical thinking questions again.

Google's decision to enter the Chinese Internet market was clearly nonprogrammable, and it was high in uncertainty and risk. Entering any huge and growing market, even at home, is always a risk, but the Chinese government's restrictive control of Internet operations based within its borders adds another layer of potential hazard that Google's executives had to carefully calculate. The decision clearly brought conflict to, and probably within, the company, as debates about the possible outcomes of its choice continue. The scope of the decision is vast, with China poised to become the world's largest Internet market in a very short time, and its effects will extend far into the future if Google's offerings in China gain prominence.

Google's decision differed from Yahoo!'s and Microsoft's in coming a few years later, after the first two companies had gained some experience in the Chinese market. Google had the opportunity to learn from its competitors' mistakes and has so far chosen to base only one of its Chinese-language operations in China, where it must operate under government scrutiny. Google's executives also had a shorter time horizon in which to make their decision than the other companies did, since competition from them and from Chinese Internet providers will continue to grow with the market.

Management Strategy and Decision Making

A new variant on the job of marketing is the *creative director* position. Companies as diverse as Marvel Enterprises (the publisher of Marvel Comics), Leo Burnett, and Bang and Olufsen all have creative director or chief designer positions. At Burger King, the "chief concept officer" is Denny Marie Post, a 48-year-old executive with more than 25 years of marketing experience behind her. Prior to working at Burger King, she was the chief innovation officer for KFC, Inc.[1]

Post points out the importance of combining creativity with a more formal decision-making process when she describes the development of the Enormous Omelet Sandwich. This sandwich, a combination of two eggs, sausage, cheese, and bacon, boosted Burger King breakfast sales by 20 percent when it was introduced in March, 2005.[2]

The idea for the sandwich occurred during a brainstorming session in the Burger King test kitchen. Three or four of the creative staff were looking at a new mold for eggs. The mold was rectangular rather than circular, and as Post tells it, "I said, 'What if we put something between it and made it like an omelet? Like bacon.' Somebody else said we could use a bun from lunch and dinner, and before you know it, about three or four of us had built it."[3] But just having a good idea and building on it wasn't enough for Post. She knew that before Burger King invested money in a new product, there had to be some proof that the product would work. Getting the Enormous Omelet Sandwich into the hands of consumers required that Post use all four of the last stages of the decision-making process.

Evaluating Alternatives

Post uses a "concept screening process" to separate good ideas from the bad. Every food idea is run past a group of Burger King's most devoted customers. They evaluate each idea, just by looking at a description and a picture of the proposed food item. In this way, Post can tease out the good alternatives from the ones that are less likely to sell. She points out that of the 500 ideas run past the group in a given year, only 120 will receive further consideration. So, the first step in evaluating the Enormous Omelet Sandwich was to see how it fared with this important group of evaluators.

Choosing the Best Alternative

It isn't always easy to settle on one or two ideas for implementation. Post points out that when Burger King was testing the Enormous Omelet Sandwich, they were also testing a breakfast sandwich which included a biscuit and pepper-jack cheese. Although the other sandwich made it through several rounds of testing, in the end, evaluators decided that most people's taste buds weren't ready for pepper-jack anything at breakfast. Post used an optimizing strategy to select the best product, based on multiple criteria.

Implementing the Decision

Implementing the decision involved not only getting stores ready to produce the new product (which required the special egg molds discussed earlier), but also getting customers ready to buy the new product. Burger King started by targeting a specific market—16-to-24-year-old males who want to be "satisfied" after eating a sandwich, and who don't care much about calorie content or nutrition. They then commissioned their advertising agency, Crispin Porter + Bogusky, to create new commercials featuring "The King," a Burger King advertising mascot.[4] Finally, they created print and other media advertising to support the television ads designed to appeal to their target demographic.

An important part of implementation is being willing to stand up for decisions, even when those decisions are questioned by others. Denny Marie Post appeared on multiple television news and talk shows in 2005 to defend Burger King against charges that it was contributing to a growing obesity crisis in the United States. At 730 calories per sandwich with 47 grams of fat, the Enormous Omelet Sandwich was characterized by one ABC reporter as a "gut buster" and other reporters pointed out that the sandwich was basically a heart attack waiting to happen. Post countered these claims by informing the media that Burger King also offered low fat food options, and that consumer choice was the most important thing in the long run.[5]

Evaluating the Decision

Denny Marie Post watched sales carefully after the introduction of the new sandwich. As noted above, they were up for the first two months by 20 percent. They remained high throughout the year, and Burger King credits the Enormous Omelet Sandwich with helping to save the company.[6] In fact, the sandwich was so successful, that a second sandwich, the Meat'normous Omelet Sandwich, was introduced in the fall of 2005.

Source: [1]Burger King Company Information Web site, http://www.bk.com/CompanyInfo/bk_corporation/executive_team/post.aspx, April 13, 2006; [2]Bruce Horovitz, "Restaurant Sales Climb with Bad-For-You Food," *USA Today*, May 12, 2005; [3]Michael Prospero, Fast Talk: Creative to the Core, *Fast Company*, December 2005, p. 30; [4]*South Florida The Business Journal*, "'Enormous' Launch Adds to Burger King Breakfast Menu," March 28, 2005, April 13, 2006, http://www.bizjournals.com/southflorida/stories/2005/03/28/daily1.html; [5]Amy Menefee, "Networks Hound Burger King for Launching 'Enormous Sandwich,'" Free Market Project, April, 1, 2005, April 13, 2006, http://www.freemarketproject.org/news/2005/news20050401.asp; [6]*QSR Magazine*, "Best of 2005," http://www.qsrmagazine.com/issue/84/best/menu.phtml, April 13, 2006.

Summary of Learning Objectives

Decision making is the process of identifying and resolving problems and taking advantage of opportunities. It involves understanding the underlying causes of a problem or nature of an opportunity and implementing an effective plan or solution. This chapter's discussion will help future managers, work teams, and employees make better, more effective decisions. The ideas presented in the chapter to meet each of the learning objectives is summarized below.

1 Recognize the nature of management decisions: programmability, uncertainty, risk, conflict, decision scope, and crisis situations.

- **Programmability** refers to whether the problem is well defined based on past experience or whether there are no established procedures for making a unique decision.
- **Uncertainty** means that incomplete information is available to make a decision.
- **Risk** varies with the level of uncertainty associated with the decision outcome. Under a state of risk, the availability of each alternative and its outcome are associated with a probability estimate.
- **Conflict** occurs when there are disagreements about goals and priorities that affect the selection of the solution. Conflict is a normal part of the decision-making process when diverse interests are competing to control the outcome.
- **Decision scope** involves the effect and time horizon of the decision.
- In a **crisis** situation there is a small amount of time to make a decision that can impact the survival of the organization.

2 Utilize the six steps of decision making.

- Decision making involves a step-by-step process that unfolds in sequential stages:
- *Identify and diagnose the problem*. Understand the underlying causes of the problem before attempting to form possible solutions.
- *Generate alternative solutions*.
- *Evaluate the alternative* solutions in light of the decision criteria. The decision criteria should be related to performance goals.
- *Choose the best alternative* solution by either **optimizing** (selecting the optimally best solution) or **satisficing** (selecting the first alternative that meets the minimum criteria).
- *Implement the decision*. This means putting the solution into practice and establishing controls to make sure it works the way it is expected to work.
- *Evaluate the results*. Decision evaluation involves gathering information and learning if the decision is on target to reach its goals. If not, modifications should be made to ensure the goals are reached.

3 Apply the criteria of quality and acceptance to a decision.

- **Decision quality** is based on factual information such as costs, revenues, or profits.
- **Decision acceptance** is based on people's feelings. Decision acceptance happens when people who are affected by a decision agree with what is done.

4 Reap the benefits and avoid the problems of group decision making.

- The decision-making process is likely to reside within a group when employee commitment to the decision outcome is critical to the successful implementation.

- Group decision-making can be beneficial to the *quality* of the decision by involving more people who have a greater diversity of ideas and opinions, and it can enhance decision *acceptance* by giving more people a voice in the decision.
- Disadvantages of group decision making are having to deal with dominant individuals or forceful factions and **groupthink**, where the group avoids meaningful critical evaluation of solutions in favor of maintaining social harmony and cohesion.

5 Develop time management skills to generate adequate time to make decisions.

- One way to manage time is to eliminate or minimize "time wasters," activities that squander time.
- Another way to manage time is to be proactive and anticipate problems before they become pervasive by "working smarter, not harder."

6 Know when to delegate, and how to do so wisely.

- When a manager **delegates** decision-making authority, subordinates make decisions.
- The most important reason for a manager to delegate is that it gives the manager more time to spend on more important tasks and decisions.

Discussion Questions

1. What is the difference between a programmed and nonprogrammed decision? Consider a programmed decision and a nonprogrammed decision you have made recently. Compare and contrast the approaches you used to make these two decisions.
2. Can you teach people to make decisions? What types of decisions are useful for giving people experience in decision making? What types of decisions should be avoided in teaching trainees about decision making?
3. What are the advantages of delegating decision making to front-line employees and teams? Are there any disadvantages to this approach to decision making?
4. Should only top executives, such as the CEO, be involved in making strategic decisions? Can you think of a tactical or operational decision that could benefit from the involvement of the CEO or another top executive? What are the drawbacks of involving CEOs in tactical and operational decision making?
5. How can electronic communications such as the Internet and e-mail be used to improve the decision-making process? Give some examples.
6. Define the following decision-making errors and identify ways to correct for them:
   a. Poor problem identification.
   b. Solution focus.
   c. Premature evaluation.
   d. Groupthink.
   e. Overemphasis on objective data without considering gut feelings.
   f. Omission of a way to monitor and control the decision.
7. Think of a decision in which you used an optimizing criterion for selecting the best decision alternative, and another decision in which you used a satisficing criterion. What factors influenced you to optimize instead of satisfice? Which ones affected your choice to satisfice instead of optimize?
8. Under what conditions is it better to involve a group of employees in decision making, rather than an individual manager? What roles should a manager or leader take in the group decision-making process?

Management Minicase 6.1
Circuit City's Decision to Lay Off Experienced Employees Backfires

In 2007, Circuit City, a large U.S. consumer electronics retailer, was facing strong competition from larger rivals such as Best Buy and Costco, which forced Circuit City's top management to seek ways to economize on operational costs. The result was an extraordinary decision to lay off 3,400 people, or about 8 percent of its work force: not because they were doing a bad job and not because the company was eliminating their positions, but rather because executives determined that the workers were being paid too much and that the company would replace them with new employees who would be paid less.

The laid off employees worked in the company's stores and warehouses, selling electronics, unloading boxes and related tasks. They generally earned $10 to $20 per hour.

Eighteen months later Circuit City filed for Chapter 11 bankruptcy protection just before the holiday shopping season at the end of 2008. At the time of the bankruptcy filing, the chief financial officer of the retailer attributed the company's poor financial position to an erosion of vendor confidence, decreased liquidity, and the global economic crisis. Recently, suppliers affected by the global credit crunch had tightened terms of credit they extended to the retailer, sometimes requiring up-front payments before shipping goods. In early 2009, a few months after filing for bankruptcy Circuit City went out of business and its assets were liquidated to creditors.

Wall Street analysts believed one of the main reasons for the rapid demise of Circuit City was that it had basically destroyed customer loyalty among its best customers by laying off the most experienced sales staff, which also undermined employee morale and greatly reduced the service provided to customers. Without its top sales staff, Circuit City could not sustain its sales revenues in challenging economic times.

DISCUSSION QUESTIONS

1. When making decisions it is important to examine reasonable alternatives before settling on the best alternative for the decision at hand. What reasonable alternatives could top management of Circuit City have considered to laying off their most experienced employees? Was there a better alternative than a layoff at Circuit City? Explain the basis for your choice.

2. Why do you think companies, such as Circuit City, that are facing economic challenges so often choose to lay off employees rather than explore other alternatives that might produce better long-term results?

Sources: Based on P. Kavilanz, "Circuit City to Shut Down," *CNNMoney*, January 16, 2009. www.cnn.com; S. Rosenbloom, "Circuit City to Shut Down," *The New York Times*, January 16, 2009. www.nytimes.com/2009/01/.../17circuit.html; C. Mathews, "Lessons from Circuit City's Bankruptcy," January 17, 2009. www.teleread.com; D. Leonhardt, "3,400 Layoffs Send a Message to Millions," *The New York Times*, April 4, 2007. www.nytimes.com/gst/fullpage.html.

Management Minicase 6.2

Merck's Decision to Withdraw Its Vioxx Drug from the Market

By the time Merck, a leading pharmaceutical firm, withdrew its pain relief drug Vioxx from the market in 2004, more than 100 million prescriptions had been filled in the United States alone. Researchers estimate that Vioxx may have been associated with as many as 25,000 heart attacks and strokes, and more than 1,000 claims have been filed against the company. Evidence of the drug's risks was available as early as 2000, when the *New England Journal of Medicine* reported evidence that linked Vioxx to a greater risk of heart attacks and strokes. In one of Merck's own reports to federal regulators it showed that 14.6 percent of Vioxx patients suffered from cardiovascular problems while taking the drug and 2.5 percent developed serious problems including heart attacks. So why did so many doctors keep prescribing it?

The answer is that without realizing it, decision makers ignore certain critical information due to a phenomenon called *bounded awareness*—when cognitive blinders prevent a person from seeing, seeking, using, or sharing highly relevant, easily accessible, and readily understandable information during the decision-making process. Doctors that prescribed Vioxx, for example, in many cases received positive feedback from the patients. So, despite having access to information about the risks, physicians may have been blinded to the actual extent of the risks. To make matters worse, Merck heavily advertised Vioxx to customers by using media such as television to stimulate the demand for the drug so that by 2004 it became one of the firm's most profitable products. One must also wonder why Merck's executives allowed the drug to remain on the market for several years after the published research reported that there were problems with the drug.

Bounded awareness, an impediment to effective decision making, can occur at three stages in the decision-making process. First, decision makers may fail to see or look for important information that is needed to make a sound decision. Second, they may fail to use the information that they do see because they are not aware of its relevance. Third, decision makers may fail to share information with others, which limits the organization's awareness.

When making decisions in which a bad decision can have disastrous consequences, it is a good idea for executives to broadly collect information from many sources and share information with diverse people who bring different perspectives to the decision-making process. Had this approach been taken, disasters such as the terrorist attack on the World Trade Center or the *Challenger* space shuttle explosion might have been avoided because in both these situations decision makers had information that predicted these events yet in the decision-making process this information was not used.

DISCUSSION QUESTIONS

1. Why do you think the decision makers at Merck failed to use the information that indicated that the Vioxx pain relief drug was linked to increased risk of heart attacks and strokes?

2. What practices should Merck develop to improve its decision-making process in order to avoid future product recalls such as the situation with Vioxx, which is likely to cost the company billions in legal costs to settle with customers as well as tarnish its reputation as a leading drug company?

3. Why do you think so many doctors failed to use the published information about the risks to their patients of using Vioxx and instead continued to prescribe this drug? What should doctors do to improve their decision making when it concerns prescribing drugs to patients?

Sources: Based on M. Bazerman and D. Chugh, "Decisions without Blinders," *Harvard Business Review*, January 2006, pp. 88–97; M. Watkins, and M. Bazerman, "Predictable Surprises: The Disasters You Should Have Seen Coming," *Harvard Business Review*, March 2003, pp. 72–80; and M. Bazerman, *Judgment in Managerial Decision Making*, 6th ed. New York: Wiley, 2005.

Individual/Collaborative Learning Case 6.1

Intel Recalls the Pentium Chip

In the fall of 1994, cofounder Andrew Grove was riding high as CEO of Intel, the largest and most profitable semiconductor company in the world. Intel's chips were found in 80 percent of the personal computers in the world. In its twenty-sixth year of making computer chips, it was anticipating a record $10 billion dollars in sales and 30 percent growth.

Intel was beginning full-scale production of the Pentium, its newest microprocessor chip. This chip's superior performance promised a bright future for the company. In the previous year, Grove began a massive advertising campaign for Intel chips, which elevated public awareness of Intel and differentiated the products that contained its chips.

In the midst of these positive circumstances, a troubling event occurred. A bug was discovered in the Pentium chip that could cause mathematical errors during processing. The bug caused a division error once every 9 billion times. At this rate a typical user of spreadsheet software on a Pentium-controlled computer would run into the problem once every 27,000 years of use. Intel scientists were aware of this error in June 1994, but because it would cause an error so infrequently, they did not consider it to be a material flaw and put the problem on the back burner, while the company continued to ship the Pentium chip.

When individual users encountered the error and turned to Intel for help, however, they were not happy with Intel's response to the problem or to their requests for replacement chips. The company's policy was to replace chips only after assessing each individual's problem. Customers who claimed their computers handled a lot of division functions were given replacement chips, while others might or might not have their chips replaced.

Users affected by the chip's flaw began posting information about the error on the Internet in late October; it was picked up by a trade newspaper, which ran a story about it on the front page; other trade papers ran the story as well. Three weeks later when CNN, the cable news network, wanted to question Intel executives about the bug on television, a media frenzy occurred. Stories appeared in major newspapers with headlines such as, "Flaw Undermines Accuracy of Pentium Chips."

The crisis mushroomed in mid-December, when IBM announced that it would stop shipments of all Pentium-based computers. Because IBM was a key player in the computer industry, its action attracted a lot of attention. Intel customers clamored to find out what Intel was going to do with the Pentium chips that it had already sold to them.

After the events of the fall, Grove knew he had to make a decision on the Pentium chip. Should Intel spend millions of dollars to replace the flawed chip for all users, or should it counter what the company felt were overly negative reports from the media with a more moderate response?

CRITICAL THINKING QUESTIONS

1. Why do you think the media paid so much attention to the error in the Pentium chip, which occurred only once in every 9 billion divisions? Was the margin for accuracy high enough for the typical customer of a personal computer? Explain.
2. Why would Intel release the flawed Pentium chip to the market instead of delaying its introduction until the flaw was fixed?
3. Why do you think Intel treated early customer complaints about the Pentium error by relying on standard Intel customer complaint procedures—a programmed approach to decision making?

COLLABORATIVE LEARNING EXERCISE

Assume it is 1994. With a partner or small group, identify the true nature of the problem Intel CEO Andrew Grove faced. Recommend a course of action to Grove, considering the following alternatives. Should all the Pentium chips be replaced at a cost of $500 million? Or should he run an aggressive media campaign to tell Intel's side of the story, spelling out how trivial the flaw is and trying to convince customers that they are highly unlikely to be affected by it? Support your recommendation.

Source: Based on A. Grove, *Only the Paranoid Survive*. New York: Currency Doubleday, 1996, pp. 11–16; J. Markoff, "Chip error continuing to dog officials at Intel," *The New York Times*, December 6, 1994. www.nytimes.com; A. Wolfe, "Intel fixes a Pentium FPU glitch," *Electronic Engineering Times*, November 7, 1994. www.davefag.com/opinions/.../pentuim.html

Internet Exercise 6.1

Decision Making at Coca-Cola

www.cocacola.com

Coca-Cola CEO Roberto Goizueta acted decisively after making a mistake with the launch of the New Coke product in 1985. In this exercise you will learn more about the Coca-Cola Company and what it stands for. Visit the Coca-Cola Web site and explore the "Our Company" and "Investors" areas there, and then answer the following questions:

1. What are the key values at Coca-Cola? What do these values reveal about the Coca-Cola Company?

2. Coke sponsors many sporting events, such as World Cup Soccer, National Football League, National Basketball Association, Tour de France bicycle race, Rugby World Cup, and the Olympic Games. Why is Coke so involved with sponsoring these events? What benefits do you think Coke receives from these sponsorships?
3. Who is the current CEO of Coca-Cola? How has Coke's market valuation changed since 1997, when it was valued at $180 billion?

Manager's Checkup 6.1

Determining Decision Risk and Uncertainty Preferences

What is your preference with regard to taking risks when making decisions? Consider the following statements and mark each "True" or "False" to indicate whether you agree or disagree with the statement.

_____ 1. I buy a pizza at the same restaurant every month because I know the pizza will always be prepared the same way.

_____ 2. If I need help preparing my income taxes I will hire someone with a CPA because a certified accountant will have the knowledge needed to do the job.

____ 3. With the growing consumer market in India, products should sell well there.

____ 4. The lease on the store is expensive, but the good location in the mall should provide enough business to cover the cost in about six months.

____ 5. If two dentists are both considered to be reliable and say they can do the root canal work on my tooth, I will go to the dentist that charges $100 dollars less for the dental work.

____ 6. If I do not invest in this business opportunity right away I will miss a golden opportunity.

____ 7. If I know a colleague always eats lunch in the company cafeteria at noon, I am certain to meet him there at 12:15 pm to discuss a problem.

____ 8. My company does not offer health insurance and since I am young and healthy I think it makes sense to go without buying health insurance.

____ 9. Switching our source of energy in our business from burning coal to wind energy will be more expensive but our customers should be more loyal because our product is less harmful to the environment.

____ 10. The store around the corner does not carry my favorite brand of beer and even though it is more convenient to buy my beer there, instead I go to a store that is ten miles away because it always has my favorite brand of beer in stock.

Scoring: "True" answers to statements 1, 5, 7, and 10 indicate a preference for certainty. "True" answers to statements 2, 4, and 8 indicate an acceptance for risk. "True" answers to statements 3, 6, and 9 indicate an acceptance of uncertainty.

Endnotes

1. C. M. Pearson and J. A. Clair, "Reframing Organizational Crisis," *Academy of Management Review* 23 (1998), 59–76.
2. E. Leonard, "The Only Lifeline Was the Wal-Mart," *Fortune*, October 3, 2005, pp. 74–80.
3. L. Gerstner, *Who Says Elephants Can't Dance? Leading a Great Enterprise through Dramatic Change* (New York: HarperBusiness, 2002).
4. N. R. Maier, *Psychology in Industrial Organizations*, 4th ed. (Boston: Houghton Mifflin, 1973).
5. A. A. Thompson and A. J. Strickland, (1998). *Strategic Management: Concepts and Cases*, 10th ed. New York: Irwin/McGraw-Hill.
6. S. P. Robbins and M. Coulter, *Management*; 5th ed. (Upper Saddle River, NJ: Prentice Hall, 1996), pp. 196–197.
7. D. Ariely, *Predictably Irrational: The Hidden Forces that Shape our Decisions* (New York: HarperCollins Publishers, 2009).
8. M. Gladwell, *Blink: The Power of Thinking without Thinking*, (New York: Little, Brown and Company, 2005).
9. J. Hammond, R. Keeney, and H. Raiffa, "The Hidden Traps of Decision Making," *Harvard Business Review*, January, 2006, pp. 118–126.
10. Ibid.
11. H. A. Simon, *Models of Man* (New York: Wiley, 1957).
12. M. Bazerman and D. Chugh, "Decisions without Blinders, *Harvard Business Review*, January 2006, pp. 88–97.
13. M. D. Cohen, J. G. March, and J. P. Olsen, "The Garbage Can Model of Organizational Choice," *Administrative Science Quarterly* 17 (1972), 1–25.
14. R. H. Hall, *Organizations* (Upper Saddle River, NJ: Prentice Hall, 1999).
15. A. Rowe and R. Mason, *Managing with Style: A Guide to Understanding, Assessing, and Improving Your Decision Making* (San Francisco: Jossey-Bass, 1987).
16. A. L. Delbecq, A. H. Van de Ven, and D.H. Gustafson, *Group Techniques for Program Planning* (Glenview, IL: Scott Foresman, 1975).
17. M. Mauboussin, "What Good Are Experts?", *Harvard Business Review*, February, 2008. 43–44; R. Duboff, "The Wisdom of (Expert) Crowds, *Harvard Business Review*, September, 2007, p. 28.
18. M. Mankins, "Stop Wasting Valuable Time," *Harvard Business Review*, September 2004, pp. 58–65.
19. R. E. Quinn, S. R. Faerman, M. P. Thompson, and M. R. McGrath, *Becoming a Master Manager*, 3rd ed. (New York: John Wiley & Sons, 2003).

7

Learning Objectives

1 Explain how the firm's external environment should be examined as part of the strategic management process.

2 Explain how the firm's internal environment should be examined as part of the strategic management process.

3 State the meaning and purpose of the firm's strategic intent and mission.

4 Understand how the strategy formulation process helps the firm achieve its mission.

5 Describe the issues that should be considered in strategy implementation.

6 Understand how the outcomes of the strategic management process should be assessed.

The Universe of iPod and iPad

It's not unusual these days to spend a few hundred dollars on an iPod or an iPad. In one recent year Apple sold 32 million of its digital music players, or one every second. But as good as that news is, the story of the iPod universe may be even better for Apple and for the dozens of firms licensed to create accessories for its hottest new product. For every $3 spent on an iPod, at least $1 was spent on an iPod accessory, which means that each player spins off about three or four additional purchases. The sales of accessories for iPod has already exceeded $1 billion annually. Less than five years ago a manufacturer of about a dozen iPod accessories exclaimed, "I've never seen anything like it in my career." Little did he know that Apple would revolutionize the market over again with a gadget called the iPad, which does Web browsers, e-mail, photos, music, movies, games, word processing, spreadsheets, presentations, e-books, and more. According to a consumer report, "You can pick it up. You can rest it in your lap. You can pass it around. You can leave it on a coffee table. You can tuck it in a bag. You can one-hand it while reading on a train." Perhaps even more than the iPod, the iPad should generate a whole new generation of accessories (such as textbooks, video, course materials, games, and office productivity services) expected to exceed more than $2 billion dollars in sales per year during 2012–2016.

Strategic Management

Sources: Based on S. Fry, "On the mothership: A Confessed Apple fanblog gets finger time with the iPad—and facetime with Steve Jobs," *Time*, April 12, 2010, p. 111; L. Grossman, "Launch iPad. It is here, it is hot. But what on earth is the iPad for? *Time*, April 12, 2010, pp. 36–40. Laurie J. Flynn, "Apple Offers Hi-Fi System to Use iPod in the Home," *New York Times*, www.nytimes.com, March 1, 2006, Joe Nocera, "Good Luck with That Broken iPod," *New York Times,* February 4, 2006, p. C1; Damon Darlin, "The iPod Econsystem: Add-Ons Have Become a Billion-Dollar Bonanza," *New York Times*, www.nytimes.com, February 3, 2006.

CRITICAL THINKING QUESTIONS

1. *How has Apple's strategy of encouraging the manufacturer of accessories helped boost the success of its products?*
2. *What role does strategic management play in Apple's decision to encourage other manufacturers to ride on its gadgets success?*
3. *What will be the result of Apple's more aggressive entry into the accessory market?*

Its savvy in the accessories market may be one of the reasons Apple isn't hurting very much from the effects of one of its other strategies: providing minimal customer support.

We'll revisit these questions at the end of the chapter in our Concluding Thoughts, after you've had a chance to read about strategic management.

■ The Strategic Management Process

It is the job of top-level management to chart the course of the entire enterprise. The strategic management process includes analysis of the internal and external environment of the firm, definition of the firm's mission, and formulation and implementation of strategies to create or continue a competitive advantage. These efforts steer the organization in a particular direction and require large resource commitments, which is why strategic management is generally the responsibility of top executives.

Reversing strategic decisions can be costly, so most firms take a long-term perspective when making these choices. For instance, in the mid-1990s, Ford CEO Alex Trotman announced "Ford 2000," a new strategic direction for the firm. The strategy spelled out all the new cars and trucks Ford would manufacture in the following 10 years and the resources required to produce them. It called for reducing the number of basic designs or platforms from 24 to 16 and increasing the number of models produced from them by 50 percent. To save on costs and increase quality, Ford would revamp its design and manufacturing process on a worldwide basis. All North American and European engineering operations were consolidated in five vehicle development centers, each of which had a global mission.

Five years later, Ford realized that although centralized worldwide responsibility for functions such as product development, purchasing, design, and manufacturing generated significant cost savings, it also resulted in less customer responsiveness at the local level. Jacques A. Nasser, who became CEO following Trotman, made significant adjustments to Trotman's plan by restoring much of the power that had been stripped away from regional Ford managers: "The central idea is to create bite-size, highly accountable regional brand units that can get to their target customers' tastes and needs."

Yet Nasser lasted only two years on the job. According to his successor, Bill Ford (whose great-grandfather was Henry Ford), Nasser was fired by the Ford family (which still controls one-third of Ford's shares) for "pursuing strategies that were either poorly conceived or poorly timed." Bill Ford decided to centralize many of Ford's activities in order to avoid duplication and focus the company's attention on launching new products, saving on costs, and eliminating low-margin vehicles. Unfortunately, by 2006, it had become evident that this strategy was not producing the intended results. Ford's market share dropped precipitously and its U.S. auto sales have been declining about 5 percent a year. In late 2006, Bill Ford stepped down as Ford's situation continued to deteriorate. Besides draconian reductions in workforce, Ford's new CEO Allan Mullaby (who spent most of his career at Boeing) decided to emphasize production of cars that run on ethanol (which is distilled from corn and grain)—a market niche with little competition from Japanese car makers—and "nostalgia" cars (such as the Mustang) to appeal to baby boomers.[1] It remains to be seen at the time of this writing if this strategy will work; if not, Ford may need to once again revise its strategic plans. One strong indication that Ford is in the right track is that it is the only American car manufacturer that was not bailed out by the federal government during the economic turmoil of 2008–2011.

The experience at Ford demonstrates another key attribute of strategic management: For a strategy to be successful, a firm must be flexible and make changes to the plan based on experience. Strategic management involves both long-range thinking and adaptation to changing conditions. However, each change also carries risk. Some of these issues are explored in greater detail in Chapter 8.

Strategies should be designed to generate a sustainable competitive advantage. This means that competitors will be unable to duplicate what the firm has done or will find it too difficult or expensive. When competitors ultimately learn how to copy the strategy, the firm should modify or reformulate the strategy to stay ahead. American Express was a pioneer in the credit card business in the 1950s. The card charged an annual fee and all purchases had to be repaid within a month of billing. For almost 25 years, the American Express card was a worldwide symbol of prestige. American Express posted high earnings year after year. Soon, competitors such as Visa and MasterCard entered the industry with card features that were more convenient to customers, such as no annual fees, installment payment plans, air travel insurance, and extended warranties on purchases. These cards were also differentiated based on prestige, with different-colored cards for varying credit limits. American Express began to lose its competitive advantage. In the late 1990s, American Express's CEO, Harvey Golub, and president, Kenneth Chenault, launched a fierce counterattack against Visa and MasterCard, introducing a wide variety of cards for different market segments with many features that matched or surpassed those of the competitors. American Express has launched about 20 new cards including a consumer-friendly "Blue card" with an electronic smart chip embedded in it that could contain account information. American Express summarized its new strategy as "to earn 100 percent of plastic spending of all target U.S. individuals and their households by providing a wide range of payment options (charge and lending cards) . . . offering a portfolio of products tailored to the needs of specific customer groups."[2]

In the automotive sector, the truck and SUV segments were General Motors' golden goose, bringing in almost twice as much profit per vehicle as compared to cars. Asian manufacturers such as Nissan and Honda quickly entered this attractive market and have already conquered more than a third of the light truck and SUV market in the United States. GM's profits have dropped accordingly. A major challenge facing GM is how to modify or reformulate its strategy now that its golden goose has been stolen by competitors capable of producing these vehicles at much lower costs.[3]

As a last example of how imitation by competitors tends to erode profits, and why firms must be on constant alert to be able to respond, Whole Foods (a supermarket chain) has increased its earnings at a nearly 20 percent annualized clip since the early 1990s, at a time when most other chains were stagnant or making modest profit gains. It has done so by targeting a growing market niche of consumers willing to pay more for organic food (for instance, chicken without hormones and bananas without pesticides). But by 2012, most other large supermarket chains, such as Safeway, Albertson's, and Fry's, have copied the Whole Foods approach. Investors are currently wondering how Whole Foods will be able to respond to this competitive challenge in years to come.[4] What investors think of a company's competitive strategy is a critical issue for most firms, since in the long run, a firm must earn at least average returns if it hopes to stay in business. Investors are likely to withdraw their funds from firms with below-average earnings.

In this chapter, we discuss the major aspects of the strategic management process and how this process affects the firm's competitive advantage. Figure 7.1 shows the interdependent parts of the strategic management process that firms must manage to win battles in a global marketplace that grows more ferocious every year. First, the firm needs to analyze its external and internal environments. Second, information gathered from this analysis serves as a basis of a statement of strategic intent and mission. Next, company leaders formulate and implement

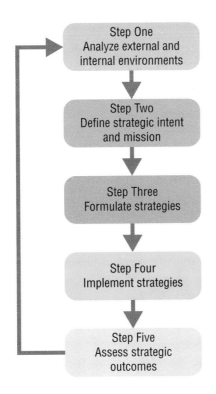

FIGURE 7.1

Components of the Strategic Management Process

Step One
Analyze external and internal environments

Step Two
Define strategic intent and mission

Step Three
Formulate strategies

Step Four
Implement strategies

Step Five
Assess strategic outcomes

strategies that will allow the firm to achieve sustained superior performance in light of its strategic intent and mission. Last, the executive team should periodically assess the outcomes of strategic plans. *Strategic outcomes* refer to intended and unintended results. Intended results can include higher profits, more focus on products or services, and increased stock price; unintended results can be lower customer responsiveness, higher cost, and improved productivity. The strategic outcome information in turn feeds into the analysis of the internal and external environment, which may lead to redefinition of strategic intent and mission, strategy formulation, and implementation.

As indicated in the case of Ford Motor Company, strategic management is a dynamic process. Adjustments may be necessary after examining strategic outcomes. For the sake of clarity, each step in Figure 7.1 is discussed separately, but it is important to remember that the various components of the strategic management process are closely linked to one another.

■ Step One: Analyzing External and Internal Environments

SWOT analysis
A strategic management tool to evaluate the firm, which is accomplished by identifying its strengths and weaknesses and identifying its opportunities and threats.

One commonly used strategic tool is a **SWOT (strengths-weaknesses-opportunities-threats) analysis**. The objective is to analyze factors from both within and outside the organization that may influence success. The external and internal factors to be considered in the SWOT analysis are discussed next. SWOT enables managers to identify organizational strengths (S) and weaknesses (W), and environmental opportunities (O) and threats (T). A properly conducted SWOT analysis generates information which helps a firm respond to various strategic challenges. SWOT does not tell the firm what strategies to pursue; instead it provides input for strategic decisions. Skills for Managing 7.1 "Will Harley-Davidson Hit the Wall?", shows a summary of a SWOT analysis for the motorcycle manufacturer. Based on this SWOT information, executives at Harley-Davidson must consider whether or not to redefine the company's strategic intent and mission. For instance, the management team should consider broadening the firm's mission to incorporate a wide array of two-wheel vehicles, not only large motorcycles, reformulating strategies to diversify its product mix, and changing strategy implementation protocols such as opening franchises in newly developing markets.

Figure 7.2 summarizes the factors that should be considered in an analysis of the firm's external and internal environments. Each of these is discussed in turn next.

The External Environment

In strategic management, the world around the company must be considered as carefully as the world inside the company. Company leaders must study the external environment in order to identify opportunities and threats in the marketplace, avoid surprises, and respond appropriately to competitors' moves. Bill Gates's observation may explain why Microsoft controls 93 percent of the world market for PC operating systems: "Why have we doubled our R&D on Windows in the last three years? Because we know that unless we do that we will be replaced. . . . Somebody makes something better? The demand can shift to that person overnight."[5] A major challenge for company executives is to gather accurate market intelligence in a timely fashion and transform it into usable knowledge that may be used to gain a competitive advantage.

FIGURE 7.2

Step One of the Strategic Management Process: Analyze External and Internal Environments

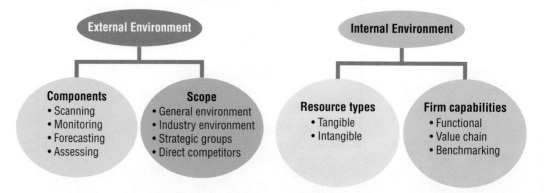

SKILLS FOR MANAGING 7.1

Will Harley-Davidson Hit The Wall? Identifying Strengths, Weaknesses, Opportunities, and Threats

Every year, Harley owners around the country get together for rallies, with up to 20,000 bikers at some events. For instance, there are local and national rallies to celebrate Elvis' birthday, sports events, and unveiling of new Harley-Davidson racing bikes. Some would be hard-core guys with big tattoos and bad tempers, the sort who once typified the Harley customer. But most are upper-middle class professionals earning salaries of more than six-figures on average, riding $17,000 motorcycles (the typical cost of Harley's biggest bike, a cruiser), and pledging fealty to an open-road cult that doubles as a highly profitable $5 billion-a-year company.

This is the motorcycle world that Harley-Davidson has reinvented, one that seems—and is—a century removed from the Milwaukee shed where William Harley and Andrew Davidson first collaborated in 1903. To continue riding this success in the new millennium, top executives at Harley-Davidson believe that the time has come to analyze the company's strengths, weaknesses, opportunities, and threats (SWOT) in order to formulate and implement future strategies. The results of the SWOT analysis are summarized below.

Strengths

- *Customer Loyalty.* Harley today is more of a fraternity than a producer of machinery. Buying a Harley makes you part of a ready-made motorcycle gang consisting of 600 U.S. HOG chapters, operated under the dealers' aegis. Style is as important as speed. On dealer floors, leather-draped mannequins outnumber the bikes. Harley has artfully parlayed the romance of the road and the independence of the biker to capture baby-boomers. The company's core customers have reprised their 1960s rebelliousness through a product that bespeaks their middle-aged success.
- *Brand Recognition.* Even though it sells a niche product, Harley consistently ranks among the 10 best-known American brands, in the company of Coca-Cola and Disney.
- *Top Growth Stocks.* Harley ranks among America's top growth stocks since its 1986 IPO. Its 37 percent average annual gain runs just behind the 42 percent pace of another 1986 debutant: Microsoft.
- *Strong Dealer Networks.* The people who catch Harley fever will be directed to a hometown dealer. A Harley dealer is never too far away. Many offer "Rider's Edge" courses for novices.

Weaknesses

- *Limited Product Line.* Most of the company's revenues are tied to the big cruiser bike.
- *Quality.* Harley hasn't built better bikes than its four main Japanese competitors and the company once had persistent quality problems. There is still room for improvements in quality.
- *Limited Cross-Cultural Appeal.* The firm has been primarily USA-centric and is strongly associated with the American culture. This has limited its international sales in the past,

although in recent years foreigners seem to find this symbol of America as a curious and attractive differentiating feature.

Opportunities

- *International Markets.* As foreign markets continue to expand, primarily, in developing countries such as India and China with a growing middle class, there may be an excellent outlet for the firm's products.
- *Youth Market.* Harley-Davidson appeals primarily to those over 45. Thus, there is an excellent market opportunity if the firm can develop products that appeal to prospective younger buyers.

Threats

- *Narrow Market Niche.* As the customer base has grayed, the average age of a Harley rider has risen from 38 to 46. Yet, the prime age for motorcycle customers is 35 to 44. In addition, 91 percent of buyers are males, further limiting the customer base.
- *Generation Gap.* Harley's appeal still lies more in image than in performance, but fashion-driven companies are vulnerable to changes of fashion and generation. The future of Harley's business is in the new generations, not exactly the forte of a company attuned to baby-boomer rhythms and values. Naturally the boomers' kids want to ride anything but the old man's model. They may be drawn to machines that are the anti-Harley.
- *Customer Resistance to Change.* Making changes is tricky for a company with Harley's cult following: They risk alienating currrent customers. The V-Rod's water-cooled engine is a big departure from Harley's traditional air-cooled one, and to some uneasy riders a portent of additional unwelcome changes to come. "If they ever do anything with that [roaring] sound, they've lost their customer base," according to an industry consultant.
- *Strong Signs of Weakening Demand.* The customer waiting list for new motorcycles has shrunk from as much as two years to a matter of months. Dealer premiums that used to range between $2,000 and $4,000 have disappeared for most models.

Source: Based on D. Oosterwal, *The Lean Machine: How Harley-Davidson Drove Top Line Growth*, New York: Amacon; R. A. D. Aveni, (2010). *Beating the commodity trap: How to maximize your competitive position*. Boston Mass., Harvard Business Press; H. O. Awa and S. E. Kalu (2010), "Repositioning the non-incremental changes and business strategic windows correlates," *International Journal of Business and Management*, 5(2), 15–26; L. G. Zomerdijk and C. A. Voss (2010), "Service design for experience—centric services." *Journal of Service Research*, 13 (1), 67–82; K. Nuttavuthisit (2010), "If you can't beat them, let them join: The development of strategies to foster consumers' co-creative priorities." *Business Horizons*, April 15, 2010, 19–26. J. Helyar, "Will Harley-Davidson Hit the Wall?" *Fortune*, August 12, 2003, pp. 120–24; www.harley-davidson.com.

Managers at Coke and Pepsi must now consider a new threat to soda's dominance as the quintessential American drink. Sales of soda have begun to decline as alternatives like bottled water and sports drinks like Red Bull, Gatorade, Powerade, and Full Throttle have grown in popularity. The shift comes about as consumers begin to worry about the problem of obesity and look for healthier and more varied choices.

scanning
The analysis of general environmental factors that may directly or indirectly be relevant to the firm's future.

monitoring
Observing environmental changes on a continuous basis to determine whether a clear trend is emerging.

forecasting
Predicting what is likely to happen in the future, the intensity of the anticipated event, its importance to the firm, and the pace or time frame in which it may occur.

assessing
Evaluating the environmental data received to study the implications for the firm.

Components of External Analysis

Studying the external environment requires managers to tap into a variety of sources, including the media, online information, journals and trade magazines, and other sources. There are four components of an external analysis: scanning, monitoring, forecasting, and assessing.

SCANNING   Analysis of general environmental factors that may be relevant to the firm's future is referred to as **scanning**. The primary objective is to identify early signs of emerging trends and changes in the environment that may result in an opportunity or a threat. For instance, when there were fewer college-age students, many private universities stayed afloat by targeting senior citizens, foreign students, and working adults. Colgate-Palmolive also looked at changing demographics before launching Total, which has become the top-selling toothpaste in the United States. It contains triclosan, a broad spectrum antibiotic (effective against bleeding gum disease, making it a hit among aging baby boomers).[6] Also, many corporations have adapted products and marketing campaigns to segmented markets to take advantage of ethnic diversity. The Internet is having a major effect on the way firms sell their products and services worldwide. It can also change the competitive landscape almost overnight.

MONITORING   Observing environmental changes on a continuous basis to determine whether a clear trend is emerging is referred to as **monitoring**. For example, recent data appears to contradict the belief that the future of North American business lies in design and innovation, while less developed countries will compete primarily through less skilled, lower-cost operations. In fact, countries such as India, China, and Brazil are quickly becoming "first world" in some high technology industries, showing high degrees of creativity, design, and innovation.[7] Monitoring can reduce the firm's level of uncertainty by interpreting current or past environmental information that is consequential to strategic decisions and that might require a response. Monitoring can reduce the level of uncertainty by keeping them aware of such events as elections, currency stability, lower inflation, and savings rates.

FORECASTING   In **forecasting**, the firm attempts to predict what is likely to happen in the future, the intensity of the anticipated event, its importance to the firm, and the pace or time frame in which it may occur. Some firms routinely delay investing in new information technology based on forecasts of lower costs relative to the amount of computer power that may be purchased. However, these investments can only be postponed for so long before the firm is at a disadvantage. As discussed in Chapter 2, firms that expand internationally attempt to predict a host of variables that may have a direct effect on return on investments. These variables include political and legal change, economic conditions, and currency convertibility.

Forecasts can be wrong, so a firm needs to retain strategic flexibility to make necessary adjustments. Continuous scanning and monitoring of the environment can provide valuable feedback about whether a firm needs to reconsider its position.

ASSESSING   Evaluation of environmental data received to study the implications for the firm is the process of **assessing**. Without an accurate assessment of consequences, the firm can make major blunders. For instance, when the cost of resin, a key raw material, increased, the management team at Rubbermaid thought that the company's well-recognized brand name and strong market presence would allow it to pass the increased costs on to customers. To their surprise, relatively unknown competitors such as Sterilite did not increase prices and quickly took away some of Rubbermaid's market share. Wal-Mart, which accounted for more than 15 percent of Rubbermaid's total household product sales, deleted Rubbermaid from its promotional materials and replaced it with Sterilite.

Rubbermaid is not alone.[8] Extended warranties represent the most profitable line of business for Best Buy and Circuit City (which has now filed for bankruptcy). Unfortunately for these two firms, Wal-Mart put a big dent in their earnings by offering warranties that are

50 percent less expensive on average. Wal-Mart, with its over $300 billion in sales and approximately 1.5 million employees, is the biggest employer in 21 states, with more people in uniform than the U.S. Army. And Wal-Mart "is pressuring everyone from Bloomingdale's to Banana Republic to compete on price as well as image."[9] Circuit City could no longer compete and is now defunct.[10]

Scope of the External Analysis

Analysis of the environment requires thinking on several levels. Managers can examine the environment at four different levels, including the general environment, the industry, strategic groups, and direct competitors.

THE GENERAL ENVIRONMENT   Broad environmental forces may have an impact on a firm even though their consequences may not be apparent or the effect may not be immediate. For instance, most population growth is occurring in third world countries. This means that a huge middle class is developing in such poor countries as India and China. This may represent a market opportunity for some Western firms.[11] The population of the United States and many Western countries is aging rapidly as a result of increasing life expectancies and declining birth rates. Some automobile manufacturers anticipate that the demand for trucks, sport utility vehicles, and vans has peaked, because older people prefer more comfortable cars with a plush feel to them. This has implications for R&D investments, car design, and manufacturing processes.

Sometimes changes in the general environment may be abrupt and unpredictable. For instance, Boeing expected to earn $2.6 billion on sales of $47 billion by the end of 1997. Boeing ended up losing $348 million, in large measure because of a sudden economic crisis in Asia, where it had 35 percent of its backlogged orders. A few years later, Boeing had almost recovered. Then came the terrorist attacks of September 11, 2001. Once again, profits plummeted as most airlines in the United States and abroad were faced with empty flights. By 2006, Boeing was entering a boom period after booking a record order for 1,002 new planes[12] and landing a big new commercial satellite customer (Mobile Satellite Ventures) with an order valued at between $500 million and $1 billion.[13] Then the severe recession of 2008–2012 hit, with most airlines around the world canceling orders for new planes.

The general environment may be broken down into individual segments. These segments include demographic trends, economic conditions, political/legal forces, sociocultural conditions, technological changes, and globalization. Each of these is discussed next. They are not independent segments. A change in one, such as globalization, is likely to affect others, especially sociocultural conditions.

Subway's "Eat Fresh" and dieter Jared Fogle helped propel the fast food restaurant past the big guys—namely McDonald's and Burger King. By recognizing the changing environment of its consumer— the desire for healthier fast food—Subway has become a number one franchise.

Demographic Trends   The study of population characteristics and trends is demographics. Some may have a direct impact on both current and future business opportunities. These include population size, age distribution, ethnic mix, levels of labor force participation by women and the size and composition of families.

A full chapter in the book (Chapter 11) is devoted to population diversity issues both in the United States and overseas. Demographic information can be useful when formulating strategies. For instance, electronic commerce was touted by many as the wave of the future in the late 1990s. Numerous investors rushed to pump money into Internet stores only to see the majority of them go bankrupt in less than two years. Surprisingly, by the middle of this decade electronic commerce is flourishing as exemplified by the case of Zappos, a shoe online retailer (see Management Close-Up 7.1, "Surviving and Doing Well After an Industry's Collapse."). A major reason for this turnaround is that the demographic characteristics of those using the Internet have changed considerably in the past five years. There are now more women who are Internet users than men. This trend is relevant for e-commerce because women do most of the household shopping. Other firms that have taken advantage of demographic changes include Cochlear Ltd. (which produces ear implants to improve hearing)[14] and condo developers (which have seen condo values remain more stable than single-family homes during the most recent recession of 2008–2012.).[15] How? By targeting a rapidly graying population (more on this when we discuss diversity in Chapter 11). Skills for Managing 7.2,

Surviving and Doing Well After an Industry's Collapse

Most dot-com firms have failed, yet Zappos.com's blue-ribbon customer service has taken over a large segment of the shoe market more than 12 years after the dot-com crisis occurred. Zappos, which was launched by a young entrepreneur named Tony Hsieh, sells shoes online, differentiating itself by its selection—some 100,000 styles and more than 600 brands, from Bass to Givenchy—and a near-fanatical devotion to customer service. Shipping and return shipping are free; most repeat customers get upgrades to free overnight or second-day delivery. The company has a 365-day return policy and promises to pay 110 percent of the difference if a customer finds a better price for the same item elsewhere. "With Zappos, the shoe store comes to you," says Pamela Leo. a customer in Monlclair, New Jersey. "I can try the shoes on in the comfort of my own home. I can tell if the shoes I want will really work with a particular suit. It's fabulous."

At Zappos, a customer-service team makes sure that every customer e-mail gets a response. Customer-service employees don't use scripts and aren't pressed to keep calls short. Hsieh says customer loyalty is so important to the company culture that the call center and headquarters have to be in the same place—Las Vegas. Every new hire spends a week in the Kentucky warehouse before starting work. Staff is treated well: Health insurance premiums are 100 percent company-paid (though employees contribute to dependents' premiums). All 650 employees, from execs to warehouse workers, get a free lunch every day.

The warehouse is open 24/7, so customers can order shoes as late as 11 p.m. and still get next-day delivery. "If customers know that they're going to get the best service from Zappos and they're going to get it overnight, then anytime we're going to add a product category, our customers will be loyal to us," says Hsieh.

Customer's testimonials abound on the Zappos Web page, which has a section on "what our customers are saying." For instance, one customer notes: "These shoes made my trip to Argentina that much more enjoyable. I needed a pair of shoes that I could walk great distances in and stand in for several hours at a time. These were my answer. They have great support, and give the feeling that one is walking on air. They did get dirty, when we went rappelling. Although you are not supposed to, I washed them on gentle cycle in my front loader washing machine. No harm, no foul. I highly recommend them."

Source: Based on J. Levine (2010), "Invisible branding." *Design Management Review*, 20 (4), 32–37; C. Hancock (2010), "You are connected, now, what are you going to do about it? *Design Management Review*, 21 (1), 62–67; J. Kolko (2010), "Abductive thinking and sensemaking; the drivers of design synthesis," *Design Issues*, 26 (1), 15–27; Zappos Web page, www.zappos.com; K. Welsul, "A shine on their shoes." *BusinessWeek*, December 5, 2005, p. 84.

"Business Implications of an Increasingly Older Population," challenges you to assess the effects of a rapidly aging population on business and the strategies firms may adopt to deal with that demographic change.

Economic Conditions   The economy of a region surrounding a company has a major impact on the strategic success of that company. Local companies are affected by local economic conditions, regional firms by regional conditions, and national companies by both national and international economic concerns. A sharp economic downturn in Asia during 1999–2003, for instance, had a major negative effect on financial institutions in the United States as well as on most larger American manufacturing firms. And conversely, the financial crisis that originated in the United States around September 2008 had a damaging effect on most economies around the world during subsequent years.

SKILLS FOR MANAGING 7.2

Business Implications of an Increasingly Older Population

In the richest countries of the world such as in North America and Western Europe, the population is aging rapidly. By 2020, it is estimated that approximately 35 percent of the population will be over 65, and about half will be 50 and older. A recent survey (Wiles, 2003) shows that various age groups have different attitudes toward life, including the willingness to take risks with investments or try new things. While 43 percent of those under 40 are willing to take substantial or above average risk, only 18 percent of those 58 or older are willing to do so.

In this exercise, the class is divided into groups of five. Each group chooses a well-known firm for analysis. It could be an investment bank, a brokerage house, a retailer, an educational institution, or a high-technology organization, for example.

1. Each group should first assess how the aging of the population is going to affect the business in the next 20 years.
2. Then each group must provide recommendations for dealing with any anticipated population effects they have identified.
3. A spokesperson from each group should then present the results of the group deliberations to the entire class.

In the modern world, most firms are highly interdependent. The ups and downs in one economic sector are likely to have a ripple effect on other sectors. For this reason, company leaders should be attuned to changes and trends in the economic environment.

Political/Legal Forces   The segment of the environment in which government policies and actions take place also has major effects on firms. Local, state, and federal governments along with the judicial system constantly issue a flurry of new regulations or reinterpretations of past regulations. Passage of the Health Care Act in 2010, to be implemented during 2011–2018, is likely to have a positive financial effect on some firms (such as small businesses and the self-employed) and a negative effect on others (for instance AT& T's top executives have vociferously complained about the cost to AT & T of complying with the Act).[16] Regulatory changes introduced by sovereign governments overseas compound the complexity of political/legal forces. When President George Bush decided to impose a 30 percent tariff on imported steel, other countries quickly responded with a tariff of their own on select American products. Mexican truck drivers are unable to enter the lucrative U.S. transportation market (as stipulated in the NAFTA accords drawn up almost 20 years ago; see Chapter 2) mainly due to political pressure on the part of the American Teamsters Union, which claims that Mexican trucks are unsafe.

Technological changes are occurring so fast that the legal system is having a hard time keeping up. Company leaders seek to develop political strategies to influence evolving legislation that covers new technologies. For instance, there is still no answer to a seemingly simple question: If a consumer buys an item on the Internet, which government entity has the right to collect a sales tax on that item, the state government, local government, or perhaps even a foreign government? As another example, a 120-year-old body of antitrust legislation, including the Sherman Act, designed to prevent monopolies, seems to be outmoded in the Digital Age. This became clear when Microsoft was charged with antitrust violations in the late 1990s under the Sherman Act for monopolizing computer operating systems, thereby engaging in unfair competition against competitors such as Netscape Communication Corp. and Intuit. At least for now Microsoft has won the legal battle, and its dominant position in the operating systems arena has strengthened considerably. Microsoft now controls 93 percent of new PC operating systems, up from 86 percent in 1997, and 96 percent of browsers, up from 67 percent in 1999. As noted by one observer, "From its inception, this case was supposed to prove that trustbusting is still relevant in the Digital Age. When the Justice Department sued the company in 1998, it argued that the century-old Sherman Antitrust Act could be applied swiftly and predictably to police high-tech monopolies. These claims now look pretty dubious."[17]

Part of the reason Microsoft was able to influence the court was a strong consumer preference for a common operating system. In other words, isn't it nice to send and open an attachment in the same manner in Washington, D.C., as you would in Moscow? As the digital economy evolves, antitrust legislation may need to change accordingly in order to accommodate these "natural monopolies" in which consumers have reasons to prefer unified technical standards. But how well a company fares under various political/legal forces also depends on a firm's strategy. For instance, almost 10 years after it was charged with antitrust violations, a poll of 940 senior executives in 68 countries ranked Microsoft as one of the top three most innovative companies around the world.[18] In the end, favorable public perceptions are likely to shelter a firm from political interference.[19]

Sociocultural Conditions   This part of the environment consists of the norms, values, and preferences of a society. These change over time, and vary by country or even by geographical area within a country. In general, firms are more likely to succeed if they can adapt products and services to prevalent sociocultural conditions. For instance, McDonald's has surprised many of its competitors by being able to crack the fastidious French market by adapting its menu and the look of its restaurants to French taste. McDonald's suffered declining sales in the United States during the past decade because many people were becoming leery of unhealthy fried fast food. McDonald's responded by introducing upscale organic coffee, healthier menus, leather sofas, soft lighting, and wireless Internet access.[20] These changes seem to be having a favorable impact on McDonald's bottom line in the United States.

Barbie Dolls, which are produced by Mattel, became a hit in the 1950s by capturing children's imaginations through what American society considered universal signs of beauty at the

Technological changes have had a tremendous impact on the newspaper industry. Managers have seen the newspaper medium grow old before their eyes as readers and advertisers turn to television, Webcasts, and podcasts for news and entertainment, just as the costs of printing and distribution have risen.

time: blond hair, blue eyes, large breasts, pale white skin, long legs. As the civil rights movement took hold in the 1960s, large numbers of non-European immigrants entered the United States, and international markets became more diverse, Mattel had little choice but to change Barbie or see its market slowly disappear. Barbie now comes in all colors and ethnic types, appealing to a wider variety of prospective buyers.

Technological Changes   The segment of the environment in which new knowledge is created and transformed into innovative products, services, or inputs is the technological environment. As the knowledge base increases, it is easier to create new knowledge or recombine existing knowledge to develop new products, processes, and materials. It took society thousands of years to create the first computer. Yet, it wasn't long ago when mainframe computers in 4,000 square feet of floor space could do less than a contemporary 2×2, one-pound personal computer can do now. In some product lines, such as software, the life cycle is measured in months, because new software quickly makes prior software obsolete.

By increasing productivity, technology can greatly decrease production costs. This, in turn, is reflected in product prices. DVD players were considered a luxury around the year 2000 with prices generally exceeding $1,000 dollars each. They now are priced as low as $35, and many have better features than their more expensive predecessors. Blu-Ray DVD players now cost one-fifth of their original prices and may be purchased in some electronic stores for under $150. A similar downward price spread is found for the flat, widescreen TVs, which not long ago sold in the $4,000–$12,000 range and can now be purchased for $600 or less. A similar trend is likely to occur for the three-dimensional TVs now entering the market for the first time.

More than ever before, firms must keep abreast of technological changes to remain competitive. For instance, for more than 100 years AT&T drew most of its revenues from residential landline phone businesses. But since the mid-1990s, this source of revenue has steadily declined due to cell phones and the Internet. A reborn AT&T now aims to deliver TV, Web, and wireless services hoping that these items will soon account for 90 percent of its revenues.[21] Bill Gates, the founder of what is possibly the most economically powerful business organization in history, is fond of saying that "Microsoft is three months away from bankruptcy." As noted earlier, he is referring to the constant fear that a competitor will develop a better and cheaper technology that will quickly replace Microsoft's market dominance. While this is unlikely to happen any time soon, it is not as farfetched as it may seem. For instance, the free Linux operating system, an alternative to Microsoft's software, is rapidly catching on and threatening Microsoft as a result.[22] As another case in point, Google seems to have come out of nowhere to put enormous pressure on its main competitor, Yahoo, quickly surpassing it on advertising sales.[23]

Globalization   In a world that continues to get smaller, firms are becoming increasingly dependent on foreign markets for raw materials as well as for processing and the sale of products and services (see Chapter 2). In many cases, it is difficult to define what is "domestic" and what is "foreign," as companies divvy up production processes and other essential activities, such as R&D and marketing, across different countries. These borderless strategic alliances and joint ventures with various ownership configurations are increasingly more common even among firms that are fierce competitors (such as the alliance between Japan's Sony, headed by Welsh-born executive Sir Howard Stringer, and Korea's Samsung to produce flat panel technology.[24] For instance, is Mazda a Japanese firm even though Ford Motor Company is its major shareholder and Ford's executives play an active role in managing the company? Did DaimlerChrysler (now dissolved) become a German or an American firm after Daimler from Germany bought Chrysler, even though most of Chrysler's facilities are in the United States and Mexico? Should Toyota's plants in Kentucky be considered Japanese or American even though they are completely staffed by Americans?

THE INDUSTRY ENVIRONMENT   An industry is composed of a group of firms with products that can substitute for one another. In the computer industry, the consumer may substitute an IBM PC for an Apple Macintosh. The industry environment has a direct effect on a firm's strategic competitiveness. This input is greater than the general environment, because firms within an industry are competing for a share of the same market.

The best-known framework for analyzing the industry environment was developed by Harvard professor Michael Porter.[25] According to this framework, the Five Forces within an industry are: the threat of new entrants, the threat of substitutes, suppliers, customers, and intensity of rivalry among competitors.

LOC-In 1 Learning Objective Check-In

Marketway is a company whose purpose is to deliver the latest information about firms' environments—essentially, they contract jobs to perform external analyses for other firms. Marketway advises many manufacturing clients, as well as service-based firms; For instance, it recently worked with a car manufacturer to consider the impact of declining birth rates and an aging population on the types of cars it should begin designing in the near term.

1. From an external analysis perspective, the aging population in Western countries demonstrates a _____.
   a. demographic trend
   b. political/legal force
   c. sociocultural condition
   d. technological change

2. The example in the scenario above focuses on an issue that is part of the car manufacturer's _____.
   a. immediate environment
   b. industry environment
   c. general environment
   d. tactical environment

The Threat of New Entrants   New competitors can change an industry overnight. Unless product demand is increasing, a new entrant is likely to take away part of the market and earnings enjoyed by existing firms.

The threat of new entrants decreases as barriers to entry and fear of retaliation by current industry participants increase. Obstacles that serve as roadblocks to prevent new companies from becoming part of an industry are called *barriers to entry*. Examples include the following.

- The government can restrict entry. For instance, trucking and liquor retailing are regulated. The costs of complying with government regulations discourages some potential entrants, and requirements such as liquor licenses may serve to limit the number of operating establishments a governmental body will allow.
- Intellectual property that is legally protected may keep firms out of the industry. For instance, Kodak could not enter the field of instant photography until the basic patents held by Polaroid had expired.
- Capital requirements may be so high that few firms have the resources to enter and few, if any, financial institutions are willing to lend them money. This would be the case for a new firm trying to enter the automobile manufacturing industry.
- If strong brand identification already exists within the industry, prospective entrants would have to spend heavily in marketing to overcome a consumer's natural inclination to purchase familiar brands.
- New entrants may not enjoy the cost advantages that help existing firms remain profitable. These include economies of scale from large size, favorable locations, and existing plants and equipment.
- New entrants may find it difficult to enter established distribution channels. For instance, they may have to use costly marketing campaigns, price breaks, and easy credit to get space on supermarket shelves.

Competitors may also be reluctant to enter a market if they believe that existing firms will react strongly. For instance, a new airline has low probability of surviving for very long because existing airlines use fare wars, premiums for passengers flying certain routes, and easy upgrades to first class to beat the competition. New airlines still enter the market from time to time, but many entrepreneurs and investors have probably been dissuaded from launching a new carrier because of fears of retaliation.

At the same time, the Internet is eroding barriers to entry by allowing new firms access to a global customer base. One observer notes that the Web is making high-end fashion as accessible to shoppers in Peoria as to those in Paris.[26]

The Threat of Substitutes   Technological changes may lead to the discovery and manufacturing of new products that supplant existing products. Higher quality, lower costs, more features, and safety considerations may induce consumers to shift preferences from the old to the new as shown in the following examples: Cheaper hardened plastics can now be used for automobile chassis in place of metal, posing a major threat to steel and aluminum companies that depend on the automobile industry for a substantial portion of their revenues. Likewise, cellulose, Styrofoam, and rock wool are increasingly replacing traditional fiberglass as insulation. Kodak has never recovered from the change from operating in a world of film where profit margins were high and product cycles were lengthy to living in the low-margin digital world where products continually change.[27] As a last example, people's music-buying habits have increasingly shifted toward musical downloads and as a result CD sales have dropped from 730 million units in 2000 to an estimated 400 million units at the present time.[28]

Suppliers   It is almost impossible to find a self-sufficient firm. Firms purchase inputs from suppliers and transform them to create products or services. Human resources are supplied by universities, trade schools, and other firms; raw materials are obtained from distributors, wholesalers, trading houses, and mining companies; and capital is supplied by banks, individual investors, and venture capitalists.

Suppliers can affect the cost of inputs, such as when a strong union sets a high wage for a particular craft. Dependence may pose a major threat to the firm if the skills are essential to the firm's production process. In other words, greater dependence on a particular supplier increases the power of that supplier to impose terms on the buyer. This dependence increases if the buyer has few other sources of supply, the supplier has many other buyers, satisfactory substitutes for the input are not available, or the cost of changing suppliers is significant.

Customers   Another major force in the industry is customers, who look for higher quality and the best service at the lowest price. Customers enjoy more bargaining power and negotiate better terms when they purchase a large portion of the firm's output, the product is important to them, close substitutes are easily available, and the products are relatively standardized or undifferentiated.

Intensity of Rivalry among Competitors   Firms use price, product differentiation, and product innovation to improve their market positions. Product differentiation includes extended warranties, "free" options, customer service, and user friendliness. Product innovations are new features that competitors don't yet offer. Typically one firm's action causes a reaction from other firms. A firm that makes a bold move to capture more of the market can expect retaliation from other players in the industry. Airlines, for instance, almost always match the price cuts of competitors, and they are quick to imitate any differentiating features of competitors. For example, Independence Air was launched in 2004 as a discount airline flying 50-seat jets but had to close down shortly thereafter as rivals such as United, Delta, and US Airways added flights and dropped ticket prices to combat the upstart.[29] Investors in Independence Air lost about $300 million in its short history and its 2,700 employees ended up in unemployment lines. When Continental credited triple miles rather than actual miles flown as part of its frequent-flyer program, most major airlines promptly followed suit. Robert Crandall, CEO of American Airlines, summarized the competitive environment of the industry as "intensely, vigorously, bitterly, savagely competitive."[30]

The intensity of competitive rivalry increases with the number of competitors. Other factors that cause competitive rivalry to increase are slow industry growth, unused productive capacity, undifferentiated services, and high exit barriers, such as major costs incurred by a firm in purchasing specialized plant and equipment.

SKILLS FOR MANAGING 7.3

Conducting an Environmental Analysis

Class is divided into groups of five. Each group is asked to think about a new business they would like to start. Be as specific as possible. Then group members determine which environmental characteristics are most likely to influence the future success of the chosen business and that they should be concerned about. This environmental analysis should consider the four levels discussed in this chapter, namely the general environment, industry environment, strategic groups, and direct competitors.

STRATEGIC GROUPS The management team must also examine the opportunities and threats in the external environment by focusing on the moves of competitors that follow similar strategies. A *strategic group* consists of a cluster of firms within an industry that tend to adopt common strategies of technological leadership, quality standards, prices, distribution channels, and customer service.[31] Ford, Chevrolet, and Toyota are in a different cluster than Mercedes, BMW, and Rolls-Royce. Similarly, Wal-Mart and Target are more likely competitors to Kmart than to Dillard's and Macy's. Such groups may be difficult to identify, and firms may have products that could belong to different strategic groups. However, many managers find it useful to closely track the behaviors of their closest competitors within the industry.

COMPETITOR ANALYSIS It is helpful to conduct a detailed study of each company that management considers a major competitor. Company leaders obtain data from a variety of sources including trade fairs, court records, annual reports, and competitor brochures. These data may be used to make educated inferences about competitor's goals and objectives, current strategies, strengths and weaknesses, and possible competitive moves. Deloitte & Touche estimates that 58 percent of firms have a formal process for obtaining competitor intelligence information, and that the rest use informal methods.[32]

Skills for Managing 7.3, "Conducting an Environmental Analysis," challenges you to identify the external factors that are most likely to impact the success of a business of your choice.

The Internal Environment

Have a look back at Figures 7.1 and 7.2. We now turn to analysis of the firm's internal environment, the second component (see Figure 7.2) of Step One of the strategic management process outlined in Figure 7.1. Every company has something that it does well. These are called "core competencies." Along with an analysis of the external environment, company executives should identify the internal resources, capabilities, and knowledge the firm has that may be used to exploit market opportunities and avoid potential threats. The **resource-based view** argues that basing a business strategy on what the firm is capable of doing provides a more sustainable competitive advantage than basing it on external opportunities. This is so because "customer preferences are volatile, the identity of customers is changing, and the technologies for serving customer requirements are developing rapidly, [so] an externally focused orientation does not provide the constancy of direction to act as a secure foundation for formulating long-term strategy."[33]

Since 1948 Honda has successfully used its expertise in the design and development of engines to manufacture and sell motorcycles, cars, and such gasoline-based engines as ground tillers, lawn mowers, pumps, and chainsaws. Likewise, 3M has used its knowledge of adhesive and thin-film technology for more than three generations to produce a broad range of successful products including Scotch Tape, magnetic tape, Post-it Notes, and adhesives that help heal minor cuts.

While a thorough understanding of company resources and capabilities can help the management team select a strategy that exploits these internal assets, no company can remain in business for very long unless there is a market for its products and services. Thus, even firms that base strategies on the internal environment must continuously monitor the external environment to devise appropriate responses to external opportunities and threats. Firms such as Sony, Black & Decker, Marks & Spencer, BMW, Motorola, and Intel attribute much of their long-term

resource-based view
A strategic management viewpoint that basing business strategy on what the firm is capable of doing provides a more sustainable competitive advantage than basing it on external opportunities.

Some U.S. automakers are hoping their internal resources will help them meet the continuing stiff competition from Japan. *Consumer Reports* recently named all Japanese cars as its top picks for the year, but Dodge, for one, still believes in the appeal of its classic models like the Charger and Challenger (pictured here), which are selling for top dollar in record numbers.

tangible resources
Assets that can be quantified and observed, including financial resources, physical assets, and manpower.

intangible resources
Resources that are difficult to quantify and include on a balance sheet, which often provide the firm with the strongest competitive advantage.

success to the ability to link information from the external environment, such as changing consumer tastes, shifting demographics, competitor's intelligence information, and new technologies, to internal resources and capabilities.

Resource Types

Many ingredients must be combined effectively to create an advantage for the company. These resources include a wide spectrum of inputs that firms use to deliver products and services. Capital, equipment, talents of employees and managers, patents, and brand names are key resources that may be *tangible* or *intangible*.

TANGIBLE RESOURCES   Financial resources, physical assets, and workers are all **tangible resources** that can be observed and quantified. A strategic assessment of tangible resources should enable management to efficiently use them to support the company and to expand the volume of business. The management team may also be able to find more profitable uses for tangible resources.

INTANGIBLE RESOURCES   Items which are difficult to quantify and include on a balance sheet often provide the firm with the strongest competitive advantage. These **intangible resources** are invisible and not obvious, and are difficult for competitors to purchase or imitate. The three most strategically important intangible resources are the firm's reputation, technology, and human capital.

Reputation   Other things being equal, consumers tend to buy products or services from a firm that is held in high regard. Many customers are even willing to pay more for that firm's recognizable brand. Reputation reduces uncertainty and risk. For years, IBM was able to sell personal computers at prices which were 50 percent more than competitors because the IBM name was synonymous with reliability and excellent customer service. When Nestlé acquired the British chocolate manufacturer Rowntree in the late 1980s, the bid price exceeded the book value of Rowntree's assets by more than 500 percent, an indication of the value of Rowntree's brand names Kit Kat and After Eights. Harley-Davidson stock went up faster than competitors' during the 1990s because the Harley name supported a price premium of about 40 percent above that of comparable motorcycles. Some of the most widely recognized brands around the world include Coca-Cola, Microsoft, IBM, GE, and Nokia.

Technology   Valuable patents, copyrights, and trade secrets that competitors don't have are all examples of the various technological advantages companies can enjoy. Also, the ability to create new technology faster than competitors or to make more efficient use of existing technology creates a sustained advantage. For example, Affymetrix, Inc., based in Santa Clara, California, pioneered a technology that allows up to 60,000 gene sequences to be scanned in one step. Licensing this technology to pharmaceutical companies enabled them to more precisely target certain drugs to meet the needs of the patient; and it may eventually alter the treatment of many types of cancer.[34] Firms that produce approximately 1,500 or more patents each year include Sony, Toshiba, Hitachi, Intel, Samsung Electronics, Micron Technology, Hewlett-Packard, Canon, Matsushita Electric, and IBM.[35]

Human Capital   The skills, knowledge, reasoning, and decision-making abilities of the workforce which support a firm's innovation and productivity reflect the value of the human capital present in the company (more on this in Chapter 10). Human capital can provide a very strong core competence that other firms cannot imitate in the following ways:

- Knowledge resides in people's minds, so it is unique to the employees in each firm.
- The ability to harness human resources depends on the integrated achievement of interdependent individual employees and their willingness to collaboratively use their talents to

support the firm's mission. That is, capabilities are created from teams of people working together, which represents an asset that is specific to the firm.

- It takes a long time to develop a core competence. Competitors are unlikely to assume the cost and risk of trying to duplicate it.
- The organization's culture may play a key role in how well people work together to achieve organizational objectives. Culture is idiosyncratic to each organization, which means it is a unique competitive factor.

Analyzing the Firm's Capabilities

Successful organizations excel or have the potential to excel in a specific activity. The Federal Express guarantee of next-day delivery anywhere within the United States is such a competitive advantage. British retailer Marks & Spencer ensures a high and consistent level of product quality across a wide range of merchandise through meticulously managed supplier relationships. General Electric reconciles control, coordination, flexibility, and innovation in one of the world's largest and most diversified corporations.

Company leaders can choose from three approaches to examine their capabilities. The first analyzes organizational capabilities for each of the major functional areas of the business. Table 7.1 is an example of how a **functional analysis** is conducted. This type of approach is easy for most people to understand, and provides the basis for meaningful discussion of the firm's strategy.

functional analysis
A strategic management approach that establishes organizational capabilities for each of the major functional areas of the business.

TABLE 7.1 Analyzing Capabilities by Functional Areas

Functional Area	Capability	Examples
Corporate management	Effective financial control systems	Hanson, Exxon
	Expertise in strategic control of diversified corporation	General Electric, ABB
	Effectiveness in motivating and coordinating divisional and business-unit management	Shell
	Management of acquisitions	ConAgra, BTR
	Values-driven, in-touch corporate leadership	Wal-Mart, FedEx
Information management	Comprehensive and effective MIS network, with strong central coordination	American Airlines, L. L. Bean
Research and development	Capability in basic research	Merck, AT&T
	Ability to develop innovative new products	Sony, 3M
Manufacturing	Speed of new product development	Canon, Mazda
	Efficiency in volume manufacturing	Briggs & Stratton
	Capacity for continual improvements in production processes	Toyota, Nucor
	Flexibility and speed of response	Benetton, Worthington Industries
Product design	Design capability	Pinifarini, Apple
Marketing	Brand management and brand promotion	Procter & Gamble, PepsiCo
	Promoting and exploiting reputation for quality	American Express
	Responsive to market trends	The Gap, Campbell Soup
Sales and distribution	Effectiveness in promoting and executing sales	Microsoft, Glaxo
	Efficiency and speed of distribution	FedEx, The Limited
	Quality and effectiveness of customer service	Walt Disney Co., Marks & Spencer

Source: Adapted from R. M. Grant, *Contemporary Strategy Analysis,* copyright © 2010. Reprinted with permission of Wiley-Blackwell Publishing.

value-chain analysis
Strategic management analysis that breaks the firm down into a sequential series of activities and attempts to identify the value-added of each activity.

The second method breaks the firm down into a sequential series of activities and attempts to identify the value-added of each activity. Professor Michael Porter refers to it as a **value-chain analysis**. Porter distinguishes between primary activities, concerned with the transformation of inputs and outputs (such as materials handling, purchasing, inventory holding, machining, and packaging), direct customer contact (such as sales, marketing, and customer service), and support (such as administrative assistance and human resource management). In other words, rather than analyzing the firm's capabilities in terms of what different functions contribute, Porter suggests that it is better to identify those activities that create value and those that do not. This approach has the distinct advantage of focusing the analysis on value creation. That is, it can help managers determine the extent to which the value created by a particular activity is greater than the cost incurred to create that value. This is referred to as "margin."

While theoretically useful for understanding competitive advantage, the value chain concept is difficult to apply in practice. For one thing, it may be impossible to meaningfully assess the net value added (margin) of singular activities. Company activities tend to be so intertwined that they are seldom carried out in isolation. For instance, customer service, which is a primary activity, is unlikely to be superior if product quality is deficient (a production issue, which is also a primary activity) or if recruits are poorly trained (a human resource issue, a support activity). Making those comparisons in relation to competitors is even more difficult because this information is very hard to obtain.

benchmarking
A strategic management approach that assesses capabilities by comparing the firm's activities or functions with those of other firms.

A third approach assesses capabilities by comparing the firm's activities or functions with those of other firms. This approach, normally referred to as **benchmarking**, has four stages:

1. Identifying activities or functions that are weak and need improvement.
2. Identifying firms that are known to be at the leading edge of each of these activities or functions.
3. Studying the leading-edge firms by visiting them, talking to managers and employees, and reading trade publications to ascertain how and why they perform so well.
4. Using the information gathered to redefine goals, modify processes, acquire new resources, and engage in other activities to improve the firm's functions.

Benchmarking has been used as an important strategic tool by a number of well-known companies. It played a central role in the revitalization of Xerox during the 1980s. Detailed comparisons of Xerox copiers and those of competing manufacturers revealed that Japanese rivals made copiers at half the cost in half the time and with half as many workers. Xerox's defects per thousand in assembly were 10 to 30 times greater than those of Japanese competitors. The result was the establishment of a continuous program of benchmarking in which every Xerox department is encouraged to look globally to identify "best in class" companies against which to benchmark. Similarly, ICL, the British computer subsidiary of Fujitsu, benchmarks against the manufacturing processes of Sun Microsystems and the distribution system of the retailer Marks & Spencer. As a last example, in the years 2006–2009 Volkswagen was losing about $1.2 billion a year in its North American operation, a huge amount putting the survival of VW in question. A benchmark analysis by VW identified what might be a major reason behind these appalling losses. Wolfgang Bernhard, head of the German automaker's Volkswagen brand,

---

LOC-In 2   **Learning Objective Check-In**

1. Eliza is an executive in a large business unit at her firm. In an effort to better understand the sustainable competitive advantages of her particular business unit, she and the rest of her executive team have chosen to focus on what the firm is capable of doing. They believe, based on customer trends and rapid development of technology, that basing their business strategy on capabilities instead of external factors will provide a more sustainable competitive advantage. Eliza and her team subscribe to the _____ .
   a. SWOT analysis method
   b. functional analysis view
   c. resource-based view
   d. planning view

summarized the results of the study as follows: "Volkswagen takes twice as many hours to assemble a car as its most productive rivals, and it labors at a cost disadvantage of a couple thousand dollars per vehicle in the U.S. market."[36] Now, as discussed in the introductory vignette in Chapter 1, Volkswagen's objective is to be ahead of Toyota in the United States in market share by 2018, using as a springboard its reputation for high quality and reliability, and taking advantage of Toyota's recent tarnished image.

In the end, all approaches used to analyze the firm's capabilities have advantages as well as disadvantages. And while there is no model or rule that is clearly best for every situation, having an understanding of all of these perspectives (functional, value chain or benchmarking) can help strategists make better decisions and form higher quality strategies.

■ Step Two: Strategic Intent and Mission

The second component of the strategic management process (following the analysis of the external and internal environments) consists of formal statements of strategic intent and mission. (See Figure 7.3.) **Strategic intent** is internally focused, indicating how the firm will use its resources, capabilities, and core competencies. It guides future actions and focuses employees' attention on using their talents to outdo competitors. Several large firms express their strategic intent as follows:

- Unocal Corporation: "To become a high performance multinational energy company—not the biggest, but the best."
- Eli Lilly and Company: "It is our strategic intent that customers worldwide view us as their most valued pharmaceutical partner."
- Intel: "We intend to become the premier building block supplier to the computer industry."
- Microsoft: "To provide the Yellow Pages for an electronic marketplace of online information systems."[37]

A firm's **strategic mission** flows from its strategic intent, defining the company's external focus in terms of what will be produced and marketed, utilizing the firm's internally based core competence. Figure 7.4 reproduces Chevron's strategic mission statement, which is distributed to all employees.

This is a good point to remind you again that even though the components of the strategic management process have been presented one step at a time (following the model in Figure 7.1), they are not completely separate from each other nor do they cover every element. This is particularly true in the case of the firm's strategic intent and mission. For a brand new entrepreneurial firm being built from the ground up, the strategic management process is fairly straightforward. First, the entrepreneur looks for opportunities in the environment, and then defines strategic intent and mission to take advantage of those opportunities. For instance, according to legend, Kenmons Wilson became irate at shoddy accommodations during a family vacation in the early 1950s, and sitting at night in a hotel room he dreamed up a new business whose mission would be "to provide comfortable, child-friendly, inexpensive lodging." This led to a motel chain offering customers high-quality accommodations anywhere in the world. Wilson built the first

strategic intent
The firm's internally focused definition of how the firm intends to use its resources, capabilities, and core competencies to win competitive battles.

strategic mission
The firm's externally focused definition of what it plans to produce and market, utilizing its internally based core competence.

FIGURE 7.3

Step Two of the Strategic Management Process: Define Strategic Intent and Mission

FIGURE 7.4

A Strategic Mission Statement: The Case of P&G

Source: From http://www.pg.com/annualreport2009/letter/purpose-growth.shtml.

Purpose-Inspired Growth Strategy: "Where to Play" Choices

Our single, unifying growth strategy is tightly linked to our Purpose: "We will grow by touching and improving the lives of more consumers in more parts of the world…more completely."

Specifically, we will:

- Grow our leading global brands and core categories—with an unrelenting focus on innovation.
- Build business with underserved and unserved consumers.
- Continue to grow and develop faster-growing, structurally attractive businesses with global leadership potential.

We will create abundant growth opportunities in each of these areas.

Holiday Inn in Memphis in 1952. At the time of his death in 2003 there were 3,000 motels worldwide bearing the Holiday Inn name.[38]

As firms mature, however, the strategic management process is not as clear-cut. Why? Very few firms can radically change their strategic intent and mission in search for new opportunities in the external and internal environment. Most established companies have invested large sums of money in plant, equipment, and human resources to accomplish a mission. Thus, they are more likely to focus on those aspects of the environment that are relevant to their already existing strategic intent and mission. Another way of looking at it is that the firm's strategic intent and mission restrict how managers view the environment. Over the long term, however, a firm whose strategic intent and mission are incongruent with the environment is unlikely to continue to be successful, and may face extinction. Think of what would have happened to DuPont had it remained faithful to its original mission in the 19th century: the production of dynamite for use in coal mines. Instead, by diversifying into a variety of chemicals, DuPont seized on new opportunities as they became available and grew and prospered as a result.

LOC-In 3 Learning Objective Check-In

1. Adriatics is a software development firm that specializes in research and intense-weather data gathering tools. For example, their highly sensitive tools can be used in tornadoes or hurricanes or in underwater environments. Adriatics' _____ is to develop the most advanced intense-weather data gathering tools in the industry, whereas its _____ is to make marketable the tools and research software it develops and offer them to the world at the best value possible.
   a. strategic mission; strategic intent
   b. vision statement; strategic mission
   c. strategic intent; vision statement
   d. strategic intent; strategic mission

■ Step 3: Strategy Formulation

Strategy formulation, the third component of the strategic management process (see again Figure 7.1), is the design of an approach to achieve the firm's mission. An effectively formulated strategy integrates, marshals, and allocates the firm's internal resources and makes appropriate use of external environmental information. The idea is to formulate a mission-consistent strategy that will lead to sustained superior performance. For instance, as shown in Management Close-Up 7.2, a growing number of firms use innovation labs as a strategy to stay ahead of competitors in a rapidly changing environment. Strategy formulation takes place at the corporate and business-unit levels (see Figure 7.5).

Corporate-Level Strategy

Strategy formulation begins with an overall approach to the direction of the organization. A **corporate-level strategy** encompasses the number of businesses the corporation holds, the

strategy formulation
The design of an approach to achieve the firm's mission.

corporate-level strategy
The corporation's overall plan concerning the number of businesses the corporation holds, the variety of markets or industries it serves, and the distribution of resources among those businesses.

MANAGEMENT CLOSE-UP 7.2   THEME: **DEALING WITH CHANGE**

Innovation as a Key Part of Strategy Formulation

The need for speed in innovation in order to achieve a company's mission stretches beyond high-tech companies. Outfits as varied as Mattel, Steelcase, Boeing, Wrigley, Procter & Gamble, and even the Mayo Clinic now use so-called innovation labs to shatter bureaucratic barriers that have grown up among inventors, engineers, researchers, designers, marketers, and others. In these labs, teams of people from different disciplines gather to focus on a problem. They brainstorm, tinker, and toy with different approaches—and generate answers that can be tested on customers and sped to the market. Often this process involves the application of knowledge from one area into a totally different domain. For instance, the Mayo Clinic developed a process to catch 95 percent of brain aneurysms (which are usually fatal when they pop) through the use of "business intelligence" software created by IBM. Although this type of business software has been around for decades in supply chain and inventory management, the Mayo Clinic's application of it to *the health field* is fairly new (around 2010).

A central tenet of the innovation lab movement is that layout and design are crucial. Mattel Inc.'s preschool toy unit, Fisher-Price, has its center at company headquarters in East Aurora, New York, but it's clearly a separate part of the operation. Called "the Cave," the center boasts bean-bag chairs, comfy couches, and adjustable lighting that make people feel as if they are far from the office. Teams of staffers from engineering, marketing, and design meet there with child psychologists or other specialists to share ideas. After observing families at play in the field, they return to brainstorm—or "sketch-storm," as they call it. Then they build prototypes of toys from foam, cardboard, glue, and acrylic paint.

In an innovation lab that involved child psychologists, sociologists, software specialists, and marketing personnel Mattel, Inc. recently came up with the idea of a virtual world "Barbie girls ™" designed for 6–16 years old with Internet access. By 2011 it had approximately 17 million registered users.

Sources: Based on: www.Mattel.com (2011); www.fisher-price.com (2011) ; J. D. Wineman, F. W. Kabo, and G. F. Davis (2009); "Spatial and Social Networks in Organizational Innovation." *Environment and Behavior*, 41 (3), 427–442; C. Neuman and J. Srinivasan (2010), *Managing Innovation for the Land of Ideas and Talent*, Springer Publishing Co.; B. A. Lundwall, (2010). *National Systems of Innovation*, Anthem Press (2010); J. Fortt (2010), "Software that saves money and lives." *Fortune*, 2010, March 22, p. 28; J. Weber, S. Holmes, and C. Palmeri, "Mosh Pits of Creativity," *BusinessWeek*, November 7, 2005, pp. 98–101.

diversification strategy
A firm's strategic plan to create and manage a mix of businesses owned by the firm.

portfolio analysis
An approach to classify the processes of a diversified company within a single framework or taxonomy.

variety of markets or industries it serves, and the distribution of resources among those businesses. For instance, the Wm. Wrigley Jr. Company focused almost exclusively on the chewing gum market. Seagram, on the other hand, diversified from its core beverage business by acquiring MCA in the entertainment industry. This is called a **diversification strategy**.

Corporate diversification strategy addresses two questions: (1) What business are we in? (2) What businesses should we be in? Corporate diversification may be analyzed in terms of portfolio mix, diversification type, and diversification process. Each of these is discussed in turn.

PORTFOLIO ANALYSIS The basic idea of **portfolio analysis** is to classify the businesses of a diversified company within a single framework or taxonomy. Two of the most widely applied techniques are the McKinsey-General Electric Portfolio Analysis Matrix and the Boston Consulting Group's Growth-Share Matrix.

McKinsey-General Electric Portfolio Analysis Matrix   This model has two sides, and classifies all businesses held by a diversified corporation (see Figure 7.6). The horizontal side refers to the health of the business unit in terms of markets (using indicators such as the domestic or global market share of the business, its competitive situation, and its level of profitability). The vertical side reflects the attractiveness of the industry of the business unit along the dimensions of market size, market growth, and industry profitability. This two-dimensional matrix is used to classify all the business units of a diversified corporation. Then the matrix is used as a diagnostic tool to make recommendations, such as:

- When a business unit ranks high on both dimensions (see quadrant 9), it means that it has an excellent future and should be "grown" (i.e., more resources should be allocated to it).
- When a business unit ranks low on both dimensions (see quadrant 1), it means that future prospects are poor and should be "harvested" (i.e., the corporation should squeeze all the possible profits out of it without doing much in terms of additional resources devoted to it).
- When a business unit falls in the middle (see quadrants 3, 5, 7), it becomes a candidate for a "hold" strategy (corporation adopts a "wait and see" attitude, but continues to allocate sufficient resources to maintain current level of activity).

Boston Consulting Group's Growth-Share Matrix   This approach (also known as the BCG Matrix) applies a similar method to that of the McKinsey-General Electric Portfolio Analysis Matrix except that the horizontal axis refers to the business unit's market share and the vertical axis refers to the annual real rate of market growth (see Figure 7.7). The strategic recommendations of the BCG Matrix approach are also quite direct and simple:

- A business unit that is both low in market share and low in market growth (a "dog") should be divested as soon as possible.
- If a business unit has a high market share in a market with low growth potential (a "cow"), it should be "milked" as much as possible with only limited additional resources devoted to it.

FIGURE 7.6

The McKinsey–General Electric Portfolio Analysis Matrix

Source: From R. M. Grant, *Contemporary Strategy Analysis,* copyright © 2010. Reprinted with permission of Wiley-Blackwell Publishing.

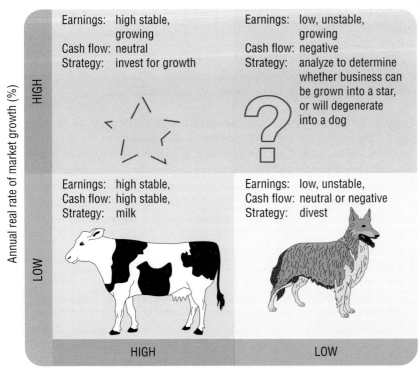

FIGURE 7.7

The Boston Consulting Group's Growth-Share Matrix

Source: From R. M. Grant, *Contemporary Strategy Analysis,* copyright © 2010. Reprinted with permission of Wiley-Blackwell Publishing.

- If a business unit has both a high market share and operates in a growing market (a "star"), the corporation should greatly invest in it to fuel additional growth.
- If a business unit has a low market share but operates in a growing market (a question mark), additional analysis is necessary to decide whether or not more responses should be channeled its way.

The main advantage of the portfolio approach (which includes both the McKinsey-GE Matrix and the BCG Matrix) to examine the businesses a diversified corporation holds is that it can combine several elements of strategically useful information in a single framework. This simplicity also has its downside. Portfolio models assume that each business unit operates independently. Often business units are not "stand-alone" profit centers. Many do (or should) share valuable resources. Corporate executives may also acquire or sell business units without considering the effects this may have on the rest of the corporation's core business. Within each business unit, managers may have an incentive to "play by the numbers" to avoid their unit's being placed in the "harvest" or the "dog" categories.

Canon suffered from most of the problems noted in the previous paragraph. The company was managed with a typical corporate portfolio mentality. Canon had a dozen major independent divisions, or profit centers with a great deal of duplication of activities that could have been shared (such as R&D and purchasing). Canon divisions "operated like individual fiefdoms, obsessed with building sales numbers at any costs."[39] Fujio Mitarai decided to change this portfolio scheme upon taking over as CEO in the late 1990s. Since then Canon has done remarkably well. Now, there are four key divisions: copiers, printers, cameras, and optical equipment. Each cooperates rather than competes with the others. To underscore that all divisions are part of one company, Mitarai introduced consolidated balance sheets, in which profits and losses are reported at the corporate level, not at the business-unit or divisional level. To keep communication flowing across divisions and reinforce a sense that all divisions are part of one company, Mitarai frequently holds an informal board meeting at 7:45 a.m. to have division executives debate the company's direction. He also holds daily lunch meetings with senior managers of various divisions and monthly meetings for 800 lower-level managers.

As a final comment, portfolio matrices may create the illusion of objectivity when in fact a considerable amount of personal judgment is involved when classifying businesses into particular boxes. As noted by one observer, "Is BMW's North American auto business a 'dog' because it holds less than 1 percent of a low-growth market or a cash 'cow' because it is market leader in the luxury car segment?"[40]

TYPES OF DIVERSIFICATION Firms may be classified according to the mix of businesses owned by the firm. Four major types of business mix are concentration strategy, vertical integration strategy, concentric diversification strategy, and conglomerate diversification.

concentration strategy
A form of diversification strategy that focuses on a single business operating in a single industry segment.

Concentration Strategy A firm following the **concentration strategy** focuses on a simple business operating in a single industry segment. A firm is classified as a single business if 95 percent or more of its total sales come from that business. A concentration strategy allows the firm to become the best at a particular competency, which may provide a sustained competitive advantage. For example, Research in Motion, Ltd. (RIM) has been a leader in the wireless e-mail gadget, with all of its profits derived from one highly successful product: The BlackBerry. The disadvantage of a concentration strategy is that a firm assumes a higher degree of risk when most earnings come from a single source. In the case of RIM, Motorola, Nokia, Palm, Inc., Samsung Electronics, Hewlett Packard Co., Apple, and Siemens have entered the BlackBerry's market, introducing an array of inexpensive wireless e-mail devices with beefed-up features.[41]

vertical integration strategy
A form of diversification strategy in which a firm integrates vertically by acquiring businesses that are supply channels or distributors to the primary business; producing its own inputs is backward integration, and distributing its own outputs is forward integration.

Vertical Integration Strategy Another method to grow quickly is to buy the company that sells you supplies. Or set up retail outlets to sell your own goods and services, rather than going through others. In **vertical integration**, a firm acquires businesses that are supply channels or distributors to the primary business. Producing its own inputs is called *backward integration*, and distributing its own outputs is *forward integration*. Either may give the firm greater control and allow it to reduce costs and uncertainty. For instance, Time Warner acquired Turner Broadcasting in part to help distribute Turner's classic movies and also so that the Turner cartoon network would show Warner Brothers cartoons. A potential disadvantage of a vertical integration strategy is that the firm may be unfamiliar with the business of suppliers or distributors, and make mistakes as a result.

concentric diversification strategy
A form of diversification strategy in which the firm expands by creating or acquiring new businesses that are related to the firm's core business.

Concentric Diversification Strategy In **concentric diversification**, the firm expands by creating or acquiring new businesses related to the firm's core business. This would be the case, for instance, when Compaq was purchased by Hewlett-Packard about a decade ago. Concentric diversification strategies offer two advantages. First, it may be possible to reduce costs, because two similar businesses may share HR departments, shipping processes, inventory systems, or other activities. Second, the core competency of the original company can be transferred to the newly acquired company. Two potential disadvantages of this strategy are that business-unit managers do not always cooperate with one another and that corporate headquarters may not be able to effectively manage the interrelationships among the business units.

conglomerate diversification
A form of diversification strategy that involves managing a portfolio of businesses that are unrelated to each other.

Conglomerate Diversification **Conglomerate diversification** involves managing a portfolio of businesses that are unrelated to each other. For instance, Union Pacific Corporation's original focus was building and managing railroads. It has now expanded into oil and gas exploration, mining, microwave technology, fiber optic systems, waste disposal, trucking, and real estate. One advantage of conglomerate diversification is that risks are spread across different markets and industries so that potential downturns in one business segment may be offset by higher earnings from other business units.

Research suggests that as a whole conglomerates are not as profitable as the other types of corporate diversification strategies.[42] The main problems appear to be that conglomerate diversification does not build on a firm's core competencies and that corporate executives do not have sufficient knowledge to effectively manage disparate business units.

PROCESS OF DIVERSIFICATION A firm's corporate diversification strategy may also be examined in terms of the way it diversifies. Diversification occurs by acquisition and restructuring, and by internationalization.

acquisition
The process of purchasing other firms.

merger
The process of integrating two firms.

Acquisition and Restructuring Strategies The primary means for conducting a diversification strategy are through **acquisition**—purchasing other firms—and **merger**—integrating two firms. Firms engage in mergers and acquisitions to gain greater market power, move into new markets, avoid the cost of new product development, and spread business risks. Among the problems that can arise are failure to integrate different corporate cultures, overvaluation of the target firm, inability to achieve successful synergies between the firms, and increased inefficiencies and poor cost controls attributed to large size. For example, a recent survey suggests that companies that are merging often focus on cost-cutting, not consumer service.[43]

International Strategy Firms are increasingly moving some manufacturing operations overseas. Even small companies seek to secure access to markets outside domestic borders. Firms internationalize for a variety of reasons, including a desire to increase market size, share resources and knowledge between units, lower costs, and spread business risks across diverse markets. Internationalization issues were discussed at length in Chapter 2.

Business-Level Strategy

Once company leaders determine a diversification strategy, they must decide how to compete in each business area or market segment. This is referred to as *business-level strategy*. For instance, Kmart and Wal-Mart have traditionally emphasized the low-cost end of the retail market while Dillard's and Dayton's have focused on high-quality, higher-priced leading-edge fashion.

There are two basic choices when selecting an industry position. One is to try to achieve lower cost than rivals. The other is to try to differentiate products and command a premium price. Providing products and services that are less expensive than those of competitors is referred to as **cost-leadership strategy**. Delivering products and services that customers perceive to be different and better is a **differentiation strategy**.

cost-leadership strategy
Providing products and services that are less expensive than those of competitors.

differentiation strategy
Delivering products and services that customers perceive as unique.

A cost-leadership strategy requires the firm to carry out its activities more efficiently than competitors, passing along cost savings to consumers in the form of lower prices. Firms may reduce costs through large-scale efficient facilities, low overhead, fast turnover of inventories, volume buying of needed inputs, state of the art technology, plants located in low-wage countries, and "build to order systems." Because their profit margins are low, such firms need to sell large volumes to earn acceptable returns. For example,

- Toys 'R' Us secured a large market share in the toy retailing industry in the United States and overseas by charging 10 percent to 15 percent less than competitors. Its efficient distribution system, volume purchasing, and large stores have given the firm the necessary cost advantage to undercut the competition.
- Unifi, Inc., one of the most efficient producers of filament polyester and nylon fiber, dominated its market by being a leader in manufacturing technologies, allowing it to underprice its competitors.
- Southwest Airlines was able to maintain high profitability in an industry where being in the red is not uncommon. It specializes in no-frills, low-price fares on selected "short-hop" routes and a highly versatile workforce willing to perform multiple jobs. A single employee may serve as a bag handler, front desk representative, ticket collector, and steward. Southwest maintains its low-cost strategy while outperforming all other U.S. carriers in terms of on-time performance, baggage handling, and number of complaints.

A differentiation strategy requires a firm to continuously invest in the creation of new products or add new features to existing products so that customers believe the products are different and better than those offered by competitors. The challenge for these firms lies in selling products at a price that customers are willing to pay. For instance, consumers may be willing to pay three times as much for a Gucci or an "Oscar de la Renta" brand item than for an equally attractive off-label version of the same item. The consumer may justify what seems like an irrational choice citing a combination of higher prestige, perceived better design, and presumed higher quality of the more expensive brands.[44]

Commonly recognized differentiated products include:

- Toyota's Lexus: the relentless pursuit of perfection.
- Ralph Lauren's and Tommy Hilfiger's clothing lines: image.
- Caterpillar: a heavy equipment manufacturing firm committed to providing rapid delivery of spare parts to any location in the world.
- Maytag appliances: product reliability.

- McKinsey & Co: the highest priced and most prestigious consulting firm in the world.
- Rolex watches: prestige and image.
- Gateway: low-cost PCs for home use.
- Google: comprehensive Web surfing.

LOC-In 4 Learning Objective Check-In

Sing Brand Foods is a corporation that has six different business units, including Gregory's, an upscale chain of restaurants popular throughout the Midwest.

1. Executives involved in _____ most likely work at the corporate level.
   a. differentiation strategy
   b. cost leadership strategy
   c. restaurant staffing decisions
   d. the diversification process

2. Executives involved in _____ make decisions regardining the strategy formulation at Gregory's.
   a. portfolio analysis
   b. differentiation strategy
   c. diversification type decisions
   d. horizontal diversification strategy

■ Step 4: Strategy Implementation

An idea is nothing until it becomes an action. The fourth key component of the strategic management process is strategy implementation (see Figure 7.1). Even the best conceived strategies are of little value if they are not implemented effectively. For instance, a few years ago Blockbuster Inc. ditched late fees to compete more effectively with video-by-mail chains such as Netflex Inc., which allows consumers to pay a flat monthly fee and retain movies for as long as they want. But the wisdom of Blockbuster's move was soon put into doubt since those late fees accounted for $250–300 million a year (or about 15 percent of Blockbuster's annual revenue).[45]

To implement formulated strategies successfully, company executives must consider strategic leadership, organizational structure and controls, cooperative strategies, global strategies human resource strategies, and corporate entrepreneurship and innovation (see Figure 7.8).

Strategic Leadership

Effective leadership plays a fundamental role in the relative success or failure of a firm (see Chapter 13 on leadership). This is particularly true for top executives who are responsible for charting general implementation plans, making key resource allocation decisions, and delegating day-to-day operations. In the opinion of three well-known management authors, "By word and/or personal example and through their ability to dream pragmatically, effective strategic leaders meaningfully influence the behaviors, thoughts, and feelings of those with whom they work."[46] Management Is Everyone's Business 7.1 on page 219 provides a set of recommendations for those who are expected to play a managerial role as part of the strategic management process.

FIGURE 7.8

Step Four of the Strategic Management Process: Implement Strategy

MANAGEMENT IS EVERYONE'S BUSINESS   7.1

WORKING AS A MANAGER   An effective manager must be proactive in responding to evolving challenges and opportunities rather than be overtaken by events. Learning to think strategically forces managers to be on the alert for changes in the external and internal environments, to modify the firm's strategic intent, mission, and formulated strategy when necessary, and to effectively implement the new or redefined strategies.

As a manager, you should:

- Be continuously alert to changes in the environment (such as new technologies, potential competitors, changes in customer preferences) that may be relevant to the entire organization or your particular unit.
- Always think ahead and try to envision the prospect the entire organization or your unit may be facing in the short term (say, less than a year), mid-term (say, between 1–5 years), and long term (say, 5 years or more). In other words, don't assume present conditions will stay the same in the future (most likely they will not!).
- Even if not done as a formal exercise (although it is highly advisable from time to time) managers should conduct a strengths-weaknesses-opportunities-threats (SWOT) analysis for their areas of responsibility.
- Identify those unique resources available in your areas of responsibility that are rare and difficult to imitate by competitors and that can be mobilized to stay ahead of the game. This could be as broad as organizational culture (for instance, an entrepreneurial orientation) or specific (concrete set of talents and skills possessed by individual employees).
- Be input driven, continuously seeking ideas and feedback from subordinates, peers, and other managers.
- Don't take things for granted and don't hesitate to question assumptions (for instance, about markets, technology, legal issues) that may be driving your decisions.
- Be flexible to change course if necessary but do not overact as such changes may be costly and risky.
- Be keenly aware that short-term gains (for instance, increasing profitability by cutting R&D expenditures or massive layoffs) may be more than offset by long-term losses (for instance, fewer new products and migration of key talent to competitors). To be strategic, you must have a long-term view of your actions and decisions!
- Being data driven has the advantage of objectivity but too much "bean counting" may have negative strategic value as the complexity of strategic issues can seldom be summarized in a set of quantifiable indicators.

Organizational Controls

A company's board of directors is expected to monitor the actions and decisions of top executives to ensure that they act in the best interest of the firm. Until recently, boards of directors operated freely, with little government supervision. The Sarbanes-Oxley Act of 2002 has changed most of that. Crafted by Congress in the aftermath of financial collapses at corporations like Enron, Global Crossing, and WorldCom, the act outlines a set of accountability standards by public companies in the areas of financial reporting and disclosure, audits, conflict of interest, and governance. While differences of opinion abound, particularly when it comes to the added compliance cost for companies (paying for auditors, paperwork, administrative expenses and such) most observers believe that Sarbanes-Oxley has had positive effect by preventing some of the worst corporate abuses.[47] Chapter 16 deals with control issues in greater detail.

Organizational Structures

Below the top-executive level, firms have many choices for organizing the work that needs to be done to implement a particular strategy. Implementation begins with defining roles for different individuals and establishing procedures, reporting relationships, chains of command, decision-making processes, and organizational forms (collectively known as organizational structures). Chapter 9 is devoted entirely to managing the structure and design of organizations.

Organizational structure is critical to strategy implementation because "through structure, managers largely determine what a firm does and how it completes that work, given its chosen strategies. Strategic competitiveness can be attained only when the firm's selected structure is congruent with its formulated strategy"[48]

While organizational structures help in providing for an orderly execution of strategies, most successful firms tap the collective knowledge of employees through the use of teams that might cut across job titles, departments, functional areas, business units, levels, and the like. The strategic management process should be an organizationwide effort rather than a top-down exercise. Management Is Everyone's Business 7.2 provides a list of recommendations that teams should consider as part of their role in the strategic management process.

Cooperative Strategies

cooperative strategies
Establishing partnerships or strategic alliances with other firms.

Cooperative strategies involve establishing partnerships or strategic alliances with other firms. For instance, Procter & Gamble and General Electric cooperated to develop a jet engine for Boeing's new jumbo jet. Although the companies were fierce competitors over the years, senior executives indicated that "neither of us [was] prepared to make the enormous financial, personnel, and technical investment required to develop an all-new engine in an uncertain environment." Additionally, according to a Boeing executive, "using our complementary skills and resources we can produce an engine that meets the requirements of Boeing and our airline customers in a more timely fashion and at lower cost and risk."[49] Recently many major airlines have been sharing ticket sales to make travel easier.

Strategic alliances can serve a number of purposes. Firms may combine resources, capabilities, and core competencies to gain market power, overcome trade barriers, learn from each other, pool resources for expensive and risky projects, compete more effectively in a particular industry, and speed up entry into new markets. Strategic alliances also allow a firm to create and disband projects with minimal paperwork.

MANAGEMENT IS EVERYONE'S BUSINESS 7.2

WORKING AS A TEAM   The strategic management process generally involves teams of managers and employees from different areas who bring their perspectives and expertise to bear on the issues facing the firm. An important factor in the success of the strategic management process is how well the firm can mobilize and integrate the efforts of managers and employees to identify relevant environmental trends, define or redefine firm strategies, and support the successful implementation of those strategies.

This all means that organizations should:

- Form strategy-making teams either on a continuous basis or from time to time by bringing together employees from different functional areas (marketing, manufacturing, human resources), background (technical, managerial, sales), organizational levels (for instance, top executives as well as first-line supervisors), and various parts of the organization (departments, business units, divisions). Such diverse teams can bring to bear a wide field of vision on the strategic challenges facing the organization.
- Create scanning and monitoring teams that gather, filter, and interpret environmental information and what this might mean to the organization. Ideally, such teams should be composed of individuals akin to different parts of the environment (for instance, customer needs, global trends, technological innovations).
- At any level within the organization, teams should be created as needed to analyze strengths-weaknesses-opportunities-threats affecting the unit in question (the unit might be the entire organization at one extreme or a specific department at the other extreme). The broader the unit in question, the greater the need to increase diversity within the team to ensure that multiple perspectives are part of the process.
- Ensure that strategy formulation leads to proper implementation by securing the collective commitment of employees to the adopted strategy. The more employees work in teams as part of this process, the more likely they will accept and fully support strategic decisions, particularly those requiring significant changes affecting their lives. Teams can also offer top managers a better sense of limitations or constraints being faced, as well as information about resources they might not be aware of.
- Blend cultures of units involved in mergers and acquisitions by creating teams that can effectively draw bridges across disappearing organizational boundaries. Mergers and acquisitions often fail because financially driven executives tend to ignore or underestimate the difficulties involved in managing cultural integration.

MANAGEMENT IS EVERYONE'S BUSINESS 7.3

WORKING AS AN INDIVIDUAL Individual employees are more likely to make greater contributions to the firm if they engage in activities that have strategic value. If the firm's strategic objective is to increase market share by underpricing competitors, the employee can suggest easy-to-cut costs or easy-to-reduce inefficiencies. The employee can also be attuned to changes in his or her areas of expertise and advise management on the strategic implications of those changes, Lastly, employee success depends on the ability to adapt to the firm's strategic change.

This means that you as an individual should:

- Learn about the strategies of your entire organization and how your unit fits into it. Much of this information may be obtained through company publications, business media, and the Internet. You can also ask your supervisors directly. If you do so with a sincere "I want to contribute more" attitude, they are likely to respond to you positively.
- Develop skills attuned to the strategy of the organization and strategic redirections that might be taking place. This will make you more valuable as an employee.
- Behave in a manner consistent with the strategy of the organization and the role of your unit as part of the big picture.
- Volunteer with a positive attitude to participate to the extent you can in your firm's strategy formulation and implementation. Many firms now encourage technology employees to use Web technology to provide input and ideas that may be valuable to those who make strategic decisions.

Human Resource Strategies

The policies and practices of the human resource department should also support the firm's overall strategy (see Chapter 10 on human resource management). Who gets recruited, how performance is evaluated and rewarded, how training is conducted, and how career advancement is managed should be consistent with the strategic mission of the firm. For example, a company that wants to be innovative in various markets would want to develop human resource policies that stimulate rather than dissuade employees from taking risks. This may require greater tolerance for failure, more subjective assessment of performance, more incentives for taking risks, and the hiring of managers with track records of making risky but prudent decisions. These policies are likely to influence how individual employees see their role as part of the strategic management process. Management Is Everyone's Business 7.3 offers a set of tips that an individual employee might consider to become a contributor to the implementation of his or her firm's strategy.

Corporate Entrepreneurship and Innovation

Competitive pressures require firms to be innovative (see Management Close-Up 7.2 "Innovation as a Key Part of Strategy Formulation"). High returns and investments in innovation tend to go hand in hand. Innovation contributes to a sustainable competitive advantage if (1) it is difficult or costly for competitors to imitate, (2) customers can see a value in the innovation, (3) the firm enjoys a time advantage over the other company, and (4) the firm is capable of commercializing the innovation.

Research and development is necessary for firms in high-technology markets such as computers, electronics, and pharmaceuticals. However, firms also need to encourage entrepreneurship, supporting employees who are willing to take risks and be aggressive, proactive, and creative and can see opportunities where others perceive problems.

LOC-In 5   Learning Objective Check-In

1. There is a fairly strict hierarchy at Pierpont Stores. The board of directors, for example, monitors the actions and decisions of all the top executives in the company to make sure they are acting in the best interest of the firm and its various stakeholders, particularly shareholders. Below the board, there are certain chains of command that can appear stifling to some on the outside, but actually prove quite effective for this particular company. The of the board of directors and the internal chains of command is to _____ .
   a. implement strategy effectively
   b. safeguard against competitive influence
   c. develop the best alternatives for developing strategy
   d. evaluate the effectiveness of strategies used in the past

FIGURE 7.9

Step Five of the Strategic Management Process: Analyze Strategic Outcomes

stakeholders

The groups or individuals who have an interest in the performance of the enterprise and how it uses its resources, including employees, customers, and shareholders.

■ Step 5: Strategic Outcomes

The fifth and final step of the strategic management process is an analysis of the strategic outcomes, or the end result of the entire process. (See Figure 7.9, which corresponds to the last stage shown in Figure 7.1.) Company leaders should periodically assess whether the outcomes meet expectations. This information should be used to determine whether or not company strategies are successful.

A firm must first and foremost cater to the desires of its primary stakeholders. **Stakeholders** are the individuals and institutions who have vested interests in the performance of the firm. In a capitalist system, the main stakeholders are the people who own stock in the company and who are the major suppliers of the firm's capital. These stakeholders expect to earn at least an average return on their investment, although they would prefer the return to be as high as possible. If lenders are dissatisfied, they can make it more costly for the firm to raise capital and may increase the number of restrictions on the company's borrowing. Shareholders who are unhappy with the firm's stock performance can sell stock and invest their money in other firms. Because the firm depends on investors and stockholders, its highest priority when analyzing strategic outcomes is the needs of those constituencies.

At the same time, the firm's managers should consider the desires of other people who are affected by a firm's actions. At times, the interests of these other stakeholders may conflict with those of shareholders. For instance, customers prefer products with great reliability, more features, and low price. Employees would like a greater share of the company's profits. The community may want the firm to invest in projects of social interest. That is, what appears to be a good outcome for some stakeholders may have negative consequences for other stakeholders, and this might raise important ethical concerns. This would be the case, for instance, of patients who benefit from low complication rates and shareholders who receive higher returns in certain hospitals at the expense of difficult-to-treat patients who might be denied treatment (see Management Close-Up 7.3, "Making It Easy to Size Up a Hospital"). The firm should try to find win–win

MANAGEMENT CLOSE-UP 7.3   THEME: **ETHICS**

Making It Easy to Size Up a Hospital

Few decisions are more important than what hospital you should choose to treat a serious illness. In recent years several independent bodies rank hospitals on such factors as complication rates, mortality rates, cost, and overall quality of service. Thus, for instance, according to the rating service Health Grades, patients have a 52 percent lower chance on average of dying for the same procedure at top-rated hospitals than at lower-rated hospitals. Across all 17 procedures and diagnoses, Health Grades concludes that a patient has a 71.64 percent lower chance of dying in a 5-star rated hospital compared to a 1-star rated hospital.

Not everyone agrees that this type of hospital rating is a good idea. Many doctors feel that such systems may inadvertently induce hospitals to compete in less than ethical ways in order to appease potential investors and shareholders. For instance, a hospital may be tempted to refuse difficult-to-treat patients to reduce reported complication rates. And hospitals that accept the most critically ill patients may be penalized since they an likely to score lower on complication rates and expenses.

Source: Based on: http://www.healthgrades.com, "2010 Fall Ratings;" 2011; http://myhealthcareadviser.com, 2011; http://www.consumerhealthratings.com, 2011.

situations for as many stakeholders as possible. For instance, higher quality products at a lower price may benefit investors if the firm's market share increases. Employees may also benefit if the company enjoys greater ability to pay and offers them greater job security.

Some of the standard measures of strategic success include:

- Profits
- Growth of sales/market share
- Growth of corporate assets
- Reduced competitive threats
- Innovations that fuel future success

It is vital for the executive team to assess both the short term and long range when assessing strategic outcomes. Long-term success should be the ultimate criterion when studying strategic outcomes.

LOC-In 6 Learning Objective Check-In

ARTRON is a publicly held company. It has upwards of 1,500 investors who hold a direct interest in the firm's performance and profitability. ARTRON has manufacturing facilities in eight different locations on the West Coast. It provides an average of 130 jobs in each of those communities and gives back to the community through direct philanthropic investments in important causes like education.

1. Those investors who have an interest in the firm's profitability are called _____.
   a. stakeholders
   b. shareholders
   c. activists
   d. interested parties

2. The children and adults who benefit from the philanthropic efforts of ARTRON in different communities are considered the company's _____.
   a. shareholders
   b. social activists
   c. administrators
   d. stakeholders

CONCLUDING THOUGHTS

At the beginning of the chapter you read about Apple's strategy for helping the market for accessories to thrive through the effort of outside manufacturers and marketers. Now that you've had a chance to read the chapter, let's revisit the questions posed there.

Apple's strategy to allow the manufacture of all kinds of iPod and iPad accessories has helped other manufacturers earn revenue, but it has also helped Apple itself by keeping the sleek little electronic gadgets at the peak of coolness among its customers. Already valued for their design appeal as well as their functionality, the iPod and iPad now stand at the center of a

universe of affordable products to personalize them and broaden their use. Apple's decision to foster the creation of that universe has proved a wise one, since the existence of covers, speakers, ports, headphones, and other gear clearly plays into the iPod and iPad purchase decision, giving them an advantage no other gadgets have.

Apple's own entry into the accessories market could well prove quite successful, since the company has waited for other manufacturers to establish the market and carry some of the initial risk of introducing a whole new product category. Now it's time for Apple to capitalize on its own resources.

FOCUSING ON THE FUTURE: Using Management Theory in Daily Life

Strategic Management

In Chapter 5, you saw how Mary Kelley and Robert deStefano used the action planning model to start their business, Sleep Garden, Inc. Now let's look at how Mary and Robert used Porter's Five Forces for analyzing the industry environment of their new venture.

Threat of New Entrants

Fortunately, Sleep Garden faced few threats to entry. Almost all government regulation of sleep aids centers on ingestibles—drugs are highly regulated, and herbs, while they have not been regulated in the past, are coming under more scrutiny now. By contracting with their own yoga instructor and composer, Robert and Mary avoided intellectual property constraints, although they have to be careful that their creative properties are not imitated or duplicated by others. Mary has provided the funding for the new venture, and that was a constraint—if she had not had the money available to keep the company going for the past several years, it could easily have folded. While drug products like "Ambien" and "Lunesta" have strong brands, they do not directly compete with such Sleep Garden products as "zMusic" or "zYoga." As a new, small company, Sleep Garden did not have things like existing plants or economies of scale, but they leveraged the resources they had. For example, they found manufacturers who were willing to produce short runs of their products and stores which saw the products as natural tie-ins to their existing customer base.

Threat of Substitutes

Sleep is big business today, and there are many products on the market designed to help people sleep. Fortunately for Mary and Robert, most of the products are either scientific (drug based) or artistic (white noise or new-age music CDs) but virtually none combine both scientific research and art. The uniqueness of a nondrug, clinically tested product set them apart from their competitors. However, the two entrepreneurs still faced the challenge of clearly defining their target market, and then identifying the best channels for reaching that market. While one of their original objectives was to make their products available to a mass market, they found that mass market advertising in print and radio did little for them. Instead, they found that their products sold well in upscale, natural (organic) food stores such as Whole Foods. People in these stores responded to the idea of a "natural" sleep aid. A different marketing channel involved positioning their products as an in-room spa experience, and for this, they contacted high-end resorts and hotels. Clients in these places are looking for pampering and expect a product that comes with "extras" and attractive packaging.

Suppliers

There are many companies that manufacture CDs and DVDs in the United States today. Because of this, Mary and Robert were able to keep their manufacturing costs relatively low, a boon for a new business. However, postproduction editing, scoring, and rerecording can make or break a video product. While there are many postproduction studios, Robert felt that only one offered the quality of services that would make their "zYoga" DVD stand out. For that reason, the postproduction supplier had more power and was able to command a higher price than a less skilled supplier. Similarly, Robert and Mary had to pay more to a supplier that designed the merchandising units used to display Sleep Garden products, because there are few companies which produce this type of "product furniture."

Customers

One of the most important things Mary and Robert learned as they built their business was the power not only of end customers, but of intermediate customers—the brokers and distributors who actually get product into the hands of consumers. Many stores will deal only with brokers, and each broker used shaves a bit of profit off a given product. End users have little power over price or packaging, but retailers have a great deal of power, and the bigger the retailer is, the more power they have. For example, it is an entirely different process to get product into an individual grocery store than it is to get product into an entire chain of stores such as CVS or Wal-Mart. The bigger the chain, the more power they have over products, packaging, and pricing. But even small retailers can impact the way a product is sold. For example, Robert and Mary purchased merchandisers so that retailers wouldn't have to move other products off store shelves in order to get Sleep Garden products in stores.

Intensity of Rivalry among Competitors

While rivalry is intense in the drug segment of the sleep market, Mary and Robert were relieved to find that they had few head-to-head competitors in their side of the industry. This made a friendlier environment for their business.

By analyzing industry forces prior to incorporating their business, Robert and Mary had a clear picture of the challenges that would face them in getting their product to market. While these challenges evolved and changed overtime, continual monitoring enabled the Sleep Garden executives to modify their strategy accordingly.

Summary of Learning Objectives

1 Explain how the firm's external environment should be examined as part of the strategic management process.

- There are two important considerations when examining the external environment. Analysis *components* are scanning (tracking the environment for changes), monitoring (observing environment to determine if clear trends are emerging), forecasting (trying to predict what is likely to occur in the future), and assessing (evaluating consequences of environmental data to the firm).
- Environmental forces may be examined at different levels of specificity, or *scope,* including the general environment (such as demographic changes, economic forces, and sociocultural conditions which might impinge upon the firm), the industry environment (tracking groups of firms with products/services that can serve as substitutes for one another), strategic groups (observing the behavior of cluster of firms within the industry that tend to adopt common strategies), and direct competitors (studying the moves and countermoves of select sample of firms believed to be key competitors).

2 Explain how the firm's internal environment should be examined as part of the strategic management process.

- *Resource analysis.* Focuses on the tangible and intangible resources that provide the firm with core competencies that are difficult for competitors to imitate.
- *Capabilities analysis.* Focuses on what the firm can do better than competitors, which might be analyzed *by function* (such as marketing and human resources), value added of various activities **(value-chain analysis)**, and **benchmarking** (comparing the firm's activities and/or functions with those of firms known for best practices).

3 State the meaning and purpose of the firm's strategic intent and mission.

- **Strategic intent.** Statement of how the firm would like to use its resources and capabilities.
- **Strategic mission.** A definition of the firm's external focus in terms of what it will produce and market.

4 Understand how the strategy formulation process helps the firm achieve its mission.

- **Corporate-level strategy** refers to strategic decisions concerning number of businesses, the variety of markets or industries in which the firm operates, and the distribution of resources across those businesses. Analysis can proceed in three ways:
  - *Portfolio analysis.* Creation of a taxonomy to classify various businesses owned by the corporation by their revenue potential (for instance, those which are low in market share and low in market growth versus those which are high in market share and that operate in a growing market).
  - *Diversification type.* The company may choose to hold a single business competing in one industry segment (concentration strategy), diversify by setting up or acquiring firms that serve the primary business (vertical integration strategy), create or purchase new businesses related to the core business (concentric diversification), or manage a portfolio of unrelated businesses (conglomerate diversification).
  - *Diversification process.* Focuses on how the firm should diversify such as purchasing other firms (acquisition), integration of two firms (mergers), and internationalization (moving some of its operations overseas).
- **Business-level strategy** involves decisions on how to compete in a given industry. The two major choices are competing with price (by being a low cost producer or *cost leader)* and on special features that command a price premium *(differentiation).*

5 Describe the issues that should be considered in strategy implementation.

- The formulated strategy must be implemented effectively, and feedback from the implementation process should be used to adjust the formulated strategy.

- Effective strategy implementation requires a corporate governance system (to ensure that executives make decisions that are most beneficial to the firm), a system for completing the necessary work (organizational structure and controls), functional strategies (to support the overall strategy), and strong leadership at the top as well as entrepreneurial activities at lower organizational levels.

6 Understand how the outcomes of the strategic management process should be assessed.

- An analysis of how the firm's *shareholders* are being served; at a minimum shareholders should earn an average return on their investment.
- A consideration of the extent to which the needs of other **stakeholders** who might be affected by the firm's actions are being satisfied.
- An analysis of short-term and long-range results.

Discussion Questions

1. Some argue that the business environment changes so quickly that we are entering a period of "hypercompetition," which will make it difficult to establish long-term strategic objectives. Do you agree? Identify five major forces that accelerated environmental change at the turn of the century.

2. Scan business publications such as *BusinessWeek, The Wall Street Journal,* and *Fortune.* From these publications' articles, select a firm that has been affected by each of the following: the general environment, the industry, strategic groups, and direct competitors. Explain the reason for your choice and show how that particular segment of the environment affects the firm you have chosen.

3. Why should most firms develop their strategic mission following a rational process that incorporates internal and external environmental data? Explain.

4. Going back to Management Close-Up 7.3, if you were a hospital administrator, how would the availability of "hospital performance" data affect your behavior? Explain.

5. In what situations do you believe that strategy formulation leads to strategy implementation? In what situations do you believe that strategy implementation plays an equal role with strategy formulation as a source of competitive advantage? Explain.

6. In what situations do you believe that the external environment of the firm is more important than the internal environment as a determinant of the firm's profitability? Explain.

7. Norway has passed a law that a minimum of 40 percent of members of boards of directors must be women.[50] This represents a dramatic change as only a handful of women were on such boards prior to the passage of this law. Why do you think Norway passed such a law? Based on what you have learned in this chapter, is this a good policy? Explain your answer.

Management Minicase 7.1

Why Would Microsoft Sell the Xbox at a Loss?

Despite all the hype surrounding the Xbox 360 when it was introduced back in 2005, it is estimated that Microsoft incurred losses of $1.26 billion by launching the console. A tear-down analysis by market researcher iSuppli of the high-end Xbox 360, which contains a hard drive, found that the materials cost Microsoft $470 before assembly. Chips alone account for 72 percent of that. The console sells at retail for $399, for a loss of $71 per unit. Other items in the box, such as the power supply, cables, and controllers, add S55 more to Microsoft's cost, pushing its loss per unit to $126.

Yet in 2010 Microsoft CEO Steve Ballmer noted, "We are not even halfway through the current console generation lifecycle and believe Xbox 360 will be the entertainment center in the home for long into the next decade." The new Xbox 360 (called the "Natal Xbox") hit store shelves in 2010 and a future Xbox is planned probably for 2016 and possibly sooner.

DISCUSSION QUESTIONS

1. Based on what you have learned in this chapter, why would a company such as Microsoft develop, produce, and sell a product at a loss? Do you think this is a deliberate strategy? If so, is it rational? Explain your answer.

2. Do you think demographic trends are likely to support or hinder the market for this type of product? More broadly, what do you see as opportunities and threats in this market? Explain your answer.

3. From a resource-based perspective, do you think Microsoft's core competencies are likely to give the company a competitive advantage in the game consoles market in the future? Explain your answer.

Sources: Based on http://gizmodo.com, 2011; http://www.videogames blogger.com, 2011; http://www.cinemablend.com/games, 2011; A. Hesseldahl, "For Every Xbox, a Big Fat Loss," *BusinessWeek,* December 5, 2005, p. 13. Updated by authors in 2006.

Management Minicase 7.2

Why Are Rebates Becoming so Popular?

Mail-in offers are everywhere these days. Shoppers hate collecting all the paperwork, filling out the forms, and mailing it all in to claim their $10 or $100. But no matter how annoying rebates are for consumers, the country's retailers and manufacturers love them. Probably between 25–50 percent of computer gear, cell phone cameras, camcorders and high definition TVs are sold with some form of rebate, and this trend seems to be accelerating during this second decade of the 21st century.

Why are rebates becoming so popular among retailers? A not-so-well-kept secret is that 40 percent of all rebates never get redeemed, either because the customer did not bother to send it in by the deadline or the request gets rejected (for instance, the consumer forgot to include a required part of the box that included a particular code or inadvertently discarded the box). This all translates into several billion dollars of added revenue for retailers and suppliers every year.

DISCUSSION QUESTIONS

1. Do you think that use of rebates offers a company a cost-leadership advantage? Why or why not? Explain your answer.
2. How would you analyze the expanding use of rebates from a competitive dynamic perspective? Explain your answer.
3. Do you think that heavy reliance on rebates to drum up customers may be considered an unethical business strategy? Should federal law regulate use of rebates in the future? Explain your answer.

Sources: Based on G. Martin-Herran, S. Simon-Pierre, and G. Zaccour (2010), "The dilemma of pull and push-price promotions," *Journal of Retailing*, 86 (1), 51–58; M. F. Gorman (2010), "Management insights," *Management Science*, 56 (1), iv–vii. B. Grow, "The Great Rebate Runaround," *BusinessWeek,* December 5, 2005, pp. 34–39.

Individual/Collaborative Learning Case 7.1

Analyzing Threats: Can Walgreen Co. Survive?

Almost half of all Americans live within two miles of a Walgreens store (the density of its stores can reach Starbuckian levels—downtown San Francisco has 21 stores within a one-mile radius)!

Walgreens had in excess of 7,200 drugstores spread across all 50 states and Puerto Rico in 2011, more than double the number in 2005. Walgreens is one of a handful of Fortune 500 firms whose stock has consistently outperformed the 5½ P 500 during the past 35 years or so.

Yet, past performance is no guarantee of future results, and Walgreens faces some vicious multifront battles in the future. First, there is Walgreens' biggest traditional rival, CVS, which has been expending rapidly. Second, there is the rise of low-cost mail-order prescriptions, which represents a profound shift in the way Americans buy their medicines. The problem for Walgreens is that all the operational excellence in the would is useless if customers have no compelling reason to enter your store. Mail order is now the fastest-growing sales channel for prescription drugs. Mail order threatens not only the chains' bread-and-butter prescription business (which in Walgreens' case makes up 63 percent of total sales) but also the higher-margin "front-end" general merchandise. That is because customers who receive drugs in their mailbox are less likely to visit their local drugstore to shop for things like film, cosmetics, candy, and small appliances and instead go to stores like Target, Wal-Mart, or the local supermarket.

CRITICAL THINKING QUESTIONS

1. Using the material presented in the chapter, how would you explain Walgreens' success story in the past? Do you think Walgreens can overcome the challenges discussed in this case? If so, how? Explain your answer.
2. If you were asked to analyze Walgreens' capabilities, how would you go about conducting such a study? What kind of data would you obtain? Explain your answer.
3. Describe Walgreens' industry environment using Porter's Five Forces framework as discussed in this chapter.

COLLABORATIVE LEARNING EXERCISE

You have been appointed to an advisory task force of the board of directors at Walgreens to provide a set of recommendations to help the company overcome the challenges discussed in the case. Each task force will have approximately five students and meet for approximately 20 minutes. Each task force is then expected to justify its recommendations to the chairman of the board (represented by the instructor of your class).

Sources: Based on http://en.wikipedia.org, "The Walgreen Company," 2011; http://investor.walgreens.com, 2011; http://www.chicagotribune.com, "Walgreen Co., News and photos," 2011; M. Boyle, "Drug Wars," *Fortune,* June 13, 2005, pp. 25–36.

Internet Exercise 7.1

Internet Strategies

During the past 15 years or so all "unhire" firms and an increasing number of bricks-and-mortar companies rely on the Internet as a normal part of their operations. Many of these have discovered, however, that the Internet is no panacea. Choose any five firms and analyze how they use the Internet to achieve their strategic objectives. Answer the following questions:

1. After comparing and contrasting the different firms, how effectively do you think they use the Internet from a strategic perspective?
2. Is the Internet an appropriate medium to achieve a sustainable competitive advantage? Support your conclusions using the materials discussed in this chapter.

Endnotes

1. "Wall Street 2010: What's changed. What hasn't. What should." *Fortune,* May 2, 2010, 161 (6), 190–202; J. McCraken, "Ford Focuses on Market-Share Slide," *The Wall Street Journal,* February 17, 2006, p. A-1; K. Lundegaard, "Ford, GM Make Big Push to Promote 'Flex-Fuel' Vehicles," *The Wall Street Journal,* January 10, 2006, p. B1; J. B. White and J. McCracken, "Troubled Legacy: Auto Industry, at a Crossroads, Finds Itself Stalled by History," *The Wall Street Journal,* January 7, 2006, p. B1; S. Silke, "Most Automakers See Their Sales Fall in December," *USA Today,* January 5, 2006, p. B1; M. Maynard, "Is There a Future in Ford's Future?" *New York Times,* January 8, 2006, p. 3; A. Taylor III, "Ford: The Hamlet of Dearborn," *Fortune,* October 17, 2005, p. 36; G. Chon, "GM and Ford Lose More Market Share," *The Wall Street Journal,* January 5, 2006, p. A13.
2. www.americanexpress.com.
3. Hitt et al. (2011) (see reference list) G. Zuckerman, I. McDonald, and L. Hawkins, "If GM's Big Yield Vanishes, Investors May Do the Same," *The Wall Street Journal,* January 12, 2006, p. C1; M. Maynard, "Toyota Shows Big Three How It Is Done," *New York Times,* January 3, 2006, p. C1.
4. I. McDonald, and J. Adamy, "Whole Foods Fare's Pricey" *The Wall Street Journal,* January 3, 2006, p. C1.
5. *San Jose Mercury News,* "Gates Too Busy to Define Government," *Arizona Republic,* May 2, 1998, p. E1.
6. www.colgate.com, 2006.
7. Valeen & McNamara (2010) (see reference list) R.L. Martin, "What Innoviation Advantage?" *BusinessWeek,* January 16, 2006 p. 102.
8. A. Serwer, "Bruised in Bentonville," *Fortune,* April 18, 2005, p. 84; R. Berner "Watch Out, Best Buy and Circuit City," *BusinessWeek,* November 21, 2005, p. 46; T. P. Coates, "Wal-Mart's Urban Room," *Time,* September 5, 2005, p. 44.
9. J. Useem, "One Nation under Wal-Mart," *Fortune,* March 3, 2003, p.65.
10. S. Lohr, "Just Googling It Is Striking Fear into Companies," *New York Times,* November 6, 2005.
11. Wonacott, 2006.
12. Lundsford and Michales, 2006.
13. Pasztor and Christie, 2006.
14. "Wall Street 2010: What's changed. What hasn't. What should." B. Einhorn, "Listen: The sound of Hope," *BusinessWeek,* November 14, 2005, p. 68.
15. K. Durham, and R. A. Smith, "Behind Zooming Conddo Prices," *The Wall Street Journal,* August 18, 2005, p. A-1.
16. M. Barboso, "State Mandate for Wal-Mart on Health Care." *New York Times,* January 13, 2006, p. A-1.
17. D. Carney, "Uncle Sam's Trustbusters Outguneed and Outmoded." *BusinessWeek,* November 18, 2002, pp. 44–45.
18. B. Acohido, and E.C. Baig, "Gates Shares Spotlight with New Windows," *USA Today,* January 5, 2006, p. B-1.
19. Ibid.; R.A. Guth, "Microsoft Palm Unite to Fight Blackberrt," *The Wall Street Journal,* November 18, 2005, p. B1.; R.A. Guth, "Getting Xbox to Market," *The Wall Street Journal,* September 27, 2005, November 18, 2005 p. B1; D. Barboza and T.Zeller Jr., "Microsoft Shuts Blog's Site after Complaints by Beijing," *New York Times,* January 6 2006, p. C3.
20. "The Big Picture," *BusinessWeek,* December 5, 2005, p. 16.
21. D. Grant, and A. Latour, "Changing Channels," *The Wall Street Journal,* November 21, 2005, p. A-1.
22. Tuggle & Sirmon (2010) (see reference list) S. Hamm, J. Greene, and A. Reinhardt, "What Is a Rival to Do Now?" *BusinessWeek,* November 18, 2002, pp. 44–46.
23. R. Farzad, and B. Elgin, "Googling," *BusinessWeek,* December 5, 2005, p. 61
24. P. Dvorak, and E. Ramstad, "TV Marriage: Behind Sony-Samsung Rivalry, an Unlikely Alliance Develops," *The Wall Street Journal,* January 3, 2006, p. A-1.
25. M. E. Porter, *Competitve Advantage* (New York: Free Press, 1990).
26. W. Echikson, "Designers Climb onto the Virtual Catwalk," *BusinessWeek,* October 11, 1999, pp. 164–166.

27. W. M. Bulkeley," Kodak Swings to $1.03 Billion Loss," *The Wall Street Journal,* December 21, 2005, p. A1.; W.C. Symonds, and D. Burrows, "A Digital Warrior for Kodak," *BusinessWeek,* May 23, 2005, p. 42.
28. K. Barnes, "Alburn Sales Slump as Downloads Rise," *USA Today,* January 5, 2006, p. D-1.
29. M. Adams, "Independence CEO Says He Doesn't Regret Gamble," *USA Today, January* 5, 2006, p. B-5.
30. Palfreyman (2010) (see reference list) R. A. D'Aveni, "Coping with Hyper-competition: Utilizing the New 75's Framwork, " *Academy of Management Executive* 9, no. 3 (1995): 54.
31. Palfreyman (2010) (see reference list) M. S. Hunt, *Competition in the Major Home Appliance Industry* (Cambridge, MA: Harvard University Press, 1972).
32. M. A. Hitt, R. D. Ireland, and R. E. Hoskisson, *Strategic Management* (New York: Irwin/McGraw-Hill, 2001).
33. R. M. Grant, *Contemporary Strategy Analysis* (Malden, MA: Blackwell, 1998), p. 129.
34. U. Kher, "The Workhorse of Genomic Medicine, " *Time,* January 15, 2001, p. 62.
35. www.canon.com, 2006.
36. J. White, and S. Power, "VW's Bernhard Says Labor Costs Dent Profit, " *The Wall Street Journal,* January 9, 2006, p. A10.
37. Michael Hitt, R. Duane Ireland, and Robert E. Hoskisson, *Strategic Management: Competitiveness and Globalization* (Cincinnati, OH: South-Western Publishing, 2011), p. 26.
38. Moskowitz et al. (2010) (see reference list) N. Stein, "America's Most Admired Companies, " *Fortune,* March 3, 2003, pp. 81–98.
39. I. M. Kunii, "Making Canon Click" *BusinessWeek,* September 16, 2002, pp. 40–42.
40. R. M. Grant, *Contemporary Strategic Analysis* (Malden, MA: Blackwell, 2008).
41. M. Heinzl, "A New Crop of Gadgets Challenge the BlackBerry," *The Wall Street Journal,* November 2, 2005, p. D-1.
42. Hitt et al. (2011) (see reference list) K. Hughes and C. Oughton, "Diversification, Multimarket Contact, and Profitability," *Economics* 60 (1993): 203–224; C. W. L. Hill, "Diversification and Economic Performance: Bringing Structure and Corporate Management Back into the Picture," in R. P. Rumelt et al. (Eds.), *Fundamental Issues in Strategy* (Boston: Harvard Business School Press, 1994), pp. 297–321.
43. "Upfront," *Business Weak,* August 6, 2001, p. 7.
44. S. Carey, "As Airlines Pull Out of Dive, Limited Charts Its Own Course," *The Wall Street Journal,* January 13, 2006, p. A-1.
45. K. Richardson, "Blockbuster's Backbreaker: No-Late-Fee Policy," *The Wall Street Journal,* January 5, 2006, p. B1.
46. Hitt, Ireland, and Hoskisson, *Strategic Management: Competitiveness and Globalization,* p. 383.
47. J. Shambora (2010). "The directors". *Fortune,* 2010, May 3, 170–183. D. Gullapalli, "Living with Sarbanes Oxley," *The Wall Street Journal,* October 17, 2005, p. R1; A. Borrus, "Learning to Love Sarbanes-Oxley," *BusinessWeek,* November 21, 2005, p. 126; R. Sorkin, "To Battle, Armed with Shares, Big Holders Wield Their Shares to Push for Corporate Change," *New York Times,* January 6, 2006, p. C1; M. Jacoby, "The Global Agenda," *The Wall Street Journal,* October 17, 2005, p. R7; J Burns, "Board Members Find Independence," *The Wall Street Journal,* January 12, 2006, p. C11; J. Weber, S. Holmes, and C. Palmeri, "Older Workers May Have a Hard Time Giving Up Private Offices," *BusinessWeek,* November 7, 2005, p. 100.
48. Hitt, Ireland and Hoskisson, *Strategic Management,* p. 347.
49. Ibid., p. 28.
50. Tuggle & Sirmon (2010) (see reference list) R. Berstein, R. "Men Chafe as Norway Ushers Women into Boardroom," *New York Times,* January 12, 2006, p. A-3.

8

Learning Objectives

1 Explain the economic importance of entrepreneurship.

2 Identify the key characteristics and skills of entrepreneurs.

3 Recognize the basic ingredients needed to effectively start and manage an entrepreneurial venture.

4 Differentiate among the legal forms of organizing an entrepreneurial venture.

5 Identify alternative forms of entrepreneurship.

6 Describe innovation and demonstrate why it is important for business success.

Starting a Company in the Kitchen

Jim Koch was working at the Boston Consulting Group when he began brewing beer in his kitchen. Brewing beer was natural for Jim Koch since his father and grandfather worked in the brewing business. The result of his kitchen experiments was the first batch of Samuel Adams Boston Lager, which was created to use only the finest natural ingredients and become a handcrafted full-flavor beer for the discriminating beer drinker who preferred quality over the bland tasting industrially produced beers of the major beer companies. Before long, Koch raised $250,000 to fund and launch the Boston Beer Company in 1985. Shortly after the launch the Samuel Adams brand won recognition as the best beer by the attendees at the Great American Beer Festival in Denver in which 93 regional and national beers competed. At the time he launched Boston Beer Company there were only about 10 micro brewers in the United States due to the market dominance of large corporations such as Anheuser-Busch, Miller, and Coors.

Jim Koch is recognized as a pioneer in the renaissance in American taste for flavorful, traditional beer, as the success of the Samuel Adams brand became an inspiration for other small brewers to launch businesses. By 1995, hundreds of micro brewers had sprouted up all over the country and as of 2009 the total of micro brewers numbered 1,500. Today, Boston Beer Company is the largest

Entrepreneurship and Innovation

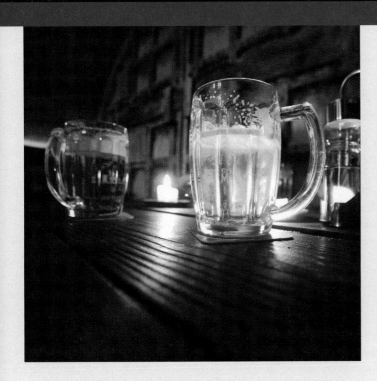

micro brewer and sells over one million barrels of Boston Beer products with $415 million in sales, but still accounts for less than one percent of the total U.S. beer market.

The company thrives under the guidance of Jim Koch, who to this day tastes every batch of beer brewed to ensure it meets his high standards. In 1995 the Boston Beer Company went public selling shares of common stock on the New York Stock Exchange. The company employs over 300 people who are just as passionate as Jim when it comes to making a full-flavored beer out of the finest ingredients. With this level of growth, Boston Beer Company is concerned about holding onto its official designation as a craft beer, which provides tax advantages to smaller brewers who produce fewer than two million barrels of beer annually.

Sources: J. Hyatt, "Beer Baron," *Newsweek*, May 24 & 31, 2010, p. 54; J. Daly, "Sam Adams Beer Pleads to Keep Craft Status," *Huffington Post*, June 14, 2010, www.huffingtonpost.com; www.bostonbeer.com, accessed July 1, 2010.

CRITICAL THINKING QUESTIONS

1. *Boston Beer Company has grown over the years to become the largest brewer of craft beers. What concerns and potential threats could the company face if it continues to grow and account for a larger share of the U.S. beer market?*

2. *Jim Koch did not start to launch a business as an entrepreneur until he achieved some success in a different career as a business consultant. What are the advantages to an entrepreneur of working for someone else as an employee and achieving some success in business prior to starting a new enterprise?*

MANAGER'S NOTEBOOK 8.1

Skills for Managing Entrepreneurships

The following are critical skills that entrepreneurs use to create, grow and develop new ventures.

- *Opportunity recognition.* Entrepreneurs have a knack for being able to identify opportunities that can potentially result in a profitable new business, product, or service. This opportunity needs to be robust enough to meet an unsatisfied need in the market that makes it worthwhile for the entrepreneur to commit resources to pursue it.
- *Entrepreneurial implementation skills.* Successful entrepreneurs have a high need for achievement, internal locus of

control, are risk takers, and are self-confident about their ability to master unforeseen challenges.
- *Networking skills.* Networking skills are critical to obtaining financial capital, business and technical knowledge, retail shelf space, and other resources required to start a business.

Sources: Based on S. Shane, "Prior Knowledge and Discovery of Entrepreneurial Opportunities," *Organization Science*, 11, (2000), pp. 448–69; N. Lindsay and J. Craig, "A Framework for Understanding Opportunity Recognition: Entrepreneurs versus Private Equity Financiers," *Journal of Private Equity*, 6 (2002), pp. 13–24; M. Rodgers, "Networks, Firm Size and Innovation," *Small Business Economics*, 22 (2004), pp. 141–53.

We'll look at these questions again at the end of the chapter in our Concluding Thoughts, after you've had a chance to learn about entrepreneurs and Innovation.

Creating a new enterprise can be one of the most exciting management challenges. Numerous entrepreneurs have built successful companies by discovering and meeting unmet needs. Many kinds of people start businesses. Men, women, minorities, immigrants—all can and do become entrepreneurs. As a result, entrepreneurship is becoming a popular field of study for many university business students.

Today's entrepreneurs face a variety of challenges. They must find answers to such questions as: Do I have the right skills and abilities to become a successful entrepreneur? What type of business should I start? How can I raise capital to grow the business? Which markets should my business compete in? How much growth and what rate of growth is desirable? Manager's Notebook 8.1 presents the basic entrepreneurial skills needed to successfully launch a new business venture. This chapter explores questions and issues about starting and growing a business. The first issue is describing what entrepreneurship is and is not.

■ What Is Entrepreneurship?

entrepreneurship
The process of creating a business enterprise capable of entering new or established markets by deploying resources and people in a unique way to develop a new organization.

entrepreneur
An individual who creates an enterprise that becomes a new entry to a market.

The process of creating a business enterprise capable of entering new or established markets is **entrepreneurship**. Successful entrepreneurship requires deploying resources and people in unique ways to develop a new organization. An **entrepreneur** is an individual who creates an enterprise that becomes a new entry to a market. Broadly stated, an entrepreneur is anyone who recognizes an opportunity, undertakes some project, and bears some risk.[1]

Entrepreneurship Myths

Entrepreneurs have received considerable attention from the business and popular press in recent years. Still, many misconceptions remain concerning entrepreneurs and what they do in order to succeed. We next consider some of these myths and contrast those with the common reality faced by most entrepreneurs.[2]

MYTH 1: ENTREPRENEURS ARE BORN, NOT MADE One common belief is that entrepreneurs possess certain innate traits that are different from regular people. In fact, many types of people with different personality characteristics have become successful entrepreneurs. Many of them studied entrepreneurship as a discipline before launching a business. Business schools offer courses in entrepreneurship that provide opportunities to learn and practice skills that are useful to entrepreneurs.

MYTH 2: IT IS NECESSARY TO HAVE ACCESS TO MONEY TO BECOME AN ENTREPRENEUR A second common myth is that only wealthy people, or those who have access to wealthy people, can start businesses. The truth is, however, that many companies have been started by people with few resources. These entrepreneurs accumulated capital by putting in long hours without pay and reinvesting the profits of the business into expansion. For example, Hewlett-Packard, the giant electronics company, was started in a Palo Alto, California, garage in 1940 by two Stanford University students with a few hundred dollars and an order for sound equipment from the Walt Disney Company.

MYTH 3: MOST ENTREPRENEURS ARE YOUNG PEOPLE UNDER 30 YEARS OF AGE It is true that some of the most celebrated entrepreneurs were young when they started their business. Bill Gates (Microsoft), Steve Jobs (Apple), Michael Dell (Dell Computer), and Mark Zuckerberg (Facebook) either dropped out of college to start their business or started it (Facebook) while they were still students. However, not all successful entrepreneurs were young when they got started. Harland Sanders started franchising Kentucky Fried Chicken when he was 65, and Herb Kelleher was 40 when he founded Southwest Airlines.[3]

MYTH 4: ENTREPRENEURS BECOME SUCCESSFUL ON THEIR FIRST VENTURE People tend to remember entrepreneurial successes. Many times, however, failure is a key part of the learning process. By failing, entrepreneurs learn lessons that eventually lead to the creation of successful ventures. Nolan Bushnell, the entrepreneur who is best remembered for starting the videogame company Atari, failed at several different businesses but he persisted and learned from his mistakes. Likewise, initial business ventures of Richard Branson, founder of Virgin Records, include a failed magazine launch.[4]

A Distinction Between an Entrepreneurial Venture and a Small Business

A **small business** is any company that is independently owned and operated, is small in size, and does not dominate its markets. For research purposes, the U.S. Small Business Administration defines a small business as employing fewer than 500 employees. Small businesses do not always grow into medium-sized or large businesses. Some small-business owners prefer to keep their operations modest.

One of the most important goals of an entrepreneur, on the other hand, can be growth. An entrepreneurial venture may be small during its early stages, but the goal may be to become a medium-sized firm of 100 to 499 employees or a large firm with 500 or more employees. Giant firms like Wal-Mart, Home Depot, Microsoft, and Intel started as entrepreneurships with the goal of becoming dominant companies in their markets. At the start, however, a small business and an entrepreneurial venture may be hard to tell apart. For a small business owner, stability and profitability are the ideal situation. For the entrepreneur, growth and a greater presence in the market can be important objectives.

small business
Any business that is independently owned and operated, that is small in size, and that is not dominant in its markets.

■ The Importance of Entrepreneurship

According to the latest figures compiled by the U.S. Census Bureau, the number of U.S. businesses increased by 10 percent between 1997 and 2002, with approximately 23 million businesses operating in the United States by the end of 2002.[5] An average of 500,000 new businesses were created in the United States between 2000 and 2009, according to the Kauffman Foundation, an organization that sponsors entrepreneurship research.[6] The economies of the United States and many other countries depend on the creation of new enterprises. Entrepreneurship creates jobs, stimulates innovation, and provides opportunities for diverse people in society.

Job Creation

Entrepreneurship and the creation of small businesses have surprising impacts on the creation of new jobs. Young companies, defined as those younger than six years old, provide a large share of the new jobs in the United States. In 2007 young companies accounted for 64 percent of new jobs according to a 2009 survey by the Kauffman Foundation.[7]

Innovation

Entrepreneurships are responsible for introducing a major proportion of new and innovative products and services that reach the market. They are often started by visionary people who develop an innovative way to do something faster, better, cheaper, or with improved features. Entrepreneurships often pioneer new technologies designed to make older technologies obsolete. This was the case when Apple Computer pioneered the first commercial personal computer and challenged the computing technology of the 1970s, which was based on centralized, mainframe computers. Eventually, the personal computer became the dominant technology and spawned, a huge market for computer components, software, systems, and services.

Apple created another successful product based on innovation when it launched the iPhone in 2007. The iPhone is a smart phone that has the ability to transmit voice and text, and act as an Internet client with e-mail, video, and Web browsing capabilities. The smart phone also has thousands of applications that are available including games, references, navigation software, and social networking.

Opportunities for Diverse People

People of diverse backgrounds who have experienced frustration and blocked career paths in large corporations can improve their economic status and develop interesting careers by becoming entrepreneurs. Entrepreneurship provides an attractive alternative for women who bump up against the glass ceiling in male-dominated firms. Many female corporate executives have left their firms to become entrepreneurs to: (1) balance work and family responsibilities; (2) obtain more challenge and autonomy; and (3) avoid unpleasant organization politics.

Similarly, increasing numbers of blacks, Hispanics, and Asian Americans have launched successful entrepreneurial efforts. Entrepreneurship can provide anyone, particularly in the United States, an alternative to the corporate career path. The most recent U.S. Census Bureau data indicates that business ownership by minorities and women has increased significantly.[8] For the period 1997 to 2002, the number of black-owned businesses increased by 45 percent, Hispanic-owned businesses increased by 31 percent, and Asian-owned businesses increased by 24 percent. Female-owned businesses for the period increased by 20 percent.

LOC-In 1   Learning Objective Check-In

Jess, Carol, and Kate are all women entrepreneurs. Jess has three kids and is a single mother. Kate was a former corporate manager who worked in a male-dominated firm and was not advancing to top executive status despite years of hard work. Carol, diplomatic to a fault, simply wanted to remove herself from the cutthroat environment of the corporate world in which she worked previously to start her own company and still serve top clients.

1. Jess removed herself from the corporate world to enter entrepreneurship in order to _____.
   a. make strategic decisions at a firm
   b. avoid unpleasant organization politics
   c. balance work and family responsibilities
   d. obtain more autonomy

2. Carol chose entrepreneurship because she wanted to _____.
   a. make strategic decisions at a firm
   b. obtain more autonomy and challenge at work
   c. balance work and family responsibilities
   d. avoid unpleasant organization politics

3. Kate chose entrepreneurship because she wanted to _____.
   a. avoid unpleasant organization politics
   b. advance beyond the "glass ceiling"
   c. obtain more autonomy and challenge at work
   d. achieve personal fulfillment through innovation

■ Entrepreneurial Characteristics and Skills

There are many motives for starting a new business. Some entrepreneurs learn from successful family role models. A few stumble onto an entrepreneurial career path by inventing a new product and building a business around it, as did Steven Jobs and Steve Wozniak with the first prototype of the Apple computer. Others become dissatisfied with corporate careers and discover that entrepreneurship provides an attractive set of challenges and rewards. Jim Koch, the founder of Boston Beer Company, who was discussed in the vignette at the start of this chapter, left a successful corporate career to become an entrepreneur. David Neeleman founded JetBlue Airways after working as an executive at Morris Air and Southwest Airlines, and was fired from the latter company. Next we will examine characteristics of entrepreneurs followed by the skills of entrepreneurs.

Characteristics of Entrepreneurs

Some key characteristics associated with entrepreneurship are a high need for achievement, an internal locus of control, the willingness to take risks, and self-confidence.

People with a *high need for achievement* have a strong desire to solve problems on their own. They enjoy setting goals and achieving them through their own efforts, and like receiving feedback on how they are doing. These characteristics help entrepreneurs to be more proactive and anticipate future problems, needs, or changes.

An entrepreneur is likely to have an **internal locus of control**, with a strong belief in his or her ability to succeed. When a person with an internal locus of control fails or makes a mistake, the individual is likely to accept responsibility for the outcome and try harder, rather than searching for external reasons to explain the failure. Entrepreneurs are persistent and motivated to overcome barriers that would deter others. People with an **external locus of control** believe that what happens to them is due to luck, fate, or factors beyond their control. When people with an external locus of control fail, they are more likely to feel helpless and are less likely to sustain or intensify their goal-seeking efforts.

An entrepreneur takes on some level of risk when trying to start a new venture. In some cases, entrepreneurs may risk a substantial portion of their own capital as well as funds contributed by family, friends, and other investors. The entrepreneur may leave the security of a corporate career and still be uncertain that the new venture presents a better opportunity. However, entrepreneurs, as a group, may not face quite as much risk of failure as previously thought. Current data indicates that 67 percent of new ventures are successful after four years.[9]

Entrepreneurs feel certain they can master the skills needed to run a business and that they can overcome unforeseen obstacles. This self-confidence can be used to energize and motivate others. Self-confidence enables entrepreneurs to improvise and find novel solutions to business problems that might discourage people who are more self-critical.

Michael Dell, the entrepreneur who founded Dell Computer, exhibits all of these characteristics. His background and reasons for launching his company are described in Management Close-Up 8.1.

Entrepreneurs acquire these characteristics in various ways. Some learn them from family role models. Others are exposed to entrepreneurs in school, work, or social activities. Most people have opportunities to develop entrepreneurial characteristics by imitating others who have these characteristics.

Entrepreneurial Skills

Just as there are certain personal characteristics that are likely to be found in entrepreneurs, there are also skills which are related to success. An entrepreneur utilizes a variety of business skills to create and operate an enterprise. Among these are negotiation skills, networking skills, and leadership skills.

NEGOTIATION SKILLS Whenever an exchange of goods or services between two or more parties takes place, quality negotiation skills are helpful. A party who applies negotiation skills effectively ensures favorable terms for both parties by finding common ground. This problem-solving style of negotiation, also referred to as *win-win* negotiating, requires the individual to act in good faith to forge a relationship based on trust and cooperation. This makes it easier to discover a basis of exchange that is attractive to both parties. More information on negotiation skills is provided in Chapter 13.

Earl G. Graves, Sr., chief executive officer of Earl G. Graves Ltd., founded Black Enterprise in 1970. His vision was to create a link of commerce and communication between the black professional class and American industry.

internal locus of control
A strong belief in one's own ability to succeed, so that one accepts responsibility for outcomes and tries harder after making mistakes.

external locus of control
A strong belief that luck, fate, or factors beyond one's control determine one's progress, causing feelings of helplessness and decreasing intensity of goal-seeking efforts in the face of failure.

MANAGEMENT CLOSE-UP 8.1   THEME: **CUSTOMER FOCUS**

Michael Dell, Founder and CEO, Dell Computer Corporation

Michael Dell is founder and CEO of Austin-based Dell Computer Corporation, a widely recognized U.S. computer company with over 96,000 employees and over $53 billion in revenues for 2010. With a net worth of $13.5 billion, he is the wealthiest person in Texas. Dell's idea was to sell computers directly to the customer by telephone, avoiding costly middlemen and saving the customer money. Rather than building computers to distribute to retail outlets and carrying large inventories of finished computers and parts to build them, he built computers to order. The company saved money by having a lean, just-in-time inventory of parts from suppliers. Michael Dell pioneered the use of the Internet as a distribution channel for selling computers, and Dell now sells more computers on the Internet than any other company.

Dell was born into a Houston family of high achievers. His father was an orthodontist, his mother a stockbroker. When Michael was 8 years old he applied for a high school equivalency exam, and by age 13 he started a mail order stamp-trading business. When Dell was 16 he started selling subscriptions to the *Houston Post* by phone and became salesman of the month shortly after. A year later he was earning $18,000 annually supervising fellow high school students as they sold subscriptions.

At a young age Dell became very interested in computers. While spending a lot of time around computer retail stores, he realized that these stores were charging up to a 40 percent markup on their products. Even though these stores were charging a high amount for their computers, their service was not very good. Dell realized that he could buy the products directly from the manufacturer, sell them cheaply to the customer, provide better service, and completely eliminate the retail store.

Dell decided to start his computer business when he was just a freshman at the University of Texas at Austin. Working out of his dorm room, Dell sold computers built to order to interested buyers. Three months later, Dell had racked up sales of $181,000. Two years later, when Dell turned 20, the company reached $34 million in sales.

Michael Dell has remained at the helm of Dell Computer from the start, becoming one of the youngest CEOs of a major U.S. corporation while still in his twenties.

Sources: A. Serwer, "Michael Dell Rocks," *Fortune,* May 11, 1998, pp. 59–70; A. Serwer, "Michael Dell Turns the PC World Inside Out," *Fortune,* September 8, 1997, pp. 76–86; D. F. Kuratko and R. M. Hodgetts, *Entrepreneurship,* 2nd ed., Fort Worth: Dryden Press, 1992, p. 72; Dell Inc. Web site, "Facts about Dell," www.dell.com, accessed July 3, 2010.

Entrepreneurs use negotiation skills to obtain resources needed to launch and maintain a company. Among the situations that require negotiation skills are:

- Borrowing money from a bank at good terms to finance business expansion.
- Locking into an attractive, long-term lease to control office space expenses.
- Obtaining a low price on raw materials from a supplier to gain a cost advantage over competitors.
- Negotiating employment contracts to attract and retain key executives.

NETWORKING SKILLS Gathering information and building alliances requires quality networking skills. These are applied to both personal and business networks.

personal network
The relationships between an entrepreneur and other parties, including other entrepreneurs, suppliers, creditors, investors, friends, former colleagues, and others.

A **personal network** is based on relationships between the entrepreneur and other entrepreneurs, suppliers, creditors, investors, friends, former professors, and others. These personal contacts can help an entrepreneur make effective decisions by providing information that reduces uncertainty for the business. For example,

- A fellow entrepreneur can help locate a wealthy interested private investor (sometimes referred to as a "business angel") to provide scarce capital.
- A former professor may provide free technical consulting advice and student volunteers to help develop a marketing strategy for the new venture.
- A banker may be able to locate a skilled executive who could provide complementary management skills to the entrepreneurship at a critical stage of growth.
- Talks with fellow entrepreneurs who have been through the process of building a business from the ground up can provide invaluable feedback and emotional support.

Entrepreneurs build personal networks by actively seeking out individuals with similar interests, staying in touch with them, and looking for opportunities to make the relationship

SKILLS FOR MANAGING 8.1

Networking Skills

Reflect on a meeting of a professional student club or organization that you have recently attended.

1. What was your purpose for attending this meeting?
2. Did you have any specific goals in mind in terms of the kinds of people you hoped to meet and how you hoped to benefit from the meeting?
3. How many people did you meet at the meeting?
4. How many of these new acquaintances did you connect with so that there was a possibility for a relationship to emerge?
5. How many people did you follow up with a phone call after the meeting?
6. What was the basis of your relationship with these new contacts?
7. Have you continued to keep in touch with these new contacts? If not, why not?

Instructions: Answer the preceding questions individually. Then form small groups of four to five students. Share your experiences in networking with each other. Then work together to answer the following questions. If time permits, attend a professional meeting after developing some network strategies and report back to the group with your experiences.

Discussion Questions

1. What are some effective practices that can be used to network with other people?
2. How can you avoid getting entangled in too many fruitless network relationships that are not mutually beneficial?
3. What are some ways to keep your network vital so that you can feel free to tap your network for opportunities when the time comes and you are in need of help?

Source: From *Entrepreneurship,* by M. J. Dollinger. Copyright © 1995 The McGraw-Hill Companies, Inc. Reprinted with permission.

---

mutually satisfying. By being responsive to the needs and interests of the people in their personal networks, entrepreneurs build trust and goodwill. A personal network can be formed through participation in professional societies, business clubs, charitable organizations, trade fairs, and networks of entrepreneurs. Skills for Managing 8.1 presents an opportunity to analyze and improve your networking skills.

Networking skills can come in handy in developing useful business alliances. A **business network** is a set of alliances forged with other businesses to achieve mutually beneficial goals. A larger company may enter a partnership with a small entrepreneurship in order to gain some of the benefits of the new and innovative product or service the entrepreneurship is developing. Through licensing agreements that provide limited access to the technology or strategic alliances to pool resources, a new company may gain access to a larger corporation's marketing and finance professionals or may obtain capital to help enter markets that are difficult to reach. This includes acquiring shelf space in Wal-Mart or having a national direct sales force call on customers.

business network
A firm's alliances formed with other businesses to achieve mutually beneficial goals.

Microsoft entered a strategic alliance with IBM in 1980 to provide DOS-based operating systems for the new IBM personal computer. This strategic alliance ensured the success of Microsoft and greatly enabled it to set the technology standard for personal computer operating systems, which resulted in huge profits for Microsoft.

LEADERSHIP SKILLS Quality leaders provide a shared vision for others to work toward common goals. As leaders, entrepreneurs inspire and motivate employees to do what is good for the enterprise, even when it is not in their short-term interests. For example, employees in a start-up company are likely to work extremely long hours for modest pay. The entrepreneur depends on leadership skills to bolster employee morale and guide the enterprise toward the objectives, overcoming obstacles that stand in the way.

Starting a business is a difficult prospect. In addition to possessing certain personal characteristics and skills, there are steps that an entrepreneur should take to help assure the success of the new business. Management Is Everyone's Business 8.1 offers some simple but important recommendations that should enhance your success as an individual entrepreneur.

MANAGEMENT IS EVERYONE'S BUSINESS 8.1

WORKING AS AN INDIVIDUAL When starting a business, an entrepreneur is likely to encounter unforeseen difficulties that require the assistance of experts who can offer useful advice to the nascent entrepreneur. Many start-up firms form advisory boards to provide advice and a sounding board for an entrepreneur to discuss possible alternatives when facing a challenging business decision. An **advisory board** is a panel of experts that offer advice and counsel to an entrepreneur on a regular basis. The advisory board has no legally binding duties to the business and the advice it gives is nonbinding. Here is an example of a problem that an entrepreneur may present to an advisory board when seeking advice: The entrepreneur has developed a video game and is wondering whether it would be better to partner with a large corporation to market the game or sell the video game directly to customers.

■ Starting and Managing an Entrepreneurial Venture

An entrepreneurial venture begins with an idea. The next steps are developing a business plan, selecting the most appropriate type of legal structure to operate under, obtaining financing, and dealing with growth and expansion. Many entrepreneurial ventures are new businesses, rather than being franchises or spin-offs.

New Business Ideas

Entrepreneurs get ideas for new businesses from many different sources, including

- Newspapers, magazines, and trade journals that identify market trends.
- Inventions or discoveries that provide products or services faster, better, cheaper, or with more features. Corporations like the 3M Company give technologists unstructured time to experiment, hoping for the discovery of the next Post-it Notes.
- Trade shows and exhibitions, where new products and innovations are displayed.
- Hobbies, such as jogging, bicycling, or skiing, as was the case with new companies that marketed running shoes (Nike), mountain bicycles (Cannondale), and snowboards (Burton).
- Family members, including children, such as in the design of video games, educational toys, and the baby jogger that lets people combine jogging with taking the baby out.
- Entrepreneurship courses in business schools. Babson University in Wellesley, Massachusetts, sponsors a business plan contest between teams of business students who compete for prize money. Student entrepreneurs with promising business plans are likely to attract the attention of investors.

Why Entrepreneurs Fail

Entrepreneurial ventures can fail if the business idea is poorly implemented. The most common reasons for business failure include:

- *Lack of capital.* When an entrepreneur underestimates the need for capital and assumes more debt than can be repaid, the new business is in trouble. Many businesses fail because investors do not purchase enough stock during the initial public offering to cover accumulated debts.
- *Poor knowledge of the market.* An entrepreneur can miscalculate the appeal of the product or service. This often occurs when an inventor "falls in love" with an invention and expects consumers to do so as well.
- *Faulty product design.* Design or other features of a product can be rejected by consumers. This was the case with word processing products sold by Wang Computer, which were linked to mainframe computers and were much more expensive than rival products that were driven by personal computers. Wang was unable to sell enough of its products and went out of business.
- *Human resource problems.* Entrepreneurs may select employees who do not support the goals of the business. In a family business, there is the potential for divorce or sibling rivalry to divide workers into feuding factions.

- *Poor understanding of the competition.* Entrepreneurs should study their competitors and try to understand their interests. Firmly entrenched businesses may react aggressively and use price cuts or special discounts to try to drive new competitors out of business.

Sometimes businesses exit the market for reasons other than failure. An entrepreneur may sell the business to a competitor for a good price or close it because a more attractive business opportunity has come along.

LOC-In 2   Learning Objective Check-In

1. Carlita has always had trouble using the standard adjustable headphones that come with electronic devices she has purchased in the past. They are either too stiff or too loose, or else they do not adjust to be small enough. Carlita has an idea for developing easily adjustable audio and video equipment for adults and children for use with standard electronic equipment, including video game equipment. She thinks that she might be able to turn her idea into a new business venture. The source of Carlita's idea is _____.
   a. newspapers, magazines, and trade journals
   b. inventions or discoveries
   c. trade shows and exhibitions
   d. personal hobbies or discoveries

Business Plan

Once an entrepreneur develops an idea for a new business venture, the next critical step is to prepare a **business plan**, which is a blueprint that maps out the business strategy for entering markets and explains the business to potential investors. A business plan details the strategies and tactics needed to minimize the enterprise's risk of failure, which is highest during the early stages.

Key components of the business plan include:

- A description of the product or service.
- An analysis of market trends and potential competitors.
- An estimated price for the product or service.
- An estimate of the time it will take to generate profits.
- A plan for manufacturing the product.
- A plan for growth and expansion of the business.
- Sources of funding.
- A plan for obtaining financing.
- An approach for putting an effective management team in place.

A detailed outline for creating a business plan appears in Figure 8.1.

> **business plan**
> The business's blueprint that maps out its business strategy for entering markets and that explains the business to potential investors.

Legal Forms

Entrepreneurs can select from three different legal forms when launching a new enterprise. The legal forms are a proprietorship, a partnership, and a corporation. An entrepreneur should consider tax implications, willingness to accept personal liability, and the ease of raising capital for the business before making this important decision.

PROPRIETORSHIP Many new businesses are owned by single individuals. **Proprietorships** are easy to form and require a minimum of paperwork. The owner keeps all of the profits and makes all of the important decisions without having to get the approval of co-owners.

A proprietorship is limited to one person, which restricts the owner from obtaining more than limited amounts of credit and capital. Another drawback is that the sole owner has unlimited liability, which means that the personal assets of the owner may be at stake in a lawsuit. About 74 percent of all U.S. businesses are proprietorships, though revenues and profits are relatively small compared to other forms of ownership.

> **proprietorship**
> A form of business that is owned by one person.

PARTNERSHIP An association of two or more persons acting as co-owners of a business creates a **partnership**. Each partner provides resources and skills and shares in the profits. A partnership

> **partnership**
> A form of business that is an association of two or more persons acting as co-owners of a business.

FIGURE 8.1

Outline of a Business Plan

Source: From *Entrepreneurship,* 4th ed., by R. Hisrich and M. Peters. Copyright © 1998 The McGraw-Hill Companies, Inc. Reprinted with permission.

Introductory Page
- Name and address of business
- Name(s) and address(es) of principals
- Nature of business
- Statement of financing needed
- Statement of confidentiality of report

Executive Summary
- Three to four pages summarizing the complete business plan

Industry Analysis
- Future outlook and trends
- Market segmentation
- Industry forecasts

Description of Venture
- Product(s)
- Service(s)
- Size of business
- Office equipment and personnel
- Background of entrepreneurs

Production Plan
- Manufacturing process (amount subcontracted)
- Physical plant
- Machinery and equipment
- Names of suppliers of raw materials

Marketing Plan
- Pricing
- Distribution
- Promotion
- Product forecasts
- Controls

Organizational Plan
- Form of ownership
- Identification of partners or prinicipal shareholders
- Authority of principals
- Management-team background
- Roles and responsibilities of members of organization

Assessment of Risk
- Evaluate weakness of business
- New technologies
- Contingency plans

Financial Plan
- Pro forma income statement
- Cash flow projections
- Pro forma balance sheet
- Break-even analysis
- Sources and applications of funds

Appendix
- Letters
- Market research data
- Leases or contracts
- Price lists from suppliers

can raise more capital than a proprietorship and can provide complementary skills that can create more opportunity for the enterprise. For example, one partner of a small Los Angeles law firm is skillful at generating new clients from his extensive networks in the local bar association, while the other is skilled at providing meticulous legal research that results in a high court success rate. The synergy between these two law partners results in more profits than would be possible if each were operating alone.

While partnerships are easy to start and are subject to few government regulations, they do have some drawbacks. Each partner is responsible for the acts of the other partners. If one partner makes a bad business decision, the other partners are liable. In other words, each owner's personal assets are at risk in a lawsuit or to pay off debts. If the partners disagree about important goals of the business, the firm may become paralyzed or fail. If one of the partners dies, a partnership will be in jeopardy unless provisions for the other partners to buy out the deceased partner's share have been made. Nonetheless, some large and successful businesses use the partnership legal structure. Large accounting firms such as PriceWaterhouseCoopers have more than 1,000 partners in offices around the globe.

corporation

A form of business that is a legal entity separate from the individuals who own it.

CORPORATION A **corporation** is a legal entity separate from the individuals who own it. A corporation receives limited rights to operate from the state or government that provides its charter. A corporation is more complex and costly to form and operate than a proprietorship or a partnership. Since its activities are regulated by the government, many records must be kept and regularly filed with the government.

MANAGEMENT IS EVERYONE'S BUSINESS   8.2

WORKING AS A TEAM   More than half of all entrepreneurships are started by a team of founders, not just a single individual. Google (Sergey Brin and Larry Page), Apple (Steve Jobs and Steve Wozniak), Microsoft (Bill Gates and Paul Allen), Yahoo! (Jerry Yang and David Filo), Sun Microsystems (Vinod Khosla, Andy Bechtolsheim, and Scott McNealy), and Cisco Systems (Len Bosack, Sandy Lerner, and Richard Troiano) were all founded by teams of two or more entrepreneurs. In general, new ventures started by a team have an advantage over those started by an individual because a team brings more talent, resources, ideas, and professional contacts to a new venture than does a single entrepreneur. However, there are a few key factors that should be considered when forming a team of founders to start a business. First, it is advantageous if the team has worked together prior to starting a business so that there is a basis of trust and an experience of working together that can be applied to the start-up situation. Next, it is advantageous for the members of the founding team to have complementary sets of skills so that they can draw on different types of expertise when starting a new business. For example, one founder may have a strength in technology know-how and the other founding partner may have deep knowledge of sales and marketing. Finally, it is important to avoid having too many people on a team of founders, with four considered to be an upper bound. Having too many founders on a team creates potential for conflict and miscommunication, which can be disruptive to the business.

The benefit of forming a corporation is limited liability. If the corporation is sued, corporate assets are at risk, but the personal assets of the owners are not. A corporation is separate from the owner. When the owner dies, the corporation continues. Corporations are able to raise more capital than any of the other legal forms of enterprise. Corporations are able to raise capital through the sale of shares of stock to the public or through loans and bonds.

Besides incorporation fees and the additional record-keeping expenses, many corporations are doubly taxed by the government. The corporation pays taxes on its profits, and the owners pay taxes on their dividends. Some other countries do not have this double taxation system, and some firms find it attractive to incorporate in countries that offer advantageous tax treatment. The advantages and disadvantages of partnerships and corporations are summarized in Table 8.1. In addition, Management Is Everyone's Business 8.2 provides some guidelines for forming a founding team for a start-up business.

TABLE 8.1 Partnership and Corporation Forms of Ownership

Advantages	Disadvantages
Partnership	
Ease of formation	Unlimited liability for firm's debt
Direct share of profits	Limited continuity of life of enterprise
Division of labor and management responsibility	Difficulty in obtaining capital
More capital available than in a sole proprietorship	Partners share responsibility for other partners' actions
Less governmental control and regulation	
Corporation	
Owners' liability for the firm's debt limited to their investment	Extensive government regulation of activities
Ease of raising large amounts of capital	High incorporation fees
Ease of transfer of ownership through sales of stock	Corporate capital, profits, dividends and salaries double-taxed
Life of enterprise distinct from owners	Activities limited to those stated in charter

Sources: Based on W. Megginson et al., *Small Business Management,* 2nd ed., New York: Irwin/McGraw-Hill, 1997, pp. 74, 78; D. F. Kuratko and R. M. Hodgetts, Entrepreneurship, 2nd ed., Fort Worth: Dryden Press, 1992, p. 208; E. McKinney, "Partnership vs. Corporation," 2010, www.ehow.com/.

The Kauffman Foundation's Collegiate Entrepreneurship site serves as a repository for the growing amount of information about cross-campus entrepreneurship programs. The foundation's Kauffman Campuses initiative seeks to transform the way colleges and universities make entrepreneurship education available across their campuses, enabling any student, regardless of field of study, to access entrepreneurial training.

debt financing
A means of obtaining financial resources that involves obtaining a commercial loan and setting up a plan to repay the principal and interest.

bankruptcy
A legal procedure that distributes company assets to creditors and protects the debtor from unfair demands of creditors when the debtor fails to make scheduled loan repayments.

equity financing
A means of obtaining financial resources that involves the sale of part of the ownership of the business to investors.

Sources of Financial Resources

Entrepreneurships require capital to get started. The two principal means of obtaining the resources to fund a new business are debt financing and equity financing. Factors favoring one type of financing over the other include the value of the firm's assets, the interest rate, and the availability of investor funds.

DEBT FINANCING Commercial loans are a common form of **debt financing**. Company leaders must set up a plan to repay the principal and interest. The schedule to repay the loan may be short term, lasting less than one year, or long term. Commercial banks are the principal source of debt financing.

The bank establishes a repayment schedule for the loan and secures the loan with company assets such as inventories, equipment, and machines or real estate. Failure to make the scheduled loan repayments can lead to **bankruptcy**, a legal procedure that distributes company assets to creditors and protects the debtor from unfair demands of creditors. Bankruptcy can hurt the reputation of an entrepreneur and make it difficult to obtain future business loans.

An entrepreneur must be careful not to take on too much debt. Excessive debt will result in most of the company's positive cash flow going to retiring the debt rather than growing the business. New ventures that have uncertain cash flows during start-up may not be able to qualify for debt financing.

Other sources of debt financing for more specific purchases are:

- Equipment manufacturers (for example, a computer firm may debt finance a computer system).
- Suppliers (credit may be given on supplies for a fee).
- Credit cards (some businesses were started by overextending several of an owner's credit cards, an expensive way to obtain financing).

EQUITY FINANCING As a business grows, an entrepreneur will most likely combine a mix of debt and equity sources of capital. **Equity financing** is raising money by selling part of the ownership of the business to investors. In equity financing, the entrepreneur shares control of the business with the investors. Equity financing does not require collateral. Sources of equity financing include private investors, venture capitalists, and public offerings in which shares of stock are sold.

Early in the growth of a business, the risk of failure may be great. At this stage, private investors and venture capitalists may be willing to provide equity financing. **Venture capitalists** specialize in making loans to entrepreneurships that have the potential for rapid growth but are in high-risk situations with few assets and would therefore not qualify for commercial bank loans. Venture capitalists manage pools of money provided by wealthy individuals and institutions seeking to invest in entrepreneurships. High-technology businesses such as software, telecommunications, and biotechnology are particularly attractive to venture capitalists because they anticipate high financial returns from their investment. Microsoft, Compaq Computer, and Intel were started with venture capital financing and made fabulous returns for early investors. Venture capitalists also provide management knowledge, contacts to hire key employees, and financial advice.

Public offerings raise capital by selling securities in public markets such as the New York Stock Exchange and NASDAQ. A public offering can provide large infusions of cash to fuel rapid internal growth or to finance a merger or acquisition. One drawback of a public offering is that publicly traded companies must disclose a great deal of information, including quarterly reports on income, balance sheet assets, and use of funds. Competitors can exploit weaknesses that are disclosed in these reports. After a public offering, management decisions are under a higher level of public scrutiny. There is a lower tolerance for management mistakes, and there is increased shareholder pressure for dividends and predictable quarterly profits. Unhappy shareholders can sell their shares, driving down the value of the company. Public offerings generally do not take place until an entrepreneurship achieves a critical mass of about $10 million to $20 million in annual revenue.

Managing Growth

Entrepreneurs manage business growth by establishing benchmarks based on market data and a thorough analysis of the firm's ability to handle increased demand without sacrificing quality. A business plan is an invaluable tool for planning growth targets. These milestones can be used to pace company expansion. The growth of a business reflects the success of the entrepreneurial effort, but can also place stress on the entrepreneur to become an effective manager.

Too much growth can put an unbearable strain on the operations of a business. A company that grows too quickly may experience the following:

- The company spends most of its available cash on expansion and has difficulty meeting obligations to creditors. The result is a cash flow crisis.
- Employees are likely to experience stress from such rapid changes as moving to new jobs without training, adjusting to new supervisors and colleagues, and making frequent changes in office locations.
- Accounting and information systems that worked well when the firm was smaller must be replaced with more complicated and sophisticated systems. Current personnel may not be capable of operating these systems, and information may not be available when it is needed.
- Management may no longer be competent to manage a larger or more diverse portfolio of business units or product lines. The board of directors may replace the chief executive officer or other key executives with more experienced managers. To make matters worse, the founder may resist stepping down. In 1985 Steve Jobs, the founder of Apple Inc., was asked to leave by its board, which felt his leadership style was not appropriate for the large company that Apple had become. (Jobs, always the entrepreneur, started another company. In 1997 he returned to Apple—by then under different leadership—with the technology he had developed in the interim and sold it to Apple for $400 million.)

Unchecked growth can threaten the survival of a business venture. For example, James L. Bildner, the founder of J. Bildner & Sons Inc., a specialty food business, expanded rapidly from a single store to a chain of 20 stores after a public offering in 1986. The company ran out of cash because it had built too many stores. Employees started leaving and operations became chaotic.

venture capitalists
Financial investors who specialize in making loans to entrepreneurships that have the potential for rapid growth but are in high-risk situations with few assets and would therefore not qualify for commercial bank loans.

public offerings
A means of raising capital by the sale of securities in public markets such as the New York Stock Exchange and NASDAQ.

LOC-In 3 Learning Objective Check-In

Janet's Scallops is a new business that Janet Phillips wants to start within the coming year. She will own the business herself, keeping all the profits and assuming all the risk personally. Furthermore, Janet will obtain a short-term commercial loan and will repay the principal and interest on that loan. If the company grows as she hopes it does, Janet plans to entertain the idea of another type of financing by which she will sell part of the ownership of the business to investors.

1. Which of the following best describes the type of legal form that Janet's business will assume?
   a. Proprietorship
   b. Corporation
   c. S-Corporation
   d. Partnership

2. Which of the following best characterizes the type of financing Janet plans to use in the beginning of her business?
   a. Equity financing
   b. Public offerings
   c. Venture capitalists
   d. Debt financing

3. Which of the following represents the type of financing option Janet will entertain if the business is successful and grows in the future?
   a. Debt financing
   b. Venture capitalists
   c. Equity financing
   d. Public offerings

Too many new stores, ineffective new products, attempts to hire too many new people at once, and lack of controls made everything worse. The company experienced large losses, inventory control problems, and the departure of loyal customers. This crisis could have been avoided if the management team had pursued less aggressive growth. Sometimes managers should turn down growth opportunities in an expanding market rather than lose control of the operation.

■ Alternative Forms of Entrepreneurship

This chapter has focused on *independent entrepreneurship*. Alternatives to this form of entrepreneurship are intrapreneurship, spin-offs, and franchising. In general, these alternative forms involve smaller risks than independent entrepreneurship.

Intrapreneurship

intrapreneurship
A form of business organization in which new business units are developed within a larger corporate structure in order to deploy the firm's resources to market a new product or service; also called corporate entrepreneurship.

The development of new business units within a larger corporate structure in order to deploy the firm's resources to market a new product or service is **intrapreneurship**, or *corporate entrepreneurship*. Some large companies develop cultures that foster innovation and the nurturing of new businesses. The 3M Company maintains a corporate goal that requires over 30 percent of corporate sales to come from products less than four years old. The technical staff is encouraged to devote 15 percent of its time to experimentation in new product designs that are peripheral to the projects they have been assigned to work on. These policies support a culture of innovation that has resulted in a steady stream of internally developed new products at the 3M Company.

When Apple showed the world that there was a large market for personal computers, IBM saw the need to design its own personal computer to challenge the Apple computer. The IBM Personal Computer was developed in a separate business unit located in Florida and isolated from the rest of the company. To build, test, and market launch the IBM PC in only 12 months, the IBM Personal Computer unit used standard electronic components and systems, rather than using all-IBM manufactured components as was typical in the company.

In the 1990s the National Broadcasting Company (NBC), the television network owned by General Electric, launched CNBC, a cable television network that provided financial news 24 hours a day. The launch coincided with the 1990s bull market that generated a large demand for televised financial news. Within a few years CNBC was profitable and successful, attracting a highly desirable audience of wealthy executives and investors.

An advantage of intrapreneurship is that the company provides funding and corporate resources that an independent entrepreneur cannot gather. The intrapreneuring corporate engineer or manager does not have to abandon a corporate career to manage the new venture. On the other hand, a successful *intrapreneur* within a corporation usually does not receive the financial rewards that might be generated by an independent entrepreneurship.

Spin-Offs

spin-off
An independent entrepreneurship that produces a product or service that originated in a large company.

Sometimes a new product developed by a corporation does not fit with the company's established products. A group of managers may decide to create a new business for this product rather than forgo the opportunity to market it. A **spin-off** is an independent entrepreneurship that produces a product or service that originated in a large company. Spin-offs are typical of technology companies, which must develop a steady stream of new products to keep up with competitors. Some of the new technologies do not fit with the company's core competencies, providing the opportunity for spin-offs.

Xerox's Palo Alto Research Center (PARC) is a laboratory located in California's Silicon Valley that develops new optical imaging products that fit with the core competencies of Xerox. Occasionally, new technologies that do not fit with other Xerox products are spawned in this research laboratory. Xerox encourages the formation of spin-offs when the technology has commercial potential. In some cases, Xerox forms a partnership with the managers who start the spin-off. For example, when a security product that encrypts messages for cellular phones was developed in the PARC laboratories, Xerox created a spin-off called Semaphore Communications to manufacture and market the device.

Franchises

When a business with an established name and product is sold to additional owners along with the rights to distribute the product, a franchise operation is created. Franchising is particularly prevalent in the retail service sector of the economy, such as in the restaurant, hotel, and retail businesses. McDonald's, Taco Bell, Subway, Quality Inn, Dunkin' Donuts, Radio Shack, and Midas are well-known franchises. Franchising can also occur in unexpected situations.

In franchising, an entrepreneur assumes fewer risks because the franchise can provide: (1) a product or service with an established market and favorable image; (2) management training and assistance in operating the business; (3) economies of scale for advertising and purchasing; (4) operating and structural controls; and (5) financial assistance. The franchising company sells the distribution rights for a limited geographic area to the entrepreneur for a fee plus a share of the revenues.

Sometimes franchising companies fail to provide promised services. The franchise company may oversell franchise rights in a geographic location, making it difficult for an entrepreneur to profit. Such conflicts of interests can result in lengthy courtroom battles.

LOC-In 4 **Learning Objective Check-In**

1. Walton's is a large corporation in which new business units are developed within the larger corporate structure in order to deploy Walton's resources to market new products and services. This is an example of _____.
   a. proprietorship
   b. intrapreneurship
   c. spin-offs
   d. a franchise

■ Innovation

Innovation is a key to long-term success. Exploring and developing new technologies and new ways of doing things are vital to the future viability of an organization.[10] Entrepreneurs often pursue innovative ideas in their new business ventures. They may come up with ideas and pursue them when an organization decides that the time and cost of development are just too great.

However, as pointed out earlier, entrepreneurship is often about rather modest and incremental change to a product or service, rather than a radical change. Further, larger organizations may embrace and encourage innovation. While innovation and entreprenuership are related concepts, they are basically separate and distinct issues. Whether you have entrepreneurial aspirations or want to work in a corporate environment, you are likely to find yourself in situations that call for *innovation.*

What Is Innovation?

Fundamentally, innovation is doing something differently. As Michael Tushman, professor of management at Harvard Business School, describes it,[11] innovation can involve *radical* or *incremental* change. Radical innovations often make prior technologies obsolete. For example, digital compact discs have all but replaced cassette tapes and require a compact disc player to use them. Alternatively, incremental innovations are generally improvements of existing products that usually do *not* render prior products or technologies obsolete. Examples include smaller cell phones or even Caffeine-Free Coke. So while it may be difficult to find cassette tapes in your local record store due to the radical innovation of the CD, both Coke and Caffeine-Free Coke can easily be had at your local supermarket.

Whether a change is radical or incremental, it is not just the change that is important or that defines an innovation. Certainly, the change or invention is a critical component, but an invention, by itself, does not make for innovation. A description of innovation used by 3M, a company known for innovation, is a new idea together with action or implementation that has a bottom-line impact.[12] In other words, an innovation is more than just a novel idea or product;

an innovation has to add value and somehow result in positive gain or improvement. Without adding value, a new idea or product could be just a novel invention, but would not qualify as an innovation. To be an innovator, you must find a way to implement your idea as a cost-effective or commercially viable product or service. Consider, for example, the Segway people mover. It is, no doubt, a novel invention, but a couple of years after its creation, can it be considered an innovation? At the time of its creation, Segway supporters envisioned cities being redesigned to accommodate the machine and the use of the Segway as a replacement for the automobile for short trips.[13] Today, Segways are being used in only limited situations and chances are, you do not see any of them in regular use. The Segway is a neat invention, but it hasn't had a socioeconomic impact—it hasn't changed people's lives or what they buy. Novelty without a tangible return is not an innovation. In contrast, going from diapers to disposable diapers may have been a mundane and simple change, as inventions go, but it has proven to be major innovation.[14]

LOC-In 5 Learning Objective Check-In

1. William thinks he has developed a composite material that could replace glass windows in houses where tornadoes are prevalent. While the material is more expensive than glass, it is 100 times more durable, and is practically shatter-proof. As an added bonus, it is naturally UV-resistant due to one of the chemicals used in producing the product. Given what you know about William's material what kind of innovation do you think it represents for people living in tornado areas of the country?
   a. Incremental
   b. Distributive
   c. Radical
   d. New generation

The Importance of Innovation

Innovation is playing a more important and central role in many organizations. A recent survey of senior executives from around the world concluded that innovation has become essential to success in their industries.[15] The importance being placed on innovation may reflect a shift in the economic paradigm. In recent years the focus has been on quality and consistency of execution. However, business success may now be more tied to providing innovations that respond to customer needs. In broad terms, you might think of the current situation as shifting from quality and price as key drivers to creativity.[16] It is not that quality and price are irrelevant; it is that they are assumed. What can differentiate and underlie success in the marketplace is innovation. One of the best examples of a company that is succeeding based on creativity and innovation is Apple. The company is continually bringing new innovations to its iPod, reducing size and increasing capability to include video.

Steve Jobs, CEO of Apple which he cofounded in 1976, is widely credited with nurturing the company's distinctive brand of creativity and innovation, blended with sleek and groundbreaking product design.

The Innovation Process

The management of innovation needs encouragement and support for both *invention*, which deals with discovery, and for *application*, which involves the act of utilization. Managers need to provide environments that stimulate creativity, which culminates in a pipeline of new products or improvements to ongoing products. One of the key challenges for managers in the process of innovation is in establishing a set of procedures that separates the good ideas, which should be commercialized into products and services of value to the firm, from the less desirable ideas, which are not commercially feasible for investing resources for further development.

One approach that describes a set of procedures for the innovation process is called the *wheel of innovation*, which was developed by Gary Hamel, a consultant and professor at the London Business School.[17] The wheel of innovation consists of five steps:

1. *Imagining*—thinking about new ways of doing something or extending existing ways.
2. *Designing*—testing ideas at the conceptual level by discussing them with colleagues, customers, clients, or technical experts; building models or prototypes that can be tested.
3. *Experimenting*—examining the practical use of the idea and its financial value through experiments and feasibility studies.
4. *Assessing*—identifying the strengths and weaknesses of the idea, its costs and benefits, and potential markets, and how it will be used by customers; making constructive changes based on the assessments.
5. *Scaling*—deploying resources and developing new processes to produce the innovation on a commercial basis; incorporating what has been learned into the production and marketing of the product or service.

An important goal of the innovation process is for successful innovation to occur that meets the needs of the organization and its customers in the marketplace. Companies that depend on innovation as a source of competitive advantage develop strategic measures of innovation to which executives are held accountable for achieving. One measure that drives innovation at General Electric and Procter & Gamble is to track the percentage of a company's annual revenues that come from new products that were developed within recent years.

CONCLUDING THOUGHTS

After the story about how Boston Beer Company started in Jim Koch's kitchen, where he developed the Samuel Adams Boston Lager brand and grew it to be the largest craft beer company in the U.S, we asked some critical thinking questions about the concerns related to the decision to continue to grow an entrepreneurship and the importance of experience in the background of successful entrepreneurs. Now that you have read the topics on entrepreneurship and innovation, it is time to revisit those two introductory questions. First, additional growth of Boston Beer Company needs to be managed and thought out carefully. Since Boston Beer Company competes in the craft beer market segment, it serves a niche market and needs to maintain control over the high quality of its beer or it could lose its loyal, core customers who pay a premium price to enjoy the product. Further, Boston Beer Company has already attained the distinction of being the largest craft beer brewer in the United States. With a significant increase in future growth, Boston Beer Company could be perceived as a threat by the giant multinational beer brewers, such as Anheuser-Busch, which might retaliate aggressively in how they price their products or launch "me too" products that compete directly with the brands of Boston Beer Company and use their massive advertising budgets to persuade customers to switch to their new brand of beer. It is likely to be in the best interests of Boston Beer Company to not awaken the sleeping giants in the beer industry and not be perceived as a threat to them by taking away a chunk of their market share due to growth.

Second, Jim Koch decided to become an entrepreneur after he already had experience as a management consultant. As explained earlier in the chapter, many entrepreneurs build on successful earlier career experiences to gain confidence and use their knowledge to recognize opportunities and start a new business. A clear advantage of first working for an employer before launching a business is that one can learn how to avoid key mistakes in a business without having one's personal resources at risk if a costly mistake is made. By working in industry first as an employee, a future entrepreneur can also develop a powerful network of friends and allies in the industry and build a positive reputation as a dependable and professional employee. This social capital that is formed in professional life can be useful to draw on resources for support that will be needed from members of the network after the decision is made to start a new business.

FOCUSING ON THE FUTURE: Using Management Theory in Daily Life

Entrepreneurship and Innovation

Dave Moore is the pastor of the New Summit Presbyterian Church—not someone most people would think of as an entrepreneur. And yet, in bringing a new church from zero members to over 300, in an environment where two-thirds of all new churches fail, he has had to use each of the following five management tactics to maximize innovation.

Capability

When Dave arrived in Lee's Summit, Missouri, he found 10 people who were interested in being part of a new church. A few of these people had been asked to be part of the new church by the Presbytery—they were "doing their duty to the denomination." Others wanted to start a new church in the area where they lived. Regardless of their initial reasons for joining, Dave recognized that he needed to build on the capabilities of each of these 10 people if the endeavor was to succeed. As he puts it, "I wanted to honor the gifts and passions of everyone involved—the first members, our emerging church leaders, and everyone else who would become part of our organization."

Based on a demographic study of the area, Dave determined that people who were likely to consider joining a new church would look at three key areas: (1) overall environment, including the structure of services and teaching; (2) music; and (3) child care. With these in mind, he asked people to consider where they could best contribute. Responses came in quickly. One member offered to do all the publicity for the new church, another to handle the technology needed in the church office and during services, another to run the day care center, and another to set up seating for services. In addition to these somewhat obvious tasks, Dave found that his other members could contribute expertise on financing and real estate development, accounting and budgetary controls, marketing, planning and the other business functions related to running any organization. One critical area remained understaffed—music. To handle this issue, Dave and the members of the church decided to hire a part-time Music Director.

As New Summit grew, new needs for people with specialized capabilities emerged. Overtime, Dave and the other members of the church created a new full-time position for a church secretary. They also identified four primary "quadrants" for church activities: gather (evangelism), inspire (worship), equip (training), and send (mission work). These quadrants (and their associated teams) were developed as a direct result of Dave's reading and study of Margaret Wheatley's book *Leadership and the New Science*—a theoretical work which proposes that the "core identity" of any person or organization is more important than having policies or procedures. Each of these activities now has a leadership position associated with it. The vision for the future is that as the church grows, these leadership positions will be staffed with full-time people. Finally, 10 elders of the church serve as a "board of directors" and handle major financial and managerial decisions.

Culture

Balancing innovation and tradition is not an easy job in any church, and it can be especially difficult when the church is a new venture. At first, the church services were held in a rented school auditorium. As the congregation grew, they were able to acquire a large piece of land on which to build their sanctuary. But what kind of building should go up? Tradition called for a steepled structure where people would congregate on Sundays for an hour or two. But since caring for one another and the community were integral parts of the New Summit vision and mission statements, after much deliberation, a different kind of structure was raised—a large, open space that could accommodate child care and after school activities as easily as traditional worship.

This issue was recently faced again, as the church members and elders started the process of putting up a second building. Cognizant of the fact that new buildings cost $100 to $150 a square foot in their area, the group again had to weigh the traditional with the innovative. They found that while stained glass and an organ "spoke to" people in earlier times, today's congregants speak a different language—one that is more digital and visual. Money that might have been spent on pews is now being spent on projection systems, and rather than stained glass, people respond to images of classic paintings projected on blank walls. The interesting thing about this new technology is that it allows for a marriage of tradition and innovation. For example, in one recent service, classic paintings of the crucifixion were blended with images from a current movie—Mel Gibson's "The Passion of the Christ."

Dave says that he is constantly seeking ways to "talk to people in their own language." But he also realizes that this new language may not appeal to everyone. His research shows that his church is more likely to appeal to people who do not normally go to any church. It is harder to get past the expectations and past experiences of people who are "traditionally churched" because they have a different image of what church "should be." Dave challenges congregants who want a more traditional service to take responsibility for putting it together, but he also reaches out to them by trying to include at least one more traditional hymn in each service, and by retaining key elements of the service that can act as a touchstone for traditionalists.

Cash and Recognition

Dave and the other leaders of New Summit have a large number of volunteer workers to motivate, and they need to be creative with rewards for those workers. While the tasks themselves can be rewarding, and there is always the promise of an eternal reward, it can be a challenge to sustain day-to-day motivational levels. Recently, Dave instituted a new program called "Kingdom Assignments." This program, created by Pastor Dennis Bellesi at the Coast Hills Community Church in Aliso Viejo, California, challenges congregants by providing them with $100 to "further the Kingdom of God" in any way they see fit. As Dave points out, the purpose of the exercise is to let people know that "the ministry that you are going to participate in has yet to be discovered, and you have a significant part in discovering it." The program is motivating both because of the recognition people receive in the church for their projects, and also because it gives people the opportunity to have complete control over a project of their own choosing. This is a key component of intrinsic motivation.

Customer Orientation

Lee's Summit is a "bedroom community" of 80,000 people. Some demographers classify it as a "hopes and dreams" community. People in Lee's Summit want a meaningful career, a meaningful marriage, good relationships with friends, financial security, and a good education for their children. It is a safe community where people rarely worry about crime and drugs. But it is also a community in which people do not go to church on a regular basis. Dave asked his staff at New Summit to survey every church in the area and find out how many people the sanctuary could hold when filled to capacity. They estimated that if every sanctuary was filled to capacity twice every Sunday, there would still be 50 percent of the people in Lee's Summit who would not have a place to sit.

The survey indicated a need for a new church, but Dave had to take his customers' needs into account to attract them to that church. As he puts it, "We wanted to attract people to our services, so we said, 'Come as you are. We'll accept you, we'll speak your language, we'll take care of your kids, we'll have topics that are relevant to you, and we'll provide a place to enrich all of the relationships in your life.'" He soon found that it wasn't just Sunday morning services that attracted people, but activities they could enjoy, both as adults and as a family. Soon the new church was buzzing with everything from small group meetings to building Habitat for Humanity houses— anything and everything that might attract people and draw them away from Sunday morning soccer games and other competitors for their time and efforts.

Cut Losses

When is it time to pull the plug on an innovative idea? While Dave learns as much from ideas that work as those that don't work, he watches carefully to be sure that he is not committing too many resources to a failed innovation. For example, New Summit hired a youth director at one point. It made sense at the time, because of the number of growing families, and it was a popular decision with the congregation, but it was also fraught with problems. Nationally, most youth directors are underpaid and do not stay in their jobs for more than two years. Despite Dave's best efforts to anticipate and deal with these problems, the new youth director simply didn't work out, and left after one year of service. Dave used the opportunity to reevaluate the position and decided that it would be better to put the church's resources into a full time "equipping minister" whose focus would be on training people of all ages to help them to discover their gifts.

Summary of Learning Objectives

Entrepreneurship and innovation are critical to the continued competitiveness and economic vitality of any developed economy that hopes to remain a player in today's global marketplace. Entrepreneurship refers to the process of creating an enterprise capable of entering new or established markets. Innovation refers to the translation of knowledge into products or services that add value. Both the opportunities created through entrepreneurship and the new value and bottom-line impact of effective innovation are needed for long-term economic prosperity. This chapter's discussion should help you to promote entrepreneurship and innovation as a manager, team member, and individual employee. The chapter's learning objectives and the related chapter discussion points are summarized below.

1 Explain the economic importance of entrepreneurship.

- Entrepreneurship is responsible for much of the job creation in the U.S.
- Innovation and entrepreneurship go hand in hand bringing new products to market.
- Entrepreneurship brings opportunities to minorities and women.

2 Identify the key characteristics and skills of entrepreneurs.

- Entrepreneur's have an **internal locus of control**—a belief in one's own ability to succeed.
- Negotiation skills, networking sills, and leadership skills are critical to successful entrepreneurs.

3 Recognize the basic ingredients needed to effectively start and manage an entrepreneurial venture.

- New business ideas can come from a variety of sources.
- The business plan maps out the business strategy.
- Selecting the right form of business is crucial—**proprietorship, partnership, corporation.**
- Obtaining financing is often **debt financing** or equity financing.
- Growth must be managed.

4 Differentiate among the legal forms of organizing an entrepreneurial venture.

- Proprietorship—owned by one person.
- Partnership—association of two or more persons acting as co-owners.
- Corporation—a legal entity separate from individual owners.

5 Identify alternative forms of entrepreneurship.

- Intrapreneurship—new business units developed within a larger corporate structure.
- Spin-offs—independent entrepreneurship that originated in a large company.
- Franchises—an established business that sells distribution rights to additional owners.

6 Describe innovation and demonstrate why it is important for business success.

- Innovation
  - New Idea
  - Business Results
- Key to success in creativity-driven market

Discussion Questions

1. How does an entrepreneurial business differ from a small business? What are the similarities?
2. What are the differences between an entrepreneur and a manager?
3. What is the significance of entrepreneurship to the U.S. economy?
4. Identify the important personal characteristics of entrepreneurs. Do you think only people with these characteristics should become entrepreneurs? What problems does this approach present? What alternatives could be used to encourage people to choose an entrepreneurial path?
5. Compare and contrast debt financing and equity financing as ways of starting a new business. Does one have an overall advantage over the other? What situation is more favorable to the use of debt financing? Which situation favors equity financing?
6. Why is growth important to an entrepreneurial business? How can rapid growth be detrimental to its survival?
7. Can an individual be an entrepreneur yet work within a large corporation? Explain your answer.
8. What are the advantages of starting a franchise business (such as a McDonald's) instead of an independent entrepreneurial business? What are the disadvantages?
9. What is the purpose of a business plan for an entrepreneurial effort? Some successful businesses are started without any business plan and operate according to the gut instincts of the entrepreneur. What do you think accounts for the success of businesses that are run "by the seat of the pants" without any formal planning?
10. Describe what is meant by the statement that an invention is not necessarily an innovation. Can you provide any examples of inventions that may not be innovations?

Management Minicase 8.1

From a Pretzel Stand to a Franchise Business at Auntie Anne's

Auntie Anne's began in Lancaster, Pennsylvania, often called the "Heart of Amish Country." It all began at a farmer's market in 1988. Having no money, but wanting to help her husband open a free family resource and counseling center, Anne Beiler borrowed $6,000 to buy a concession stand in the farmer's market to sell the original Auntie Anne's pretzels, lemonade, and other goodies. Anne tasted the soft pretzel recipe and decided it just wouldn't do at first. Her husband, Jonas, helped her modify the recipe, and pretzels were an instant success. Eventually, they eliminated pizza and ice cream and focused on pretzels. At first, friends and family asked if they could sell the pretzels at other locations. By the time there were 40 different locations, Anne decided they needed to turn what they had into an official business. They considered several options, including a sole proprietorship, a partnership, and a corporation. The alternative they settled on, however, was the franchise.

The Beilers looked to outside help in setting up an official franchise. A franchise is an arrangement where there is less risk for the potential partners who purchase the rights to operate a unit of the business in a restricted geographic area. There is also marketing assistance provided to all of the partners. There is high brand recognition cultivated by the franchise company. There is also good training, which is managed by the franchise company. Disadvantages to franchising include high start-up costs, shared profits, management regulations (also seen as an advantage for Auntie Anne's because of quality-control support), restrictions on selling (owners of a franchise cannot sell it to anyone they want), and fraudulent franchisers.

The company in 2008 supported over 300 franchisees with over 1,050 locations in 21 countries worldwide. Auntie Anne's reported sales revenues of $333 million in 2008. Anne Beiler is an inspiration for many women because she serves as a good example of how an individual can develop a company and be successful.

DISCUSSION QUESTIONS

1. Why do some people decide to buy a franchise business to operate, such as an Auntie Anne's franchise, instead of starting their own business from scratch?
2. Anne Beiler is a successful female entrepreneur who built a large business from a small stand in a farmer's market. However, female entrepreneurs often encounter barriers in growing a business. What factors contributed to Anne Beiler's success as an entrepreneur?

Sources: Auntie Anne's Web site, "Fact Sheet," www.auntieannes.com, accessed July 3, 2010; "Auntie Anne's," www.wikipedia.org/wiki/Auntie_Anne's, accessed July 3, 2010.

Management Minicase 8.2
An Innovation Marketplace on the Internet

If a company is unable to solve a challenging problem on its own, why not post it on the Internet and see if someone else can come up with a good solution? This simple idea was the basis of a business concept that was conceived by three scientists working at Eli Lilly, a pharmaceutical company. The three scientists brainstormed the idea during a session that was focused on exploring the application of the Internet to business. Ultimately they launched the business in 2001 as an independent startup and called it InnoCentive.

Companies that are interested in using the innovation service provided by InnoCentive post their problems on the firm's Web site. Solvers consist of a list of 200,000 engineers, scientists, inventors, business people, and research organizations in more than 200 countries that are invited to solve the problems posted on the Web site. Solvers who deliver the most innovative solutions receive financial rewards ranging up to one million dollars. The cash awards for solving challenging problems are typically in the $10,000 to $100,000 range. To date, over $3 million in awards have been made to problem solvers. As of 2009 over 400 problems posted on the Internet have been solved in disciplines such as chemistry, life sciences, computer science, and clean technology.

InnoCentive has over 60 corporate clients who seek innovative solutions to problems that include such companies as Procter & Gamble, Eli Lilly, SAP, and Dow AgroSciences. In one case, a partnership between InnoCentive and SCA, a Swedish maker of personal hygiene products, resulted in an average return on investment of 74 percent with a payback period of less than three months when SCA posted its problems on InnoCentive's Web site. InnoCentive takes care to post problems in a generic way to protect a company's intellectual property and it only pays for significant results to solving the problem rather than for the effort.

DISCUSSION QUESTIONS

1. InnoCentive has developed a service for client companies that outsources creative problem solving and innovations to outside problem solvers, who might live anywhere in the world such as India, China, or Russia. What guidelines to follow for choosing the type of problems to be posted on the Internet would you suggest to a company that is going to use this service? What type of problems do you think would be preferable to solve internally (and not post on the Internet) using the company's own employees to develop a solution.
2. The problem solvers receive financial rewards for solving the problems posted on the Internet. Can you suggest a method for determining a fair monetary prize for the problem solver who successfully solves a problem posted on the Internet?

Sources: Based on "A Market for Ideas," *The Economist*, September 19, 2009, pp. 75–76; InnoCentive Company Overview, 2010, www.businessweek.com; InnoCentive Web Site, "About InnoCentive," 2010, www.innocentive.com.

Individual/Collaborative Learning Case 8.1
Running a Sole Proprietorship

The most common form of business ownership in the United States is the sole proprietorship. One such business was L. A. Nicola, a Los Angeles restaurant owned by Larry Nicola. Located away from diners' row, the restaurant attracted clientele for one major reason: great food. As with his later restaurants, Nicola made the menu choices and, in his role as chef, saw that the food was cooked to perfection. He kept on top of new industry trends and knew how to change the menu to reflect the emerging tastes of customers. For example, before health foods became a fad, L. A. Nicola had cut down on sauces and fatty foods and was offering leaner cuisine.

Nicola gets out into his restaurants and works the crowd. He ensures that everything is running smoothly, greets old customers, and welcomes new ones. From his L. A. Nicola venture he went on to open other California restaurants.

What does Nicola like best about being a sole proprietor? He says it is the freedom of choice to do things his own way. If he sees something going wrong, he can correct it. If a customer is not getting proper service, Nicola will intervene and help the waiter out or assign a second waiter to the area. If a customer's food has not been cooked to his or her taste, Nicola can send it back to the kitchen and personally supervise the preparation.

Nicola is not alone in his desire for freedom in running things his own way. In recent years more and more sole proprietorships have been formed by individuals who used to work for other companies and have now broken away and started their own businesses. In the restaurant industry, chefs with an entrepreneurial spirit often first learn the business through experience and then open their own restaurants. Since chefs are usually the people who know the most about restaurants, they have a distinct advantage in starting a new business—the operation cannot succeed without them.

CRITICAL THINKING QUESTIONS

1. Why is the sole proprietorship business form so popular with people who want to start a business?

2. What type of liability do sole proprietors have if their business suffers a large loss?

3. If Nicola decided to raise $1 million and expand his restaurant, could he do this as a sole proprietor or would he have to form a partnership or corporation? Explain.

COLLABORATIVE LEARNING EXERCISE

One of the drawbacks of a proprietorship is that the responsibilities of operating the business are the proprietor's alone. It is difficult to take vacations, and sole proprietors tend to be workaholics who average 61 hours of work per week. Stress, burnout, and neglected families are occupational hazards. Further, there is no one in the business to provide guidance, since the business is owned and operated by one person. The business owner may make a serious blunder in the business strategy and may not become aware of it before it is too late to recover. Meet in a small group to develop tactics that would be useful to entrepreneurs for dealing with these challenges for sole proprietors.

Sources: Based on D. F. Kuratko and R. M. Hodgetts, *Entrepreneurship*, 2nd ed., Fort Worth: Dryden Press, 1992, pp. 220–221; R. R. Roha, "Home Alone," *Kiplinger's Personal Finance Magazine*, May 1997, pp. 85–89; D. Zahorsky, "Sole Proprietorship: The Right Business Structure?" 2010, www.sbinformation.about.com/.

Internet Exercise 8.1

How the Kauffman Foundation Supports Entrepreneurship

www.kauffman.org
Visit the Web site of the Kauffman Foundation at: www.kauffman.org. The Kauffman Foundation supports entrepreneurship activities for students and entrepreneurs. Explore the Web site and answer the following questions:

1. What kind of student entrepreneurship activities at universities are supported by Kauffman Foundation funding? Which universities were supported?

2. What kinds of research on entrepreneurship does the Kauffman Foundation sponsor? Is the sponsored research applied or basic and theoretical research? Who is the intended audience for the research studies that are supported by the Kauffman Foundation?

Manager's Checkup 8.1

Should You Start Your Own Business?

Do you have what it takes to be self-employed and operate your own proprietorship? Answer the following questions with either a "yes" or a "no."

1. Do you consider yourself to be highly self-motivated?	Yes	No
2. Are you a skilled multitasker who can juggle different tasks and perform them well?	Yes	No
3. Are you willing to work long hours to build your business even if it means sometimes working on weekends and holidays?	Yes	No

4. Are you able to work by yourself for extended periods of time without having any co-workers to chat with?   Yes _____ No _____

5. Are you prepared to support yourself without the security of having a regular paycheck and deal with having a variable income based on the success of the proprietorship?   Yes _____ No _____

6. Are you willing to give up some of the employee benefits you had when you worked at a large company such as paid vacations, paid holidays, and education benefits?   Yes _____ No _____

Scoring: Give yourself one point for each "yes" that you answered. A score of four points or higher suggests that being a self-employed owner of a proprietorship may be a career option that would be worthwhile for you to consider. A score of less than three points suggests that you might be more comfortable working as an employee in an established organization, and it would be preferable to postpone starting your own business until a later date.

Endnotes

1. R. A. Cherwitz, and C. A. Sullivan, "Intellectual Entrepreneurship: A Vision for Graduate Education," *Change*, 34 (2002): 23–28.
2. National Commission on Entrepreneurship, "Five Myths about Entrepreneurs: Understanding How Businesses Start and Grow," www.ncoe.org, accessed February 19, 2003.
3. *The Economist*, "Global Heroes: A Special Report on Entrepreneurship," March 14, 2009, p. 5.
4. National Commission on Entrepreneurship, op cit.
5. http://www.census.gov/scd/sbol.
6. A. Bluestein and A. Barrett, "Bring on the Entrepreneurs!," *Inc. Magazine*, July/August, 2010, p. 78.
7. Ibid.
8. K. E. Klein, "Minority Startups: A Measure of Progress," *BusinessWeek Online*, August 25, 2005.
9. J. Hopkins, "Start-Up Succeeding Study Says," *The Arizona Republic*, February 24, 2003, p. D1.
10. C. Barrett, "Good Times and Bad: Innovation Is Key," *Information Week*, January 27, 2003, p. 20.
11. J. Eckberg, "Innovation Spells Success," *Cincinnati Enquirer*, October 14, 2002, p. B6.
12. B. Nadel, "Unraveling the Mysteries of Innovation," *Fortune*, 152 (2000): 554–56.
13. D. Patnaik, "The True Measure of a Good Idea," *BusinessWeek Online*, December 21, 2005.
14. Ibid.
15. B. Nussbaum, R. Berner, and D. Brady, (2005). "Get Creative! How to Build Innovative Companies," *BusinessWeek Online*, August 1, 2005.
16. Ibid.
17. G. Hamel, *Leading the Revolution*, (Boston: Harvard Business School Press, 2002).

9

Learning Objectives

1 Identify the vertical and horizontal dimensions of organization structure.

2 Apply the three basic approaches— functional, divisional, and matrix—to departmentalization.

3 Develop coordination across departments and hierarchical levels.

4 Use organization structure and the three basic organization designs—mechanistic, organic, and boundaryless—to achieve strategic goals.

5 Develop an awareness of strategic events that are likely to trigger a change in the structure and design of an organization.

United and Continental Airlines Announce a Merger

In 2010 United Airlines and Continental Airlines announced their intention to merge their operations in a $3 billion deal to form the world's largest airline. The merged combination of the two airlines will account for 40 percent of the U.S. passenger traffic across the Atlantic and 53 percent of all traffic on Pacific routes. In the U.S. the two airlines have overlapping nonstop flights in 13 markets. United is buying Continental, and the combined company will keep the United name and be based in Chicago. Jeffrey A. Smisek, Continental's chief executive, would run the merged company.

The U.S. airline industry in the first decade of the 21st century has accumulated $60 billion in losses and shed 160,000 jobs, according to the Air Transport Association, a Washington trade group. United and Continental each suffered losses for the past two years, and as borrowers they have both received poor credit ratings. The U.S. airline industry has been plagued by a necessity to book over capacity, which has led to clogged airports and delays on the tarmac as planes wait to take off and for landing slots to open up. Mergers are one way that airline executives can improve efficiency. The synergy of an airline combining United and Continental could lead to improvements in

Managing the Structure and Design of Organizations

revenue and costs, and give the airline better access to credit and equity markets.

The logistics of running the merged airline can be expected to be enormously challenging. The main fleets of the two carriers consist of 700 aircraft. Continental flies only Boeing planes, while United flies both Boeing and Airbus planes. Flying planes from different manufacturers requires separate maintenance procedures, staff training, and spare parts. The combined workforces of the two carriers amount to more than 88,000 employees. Other than the consolidation of administrative personnel, management does not plan to have large cuts in staff. Yet it still could face difficult negotiations with the unions that represent pilots, flight attendants, and maintenance workers which can create major stumbling blocks to a successful merger.

A key task in implementing a merger between airlines has been to synchronize work rules and consolidate union seniority lists into a single worker roster. Since seniority determines which pilots get to operate higher-paying aircraft assignments and better working hours, sorting out the seniority roster can result in strong resistance from the pilots who fare worse under the combined roster. US Airways, for instance, continues to fail to get workers to agree to unified contracts, five years after its merger with America West. Maintaining two sets of work rules has kept US Airways from profiting from some of the planned economies of this merger.

The two chief executives of United and Continental Airlines claim that the combined carrier should benefit from savings of at least $1 billion a year and from substantial extra revenues once operational integration is completed in 2013.

Sources: "Love is in the Air: UAL and Continental Agree to Merge," *The Economist*, May 8, 2010, p. 64; M. Schlangenstein, M. Credeur, J. Hughes, and J. Bliss, "United and Continental Reach for the Sky," *Bloomberg BusinessWeek*, May 10–16, 2010, pp.19–20; P. Barrett, "The Departed: A Merger of United and Continental Makes Sense, but Can it Bring Back the Business of Flying? *Bloomberg BusinessWeek*, May 10–16, 2010, pp. 7–8; J. Mouawad and M. de la Merced, "United and Continental Said to Merge," *The New York Times*, May 2, 2010. www.nytimes.com/2010/05/.../03merger.html.

CRITICAL THINKING QUESTIONS

1. *What changes in the structure of the organization formed by the two combined airlines are related to the reasons for the merger?*

2. *Which coordination mechanisms will be useful to align the units of the merged companies into a more coherent and unified organization?*

Organization Structure and Design

- *Understanding the chain of command.* Some organizations are structured in a hierarchical fashion. In these organizations, employees are expected to respect and follow the chain of command, that is, the directives of top managers. Other organizations are less hierarchical and permit individuals in the lower ranks to initiate and implement ideas without the approval of their bosses.
- *Understanding the dimensions of organization structure.* Some of the factors that affect the design of an organi-

zation include size (large or small), emphasis on teams or individuals, degree of change in the work environment, and broad versus narrow spans of supervisory control. By understanding the key dimensions of organization structure, you can get an idea of what it would be like to work in an organization so that you can choose a work environment in which you can make your most valuable contributions.

---

organizing
The management function that determines how the firm's resources are arranged and coordinated; the deployment of resources to achieve strategic goals.

At the end of the chapter in our Concluding Thoughts, we will revisit the critical thinking questions regarding the decision to merge United and Continental Airlines.

Many strategies and key business decisions have profound effects on the structures and designs of various organizations. A change in strategic direction due to a merger or acquisition or a change in competitive strategy requires the management team to rethink how to deploy company resources. **Organizing** is the deployment of resources to achieve strategic goals, and is reflected in: (1) the organization's division of labor that forms jobs and departments, (2) formal lines of authority, and (3) the mechanisms used for coordinating diverse jobs and roles in the organization.

Organizing follows the formulation of strategy. While strategy indicates *what* needs to be done, organizing shows *how* to do it. This chapter begins by examining the vertical and horizontal dimensions of organization structure. It then examines ways to coordinate organizational units so that they move in the same direction toward meeting organization goals. Finally, it identifies different approaches to organization design.

Skills for Managing 9.1 lists the key skills for managing organizing.

■ The Vertical Dimension of Organization Structure

organization structure
The formal system of relationships that determines lines of authority and the tasks assigned to individuals and units.

vertical dimension
The element of who has the authority to make decisions and who supervises which subordinates.

horizontal dimension
The element of dividing work into specific jobs and tasks and assigning jobs into units.

unity of command
The management concept that a subordinate should have only one direct supervisor.

Organization structure is a formal system of relationships that determines lines of authority (who reports to whom) and the tasks assigned to individuals and units (who does what task and with which department). The **vertical dimension** of organization structure indicates who has the authority to make decisions and who is expected to supervise which subordinates. The **horizontal dimension** is the basis for dividing work into specific jobs and tasks and assigning those jobs into units such as departments or teams.

Unity of Command

The concept of **unity of command** is based on one of Fayol's 14 principles of management (see Chapter 1): a subordinate should have only one direct supervisor. Multiple bosses may give a subordinate conflicting instructions or goals. In unity of command, a decision can be traced back from the subordinates of the manager who made it.

Exceptions to the unity of command principle are sometimes necessary. For example, computer programmers in software firms are often assigned to different projects as the need arises. They are supervised by a project manager who coordinates the people and resources on the project and by a functional manager, the manager of information technology (IT), who supervises the IT department. This violation of the unity of command principle makes it critical for both managers to coordinate goals and priorities to avoid causing confusion.

Authority, Responsibility, and Accountability

authority
The formal right of a manager to make decisions, give orders, and expect the orders to be carried out.

Managers, teams, and employees have varying amounts of authority, responsibility, and accountability based on where they are in the vertical structure of the organization. **Authority** is the formal right of a manager to make decisions, give orders, and expect those orders to be carried out. A manager is an agent of the owners of the business. The role of the manager encompasses decision-making authority to manage the workforce, resources, and assets of the business in the owners' best interests. Authority is given to the position of the manager, not the person. It originates at the top of the organization based on the property rights of the owners and flows down the vertical organizational hierarchy from top executives to middle managers to supervisors and operative employees. Consequently, positions at the top of the hierarchy have more authority than positions at lower levels.

Responsibility is the duty to perform assigned tasks. All employees are expected to accept these responsibilities as a condition of employment. Ideally, a manager's responsibilities are matched with the appropriate amount of authority so that the manager is in "control" of the task. The manager may *delegate,* or transfer responsibility to a subordinate or team, but the manager is still in control because the subordinate or team is subject to his or her authority. Managers delegate decision-making authority for some tasks in order to give themselves more time to focus on the most important tasks and decisions. Chapter 6, on decision making, listed the steps that lead to effective delegation skills. Management Is Everyone's Business 9.1 offers some advice on how you can manage your work responsibilities more effectively given a limited amount of time to do them.

Sometimes managers are given responsibility without equal levels of authority. This situation is common in organizations in which managers must work with managers of other units or with customers outside of the organization. For example, the vice president of global learning solutions at Alcatel-Lucent, a manufacturer of telecommunications equipment, is responsible for disseminating employee development courses to various business units throughout the large corporation. This

New York City Mayor Michael R. Bloomberg promised voters an overhaul of the city's troubled public school system, but his subsequent dismantling of the system's central bureaucracy was controversial. The principals' union opposed the mayor's plan on the grounds that it stripped principals of their authority.

responsibility
The manager's duty to perform assigned tasks.

MANAGEMENT IS EVERYONE'S BUSINESS   9.1

WORKING AS A MANAGER   Here are some suggestions that should help you manage your work responsibilities more effectively.

- *Establish priorities.* Priorities include both urgent and important tasks. Spend as much time as possible doing things that are important but not urgent. Otherwise you will find you have neglected important tasks such as training and learning opportunities (and your skills become obsolete) because you've only attended to the urgent tasks as you "put out fires." Schedule self-improvement and other learning opportunities as priorities in your weekly or monthly schedule. If you don't, you'll find yourself attending to the less critical but more urgent activities that arise that will preclude improving your skills.

- *Delegate lower priority tasks to subordinates.* Tasks that are of a lower priority can be delegated to subordinates which frees up time for you to concentrate on more demanding ones. However, it is important to be able to identify the right subordinates who have the skills and work habits to do the delegated task effectively with a minimum amount of your supervision. Otherwise you may end up spending more time reworking the delegated task, which is counterproductive.

- *Give yourself thinking time.* Close your door if possible and spend an hour each day working without the interruptions of people, phones, or e-mail. Schedule the most crucial, creative tasks when you have the most energy, and use your downtime when you tend to tire to open mail or return phone calls.

- *Use the informal organization to get things done.* The *informal organization* is a network of social groups that are formed based on friendships or interests between employees. Most typical, *friendship groups* within an informal organization are groups of employees who meet for lunch, or meet after work for drinks, sports, or other activities. You can use the informal organization to solve work-related problems and gather information that may not be available through formal processes. For example, you may learn while playing golf with some company executives who are part of a friendship group that corporate headquarters is about to enact a freeze on hiring new employees within a week. Knowledge of this suspension of hiring may enable you to urgently conclude employment negotiations with a desirable employee being recruited and bring the individual on board before the hiring freeze is formally announced.

Sources: Based on J. Welch, *Winning* (New York: HarperBusiness, 2005); S. Covery and R. Merrill, "New Ways to Get Organized at Work," *USA Weekend,* February 6,1998, p. 18; J. Segal, L. Horowitz, E. Jaffe-Gill, M. Smith, and R. Segal, "How to Reduce and Manage Workplace Stress," November, 2008. www.helpguide.org/mental/work_stress_management.htm.

accountability
The expectation that the manager must be able to justify results to a manager at a higher level.

management by objectives (MBO)
A goal-setting program for managers and subordinates.

line authority
The manager's control of subordinates by hiring, discharging, evaluating, and rewarding.

chain of command
The superior–subordinate authority relationship.

line managers
The management level that contributes directly to the strategic goals of the organization.

staff authority
Management function of advising, recommending, and counseling line managers.

staff managers
Mangers who assist line managers to achieve bottom-line results.

organization chart
A graphic depiction that summarizes the lines of authority in an organization.

executive does not have the authority to control whether or how business-unit managers use the training services with their own employees. Instead, the executive must "market" the training courses to various business units in order to effectively fulfill the responsibility of the position.

A manager may delegate responsibilities to subordinates, but he or she remains accountable for the actions of subordinates. Managers hold the ultimate responsibility for tasks they delegate. **Accountability** means that a manager or other employee with authority and responsibility must be able to justify results to a manager at a higher level in the organizational hierarchy. One way managers are held accountable for the performance of their units is in periodic performance appraisals. For example, a **management by objectives (MBO)** program can be used to compare planned goals with achieved results. Employees receive rewards based on meeting or exceeding expected results.

There are two distinct types of authority: line and staff authority. **Line authority** entitles a manager to directly control the work of subordinates by hiring, discharging, evaluating, and rewarding them. It is based on superior-subordinate authority relationships that start at the top of the organization hierarchy and extend to the lowest level. This provides what is called the **chain of command**. **Line managers** hold positions that contribute directly to the strategic goals of the organization. For example, the line managers of a manufacturing firm include production managers and sales managers who contribute directly to the bottom line.

Staff authority includes giving advice, making recommendations, and offering counsel to line managers and other members of the organization. Staff authority is based on expertise and is not directly related to achieving the strategic goals of the organization. **Staff managers** help line managers achieve bottom-line results, but they contribute only indirectly to outcomes. For example, the accounting, legal, and human resource management staffs of a manufacturing firm provide specialized advice on cost control, federal regulations, and staffing requirements to line managers.

The key to knowing whether a position has line or staff status is the organization's strategic objectives. In an accounting firm, the accountants have line authority since their work directly contributes to the bottom line, whereas accountants in a manufacturing firm are used in an advisory capacity and thus are classified as having staff authority.

An **organization chart** summarizes the lines of authority in an organization. In the organization chart seen in Figure 9.1, authority flows in a vertical downward direction starting with the president, who has authority over the vice president, who in turn supervises several department heads. The department heads manage the supervisors, who have authority over the operatives. Each box represents a position in the organization occupied by one person. Each horizontal level

FIGURE 9.1

A Formal Organization Chart

MANAGEMENT IS EVERYONE'S BUSINESS   9.2

WORKING AS AN INDIVIDUAL   While formal power and influence in an organization are often structured to flow in a top-down direction, this does not mean that you cannot influence your boss by managing your relationship with him or her. For example, you can

- Make yourself indispensable by anticipating your boss's need for support and by providing it without being asked.
- Look for ways to show loyalty by speaking well of your boss to others.
- Develop a trusting relationship by being dependable, consistent, and honest. Do your work well and look for ways to exceed your boss's expectations.
- Keep your boss well informed.

of boxes represents a level of authority in the organization. Management Is Everyone's Business 9.2 shows you how you can influence your boss despite the fact that authority flows in a vertical downward direction in an organization's formal structure.

Span of Control

A critical feature of the vertical structure of an organization is the number of subordinates who report to a manager. This is called the **span of control**, and it determines the number of managers and number of levels of management in an organization. A manager with a small span of control supervises a small number of subordinates (about five or six on average) and can closely monitor the work of each subordinate. Small spans of control are usually associated with many levels of management, which gives rise to a tall vertical organization structure.

A tall vertical structure may have too many levels of management separating front-line employees from top executives. It may cause the organization to perform inefficiently because the company is not being responsive to the needs of customers. When a top executive is required to go through numerous intermediaries to learn what is happening at the operational level of the business, information often gets distorted and poor decisions result.

Larger spans of control (ranging from 10 to 20 or more subordinates) mean more responsibility is pushed to lower levels. A manager with a large span of control may not be able to directly monitor the behavior of all subordinates. However, using management information systems, which provide systematic feedback on employee performance, and work teams, in which monitoring activities are performed by peers on the team, managers can effectively supervise many subordinates.

Large spans of control result in fewer management levels. Executives at well-managed companies such as General Electric and Nucor (one of the most productive steel companies in the world) take pride in having fewer levels separating top management from first-level operative employees who deal with customers or produce the product. A large span of control works best when there are routine tasks, highly trained subordinates, competent managers, similar jobs with comparable performance measures, and subordinates who prefer autonomy.

Centralization and Decentralization

Centralization and decentralization are related to the degree of concentration of decision authority at various levels of the organization. **Centralization** means that decision-making authority is located at the top of the organization hierarchy. Centralized companies can coordinate activities in a consistent way across diverse units or departments of an organization.

With **decentralization** decision-making authority is pushed to lower levels in the organization. Decentralization is often more effective in rapidly changing environments where it is necessary to be responsive to changing customer needs and tastes. Decentralized decision-making authority spurs innovation and risk taking by allowing individuals to control resources and engage in experimentation without having to obtain the approval of higher authorities.

In recent years decentralized decision authority has become relatively common in organizations. Decentralization permits greater utilization of the talents and abilities of managers and teams of employees and makes it possible to be more responsive to the needs of customers. By maintaining a highly decentralized structure, the 3M Corporation has become one of the world's most

span of control
The feature of the vertical structure of an organization that outlines the number of subordinates who report to a manager, the number of managers, and the layers of management within the organization.

centralization
The location of decision authority at the top of the organization hierarchy.

decentralization
The location of decision authority at lower levels in the organization.

When Sir Howard Stringer took over as CEO of the Sony Corporation, he quickly announced a series of important changes designed to stem losses at the huge Japanese electronics maker. The biggest change was the creation of 13 product-category units intended to centralize control of product development. The new units are empowered to cross-fertilize ideas and communicate across Sony's famously autonomous divisions. The computer and entertainment subsidiary will build new PlayStation consoles, for instance, with microprocessors co-produced in the semiconductor division and content from Sony's movie and music units.

innovative companies with more than 60,000 diverse products such as Scotch Tape, Post-it Notes, video recording tape, reflective highway signs, and computer storage diskettes. One of the keys to the high rate of innovation at 3M is its 40 autonomous product divisions and other business units that are purposely kept small. Managers of these divisions and units have the authority to run their establishments as they see fit.

There is a trade-off between centralization and decentralization. Centralization allows management to coordinate the various parts of the organization in a consistent manner. Decentralization provides greater flexibility to respond to change. IBM used a centralized structure for many years because building mainframe computers required the expenditure of vast sums of money and the coordination of units that built and designed hardware and software components. However, IBM moved significantly in the direction of decentralization as its dependence on mainframe computers diminished and as its consulting services began to provide a significant portion of its total revenues. Decentralized decision authority made IBM more flexible and responsive to customers.

Formalization

The degree of written documentation that is used to direct and control employees is the level of **formalization** present. An organization with high formalization provides employees with many documents that specify the "right way" to conduct business with customers or interact with other employees. These documents include policy manuals, job descriptions, procedures, memos, and rule books. A high degree of formalization encourages employees to do their jobs in standardized and predictable ways.

Other organizations choose a low degree of formalization, with few rules and regulations, which encourages employees to improvise. This is especially useful when customer needs and conditions are subject to change. For example, Nordstrom, a retail store that serves affluent customers, has an employee handbook that consists of a single page with one rule: "Use your good judgment in all situations."

LOC-In   1   **Learning Objective Check-In**

Ballard Company has a strict management philosophy that each subordinate in the firm—at any level—should have only one direct supervisor. Ballard also uses a goal-setting program, wherein managers and subordinates compare planned goals with achieved results. When the employees meet or exceed expectations, they receive appropriate rewards.

1. The concept that a subordinate should have only one direct supervisor is called _____.
   a. unity of comnand
   b. unity of management
   c. span of control
   d. accountability

2. Ballard Company's goal-setting program can also he called _____.
   a. line authority
   b. control-based management
   c. management by objectives
   d. staff authority

---

formalization
The degree of written documentation that is used to direct and control employees.

departmentalization
The horizontal basis for organizing jobs into units in an organization.

■ The Horizontal Dimension of Organization Structure

The horizontal basis for organizing jobs into units in an organization is called **departmentalization**. The three basic approaches to departmentalization are functional, divisional, and matrix.

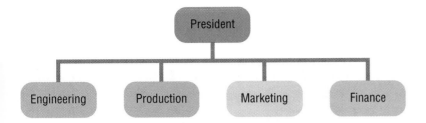

FIGURE 9.2
Functional Departmental Structure

Functional Structure

A **functional structure** places similar jobs into departments. For example, the departments in Figure 9.2 are engineering, production, marketing, and finance. The president integrates the activities of these departments so that each department's efforts are aligned with organizational goals and objectives.

The functional approach works best in small to medium-sized companies operating in somewhat stable business environments without a great deal of change and uncertainty. The functional structure has several advantages. Decision authority is centralized at the top of the organization hierarchy. Career paths foster professional identity with the business function. Because this approach permits employees to do specialized tasks, it creates a high degree of efficiency.[1] A functional form of structure causes employees to develop specialized expertise in a functional area of the business, such as finance or marketing.

In a company with a functional form of structure, an employee in the finance department of a telecommunications company, for example, can specialize in providing financial assistance to small-business clients who purchase small phone systems. The employee can advance within the finance department by building a depth and breadth of knowledge in finance and identifying professionally with the field. The individual may be promoted to a position that provides financing to corporate clients who purchase larger, more sophisticated phone systems. The result of serving a variety of clients is that the employee eventually becomes a financial expert.

The disadvantages of the functional departmental structure include communication barriers and conflicts between functional departments. It may be difficult to coordinate products and services, which could result in diminished responsiveness to the needs of customers. When employees are assigned to functional departments, they tend to identify with the functional departmental goals rather than with organizational goals or customer needs. This could lead to departmental conflict. Anyone who has called a large corporation looking for service only to be put on hold and transferred several times by indifferent employees has experienced one of the disadvantages of a functional organization.

Engineers who work in an engineering department may provide a "state of the art" technical design that is difficult to manufacture and that contains features that are not desired by the targeted customer. In this case, engineering goals are at odds with production and marketing goals. If the top executive does not have time to manage the conflict among the engineering, marketing, and production departments, the product development cycle may slow down as the departmental managers try to work out their differences. By the time these differences are ironed out the product may be late to market and potential sales revenues are lost.

Divisional Approach

The **divisional approach**, sometimes called the *product approach*, organizes employees into units based on common products, services, or markets. The divisional approach is used when a company produces many products or provides services to different types of markets, such as regional, domestic, and international markets, that require specialized knowledge. In the divisional approach key functional activities are present in each division and are coordinated by a general manager responsible for generating divisional profits.

Figure 9.3 shows a hypothetical computer company structured into three divisions: computer, software, and consulting services. The division structure allows employees to develop expertise in both a function and a line of products or services. A salesperson in the computer division can develop specialized product knowledge in selling computer systems without

functional structure
A departmentalization approach that places similar jobs into departments.

divisional approach
A departmentalization approach, sometimes called the product approach, that organizes employees into units based on common products, services, or markets.

FIGURE 9.3

Divisional Organization Structure

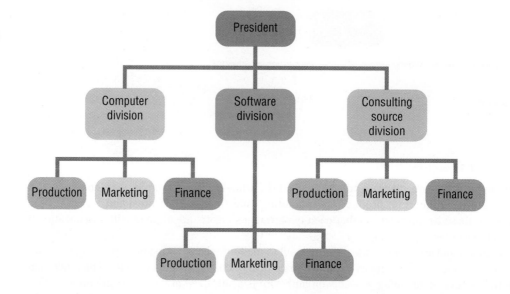

General Motors was one of the companies that pioneered the division structure, creating divisions based on its different automobile brands (Chevrolet, Buick, and Cadillac). Hewlett-Packard has used the division structure to reinforce its entrepreneurial culture so that employees identify with smaller units within the large company. Hewlett-Packard expects that keeping the divisions small will encourage employees to innovate new products. Large consumer products companies such as PepsiCo, Procter & Gamble, Johnson & Johnson, and Colgate-Palmolive also use the division structure to create opportunities for managers to learn the skills of operating a unit of the company from a profit-and-loss perspective. The most successful division managers (judged by the profitability of their divisions) are identified as likely candidates for executive leadership roles.

GEOGRAPHIC-BASED DIVISIONS   A variation of the product-based divisional structure organizes divisions by geographic region. **Geographic-based divisions** allow an organization to focus on customer needs that may vary by geographic region or market. In this approach to organizing, the functional business activities are coordinated by a division manager, who is responsible for products or services provided to a specific area. Figure 9.4 shows the organization of a fast-food company with United States and Canadian, Latin American, European, and Asian divisions. This structure allows each division manager to satisfy customer tastes and preferences in the region. Thus, American and Canadian menus may focus on hamburgers, a favorite North American food; the menu may add chicken burgers in India, since beef is a forbidden food for many Indians, and noodle soup in China; and the European menu may make wine available to French, Italian, and Spanish customers who customarily drink wine with meals.

CUSTOMER-BASED DIVISIONS   Another variation of the product-based divisional structure organizes divisions by particular types of customers or clients. Customer-based divisions allow an organization to focus on customer needs within a basic functional structure. With customer divisions, each department contains employees who perform functional tasks for a specific type

geographic-based divisions
A variation of the product-based departmentalization structure in which divisions are organized by geographic region.

FIGURE 9.4

Geographic-Based Organization Structure

of customer. The division manager coordinates the business activities for a specific type of customer. Figure 9.5 shows the organization of a bank that organizes its banking services into divisions that serve personal banking customers, small business banking customers, and corporate banking customers. Each customer division provides a different array of services that are relevant to it. For example, Wells Fargo Bank, a large San Francisco-based commercial bank, has organized its banking services into a customer-based structure.

CONGLOMERATE   The *conglomerate* is another variation of the product-based divisional structure and is made up of a set of unrelated businesses. Each business is run independently from the other businesses by a general manager who has profit and loss responsibility. Figure 9.6 shows a conglomerate that consists of four business groups: aircraft engines, medical systems, financial services, and plastics. Companies that use the conglomerate structure include United Technologies Corporation (helicopters, air conditioners, aircraft engines, and elevators), Honeywell (aerospace, automation and control solutions, specialty materials, and transportation systems), ITT (electronic components, defense electronics and services, fluid technology, and motion and flow control), and General Electric (financial services, media, health care, industrial products and infrastructure technologies). The executives in the company headquarters oversee all the businesses and make decisions concerning allocating corporate resources to businesses and decisions related to buying and selling businesses.

General Motors broke its corporate structure into several divisions based on automobile brands, each with its own management.

ADVANTAGES AND DISADVANTAGES OF THE DIVISIONAL APPROACH   The divisional approach has several advantages, including:

- Coordination among different business functions.
- Improved and speedier service.
- Accountability for performance.
- Development of general manager and executive skills.[2]

Bringing all the functional areas together to focus on a line of products reduces barriers that inhibit coordination among marketing, finance, production, and other functions. Employees identify with products and customers rather than with professional business disciplines. This allows the company to provide better quality products and services and employees are more responsive to customers. Division managers have bottom-line profit responsibility, which

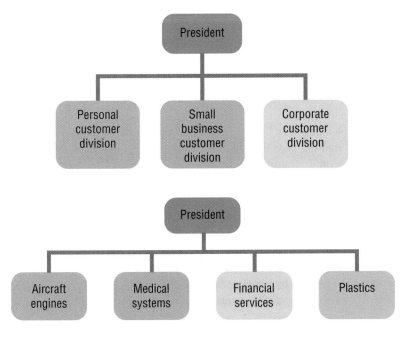

FIGURE 9.5

Customer-Based Organization Structure

FIGURE 9.6

Conglomerate-Based Organization Structure

prepares them to operate larger units or assume higher level corporate responsibilities. In a sense, the division managers are running a smaller company within the company, which motivates them to meet performance goals for the unit.

The disadvantages of the divisional approach include:

- Duplication of resources by two or more departments.
- Reduced specialization in occupation skills.
- Competition among divisions.[3]

The price an organization pays for the better coordination of the functional areas within the division is that some efficiencies are lost due to the duplication of employee roles within divisions. For example, each division may have its own direct sales force, which is more costly to support than a single sales force serving the entire organization. Further, employees operating within the division structure may not be able to specialize in their functional areas to the degree needed to provide specific competencies. Thus, each division may employ one or two human resource management generalists who know a little bit about payroll, benefits, and basic employment policies but are incapable of designing specialized performance appraisal systems for supervisory personnel. Consequently, each division may hire expensive outside consultants to perform this activity. Finally, coordination and cooperation between divisions may be problematic, resulting in further inefficiencies. When divisions compete for corporate resources, office politics may inhibit cooperation or sharing of information between divisions. At General Motors, auto sales gains in the new Saturn division came at the expense of some lost sales in the Chevrolet division. Executives in the Chevrolet division in the 1990s engaged in politics at the corporate level to make sure their Saturn "rival" did not receive corporate funds to produce a proposed Saturn minivan or sport utility vehicle, which at that time was the fastest growing segment in the auto industry.

In general, the divisional structure is best suited to medium to large-size firms with a variety of products in environments with moderate to high levels of uncertainty. The divisional structure provides flexibility to allow an organization to respond to rapidly changing market conditions. However, provisions for integration between the divisions must be developed to take full advantage of the division structure. Methods to integrate across divisions are discussed later in this chapter.

Matrix Approach

matrix approach
A departmentalization approach that superimposes a divisional structure over a functional structure in order to combine the efficiency of the functional approach with the flexibility and responsiveness to change of the divisional approach.

The **matrix approach** superimposes a divisional structure over a functional structure in order to combine the efficiency of the functional approach with the flexibility and responsiveness to change of the divisional approach. Each employee in a matrix unit reports to two bosses—a functional manager and a product or project manager. This means that there are dual lines of authority in the matrix organization. As seen in Figure 9.7, there is a vertical chain of command for the functions of finance, operations, manufacturing, and sales and marketing. There is a lateral chain of command for the three regions. An engineer who is assigned to work in region A will report to both region manager A and the vice president of engineering applications.

The matrix approach originated in U.S. defense companies so that employees with scarce technical skills could work on one or more projects that were under time pressures for completion. The project manager is responsible for coordinating budgets, personnel, and resources in order to bring the project in on time and within budget. The functional manager is responsible for allocating specialists to projects, making sure their skills are current, and evaluating their performance according to professional standards. The National Aeronautics and Space Administration (NASA) has used matrix structures to assign space scientists to various projects such as weather satellite or space shuttle programs. Dow Corning has used matrix structures to give marketing specialists broader exposure to different products.

The advantages of the matrix approach include:

- Efficient utilization of scarce, expensive specialists.
- Flexibility that facilitates starting new projects and ventures quickly.
- Development of cross-functional skills by employees.
- Increased employee involvement in management decisions affecting project or product assignments.[4]

FIGURE 9.7

Matrix Organization Structure

The key advantage is that flexibility makes it easier to start new projects or business ventures quickly with a minimum of bureaucratic inertia. Further, talented specialists can be utilized more efficiently under this approach.

The disadvantages of the matrix form include:

- Employee frustration and confusion as a result of the dual chain of command.
- Conflict between product and functional managers over deadlines and priorities.
- Too much time spent on coordinating decisions in meetings.[5]

One of the main problems with the matrix structure is that the product manager and functional manager may not agree on priorities or resource allocations, leading to conflict. Employees who have two bosses with different priorities may feel stressed and powerless to please both. The result may be another disadvantage, too much time devoted to meetings to coordinate various agendas and resolve conflicts.

LOC-In 2 Learning Objective Check-In

1. Janet, Trina, and Jim work in the finance department at SamCo, a utility company. Janet specializes in capital credits, while Trina works in remittance, and Jim works on projects dealing with business clients. While the finance department is specialized, it is also somewhat isolated from the other departments, despite the fact that they affect the entire business's operations. What kind of departmentalization does SamCo use?
   a. Matrix structure
   b. Divisional structure
   c. Functional structure
   d. Conglomerate structure

■ Coordination Mechanisms

No matter whether the functional, divisional, or matrix approach to horizontal structure is selected, each requires **coordination** to link activities so that diverse departments or divisions work in harmony and learn from each other. For example, an innovation in customer service in

coordination
Linking activities so that diverse departments or divisions work in harmony and learn from each other.

one division can quickly be diffused throughout the organization so that gains in customer satisfaction spread throughout the entire organization. The Wal-Mart "greeter" who welcomes customers entering the store began as an experiment in one store and spread throughout the organization when customers responded positively to being greeted. Coordination also allows units to align departmental goals with organizational goals so that interdepartmental goal conflicts are avoided or resolved. Coordination mechanisms include meetings, organizationwide reward systems, teams and task forces, liaisons, integrating managers, and the organization's culture.

Meetings

strategic meeting
Bringing people from different departments or divisions together to synchronize plans and objectives and to coordinate activities.

To achieve harmony in pursuing organizational goals, individual employees must "be on the same page" as their leaders and their co-workers. One way to achieve this harmony is to organize a **strategic meeting** to synchronize plans and objectives. Representatives of each unit attend the meeting and participate in the formulation of policies that are designed to align the activities of the various departments. Such meetings may occur at the division level (involving functional managers) or at the corporate level (typically involving division managers). They provide opportunities for face-to-face contact so that managers can learn to trust and collaborate with one another. For example, Pearson Prentice Hall the publisher of this text, holds a marketing-strategy meeting twice a year to discuss sales and marketing policies and strategies for marketing its textbooks to colleges. Editorial, production, marketing, and sales managers exchange information about books and ideas for new projects that may serve unmet needs in the market. Chapter 14 examines meetings in greater detail.

Organizationwide Reward Systems

profit sharing
Providing a share of a company's profits to the employees in the form of a bonus.

Another approach to coordinating activities of people from different departments is to provide a reward based on organizationwide profits. **Profit-sharing** plans pay a share of the company's profits to the employees in the form of a bonus. In a typical plan, the size of the bonus check is tied to quarterly profits.

Profit sharing creates a "we're in this together" mentality which nurtures collaboration between departments. As a result of profit sharing at Hewlett-Packard, for example, new technologies developed in one division can be shared with other divisions and fashioned into new products. Profit sharing bonuses have averaged around 15 percent of base salaries at Hewlett-Packard. An employee earning an annual salary of $50,000 may earn an additional $8,000 in a typical year. Profit sharing can also be used to encourage cooperation between people at different levels of the hierarchy. For example, pay raises of both union and management personnel at Ford are tied to a profit-sharing plan. The result has been better labor relations and a total absence of work stoppages in recent years.

Task Forces and Teams

task force
A temporary interdepartmental group formed to study an issue and make recommendations.

One of the keys to an effective workforce is teamwork. A **task force** is a temporary interdepartmental group formed to study an issue and make recommendations. The issue typically has organizationwide implications, and the task force gathers input from different departments. For example, the University of Colorado's diversity task force consists of representatives from all nine colleges. The group provides recommendations on how to make the culture of the university welcoming to people from diverse backgrounds.

problem-solving team
A group representing different departments that solves problems; sometimes called a *parallel team.*

A **problem-solving team**, sometimes called a *parallel team,* is a special type of group. A representative group from different departments is formed to solve problems such as quality improvement, workplace safety, and employee grievances. A problem-solving team can operate either on a temporary or a continuing basis. A problem-solving team at Federal Express improved the process of package sorting, providing savings in labor costs. At Ford, problem-solving teams made improvements in the quality of employee work life, which ultimately resulted in improved product quality. For more information, see Chapter 13, "Managing Teams." Management Is Everyone's Business 9.3 offers some advice on how you can coordinate the efforts of two or more teams working in parallel to solve a complex problem.

MANAGEMENT IS EVERYONE'S BUSINESS 9.3

WORKING AS A TEAM There are occasions when several teams are working in parallel to solve a complex problem and will need to have their efforts coordinated. For example, one of the authors of this text is familiar with a university that developed an honesty policy for students and formed a number of different student teams to work on different aspects of the honesty policy. Different teams were assigned to (1) develop a code of ethical student conduct, (2) write an honesty policy for students that they are expected to sign as a condition of admission to the university, (3) scan the external environment to learn from other universities' experiences with administering an honesty policy, and (4) set up a mechanism to enforce the honesty policy run by the students to hear cases of alleged student dishonesty and determine how infractions of the policy will be treated. Here are some coordinating mechanisms that would be useful when several teams are working in parallel on a complex problem:

● Form a steering committee composed of representatives from each team. The *steering committee* oversees the overall process of managing the entire problem. Team representatives are selected for the steering committee. These individuals report the progress of their specific team to the entire steering committee so that this information can be brought back to the other teams. Useful knowledge or best practices that are used by one team can be shared with all the teams.
● When only a few teams are working in parallel it may be useful to assign a *boundary spanning role* to an individual who is a member on both or several teams. The person in the boundary spanning role tells the members of a specific team what the other teams are doing and helps to coordinate their efforts. This helps to reduce redundant efforts and share information that all teams may find beneficial to achieving their goals.

Liaison Roles

A **liaison role** is used to facilitate communications between two or more departments. Liaisons are useful in situations where it is necessary to continuously coordinate between departments in order to improve the quality of communication and resolve misunderstandings and conflicts.

A software systems specialist from the information technology (IT) department may be assigned to coordinate contact between the IT and the marketing departments. When the IT department makes a decision involving the purchase of new computer software or decides to get rid of old software, the IT liaison meets with the marketing department to obtain input. Without the IT liaison, the IT experts may unknowingly discard software in the middle of a critical task, or they may purchase software that is not "user friendly" for the marketing people. Liaison roles reduce the likelihood of making decisions that do not represent the interests of other departments.

liaison role
A management role used to facilitate communications between two or more departments.

Integrating Managers

Many times the job of coordination is assigned to a specific individual. For example, an **integrating manager** position may be created to coordinate the work of several different departments. The integrating manager is not a member of any of the departments whose activities are being coordinated. These managers have job titles such as project manager, product manager, or brand manager. They use negotiation and persuasion skills to influence functional managers to provide resources and to influence employees to be committed and motivated to achieve the product or project goals on time and within budget.

A **project manager** coordinates work on a scientific, aerospace, or construction project. When the Denver International Airport was being built, a project manager coordinated construction in each of five project management areas: site development (earth-moving, grading, and drainage); roadways and on-grade parking (service roads, on-airport roads, and off-airport roads connecting to highways); airfield paving; building design (baggage handling, concourses, terminal, and parking); and utility systems and other facilities (electrical transmission, oil and gas line removal and relocation).

Matrix organization structures utilize **product managers**. These individuals coordinate the development of new products. They also negotiate with various functional managers for resources (people, finances, technology) and keep the product moving so it can be released to the market on time. The product manager must be a champion for the new product during the budget planning process, so that the product receives the resources needed to finish the project. New

integrating manager
A management position designed to coordinate the work of several different departments: the integrating manager is not a member of any of the departments whose activities are being coordinated.

project manager
A management role that coordinates work on a scientific, aerospace, or construction project.

product managers
A management role that coordinates the development of new products.

products without champions are vulnerable to critics who support diverting resources to areas that offer more immediate cash returns.

Brand managers coordinate the ongoing activities of branded consumer products such as food, soap and cleaning products, toiletries, and over-the-counter medicines. A brand manager coordinates the activities of marketing, advertising, sales and pricing, production, accounting, control, packaging, and product research. The brand manager makes sure the work of people in these different functional areas is aligned with the strategy for the product.

brand managers
A management role that coordinates the ongoing activities of branded consumer products.

Organizational Culture

The system of shared values, assumptions, beliefs, and norms that unite the members of an organization is the company's culture. It reflects employees' views about "the way things are done around here." **Organizational culture** influences people to share values, and that translates into a commitment to working together to achieve important goals. Culture gives employees an internal gyroscope that directs them to do things that make the entire organization more effective.[6] For more information see Chapter 4, "Managing Organizational Culture and Change."

organizational culture
A system of shared values, assumptions, beliefs, and norms that unite the members of an organization.

■ Organization Design

The structure of a company must match the firm's strategies in order to operate at peak levels. **Organization design** is the selection of an organization structure that best fits the strategic direction of the business. The three basic organization designs are mechanistic, organic, and boundaryless (see Table 9.1). These designs incorporate the vertical and horizontal structural elements covered earlier in this chapter.

organization design
The selection of an organization structure that best fits the strategic goals of the business.

TABLE 9.1 Mechanistic, Organic, and Boundaryless Deigns

Mechanistic	Organic	Boundaryless
Rigid hierarchical relationships	Collaboration (both vertical and horizontal)	Collaboration (vertical and horizontal, as well as customers, suppliers, and competitors)
High formalization	Low formalization	Same as organic
Top-down communication	Informal communication	Same as organic
Centralized decision authority	Decentralized decision authority	Same as organic
Narrowly defined specialized jobs	Broadly defined flexible jobs	Same as organic
Emphasis on individuals working independently	Emphasis on teams	Emphasis on teams that also may cross organization boundaries

Sources: Based on S. P. Robbins and M. Coulter, *Management,* 8th ed. Upper Saddle River, NJ: Prentice Hall, 2005, p. 245; L.R. Gomez-Mejia, D. B. Balkin, and R. L. Cardy, *Managing Human Resources,* 6th ed. Upper Saddle River, NJ: Pearson Prentice Hall, 2010, p. 51.

Before the most appropriate design can be selected, management should determine how to best deploy the organization's assets and develop a strategy for the business. (For more information on how organizations develop strategies that improve firm performance, see Chapter 7.) As the strategic direction changes, so do the structural elements that make up the design.

Strategic factors that affect the choices of organization design include:

1. *Organization capabilities.* The activities that the company does best are likely to be retained, while under certain strategic conditions (for example, a cost leadership strategy) the activities that are peripheral to the core mission of the business may be contracted out to more efficient suppliers.

2. *Technology.* The type of technology the firm uses to produce its product or service has an effect on the organization design. For example, an electronic components company that utilizes mass production technologies for manufacturing its integrated circuits in an expensive fabrication plant is likely to be structured on a centralized basis to take advantage of plant efficiencies while a fast food company utilizing service technologies will be structured on a decentralized basis in order to respond to local customer tastes and needs. Here are some different categories of technology that can affect the choice of organization design:

   ■ *Manufacturing technology* converts products from raw materials. One type of manufacturing technology is *small-batch technology,* which produces custom-made products for customers or products produced in small quantities. Luxury pleasure boats or women's high fashion clothing uses this type of technology. *Mass production technology,* another type of manufacturing technology, produces standardized products using an assembly line with a heavy reliance on automated machines such as robots. Automobiles and consumer electronics use this type of technology. The most sophisticated and complex form of manufacturing technology is *continuous process technology* in which the entire work flow is automated. The manufacturing process runs continuously and employees simply monitor the machines that control the process. Chemicals manufacturing and petroleum refining use this type of technology.[7]

   ■ *Service technology* provides services to customers, which makes contact with the customer a critical feature of this technology. Service firms tend to be structured on a decentralized and flexible basis in order to respond to each customer's needs. Consulting, medical firms, law firms, hotels, restaurants, and banks utilize service technologies in order to provide service to their customers.[8]

   ■ *Digital technology* uses the Internet to provide a customer with faster service, at a lower price, and with more choices. Businesses that use digital technology include search engines such as Google, booksellers such as Amazon.com, and trading communities such as eBay. Organizations that use digital technology tend to be structured on a decentralized and flexible basis in order respond quickly to a customer's needs.[9]

3. *Organization size.* As organization size increases, so do work specialization and the need to coordinate the work of diverse employees. Large organizations need more coordinating mechanisms than small ones.

4. *Environmental turbulence.* Organizations that operate in turbulent environments require different designs than organizations that operate in more stable environments in which change happens gradually. Turbulent environments are characterized by dynamic change due to market, technological, political, and regulatory or social forces.[10] Under conditions of rapid change, on-the-spot decisions are made, and lower level employees need the authority to make decisions. Decentralized structures that delegate authority to lower-level employees are used in turbulent environments to enable decisions to be made by those who are closest to the customer or the source of change.[11] An organization with a predictable and stable environment is more likely to have a structure with greater centralization. Figure 9.8 shows that the strategic factors that influence the choice of organization design ultimately affect organization performance.

Mechanistic Organizations

A **mechanistic organization design** emphasizes vertical control with rigid hierarchical relationships, top-down "command and control" communication channels, centralized decision

mechanistic organization design
A management design based on the classical perspective of management, emphasizing vertical control with rigid hierarchical relationships, top-down "command and control" communication channels, centralized decision authority, highly formalized work rules and policies, and specialized, narrowly defined jobs; sometimes called a *bureaucratic design.*

authority, highly formalized work rules and policies, and specialized, narrowly defined jobs. It is based on many of the classical management principles that were described in Chapter 1. The organization has a tall pyramid shape with numerous levels of management. Managers have small spans of control and closely supervise subordinates.

A mechanistic organization design is best suited to a stable and relatively predictable environment. It depends on managers making decisions and frontline workers executing the decisions by doing repetitive tasks. While industry is moving away from this design, it is still applied in government agencies, labor unions, and some family businesses.

Organic Organizations

organic organization design
A management design that is focused on change and flexibility, emphasizing horizontal relationships that involve teams, departments, or divisions, and provisions to coordinate these lateral units.

A focus on change and flexibility requires a more **organic organization design**. Such a design emphasizes horizontal relationships involving teams, departments, or divisions and provisions to coordinate these lateral units. Organic organizations are relatively decentralized and low in specialization, formalization, and standardization. Employees have more leeway in dealing with changing customer needs or technological challenges. The span of control is larger than in a mechanistic organization, and managers are less inclined to closely supervise subordinates. The organic design has fewer levels of management separating front-line employees from the executives. Its shape is flatter in appearance.

An organic organization design is most effective in turbulent and uncertain environments. Organic designs are beneficial for nurturing creativity and innovation, where employees are more likely to spend their time thinking and planning. Organizations that use organic design include high technology, entertainment and media, financial services, and consumer goods companies. Many entrepreneurships adopt organic designs from inception because management anticipates future growth in a highly uncertain environment. As deregulation has heated up the competitive landscape, public utilities, airlines, and telecommunications companies are also moving toward the use of organic designs.

Home Box Office (HBO) plays movies and produces programs with adult topics. HBO has benefited from the flexibility and decentralization of an organic design. Its corporate parent, Time Warner, has given HBO writers creative and artistic freedom of expression. With the organic design, HBO is physically removed from the rest of the Time Warner corporation, which also contains the larger Warner Brothers operating under the pressure of ratings-driven broadcast schedules.[12] HBO programs, on the other hand, are directly paid for by subscribers. This allows HBO to produce more controversial and cutting-edge television content than is possible under traditional television broadcasting constraints. Partly due to the independence provided within an organic design, HBO programs such as *The Sopranos* and *Sex and the City* have won many Emmy television industry awards for quality. Moreover, HBO has also become a highly profitable business for Time Warner.

Some organizations have a hybrid design in which mechanistic and organic designs are used in different parts of the organization. For example, McDonald's utilizes a mechanistic design at its Chicago-area headquarters, where corporate functions such as training, marketing, and advertising are centralized. Managers are arranged in a hierarchy with an emphasis on vertical reporting relationships. However, within the geographical regions of McDonald's, the company applies an organic design so that divisions can be more responsive to changing customer tastes. Figure 9.9 arranges the basic types of organization structures from highly mechanistic to highly organic.

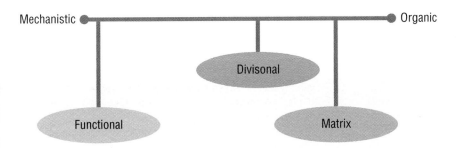

FIGURE 9.9

Organization Structures: From Mechanistic to Organic

Boundaryless Organizations

Recently a newer form of organizational structure has emerged in response to changing technologies and evolving marketplace relationships. A **boundaryless organization design** eliminates internal and external structural boundaries that inhibit employees from collaborating with each other or that inhibit firms from collaborating with customers, suppliers, or competitors. This design has many of the features of organic design, but it uses a flexible structure that makes it possible to overlap with other organizations so that seamless cooperation between organizations results in better service to the customer. By using teams that span organization boundaries, a boundaryless organization may share employees with a supplier through a joint venture; use its sales force to sell a partner's products; share a patented manufacturing process with a customer through a licensing agreement; or buy a large block of a competitor's stock to gain the right to use the competitor's technology. Such cooperative arrangements enable a boundaryless organization to improve the speed with which it reacts to change and uncertainty in the environment.

One of the first executives to use the boundaryless organization design was Jack Welch, the former CEO of General Electric. Welch was the architect of a bold plan to redesign General Electric, a large, diversified corporation, so that each of its divisions would operate with a minimum of bureaucracy. Hierarchies were flattened and vertical functional silos were broken down.

- At its locomotive division in Erie, Pennsylvania, GE formed a partnership with a paint supplier to improve the consistency of the paint used on its locomotives. Team members from GE and the paint supplier collaborated to reduce painting time and improve quality.
- GE Capital's Global Consumer Finance business worked with top global retailers such as Wal-Mart to deliver financial services to their customers.
- GE signed a 10-year maintenance agreement with British Airways in 1998. GE and British Airways maintenance crews work together on maintenance and overhaul projects.

Other companies have followed GE's lead. Boundaryless designs have been used to: (1) enter foreign markets, (2) manage the risk of developing new technologies, and (3) pool resources to compete in an industry with high financial entry barriers. For example,

- Airbus Industries utilizes a boundaryless design that consists of a partnership of four firms from France, Germany, England, and Spain that collaborated to market and develop commercial jet aircraft. The group competes with Boeing, the world's leading producer of passenger jets.
- Paramount and Twentieth Century Fox combined to produce, market, and distribute the enormously expensive epic movie *Titanic,* which broke box office records in the late 1990s. The production costs of the movie were higher than any single film company could risk alone.
- General Motors and SAIC Motor Corp., a Chinese automobile manufacturer, have formed a partnership to build and market cars for the rapidly growing Chinese market, which became the world's largest auto market in 2009.[13]
- Apple, Inc. and AT&T partnered to bring the iPhone to market. The iPhone is a smart phone that functions as a camera phone (including text messaging and visual voicemail), a portable media player, and an Internet client (with e-mail, Web browsing, and WiFi connectivity).[14]

boundaryless organization design

A management design that eliminates internal and external structural boundaries that inhibit employees from collaborating with each other or that inhibit firms from collaborating with customers, suppliers, or competitors.

Where Can You Do Your Best Work?

Different types of organization design provide different environments for working and managing. This exercise lets you assess your preferences with respect to different structural dimensions of an organization.

First answer the following questions individually. Then, in groups of four to five people, share your responses with each other. Finally, complete the group discussion questions that appear at the end of the exercise and be ready to share your group's answers with the class.

1. Would you rather work in a large (more than 1,000 employees) or small (fewer than 100 employees) organization? Why?
2. Do you prefer to have frequent (on a daily basis) interactions with your boss, or would you prefer infrequent (once or twice per month) interactions with your boss?
3. Do you prefer to work primarily as part of a team or as an individual?
4. Do you prefer to be a specialist in a company (knowing a lot about a highly specialized function or business process), or do you prefer to be a generalist (having a broad scope of knowledge of different facets of the business, but not specializing in any of them)?
5. Do you prefer a job that is constantly changing and requires continuing training and education to keep pace

with change, or do you prefer a job with stable content that lets you develop work routines that are predictable after you master the job skills?
6. Do you prefer working cross-functionally with people you have no line authority to influence, or do you prefer working in vertical relationships with people who are either subordinates or superiors, located up or down the chain of command?

Discussion Questions

1. What are the advantages of working in a mechanistic organization, an organic organization, and a boundaryless organization? You may want to refer to Table 9.1.
2. What are the disadvantages of working in a mechanistic organization, an organic organization, and a boundaryless organization?
3. Do group members agree or disagree that one design is superior to the others for providing the best work environment? Does organization design matter when it comes to choosing a company to work for? Are there certain designs that one should avoid when searching for a job?
4. What conclusions about your career path and goals can you draw from this discussion?

A type of boundaryless design that has been adopted by many multinational firms in recent years is the network design. The *network design* consists of a series of strategic alliances or relationships that a company develops with suppliers, distributors, or manufacturers in order to produce and market a product. A *strategic alliance* is an agreement between two or more companies to collaborate by sharing or exchanging resources to produce and market a product (see Chapter 2 for more on strategic alliances). For example, Hewlett-Packard and Canon formed a network design to produce laser printers that has endured for over 15 years. Hewlett-Packard provides its computer technologies and know-how which is combined with Canon's knowledge of imaging and laser technology. By sharing the knowledge and technologies, the laser printers that are marketed by Hewlett-Packard own a dominant share of the market.

LOC-In 4 Learning Objective Check-In

1. Tip Tops, Incorporated, is an external marketing consulting firm whose industry is always changing. In addition, it never has two clients who are exactly alike, and while it can apply some of the same techniques across clients, there is no "template" for the way it provides services. Lastly, the technological climate also changes rapidly in this industry. Given what you know about Tip Tops, which type of organization design would be most appropriate for this firm?
   a. Mechanistic organization
   b. Organic organization
   c. Boundaryless organization
   d. Task-based organization

MANAGER'S NOTEBOOK 9.1

Is Your Organization Design Functioning Effectively?

Managers should be aware of symptoms that indicate a malfunctioning organization design. Here are some of the most important. If one or more of these exist, managers are advised to consider making changes to the organization's structure.

- *The organization design focuses employees on work that uses noncritical skills rather than emphasizing the opportunity to use their strengths.* The design should provide the opportunity for highly skilled employees to do the work that they do best, rather than being bogged down by less critical tasks of lesser value. For example, sales and marketing people may be spending too much time attending required staff meetings to coordinate with others on projects within a matrix structure. Disappointing sales results may be the result of using a structure that keeps salespeople away from their customers by forcing them to attend regular meetings. The matrix structure may be diverting salespeople from making their most valuable contributions to company performance.

- *The organization design has too many levels in the hierarchy.* Too many management levels inhibit the responsiveness of employees in an organization. Consequently they do not serve customers, because they are oversupervised and do not have enough autonomy. Employees' contacts with customers are limited, because they must obtain management approval to take action. Instead, the structure should help them show initiative and adopt standardized procedures in order to please a customer. A good rule to use is to ask if the managers at higher levels are adding value to or taking value away from the business activity. Value is added when they

improve quality or consistency. Managers take value away by slowing down the process of giving service to the customer or by taking away the initiative of lower-level employees to better serve customers. By giving additional authority to lower-level employees who have direct contact with customers, organizations provide better service. The executive team may also learn that they need fewer levels of managers to supervise employees.

- *The organization design is not flexible enough to accommodate changes in strategy or the environment.* A well-designed structure should allow the organization to be innovative and adapt to changing circumstances. For example, if a new product takes off unexpectedly and is in high demand in a fast growing market, this market jolt is likely to result in a reallocation of company resources devoted to producing the successful new product. The current organization design should be able to accommodate a decision made to reallocate capital, people, and technology to satisfy the surging demand for the new product. A flexible design, like a tree bending in the wind, should be able to deal with an unexpected jolt from the environment.

Source: Based on M. Goold and A. Campbell, "Do You Have a Well-Designed Organization? *Harvard Business Review*, March 2002, pp. 117–124; R. Sanchez and J. Mahoney, "Modularity, Flexibility and Knowledge Management in Product and Organization Design, *Strategic Management Journal*, 17, Winter, 1996, pp. 63–76; D. Lei, M. Hitt, and J. Goldhar, "Advanced Manufacturing Technology: Organization Design and Strategic Flexibility," *Organization Studies*, 17 (3), 1996, pp. 501–23.

How do you know if your organization has the optimal design? Manager's Notebook 9.1 provides some important symptoms to let managers become aware of a malfunctioning organization design.

Redesigning Organizations

As a firm's strategy changes, organization structure and design also change to support the implementation of the new strategy. In a sense, organization design can be considered a continuous work in progress. An organization is *redesigned* to enable the firm to more effectively use its technology, assets, and human resources to accomplish strategic goals. The key strategic events that are likely to trigger change in the structure and design of an organization are mergers, acquisitions, and divestitures.

MERGER   When two independent companies agree to combine their assets and form a single organization a **merger** has taken place. In many cases, companies that compete in the same industry merge to create a larger entity with greater economies of scale. Redundant facilities such as corporate headquarters or back-office operations can be disposed of to create a more efficient operation.

merger
The process of integrating two firms.

There were numerous bank mergers in the 1990s. California-based Wells Fargo and Midwest-based Northwest Banks merged operations and decided to use the Wells Fargo name for the emergent organization. Citicorp, the largest U.S. Bank, merged with Travelers Group, a leading insurance company, to create a global financial giant called Citigroup. The merger in 2008 between InBev, a Belgium-based beer company, and Anheuser-Busch, the largest U.S. brewer, formed the world's largest brewer, uniting the maker of Budweiser and Michelob with the producer of Stella Artois and Bass. The merged firm is called Anheuser-Busch InBev and in 2009 had annual sales of $36.8 billion.[15]

acquisition
The process of purchasing other firms.

ACQUISITION An **acquisition** takes place when a firm buys all or part of another business. The acquiring firm may use cash or trade some of its stock to purchase the acquired firm. In the 1980s, many companies acquired businesses in unrelated industries as part of a strategy of diversification, as when Phillip Morris, a tobacco company, acquired Kraft and General Foods.

In the corporate applications software industry Oracle, the world's second largest software company, spent $10.3 billion to acquire PeopleSoft Inc. in 2004 and $5.8 billion to acquire Siebel Systems Inc. in 2005. These acquisitions enabled Oracle to realize a strategy that will allow it to help its corporate clients run everything from accounting and sales to customer relations and supply-chain management with its software.[16]

divestiture
The corporate process of selling a business in order to generate cash, which the corporation can better deploy elsewhere, or to refocus on a core business which is better understood by management.

DIVESTITURE A **divestiture** occurs when an organization sells a business in order to generate cash. The goal is to better deploy the funds elsewhere, or to refocus on a core business which is better understood by management. General Electric divested many business units that did not fit with its boundaryless organization strategy and high performance expectations. GE acquired others (such as the NBC television network) that better fit with the company's strategy. The redesign helped General Electric become a flatter and more competitive company and increased its market value from $12 billion in 1981 to $346 billion in 2006.

downsizing
A management strategy used to reduce the scale and scope of a business to improve its financial performance.

Many corporations that increased their size through mergers and acquisitions in the 1970s and 1980s found that the complexity of managing the new business units led to disappointing earnings. In the late 1980s and the 1990s, many corporate divestitures took place, and **downsizing** (a strategy used to reduce the scale and scope of a business to improve its financial performance) became common. Management Close-Up 9.1 shows how Sara Lee adopted a strategy of divestiture to add value.

LOC-In 5   Learning Objective Check-in

Scottsdale Company, a producer of high-end lawn and garden equipment, including some chemical products, is anticipating one of two alternatives that will be affected by its near-term strategy, which is to expand the company. The first alternative is to agree with Pro-Gene, a fertilizer company to combine the assets from both companies and form a single organization. If this alternative is chosen, the new firm will be able to eliminate some of the administrative operations and even consolidate manufacturing facilities in some cases. The second, alternative is to actually purchase some smaller firms along Scottsdale's supply chain, particularly at the back end.

1. If Scottsdale chooses the first option, it would be engaging in _____.
   a. acquisition
   b. a divestiture
   c. task forces
   d. a merger

2. If Scottsdale chooses the second option, it would be engaging in _____.
   a. a divestiture
   b. acquisition
   c. a merger
   d. centralization

MANAGEMENT CLOSE-UP 9.1

Deverticalizing Sara Lee

Many large consumer goods companies have embraced outsourcing. For example, Nike doesn't make any shoes. Pillsbury's Green Giant line of canned vegetables are not actually canned by the Minneapolis, Minnesota, food company—Seneca Foods does it for Pillsbury. Outsourcing lets companies concentrate on sales, marketing, and improving their brands while the actual manufacturing of their products is done by other companies.

In 1949 a Chicago baker perfected cheesecakes that kept their quality after being frozen. Charles Lubin, the baker, named his shop after his eight-year-old daughter, Sara Lee. Today Sara Lee is a top multinational corporation whose products are sold in over 140 countries. Globally, the company is first in the packaged meats industry, and it is ranked first in the United States for frozen baked goods, intimate apparel, and socks.

Since 1997, however, Sara Lee has sold or closed more than 100 plants while maintaining its position in its markets. The corporation surprised everyone with its decision to sell its manufacturing operations and outsource the work. The corporation wanted to focus on developing new products and promoting its brands instead of manufacturing them. Senior management called the divestiture action "deverticalizing" the company's organization, with its brands being made by suppliers according to Sara Lee's specifications.

Sara Lee will be focusing on marketing brands in the baked goods and packaged meats categories, which include the Sara Lee brand cheesecakes and other desserts, Jimmy Dean sausages, Ball Park franks, and Earth Grains breads. It plans to divest other products that do not fit into its targeted product categories. In 2005 it announced that it had put its brands in the intimate apparel products category up for sale, including Hanes underwear, Wonderbras, and Playtex panties. By narrowing its focus on branded food products Sara Lee expects that it will be better able to innovate and boost profit margins.

Sources: Based on "Sara Lee: Chock full o' Brands," *The Economist,* November 12, 2005; P. Eogoi, "Sara Lee: No Piece of Cake," *BusinessWeek,* May 26, 2003, pp. 66–68; "Separate and Lift," *The Economist,* September 20,1997, p. 69.

CONCLUDING THOUGHTS

In the introductory vignette at the beginning of the chapter we presented some critical thinking questions related to aspects of organization structure formed by the merger of two airlines, United and Continental. Now that you have had the opportunity to learn about managing organization structure and design, let's reexamine the questions that were raised in the vignette.

First, the merged organization will have combined the assets of both airline companies, enabling it to have greater bargaining power to purchase aircraft or aviation fuel at favorable prices as well as secure a stronger credit rating with more attractive rates from lenders. The new structure should enable the merged organization to obtain cost savings by eliminating administrative overhead by reducing corporate headquarters staff and eliminating redundant management positions.

The coordination mechanisms that should be useful for aligning the units of the merged companies into a more coherent unified organization should include meetings, organization culture, and organizational reward systems. Meetings that bring together representative employees from each organization can be set up to discuss organizational values, strategic goals, and plans that can be established to coordinate the efforts of employees from both companies. The emergent organization culture of a merged firm based on shared values, beliefs, and norms will unite employees around a common way of doing things. The organizational reward system, such as profit sharing, will tie all the employees in the merged company to a common fate and share part of the financial success with employees. The sharing of financial success with all employees should nurture a collaborative spirit between different organizational units in the merged structure.

FOCUSING ON THE FUTURE: Using Management Theory in Daily Life

Managing the Structure and Design of Organizations

Andy Bryant, the CFO of Intel, manages Finance, Information Technology (IT), and Human Resources (HR) for his company. His integrated role mirrors the team roles he assigns to his Finance personnel. They now work in cross-functional teams with employees from Operations. Together, Finance and Operations employees have developed a business partnership, and both departments are involved in the development of new products, improving the efficiency and effectiveness of operations and increasing productivity and profitability.[1]

Under Bryant, the Finance Department underwent an organizational redesign. The first step in the process was to develop a strategic vision for the department that mirrored the strategic vision of Intel as a whole. Intel's Finance Vision and Charter is as follows:

Vision:

Intel Finance is a full partner in business decisions to maximize shareholder value.

Charter:

- Maximize profits by providing effective analysis, influence, leadership, and control as business partners.
- Keep Intel legal worldwide while maintaining high standards of professionalism and integrity.
- Protect shareholder interests by safeguarding the assets of the Corporation.
- Deliver world-class services and productivity.
- Develop effective leaders and partners through career opportunities that foster improved performance and professional growth.[2]

This strategic vision highlights several key points: (1) Finance has an interest in the business, and they take the "bottom line" seriously; (2) Finance expects to partner with others in the corporation for the betterment of the company as a whole; and (3) employees in finance are professionals, and they need to be on the cutting edge of their industry as well as being involved in the overall business of the company. These points brought Bryant to the next step in the organizational design process—setting up an organizational structure that matched the strategy. Bryant chose a modified matrix for his organizational structure.

To address the first and second points, Bryant made sure that each Finance employee was assigned to a particular project or area of operations. Financial professionals working in a specific operational unit are expected to know everything about that unit—from understanding the manufacturing process to learning how the unit markets and sells its product or products.

In acknowledgment of the third point, all Finance employees report to a Finance Manager, along with an operations manager. In most organizations, financial staffers are embedded in operating units. Intel's structure allows Finance employees to gain an overview of the company's entire financial picture, and have access to financial competencies that they would not get in a standard decentralized structure.

In setting up this new organizational design, Bryant also paid attention to corporate culture. He knew that the role of the Finance employees was an advisory one—the final decision on any operational issue had to stay with operations or general managers. To avoid the conflicts inherent in such a structure, he insisted that his Finance employees understand not only finance, but also the business of the group they were supporting, how to influence and persuade others without a command position, and when and how to proactively address issues. The bottom line was that if Finance was to be considered to be a true partner, and to be included in the strategic decision-making process, Finance employees had to be able to provide information to operations that was useful in running a business, not just interesting. Operations managers want bottom-line information, presented succinctly and clearly. They don't want huge piles of reports, and they don't want financial analysts to do every report that is requested—just those that will really add value to the operation. Operations managers expect Finance professionals to have an opinion and to express that opinion in a way that brings both groups closer to agreement.

A key component of any organizational design intervention is to measure results. At Intel, Finance measures results based on whether they have effectively changed business practices, and whether or not those changes increase corporate savings and/or profitability.

Interestingly, Andy Bryant's own leanings toward the operations side of the business may have prompted his desire to create better relations between his team and operations. As he notes in a recent interview, "I have tried three different times to, leave Finance for operations.[3] He also points out that ex-CEO Andy Grove prevented that move each time, finally telling Andy, "you need to do what's in the best interest of the company."

Sources: [1] PriceWaterhouseCoopers, "Global Best Practices," http://www.globalbestpractices.com/Home/Document. aspx?Q=273,4537,205, D39Fo85F-3BCD-4C5C-B6FC-6859i8BC2iB6; [2] R. R. Boedecker, and S. B. Hughes, "Best Practices in Finance: How Intel Finance Uses Business Partnerships to Supercharge Results," *Strategic Finance,* October 2005, pp. 26–34; [3] Don Durfee,"Intel's Andy Bryant," *CFO,* November 2005, pp. 48–51.

Summary of Learning Objectives

Organizing is a process that involves the deployment of resources to achieve strategic goals. **Organization structure** is the development of a formal system of relationships that determine lines of authority and the tasks assigned to individuals and units. This chapter's discussion will help future managers, work teams and employees better understand the importance of organizing. The content presented in this chapter to meet each of the learning objectives we set out at the start of the chapter is summarized below.

1 Identify the vertical and horizontal dimensions of organization structure.

The **vertical dimension** of organization structure is concerned with who has the authority to make decisions; it involves

- **Unity of command:** each subordinate should have only one supervisor.
- **Authority:** the formal right of a manager to make decisions and give orders that are carried out by others.
- **Responsibility:** the duty to perform a task that has been assigned.
- **Delegation:** a transfer of responsibility to a subordinate or team subject to the authority of the manager.
- **Line authority:** direct control over the work of subordinates.
- **Staff authority:** advising, recommending, and counseling other managers and personnel in the organization.
- **Span of control:** the number of subordinates who directly report to a manager.
- **Centralization:** decision authority concentrated at the top of the organization hierarchy.
- **Decentralization:** decision authority pushed to lower levels in the organizational hierarchy.
- **Formalization:** the amount of written documentation that is used to direct and control employees.

The **horizontal dimension** of organization structure is **departmentalization**, which is the basis of the deployment of employees into jobs in units that are called departments.

2 Apply the three basic approaches—functional, divisional, and matrix—to departmentalization.

- The **functional structure** of departmentalization assigns people with similar skills to a department such as accounting or marketing. It is highly efficient because it permits employees to do specialized tasks.
- The **divisional approach** organizes employees into units based on common products, services, or markets. It improves coordination between different business functions and allows for faster services to customers.
- The **matrix approach** combines the efficiency of the functional approach with the flexibility and responsiveness of the divisional approach. The matrix approach greatly facilitates starting new projects and ventures, and it efficiently utilizes the talents of scarce specialists.

3 Develop coordination across departments and hierarchical levels.

As organizations grow and become more complex, there is a greater need for **coordination** mechanisms to link activities between departments. Some key coordination mechanisms include the following:

- **Strategic meetings:** face-to-face gatherings of departmental or division managers to coordinate overarching organizational objectives.
- **Organizationwide reward systems:** rewards that are based on organizationwide results that strengthen collaboration between departments.
- **Task forces:** ad hoc interdepartmental groups that are formed to study a specific problem and make recommendations.
- **Problem-solving teams:** groups representing different departments that solve problems on either a temporary or permanent basis.
- **Liaison role:** a position held by an individual that is used to facilitate communications between two or more departments.
- **Integrating manager:** a manager who is responsible for the success of a project or product and who coordinates the work of people from different departments.

- **Organization culture:** a system of shared values, assumptions, beliefs, and norms that give the members of an organization a common understanding about "the way things are done around here."

4 Use organization structure and the three basic organization designs—mechanistic, organic, and boundaryless—to achieve strategic goals.

Organization design involves selecting an organization structure that best fits the strategic goals of the business. Managers can design organization goals that are mechanistic, organic, or boundaryless.

- **Mechanistic designs** emphasize vertical structure and use top-down "command and control" communication channels with a high level of formalization.
- **Organic designs** emphasize horizontal relationships involving teams and rely on coordination mechanisms to keep everything under control. There is more flexibility and less formalization in an organic design than in a mechanistic design.
- **Boundaryless designs** eliminate structural boundaries between organizations and units within them so that employees can develop collaborative relationships with customers, suppliers, and sometimes competitors. While sharing some similarities with the organic design, the boundaryless design uses teams to span oragnizational boundaries with other firms to more quickly respond to change and uncertainty in the environment.

5 Develop an awareness of strategic events that are likely to trigger a change in the structure and design of an organization.

The key strategic events that are likely to trigger a change in the structure and design of an organization are mergers, acquisitions, and divestitures.

- A **merger** takes place when two independent companies agree to combine their assets and form a single organization. In many cases these merging firms compete in the same industry and achieve efficiencies based on size.
- An **acquisition** takes place when a firm buys all or part of another business. The acquisition may be in the same industry or a different one than that of the acquiring firm.
- A **divestiture** occurs when an organization sells a business in order to generate cash.

Discussion Questions

1. What would it be like to be a department manager in a functional organization structure? In a divisional approach to organization structure? In your comparison discuss responsibilities, skills, competencies, and decision-making authority.

2. How do responsibility, authority, and accountability differ? What happens to responsibility, authority, and accountability when a manager delegates work to a subordinate?

3. What are the advantages and disadvantages of centralization and decentralization? You are the CEO of a diversified food company with four divisions that produce breakfast cereals, cookies, salty snack foods, and fruit juices under different brand names. Give an example of a situation where centralized decision authority would be more effective to use. Give an example where decentralized decision authority would be more effective to use. Justify your answers.

4. What issues or problems would an organization encounter with a matrix structure? Would you like to work in a matrix organization structure? Why or why not?

5. Your organization is organized with functional departments. It has encountered the following problems. What

coordinating mechanism would you select to manage each problem? Justify your selection.

a. The number of workplace accidents has increased greatly in all the departments.

b. Departments are competing with each other for budgets and other scarce resources, resulting in dysfunctional conflict.

c. The research, engineering, manufacturing, and marketing departments disagree on product specifications and performance features, and new products are being delivered too late to market as a result.

6. How are teams used in the organic design? What about in the boundaryless design?

7. Does an organization in a turbulent environment require more horizontal relationships than one in a stable environment? Explain.

8. Why does the structure of an organization follow the development of the organization strategy, rather than the strategy following the development of the structure?

Management Minicase 9.1

Decentralization Works at Johnson & Johnson

Johnson & Johnson has relied on decentralization as a good way to spark innovation and train corporate leaders, according to William Weldon, CEO of Johnson & Johnson, a health-care products company that makes such brands as Band-Aids, Tylenol, and Splenda. Johnson & Johnson's commitment to innovative products has led to 76 consecutive years of sales increases, 25 consecutive years of adjusted earnings increase, and 47 consecutive years of dividend increases for shareholders.

Decentralization has helped Johnson & Johnson develop leaders. Because managers know they can operate a business unit profitably, they try hard for the top jobs at the company's best businesses. Johnson & Johnson has 250 operating companies in 57 countries and generated annual revenues of $63.7 billion in 2008. All these separate businesses create a wide range of development opportunities for mangers at Johnson & Johnson.

A decentralized approach helps innovation "in that it allows different people with different skills, different thoughts, to bring together different products and technologies to satisfy the unmet needs of patients or customers," according to CEO Weldon. One example of this kind of innovation happened when Johnson & Johnson brought together individuals from its medical products division with its drug business. The combined efforts of these specialists generated the idea of putting a drug on a stent to treat cardiovascular disease, which was a major breakthrough.

DISCUSSION QUESTIONS

1. What are the advantages of using a decentralized organization structure at Johnson & Johnson? What is the basis of organizing employees into units at Johnson & Johnson?
2. Can you think of any inefficiencies or drawbacks to Johnson & Johnson's emphasis on decentralization?

Sources: Based on Johnson & Johnson Web site, "Company Overview," 2010. www.jnj.com/company-overview.cfm; G. Colvin and J. Shambora, "J&J: Secrets of Success," *Fortune*, May 4, 2009, pp. 117–21; P. Galuszka, "Johnson & Johnson CEO: Decentralization Works," July 2, 2008. www.blogs.bnet.com/ceo/?p=1199.

Management Minicase 9.2

Restructuring the 3M Company for Growth and Profitability

The 3M Company of 2003 bore a resemblance to the "old IBM" of the 1980s, which was a place of lifetime employment for tinkerers, coddled from postgraduate life to the grave, and who might or might not eventually turn out commercial products. They read the company's weekly newspaper that provided features about cooking classes, stamp collecting, and volunteerism. In other words, life at 3M was cushy and undemanding for its employees.

Complacency begat financial disappointments. Between 1992 and 2002 sales crept ahead at an average of 1.6 percent and profits increased 4.9 percent a year. The 3M Company generated $16 billion in sales in 2002. The 3M Company's product lines focused on industrial and consumer goods such as abrasives, glues, and various types of tapes with adhesive qualities. Starting in 2001, CEO James McNerney formulated a strategy of diversification to refocus 3M on faster-growing markets that could provide better performance in terms of growth and profitability to investors. McNerney used a two-pronged approach to realize these goals. First, he reduced operating expenses by $500 million, mostly by laying off 6,500 of 3M's 75,000 workers. He slashed inventories and accounts receivable by $675 million and trimmed debt. Profitability jumped 38 percent to $2 billion due to these efforts.

Second, CEO McNerney decided to reposition 3M as more of a health care company, building on the health unit's 22 percent of revenue and 27 percent of operating income. Until now, 3M's medical products have been mostly low tech, such as skin patches or inhalers, or service based, including software used to code medical procedures for Medicare reimbursement. Scientists in 3M's laboratories are developing medications to treat respiratory, cardiovascular, skin, and sexually related diseases. The company is an important supplier of materials to repair and replace teeth, and the CEO wants to branch into such areas as fluoride treatment and products to stem periodontal disease. With the U.S. population aging, the $12 billion restorative dental care market is expected to reach $21.5 billion in 10 years. McNerney is also looking for acquisitions in expanding industries. He recently completed a $680 million acquisition of Corning's precision lens business, which makes parts for projection TVs.

The 3M Company had 148 plants in 60 countries with 53 percent of sales outside the United States. At any given time there were 1,500 products in development. Many never made it further. The company's organization chart was bewildering. Mixing faster-growing businesses with low-tech slowpokes made it impossible to evaluate performance, a frequent complaint from the investment community. McNerney has asked researchers to focus the $1 billion they spend annually on their best ideas, ones that have a sales potential of $100 million or more in annual sales. He is also asking 3M employees to think more like their customers—a novel idea in this organization.

DISCUSSION QUESTIONS

1. The CEO at 3M has formulated a new strategy of diversification with increased growth and profitability. In what ways will the new strategy affect the organization structure at 3M? How will it affect the vertical dimension of organization structure? Will it be flatter or taller? How will it affect the horizontal dimension of organization structure? Will 3M need to change the basis for its allocation of departments?
2. The CEO is asking the scientists at the research laboratories at 3M to focus on research projects that could result in $100 million or more annual sales. Will this new policy result in a more centralized or decentralized research and development unit at 3M?
3. With the changes in structure that are likely to follow the diversification strategy that calls for higher performance in terms of growth and profitability, what type of coordination mechanisms do you think will best enable 3M management to link activities between diverse departments or divisions. Do you think that the portfolio of 3M products and services is becoming more diverse or less diverse? Justify your answers.

Source: Adapted from M. Tatge, "Prescription for Growth," *Forbes*, February 17, 2003, pp. 64–66.

Individual/Collaborative Learning Case 9.1

Fast Food's Yummy Secret

It is one of the biggest companies in one of the biggest industries in America. Its brand names are viewed from highways and city streets throughout the world. From its base in Louisville, Kentucky, it oversees the opening of three new restaurants, one of them in China, every day. It does over $11 billion in annual sales in 2009 and yet few customers have ever heard of it.

However, if they know KFC (previously Kentucky Fried Chicken), or Pizza Hut, or Taco Bell, then they know Yum! Brands. The parent of those three fast-food chains, it has 37,000 restaurants around the world, more than McDonald's. With 2950 KFC restaurants and 460 Pizza Huts in China in 2005, Yum! owns two of the best-known brand names in the world's most populous market. This is not bad for a company that Pepsi-Cola got rid of in 1997 in a spin-off because it did not fit with Pepsi's beverage and snack foods units.

A spin-off occurs when the corporate parent, Pepsi in this case, decides that the businesses in the proposed spin-off could be better managed as an independent company rather than as a unit within the structure of a larger corporation. It is expected that the spin-off will produce more wealth for shareholders as an independent firm and so the shareholders could potentially benefit from the spin-off. Pepsi shareholders received shares in Yum! Brands after the spin-off was completed.

After the spin-off the morale of the franchise owners of the restaurants at Yum! increased substantially—one of the reasons was that restaurant managers received stock options. The managers treated the restaurant crews better too. Kitchen employees were retained on average twice as long after the spin-off, reducing training and recruiting costs. Under Pepsi, the three restaurants acted more like rivals, with each buying its own advertising through different agencies. After the spin-off the restaurants collaborated by using a single ad agency and gained better deals by leveraging Yum!'s greater size.

CRITICAL THINKING QUESTIONS

1. What is the difference between a spin-off and a divestiture?
2. Why do you think that Pepsi management decided it would be more beneficial to spin off the fast-food restaurant businesses from the rest of the company? How does the fast-food restaurant business differ from the business of producing beverages such as Pepsi-Cola or selling snack foods such as corn chips?

COLLABORATIVE LEARNING EXERCISE

With a partner or a small group try to develop additional ways that collaboration between the three fast-food restaurants, KFC, Pizza Hut, and Taco Bell can be beneficial to Yum! Brands. How can collaboration achieve more customers for the restaurants? Save costs with supplies? Enter new markets? Achieve better relations with employees? Generate higher levels of brand awareness? Offer better service and food to the customers? Why do you think there was less collaboration between the restaurants when they were organized within the Pepsi corporate structure before the spin-off was completed? Be prepared to share your findings with other members of your class.

Source: Based on "Special report: Yum! Brands: Fast Food's Yummy Secret," *The Economist,* August 27, 2005, pp. 60–62; Yum! Brands Web site, "Yum! FAQs," 2010. www.yum.com/investors/faqs.asp; "Taking the hill less climbed," *The Economist*, October 31, 2009, p. 76.

Internet Exercise 9.1

PepsiCo: A World Leader in Food and Beverages

www.pepsico.com

PepsiCo is a world leader in convenient foods and beverages. It has organized a powerful portfolio of branded foods and beverages based on developing some brands internally and through acquiring other brands and managing them effectively as assets. Visit the PepsiCo Web site and click on the "company" and the "history" features in order to answer the following questions:

1. What are the important brands that PepsiCo owns? Which ones did they acquire? Which ones did the company develop internally?
2. How are the beverages organized into groups?
3. How are the convenient foods organized into groups?

Manager's Checkup 9.1

Do You Follow the Chain of Command?

Would you fit into the traditional hierarchical structure of a corporation? Would an organization that puts a low priority on hierarchical relationships be more your style? This exercise can indicate your ability to manage within an organization that expects allegiance to the chain of command.

Consider the following statements and mark each as "True" or "False" to indicate whether you agree or disagree.

_____   1. When something bothers me at work, I go straight to top management.

_____   2. The only way to get what you need is to talk to the owner of the company.

——— 3. If my supervisor behaved in a way that offended me, I would speak directly to his or her boss.

——— 4. Although I feel comfortable delegating responsibility to my employees. I follow up to make certain they have accomplished the tasks they were assigned.

——— 5. If I suspected my boss were engaging in unethical behavior, I would speak to someone in the human resources department in strict confidence.

——— 6. I will not mention a potential promotion to my star employee until I have received approval to do so from upper management.

——— 7. If I wait for the required approval from human resources to begin interviewing candidates for the new position that is open, it will be months before I can get anyone on board to help with this project. So I am going ahead with the interviews.

——— 8. If I suspected my boss were having emotional problems, I would speak to his or her best friend, who also works at the company.

——— 9. If a customer made a special request I did not have the authority to approve, I would politely explain that I'd get back to him or her as soon as possible.

——— 10. If a friend of mine wanted to apply for a job at my organization, I'd sneak her past human resources to speak with my boss.

Scoring: "True" responses to statements 4, 5, 6 and 9 indicate an ability to follow the chain of command. "True" responses to statements 1–3, 7–8 and 10 indicate an inability to follow the chain of command.

Source: From *Management of Organizations,* by P. M. Wright and R. A. Noe. Copyright © 1996 The McGraw-Hill Companies, Inc. Reprinted with permission.

Endnotes

1. D. Robey and C. A. Sayles, *Designing Organizations* (Burr Ridge, IL: Irwin, 1994).
2. Ibid.
3. Ibid.
4. R. C. Ford and W. A. Randolph, "Cross-Functional Structures: A Review and Integration of Matrix Organization and Project Management," *Journal of Management* 18 (1992): 267–294.
5. R. L. Daft, *Management*, 4th ed. (Fort Worth: Dryden Press, 1997).
6. K. A. Frank and K. Fahrback, "Organization Culture as a Complex System: Balance and Information Models of Influence and Selection," *Organization Science* 10 (1999): 253–277.
7. S. Brown and K. Blackmon, "Aligning Manufacturing Strategy and Business-Level Competitive Strategy in New Competitive Environments: The Case for Strategic Resonance," *Journal of Management Studies* 42 (2005): 793–815; J. Woodward, *Industrial Organizations: Theory and Practice* (London: Oxford University Press, 1965).
8. S. Das, "Designing Service Processes: A Design Factor Based Process Model," *International Journal of Services Technology and Management* 7(1) (2006): 85.
9. B. Evans, "Google Becomes an Irresistible Force," *InformationWeek*, December 19–26, 2005, p. 76; S. Smith, "A Date with Digital," *Mediaweek*, September 12, 2005, pp. 38–39.
10. M. S. Kraatz and E. J. Zaja, "How Organizational Resources Affect Strategic Change and Performance in Turbulent Environments: Theory and Evidence," *Organization Science* 12 (2001): 632–657.
11. G. R. Jones, *Organizational Theory*, 2nd ed. (Reading, MA: Addision-Wesley, 1998).
12. *The Economist*, "How to Manage a Dream Factory," January 18, 2003, pp. 73–75.
13. N. Shirouzu and P. Ho, "GM, SAIC Reshape Partnership," *Wall Street Journal*, December 5, 2009. www.wsj.com.
14. J. Fortt, "Life After iPhone," *Fortune*, January 19, 2009, p. 34.
15. D. Foust, "Looks Like a Beer Brawl," *BusinessWeek*, July 28, 2008, pp. 52–53.
16. S. Lacy, "The Hardest Job in Silicon Valley," *BusinessWeek*, January 23, 2006, pp. 65–66.

10

Learning Objectives

1 Explain the role of human resource management in achieving a sustainable competitive advantage.

2 Identify the key factors in the environment affecting the management of human resources.

3 Describe the human resource planning process.

4 Explain the key components of staffing and their importance.

5 Describe how training and career development provide employees with tools to succeed once they are hired.

6 Identify the purposes of performance appraisal and how it might be conducted.

7 Describe the key objectives of the compensation system and its components.

Hire a Hero

Every employer wants to hire the right people for the right jobs. Lately some companies are doing that by targeting veterans coming home from the wars in Iraq and Afghanistan. For example, Toyota has launched a Hire-a-Hero program to help returning soldiers find jobs. Members of all the U.S. military branches can search a special Toyota Web site for job opportunities at more than 1,400 Toyota and Lexus dealerships anywhere in the country and at the automaker's corporate and manufacturing facilities. Army, Navy, Air Force, Marines, Coast Guard, and National Guard personnel can search job information on the Web site by city and state and then contact the hiring dealers or managers directly. Web sites associated with the military branches are cross-linked to the Toyota and Lexus Web sites as well, making it easy for military men and women to find the hundreds of jobs that are listed there.

Skill, discipline, commitment, and leadership ability are only a few of the advantages Toyota hopes to gain by hiring veterans. Many military personnel return from the service with specialized technical training that's highly sought after in the automotive industry and that translates readily into the civilian workplace. Don Esmond, senior vice president of Toyota Motor Sales, U.S.A., and a Vietnam veteran, says. "Our dealers have found that the men and women of the U.S. military make up one of the best talent pools in America."

Human Resource Management

Launched a few years ago when Esmond decided to develop a hiring program in California for guardsmen and reservists returning from service in Iraq and Afghanistan, Hire-a-Hero earned Toyota the federal government's Secretary of Defense Freedom Award. Since its beginning, Hire-a-Hero has expanded to include veterans of all branches and now also includes a $1.25 million scholarship program for children of current and former Marines.

Besides hiring veterans, Toyota also looks out for those who become employees first, soldiers next. While some reservists called to active duty have lost their employment benefits or even their jobs while serving in the military, "that's something that will not happen at Toyota," said a company spokesperson. "The company makes up the difference in their citizen-soldier's pay, maintains their health care benefits and continues paying into their pension plan." Care packages for the wounded, specially equipped vans for the Paralyzed Veterans of America, and an

ombudsman to help Guard and Reserve employees' families are other Toyota initiatives for its military employees.

"The Hire-a-Hero program is a tool to make members of the military aware of job opportunities available at independently owned Toyota and Lexus dealerships," Toyota's spokesperson says. "The company benefits by hiring a diverse group of individuals who have typically demonstrated commitment and responsibility and have attained skills and leadership abilities while on military duty."

Bill Lester. who races a Toyota Tundra with a Hire-a-Hero logo at NASCAR, echoes the thought. "All of these men and women are heroes to me," he says, "and it's an honor to help inform them about Toyota and Lexus job opportunities when they decide to return to civilian life." A more intangible advantage of this policy to the Japanese automaker is in developing political goodwill in the United States, particularly when Toyota ran into some rough patches this decade with mechanical troubles followed by accusations by some politicians that Toyota had not been truthful to the American public. This policy fits nicely with the Obama administration's expansion of benefits and services for veterans by, in his words, "taking care of the people who have protected our freedom over time."

Sources: Based on E. O'Keefe, "Hiring to expand veteran's services," *Washington Post*, February 23, 2010, A-1 ; http://newsday.com "Toyota counting on veterans at Congress hearing," 2010; http://www.workforce.com "HR Management," 2011; http://www.workforce.com, "Toyota on a military mission," 2011; www.etoyota.com/joblink/main.asp, accessed March 16, 2006; Rudi Williams, "Toyota Helps Guards, Reservists Find Jobs," www.americasupportsyou.mil, February 27, 2006; "Toyota's Hire a

Hero Program Debuts at Richmond," www.theautochannel.com, September 8, 2004; "Toyota's 'Hire a Hero' to Aid Veterans' Return to Civilian Workforce," Toyota press release, n.d., www.glassbytes.com, accessed March 16,2006.

CRITICAL THINKING QUESTIONS

1. *How does the Hire-a-Hero program help Toyota attract and retain skilled employees despite a shortage of technically trained and committed labor?*

2. *Why is effective management of human resources critical to achieving a sustainable competitive advantage?*

3. *What are some of the advantages for a foreign multinational firm to follow this type of Hire-a-Hero program in the United States?*

We'll revisit these questions in our Concluding Thoughts at the end of the chapter, after you have had a chance to read about the challenges of human resource management.

■ The Importance of Human Resource Management

The heart and soul of practically every company is its employees. Human resource issues are crucial at every level of the organization. Even entry-level supervisors play a vital role in HR practices. They are part of the selection process, and then train, coach, and evaluate employees.

The Human Resources Department supports managers in carrying out HR responsibilities. The HR department may conduct a pay survey to determine a salary range for a given position, inform managers about changes in employment law, develop a form to evaluate employees, or determine if applicants meet minimum position requirements. But in the end, it is managers who determine a prospective employee's salary subject to budget constraints, ensure that the law is being applied correctly, assess a subordinate's performance, and make final hiring decisions. For this reason, there is an old saying among HR professionals: "Every manager is a personnel manager." Management Is Everyone's Business 10.1 shows some of the implications of this for those with managerial responsibilities. And as we have discussed in prior chapters, teams of employees are playing a larger role in most organizations. This is particularly true in HR decisions as outlined in Management Is Everyone's Business 10.2.

MANAGEMENT IS EVERYONE'S BUSINESS 10.1

WORKING AS A MANAGER Many if not most management problems are a result of poor human resource practices. Indicators that something is wrong with HR practices include inability to recruit top talent, loss of key employees to competitors, costly lawsuits, internal conflicts that sap the organization's time and energy, low innovation by employees afraid of taking risks or with outdated skills, and little concern for quality. By diagnosing the cause of these problems, managers may be able to design and implement appropriate HR programs in collaboration with the HR department or external consultants to help the firm gain or maintain an edge against its competitors. As a manager you should:

- Ensure that human resource practices in your unit are congruent with overall organizational strategies.
- Be attuned to major changes in the law at federal, state, and local levels that might affect human resource practices in your unit. Remember, ignorance of the law is no excuse!
- Try to be consistent in your treatment of employees when it comes to discipline, appraisals, pay decisions, and so on.
- Make sure that personnel decisions concerning selection, training, appraisals, compensation, and so forth are job-related. This is important both legally and in order to maintain employee morale.
- Help employees grow in their jobs by giving them helpful/constructive feedback and challenging assignments.

MANAGEMENT IS EVERYONE'S BUSINESS   10.2

WORKING AS A TEAM Employees working in teams often take over HR functions that have tradition-ally come under the purview of supervisors. For instance, peers may evaluate each other, allocate rewards, decide who should be on the team, interview candidates, and organize their own work flow. The firm needs to provide adequate support so that teams are able to perform these HR functions. Ultimately, the firm is responsible for the team's actions. For instance, the firm is liable for discriminatory practices or sexual harassment within teams even if managers do not condone such practices. Team members should:

- Play a major role in supporting each other through training, information exchange, helpful feed-back and such.
- Comply with all pertinent laws pertaining to sexual harassment, various forms of discrimination, violation of overtime laws (for instance, by expecting hourly workers to meet after they have complied with a 40-hour week), and so on.
- Be aware and try to reduce biases that might make certain team members uncomfortable (for instance, cracking jokes about people from other disciplines or backgrounds) and that could even lead to unfair judgments in appraisals, assignments, and incentive allocation.
- Seek assistance from the Human Resource Department if there are issues within the team that might benefit from professional advice and intervention (for instance, members who are per-ceived to be freeriders).

LOC-In   1   Learning Objective Check-In

1. Luis is a manager who tries to make sure that the ways he treats employees when it comes to discipline, appraisals, and pay decisions are consistent. He also strives to ensure that selection and training decisions are job related. This is important not only because of the morale of his workers, but because of legal issues as well. Luis is practicing good _____ practices as a manager.
   a. strategic
   b. operational
   c. human resources
   d. information

This chapter describes the human resource skills you will need to help an organization become more productive, comply with legal requirements, and gain or maintain a competitive edge in the marketplace.

▮ Environment of Human Resources

Managers need to constantly monitor the external environment for opportunities and threats affecting human resources and be prepared to react quickly to these changes. Major environmen-tal considerations include workforce diversity, legislation, globalization, competitive forces, and labor unions.

Workforce Diversity

The U.S. workforce is rapidly becoming more diverse. Company leaders can take advantage of diversity in order to succeed. African Americans, Asian Americans, Hispanics, and other minori-ties make up approximately one-third of the U.S. workforce. At least 11 million undocumented workers are also estimated to be working in the United States. In large urban centers where most business activity takes place and corporate headquarters are usually located, the workforce is often 50 percent to 75 percent nonwhite. Women represent almost half of the workforce, and women with children under six years of age are the fastest growing segment. The workforce is aging, includes a larger proportion of disabled employees, and a growing number are openly homosexual.

In 2011, the proportion of the U.S. population that is foreign born reached almost 12 percent. In some urban areas, such as New York, Los Angeles, and Miami, this proportion is probably closer to one third of the population. This historic high is more than double what it was in 1970 and a third higher than it was in 1990.[1] Unlike early immigrants who came from Europe, recent immigrants come from every corner of the world.[2] Clear-cut racial distinctions are also blurring as intermarriage of different groups has steadily increased. The resulting large population of biracial children "view the world from the wondrous, troubling perspective of insider/outsider."[3]

Employees and managers need to work effectively with people who are different from them. The HR department is responsible for facilitating this process. Many HR departments organize diversity training workshops for managers and employees to enable them to better relate to customers and one another. Some HR departments hire a manager of diversity who is responsible for dealing with the day-to-day issues of managing a diverse workforce.

Globalization

In order to grow, many firms enter the global marketplace as exporters, overseas manufacturers, or both. Even those that choose to remain in the domestic market are not insulated from foreign competition. Human resources plays a central role in this process. A firm may restructure the top-management team and decentralize operations to meet the global challenge, use cheaper foreign labor to reduce costs, or promote managers with foreign experience and language skills. The HR department can organize international training programs, offer financial incentives for managers to export the company's products, and identify the appropriate mix of foreign (or *expatriate*) and local managers in overseas operations.

Legislation

Over the past 40 years, federal, state, and local governments have passed many laws to protect employees and ensure equal employment opportunity. Company leaders must deal effectively with applicable government regulations. The HR department plays a crucial role by monitoring the legal environment and developing internal systems such as supervisory training and grievance procedures to avoid costly legal battles. Key legislation and executive orders are summarized in Table 10.1.

Most work-related laws are designed to prevent **discrimination**, the unfair treatment of employees because of personal characteristics that are not job-related. Title VII of the Civil

discrimination
The unfair treatment of employees because of personal characteristics that are not job-related.

TABLE 10.1 Key Legislation Affecting Human Resources

Law	Year	Description
Workers compensation laws	Various	State-by-state laws that establish insurance plans to compensate employees injured on the job
Social Security Act	1935	Payroll tax to fund retirement benefits, disability, and unemployment insurance
Wagner Act	1935	Legitimized labor unions and established the National Labor Relations Board
Fair Labor Standards Act	1938	Established minimum wage and overtime pay
Taft-Hartley Act	1947	Provided protection for employers and limited union power; permitted states to enact right-to-work laws
Landrum-Griffin Act	1959	Protects union members' right to participate in union affairs
Equal Pay Act	1963	Prohibits unequal pay for the same job
Title VII of Civil Rights Act	1964	Prohibits employment decisions based on race, color, religion, sex, or national origin
Executive Order 11246	1965	Same as Title VII, also requires affirmative action
Age Discrimination in Employment Act	1967	Prohibits employment decisions based on age of persons aged 40 or older
Occupational Safety and Health Act	1970	Establishes safety and health standards for organizations to protect employees
Employee Retirement Income Security Act	1974	Regulates the financial stability of employee benefit and pension plans

Law	Year	Description
Vietnam-Era Veterans Readjustment Act	1974	Prohibits federal contracts from discriminating against Vietnam-era veterans
Pregnancy Discrimination Act	1978	Prohibits employers from discriminating against pregnant women
Job Training Partnership Act	1982	Provides block money grants to states to pass on to local governments and private entities that provide on-the-job training
Consolidated Omnibus Budget Reconciliation Act (COBRA)	1985	Requires continued health insurance coverage paid by employee following termination
Immigration Reform and Control Act	1986	Prohibits discrimination based on citizenship status; employers required to document employees' legal work status
Worker Adjustment and Retraining Act (WARN)	1988	Employers required to notify workers of impending layoffs
Drug-Free Workplace Act	1988	Covered employers must implement certain policies to restrict employee drug use
Americans with Disabilities Act (ADA)	1990	Prohibits discrimination based on disability
Civil Rights Act	1991	Amends Title VII; prohibits quotas, allows for monetary punitive damages
Family and Medical Leave Act	1993	Employers required to provide unpaid leave for childbirth, adoption, illness
Health Care Reform Act	2010	Provides health coverage to most Americans by 2018

Source: From *Managing Human Resources* by Gomez-Mejia, et al. Copyright © 2012. Reprinted by permission of Pearson Education, Inc., Upper Saddle River, NJ.

Rights Act of 1964 is considered the most important legislation on this matter. Title VII prohibits firms from basing "compensation, terms, conditions, or privileges of employment" on a person's race, color, religion, sex, or national origin. The central provisions of Title VII appear in Table 10.2.

Interpretations of the Civil Rights Act led to a legal definition of a **protected class** of groups of people who suffered widespread discrimination in the past and who are granted special protection by the judicial system. These include African Americans, Asian Americans, Hispanic Americans, Native Americans, and women. **Affirmative action** aims to accomplish the goal of fair employment by urging employers to make a conscious effort to hire members from protected classes. In affirmative action programs, employment decisions are made at least in part on the basis of demographic characteristics such as race, sex, or age. These programs are controversial because some people believe that only "blind" hiring practices are fair and that the programs may result in hiring quotas that hurt people who are not members of protected groups. This, in effect, penalizes them for the errors of their parents and grandparents. A series of Supreme Court decisions indicate that employment decisions cannot be made solely on the basis of protected class status; people should be "essentially equally qualified" on job-relevant factors before protected class status is permitted to play a role. The Supreme Court in a 2003

protected class
The legal definition of specified groups of people who suffered widespread discrimination in the past and who are given special protection by the judicial system.

affirmative action
A federal government-mandated program that requires corporations to provide opportunities to women and members of minority groups who traditionally had been excluded from good jobs; it aims to accomplish the goal of fair employment by urging employers to make a conscious effort to hire members of protected classes.

TABLE 10.2 Central Provisions of Title VII, Civil Rights Act of 1964

Section 703. (a) It shall be an unlawful employment practice for an employer—(1) to fail or refuse to hire or to discharge any individual, or otherwise to discriminate against any individual with respect to his compensation, terms, conditions, or privileges of employment, because of such individual's race, color, religion, sex, or national origin, or (2) to limit, segregate, or classify his employees or applicants for employment in any way which would deprive or tend to deprive any individual of employment opportunities or otherwise adversely affect his status as an employee, because of such individual's race, color, religion, sex, or national origin.

Source: Title VII, Civil Rights Act of 1964.

ruling reaffirmed the notion that protected class status may be considered in retention decisions but prohibited the use of such explicit criteria as quotas or added points in an exam based on a person's race, ethnic status, or gender.

Two forms of discrimination are considered illegal and may result in substantial fines and penalties for employers and/or in a court-imposed affirmative action plan. The first form of discrimination, **disparate treatment**, occurs when an employer treats an employee differently because of his or her protected class status. The second form of discrimination, **adverse impact** (also called *disparate impact),* occurs when the same standard is applied to all applicants or employees but that standard affects a protected class more negatively. For instance, a minimum height requirement for police tends to automatically disqualify more women than men. If a protected class suffers from adverse impact, then the firm may be required to demonstrate that the standards used were job-related and that alternative selection methods were too costly or unreliable.

The Equal Employment Opportunity Commission (EEOC) was created by the Civil Rights Act of 1964 to initiate investigations in response to discrimination complaints. An individual bringing a complaint to court must prove that there is *prima facie* ("on its face") *evidence* of discrimination. In the case of disparate treatment, a plaintiff can establish prima facie discrimination by showing that he or she was at least as qualified for the job as the person who was hired. In the case of an adverse impact lawsuit, the EEOC has established *the four-fifths rule* for prima facie cases. This means that the hiring rate of a protected class should be at least four-fifths of the hiring rate of the majority group. For example, a firm may hire 50 percent of all its white male job applicants but only 25 percent of all African-American male job applicants. Using the four-fifths rule, there is prima facie evidence of discrimination because four-fifths of 50 percent is 40 percent, which exceeds the 25 percent hiring rate for African-American men.

Once a plaintiff has established a prima facie case, the accused organization must demonstrate that illegal discrimination did not occur. This can be difficult to prove. There are three basic defenses that an employer can use:

1. **Job relatedness** is the most compelling defense. Here the firm shows that decisions were made for job-related reasons. The HR department can help demonstrate job relatedness by preparing written documentation to support and explain the decision.
2. The organization may claim a **bona fide occupational qualification (BFOQ)**, a personal characteristic that must be present to do the job. An example is the need for a female actor for a woman's part in a movie. This option is severely restricted as a justification to discriminate.
3. The final basis to justify disparate impact is **seniority**. In companies with a well-established seniority system, more senior workers may receive priority, even if this has an adverse impact on protected class members.

As illustrated in Table 10.1, other federal legislation influences HR decisions. For instance, the **Drug-Free Workplace Act** requires employers to implement policies that restrict drug use, and the **Family and Medical Leave Act** requires employers to provide unpaid leave for childbirth, adoption, and illness. In most large firms, the HR department is responsible for keeping track of changes in legislation that affects human resources and for developing steps to comply with various laws. This role is crucial because the law may be enforced differently for each firm. For example, many firms require drug testing of all employees, but some require testing only at the time of hiring or at random times. Organizations must also be flexible to respond to changing circumstances in enforcing the law. For example, the Air Force used to randomly test 65 percent of its cadets for drug use. The Air Force has recently decided to increase that percentage and do more testing on weekends, because some of the new recreational drugs, such as Ecstasy, pass through the body quickly.[4]

Sexual harassment, a violation of the Civil Rights Act, has become a highly visible issue. There are two forms of sexual harassment. The first involves sexually suggestive remarks, unwanted touching, or any other physical or verbal act that creates what is called a "hostile environment," for either gender. The second type is called *quid pro quo* harassment, in which sexual favors are sought and/or granted in exchange for company rewards, such as pay raises, promotions, or more choice job assignments. To avoid liability, a company must develop an explicit policy against sexual harassment and a system to investigate allegations. Managers must be made aware that this type of behavior will not be tolerated and may result in severe penalties, including termination. They must also be educated about sexual harassment policies, for instance, in special workshops.

disparate treatment
A form of discrimination that occurs when an employer treats an employee differently because of his or her protected class status.

adverse impact
A form of discrimination, also called disparate impact, that occurs when one standard that is applied to all applicants or employees negatively affects a protected class.

job relatedness
A defense against discrimination claims in which the firm must show that the decision was made for job-related reasons.

bona fide occupational qualification (BFOQ)
A defense against discrimination in which a firm must show that a personal characteristic must be present to do the job.

seniority
A defense against discrimination in which companies with a well-established seniority system can give more senior workers priority, even if this has an adverse impact on protected class members.

Drug-Free Workplace Act
Federal legislation that requires employers to implement policies that restrict drug use.

Family and Medical Leave Act
Federal legislation that requires employers to provide unpaid leave for childbirth, adoption, and illness.

sexual harassment
A form of discrimination that is broadly interpreted to include sexually suggestive remarks, unwanted touching, any physical or verbal act that indicates sexual advances or requests sexual favors, a promise of rewards or hidden threats by a supervisor to induce emotional attachment by a subordinate, and a "hostile environment" based on sex.

Many state and local governments have also passed laws that restrict organizational discretion in the use of human resources. An important law is a limitation on **employment at will**, a longstanding legal doctrine stating that unless there is an employment contract (such as a union contract or an implied contract), both employer and employee are free to end the employment relationship whenever and for whatever reasons they choose. Most states have written employment laws that allow terminated employees to sue if they can show that they have been wrongfully discharged. One common ground is lack of good faith and fair dealing, such as firing a worker shortly before he or she becomes eligible for a retirement plan.

Probably one of the most contentions pieces of legislation in the United States affecting HR policies for years to come was passed by congress in 2010 without a single Republican vote. Known as the Health Care Reform Act, it is intended to provide universal health insurance coverage for practically all Americans by 2018. Until now most Americans obtained health insurance through their employers; the act is intended to provide coverage for most individuals regardless of their employment status and the particular firm they work for. This might make employees more mobile as before the act they were subject to exclusion from insurance coverage due to preexisting health conditions (for themselves or any family member, let's say the wife's pregnancy) if they were to quit their job; now insurance companies will be required to provide coverage for employee and family regardless of prior health conditions.

Manager's Notebook 10.1 lists some interview questions that, if asked, could be interpreted as violating employment law.

employment at will
A very old legal doctrine stating that unless there is an employment contract (such as a union contract or an implied contract), both employer and employee are free to end the employment relationship whenever and for whatever reasons they choose.

Unions

In 1945, about 35 percent of the labor force belonged to unions. Since then, union membership has been declining steadily, reaching a low of approximately 10 percent in 2011.[5] If the present trend continues, this percentage will drop to approximately 8 percent by 2015. Strong employer challenges to unions, plant closures, international competition, and a shrinking manufacturing sector have all contributed to the decline in union membership. Unions are still influential in some sectors, such as automobile manufacturing; even there, however, unions have been more willing to work closely with management in such areas as quality control, cross-training, and innovative compensation systems to meet global challenges.

U.S. employees generally seek representation from a union for one or more of the following reasons:

- Dissatisfaction with certain aspects of their job (such as poor working conditions or pay that is perceived to be low).
- A belief that as individuals they lack influence with management to make needed changes, and that by working together through concerted action they can put greater pressure on management to make concessions.

MANAGER'S NOTEBOOK 10.1

Nine Don'ts of Interviewing

1. Don't ask applicants if they have children, plan to have children, or have child care arrangements made.
2. Don't ask an applicant's age.
3. Don't ask whether the applicant has a physical or mental disability that would interfere with the job. (Employers can explore the subject of disabilities only after making a job offer that is conditional on the applicant's satisfactory completion of a required physical, medical, or job-skills test.)
4. Don't ask for identifying characteristics, such as height and weight.
5. Don't ask marital status, including asking a female candidate her maiden name.
6. Don't ask applicants about their citizenship.
7. Don't ask applicants about their arrest records (employers may ask whether a candidate has ever been convicted of a crime).
8. Don't ask applicants if they smoke (employers can ask whether applicants are aware of legislative restrictions against smoking and whether they are willing to comply with them).
9. Don't ask applicants if they are HIV-positive or have AIDS.

Source: From *Managing Human Resources* by Gomez-Mejia, et al. Copyright © 2012. Reprinted by permission of Pearson Education, Inc., Upper Saddle River, NJ.

- A belief that the union can equalize some of the power between workers and management, so that the company cannot act unilaterally.
- Job insecurity and the conviction that unions can protect workers from arbitrary layoffs by establishing a set of rules that management will abide by. For instance, a unionized firm may stipulate that layoffs will be done in order of seniority.
- The need to establish formal grievance procedures, administered by both the union and management, whereby individual workers can appeal managerial decisions that they believe are unfair.

labor contract
A written agreement negotiated between union and management.

The agreement between the union and management is written in a document called the **labor contract**. In addition to specifying pay schedules, fringe benefits, cost of living adjustments and the like, the labor contract gives employees specific rights. If an employee believes his or her rights have been violated under the contract, the individual can file a grievance against the company. For instance, an employee who believes that he or she was overlooked for promotion may try to remedy this perceived unfairness by filing a grievance, hoping to be reconsidered for the promotion.

Labor unions were largely unprotected by law in the United States until 1935. Crafted by Congress during the Great Depression, the Wagner Act (1935), also known in union circles as the "Magna Carta of Labor," facilitated the establishment and expansion of unions. The Wagner Act created the National Labor Relations Board (NLRB), which is responsible for supervising union elections through secret ballots by workers. The NLRB also determines whether or not a union or management group has engaged in unfair labor practices. For example, firing union sympathizers is an unfair practice, as is a union's calling for a strike while a labor contract is still in effect. The Wagner Act tried to equalize the power of unions and management. After World War II, however, there was a widespread perception that unions had become too powerful, and in some cases corrupt.

The Taft-Hartley Act (1947) specified a set of unfair labor practices by unions along with the remedies that the National Labor Relations Board may take if the union is found guilty of engaging in those practices. Unfair union practices include causing an employer to pay for services that are not performed (a practice often called *featherbedding*) or refusing to bargain in good faith for a new contract.

Twelve years later, the Landrum-Griffin Act (1959) allowed the federal government, through the Department of Labor, to regulate some union activities. Landrum-Griffin was enacted because a few unions experienced problems with corrupt leadership and had misused union funds. Among other things, Landrum-Griffin requires each union to report its financial activities and the financial interests of its leaders to the Department of Labor.

Labor relations tend to be country specific and reflect the sociocultural and historical milieu of each nation. For instance, in the United States labor relations are characterized by:

business unionism
Unions that focus on "bread and butter" issues such as wages, benefits, and job security.

job-based unionism
Unions that are organized by type of job.

collective bargaining
Negotiations between union and management with little, if any, government involvement.

voluntary contracts
Because both parties enter the labor contract freely, one party can use the legal system to enforce the terms of the contract if the other party does not fulfill its responsibilities.

- **Business unionism.** Unlike most other countries where unions are ideological and often tend to pursue political goals, U.S. unions focus on "bread and butter" issues such as wages, benefits, and job security.
- **Job-based unionism.** In contrast to unions in many other countries, which tend to be organized according to political persuasion, U.S. unions tend to be organized by the type of job. Truck drivers are often members of the Teamsters Union and many public school teachers are members of the National Education Association. This is in line with the American notion that interest groups represent the desires of particular constituencies.
- **Collective bargaining.** Under the U.S. collective bargaining system the government takes a neutral or nonintervention role, allowing the players to make the rules that govern their particular workplace. In most other countries, the government is closely involved in labor-management relations. For instance, for almost 70 years the Partido Revolucionario Institucional (PRI) governed Mexico, and unions were an integral part of the government machinery.
- **Voluntary contracts.** Because both parties enter into the labor contract voluntarily, in the United States one party can use the legal system to enforce the terms of the contract if the other party does not fulfill its responsibilities. In many other countries, such as Italy and Sweden, working conditions and employee benefits are codified into labor laws. These laws are enforced by the central government and labor unions often put direct pressure on

the government to modify legislation affecting workers. General strikes to force the government's hand are common around the world, but unheard of in the United States. Recently, unions in France called for a general strike to force the government to pass a 35-hour working week. Likewise, unions in Spain recently called for a general strike to force the government to pass legislation that would make it costly for firms to lay off workers.

■ **Adversarial relations.** U.S. labor laws view management and labor as natural adversaries who want to have a larger share of the firm's profits and who must reach a compromise through collective bargaining. When asked about the objectives of the labor movement, Samuel Gompers (considered the founder of the AFL-CIO) responded with one word: More! For this reason, rules have been put in place so that the pie can be divided peacefully through orderly negotiations. In some other countries, the labor relations system stresses cooperation rather than competition between management and labor. For instance, the German system uses work councils and codetermination to involve workers in decisions at all levels of the organization. Even a company's board of directors generally will include union members. This would be seen as a conflict of interest in the United States. In Japan, enterprise unions work closely with companies for mutual benefits and the union generally has complete access to the company's financial records.

adversarial relations
U.S. labor laws view management and labor as natural adversaries who want to have a larger share of the firm's profits and who must reach a compromise through collective bargaining.

LOC-In 2 Learning Objective Check-In

Hillary, an Asian American, comes from a group of people who suffered widespread discrimination in the past. She has suffered some discrimination from her previous employer, who treated her differently because of her ethnicity. For example, he never assigned her to work with clients, and gave her most of the "backroom" assignments. Hillary is a very capable worker, who has benefited from a government-mandated program that required her new employer to give a conscious effort in hiring Asian Americans, among others.

1. Hillary is a member of a _____ in the United States.
   a. protective class
   b. protected class
   c. control group
   d. direct hire program

2. Hillary's previous employer was practicing _____.
   a. disparate treatment
   b. adverse impact
   c. disparate impact
   d. legal discrimination

3. Hillary is a beneficiary of _____.
   a. protective class status
   b. adverse impact
   c. affirmative action
   d. discrimination in the workplace

■ The Human Resource Management Process

Figure 10.1 on page 292 introduces the key components of the human resource management process. The input that drives the entire process is **strategic HR planning (SHRP)**, which is the development of a vision about where the company wants to be and how it can utilize human resources to get there. By forcing managers to think ahead, SHRP can help a firm identify the difference between "where we are today" and "where we want to be," and to implement human resource programs (often referred to as **HR tactics**) to achieve its vision.

The ultimate objective of SHRP is creating a *sustained competitive advantage. A* common view held by HR managers is based on the **contingency theory** notion that no HR strategy is "good" or "bad" in and of itself but rather depends on the situation or context in which it is used. According to this approach, the consistency or compatibility between HR strategies and other important aspects of the organization, which is known as *fit,* leads to better performance. The

strategic HR planning (SHRP)
The development of a vision about where the company wants to be and how it can use human resources to get there.

HR tactics
The implementation of human resource programs to achieve the firm's vision.

contingency theory
The management theory that there is no "one best way" to manage and organize an organization because situational characteristics, called contingencies, differ; also, the view that no HR strategy is "good" or "bad" in and of itself but rather depends on the situation or context in which it is used.

FIGURE 10.1

The Human Resource Management Process

lack of a fit creates inconsistencies that reduce performance. Management Close-Up 10.1 on page 293 shows how HR strategies fit with the overall business strategy of Genentech.

Human Resource Planning

Human resource planning (HRP) is the process organizational leaders follow to ensure that the company has the right number and the right kinds of people to meet output or service goals. Figure 10.2 summarizes the HRP process. The first step is forecasting **labor demand**, or how many and what type of workers the organization will need in the future. Labor demand is likely to increase as the demand for the company's products increases and to decrease as productivity increases, since fewer labor hours will be needed to produce the same level of output. However,

labor demand
The forecast of how many and what type of workers the organization will need in the future.

FIGURE 10.2

Human Resource Planning

Source: From *Managing Human Resources* by Gomez-Mejia, et al. Copyright © 2012. Reprinted by permission of Pearson Education, Inc., Upper Saddle River, NJ.

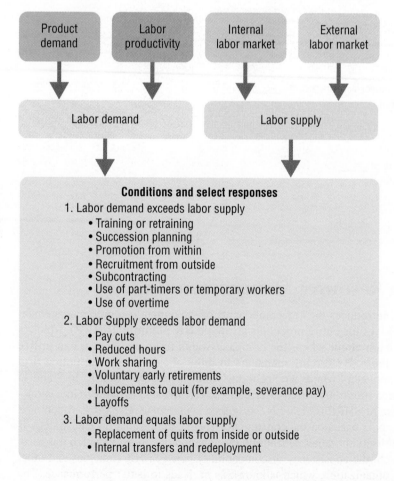

Genentech: Supporting Innovation with HR Practices

Genentech—a biotech company with over 8,000 employees located in San Francisco—has been chosen on several occasions as "The Best Place to Work" by *Fortune* magazine. People at Genentech are driven by a passion to find new drugs for millions of patients who need them, particularly cancer patients.

Human resource strategies at Genentech are designed to accomplish the firm's mission: serving the sick through revolutionary drug discoveries. These HR strategies are summarized below:

- Genentech has created a university-style working environment that facilitates interaction, and this in turn fosters creativity. With its storybook view of San Francisco Bay, the place feels more like a college campus than a pillar of the Fortune 500. Signs point to the North Campus, down by the water, and the South Campus, up on the hill. Employees don't get assignments, they get "appointments." They traverse the grounds by shuttle bus and bicycles provided by the company. Every Friday night there's at least one "ho-ho"—Genentechese for kegger— a tradition that began in the 70s when the workforce was mostly a handful of rowdy postdocs barely out of grad school. At Genentech, every milestone calls for a party and a commemorative T-shirt—and on very big occasions, very big celebrity bands. A year and a half ago, after an unusual run of FDA approvals, the parking lot in front of Building 9 became the site of a rock concert featuring Elton John, Mary J. Blige, and Matchbox 20.
- Genentech minimizes power differentials and symbols of authority that create barriers among employees. For instance, at Genentech nobody dresses up, except on Halloween. This even includes CEO Levinson, often seen in tennis shoes and a black "CLONE or DIE" T-shirt. There are no fancy titles, all offices look alike and regular employees as well as top executives use low-end, metal office furniture.
- Genentech gives employees substantial freedom to pursue their own interests in order to foster creativity and reinforce a "can do" mentality. For example, it tells scientists and engineers to spend fully 20 percent of each work week pursuing pet projects.
- Genentech encourages employees to take risks. As it often happens, what look like promising projects have to be canceled because they don't work or other priorities take their place. In those cases, not only are the researchers not fired; they usually have a say in their next assignments.
- Genentech awards sabbaticals to employees to avoid burnout.
- Genentech has been extremely generous in sharing its success with employees. Ninety-five percent of workers are shareholders, and they have benefited handsomely from the soaring stock.
- Genentech invests a lot of lime, effort, and money in its orientation program to acculturate the rookies. New-hire orientation includes patient lectures, history lessons by old-timers, in-depth sessions on the company's goals, its science—and the fact that the place works "because of all the thousands of little decisions that are made very day," says HR Vice President Denise Smith-Hams.
- Genentech polls its workers weekly to ferret out complaints and monitor any problem areas that might need attention before these grow worse.

Genentech scientists enjoy the collaborative, nonhierarchical work atmosphere. The San Francisco biotech lab was recently chosen as *Fortune* magazine's #1 best place to work in the United States. Ninety-five percent or employees are company shareholders, and no one wears a tie.

- Lastly, Genentech pours tremendous energy into hiring people with the kind of passion it feels it needs to accomplish its strategic goals. In fact, it can take five or six visits and 20 interviews to snag a job. In 2008 the Swiss pharmaceutical company Roche acquired all of Genentech stock in a $46.8 billion deal. Some observers wonder whether Genentech entrepreneurial culture, supported by the HR practices described above, will survive over time under the Roche umbrella, even though Roche has vowed to preserve it. Roche-Genentech is now a huge company, one of the seventh largest pharmaceutical companies in the United States with revenues exceeding $17 billion yearly. Even Roche chairman Franz Humer, who drove the deal, had said a few years before the acquisition, "if we owned all of Genentech we would kill it." (He obviously had a change of heart later when Roche made the decision to acquire Genetech, but it will take several years to see whether this was a wise decision).

Source: Based on C. Scott (2010), "Never again," *Nature Biotechnology*, 28, 131–42; F. T. Mongiol, Jr. (2010), "The human element of supply chain security"; http://www.books.google.com; B. Morris, "No. 1 Genentech". *Fortune*, January 23, 2006. pp. 80–86.

labor supply
The availability of workers with the required skills to meet the firm's labor demand.

skills inventory
A human resource inventory that keeps track of the firm's internal supply of talent by listing employees' education, training, experience, and language abilities; the firm can use this information to identify those eligible for promotion or transfer before trying to fill the position from the external market.

the demand for various types of workers (for example, factory versus clerical) may not increase or decrease at the same rate, so this forecast must be performed for various employee groups.

The second part of the HRP process entails estimating the **labor supply**, or the availability of workers with the required skills to meet the firm's labor demand. The labor supply may come from the internal labor market inside the firm or from the external labor market outside the firm. Many firms keep track of the internal supply of talent by generating a human resource inventory called a **skills inventory**. Employees are asked to list their education, training, experience, and language abilities. This information is used to identify those eligible for promotion or transfer before trying to fill the position from the external market. Such a process can reduce recruitment costs and increase employee commitment to the firm.

As shown in Figure 10.2, the HR planning process may lead to very different organizational responses. If labor demand exceeds supply, the firm may in vest in training workers, promoting from within, and actively recruiting employees to meet projected needs. On the other hand, if there is an excess labor supply, the HR department may plan cutbacks in the workforce through work sharing, voluntary early retirements, and layoffs.

Through careful planning some firms develop creative means to avoid or minimize layoffs, which are costly in terms of employee morale and loss of human capital. For example, these firms have been able to minimize layoffs in past recessions by using alternative ways to save money:

- Hewlett-Packard delayed employee raises for several months and awarded no bonuses for its top executives.
- First Union asked employees to limit the number of color copies they make and restricted first-class travel to redeye flights.
- Charles Schwab cut salaries for senior executives and gave smaller bonuses to the rank and file. The brokerage firm also rationed travel and entertainment dollars and reviewed advertising contracts.
- Xerox grounded corporate jets and cut back on catered food and free coffee to prevent more layoffs.[6]

LOC-In 3 Learning Objective Check-In

Morristown Motors usually recruits from the four regional trade schools to fill its entry-level certified mechanic positions. In recent years, the company has been experiencing higher levels of service orders from its clients and has even expanded its client base by about 15 percent every two years. The firm is considering hiring more entry-level mechanics in future years than it has in the past. Fortunately for the firm, this profession has grown popular in the region, and the schools are turning out more qualified applicants each year.

1. Because the firm is expanding, Morristown's hiring manager can forecast an increase in the firm's _____.
   a. cost of new hires
   b. labor demand
   c. labor supply
   d. contingency theory

2. Because the region's schools are turning out more qualified applicants each year, Morristown's hiring manager can forecast an increase in the firm's _____.
   a. cost of new hires
   b. labor demand
   c. labor supply
   d. cost of recruiting workers

recruitment
The process of generating a pool of qualified candidates for a particular job.

job specification
The knowledge, skills, and abilities needed to successfully perform the job.

job analysis
The systematic gathering and organizing of information about the tasks, duties, and responsibilities of various jobs.

Staffing Process

Human resource planning guides the staffing process, or the hiring of employees to meet the firm's labor needs. The staffing process has three components: recruitment, selection, and socialization, or orientation.

RECRUITMENT Generating a pool of qualified candidates for a particular job is the **recruitment** component of staffing. It requires a **job specification**, which identifies the qualifications necessary for effective job performance. Most firms conduct a **job analysis** in which they systematically gather and organize information about the tasks, duties, and responsibilities of various jobs. While there are many job analysis techniques, virtually all of them lead to a **job description**, which is a formal document that identifies, defines, and describes the duties, responsibilities, and working conditions associated with a job. A properly conducted job analysis ensures that the hiring process is job-related in case of a legal challenge.

Once the qualifications for effective job performance have been identified, the HR department looks for recruitment sources that are most likely to produce the best candidates. Most searches start with current employees, utilizing skill inventories if available. The second major source of recruits is referrals from current employees. Both sources give HR more information about applicants than would going outside. One disadvantage is that the firm may not attract a diverse pool of applicants, creating potential equal employment opportunity (EEO) problems. Other sources of recruits include former employees, advertisements, employment agencies, colleges, and customers. Recruitment over the Internet is becoming more prevalent and occurs at broad job search engines such as Monster.com, which includes all types of positions. Specialized job search engines such as Dice.com target information technology professionals; Dice.com is advertised as "a high-traffic job board with over 350,000 IT professionals searching every week."[7]

One way to increase recruitment effectiveness is a *realistic* **job preview** in which potential applicants are provided with honest information about the positive and negative aspects of the job. It can reduce selection expenses because individuals can "self-select" into or out of positions based on realistic job information.

An emergent trend to attract potential recruits without incurring additional costs (such as higher salaries) is to offer prospective candidates greater work flexibility than offered by other employers. This approach is being used by Best Buy apparently with great success (see Management Close-Up 10.2, "Reworking Work").

job description

A formal document that identifies, defines, and describes the duties, responsibilities, and working conditions.

job preview

Information about the positive and negative aspects of the job that is provided to potential applicants.

MANAGEMENT CLOSE-UP 10.2   THEME: **DEALING WITH CHANGE**

Reworking Work

There is a growing trend for firms to allow employees to decide how, when, and where they get the job done. Approximately 45 percent of U.S. employees now determine their own starting and quitting time around a core of regular working hours. Best Buy, for instance, has introduced a program called "Results-Only Work Environment" or ROWE. In ROWE, most of the rules, restrictions, and expectations of a traditional work environment—such as keeping regular hours and showing up in the office every morning—are discarded. Salaried employees are only required to work as many hours as necessary to get the work done and they are given much freedom to decide when and where.

The freedom, employees say, is changing their lives. They don't know if they work fewer hours—they've stopped counting—but they are more productive. That's welcome news for a company that hopes its employees will give it a competitive edge. And employees have adapted well to the new system.

Best Buy uses its new work flexibility approach as a major selling point to convince people to apply for jobs and get those who pass the selection screening to sign up. Employees report in attitude surveys that they have better relationships with family and friends, express more loyalty to the company and feel more focused and energized about their work.

Sources: Based on P. J. Kiger (2010), "Throwing out the rules of work," http://www.workforce.com, 2011; A. Kjerulf, "Chief Happiness Officer," http://positivesharing.com, 2010; E. Diener, J. F. Helliwell, and D. Kahneman (2010), "International differences in well being," in: A. E. Clark (ed) (2010), *Work, Jobs and Well Being Across the Millennium*. London, U.K.; Oxford University Press; J. Thottam, "Reworking Work." *Time*, July 5, 2005, pp. 50–55.

The flexible nature of Jennifer Janssen's job in the finance department of Best Buy demonstrates the company's commitment to an experiment in turning around its former high-stress culture. Flexible hours, working from home, increased autonomy, and goals that focus on accomplishments rather than time spent at the desk are transforming the lives of the electronics retailer's employees.

FIGURE 10.3

Performance Consequences of Selection Decision

Selection decision

	Hire	No hire
High	1 — Right decision	2 — Wrong decision
Low	3 — Wrong decision	4 — Right decision

Future performance

FIGURE 10.3

Performance Consequences of Selection Decision

selection

The screening process used to decide which job applicant to hire.

validity

The measurement of how well a technique used to assess candidates is related to performance in the job.

content validity

The measurement that the selection process represents the actual activities or knowledge required to successfully perform the job.

empirical validity

Statistical evidence that the selection method distinguishes between higher and lower performing employees.

reliability

The consistency of results from the selection method.

SELECTION An effective recruitment effort should create a pool of qualified applicants. As the word implies, **selection** is the screening process used to decide which individuals to hire. The ultimate objective is to hire people who will perform well based on the criteria the firm uses to evaluate employees. No selection process is foolproof. Some hires will turn out to be mistakes and other candidates who would have made good employees may be rejected. An organization with a high proportion of individuals who fall into these categories, as shown in Figure 10.3, is likely to see much lower job performance on average than an organization that consistently makes the right hiring decisions.

Valid and reliable selection techniques help reduce the proportion of errors and increase the proportion of correct hiring decisions. **Validity** is how well a technique used to assess candidates is related to performance in the. job. A technique that is not job-related is useless and, as noted earlier, is also illegal if it results in discrimination. In fact, documenting validity is essential to a legal defense of job discrimination.

Validity can be demonstrated in two ways. **Content validity** means that the selection process represents the actual activities or knowledge required to successfully perform the job. Many firms require applicants to perform tasks similar to those they will carry out on the job if hired. For instance, if a minimum requirement for a job is possession of a valid pilot's license, a flight simulator may be used to select the best pilot. **Empirical validity** means that there is statistical evidence that the selection method distinguishes between higher and lower performing employees. For instance, a selection method that consistently predicts which individuals fall into boxes 1 and 4 in Figure 10.3 would have high empirical validity. Lack of empirical validity means that the selection method cannot predict who is going to be a better or worse performer.

Reliability It is important to measure the consistency or **reliability** of results of the selection method. For instance, if multiple interviewers reach entirely different conclusions about each job applicant, the method is not reliable. Or if test scores for the same applicant vary dramatically from one day to the next, the test is not reliable. In other words, reliability is an indicator of how much random error there is in the measure being used. Lack of reliability is equivalent to a speed indicator on a car that is 10 to 30 miles per hour above or below the actual speed. Because the reading is unreliable, the position of the speed needle is not helpful in assessing how fast the car is traveling.

Selection Tools as Predictors of Job Performance An organization may use a variety of selection tools to screen out applicants and attempt to increase the proportion of good performers, as shown in Manager's Notebook 10.2. Besides the technical aspect of the selection procedures discussed earlier (namely validity and reliability) firms should also consider applicant acceptance of the selection procedure. A procedure that applicants believe is inappropriate or perceived to be arbitrary is likely to generate complaints and some of these complaints may result in costly litigation. Table 10.3 shows how applicants rate the effectiveness and fairness of selection methods in the United States and Netherlands, suggesting that even when comparing two similar Western countries, cultural differences play a role in these perceptions.

MANAGER'S NOTEBOOK 10.2

Selection Tools

- *Application forms* are used almost universally. They provide information that shows whether the candidate meets minimum qualification requirements as identified in the job analysis. Firms can also use information from application forms to determine whether the applicant would qualify for other openings when they occur. A *biodata form* asks a series of specific questions about the candidate's background, experiences, and preferences. Biodata have been found to have moderate validity in predicting job performance.
- *Letters of recommendation* typically are very positive—most people are reluctant to put negative information in writing. Their value thus is limited as a predictor of future performance, but they still may be helpful, particularly in finding a job match for the employer.
- *Ability tests* measure a wide range of abilities, from manual dexterity to verbal skills. *Cognitive ability tests* measure reasoning skills in a particular area, such as math or writing, and may be a good predictor of job performance. *General cognitive ability* tests measure general intelligence or ability to learn. Ability tests can be valid, but they may also be culturally biased and result in a disproportionate number of minorities being rejected.
- *Performance simulation tests* attempt to mimic the job experience and are based on actual job behaviors or *work samples.* These tests are particularly helpful for hiring managers. An *assessment center* is a set of simulated tasks, such as making business decisions with limited information. *In-basket exercises* provide memos, reports, requests, data, and messages for candidates to work through. Candidates can then be evaluated by the quality of their decisions and of their process. Performance simulation tests are highly predictive for managerial jobs and may identify hidden strengths and weaknesses.
- *Personality tests* are used to measure enduring traits, such as extroversion, that can affect how applicants relate to others and their basic outlook on life.
- *Psychological tests* gauge an individual's values, motivation, attitudes, and so on. These tests ask questions such as, "To what extent do you agree that luck plays a key role for success in life?" These types of tests are used to select employees who presumably are more motivated, more open to new experiences, and more capable of working independently without close supervision. The validity and reliability of a particular test or situation may not have been established, however, and the firm must be careful not to delve into applicants' personal lives.
- *Honesty tests* are growing in use among retail chains, banks, and other service-sector companies to screen out applicants who may steal from the employer.
- *Interviews* are the most frequently used selection technique. Ironically, the interview is often unreliable and a poor predictor of job performance. Interviews are subject to many overt and subtle biases, but they can be a useful selection device. Excellent guides are available to help managers be objective during the interview process and keep it job-related. For example, the National Federation of Independent Business and the Atlantic Legal Foundation recently developed a handbook on federal employment laws, including a list of questions managers should never ask in job interviews.
- *Physical exams* once were widely used, but their use has declined. Employers cannot discriminate on the basis of disability. Furthermore, social attitudes toward the disabled have changed dramatically in recent years. Employers are more willing to hire employees with overt physical problems that are easily spotted in a cursory physical exam. The cost of physical exams has increased enormously, and employer health insurance programs such as health maintenance organizations typically do not exclude prior conditions that may be uncovered during a physical examination.

Sources: Based on C. J. Konig, U. Christine Klehe, and M. Berchtold (2010), "Reasons for being selective when choosing personnel selection procedures." *International Journal of Selection and Assessment*, 18 (1), 17–27; J. C. Cerrito and G. N. McLean (2010), "Developing content validity selection procedures," *Performance Improvement*, 49 (2), 29–35; L. R. Gomez-Mejia, D. B. Balkin, and R. Cardy, *Managing Human Resources* (2012), Upper Saddle River, NJ: Prentice Hall.

LOC-In 4 Learning Objective Check-In

Sydney Corp's engineering department conducts analysis in which they systematically gather and organize information about the tasks and responsibilities of each of its engineering positions. This is meant to help develop a formal document that identifies and defines these duties and responsibilities, as well as any working conditions associated with each job. These factors help Sydney Corp. in generating a pool of qualified candidates for each of these jobs.

1. In the example, the _____ systematically gathers and organizes information about the tasks and responsibilities of each position.
   a. HR strategy
   b. job specification
   c. job description
   d. job analysis

2. The _____ is the formal document discussed in this example.
   a. contingency plan
   b. job specification
   c. job analysis
   d. job description

3. _____ involves generating a pool of qualified applicants for a particular job.
   a. Contingency planning
   b. Recruitment
   c. Job analysis
   d. Job placement

If properly conducted, interviews can provide useful information and help select the best candidates. Skills for Managing 10.1 provides an exercise to sharpen your interviewing skills by applying a set of good interviewing practices.

Interviews are the most often used screening tool, but they, too, have a variety of problems, which are shown in Table 10.4.

To avoid some of these shortcomings, many organizations are turning to a particular type of interviewing technique known as the *situational* or *behavioral interview*. This type of interview requires that the applicant role-play a particular situation—for instance, calming down an irate customer. Behavioral interviews seem to do a much better job of predicting future performance than other selection methods. On the other hand, when professionally conducted with the help of a consultant, these interviews can be rather expensive, costing between $245 and $500 per

TABLE 10.3 Cross-Cultural Perceptions of Selection Tools

The following table presents 10 major types of selection methods. For each method, an average score is listed for 150 U.S. respondents and 167 Dutch respondents. These average scores are the mean ratings given by respondents regarding the perceived effectiveness and fairness of each method. These evaluations were made using a rating scale of 1 (least favorable) to 7 (most favorable).

	Average Perception	
Selection Method	United States	Netherlands
Interviews	5.39	5.08
Resumes	5.37	4.68
Work-sample tests	5.26	5.10
Biographical information	4.59	4.24
Written ability tests	4.50	4.15
References	4.38	4.34
Personality tests	3.50	4.42
Honesty tests	3.41	3.26
Personal connections/network	3.29	3.04
Graphology	1.95	1.95

The table shows that in the United States job-focused measures are viewed more favorably than person-focused measures—personality tests, honesty tests, graphology, and getting a job based on who you know. As with the U.S. respondents, the Dutch viewed graphology, personal contacts, and honesty tests less favorably than other methods. However, they viewed personality tests more positively than did their U.S. counterparts. The more positive Dutch reaction to personality tests may be due to the Netherlands having a culture that is more accepting of personality being a legitimate concern of employers because it purportedly influences how well employees will blend with their peers. In the United States personality tends to be viewed as a private, nonjob-related matter that employers should not use to determine who to hire or reject (except perhaps in some very specific cases, such as sales).

Source: Adapted with permission from L. R. Gomez-Mejia, D. B. Balkin, and R. Cardy (2012) *Managing Human Resources*, Pearson Education, Upper Saddle River, NJ

SKILLS FOR MANAGING 10.1

Interviewing Skills

The objective of the interview is to elicit information from applicants so that the company can choose the applicant who is best qualified to perform the tasks the job requires. This exercise helps you develop interviewing skills for selection purposes.

In this exercise, an interviewer for a large retail store is on campus to recruit students for management trainee jobs after graduation. There are several job openings. The exercise proceeds through the following steps:

1. The class is divided into pairs of students. One student in each pair will act as interviewer and the other will play the role of applicant. The applicant should create a curriculum vitae (either real or fictitious) before class and provide a copy to the interviewer.
2. The interviewer from each pair interviews the applicant for 10 minutes in front of the entire class.
3. The class rates each pair using the interviewer skills checklist. For each item in the checklist, assign a rating of o (very poor) to 10 (outstanding).
4. At the end of each interview, the class discusses how effective it was by answering the discussion questions at the end of this exercise.

Interview Skills Checklist

Rate each of the following skills demonstrated by the interviewer on a 0 (very poor) to 10 (outstanding) scale. Maximum = 100.

_____ Was the interviewer prepared? (Lack of preparation is the most common, and costly, mistake interviewers make. Use the interviewee's resume to create an interview agenda and review it before the interview.)

_____ Did the interviewer put the applicant at ease? (Few things are more unsettling to an applicant than being ushered into an office and waiting for the interviewer to be ready. Greet applicants, and put them at ease with some pleasant small talk before moving on to the interview questions.)

_____ Did the interviewer make snap judgments or treat the applicant as a stereotype? (Stereotyping is bad for the manager and bad for the company. Curb your tendency to rush to judgment. Always keep in mind that you are dealing with an individual, not a type.)

_____ Did the interviewer ask results-oriented questions? (Ask questions that will uncover not only what the job candidate has done but also what the results of the person's actions have been.)

_____ Did the interviewer allow the applicant to pause? (Many interviewers jump in during any pause in the dialogue to discuss their own views on management and the company. The applicant may be absorbing information before forming a question or comment, which the interviewer should wait for.)

_____ Did the interviewer stick to job-related issues? (The interviewer's questions should be directly relevant to the tasks the employee is expected to carry out in the future.)

_____ Did the interviewer avoid questions that may increase the risk of being sued for discrimination in hiring? (Litigious questions include queries about children, disabilities, age, and maiden name, as well as seemingly innocent questions such as, "Are you originally from this area?" which may be misused or misinterpreted.)

_____ Did the interviewer ask simulated questions? (These are questions that try to elicit from candidates how they would respond to particular work situations.)

_____ Did the interviewer establish two-way communication? (The applicant should be given a chance to ask questions about the job, the company, and the long-term career prospects within the company.)

_____ Did the interviewer close definitively? (Don't let the session drift on until both parties begin to flounder about or lose interest; don't close it abruptly when interrupted by a phone call or a colleague. Plan a time limit and bring the interview to a natural close rather than letting an outside event terminate the conversation prematurely.)

Discussion Questions

1. Assess the effectiveness of the interviewing approach used by various interviewers. How well did the applicants handle the questions raised by the interviewers?
2. Use the skills checklist total to determine whether a particular interviewer was better than others. Did one applicant handle the interview questions better than the others?

Source: Reprinted from *88 Mistakes Interviewers Make and How to Avoid Them* by Auren Uris. Copyright © 1988 AMACOM Books. Reprinted with the permission of AMACOM Books, via Copyright Clearance Center.

interview. Yet, the investment may be worthwhile for many critical positions. Skills for Managing 10.2 asks you to practice developing and conducting this type of interview.

Another recent trend in personnel selection in the United States is allowing the applicant to display his or her skills by performing certain jobs, often for little or no pay. The performance is used as the basis for hiring instead of written paper-and-pencil exams or other types of tests. This selection practice is routine in some countries. For instance, German firms have long relied on apprenticeships (roughly similar to what are called "internships" in the United States) to make hiring decisions; the firm keeps only those who performed well during the trial period.

TABLE 10.4 Common Problems with Selection Interviews

1. Interviewers may not agree on their assessment of a candidate—their evaluation thus may say more about the interviewers than their subject.

2. The interviewer may form an overall impression of the applicant in the first two or three minutes of the interview. Snap decisions reduce the validity of the interview, because judgments are made based on very limited information.

3. Interviewers may hold a stereotype of the ideal candidates and give lower assessments to individuals who don't fit it.

4. The interview may proceed haphazardly depending on the applicant's response to open-ended questions, such as "Where would you like to be 10 years from now?" and "Tell me about yourself." The applicant's answers may trigger questions different from those asked of other candidates, with different information thus available for evaluating them.

5. The interviewer may view more favorably those candidates who are like himself or herself in terms of background, attitudes, gender, ethnicity, and so on.

6. The order in which applicants are interviewed may affect the evaluation.

7. What an interviewer perceives as negative information, such as an applicant revealing an upcoming marriage to someone who works in a different state, may outweigh the positive information.

8. The interviewer's style may affect the applicant's responses. For instance, an aggressive interviewer may intimidate an individual who is shy, even if this trait is not job-related.

9. The interviewer may not make careful written notes of the information provided by the applicant and may just have a global perception of the applicant after the interview has concluded.

Source: From *Managing Human Resources* by Gomez-Mejia, et al. Copyright © 2012. Reprinted by permission of Pearson Education, Inc., Upper Saddle River, NJ.

ORIENTATION An *orientation program* helps new employees to learn more about the company and what is expected of them in the job. The program should also be designed to help reduce the initial anxiety of the transition into the company. An orientation program should also familiarize employees with co-workers and provide the opportunity to systematically learn about work rules, personnel policies, benefits, equipment, location of the copy room, as well as how to get supplies.

Several studies show that most people find starting a new job to be stressful. Stress may be compounded by other changes in a person's life, such as having lost a previous job, going through a divorce, or moving into a new town. One important function of orientation is to help employees cope with stress. John Wanous, a well-known researcher, suggests using the Realistic Orientation Programs for New Employee Stress, or ROPES, which provides realistic information about the job and the organization, gives general support and reassurance, demonstrates coping skills, and identifies potential stressors. This program helps employees become fully functional more quickly and reduces turnover.[8]

SKILLS FOR MANAGING 10.2

Create and Conduct Your Own Behavioral Interview

Assume that you are part of a team of four managers asked to develop a situational or behavioral interview for the following positions:

- Customer representative
- First-line supervisor of a clerical pool
- Human resource director
- Marketing director

Once you develop a behavioral or situational interview for each, you are asked to role-play one or two interviews for each position. The instructor will then assign students to serve as interviewees. At the end of the exercise, the entire class will discuss the effectiveness of the behavioral interview.

Employee Training

Training is a planned effort to provide employees with specific skills to improve their performance. Effective training can also improve morale and increase an organization's potential. Poor, inappropriate, or inadequate training can be a source of frustration for everyone involved. Unfortunately, training programs often are affected by passing fads. For example, many firms in the late 1990s sent key employees to newly developed e-commerce programs that were offered in business schools at Carnegie-Mellon in Pittsburgh, Old Dominion in Norfolk, Virginia, Stanford in Palo Alto, and dozens of other colleges and universities. By 1999, these schools were earning at least $24.3 million in revenue from such courses. In 2001, many of the programs were struggling and companies doubted their value as Internet business faltered. Companies also suspected that e-commerce training, instead of being something new or unique, was really a principles-of-marketing course in a different format.[9] During this decade there is renewed interest in Internet-based training but there is greater sensitivity as to when it might be appropriate (for instance, a step-by-step technical training course) and when it might not (for instance, human relations training for supervisors).

For a training program to be effective, it must encompass the entire training process, which consists of three major phases. As shown in Figure 10.4, the first phase is **needs assessment**, a determination of whether training is needed. This requires an examination of the organization's plans to expand, diversify into new products, establish an overseas joint venture, or undertake other activities that may require employees with additional skills.

Next is the **development and conduct of training phase**. Making sure that training solves an organizational problem or need is critical to ensuring that it will be beneficial to the company. The first major decision is the location of the training. **On-the-job training (OJT)** takes place in the actual work setting under the guidance of an experienced worker, supervisor, or trainer. Job rotation, apprenticeships, and internships are all forms of on-the-job training. For instance, new hires at Baptist Health Care wear an ID badge sticker for the first 90 days so that co-workers can offer a helping hand.[10] At Sherwin Williams about 600 new college hires receive training in different divisions and functions each year. **Off-the-job training** takes place away from the employment site. Common examples are formal courses, simulations, and role playing. One major advantage of off-the-job training is that employees can concentrate on the training without the interruptions that are likely to occur on the job, which facilitates learning and retention. A variety of presentation techniques and approaches may be used for off-the-job training:

- *Slides* and *videotapes* are relatively inexpensive. They can be an excellent way to stimulate discussion and raise questions. An HR representative should be available to offer more detailed explanations.
- *Computer-assisted instruction (CAI)* lets trainees learn at their own pace— the computer is always available and never becomes tired, bored, or irritable. CAI programs will limit flexibility in that the computer cannot answer questions that have not been

needs assessment
A training tool that is used to determine whether training is needed.

development and conduct of training phase
A stage in the training process that ensures training will solve an organizational problem or need; this step is critical to ensuring that training will be beneficial to the organization.

on-the-job training (OJT)
Training that takes place in the actual work setting under the guidance of an experienced worker, supervisor, or trainer.

off-the-job training
Training that takes place away from the employment site.

FIGURE 10.4

The Training Process

Source: From *Managing Human Resources* by Gomez-Mejia, et al. Copyright © 2012. Reprinted by permission of Pearson Education, Inc., Upper Saddle River, NJ.

Needs assessment phase
- Organization needs
- Task needs
- Person needs

Development & conduct of training
- Location
- Presentation
- Type

Evaluation

preprogrammed, and some employees may not be comfortable or well versed in using computers effectively.

- *Classroom lectures* provide specific information and raise issues for group discussion, facilitating problem solving. However, people may forget what they learn in a lecture unless they practice it.
- *Simulations* duplicate tasks or activities normally encountered on the job. Firms use simulations when the information to be mastered is complex, the equipment used on the job is expensive, and the costs of making the wrong decision are high.
- *Virtual reality* provides three-dimensional electronic environments for tasks that require rehearsal and practice or the visualization of objects and processes where many factors need to be monitored simultaneously.
- *Vestibule training* provides training on the same equipment the employees will use at work. They can learn how to use the equipment without disrupting ongoing operations at the workplace.
- *Cross-functional training* trains employees to work effectively with employees in other areas. Two commonly used forms of cross-functional training are *team training,* which helps employees learn to work effectively in groups, and *brainstorming,* which helps employees learn creative problem solving by encouraging them to generate ideas openly, without the fear of judgment.

On-the-job training is more appropriate in certain situations. Manager's Notebook 10.3 lists some situations when OJT should be used.

The final phase of the training process is **evaluation**. From time to time, an organization should reexamine training methods to determine whether they provide the expected benefits and meet the needs identified in phase I. Effectiveness may be measured in monetary terms (e.g., dollars saved by reducing the number of defects) or nonmonetary terms (e.g., fewer employee complaints). The most important consideration is that the evaluation criteria should reflect the needs that the training was supposed to address.

In recent years, many companies have introduced ethics training programs or require that prospective hires, particularly middle- and top-level executives, show evidence that they have undergone such training. This is clearly one of the most rapidly growing areas in executive training programs, whether conducted in-house or by educational institutions. For instance, one such program requires that the trainee actually visit with executives who are in prison to learn firsthand what landed them there.

evaluation
The organization's reexamination of whether training is providing the expected benefits and meeting the identified needs.

MANAGER'S NOTEBOOK 10.3

When to Use OJT

Ask these questions when deciding whether on-the-job training should be undertaken. If your answer is "yes," the training generally should be done on the job.

1. Is participatory learning necessary?
2. Is one-on-one training called for?
3. Does only a small group of employees need training?
4. Is the cost of training the employees away from the job more than the benefit expected from the training?
5. Is the training not appropriate for a classroom setting?
6. Are safety factors and equipment requirements not available away from the job site?
7. Does the training have to be done immediately?
8. Does the training have to be done to meet new safety requirements that have just been implemented?
9. Is disrupting ongoing work by pulling employees away from the job too costly?

10. Is the training designed for an infrequently performed task?
11. Does the employee have to meet defined standards to obtain certification or qualification?
12. Is the equipment needed for training too large to move or not moveable?
13. Is the equipment needed for training too fragile or carefully calibrated to move?
14. Are the materials required for training also part of the overall job site?
15. Are the training procedures or equipment too dangerous to use off site?
16. Does the training involve sensitive information that must be kept in a secure environment?

Source: From C. A. Mullaney and L. D. Trask, "Show Them the Ropes," *Technical & Skills Training,* October 1992, pp. 8–11. Reprinted with permission.

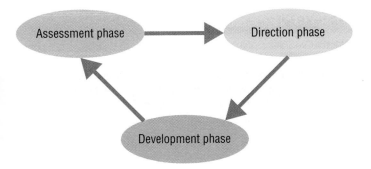

FIGURE 10.5

The Career Development Process

Source: From *Managing Human Resources* by Gomez-Mejia, et al. Copyright © 2012. Reprinted by permission of Pearson Education, Inc., Upper Saddle River, NJ.

Career Development

Career development is a long-term effort in which the organization helps employees utilize their full potential. It is not a one-shot training program or a series of workshops. Instead there are three major phases—assessment, direction, and development—as shown in Figure 10.5.

ASSESSMENT   The **assessment phase** involves helping employees choose career paths that are realistically attainable and fit with the employee's temperament and personality. The assessment phase includes determining what obstacles they need to overcome to succeed. Some companies use a combination of tools to accomplish this, including performance appraisal data from supervisors, psychological tests, assessment centers, interest inventories, and skill inventories.

DIRECTION   The next phase, the **direction phase**, includes determining the steps employees must take to reach their career goals. Appropriate direction requires understanding of the *sequence* of jobs employees are expected to fill over time—that is, identifying jobs that are logically connected and that offer increasing responsibility. A job analysis may provide a sound basis for creating a logical career path so that skills learned on a job prepare the employee for the next higher level of responsibility. The **career path** presents the steps and a plausible time frame for accomplishing them.

Firms use a variety of approaches to assist employees in the direction phase, including:

- *Promotability forecasts,* judgments by managers about the advancement potential of subordinates.
- *Succession planning,* the identification and development of replacements for jobs that are expected to open up.
- *Individual career counseling,* one-on-one sessions to examine the person's present and possible next career stages.
- *Job posting systems,* in which all vacancies are listed on a bulletin board, in a company newsletter, or in a phone recording or computer system.
- *Career resource centers,* where career development materials such as workbooks, tapes, and texts are located in a central location, such as the HR department.

DEVELOPMENT   The final phase, the **development phase**, outlines actions designed to help the employee grow and learn the necessary skills to move along the desired career paths. Some common programs include:

- **Mentoring,** or the developmental activities carried out by more seasoned employees to help those who are learning the ropes. Mentoring takes many forms, including role modeling, sharing contacts, bouncing ideas, advising, and giving general support. It may be formal or informal. Most firms expect senior employees, particularly those in managerial positions, to act as mentors.
- **Coaching,** which is the ongoing, mostly spontaneous, meetings between managers and employees to discuss career goals, roadblocks, and opportunities.
- **Job rotation** is a formal program in which employees are assigned to different jobs to expand their skills base and to learn more about various parts of the organization.
- **Tuition assistance programs,** which support the employee's education and development by covering the cost of tuition and other fees for seminars, workshops, and continuing education programs.

assessment phase
A career development step in which employees are helped to choose personally fitting career paths that are realistically attainable and to determine any obstacles they need to overcome to succeed.

direction phase
The step in career development that involves determining the steps employees must take to reach their career goals.

career path
The steps for advancement to a career goal and a plausible time frame for accomplishing them.

development phase
A career development step in which actions are designed to help the employee grow and learn the necessary skills to move along the desired career path.

mentoring
Developmental activities carried out by more seasoned employees to help those who are learning the ropes.

coaching
Ongoing, mostly spontaneous, meetings between managers and their employees to discuss career goals, roadblocks, and available opportunities.

job rotation
A formal program in which employees are assigned to different jobs to expand their skills base and to learn more about various parts of the organization.

tuition assistance programs
Support by the firm for employees' education and development by covering the cost of tuition and other fees for seminars, workshops, and continuing education programs.

MANAGEMENT IS EVERYONE'S BUSINESS 10.3

WORKING AS AN INDIVIDUAL   Whether you are a manager or an employee, to a large extent your success depends on your ability to take advantage of the HR opportunities the firm offers. You need to use appraisal feedback constructively, take courses to keep your skills up to date, learn the important criteria for promotion and pay allocation decisions, and join teams that best complement your interests. In the end, it is your responsibility to make the "right moves" to position yourself well. What it takes to succeed may vary by firm; successful individuals learn how to identify this and act accordingly. As an individual employee you should:

- Assume responsibility for your own career, making your superiors know what you would like to do in the future and how you could contribute more.
- Try to develop skills that fit with the organization's needs, going beyond the demands of your present position. Most firms value employee potential to do things that might not be in current job description.
- Cooperate within your peers, always lending a helping hand. Most firms highly value employees who are seen as team players.
- Show respect for those around you, regardless of how different they are from you.
- Try to develop a reputation as a "can do" person who will to his or her best to solve problems and unexpected issues without close supervision.

Management Is Everyone's Business 10.3 offers a set of recommendations that individual employees might wish to follow to enhance their career success within the organization.

Performance Appraisal

One of the keys to both individual and organizational success is providing quality feedback about individual performance. Performance appraisals have three important objectives. First, they open two-way communication channels so that supervisors may convey to employees what is expected of them and employees have an opportunity to tell supervisors what is on their minds. Second, they provide constructive feedback to employees so that positive steps may be taken to capitalize on strengths and reduce weaknesses; performance appraisal is an integral part of the career

---

LOC-In 5 Learning Objective Check-In

Gene is a manager who works in the HR department: He helps coordinate various programs for his firm. For instance, he coordinates a program that familiarizes workers with the firm by providing them the opportunity to learn about rules, policies, benefits, and which resources are available in a particular job. Gene also coordinates programs with each functional department whereby new hires or veteran workers who are entering new phases in their careers with the orgization can learn job-specific methods for completing assigned tasks. Lastly, Gene helps consult with employees, one-on-one, in determining the steps they must take to reach their career goals.

1. What is the first type of program Gene is involved in coordinating?
   a. Bureaucratic management
   b. Orientation
   c. On-the-job training (OJT)
   d. Assessment

2. The _____ program allows each functional department to ensure that workers are up to date with job-specific methods for completing their work.
   a. contingency plan
   b. training
   c. orientation
   d. career development

3. Gene's consultation with individual workers is part of the _____ phase of career development.
   a. performance appraisal
   b. assessment
   c. development
   d. direction

SKILLS FOR MANAGING 10.3

Performance Appraisal Feedback Skills

Constructive feedback is critical to effective performance management, with evaluative communication directed at the employee's performance and not at the person. Skills in providing feedback can help you uncover reasons for a performance problem and create an effective solution and performance improvement. This exercise, which helps you develop feedback skills, begins with the following steps:

1. The class is divided into pairs of students. One student in each pair will act as supervisor and the other will play the role of the employee.
2. Each student pair will meet outside class to prepare and discuss a performance problem, based on any personal work experiences, experiences heard from other people, or personal observation.
3. In front of the class, the supervisor and employee in each pair discuss the performance problem for 10 minutes. The class rates each of the supervisor-employee pairs using the performance feedback skills checklist. For each item in the checklist, students in class will assign a rating of 0 (very poor) to 10 (outstanding).
4. At the end of each pair's meeting in front of the class, the class discusses the feedback approaches used and then answers the discussion questions at the end of this exercise.

Performance Feedback Skills Checklist

Rate each of the following skills demonstrated by the supervisor-employee pair from 0 (very poor) to 10 (outstanding). Maximum = 100.

_____ Did the pair present perceptions, reactions, and opinions as such and not as facts?

_____ Did the pair refer to the problem relative to performance, behavior, or outcomes, not to the individual as a person?

_____ Did the pair provide feedback in terms of specific, observable behavior, not general behavior?

_____ Did the pair talk in terms of established criteria, probable outcomes, or possible improvement, as opposed to being good or bad?

_____ Did the pair discuss performance and the specific behaviors that appear to be contributing to or limiting full effectiveness?

_____ Did the pair avoid overload terms (for example, _crabby, mess-up, rip-off,_ or _stupid)_ that can produce emotional reactions and defensiveness?

_____ Did the pair concentrate on things that the employee or supervisor can control, and focus on ways the employee can use the feedback to improve performance?

_____ Did the pair react defensively or emotionally rather than trying to convince, reason, or supply additional information?

_____ Did the pair give each other feedback in a manner that communicates acceptance of the employee as a worthwhile person and of that person's right be an individual?

_____ Was feedback tied to specific development plans that could capitalize on strengths and minimize performance weaknesses?

Discussion Questions

1. Describe the feedback approach used by various supervisors. Was there an approach that you felt was particularly effective or ineffective? Why?
2. Use the checklist to determine if a particular pair was more effective than others. If there is significant disagreement in the class, discuss the reasons why.

---

development process. (See Skills for Managing 10.3.) Finally, a performance appraisal helps the manager decide who should be paid more based on individual contributions. The numerous techniques that measure performance can be classified by the type of judgment required (relative or absolute). They can also be classified by the focus of the measure (trait, behavior, or outcome).

JUDGMENT APPROACHES TO PERFORMANCE APPRAISAL Performance appraisals may use relative judgment or absolute judgment approaches.

In **relative judgments**, employees are compared to one another. Supervisors may be asked to rank subordinates from best to worst, or they may be asked to create _a forced distribution_ by classifying a given percentage of employees into various groups, such as exceptional, standard, room for improvement, and not adequate.

relative judgments
A performance appraisal approach in which employees are compared to one another.

The advantage of the relative judgment approach is it requires supervisors to make difficult choices. Supervisors who want their subordinates to like them typically prefer to rate most as excellent, which may not be valid. The relative judgment approach has serious disadvantages, however. Performance distributions may vary among units: the performance of a person at the top in one unit may rank at the bottom of another. These systems can force managers to make unrealistic performance distinctions, which creates dissatisfaction in the workforce. They may also reduce cooperation among workers, which will have a negative impact on the performance of the entire unit.

absolute judgments
A performance appraisal approach in which the performance of employees is evaluated against performance standards, and not in comparison to each other.

Appraisal methods using **absolute judgments** evaluate the performance of employees against performance standards, and not in comparison to other employees. There are several advantages to this approach. The evaluation data are comparable from one unit to another. Employees are more likely to cooperate with one another since individual ratings that are high are not a threat to the other workers. From a developmental perspective, the supervisor can provide more constructive feedback since the evaluation is centered on job requirements. Absolute judgments are also easier to defend legally than relative judgments; the firm can show that each employee's evaluation is based on performance dimensions that measure success on the job.

Absolute judgments are based on the performance appraisal interview, which also provides a manager the opportunity to help employees deal with behavioral problems that make them less effective. An estimated 19 million U.S. citizens suffer from depression each year, and most receive no treatment.[11] The regularly scheduled appraisal interview may provide the supervisor with a mechanism to help depressed employees seek professional help without the employees feeling that they are being singled out.

Measurement Approaches to Performance Appraisal

Performance appraisals may also be based on focus of the measures approaches. These appraisals assess different aspects of employee characteristics and focus on specific data.

trait appraisal instruments
Performance appraisal tools that evaluate employees based on consistent and enduring worker characteristics.

Trait appraisal instruments evaluate employees based on characteristics that tend to be consistent and enduring, such as decisiveness, reliability, energy, and loyalty. Because people routinely make trait judgments about others, they can be a powerful way of describing people. This type of appraisal instrument also has several disadvantages, such as ambiguity (what does it take to be loyal?) and propensity for conscious or unconscious bias (the supervisor may feel that women are more emotional than men and therefore rate the trait differently). It is also difficult to defend legally, given that assessment of traits focuses attention on the person rather than on job performance.

behavioral appraisal instruments
Performance appraisal tools that assess certain employee behaviors, such as coming to work on time.

Behavioral appraisal instruments assess certain employee behaviors, such as coming to work on time, completing assignments within stipulated guidelines, and getting along with co-workers. A *behavioral observation scale* is one type of behavioral appraisal instrument in which various behaviors are listed and supervisors record the frequency of their occurrence.

behavioral anchored rating scales
Performance appraisal tools that assess the effectiveness of the employee's performance using specific examples of good or bad behaviors at work.

Behavioral anchored rating scales assess the effectiveness of the employee's performance using specific examples of good or bad behaviors at work, often referred to as *critical incidents*. The main advantage of this approach is that it is closely focused on concrete aspects of job performance. Employees may more clearly understand why they received a particular rating and what they need to do to improve their performance. This approach is easier to defend legally. One drawback to using this approach is that the instrument is expensive to develop. They become more difficult to apply in companies with a wide variety of jobs, especially if those jobs frequently change.

outcome appraisal instruments
Performance appraisal tools that measure workers' results, such as sales volume, number of units produced, and meeting deadlines.

Outcome appraisal instruments measure results, such as sales volume, the number of units produced, and meeting deadlines. Setting quantitative measures of performance for most jobs is subjective. The most prevalent outcome-oriented approach focuses on goals agreed to by the employee and supervisor. Management by objectives (MBO) is one technique widely used for this purpose (see the planning chapter, Chapter 5, for a more extensive description of these programs). In MBO programs, employees and supervisors agree on a set of goals to be accomplished for a particular period. Performance is then assessed at the end of the period by comparing actual achievement against the agreed-upon goals. This approach provides clear direction to

LOC-In 6 Learning Objective Check-In

1. Phil evaluates his employees by comparing them to one another. This can be difficult for him, but he realizes that it forces him to make choices regarding who really contributes the most or the least to the team. This method sometimes calls for the use of a forced distribution.
   a. Absolute judgment
   b. Relative judgment
   c. Trait appraisal
   d. Behavioral appraisal

employees, reduces subjectivity, and allows individual goals to be established (for instance, objectives for new workers may be less challenging than those set for senior employees). As we saw in Chapter 5, MBO also has drawbacks in that it can be manipulated—employees and managers may set conservative goals to lessen the risk of not reaching the target. Some aspects of a job that are difficult to measure quantitatively, such as cooperating with other units or departments, may not be made part of the evaluation and thus may be ignored by the employee.[12]

Compensation

The three key objectives of any compensation system should be to attract high-quality workers from the labor market, retain the best employees the company already has, and motivate employees to work harder and to help the company achieve its strategic goals.

As illustrated in Figure 10.6, an employee's total compensation package is made up of three components. The first is **base compensation**, or the fixed amount of money the employee expects to receive in a weekly or monthly paycheck or as an hourly wage. The second is **pay incentives**, or the compensation that rewards employees for high performance. Incentives may be based on employees' own contributions or the performance of the team, business unit, or entire company. They are generally paid out as a percentage of base compensation. Pay incentives are often referred to as *variable pay* because the amount is contingent on or varies according to changes in performance. Incentive plans include one-time-only bonuses, pay raises (*merit pay* increases), profit sharing, and company stock or stock options. For instance, 19,000 engineers and technical workers at Boeing each recently received a $1,000 bonus after meeting a deadline for delivery of Boeing's 491st commercial jetliner.[13] The third component of total compensation is **benefits**, or *indirect compensation,* which accounts for almost 40 percent of the typical total compensation package. Benefits include health insurance, pension plans, unemployment insurance, vacations, and sick leave.

Compensation is a major cost for most firms. Labor costs may be as high as 60 percent in some manufacturing environments and even higher in service organizations. For instance, personnel costs reach 80 percent of the total budget of the U.S. Postal Service. This means that how well compensation dollars are allocated is likely to have a significant effect on firm performance. The design of the compensation system should fit with the firm's strategic objectives, the firm's unique characteristics, and the company's environment. Pay should also exhibit internal equity and external equity, and match employee contributions.

FIT WITH THE FIRM'S STRATEGIC OBJECTIVES The reward system should help implement the firm's strategy. A firm trying to expand its market share may pay the sales force on commission in order to generate more sales, while a firm trying to create customer loyalty in a narrow market segment may pay the sales force primarily on salary to focus on existing customers as well as on new business. This requires strong collaboration between top executives, who are responsible for strategy formulation, and the HR department, which designs the compensation program.

Compensation practices that best support the firm's business strategy are called **strategic compensation**. For instance, Ford, a pioneer in quality improvements since the 1980s, made it a core of its business strategy and summarizes it in its motto: "Quality Is Job One." A rash of quality-related problems surfaced in 2000, however, culminating with the recall of Firestone tires used in Ford vehicles and safety concerns with Ford Explorer. To prevent these problems from recurring, Ford executives' bonuses were tied to improving customer satisfaction more quickly than its rivals in the industry, based on consumer surveys and other data.[14]

base compensation
The fixed amount of money the employee expects to receive in a paycheck weekly or monthly or as an hourly wage.

pay incentives
Compensation that rewards employees for good performance, including variable pay and merit pay.

benefits
A compensation component that accounts for almost 40 percent of the typical total compensation package and includes health insurance, pension plans, unemployment insurance, vacations, sick leave, and the like.

strategic compensation
Compensation practices that best support the firm's business strategy.

FIGURE 10.6

Components of Total Compensation

Source: From *Managing Human Resources* by Gomez-Mejia, et al. Copyright © 2012. Reprinted by permission of Pearson Education, Inc., Upper Saddle River, NJ.

To Fight Rising Costs, Hospitals Seek Allies in the Operating Room

A new trend in hospitals is to share some of the cost savings from increased efficiencies with its physicians. Thus, for instance, two hospitals in New York City run by Continuum Health Partners, Inc. (CHP) provide to the "responsible physician" incentives of up to 25 percent of the cost savings for each inpatient each year. These amounts are to be determined based on cost improvement (compared to expenses on that patient in the prior year) and relative performance (compared to a "best practice norm" derived from cost figures for treatment of similar conditions by other providers in the CHP system).

Until recently, some cardiologists at the Pinnacle Health System hospital group in Pennsylvania would inflate a new artery opening balloon each time they inserted a stent into a patient's clogged arteries. Now, if they can, these doctors will use a single balloon throughout a patient's procedure.

That simple step, which the doctors say poses no additional risk to patients, saves at least a couple of hundred dollars a procedure.

PinnacleHealth says it saved 5 percent last year in cardiology supplies by conserving on balloons and getting cardiologists to agree, when feasible, to use stents, pacemakers, and other cardiac devices that it buys at a negotiated volume discount. Those savings equaled about $1 million, which the hospital split with doctors. "This is just common sense," said Dr. Ken May, whose 17-doctor cardiology practice is among the groups involved.

On the other hand many feel that such programs could tempt doctors to put money matters ahead of the interest of the patients. "We believe that gainsharing would have an immediate and significant negative effect on public health by encouraging the use of the least expensive option without consideration of long-term effects or overall health economics," said Martin J. Emerson, chief executive of American Medical Systems, a maker of pelvic devices based in Minnetonka, Minnesota.

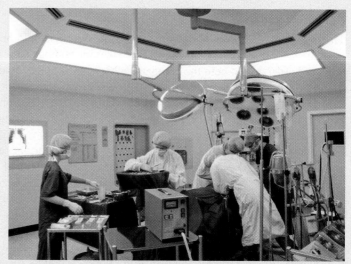

Gainsharing is one of the ways in which hospitals are teaming up with doctors to save costs in ways that don't affect patient care. While the idea, which splits the cost savings between the doctors and the hospital, has its critics and potential downsides, it does appear to be gaining support.

Source: Based on American Hospital Association (2010), "Trend Watch," February, p. 5; D. E. Steckler, F. Epstein, and R. N. Riner (September, 2009), "Physician-Hospital alignment; Finding the sweetspot," http://www.invasivecardiology.com; R. Averill, N. Goldfield, J. C. Vertrees, E. C. McCullough, R. L. Fuller, and J. Eisenhandler (2010), "Achieving cost control, care coordination, and quality improvement through incremental payment system reform," *Journal of Ambulatory Care Management*, 33 (1), 2–23; R. Abelson, "Dr. Saves-a-Lot," *The New York Times*, November 1, 2005, pp. C-1 and C-5.

Firms should be aware that incentives can help support strategic objectives but they may raise potential ethical issues, if employees and managers try to manipulate the system to get the incentives. Or there may be unintended consequences. This is a fear expressed by some with the incentive plan being introduced by some hospitals to have doctors share in cost savings (see Management Close-Up 10.3, "To Fight Costs, Hospital Seek Allies in the Operating Room").

FIT WITH THE FIRM'S UNIQUE CHARACTERISTICS AND ENVIRONMENT Company leaders must consider the organization's needs along with the firm's environment when designing a compensation program. A labor-intensive company with a highly unstable demand for products may provide more incentives and less in base pay to reduce financial risks, because base pay requires a fixed financial commitment.

What is important to one firm may be almost irrelevant to another. A high-tech firm that provides generous compensation to managerial and marketing personnel and underpays its research and development staff may lose the ability to innovate because competitors have stolen the company's best talent. On the other hand, a manufacturing firm producing a standard commodity that has changed little over the years, such as coat hangers, may not need to pay a premium for innovative talent.

internal equity
The perceived fairness of the pay structure within a firm.

job evaluation
A rational, orderly, and systematic judgment of how important each job is to the firm and how each job should be compensated.

INTERNAL EQUITY The perceived fairness of the pay structure within a firm is termed **internal equity**. A common procedure called **job evaluation** is intended to provide a rational, orderly, and systematic judgment of how important each job is to the firm. The key input to job evaluation is the job analysis, which was discussed earlier. Most firms use committees (which may include manager, employees, consultants, and union members) to examine the job analysis data to make that judgment. After applying a set of evaluation criteria called **compensable factors**, such as responsibility, educational requirements, and problem-solving potential, the committee develops a hierarchy of jobs in terms of their relative importance. To simplify matters, some firms group jobs into grade levels, where jobs at higher grade levels are considered to be more important than those at lower levels. Table 10.5 is an example of the pay structure of a large restaurant that uses grade levels.

compensable factors
A set of evaluation criteria used in job evaluation.

EXTERNAL EQUITY   The perceived fairness of the compensation employees receive relative to what other companies pay for similar work is termed **external equity**. HR departments often use market surveys to study external equity. An organization may conduct its own salary surveys, but most purchase commercially available surveys. Information about these surveys may be obtained over the Internet. HR.com offers timely information on compensation and benefit surveys available to employers. The purpose of these surveys in most job-based compensation systems is to determine pay ranges for each grade level.

external equity
The perceived fairness of the compensation employees receive relative to what other companies pay for similar work.

EMPLOYEE CONTRIBUTIONS   One important element of an employee's level of contribution to the company is the job he or she holds.

As discussed earlier, employees with more responsible positions generally contribute more to the organization, which is why they get paid more. Another key factor is how effectively employees perform their tasks. To attract, retain, and motivate high performers and to be fair to all workers, a company should reward employees based on their relative levels of performance.

Most firms reward employees based on their individual contributions. Companies may use piece rates, special awards, stock, bonuses, and merit pay. Merit pay increases, which are based on the supervisor ratings of employee performance and normally given once a year, are by far the most popular and are used by almost all companies.

TABLE 10.5 Pay Structure of a Large Restaurant Developed Using a Job-Based Approach

	Jobs	Number of Positions	Pay
GRADE 6	Chef	2	$23.50–$34.00/hr.
GRADE 5	Manager	1	$14.50–$24.00/hr.
	Sous-Chef	1	
GRADE 4	Assistant Manager	2	$10.50–$15.00/hr.
	Lead Cook	2	
	Office Manager	1	
GRADE 3	General Cook	5	$9.50–$11.00/hr.
	Short-Order Cook	2	
	Assistant to Lead Cook	2	
	Clerk	1	
GRADE 2	Server	45	$9.00–$10.00/hr.
	Hostess	4	
	Cashier	4	
GRADE 1	Kitchen Helper	2	$8.50–$9.25/hr.
	Dishwasher	3	
	Janitor	2	
	Busser	6	
	Security Guard	2	

Source: From *Managing Human Resources* by Gomez-Mejia et al. Copyright © 2012. Reprinted by permission of Pearson Education, Upper Saddle River, NJ

LOC-In 7 Learning Objective Check-In

Jeff's firm pays him $84,000 per year, up to $500 per quarter in quarterly performance bonuses, and a prearranged set of factors like 80 percent of health insurance costs, a fully matched 401(k), various work-associated insurances, and 20 days of personal leave to include vacation or sick leave.

1. What does the $84,000 represent in terms of Jeff's total compensation package?
   a. Pay incentives
   b. Benefits
   c. Base compensation
   d. Company goodwill

2. What does the potential $500 per quarter represent in terms of Jeff's total compensation package?
   a. Pay incentives
   b. Profit sharing
   c. Benefits
   d. Base compensation

3. What does the range of fringe components, including personal leave and health insurance, represent in terms of Jeff's total compensation package?
   a. Base compensation
   b. Pay incentives
   c. Benefits
   d. Company goodwill

CONCLUDING THOUGHTS

Thinking back to the introductory vignette and the questions raised at the beginning of this chapter, Toyota benefits from its Hire-a-Hero program because it creates a direct line of communication with returning veterans who have many of the types of technical skills and training the company is looking for in its employees. Leadership and commitment are other pluses that many veterans bring to the workplace, and Toyota makes a practice of supporting and rewarding its military and ex-military employees in return for their dedication and expertise.

If Toyota does better, so will its employees. In the end, nothing will make a company more successful than carefully selecting and placing the right people for the right jobs, ensuring that employees learn their jobs well, seeing to it that they will all have futures in the company, treating them fairly, and compensating them well.

As noted in Chapter 2, multinational firms are subject to the risk of government meddling as politicians may find the foreign firm an easy target for drumming up popular support. Actions such as the Hire-a-Hero program can help the foreign firm, Toyota in this case, foster positive attitudes in the local population towards the firm.

FOCUSING ON THE FUTURE: Using Management Theory in Daily Life

Human Resource Management

Brendan Geary is the Director of Compensation and Benefits at Panalpina, a freight forwarding and logistics services company. The company, which has headquarters in both Switzerland and the United States, is truly global, operating 500 branches in 80 countries, with partnerships in an additional 60 countries. In addition to freight forwarding, Panalpina offers supply chain management advice based on over 100 years of intercontinental air freight and ocean freight experience. With 13,000 employees scattered worldwide, Brendan is acutely aware of factors influencing the environment of Human Resources, and the compensation and performance management programs he designed contain many of the "best practice" features described in Chapter 10.

Human Resource Environment

Two factors of the Human Resource environment that influence Brendan's work with Panalpina on a daily basis are globalization and legislation.

Globalization

Panalpina managers often take on assignments in other countries, and Brendan must structure their benefits and compensation accordingly. Compensation strategies vary by geographic area. In Europe, for example, managers typically receive less take-home pay, but their pensions and health benefits are strong, in part due to the high taxes that support socialized medical programs. In the United States, less money is spent on pensions and health benefits, but take-home pay is much higher. Brendan must determine whether an executive is making a permanent move or a temporary one when setting up that employee's compensation package. If the move is permanent, he tries to bring compensation in line with local practices as quickly as possible, but if the move is temporary, he adopts a compensation strategy which is consistent with practices in the executive's home country.

Legislation

In terms of legislation, Brendan spends the majority of his time dealing with issues related to the Fair Labor Standards Act (FLSA) and the Family Medical Leave Act (FMLA.) The FLSA distinguishes exempt from nonexempt employees and establishes guidelines for minimum wages. In 2004, the law was amended, and new guidelines were established to clarify the duties associated with jobs that are exempt from being paid overtime. In the last year, Brendan has had to deal with one lawsuit (settled out of court) and three labor commissioner hearings about overtime issues. He finds that the bottom line for determining if an employee is exempt is whether or not that person "regularly makes independent judgments in their work."

The Family Medical Leave Act presents a different challenge for Brendan, one that is primarily related to reporting requirements. Because the FMLA requires that employees be given up to 12 weeks of unpaid leave a year to care for themselves or a family member, and because that leave can be taken in daily and/or hourly increments, Brendan finds that it is critical to monitor FMLA leave closely. Employees who request time off must clarify whether they are taking FMLA time and when they are planning to return to work. By law, an employee's job must be held open for him or her for the 12 weeks he or she is on FMLA leave. Unfortunately, some employees abuse the FMLA guidelines and try to take far more than the 12 weeks to which they are entitled. To deal with this issue, Brendan utilizes a third party administrator who tracks FMLA leaves throughout Panalpina.

Compensation

Obviously, as Director of Compensation and Benefits, Brendan must create compensation programs that will attract high quality applicants, retain the best employees the company already has, and motivate employees to work harder and help the company achieve its strategic goals. Brendan recently changed the sales compensation program, keeping in mind the following key design components.

Fit with the Firm's Strategic Objectives

One of Panalpina's primary strategic objectives is organic growth—expanding the company's overall revenues in a natural fashion. In a freight forwarding company, this means utilizing existing trade lanes whenever possible, and bringing in business that fills identified trade lanes to capacity. When Brendan was hired, all Panalpina sales personnel received their incentive compensation based on simple incremental gross profit on different product lines. But Brendan knew that some sales were more in line with the company's strategic objectives than others. Therefore, he created a sales compensation plan that offers increased rewards for selling to clients on existing trade lanes, for selling to larger rather than smaller clients, and for identifying clients who can "fill out" cargo planes and ships to capacity.

Fit with the Firm's Unique Characteristics and Environment

As noted above, the global character of Panalpina makes it imperative that compensation programs are designed with regional standards in mind. For the sales compensation program, this means adjusting salary and commission components to fit with local norms. Salaries differ depending on geographic location.

Internal Equity

The salary component of sales compensation is adjusted so that all sales personnel receive equivalent starting salaries. This means that salaries have to be adjusted using geographic pay differentials to reflect the underlying economic conditions of the area in which the salesperson is working. This keeps perceptions of pay equitable across the organization. On the incentive side of the mix, pay is tied directly to results, so it is easy for salespeople to see how their inputs relate to outcomes and see the overall fairness of the system. Rather than spending a lot of time on job evaluation studies, Brendan allows the market to determine the value of jobs to the organization.

External Equity

Panalpina does not do traditional job evaluation studies—instead, Brendan focuses his compensation strategy on external market data and works to ensure that all salaries in the company are market driven. Job salaries are benchmarked by participating in sponsored compensation surveys or purchasing compensation survey information from a consulting company like Watson Wyatt.

Employee Contributions

All compensation systems at Panalpina are tied to employee contributions. As noted above, sales personnel receive incentive compensation which is directly linked to the amount of money they bring into the company in sales. Salaried employees participate in an annual review process, where their performance is rated based on goal setting and competency components. This rating is incorporated into a merit pay program, which uses a merit matrix to establish the rate of salary increase associated with each performance rating level. High potential and especially talented employees receive extra compensation reviews to be sure that they are being paid for their contributions to the company.

Summary of Learning Objectives

1 Explain the role of human resource management in achieving a sustainable competitive advantage.

- The business strategy of the firm should guide human resource strategies, which in turn provide the basis for HR programs in effectively implementing those strategies.
- All managers are responsible for making human resources decisions, while the human resource department provides the necessary support so that managers can hire the best talent, train employees, assess performance, and reward contributions.

2 Identify the key factors in the environment affecting the management of human resources.

- The workforce is becoming increasingly diverse in terms of race, ethnicity, gender, age, and such.
- Globalization is widening the labor market from which firms recruit and requires greater HR involvement in preparing employees to compete in that environment.
- Legislation that affects human resource management, primarily discrimination issues, is constantly being interpreted at federal, state, and local levels.
- Labor unions have been declining in strength in the United States but still remain strong in certain industry sectors and in many countries around the world.

3 Describe the human resource planning process.

The process involves two steps:

- Forecast of **labor demand:** An estimate of how many and what kinds of workers will be needed in the future.
- Forecast of **labor supply:** An estimate of the availability of employees with required skills.

4 Explain the key components of staffing and their importance.

- **Recruitment.** Firms can greatly improve the quality of the workforce by generating a good pool of applicants.
- **Selection.** Firms can hire better employees by developing selection programs that are job related and capable of predicting who is most likely to be a good performer.
- The *orientation program* can ease the entry of employees into the company so that they become fully functioning in the shortest time possible.

5 Describe how training and career development provide employees with tools to succeed once they are hired.

- *Training* provides employees with specific skills to enhance their job performance.
- *Career development* offers long-term growth so that employees can use their abilities to the maximum during their employment with the firm.

6 Identify the purposes of performance appraisal and how it might be conducted.

- *Developmental purpose.* The performance appraisal system can help identify employee weaknesses that should improve through training and career development as well as strengths that may be channeled to better utilize the employee's talents.
- *Recognition purposes.* The appraisal system may provide important input to reward employees (for instance, through promotions and salary adjustments) based on their relative contributions.
- *Appraisal means.* Employees' performance may be judged by comparing them to one another or by evaluating performance relative to an establishment performance standard. The focus of the appraisal may be traits (such as decisiveness and reliability), behaviors (such as using examples that illustrate good or bad behaviors at work), and outcomes (measuring observed results). All approaches have advantages and disadvantages so it is important to be aware of their pros and cons as discussed in this chapter.

7 Describe the key objectives of the compensation system and its components.

- A well-designed compensation system should serve to attract, retain, and motivate good employees.
- The compensation system allocates pay based on the importance of the job, how well employees perform their assignments, and the pay for similar positions in the labor market.
- The compensation package is made up of three components: **base compensation** or salary, **pay incentives** (amounts may vary by year, usually depending on performance), and **benefits** (such as health insurance, pension plans, unemployment insurance and so on).

Discussion Questions

1. Many firms today subcontract to external consultants part of the work that traditionally was conducted in the HR department. Why do you think this is happening?
2. What do you foresee as the major forces affecting human resources in the future? Do you see those forces as threats or opportunities for firms? Why?
3. A cynic might argue that most firms do not hire employees following the practices outlined in this chapter (job analysis, realistic job previews, and the like), but they still manage to have an effective workforce. Some go even further and argue that those practices tend to create an expensive bureaucracy with doubtful benefits. Do you agree? Why or why not?
4. Going back to Management Close-Up 10.2, do you think the flexible work plan developed by Best Buy may be used in most firms? What are some of the challenges employers are most likely to face if they implement such programs?
5. Should a firm use an objective or a subjective performance appraisal system? What factors determine which type of system a company should use? Explain.
6. Going back to Management Close-Up 10.3, do you believe that incentive programs such as the one described should be used in the medical industry? Why or why not?

Management Minicase 10.1
Rewards for Good Teaching?

According to one analyst:

> Good teachers matter. This may seem obvious to anyone who has a child in school or, for that matter, to anyone who has been a child in school. For a long time, though, researchers couldn't actually prove that teaching talent was important. But new research finally shows that teacher quality is a close cousin to student achievement: A great teacher can cram one-and-a-half grades' worth of learning into a single year, while laggards are lucky to accomplish half that much. Parents and kids, it seems, have been right all along to care whether they were assigned to Mrs. Smith or Mr. Brown.

Consistent with this view, a growing number of jurisdictions are supporting the use of incentives to attract, retain, and motivate the most effective teachers. A case in point is that of the City of Houston, Texas.

Over the objections of the teachers' union, the Houston Board of Education unanimously approved the nation's largest merit pay program, which calls for rewarding teachers based on how well then students perform on standardized tests.

The $14.5 million program, which immediately replaces a model with lower incentives, would distribute up to $3,000 annually per teacher and up to $25,000 for senior administrators.

Abelardo Saavedra, the Houston superintendent of schools, praised the vote, saying that it "will ensure that the academic growth of each child is important and will be compensated." Houston business leaders also supported the change.

But Gayle Fallon, president of the United Federation of Teachers, which represents about 40 percent of the district's 12,300 teachers,

condemned the program as misguided. In its place, Ms. Fallon called for across-the-board raises to lift Houston from what she said was the low-paying end of area school districts. "No one has been able to show us one ounce of research that paying teachers for test scores improves performance," she said.

DISCUSSION QUESTIONS

1. What are the pros and cons of rewarding teachers for student test results? What side do you mostly agree with (pros or cons?). Explain your answer.
2. Do yon think it is fair to pay teachers a stipend up to $3,000, principals up to $6,000, and executive principals/regional superintendents up to $25,000? Explain your answer.
3. If you were to suggest a performance appraisal system for teachers, how would you do it? Would you tie the resulting appraisals to pay and if so, how would you do it? Explain your answers.

Source: Based on M. Gryphon, "Better teachers: A lesson plan," http://www.cato.org, 2011; L. Langbein (2010). "Economics, Public Service Motivation and Pay for Performance." *International Public Management Journal*, 13 (1), 9–23; D. B. Gratz (2010). *The Peril and Promise of Performance Pay: Making Education Compensation Work*, New York, NY; Rowman & Littlefield; J. Caillier (2010), "Paying teachers according to student achievement: Questions regarding pay-for-performance models in public education," *The Clearing House*, 83 (2), 58–61; R. Blumenthal, "In Houston, Teachers Get Merit Pay," *New York Times*, January 13, 2006, p. A-12.

Management Minicase 10.2
Balancing Family Issues and Work

A growing number of companies are launching initiatives so that employees can balance their family and work life. The most common initiatives include:

Redesigning Work

Many companies are redesigning how the work is to be done and involve employees in designing how to make their own lives more livable while still getting the job done. They eliminate tasks that are redundant, reassign some employees to positions that offer scheduling flexibility or the possibility for remote work, and look for ways to save time—some of which goes back to employees.

Alternative Work Arrangements

Alternative work arrangements like flextime (altering starting and ending times), job sharing, telecommuting, reduced work schedules, and compressed work weeks are now becoming standard in many organizations.

Leave

More employees are putting all their paid leave days—sick leave, personal leave, funeral leave, parental leave, floating holidays, and so on, into what most call a "Paid Time Off Bank," from which employees "withdraw" a certain number of days each year.

Time-Saving Assistance

Concierge services, onsite shopping, consumer resources, buying, leasing and maintaining cars, home repairs, real estate listings, house cleaning, and other services that help employees save time are gaining in popularity again as the economy surges ahead.

Emotional Well-being

Most employers offer the services of an Employee Assistance Program (EAP). Developed in the early 1970s to help with employees' alcoholism and addiction issues, their mandate has grown. Still the experts in alcohol and drug intervention assistance, counseling for gambling and eating disorders, these programs also provide counseling for grief and loss, personal relationships, work relationships, marriage and family issues, divorce and separation, mental health issues, violence and crisis, work-life balance, and stress management.

Financial Assistance

Sometimes included in EAP services, financial counseling is growing in importance. Companies are offering assistance with budgeting, credit and collections, home buying and renting, saving and investing, retirement planning, insurance, and taxes. Many offer low-interest loans for housing, college, and personal emergencies.

Legal Assistance

Many employers offer the services of a lawyer to talk with employees about wills, consumer protection, estate and probate law, family and elder law, real estate issues, living wills, and other legal issues. Some subsidize the service and some arrange for lower group rates.

Relocation

It pays to offer as much assistance as possible to make sure relocation is a success. Most offer help with selling current homes and finding housing in the new location. Many help spouses to find a job and assist with school issues, childcare, financial counseling, and transportation. They also have well-organized programs, including support groups, for expatriates returning from overseas.

Health Benefits

Health insurance may be the most important work-life benefit of all. As costs skyrocket, more employers are switching to consumer-driven plans, offering employees the option of a high-deductible, lower cost health savings account.

Wellness

Fitness programs, disease prevention, smoking cessation, obesity programs, nutrition and diet assistance all have a measurable payoff in keeping employees healthier, which not only cuts healthcare costs but raises productivity and reduces absenteeism.

Parenting, Childcare, and Child Development

When the field of work and family was first invented, in the mid-1980s, childcare was pretty much its sole focus, and it's still an important piece of keeping a work force productive. It includes helping those who want to be parents with infertility counseling and financial assistance, and even, in some cases, in-vitro fertilization. It often means helping new parents with adoption leave and financial assistance, and of course finding or providing regular and after-school care, summer care, backup, and sick child care. Most companies now offer parenting seminars and support groups. Some provide summer programs for older children and teens and many offer college support of various kinds. There's special help for single parents and support groups for blended families.

Exceptional Care Giving, Eldercare, Special Needs Children

There are now about 120 million caregivers in the United States and an estimated 60 percent are also in the workplace. As the boomer generation move into their 60s, both of those numbers will grow very fast. Therefore, more companies will provide or facilitate the services of geriatric care managers, help find or provide elder-care, backup care or caregiving assistance, along with resources for emergencies, special needs children, disabled adults, legal or financial resources and information, needs assessment, evaluation of eldercare facilities, caregiver support groups, and eldercare fairs.

Handling Family Issues in the Office

"People who are running copies of soccer schedules on the company copiers do not give it a second thought, because they're also using their home resources to do work—the home PC, the phone, a room in the house, paper, and personal time," says Jeff Saltzman, chief executive officer at Sirota Survey Intelligence, Purchase, New York, which surveys 1.5 million employees annually on work issues. Thus, if a big project for a sports team or dance troupe needs a graphic design or photocopying, parents may opt to do it at the office because the technology often is better.

DISCUSSION QUESTIONS

1. Should employers have explicit policies on family-related uses of time and equipment while at work or should this issue be handle informally on a one-to-one basis? Explain.
2. Should employers give employees credit for work done at home even if this is very difficult, it not impossible, to monitor? Explain your answer.
3. Talk to some of the people you know and ask them about the availability of the programs described above in their organization. What is their perception about the effectiveness of these programs?

Sources: Adapted from WFC Resources, *Work-Life and Human Capital Solutions,* "Overview: What is work life," 2011, http://www.workfamily.com/aboutworklife/aboutworklife.htm; Also based on S. Shellenberger, "Work and Family," *The Wall Street Journal,* October 20, 2005, p. D-1; *Work & Family Life,* "Balancing job and personal responsibilities," http://www.workandfamilylife.com, 2011.

Individual/Collaborative Learning Case 10.1

How to Reduce Turnover

At Applebee's, Overland Park, Kansas, managers must divide hourly workers into "A" players, the top 20 percent; B, the middle 60 percent; and C, the bottom 20 percent. The managers then are eligible for merit raises and bonuses based on how well they retain employees in the top 80 percent. The practice is unusual in the restaurant industry, where managers tend to worry more about staffing the next shift than career development and performance evaluation.

Applebee contracted a consulting firm named TRABON to develop a Web-based tool to manage the performance resources of thousands of employees in hundreds of locations. The program tracks key financial, guest, and people performance indicators. Associates at all levels have unprecedented visibility to clear, concise, and accurate information. Each measure of performance is evaluated against targets twice a year and given a performance rating ranging from outstanding to unacceptable.

CRITICAL THINKING QUESTIONS

1. Do you think Applebee's approach to reducing employee turnover is fair and reasonable? Is it likely to engender too much stress on employees low paying jobs? Explain your answer.
2. Some people believe that the key to retaining good workers in low-paying jobs is to offer them flexibility in scheduling

rather than financial incentives. Do you agree? Explain your answer.
3. Do you think a system such as that used by Applebee's should be adopted by other fast-food restaurants such as McDonald's, Burger King, Taco Bell, and others? Why or why not? Explain your answer.

COLLABORATIVE LEARNING EXERCISE

A large hotel and restaurant chain has been experiencing turnover rates of 250 percent a year, on average. You are part of a consultant group (consisting of 4–6 students selected by the instructor) responsible for developing a proposal to identify the causes of the problem and to develop a set of suggestions to try to reduce turnover. After each team meets for about 20 minutes, class will reconvene and each team will present its recommendations to the instructor. This should be followed by an open class discussion.

Source: Based on Trabon "Applebee's International," www./trabonsolutions.com, 2011; http://www.workforce.com, "Applebee's turnover recipe," 2011; http://www.amrestapplebees.com, "What makes a successful Applebee's Manager?" 2011. E. White, "How to Reduce Turnover," *The Wall Street Journal,* November 28, 2005, p. C-3.

Internet Exercise 10.1

Help on the Web

www.hr.com
HR.com provides extensive and current information, updated almost daily, on all facets of human resource management, including compensation and benefits, staffing, legal issues training and development, and labor relations. Explore the Web site and answer the following questions.

1. How can you use this information to become more effective as a manager? As a team member? In managing your own work? Explain.
2. What specific examples can you draw from this Web site that illustrate how this information may be beneficial to you in these different roles?

Endnotes

1. Storey et al. (2010) (see reference list) "USA Today Snapshots," *USA Today,* January 17, 2001, p. 1A.
2. D. Gonzalez, "World's Cultures Converge in State," *The Arizona Republic,* January 8, 2001, p. A1.
3. Rebecca Walker, *Black, White and Jewish: Autobiography of a Shifting Self* (New York: Riverhead Books, 2001).
4. T. Kenworthy, "Air Force Academy Hit by Drug Scandal," *USA Today,* January 16, 2001, p. 3A.
5. Moskowitz et al. (2010) (see reference list) "Companies Try Creative Cutbacks: Managers Hope to Avoid Drastic Step of Layoffs." *USA Today,* January 8, 2001, p. D1.
6. www.latestandgreatest5@hrpomotions.com.
7. J.P. Wanous, *Organizational Entry,* 2nd ed. (Reading, MA: Addison-Wesley, 1992).
8. S. Armour. "Degrees in e-Commerce Seem Less Dazzling," *The Wall Street Journal,* January 16, 2001, p. B1.
9. F. Golden, "Probing the Chemistry of the Brain," *Time,* January 15, 2001, p. 55.
10. Moskowitz et al. (2010) (see reference list) "The 100 Best Companies to Work For," *Fortune,* January 23, 2006, pp. 89–108.
11. L. M. Gomez-Mejia, D. B. Balkin, and R. Cardy, *Managing Human Resources* (Englewood Cliffs, NJ: Prentice Hall, 2012).
12. "Boeing Engineers to Get Bonuses," *USA Today,* January 8, 2001, p. A3.
13. G. L. White, "Ford Admits Last Year's Quality Snafus," *The Wall Street Journal,* January 12, 2001, p. A3.
14. T. Larimer, "Rebirth of the Z," *Time,* January 15, 2001, pp. 42–44.

11

Learning Objectives

1 Explain the meaning and benefits of employee diversity.

2 Develop an awareness of the unique perspectives, problems, and issues of diverse employee groups.

3 Understand demographic trends in the labor force and their managerial implications.

4 Describe the challenges firms may face in the management of diversity.

5 Describe various approaches that managers may use to enjoy the benefits of employee diversity and meet the challenges associated with diversity.

Eleven Decades of Ensuring that Employee Diversity Equals Corporate Success

From its inception more than a century ago, at a time when employee diversity was an alien concept, IBM has embraced workforce diversity as a fundamental value. IBM's commitment to workforce diversity can be traced back to 1899, when it hired its first female and black employees—20 years before women's suffrage, 10 years before the founding of the NAACP, and 36 years after the signing of the Emancipation Proclamation.

In the early 1950s, when racial discrimination was perfectly legal and the norm in the South, Thomas Watson, IBM founder and CEO, wrote a policy statement stating IBM's commitment to fairness and inclusion. During negotiations with the governors of two southern states regarding the building of IBM plants, Watson said there would be no "separate but equal" racial policies at IBM. To ensure the governors took him seriously, he wrote a letter to his management team in 1953 and made the letter public. As a result, he said, both governors responded by choosing payroll and tax dollars over bad social policy. Six decades later, IBM continues at the forefront of diversity. According to IBM's Chairman and CEO, Sam Palmisano, "diversity policies lie as close to IBM's core as they have throughout

Managing Employee Diversity

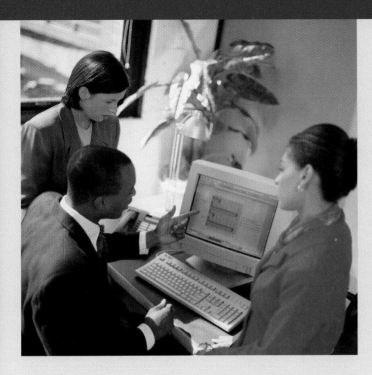

our heritage. Today, we're building a workforce in keeping with the global, diverse marketplace, to better serve our customers and capture a greater share of the on demand opportunity."

Commitment to diversity is far more than a public relations act for IBM. This is exemplified by the following:

- IBM purchases about $1.5 billion in supplies from minority-owned firms.
- IBM has eight task forces designed to make diverse employees feel welcomed and valued at IBM and to focus on the various constituencies as customers. These include Asian, Black, Gay/Lesbian/Bisexual/Transgender, Hispanic, men, Native American, people with disabilities, and women.

- IBM invests heavily in supporting initiatives to ensure all of its employees use their full potential. These initiatives include "Black Executive Forums" (to mentor black managers), "Multicultural Techies Inside Track" (to reduce voluntary attrition of minorities at IBM), "Women Perfectly Suited to Fulfill IBM's On Demand Strategy" (to prevent subtle ways women can be excluded in the corporate environment), and the "Hispanic Task Force to Bridge Digital Divide" (to facilitate the recruitment, training, and mentoring of Hispanics).
- IBM has an extraordinarily extensive corporate Web site dedicated to diversity issues, which is continually updated. At the time of this writing (2011), 25 densely packed Web pages fall under the IBM diversity icon. Diversity information is divided into 11 areas (Asians, Blacks, Gay/Lesbian/Bisexual/Transgender, Hispanic/Latino, mature adults, people with disabilities, and so on).
- IBM has received over 150 national and international prestigious awards for successful management of diversity during the past decade, including the "DiversityInc's Top Ten Global diversity list," "Working Mother Magazine—Best Companies for Working Mothers—Top 10 Recipient," "Top Ten Best Companies for Asian Americans," "National Society of Black Engineers Employee of Choice," "Business Leadership Award from Equality Forum," "Top Five Companies in Terms of

Lesbian/Gay, Friendliness," "Society of Hispanic Professional Engineers Employer of the Year," "National Science Foundation—Diversity Award," "American Society on Aging—Business of the Year Award," and "Top Company for Women Executives," plus many, many others.

Source: Based on "Diversity 3.0, Leveraging our differences for innovation, collaboration, and client success," http://www-03.ibm.com, 2011; "NAFE 2010 Top 50 companies for Executive Women," http://www.Nafe.com, 2011; V. J. Racanelli "The World's Most Respected Companies," http://www.online.barrons.com, 2011; "Awards and Recognition," http://www-03.ibm.com, 2011; "IBM workforce diversity policy," http://www-03.ibm.com, 2011; "Diversity Management," http://www.diversityinc.com, 2011; T. Childs, "Managing Workforce Diversity at IBM," *Human Resources Management*, 114 (1) (Spring 2005), pp. 73–77.

CRITICAL THINKING QUESTIONS

1. *Why do most executives believe that effective management of diversity is critical to business success?*

2. *What are the most difficult challenges firms face in managing employee diversity? What can they do to deal with those challenges?*

We will be revisiting these questions again in our Concluding Thoughts at the end of the chapter after you have had an opportunity to read the following discussion on managing diversity.

■ The Meaning of Diversity

diversity
The wide spectrum of individual and group differences.

The term **diversity** describes a wide spectrum of differences between people. On an individual level, a person's sexual preference, disability status, or many other characteristics may cause the individual to be perceived as different. Groups of individuals share characteristics that distinguish them from other groups. Some of the characteristics, such as race, age, and gender, cannot be controlled by the individuals involved. Others, such as occupation, political party membership, and religion, may be changed through conscious choice and deliberate effort.

The crucial fact to bear in mind about diversity, however, is that although the attitudes, life interests, expectations, and norms of behavior of groups may differ on average, the differences between groups are smaller than the differences within groups. Classifying people into such typologies as black or white, male or female, and gay or straight often leads to false stereotypes because it incorrectly assumes that group averages or characteristics apply to every individual in the group.

In Figure 11.1, the curve for veterans shows that people who have been in the armed forces tend to be more accepting of an authoritarian management style than nonveterans. However, the figure does not prove that a particular veteran is more accepting of an authoritarian management style than a particular nonveteran. About half the veterans—those below point D on the curve—are less accepting of authoritarianism, and there is a great deal of overlap between veterans and nonveterans on this trait. This is true of almost all psychological traits.[1] In other words, only a

FIGURE 11.1

Group versus Individual Differences on Acceptance of Authoritarian Leadership

Source: From *Managing Human Resources*, by Gomez-Mejia, et al., copyright © 2012. Reprinted by permission of Pearson Education, Inc., Upper Saddle River, NJ.

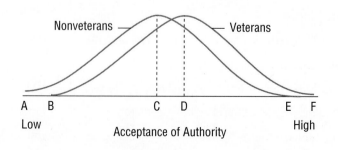

relatively small amount of employee diversity is explained by group membership. This is an important point to keep in mind. While managers need to be alert to diversity in their employees, the effective manager views employees as individuals, not as members of a particular group.

Currently, American-born white males constitute only 15 percent of new entrants to the workforce. The rest are women, immigrants, and minorities. Women now represent about half of the workforce, and nonwhites comprise about a third of the working population. In many parts of the country, the numbers are even more striking. Almost a third of New York residents are foreign born, Miami is two-thirds Hispanic, San Francisco is one-third Asian, and 80 percent of Detroit residents are African Americans. The Hispanic community in the United States is increasing by 1.7 million a year. In seven of the largest states (including California, Texas, Florida, and New York) 20 percent or more of the population speaks a foreign language at home; in an additional 16 states, the proportion of nonnative English speakers exceeds 10 percent.[2]

One in ten Americans is of Hispanic origin.

In this chapter, you will be able to develop some skills that will positively affect your ability to relate to employees of different backgrounds. While these skills are important for everyone, they are crucial for those with managerial responsibilities, as summarized in Management Is Everyone's Business 11.1.

Advantages of Employee Diversity

As noted in Figure 11.2, a firm can derive many benefits from a heterogeneous workforce. First, however, company leaders must help employees avoid misunderstandings, ill feelings, and marginalization of those who do not fit into the dominant groups. Some of the most important potential benefits of diversity are better market access, global competitiveness, greater creativity, and improved team performance.

MARKET ACCESS A diverse employee base allows a firm to tap into profitable markets. Utilizing employees who are attuned to these markets gives the firm a competitive edge. Women, older Americans, African Americans, Hispanics, and Asian Americans have more buying power than in the past. They expect businesses to provide products and services that meet their needs. As Deborah Yarborough, a manager at Silicon Graphics, points out, if they "don't feel respected and listened to, they will take their business elsewhere."[3]

MANAGEMENT IS EVERYONE'S BUSINESS   11.1

WORKING AS A MANAGER Today's labor force is highly diverse. If effectively managed, this diversity can provide the organization with a powerful competitive edge. It can foster creativity, improve problem solving, provide greater flexibility, and make a firm more attractive to a broad labor market. But if diversity is not effectively managed, there may be misunderstandings and poor communication, which have negative effects on productivity and teamwork. For you as a manager, this means that you should:

- Treat people consistently yet try to understand their perspectives.
- Realize that people interpret reality through the lens of their prior experiences.
- Avoid stereotyping employees—and you should never relate to employees based on preconceived notions of the group to which they belong.
- Make diversity work for you by considering the viewpoints of employees who might have a unique perspective of the issues at hand.
- Try to provide an example to other employees that you value diversity, and be an example that you avoid behaviors (such as crude jokes) that are offensive to some.
- Show respect to all the people who work for you regardless of their differences.
- Encourage employees to take advantage of diversity initiatives offered by the firm.
- Be fair to all employees but also consider giving opportunities to employees who have the potential to succeed yet come from disadvantaged backgrounds.

FIGURE 11.2

Benefits from a Heterogeneous Workforce

Many companies have successfully tapped into diverse markets. Hispanic, Asian, and female community development officers from First Community Bank Boston present seminars to diverse communities in order to develop market opportunities. The bank also provides translation, advertising, an 800 line for people who do not speak English well, and modification of loan application procedures to make them less threatening to non-Anglo groups.[4] As described in Management Close-Up 11.1, other banks are targeting services to minority groups. These companies are able to develop those market niches to attain a sustainable competitive advantage. Avon has a workforce that is almost a third minority. The marketing team at Avon discovered a niche in an industry that had been largely ignored: the beauty needs of women of color. The company introduced a highly profitable cosmetic line for black women back in 1999 which is still selling well almost a decade later.[5] At both American Express Co. and Merrill Lynch & Co., African American female employees attempt to attract black investors by holding workshops and networking receptions in such venues as African-American museums. Within two years of launching the program, 68 percent of new business at American Express has come from African-American clients.[6] Upon the advice of several older employees approaching retirement, in the mid-2000's Motorola decided to romance the rapidly growing over-55 market by making phones with features that aging consumers like, such as a zoom function to bump up the font size on the tiny screen and internal speakers that can be connected to hearing aids.[7]

MANAGEMENT CLOSE-UP 11.1

THEME **CUSTOMER FOCUS**

Tapping a Market That Is Hot, Hot, Hot

When National City Corp. bank decided to roll out 78 new branches in Chicago two years ago, it went in knowing its market. With Hispanics expected to account for virtually all of the city's population growth over the next decade, the bank hired dozens of Spanish-speaking staffers and printed thousands of glossy pamphlets, hawking savings accounts to new immigrants and explaining the benefits of IRAs to more established Latinos. This year, the nation's 10th largest bank will double its Hispanic marketing budget, targeting middle-class Latinos with direct mail offering mortgage financing and money-market accounts, all written in Spanish. "A simple hello in Spanish," says Christian Sandoval, vice president of Hispanic marketing at National City, "can open the door to a Hispanic better than a product with a 4.5 percent interest rate." Spanish-speaking employees are always available to assist customers.

Hispanics represent a huge, largely untapped market. The monetary wealth of Hispanic families is increasing at a rate three times faster than that of the U.S. population as a whole and more than half of Hispanic households do not yet have a U.S. bank account. According to the FDIC, Hispanic families will account for more than half of the growth in retail banking during the next 10 years. With about $20 billion being wired to Latin America and the Caribbean annually, financial institutions nationwide are scrambling to take advantage of this by offering a safe, convenient way to transfer these funds (and of course make money in the process). According to Bank of America, Spanish-language advertising has brought in millions of new checking accounts from Hispanics. Some banks are even finding creative ways to attract the money of undocumented depositors. For instance, Industrial State Bank from Kansas does a healthy business by targeting Latino enclaves. In order to open accounts for the many immigrants who lack the traditional documents, such as driver's licenses and Social Security numbers, the bank accepts Individual Taxpayer Identification Numbers (ITINs) and matriculas consulares, official idenfication cards issued by the Mexican government. Similarly, Wells Fargo in California accepts the marticulas consulares to open hundreds of new accounts each year.

Source: Based on "Banking Latino Immigrants," *Hispanic Bank Markets*, http://nubank.cust.digitalwest.net, 2011; "Hispanic banking: The race is on," http://www.hispanicbusiness.com, 2011; Bank of America's "Hispanic Press Kit," http://newsroom.bankofamerica.com, 2011; Bank of America's, "Hispanic products and services," http://www.bankofamerica.com; 2011; B. Grow, "Tapping a Market That Is Hot, Hot, Hot," *Business Week*, January 17, 2005, p. 36.

INTERNATIONAL COMPETITION As discussed in Chapter 2, success increasingly depends on a firm's ability to compete on an international stage. A growing number of U.S. firms have established joint ventures with foreign companies, and many workers are employed by foreign companies and work for foreign managers. Japanese cars are produced in Kentucky, Swedish pharmaceuticals are made in Italy, and U.S. software is developed in India. Phillip Morris and Intel operate in more then 200 countries and employees speak more than 100 languages.

Firms with employee diversity in their home offices are likely to display the cultural sensitivity, understanding, and awareness that will help them succeed in the global arena. An observer has noted that "there is a growing consensus that U.S. managers are more . . . able to adapt to other cultures and environments than managers from other countries. Experts suspect that's because U.S. managers grow up leading a more diverse workforce at home."[8]

Bank of America has taken advantage of its employee diversity in a global context. The organization does business in 37 countries, and the California customer call center staff speaks more than 13 languages. This is possible because 32 million Americans speak a language other than English at home, and 8.6 million of them live in California.[9] Similarly, the DuPont Company uses its 100-plus ethnic and gender networks as a source of internal resource for global access. As a senior manager explains, "Network members have provided important insights regarding ethnic markets here in the United States as well as in other regions of the world. For example, the company recently test marketed a new hosiery fiber with women in its Asian network. In addition, African American networks helped our agricultural products business build a closer relationship with black farmers in South Africa, a major customer base for DuPont."[10]

MULTIPLICITY OF POINTS OF VIEW People from different backgrounds bring a variety of experiences, skills, abilities, and information to bear on the tasks at hand. This allows them to examine issues and problems from different angles. Research on group dynamics suggests that groups with members from a variety of backgrounds are likely to come up with more ideas and solutions than groups whose members are homogeneous.[11] Diversity is an important source of innovation that helps fuel creativity and improve a firm's competitive position in the marketplace. For example, "diverse groups of employees conceptualized product development, manufacturing and the marketing strategies" for Saturn Corporation.[12] American-born physicists are in the minority at Bell Laboratories, and the first language of biochemists at Schering-Plough's research labs is less likely to be English than Korean, Hindi, Chinese, Japanese, German, Russian, Vietnamese, or Spanish. Effective management of diversity has helped these firms become highly successful in their efforts to be innovative.

TEAM PERFORMANCE Groups consisting of people with different personality types, attitudes, ethnicity, and gender also make better decisions. A diverse team may be able to find better solutions because of the divergent thinking processes characteristic of a more diverse group of people. Diversity minimizes the phenomenon called *groupthink,* in which a homogeneous group agrees on a mistaken solution because members share a similar mind-set. The presence of team members who view the problem differently may stimulate others in the team to discover novel approaches that they would not have considered, thereby leading to better decisions. Moreover, diverse group members may learn from, emulate, and internalize the different strengths of other team members. This allows the team to conceptualize problems in a more comprehensive manner, avoiding simplistic solutions that may prove to be unsatisfactory.

Minorities make up 15 percent of the Ohio State Highway Patrol, which actively recruits its diverse workforce through campus recruiting and employee referrals and promotes minority officers to leadership positions.

The Challenges of Diversity

As summarized in Figure 11.3 potential problems can emerge when there is increasing employee diversity. These problems include pressures toward homogenization, lower cohesiveness, interpersonal conflict and tension, and confusing employee diversity with affirmative action. Firms must effectively manage these challenges in order to derive the benefits noted above.

Management Minicase 11.2 at the end of this chapter discusses how this is a particularly serious issue in some parts of the economy such as Wall Street.

FIGURE 11.3

Potential Problems that Can Emerge with Employee Diversity Management

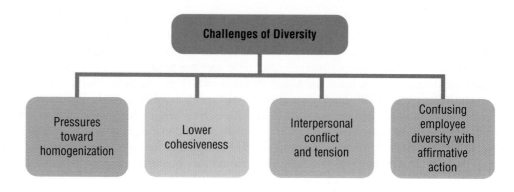

PRESSURES TOWARD HOMOGENIZATION There is a natural tendency for organizations to become demographically homogeneous because people are attracted to others they believe are similar to themselves. Indeed, as employee diversity increases, individuals segregate into groups composed of people like themselves, and dissimilar co-workers may feel pressure to leave the organization. Turnover of dissimilar employees tends to produce a **monoculture** within the firm, causing the organization to become more homogeneous. As a firm becomes more monocultural, the job satisfaction of minority employees and women decreases, which translates into higher resignation rates. On average, at all organizational levels and among all age groups, the turnover rate of minorities is 40 percent higher than that of whites, and the turnover rate of women is more than twice that of men.[13]

Dissimilar employees who stay may be segregated within the firm and kept out of the mainstream. **Ethnocentrism** may become prevalent among various groups of employees, meaning that they believe that their way of doing things, their values, and their norms are inherently superior to those of other groups and cultures. To the extent that managers are white males, their values, beliefs, motivations, and attitudes may prevent dissimilar employees from being promoted, because they do not look, act, and think in what are considered appropriate ways for individuals who aspire to responsible managerial positions. Although the exclusion of women and minorities may not be malicious or deliberate, ethnocentrism at the top makes it difficult for dissimilar groups to participate at all organizational levels. This creates a **glass ceiling**, an intangible barrier that prevents women and minorities from rising to the upper levels. Only about 3 percent of senior executives in Fortune 500 firms are women.

The prevalence of segregated groups may also lead to **segmented communication** channels within the firm. This means that communication flows are far greater within groups than between groups. For example, one study indicates that a surprising amount of communication occurs only among individuals of the same sex and ethnic status. This was found to be true among all professional groups and at all organizational levels, even at the executive level where there are few women and minorities.[14] When employee viewpoints and ideas remain confined to employees' own groups, it is difficult to establish common ground across various groups. Unfortunately, this also means that dissimilar employees may not be attuned to mainstream communication networks or be able to share their unique experiences with the rest of the company.

LOWER COHESIVENESS A measure of how emotionally close group members are and how supportive they are of each other is the degree of **cohesiveness**. Diversity may lead to a fragmented workforce with little cohesion. In the extreme, it may lead to a lack of commonality of organizational values and goals. Taylor Cox, a respected academic and consultant on diversity issues, noted that "a core of similarity among group members is desirable. Members must share some common values and norms to promote coherent actions on organizational goals. The need for heterogeneity, to promote problem solving and innovation, must be balanced with the need for organizational coherence and unity of action to provide competitive advantage."[15] Management Is Everyone's Business 11.2 includes a set of recommendations that teams should consider in order to effectively deal with these issues.

INTERPERSONAL CONFLICT AND TENSION As organizations become more diverse, mistrust, lack of understanding, and lack of mutual respect may lead to decreasing cooperation among

---

monoculture
The homogeneous organizational culture that results from turnover of dissimilar employees.

ethnocentrism
A belief that may become prevalent among majority-group employees, meaning that they believe that their way of doing things, their values, and their norms are inherently superior to those of other groups and cultures.

glass ceiling
The intangible barrier that prevents women and minorities from rising to the upper levels in business.

segmented communication
Flows of information within the firm that are far greater within groups than between groups.

cohesiveness
The emotional closeness group members feel toward each other and how supportive they are of each other.

MANAGEMENT IS EVERYONE'S BUSINESS   11.2

WORKING AS A TEAM   Despite management's best intentions, employee diversity may lead to inter-personal problems within and between teams unless all employee groups and group members learn to work effectively with one another in a climate of mutual respect. Interpersonal friction can lead to open conflict, wider mistrust and loss of respect, even chaos, and overt or subtle discrimination by those who control organizational resources. If groups become dysfunctional or segregated, the problem-solving and innovation benefits of diversity will be reduced or lost. Team members should:

- Strive to listen to the viewpoints of different individuals within the team and consider those as valid as yours.
- Resist temptation to relate primarily to people who are similar to you, disregarding the rest of the team.
- Actively seek to bring people into the team who are different, and value some degree of hetero-geneity as a good thing.
- Be careful with verbal and body language that other team members may find offensive.
- Ensure the participation of all members of the group, even those who might be shy, quiet, or afraid, and enable then to bring their ideas to the table.
- Strive to create a win-win environment within the team so that all participants, regardless of background, develop a sense of common fate within the group.

employees and poor integration of individuals who are supposed to work closely with each other. Diversity may also cause stress and interpersonal friction, making it difficult to reach agreement on issues. In extreme cases, open conflict and other problems may ensue. In countries where there is high "power distance" (see discussion of this cultural dimension in Chapter 2) it may be difficult for low power employees to participate and hence diversity may not be used as an asset.[16] Attempts to do so may even be counterproductive. On the other hand, in countries, such as the United States, where power distance is low, there is a greater likelihood of individuals' overcoming cultural barriers to communication and achieving the potential advantages in diversity.

CONFUSING EMPLOYEE DIVERSITY WITH AFFIRMATIVE ACTION   Affirmative action and employee diversity are not the same thing. As we discussed in the preceding chapter, **affirmative action** is a government-mandated program that requires corporations to provide opportunities to women and members of minority groups who traditionally here been excluded from good jobs. Introduced about 45 years ago, affirmative action programs are controversial. Some members of groups not covered by the programs have complained that affirmative action programs lead to "reverse discrimination," in which opportunity is denied to majority-group members. There is also a belief that affirmative action programs lead to lower self-esteem among beneficiaries by creating the perception that they received undeserved special treatment.

It would be difficult to prove what the real effect of affirmative action has been. It is clear that women and minorities have had more advancement opportunities since the programs were implemented. For instance, the percentage of women managers increased from 27 percent to 46 percent between 1981 and 2012. The number of African American officials, managers, technicians, and skilled craftspeople has tripled since the mid-1960s, while the number in clerical positions has quadrupled and the number in professional jobs has doubled. In 2010, 17 Hispanics occupied top executive spots among Fortune 1000 companies, when 25 years ago there were one. In 1995, not one of the Fortune 500 CEOs was a non-caucasian. At the time of this writing, 20 Fortune 500 companies are run by people of color, including five who are black, seven who are Latino, and seven who are Asian. At some of the largest blue-chip firms the progress has been remarkable. For instance, almost half of the 50 highest paid employees at Xerox are minorities, and a third of board members at General Motors are

affirmative action
A federal government-mandated program that requires corporations to provide opportunities to women and members of minority groups who traditionally have been excluded from good jobs; it aims to accomplish the goal of fair employment by urging employers to make a conscious effort to hire members of protected classes.

A diverse workforce is a key component of highly regarded firms.

minorities. One U.S. supreme court justice is black and one is a Hispanic woman. And of course we have a black president, Barack Obama; not too long ago this would have been akin to science fiction.

It may be logical to assume some of these changes are the consequence of affirmative action. On the other hand, diversity is a fact of life as well as work life. Unlike affirmative action, a *diversity program* recognizes that, as a *de facto* consequence of demographic changes in the workforce, organizations need to employ women and minorities in order to succeed. Whereas affirmative action is a political solution to societal ills, a diversity program is a human resource program that focuses on performance and competence to ensure equal opportunities in a manner blind to ethnicity and sex. Unfortunately, some employees, particularly white males, believe that *diversity* is simply another name for affirmative action. A survey found that twice as many white men as women and minorities believe that promotions of women and minorities are a result of affirmative action.[17]

Diversity programs present four related challenges to HR managers and companies. First, white males may view a program as a threat to their own opportunities for advancement. When white male executives develop a cynical view of diversity management, the program is unlikely to provide competitive advantage to the firm. Second, the perception of special treatment may undermine the formal procedures, policies, and enforcement mechanisms of the diversity program. Third, women and minorities in positions of authority may not receive as much respect from their subordinates and colleagues as do white men. Finally, the organization may not reap the benefits of employee diversity described earlier.

It is probably true that a generation ago many business leaders launched affirmative action programs somewhat begrudgingly. Government pressure and the fear of losing costly class action suits were probably their primary motives. Today, there is strong support for the idea that creating an environment of inclusion of diverse groups is a competitive business necessity. Indeed, a quick look at the Web pages of most of the Fortune 1000 firms today shows that diversity is at the forefront of policy statements made by CEOs. For instance, according to the chairman and CEO of PricewaterhouseCoopers, LLP, "we must promote diversity and inclusion to attract and retain the best talent, to maintain meaningful client relationships, to win continuously in the market place."[18] Business leaders are quick to stress that diversity policies are not intended to encourage what may be perceived as preferential quotas for particular groups.[19] Rather, the intent is to provide opportunities to employees of different backgrounds. Nevertheless, debate on these issues is likely to continue for years to come. Most Americans, including a majority of women and minority group members, reject quotas that set aside a proportion of job openings for "protected classes."[20] At the same time, most successful firms hold managers accountable for achieving diversity goals.[21]

LOC-In 1 **Learning Objective Check-In**

1. Jeanne is a U.S. manager who has always led a diverse workforce, ever since she began working at an aerospace engineering firm as a project manager in 1986. Today, that firm is highly successful versus other firms from Japan, Italy, and Canada. Jeanne suspects that this _____ is attributable to the firm's ongoing emphasis on diversity.
   a. multiplicity of points of view
   b. international competitiveness
   c. market access
   d. team performance

■ Diversity Today

The U.S. workforce has been a mosaic of diverse cultures at least since the 1880s. When large contingents of immigrants arrived from southern Europe, Poland, Ireland, and Russia, they were considered outsiders because they had different customs, did not speak English, and were not Protestants. Immigrants from Asia and from eastern and southern Europe were largely excluded under the Immigration Act of 1929 because they were considered intellectually inferior based on their performance on standardized tests during Army recruitment drives in World War I. Women were largely missing from the workforce except in elementary-school teaching, nursing, and sewing. Most clerical administrative work was performed by men. Many of the largest companies considered hiring southern Europeans, Catholics, Jews, and Irish to be a poor business practice.

Throughout successive generations, many ethnic barriers eroded, and the diverse European groups entered the mainstream. This created the myth of the "American melting pot," a belief that the United States was a country of immigrants and that diverse groups would assimilate and blend into the American culture over time. However, "in real life many ethnic and most racial groups retained their identities—but they did not express them at work. Employees often abandoned most of their ethnic and cultural distinctions while at work to keep their jobs and get ahead. *Many* Europeans came to the United States, Americanized their names, perfected their English, and tried to enter the mainstream as quickly as possible."[22]

Today the prevalent thinking is that rather than making everyone fit a common corporate mold, organizations should support, nurture, and utilize people's differences in a way that both respects employees' unique perspectives and promotes a shared vision. If a firm is going to succeed, company leaders must learn to manage a diverse workforce.

A good place to start is to be cognizant of the unique perspectives, problems, and issues of various groups. It is important to keep two things in mind. First, as discussed earlier, characteristics overlap between any two groups. Second, employees have multiple identities, some of which are more strongly felt at different moments in their lives and in different contexts. For instance, a female black Hispanic engineer from Cuba who is 50 years old and disabled may identify most strongly with women under some circumstances and with Cubans under others.

Each person's self-concept reflects a web of identities: sex, race, ethnic origins, place of birth, religion, age, sexual orientation, occupation, socioeconomic status, and so on. Seeing individuals in terms of multiple identities permits a better appreciation of their personalities in more subtle, less stereotypical, and ultimately more realistic ways. Many of the social and legal barriers that have kept ethnic groups apart have come down because there are millions of people with mixed identities. For this reason, the Census Bureau now allows Americans to classify themselves into multiple racial categories. The evidence seems to suggest that airtight racial distinctions are slowly disappearing. Currently, approximately one-fourth of blacks and more than half of Hispanics marry people outside their racial or ethnic group.[23] At the same time, specific employee groups certainly have concerns that still remain. The following is a presentation of some of these groups' concerns. Obviously, they should be considered carefully as general trends rather than the stereotyping of every member of the category. Skills for Managing 11.1 will help you counteract negative stereotypes that often exist between groups of people who perceive

---

SKILLS FOR MANAGING 11.1

Counteracting Stereotypes

Racial or ethnic, prejudice is generally based on crude stereotypes that are as old as mankind itself. The earliest records of stereotyping are Egyptian hieroglyphs about Assyrians and Babylonians. The Lydian tablets (from present day Izmir), which are just being translated, speak harshly of piratical seamen called Achaeans (Greeks). Or think of the Old Testament and the Israelite stereotyping of Philistines. The Greeks referred to all aliens as "barbarians" because they couldn't speak Greek but went "baa-baa," like sheep. The Scots and the French have, through history, been England's favorite stereotype targets. The Scots have been seen as "wild" ever since their James VI became James I of England in 1603 and brought south thousands of "thuggish" Scots on the make. Suspicion of France has been rampant ever since the Norman Conquest. More recently,

one variant of a joke in the 27-country European Union that capitalizes on national stereotypes reads something as follows, "Heaven is defined as the place where the police are British, the cooks are French, the mechanics are German, the lovers are Italian, the Spanish are in charge of leisure activities, the Dutch serve as treasurers, the Greeks maintain the museums, and it is all organized by the Swiss; conversely, hell is defined as the place where the cooks are British, the mechanics are French, the lovers are Swiss, the police are German, the Spanish are in charge of work activities, the Dutch are responsible for entertainment, the Greeks serve as treasurers, and it is all organized by the Italians."

A common thread in stereotyping is that particular groups make themselves feel better by looking down on other groups and having a laugh at their expense. Unfortunately,

(Continued)

social scientists have shown that we are all prone to stereotyping, not only because it makes our identity feel superior to others but also because our brain has a tendency to simplify reality by placing objects and people into mental categories.

Team Exercise

As noted above, humans have a tendency to lump together people who are different from them into categories, ascribing certain characteristics (often negative) to those who fit into those categories. One way to break down stereotypes is to meet people who presumably should share characteristics associated with their category (not only ethnic or tribal, but old or young, male or female) but in fact are individuals (some who might somewhat fit the stereotype, some who are the opposite of the stereotype, and many others who might fall anywhere in between). Your class will be randomly divided into groups of five. Each group will make a list of commonly held stereotypes for any one category of your choice. Please choose only one category (or one pair of opposites). Categories may include gender, age-older versus younger workers, geographic origin (for instance, those from specific states, or those from the North, South, Midwest, West, and East), urban versus rural, occupational groups (such as lawyers, teachers, or taxi drivers), university majors (such as accounting, music, or physical education

majors), union versus nonunion members, public versus private sector employees, fraternity or sorority members, those who come from high and low family incomes, blue collar versus white collar employees—as you can see your possiblities are almost endless. Then after listing the stereotypes, each team should think of examples of individuals they have known from the category or opposing categories and the extent to which those individuals differ from or fit the stereotypes.

After meeting for approximately 15–20 minutes, each group should post or write their results, and the instructor will then mediate discussion.

Sources: Adapted from based on S. Spencer, C. Logel, and P. G. Davies (2011) "Stereotype threat," *Annual Review of Psychology*, January, 26–48; S. A. Mendoza, P. M. Gollwitzer, and D. M. Amodio (2010) "Reducing the expression of implicit stereotypes: Reflexive control through implementation discussions," *Personality and Social Psychology Bulletin*, 36 (4), 512–23; L. A. Zebrowitz, M. Kikuchi, and J. M. Fellows (2010) "Facial resemblance to emotions; group differences, impression effects, and race stereotypes," *Journal of Personality and Social Psychology*, 98 (2), 175–89; B. P. Bryson and A. K. Davis (2010) "Conquering stereotypes in research on race and gender," *Sociological Forum*, 25 (1), 161–66; G. Ferraro (2010). *The Cultural Dimension of International Business*. Pearson Education, Upper Saddle River, NJ; T. Varadarajan, "At Least It Is OK to Back Away with Stereotypes," *The Wall Street Journal*, February 21, 2003, p. W-15.

themselves to be different. The Management Is Everyone's Business 11.3 provides a set of recommendations that you should apply to yourself as an individual when dealing with people who are different from yourself.

African Americans

African Americans constitute 11.3 percent of the population and 11.8 percent of the workforce in the United States. Prior to the Civil War, most African Americans were enslaved. Since then this group has suffered the most blatant forms of discrimination. Discrimination has resulted in poverty, segregated housing, fewer educational opportunities, and severe underrepresentation in managerial and professional jobs.

MANAGEMENT IS EVERYONE'S BUSINESS 11.3

WORKING AS AN INDIVIDUAL It is important to learn to work with people who are different from you. Employees who can relate effectively to members of other groups are more likely to be favorably noticed by management and placed in positions of responsibility. One of the most fundamental management skills is the ability to get work done through others. However, even those who are not interested in a managerial role will benefit from relating well to people of diverse backgrounds; support from peers will make their work easier to accomplish. As an individual employee you should:

- Show respect for other people in the organization no matter how different they are from you.
- Develop a reputation for relating well to all sorts of people; this is almost certain to help your long-term career prospects within and outside the firm.
- Avoid being overly sensitive to perceived "slights" by other employees who are different from you; perhaps you might unwittingly be blowing things out of proportion.
- Go out of your way to work with people who are different from you; you may be surprised how much you can learn and grow from the experience.
- Develop insights into your way of thinking and why you respond to certain people the way you do; perhaps you may be unaware that you are reacting to them based on prejudice and stereotypes without considering all the relevant factors.
- Volunteer to participate in diversity initiatives (such as diversity training) offered by your organization.

Until the 1960s, it was legal in the United States to segregate African Americans and create company policies that automatically eliminated them from employee selection and promotion decisions. Prestigious universities refused to admit them, creating a vicious cycle of low educational achievement, little opportunity for career advancement, and little chance to enter professional, technical, and managerial jobs. Institutionalized racism is now illegal. But many blacks believe that discrimination is still present in the corporate world today.[24]

Unfortunately, many whites do not realize that bigotry against blacks in the workplace is still a serious problem. For instance, one survey showed that half as many whites as blacks believe that there is a lack of fair treatment in promotion decisions. The discrepancy between white and minority perceptions of equal opportunity in the workplace was larger among African Americans than among any other ethnic group surveyed, including Hispanics and Asian Americans.[25] In fact, one report concluded that "a new wave of race-discrimination cases is appearing in the workplace: African Americans who feel that they are being passed over for Hispanics."[26] Bias is not always intentional; unintentional bias has been reported at numerous companies and organizations, including Amtrak, Coca-Cola, and the New Jersey State Police.

LOC-In 2   Learning Objective Check-In

1. Rose is an Asian American of Korean descent. She was very successful in business school and graduated at the top of her class. She is an outspoken young woman who has often taken the lead in the team work exercises throughout school. Carolyn, Rose's new manager, wants to make sure she is sensitive to Rose's unique needs and issues. Which of the following can Carolyn infer about Rose?
   a. Rose is qualified to perform more technical work than other workers.
   b. Rose is a hard worker and will be best utilized crunching numbers.
   c. Rose will be successful on her own, and does not need help from Carolyn in pursuing her career goals.
   d. Rose is a demonstrated leader who may prove useful in the firm's management.

Asian Americans

Asian Americans make up 3.6 percent of the U.S. population. People designated as Asian Americans include a wide variety of races, ethnic groups, and nationalities including people of Japanese, Chinese, Korean, Indian, and Pakistani descent. Asian Americans are well represented in technical fields, but despite high educational achievements, they are severely underrepresented in managerial positions and seldom make it to the upper echelons. Those Asians who head high-tech companies are often the founders of the companies. Asian Americans have been held back by the stereotype that they are too reserved to lead others and that they have limited verbal skills. Other characterizations of Asians as hardworking and deferential can end up relegating them to roles as corporate workhorses—not leaders—and keep them segregated in technical areas. Asian Americans are also subject to bigotry; in the mid-1990s, 40 percent of African Americans and Hispanics and almost a third of whites saw Asian Americans as "unscrupulous, crafty, and devious in business."[27] A survey reported by *Time* in 2006 suggests that many Asian Americans feel alienated even when they were born in the United States. They are often seen as what sociologists call "forever foreigners . . . their looks lead to a lifetime of questions like 'no, where are you really from?'"[28] As of this writing, all Asian American households, on average, have an annual median household income that is 16 percent greater than that of whites, and those Americans who trace their roots to India enjoy an income advantage over whites of more than 42 percent.[29] The perception that Asian Americans are already successful paradoxically makes some managers insensitive to their needs and problems.

Disabled Americans

It is estimated that approximately 50 million Americans have some form of disability. Among people with disabilities between the ages of 16–64, the employment rate is 55.8 percent. People with disabilities are subject to unwarranted discrimination when supervisors resist hiring them for fear that they require special equipment, training, and support. They may also be perceived as being less capable and less flexible than nondisabled employees. Once hired, coworkers may feel uncomfortable around them, making disabled employees feel isolated or patronized so that they are unable to fully integrate into a work group.

In fact, accommodating employees with disabilities is less expensive than people think. According to a report issued by the Job Accommodation Network, the typical cost of accommodating a disabled employee is $600. Disabled employees are also less prone to absenteeism and turnover than other employees.[30]

Some progress has been made over time in the hiring of people with disabilities. The National Organization on Disability reports that approximately 60 percent of this group is gainfully employed, compared to 46 percent in the mid-1980s. However, this same survey indicates that there are many more disabled people (two out of three) who are unemployed but would prefer to be working. One promising development is the use of telecommuting to increase employment of people with disabilities. The Equal Employment Opportunity Commission (EEOC) has issued a set of guidelines to encourage the hiring of disabled employees on a telecommuting basis. According to an EEOC officer, "for some people with disabilities, telework may actually be the difference between having the opportunity to be among an employer's best and brightest workers and not working at all."[31] Some organizations are also starting to provide assistance for parents of children with disabilities.[32]

Foreign-Born Americans

It is estimated that at least 10 percent of Americans are foreign born but in many large urban areas the proportion is considerably higher: approaching over one third in some cities such as Miami, Los Angeles, and New York. The statistics are not reliable, because they do not account for at least 11 million undocumented immigrants. About 820,000 immigrants enter the United States legally every year.[33] The number of illegal immigrants has slowed down considerably during the most recent downturn of 2008–2012.

Immigrants tend to be relatively young, ambitious, and upwardly mobile. Some business sectors view them as a remedy for the relatively small generation of native-born Americans now entering their thirties. Immigrants form 250,000 new households every year, fueling demand for the services of builders, brokers, bankers, and department stores, among other businesses. In Los Angeles, about a quarter of home buyers aged 25 to 44 are foreign born. More than two-thirds of California's population growth in the past 20 years can be attributed to immigrants. New York State would have lost population were it not for 475,000 newcomers.

The United States is still the land of opportunity for most of the world. At any given time, there are more than half a million foreign students in American universities. A high proportion of them choose to remain in the United States after graduation, particularly those majoring in engineering and technical fields, where they often outnumber native-born Americans.

The United States has had a love-hate relationship with immigrants for much of its history. Periodically, immigrants are denounced for taking jobs away from native-born citizens and for not assimilating into the proverbial American melting pot. Established immigrants have worried that they might have to compete with new immigrants for jobs. Such beliefs have generally been unfounded, but they have often resulted in restrictive legislation. They also expose the foreign born to resentment and discrimination, complicating other factors, such as language, culture, and race, that create barriers to their full participation at work.

Nonetheless, the United States continues to provide upward mobility for people coming to its shores. One study revealed that the earnings of the more than 25 million immigrants who arrived since the mid-1970s had reached the average income of the native-born population within 15 years of arrival. Also, the poverty rate of those who are in the country for 15 to 20 years is lower than that of people born in the United States.[34]

Another study suggests that most foreign-born immigrants do not create an economic threat to those who are native born. According to one study, the income differential between a household led by a foreign-born and a native-born resident in the United States is only about 12 percent. This is amazingly low considering the additional hurdles an immigrant faces in learning a new language, adapting to a new culture, coping with employment discrimination, and so on.[35]

It is important to note that large-scale immigration is not the exclusive province of the United States. World migration has increased dramatically during the past 30 years in many parts of the planet.[36] All one has to do is to stroll through the streets of Paris, Vancouver, Amsterdam, Johannesburg, London, Madrid, Kuwait, or San Jose to see the mix of people from different nationalities who live and work there, often with dubious legal status. During the 15-year period 1996–2011, the United States received 27 percent of the world's international migrants, yet Western Europe received almost as many (21 percent).[37] While the United States has always been a nation of immigrants, firms in many other countries are now having to adapt to such demographic changes rather abruptly.

Hispanic Americans

Nearly 28 million people, or one in ten Americans, consider themselves to be of Hispanic origin. This figure, which is based on census data, is probably a conservative estimate. Many Hispanics are afraid to identify themselves for fear of the Immigration and Naturalization Service and a general distrust of the government. A widely quoted figure is that the actual number is closer to 40 million and in some areas such as California, New York, southern Texas, and southern Florida, the proportion reaches close to one-fourth of the population.[38]

According to census figures, roughly 60 percent of Hispanics have roots in Mexico, 12 percent in Puerto Rico, and 5 percent in Cuba. Fifty-eight counties in the United States have a Hispanic majority. The largest number of Mexican Americans (2.6 million) live in Los Angeles County. The largest concentration of Puerto Ricans (900,000) live in the five boroughs of New York City. Dade County, Florida, where Miami is located, has the most Cuban Americans (600,000). However, a recent study using census figures found that Hispanics are not staying in segregated areas but rather moving to areas with few from their ethnic group such as Ford (Kansas), Texas (Oklahoma), Prince William (Virginia) and Crawford (Iowa).[39] The portion of the U.S. economy that is Hispanic is bigger than the gross national product of most Spanish-speaking countries, with 772,000 Hispanic-owned firms.[40]

"Hispanic" is not a term for a race but a label encompassing a wide variety of groups. It includes American Indians of the Southwest, whose homelands became Spanish colonies more than four centuries ago and who adopted Spanish surnames and customs, as well as immigrants from Spain, Mexico, Guatemala, Argentina, Cuba, and other Central and South American countries. At least 70 million Latin Americans are of European descent, 25 million are of African descent (mostly from the Spanish Antilles and the Caribbean basin), 10 million or so are of Asian descent from various countries, 60 million are Native Americans, and a high proportion are individuals of mixed ethnic background. Hispanic groups are diverse within their own countries as well as within the United States in terms of race, history, and economic status. What they have in common are the Spanish language, which Hispanic families tend to maintain across generations, the Catholic religion, which plays a key role in people's lives and values, and a high regard for extended family. Hispanic people tend to be family-oriented. Some cultural attributes, such as humor, a more laid-back style, chivalry, and freedom to express emotions, may also be present.

Language and skin color can pose problems for Hispanics in the workplace, particularly for recent immigrants. Many Hispanic immigrants come from an agrarian background and have limited formal education. Value differences may also cause problems. "Some Latinos see non-Latino North Americans as unemotional, insensitive, self-centered, rigid, and ambitious to the point where they live to work rather than the other way around."[41] For their part, non-Hispanics often complain that Hispanics' "punctuality, absenteeism, planning, and scheduling can be a lot more loose than one would expect."[42] Clearly these negative stereotypes do not apply to most people of either group.

Homosexuals

Estimates of the percentage of the population that is homosexual vary between 1 and 10 percent. Homosexuals are sometimes referred to as an "invisible minority" because an individual's status is not obvious unless the person declares his or her sexual orientation. Unlike race, gender, national origin, age, and disability, there is no federal antidiscrimination law protecting homosexuals, and only a handful of states offer such protection at the state level. In the fall of 2010, the Senate declined to discuss a possible repeal of this policy, although at the time of this writing, enforcement of the "don't ask, don't tell" policy seems to be in a legal limbo.

Most gays and lesbians keep their homosexuality secret for fear of jeopardizing their careers. Declared homosexuals may face intolerance and scorn from co-workers, bosses, and even clients. However, company attitudes are changing in a way that was unthinkable even a decade ago. For instance, General Motors of Canada, Hewlett-Packard, Intel, American Express, IBM, and the Walt Disney Company now make health benefits available to same-sex partners of employees. Likewise, public policy regarding homosexuals is likely to become more tolerant in the future. For instance, the state of California now grants state-registered domestic partners all of the same rights, protections, benefits, obligations, and duties as married spouses.

Older Workers

The U.S. workforce is growing older each year. The average age of the workforce is now close to 42, and the proportion of employees between 50 and 65 is currently increasing at twice the rate of the overall population. Negative stereotypes of older workers as being inflexible, resistant to learning new skills, and coasting until retirement are pervasive.

Contrary to stereotypes, older workers, particularly those in jobs requiring little physical exertion, function as well as they did 20 or 30 years earlier. They also have more wisdom and seasoned judgment. Many successful companies have implemented programs to share the knowledge and wisdom of older workers with younger employees through mentoring. In the words of an HR consultant, "these companies are striking gold in a silver mine by leveraging senior workers as knowledge champions."[43] Because the service sector has been growing more rapidly than manufacturing, physical strength and health are less important for successful performance than they were in the past. Nevertheless, older workers often suffer from discrimination in hiring and promotion decisions. Also, unlike countries in which the wisdom of older people is respected, the input of older workers in U.S. firms is often not accorded the consideration it deserves. (See Management Close-Up 11.2, "When Grey Heads Roll.") Another serious problem older workers encounter is the rising cost of health insurance and the increasing reluctance of firms to provide any sort of job-based coverage. Indeed, this has become a considerable topic of debate in the latter half of this decade, and from all indications both state and federal

---

MANAGEMENT CLOSE-UP 11.2

THEME: **ETHICS**

When Grey Heads Roll

One of the growing ethical issues issues this decade is whether organizations systematically terminate older employees in what is perhaps a short-sighted attempt to save money as these employees typically enjoy higher salaries and increased health premiums. In recent years there has been a flurry of allegations by older employees that they are easy prey of cost cutters in corporate America. Below you will find several recent examples. Keep in mind, however, that the firms involved deny that age was a factor in layoffs and the "smoking gun" needed to prove deliberate age discrimination is hard to find.

Best Buy: Layoffs According to Age?
Several weeks after being laid off last spring by Best Buy, the consumer electronics retailer, Lynette M. Steuck, a software project manager, showed up for a resume-polishing "outplacement session" of the sort commonly offered to employees recently shoved out the door. As Ms. Steuck, 51, a divorced mother, surveyed the sparely furnished conference room, she was struck by something. "It was shocking," she recalled recently. "There were probably 25 to 30 people in the session. And there were only three or four people under the age of 40."

Sprint: Legitimizing Age Discrimination through Performance Appraisals?
"It's not the blatant: 'Jones, you're too old. We're firing you,'" said Tom Osborne, a senior attorney at AARP and a co-counsel for plaintiffs in a case against Sprint. Instead, he said, companies might adopt

new employee-evaluation systems that happen to reverse the career-long high performance ranking of older employees.

In the Sprint case, thousands of people who were recently laid off contend that a subjective and arbitrary new ranking system was used to weed out older workers. Known as "forced ranking," the system requires individual departments to apply bell-curve ratings in which 30 percent of workers must be classified as subpar. "We can show statistically that when it came to rankings, those over 40 did worse than those under 40," said Mr. Egan, the lead attorney for the Sprint plaintiffs.

3M: Systematic Bias in Favor of Younger Workers?
Arbitrary management decisions are all a central assertion in the lawsuit against 3M. "We are alleging that older people are more likely to be put into the lower-ranking groups" when evaluated by managers, said Susan M. Coler of Sprenger & Lang, a law firm in Minneapolis, who represents the 3M plaintiffs. The suit also contends that younger workers were more likely than their older colleagues to receive training that led to promotions and raises.

Sources: Based on "Huge Best Buy Layoffs coming tomorrow," http://www.gizmodo.com, 2010; "Best Buy Considers layoffs," http://www.promomagazine.com, 2010; K. Jacobs "Two Best Buy Plans Layoffs at Headquarters," http://www.forbes.com, 2010; "More bad news for KC: 8,000 Sprint Layoffs," http://www.economy.kansascity.com, 2010; "Wrongful termination," http://www.fairmeasures.com, 2011; N. Alster, "When Grey "Heads Roll." *New York Times*, January 3, 2005, p. B-3.

governments are likely to become more heavily involved in health care.[44] The United States is the only industrialized country that does not offer public health insurance. This lack of coverage can be catastrophic to elderly workers.

LOC-In 3 Learning Objective Check-In

1. Harry is a 64-year-old worker who works in an office environment. He is very good at dealing with clients and has more wisdom than the average younger worker. Harry has been passed over three times in the last three years, however, and he suspects his age plays the biggest role in the decision, especially since he has the most experience, the best record, and intends to continue working well past age 65. Which of the following statements is true regarding older workers?
   a. The U.S. workforce is growing younger each year, with the average age expected to fall to 40 by 2010.
   b. The proportion of workers between 50 and 65 is increasing at twice the rate of the overall population.
   c. The manufacturing sector has been growing faster than the service sector, making older workers less useful today.
   d. Older workers seldom suffer from discrimination in hiring and promotion decisions.

Religious Diversity

Many, if not most, Americans trace their roots to immigrants who fled religious persecution and wars in Europe. Apart from those of the Jewish faith, the United States has been traditionally and overwhelmingly Christian. In recent years, however, there has been a growing non-Christian minority, with approximately 4 million Americans now professing Islamic, Hindu, Taoist, or other non-Christian beliefs. This went largely unnoticed until America's tolerance toward people of different religious backgrounds was severely tested by the terrorist attacks of September 11, 2001. A survey by the Society for Human Resource Management (SHRM) revealed that so-called "ethnic religions" such as Islam now come just after race and gender in American perceptions of "otherness."[45] Security fears due to terrorist threats have led to many complaints of "racial profiling" and discrimination by Arab Americans, as well as those who may be confused as Muslims, such as some people of East Indian descent.[46] Religious tolerance has been most severely tested in Europe in recent years, culminating with the Paris riots in 2005 and widespread protests by Muslim believers in 2006 against what they see as Western insensitivity to their faith.[47]

Many firms are now developing policies concerning tolerance for religious diversity. These policies cover such issues as permissible garments at work, religious holidays, potential harassment or ridicule based on one's faith, and the display of religious symbols on company premises.

Undocumented Workers

There are at least 11 million workers in the United States who are here illegally or without immigration papers. Approximately 57 percent come from Mexico, and the remaining 43 percent from various countries around the world. In many sectors (particularly construction, agriculture, services, and parts of manufacturing) undocumented employees do much of the work.[48] Let's take, for instance, the case of Chesapeake Bay seafood processors. These processors claim that they would face catastrophe if they did not have access to alien workers: "These workers have come to dominate shellfish processing over the past decade, doing dirty, repetitive work that machines can't and Americans won't. The work is unpleasant. Picking crabs, for instance, requires scraping off the gills, cleaning out the organs, breaking off the mouth, and prying meat out of tiny cavities. All that must be repeated up to 600 times a day, yielding a daily wage that might reach $120 on a good day."[49]

The U.S. "love-hate" relationship with immigration is nothing new, although this contradiction has become more pronounced in recent years as so-called illegal immigration has greatly outpaced legal immigration. Part of the problem is that immigration laws have become so restrictive that it is nearly impossible for a prospective unskilled or semiskilled immigrant to obtain a working visa in the United States (unless married to a U.S. citizen). But on the other hand, there is undoubtedly a huge demand for their services in many sectors. This creates a situation of increasing tension and potential abuses.[50] Also, children of these undocumented workers are often born and raised in the United States, so they are "full blown" Americans, yet face an uncertain future because of their parents' legal status.[51]

This is an issue that will loom large in public debate for years to come. At the core of this debate lies the need to balance humanitarian concerns, employer demand for labor, potential incentives for American firms to export jobs overseas (which might occur if U.S.-based firms did not have access to a supply of cheap labor at home), inflationary pressures (prices of basic commodities and services are likely to rise if this alien workforce were to disappear), the question of fair versus expedient application of immigration laws, border security, and the desires of various political constituencies. Certainly, this is not an easy feat! What almost everyone agrees on, however, is that the current system is not working, creating a lot of frustration on all sides.[52] For instance, in 2010 the State of Arizona passed the toughest immigration law in the country (if not in the world) declaring undocumented immigrants as criminals and requiring police to question people about their immigration status if officers suspect they are in the United States illegally (which of course raises the ugly specter of racial profiling for people with foreign accents, those with darker skins, those who dress in an unusual manner, and soon). In an unusual White House attack on state legislation President Obama wasted no time in harshly criticizing the measure and a federal judge has declared unconstitutional some of its key provisions (although the state of Arizona is appealing this decision at the time of this writing).

Women

As noted earlier, the labor force is half female, and 40 percent of the U.S. workforce consists of families in which both spouses are working. In recent years women have successfully entered many occupations previously reserved for men such as law, medicine, police, and even firefighting (see Management Close-Up 11.3). However, women continue to face several problems at work. Those who want families may be seen as not being committed to their careers. Firms in the United States, unlike much of the industrialized world, are not required by law to provide maternity leave. Women continue to have primary responsibility for child rearing and most household duties. Only a tiny percentage of firms offer day care job sharing, and reduced hours for employees with young children. This situation causes many women in their 20s and 30s to withdraw from the workforce or curtail their work-related activities at crucial times in their careers. For instance, only 38 percent of women who graduate from Harvard Business School are expected to be working full time in professional careers 20 years after graduation (based on historical records from the early 1980s to the 2000s).[53]

The glass ceiling makes it hard for women to move beyond a certain level in the corporate hierarchy. Women have limited access to the "old boys' network," the informal relationships that

---

MANAGEMENT CLOSE-UP 11.3   THEME: **DEALING WITH CHANGE**

On Engine 22, Women Who Answer the Bell

When the crew from Fire Engine Company 22 raced off at 7:50 a.m. the other day for the first call of their 24-hour shift, a woman reporting chest pains, their big red rig was primed for action but missing a typical feature: a man.

The four members of Engine 22, Division A, a captain, an engineer, a firefighter-paramedic, and a firefighter, protect the Point Loma neighborhood of San Diego, an affluent peninsula on the Pacific-Ocean. They are one of the few crews in the nation made up entirely of women, winding up together last October, as the captain, Joi Evans, said, because of "the way the cards fell."

Together they work, cook, shop, train and sleep in small dorm rooms in the station house, around the clock for 10 days a month, at a time when women are making some inroads into the fire service nationwide but are still only a sliver of the front line in one of the most physically grueling and male-dominated professions.

Fewer than 4 percent of the nation's firefighters are women, and more than half of paid fire departments have never hired a female firefighter, according to a 2010 report issued by Cornell's Institute for Women and Work. "Women are not getting recruited and hired because of an occupational culture that is exclusionary and supportive of unequal employment practices in recruiting, hiring, assigning, and promoting women generally—and women of color in particular—in fire service", noted the director of the Institute and one of the report's coauthors.

Sources: Based on "Women in Fire and emergency services," http://www.i-women.org, 2011; S. Lang, "Women firefighters can take the heat, but too few firehouses give them the chance, study finds," *Chronicle Online*, http://www.news.cornell.edu, 2011; A. M. Denissen (2010), "The right tools for the job: constructing gender meanings and identities in the male-dominated building trades," *Human Relations*, March, 2010, 1–19. S. Kershaw, (2006, Jan. 23). "On Engine 22, It Is Women Who Answer the Belt, *New York Times*, January 23, 2006, p. A-14.

exist among managers and executives in which much important communication occurs. Significant decisions, such as who will be promoted, are often made through loose coalitions that are part of this informal network.

Women face sexual harassment at work far more often than men. Unwanted sexual advances, even if they are not overt, may cause women to quit their jobs. When a woman refuses, resists, or challenges such pressures, she often jeopardizes her future with the department or company. Sexual harassment is discussed in more detail in Chapter 10.

Finally, men and women may have somewhat different communication styles. They may attach a meaning that is different from the one that a person of the opposite sex intended to convey (see Figure 11.4). This increases the odds of miscommunication and conflict. Since more men are in powerful positions than women, this works against a woman's upward advancement.

LOC-In 4 Learning Objective Check-In

1. Chris, Kim, and Jamal were co-workers in the finance department. Chris and Jamal often went to lunch together, shared information, and coordinated with one another on difficult or complementary projects. Yet Kim often wondered why she was not a part of the _____. Eventually, Kim resigned from her position in the department. It became clear to her, from daily experience and tensions and discussions with previous employees, that women were not a welcome part of the finance department.
   a. diversity resources
   b. management structure
   c. communication flow
   d. negotiation process

FIGURE 11.4

Men and Women, Divided by Language

Source: Adapted from R. D. Bucher, *Diversity Consciousness* (Upper Saddle River, NJ: Prentice Hall, 2000), p. 130.

Deborah Tannen is a professor of linguistics, the science of language. In her research, Tannen has focused on the different communication styles of men and women. She has written extensively on this subject. Her books, titled *You Just Don't Understand, That's Not What I Meant,* and *Talking from 9 to 5,* offer examples of gender differences:

- Men tend to engage in report talk, women in rapport talk. Report talk is a way of showing one's knowledge and skill. Rapport talk allows one to share with others and develop relationships.

- When making requests, women tend to be indirect. A female supervisor might ask: "Could you do this by 5 pm?" Something more direct and to the point is more typical of a male supervisor: "This needs to be done by 5 pm."

- Women have a greater information focus. They do not hesitate to ask questions in order to understand something. Men have more of an image focus. Even though men may be unclear about an issue, they may forgo asking questions, to preserve their image or reputation.

- Women often say "I'm sorry" to express concern about something. Men, on the other hand, may interpret this to mean that women are accepting blame or responsibility. This is not at all what women have in mind.

- People tend to judge men for what they say and do. Women are often judged by how they look and dress.

- For women, tears may be a way of expressing valid emotions. For men, they are a sign of weakness and immaturity.

Tannen makes the point that these differences do not apply to all men or women in all situations. By realizing that differences such as these may exist, we lessen the chances of miscommunication and conflict.

■ Building on Diversity

Organizations can choose from a number of strategies for improving the management of diversity. Several of these, which are summarized in Figure 11.5, are discussed next.

Top Management Commitment

Lower-level managers and employees are unlikely to take diversity seriously if they believe that senior executives are not giving the management of diversity a high priority. Some CEOs take active and visible roles in diversity management, attending multiple meetings on diversity issues, while others merely make an internal announcement about the program. At Sara Lee, top executives played a major role in a three-day conference on diversity, launching several diversity initiatives. Similarly, the top nine officers of Bank of America attended a three-day off-site meeting on how to improve the management of diversity. The meeting involved all of the bank branches and was attended by a cross-section of employees from various geographic areas, job levels, racial groups, ages, and sexual orientations. Attendees examined the following issues:

1. How can we develop all employees so that they are ready for opportunities that arise in the company?
2. How can we be sure that minorities and women gain access to better jobs as they become available?
3. How can we make sure that we give minorities and women opportunities without discriminating against white men?
4. How can we show all employees that we value their contributions?
5. How can we change attitudes of both employees and customers?
6. Will the same approach work for new employees and those with many years of service?[54]

Linking Diversity Initiatives to Business Strategies and Objectives

If diversity management is perceived only as a program emanating from the Human Resource Department with lip service support from top management, it is unlikely to be effective. Announcing a diversity program without giving it corporate support could give employees the impression that the company is simply going through the motions, which would be counterproductive. This was alleged to be the situation at Texaco in 1996 before the firm had to make drastic moves in response to public scandal.

FIGURE 11.5

How Organizations May Build on Diversity

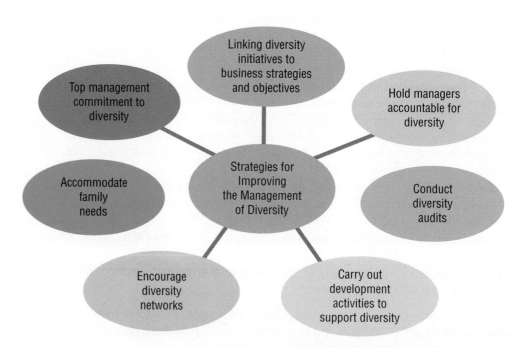

Employee diversity objectives should be key components of corporate mission statements and company strategies. Companies whose leaders have incorporated management of diversity into their mission statements include Inland Steel, FMC Corporation, Digital Equipment Corporation, and NASA. Hewlett-Packard has a comprehensive diversity model that considers external and internal forces and that includes corporate objectives and diversity goals and objectives. FMC has produced a *Diversity Handbook for Managers,* with guidelines and examples to create a tight link among business strategy, human resources strategy, and the management of diversity. Topics covered include new management orientation, diversity briefings for senior management, networking groups, developmental assignments, linking diversity performance to other corporate objectives, and benchmarking with other companies.

Management Responsibility and Accountability

People tend to invest time and effort in things that are measured and rewarded. "Diversity is not likely to become part of management and employee priorities without real accountability for specific objectives."[55] General Electric, Inland Steel, Hewlett-Packard, and other companies hold their managers accountable for employee diversity by making it part of their performance appraisals and merit pay. Some companies link a significant amount of a manager's financial reward to effective handling of diversity issues. For example, one-fifth of managers' annual bonuses at Harvard Pilgrim Health Care is directly tied to meeting measurable diversity objectives.

Firms use a variety of accountability tools to ensure the implementation of diversity strategies. These include written and verbal **360-degree feedback** (multirater feedback from peers, suppliers, other levels of management, and internal and external customers), employee surveys, performance appraisals, and self-evaluations. General Electric has managers assess their own performance on key diversity practices, including recruitment objectives, support of work/life balance programs, and involvement in outreach programs.

360-degree feedback
Multirater feedback from peers, suppliers, other levels of management, and internal and external customers.

Diversity Audits

Before launching a new diversity initiative or designing an intervention to fit a situation, it is important to ascertain why things are the way they are, which things should stay the way they are, and which should be changed. A diversity audit can help reveal possible sources of bias, and the indicators or factors used in the audit can also be used to measure whether corrective actions have the desired effects. For instance, if the percentage of women who quit each year in a particular division is twice as high of that of men, this could indicate that there is a problem that should be examined further.

Developmental Activities

Besides measuring and rewarding diversity efforts, companies also offer developmental opportunities to managers and employees to improve diversity management. The most common activities are diversity training, senior mentoring, apprenticeships, and diversity learning labs.

DIVERSITY TRAINING Many programs can improve awareness of diversity issues. Managers and employees should learn about specific cultural and gender differences to help them respond in the workplace. At the information services company EDS, for example, employees attend diversity awareness workshops that focus on working together with people of different race, sex, religion, age, and social status, people with disabilities, and so on. Besides improving customer satisfaction with the company, these workshops have increased the pool of applicants for the company.[56] However, any firm using diversity training programs needs to be very careful that these are not perceived as a medium to reinforce stereotypes or as an opportunity to vent hostility toward a particular group, such as white males. Figure 11.6 shows a list of issues, according to the Society for Human Resource Management, that should be considered in diversity training.

SENIOR MENTORING Some firms have implemented senior mentoring programs in which managers and senior employees are encouraged to identify women and minorities with

FIGURE 11.6

Issues to Consider in Diversity Training

Source: Society for Human Resource Management, *HR Resources*, 2011 http://www.shim.org/diversity.

- Diversity is about each person coming to terms with his or her attitudes, beliefs, and expectations about others and gaining comfort with differences.
- Diversity is big enough to include everyone: young and old, homeless and affluent, immigrant and native, white and black. Diversity goes beyond race and gender.
- No one is or should be the target for blame for current or past inequities. All human beings have been socialized to behave in certain ways, and all of us are at times both perpetrators and victims of discrimination and stereotypes.
- Human beings are ethnocentric—they see the world through their own narrow view and judge the world by what is familiar to them.
- The human species resists change. This makes the constant adaptation required for diversity difficult for people already overwhelmed by staggering transitions in today's organizations.
- Human beings find comfort and trust in likeness. There is a tendency to seek the company of those most similar to ourselves.
- It is difficult for people to share power. History shows that it is rarely done voluntarily and without a reason that will somehow benefit those dominating the pool of wealth.

promising careers. The mentor is responsible for coaching the employee, offering a nurturing environment, and facilitating the employee's career progress. Marriott, for instance, has made senior mentoring available to disabled employees for many years. Honeywell and 3M team up experienced executives with young women and minorities to give them advice on career strategies and corporate politics. General Electric recently introduced a buddy system to assist new employees with their transition to GE.

APPRENTICESHIPS Apprenticeship programs groom prospective employees before they are hired on a permanent basis. For instance, General Electric provides scholarships and internships to minority students, many of whom become a permanent part of GE's workforce at a later date.

DIVERSITY LEARNING LABS Diversity learning labs improve knowledge and insight about market niches of diverse client populations. American Express has established 15 diversity learning labs that "receive concentrated funding, resource and training support from the region and corporate office. They are focused on diverse segments in the African-American, gay and lesbian, Hispanic, and women's market. The labs are not only experiencing increased diverse client acquisition but are also surfacing key learning such as strong project management experience in diverse segments."[57]

LOC-In 5 Learning Objective Check-In

Poston Company conducts on-site programs that improve the employees' awareness of diversity issues. These programs help managers and employees learn about specific cultural and gender differences to help them respond better in the workplace. Another method Poston Company uses to manage diversity internally is programs that groom prospective employees before they are hired on a permanent basis. They achieve this by providing internships to a variety of targeted student groups, many of whom become a permanent part of the workforce following the internships.

1. The programs employees attend that help them with the awareness of and appropriate responses to cultural and gender differences are collectively called _____ .
   a. diversity training
   b. administrative management
   c. behavioral training
   d. apprenticeships

2. The internships at Poston Company that groom prospective employees before they are hired on a permanent basis at the company represent _____ .
   a. senior mentoring programs
   b. apprenticeships
   c. diversity learning labs
   d. diversity training sessions

Encouraging Diversity Networks

The corporate environment can be insensitive, cold, or even hostile to the needs of many women and minorities. Support groups offer a nurturing environment to employees who otherwise may feel excluded from the corporate mainstream or lost in a bureaucracy run by people dissimilar to them. Companies with support groups for women, homosexuals, and/or racial and ethnic minorities include Allstate, Avon, Digital Equipment, and Xerox. DuPont is reported to have more than 100 such networks. Apple headquarters in Cupertino, California, has a Jewish cultural group, a gay/lesbian group, and women's groups.

Microsoft has a large number of support groups representing a variety of constituencies, such as Attention Deficit Disorder, Deaf and Hard of Hearing, Single Parents, and Working Parents, in addition to various ethnic groups.[58] Despite their potential value in promoting diversity, it is important to make sure that these support groups do not become "self-contained units" that separate particular kinds of employees from the rest. This inadvertently creates conflict and a "we versus them" mentality.

Company leaders may actively encourage or even require employees, particularly those in responsible professional and managerial positions, to become part of international teams. The growing global economy and increasingly diverse customers and markets justify such added expenses as travel, long-distance calls, and extra time. Intel Business Practices Network makes use of global teams. "Teams are multicultural/multifunctional, often involving people across three to five geographies—domestically and internationally. . . . The global team approach has paid off in a short time to market innovative ideas and product design."[59]

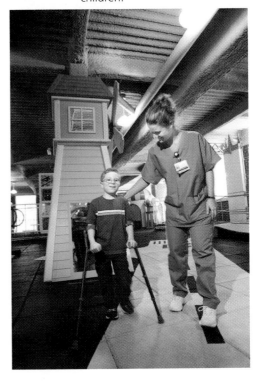

Though much remains to be done, some companies are trying to help employees meet the needs of work and family by providing child care and other support services, such as special help to parents of disabled children.

Accommodating Family Needs

Although 8.7 million single mothers and 1.4 million single fathers are in the workforce, as are more than half of women with young children, most companies are not family-friendly. Men as well as women find it difficult to balance family and career. Being responsible for child care results in less opportunity for advancement for employees of both sexes.

This is starting to change. Many executives now realize that the benefits of accommodating employees' family needs can exceed the cost and inconvenience. Family-friendly policies expand the pool of applicants so that the firm can recruit better employees, improve morale, and reduce turnover and absenteeism. Because workers have fewer worries and distractions, they can concentrate on their jobs and better use their talents.

Some of the options available to organizations to help employees handle family and career simultaneously include:

1. Day care assistance—for instance, Merck and Campbell Soup have day care centers at the workplace. One company, Massachusetts-based Bright Horizons Family Solutions, runs round-the-clock child care facilities for Toyota in Kentucky and S. C. Johnson in Wisconsin and two Ford Motor Co./United Auto Workers Family Service Learning Centers, and is currently developing child care facilities for 11 more firms.[60]
2. Flexible work schedules and arrangements.
3. Compressed work weeks—for example, working four 10-hour days instead of five 8-hour days.

4. Job sharing—two part-time workers share one full-time job. A survey of more than 1,000 companies by consulting firm Hewitt Associates indicates that 28 percent of the organizations surveyed offer job sharing, up from just 12 percent in 1990.[61]
5. Telecommuting—full-or part-time employees work at home, maintaining their connection to the office via fax, phone, and computer.
6. Care assistance for elderly dependents.
7. Paid time off to care for family members who are ill.
8. Paid parental leave.
9. Keeping relocations to a minimum.
10. Giving a high priority to finding a position for a spouse within the company.
11. Providing job search assistance to relocated spouses.

CONCLUDING THOUGHTS

At the beginning of the chapter, we asked why most executives believe that effective management of diversity is critical to organizational success. This belief IBM has put into practice since the 19th century, even though the term "employee diversity" was probably coined for the first time in the 1980s. Besides the moral argument that it is the right thing to do, most executives now believe that effective management of diversity is "all business" and that it represents a pragmatic response to demographic changes. These executives argue that effective management of diversity is good as well as necessary for business because (1) changes in technology and competition make diverse thinking a necessity; (2) minorities make up a majority of the labor market in many parts of the country, and, to be competitive, firms need to retain and motivate minority employees; and (3) companies are wooing customers from all corners of the globe, and they need the help of executives who can function in different cultures.

A major challenge organizations face is how to balance the need for greater workforce diversity with the perception that this diversity comes at the expense of the dominant group. In other words, it is important to actively support employee diversity in such a way that everyone sees it as a win-win situation. Managers should devote considerable time and resources to ensuring that diversity efforts are inclusive rather than exclusive and that employees come to appreciate and respect the contributions of other employees who may not be like or look like them.

FOCUSING ON THE FUTURE: Using Management Theory in Daily Life

Managing Employee Diversity

Roxana Carbajal is a Human Resource Director at an Embassy Suites Hotel, which is owned by the Hilton Hotel Corporation. She currently serves approximately 145 employees, of whom only 3–4 percent are "nonminority." Eighty percent of the employees speak Spanish, 7 percent Mandarin, 3 percent Cantonese, 8 percent Tagalog (Filipino), 1 percent Hindi, and 1 percent German. Roxana was hired in part because she is bilingual—and also because she knows how to maximize the performance of a diverse workforce.

The Hilton Hotel Corporation has a wide variety of diversity initiatives and policies, ranging from a formal mission statement through diversity training programs, mentoring, and even diversity performance measurements at the hotel level. Roxana's job is to be sure these programs and policies are carried out in the day-to-day activities of her hotel.

The Workforce Diversity Mission Statement is "to create and maintain a diverse work place culture that strengthens the business value of the corporation and affirms Hilton Hotels Corporation as an industry leader in the global market."[1] In Roxana's world, this means that she must attract and hire a diverse workforce, and then create an environment in which everyone focuses on creating a first-class destination for world travelers. Put in a different way, it is the responsibility of the Human Resource Director to create "a workforce that reflects diversity of our hotel guests, appreciates uniqueness of each guest, and values contributions of all fellow team members."[2] Roxana starts this process by advertising open positions widely and using Equal Employment Opportunity agencies such as the California Employment Development Department to get the news of job openings to a diverse set of applicants. When interviewing new applicants, Roxana uses a structured interview process, which is less likely to be unfairly discriminatory than an unstructured interview.

Once they are hired, Roxana ensures that all new employees receive orientation training that incorporates information on working with diverse co-workers and serving a diverse clientele. One of the most important messages of the program is to communicate the "Embassy Way." Every employee is expected to recognize guests promptly, use their first names, and smile at them. This form of homogenization helps to ensure a consistent experience for guests, and it also brings diverse co-workers closer together. In addition to diversity training, all hotel employees and managers go through "Harassment Free" training, as well as additional customer service training. Again, all training serves to make employee behavior more consistent and to make employees and managers aware of diversity issues.

According to the "Hilton Family" HR procedural manual (which covers the Hilton, Conrad, DoubleTree, Embassy Suites, Homewood Suites, Hampton Inn, Grand Vacations Club, Scandia, and Hilton Garden Inn hotels)

- Each year, management at all Hilton-owned and managed hotels must have a specific written set of performance goals established to measure diversity performance.
- A set of specific written performance goals must be in place for all corporate management staff for annual measurement of their diversity performance.
- Diversity performance measurements must be attached to annual bonus calculations for both hotel and corporate management.

Sources: [1]Hilton Hotels Corporation, "Diversity Programs" http://cvmsolutions.com/hilton, accessed April, 2010; [2]ibid.

Summary of Learning Objectives

1 Explain the meaning and benefits of employee diversity.

- The term *diversity* refers to differences among people that are either inborn (such as race and gender) or chosen (such as occupation and religion).
- The benefits of employee diversity include better access to differentiated markets, greater competitiveness on a global scale, more creative problem solving within the firm, and enhanced team performance.

2 Develop an awareness of the unique perspectives, problems, and issues of diverse employee groups.

- African Americans, Asian Americans, the disabled, the foreign born, homosexuals, Hispanics, older workers, those who hold different religious views, and women often face unique problems in the workplace, and firms need to take their problems into account to improve the management of diversity.
- Managers should avoid making inferences about a specific individual based on demographic group characteristics because there is a great deal of overlap between groups on most psychological traits.

3 Understand demographic trends in the labor force and their managerial implications.

- The U.S. workforce is increasingly diverse in terms of gender, race, ethnicity, expressed sexual orientation, age, and so on. Currently, American-born white males constitute only about 15 percent of new entrants to the workforce and by the middle of the 21st century more than half of the workforce is likely to be non-white.
- Firms that can manage employee diversity effectively, and do it better than other firms, are likely to enjoy a competitive advantage.

4 Describe the challenges firms may face in the management of diversity.

- Some people erroneously believe that effective management of employee diversity means that minorities and women receive special treatment.
- If not properly managed, diversity may negatively result in pressures to induce dissimilar employees to leave the firm, segregating them, limiting communication flow, and preventing their career advancement.
- When diverse employees do come together, a firm's cohesiveness may diminish while interpersonal conflict and tension could intensify if this is not understood and headed off.

5 Describe various approaches that managers may use to enjoy the benefits of employee diversity and meet the challenges associated with diversity.

- Improving the utilization of employee diversity includes obtaining top-management commitment, linking diversity initiatives to business strategies and objectives, holding managers responsible for diversity results, conducting diversity audits, implementing a variety of developmental activities, fostering the establishment of employee diversity networks, and offering family-friendly programs to help employees accommodate work and family life.
- It is important to actively support employee diversity in such a way that everyone sees it as a win-win situation.
- Managers should devote considerable time and resources to ensure that diversity efforts are inclusive rather than exclusive and that employees come to appreciate the respect the contributions of other employees who may not be or look like them.

Discussion Questions

1. Look back at Management Close-Up 11.1 on tapping the Hispanic market for banking services. How would you develop a plan to take advantage of employee diversity in order to sell *your* product or services to particular market segments? Explain your answer.
2. Going back to Management Close-Up 11.2, what ethical responsibilities if any should a company have with older employees? Explain your answer.
3. Look back at Management Close-Up 11.3 on women firefighters. Why do you think women are still severely underrepresented in many fields (even though much progress has been achieved in the last 20 years or so)? Explain your answer.

4. Of all the challenges of diversity discussed in this chapter, which do you think is the most serious? Explain why.
5. What do you see as the connection between affirmative action and the management of employee diversity? How are they similar? How are they different?
6. How would you know whether your firm was doing a good or a bad job of managing employee diversity? What type of data would you need to answer this question?
7. Of all the initiatives for improving the management of diversity discussed in this chapter, which do you consider the most important? Why?

Management Minicase 11.1
We Are All Getting Older!

A rapidly aging workforce in the developed countries has become a key concern as expressed by the labor ministers of the United States, Canada, United Kingdom, France, Germany, Italy, Japan, and Russia, who recently met in London. Unless something radical happens in another generation (around 2040) almost half of the population in the developed world will be 50 years old or older and more than one-fourth will be over 65. Here is how some countries and organizations are trying to meet this challenge.

The Graying Baby Boom Generation around the World

Jenni Francois doesn't have the world's most glamorous job. For 20 years she has commuted 45 minutes to the office of insurer Macif in Agen, France, where she punches data into a computer. But in the not-too-distant future, Francois and hundreds of millions of people like her in the industrialized world could look back at the early 21st century as the beginning of the end of a wonderful era, when even average workers could retire in reasonable comfort in their still-vigorous 50s. Thanks to France's pension system, Francois, 58, is in "pre-retirement." For three years, she has worked two days a week and still collects 1,500 a month—over 70 percent of her old full-time salary. Her pay will dip only slightly when she reaches 60. "The system is great for me," Francois says. "I think it should be every worker's right."

It's already clear that the system will be far less generous to future retirees in France and elsewhere. And the message isn't going down easy. Despite a national wave of strikes, France has enacted new rules requiring people to work longer to qualify for the benefits to avert a fiscal crunch. Italy, Germany, Japan, Finland, South Korea, Brazil, and Greece all have moved to or proposed to trim benefits, raise retirement ages, and hike workers' pension contributions. To counter the pension crisis. China is likely to gradually boost the retirement age, now 55 for women and 60 for men, to 65 by 2030. It might further loosen the one-child policy. Meanwhile, even those with two children, like Ms. Wang, worry. "I'm considering finding another job," says Wang. "I might work as a cook for construction workers, but I know that will be very tiring." For now, too many of China's wannabe retirees may have to labor on into their golden years.

Help Wanted: Older Workers Please Apply

In a push to recruit older workers, Home Depot, the hardware chain, now offers "snowbird specials": winter work in Florida and summers in Maine. Borders bookstores lure retired teachers to sales jobs with discounts and the promise of reading and discussion groups. Pitney Bowes, the business services company, pays tuition for courses in computer programming as well as spare-time skills like golf and flower arranging. Some companies like Wal-Mart are making their pitches at senior centers and others are sending company brochures to churches and community libraries and posting their attractions on Web sites. AARP, the advocacy group for older people, recently put on its Web site links to 13 "featured employers" including MetLife, Pitney Bowes, Borders, Home Depot, Principal Financial, and Walgreen that are recruiting older workers with offers of health benefits, training, and flexible work schedules. More than 71,000 people have used the Web site in a recent month to seek job information.

In industries with labor shortages, like nursing, older workers already have an edge. Nurses, who typically retire at 53, are being recruited at high rates, says Peter Buerhaus, associate dean of the school of nursing at Vanderbilt University. "They are probably the fastest-aging work force in the country." More than 70 percent of nurses hired in recent years are over 50.

Battling the Brain Drain

As older workers retire in droves, organizations are trying to find ways to prevent their crucial knowledge from leaving with them.

Consider the chilling example of the National Aeronautics and Space Administration. Way back in the 1960s, it spent $24 billion (in 1969 dollars) and at one point employed 400,000 people—to send 12 astronauts to the moon. But in the 24 years since the Apollo program ended, the engineers who carried crucial know-how in their heads, without ever passing it on to colleagues, have retired or died (or both). At the same time, important blueprints were catalogued incorrectly or not at all, and the people who drew them are no longer around to draw them again. So to fulfill NASA's desire to return to the moon in the next decade, NASA is essentially starting all over again. Estimated cost to taxpayers in current dollars: $100 billion.

Now more and more organizations—among them General Electric, Dow Chemical, and Northrop Grumman—are working on ways to capture their oldsters' knowledge and disseminate it to younger workers before it's too late. Defense contractor Northrop Grumman has created what are called communities of practice—companywide groups that meet, in person and online, to share information. "Social networks, people building connections across divisional boundaries, are where the breakthrough innovations are coming from," Schaffar says. "We're seeing a crop of young, emerging leaders coming out of these groups."

Still another mechanism for transferring expertise is something General Electric calls "action learning teams." Action learning teams put people together from several disciplines— manufacturing, sales, marketing, legal, finance—to solve particular problems. The hand-picked young managers who participate, along with older and presumably wiser colleagues, "get exposed to very big projects and issues, but with a safety net. You learn by doing, and you get continuous feedback on your performance." One advantage of the teams, says Bob Corcoran, GE's chief learning officer, is that they "encourage people to learn a lot about a lot of things, not just their own jobs. It reduces the likelihood that when boomers do retire, you'll be left saying, 'Gee, old Alex was the only person here who knew how to do this.'"

There is another approach companies are taking: pooling resources. For example, four years ago, Procter & Gamble started worrying that boomers retiring in masse would decimate their R&D department. Eli Lilly, with which P&G had done some joint research projects, had the same concern. So the two companies formed Yourencore.com, an online network of retired and semiretired research scientists and engineers that matches available brains with short-term R&D projects. Two more employers, Boeing and National Starch & Chemical, recently joined the group, which draws on a database of 470 scientists. The folks who sign on with Yourencore are paid an hourly rate for their project work and often do their own consulting and teaching on the side.

DISCUSSION QUESTIONS

1. What are some of the common issues in the scenarios described? Explain.
2. What do you see as the key implications of a population that is getting older to the practice of human resources? Explain.
3. Some people argue that the United States is a "youth loving" society and that for this reason organizations often do not value the wisdom of older workers. Do you agree?

Sources: "Global demographic changes," http://www.w3.org, 2011; J. Hennens, "Online communities are getting old," http://blog.vovici.com, 2011; "Chao Addresses Challenges of Aging workforces at Conference," *Newsline,* April 27, 2005 http://resourcespro.worldatwork.org/; P. Engardio, C. Matlack, G. Edmondson, I. Rowley, C. Barraclough, G. Smith, "Global Aging: Now, the Geezer Glut," *BusinessWeek,* January 31, 2005, pp. 44–47; M. W. Walsh, "When Your Pension Is Frozen," *New York Times,* January 22, 2006, p. A-1; M. Freudenheim, "Help Wanted: Older Workers Please Apply," *New York Times,* March 23, 2005, P A-1; A. Fisher, "How to Battle the Coming Brain Drain," *Fortune,* March 31, 2005, pp. 21–128; J. Helyar, "50 and Fired," *Fortune,* May 10, 2006, pp. 78–86.

Management Minicase 11.2
Despite Past Cases, Wall Street Has Yet to Shake a Boys' Club Image

Six women who are senior bankers at Dresdner Kleinwort Wasserstein services have sued the investment bank for $1.4 billon on behalf of 500 women who work at Dresdner Kleinwort, contending that they were denied equal bonuses and promotions that went to men with less experience.

The complaint, brought by three directors and three vice presidents—all still working at the bank—also cites instances of lewd behavior toward the women, entertainment of clients at a strip club, and repeated examples of scaled-back opportunities for women after they returned from maternity leave. Women account for less than 2 percent of the company's managing directors. Other Wall Street firms that have recently faced similar charges include Merrill Lynch, Morgan Stanley, and Salomon Smith Barney. In an explosive book titled "The Manhattan Madam: Sex, Drugs, Scandal & Greed Inside America's Most Successful Prostitution Ring," Kristin Davis paints a vivid and behind-the-scenes look at the sexist macho culture of leading Wall Street firms.

DISCUSSION QUESTIONS

1. Why do you think in some industries such as the one discussed women are so under-represented in managerial positions? Explain.
2. If you were an executive in another Wall Street firm and saw these data and allegations being made against other firms, what steps if any would you take to ensure this does not occur at your company? Explain.
3. Some people argue that overt discrimination is a thing of the past and that a company trying to make money has no reason to discriminate. Do you agree? Explain.

Source: Based on "Former Manhattan Madam Kristin Davis dishes insider information on flip side of Wall Street boysclub," http://www.image.examiner.com, 2011; S. Antilla, "In the companies of men: A rash of gender-discrimination suits suggests the Morgan Stanley payout may be only the beginning," *New York Magazine*, http://www.nymag.com, 2010; "Women and Wall Street," *New York Times*, August 13, 2006, A-1; J. Anderson. "Six Women at Dresdner File Bias Suit," *New York Times*, January 10, 2006, p. C-1.

Individual/Collaborative Learning Case 11.1
Approaching a Demographic Milestone

The Census Bureau estimates that with a baby being born every 8 seconds, someone dying every 12 seconds, and the nation gaining an immigrant every 31 seconds on average, the population is growing by one person every 14 seconds. At that rate, the total is expected to exceed 390 million by the year 2040. Compare this to a total population of 200 million in 1970.

Demographers do know that the United States, which ranks third in population behind China and India, is still gaining people while many other industrialized nations are not. (Japan, officials there announced that it has begun shrinking.) Driven by immigration and higher fertility rates, particularly among newcomers from abroad, the United States' population is growing by just under 1 percent annually, the equivalent of the entire population of Chicago (2.8 million). While 84 percent of the U.S. population was Caucasian in 1970, by 2011 this percentage was down to an estimated 65 percent, and by 2030 it would probably be under the 50 percent mark. However, racial classifications are becoming less meaningful as intermarriage has increased dramatically and a greater percentage of the population includes people with mixed ancestry (with the president of the United States, Barack Obama, serving as a prime example).

CRITICAL THINKING QUESTIONS

1. What do you see as the main implications for U.S. firms of the trends discussed above? How are they likely to affect the practice of management? Explain.

2. Do you think that most Americans in general and U.S. firms in particular have handled the changing demographics well during past decades? How about the future? Explain.
3. Some people strongly argue that increased workforce diversity gives American firms a global competitive edge. Do you agree? Why or why not?

COLLABORATIVE LEARNING EXERCISE

The class is divided into groups of five. Each group is expected to develop a set of recommendations that companies should consider in light of the trends discussed above. After meeting for approximately 15–20 minutes, groups will reconvene and present their conclusions to the entire class with the instructor as moderator.

Source: Based on "Demographic change and local government: Overview of issues," http://www.mrsc.org, 2011; "Population profile of the United States," http://www.census.gov, 2010; S. Roberts. "Come October, Body Count Will Make 300 Million or So," *New York Times*, January 13, 2006, p. A-1.

Internet Exercise 11.1

Managing Employee Diversity

www.fortune.com

Choose four or five of the companies listed in *Fortune's* "America's Best Companies for Minorities," published annually (www.fortune.com). Search the Internet for information about them, Use the companies' Web sites and other sites. Use this information to answer the following questions:

1. What advantages have accrued to the firms as a result of their effective management of employee diversity?
2. Are there common approaches to managing employee diversity among the companies you've chosen? what strategies are unique to any of the companies? What reasons, such as industry, geographical location, size, and history, might lie behind these unique strategies?
3. Could other firms apply the diversity-related policies and practices used by the firms you've chosen? Why or why not?
4. *Fortune* rates the firms "the best" in their diversity efforts following specified criteria which are noted in the published annual report. What criteria would you use to evaluate a company's diversity efforts? How would you rate the firms you've chosen to investigate based on your criteria?

Endnotes

1. L. R. Gomez-Mejia, D. B. Balkin, and R. Cardy, *Managing Human Resources* (Englewood Cliffs, NJ: Prentice Hall, 2012).
2. C. Crossen, "How U.S. Immigration Evolved as the Nation Grew and Changed," *The Wall Street Journal*, January 9, 2006, p. B-3; S. Roberts, "Come October, Body Count Will Make 300 Million or So," *New York Times*, January 13, 2006, p. A. 1.
3. Stead & Elliot (2010) (see reference list) M. L. Wheeler, "Capitalizing on Diversity," *BusinessWeek*, December 14, 1998, special advertising section.
4. Ibid.
5. G. Colvin, "50 Best Companies for Asians, Blacks, and Hispanics," *Fortune*, July 19, 1999, pp. 52–59.
6. R. O. Crockett, "African-Americans Get the Investing Bug," *BusinessWeek*, May 24, 1999, p. 39.
7. C. Prystay, and S. Ellison, "Time for Marketers to Grow Up?" *The Wall Street Journal*, February 27, 2003 p. B-1.
8. D. Jones, "U.S. Managers Earn Global Credentials," *USA Today*, February 26, 1997, p. A1.
9. Johnson et al. (2010) (see reference list) M. L. Wheeler, "Diversity: Making the Business Case," *BusinessWeek*, December 9, 1996, special advertising section.
10. Ibid.
11. V. I. Sessa, S. E. Jackson, and D. T. Rapini, "Workforce Diversity: The Good, and Bad, and the Reality." In G. Ferris, S. D. Rosen, and D. T. Barnum (Eds.), *Handbook of Human Resource Management* (Cambridge, MA: Blackwell, 1995), pp. 263–282.
12. Wheeler, "Diversity."
13. http://www.SHRM.com/diversity, 2011 T. H. Cox, and S. Blake, "Managing Cultural Diversity: Implications for Organizational Competitiveness," *Academy of Management Executive* 5, no. 3 (1991): 45–46.
14. M. C. Fine, P. L. Johnson, and S. M. Ryan, "Cultural Diversity in the Workplace," *Public Personnel Management* 19, no. 3 (1990): 305–319.
15. Wheeler, "Diversity."
16. G. S. Van Der Vegt, E. V. Ulert, and X. Huang, "Location Level Links between Diversity and Innovative Climate Depend on National Power Distance," *Academy of Management Journal*, 48(6), (2005): 1171–1182.
17. Fine, Johnson, and Ryan, "Cultural Diversity in the Workplace."
18. www.businessweek.com, 2006.
19. http://www.SHRM.com/diversity, 2011 R. O. Crockett, "The Changing Landscape," *BusinessWeek*, January 27, 2003, p. 96.
20. H. Fineman, and T. Lipper, "Spinning Race," *Newsweek*, January 23, 2003, pp. 27–38.

21. C. Hastings, "Engaging in a Growing Workforce." *Workspan*, April 2003, pp. 35–39.
22. T. S. Bateman and S. A. Snell, *Management: Building Competitive Advantage*, 4th ed. (Burr Ridge, IL: Irwin, 1999), p. 320.
23. L. R. Gomez-Mejia, D. B. Balkin, and R. Cardy, *Managing Human Resources*. (Englewood Cliffs, NJ: Prentice Hall, 2012).
24. H. Green, "Chocolate Mess," *BusinessWeek*, January 16, 2006, p. 14; M. Jordan, "Blacks vs. Latinos at Work," *The Wall Street Journal*, January 24, 2006, p. B-1.
25. "Research National Phone Poll," *Chattanooga Times*, March 4, 1994, p. 1.
26. Jordan, "Blacks vs. Latinos."
27. http://www.SHRM.com/diversity, 2011 "Research National Phone Poll"; Stephanie Mehta, "What Minority Employees Really Want," *Fortune*, July 10, 2000, p. 180.
28. J. Chu, and N. Mustafa, "Between Two Worlds," *Time*, January 16, 2006, p. 67.
29. Ibid.
30. Briefs, *Workforce Strategies*, 4(2) (February 22, 1993): WS-12.
31. Y. Armendariz, "Disabled Workers Can Telecommute," *Arizona Republic*, February 10, 2003, p. D-3.
32. Brummelhuis et al. (2010) (see reference list) S. Shellenbarger, "You Can Work from Home—Can You Coach Little League from the Office?" *The Wall Street Journal*, October 20, 2005, p. D-1.
33. R. Alonso-Zaldivar, "Immigrants at 7 million, Revised INS Report Says," *Arizona Republic*, February, 2003 p. A-5.
34. L. Koss-Feder, "Spurred by the Americans with Disabilities Act," p. 82.
35. J. Kanman, and H. Rozenberg, "Survey Looks at Residents with Recent Foreign Roots," *Arizona Republic*, February 7, 2002, p. A-8.
36. Pitts et al. (2010) (see reference list) R. Doyle, "Assembling the future," *Scientific American*, February 2000, p. 30.
37. L. R. Gomez-Mejia, D. B. Balkin, and R. Cardy, *Managing Human Resources*. (New York: Prentice Hall, 2012); Crossen, "How U.S. Immigration Evolved."
38. Gomez-Mejia, Balkin, and Cardy, *Managing Human Resources*.
39. Overberg, El Nasser, 2005.
40. Manley (2010) (see reference list) R. Mendosa, "The $152 Billion Engine," *Hispanic Business*, October 1996, pp. 28–29; R. Mendosa, "A Downward Count," *Hispanic Business*, October 1996, p. 18.
41. Gomez-Mejia, Balkin, and Cardy, *Managing Human Resources*.
42. E. Banach, "Today's Supply of Entry Level Workers Reflect Diversity," *Savings Institution*, September 1990, p. 74.
43. Pitts et al. (2010) (see reference list) D. S. Fellows, "Striking Gold in a Silver Mine: Leveraging Senior Workers as Knowledge Champions," *Worldatwork Journal*, 10(4), (2001): 1–12.
44. http://www.SHRM.com/diversity, 2011; C. J. Levy, "The New Corporate Outsourcing," *New York Times*, January 29, 2006, p. D-1; R. Bernstein, "The Undoing of a Done Deal," *BusinessWeek*, February 13, 2006, p. 54; K. Greene, "Bye-Bye Boomers?" *The Wall Street Journal*, September 20, 2005, p. B-1; M. W. Walsh, "When Your Pension Is Frozen," *New York Times*, January 22, 2006, p. A-1; J. Helyar, "50 and Fired," *Fortune*, May 10, 2006, p. 78-86; "Aging Workforce Presents New Opportunities, Challenges for Employers," *Workspan*, November 2, 2005, p. 16; P. Coy, "Surprise! The Graying of the

Workforce Is Better News than You Think," *BusinessWeek*, June 27, 2005, p. 78; R. Pear, "Bush to Propose Vast Cost Savings in Medicare Plan," *New York Times*, February 4, 2006, p. B-1.

45. "Talking to Diversity Experts," 2003, www.fortune.com/sections.
46. Ameer, 2006.; Anna, 2006.
47. Abserhan et al. (2010) (see reference list) D. Bilefsky, "Denmark Is Unlikely Front in Islam-West Culture War," *New York Times*, January 8, 2006, p. 3; A. Cowell, "More European Papers Print Cartoons of Muhammad, Fueling Dispute among Muslims." *New York Times*, February 2, 2006, p. A-3; A. Cowell, "Cartoons Force Danish Muslims to Examine Loyalties," *New York Times*, February 4, 2006, p. B-1; M. Champion, "Muslim Outrage Mounts Over Cartoons in EU," *The Wall Street Journal*, February 3, 2006, p. B-2; A. Aji, "Syrians Burn Embassies over Cartoons," *Arizona Republic*, February 5, 2006, p. A-11; S. Nassauer, "France's New Race Relations," *The Wall Street Journal*, January 9, 2006, p. A-11.
48. Gomez-Mejia, Balkin & Cardy (2012) (see reference list) P. Magnusson, "Wipsaved on the Border," *BusinessWeek*, October 10, 2005, pp. 64–66; B. Grow, "Tapping a Market That Is Hot, Hot, Hot," *BusinessWeek* January 17, 2005, p. 36; B. Grow, "Embracing Illegals," *BusinessWeek*, July 18, 2005, p. 55; J. Millman, "Changing Face of Immigrants," *The Wall Street Journal*, January 24, 2005, p. A-4; J. C. McKinley, "Mexican Pride and Death in U.S. Service," *New York Times*, March 22, 2005, p. A-6; J. C. McKinley, "At Mexican Border, Tunnels, Vile River, Rusty Fence," *New York Times*, March 23, 2005, p. A-8; C. Leduff and E. Flores, "The Everymigrant's Guide to Crossing the Border Illegally," *New York Times*, February 9, 2005, p. A-16; N. Thornburgh, "Inside the Lives of the Migrants Next Door," *BusinessWeek*, February 6, 2006, pp. 36–46; L. Valdez, "Migration a 2-Nation Concern," *Arizona Republic*, February 5, 2006, p. D-1.
49. D. A. Fahrenthold, "Cap on Migrant Workers Hurting Seafood Processors," *Arizona Republic*, January 16, 2005, p. A-16.
50. L. Greenhouse, "Broad Survey of Day Laborers Finds High Level of Injuries and Pay Violations," *New York Times*, January 22, 2006, p. A-17.
51. Gomez-Mejia, Balkin & Cardy (2012) (see reference list) B. Kiviat, "Dessi Dollars. Inside Business Issue," *The Wall Street Journal*, August 2005, pp. A21–A23; R. L. Swarns, "Chamber and Two Unions Forge Alliance on Immigration Bill," *The Wall Street Journal*, January 19, 2006, p. A-15; Valdez, "Migration a 2-Nation Concern."
52. T. Egan, "Wanted: Border Hoppers," *Arizona Republic*, April 1, 2005, p. A-12.
53. J. Welch, and S. Welch, "What Is Holding Women Back," *BusinessWeek*, February 13, 2006, p. 100.
54. Wheeler, "Diversity."
55. Ibid.
56. Ibid.
57. Ibid.
58. Gomez-Mejia, Balkin, and Cardy, *Managing Human Resources*.
59. Wheeler, "Diversity."
60. A. Ashton, "Around-the-Clock Child Care," *Working Women*, February 2002, p. 14.
61. Wilkinson et al. (2010) (see reference list) A. M. Newman, "Fair shares," *Working Women*, February 2002, pp. 64–71.

12

Learning Objectives

1 Explain what makes leaders unique.

2 Distinguish between management and leadership.

3 Recognize how leaders use different power bases to exercise influence.

4 Differentiate effective and ineffective leaders.

5 Use individualized goals to increase employee motivation.

6 Apply basic reinforcement principles to stimulate desired employee behaviors.

7 Become aware of the role of needs in employee motivation.

8 Recognize assumptions about people and perceptions that may affect employee treatment and motivation.

9 Use work design as a means of employee motivation.

Management Beyond 2020: *Leadership*

A year after Vincent Sollitto was hired as CEO for Photon Dynamics, a San Jose, California, maker of test and repair systems for the flat-panel display industry, the Asian economic crisis threatened the company's survival. Three of Photon's key executives quit, and staff cost-cutting measures included laying off 7 of the company's 100 employees as well as postponing pay raises. How could Sollitto motivate his staff to stay with the company and work harder than ever to make the company successful again?

Sollitto kept his worries about the company's future from employees as he set about involving them in the company's recovery. Sollitto promised his remaining employees that their jobs were safe and promised financial rewards when the company was profitable again. The company brought outsourced projects back in house to keep the staff working and to reduce costs. At weekly companywide meetings, Sollitto answered employee questions and discussed rumors. He continued longstanding traditions, such as free coffee, tea, and popcorn, and the monthly group birthday party.

Sollitto's efforts kept Photon's employee turnover rate at a relatively low 15 percent. When the market improved and Photon recovered, many employees profited handsomely from his options plan. They continue to enjoy top benefits and the company has more than doubled its staff.

Leading and Motivating Others

Sollito was later hired as CEO of Syntax-Brillian, the fastest growing manufacturer of rear-projection HD TVs targeted at high-end video/audio users.

It would have been impossible for then Microsoft Chairman and CEO Bill Gates (pictured here) to stay on top of every issue in every business unit or subsidiary. His leadership was based on providing strategy and direction so that the firm could move fast enough to stay in step. Companies that operate from a central authority and ignore the individual are shortsighted, according to Gates, who sees a parallel in NASA's original design of a manned space capsule. The capsule was designed without manual guidance systems under the assumption that the central aviation system would fly the spacecraft, not the astronauts. The U.S. astronauts were veteran combat and test pilots, and they voiced their concerns that the aviation systems would fail. NASA capitulated and added back-up manual controls that would allow the astronauts to fly the space capsule manually. The astronauts were right. Several of the individual astronauts took over and flew the spacecraft when the central aviation system failed. Indeed, the first landing on the moon would have been a failed mission if only the central authority, and not the individual, had the power.

Being "one of the world's boldest thinkers" wasn't enough for Compaq CEO Eckhard Pfeiffer, who was honored as such by the University of Houston in May 1999. A week later, Pfeiffer was fired by Compaq's board. Pfeiffer's stiff leadership style did not mesh with Compaq's culture and the needs of its employees. Former Compaq chief strategist Robert Stearns described the atmosphere at Compaq: "It felt like we were the Olympic dream team of the PC industry, but over a period of about three years, most of the real players were either forced out or left in disgust." When key personnel were hired by competing companies. Pfeiffer reacted defensively, saying, "I delegated authority and responsibility to a point that exceeded some people's ability to fully live up to that expectation."

When Pfeiffer offered executive perks at the company that had always had an egalitarian culture, he created feelings of inequity among the employees, who felt that these rewards reinforced the wrong things. For example, even though reserved parking spaces had never been assigned, Pfeiffer built an executive parking garage. He repeatedly remodeled the executive floor and he restricted access to it.

Although Pfeiffer talked constantly about Compaq being number one, he lost touch with employees. The Compaq board reacted to the large but unprofitable company Pfeiffer was in charge of by asking him to resign. Compaq never seemed to recover after these turbulent years. It was later acquired by Hewlett Packard, which in 2009 sold most of Compaq's former headquarters to the Lone Star College System.

Sources: Based on http://www.news.ecoustics.com, "Brillian President and CEO, Vincent Sollito, to speak at upcoming USDC investment conference," 2011; "Digital Hollywood," http://www.digitalhollywood.com, 2011; "About Photon dynamics," http://www.newsblaze.com, 2011; "Compaq Management," http://www.thinkingmanagers.com, 2011; C. Hymowitz, "Crises Test a CEO's Leadership Ability," 2010, *The Wall Street*

Journal careerjournal.com; B. Schlender, "e-Business According to Gates," *Fortune*, April 12, 1999, pp. 75–80; D. Kirkpatrick, "Eckhard's Fall, but the PC Rocks On," *Fortune*, May 24, 1999, pp. 153–161; C. Edwards, P. Burrows, and J. Greene, "Microsoft and Intel: Moving In On PC Makers' Turf," *Business Week*, January 15, 2001, p. 41.

CRITICAL THINKING QUESTIONS

1. *What are some of the commonalities that you see among the leaders described in the introductory vignette? What are some of the differences?*

2. *Based on the introductory vignette, why do you think some leaders succeed over the long term while others fail?*

3. *What do you see as the relationship between being an effective leader and motivating others?*

There is an increasing realization that leadership style affects employee motivation, which in turn determines a firm's long-term performance prospects. This chapter examines what makes a person an effective leader and how managers can motivate employees to contribute more. These issues represent two sides of the same coin. A manager cannot be an effective leader unless subordinates are willing to do their best to accomplish organizational goals. If managers want to provide strong leadership, they must also be concerned with employee motivation. This chapter will help you develop skills to lead people to accomplish organizational objectives and induce them to use their talents to the maximum.

■ What Makes an Effective Leader?

When Anne Mulcahy took over as CEO of Xerox, the company was facing bankruptcy. She attributed her success of saving the company to focusing on client services rather than finances.

Almost everyone would agree that strong leadership is necessary to ensure organizational success. However, there is no simple, agreed-on definition of *effective leadership*. Some think that such personal characteristics as charisma, perseverance, and strong communication skills make other people want to follow a leader. Thomas Watson of IBM, Alfred Sloan of General Motors, and former presidents Ronald Reagan and John F. Kennedy are seen by many as the embodiment of these traits. Others think of effective leadership as "being at the right place at the right time," that is, as the fit between the leader's message and the situation. In the business community, Lee Iacocca's authoritarian, brassy, and opinionated style contributed to his image as a savior of bankrupt Chrysler Corporation in the early 1980s, but after Chrysler became the U.S. auto company that earned the most profit per vehicle, these same attributes were seen by many as egotistical, capricious, and unresponsive to the needs of employees and consumers. By an ironic twist of history, in 2012 many Chrysler employees, union members, and investors wished Iacocca would come back from retirement— Chrysler had experienced a disastrous merger with German car manufacturer Daimler. These two companies split in late 2007, and Chrysler declared bankruptcy in 2009 as the company had lost billions of dollars and laid off almost half of its workforce. Soon after Fiat purchased most of Chrysler stock and now effectively controls Chrysler.[1]

Almost everyone would agree that an essential part of being an effective leader is the ability to influence other people. A

MANAGER'S NOTEBOOK 12.1

Management Skills for Leadership

- *Influence skills.* Leaders direct people toward a goal or end result. A manager may have formal power to use rewards and punishment to induce compliance, but the best leaders make people want to do things.
- *Delegation skills.* A good leader assigns others responsibility to get the work done. Inability to delegate is likely to lead to lower employee motivation. When employees no longer search for the best way to do things, the leader loses influence.

- *Flexibility skills.* To be an effective leader, you must adapt to the situation confronting you and the characteristics of the individuals you wish to lead. What works in one situation or with one person may not work in others.
- *Motivational skills.* To be successful requires creating a work environment in which employees are fully dedicated to the task at hand and want to contribute more.

---

leader should have vision—ideas or objectives that clarify to others where they should be headed. The vision may be ill conceived, inaccurate, or selfish, or it may identify opportunities that others have failed to see. Although it can take years to assess whether the vision is "good" or "bad," without vision there is little hope of energizing people to act. The leader needs to "sell" the vision by articulating it in a compelling and persuasive manner so that people are inspired to overcome obstacles and keep moving toward the ideal future. The leader must work with followers to establish appropriate implementation activities to support the accomplishment of the vision and to induce them to use their personal initiative and talents in achieving the vision. Stephen M. Case, former AOL Time Warner's CEO, noted, "In the end, a vision without the ability to execute is probably a hallucination."[2] Ironically, the merger that he led between AOL and Time Warner ended in a crash in late 2009. In the words of one expert, "the trail of despair in subsequent years included countless job losses, the decimation of retirement accounts, investigations by the Securities and Exchange Commission and the Justice Department, and countless executive upheavals." Today the total value of both companies is about one-seventh of their worth on the day of the merger.

Management versus Leadership

Not all leaders are managers; not all managers are leaders. According to one observer, "Management is about coping with complexity. Good management brings about order and consistency by drawing up formal plans, designing rigid organizational structures, and monitoring results against the plans.[3] While leaders exercise influence in a more informal and unstructured manner, managers occupy formal decision-making positions in the organization. Management jobs can provide the opportunity for leadership, and managers are more likely to be effective by combining formal authority to make decisions and allocate resources with the ability to motivate subordinates. Table 12.1 lists leadership practices of managers.

Power and Leadership

The ability to influence other people means that leaders have power. Managers have certain powers, such as the power to give pay raises or fire employees for insubordination, and a manager who is a good leader will use power wisely. Central to power is the willingness of followers to act in accordance with the leader's wishes. In a well-known work on power, J. French and B. Raven proposed five ways in which people may be induced to follow a leader:[4]

1. **Coercive power** is based on fear that the leader may cause people harm unless they support him or her. Intimidation and anxiety may induce people to go along with the actions, attitudes, or directives of a superior even if they disagree. Even if a leader does not use overt threats, the possibility of retaliation such as a poor recommendation to a prospective employer may induce compliance.

coercive power
Power based on the fear that the leader may cause people harm unless they support him or her.

TABLE 12-1 Practices Associated with Leadership by Managers

Defining Goals and Objectives for Unit that Are Consistent with Those of Organization

Facilitating Task Completion within Unit
- Planning and Organizing
- Problem Solving
- Clarifying Issues
- Providing Direction

Supervising
- Delegating work activities to subordinates
- Monitoring the activities and performance of subordinates
- Managing potential conflicts as they arise

Rewarding
- Providing praise and recognition for good work
- Offering opportunities for subordinates to do work that provide intrinsic satisfaction
- Reinforcing good behavior and desired outcomes with financial rewards
- Creating a climate where subordinates believe that rewards are fair and well justified

Meeting Personal Needs of Subordinates
- Acting friendly and providing emotional support
- Identifying the personal needs of subordinates that are most likely to motivate them in a particular direction (for instance, desire for recognition, desire for greater power and influence, desire for autonomy)
- Showing care, compassion, and sympathy when the situation demands it
- Encouraging subordinates participation in decision making, taking into account their views before making major decisions that affect them
- Doing things that help subordinates achieve their career goals

Acting as Boundary Spanner
- Maintaining contacts with people outside the unit (superiors, managers of other units, suppliers important people in the profession, and others) who can facilitate the work of the unit and provide advice and resources as necessary
- Disseminating relevant information about the unit so that other people realize what the unit is doing
- Representing the unit to outsiders (giving presentations, attending meetings, going to professional conferences and the like)

reward power
Power derived from the belief that the leader can provide something that other people value so that they trade their support for the rewards.

legitimate power
The legal or formal authority to make decisions subject to certain constraints.

expert power
Power deriving from the leader's valued knowledge or skills, which other people recognize as worthy of respect.

referent power
Power derived from the satisfaction people receive from identifying themselves with the leader.

2. **Reward power** means that the leader can provide something that other people value so that they trade their support for the rewards. Rewards may be financial (such as promotion with higher pay) or psychological (such as greater status from being perceived as close to the leader).

3. **Legitimate power** comes from the legal or formal authority to make decisions subject to certain constraints. For instance, in most universities the chair of an academic department has the legitimate power to write an annual evaluation of each faculty member to be used to allocate merit pay, assign teaching schedules, and establish differential teaching loads. Few department chairs have the legitimate power to hire or terminate full-time faculty.

4. **Expert power** derives from the leader's unique knowledge or skills, which other people recognize as worthy of respect.

5. **Referent power** is based on the satisfaction people receive from identifying themselves with the leader. They are willing to grant power to the leader because they see him or her as a role model.

These power bases are not independent. Employees may comply with the wishes of a person they admire (referent power) who is a division head (legitimate power) with formal authority to promote (reward power) or terminate employees (coercive power) and who has expertise about a particular product line (expert power). Leaders typically prefer to emphasize some of these sources of power more than others. For instance, some supervisors motivate subordinates by serving as an example (referent power) even if they have the authority to induce compliance through punishment (coercive power) or financial incentives (reward power).

LOC-In 1 **Learning Objective Check-In**

1. Andy tries to cultivate a close professional relationship with his staff in the engineering department. A certain clique has even been established as a result of this. Either workers are close to Andy, or they are not. Those who are close often feel a sense of higher status in the office because they are "in" with the boss. Andy is exercising _____.
   a. expert power
   b. reward power
   c. legitimate power
   d. coercive power

■ Why a Person Becomes a Leader: Traditional Explanations

For many years, academics have tried to identify the factors that account for the ability to influence other people to comply with the leader's wishes. The three major traditional approaches to understanding leadership are the trait approach, the behavioral approach, and the situational approach.

Trait Theories

What sets Napoleon Bonaparte, Franklin Delano Roosevelt, Mohandas Gandhi, Margaret Thatcher, Golda Meir, Cesar Chavez, and Nelson Mandela apart from the crowd? When we think about leaders, certain traits or personal characteristics come to mind, such as self-confidence, determination, and communication skills. Researchers have tried to find a personality profile or set of characteristics that distinguishes leaders from nonleaders. Surprisingly, the trait approach has not been successful in explaining leadership. Instead, such factors as the needs of followers, cultural norms, prior group history, and situational variables come into play. Nevertheless, cumulative research suggests that certain traits, most of which can be learned, increase the likelihood of becoming a leader, although they don't guarantee it. These include ambition; energy; the motivation or desire to lead; intelligence; integrity, or high correspondence between actions and words; a "can-do attitude," or self-confidence; the ability to grasp and interpret large amounts of information; and the flexibility to adapt to the needs and goals of others.[5]

Behavioral Theories

Behavioral theories attempt to identify what good leaders do. Broadly speaking, these theories either map out the behavioral dimensions of leadership or describe leadership styles.

BEHAVIORAL DIMENSIONS Two classic studies conducted at Ohio State University and the University of Michigan in the 1940s and 1950s uncovered two dimensions that summarize how subordinates describe most leadership behaviors.[6] The first dimension refers to the concern that the leader has for the feelings, needs, personal interest, problems, and well-being of followers; it was called **consideration** (at Ohio State) or *employee-oriented behaviors* (at the University of Michigan). The second dimension, which refers to activities designed to accomplish group goals, including organizing tasks, assigning responsibilities, and establishing performance standards, was labeled **initiating structure** (at Ohio State) and *production-oriented behaviors* (at the University of Michigan).

Using these two dimensions, researchers R. R. Blake and J. S. Mouton developed a tool to classify managers based on leadership behaviors in a model called the **managerial grid**.[7] As illustrated in Figure 12.1, the vertical axis of the managerial grid is a scale of 1 to 9 for concern for people, and the horizontal axis is a scale of 1 to 9 for production. Presumably, the "ideal" behaviors fall in the 9,9 quadrant; that is, leaders who are high on concern for production and high on concern for people tend to achieve optimal subordinate performance and satisfaction. In other words, the most effective managers relate well to their followers and can efficiently delineate what needs to get done. While the managerial grid is used by practitioners and management trainers because of its simplicity and intuitive appeal, there is little empirical evidence to indicate that a 9,9 approach is best in all situations.

consideration
The behavioral dimensions of leadership involving the concern that the leader has for the feelings, needs, personal interest, problems, and well-being of followers; also called employee-oriented behaviors.

initiating structure
The behavioral dimension of leadership that refers to activities designed to accomplish group goals, including organizing tasks, assigning responsibilities, and establishing performance standards; also called production-oriented behaviors.

managerial grid
A system of classifying managers based on leadership behaviors.

FIGURE 12.1

The Managerial (Leadership) Grid

Source: From *Grid Solutions*, by Robert R. Blake and Anne Adams McCanse (formerly *The Managerial Grid Figure* by Robert R. Blake and Jane S. Mouton), Houston: Gulf Publishing Company, p. 29. Copyright 1991 by Scientific Methods, Inc. Reproduced by permission of Grid International, Inc.

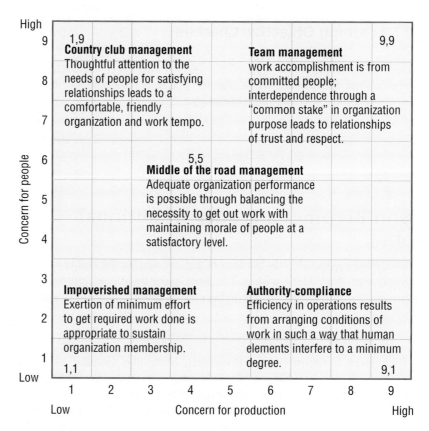

Leadership Style

A classic study defined two leadership styles or decision-making approaches: the autocratic style and the democratic style.[8] Leaders who use the *autocratic* style make decisions on their own and announce them as a done deal. A *democratic* leader actively tries to solicit the input of subordinates, often requiring consensus or a majority vote before making a final decision. This early study found that a democratic style resulted in higher subordinate satisfaction with the leader but that an autocractic approach resulted in somewhat higher performance. The performance advantage associated with an autocratic style tends to disappear when the leader is not present to monitor subordinates. A *laissez-faire* style, in which a leader avoids making decisions, results in both low satisfaction and low performance.

Contingency Theories

Subsequent research on leadership questioned the "one best way" approach suggested by the behavioral theories, and a contingency, or "it depends," approach began to replace the simplistic view that a particular set of behaviors or decision-making style separates good from bad leaders. The key point of the contingency approach is that leadership success depends on the fit between the leader's behavior and decision-making style and the requirements of the situation. One author illustrated how leadership effectiveness was dependent on the situation as follows:

> Bob Knight, the men's head basketball coach at Indiana University, consistently uses an intense, task-oriented leadership style that intimidates players, officials, the media, and university administrators. But his style works with the Indiana teams he recruits. Knight has one of the most impressive win-loss records of any active major college basketball coach. But would this same style work if Bob Knight was counsel-general of the United Nations or project manager for a group of Ph.D. software designers at Microsoft? Probably not![9]

Bob Knight's leadership style ultimately resulted in his being asked to resign by the university because of numerous complaints about his behavior, indicating that the fit between him and the university was no longer optimal.

Several theorists have attempted to isolate critical situational factors that affect leadership effectiveness. The include Fiedler's contingency model and the path–goal model.

FIEDLER'S CONTINGENCY MODEL   According to Fiedler's contingency model of leadership effectiveness, three aspects of a situation are determinants of which leader behavior or style is suitable:[10]

- *Leader-member relations:* The extent to which the leader is well liked and enjoys the trust, support, and respect of subordinates.
- *Task structure:* The extent to which the leader delineates which "what, how, and why" work tasks are performed.
- *Position power:* The degree to which the leader has the authority to reward and punish subordinates.

According to Fiedler, the better the leader–member relations, the more highly structured the job, and the stronger the position power, the more control or influence a leader enjoys.

Fiedler identified two major leadership styles. **Task-oriented leadership** emphasizes work accomplishments and performance results; **relationship-oriented leadership** focuses on maintaining good interpersonal relationships. Fiedler contends that task-oriented leaders are more effective in situations that are very favorable and very unfavorable. The most favorable cases correspond to situations where at least two of the three determinates noted above are postive, and the most unfavorable cases correspond to situations where all three determinants are negative. For situations in the middle categories, which are of moderate difficulty, a relationship-oriented leader performs better. (see Figure 12.2).

As a whole, empirical evidence supports the main ideas of this model.[11] However, the implication that leaders must be assigned to a situations that suits their style makes the model somewhat controversial because it implies that leaders cannot change their style. The emphasis on a fit between the leader and the situation makes it difficult to translate the theory into practice. Work environments change often, and there is no easy way to assess on an ongoing basis how good the leader–member relations are, how structured the task is, and how much position power the leader actually enjoys.

PATH-GOAL THEORY   A contingency model of leadership that has gained wide acceptance and enjoys substantial empirical support was developed by Robert House, who labeled **Path-goal theory** because of its focus on how leaders influence subordinate's perceptions of work goals and path to achieve those goals.[12] The crux of the theory is that it is the leader's job to help followers achieve their goals and to influence followers to ensure that their goals are consistent with the overall objectives of the group or organization.

The theory specifies four leadership behaviors, as seen in Figure 12.3. The *directive leader* establishes expectations for followers, determines targets to attain, organizes tasks, sets

task-oriented leadership
A leadership style that emphasizes work accomplishments and performance results.

relationship-oriented leadership
A leadership style that focuses on maintaining good interpersonal relationships.

path-goal theory
A contingency model of leadership that focuses on how leaders influence subordinates' perceptions of work goals and the path to achieve those goals.

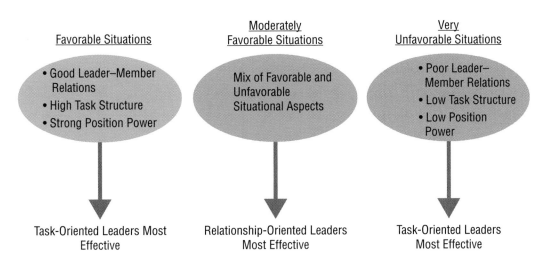

FIGURE 12.2

Key Findings from Fiedler's Contingency Model

FIGURE 12.3

The Path–Goal Framework of Leadership

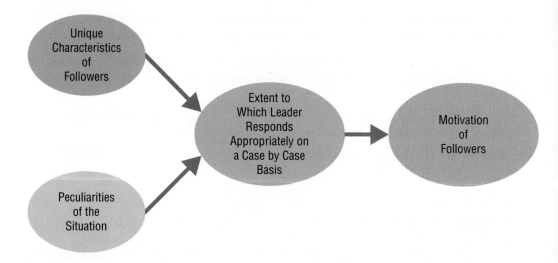

deadlines and schedules, and closely monitors progress. These behaviors are similar to the initiating structure and the autocratic styles discussed earlier. For instance, Thomas M. Siebel was the brash CEO of Siebel Systems Inc., a Silicon Valley maker of software used to manage customer relations. Siebel was almost obsessed with inspecting everything to make sure it is done right. His philosophy was, "No software gets written until customers weigh in. Outside consultants routinely poll clients on their satisfaction, and [employee] compensation is heavily based on those reports." Siebel's direct approach was unusual for Silicon Valley, but his firm had a third of the market for customer-management software, a market Siebel shared with Oracle.[13] Siebel retired from the company as one of the richest men in the world and Oracle acquired Siebel Systems in 2006. Siebel has pledged $100 million to his alma mater, the University of Illinois at Urbana-Champaign, upon his death.

LOC-In   2   Learning Objective Check-In

Caroline tailors her leadership style to the situation at hand. She operates fairly consistently around all the people in her department. Caroline operates very effectively when there is an important deadline that needs to be reached by the group, especially if it represents a serious challenge or opportunity for the team to do well.

1. Caroline best demonstrates _____.
   a. path-goal theory
   b. trait theory
   c. Fiedler's Contingency Model
   d. Maslow's hierarchy of needs

2. In the example above, Caroline is a _____.
   a. relationship-oriented leader
   b. task-oriented leader
   c. supportive leader
   d. participative leader

The *supportive leader* is warm and friendly and shows concern about the problems and needs of subordinates. This is the same as consideration factor described before. The *participative leader* actively elicits subordinates' input and opinions and uses them to make decisions that affect the group. This is similar to the democratic leadership style discussed earlier. A classic example of a highly successful participative leader was William Hewlett, the Silicon Valley and computer-age pioneer who cofounded Hewlett-Packard in a garage in 1938. Shortly before his death in 2001 at age 87, he said that he was proudest of his personal relationship and camaraderie with employees. One observer recalled, "Despite his position and wealth, Hewlett delighted in working side-by-side with employees or playing penny-ante poker with them."[14]

The *achievement-oriented leader* is primarily concerned with motivating people by setting challenging goals, coaching subordinates to perform at their highest level, and rewarding those who meet or exceed their targets. House believes that leaders are flexible enough to exhibit all four of these behaviors and that their effectiveness depends on their ability to use the behavior appropriate to the particular circumstances.

Path-goal theory proposes two key factors that determine which leadership behaviors are most appropriate. The first, the **situational context**, refers to factors outside the control of the subordinate, such as the tasks defining the job, the formal authority system of the organization, and the work group. The second, the personal characteristics of the follower, are the attributes of the subordinate such as experience and perceived ability or self-confidence. Effectiveness is defined in terms of the performance of subordinates and the extent to which followers perceive a leader's behavior as increasing their present or future satisfaction. A leader's behavior is more effective if it is congruent with the situation and the personal characteristics of subordinates.

situational context
The factors that are outside the control of the subordinate such as the tasks defining the job, the formal authority system of the organization, and the work group.

Many propositions have been derived from this theory and have been supported empirically. Based on personal characteristics of followers, the following leadership styles are effective:

- Subordinates who are highly authoritarian prefer a directive leadership style because to them this commands respect.
- Subordinates who believe they control their own destinies are more satisfied with a participative leadership style because it gives them more opportunity to influence decisions that affect their lives. Those who believe their destiny is in the hands of others prefer a more directive style.
- Supportive and participative leaders improve satisfaction and enhance group performance of subordinates with high perceived ability who don't wish to be told what to do and those with considerable experience who are capable of offering valuable input.
- Based on fit with the situational context, the effective leadership styles are as follows:
- Directive leadership improves followers' satisfaction when the tasks are ambiguous and stressful because it helps clarify the situation.
- Supportive leadership increases subordinates' satisfaction when the tasks are clearly structured and laid out. Employees see directive leader behavior as patronizing or insulting when they already understand what needs to get done.
- Achievement-oriented leadership increases subordinates' satisfaction and group productivity when the organization can provide rewards contingent on the performance of the group.

■ Contemporary Leadership Issues

The classical approaches examined above attempt to identify the factor that predict leadership effectiveness. During the 1980s and 1990s, several studies reexamined many of the same issues. Seven contemporary perspectives on leadership effectiveness are attribution theory, substitutes for leadership, charismatic leadership, transformational leadership, postheroic leadership, self-leadership, and emotional intelligence. Most of them attempt to explain how leaders are able to lead organizations to attain outstanding accomplishments such as the founding and growth of successful entrepreneurial firms, corporate turnarounds in the face of overwhelming competition, military victories in the face of superior forces, and leadership of successful social reform for independence from colonial rule or political tyranny.

These theories also attempt to explain how certain leaders are able to achieve extraordinary levels of followers' motivation, admiration, respect, trust, commitment, dedication, loyalty, and performance. They stress symbolic and emotionally appealing leader behaviors—visionary, frame alignment, empowering, role modeling, image building, exceptional, risk taking, and supportive behaviors, for example—as well as cognitively oriented behavior—adapting, showing versatility and environmental sensitivity, and intellectual stimulation, for example. Finally, these theories hold that leaders affect follower self-esteem and motivation and that followers identify with the leader's vision and values.[15]

Attribution Theory

attribution theory
The idea that the major function of the leader is to be blamed or given credit for a bad or a good situation, even if the leader has little or no control over the factors that led to the results.

According to **attribution theory**, a major function of the leader is to be blamed or given credit for a bad or a good situation, even if the leader has little or no control over the factors that led to the results. In other words, leaders serve people's need to fix responsibilities for whatever is happening. When an organization's performance is good or bad, members are likely to make leadership attributions. This helps explain why CEOs are likely to be terminated when profits decline and presidents aren't reelected when unemployment and inflation are high. CEOs get credit when the company is doing well, and presidents get higher approval ratings when unemployment and inflation drop, even if they had little or nothing to do with the results. This view is similar to the older view that managers are given authority and get paid accordingly in exchange for accepting responsibility for everything that happens in their area.

This practice remains common at the executive level. Approximately 20 percent of CEOs at the largest U.S. companies are replaced during a given year, typically after stock prices fall or the company has failed to meet its performance goals.[16] For instance, the termination of CEOs picked up quickly during the deep recession of 2008–2011 even though economic problems and slow U.S. sales hurt almost every company during the same period.[17] Negative leader attributions may be deserved, but leaders are often used as scapegoats in adverse circumstances. Therefore, a firm's management may forgo pursuing potentially highly profitable but somewhat risky ventures to safeguard their own jobs.

Leadership Substitute

leadership substitute view
The leadership theory that contends that people overestimate the effect of leaders even when leader behaviors are irrelevant, so organizations need to develop mechanisms to replace or substitute the influence role assigned to leaders.

The **leadership substitute view** contends that people overestimate the effect of leaders even when leader behaviors are irrelevant, so organizations need to develop mechanisms to replace or substitute the influence role assigned to leaders. For example, having people participate in teams or giving them interesting tasks that require close cooperation increases satisfaction levels and personal commitment. Because team members will pressure those who shirk their share of the work, there is less need for a leader who exhibits high consideration and initiating structure. A growing number of firms, for instance, have been able to cut back on the number of supervisors by implementing programs in which employees and the firm share in savings attributed to cost-reduction suggestions made by workers organized in teams.

Many firms rely on group decision making in which employees play the leadership role, especially in firms that rely on continuous innovation to keep a competitive advantage. For instance, Merck & Co. is one of the largest pharmaceutical firms in an industry where one blockbuster drug can sway the fate of an entire company. Merck continuously monitors hundreds of ideas floating around its labs to decide where the company will make its big bets. The company's decision-making process regarding new products, modeled on that of the National Institutes of Health, has evolved into committees of scientists who consider each other's work. This system of peer review fosters lively debate about what Merck should be doing.[18]

Charismatic Leadership

charismatic leader
A leader who can engender a strong emotional attachment from followers; charisma is associated with admiration, trust, and a willingness to believe what the leader says.

To most people, a **charismatic leader** is one who can engender a strong emotional attachment from followers. Charisma is associated with admiration, trust, and a willingness to believe what the leader says. Table 12.2 lists key characteristics of charismatic leaders.

TABLE 12.2 **Characteristics of Charismatic Leaders**

- Propose major changes to a status quo that is deemed unsatisfactory.
- Offer a strategic vision that inspires other people to be energized and optimistic, convinced that the status quo can be improved or even changed radically for the best.
- Carefully assess the needs of followers, motivating them to meet those needs by accomplishing the leader's vision.
- Project self-confidence, often providing an example to others of self-sacrifice.
- Provide an idealistic role model for followers to imitate.

SKILLS FOR MANAGING 12.1

Power and Influence

Class is divided into groups of five. Members of each group are asked to identify five people who have each had a major influence on their lives. Then explain the kind of power used by each of these individuals and the extent to which the type of power used had a positive or negative effect on behavior. There is no need to provide specific names. It is possible to note more than one power base for each person but make sure to list these in order of importance.

	Power Base Used	Positive or Negative
Person 1	_____	_____
	_____	_____
Person 2	_____	_____
	_____	_____
Person 3	_____	_____
	_____	_____
Person 4	_____	_____
	_____	_____
Person 5	_____	_____
	_____	_____

Charismatic leaders tend to obtain high levels of employee performance in rapidly changing, threatening, or crisis situations. However, they "may become a liability to an organization once the crisis and need for dramatic change subside. Why? Because then the charismatic leader's overwhelming self-confidence often becomes a liability. He or she is unable to listen to others, becomes uncomfortable when challenged by aggressive subordinates, and begins to hold an unjustifiable belief in his or her 'rightness' on issues."[19] Most experts believe that managers can be trained to acquire charismatic skills that allow them to foster greater emotional involvement, positive attitudes, and a willingness to go beyond the call of duty among subordinates, all of which may lead to higher performance.[20] An example of a charismatic leader is Steve Jobs, founder of Apple, who was fired by the company's board at one point for his brash leadership style yet was called back years later as a savior when Apple got into deep financial trouble (see Management Close-Up 12.1, "Steve Job's Charisma Made Apple No. 1").

Transformational versus Transactional Leadership

Most classical leadership theories are concerned with **transactional leaders**, who use legitimate, coercive, or reward powers to elicit obedience. Transactional leaders do not generate passion and excitement, and they do not empower or inspire individuals to transcend their own self-interest for the good of the organization. **Transformational leaders**, on the other hand, attempt to instill in followers the ability to question standard modes of operation. They are capable of revitalizing organizations by tapping people's reservoir of creativity. While transformational leaders are charismatic, they also inspire people, provide them with intellectual stimulation, and give followers individualized consideration. Table 12.3 lists, the characteristics of transactional leaders while Table 12.4 lists the characteristics of transformational leaders.

In addition to articulating a vision and communicating that vision to subordinates, transformational leaders build trust by being dependable, consistent, and persevering. "They do not feel

transactional leaders
Leaders who use legitimate, coercive, or reward powers to elicit obedience and attempt to instill in followed the ability to question standard modes of operation.

transformational leaders
Leaders who revitalize organizations by instilling in followers the ability to question standard modes of operation.

Steve Jobs' Charisma Made Apple No. 1

Born in 1955, Apple's CEO Steve Jobs is a practical visionary who has the idea of changing the world by introducing new electronic gadgets that he believes customers will love. According to an industry observer, "Apple never holds focus groups. It doesn't ask people what they want; it tells them what they are going to want next." Starting with the Macintosh, Jobs imagined a wide array of consumer electronics that eventually became market hits, including the MacBook Air, the iPod and more recently the iPad. In the past Jobs has referred to himself as a "lead gladiator." He repeatedly talks about his team in revolutionary prose, sometimes using violent imagery, encouraging them to see themselves as outlaws who will turn the industry upside down. He talks about his projects in almost evangelical terms. In an interview, Jobs described the development team for the Macintosh as souls who were "well grounded in the philosophical traditions of the last 100 years and the sociological traditions of the 60s." The Macintosh team pursued their project through grueling hours and against formidable odds. "The machine's development was, in turn, traumatic, joyful, grueling, lunatic, rewarding, and ultimately the major event in the lives of almost everyone involved."

Time recently described Steve Jobs as confident, assured, and open. His personal magnetism is overwhelming. And his view of the customer is that he knows what is best for them and the objective of his development team is to come up with products that create rather than meet a consumer need. In Steve's own words, "sure, what we do has to make commercial sense but it's never the starting point. We start with the product and the user experience… I think the experience of using an iPad is going to be profound for many people. I really do. Genuinely profound."

Fortune magazine describes Jobs' charismatic leadership style as follows: "Jobs is a wickedly smart, inspiring, inspired perfectionist of a man who has turned much of what he touches into gold. His influence on global culture cannot be underestimated. On the surface it seems he makes mere amusements: tiny music players and touchable phones and candy-colored laptops. Yet those things have rocked multibillion-dollar companies and changed the way the world buys music, accesses information, and designs products ranging from home appliances to cars. Every day, several times a day, some student, entrepreneur, industrial designer, or CEO looks at a problem and wonders: What would Steve Jobs do?"

Sources: Based on S. Fry, "On the Mothership. A confessed Apple Famboy gets finger time with the iPad and face time with Steve Jobs," *Time*, 2010, April 12, 40–41; L. Grosman, "Launch iPad. It is here, It is hot; But what on earth is the iPad for?" *Time*, 2010, April 12, 36–42; P. Burrows, "Apple's endlessly expanding universe," *BusinessWeek*, 2010, April 26, 93–98; "Steve Paul Jobs," http://www.ei.cs.vc,edu, accessed April, 2010; S. M. Mehta "Why him?" *Fortune*, 2009, November 23, 89–92.

TABLE 12.3 Characteristics of Transactional Leaders

- Offer reward to followers in exchange for complying with the leader's wishes and directives.
- Closely monitor followers to ensure that performance problems are detected and if necessary penalize followers for these problems.
- Establish a relationship with followers that is utilitarian and calculative, whereby each party seeks its own benefit rather than trying to reach an ideal.

TABLE 12.4 Characteristics of Transformational Leaders

- Inspire other people to follow a vision articulated by the leader.
- Make followers feel good and proud about identifying with leader.
- Make followers trust the leader, sacrificing themselves if necessary to accomplish the leader's agenda.
- Make followers question status quo, buying into the leader's solutions to problems associated with current state of affairs.
- Make followers feel that their individual needs and abilities are understood by the leader and that the leader empowers them and energizes them to get better.

self-important or complacent: rather, they recognize their personal strength, compensate for their weaknesses, nurture their skills and continually develop their talents, and know how to learn from failure. They strive for success rather than merely trying to avoid failure."[21] Overall, transformational leadership is more likely than transactional leadership to reduce turnover rates, increase productivity, and improve employee satisfaction.[22]

Postheroic Leadership

The **postheroic leadership perspective** holds that most top executives, no matter how good they are, are limited in what they can do to solve problems. Given rapid changes in technology, competitive threats, and market shifts, it is doubtful that a single leader can make the difference between success or failure. In other words, a firm cannot depend on a hero to act as a savior.

Postheroic leaders spread leadership responsibilities throughout the firm instead of centralizing leadership in key individuals. They (1) make people responsible for their own performance, (2) create an environment in which each person can figure out what needs to be done and then do it well, (3) point the way and clear the path so people can succeed, and (4) give people the credit they deserve. Their role is to coach and develop individual capability and competence and to challenge every individual to continually improve abilities and make greater contributions.

Lance Armstrong, cyclist and founder of the Lance Armstrong Foundation, works hard and is optimistic. As a result, both his team and staff emulate the same behaviors.

Self-Leadership

Like the postheroic leadership perspective, **self-leadership** stresses the individual responsibility of employees to develop their own work priorities aligned with organizational goals. The manager is a facilitator who enhances the self-leadership capabilities of subordinates, encouraging them to develop self-control skills. This leadership approach is far more decentralized than traditional leadership, which focuses on the supervisor as the pivotal figure.

There are two important mechanisms to foster self-leadership within the firm. The first is **empowerment**, or the process of transferring control of individual work behavior from the supervisor to the employee. Employees must be provided with skills, tools, support, and information so that authority and responsibility can be successfully delegated to them. The second key vehicle is **role modeling**, whereby managers serve as examples of the behaviors they would like employees to emulate. Role modeling is more likely to be effective if workers can see a link between adopting the desired behaviors and positive outcomes, such as higher pay, a promotion, and public recognition.[23]

Leadership and Emotional Intelligence

In two groundbreaking bestsellers, psychologist Daniel Goleman drew on a wealth of research to argue that successful leaders need **emotional intelligence**, or the attributes of self-awareness, impulse control, persistence, confidence, self-motivation, empathy, social deftness, trustworthiness, adaptability, and a talent for collaboration.[24] "Effective leaders have a knack for articulating a mission or a goal and knowing how to bring everyone on board to get it accomplished. Can you take the pulse of a group, understand its unspoken currents of thought and concerns, and communicate with people in terms they can understand and embrace? That is great leadership. And it takes huge intelligence."[25] Often when people who are promoted on the basis of technical ability fail in their new jobs, it's because they lack emotional competencies that are crucial at the higher level.

Refer to Internet Exercise 12.2 at the end of this chapter if you wish to take an online test to assess your emotional intelligence. According to Goleman, "Emotional intelligence can be learned, and in fact we are each building it, in varying degrees, throughout life. EQ is nothing more or less than a collection of tools that we can sharpen to help ensure our own survival."[26]

Leader–Member Exchange: Relationships between Leaders and Followers

According to this perspective the relationship between each follower and the leader is unique. In some cases the relationship is characterized by mutual trust, commitment, loyalty, and strong liking. Because the leader is positively predisposed toward the subordinate the latter is afforded an unusual amount of latitude or discretion to use his or her judgment on the job. In turn the

postheroic leadership perspective
The view that most top executives, no matter how good they are, are limited in what they can do to solve problems, so that leadership responsibilities are spread throughout the firm.

self-leadership
Leadership that stresses the individual responsibility of employees to develop their own work priorities aligned with organizational goals; the manager is a facilitator who enhances the self-leadership capabilities of subordinates, encouraging them to develop self-control skills.

empowerment
The process of transferring control of individual work behavior from the supervisor to the employee.

role modeling
The leadership mechanism in which managers serve as examples of the behaviors they would like employees to emulate.

emotional intelligence
The attributes of self-awareness, impulse control, persistence, confidence, self-motivation, empathy, social deftness, trustworthiness, adaptability, and a talent for collaboration.

subordinate enjoys that freedom, feels happier for being special, and becomes highly supportive of the leader. Subordinates that fall into this category are said to be in the "in-group." Those in the "out-group" tend to have a more distant, impersonal relationship with the leader and the level of trust between the parties is low. Because the loyalty of the "out-group" subordinate is in question the leader tends to be more directive, controlling, and critical of him or her. Understandably those in the "out-group" are less satisfied and perform at lower levels (at least as perceived by the leader) than those in the "in-group." This tends to create a vicious cycle where those in the "out-group" become more antagonistic toward the leader and the leader responds accordingly. Research suggests that in the long run the most effective leaders are capable of developing special relationships with many subordinates so that few, if any, subordinates feel that they are in the "out-group." In short, good managers should strive to have as many "in-group" members as possible.

LOC-In 3 Learning Objective Check-In

James is a very effective manager who consistently has a capable and effective staff. He encourages his subordinates to develop self-control skills and is a firm believer in the empowerment of his staff. His subordinates often say that they look to James as a successful role model whose goals are aligned well with the goals of the organization.

1. Which leadership perspective best reflects James' attitude?
   a. Transformational leadership
   b. Substitute leadership
   c. Self-leadership
   d. Transactional leadership

2. James pursues a(n) _____ in his approach to his role at work.
   a. dispersed theory of leadership
   b. person-based theory of leadership
   c. exchange theory of leadership
   d. situational theory of leadership

■ Motivation

The one thing all leadership theories agree on is that effective, direct, and sustain subordinates' efforts; that is, they are capable of motivating people to do their best. Performance depends on personal ability and on the opportunities afforded by the organization for employees to use their talents. A highly motivated employee in a boring, repetitive job is likely to get frustrated and either leave the firm or become a malcontent. A person with little mathematical ability is unlikely to become a top-flight engineer, regardless of how hard he or she tries. But a high level of motivation increases perseverance to use talent to the maximum, and this attitude makes an employee more valuable to the firm. In many cases, high motivation compensates for lower ability by making employees eager to learn.

To motivate employees, managers need to set challenging goals, reinforce desired behaviors, satisfy employees' needs, design jobs that are interesting and offer opportunities for incumbents to use their talents, provide performance-contingent rewards that people value, and be fair. There are several well-known theories that focus on different aspects of motivation. Together they help explain what makes people work harder and what managers can do to facilitate and stimulate high performance.

Goal-Setting Theory

Hundreds of studies have demonstrated that people are more highly motivated when they have concrete objectives or targets to achieve.[27] These studies suggest that three important aspects of goals energize people to try harder. First, employees need to believe that the goals are good, that is, they should "buy into" the goals. One effective way to increase goal acceptability is to have employees and supervisors jointly set the goals in a participative fashion. Second, the targets set should challenge people to "stretch" their abilities, but they should also be realistic. Unattainable goals frustrate and demoralize employees. Third, goals should be specific, quantifiable, and measurable to give people clear direction on how to focus their efforts so they can concentrate on meeting or exceeding the established targets.

Goal setting must be carefully done. In most jobs, successful performance depends on the accomplishment of intangible tasks or duties that cannot be easily quantified or translated into a neat set of targets or objectives. The evaluation and reward system needs to be flexible enough to prevent employees from single-mindedly focusing on the achievement of measurable performance objectives at the expense of other key elements of job success.

Consider the following goal-setting failures:

1. Several airlines experienced deteriorating customer relations and a large number of no-shows when their sales representatives' pay was based on the number of bookings.
2. In a Midwestern state, paying snowplow operators on a per-mile basis resulted in many roads packed with snow and ice because it was easier to cover more miles and get paid more by disengaging the snow-removal equipment.
3. In some academic departments, faculty may avoid teaching because pay, promotion, and tenure are based only on having research published in leading journals.
4. Top executives are frequently accused of maximizing short-term gains to trigger larger annual bonuses at the expense of long-term performance.
5. A major reason behind the banking collapse in recent years may be attributed to goals that encourage financial institutions and mortgage brokers to make risky loans in order to meet challenging performance targets (see Individual-Collaborative Learning Case 12.1 at the end of this chapter "What Caused the So-called 'Financial Meltdown' of 2008–2011?").

One well-known approach to implementing goal theory is management by objectives (MBO). In an MBO system, employees and supervisors agree on a set of measurable goals to be accomplished within a certain amount of time. MBO allows the firm to implement overall organizational objectives by breaking these down into specific objectives assigned to different units and individuals in the firm. As depicted in Figure 12.4, the objectives for the entire firm "cascade down" to the divisional, departmental, and individual levels.

Management by objectives has several advantages. First, it results in a hierarchy of objectives that links specific objectives with each succeeding organizational level. Second, each person knows exactly what is expected of him or her. This makes it easier to evaluate and reward employee contributions by comparing them to agreed-on goals. Third, because employees and managers jointly participate in the goal setting, MBO facilitates the flow of work-related information from the bottom up as well as the top down.

One drawback of MBO has already been discussed: in many jobs the most important tasks cannot be easily quantified. By emphasizing what can be measured, an MBO system may cause people to lose sight of crucial behaviors that have no clear metrics, such as being patient and friendly with customers. Another drawback is that MBO systems may encourage people to play it safe by choosing less challenging goals that are more easily attainable. This risk-reduction strategy makes sense from the employee's perspective if job security and organizational rewards are contingent on the achievement of agreed-on goals.

Reinforcement Theory

Probably the best established principle in the social sciences is the *law of effect,* first enunciated by psychologist Edward Thorndike: behaviors that are rewarded tend to be repeated.[28] Behavior is encouraged or discouraged depending on the consequences. Three key consequences, as seen in Figure 12.5, are:

1. **Positive reinforcement**: a pleasurable stimulus or reward following a desired behavior that induces people to continue the behavior. For instance, people are likely to spend more times in the office if they feel it will help them earn promotions even though it may not increase their overall productivity. Withdrawing or failing to provide a reinforcer for behavior reduces motivation, and the behavior is "extinguished," or discontinued.
2. **Negative reinforcement**: the removal of unpleasant consequences associated with a desired behavior, resulting in an increase in the frequency of that behavior. For instance, if employees feel that being creative at work will not lead to reprimands for not following procedures, they are more likely to try new ways of doing things and become more entrepreneurial.

positive reinforcement
A pleasurable stimulus or reward following a desired behavior that induces people to continue the behavior.

negative reinforcement
The removal of unpleasant consequences associated with a desired behavior, resulting in an increase in the frequency of that behavior.

FIGURE 12.4

Cascading Objectives

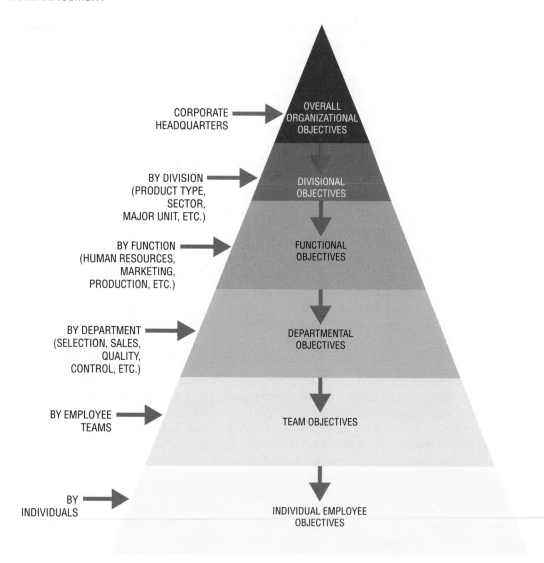

CORPORATE HEADQUARTERS → OVERALL ORGANIZATIONAL OBJECTIVES

BY DIVISION (PRODUCT TYPE, SECTOR, MAJOR UNIT, ETC.) → DIVISIONAL OBJECTIVES

BY FUNCTION (HUMAN RESOURCES, MARKETING, PRODUCTION, ETC.) → FUNCTIONAL OBJECTIVES

BY DEPARTMENT (SELECTION, SALES, QUALITY, CONTROL, ETC.) → DEPARTMENTAL OBJECTIVES

BY EMPLOYEE TEAMS → TEAM OBJECTIVES

BY INDIVIDUALS → INDIVIDUAL EMPLOYEE OBJECTIVES

FIGURE 12.5

Consequences of Reinforcement

Source: Reprinted with permission of J. M. George and G. R. Jones (2011), *Understanding and Managing Organizational Behavior*, 6th ed. Pearson Prentice Hall, Upper Saddle River, NJ.

Technique	How Consequence Is Administered	Effect on Behavior	Example
Positive reinforcement	Positive consequence is given when desired behavior is performed	Increases probability of desired behavior	Employee is praised for cleaning up work station
Negative reinforcement	Negative consequence is removed when desired behavior is performed	Increases probability of desired behavior	Supervisor complains about messy work station and stops only when worker cleans it
Extinction	Positive consequence is removed when undesired behavior is performed	Decreases probability of undesired behavior	Manager refrains from laughing at a subordinate's disruptive jokes when the two have important matters to discuss
Punishment	Negative consequence is given when undesired behavior is performed	Decreases probability of undesired behavior	Manager criticizes subordinate for telling disruptive jokes when the two have important matters to discuss

3. **Extinction**: the removal of positive consequences when undesired behavior is performed.
4. **Punishment**: an aversive or unpleasant consequence following an undesired behavior. This leads to a decrease in that behavior. However, their avoidance of undesired behaviors through punishment does not mean that people will engage in desired behaviors. For instance, a boss who yells at people for being late may provoke employees to show little initiative to try their best once they clock in. In fact, they may resent the boss and try to get even whenever they can. The threat of punishment for undesired behaviors is more effective than the actual use of punishment because punishment decreases undesirable behaviors only temporarily and may create anger and resentment, which hurt communication and undermine good will and personal initiative.

Some companies use an elaborate system of rewards. For example, sometime ago Honeywell IT implemented a "multitier reward program." Features of Honeywell's program included the following:

- Each quarter, each employee can award a $10 gift certificate to up to four employees who are perceived as doing a good job, helping out, and so on.
- Honeywell chooses three employees who used the certificates in a quarter to receive $50 gift certificates.
- Team leaders can award up to $200 to either individuals or teams based on five different criteria, such as leadership, commitment, and customer focus.
- Employees can nomiate individuals or teams for quarterly organizational awards for excellence in the same categories. A committee reviews the nominations to select those that went significantly above and beyond.

Reinforcement theory indicates the managers should link desirable outcomes (such as pay raises or promotion) to the behaviors they want to encourage. They should also try to reduce undesirable outcomes associated with the behaviors they wish people to exhibit. For instance, providing day care facilities may prompt more women to accept jobs that require frequent travel and unpredictable schedules.

Need Theories

According to need theories, people are motivated to satisfy their needs, and the more a firm can provide the means to meet needs, the harder employees will work to obtain those satisfiers. Three well-known theories attempt to specify what the most important human needs are: Maslow's hierarchy of needs, ERG theory, and McClelland's set of needs.

MASLOW'S HIERARCHY OF NEEDS According to Abraham Maslow, people tend to satisfy their needs in a specified order, from the most to the least basic, as seen in Figure 12.6. In ascending order, the needs are:

- *Physiological needs,* such as food and shelter.
- *Safety* or *security needs,* such as danger avoidance, steady jobs, and a healthy work enviroment.

extinction
The removal of positive consequences when undesired behavior is performed.

punishment
An aversive or unpleasant consequence following undesired behavior.

Maslow's hierarchy of needs
The theory that people tend to satisfy their needs in a specified order, from the most to the least basic.

LOC-In 4 **Learning Objective Check-In**

Heidi is using what she knows about what drives her staff's efforts to make subtle changes to the way the firm manages them, including their compensation packages. First, she is considering salaries, fringe benefits, working conditions, and how the staff relate to their supervisors. While she realizes these will not motivate people to do a good job, she understands that they can cause dissatisfaction if they are inadequate. Beyond these factors, Heidi is developing ways to give her staff more responsibility and challenges, as well as recognition for jobs well done.

1. Fringe benefits, working conditions, and interoffice relationships are _____.
   a. process factors
   b. extrinsic motivators
   c. self-actualization factors
   d. intrinsic motivators

FIGURE 12.6

Maslow's Hierarchy of Needs Theory

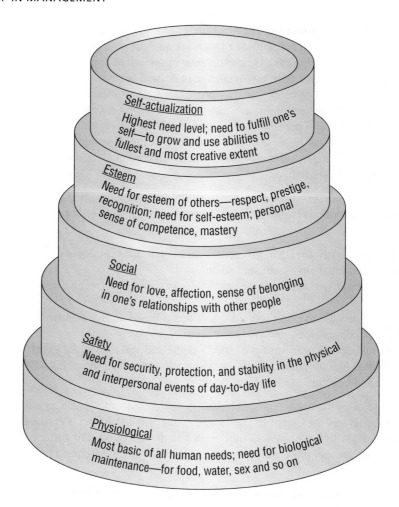

Self-actualization
Highest need level; need to fulfill one's self—to grow and use abilities to fullest and most creative extent

Esteem
Need for esteem of others—respect, prestige, recognition; need for self-esteem; personal sense of competence, mastery

Social
Need for love, affection, sense of belonging in one's relationships with other people

Safety
Need for security, protection, and stability in the physical and interpersonal events of day-to-day life

Physiological
Most basic of all human needs; need for biological maintenance—for food, water, sex and so on

2. When Heidi gives her staff more responsibilities within their jobs, she will be addressing their
   _____.
   a. physiological factors
   b. intrinsic motivators
   c. process factors
   d. extrinsic motivators

- *Social needs,* such as friendships, supervisory support, sense of belonging and affection.
- *Esteem needs,* such as personal pride, a positive self-concept, and status.
- *Self-actualization,* or the desire to use one's potential to the maximum.

Maslow argues that each lower level need has to be satisfied before the next higher level need becomes salient or motivating.[29] For instance, a hungry person is highly motivated to do whatever it takes to secure food, even taking actions that jeopardize safety, such as accepting a dangerous job or stealing the food. A person who is deprived of nourishment is not likely to be overly concerned with social status.

The policy implication of Maslow's hierarchy is that providing additional rewards to meet a need will motivate people only if the need has not already been satisfied. Also, when lower level needs are not satisfied, providing rewards for a higher level need will not motivate people. According to Maslow, the only need that can never be fully satisfied is *self-actualization,* at the top of the hierarchy. This is the case because people can keep developing and learning as long as they have the opportunity to do so, such as in an interesting and challenging work environment that continues to promote personal growth.

One the whole, empirical research has failed to support the notion that needs operate in the precise sequence that the steps imply. However, there is general agreement about two important points: (1) a dominant or salient need will motivate people more than a less important or weaker need, and (2) managers should strive to provide people with opportunities for self-actualization, since personal growth is likely to keep people interested in learning and developing their talents over time. In other words, rewards associated with lower level needs (e.g., higher pay) can only go so far in motivating people unless the work itself is stimulating and exciting.

ALDERFER'S ERG THEORY Clayton Alderfer revised Maslow's theory to make the needs and the sequence of needs less rigid. Alderfer's revised need hierarchy is called **ERG theory**, referring to three groups of core needs: existence, relationships, and growth.[30] The *existence group* is concerned with material requirements for survival, corresponding to the physiological and safety needs in Maslow's hierarchy. The *relationship group* of needs involves people's desire for social support, interpersonal relationships, and favorable recognition by others. These needs roughly correspond to Maslow's social and ego (or esteem) needs. Alderfer postulates a third set of needs that he refers to as *growth,* or people's intrinsic desire to use and develop their talents. This set closely overlaps Maslow's self-actualization category, although it also includes some elements of the ego category such as the drive to achieve.

> **ERG theory**
> A theory of needs based on three core groups: existence, relationships, and growth (ERG).

The key difference between these two theories is not that Alderfer collapses five needs to three. Rather, Alderfer does not assume a rigid hierarchy in which one need has to be satisfied before other needs can become operative. Instead, according to Alderfer, all three need categories can operate simultaneously. Also, Alderfer claims that if a higher order need is not being met, people may demand more rewards to satisfy lower level needs. Cross-cultural evidence suggest that Alderfer's view of needs is more universally valid than Maslow's. For instance, workers in Spain and Japan are likely to place social needs before physiological requirements.

McCLELLAND'S NEEDS David McClelland also identified a set of important needs that motivate people.[31] The most important needs for managers are the needs for achievement, power, and affiliation. The **need for achievement** is a strong drive to accomplish things, in which the individual receives great satisfaction from personal attainment and goal completion. Most U.S. managers believe that the need for achievement is important to success, and visible signs that a person is achievement-oriented are important in upward movement within organizations. Ironically, some research suggests that effective general managers do not typically have a high need to achieve because people with high achievement needs are more interested in personal gains than in helping others do well.[32] Instead, high achievers tend to be more successful at entrepreneurial activities such as running their own businesses, launching new projects, or leading self-contained units within a large firm. McClelland claims that people can be trained to increase the need for achievement.

> **need for achievement**
> The drive to accomplish things, in which the individual receives great satisfaction from personal attainment and goal completion.

The **need for affiliation** is the a strong desire to be liked by others, to receive social approval, and to establish close interpersonal relationships. Research suggests that a low need for affiliation is associated with managerial success.[33] This is so because an important part of the manager's job is to make tough decisions that will displease some people.

> **need for affiliation**
> The desire to be liked by others, to receive social approval, and to establish close interpersonal relationships.

The **need for power** is the desire to influence or control other people. Managers have a strong drive to have an effect, to be in charge, and to compete against others. To the extent that an individual does not want power purely for the pursuit of personal goals and does not place prestige and influence ahead of effective performance, the strength of this need is an important predictor of success in managerial jobs.

> **need for power**
> The desire to influence or control other people.

One particularly controversial part of this theory is that a high need for achievement in a national population is necessary to launch and sustain a high level of economic development. However, empirical data suggest that a high achievement need is not universal among industrialized nations.[34] For instance, security is a more important motivator among many Greek and Japanese managers, and social needs are often paramount in Scandinavian countries. In most Latin countries, an important part of achievement is the ability to reward friends and families, practices that may be viewed as corrupt in Anglo-American countries. The point is that needs and their importance vary significantly from one society to another.

Human Relations Perspective

The central concern of the human relations perspective on motivation is how subordinates respond to supervisory treatmet and, more specifically, how supervisors influence motivation by

Theory X
A negative perspective on human behavior.

Theory Y
A positive perspective on human behavior.

the way they deal with employees. A classical human relations approach to understanding employee motivation is that of Douglas McGregor.[35] According to McGregor, a manager's assumptions about human nature determine how the manager will view employees, interpret their behavior, and relate to them. McGregor postulated two distinct and opposite perspectives, a negative view he called **Theory X** and a positive view he called **Theory Y**.

Managers who rely on Theory X hold the following set of assumption:

- Employees dislike work and will try to avoid it if they can.
- Since work is unpleasant, employees need to be coerced, threatened with punishment, and closely supervised to perform effectively.
- Employees prefer to be directed or told what to do, thus avoiding responsibility.
- Most workers have little ambition and desire security more than anything else.

At the opposite extreme, managers who hold Theory Y assumptions believe that:

- Work can be pleasurable and may be enjoyed as much as rest or play.
- Employees are capable of exercising self-control and acting independently if they are committed to achieving organizational goals.
- Given the opportunity, the average employee will eagerly accept and seek responsibility.
- The ability to innovate and be creative is widely distributed in the population, and it is not limited to those in management positions.

Theory Y managers rely on participative decision making, offer emplyees responsible and challenging assignments, and treat people with respect, all of which tend to maximize an employee's job motivation. McGregor believed that managers who hold Theory Y assumptions are more likely to motivate emploes than managers with Theory X views. While the theory is intuitively appealing, it is difficult to test empirically because it is essentially prescriptive and a statement of philosophy.

Work Design Theories

intrinsic reward design theory
The perspective that a potent motivator for work is the intangible reward people derive from performing well in a job they find interesting, challenging, and intriguing and that provides an opportunity for continued learning.

Work design theories focus on the work itself rather than the supervisor, the company, or extrinsic rewards as the primary source of motivation. **Intrinsic reward design theories** contend that the satisfaction people derive from performing well in a job they find interesting, challenging, and intriguing and that provides an opportunity for continued learning is a potent motivator. These intrinsic rewards appeal to the higher level needs that Maslow, Alderfer, and McClelland felt are most important to propel people to use their talents to the maximum on a continuing basis. The two best known motivational theories that focus on the work itself are Herzberg's two-factor theory and the Hackman-Oldham model of job design.

HERZBERG'S TWO-FACTOR THEORY According to Frederick Herzberg, two major sets of factors affect employee performance.[36] The first set, which Herzberg labeled *hygiene factors*, corresponds to the lower level needs in Maslow's theory. Hygiene factors are contextual or extrinsic aspects of jobs, such as salary, fringe benefits, company policies, working conditions, and interpersonal relations with coworkers and supervisors. They can make people dissatisfied if they are inadequately met, but they will not motivate people to do a good job.

Assuming the hygiene factors are well managed, the key is to provide workers with *motivators,* or intrinsic rewards derived from the work itself, that provide continuous stimulation to strive for the best possible performance level, as shown in Figure 12.7. According to Herzberg, such motivators include the nature of the work, responsibility for a task well done, feedback and recognition, opportunities for personal growth and learning, and feelings of achievement derived from task completion. Herzberg contends that these motivators increase job satisfaction, and that removing dissatisfying characteristics from a job does not necessarily make the job satisfying.

The notion that the two sets of factors are distinct and the statement that only intrinsic factors motivate people are controversial. A raise is an extrinsic reward, or a hygiene factor, and it may also be a strong form of recognition (an intrinsic reward, or a motivator factor). Although the pure form of the theory has not been supported by most studies, Herzberg's work has been widely read, and many managers believe that it is a helpful way to analyze motivational problems at work. It reminds managers that intrinsic rewards are too often ignored.

HACKMAN-OLDHAM MODEL Herzberg's theory served as an impetus for more sophisticated explanations of how managers can design jobs to make them intrinsically interesting for

What Prevents People from Becoming Dissatisfied at Work?   What Makes People Satisfied and Motivated at Work?

FIGURE 12.7
Herzberg's Two-Factor Theory

Hygiene Factors

Motivational Factors

- Good pay and benefits
- Good supervisors
- Excellent working conditions
- Fair and effective rules, regulations, and policies

- Opportunities for achievement
- Enjoyment of work challenges
- Taking responsibility for their work
- Receiving recognition for good work
- Autonomy

SKILLS FOR MANAGING

How Close Do Your Results Come To Those Found By Herzberg?

Class is divided into groups of five. Either based on experiences of group members or based on interviews of working people known to members of the group (could be relatives, friends, acquaintances, and such) think of job situations associated with high levels of motivation. Take a look at the list of so-called "hygiene" and "motivator factors" in Figure 12.7 and assess the extent to which doing well in each of those areas increases motivation at work. Did you find that doing well in only some factors made people more highly motivated and that doing well in only some other factors prevented them from being unhappy at work? What motivational implications did your group discover based on your analysis?

employees. For example, the Hackman-Oldham approach, proposed a more complete model of job design. According to this model, the way jobs are designed (for instance, variety of skills required, autonomy, and feedback) produces critical psychological states (such as experienced meaningfulness of the work), which in turn affect key personal and work-related outcomes.[37]

The outcomes include high internal drive to succeed, attention to quality, satisfaction with the work itself, and low rates of absenteeism and turnover. For these outcomes to occur, employees must feel that their jobs are meaningful, that they can accept personal responsibility for a job well done, and that they receive accurate feedback that tells them how well they do their jobs. Hackman and Oldham refer to these conditions as *psychological states* and indicate that these states are more likely to be present when jobs are designed so that employees utilize a greater variety of skills; are responsible for completion of a whole, identifiable piece of work; have an opportunity to perform tasks that have a positive effect on the lives of others; enjoy autonomy and discretion in decision making; and can learn where they stand by receiving accurate information about job performance. Providing all five of these core dimensions in a single job results in *job enrichment*, which allows a person to grow and develop.

LOC-In   5   Learning Objective Check-In

Lauren suspects her workers are getting bored from monotony on the job. She is considering moving the workers to different tasks, periodically to increase the overall complexity of their jobs, and to add some variety to their tasks. In addition to this, she intends to expand the scope of their jobs by giving workers responsibility for more tasks. Once the workers have more tasks to work on, Lauren knows there will be a greater need for day-to-day planning and organization of these tasks. She knows her workers well and trusts their ability to organize their own work to a great degree. This is why she intends to allow them greater involvement in the way they organize their schedules.

1. The decision periodically to move workers to different tasks reflects _____.
   a. job rotation
   b. job enrichment
   c. job emprowerment
   d. job empowerment

2. The decision to expand the scope of workers' jobs reflects _____.
   a. job enrichment
   b. job rotation
   c. job enlargement
   d. job empowerment

3. The decision to give workers more control over the increased number of tasks will have responsibility for reflects _____.
   a. job enrichment
   b. job enlargement
   c. job rotation
   d. job development

A supportive leadership style is necessary for job enrichment to work. The leadership notion of *empowerment*, discussed earlier, is consistent with the idea that enriched jobs create conditions most likely to motivate employees to achieve favorable results. Managers who empower employees give them greater responsibility, freedom, and influence to set performance standards, reducing the need to monitor and control their behavior through close supervision.

The Role of People's Perceptions

Important aspects of motivation are how people perceive that certain work behaviors will be rewarded and how fair or equitable the rewards are. Two well-known motivation theories focusing on beliefs are expectancy theory and equity theory.

EXPECTANCY THEORY One of the most widely accepted explanations of motivation is Victor Vroom's **expectancy theory**.[38] According to this theory, the strength to act in a particular way depends on people's beliefs that their actions will produce outcomes they find valuable and attractive. For instance, employees work harder if they believe that hard work will lead to better performance appraisals and promotion. As illustrated in Figure 12.8, the theory examines three linkages:

- *Effort–performance relationship:* The subjective probability or expectancy that exerting more effort will improve performance. The term *subjective* is crucial to the theory because people may underestimate or overestimate the extent to which working harder will lead to better performance.

expectancy theory
The view that having the strength to act in a particular way depends on people' beliefs that their actions will produce outcomes they find valuable and attractive.

FIGURE 12.8

Expectancy Theory of Motivation

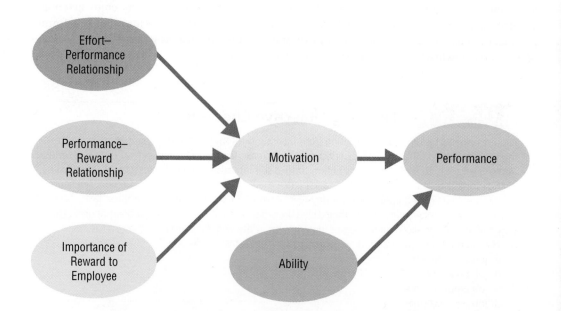

- *Performance–outcome (reward) relationship:* The degree to which individuals expect that performing at a certain level will lead to outcomes or rewards they find attractive.
- *Valences (importance of rewards to achieve personal goals):* The extent to which rewards that are contingent on performance satisfy an individual's personal goals or needs.

Expectancy theory helps explain why some people merely do the minimum necessary to get by while others seem to put all they have into their jobs. First, expectancy theory recognizes that there is no universal way to motivate people, because personal beliefs and perceptions play a major role in how people see the linkage of effort, performance, outcomes, and the attractiveness of those outcomes. These beliefs may be influenced by the organization (for instance, through training and incentive programs), but factors such as family background, culture, educational level, and personality are likely to play a role. Second, many employees may not give a maximum effort because they don't think it will be properly assessed by the organization. For instance, supervisors often don't differentiate high from low performers or may include personal factors in their evaluations (see Chapter 11). Third, organizations are often afraid to reward people based on performance because measuring performance is difficult and because people disagree about the accuracy of the performance assessment, particularly when it is not favorable. Last, rewards that are individualized are more motivating. Not all employees want the same thing. For instance, a working mother may place a high value on a flexible work schedule and may work harder to obtain flexibility. The hope of a better retirement package may induce a 55-year-old to be a key contributor at a time when other people are slowing down. Unfortunately, many managers are limited in the rewards they can provide, and few organizations allow rewards to be tailored to meet individual needs.

EQUITY THEORY According to **equity theory**, people develop beliefs about the fairness of the rewards they receive relative to their contributions.[39] Equity theory proposes that people's perceptions of fairness depend on their personal assessment of outcomes and inputs. *Outcomes* are rewards such as recognition, promotions, and pay. *Inputs* are contributions such as effort, education, and special skills. Employees have a general expectation that the outcomes or rewards they receive will be proportionate to the inputs they provide. People make this judgment not in an absolute sense but by using others as a reference point. A comparison person may be a coworker inside the firm or a friend who works for a different company. The relationship is summarized in the ratio

equity theory
The view that people develop beliefs about the fairness of the rewards they receive relative to their contributions.

$$\frac{\text{Personal outcomes}}{\text{Inputs}} \quad \text{versus} \quad \frac{\text{Others' outcomes}}{\text{Inputs}}$$

Fairness is achieved when the ratios are equivalent. Ratios that are not equivalent produce a psychological state called *cognitive dissonance,* which creates dissatisfaction and results in attempts to bring the ratios back into balance.

People who perceive that they are being inequitably treated can use one of four methods to attempt to change the ratios, or they can mentally reassess the situation and decide that it is equitable after all. One option is to reduce inputs by cutting back on the level of effort, and if the

LOC-In 6 **Learning Objective Check-In**

1. Don sees that his staff are constantly chatting and comparing the fairness of different individuals' compensations. Don manages factors like fairness according to _____ which suggests that his staff's perceptions of fairness depend on their personal assessments of their recognition and rewards as well as their contributions, backgrounds, and education.
   a. strategy theory
   b. MBO
   c. goal-setting theory
   d. equity theory

FIGURE 12.9

Motivations Associated with Commitment at Work

Source: Based on R. E. Johnson, C. H. Chang, and L. Q. Yang (2010). "Commitment and motivation at work: The relevance of employee identity and regulatory focus." *Academy of Management Review*, 35 (2), 226–45.

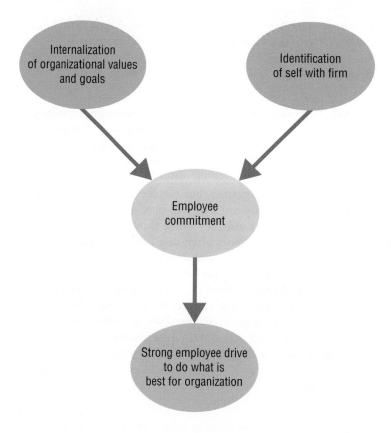

imbalance becomes too great, to leave the firm. A second option is to influence the outcomes. For instance, the employee may document what he or she has accomplished to persuade the boss to provide a raise or a promotion. Third, a person can decrease others' outcomes. For instance, a dissatisfied employee may spread rumors about people in order to reduce their outcomes. Finally, a person who feels that he or she is getting more than deserved may increase effort levels to reduce the dissatisfaction resulting from guilt.

Equity theory thus makes two important observations. First, motivation largely depends on perception of fairness in the exchange process between what the person contributes and what the person receives. Second, people are constantly comparing themselves to others, and the way they see their input–outcome exchange relative to others will affect their behavior.

Commitment and Motivation

More recent motivation models argue that the commitment that individuals feel toward the organization can make a big difference in their willingness sacrifice and be fully dedicated to the achievement of organizational goals (see Figure 12.9).

One driver of motivational commitment is internalization or doing your best because the values and goals of the organization have been integrated into the self. A second important driver of motivational commitment is identification or the desire to do your best because your self-esteem is closely tied to how well the organization achieves its objectives. Neither one of these motives is driven by desire to acquire rewards or avoid punishment as in the more utilitarian perspective that underlies reinforcement and expectancy theories. In fact too much emphasis on rewards and punishment may be detrimental to internalization and identification (the two motivational commitment mechanisms) because the individual might develop an egotistical, calculative "what is in it for me" attitude that preempts spontaneous "good citizenship" behaviors. Management Close-Up 12.2 illustrates how the CEO of Molson Coors, Peter Swinburn, is trying to create a corporate environment that increases employee commitment, thus providing a competitive advantage via a more motivated workforce to one of the largest brewers in the world.

MANAGEMENT CLOSE-UP 12.2   THEME: **DEALING WITH CHANGE**

How Molson Coors Is Trying to Increase Employee Commitment in the Midst of Fast Growth

During the past five years or so Molson Coors has become one of the largest brewers in the world, with such well-known brands as Molson Dry, Coors Light, Miller, and Carling. Most of this growth has occurred through a program of aggressive acquisition of other brewers and joint ventures around the world. This has created a major challenge for Molson Coors of how to blend at least 10 very different corporate cultures into one. CEO Peter Swinburn has made it a high priority to forge a cohesive corporate culture out of this mishmash. He is convinced that this will make employees more committed to doing high quality productive work by internalizing Molson Coors' values. To accomplish this, Swinburn is encouraging employees and managers to get together more frequently, and he has set up a site similar to Twitter, which is now used by 2,000 or so employees, to interact and collaborate on projects. "The challenge is getting a staff of 15,000 workers on three continents to think as one. There are different languages and work practices. The U.S. and British operations even disagree over the proper size for a beer barrel. (It was 117 liters in the U.S. and 163 in the U.K.)".

Sources: Based on *BusinessWeek*, "Yammering is good," 2010, March 1, pp. 37–38; "Molson Coors is Icecold with less froth," www.ethicalcorp.com, accessed April, 2010; "Peter Swinburn's profile," *Forbes Online*, http://www.forbes.com, accessed April, 2010; http://www.molsoncoors.com, accessed April, 2010.

MANAGEMENT IS EVERYONE'S BUSINESS   12.1

WORKING AS A MANAGER. The manager may influence subordinates by being recognized as an expert, by using rewards, by meeting the needs of subordinates, and by helping subordinates achieve their objectives. The manager can help forge a vision for the group but may also develop that vision by encouraging subordinates to provide their own ideas. For the manager to be an effective leader he or she has to be flexible enough to adapt to the uniqueness of each subordinate.

Effective managers:

- Energize employees to contribute as much as possible.
- Provide a sense of direction to channel employee efforts for the benefit of the organization.

Employees are more likely to accept the influence of managers they respect and believe. Managers can earn respect and credibility by tapping the reservoir of ideas and expertise of subordinates and by motivating them to fulfill a vision.

Working as a Team

A team is more likely to be effective if it has a leader that is capable of coordinating the activities of the team and meeting the needs of team members. In many cases the team leader is not appointed but emerges naturally from within the group.

Self-managed work teams need to provide leadership to unify the activities of the group. This involves setting objectives, dividing tasks to be accomplished, setting up evaluation procedures, and in some cases distributing rewards based on individual contribution. All team members may participate in this process, and the team's coordinator might not be the most influential person. The effectiveness of the team might largely depend on its ability to lead itself.

Working as an Individual

Individual employees are more likely to help their career chances if they show an ability to work independently while at the same time making superiors "look good" by helping them to achieve their objectives. Employees are more likely to do this well if they:

- are aware of how their personal traits pose strengths or weaknesses in light of the tasks to be accomplished;
- make a point to show that they can do things beyond what is expected; and
- set challenging goals for themselves and reward themselves for achieving their goals.

In other words, employees are more likely to succeed if they can manage themselves without relying on others to motivate them and define their tasks. Employees can become self-leaders by finding opportunities in their work environment, showing initiative, encouraging others to do their best, and generating enthusiasm for the tasks at hand. Individuals may also motivate themselves by setting challenging goals, choosing tasks that meet their needs, and reinforcing the achievement of milestones (such as taking a short vacation).

CONCLUDING THOUGHTS

The examples provided in the introductory vignette suggests that leadership and motivation are two sides of the same coin. A person is not a leader unless this individual is capable of creating the conditions that induce other people to achieve goals and objectives that flow from the leader's vision. Being a bold thinker is not enough for a leader to be effective and retain a leadership position. Coming up with challenging goals and visionary statements is the easiest part; the toughest part for a leader is to persuade other people to rally behind him or her and be willing to self-sacrifice and persevere over the long haul to support the leader's agenda. For this to happen, the leader must be able to accurately pinpoint and satisfy the needs of followers, make the work place an exciting place to be, offer opportunities for personal advancement, provide rewards that are perceived as fair, and induce employees to identify with the firm and adopt organizational values as their own. Management Is Everyone's Business 12.1 summarizes the implications of the concepts discussed in this chapter for managers, teams, and individual employees.

Summary of Learning Objectives

A variety of approaches may be used to improve leadership effectiveness and induce employees to work harder to accomplish organizational goals. Leaders are expected to forge a vision, sell that vision to others, and take the necessary steps to support its accomplishment. One critical aspect of effective leadership is inducing subordinates to work harder to accomplish organizational objectives. The chapter material relevant to each of the learning objectives presented at the start of the chapter is summarized below.

1 Explain what makes leaders unique.

- Personal characteristics such as charisma, perseverance and strong communication skills
- Being in the right place at the right time
- Ability to influence other people
- Developing a vision
- Selling the vision to others
- Working with followers to establish appropriate implementation activities

2 Distinguish between management and leadership.

- Management is about implementation and control
- Leadership is about vision and inspiration

3 Recognize how leaders use different power basis to exercise influence.

- Coercive power
- Reward power
- Legitimate power
- Expert power
- Referent power

4 Differentiate effective and ineffective leaders.

- Person-based theories
  - Trait theory
  - Behavioral theories
- Consideration and initiating structures
- Managerial grid
- Leadership style
- Contingency theories (best leadership approach may depend on the situation)
- Relationship and exchange theories

5 Use individualized goals to increase employee motivation.

- Maximize goal acceptability by taking a participative approach to setting goals
- Set challenging but realistic goals
- Goals should be specific, quantifiable, and measurable

6 Apply basic reinforcement principles to stimulate desired employee behaviors.

- *Positive reinforcement.* Follow desired behaviors with rewards.
- *Negative reinforcement.* Remove negative conditions following desired behavior.
- *Punishment.* Follow undesired behavior with unpleasant consequence.
- *Extinction.* Withhold a reward that used to be linked with the behavior.

7 Become aware of the role of needs in employee motivation.

- *Maslow's Hierarchy of needs.* People experience needs in a particular order.
- *Alderfer's ERG Theory.* Three groups of core needs (existence, relationship, growth) that are not ordered
- *Mclelland's Needs.* Identifies needs for managers to consider (need for achievement, need for affiliation, need for power)
- *Herzberg's Two-Factor Theory.* Hygiene factors (extrinsic factors) and motivators (intrinsic factors)
- General implication of need theories is that needs energize action, and knowing the needs of your workers can help you to align rewards so that motivation and desired performance are maximized.

8 Recognize assumptions about people and perceptions that may affect employee treatment and motivation.

- *Expectancy theory.* Remove barriers so that employee expects that he or she can perform the tasks if they put in the effort; establish clear links between task performance and rewards; offer rewards that are positively valued by workers.
- *Equity Theory.* Make outputs proportionate to inputs; establish fairness in outcome/impact ratios so that comparisons with others results in the conclusion that treatment is equitable.

9 Use work design as a means of employee motivation.

- *Job characteristics model.* Design enriched jobs.
  - Skill variety
  - Task identity
  - Task significance
  - Autonomy
  - Feedback
- Identify characteristics of job design that can affect worker motivation
  - Job enlargement
  - Job rotation
  - Job enrichment

Discussion Questions

1. Do you agree that managers and leaders are different kinds of people? Why or why not?
2. Some people argue that organizations need to put in place mechanisms to prevent informal leaders from imposing their own agenda on others. Do you agree? Why or why not?
3. Think about some people you have met who are excellent leaders and some who have been entrusted with a leadership position yet are highly ineffective. Use the theories discussed in this chapter to analyze what made those individuals effective or ineffective as leaders.
4. Consider a time when you were highly motivated to do your best at something (such as a particular task, a job, a course). Based on the theories discussed in this chapter, analyze what made you feel that way. Would the same motivation affect you in a different situation?
5. Some people aruge that employees are either highly motivated or they are not, and there is little the firm can do to change that the predisposition. Do you agree? Why or why not?

6. If you were forced to choose, which of the motivational theories discussed in this chapter do you think is most likely to account for employee motivation? Explain your rationale.

7. On average, U.S. workers spend about 20 percent more time at work and devote less time to leisure in comparison with other industrialized countries such as Japan, Great Britain, France, and Germany. This gap seems to be increasing.[40] How would you explain this phenomenon? Support your answer in light of the material discussed in this chapter.

Management Minicase 12.1
Executives for Rent

It used to be that temporary employment agencies provided support for companies that needed clerical help. But today there is a thriving cadre of executives who are hired for short-term assignments.

Jon Osborne, VP of research at Staffing Industry Analysts, estimates that the market for contingent management jobs will grow 90 percent over the next decade, to $26.6 billion. Littler Mendelson, the giant employment-law firm, forecasts that as much as 50 percent of all hiring in the near future will be for contingent positions.

It is estimated that approximately 5.6 million "executive temps" are at work every business day, earning between $200 and $1,500 a day, depending on local business conditions and the temp's background. In most cases the temp executive is responsible for a number of subordinates, the majority of whom are regular employees, some of whom may have been working there for 10 years or more.

DISCUSSION QUESTIONS

1. Do you think a temporary executive may be an effective leader? What types of skills should this person have to inspire and motivate subordinates?

2. Make a list of challenges a temporary executive is likely to face when put in charge of a team of employees in the temporary assignment. How should this person deal with these challenges? Explain.

3. What factors do you think account for the trend of hiring temporary executives? Explain.

4. If you were a temporary executive, how would you see your work identity? As a freelancer? As a "mercenary"? As a person with multiple identities that change as you change employers? Would this affect how you interact with employees? Explain your answer.

Sources: Based on J. McGregor, "How to become an exec-for rent," *Fortune,* 2010, March 22, 41–44; M. Piturro, "The temporary executive," http://www.journalofaccountancy.com, 2011 ; http://www.interimmanagers.com, 2011.

Management Minicase 12.2
Does Money Motivate?

Stock options, with their potential for huge financial reward, have frequently been used by firms as a major motivator to get employees to work harder. Matt Ward's San Francisco consulting firm, WestWard Pay Strategies, designs stock plans for tech companies. Ward says, "Silicon Valley is the economic engine of the world, and options are the fuel."

Stock options became big news more than 30 years ago, when some big name firms first went public, including Oracle, Sun Microsystems, Silicon Graphics, Adobe Systems, Informix—and Microsoft. Already hugely successful, Microsoft didn't need the money from going public. If had to go public so its employees could take advantage of the stock and stock options they'd been given over the company's 11-year lifetime, Options have driven Microsoft's compensation system and finances ever since. In the first three months of 1997, for example, employees realized $32,000 each from their stock options—and another $1 million per employee was outstanding.

Corporate executives in other industries and areas started to use stock options as a motivational tool in the late 1990s. Growth companies like Home Depot and Statbucks provided them, as did Warner-Lambert, Citicorp, and Merrill Lynch. General Mills, gave options to almost 10,000 employees, and 800 managers could and did choose even bigger options over pay raises. By 2000, there were at least 15 times more employees receiving stock options than a decade earlier.

The idea behind options is very simple: to link employees' and managers' fortunes to those of the firm, for better—and for worse. During the 1990s, millions of employees benefited greatly from stock options. Relatively few options holders thought about how much risk they were taking. By 2001, an estimated 52 percent of employees' options had lost 10 percent or more of their value, and 11 percent of employees holding stock options realized that they had become worthless. For instance, Xerox employees holding stock saw its value plummeting almost 90 percent in less than a year.

For a while, stock options lost their luster but it wasn't long before they regained their popularity as stock prices shot up during 2005–2008. Then the worst happened in 2008, when the Wall Street crisis hit in September of that year and stock options in many firms lost 50 percent or more of their value. It seemed that stock options were doomed forever, yet by 2011 stock options had regained much of their lost value and many companies began to offer them once again to eager employees who bet the market would go even higher.

DISCUSSION QUESTIONS

1. Do you believe that stock options can motivate employees to work harder? Should employees be held responsible for factors beyond their control, such as gyrations in stock prices? Answer this question in light of the motivational theories that are discussed in this chapter.

2. Some people argue that stock options provide an effective mechanism to foster self-leadership within the firm. Do you agree? Why or why not?

3. Which employee needs in Maslow's hierarchy or Alderfer's ERG theory, if any, are met through stock-option plans? Explain your answer.

Sources: Based on M. Dorning, "Why the Obama plan is working," *BusinessWeek,* April 19, 2010, 29–36; Bloomberg Survey, "Indicators now point in the right direction: The stock and bond markets have returned to health and the consensus outlook is far brighter," *BusinessWeek,* April 19, 2010, chart on stock values, p. 30; J. Fox, "The Next Best Thing to Free Money," *Fortune,* July 7, 1997, pp.52–62; R. Kanetsar and J. Stern, "Get Rich.Com," *Time,* September 27, 1999, pp. 65–78; D. Sparks. "Options Put Grants in a Jam," *BusinessWeek,* January 15, 2001, pp. 68–69; L. Lavelle, "Undermining Pay for Performance," *BusinessWeek,* January 15, 2001, pp. 70–71; G. Smith, "Are High-Tech Stocks Headed for More Turmoil?" *BusinessWeek,* February 5, 2001, p. 50; M. Mandel, "The New Economy's Cruel Math," *BusinessWeek,* February 5, 2001, pp. 42–43.

Management Minicase 12.3
Working in Heaven?

The 6,000 employees at SAS in North Carolina (chosen by *Fortune* as one of the 50 "best companies to work for" every year since the mid-1990s) are pampered by a variety of perks to make work enjoyable. These includes massages on the 66,000 square foot recreation and fitness center, a billiards hall, hair salon, manicurist, zen music, free biscuits, a 35-hour workweek, no monitoring of sick leave or absences, flexible work hours, and subsidized daycare for 600 children, among others. Turnover rate is extremely low (2 percent per year), less than one-tenth of the industry average, and the average number of absences per employee is an incredibly low: two per year. SAS seems to accomplish this without offering stock options, with salaries that are relatively low by industry standards, and with very little use of disciplinary procedures to keep employees in line.

Garrett Brown, 32, a desktop support specialist for DWL Inc., recently spent the day in simulated dogfights in a World War II Spitfree replica. Even better, he gets an extra $1,000 each year to do it.

DWL is a privately held Toronto customer-relationship management consulting firm founded in the late 1990s, with clients such as Body Shop International and National Life Insurance. Being sure people have fun is part of DWL's day-to-day management. Top executives believe encouraging fun helps morale and retention among the 300 employees, and the company is spending about $500,000 a year on this belief. The company offers $1,000 annually to each employee to do something fun. Trips and cruises are common uses for the money. One employee surprised his father with a trip to a favorite fishing camp. Another bought a guitar, and still another signed up for cooking lessons.

At year's end, the company posts photos of the activities—the more colorful, the better. Sometimes the photograph tells it all. For example, one employee's wife coaches high school girls' volleyball. The employee used his money to tag along on one of his wife's trips to the Caribbean with the girls. His photo of 15 volleyball players carrying him on the beach impressed the panel of five employees voting on who had the most fun during the year.

The winner is awarded $5,000 for next year's activity; two runners-up each receive $2,000. Last year's winner used the money for his avocation: video art. Though he enjoys producing videos, there isn't much local interest in it, so the employee used the money to produce a video and travel to its showing in Amsterdam.

Mark Mighton, VP of Sales Operations, invented the program and earned the informal title of Director of Fun. He reviews the employees' applications for the annual grant, which are usually informal e-mails. About 90 percent of the applications are accepted immediately; the other 10 percent usually are approved on the second try. The typical reason for rejection is that the idea didn't involve having enough fun—a new TV, a mortgage payment, a new bathroom sink, and anything job-related will be rejected. Mighton sets an example with his own choices—his African safari was paid for in part by the fun fund.

Justin La Fayette, DWL's CEO and founder, wants everyone to participate to keep work in perspective and to offset the "north of 50-plus, 60-plus hours a week for extended periods" so many employees put in. He sees the fun fund as a way of keeping work and leisure balanced and believes that it is a key factor in the 98 percent retention rate the company boasts as well as powerful employee motivator. Workers themselves make decisions on how they can best contribute to the company's success and are rewarded both by jobs that are more exciting and by the opportunity and the means to enjoy their time outside the office.

DISCUSSION QUESTIONS

1. Based on the material you read in this chapter, how would you characterize the motivational and leadership approach used by SAS and DWL Inc.? Explain.

2. Do you think that the motivational and leadership style at SAS and DWL Inc. would be successful in most situations? Why or why not? If not, explain under what situations it may work better.

3. Of all the motivation theories discussed in this chapter, which one(s) seem to be applied by SAS and DWL Inc. to boost employee morale? Explain.

Sources: Based on D. A. Kaplan, "#1 SAS: How do you build a tech powerhouse without offering any stock options?" *Fortune,* 2010, February 8, 57–64; M. Moskowitz, R. Levering, and C. Tkaczyk "100 best companies," *Fortune,* 2010, February 8, 75–92; http://www.sas.com; D. R. Khurallah, "Where Having Fun Really Pays," *Information Week,* January 15, 2001, p. 87.

Individual/Collaborative Learning Case 12.1
What Caused the So-called "Financial Meltdown" of 2008–2011?

Many experts blame a combination of incentive systems and ethical lapses among corporate leaders in the financial sector for the world's economic troubles in recent years. Banks and financial institutions rewarded top executives for revenues generated. Hence, a high proportion of mortgages were given out with little or no down payment, thinking that prices would keep on rising at a fast clip. The broker who handled the transaction had an incentive to encourage mortgage applicants to overstate their income and to look the other way for troublesome signs that the applicant may not be able to make timely payments. The broker received a fee at the time of escrow closing and bore no personal risk if the mortgage defaulted after that point in time. The banks in turn would sell the mortgage quickly to other entities around the world or split it up into exotic, small pieces called "instruments" or "derivatives" that other brokers would then sell down the line to dispersed or atomistic investors. Very few people understood the process. In the meantime, top executives reaped huge bonuses as the volume of these transactions increased. Borrowers faced little personal risk for overstating income (because down payments were minimal) and as long as housing prices were rising they had everything to gain and very little to lose.

In what is perhaps the most extreme case of some of these practices, top executives at Goldman Sachs were charged with fraud in 2010 by the Securities and Exchange Commission (SEC) for misleading investors on securities linked to subprime mortgages. "Their products were new and complex but the deception and conflicts are old and simple, with greed as the prime motivator," said the SEC enforcement chief. Some of the "hedge fund" managers involved in these transactions made over $4 billion in a single year. While Goldman Sachs vigorously denies doing anything illegal *BusinessWeek* refers to this incident as "one small, rotten potato in a large and smelly field."

CRITICAL THINKING QUESTIONS

1. How would you describe the leadership style and the motivational approach used by some of the financial sector firms in light of the theories discussed in this chapter? Explain.

2. One critic argues that it is unfair to question the activities sponsored by these corporate leaders after the fact. At the time these things happened they were standard practices in the industry. Who would have ever thought that home prices would collapse by as much as 50 percent in some cities? Do you agree with this assessment? Why or why not?

3. Do you believe that it is a good idea to rely heavily on financial incentives to motivate top executives, managers, and employees? Do you see any potential danger with using money as a motivator? Explain.

COLLABORATIVE LEARNING EXERCISE

Students form groups of four or five. Each group is asked to provide a set of recommendations to leaders in the financial industry to avoid the problems discussed above. Specifically, the group members should think of motivational approaches that would prevent these sorts of problems from arising again.

Sources: Based on J. Weld, "Goldman slapped," *BusinessWeek*, May 2, 2010, p. 13; M. Lewis, "A message to Wall Street's fabulous fabs," *Business Week*, 2010, May 2, p. 15; G. Zuckerman et al, "Goldman Sachs charged with fraud," *Wall Street Journal*, http://online.WSJ.com, 2010; C. Harper, "Goldman Sachs clients—just pledge undercut by SEC; http://www.businessweek.com, 2010; A. Jones, "A crash course on the financial meltdown," http://motherjones.com, 2011.

Individual/Collaborative Learning Case 12.2
Motivating Low-Wage Workers

Mini Maid Inc., a chain of more than 100 franchises in 24 states offering residential maid service, is owned by Leone Ackerly. In the 24 years since she started the firm, Ackerly has developed a philosophy of mutual respect that motivates a low-wage workforce and improves customer service and productivity.

Most Mini Maid employees are women who grew up on welfare, according to Ackerly They typically are in their twenties and have little education or skills; many have been abused. Ackerly learned that many of her workers felt they were not respected, but when given respect they changed for the better. Ackerly doesn't care that previous employers looked down on her workers. Even though most of them start working at Mini Maid just for the paychecks, "We ask them to look at us as their partners in a team effort. We tell them, 'this is what we give you; this is what you give us.' Right off the bat, the new employee feels that she is an important part of our company. What happens at this point is that they begin to listen."

Ackerly checks applicants' backgrounds before hiring them—a police record or history of drug use means they won't be offered a job. She presses charges against any maid caught stealing. She expects her employees to be punctual, clean and neat, and polite, and she gives them discipline, standards, and structure.

She has found that fair and honest dealings with employees are returned in kind. If they respect their manager, they do a better job representing the company. Ackerly provides workers with an attendance bonus each pay period for coming to work every day, on time, and in uniform. The extra motivation and reward encourage good work habits. The results go beyond the job. Over the years, Ackerly's workers have learned to apply the concept of mutual respect to their family lives.

Besides respect, low-wage workers need to feel recognized, says consultant Rosalind Jeffries. The self-esteem of a low-wage worker typically is very low, and the pat on the back and expression of thanks go a long way as motivators. Fine Host Corp., a food service in Greenwich, Connecticut, hires contract workers to bus tables and cook and serve food, and has found that recognition is key to keeping them motivated. Fine Host president and CEO Richard Kerley understands that the employees are the ones who can drive customers away, and he knows that recognition is relatively easy to give. "Though there may be economic restraints on what we pay them, there are no restraints on the recognition we give them." His company gives employee awards and puts their names on company buildings in recognition of good work. Also, the employees receive framed certificates when they complete training courses. Kerley believes companies like his must show people they are appreciated.

Irving Edwards is CEO of All Metro Health Care in Lynbrook, New York, a company that employs home health aides. The company sponsors an award for caregiver of the year and occasionally sponsors essay contests for its workers, complete with prizes. Gifts such as watches and blenders are given to employees when they score high in a quarterly training game. Health aides who are asked to work on holidays know the company will serve them food at the office, too.

ServiceMaster, with more than 20,000 housecleaning and lawn care workers, found one way that its employees would have more take-home pay and earned employee loyalty in return. Many of its employees do not have checking accounts and had to pay a fee to check-cashing services in order to cash their paychecks. ServiceMaster provides a company-sponsored bank account and ATM cards. For $1 a month, employees can have their paychecks deposited every week and they can then withdraw money with ATM cards, bypassing the expensive check-cashing services. For example, Araceli Perez is a ServiceMaster employee in Santa Clara, California, who saves $15 to $20 a month by no longer having to pay check cashers.

CRITICAL THINKING QUESTIONS

1. How would you describe the motivational techniques used by these firms in light of the theories discussed in this chapter? Explain.
2. One critic argues that a growing trend is for firms to try to motivate workers the "cheap way"—a pat on the back or an inexpensive certificate—but that these actions make employees more cynical rather than more highly motivated? Do you agree with this assessment? Why or why not?
3. Do you believe that workers can be motivated for the long haul with nonfinancial rewards that appeal to their self-esteem? Why or why not?
4. According to a recent survey "Low-paid workers who are given more autonomy and flexibility at work let fewer negative events at home impact their productivity at work—more so than higher-paid workers who get autonomy and flexibility." How would you explain these findings?

COLLABORATIVE LEARNING EXERCISE

Students form groups of four or five and assume the role of manager for Mini Maid. The task is to outline a short speech to be given to new employees that explains "what we give you, and what you give us." Special attention should be paid to ways to sustain motivation. Post or display completed outlines and compare.

Sources: Based F. Sharpe, "Guide to Manage Minimum Wage Workers," http://www.business.com; 2011; B. Hunsberger, "Motivating low wage workers," http://blog.oregonlive.com, 2011; "Tips for motivating low wage workers," http://www.workforce.com, 2011; R. Maynard, "How to Motivate Low Wage Workers," *Nation's Business,* May 1997, pp. 35–40; "The Pay Is in the Bank," *BusinessWeek,* January 29, 2001, p. 10.

Internet Exercise 12.1

Leading the Pack

www.businessweek.com

In January of each year *Business Week* identifies top managers and entrepreneurs as exemplary leaders and justifies its choices. Visit the *Business Week* Web site (www.businessweek.com) and enter "Top 25 Managers" as a search term to access a articles from the January issue. Use the results of your search to answer the following questions:

1. Develop a list of 3–10 characteristic that these people have in common.
2. How do differences in leadership style contribute to success?
3. How did the firm's context or situation affect the leadership style among *Business Week's* top leaders?

Internet Exercise 12.2

Test Your Emotional Intelligence

Go to http://discoveryhealth.queendom.com/questions/eiq_abridged_1.html and complete the questionnaire that measures your emotional intelligence. The program will then score it for you. Do you agree that this is an accurate representation of emotional intelligence? How else would you measure it? How can a firm use emotional intelligence information to help improve the quality of its leaders? Explain.

Endnotes

1. http://www.chrysler.com, 2011; http://www.automotive.com, 2011 J. R. Healey, "Chrysler Again Runs Low on Financial Fuel," *USA Today,* January 30, 2001, p. 1B; D. Goodman, "Can Chrysler Survive?" *Arizona Republic,* January 30, 2001, p. D1.
2. Podsakoff et al. (2010) (see reference list) J. E. Garten, "The Mind of the CEO," *Business Week,* February 5, 2001, p. 107. Cited in T. Arango "How the AOL-Time Warner merger went so wrong," http://www.nytimes.com, 2011.
3. S. P. Robbins and T. Judge, *Organizational Behavior,* (Englewood Cliffs, NJ: Prentice Hall, 2011).
4. J. French and B. Raven, "The Bases of Social Power," in D. Cartwright (ed.), *Studies in Social Power* (Ann Arbor, MI: Institute for Social Research, 1959).
5. Rowold & Heinitz (2010) (see reference list) R. G. Lord, C. C. DeVader, and G. M. Alleger, "A Meta-analysis of the Relation between Personality Traits and Leadership

Perception," *Journal of Applied Psychology* 71, no. 3 (1986): 402–410; D. A. Kenny and S. J. Zaccaro, "An Estimate of the Variance due to Traits in Leadership," *Journal of Applied Psychology* 68, no. 4 (1983): 678–685; D. a. Kenny and B. W. Hallmark, "Rotation Designs in Leadership Research," *Leadership Quarterly* 3, no. 1 (1992): 25–41; J. L. Denis, "Becoming a Leader in a Complex Organization," *Journal of Management Studies* 37, no. 8 (2000): 1063–1099; B. O'Reilly, "What It Takes to Start a Startup," *Fortune,* June 7, 1999, pp. 135–139; "The Top 25 Managers of the Year," *Business Week,* January 8, 2001, pp. 60–79.

6. Steers et al. (2010) (see reference list). Mabey & Finch-Lees (see reference list) S. Kerry, C. A. Schriesheim, C. J. Murphy, and R. M. Stogdill, "Toward a Contingency Theory of Leadership Based upon the Consideration and Initiating structure Literature," *Organizational Behavior and Human Performance,* August 1974, pp. 62–82; and R. Kahn and D. Katz, "Leadership Practices in Relation to Productivity and Morale," in D. Cartwright and A. Sander (eds.), *Group Dynamics: Research and Theory* (Elmsford, NY: Row, Peterson, 1960).

7. R. R. Blake and J. S. Mouton, *The Managerial Grid* (Houston: Gulf, 1964).

8. R. White and R. Lippit, *Autocracy and Democracy: An Experimental Inquiry* (New York: Harper & Brothers, 1960).

9. Robbins, *Organizational Behavior,* p. 419.

10. F. E. Fiedler, *A Theory of Leadership Effectiveness* (New York: McGraw-Hill, 1967): F. E. Fiedler, "Validation and Extension of The Contingency Model of Leadership Effectiveness," *Psychological Bulletin* 76 (1971): 128–148.

11. L. H. Peter, D. D. Hartke, and J. T. Pohlmann, "Fiedler's Contingency Theory of Leadership: An Application of the Meta-analysis Procedures of Schmidt and Hunter," *Psychological Bulletin,* March 1985, pp. 274–285; and C. A. Schriesheim, B. J. Tepper, and L. A. Tetrault, "Least Preferred Co-worker Score Situational Control, and Leadership Effectiveness: A Meta-analysis of Contingency Model Performance Predictions," *Journal of Applied Psychology,* August 1994, pp. 562–573.

12. Mabey & Finch-Lees (2009) (see reference list) R. J. House, "A Path Goal Theory of Leader Effectiveness," *Administrative Science Quarterly* 16 (1971): 321–338; R. J. House and T. R. Michell, "Path Goal Theory of Leadership," *Journal of Contemporary Business* 3 (1974): 81–97; R. House, "Weber and the Neo-charismatic Paradigm," *Leadership Quarterly* 10, no. 4 (2000): 15–26; R. House, P. J. Hanges, A. Quintanilla, P. W. Dorfman, M. W. Dickson, M. Javidan, et al., *Advances in Global Leadership* (Greenwich, CT: JAI Press, 1999), pp. 100–185.

13. "The best and worst managers of the year," *Business Week,* January 10, 2005.

14. "Pioneer Hewlett Dies at 87," *Arizona Republic,* January 13, 2001.

15. Mabey & Finch-Lees (2009) (See reference list) R. J. House and R. Aditya, "The Social Scientific Study of Leadership: Quo Vadis?" *Journal of Management* 23, no. 3 (1997): 409–475.

16. G. Koretz, "Economic Trends," *Business Week,* February 5, 2001, p. 30.

17. E. Iawata, "Exec Shuffle May Not Prevent Gateway Crash," *USA Today,* January 31, 2001, pp. 3–13.

18. G. Harris, "The Cure," *The Wall Street Journal,* January 10, 2001, p. A1.

19. Robbins & Judge *Organizational Behavior,* p. 438.

20. House and Aditya, "The Social Scientific Study of Leadership."

21. T. Bateman and S. Snell, *Management: Building Competitive Advantage,* 4th ed. (New York: Irwin/McGraw-Hill, 2000).

22. Galvin & Balkundi (2010) (see reference for list); Rowold & Heinitz (2007) (see reference for list); B. M. Bass and B. J. Avolio, "Developing Transformational Leadership: 1992 and Beyond," *Journal of European Industrial Training* January 1990, p. 23; B. Bass, B. Avolio, and L. Goodheim, "Biography in the Assessment of Transformational Leadership at the World Class Level," *Journal of Management* 13 (1987) 7–20.

23. Podsakoff, Podsakoff, and Kustova (see references).

24. N. S. Schuttle et al. (2010); M. J. Sanchez-Ruiz (2010); K. J. Gardner (2010) (all in reference list) D. Goleman, *Emotional Intelligence* (New York: Bantam Books, 1995) D. Goleman, *Working with Emotional Intelligence* (New York: Bantam Books, 2000).

25. Goleman, *Working with Emotional Intelligence,* p. 297.

26. Goleman, *Working with Emotional Intelligence,* p. 299.

27. Wilkinson et al. (2010); Podsakoff et al. (2010); Tsung-Hsien et al. (2010); (all in reference list) P. C. Early, T. Connolly, and G. Ekegren, "Goals, Strategy Development, and

Task Performance: Some Limits on the Efficacy of Goal Setting," *Journal of Applied Psychology* 74 (1989): 24–33; C. E. Shalley, "Effects of Productivity Goals, Creativity Goals, and Personal Discretion on Individual Creativity," *Journal of Applied Psychology* 76 (1991): 179–185. Most of these studies are based on the pioneering work of E. Locke, "Toward a Theory of Task Motivation and Incentives," *Organizational Behavior and Human Performance* 3 (1968): 157–189. For practitioner perspective, see J. W. Marcum, "Out with Motivation, in with Engagement," *National Productivity Review* 19, no. 4 (Autumn 2000): 57–60.

28. E. L. Thorndike, *The Fundamentals of Learning* (New York: AMS Press, 1971).
29. A. H. Maslow, "A Theory of Human Motivation," *Psychological Review*, July 1943, pp. 370–396.
30. C. Alderfer, *Existence, Relatedness, and Growth: Human Needs in Organizational Settings* (Glencoe, IL: Free Press, 1972).
31. D. McClelland, *The Achieving Society* (New York: Van Nostrand Reinhold, 1961).
32. Ahmed (2010) (see reference list) R. E. Boyatzis, "The Need for Close Relationships and the Manager's Job," in D. A. Kolls, I. M. Rubin, and J. M. McIntyre (eds.), *Organizational Psychology: Readings on Human Behavior in Organizations,* 4th ed. (Englewood Cliffs, NJ: Prentice Hall, 1984).
33. D. C. McClelland and R. Boyatzis, "Leadership Motive Pattern and Long-Term Success in Management," *Journal of Applied Psychology* 67 (1982): 737–743.
34. Ferraro (2010) (see reference list) N. Adler, *International Dimensions of Organizational Behavior*, 3rd ed. (Cincinnati, OH: South-Western Publishing Co., 2008); G. Hofstede, *Culture's Consequences: International Differences in Work Related Values* (Beverly Hills, CA: Sage, 1980).
35. D. McGregor, *The Human Side of Enterprise* (New York: McGraw-Hill, 1960).
36. F. Herzberg, B. Mausner, and B. Snyderman, *The Motivation to Work* (New York, John Wiley & Sons, 1959).
37. Ismail et al. (2010) (see reference list); Tsung-Hsien et al. (2010) (see reference list); Kim et al. (2010) (see reference list); Gagne et al. (2010) (see reference list) J. R. Hackman, G. Oldham, R. Janson, and K. Purdy, "A New Strategy for Job Enrichment," *California Management Review* 16 (1975): 57–71.
38. V. H. Vroom, *Work and Motivation* (New York: John Wiley & Sons, 1964); H. J. Arnold, "A Test of the Multiplicative Hypotheis of Expectancy-Valence Theories of Work Motivation," *Academy of Management Journal*, April 1981, pp. 128–141.
39. J. S. Adams, "Inequity in Social Exchanges," in L. Berkowitz (ed.), *Advances in Experimental Social Psychology* (New York: Academic Press, 1965), pp. 267–300; S. Ronen, "Equity Perception in Multiple Comparisons: A Field Study, *Human Relations*, April, 1986, pp. 333–346; T. P. Summers and A. S. DeNisi, "In Search of Adam's Other. Reexamination of Referents Used in the Evaluation of Pay," *Human Relations*, June 1990, pp. 495–511.
40. M. Memmotl, "Reich Knows High Cost of 'Success': He Paid It," *USA Today*, January 8, 2001, p. A1.

13

Learning Objectives

1 Translate the benefits teams provide into competitive advantages.

2 Identify the different types of teams—self-managed, parallel, project, and virtual.

3 Track the stages of team development that occur over the life of a project and help the team perform effectively.

4 Recognize the key roles that team members must play to ensure high performance.

5 Master the skills to detect and control team performance problems.

6 Manage team conflict through negotiation.

Rapid-Response Teams Save Lives at Tenet Healthcare Corporation
www.tenethealth.com

Rapid-response teams avert life-threatening medical catastrophes by aggressively deploying experienced clinical staff to the bedside if a patient's condition becomes ambiguous enough to raise concerns. The teams provide assistance before a situation escalates into a critical event that could lead to serious complications, days in an intensive-care unit (ICU), or even death. Although the teams operate in various modes at hospitals across the country, they often include an ICU nurse, a respiratory therapist, and a hospital staff person. Rapid-response teams are one of six interventions that have been recommended as practices that should be used to reduce thousands of avoidable deaths at American hospitals each year.

Managing Teams

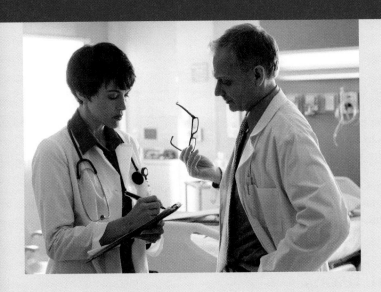

One research study has reported that rapid-response teams in hospitals produced substantial cost savings by reducing by 75 percent the number of patients admitted to the ICU, which has resulted in savings of millions of dollars.

Sources: C. Becker, "Fast Start for Hospitals," *Modern Healthcare*, December 19–26, 2005, pp. 8–9; J. Molyneux, "Do Rapid Response Teams Save Lives?" *American Journal of Nursing*, March, 2009, p. 19; "Rapid Response Teams: The Case for Early Intervention," *Institute for Healthcare Improvement*, 2007, www.ihi.org.

CRITICAL THINKING QUESTIONS

1. *What are the benefits of using rapid-response teams to provide medical services to patients in a hospital? How does the use of rapid-response teams compare to a more traditional approach to providing care to patients who have problems with their vital medical signs?*

2. *What type of team most closely matches the rapid-response teams at Tenet Healthcare Corporation? There are four types of teams to choose from: self-managed teams, project teams, parallel teams, or virtual teams. Justify your choice.*

In addition to saving lives, rapid-response teams are credited with helping hospitals increase nursing job satisfaction by taking away a layer of stress. At Tenet Healthcare Corporation the teams have provided a strong morale boost for nurses, according to its senior vice president for clinical quality and chief medical officer. Aproximately 80 percent of Tenet's 69 hospitals have rapid-response teams on one or more units.

Skills for Managing Teams

- *Conflict management skills.* Conflict is a natural part of the growth and development of a team. Team members need to be able to recognize the difference between functional conflict, which stimulates team performance, and dysfunctional conflict, which can undermine effectiveness. Different situations call for different approaches to managing conflict.
- *Negotiation skills.* The *win–win* approach to negotiation is a way to develop a solution that satisfies the needs of both parties. This type of negotiation is particularly

effective when it is important to maintain long-term relationships, which is the case with teams.
- *Skills for handling difficult team members.* In cases in which a team member is preventing the team from performing to potential, it is crucial to deal with and motivate the difficult person. Two types of difficult people you are likely to encounter on a team are the "free rider," who tries to get away with doing as little work as possible, and the "nonconforming high performer," who performs well as an individual but does not work well with other people.

At the end of the chapter in our Concluding Thoughts we will revisit these critical thinking questions regarding the use of rapid-response teams at Tenet Healthcare Corporation.

Many U.S. companies that employ knowledge workers are increasingly using teams to fully engage and empower workers to take advantage of their specialized knowledge. As more work is being performed by teams, the ability to manage them has become an increasingly important skill. This chapter examines the management of teams, beginning with the reasons companies use teams and the different types and design aspects of teams. Key topics include the behavioral issues that must be identified and administered, problems that need to be addressed along with ways to deal with them, and the critical skills needed to effectively manage teams such as those outlined in Skills for Managing 13.1.

■ The Benefits of Teams

In this new millennium, many tasks are far too complex to be completed by a single individual. As a result, the success of various teams and groups directly affects the success of the overall organization.

team
A small number of people with complementary skills who are committed to a common purpose, a set of performance goals, and an approach for which they hold themselves mutually accountable.

A **team** is a small number of people with complementary skills who are committed to a common purpose, a set of performance goals, and an approach for which they hold themselves mutually accountable. Team members interact with each other on a regular basis. A team can be as small as two people, such as a telephone company's sales team, composed of a customer service representative and a customer service engineer. Larger teams may be responsible for taking charge of core business processes such as order fulfillment, customer service, or procurement of raw materials and supplies. When the size of a team exceeds 25 members the individuals have difficulty interacting intensively. The range of team size for high-performing teams is between 5 and 12 members. This range in size allows for teams to be large enough to take advantage of the different skills of members and small enough to provide a feeling of community and cohesion among the team members.[1]

Teams share performance goals. Individuals on teams are mutually responsible for end results. The teams at the hospitals discussed in the opening vignette are responsible for patient care. If one person on the team is negligent, all team members are responsible for and affected by the poor care given to the patient.

synergy
When individuals blend complementary skills and talents to produce a product that is more valuable than the sum of the individual contributions.

A quality team environment produces **synergy**, which results when individuals blend complementary skills and talents to produce a product that is more valuable than the sum of the individual contributions. Teams can energize and motivate individuals to perform at consistently high levels, another aspect of synergy.

work group
A group whose members are held accountable for individual work, but are not responsible for the output of the entire group.

A **work group** differs from a team. Members of a work group are held accountable for individual work, but they are not responsible for the output of the entire group. For example, a group of accountants in an accounting firm may meet occasionally to discuss auditing procedures. Still,

TABLE 13.1 Team Characteristics Compared to a Working Group

Characteristic	Team	Working Group
Purpose	Teams exist to achieve a shared team goal	Groups support organizational goals
Accountability	Individual and team work	Individual work assignments
Leadership	Shared leadership roles	Strong, clearly focused leader
Membership tenure	Teams are bounded and stable over time	Group membership is more variable over time
Voice of members over work procedures	Team members are highly engaged in discussing team procedures and tactics	Variable input from group members is solicited by the group leader

Sources: Based on L. Thompson, *Making the Team*, 3rd ed., Pearson, Upper Saddle River, NJ, 2008; J. R. Katzenbach and D. K. Smith, "The Discipline of Teams," *Harvard Business Review*, July–August, 2005, pp. 162–171; D. Coutu, "Why Teams Don't Work," *Harvard Business Review*, May, 2009, pp. 99–105.

each accountant works individually with clients, and the firm holds the accountant responsible only for that work. The accountants are part of a group, not a team.

Table 13.1 lists the differences between a team and a work group. Team members hold themselves mutually accountable for team goals, and leadership responsibilities are shared among the members of the team. They openly discuss goals and procedures with each other until they reach a consensus. A work group is more likely to have a strong, directive leader who seeks input from group members and then delegates work to various individuals to complete.

Effectively managing teams makes it possible for companies to achieve important strategic business objectives, which may result in competitive advantages. The benefits of using teams include lower costs and higher productivity, quality improvements, speed, and innovation.[2] Each is described next in further detail.

Costs and Productivity

When a company delegates management work to teams, team members do many of the things that were formerly carried out by the supervisor, and the organization needs fewer supervisors. Companies can save on the labor cost of surplus supervisors and middle managers. In addition, cross-training team members to have a broad set of competencies allows a significant reduction of the total number of employees required.

Before organizing its auto assembly plants into teams, Ford Motor Company hired more skilled production workers than needed in order to have substitutes available. Using teams meant that cross-trained workers were available to cover for absent employees, making the plants more productive. This allowed Ford to abandon the practice of stockpiling employees.

Quality Improvements

The responsibility for quality now rests with team members who assemble the product or provide the service rather than on an inspector who judges quality after the product is completed. This self-inspection, or "do it right the first time," approach to quality has several advantages. It saves the company money on defective products and wasted raw materials. It can also greatly reduce the labor cost of hiring quality specialists who inspect the work of others.

Quality management experts such as W. Edwards Deming recommend using teams that include employees who deal directly with customers. The goal is to achieve continuous quality improvements.[3] "Small wins" in quality delight customers. These new work methods and practices can be rapidly disseminated throughout the company by quality teams that inform other organizational members about them. Levi Strauss, the manufacturer of casual clothing, used teams to reduce defects in its clothing by 25 percent. The Saturn division of General Motors used self-managed teams to achieve one of the highest levels of customer satisfaction of any U.S. auto manufacturer.[4]

Speed

The responsiveness of a company to the needs of the customer is a vital area of concern. Improved speed reduces the time it takes to fill a customer order. It can shorten the time required to develop a new product. Speed can also improve the responsiveness of a company, such as how quickly an electric company restores service when a power transmission line is downed in a severe storm.

Teams can reduce the time needed to respond to customers. When teams are organized around important business processes, the time to complete the processes can be greatly reduced. A **business process** is a value-adding, value-creating activity such as product development or order fulfillment. Teams reduce barriers between departments that slow the flow of work. An example of such a barrier is the handoff from a bank loan officer to a credit analyst who then lets the paperwork sit for many days before examining the creditworthiness of the customer.

Many companies have taken advantage of improved speed. Kodak cut product development process time in half by using concurrent engineering teams composed of employees with cross-functional skills. Motorola used multiskilled production teams to manufacture a custom paging device within two hours of placement of an order. Southwest Airlines turns around an aircraft from landing to takeoff in 20 minutes by using customer service teams to unload, service, and load the aircraft. This is one-third the time it takes competitors to load and unload planes.

Innovation

The ability to create new products and services can be enhanced with the use of teams. Teams allow companies to innovate more quickly. In high-technology industries, being first to market with a unique or improved product provides a powerful competitive advantage. A cross-functional team composed of people who have knowledge of the market, technologists, and experts in production reduces the cycle time for product development. It is no coincidence that companies known for innovation such as Microsoft and Hewlett-Packard intensively utilize teams in their product development processes. Moreover, recent research reveals that teams composed of members with diverse work experience backgrounds are more innovative and more likely to share information than teams composed of people with similar kinds of work experience.[5]

When engineers at Boeing designed its innovative 777 aircraft, the company's management group relied exclusively on more than 200 teams to design and build major components of the plant. The teams included representatives from nearly every function, including customers and suppliers. They made it possible for the company to build the aircraft right the first time and not incur the cost of altering the configuration after the fact.

Management Close-Up 13.1 explains how AES Corporation employs teams to achieve and sustain a position as a leading power company.

■ Types of Teams

Just as a mechanic looks for the right tool to do a job, management must identify the right type of team to complete a task or project. The four types of teams normally found in organizations are self-managed teams, project teams, parallel teams, and virtual teams. Each differs in terms of duration (a few months or less compared to several years or more) and the amount of time

---

business process
A value-adding, value-creating activity such as product development or order fulfillment.

LOC-In 1 Learning Objective Check-In

1. Guard Smart Inc. has a matrix structure with a highly developed workforce. The employees receive training to ensure they are current in their respective specialties. To maximize their effectiveness, the employees are all committed to common purposes, depending on which people they are working with at a particular time. The performance goals and approach for achieving them are common among workers, and, perhaps most important, they hold themselves mutually accountable for reaching these goals. Guard Smart employees operate in _____.
   a. SDWTs
   b. teams
   c. work groups
   d. focus groups

MANAGEMENT CLOSE-UP 13.1

Teams Give AES Corporation a Competitive Advantage

The AES Corporation is a successful global developer and operator of electric power and steam plants. Company sales are more than $14.6 billion per year and AES has over $39.5 billion in corporate assets across 26 countries. The company has never formed corporate departments or assigned officers to oversee project finance, operations, purchasing, human resources, or public relations. Instead, these functions are handled at the plant level, where plant managers assign them to volunteer teams.

The front-line employees on teams at AES develop expertise in domains such as finance. They also receive the responsibility and authority to carry out required tasks. While mistakes are sometimes made while learning, the overall results are impressive. The AES team structure saves on management costs because the company has only five managerial levels. This allows AES to optimize the time of specialized staff members such as financial experts. For example, when the company developed a $400 million plant in Cumberland, Maryland, a team of just 10 people obtained more than 36 separate permit approvals and negotiated the complex financing, including tax-exempt bonds and contracts with 10 different lenders. Normally, projects of this scope require hundreds of employees, each with narrow and specific tasks to perform. The savings, increased speed, and flexibility of the AES team-based approach are clear and constitute a key source of the company's competitive advantage.

AES volunteer teams perform tasks that might normally be handled by traditional departments.

Sources: "AES Corporation: The Global Power Company," www.aes.com (2010): J. Pieffer, *The Human Equation: Building Profits by Putting People First.* Boston: Harvard Business School Press, 1998, p. 77; "Fortune 500: Largest U.S. Corporations," *Fortune*, May 3, 2010, pp. F1–F26.

members are expected to commit to the activities of the team (full-time or part-time). Figure 13.1 shows where each of these teams fits in terms of duration and time commitment.

Self-Managed Teams

A **self-managed team (SMT)**, which is sometimes called a *process team*, is responsible for producing an entire product, component, or service. These teams are formalized as part of the organization's structure. Employees are assigned to them on a full-time basis and they have a longer duration. SMTs utilize employees whose jobs are similar but who may have different levels of skill. Team members combine skills to produce an important organizational outcome, such as an

self-managed team (SMT)
Sometimes called a *process team,* a group that is responsible for producing an entire product, component, or service.

FIGURE 13.1

Team Characteristics

Source: Based on material from *Compensation for Teams: How to Design and Implement Team-Based Reward Programs* by Steven E. Gross. Copyright © 1995 The Hay Group, Inc. Adapted with the permission of the publisher, AMACOM Books, a division of American Management Association International, New York, NY. All rights reserved. http://www.amacombooks.org.

MANAGEMENT IS EVERYONE'S BUSINESS 13.1

WORKING AS A TEAM It takes time for a team to earn the right to manage itself. It is not realistic to expect a team to start out with the ability to manage itself. Here are some indicators that show that a team is moving in the direction of becoming a self-managed team.

- A team is being given more and more responsibilities by management as it proves itself capable of handling every responsibility that it receives.
- Team members have developed processes for working out their differences so that most of the team's time can be devoted to performing its work.
- The style of the team leader is changing from that of being a directive leader who monitors and controls the work of team members to that of a coach who provides feedback and encourages team members to be proactive and make their own decisions.
- The team has many capable members who each have the potential to lead the team if called upon to do so.

automobile engine (production process) or the installation of a computer system for a customer (customer service process).

Self-managed teams have authority to make many decisions traditionally reserved for supervisors or managers. For example, team members at General Motors's Saturn facility in Spring Hill, Tennessee, schedule work, hire new team members, select appropriate work methods, manage budgets, schedule delivery of raw materials, and maintain quality standards for the work output. There are no supervisors. Each team literally manages itself. Other SMTs utilize a supervisor or manager to direct the work, but this supervisor is a coach rather than a traditional boss who tells subordinates what to do. The SMT or process team concept requires empowerment in order to engage each worker's best mental and physical efforts.

SMT members need to be trained in a variety of skills to become fully functional. These include:

1. *Technical skills.* Team members must be cross-trained to rotate between different tasks or workstations. Cross-training team members offers the SMT greater flexibility to provide speed, efficiency, and quality.

2. *Management skills.* Members of the SMT have the authority to make management decisions. Therefore, they need training in such skills as budgeting, scheduling, time management, planning, goal setting, and judging the performance of peers.

3. *Interpersonal skills.* Team members need effective interpersonal skills to form the team and sustain its performance. They must be able to communicate ideas persuasively, negotiate when there are differences of opinion, and manage conflict when emotions are aroused over important differences in goals. Two important interpersonal skills necessary for all types of teams, conflict management and negotiation, are examined later in this chapter.

Management Is Everyone's Business 13.1 shows how to know when a team is making progress in becoming a self-managed team.

project team
A group that works on a specific project that has a beginning and an end.

Saturn retains a high level of customer satisfaction by using self-managed teams.

Project Teams

A **project team** works on a specific project that has a beginning and an end. Team members work full-time until the project is complete and then disband to work on other projects, possibly with different team members. A project team is composed of members from different functions (such as marketing, production, and finance) or different technical disciplines (such as biology, chemistry, and mathematics). Members collaborate to complete the project. A key criterion for judging project team performance is meeting or exceeding deadlines or important milestones leading to completion.

Project teams have many uses. The Mobil energy company used project teams to reengineer key business processes in order to bring employees closer to the customer. At Massachusetts General Hospital in Boston, the trauma center uses a project team composed of doctors, nurses, interns, and technicians to treat accident victims. The speed at which the trauma center team can respond to the patient's medical condition can make the difference in saving a life.

Parallel Teams

Parallel teams are sometimes called *problem-solving teams* or *special-purpose teams.* These teams focus on a problem or issue that requires only part-time commitment from team members. The employee spends a few hours per week with the parallel team. The remainder of the time is spent working as an individual contributor in a functional department such as accounting. The parallel team does not alter the structure of the organization. Instead, a team is formed to solve a specific problem. When the problem is solved the team is likely to be disbanded. The team may be of short or long duration.

Parallel teams can make important contributions to organizations. *Suggestion teams* offer work method improvements or find new ways to please and delight customers. *Safety teams* reduce accidents and such common work maladies as back injuries or repetitive motion strain. *Selection committees* recruit and select job applicants for professional organizations such as law, accounting, or consulting firms. *Grievance committees* settle employee relations problems.

American Airlines involves nearly the entire workforce in parallel teams. Its 3,500 seven-person suggestion teams have proposed better ways to satisfy customers and save money for the company. In one three-month period, these suggestion teams developed 1,600 suggestions that were adopted, resulting in more than $20 million in cost-saving or revenue-generating improvements.

parallel teams
Sometimes called *problem-solving teams* or *special purpose teams,* groups that focus on a problem or issue that requires only part-time commitment from team members.

Virtual Teams

In order to take advantage of interactive computer technologies such as the Internet, groupware (software that permits people at different computer workstations to collaborate on a project simultaneously), and computer-based videoconferencing to enable distant people to work together, **virtual teams** may be formed. These teams are similar to problem-solving teams in that they require only a part-time commitment from team members. Virtual team members interact electronically, rather than engaging in face-to-face interaction typical of problem-solving teams.

Virtual teams permit organizations to link individuals who would otherwise be unable to work together. The most talented technical staff can work on problems that require their special skills. This can be a strategic advantage. Accenture, a global firm that provides information technology (IT) consulting services, can deploy a top IT consultant in the Chicago office and Accenture colleagues from the London and Amsterdam offices to work for a client in Belgium. Using the virtual team saves valuable time and the costs of travel, lodging, and downtime.

virtual teams
Groups that use interactive computer technologies such as the Internet, groupware (software that permits people at different computer workstations to collaborate on a project simultaneously), and computer-based videoconferencing to work together regardless of distance.

LOC-In 2 Learning Objective Check-In

Mr. Fisher has been considering some changes to make the team setup at his company more effective. Right now, teams are used only when there is a specific project that has a beginning and an end. Mr. Fisher sees the need for a different type of team that could operate on an ongoing basis with part-time commitment from certain employees. For example, one team would be tasked with focusing on safety issues, which have had an increasing impact on the firm since its recent expansion. It is important that these employees be on-location so they can assess risks and observe safety issues at the site in person.

1. Mr. Fisher's company currently uses a(n) _____ structure.
   a. parallel team
   b. project team
   c. virtual team
   d. SMT

2. A(n) _____ would be appropriate for addressing the safety issues that the company has been facing recently.
   a. project team
   b. virtual team
   c. parallel team
   d. SMT

Virtual teams also make it possible for companies to cross organizational boundaries by linking customers, suppliers, and business partners to improve the quality and increase the speed with which a new product or service is brought to the market. For example, textbook authors who are university professors form a virtual team with the publishing company's editors and self-employed specialists who design the book and create the graphics.

Because members of virtual teams interact with each other via computers and other forms of electronic communications technology there can be a greater potential for misunderstandings to occur than with other types of teams that have the benefit of face-to-face communication. Therefore several management practices for virtual teams are suggested:[6]

- There should be clear team goals and team roles provided that are not in conflict with commitments to other organization units.
- There needs to be a careful implementation of efficient communication and collaboration processes that prevent misunderstandings and conflict between team members.
- It is important to have orientation workshops and other forms of training offered to those who are expected to work in virtual teams as a way to prepare them for the challenges of this type of work.

■ Managing Team Performance

Team performance requires vigilant management. Teams do not always perform effectively, possibly because of a lack of team spirit, a disruptive team member, or a lack of commitment to team goals. Factors that need to be taken into account in managing effective team performance are the stages of team development, the roles of team members and leaders, and team member behaviors.

Stages of Team Development

Before a team can get started, planning and organizing must take place so that all members understand their roles and how they contribute to achieving team objectives. There are five stages of development: forming, storming, norming, performing, and adjourning.[7] These stages occur in sequence, although they may occur rapidly when a team is under strong time pressure.[8]

FORMING   When team members meet for the first time to get acquainted and discuss expectations the group is in the **forming stage**. Basic ground rules are established: What is the purpose of the team? How often will it meet? Should everybody expect to participate?

It is important for team members to begin to develop social bonds during the forming stage. Team leaders may organize a social activity to help members interact and build relationships.

STORMING   Team members voice differences about team goals and procedures during the **storming stage**. Differences may involve goal priorities, the allocation of team resources, fair work procedures, role expectations, or the selection of a team leader. These are important issues. All team members must be comfortable with the decisions before the team can perform its task.

Conflict is a normal part of team development. It should be out in the open and not suppressed. Coalitions often form during the storming stage. These subgroups may compete for dominance in setting the team agenda. Such conflict must be managed so that the team can move forward. If it is not properly managed, conflict can halt team development, leading to failure. Team leaders play an important role by defusing the negative aspects of conflict and tapping creative energies so that harmony and cohesion are achieved.

NORMING   Conflict resolution and agreement over team goals and values emerge in the **norming stage**. Team members finally understand their roles and establish closer relationships, intensifying the cohesion and interdependence of members. At

forming stage
The first stage of team development, which brings the team members together so they can get acquainted and discuss their expectations.

storming stage
A stage in team development in which team members voice differences about team goals and procedures.

norming stage
A stage in team development that is characterized by resolution of conflict and agreement over team goals and values.

Seagate Technology, which makes computer storage hardware, flies about 200 employees to New Zealand each year for an annual week of intense team-building exercises that climax with a day-long race in which team members kayak, hike, ride bikes, swim, and rappel down a cliff. CEO Bill Watkins says the exercises break down barriers and make better team players.

this point, the members begin to develop a team identity rather than seeing themselves as individuals. The team is in agreement about how to deal with and sanction members who violate important team rules and procedures.

PERFORMING   The **performing stage** is characterized by a focus on the performance of the tasks delegated to the team. Team members collaborate to capture synergies between individuals with complementary skills. When situations change and new tasks and priorities emerge, the team adjusts its tactics. When the team receives critical feedback, it has the flexibility to learn from mistakes and make improvements.

performing stage
A stage of team development that is characterized by a focus on the performance of the tasks delegated to the team.

The performance stage of team development can be viewed as the payoff of the investment of time and effort by team members. Forcing a team to perform before it has its house in order (by skipping some stages or spending too little time on the earlier stages) is likely to result in a malfunctioning group that is unable to achieve performance expectations.

ADJOURNING   Teams that are designed to disband reach the **adjourning stage** in which the team has completed its work. Team members feel satisfaction about the completion of the team's goals, but they are also anxious about possible new assignments and about separating from friends they made while on the team.

adjourning stage
A stage of team development in which teams complete their work and disband, if designed to do so.

It is a good idea to have a ceremony to celebrate the end of the project or mission when the adjourning stage is reached, especially if the team's work was successful. Team members benefit from feedback on lessons learned that they can apply to future assignments. Teams and outstanding contributors can be recognized in various ways:

1. When a team completed an important project, the owner of Five Star Speakers, a training company in Kansas, closed the office for a half day and took the entire staff to a movie and to a restaurant for coffee afterward.
2. After a team successfully achieved an important deadline at The Gap, headquartered in San Bruno, California, the manager gave a gift certificate for a facial or massage at a spa to each team member.
3. Team members at Naval Publications and Forms Center in Philadelphia preserve the memory of a completed team project with a specially designed pin.[9]

LOC-In   3   Learning Objective Check-In

Bryan, Jackie, and Jenna are members of a virtual team. In April, the team members established ground rules for the team and developed a specific purpose they all agreed on. They went to dinner and got to know one another's professional backgrounds more completely. At the third meeting, in July, Bryan voiced some concerns about the priorities that had been established at the April meeting. Based on what they learned in May, he reasoned, they really should reconsider their priorities, at least for the short term.

1. Which of the following stages represents the April period in which the members had their first meeting, where they established ground rules?
   a. Adjourning
   b. Norming
   c. Performing
   d. Forming

2. In which stage did Bryan voice his concerns to the team?
   a. Forming
   b. Norming
   c. Storming
   d. Performing

Roles of Team Members

Roles are expectations regarding how team members should act in given situations. Effective team performance requires the enactment of two roles, the task-facilitating role and the relationship-building role. It is difficult to enact both of these roles equally. Most team members emphasize one or the other.

roles
Expectations regarding how team members should act in given situations.

task-facilitating role
The team-member role with the priority of helping the team accomplish its task goals.

relationship-building role
The team-member role that focuses on sustaining harmony between team members.

The **task-facilitating role** places a priority on helping the team accomplish its task goals such as improving quality, satisfying customers, or developing new ideas. Some of the ways team members enact the task-facilitating role include:

1. *Direction giving:* Identifying ways to achieve goals and providing goal clarification.
2. *Information seeking:* Asking questions, identifying knowledge gaps, and requesting other members' opinions.
3. *Information giving:* Providing facts and data, offering judgments.
4. *Coordinating:* Pulling ideas together and helping others understand team members' suggestions and opinions.
5. *Summarizing:* Combining ideas made by team members and drawing conclusions.

The **relationship-building role** focuses on sustaining harmony between team members. This role facilitates improved interpersonal relationships and sustains team morale. The relationship-building role involves:

1. *Supporting:* Praising team members' ideas and recognizing their contributions.
2. *Harmonizing:* Mediating the differences between team members and identifying compromises.
3. *Tension relieving:* Using humor to put others at ease.
4. *Energizing:* Exuding enthusiasm and good spirits to motivate others.
5. *Facilitating:* Acting as a catalyst to smooth interactions between individuals who have difficulty communicating with each other.

Both the task-facilitating and relationship-building roles must be enacted. Some team players must focus on team objectives while others concentrate on maintaining team morale. If they do not, the team is likely to perform inadequately. If all members select the task-facilitating role, for example, the team will not develop past the norming stage because it will not get past the interpersonal conflicts that arise at this point of development.

The Role of the Team Leader

Most teams have leaders who help the teams progress through the stages of development and reach their objectives. Leaders help teams balance task-facilitating and relationship-building roles. They also deal with individuals who cause problems, such as people who dominate discussions, take unrealistic positions, or are so critical they stifle creativity. Their style of leadership is typically similar to that of a coach who: (1) provides feedback to team members ("I like how you answered that customer question"); (2) expresses a shared vision for the team ("Let's see if we can make zero defects for the entire week"); and (3) supports team members ("Tell me what resources you need to achieve our goal, and I will find mem for you"). Manager's Notebook 13.1 lists ways to be a successful team leader.

LOC-In 4 **Learning Objective Check-In**

Averly is a team member who happens to work in the records department. He is responsible for providing facts and data that pertain to issues of importance to the company's employees and, sometimes, offering an interpretation of the data. Jenny is another team member, who understands the varied personalities within the team. She is always smoothing the interactions between several of the individuals who have difficulty communicating with each other.
1. Averly is demonstrating the _____ of team members.
   a. team leader role
   b. relationship-building role
   c. task-facilitating role
   d. energizing role
2. Jenny is demonstrating the _____ of team members.
   a. relationship-building role
   b. task-facilitating role
   c. team leader role
   d. supporting role

MANAGER'S NOTEBOOK 13.1

Effective Ways to Enact the Role of Team Leader

How can a team leader positively influence team processes and outcomes?

- *Take care of team members.* Set an example of how you want team members to treat one another and customers. If the leader is self-focused, the resulting negative example for other team members will make the team less effective. Be a strong advocate for team members with management when it is justified, even when it may mean taking the heat for their mistakes or the mistakes of the team as a whole. Your loyalty to the team members will be paid back when they need to make personal sacrifices to reach team goals in high-pressure situations.

- *Communicate with team members.* Effective team leaders are good communicators. Include the entire team in the communication loop by letting team members know what other managers want them to know. Listen to the concerns of team members as well, and communicate their ideas or comments to higher level managers who can respond to these concerns by making changes. Facilitate good feedback and participation from all team members so that effective team decisions can be made.

- *Share power with the team.* Effective team leaders embrace the concept of teamwork in deeds as well as words. Share the power, information, and responsibility with the team members. Have faith in their decisions, even when they might not be the ones you would have made.

- *Learn to relax and admit your ignorance.* Team leaders aren't expected to know everything, and they cannot always be in control. Overcome the fear of looking vulnerable by not knowing the answer to a question—leaders who admit and learn from mistakes earn the respect of team members faster than those who act as if they were always in control. Being open and vulnerable also serves to build trust and improve team relationships. Team members will respond by opening up to each other, which will strengthen team members' bonds with each other.

Source: From *The Leadership Experience*, 3rd ed., by R. L. Daft. Copyright © 2005. Reprinted with permission of South-Western, a division of Thomson Learning: www.thomsonrights.com. Fax 800 730–2215.

Some teams are led by supervisors or managers, who are expected to adjust their leadership style to work effectively with a team composed of subordinates. Parallel teams and project teams are likely to have a manager or supervisor in the role of the team leader. Other teams, especially self-managed teams, may have leaders selected from the ranks. This "lead employee" may be chosen by peers or by management. Some teams are "leaderless," generally those composed of highly motivated and experienced employees. In a sense, all team members are leaders on a leaderless team.[10] Each of the four musicians who make up the Tokyo String Quartet, one of the world's finest chamber music ensembles, is a skilled virtuoso soloist, and the quartet operates more or less as a leaderless team. The automobile manufacturing plants at both Saturn and Chrysler use self-managed teams in their manufacturing process. In particular, the self-managed teams at Saturn do not have a direct supervisor, while at Chrysler a supervisor acts as a "facilitator" or coach.

Management Is Everyone's Business 13.2 explains why it is important for managers to consider the size of the team when forming teams to do specific tasks.

Behavioral Dimensions of Effective Teams

Members of effective teams share several behavioral characteristics. They are cohesive with each other, select high performance norms, cooperate, exhibit interdependence, and trust one another.

COHESIVENESS   The extent to which members feel a high degree of camaraderie, team spirit, and sense of unity is the degree of **team cohesiveness**. Individuals who are part of a cohesive team are concerned about the welfare of teammates as well as the team as a whole. When teams lack cohesion, individuals are less likely to enjoy meetings or social events and to work toward team goals. Members of teams that display cohesiveness are more likely to communicate with and influence each other. This is particularly beneficial when members have a strong attachment to high team performance.

There are ways to positively influence team cohesiveness:

1. Provide ample opportunities for team members to interact with each other during the early stages of team development. Social activities such as ice breaker exercises help stimulate interaction.

team cohesiveness
The extent to which team members feel a high degree of camaraderie, team spirit, and sense of unity.

MANAGEMENT IS EVERYONE'S BUSINESS   13.2

WORKING AS A MANAGER   When you are a manager and are asked to form one or more teams with employees in your unit, the size of the team is an important factor to consider. According to Professor Richard Daft, a leadership expert at Vanderbilt University, the optimal size of a team is about 7 employees, although a range of 5 to 12 is associated with high performance. Teams within this range of size are large enough to take advantage of diverse employee skills and are small enough to allow individuals to feel an intimate part of a community. It is also easier for individuals in larger teams greater than 12 to shirk their duties without being noticed. Here are some additional reasons why it is a good idea to restrict the size of teams to about 12 employees as an upper bound.

- Research indicates that small teams tend to be more cohesive than larger teams, which is a necessary ingredient for a team to achieve high performance.
- Large teams tend to have more disagreements and differences of opinion. Subgroups are more likely to form and they can be sources of conflict.
- Team leaders of large teams are likely to have greater demands placed on them because there is less team member participation.

Source: From *The Leadership Experience*, 3rd ed., by R. L Daft. Copyright © 2005 South-Western, a part of Cengage Learning, Inc. Reproduced with permission. www.cengage.com/permissions.

---

2. Ensure that all team members have a voice in determining team goals. When the goals are attractive to all members, individuals are more motivated to participate in activities that intensify team cohesion.
3. Celebrate successful team outcomes with rewards for team members or recognize outstanding individual contributions to the team with an awards ceremony. These celebrations build team spirit.[11]

A good example of a highly cohesive team is given in Management Close-Up 13.2, which examines the rigorous training experienced by the Navy SEALs, an elite military unit.

team norms
Shared beliefs that regulate the behavior of team members.

NORMS   The shared beliefs that regulate the behavior of team members are its **team norms**. They represent the values and aspirations of the members and are likely to be formed during the forming and norming stages of development. Teams enforce norms with rewards and sanctions.

MANAGEMENT CLOSE-UP 13.2   THEME: **DEALING WITH CHANGE**

Navy SEALs Are Highly Cohesive and Effective Teams

Some examples of high-performing teams occur outside the world of business in fields such as sports, medicine, and the military. The U.S. Navy SEALs are an elite team of individuals in the military who perform dangerous missions for the Navy. For example, one team of Navy SEALs went behind enemy lines to rescue Private Jessica Lynch who was captured during the war between the United States and Iraq in 2003. Other teams of Navy SEALs advanced on Taliban strongholds in Afghanistan during the 2001 war and called in devastating jet bomber firepower that blasted enemy troop concentrations.

While the first four weeks of Navy SEAL training is grueling, they pale in comparison with the fifth week known as hell week. During hell week, recruits swim many miles in cold water in the Pacific Ocean, they row rubber boats for hours on end, they run obstacle courses over and over, they perform grueling calisthenics using 300-pound logs, and they sustain personal insults from trainers. During the entire hell week, recruits sleep perhaps four hours.

About 30 percent of the recruits drop out during the five-day, hell-week experience. This commitment is needed because hell week is followed by months of rigorous underwater training, weapons training, explosives training, parachute training, and a six-month probationary period. The ultimate success rate for recruits is about 30 percent.

Highly cohesive teamwork is essential because SEALs never operate on their own and team members identify totally with the group. Navy SEALs will never leave the battlefield if a fallen SEAL remains. The SEALs show us that rigorous training and a strong sense of cohesion among team members can produce highly effective outcomes.

Sources: Based on J. Morse, B. Bennett, S. Donnelley, and M. Hequet, "Saving Private Jessica," *Time*, April 14, 2003, pp. 66–67; S. Foster, Managing Quality (Upper Saddle River, NJ: Prentice Hall, 2001) pp. 333–334; K. Labich and E. Davies, "Elite Teams Get the Job Done," *Fortune*, February 19, 1996, pp. 90–98.

It is important for teams to develop and enforce norms to govern the behavior of employees who avoid doing their fair share of the work. When a team is cohesive but has weak performance norms, members are likely to tolerate loafers rather than confront them, making failure more likely. A cohesive team with high performance norms has low tolerance for poor performance and is more likely to be effective. A shirker will feel that all team members are monitoring his or her behavior just as a supervisor would, making it uncomfortable to resist improving performance.

One way to ensure that team members have high performance norms is to select high-performing individuals as members of the team. Students in a management course that required team projects took this approach when they asked their professor to let them form their own teams so they could avoid conflicts with students who expected the rest of the team to do most of the work.

Team performance norms vary according to the mission of the team. At Microsoft, teams of software developers expect to work 80 or more hours a week to complete projects on time. A software developer insisting on a 40-hour weekly schedule would not last very long at Microsoft. Team performance norms influence quantity, quality, attendance at meetings, and open discussion of topics. Teams prohibit taking phone calls at meetings. And norms indicate that the team is more important than any individual, so it is better to be a team player than a star.[12]

COOPERATION The willingness to share information and help others reflects the level of **cooperation** in the team. Team members who help achieve goals exhibit useful cooperative behaviors. These behaviors are sometimes at odds with **competitive behaviors**, which view other people as rivals for a limited pool of resources and focus on individual goals, noncollaboration with other employees, and the withholding of information. It is up to the team to nurture cooperative behavior by enforcing norms that reward cooperation and sanction competitive behavior. Rewarding team outcomes can help raise the level of interdependence among team members.

INTERDEPENDENCE The extent to which team members depend on each other for resources, information, assistance, or mutual support to accomplish their tasks[13] is the degree of **interdependence** present. Tasks that involve teams of musicians giving an orchestral concert or actors giving a theatrical performance require a high degree of interaction and exchange—consequently these tasks are highly interdependent. On the other hand, tasks that involve a dock team unloading boxes of fresh fruit from a large trailer truck require lower levels of interaction, exchange, and interdependence. Three types of interdependence affect teams: pooled, sequential, and reciprocal.

Pooled interdependence is found in teams requiring the lowest amount of reliance on other members. Team members have significant aspects of their jobs where they are relatively independent from one another. With pooled interdependence, team members share some common resources such as fax and copy machines, clerical supplies, and secretarial support, but most of the work is performed independently. Real estate agents in the same branch office may share office space, supplies, copy and fax machines, and the same clerical person, but nonetheless do most of their selling activities independently. Teamwork still matters when pooled interdependence is present. Anyone who has experienced an urgent need to copy an important document for a customer and found the copy machine in a state of disrepair due to the harsh treatment it received from the last user will attest to the need for teamwork.

Sequential interdependence is a series of hand-offs of work flow between team members in which the output of one team member becomes the input of the next team member, and so forth. Each team member in the sequence of exchanges depends on all previous team members to do their portion of the work correctly or else the entire team performance falls short of expectations. For example, automobile insurance companies often organize claims adjustment processes as a sequence of steps acted on by different claims specialists. An insurance team handles an automobile accident claim starting first with the insurance agent who collects accident information from the customer. The agent hands the accident claim over to the accident investigator who inspects the damage to the car and writes a claims report. Finally the case is sent to an accident claims adjuster who coordinates the claims of other parties involved in the accident and determines the payout to the customer. A mistake assessing the damage to the car by the accident investigator diminishes the performance of the entire claims adjustment team, because either an over- or underpayment will be made.

cooperation
Team behavior that is manifested in members' willingness to share information and help others.

competitive behavior
Team behavior that views other people as rivals for a limited pool of resources and focuses on individual goals, noncollaboration, and the withholding of information.

interdependence
The extent that team members depend on each other for resources, information, assistance, or mutual support to accomplish their tasks.

pooled interdependence
Team behavior where team members share common resources such as fax and copy machines, supplies, and secretarial support, but most of the work is performed independently.

sequential interdependence
A series of hand-offs of work flow between team members in which output of one team member becomes the input of the next team member, and so forth.

reciprocal interdependence
The greatest amount of interdependence that occurs when team members interact intensively back and forth with each other until their work is judged to meet performance standards.

The greatest amount of interdependence, **reciprocal interdependence**, occurs when team members interact intensively back and forth with each other. The output of team member X becomes the input of team member Y, and the output of team member Y returns as the input to team member X. This series of reciprocal exchanges of work between team members continues until the work is judged to meet performance standards. Projects involving research and scientific work are often organized with teams that are characterized by reciprocal interdependence. Software development teams consist of: (1) software design experts that create the computer code, (2) software testing experts that test the software for bugs that reduce the reliability of the software, and (3) technical writers that create technical manuals that explain to customers how to use all the different applications that are built into the software. Software designers, testers, and writers are reciprocally interdependent, as can be demonstrated when software bugs are discovered by testers. The presence of a software bug is a flaw in the code which results in a need to make a modification to the code by the designers. The software code modification may in turn result in the need for revisions to be made to the computer user manual by the technical writers. Each time a software bug is located, this cycle of change is repeated until all the bugs are eliminated.

Research on team performance has revealed that high levels of task interdependence which require interactions between team members to obtain critical resources correspond to higher levels of performance. Team members that are highly dependent on one another develop solutions more quickly, finish more tasks, and perform better than those on teams whose members are not highly dependent upon one another.[14] Figure 13.2 illustrates the three types of interdependence between three employees, X, Y, and Z doing tasks that result in producing an output that is dependent on their collective efforts.

TRUST Team members are mutually accountable. If one member makes a serious error, it reflects on the performance and reputation of all team members. **Trust** is the willingness of one person to increase his or her vulnerability to the actions of another person whose behavior he or she cannot control.

trust
The willingness of one team member to increase his or her vulnerability to the actions of another person whose behavior he or she cannot control.

All teams require trust between members. Self-managed teams require the highest degree of trust. Supervision of a self-managed team is performed by team members who are mutually vulnerable. They evaluate, reward, and even discipline each other. When trust is present, there is a much greater likelihood that team members will cooperate to complete critical tasks.

FIGURE 13.2

Types of Interdependence

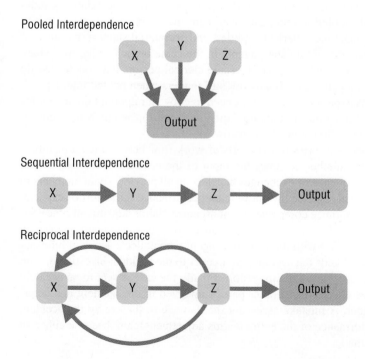

Pooled Interdependence

Sequential Interdependence

Reciprocal Interdependence

Trust can be created among team members by:

1. *Communicating openly.* At team meetings and in face-to-face conversations, strive to be open and honest. Share thoughts and feelings with team members when they relate to the business of the team.
2. *Sharing credit with others.* Do not take credit for more than your fair share of the team's success. Be generous with praise and recognition for the contributions of other teams.
3. *Reciprocating help from teammates.* Look for ways to help teammates, and reciprocate goodwill so teammates feel that their efforts are appreciated.
4. *Avoiding acting purely out of self-interest.* Find ways to align your needs with the interests of the team and other team members.

■ Team Performance Problems

Several problems within teams make it difficult to succeed. Trust and cooperation are absent or weak in malfunctioning teams and performance suffers. Managers and team members must try to determine the cause of poor team performance and implement changes to improve it. Manager's Notebook 13.2 identifies typical team performance problems a manager can expect to encounter. Three of the most challenging problems are free riders, the nonconforming high performer, and the lack of rewards for teamwork.

free riders
Individuals who find it rational to withhold effort and provide minimum input to the team in exchange for a full share of the rewards.

Free Riders

Individuals who find it rational to withhold effort and provide minimum input to the team in exchange for a full share of the rewards are known as **free riders**, which is also called *social*

MANAGER'S NOTEBOOK 13.2

Threats to Effective Team Performance

1. *Free riders.* Free riders do not participate in team efforts, but they expect to take credit for team success and receive a full share of team rewards. Free riders can quickly reduce team morale and productivity if their behavior is tolerated.

2. *Dysfunctional team conflict.* Teams can become dysfunctional if some members take a personal dislike to others or engage in political maneuvers and games. Factions within the team that compete for power by rewarding friends and punishing enemies are often the result. Infighting among these factions redirects team energies to political goals of the factions rather than the performance goals of the team and the organization.

3. *Groupthink.* Groupthink is a malady that happens when the team is intolerant of a healthy diversity of opinions—teams come to value agreement and consensus and avoid the functional conflict over real differences that can positively influence the team's performance. Groupthink undermines the purpose of most teams: the combination of people with different skills and experiences to create something more valuable than what the individual could have accomplished alone.

4. *Self-management opposition.* Team members may not want to be self-managed. Some teams are composed of individuals who prefer to have leaders direct and inspire them and who prefer less involvement in the actual decision making. Teams that desire a strong leader but who are forced to become self-managing typically will not be successful.

5. *Insecure supervisors.* Many team initiatives are derailed by supervisors and managers who feel threatened by any proposed change. Some supervisors may feel that self-managed teams reduce their status when the teams take on some of the supervisor's responsibilities. These supervisors may resist and undermine the success of self-managed teams. Unless supervisors have a reason to support teams, they may meet this approach with strong resistance.

6. *Disruptive high performers.* A high-performing team member may demand special treatment and treat other team members disrespectfully. Disruptive high performers often cost the team more in terms of cohesiveness and total outcome than their special talents warrant.

7. *Lack of teamwork rewards.* An organization that expects people to work productively in teams might nevertheless reward employees based on their individual contributions. This bias toward individual performance rather than team performance reinforces competition among team members to be seen as individual achievers rather than cooperative workers. It creates strong disincentives for teamwork to take place.

Source: Based on A. Sinclair, "The Tyranny of Team Ideology," *Organization Studies* 13 (1992): 611–626; L. R. Gomez-Mejia and D. B. Balkin, *Compensation, Organizational Strategy, and Firm Performance.* Cincinnati: South-Western, 1992; J. Eichenberg, "Investigating Sales Team Performance Problems—Diagnose the Root Problem to Tackle the Issues," *Corp Magazine*, 2010, www.corpmagazine.com.

loafing or *shirking*. It takes place because individuals can hide behind the collective effort of the team and get "lost in the crowd." When free riders are tolerated, other members may reduce their efforts ("Why should I work hard when free riders profit at my expense?") and team productivity suffers as a result.

Free riders take advantage of the difficulty managers face in separating out each team member's contribution to the overall outcome. Fortunately, there are a number of ways to deal with free riders before they undermine team morale. The best approach is to make it difficult for individuals to profit from free riding:

- Empower team members to have control over the recruitment and selection of new members. Front-line employees have more opportunities than managers to observe co-workers and know their work habits.
- Empower team members to have a voice in evaluating and disciplining peers who are not performing up to expectations. This makes it more difficult for free riders to loaf without consequences. For example, Unisys, a computer information systems company, requires that performance reviews be carried out by the team leader and three peers chosen by the employee. A poor evaluation may result in a diminished team bonus for the poorly performing member.
- Ensure that high performance norms are established early in the life of the team so that each member clearly understands performance expectations. Social controls, such as shunning those who violate performance norms, are more effective at eliminating free riding than monitoring by the supervisor. Managers can influence the development of norms by articulating a shared vision and mission that captures the imagination of the team and that spells out the expectation that each individual must provide a high level of effort.

The Nonconforming High Performer

Teams have procedures to deal with poor performers and individuals who violate a norm. These include disciplining the offending party through peer group pressure and giving the individual strongly worded critical feedback during a performance evaluation. A greater challenge is dealing with a high-performing team member who is individualistic and whose presence is disruptive to the team.

Sports teams and the entertainment industries have many examples of high-performing individuals with outsized egos who expect star treatment. Allen Iverson, an all-star guard on the Philadelphia 76ers professional basketball team and the league's most valuable player in 2000–2001, has been a difficult player to manage. Despite being an excellent player in games, Iverson had missed team practices as well as flights to games with team members. He also recorded songs that are disrespectful to women. Iverson's behavior had a negative impact on the team's morale, his coach, and the team's fans. In the 1990s, television actresses Roseanne, of the "Roseanne" show, and Brett Butler, the star of "Grace Under Fire," drove out a succession of writers and producers. The executive producers for these popular programs, Marcy Carsey and Tom Werner, were sometimes criticized for caving in to the stars' demands and for being inhospitable to writers. Carsey and Werner brushed aside the criticism. Such stars "have a lot on the line," says Carsey. "And any kind of nervousness, insecurity on their part is totally natural and very healthy."[15]

Must high performers conform and be treated like everybody else on the team or be asked to leave? The answer is, "it depends." Japanese corporations have a motto that "the head that sticks out gets pounded," which means that there is little tolerance for nonconforming behavior on Japanese teams. Those who ignore norms cause other members of the team to lose face, the personal dignity that is vitally important in Japanese culture. The United States has a more individualistic culture and is more tolerant of quirky behavior, even on teams.[16]

Sometimes it is better to channel the star's creative energies into the work of the team. A high performer who deserves special recognition should receive it. Some high performers simply want recognition for their contributions. Sports has most valuable player awards and film has the Oscars. There's no reason why a business cannot have a recognition event for high contributors to team success.

Some teams are less cohesive and more individualistic than others. These teams can better tolerate a nonconformist.[17] **Nonconforming high performers** can succeed on problem-solving

nonconforming high performer
A team member who is individualistic and whose presence is disruptive to the team.

MANAGEMENT IS EVERYONE'S BUSINESS   13.3

WORKING AS AN INDIVIDUAL   It is important to know how to cope with disruptive team members. Since team members are mutually dependent on each other for shared outcomes a direct confrontation with another team member can quickly escalate into a conflict and harm the performance of the team. Here are some suggestions for how to cope with team members who have annoying habits.

- Use supportive communication and collaborative approaches to deal with team behaviors that are problematic. For example, if a team member habitually arrives late and interrupts team meetings, it is a good idea to announce an odd starting time (9:43 A.M.) for the meeting to emphasize the need for promptness and establish a "latecomer kitty" for refreshments.
- A positive way to handle the "silent distractor" who reads a newspaper, rolls their eyes, or fidgets while other people are speaking is to ask the person questions and draw him or her into the conversation.
- A useful approach to deal with an individual who tries to dominate a team meeting by talking excessively would be to establish rules that allow each team member to express their input and limit the time for discussion for each item on the meeting agenda. These rules have some similarities with the nominal group technique described in Chapter 6. A team member can be assigned a role as a timekeeper to keep the agenda moving so that the meeting does not take more than the alloted amount of time.

teams, virtual teams, and project teams where the intensity of team interactions is low compared to self-managed teams. A nonconformist is less likely to upset other team members on a virtual team because they are interacting via computer terminal, while an egotistical team member may quickly get on the nerves of others on a self-managed team because there are many more opportunities for face-to-face interactions.

Management Is Everyone's Business 13.3 above offers some suggestions on how you can deal with disruptive team members in a positive way.

Lack of Rewards for Teamwork

A problem common to many organizations that utilize teams is that there are few if any rewards for teams that meet or exceed performance goals. These same organizations provide merit pay and other rewards for individual performance. When the only rewards are for individual performance, employees are likely to compete with each other for the incentive pay. This undermines the willingness to collaborate and team cohesiveness. For example, scientists at the National Institute of Standards and Technology (NIST), a U.S. government research laboratory, are expected to work on project teams with scientists from different disciplines. However, the main reward is merit pay, which rewards individual scientific contributions such as publishing research in leading scientific journals or making presentations at prestigious scientific conferences. Managers determine which scientists receive merit pay by comparing all the scientists and ranking them. These same managers have found it difficult to motivate the scientists to work on team projects that produce results for the good of the laboratory.

The lesson is that teamwork must be rewarded to strengthen and sustain team effort. Rewards can be monetary (such as a team bonus) or nonmonetary (such as a recognition). Other ways to reward teamwork include:

- Develop a "reward and recognition" committee that has a budget to recognize outstanding team performance with monetary or nonmonetary rewards that are meaningful to the team members. The committee should be composed of representatives from various teams and managers. It should design team reward policies and then administer rewards to deserving teams.
- Involving customers in the team reward process. For example, customers could nominate a team for a cash bonus or recognition reward. Xerox recognizes its customer service teams in this way.
- Using team rewards to complement pay policies that reward employees for their work as individuals. Team-based pay does not have to replace merit pay. Employees will be less likely to neglect their team responsibilities because they will be motivated to focus their best efforts on both individual and team goals in order to realize their total potential earnings.[18]

LOC-In 5   Learning Objective Check-In

1. Karyn is a team member who consistently performs above expectations on an individual basis. Her role as a team member is very important but Karyn is constantly seeking special recognition because she thinks she is doing more than her fair share. The other members tell her that the work she is doing is good but not always necessary and even disruptive. Karyn's team is highly cohesive and shuns expressions of individuality, putting team recognition ahead of personal status. Which of the following characterizes Karyn?
   a. The nonconforming high performer
   b. The free rider
   c. The loose cannon
   d. The insecure supervisor

■ Teams Management Skills

Teams must advance through stages where conflict and differences between members are normal. If members get stuck on important issues because of conflict, the team fails to achieve its potential, and performance suffers. Two management skills—conflict management and negotiation—are critical for team members and team leaders.

Conflict Management Skills

Conflict arises when members disagree over team policies, goals, or the motives and values of other team members. People are always going to have differences of opinion. Conflict is a normal part of the work of teams. But if conflict is not managed effectively, team members will focus on the dispute rather than on team performance. The first step in managing conflict is determining whether the conflict is functional or dysfunctional.

functional conflict
Conflict that stimulates team and organizational performance.

FUNCTIONAL CONFLICT   There are times when conflict stimulates team and organizational performance. We refer to this as **functional conflict**. As suggested in Figure 13.3, moderate levels of conflict can have a positive influence on the team and the organization, because:

■ *Creativity is stimulated.* Various positions can be contrasted when team members advocate differing approaches to achieving a goal. The debate can engage each member to express an opinion and even come up with a creative compromise that was not obvious until the conflict put the issues into perspective. Teams in creative fields such as advertising or consulting rely on the tensions embedded in conflict to develop innovative solutions for clients.[19]

FIGURE 13.3

Intensity of Conflict and Organizational Outcomes

Source: From L. David Brown, *Managing Conflict at Organizational Interfaces*, 1983. Printed and electronically reproduced by permission of Pearson Education, Inc., Upper Saddle River, NJ.

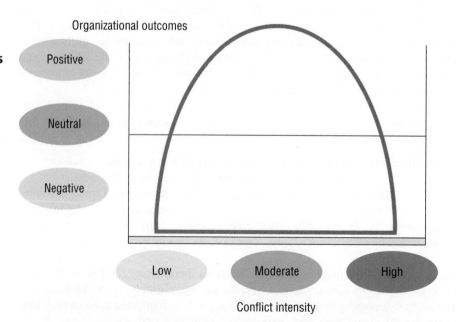

■ *Poor solutions are avoided.* People often become emotionally attached to their ideas. Disagreements over a goal or a decision alternative may lead to conflict. If the conflict is over an issue that affects team performance, the conflict is functional. When team members feel free to openly express their opinions and disagree with others, poor choices are avoided.

■ *Team members are energized.* Conflict excites and arouses individuals. Moderate conflict can energize people to exert more effort toward team goals. Debates are an excellent way to motivate students to learn about a topic in economics such as capitalism or markets. When students take sides in a highly charged debate, their motivation to learn about the topic increases.

When team members have a disagreement over ideas, plans, and projects, referred to as *task conflict,* the differences between individuals tend to be depersonalized. In many cases task conflict is functional to the team because it can stimulate creativity by forcing people to rethink problems and come up with solutions that everyone can be satisfied with.[20]

DYSFUNCTIONAL CONFLICT Some forms of conflict have negative effects on team and organizational performance. This **dysfunctional conflict** occurs when the intensity of the conflict is high, which is disruptive to team performance, or when the intensity is pervasive but too low, which results in lack of stimulation. When individuals on a team develop a personal dislike for each other based on personality clashes, anger, or interpersonal tension, there exists a *relationship conflict* within the team. Relationship conflict is dysfunctional and interferes with the team's productivity because team members are focused on reducing tension between the conflicting individuals and improving cohesion rather than working on the task at hand. Relationship conflict can appear to be a dispute over goals or resources when in reality the conflict is between people whose personalities are in conflict. Individuals in a relationship conflict may try to keep their personal dislike of each other hidden from other team members, which only allows it to simmer. It is important for the team to discover the nature of a relationship conflict so that it can find ways to manage it so that it does not disrupt team performance.

Manager's Notebook 13.2 (see item no. 3 there) introduced the idea of **groupthink**, which occurs when team members prefer to avoid conflict rather than tolerate a healthy diversity of opinions. This results in traditional and conservative decisions that are likely to be unsatisfactory and even dangerous. It is important to find ways to manage groupthink, which may be thought of as dysfunctional *avoidance* of conflict.

People tend to have different *conflict management styles,* based on placing different emphasis on concern for their own needs and concern for the needs of others. The various styles of conflict management include integrating, obliging, dominating, avoiding, and compromising. Each is appropriate in different situations. It helps to have a repertoire of conflict management styles to draw upon.

The **integrating style**, or *problem-solving style,* is used when the manager or team member can frame the issue as a problem and encourage the parties to identify the problem, examine alternatives, and agree on a satisfactory solution. The solution depends on the negotiating skills of the parties. This style enables each party to achieve its interests. The integrating style provides effective long-term solutions to conflicts, enabling the parties to come to a consensus and get on with the work. It is also time-consuming and does not work when immediate conflict resolution is needed.

An **obliging style**, or *smoothing style,* may be used when the party managing the conflict is willing to neglect his or her own needs in order to accommodate the needs of the other party. The individual decides to smooth over the conflict and focus on similarities with the other party. This style creates a win for the other party and a loss for the individual making the accommodation. It provides a short-term resolution to conflict, but the solution may give rise to resentment that may later cause a new conflict.

A **dominating style**, *ox forcing style,* may be used when the manager or team member acts in an assertive and forceful way and persuades the other party to abandon his or her objectives. The dominating style is a top-down approach to managing conflict. When time is critical and there is an emergency, this style may be the most effective way to proceed. When a verbally

dysfunctional conflict
Conflict that has a negative effect on team and organizational performance.

groupthink
Team behavior that occurs when members prefer to avoid conflict rather than tolerate a healthy diversity of opinions.

integrating style
Conflict resolution demonstrated by framing the issue as a problem and encouraging the interested parties to identify the problem, examine alternatives, and agree on a solution.

obliging style
Conflict resolution demonstrated when the party managing the conflict is willing to neglect his or her own needs in order to accommodate the needs of the other party.

dominating style
Conflict resolution used when the manager or team member acts assertively and forcefully and persuades the other party to abandon his or her objectives.

avoiding style
Conflict resolution used when the individual decides it is better to avoid the conflict rather than to deal with it.

compromising style
Conflict resolution used when the manager or team member makes some concessions to the other party and the other party is willing to reciprocate.

aggressive team member uses it to intimidate another team member during a discussion of values, the style is inappropriate and intensifies rather than mitigates conflict.

An **avoiding style** is used when the individual decides it is better to avoid the conflict rather than deal with it. It can be effective when the issues are trivial and avoiding can be used to buy time. The avoiding style will be ineffective when applied to more serious issues. If all team members have a tendency to use the avoiding style, the team is highly likely to suffer from groupthink and lag in performance.

A **compromising style** may be used when the manager or team member makes some concessions to the other party and the other party is willing to reciprocate. When this happens, a give-and-take resolution is reached. The compromising style requires the parties be able to "split the difference" over the issues in dispute. This style may be effective when resources can be shared. It may be inappropriate when values or principles are the source of the conflict. In some cases, compromise results in a solution that is of low quality and unacceptable to all team members.

APPLYING THE PROBLEM-SOLVING STYLE OF CONFLICT MANAGEMENT   The problem-solving style of conflict management offers the best opportunity for both parties in a dispute to achieve their interests. It can be used when the parties are willing to communicate openly and disclose their interests to each other. They must be able to explore different ways to reach mutually satisfying solutions. In many cases, the interests of a party may be different than that party's stated position. While a party's stated position may focus on competition over a limited resource or opportunity that each party wants, a party's interest may be reached by other means. For example, an employee's stated position in a conflict over her work schedule with a manager could be to avoid working overtime hours in order to be able to coach her daughter's soccer team, which plays games late in the afternoon. The employee's interest, which is to spend time with her daughter in the late afternoon, may be achieved with a more flexible work schedule, allowing her to do some of the work at home, which may also satisfy her manager's need for overtime work to be performed.

Applying the problem-solving approach to conflict management, a meeting should be convened at the right time and place when both parties are feeling motivated to resolve the conflict. After the problem-solving discussion between the parties gets under way, there may be times when one or both parties become angry or frustrated with each other. Time out may need to be taken at these points to allow the parties to cool down. Later, after the cooling-off period, discussions can resume until a workable resolution is achieved.

Becky, an advertising account executive, used the problem-solving style of conflict resolution with her team. Becky managed an account team at a busy advertising agency. The team worked hard and played hard. In return Becky was flexible about time off for team members. Recently, Becky felt that they were prioritizing their social lives above meeting work deadlines. Having stayed late to finalize urgent jobs for clients, she felt angry that tasks had been left for her to complete. Becky called a team meeting and calmly and assertively stated how she felt about the team's behavior. She explained that in taking on their work, her own work had not been completed on time, putting potential new business at risk. Becky asked the team for ideas to solve the problem. They all agreed that with privileges on time off came responsibilities for seeing jobs through. The result of this problem-solving discussion with the team was that Becky was able to complete her work and rely on her team to take their responsibilities seriously. Becky was able to resolve the conflict because she was able to state how her team's behavior had affected her. She explained what she wanted to happen instead and was willing to explore ideas to overcome the problem with her team.[21]

Unfortunately the willingness of both parties in a conflict to communicate openly is not always present, and this is needed for the problem-solving style to be effective. For example, at times parties in a conflict may not want to reveal their interests to each other because they have hidden agendas. The hidden agendas may be to "get even" with the other party because of real or imagined causes attributed to the other person. Problem solving in this case is pointless, because one or both of the parties are not willing to cooperate to solve the problem. In this hidden agenda situation, a different conflict management style such as the avoiding approach will be more appropriate.

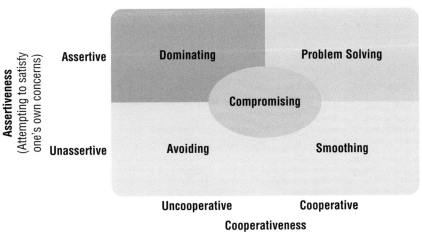

FIGURE 13.4

Five Conflict-Handiing Styles

Source: Based on K.W. Thomas, "Conflict and Negotiation Processes in Organizations," in M. D. Dunnette and L. M. Hough (eds.), *Handbook of Industrial and Organizational Psychology*, vol. 3, 2nd ed. (Palo Alto, CA: Consulting Psychologists Press, 1992), p. 668.

SELECTING A CONFLICT MANAGEMENT STYLE A useful approach to selecting a conflict management style is to examine the conflict situation according to the chart presented in Figure 13.4. The figure matches a person's combined level of assertiveness and cooperativeness to one of the five conflict management styles: problem solving, smoothing, dominating, avoiding, and compromising. Assertiveness means a person is willing to satisfy his or her own concerns. Cooperativeness occurs when a person attempts to satisfy the other party's concerns. Since conflict management is a dynamic process, a party that behaves in an uncooperative fashion is likely to be treated the same way by the other party. Therefore, styles that depend on cooperativeness such as the problem-solving and smoothing styles cannot be used. The mutual uncooperativeness enacted by the parties would result in the use of either the dominating or avoiding styles of conflict management. An assertive party will select the dominating style while a less assertive party will select the avoiding style.

When the parties strive to be cooperative with each other, they can select the problem-solving or smoothing styles, but not the dominating or avoiding styles. The problem-solving style provides the most promising opportunity to reach long-term solutions because both party's concerns are likely to be met. However, if a party in the conflict does not behave in an assertive way the smoothing style may be selected to reach a resolution. Smoothing solutions may provide a short-term conflict resolution for the unassertive party, but it will not be satisfying to this party in the long term since one's concerns were not satisfied. Finally if the parties in the conflict are only moderately assertive and cooperative as shown in Figure 13.4, a compromising style of conflict management is selected. In the compromising style the parties have moderate concern for their own interests and those of the other party. Compromises can be effective in some situations and not in others, since the compromise produces solutions that partially satisfy the concerns of each party but do not fully satisfy the concerns of either party.

Negotiation Skills

Negotiation skills are used in situations where people attempt to exchange goods and services and to find a fair price or solution. The problem-solving style of conflict management relies heavily on negotiating skills. Negotiation skills can also be used in negotiating a raise, settling on the price of a house, or agreeing on a fair procedure to allocate overtime hours.

One of the most useful negotiation skills is the **win–win style** of negotiation which is also referred to as *integrative bargaining,* as it employs the *integrative.* problem-solving style discussed in the previous section. The win–win negotiating style requires the parties to convert a potential conflict into a problem-solving process in which each party seeks to identify common, shared, or joint goals. In a sense, each party is looking for solutions that are good for everyone. This is particularly important when they are involved in a long-term working relationship. (See Skills For Managing 13.2.)

win–win style
Negotiating style requiring all interested parties to convert a potential conflict into a problem-solving process in which each party seeks to identify common, shared, or joint goals.

SKILLS FOR MANAGING 13.2

Negotiation for a Pay Raise

This exercise applies win–win negotiation skills in a business situation that is common to many managers and employees—negotiating a pay raise.

Many managers are faced with the situation where one of the employees under their supervision asks for an increase in pay. The negotiation can be sensitive. The manager and employee are likely to be in a long-term employment relationship, and if one party "wins" at the expense of the other in the context of negotiation, it could strain their working relationship. A win–win negotiation style seems to be most appropriate for this situation.

Instructions: Find one partner to work with in this exercise. One person takes the role of the employee seeking a pay raise, and the partner takes the role of the manager. Together, explore ways to turn a request for a pay raise into a win–win negotiation where the outcome is a settlement that is satisfactory to each party. Following are the constraints of the negotiation situation:

1. The manager must follow the salary guidelines provided by the policy and cannot make a special exception for this employee.

2. The employee has already received a pay raise this year but feels it is inadequate and is not due for another pay raise until next year.

3. The manager wants to preserve the motivation of this employee, who is a good performer in the unit.

Discuss how you and your partner would approach the salary negotiation and answer the following questions.

Discussion Questions

1. How should the employee frame the request for a pay raise to the manager to get a more favorable outcome? What kind of information should the employee focus on?
2. How should the manager frame the answer to the request to the employee to get a more favorable outcome? What kind of information should the manager focus on?
3. What are the areas of agreement between the two parties? What are the areas of disagreement between the two parties?
4. What are some possible solutions that would be acceptable to both parties?

To make use of the win–win negotiating style:

1. Prepare for negotiation by understanding your own needs and strengths and weaknesses. Determine your own bottom line.
2. Attempt to understand the other party's real needs and objectives. Engage in a dialogue in which both parties disclose their true preferences and priorities, rather than disguise and manipulate them.
3. Emphasize the commonalities and minimize the differences between the parties. Reframe goals as part of a larger collaborative goal. For example, the team goal of providing customer satisfaction is a common goal on which both parties agree, although they may differ on specific approaches to achieve it.
4. Search for solutions that meet both parties' goals and objectives. When parties are combative or competitive, they are more likely to focus on their own objectives and ignore those of the other party. A win–win negotiation is successful only when the needs of both parties are met.
5. Focus on building a relationship in a negotiation rather than making a onetime deal.[22]

win–lose style
Negotiating style used when there is a single issue that consists of a fixed amount of resources in which one party attempts to gain at the expense of the other.

One other style of negotiation that can be used in limited situations is the **win–lose style** of negotiation, sometimes referred to as *distributive bargaining*. The win-lose negotiating style is typically used when there is a single issue that consists of a fixed amount of resources in which one party attempts to gain at the expense of the other. Therefore, the win–lose negotiation is concerned with who will receive the most beneficial distribution of a fixed amount of goods.[23] A negotiation between a buyer and seller of a used car may take the form of a win–lose negotiation regarding the car's price. The seller is interested in obtaining the highest price and the buyer is interested in obtaining the lowest price for the car.

Win–lose negotiating styles have limited applications on teams because team members are mutually accountable and interdependent on each other to achieve their common goals. Moreover, parties involved in a win–lose negotiation are most likely to use the dominating style of conflict management. Successful win–lose negotiation outcomes depend on a party's ability to impose its will and convince its opponent that the costs of disagreement with its terms are high. The party that can impose the highest costs of disagreement to its position achieves the most concessions from the opposing party.

Behaviors typical of a win–lose style include deception, exaggerating one's strengths, threats, bluffs, and withholding information that would be helpful to the other party. A job applicant who is desperate for a job may enter into a win–lose negotiation with an employer who may use his ability to impose high costs (the threat of no job offer) on the job applicant and pressure her to take a job offer at a much lower salary than she wants. As this example shows, success in win–lose negotiation depends on the ability of each party to take advantage of and exploit the weaknesses of the other party. Win–lose negotiating styles should be used sparingly and only in exceptional circumstances. Most management processes require developing effective, collaborative, long-term relationships between employees, customers, and other parties. These relationships will be impaired when win–lose negotiating styles are used. The party that "loses" the negotiation is not likely to have positive feelings toward the "winner."

Finally, there are three common mistakes that inexperienced negotiators should be aware of and try to avoid making:

- *Do not assume that a negotiation must always result in a settlement.* When a person assumes that a negotiation must result in a settlement, the other party can take advantage by threatening to end the negotiations. This can result in unnecessary concessions being made to facilitate a settlement. It is a better practice to enter a negotiation with a resistance point in mind. The resistance point represents one's minimum acceptable position for a settlement. If the other party refuses to at least meet your resistance point in negotiations then it is better to walk away and end the negotiations.

- *Avoid becoming fixated on one particular issue in the negotiation.* Some issues are easier to settle than others in a negotiation. If the parties get stuck on an issue and find their positions frozen and lacking a settlement, it is best to move on. Settle other issues that are less difficult to agree on. In many cases the goodwill that is established between the parties when they can resolve the easier issues provides the momentum that enables the parties to collaborate and finalize the difficult issues that remain.

- *Do not assume that the other party has all the power due to greater levels of experience.* If you assume that you are powerless in a negotiation, there is a good chance you will act as if that assumption were true. You will be less apt to reach your goals. In truth, each party to a negotiation has some power—otherwise the negotiation would not take place. People negotiate because each party perceives that its counterpart controls something that it wants in an exchange. By being aware of both your interests and those of the other party, you can negotiate more confidently and increase your chances of reaching a satisfying settlement.

LOC-In 6   Learning Objective Check-In

1. Harry believes that James is receiving way more money than he should out of the team budget. Harry's reasoning is that his work is more essential to the long-term success of the team and that James's work can wait until next year to get funded. Harry and James disagree, but they agree that it is important for only one of them to proceed with the bulk of funding and that resolution must be achieved before the next disbursement of funds occurs. In this situation, it would be appropriate to use the _____ of negotiation to solve this problem.
   a. bureaucratic management style
   b. lose–lose style
   c. win–win style
   d. win–lose style

CONCLUDING THOUGHTS

After the introductory vignette at the beginning of this chapter we presented some critical thinking questions related to the use of rapid-response teams at Tenet Healthcare Corporation. Now that you have had the opportunity to learn about teams and managing teams, look back at these questions at the beginning of the chapter. The rapid-response teams provide several critical benefits to patients in a hospital. The teams provide medical intervention in time to prevent life-threatening catastrophes. The teams also boost the morale of nurses who work long hours in demanding working conditions. They reduce the level of stress experienced by nurses, who are able to provide better care to patients when their stress level is under control. Traditional approaches without the teams may have resulted in a higher mortality rate for patients and higher levels of stress and lower morale for nurses.

The type of team that most closely matches the rapid-response teams at Tenet Healthcare Corporation is the self-managed team. Tenet's rapid-response teams are given responsibility to make decisions regarding offering immediate help or seeking further medical assistance to support a patient whose vital signs are deteriorating. Characteristic of self-managed teams, there are no supervisors on the rapid-response teams and they manage themselves.

FOCUSING ON THE FUTURE: Using Management Theory in Daily Life

Managing Teams

Anne Roth is the Research Manager for the Marketing Department of a large financial-services institution. She heads a staff of four Market Research professionals. She describes her primary job as "providing customer information to my company."

Recently, Anne needed to use the win–win style of negotiation to convince her manager, the Director of Research, to authorize a study requested by Human Resources (HR). The Director had concerns because the study was being done for HR, and he did not see how the study would benefit the Marketing Department. The study was an expensive one, and he knew that it would take a large chunk of the resources he had budgeted for his department.

The requested study had two major components: a Hiring Managers Study and a New Hire Study. Both components look at the "onboarding" process in the organization—what happens in the first 90 days after a new employee is hired, and how satisfied both new employees and managers are with HR services during that time. Anne was able to work with her Director to create a study that met both the needs of the HR Department as well as the needs of the Marketing Department by using the five steps of win–win negotiations:

1. *Prepare for the negotiation by understanding your own needs and strengths and weaknesses.* Anne understood the delicacy of a situation that had multiple stakeholders and the fact that she would have to meet the needs of several parties simultaneously if the research was to be authorized. On the one hand, she knew that the research had the potential to uncover important information about how her company was incorporating new employees. She was excited about the idea of measuring and improving the flow of intellectual capital throughout the organization. She also knew that she had the resources to complete the project, once it was authorized. However, she was also conscious of her tendency to take on too much work and to not delegate work as fully as possible.

2. *Attempt to understand the other party's real needs and objectives.* Anne understood that her boss was worried about a number of things: the way the Market Research Department was perceived throughout the rest of the company, the resources available for all of the projects the Market Research Department was pursuing, and concerns about the professional status of the Market Research employees (for example, would they still be able to publish in American Marketing Association publications?). Not only did Anne have to understand her boss's perspective, but she also had to understand the needs and objectives of a number of other parties, including the Human Resource Department and the employees in her organization. The Human Resource Department wanted data from the surveys quickly, but employees were concerned about privacy, and wanted to be sure that their survey responses could not be individually identified. Anne had to take all of these needs into consideration if the project was to work.

3. *Emphasize the commonalities and differences between the parties.* Fortunately for Anne, there was one major goal shared by all of the people concerned—everyone wanted to contribute to the bottom line of the organization, and everyone agreed that getting and keeping good employees would increase their company's profitability.

4. *Search for solutions that meet both parties' goals and objectives.* In working with her boss, Anne pointed out that the research she was proposing would be seen and used throughout the organization, thereby increasing the visibility of the Market Research Department. More importantly, research costs could be justified because study results could be directly linked to increased retention, thereby demonstrating a return on investment for the monies spent on gathering the information. Finally, Anne was able to show that the research methodology used was of interest to the Market Research professional community and that internal customers were as valid a sample base as external customers. This helped to assuage her boss's professional concerns.

   To deal with the needs of the HR Department, Anne proposed a three-tiered reporting structure. For jobs that had a large enough sample size (for example tellers), research results would be reported once a month. For jobs with smaller sample sizes (for example, mid-level management), results would be reported once every six months, and for jobs with the smallest sample sizes (for example, senior executives) results would be reported once a year. While HR wanted results quickly, they also wanted those results to be accurate, and Anne convinced them that if employees thought they could be individually identified, they would not give accurate results. In a similar fashion, she was able to work with employee groups to assure them that the research would not identify them individually and to let them know that the research results would be distributed widely enough that the company would take action on the information employees shared.

5. *Focus on building a relationship in a negotiation rather than making a one-time deal.* Throughout the research process, Anne built relationships at all levels of the organization. Because the research is ongoing, she has been able to let HR know whether or not their onboarding processes are working, both from the perspective of managers and from the perspective of employees. As the research results are reported throughout the company, the Market Research Department is receiving very favorable reviews—they are now seen as the place to go for research that is cost effective, relevant, and practical. Anne's boss is impressed by the retention results in the departments where the research has been done. The company is clearly doing a better job keeping its most important asset—its employees. Finally, employees are pleased with the research outcomes because they see the company taking their opinions seriously and taking action on their concerns.

Summary of Learning Objectives

A **team** is a small number of people with complementary skills committed to a common purpose, set of performance goals, and approach for which they hold themselves mutually accountable. This chapter's discussion will help you in your future as a manager, as a member of a work team or as an employee to better understand teams and how to manage teams. The material in this chapter to meet each of the chapter's learning objectives that were presented at the outset of the chapter is summarized below.

1 Translate the benefits teams provide into competitive advantages.

- The benefits of using teams include lower costs and higher productivity, quality improvements, speed, and innovation. All of these benefits translate into competitive advantages in markets because they allow organizations to provide products and services at lower cost, higher quality, and with faster service—all sources of competitive advantage.

2 Identify the different types of teams—self-managed, project, parallel, and virtual.

Teams can be classified according to the expected duration of the team and the time commitment that team members can be expected to provide. Based on these two factors, the types of teams include:

- The **self-managed team** is responsible for producing an entire product, component, or service.
- The **project team** works on a project until completion and then disbands.
- The **parallel team** works on a particular problem that requires only part-time commitment.
- The **virtual team** works on a problem in which the members collaborate via computer.

3 Track the stages of team development that occur over the life of a project and help the team perform effectively.

There are five stages in the development of teams.

- The first stage is the **forming** stage, when people get acquainted and establish ground rules.
- Second is the **storming** stage, when team members discuss differences in goals, priorities, and values and strive to manage conflicts over these issues.
- Third is the **norming** stage, characterized by resolution of important differences in goals and values and establishment of norms governing the behavior of team members. The norms enable the team to sanction individuals who violate important team rules and procedures.
- Fourth is the **performing** stage when the team focuses on performing its important tasks.
- The last is the **adjourning** stage, the process of disbanding the team when the team's purpose is completed.

4 Recognize the key roles that team members must play to ensure high performance.

Effective team performance requires team members to play different roles to enable the team to realize its potential.

- The **task-facilitating** role puts a priority on helping the team accomplish its task goals.
- Some team members play the **relationship-building** role, which focuses on sustaining harmony between people on the team.
- The **team leader** helps the team strike a balance between the task-facilitating and relationship-building roles, and the leader must deal with deviant individuals who frustrate the team's ability to perform effectively.

5 Master the skills to detect and control team performance problems.

One of the challenges of managing teams is dealing with problems that can undermine the focus of the team. Three of the most challenging issues are:

- Dealing with **free riders,** who take credit for the team efforts while providing minimal work.
- Getting the best efforts from **nonconforming high performers,** who perform well as individuals but are difficult to work with in collaborative endeavors.
- Working around the lack of rewards for teamwork in contrast to individual performance so that the motivation of team members can be sustained.

6 Manage team conflict through negotiation.

An effective way to manage team conflict is by framing the issue as a problem and encouraging the parties to collaborate together to develop a solution that they can agree on jointly. This problem-solving approach to conflict resolution depends on the negotiating skills of the parties, which include the following:

- Understanding your strengths and weaknesses as well as those of the other party.
- Attempting to understand the other party's real needs and objectives so that the parties can enter into a dialogue and disclose their true preferences and priorities.

- Framing goals and objectives so that commonalities are emphasized and differences are minimized.
- Searching for solutions that meet the goals and objectives of each party.
- Focusing on building a relationship as a result of the negotiations rather than aiming to achieve a one-time deal.

Discussion Questions

1. Based on your personal experiences, what do you think are the advantages of teams? Which situations in a business are most likely to be most favorable for teams to perform effectively?

2. Again drawing on your own personal experiences, indicate what you think are the disadvantages of using teams. Which situations in a business are least suitable for team performance?

3. What is the role of the team leader? Should teams always have leaders? When might it be reasonable for a team to purposely leave out the role of team leader?

4. How do teams deal with individuals who violate important norms, for example, by engaging in negative conflict? Which do you think is a more effective way to sustain team performance: *(a)* the use of peer group pressure or *(b)* a supervisor who monitors and controls the behavior of team members?

5. Suppose you are working on a class project with five students, and one of the team members never shows up for your weekly meetings. Soon your project is due to be turned in to the professor. You and other team members are getting concerned about this "free rider." How should the team deal with this problem?

6. Suppose you are on a project team similar to the one in Question 5. One of the team members is very abrasive—using foul language and having a negative attitude—and is highly critical of the work of all the other team members, including you. This person also has an A (3.95) grade point average and wants to do the whole project alone and is willing to turn it in to the professor and share the credit with the whole team. The team is divided about how to respond to this offer because this team member could quite possibly achieve a better grade on the project than the team. How should the team deal with this individual?

7. Can too little conflict be a problem for a team? What are the effects on team performance of little or no conflict? In cases where there is an absence of functional conflict, how can conflict be stimulated? Which role(s) are most likely to stimulate the conflict?

Management Minicase 13.1
Companies Use Different Approaches to Encourage Teamwork

In the business world companies often develop their own unique practices to encourage their employees to treat each other as team members rather than as competitors for pay and promotions. They encourage this teamwork because it is profitable to do so. They find that when employees are collaborative the customer receives better service, resulting in more business for the company and bottom-line rewards for all. Companies develop different approaches to get their employees to collaborate with each other based on the nature of the business.

At Thrive Networks, an IT outsourcing company in Concord, Massachusetts, management decided to redesign its reward system for salespeople to reduce barriers for sales staff to collaborate. Previously each salesperson was paid almost entirely on a sales commission directly linked to individual sales performance. Individual sales commissions stimulate competitive instincts in members of the sales force so that they treat each other as competitors for customers. Interestingly, the three people in the sales force at Thrive Networks each had different strengths. Jim Lippie was a proven lead generator,

a master networker who brought in a dozen potential customers a week. John Barrows's talent was meeting with prospective clients and generating compelling proposals. Nate Wolfson's greatest skill was as a closer, the guy who could soothe last-minute concerns and make sure the papers were signed. Management reasoned that by eliminating the competition between the three members of the sales force and integrating their talents, the resulting collaborations would produce the opportunity for more deals and more rewards for all concerned.

To encourage teamwork between the sales staff the reward system was redesigned so that all sales commissions were pooled collectively and shared so that each salesperson received an equal share of the commissions once a monthly team goal was achieved. Under this team reward scheme each salesperson contributed what he did best to the overall team goal of selling IT services to customers. The results have been promising. Sales have gone up and the time to close a deal has been reduced by 30 percent.

A different approach to encouraging team behaviors among employees was adopted at Intel, the manufacturer of integrated circuit chips that power desktop and laptop computers. Intel employed many scientists and engineers that were expected to collaborate with each other on projects that would lead to the development of new products. Employees were under challenging time pressures to deliver products to market ahead of competitors. Conflicts between employees occurred with regularity causing disruptions to project schedules. Intel developed an approach suited to their needs that taught employees how to resolve conflicts by training them to use a variety of tools for handling discord. The implementation of these conflict resolution skills resulted in significant time savings on projects because little time was wasted in figuring out the best way to handle a disagreement or trading accusations of "not being a team player" since there was a clearly defined process set up that people could follow to handle the conflict.

DISCUSSION QUESTIONS

1. The redesign of the reward system for salespersons at Thrive Networks strengthened teamwork. What factors were operating in the sales environment that supported the use of team rewards?

2. Do you think servers at a restaurant would respond the same way that the sales force did at Thrive Networks and become more collaborative if management decided to pool everybody's tips from customers and give each server an individual share of the tips? What would be the ideal set of conditions at a restaurant for servers to give better customer service under a system of shared tips?

3. Why did Intel decide to teach its employees a common set of conflict resolution skills as a way to improve teamwork among its employees?

Sources: Based on J. Weiss and J. Hughes, "Want Collaboration? Accept—and Actively Manage—Conflict," *Harvard Business Review, March, 2005,* pp. 93–101; C. Cannella, "Kill the Commissions," *Inc.,* August 2004, p. 38; Thrive Networks Web site, 2010, www.thrivenetworks.com/about.us/careers.html.

Management Minicase 13.2
Whole Foods: Using Teamwork as a Recipe for Success

Whole Foods Inc. is the nation's number one chain of natural foods supermarkets. The company has more than 270 stores under the names of Whole Foods Market, Bread & Circus, Bread of Life, Fresh Fields, Merchant of Vino, and Wellspring Grocery. These stores are complete supermarkets with an emphasis on organically grown produce, fresh-baked bread, wholesome deli foods, and other health-food products. Conspicuously absent at Whole Foods stores are soft drinks in plastic containers, coupon dispensers for laundry detergent, salted potato chips, sugared cereals, and other high-sugar or high-fat products.

In the turbulent supermarket industry, Whole Foods has created a new approach to managing its employees—an approach based on teamwork and employee empowerment. Each Whole Foods store is an autonomous profit center composed of an average of 10 self-managed teams. A separate team operates each of the departments of the store, such as produce, canned goods, or the bakery. Each team has a team leader and specific team goals. The teams function as autonomous units. Members meet monthly to share information, exchange stories, solve problems, and talk about how to improve performance. The team leaders in each store form additional teams. Store leaders in each geographical region are a team and the leaders of each of the company's six regions are a team.

Why teams? Two primary benefits result from the company's emphasis on teamwork. First, teams promote cooperation among the store's employees. The teamwork approach facilitates a strong sense of community. This fosters pride and discipline in the work ethic of employees. An example of this is found in Whole Foods' hiring practices. The teams, rather than the store managers, have the power to approve new hires for full-time jobs. The store leaders provide the initial screening, but it takes a two-thirds vote of the team, after what is usually a 30-day trial period, for the candidate to become a full-time employee. This type of approval helps a team bond, which in turn facilitates a cooperative atmosphere. Another example of the ways in which teamwork promotes cooperation is

evident in Whole Foods' team meetings. Each team holds a team meeting at least once a month. There is no rank at the team meetings. Everyone is given an equal opportunity to contribute to the discussion.

The second benefit that Whole Foods realizes from its emphasis on teamwork is an increased competitive spirit among its employees. The individual teams, stores, and regions of the company compete against each other in terms of quality, service, and profitability. The results of these competitions determine employee bonuses, recognition, and promotions. To facilitate competition, the company is extraordinarily open in terms of team performance measures. At a Bread & Circus store in Wellesley, Massachusetts, a sheet posted next to the time clock lists the previous day's sales broken down by team. A separate sheet lists the sales numbers for the same day the previous year. This information is used by the teams to determine "what it will take" to be the top team for the store during a particular week. This type of competition also exists at the store level. Near the same time clock, a weekly fax is posted listing the sales of each store in the New England region broken down by team with comparisons to the same week the previous year. One note of caution has emerged from these experiences: Competition between teams can become too intense. The company had to "tone down" the intensity of the competition between teams and stores on a few occasions.

The overall results of Whole Foods' management practices have been encouraging. The company has grown from one store in 1980 to 270 stores in 2010. The profitability of the company has been strong. In 2009 Whole Foods Inc. reported $8.03 billion of sales with $147 million net income, which was a 28 percent increase in net income over the previous year. This is a strong level of performance in the competitive grocery store industry, in which low profit margins are common. Whole Foods' decision to use teamwork as a "recipe for success" represents a novel and innovative approach to management.

DISCUSSION QUESTIONS

1. Do you think Whole Foods' emphasis on teamwork could be applied to other companies in the grocery store industry such as Safeway, Kroger, or Albertson's? Why or why not? Do you think it would make a difference if the company's employees were represented by a union?

2. What are your thoughts about the Whole Foods practice of sharing team performance data with all company employees? Do you think that this practice risks creating an "overly competitive" spirit among the firm's teams and employees? Explain your answer.

Sources: Adapted from S.T. Foster, *Managing Quality*, Upper Saddle River, NJ: Prentice Hall, 2001, pp. 346–347; "Whole Foods Market," www.wholefoodsmarket.com/company/, 2010; D. McGinnn, "The Green Machine," *Newsweek*, March 21, 2005, pp. E8–E12; "Fortune 500: Largest U.S. Corporations," *Fortune*, May 3, 2010, pp. F1–F26.

Individual/Collaborative Learning Case 13.1

Managing Rewards for Teams

The following are three different reward situations you may encounter as a manager or a team member. Think about the type of reward and how it should be administered in each of these situations.

Parallel teams at Colorado General Hospital. Colorado General Hospital is a large hospital in Denver, Colorado. Employees are organized into traditional departments based on medical services: emergency room, intensive care, surgery, and so on. Support services include building maintenance, food services, and administration. Employees work in departments as individuals reporting to functional line managers. They are also placed on parallel teams or committees, such as the quality committee, safety committee, and the public relations committee. Employees spend about two hours per week on committee assignments and can expect to be a member of the committee for a two-year period before being replaced by new members. The output of the committees can be very significant, such as productivity-enhancing suggestions that result in labor or materials savings to the hospital.

Process teams at Universal Insurance. Universal Insurance provides automobile, property, and casualty insurance to its customers. The company recently underwent a major reengineering effort. The firm was restructured into core business processes, including claims administration, new product development, marketing services, and financial investment, focusing on processes that add value to the needs of the customer. Information systems technology software is applied to each process, requiring employees to learn new application software (and periodic software upgrades) that enhance employee productivity. The company has a strong culture that values quality and applies customer satisfaction as a criterion for success. Employees are given permanent assignments to self-managed process teams that are responsible for providing a core business process.

Project teams at Speedy Software. Speedy Software is a Seattle, Washington, software company that provides applications software that operates on the Internet. The market for this software is highly competitive. New products are released every year and upgrades on existing software appear even more frequently. If the company misses announced product release dates, the potential for lost profits is substantial because market share can quickly be captured by competitors who are first to market with software with better features. Therefore,

time to market is a critical factor for company success. The software engineers are organized into different project teams according to the type of software product. Engineers may work on a project very intensively for a period of 6 to 24 months and then can be reassigned to a new product. Sometimes project priorities change and a talented software designer may be shifted to a hot project before the other product is completed.

CRITICAL THINKING QUESTIONS

1. In each of the team reward situations, what size reward, measured in dollars, do you think is most appropriate? For example, should any of the teams receive a substantial reward (worth thousands of dollars)? What about more frequent small rewards ($25–$100)? In which situations would monetary rewards work most effectively? What about nonmonetary rewards, such as tickets to a sports event or dinner for two at a nice restaurant?

2. What should be the criteria for the team reward in each of the three situations? Justify your choice.

3. Should team members each receive equal amounts of the reward, or should the reward be based on each individual member's contribution to the team? Should team members who leave in the middle of a project or reward period (for example, during the middle of the fiscal year) be eligible for a full share of the team reward? How should newcomers to the team be rewarded?

COLLABORATIVE LEARNING EXERCISE

The instructor organizes the class into five- or six-member teams, each assigned to one of the team reward situations. The team develops a policy for rewarding teams in its situation which includes the following: eligibility to receive reward, basis of dividing the reward between team members, size of reward, the frequency of giving the reward to the team, and performance criteria for the reward. The teams present their policies to the class and compare the policies. The class and the instructor develop a list of conclusions that represents the best practices for providing rewards to teams.

Internet Exercise 13.1

Teamwork at Taco Bell

www.tacobell.com

Taco Bell, the Mexican fast food restaurant chain, expects its employees to work in teams starting as front-line restaurant employees serving customers and all the way up the career ladder into management. Visit the Taco Bell Web site and view the career path at Taco Bell so that you can answer the following questions. Once you are at the home page of Taco Bell you will want to click onto "careers" and next click onto "career path."

1. What type of skills for managing teams discussed in this chapter would be needed to perform as a "team member" at Taco Bell?
2. What type of skills for managing teams would be needed to perform as a "shift leader" at Taco Bell?
3. What type of skills for managing teams would be needed to perform as an "area coach" at Taco Bell?

Endnotes

1. R. L. Daft, *The Leadership Experience*, 2nd ed. (Cincinnati, OH: South-Western, 2002), p. 367.
2. J. Mathieu, M. T. Maynard, T. Rapp, and L. Gilson. "Team Effectiveness 1997–2007: A Review of Recent Advancements and a Glimpse Into the Future," *Journal of Management*, 34 (2008): 410–76; S. G. Cohen and D. E. Bailey, "What Makes Teams Work: Group Effectiveness Research from the Shop Floor to the Executive Suite," *Journal of Management*, 23 (1997): 239–90
3. W. E. Deming, *Out of the Crisis* (Cambridge, MA: MIT Press, 1986).
4. M. Sashkin and K. J. Kiser, *Putting Total Quality Management to Work* (San Francisco: Barrett-Koehler Publishers, 1993).
5. J. Bunderson and K. Sutcliffe, "Comparing Alternative Conceptualizations of Functional Diversity in Management Teams: Process and Performance Effects," *Academy of Management Journal* 45 (2002): 875–893, K. Bantel and S. Jackson, "Top Management and Innovations in Banking: Does the Demography of the Top Team Make a Difference?" *Strategic Management Journal* 10 (1989): 107–124.
6. G. Hertel, S. Geister, and U. Konradt, "Managing Virtual Teams: A Review of Current Empirical Research," *Human Resource Management Review* 15 (2005): 69–95.
7. C. J. Gersick, "Time and Transition in Work Teams: Toward a New Model of Group Development," *Academy of Management Journal* 31 (1988): 9–41.
8. A. Chang, P. Bordia, and J. Duck, "Punctuated Equilibrium and Linear Progression: Toward a New Understanding of Group Development," *Academy of Management Journal* 46 (2003): 106–117.
9. B. Nelson, *1001 Ways to Reward Employees* (New York: Workman Publishing, 1994).
10. J. Carson, P. Tesluk, and J. Marrone, "Shared Leadership in Teams: An Investigation of Antecedent Conditions and Performance," *Academy of Management Journal*, 50 (2007): 1217–234.
11. W. H. Weiss, "Teams and Teamwork," *Supervision* 59, no. 7 (1999): 9–11.
12. J. R. Katzenbach and D. K. Smith, "The Discipline of Teams," *Harvard Business Review*, March–April 1993, pp. 111–120.
13. Daft, *The Leadership Experience*, p. 368.
14. L. Thompson, *Making the Team: A Guide for Managers*, 2nd ed. (Upper Saddle River, NJ: Pearson, 2004); E. Fan and D. Grueneld, "When Needs Outweigh Desires: The Effects of Resource Interdependence and Reward Interdependence on Group Problem Solving," *Basic and Applied Social Psychology* 20 (1998): 45–56.
15. I. Berkow, "A Superstar, Iverson, Isn't a Role Model," *The New York Times*, February 2, 2001, p. C15; R. Zoglin, "Carsey and Werner, Last of the Mom-and-Pop Producers, Have a Hot Hand This Fall," *Time*, September 23, 1996.
16. T. Raz, "Taming the Savage Genius: The Delicate Art of Managing Employees Who Are Way, Way Smarter than You," *Inc.*, May 2003, pp. 33–35.
17. B. Fisher and A. Boynton, "Virtuoso Teams," *Harvard Business Review*, July–August 2005, pp. 117–123.
18. D. B. Balkin, S. Dolan, and K. Forgues, "Rewards for Team Contribution to Quality," *Journal of Compensation and Benefits* 13, no. 1 (1997): 41–46.
19. S. Joni and D. Beyer, "How to Pick a Good Fight: Strong Leaders Create the Kind of Conflict that Can Spark Creativity and Innovation," *Harvard Business Review*, December, 2009, pp. 48–57.
20. J. Varela, P. Fernandez, and M. Del Rio, "Cross-Functional Conflict, Conflict Handling Behaviors and new Product Performance in Spanish Firms," *Creativity and Innovation Management* 14 (December 2005): 355; Thompson, *Making the Team: A Guide for Managers*.
21. C. Osborne, *Dealing with Difficult People* (London: DK, 2001), p. 61.
22. J. Wecker, "Powers of Persuasion," *Fortune*, October 12, 1998, pp. 161–164; R. Lewicki and J. Litterer, *Negotiation* (Burr Ridge, IL: Irwin, 1985).
23. L. Thompson, *The Mind and Heart of the Negotiator*, 4th ed., Pearson Prentice Hall, Upper Saddle River, NJ: 2009.

14

Learning Objectives

1   Understand the communication process.

2   Eliminate barriers that distort the meaning of information.

3   Recognize the basic patterns of organizational communication.

4   Understand how to organize and run effective meetings.

5   Master electronic forms of communication.

6   Work with an organization's informal communication system.

Call Center Jobs Are Outsourced to the Home Thanks to Broadband Communications Technology

More and more companies are moving customer service jobs out of high overhead call centers and into what is possibly the lowest-overhead place in the United States: workers' homes. The widespread availability of broadband communications linked to the Internet has made it possible for people who want to work out of the home, such as stay-at-home parents, the disabled, retirees, and those caring for adults or children with special needs, to have a job that does not interfere with their lifestyle. JetBlue Airways is perhaps the most famous practitioner of using home workers-all of its 1,400 reservation agents work from home. But they are employees. Many of the new call center jobs for home workers are independent contractor positions offered by outsourcing companies. The difference is that independent contractors are expected to pay for their own health care, computer equipment, and training.

The home workers, sometimes called cyberagents, are often educated, stay-at-home workers who were previously unable to engage in paid employment because they lived in rural areas, could not afford child care, were unable to work at a job that required mandatory face-time

Managing Communication

15 minutes. Agents are paid only for the time spent on the phone. Within the United States a call center worker onsite costs about $31 per hour versus $21 per hour for a home agent. Home agents can earn $8 to $13 or more an hour and are also more productive. Willow, an outsourcing company that employs cyberagents, indicates that its home agents make sales that are up to 25 percent higher than in call centers; their customer satisfaction rates are often 40 percent better. Customers appreciate being able to have a native English speaker to communicate with. Outsource providers of call center services such as Willow expect the number of home agent jobs to increase from its current level of 112,000 in 2006 to 330,000 by 2010.

Source: M. Conlin, "Call Centers in the Rec Room," *BusinessWeek*, January 23, 2006, pp. 76–77; S. Armour, "Cost-Effective 'Homesourcing' Grows," *USA Today*, March 13, 2006; H. Clancy, "Cyber Agents: New Travel Planners Aren't Your Everyday Orbitz," *Entrepreneur Magazine*, November, 2008, www.entreprereur.com.

schedules, or had retired. More than 75 percent of home agents have some college education versus only 25 percent of employees who work in call centers. Home agents also appreciate saving money on gas and car expenses and not having to deal with commuting in traffic before starting work.

The call center work of cyberagents also provides a flexible just-in-time workforce. Shifts can last as little as

CRITICAL THINKING QUESTIONS

1. *What are the advantages to companies of using home workers who respond to customer inquiries compared to the practice of using a centralized call center staffed by employees who work onsite at the company?*

2. *What challenges do companies face managing employees who work at home providing call center services to customers?*

We will revisit these critical thinking questions in our Concluding Thoughts at the end of the chapter.

Communication is the glue that holds social organizations together. This chapter begins with a simple model of communication between two people. We then explain why it is important for the communication process to be managed to avoid misunderstandings. Next, the ways communication processes operate in organizations are described. Effective methods to manage different forms of communication in organizations and useful communication skills are also provided. This chapter will help you learn and develop skills to improve your ability to communicate with other employees, as outlined in Skills for Managing 14.1.

■ The Process of Communication

communication

The process of transmitting meaningful information from one party to another through the use of shared symbols.

facts

Bits of information that can be objectively measured or described, such as the retail price of a new product, the cost of raw materials, the defect rate of a manufacturing process, or the number of employees who quit during a year.

knowledge workers

Employees who manage information and make it available to decision makers in the organization.

feelings

An individual's emotional responses to decisions made or actions taken by other people.

Communication is the process of transmitting meaningful information from one party to another through the use of shared symbols. Communication is successful when meaning is understood. Two forms of information are sent and received in communication: facts and feelings.

Facts are bits of information that can be objectively measured or described, such as the retail price of a new product, the cost of raw materials, the defect rate of a manufacturing process, or the number of employees who quit during a year. Facts can be communicated verbally or in written documents and can also be transformed into digital symbols and stored in computer databases. **Knowledge workers** are employees who manage information and make it available to decision makers in the organization. They are the most common type of worker in the 21st century organization, and they depend on the process of communication to obtain appropriate information to do their jobs effectively.

Feelings are an individual's emotional responses to decisions made or actions taken by other people. Although feelings can be communicated verbally or in written documents, they are more likely to be communicated as nonverbal facial expressions, tone of voice, or body postures. To be effective, managers and employees must know how to interpret the feelings of others. Since managers achieve results through the actions of employees, it is important for them to take emotional reactions into consideration.

Organizations require diverse communication channels to facilitate communication among employees, managers, and customers. When messages with strong emotional content are to be received and understood, these channels must allow for face-to-face communication. Despite advances in computer technology that have created powerful ways to store, retrieve, and

FIGURE 14.1

The Communication Process

manipulate information, company leaders must still make provisions for communication *on* an interpersonal basis in order to develop trust and cohesion among organization members.

A Model of Communication

Figure 14.1 is a simple model of the communication process. Although the model illustrates communication between two people, it also applies to more complex communication situations. As the figure indicates, communication begins with a **sender**, who has a message for the **receiver**. The sender *encodes* the message and selects a **communication channel** that will deliver it to the receiver. Encoding is selecting appropriate symbols such as written words, numbers, digital symbols, sounds, or body language that can be correctly *decoded* by the receiver. The sender must anticipate the decoding skills of the receiver. For example, when a businessperson from the Netherlands does business with a U.S. executive, it is likely that all conversations and documents will be in English, because most Americans do not speak or understand Dutch, the language of the Netherlands, whereas the Dutch businessperson is very likely to speak English.

The communication channel influences the quantity and quality of information that is conveyed to the receiver. Communication channels include face-to-face conversations, group meetings, memos, policy manuals, e-mail, voice mail, videotapes, and computer printouts. Factors that influence the choice of a communication channel include the complexity of the message, the time available to compose and distribute it, the size and proximity of the audience, and the skill of the sender in using various channels. For example, some professors rely on traditional blackboard lectures because they do not have enough preparation time to create multimedia overheads.

For communication to be effective, the receiver must be able to decode the message and understand its true meaning. **Decoding** means translating the symbolic verbal, written, or visual symbols into an undistorted, clear message. The receiver may misinterpret the message if unable to decode it, perhaps because the receiver does not have the necessary skills in language or culture. For example, a U.S. buyer may insist on a written contract before agreeing to do business with a Mexican supplier. However, in Mexico, business deals are based on oral agreement, and contracts represent a lack of good faith. There are cultural differences within the United States. A simple example is the fast-talking New York sales representative who is trying to sell life insurance to a potential client in Monroe, Louisiana. The New Yorker may interpret the slower speech of the southerner as unsophisticated and less intelligent. The southerner may interpret the New Yorker's accent and fast speech as rude and untrustworthy. Other decoding problems include the use of technical jargon and the ambiguity of English words with multiple meanings. A communication channel that is rich in information, with opportunities for visual as well as verbal cues, provides a context to help the receiver select the appropriate meaning of a word with several different meanings. On the other hand, lean communication channels provide a limited context from which to select the true meaning of an ambiguously worded message.

Important messages should include opportunities for feedback from the receiver. **Feedback** allows the sender to make sure the true meaning is received. For example, if a company decides to change the basis of sales representatives' pay from salary to straight commission, communicating the change to the sales team at a face-to-face meeting is more effective than sending a memo or e-mail message because there are more opportunities for feedback and clarification. Many management problems can be avoided by using communication channels with feedback, especially when individuals are likely to feel strongly about the content the message.

sender
Individual or party that initiates communication with another individual or party.

receiver
Individual or party that receives message from sender.

communication channel
Influences the quantity and quality of information that is conveyed to the receiver. Channels of communication include face-to-face conversations, group meetings, memos, policy manuals, e-mail, voice mail.

decoding
Translating the symbolic verbal, written, or visual symbols into an undistorted, clear message.

feedback
Information received back from the receiver, which allows the sender to make sure the true meaning is received.

two-way communications
Communication channels that provide for feedback.

one-way communications
Communication channels that provide no opportunity for feedback.

noise
Anything that can interfere with sending or receiving a message.

Channels that provide for feedback are called **two-way communications,** because they allow the sender and receiver to interact. Communication channels that provide no opportunity for feedback are **one-way communications.** Although interactive communication is ideal, it is not always possible when information must be disseminated to many employees in a short period of time. IBM informs employees about the promotions of top executives in its corporate newsletter (a one-way communication channel). However, the sales force is informed about new products at a sales meeting (a two-way communication channel). As this example suggests, two-way communication channels are required for important and complex information.

Another important condition of effective communication is overcoming noise. **Noise** is anything that interferes with sending or receiving the message. Noise can distort the true meaning of the message. Sources of noise include the sender (whose accent may be difficult to understand); the communication channel (if the telecommunications system lacks bandwidth, an Internet message may be slow and frustrating); the receiver (who may have poor vision and be unable to read a memo); and the environment (time pressures may reduce availability to listen to a message). A manager at the Houston distribution center of Baxter International, a medical and health products company, receives more than 60 voice mail messages a day from customers and employees. Having many customers to satisfy and employees to supervise makes it difficult for the manager to respond to all messages promptly. However, by using some of the communication options in the voice mail system, the manager can respond to queries that require only short, direct answers.

LOC-In 1 Learning Objective Check-In

Gina wants Jerry to understand that she is no longer interested in pursuing a particular client's project. Based on the way Gina gestures to Jerry while she describes the project itself, he clearly understands what she is trying to communicate.

1. In this example, Gina is the _____.
   a. decoder
   b. receiver
   c. sender
   d. noisemaker

2. The personal conversation between Gina and Jerry represents the _____.
   a. communication channel
   b. control factor
   c. model of communication
   d. vertical communication

3. Gina's gesturing during the conversation is one way of _____ the message.
   a. decoding
   b. controlling
   c. encoding
   d. giving feedback to

Barriers to Effective Communication

The model of communication presented in Figure 14.1 suggests that barriers can disrupt the accurate transmission of information. These barriers take different forms:

1. *Sender barrier.* The sender may send a message to an audience that is not interested in the content of the message.
2. *Encoding barrier.* The sender uses a vocabulary that is too technical for the audience.
3. *Communication channel barrier.* The sender selects a communication channel that is too lean to provide the richness of information receivers need to decode the message. For example, a written memo is inadequate for explaining a change in the employee retirement plan.
4. *Decoding barrier.* The receiver does not have the decoding skills necessary to understand the message. For example, poor reading skills can prevent employees from using manuals and other reference materials.

5. *Receiver barrier.* The receiver is too busy focusing on other things to be able to accurately listen to and understand the verbal or nonverbal content of the message.
6. *Feedback barrier.* The organization has few formal communication channels with feedback loops to give lower echelon employees the opportunity to communicate their true feelings about policies.
7. *Noise barrier.* The receiver does not understand how to use time-saving features of e-mail and voice mail, resulting in message overload and unacceptable delays in responding to messages of customers and co-workers.
8. *Perception barriers.* Perception barriers occur when two individuals experience the same message differently because their mental images of the message are not identical. A receiver will fit a message into an existing pattern of experiences to make sense out of it. Sometimes the message becomes distorted during this sensemaking process. One type of perception barrier is **selective perception**, whereby the receiver focuses on the parts of the message that are most salient to his or her interests and ignores other parts that are viewed as not relevant. For example, an employee interested in a job vacancy may use selective perception to discount the fact that the job requires more work experience than the employee currently has accumulated. The result is a personal disappointment when the employee is not chosen for the job.

   Another important type of perceptual barrier is **prejudgment**, which involves making incorrect assumptions about a person due to membership in a group (based on age, race, gender or ethnicity) or about a thing (such as performance evaluation) based on earlier positive or negative experiences. For example, a manager who has a negative earlier experience with an older employee may generalize this experience to other old people. The manager may become resistant to hiring an older job applicant even if positive information is available, because the manager has already negatively prejudged the applicant. It is important to be aware of these perceptual barriers and avoid them. Prejudging older people (over 40 years of age) negatively is an illegal practice that can have costly legal implications.

selective perception
Type of perception barrier whereby the receiver focuses on the parts of the message that are most salient to his or her interests and ignores other parts that are not relevant.

prejudgment
Type of perceptual barrier that involves making incorrect assumptions about a person due to membership in a group or about a thing based on earlier positive or negative experiences.

Large, complex organizations are likely to have many barriers. These barriers can be managed by using various management practices. Senders should be educated about the necessity of learning the background of intended audiences and should gain firsthand familiarity with audiences prior to initiating communication. All members of the organization should be trained in the effective use of communication technologies to manage the flow of information. There should be a diverse mix of communication channels from lean (memos or policy manuals) to rich (videoconference and multimedia) so that senders can match the channel to the complexity of the message. The management team must make sure employees have appropriate communication skills. Key skills include listening, public speaking, and nonverbal communication skills. HR departments can either screen applicants for evidence of these skills or provide on-the-job training programs which give employees opportunities to practice and improve their communication skills.

LOC-In 2 Learning Objective Check-In

1. Steve is trying to teach a group from the company's China subunit how to use the latest phase of the software implementation that he is in charge of. While the Chinese team has learned very good spoken English from their meetings and phone conversations with the U.S. team, several among them do not know how to read and write the language very well. Steve's pamphlets, then, are useless in delivering an immediate message to the people he is trying to teach, and he will have to rely on his other presentation skills and direct training methods. Which of the following is depicted in this example?
   a. Decoding barrier
   b. Directional barrier
   c. Communication channel barrier
   d. Sender barrier

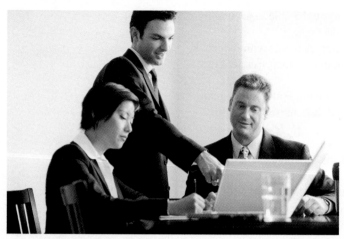

Direction and feedback from manager to employee is a form of downward communication.

downward communication
Sending a message from a high position in the organization to an individual or group lower in the hierarchy.

upward communication
Sending a message from a position lower in the hierarchy to a receiver higher in the hierarchy.

horizontal communication
Communication between a sender and a receiver at a similar level in the organization.

■ Patterns of Organizational Communications

Communication patterns in organizations are complex. Possible barriers to organizational communication include: (1) differences in employee status and power, such as communication between a subordinate and a supervisor; (2) diversity, such as cross-gender communication; and (3) differences in interests, such as a manufacturing unit focused on quality and efficiency of output and an engineering unit focused on executing a technically elegant design that may be difficult to manufacture. Organizational communication patterns operate downward, upward, and horizontally. Each direction poses specific management challenges.

Downward Communication

Downward communication frequently occurs between managers and subordinates, when the manager provides direction, feedback, and critical information to help subordinates perform at expected levels. Examples include employee performance evaluations, job descriptions, orientation of new employees, praise and recognition, company business strategies and goals, and company policies and procedures.

Upward Communication

In **upward communication**, a message is sent from a position lower in the hierarchy to a receiver higher in the hierarchy. It lets managers know how individuals, teams, and units of the company are performing. When performance deviates from expected standards, managers can make corrective adjustments.

One of the most important components of upward communication is feedback to managers about employee feelings about company policies. Organizations are likely to have barriers that filter information from subordinates before it is received by managers. Employees are well aware of the tendency to punish the bearer of bad news. It is also considered disloyal for employees to take a problem "over the head" of the boss to a higher echelon manager. Therefore, it is necessary to design special communication channels that encourage employees to express their true feelings or provide unfiltered information. Hewlett-Packard has an open-door policy that encourages employees to bring problems to any manager in the company and requires managers to resolve problems within a specified period of time. Toyota is well-known for effectively using employee suggestion systems to improve product and process quality. Besides suggestions, upward communication includes employee grievances, information about the unethical behavior of managers, accounting information, and information about the defect rate of the product.

Horizontal Communication

When a sender and a receiver are at a similar level in the organization **horizontal communication** takes place. This includes communications between team members, between different teams, and between employees in different units, such as when a safety specialist and a quality control inspector discuss proposed changes in the manufacturing process. Horizontal communication is becoming increasingly important in organizations because it involves collaboration between employees with different skills and competencies. A high proportion of communications between knowledge workers consists of horizontal communication in which information is shared. Figure 14.2 provides an illustration of the three different patterns of organizational communication: downward, upward, and horizontal.

Downsizing and reengineering have resulted in slimmer organizations with fewer levels and a greater emphasis on teams. Horizontal communication plays an important role in this environment. Interactive electronic communication technologies such as e-mail greatly facilitate horizontal communication by making it possible to establish learning communities and virtual teams

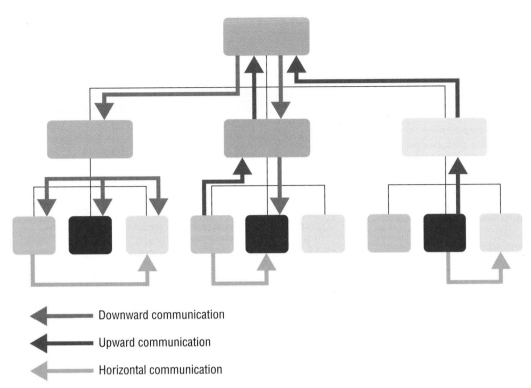

FIGURE 14.2

**Organizational
Communication Patterns**

◀━━━ Downward communication

◀━━━ Upward communication

◀━━━ Horizontal communication

of employees who work together even when separated geographically. Other examples of horizontal communication are peer performance, cross-functional new product development team meetings, self-managed work team meetings, suggestion committee meetings, and diversity task forces.

Managers and team members should have the ability to give feedback to subordinates or peers. Feedback may be communicated either horizontally (from peer to peer) or vertically (from supervisor to subordinate). All employees need feedback to improve their skills. Positive feedback lets them know they are progressing toward their goals and can be used to strengthen behaviors that are already learned. Negative feedback tells employees which behaviors should be modified to improve performance. Tips for providing feedback can be found in Manager's Notebook 14.1.

LOC-In 3 Learning Objective Check-In

Olin heads up the catalog division of a major camp gear supplier. His phone operating staff tells him that they have gotten lots of feedback from customers about a particular product, and they think that it might be worth looking into a couple of changes that could make the product better for a wider range of their customers. Olin then tells his counterpart, Joe, in the product development division what complaints were filed most frequently about the product and in what time frame they were received since the product's launch.

1. When the staff tells Olin about the complaints, this is _____.
   a. downward communication
   b. upward communication
   c. horizontal communication
   d. external communication

2. When Olin passes the information on to Joe in product development, this is _____.
   a. upward communication
   b. downward communication
   c. horizontal communication
   d. sideways communication

MANAGER'S NOTEBOOK 14.1

How to Provide Constructive Feedback to Others

Here are some useful suggestions about giving constructive feedback to peers or subordinates.

1. *Focus your feedback on specific behaviors* that were successful or that were unsuccessful. You will help motivate the employee to continue the successful behaviors and to improve the unsuccessful ones. Instead of saying "You did a great job on this project," tell the employee, "Your careful checking and rechecking caught several errors."

2. *Keep personality traits out of your feedback* by focusing on "what" rather than "who." Specify what results the person achieved or failed to achieve. Instead of saying "You don't work hard enough," tell the employee, "You used outdated figures in your report."

3. *Investigate whether the employee had control over the results* before giving feedback about unsuccessful behaviors. For example, the employee who used outdated figures in a report may have been given them by corporate headquarters and had no way of knowing they were outdated. Ask questions of the employee to find out whether unsuccessful behavior is something the employee can control. Be very cautious before offering negative feedback.

4. *Feedback should be given as soon as possible*; don't save up your feedback about both successful and unsuccessful behaviors for an end-of-the-quarter meeting, for example. Feedback given shortly after an event occurs is the most effective at changing or sustaining an employee's behaviors.

5. *Ensure privacy when giving feedback about negative behaviors*; giving it in public will cause a reaction against you by any observers. *Feedback about positive behaviors can be given in public* to recognize an employee's success. It can help motivate the employee and others.

6. *Catch people doing things right.* The more you catch people doing things right, the more right things they will do. Encourage positive behaviors by letting people know when they are doing things well.

Source: Based on S. P. Robbins and P. L. Hunsaker, *Training in Interpersonal Skills*, 2nd ed. Upper Saddle River, NJ: Prentice Hall, 1996, pp. 73–75; L. Swinton, "7 Tips for Giving Positive Feedback," *Management for the Rest of Us*, August 17, 2005, www.mftrou.com; D. Brodie, "10 Tips for Giving Effective Feedback," *Ezine Articles*, 2010, www.ezinearticles.com.

■ Managing Organizational Communications

Organizations can improve the quality of communications by providing a diverse mix of lean to rich communication channels that provide opportunities to communicate in upward, downward, and horizontal directions. Managers and employees must be trained to use the communication channels appropriately. Because communication technologies are rapidly changing, upgrading the communication skills of employees should be considered a process of continuous improvement.

information richness
The potential information-carrying capacity of data.

Communication channels vary according to **information richness**, the potential information-carrying capacity of data. Rich communication channels provide opportunities for feedback, provide a full range of visual and audio information, and personalize the message for the receiver. Rich communications channels are best for nonroutine, ambiguous, and difficult messages. Face-to-face communication provides the richest channel of communication, as displayed in Figure 14.3. Lean communication channels provide no opportunity for feedback, have a limited

FIGURE 14.3

Communication Channels Ranked by Information Richness

Sources: Robert H. Lengel and Richard L. Daft, "The Selection of Communication Media as an Executive Skill," *Academy of Management Executive* 2 (August 1988): 225–232; and Richard L Daft and Robert H. Lengel, "Organizational Information Requirements, Media Richness, and Structural Design," *Managerial Science* 32 (May 1986): 554–572.

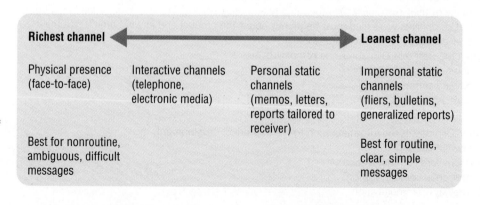

mix of information, and are impersonal. A mass-produced bulletin or flier is an example of a lean communication channel.

Face-to-Face Communication

Rich information content is possible in face-to-face communication, because there is a high level of interactivity between the sender and the receiver. Job interviews are likely to be done face-to-face. One of the most important types of face-to-face communication is the meeting.

Meetings, or gatherings of organizational members, are held to inform and train participants, solve problems, monitor and coordinate activities, delegate tasks, and create social bonds between diverse organization members. *Staff meetings* allow managers to coordinate activities with subordinates. *Corporate or business-unit meetings* address strategic issues and involve executives who formulate long-range goals. *Task force meetings* are held to discuss goals that affect a broad range of employees such as diversity in the workplace or safety. *Team meetings* are used to coordinate the work activities of members of a self-managed team, including performance goals, training new members, scheduling work, and suggesting improvements in work methods. The application of multimedia technologies that transmit video, voice, and text over satellite networks have made face-to-face meetings with globally dispersed people possible.

Face-to-face communications, such as meetings, provide an opportunity for feedback and personalized messages for receivers.

Managers can spend as much as 60 percent to 80 percent of their time in meetings. A sales manager is likely to hold regular meetings with sales representatives, attend management meetings with other sales managers, and participate in committee meetings with marketing, advertising, and promotion employees on new product development or brand management. Employees who are asked to spend more time in team-based work units require periodic meetings to form a consensus on how the team should conduct its activities. Meetings can waste time and become frustrating. It is important to manage them effectively. Manager's Notebook 14.2 lists techniques to run a meeting effectively.

MANAGER'S NOTEBOOK 14.2

Managing Productive Meetings

Here are some steps you can take to make meetings more productive:

1. Ask yourself if it's important even to schedule a meeting. If you can handle the issue with an e-mail or a memo instead, don't schedule a meeting.
2. *Schedule the meeting for an appropriate place.* Be sure the room is large enough for the participants and that they can all hear each other and the speaker. Be careful to limit the number of meeting participants to only individuals who have a good reason to attend and who are able to make contributions to the goals of the meeting.
3. *Create an agenda for the meeting* including topics and time limits, and distribute it ahead of time. The meeting participants will be able to plan their own contributions. Keeping the meeting to the agenda will ensure that all topics are covered. Plan to take careful notes during the meeting as each topic is covered.
4. *Establish rules for participation.* All participants need to have an opportunity to contribute; determine an order so that a few participants don't dominate the meeting.

5. *Follow the agenda's time limits* for each topic. Keep an eye on the clock; if a topic exceeds its allotted time, you should return to it later and go on to the next topic.
6. *Leave some open time* for topics that may not have been included on the agenda. If discussion of additional topics is expected to take more time, add them to the next meeting's agenda instead.
7. *End the meeting with a plan of action.* Discuss the steps that will be taken as a result of the meeting. Distribute a written report of the meeting and the steps to be taken based on your notes.

Sources: Based on P. Sauer, "Quick Show of Hands: Who Hates Meetings?" *Inc.,* May 2004, pp. 73–78, 112; R. Volkema and F. Niederman, "Planning and Managing Organizational Meetings: An Empirical Analysis of Written and Oral Communication," *Journal of Business Communication* 33 (July 1996): 275–293; T. Freedman, "Five Minute Tip: Managing Your Team Meetings," *ICT in Education,* May 21, 2010, www.ictineducation.org.

LOC-In   4   Learning Objective Check-In

1. Jeremy needs to delegate several tasks among his work staff, which has a busy schedule with other projects already. It is important that he does not waste time in communicating the new project's work, but it is equally important that he makes sure everyone on the staff understands his or her role. Which of the following would be appropriate for Jeremy to conduct?
   a. Corporate meeting
   b. Staff meeting
   c. Team meeting
   d. Task force meeting

Written Communication

Written communication includes memos, policy manuals, employee handbooks, company newsletters, bulletin boards, letters, and fliers. Written documents have an advantage over face-to-face communication, because messages can be revised stored and made available when needed, and disseminated in identical copies so the same message is received by all. Written communication can be personalized for a small audience or written in a generic style that accommodates a larger audience. The limitations of written communication are that there are no provisions for feedback, and the sender may not be certain if the message was received, read, and/or understood. Two popular forms of written communication are memos and company newsletters.

MEMOS   Short business messages that provide information to employees are sent in memos. They can be used to inform employees about the agenda, time, and place of a meeting; to schedule work; or to describe a change in an employment policy. A memo should be brief and to the point. Also,

- Make sure that the heading indicates: (1) the intended audience; (2) the subject of the memo; (3) the name of the sender; and (4) the date that the memo was written.
- Revise and edit the memo to eliminate misspellings and poor grammar. Make sure the message is clear and unambiguous. If the sender catches an error after the memo is distributed, it may be necessary to send a followup memo to tell the audience to disregard the previous memo. This can annoy receivers.
- Add the names of people who need to be aware of the communication to a copy list at the end of the memo. Copied individuals may not be the focus of the memo, but they need to know about it. For example, the controller who schedules a meeting of staff accountants to discuss a new way to expense research and development costs may copy the vice president of finance.
- Avoid sending memos to people who do not need to know about the content. Employees should not waste time reading memos that are not important.

COMPANY NEWSLETTERS   Many companies have short monthly or quarterly publications designed to keep employees informed of important events, meetings, and transitions and to provide inspirational stories about employee and team contributions to the business. Newsletters help foster community spirit by keeping everybody informed about what others are doing. Desktop publishing software has made the production of newsletters feasible for even the smallest companies.

A newsletter can be a one-way or interactive form of communication depending on the goals established by management. In the one-way form, a newsletter is an official downward communication from management to inform employees about company policies, procedures, and other information. In its two-way form, the newsletter is a communication channel for all directions of communication (upward, downward, and horizontal), allowing each member of the workplace to voice opinions and contribute stories of interest. Large corporations are likely to have several newsletters, with the corporate-level news from headquarters presented in a one-way version and business-unit or plant newsletters containing employee input.

Electronic Communication

Advances in electronic technology make interactive communication possible between senders and receivers, even when they are separated by physical distance and busy schedules. Electronic communication channels vary in the richness of the information that is transmitted and can include text, voice, graphics, or video. Two important forms of electronic communication are voice mail and e-mail.

VOICE MAIL   A detailed audio message that is recorded electronically and can be played back when convenient is a voice mail. Employees can play back all messages at once and answer them in a concentrated block of time so that redundant "telephone tag" calls can be avoided. Voice mail also allows a sender to set up a menu of responses to commonly asked questions, which saves additional time. Routine calls can be routed to a recorded message, and more attention can be paid to callers with nonroutine questions. Vanguard, one of the largest U.S. mutual fund companies, uses a voice mail menu to answer commonly asked questions about investments. Each customer has a special code to obtain daily mutual fund account balances and market prices of funds and to make financial transactions.

Voice mail is not always used effectively. Many organizations, including such government offices as the Social Security Administration, present a long menu of options that waste the caller's time. Some people use voice mail to screen phone calls, avoiding callers they do not want to talk to. Screening too many calls can annoy customers and block internal company communication. The following suggestions can help managers use voice mail appropriately:

- Update your personal greeting regularly. Let callers know when they can expect your return call.
- Include information in the greeting about how to reach a co-worker who can help callers if you are unavailable or if the call is urgent.
- Try to answer your phone while at your desk. Use the voice recording only for good reasons, such as being in the middle of an important meeting with a colleague.
- Check messages regularly and return calls promptly.
- Set the message capacity for one or two minutes to discourage callers from leaving overly verbose messages. For long conversations other communication channels are preferable to voice mail.[1]

ELECTRONIC MAIL   **E-mail** allows employees to communicate via written messages through personal computer terminals linked to a network. It is a fast way to distribute important business results to a large number of employees. Virtual teams of employees can work simultaneously on a document even though they may be separated geographically using e-mail attachments. E-mail is often used to exchange information (such as coordinating project activities and scheduling meetings), for social reasons (such as keeping in touch with colleagues), and to post general information that can be of use to many employees (for example, the time and place of the company picnic). The use of e-mail creates upward communication channel for employees to gain access to executives who previously may have been inaccessible to them. For example, Bill Gates, the chairman of Microsoft, makes his e-mail address known to all Microsoft employees. He reserves several hours each day to send and reply to messages.

Despite its advantages, e-mail creates challenging problems. It can contribute to information overload; numerous e-mail messages are sent to large lists of people when the message may be of interest to only a few. E-mail should not be considered private. Recent court decisions state that U.S. companies have a right to monitor the e-mail of employees.[2]

When using e-mail,

- Scan the subject heading at the beginning of the message. If the topic is of no interest to you, delete the message without reading it.
- Create electronic files to store important messages so they can be quickly retrieved when needed.
- Set up electronic lists of people who should receive the same message. For example, the project team leader should set up a list of all team members and send messages to the list rather than to each individual member.

e-mail
Electronic mail via computers.

- Assume that your e-mail will be read by management. Use other communication channels for private or controversial messages.
- Protect sensitive documents with encryption software so that private information is not accessible to hackers or other unintended receivers.
- Use e-mail to transmit factual information, and avoid using it to criticize colleagues or to communicate messages with content that will cause strong emotional reactions from the receiver.
- Avoid sending messages written in all-capitals, which is like screaming.[3]
- Reread your message before sending and check for spelling, punctuation, and grammar.
- If you won't be able to respond to an e-mail for several days, acknowledge its receipt and tell the sender when you are likely to respond.[4]

LOC-In 5 | Learning Objective Check-In

Ryan likes to stay in touch with his clients and co-workers constantly throughout the day. Sometimes, however, he has meetings to attend or other work to accomplish, and so he cannot spend all his time communicating with these important people. He wishes he could set aside a block of time to devote to using the phone and talking to clients or catching up on important internal news at the company. This would allow him to be more productive with his time.

1. _____ is one option for Ryan that would allow him to set up and record messages that could be played back when convenient.
   a. E-mail
   b. Voice mail
   c. The grapevine
   d. Informal communication

2. Which of the following would be the most appropriate way for Ryan to catch up on important company happenings throughout the day?
   a. Voice mail
   b. Team meetings
   c. E-mail
   d. Memos

In some companies e-mail is the dominant form of communcation because the employees may be spread out geographically and rarely if ever are able to meet on a face-to-face basis. That is the case at Alpine Access, a provider of outsourced call-center services based in Golden, Colorado.[5] One way to attempt to communicate emotion within an e-mail message is with the use of a *smiley,* also called an *emoticon,* which consists of a sequence of ordinary characters found on a computer keyboard that symbolize a face expressing some kind of emotion. The classic smiley shows a smiling face with a colon representing the eyes, a dash represents the nose, and a right parenthesis represents the mouth as shown in Figure 14.4 and is used at the end of a sentence to convey happiness. Other smilies as shown in the figure can represent joking around,

FIGURE 14.4

Selected Smilies Used to Convey Emotion in e-Mail

Source: D. Brake, *Dealing with e-Mail* (London: DK, 2003), p. 46; "Emoticons," *Yahoo! Messenger* 2010, www.messenger.yahoo.com; "Emoticons," *Computer User,* 2010, www.computeruser.com.

Smiley	Meaning
:-)	The basic smiley–usually indicates happiness.
;-)	Winking–usually indicates a joke or (sometimes) flirtatiousness.
:-(	Frowning–usually indicates sadness or disagreement.
:-I	Indifferent–usually indicates apathy or disinterest.
:->	Sarcastic–usually indicates insincerity or cynicism.

How Social Networking Tools Help Professionals Stay Connected

Social networking tools such as LinkedIn allow busy professionals to stay connected with each other and learn what is happening in each other's professional lives. Companies use LinkedIn and other social networking tools for hiring when job vacancies arise or for locating a good attorney or accountant who has specialized knowledge for a specific task. LinkedIn may also be used to perform due diligence on a person being considered for a job by asking former colleagues who are familiar with an individual about his or her work habits—knowledge that is not likely to be available in letters of recommendation. Currently 60 million people have registered and posted professional profiles with their employment histories on LinkedIn.

To illustrate how companies apply social networking tools, the multinational consulting firm Accenture estimated that in 2010 it plans to hire 50,000 people worldwide as telecom consultants, finance experts, software specialists, and others. The head of Accenture's global recruiting, John Campagnino, expects to identify 40 percent of the people hired at Accenture through the use of social networking tools like LinkedIn on the Internet in the coming years. One of the key advantages that companies such as Accenture see in using social networking tools is that they can do recruiting faster and cheaper online then they can with more traditional recruiting methods such as newspaper ads or flyers sent out in the mail. So to be considered for professional opportunities in the future it pays to have a profile on LinkedIn or on similar social networking sites.

Sources: Based on J. Hempel, "How LinkedIn Will Fire Up Your Career," *Fortune*, April 12, 2010, pp. 74–82; J. Swearingen, "How to Get Started with LinkedIn," *BNET*, 2010, www.bnet.com; A. McConnon, "Social networking is graduating—and Hitting the Job Market. How do Online Rolodexes Stack Up?" *IN*, September, 2007, pp. 4–6.

frowning, indifference, or sarcasm. However some people find these symbols to be childish, and, unfortunately, they are not universally understood.[6]

The **Internet** is a computer network with multimedia communication capabilities. A combination of text, voice, graphics, and video can be sent to a receiver over the Web. Companies' sites on the World Wide Web are places where potential customers can learn about products and services and place orders. The use of the Internet makes it possible for companies to serve international customers. Many universities advertise MBA programs on their Web sites to attract international students. Electronic commerce over the Internet has created many new business opportunities. Amazon.com sells books and other merchandise over the Internet. Charles Schwab, the discount broker, lets customers buy and sell stocks online. Management Close-Up 14.1 describes how Accenture uses social networking tools such as LinkedIn to identify potential new hires by examining their professional profiles posted on the Web site.

Management Is Everyone's Business 14.1 explains why virtual teams should plan to schedule periodic face-to-face meetings in order to build team spirit and trust. The payoff is a more productive team.

Internet
A computer network with multimedia communication capabilities, allowing a combination of text, voice, graphics, and video to be sent to a receiver; a network of networks, connecting hundreds of thousands of corporate, educational, and research computer networks around the world.

MANAGEMENT IS EVERYONE'S BUSINESS 14.1

WORKING AS A TEAM   If you are part of a virtual team that coordinates work over a computer network, it is important to schedule periodic face-to-face meetings in order to build team spirit and trust. Here is why.

- Face-to-face communication is a richer communication channel with many more opportunities for feedback, so that team members are able to build bonds of friendship and develop closer personal ties with each other. This social cohesion makes it easier for team members to trust one another.
- With trust, team members are willing to give people who do not meet expected task demands the benefit of the doubt, and members can depend on each other to get the job done right.
- Without trust, there can be misunderstandings, because team members are less likely to be as generous with each other when someone falls short of performance expectations, Misunderstandings can lead to dysfunctional team conflict and reduced productivity as team members are distracted from the primary tasks they should be doing.

Informal Communication

grapevine
Informal communication that takes place at the workplace.

Informal communication, sometimes referred to as the **grapevine**, is used when there are gaps in or barriers to formal communication and employees do not receive information they desire. It takes place at the water cooler or in the hallway, in the company cafeteria, in employees' offices, in the parking lot, in restaurants, and at trade shows. Job opportunities, who is being considered for a big promotion, the likelihood of downsizing, the features of a competitor's new product, and the unethical behavior of a manager are typical topics on the grapevine.

Informal communication can be a source of creative ideas. Sun Microsystems, a Silicon Valley manufacturer of computer workstations, schedules occasional Friday afternoon parties so that technical employees can visit with business-oriented employees. Ideas for new products sometimes start out as informal conversations over a beer.

Some gossip and rumors are harmful to employee morale. If employees fear that the company will soon downsize, rumors that exaggerate the true state of affairs are likely to be exchanged. This makes employees fearful of losing their jobs and negatively affects company performance. Negative rumors that disrupt employee motivation must be managed with other forms of communication.

management by wandering around (MBWA)
Dropping in unannounced at a work site and engaging employees in spontaneous conversations.

One effective way to manage rumors and misinformation is **management by wandering around (MBWA)**, dropping in unannounced at a work site and engaging employees in spontaneous conversations. MBWA can improve the level of trust between employees and management by opening up new channels of communication. Sam Walton, the founder of Wal-Mart, visited stores weekly and used MBWA to learn what front-line employees were thinking about and to see if they needed help with problems. General managers at Hewlett-Packard use MBWA to develop personal rapport with all the employees in their business units. Business units at HP contain fewer than 500 employees, to facilitate informal communication. MBWA permits the general manager to deal with potentially harmful rumors before they spread. It also helps sustain an entrepreneurial company culture that allows HP to be an innovator and technology leader. Management Close-Up 14.2 shows how companies can utilize different types of communication to develop a trusting work environment with open communications.

A pattern of informal communication that managers should be aware of occurs when employees form informal social groups called *cliques*, which may disrupt the flow of communication between employees by excluding those who are not part of the clique. Cliques form

MANAGEMENT CLOSE-UP 14.2   THEME: **ETHICS**

How Companies Communicate to Build Trust

Open communication is essential to building trust between employees and management, which leads in turn to improved sharing of information—upward, downward, and horizontally. Following are some methods that companies have used in creating a trusting environment with open communication:

1. *Communicating across borders.* Ciba Specialty Chemicals uses a satellite conference meeting to distribute its quarterly results to 5,000 employees in 14 corporate regions around the world. Employees of the specialty chemical firm can fax questions back to the board during the meeting.
2. *Using focus groups and teams to understand and resolve employee concerns.* S. C. Johnson & Son, the household cleaning goods company, holds employee focus groups and forms teams to discover and resolve issues that concern employees. The company, which employs 12,500 people around the world, also has business councils for special interest groups within the company, such as minorities, that meet and present their concerns to management.
3. *Sharing company information in meetings.* Family-owned industrial valve and seal manufacturer A. W. Chesterton holds quarterly meetings with its employees, and CEO Jim Chesterton answers questions. The company's departments, divisions, and subsidiaries also meet regularly and exchange information openly.
4. *Using a bulletin board for suggestions.* Dana Corporation employees are encouraged to post two suggestions a month on the company's bulletin board. Other workers add comments to them, and 80 percent of them are then implemented or acted on. The suggestions help the industrial manufacturer understand employee concerns and also provide valuable input for improving quality.

Source: Based on J. C. McCune, "That Elusive Thing Called Trust," *Management Review,* July/August 1998, pp. 10–16; S. Covey, "How the Best Leaders Build Trust," *Leadership Now,* 2009, www.leadershipnow.com; M. Raisanen, "How Brands Can Build Trust Among Consumers," *iMedia Connection,* 2010, www.imediaconnection.com.

LOC-In 6 **Learning Objective Check-In**

1. Serena is a sales manager who likes to stay in close proximity to all the sales representatives so she is available to help them as problems arise. She likes to put the sales reps at ease and make sure they know she is available by dropping in on them unannounced and engaging in spontaneous conversations with them. This reminds them that she is always there to help and that it is all right to have casual conversation with her about their needs and concerns. This method of communication is called _____.
   a. using the grapevine
   b. management by wandering around (MBWA)
   c. formal communication
   d. a low-richness method

---

because of friendships between employees, who are often similar to each other, which can result in the exclusion of those are are different in age, race, gender, or ethnicity. You may have seen cliques in your high school days when athletes ate lunch at one table and intellectual students ate lunch at a different table and neither group mixed with the other. The social tension between the members of the clique and the excluded employees can negatively affect team or unit performance.[7] One constructive way to deal with a clique once it is proven to be disruptive to employee morale is to reassign employees within the clique to different projects where they can form new working relationships with diverse members of the organization. Company-sponsored social events may also open up new channels of communication so that more information is shared, which may reduce some of the ways cliques block the sharing of information.

■ Communication Skills

One of the best ways to ensure effective communication is to provide opportunities for employees to develop communication skills. Skill in sending and receiving messages greatly reduces the possibility that a distorted message will be transmitted. Four key communication skills are assertive communication skills, presentation skills, nonverbal communication skills, and listening skills.

Assertive Communication Skills

Assertive communication skills enable an individual to communicate in ways that meet her or his own needs while at the same time respecting the needs and rights of others. A person who displays these skills states exactly what is wanted or needed from individuals being targeted for the message. The communicator holds himself or herself personally accountable for meeting needs. At the same time, the individual respects the needs of others and does not intrude or act childishly or manipulatively. Speaking calmly, directly, and confidently without instilling fear or anger in the other person is being assertive. The goal is to respond directly and outwardly to a problem.

A person who communicates assertively sticks to the facts, and does not communicate in a critical, subjective way. Assertive communication involves giving facts, feedback or information that makes clear the communicator's wishes, needs, wants, beliefs, or feelings. Here are some examples of speaking directly in a factual manner:[8]

- "I would like you here by eight o'clock."
- "I am quite pleased with the way the situation has been resolved."

Assertive communication includes obtaining honest feedback from others. The individual will ask direct questions or make direct statements to find out the other person's views, needs, wants, and feelings to make sure there is no misunderstanding between the two parties. Here are some examples of ways to receive direct feedback:

- "What would you prefer to do?"
- "I would like to hear your views on this."
- "What are the pros and cons on this idea from your point of view?"

passive communication
Style of communication whereby
individual does not let others know
directly what he or she wants or
needs.

aggressive communication
A forceful style of communication
with others that expresses
dominance and even anger. The
needs and wants of others are
ignored.

**passive-aggressive
communication**
Style of communication whereby
individual avoids giving direct
responses to other's requests or
feedback.

There are several less effective communication styles that people use in the workplace. This is because the communicator is either indirect or is not mindful of the needs of others or of her or his own needs. These dysfunctional communication styles include: (1) passive, (2) aggressive, and (3) passive-aggressive communication.[9] An individual who engages in **passive communication** does not let others know directly what he or she wants or needs. A passive communicator hopes that his or her needs will be met without asking. Others are expected to figure out what is needed, and, if they fail, the passive communicator becomes resentful and pouts. Passive communicators often worry about what others think about them. They do not disclose their feelings or needs for fear of offending others. Not surprisingly, passive communicators are often frustrated and moody, making them difficult to work with.

An **aggressive communication** style is a forceful approach to communicate with others that expresses dominance and even anger. An aggressive communicator ignores the needs and rights of others, and loudly proclaims what he or she wants. The aggressive communicator may coerce others by using threatening words until he or she gets what is wanted. The individual who uses this style intimidates others. The cost is damage to relationships with others, who are not likely to trust an aggressive communicator. In the long run, others begin to resent and avoid the aggressive communicator.

A **passive-aggressive communication** style avoids giving direct responses to others' requests or feedback. Instead the passive-aggressive communicator tries to "get even" with others later for real or imagined injustices. This individual fears giving direct feedback to others for the same reasons that the passive communicator does. On the other hand, the passive-aggressive communicator uses sarcasm, sniping, and indirect criticism to express anger and aggression. Often the passive-aggressive communicator manipulates others by playing on their fears or insecurities to obtain what is wanted or needed. Needless to say, passive-aggressive communication is dishonest and does not foster positive working relationships.

If a person becomes aware of a tendency to communicate in one of these three dysfunctional styles, he or she should learn and practice honest, assertive communication skills.

Presentation Skills

Presentation skills are critical in almost every job. Salespeople must present products in convincing ways to potential clients. Engineers need to present ideas persuasively to the managers who control funding. Managers must present performance results to executives, and team members may need to present ideas for quality improvement at staff meetings. Managers and team leaders often need to persuade the team or employees to do something or to accept a new policy. Basic guidelines for developing effective presentation skills include the following:

- *Prepare objectives* for your presentation. Know what you want the audience to do. Do you want them to buy a product? Invest in a new technology? Implement a new policy that controls travel expenses?
- *Organize the presentation* into several key ideas, no more than five, that will persuade the audience to act in the way you want them to. Organize your ideas in a logical sequence based on the relative importance of each idea. Use a mix of information to support your ideas, including publications, statistics, quotes from famous people, and personal anecdotes that you share with the audience.
- *Structure the presentation* into three parts: introduction, body, and conclusion. The *introduction* tells the audience what the presentation is about and what benefits they should get out of it. It should begin with a good opening, such as a story or declarative statement that grabs the audience's attention and sustains it through the rest of the presentation. The *body* is the main message and idea of the presentation. The *conclusion* summarizes the key takeaway points that the speaker wants to emphasize so that the audience will be persuaded to act.
- *Tailor the presentation* to the needs of the audience. Find out in advance who will be attending the meeting, anticipate the motivations and interests of the audience, and design the presentation to meet some of those needs and interests.
- *Establish your credibility* if the audience is not familiar with your credentials. An effective leader will introduce the speaker to establish the speaker's credentials.

- *Speak in a responsive and conversational style* that engages listeners. Nobody wants to hear a speaker read aloud or make a programmed presentation that sounds like it was memorized. Treat the audience as if you developed the presentation just for their benefit.

- *Use visual aids* such as overhead slides, charts, exhibits, or colorful posters that reinforce the verbal message. Computer programs that combine text, graphics, and color to make overhead slides are a basic part of the professional's toolkit.

- *Check your technology* ahead of time to make sure it works and assure that you know how to use it. For example, electronic devices that operate in North American that operate on 110 volts need a conversion mechanism to operate on the electric current in Europe, which has a 220 volt standard.

- *Practice your presentation skills,* which, as all performance skills, improve with effort and practice. Look for opportunities to make presentations and receive feedback. Making a presentation to a school group or a social organization or teaching a class is a good way to get additional experience.

- *Restate the key ideas* you want the audience to remember when concluding the presentation. Summarize the objectives and purpose of the talk. End the presentation with an audience appeal for action if appropriate. Also, it is always a good idea to leave some extra time at the end of the presentation for answering questions. This lets the speaker clarify any misunderstandings that members of the audience may have had concerning the message the speaker wants them to receive.

Management Is Everyone's Business 14.2 provides some suggestions on how to tell a story that makes a strong connection between the speaker and the audience so that they want to give their full attention to the presentation.

Nonverbal Communication Skills

Effective communication involves more than words. **Nonverbal communication** is sending and decoding messages with emotional content. Friendliness, respect, acceptance, rejection,

nonverbal communication
The sending and decoding of messages with emotional content. Important dimensions include body movements and gestures, eye contact, touch, facial expressions, physical closeness, and tone of voice.

MANAGEMENT IS EVERYONE'S BUSINESS   14.2

WORKING AS AN INDIVIDUAL   When speaking to an audience and attempting to persuade them to do something, it can be effective to start your presentation with a story that communicates to the listeners who you are and what you stand for. The story can be a true experience taken from your career or life that reveals to the listeners some of your strengths and perhaps also discloses a weakness or vulnerability so that you can be perceived as a sincere and authentic speaker. The punchline or takeaway point of the story should help propel the rest of your presentation in the direction you plan to go so that the audience wants to know more about what you have to tell them and learn more about who you are as a speaker. Here are some points to consider when telling a story to an audience:

- Get out from behind the podium or other props that separate you from the listeners. By removing barriers between you and the audience you can create a more intimate tone for your story so that your audience feels more engaged.
- Make eye contact with listeners to better connect with them. Use hand gestures and facial expressions to accent key points of the story.
- Raise and lower your voice appropriately to vary the pace of the story so that listeners remain alert. Avoid speaking to them in a monotone.
- Keep your storytelling focused, simple, and clear. Most stories can be told within five minutes or less. Overly long stories with many details lose the audience as well as the point of the story.
- Be authentic. Since the best storytellers talk from their hearts, do not try to fake an emotion that you do not feel. Your listeners will probably see through this, and your story will not connect with your audience.

Source: Based on S. Denning, *The Leader's Guide to Storytelling* (San Francisco: Jossey-Bass, 2005), pp. 12–18; H. Forest, "Effective Storytelling Performance Skills," *Story Arts*, 2000, www.storyarts.org; A. Simmons, "Business Story Telling, *Mind Tools*, 2010, www.mindtools.com.

By having a forward leaning posture and making direct eye contact with a speaker (photo on far left), one conveys attentiveness to the other person.

dominance, submissiveness, anger, fear, and humor are conveyed primarily by nonverbal signals. When the verbal and nonverbal messages disagree, the receiver is likely to discount the verbal message and believe the nonverbal message. For example, a sender who verbally promises to act in good faith but does not make eye contact and keeps glancing at a wristwatch is indicating lack of respect for the receiver. Important dimensions of nonverbal communication include body movements and gestures, eye contact, touch, facial expressions, physical closeness, and tone of voice.

BODY MOVEMENTS AND GESTURES Posture can indicate attentiveness or lack of interest in a conversation. In a job interview, an interviewee should lean slightly forward to indicate that he or she is attentive to the interviewer. Gestures can add or detract from the verbal message. Hand gestures help emphasize points, but fidgeting sends the message that the speaker is nervous and lacks confidence. Different cultures place different meanings on gestures. In the United States, holding the thumb and first finger in a circle means OK. In Brazil it is an insult and may provoke a fight.

EYE CONTACT Attentiveness or lack of interest on the part of the sender or receiver in face-to-face communication is conveyed by eye contact. In business communication, it is important for both parties to make some eye contact, but prolonged eye contact may be interpreted as aggressiveness or inappropriate intimacy. Use eye contact carefully in business conversations.

TOUCH A firm handshake is an enthusiastic greeting, but a weak handshake sends a negative signal, indicating low enthusiasm. Touch signals liking, acceptance, and friendship. Even more than eye contact, touch should be used sparingly in business situations. Unwanted touching in the U.S. workplace is a form of sexual harassment. Some other cultures are more permissive about touching. For example, in France it is not uncommon for employees who are good friends to greet each other with a kiss on the cheek.

FACIAL EXPRESSIONS Emotions such as happiness, satisfaction, anger, fear, and confusion are signaled by facial expressions. A confused look is feedback that the verbal message was not clearly received. Smiling conveys happiness and warmth. Along with the handshake, a smile is probably one of the most effective ways to establish a positive connection with a new acquaintance.

PHYSICAL DISTANCE Individuals regulate the physical distance between themselves and others, reserving the smallest distance (from touching to two feet away) for close, intimate friends and

SKILLS FOR MANAGING 14.2

Nonverbal Communication

Most nonverbal communication deals with feelings. Although feelings may be hidden, they are typically very potent. This exercise illustrates common nonverbal signals and explores their potency compared to verbal communication.

Form groups of four to five students. Each team works together as follows.

1. Each member of the group writes down three feelings ("happy," "irritated," and so on).
2. Each group member takes a turn trying to communicate nonverbally one of the feelings to the rest of the group. After about a minute, group members guess at the feeling. After each person's turn, he or she records how many group members guessed the correct feeling.
3. The entire class then reviews the overall level of accuracy and briefly discusses the typical accuracy of nonverbal communication.
4. In the small groups, again, step 2 is repeated except that while the person is giving the nonverbal message, he or

she also gives a different verbal message. (The verbal message need not be opposite to the nonverbal, but it must be different.)
5. The entire class group discusses the difference between the two nonverbal communication approaches.

Discussion Questions

1. How accurately were people able to understand the first round of nonverbal signals? Were more subtle or less common feelings harder to identify?
2. What happened to the level of accuracy when a different verbal signal was present?
3. When you see this happen in a real situation—different verbal and nonverbal messages are sent—which are you most likely to believe? Why?

Source: From *Organizational Behavior* by Sashkin and Morris. Copyright © 1984. Reprinted by permission of Pearson Education, Inc., Upper Saddle River, NJ.

family, and the greatest distance (4 to 12 feet) for business and casual social acquaintances.[10] Violating an individual's expectations of an appropriate social distance causes discomfort and high probability of a miscommunication.

Physical distance expectations vary between cultures. Some cultures permit closer physical distances than others. Venezuelans have much smaller distance zones for business acquaintances than U.S. workers and might consider it rude if one backs away. A public speaker who understands how to use physical distance can create a strong bond with the audience. Oprah Winfrey, the television talk show host, bonds with her audience by reducing physical distance and going into the audience to speak with audience members up close.

TONE OF VOICE Emotions such as attentiveness, friendliness, anger, or fear are transmitted by the tone in a voice. Aspects of the tone of voice that communicate different emotional states include pitch, loudness, speed, clarity of speech, and inflection. In a business setting, it is important to communicate confidence in order to establish credibility Therefore, it is a good practice to speak clearly, emphasize key words, and use variable speed and inflection at appropriate times to keep the audience interested. Avoid talking in a monotone, which conveys lack of interest to the audience and reduces their motivation to listen. The Skills for Managing 14.2 gives you an opportunity to improve your ability to understand nonverbal communication.

Listening Skills

Listening is a fundamental communication skill for understanding both the verbal content and the underlying feelings embedded in the message. Listening is an active, not a passive, activity. It requires the listener to be involved in the communication process. The listener should try to avoid judging the speaker or the message being given. Instead, the listener should focus attention on trying to understand the content of the message. An active listener indicates both verbally and nonverbally that he or she is engaged in the conversation. When the speaker is communicating a feeling, the listener can restate what the speaker is expressing, asking for confirmation. The speaker will either confirm the impression or clarify it. In either case, the speaker will be encouraged to continue the conversation. Also, by using nonverbal indicators of listening—making eye contact, nodding the head, and leaning forward, for example—the listener is encouraging the speaker to continue. Lack of feedback from the listener can discourage the speaker from sharing opinions or feelings. Passively listening may unintentionally short-circuit a conversation.

When listening to another person, the speaker's tone of voice often discloses his or her emotional state, which helps the listener understand the feelings behind the words. Aspects of the speaker's tone of voice to listen for include the pitch, loudness, and speed of the verbal message. By decoding the meaning of the speaker's tone of voice, the listener can provide feedback to the speaker that can improve the quality of communication between the two parties. Here are some examples of how to interpret and respond to a speaker's tone of voice.

- If a speaker's pitch of voice is high and strained, it indicates feelings of nervousness. A calm, reassuring response from the listener encourages the speaker to proceed speaking. On the other hand, a quick, jerky response from the listener may cut the speaker short and disrupt the speaker's train of thought. Speaking in a lower pitch that is unstrained indicates the speaker is feeling confident and has emotional composure.
- If the speaker's tone of voice is shaky and hesitant with numerous pauses, it indicates a lack of confidence and doubt. By maintaining eye contact and offering reassuring gestures such as nodding one's head, the listener encourages the speaker to go on and complete the message.
- When the speaker's voice is too loud, or on the other hand the speaker mumbles the words quietly, the listener will have difficulty understanding the message. In either case the listener has a duty to ask the speaker to reduce or increase the voice volume depending on the situation. If the speaker's voice is too loud, the listener should calmly ask the speaker to reduce the volume to a more comfortable level. This should be done in a nonjudgmental way. If the speaker speaks too softly and mumbles, making it difficult to hear the words, the listener should ask the speaker to increase the volume. In both instances the focus should be on conveying the desire to understand the speaker.

Listening is an invaluable skill for managers. By actively listening to another individual, the manager shows empathy for and understanding of the speaker's perspective, even if it is different from the manager's own position. This is critical when managers negotiate with each other or with customers to find solutions acceptable to both parties. Employees or other managers are unlikely to bring problems to managers who have weak listening skills. This is likely to undermine a manager's credibility and limit effectiveness. Manager's Notebook 14.3 presents specific ways to improve active listening skills. Management Is Everyone's Business 14.3 explains how a manager can apply listening skills to deal with an employee who is experiencing an emotionally sensitive problem.

MANAGER'S NOTEBOOK 14.3

Guidelines for Active Listening

You can show a speaker you are actively listening to the ideas and feelings that are being communicated by observing the following dos and don'ts.

Do create a supportive atmosphere.

Do listen for feelings as well as words.

Do note cues, such as gestures, tone of voice, and body posture.

Do occasionally test for understanding by asking, "Is this what you mean?"

Do demonstrate acceptance and understanding verbally and nonverbally.

Do ask exploratory, open-ended questions.

Do switch off cell phones, pagers, the television, and other sources of distraction.

Don't try to change the other's views.

Don't solve the problem for the speaker.

Don't give advice, no matter how obvious the solution may seem.

Don't pass judgment.

Don't explain or interpret others' behavior.

Don't give false reassurances.

Don't attack if the speaker is hostile to you (try to understand the source of any anger).

Don't ask questions about the "why" of feelings.

Don't check e-mail while listening to a speaker.

Source: Based on A. Cohen and S. Fink, *Effective Behavior in Organizations*, 7th ed. (Boston: McGraw-Hill Irwin, 2001); G. Kranz, *Communicating Effectively* (New York: HarperCollins, 2007); S. Boyd, "Tips to Improve Your Listening Ability," *School for Champions*, October 20, 2004, www.school-for-champions.com.

MANAGEMENT IS EVERYONE'S BUSINESS 14.3

WORKING AS A MANAGER As a manager you are occasionally likely to deal with an employee who has a problem that is highly sensitive or emotional in nature. This is the time to use your listening skills.

- First, seek to understand the nature of the problem and the perspective of the employee before telling him or her what you think about the issue or passing judgment on it. Hearing the employee out lets the person know that you are being supportive and are concerned.
- The use of listening skills lets you understand the problem from the employee's perspective so that both of you can develop a mutually beneficial solution.
- If it is necessary to give critical or negative feedback, make sure that the behavior being criticized is one that the employee is able to control. There is little value in communicating a shortcoming to a person if he or she has no control over it.
- For example, a dyslexic employee might have difficulty writing memos that are free of spelling errors. Rather than criticizing the dyslexic employee's spelling skills, a manager could encourage the employee to use the spell-checking function on a computer before distributing memos. The dyslexic employee is better able to control the spell-checking function on the computer than to correctly spell all the words in a written message.

CONCLUDING THOUGHTS

After the introductory vignette at the beginning of the chapter we presented some critical thinking questions related to the practice of using broadband communications technology to enable home workers to provide customer support services via the Internet. Now that you have had the opportunity to learn about managing communication in the chapter, let's discuss the critical thinking questions. First, one of the advantages of using home workers who respond to customer inquiries is that it opens up opportunities for workers who are highly educated, have chosen to be at home for their children, or other family members, yet have valuable skills that employers can put to good use. Home workers usually serve customers better at a lower cost than onsite call center employees, who tend to be younger, less educated, and less reliable. Home workers are more motivated and productive because they can combine work and family responsibilities without the role conflicts of traditional jobs and their inflexible schedule of work on the company premises.

Second, companies must deal with some challenges when managing employees who work at home. Supervising, coaching, and mentoring home workers can be difficult to do well. While the customer service work of home workers can be monitored electronically and corrected, an employee's need for coaching and feedback to improve performance may require face-to-face communication that can be difficult to schedule if an employee lives far from the company office. A home worker can feel isloated and detached from the company if there is no opportunity to interact with other employees. Occasional meetings organized by the company where home workers can share ideas and best practices with each other could help reduce feelings of isolation and detachment as well as improve their job skills.

FOCUSING ON THE FUTURE: Using Management Theory in Daily Life

Managing Communication

At first, you might not think that a chief financial officer would put a lot of emphasis on communication, but Todd S. Thomson, formerly the CFO of Citigroup, and now the CEO of its Global Wealth Management Division, sees communication as one of the three most critical parts of the CFO's job. Todd not only knows the power of communication for himself, but he used his knowledge of communication theory to transform the way information flowed throughout Citigroup,

In an interview with Michael Useem, the director of the Wharton Center for Leadership and Change Management, Todd suggests that there are three essential roles for a CFO. The first is to act as the "conscience of the organization"—the CFO is responsible for making sure the finances of the company are handled in the best interests of the shareholders. The second is to make sure that costs are reined in—that the organization is spending money on things that will pay off, not just on "good ideas." Finally, and perhaps most importantly, the CFO needs to be sure that he or she is "bringing the right information to the right people at the right time to make the right decisions."

Todd's communication strategy revolves around facts—identifying them, analyzing them, and getting them where they will do the most good. He recognizes the importance of horizontal, downward, and upward communication. Senior managers at Citibank engage in horizontal communication every week when they gather for their "business heads" meeting. The result of their weekly communication session is a "management information report." That report is used every week for downward communication, and it carries important messages to managers at lower levels of the organization. The emphasis of the report changes from week to week—one week it might be about cross-selling, and the next it might present an expense analysis—but the report always gives managers the information they need to assess and improve their department's performance, and it gives them a direction to emphasize in their activities for the week.

Todd places as much emphasis on upward communication as he does on downward communication. Quarterly conference calls and an annual gathering ensure that his employees have a time and space for upward communication. Like the downward communication from the business heads meeting, all information Todd gets from his employees is expected to be based on facts, not opinion. If an employee brings opinions to Thomson, he or she is sent back to "do their homework," and told to return with facts. Employees who cannot produce specific details after getting this kind of feedback do not last long in the organization.

By focusing all communications on facts, Todd is attempting to minimize both receiver and perception barriers. Todd knows his audience, and he recognizes and respects their need for getting crucial information in a form that supports business decision making. He knows that an impassioned plea will hold less weight with CEOs than a logical argument supported by detailed information. At the same time, he knows that too much irrelevant detail can also derail a presentation or report. For these reasons, he makes sure that his communications are models of targeted reporting—they focus on specific business issues, and use facts to drive discussion.

Todd further reduces receiver barriers by tailoring his presentations to his audience. For example, in the past he worked with two Citigroup CEOs who had very different styles—Sandy Weill and Charles Prince. As he explains it,

> Sandy is a "people person" and tends to manage through people. Sandy would wander around into offices—including mine—on a regular basis, and we would sit down and start talking about the business. Chuck tends to structure more formal reviews as opposed to informal discussions.

By understanding the style of each CEO and giving them information in their preferred format, Todd Thomson was able to build a good working relationship with both of them.

Useem notes that Thomson's latest job change (moving from CFO to CEO) involved a huge leap. The amount of money alone is staggering—as CFO, Todd was responsible for managing annual revenues of over $100 billion, but as CEO, he is responsible for over one *trillion* dollars worth of revenues. Likewise, the number of employees supervised jumped—from 6,000 under the CFO to 30,000 as CEO. How, then, did Todd approach such a challenging assignment?

Todd's response emphasizes another aspect of communication—listening. He points out that both jobs require one thing—getting people to believe in your vision for the company and motivating them to take action to make the vision reality. This process starts with listening—meeting people, getting them to tell you what they know about the business, and probing them for information about opportunities and issues. It is only after he has heard what his employees have to say that Thomson sets out his expectations for where the business will go and presents a strategy for getting there. The result, in his words, is,

> I find that people will follow that kind of direction. They appreciate the fact that you are listening, the fact that you set your expectations out very clearly up front, and that you have taken some time to put a strategy in place and communicate it.

Source: Based on Knowledge@Wharton, "The CFO as Company Conscience," http://leadership.wharton.upenn.edu/digest/05-05.shtml, accessed May 7, 2006; "Mastering the Four Key CFO's Roles," *Financial Executive*, July 1, 2007, www.thefreelibrary.com; R. Bacal, "Internal Communication Strategies," *Performance Management & Appraisal Help Center*, 2010, www.performance-appraisals.org.

Summary of Learning Objectives

Communication is the process of transmitting information from one party to another through the use of shared symbols. The information may take the form of facts, objective information, or feelings. This chapter's discussion will help future managers, teams, and employees better understand the importance of managing communication. The discussion in this chapter that meets each of the learning objectives set out at the start of the chapter is summarized below.

1 Understand the communication process.

- The process of communication includes a **sender** and a **receiver**. The sender encodes the message in symbols and the receiver must decode the message to receive the intended meaning.
- The sender selects a **communication channel** that can vary from rich to lean in terms of the amount of content that can be transmitted. Communication channels include face-to-face conversations, written memos, videotapes, and voice mail.
- Communication channels that provide feedback should be utilized when the content of the message is complex and important. **Noise** may interfere with the receiver's ability to accurately decode the message. Communication channels with **feedback** provisions can reduce the threat of noise-distorted messages.

2 Eliminate barriers that distort the meaning of information.

- Differences in employee status and power, diversity, and self-interest create communication barriers that must be managed for effective organizational communication to take place.
- An organization that designs a communication system with multiple communication channels and that develops communication channels that provide opportunities for feedback help the sender to clarify whether the message's content was accurately received by the receiver, which can reduce barriers to communication.

3 Recognize the basic patterns of organizational communication.
    Patterns of communication in organizations include:

- **Downward communication** in which the sender is at a high level in the organization and the receiver is at a lower level.
- **Upward communication** in which the sender is at a lower level in the organization and the receiver is at a higher level.
- **Horizontal communication** in which both the sender and receiver in the organization are at similar levels.

4 Understand how to organize and run effective meetings.
    Some ways to make meetings more effective include the following practices:

- Make sure there is a good reason for a meeting. If one can use other ways to communicate that can be substituted for a meeting such as a memo, do not schedule a meeting.
- Select a meeting place that allows everyone to hear each other and the speaker.
- Create a meeting agenda and distribute it in advance of the meeting so that everyone knows what topics the meeting will cover.
- Keep the meeting on time so that all the agenda topics are covered and if possible leave some time to cover other topics that may not be on the agenda.
- End the meeting with a plan of action.

5 Master electronic forms of communication.

Electronic forms of communication such as e-mail let employees exchange text messages and documents coded into digital symbols and transmitted over the Internet. Employees should use good judgment in deciding what kinds of messages to send with electronic communication.

- Messages with highly emotional content have a better chance of being accurately received with face-to-face communication, which provides a richer channel for sending emotional content.
- Messages that have content that is of a highly sensitive, controversial, or personal nature should not be sent over electronic communication channels because the employer has the legal right to monitor electronic communications and hold an employee responsible for the content that is sent.

6 Work with an organization's informal communication system.

Informal communication occurs in organizations when there are gaps in or barriers to formal communication and employees do not receive the information they desire.

- An effective way to work with an organization's informal communication system is with the application of **management by wandering around (MBWA),** which consists of dropping in unannounced at a work site or office to engage in spontaneous conversations with employees. MBWA can open new channels of communication between managers and employees and can also help to dispel rumors and gossip that may be harmful to employee morale.

Discussion Questions

1. Why is it important for a communication channel to have provisions for feedback? Can you think of a situation in which it may be useful to have communication without any provisions for feedback? Describe this situation.
2. What communication barriers could distort the communication between you and your professor? What are some approaches you could use to overcome these communication barriers?
3. Why are organizations today placing a greater emphasis on horizontal communications?
4. Is e-mail superior to older forms of electronic communications such as the telephone or voice mail? What are the advantages of e-mail? What are the disadvantages of e-mail? How can we manage a large volume of e-mail messages so that we are not spending too much time responding to messages each day?
5. Assume you are a manager and you overhear two employees exchanging harmful gossip about the personal life of another employee. Why do employees gossip and spread rumors about each other? How can this type of informal communication be managed? How would you handle this situation?
6. As a team leader, suppose one of the employees on your team has poor listening skills and continuously interrupts others who are speaking, becoming a source of frustration for the other team members. How would you improve this situation?
7. Research shows that in a job interview, the interviewer is likely to be strongly influenced by first impressions of the interviewee. In many cases a decision is made within the first minute of the interview. Assuming you want to make a positive impression in a job interview, how would you communicate nonverbally to create a favorable impression?
8. What is the difference between communicating assertively and communicating aggressively?

Management Minicase 14.1

Employee Blogs Are Becoming the New Virtual Watercooler

A recent trend in communications is the rapid proliferation of employee blogs, which are Web sites that let employees voice their opinions and feelings about the company where they are employed. Employees offer opinions on the blog that would not be possible on official company communication channels such as newsletters or the company e-mail system. Because the blogs are stored on the Internet, employees can express controversial opinions and remain anonymous.

A proprietor of a blog called Mini-Microsoft has been a thorn in the side of the giant software company by posting a stream of anonymous critiques of the company, the employer of the blogger. The blog pulls no punches, calling Microsoft a "passionless, process-ridden, lumbering idiot" in a recent posting. Yet the blog is also chock full of humor, intelligence, and earnest suggestions for fixing Microsoft.

While Mini-Microsoft is just one among an estimated 2,000 blogs operated by Microsoft employees, it has become a virtual watercooler for employees. Hundreds anonymously vent their frustrations there without fear of retribution. Mini has emerged as something of a folk hero. Visitors to the site and other bloggers describe Mini as both the employee most likely to save Microsoft—and most likely to be fired. Mini-Microsoft provides a fascinating example of a phenomenon that is sweeping the nation. Employee bloggers are shining a bright light on the inner workings of their companies and thrusting all sorts of bottled-up frustrations out in the open. Whispered conversations suddenly become broadcast publicly. That puts newly found power in the hands of employees for doing either good or ill to their employer. Analyst Charlene Li of Forrester Research advises companies not to try to suppress their bloggers. "You can keep it hidden, or get those voices out there and deal with the problem," she says.

There are limits to what an employee can share in a blog, however. Posting confidential employer information on a blog such as trade secrets, business strategies, or private personnel information can be prohibited by state and federal laws that protect employer rights to intellectual property and employee rights to privacy.

DISCUSSION QUESTIONS

1. Do you agree with the advice of the analyst from Forrester Research in the case who said that companies should not try to suppress bloggers? Justify your opinion.
2. What benefits can a company derive from the information posted on employee blogs by monitoring them at regular intervals?
3. Why do you think the Mini-Microsoft blog is so influential both inside and outside the company?

Sources: Based on J. Greene, "Mystery Blogger: A Rendezvous withi Microsoft's Deep Throat," *BusinessWeek,* September 26, 2005, p. 104; *The Economist,* "Blogging: Outreach and Outrage," March 11, 2006, p. 77; N. Vonk,. "A Blogger's Guide to Blogging," *Campaign,* February 17, 2006, pp. 28–29; C. Wilson, "The Blogger at Work," *T+D,* March 2006, p. 15; V. Crittenden and K. Klepper, "Social Media and the B-School," *BizEd,* May/June, 2010, pp. 72–73.

Management Minicase 14.2

Actions Speak Louder than Words All Around the World

"He wouldn't look me in the eye. I found it disconcerting that he kept looking all over the room but rarely at me," said Barbara Walters after her interview with Libya's Colonel Muamar el-Qaddafi. Like many people in the United States, Walters was associating eye contact with trustworthiness, so when Qaddafi did not make eye contact, she felt uncomfortable. In fact, Qaddafi was paying Walters a compliment. In Libya, *not* looking conveys respect. Looking straight at a woman is considered nearly as serious as physical assault.

Nonverbal communication varies widely between cultures and even between subcultures. The differences strongly affect communication in the workplace. Whether you are trying to communicate with a new Asian-American assistant, the Swedish managers who recently bought your company, the young African American college student who won a summer internship with your firm, or representatives from the French company you hope will buy your firm's new designs, your efforts will depend as much on physical cues as on verbal ones. Most Americans aren't usually aware of their own nonverbal behaviors. They have trouble understanding the body language of people from other cultures. The list of differences is endless:

- In Thailand it is rude to place your arm over the back of a chair in which another person is sitting.
- Finnish female students are horrified by Arab girls who want to walk hand in hand with them.
- Canadian listeners nod to signal agreement.
- Japanese listeners nod to indicate only that they have understood.
- British listeners stare at the speaker, blinking their eyes to indicate understanding.
- People in the United States are taught that it's impolite to stare.
- Saudis accept foreigners in Western business attire but are offended by tight-fitting clothing and by short sleeves.
- Spaniards indicate a receptive friendly handshake by clasping the other person's forearm to form a double handshake.
- Canadians consider touching any part of the arm above the hand intrusive, except in intimate relationships.
- The British and Americans wait patiently in line at a government office or a bank while the French practice line jumping as a way to improve their place in a line.
- People in Iran are expected to remove their shoes when entering a home or a mosque.
- In China, hosts will often refuse a gift many times before they accept it, and this is proper.

It may take years to understand nonverbal communication in other cultures, but there are resources to help you prepare. Books and seminars on cultural differences are readily available, as are motion pictures showing a wide range of cultures. You can always rent videos of films and TV shows from other countries. Examining the illustrations in news and business magazines can give you an idea of expected business dress and personal space. Finally, remaining flexible and interacting with people from other cultures who are visiting or living in your country will go a long way toward lowering the barriers presented by nonverbal communication.

DISCUSSION QUESTIONS

1. Explain how watching a movie from another country might help you prepare to correctly interpret nonverbal behavior from that culture.
2. Assume that one of your co-workers is originally from Saudi Arabia. You like him, and the two of you work well together. However, he stands so close when you speak with him that it makes you very uncomfortable. How would you communicate your discomfort to this co-worker?

Source: Based on C. Bovée and J. Thill, *Business Communication Today,* 6th ed. Upper Saddle River, NJ: Prentice Hall, 2000, p. 38; M. Le Baron, "Cross-Cultural Communication," *Beyond Intractability,* July, 2003, www.beyondintractability.org; C. Wu, "Cultural Gestures, *Tripod,* 2010, www.soc302.tripod.com.

Individual/Collaborative Learning Case 14.1
Selecting the Most Effective Form of Communication

You are a sales representative for a leading pharmaceutical company, which produces a full range of drugs for medical treatments to patients. You communicate on a regular basis with other sales representatives within and outside your sales region, the sales manager and the district manager, and many clients within your sales territory who are primarily physicians and directors of managed care health organizations. Since you work primarily out of an office in your home, you must depend heavily on electronic communication to stay in touch with customers, colleagues, and management. Here is some information about e-mail, voice mail, and fax to help you select the most appropriate electronic communication channel.

E-mail has the following advantages:
- It is fast and inexpensive and provides easy access to others.
- It facilitates communication with busy executives and managers.
- It provides documented evidence that a message was received.
- It is less intrusive than other forms of communication. Recipients can respond when time permits.
- Senders can communicate with large numbers of people quickly and simultaneously.
- It facilitates global communication where time zones create communication barriers.

E-mail also has disadvantages:
- Not all offices have e-mail.
- Some people are uncomfortable or inexperienced with e-mail.
- It may be awkward to use when the message contains emotional content or when a relationship of trust has not yet been established between the parties.
- It is not suitable for private or confidential messages.

E-mail tips:
- Check e-mail three or four times per day.
- Assume e-mail is not private.
- Check spelling and grammar, because e-mail represents you and your organization.

Voice mail has the following advantages:
- It is the most personal form of electronic communication.
- It allows the receiver to give a quick response.
- Your voice can convey sincerity that the written word cannot. It can ease a problematic situation.

Voice mail also has disadvantages:
- It can be frustrating to listen to a long prerecorded message with a menu of choices that may not apply to the caller's needs.
- It cannot replace a handwritten thank-you note.

Voice mail tips:
- Anticipate that you may be leaving a recorded message. Before you make the call, prepare what you want to say and avoid rambling.
- Avoid leaving the same message several times.
- The greeting you prepare on your own voice mail should communicate your availability and tell the caller how to reach a live person in case of an emergency.
- Avoid cute and humorous greetings.

Fax has the following advantages:
- It quickly delivers a close approximation to original documents.
- It is useful when a relationship is new or formal.
- It is sometimes important to use stationery with the company name on the letterhead.
- It is useful when a document requires a signature.

Fax also has disadvantages:
- Many people share fax machines and waiting is sometimes necessary.
- Confidential information may be disclosed because faxes can rarely be sent privately.
- Faxes sometimes get lost.

Fax tips:
- Always use a cover sheet that has your fax and telephone numbers.
- Avoid reading other employees' faxes.

CRITICAL THINKING QUESTIONS

1. You want to let the sales manager know which clients you will be visiting within your territory next week. Which communication channel would you select and why?
2. One of your clients complained about a late delivery of a shipment of drugs that was promised by a certain date. You must provide a response to the problem. Which communication channel would you select and why?
3. You will be attending the annual sales convention at Las Vegas, and while there you want to meet a colleague who works in the Australian subsidiary of your firm who will also attend the meeting. Which communication channel would you select to set up your meeting in advance and why?

COLLABORATIVE LEARNING EXERCISE

With a partner or small group, rank e-mail, voice mail, and fax from best to worst according to the following characteristics: richness of information, ease of use, availability, level of privacy, and speed of communication. Did everyone in your group agree on the rankings? What accounts for any differences in your rankings of these communication channels?

Source: Based on B. Pachter, "Tips for Technological Correctness," *HR Focus*, November 1996, p. 21; D. Brake, *Dealing with e-Mail*. London: DK, 2003; "Voice Mail Vs. Email," *Broken Perfection*, September 10, 2007, www.brokenperfection.com

Internet Exercise 14.1

Whole Foods, Whole Philosophy

www.wholefoodsmarket.com

Visit the Web site of Whole Foods Market, click on the "company" button, and explore the "whole philosophy" section, including the "core values," "quality standards," and "declaration of interdependence "sections of the company philosophy. Then answer the following questions:

1. What message does the Whole Foods Market company philosophy communicate to the consumer about the food products it sells?

2. What message does the Whole Foods Market company philosophy communicate to employees and job applicants about the work environment at the company?

3. Do the graphic and visual images on the Web site communicate the same or a different message to you as the text (the words) describing the company philosophy?

4. Suppose the text gave a different message to the reader than the visual images do. Which message would most likely be received by the reader? Explain your answer.

Manager's Checkup 14.1

Listening Self-Inventory

How good are you at listening? Using the following scale, circle the number that best indicates the extent to which you agree or disagree with each statement.

	Strongly Agree	Agree	Neither Agree or Disagree	Disagree	Strongly Disagree
1. I frequently glance at e-mail while another person is speaking to me.	1	2	3	4	5
2. I like people to speak without having their emotions affect the message they send to me.	1	2	3	4	5
3. I sometimes act as if I am paying attention when I am thinking about something else.	1	2	3	4	5
4. I am skilled at understanding the nonverbal messages people send when they speak.	1	2	3	4	5
5. I can complete a person's thoughts before they are able to finish verbally expressing them.	1	2	3	4	5
6. When a speaker bores me I focus my attention on other things besides the speaker.	1	2	3	4	5
7. I frequently use nonverbal gestures such as a smile to let the speaker know I am engaged in the conversation.	1	2	3	4	5
8. As soon as someone finishes talking I attempt to speak.	1	2	3	4	5

9. I often judge the speaker while he or she is speaking.	1	2	3	4	5
10. I often focus on what I want to say while another person is still talking.	1	2	3	4	5
11. The skill of a speaker's delivery makes it easier for me to listen to the content.	1	2	3	4	5
12. When I do not understand a speaker I ask him or her to clarify the message instead of guessing.	1	2	3	4	5
13. I put a lot of effort into understanding the speaker's perspective.	1	2	3	4	5
14. I frequently hear what I expect the speaker to say rather than the actual message.	1	2	3	4	5
15. Even when we disagree most people believe I understood their position.	1	2	3	4	5

Scoring

To obtain your score
  1. Total your responses to questions 1–3, 5–11, and 14   Enter total here: _____
  2. Reverse score (5 becomes 1; 4 becomes 2, etc.)   Enter total here: _____
     questions 4, 12, 13, and 15.
     Your overall score is the total of both partial scores.   TOTAL: _____

Analysis and Interpretation

Effective communicators have developed good listening skills. This instrument is designed to provide you with some insights into your listening skills.

Scores range from 15 to 75. The higher your score the better listener you are. While any cut-offs are essentially arbitrary, if you score 60 or above, your listening skills are fairly well honed. Scores of 40 or less indicate you need to make a serious effort at improving your listening skills.

Source: Based on F. M. Stone, *Supervisory Management*, January, 1989, New York: American Management Association.

Endnotes

1. D. Weeks, "Voice Mail: Blessing or Curse?" *World Traveler*, February 1995, pp. 51–54.

2. J. Fried, "Everything You Ever Wanted to Know about e-Mail," *Inc.*, October 2005, pp. 113–128.

3. M. Conlin, "Watch What You Put in That Office E-Mail," *BusinessWeek*, September 30, 2002, pp. 114–115.

4. P. Hemp, "Death by Information Overload," *Harvard Business Review*, September, 2009, pp. 83–89.

5. A. Wellner, "Lost in Translation," *Inc.*, September 2005, pp. 37–38.

6. D. Brake, *Dealing with e-Mail* (London: DK, 2003).

7. A. Wellner, "Playing Well with Others: Office Cliques Sap Morale and Kill Productivity. Does Your Firm Have Them?" *Inc.*, January 2005, pp. 29–31.

8. C. Osborn, *Dealing with Difficult People* (London: DK, 2001).

9. C. Price, *Assertive Communication* (Boulder, CO: Career Track, 1994).

10. M. Munter, "Cross-Cultural Communication for Managers," *Business Horizons*, May–June 1993, pp. 69–78.

15

Learning Objectives

1 Define operations management and its three stages: inputs, conversion, and disposition.

2 Describe materials requirements planning (MRP) and understand its use in operations management.

3 Be familiar with the conversion process tools of operations management, including Gantt charts, PERT networks, and statistical process control.

4 Explain the role quality management plays in the operations management process.

5 Understand and apply the principles of kaizen, just-in-time manufacturing, and kanban.

6 Describe management control and understand the importance of control systems.

7 Identify the major types of bureaucratic control.

When BP Lost Control of Its Drilling Operations in the Gulf of Mexico

"Who cares, it's done, end of story, will probably be fine." Thus, in an e-mail, a manager at BP, one of the largest oil companies in the world, wrote of the decision to use only a few "centralizers" when cementing into place the pipe that ran from an oil reservoir 13,000 feet below the sea floor of the Gulf of Mexico to Deepwater Horizon, the drilling rig floating 5,000 feet above it. The cement failed, considerably more likely with fewer centralizers, experts say, four days after the e-mail was sent on April 20, 2010. Oil and gas rushed up the well, causing an explosion and subsequent fire, which claimed the lives of 11 of the oil rig's crew of 126, and eventually sent the rig itself to the bottom of the ocean a mile below the surface and some 40 miles off the Louisiana coast.

On the sea floor beneath the Deepwater Horizon sat a device called a blowout preventer, capable of sealing off the well with a number of hydraulic systems, including one designed to slice right through the whole stack. Had it been activated beforehand, it should have been able to contain the pressure in the well, saving the rig. Activated after the blowout, it would have done nothing to save the rig but should still have been able to isolate the oil in the well from the sea above it. But neither of the two systems that should have activated the preventer after the blowout

Operations Management and Management Control

seems to have done so, or if they did, the preventer did not do its job. Oil continued to flow into the mutilated remains of the piping that had originally risen from the sea floor to the drilling platform.

In the aftermath of the explosion of the oil drilling rig, a leak in the underwater pipe gushed an estimated 4.9 million barrels of oil into the Gulf of Mexico over a period of nearly three months before the pipe was finally capped. The oil drifted to the marshes and beaches of Louisiana and neighboring states causing massive damage to the ecology of wetlands, fishing grounds, beaches, and the livelihood of thousands of people in the Gulf region. In this same period, the value of BP stock plunged by 50 percent. The cost of the cleanup and damages attributed to the oil spill that BP is expected to cover is estimated to be between $20 and $30 billion. BP subsequently announced a $7 billion sale of its assets to pay for the damages of the oil spill.

The oil spill in the Gulf of Mexico was not a unique experience for BP. In 2005 there was an explosion at one of BP's oil refineries in Texas City, Texas where 15 workers lost their lives and the company vowed to address the safety shortfalls that caused the blast. Next, in 2006 a badly maintained oil pipeline ruptured and spilled 200,000 gallons of crude oil over Alaska's North Slope, and the company once again promised to have better control of its operations. Despite these promises to improve, BP continues to lag behind other oil companies when it comes to the safe operations of its facilities, according to federal officials and industry analysts.

Sources: Based on *The Economist*, "Black Storm Rising: The Deepwater Horizon Disaster Will Affect Everyone from Pelicans to Politicians," May 8, 2010, pp. 69–71; *The Economist*, "The Oil Well and the Damage Done: BP Counts the Political and Financial Cost of Deepwater Horizon," June 19, 2010, pp. 65–67; J. Mouawad, "Fast-growing BP Also Has a Mounting List of Spills and Safety Lapses," *The New York Times*, May 6, 2010, p. A18; *The Economist*, "After the Leak: The Gusher in the Gulf May Soon Be Sealed. BP's Woes Will Be Harder to Cap," July 24, 2010, pp. 62–64; J. Gillis and L. Kaufman, "Oil Spill Calculations Stir Debate on Damage," *The New York Times*, August, 5, 2010, p. A16.

CRITICAL THINKING QUESTIONS

1. *Which of the three stages of operations management at BP were lacking in control based on its recent record of accidents and oil spills?*

2. *Which type of management control—feedforward, concurrent, or feedback—would be most beneficial to apply to an undersea drilling process similar to the BP oil rig and pipeline in the Gulf of Mexico?*

We will revisit these questions at the end of the chapter in our Concluding Thoughts after you have read the following pages on operations management and control management.

The heart and soul of many business operations is the production process. A new technique, such as kaizen, can greatly improve a firm's ability to deliver high quality products at a lower cost in a shorter amount of time. This chapter describes operations management methods for controlling production inputs and production processes. It also covers the concept of management control and reviews the major types of control that are used by managers.

■ What Is Operations Management?

Many organizations, both for-profit and not-for-profit, provide a product—whether a good, a service, or both. General Motors provides automobiles to its dealers, libraries provide books, and online databases provide information.

operations management
The process an organization uses to obtain the materials or ideas, the process of transforming them into the product, and the process of providing the final product to a user.

Operations management is the process an organization uses to obtain the materials or ideas, the process of transforming them into the product, and the process of providing the final product to a user. Operations management principles can be applied to a variety of departments within an organization. Typically, however, operations management refers to the firm's main product.

Operations management is closely tied to strategic management (Chapter 7) and to planning (Chapter 5).

Three Stages of Operations

Operations management consists of three stages, as shown in Figure 15.1:

1. Acquiring inputs (the materials or ideas).
2. Controlling the conversion processes (transforming the materials or ideas into the organization's products).
3. Delivering the output (providing the organization's product to the user).

Although these stages are listed separately, they are highly interrelated. The inputs a firm acquires are influenced by the production process that is available as well as by refinements based on the customers' feedback. The production process is influenced by the type of inputs, such as skilled labor, that are available. Finally, the disposition of the product is influenced by the cost of production: What market can it be priced to? And how will the good or service be distributed and delivered to customers?

Planning

The foundation of operations management is **planning**. Planning typically begins with identifying the organization's customers and their needs. Market research helps company leaders target specific groups for its product. By determining the need for a product, managers can plan for the level of resources needed, the time involved, and the objectives that the operations management process must achieve. Managing the planning process was described in detail in Chapter 5.

planning
The management function that assesses the management environment to set future objectives and map out activities necessary to achieve those objectives.

Strategic Planning

Several types of strategic management decisions are part of operations management. After determining the need for the product and the market the firm wishes to target, organizational leaders must first determine if they want to make or buy their product. As discussed in Chapter 9, outsourcing allows a firm to concentrate on marketing and new product development.

FIGURE 15.1
The Operations Management Process

A **make-buy analysis** is a tool operations managers use to help make this decision. The process begins with an assessment of whether the firm will lose or gain a competitive advantage by outsourcing the product or some aspects of the production process. Sara Lee found that outsourcing its manufacturing improved its competitive advantage. If outsourcing will hurt a firm's competitive advantage, the firm will continue making the product internally regardless of cost savings that may be obtained from outsourcing. Other factors in a make-buy analysis are the suitability of the product for outsourcing, the reasons for outsourcing, and the cost. The cost of buying the product may be less than the cost to the firm of equipment purchase and maintenance, labor and other inputs, inventory costs, administrative overhead, and so on.

Once a decision has been made to make the product, the operations manager must consider capacity, facilities, process, and layout. **Capacity** is the firm's ability to produce the product during a given period. Creating capacity that exceeds the amount of products that can be sold is inefficient because unused capacity wastes the firm's resources. Not having enough capacity to meet demand also works against the firm, as described in Management Close-Up 15.1.

make-buy analysis
An operations management tool used to help make the decision as to whether to produce an item or to purchase it.

capacity
The firm's ability to produce the product during a given period.

LOC-In 1 Learning Objective Check-In

1. Birmingham Boats Company specializes in high-quality, hand-crafted custom wooden boats. They have a very unpredictable series of projects that are waiting to be worked on at any given point in time. The resources they need to use always depend on the product that the client is requesting. Some materials, like certain woods and hardware items, are always necessary, but many custom accessories must be ordered on a project-to-project basis. _____ allows the company to manage their resource acquisition, production, and the delivery phases of the business.
   a. Communications management
   b. Operations management
   c. Functional management
   d. Information systems management

MANAGEMENT CLOSE-UP 15.1

THEME: **CUSTOMER FOCUS**

Too Little of a Good Thing

Immunex Corporation has a winner in its drug Enbrel, used to treat rheumatoid arthritis. The drug beat its optimistic 2000 sales projection by almost a third, and it became the fastest growing biological drug in history. Unfortunately, Enbrel became the largest supply shortage story in the history of prescription drugs.

Patients inject it to counteract the pain, swelling, and joint damage caused by the disease. The manufacturing process is complicated and time-consuming, however, using massive 10,000-liter tanks in sterile manufacturing plants. In spite of these quantities, the demand for Enbrel is so great that Immunex can't make enough of it. After a year on the market, it was obvious that demand would sooner or later outstrip supply. In March 2002, Immunex sent letters to doctors and to patients who were currently taking Enbrel that a shortage of two to three weeks might occur. Enbrel is a maintenance drug, not a cure. Thus, within about a month without the drug, arthritis symptoms typically return. In May 2002, the company again sent out letters informing doctors that the shortage might last longer than anticipated. In the meantime, there were approximately 20,000 people who were placed on a waiting list to receive the drug.

Enbrel's unexpected success created an overwhelming supply shortage in the drug industry. The drug was being rationed as patients across the United States were demanding it. When it wasn't available, doctors prescribed an alternative drug that required a doctor to administer it and a rigid medical regimen.

Immunex ended up being acquired by another company in July 2002. Two companies, Wyeth and Angen, now coproduce and market Enbrel. A production facility in Rhode island and a state-of-the-art production facility in Ireland now provide the production capacity needed to capitalize on demand for the drug. Demand for the drug has increased even further since Enbrel received approval as a treatment for psoriasis. For the first nine months of 2005 Enbrel accounted for $2.6 billion in global sales. Enbrel is clearly a blockbuster now that production capacity problems appear to be resolved. Unfortunately, the supply constraints did not let Immunex enjoy the economic benefits of the drug they developed.

Sources: D. Shook, "Immunex' Supply-Side Cliffhanger," *BusinessWeek*, February 8, 2001; "Delays for Enbrel Continue," www.psoriasis.org/ news/news/ 2002/20020524_enbrel.php, accessed May 20, 2003; "Alert! Enbrel Supply Shortage," http://arthritiscentral.com/enbrel/, accessed May 20, 2003; L. Loyd, "Wyeth Signs Three Biotech Product Deals—The Agreements Were an Indicator of the Direction that Major Pharmaceutical Companies Are Heading," *The Philadelphia Inquirer*, January 9, 2006, section C, p, 1.

Availability of labor and potential customers are important considerations in the facilities location for retail firms. By locating in areas with ample labor and a large customer population base, firms such as Ikea keep labor costs down and sales volume high.

facilities
The design and location of an operation.

process
How a product or service will be produced.

facilities layout design
The physical arrangement for the facility that will allow for efficient production.

inputs
The supplies needed to create a product, which can include materials, energy, information, management, technology, facilities, and labor.

materials requirements planning (MRP)
The process of analyzing a design to determine the materials and parts that it requires in the production process.

Operations management decisions also involve **facilities**, the design and location of an operation. Location decisions are based on factors such as the availability and cost of labor and energy as well as how close to suppliers or customers the facility needs to be.

Process decisions are also made regarding how a product or service will be produced. Operations managers evaluate the available production methods to see how efficiently they can achieve the operating objectives. Closely tied to process decisions are those regarding **facilities layout design**: What is the best physical arrangement for the facility that will allow for efficient production?

Once the strategic planning decisions have been made to lay the framework for producing the firm's goods or services, more focused planning must be completed for each stage of the operation.

■ Acquiring Inputs

An organization requires a sufficient supply of inputs to create various products. **Inputs** include materials, energy, information, management, technology, facilities, and labor. Individual organizations have different types of inputs. Sarnamotive Blue Water, Inc., supplies plastic products and components to the automotive industry. Sarnamotive's inputs include chemicals, natural resources, and technology. Inputs for General Motors include materials in the form of the finished products from its suppliers as well as energy, information, and so on. Dealers that sell General Motors cars have the finished automobiles as their most important input.

Managers oversee not only the selection of inputs and suppliers, but also the availability of the needed quantity of inputs, the quality of the inputs, the ability of suppliers to meet delivery dates, and the reliability of the suppliers. Obtaining supplies from foreign sources sometimes offers great dollar savings. For example, many companies purchase supplies from China due to the low manufacturing costs that are available in China. However, some companies have discovered that the quality of the parts purchased in China do not always meet the performance expectations of the firm that buys them. In the case of electronic parts that were outsourced to Chinese suppliers, some buying firms discovered that their Chinese partners sold them counterfeit parts that were substandard in performance. To manage inputs, operations mangers need to continuously monitor both the performance and costs.

Materials Requirements Planning

A product's inputs are based on its design. **Materials requirements planning (MRP)** is the process of analyzing the design to determine the materials and parts that it requires in the production process. This information is then used for purchasing, inventorying, and planning. The MRP process increasingly is tied into the firm's information technology capabilities.

While an MRP process may typically evoke images of a high technology environment and product, the process can be successfully used in low-tech situations. Consider, for example, the humble product of prepared horseradish. Silver Springs Gardens is one of the manufacturers involved in annually turning 24 million pounds of raw horseradish into 6 million gallons of prepared horseradish.[1] The company has multiple plants. Each plant traditionally had planners who determined production schedules. These planners considered account sales demand and stock on hand to manually create production orders.

Transfers of materials between plants were discussed via phone. Only after the orders were placed and negotiations were complete would the requirements for raw materials be known. Unfortunately, this process often took so long that the purchasing department did not have enough time to obtain needed materials. The manufacturer often faced having to inform customers that the company was temporarily out of stock. Silver Springs Gardens has resolved the problem and become more efficient by implementing MRP software. The software checks sales orders and stock levels automatically. It then generates production schedules and orders raw materials. The company has been able to reduce inventory levels as efficiency increased. Thus, even mundane processes can benefit from an MRP system.

Inventory

Most manufacturing operations require a stock of raw materials, inputs, and component parts on hand. Optimum **inventory** levels may be set when capacity decisions are made; the quantity of products to be created determines the amount of inventory the firm maintains. **Reordering systems** are used to help keep inventory levels more or less constant. In *fixed-point reordering systems*, the operations manager determines a minimum level of inventory; once this level is reached, inputs are reordered. In *fixed-interval reordering systems*, reordering is based on time—the operations manager determines that supplies need to be reordered every two months, for example. Just-in-time inventory levels are discussed later in this chapter.

inventory
The stock of raw materials, inputs, and component parts that the firm keeps on hand.

reordering systems
The process used to help keep inventory levels more or less constant.

LOC-In 2 Learning Objective Check-In

Scott Learning Company uses a computer system that analyzes the design of every product, which is also logged on the computers, and then determines the parts and materials that will be required for production. Once the appropriate materials are ordered, they are stored briefly in the back room until their use.

1. The program that would be appropriate for Scott teaming Company to use in analyzing product design and determining resources needed is called _____.
   a. total quality management
   b. materials requirements planning
   c. system control
   d. bureaucratic control

2. What is the name given to the goods that are in the possession of Scott Learning Company, and that are being stored before they are used?
   a. Back orders
   b. Inventory
   c. Waste product
   d. Finished goods

■ The Conversion Process

The second major stage of operations management is the **conversion process**—taking the product's inputs and converting them to the final product. The operations manager designs and controls the production system which should create high-quality, low-cost products that customers are willing to buy or use. An effective conversion process lowers the cost of creating the product or creates a better product for the same cost. Many software tools are available to help with the design and implementation of the conversion process.

conversion process
The operations management stage in which the product's inputs are converted to the final product.

Designing the Process

The conversion process typically involves several steps that may occur either at the same time or in sequence. The process will be designed to accommodate these activities. For complex operations, the conversion process is designed in subparts. An aggregate plan shows the process for the entire operation, but each subpart requires individual analysis and design. Each subpart's schedule is taken into account in a master schedule.

In designing the process, the operations manager should be careful to avoid overlooking less critical steps. Critical steps may depend on what are perceived as less important areas, but if they are not planned for, the entire process may be delayed.

Process design begins with an analysis of the general operation and identifying:

- Every major step.
- The order that the steps must take.
- The flow of the steps from start to finish, including their relationship to each other.
- The amount of time each individual step requires.

Table 15.1 shows how this information is used to set up a new bakery's baking facility. If each step were done in order, the bakery would take 11 weeks to open. Because some of the steps can be done concurrently, however, the time can be shortened to 5 weeks.

TABLE 15.1 Process Analysis Information

STEP	ORDER	RELATION TO OTHER STEPS	TIME
A. Get permit	1	None	4 weeks
B. Order equipment	1	None	1 week
C. Paint interior	2	None	2 weeks
D. Install electrical fixtures	3	Following C	1 week
E. Install floors	4	Following C	1 week
F. Install equipment	5	Following B, E	1 Week
G. Test equipment	6	Following F	1 week

Several tools are available to help analyze the steps needed to determine an efficient seqtience and also to monitor the process. Three of the best known tools are a Gantt chart, a load chart, and a PERT network.

Gantt charts
A visual sequence of the process steps used in planning, scheduling, and monitoring production.

GANTT CHARTS Developed by Henry Gantt in the early 1900s, **Gantt charts** provide a visual sequence of the process steps. A Gantt chart using the information in Table 15.1 appears in Figure 15.2.

load chart
A type of Gantt chart that is based on departments or specific resources that are used in the process.

LOAD CHARTS Another way to analyze the process is with a load chart. A **load chart** is a type of Gantt chart that is based on departments or specific resources, used in the process. Instead of the tasks listed in Figure 15.2, the load chart would list the people involved in each step and the time frame for their involvement, as seen in Figure 15.3.

FIGURE 15.2

A Gantt Chart

FIGURE 15.3

A Load Chart

FIGURE 15.4

A PERT Network

PERT NETWORKS   Another way to analyze the process, especially complex projects, is with a **program evaluation and review technique (PERT) network**. This technique was developed in the 1950s, when the work of thousands of contractors and government agencies needed to be coordinated for the Polaris submarine weapons system. A PERT network is illustrated in Figure 15.4.

FACILITIES LAYOUT   Once the major steps have been identified, the design of the actual work area is created. **Facilities layout**—the grouping and organization of equipment and employees—affects the efficiency of the production system. Workstations are arranged based on product layout, process layout, or fixed-position layout schemes.

Functions in a *product layout* are organized so that each function is performed in a fixed sequence. Employees and equipment stay in one place, or workstation, as the product moves through the system. Mass production (assembly) lines are one type of product layout system. These systems have become efficient for relatively small levels of production, but traditionally they were used for large production runs.

In *process layout,* each workstation is relatively self-contained. The product moves to the workstation needed to perform the next operation, which may not be in sequence. Process layouts are often used to create custom-made products because they offer flexibility to make product changes. This layout does reduce efficiency, making it more expensive.

In *a fixed-position layout,* remote workstations assemble the product's components, which then are brought to the production area for final assembly. Fixed-position layouts are used for complex products that are difficult to assemble and for large products that are not easily moved, such as aircraft.

FLEXIBLE MANUFACTURING   When changes are made to a product, time spent in setting up and reconfiguring the workstations is lost if the process must shut down during setup, increasing the cost and reducing efficiency. It is possible to design the process using principles of **flexible manufacturing**, which are operations management techniques that help reduce the setup costs associated with the production system. Computer-aided design, engineering, and manufacturing tools make the work process more flexible. For example, when a change in a component is needed, a computer program, not the machinery, might be modified, greatly reducing the time the machinery is not available for production and enabling more types of product to be created. The BMW factory that assembles the 3-Series automobile in Regensburg, Germany nicely illustrates how flexible manufacturing can improve efficiency. The moving assembly line where the car chassis is continuously advancing can accommodate several different models of the car simultaneously, such as the sedan, convertible, station wagon, and export versions (UK and Japanese cars have the steering wheels and instruments on the right side, while Continental European cars have these components located on the left side of the vehicle). At each assembly station smart robots with sensors have the capability of determining which version of the BMW is approaching the station, and when the robot identifies the car model the robot is programmed to search for the appropriate part

program evaluation and review technique (PERT) network
A tool for analyzing the conversion process.

facilities layout
The grouping and organization of equipment and employees.

flexible manufacturing
Operations management techniques that help reduce the setup costs associated with the production system.

Facilities layout is important in the operations management of retail outlets. At Sephora perfume stores, for instance, grand entrances are meant to suggest a "theater" of beauty. New and popular products are spotlighted near the door, and brands can pay a fee for featured retail space along the store's aisles, where the shelves at eye level produce the highest sales.

in nearby parts bins and attach the correct part in the appropriate location on the chassis, depending on the type of model being worked on.

Flexible manufacturing also involves physical layout. A Y-shaped layout, for example, is often more amenable to flexible manufacturing than a straight-line layout. While one arm of the Y is being reconfigured, processes along the other two arms can continue. In a spiral layout, workers can easily physically turn to help with other steps to keep the work flow even.

Another consideration in flexible manufacturing is how employees work. Some firms use self-managed work teams to produce an entire product or component. Team members learn all the tasks in the production process, move from job to job, and fill in for each other, thereby creating a great deal of flexibility. Team members schedule work, order materials, and hire new staff for the team. Productivity and efficiency typically increase, and the supervisor position can often be eliminated, streamlining the hierarchy.

Monitoring the Process

Operations management is a continuous function. Once the process has been designed and implemented, the systems need to be monitored and improved. *Benchmarks* that set levels of production and costs are strategic management decisions. These benchmarks are used to evaluate the production process in a number of ways.

In **acceptance sampling**, a sample of materials or products is measured against the benchmark. Based on the results of this measurement, the entire run is either accepted or rejected.

Statistical process control uses quantitative methods and procedures to evaluate transformation operations and to detect and eliminate deviations. This type of control is in wide use today. Manager's Notebook 15.1 lists several statistical process tools. By using statistical data about the process, operations managers can pinpoint problems and find solutions that address the problem. They can also see areas of improvement that will often circumvent a problem. By making the operations process more efficient, managers can also improve the firm's financial performance in most cases. Later in this chapter, systems for improving operations management quality are described in greater detail.

acceptance sampling
An operations management monitoring tool in which a sample of materials or products is measured against a benchmark.

statistical process control
An operations management monitoring tool that uses quantitative methods and procedures to evaluate transformation operations and to detect and eliminate deviations.

MANAGER'S NOTEBOOK 15.1

Statistical Process Control Tools

CHECK SHEETS Check sheets are quantity-based forms, where a check mark is made for a particular attribute. Check sheets can provide data when the attribute is tracked by time, location, or some other variable—to pinpoint workstations or processes that produce more or less than the average or that have fewer defects, for example.

PARETO ANALYSIS The concept behind Pareto analysis is that 20 percent of an operation results in 80 percent of the gap between expected and actual performance. Pareto analysis involves specifying the causes of a problem and assigning a value (such as dollars or time) to each cause based on its contribution to the problem in order to determine the causes that have the most negative effects on the operation.

PROCESS FLOW ANALYSIS Process flow analysis is a method of graphically representing the activities in a process, the exact tasks of these activities, and their organization or structure within the process. By diagramming the process, managers can identify variations and disruptions.

CAUSE-AND-EFFECT DIAGRAMS Also called *fishbone diagrams* and *Ishikawa charts*, cause-and-effect diagrams are a mechanism for identifying potential causes of problems and tracing back

through interrelationships to identify the root causes. The main cause of a problem typically is a function of other causes, which can be identified by breaking the main cause down by area.

PROCESS CAPABILITY MEASURES Certain specifications (*S*) can be defined as acceptable levels of variations, with a lower and upper limit set. By also setting acceptable variation in the process (*P*), we can evaluate the actual performance statistically as

$$C_p = \frac{\text{Specification width}}{\text{Process width}} = \frac{S}{P}$$

As the process variation narrows, the specification typically improves.

CONTROL CHARTS Control charts plot data collected over time across a set of limits for the upper and lower boundaries of acceptable performance. Points outside the acceptable limits indicate a problem that needs to be solved to improve the operation.

Source: Adapted form S. Melnyk and D. Denzler, *Operations Management*. New York: McGraw-Hill/Irwin. Copyright © 1996 McGraw-Hill Companies, Inc. Used with permission.

Another important goal of operations management is increasing the efficiency of the production process beyond the benchmarks. For example, if operations management can determine how to use fewer inputs or processes in the production system, the efficiency of the system will be improved and the operations will be more productive. Two methods are typically used to determine productivity: total factor productivity and partial factor productivity.

Total factor productivity measures how well an organization utilizes all company resources, such as capital, labor, materials, or energy, to produce its outputs, according to the equation:

$$\frac{\text{Outputs}}{\text{All inputs}} = \text{Total factor productivity}$$

total factor productivity
The measurement of how well an organization utilizes all of its resources, such as capital, labor, materials, or energy, to produce its outputs.

For total factor productivity to be valid, managers must convert all inputs to a common unit. Because inputs are typically initially measured in different units (labor may be measured in hours, materials in tons, energy in joules, for example), converting these units to their dollar cost allows them to be added.

Partial productivity measures the contribution of a single input, such as labor or materials, to the final product. The efficiency of materials would be expressed as:

$$\frac{\text{Outputs}}{\text{Materials}} = \text{Materials productivity}$$

partial productivity
The measurement of the contribution of a single input, such as labor or materials, to the final product.

The measurement of the partial productivity of labor is often used to compare the efficiency of firms within an industry.

Operations management is typically focused on the production process. The operations management approach can also be applied to other processes, such as monitoring and managing finances. Skills for Managing 15.1 is an exercise for you in applying operations management to services.

◼ Disposition of the Product

The end result of the firm's operations process is the product, whether it is a good or a service. Other areas of the firm, including marketing and sales, usually bear the responsibility for finding the user of the firm's product; actual delivery of the product may fall to customer service. Operations management, however, includes the customer-fulfillment process.

Customer fulfillment begins when an order is received, sometimes long before the firm's product will be delivered. An **order review/release (ORR) activity** is used to evaluate and track the order through the process, from creating order documentation, to material checking, capacity evaluation, and load leveling (releasing orders so that the workload is evenly distributed).

order review/ release (ORR) activity
An operations management tool that is used to evaluate and track the order through the process, including creating order documentation, material checking, capacity evaluation, and load leveling (releasing orders so that the work load is evenly distributed).

The final step of the customer-fulfillment process in operations management is the order disposition. The order must be checked to verify that it is complete. Records of labor hours, material amounts, and any problems in the production process are finalized so that the cost of producing the order can be arrived at and made available for pricing purposes.

SKILLS FOR MANAGING 15.1

Service Operations Management

Form small groups of four or five students. Each group will choose a local service industry establishment, such as the public library, a video rental establishment, a dry cleaner, or a hand car wash. The establishment can be for-profit or a non-for-profit firm. Before class, research the establishment—if possible, observe the organization in action.

1. Describe the service organization that you selected.
2. Define the target customers of that organization and what you think they value most.
3. List inputs that the service requires.

4. List the business processes that the organization uses to create its service.
5. Create a PERT network showing the business process from inputs through delivery of the service. Create a network for each process if the firm's activities require more than one process.

In class, meet with your group and share your result. Compare the PERT network each member has created. Refine the network to show an efficient process for providing the service. Each group should then present its findings to the class.

LOC-In 3   Learning Objective Check-In

Crystal Shores is in the beginning stages of another conversion process for its products. This is an ongoing cycle that begins roughly every two to seven weeks, depending on the products. There are several steps that must occur at the same time in order to achieve production in the most efficient way possible.

1. If Crystal Shores wants to use a visual tool to outline the sequence of machines and time per machine used, it could use an _____
   a. MRP
   b. Gantt chart
   c. facilities layout
   d. total factor model

2. Sometimes the products undergo changes while they are already in the middle of production. If Crystal Shores wants to minimize its downtime and reduce setup costs associated with the production system itself, it should use a _____.
   a. flexible manufacturing system
   b. product layout
   c. PERT network
   d. load chart

■ Managing Quality

During World War II, intense development in machinery and processes took place in U.S. factories to produce goods for the war effort and to use inputs more efficiently for manufacturing domestic goods. Innovations in the production process in the United States stagnated after the war, however. W. Edwards Deming, considered the father of quality management, taught Japanese firms how to use statistics to measure and improve quality—but U.S. firms had rejected his ideas. By the 1970s, firms in other countries had begun using computers to integrate manufacturing operations with strategic planning. The resulting products were better as they were being continually improved, and they became cheaper as the production process became more efficient. Their U.S. counterparts had been overtaken both in productivity and profitability.

The impact of quality improvement efforts in other countries on the U.S. economy was dramatic. Managers in the United States were forced to look hard at their operations. They began to take a second look at Deming's teachings and other means of improving quality. Quality management became an important issue to many firms by the middle of the 1980s. Company leaders began seeking a more efficient production process to lower production costs and ultimately increase profitability.

Top management must make improvement in productivity a strategic objective of the firm. Managers from different areas of the firm must work together to increase efficiency. Many of the steps to improve quality and efficiency cut across departmental boundaries.

Quality management techniques are not limited to operations management. Chapter 5 mentioned the role of the six-sigma objective in GE's planning process, and Chapter 13 emphasized the importance of quality in team performance. It is in the operations management area, however, that a quality philosophy is essential to the success of the firm. Identifying and implementing production improvements fall to operations management. Quality management, kaizen, just-in-time, and process reengineering are four methods of managing quality.

The Quality Management Approach

One of the main objectives of operations management should be to make the production sequence as effective as possible. Just what "effectiveness" means and how it can be achieved are critical issues. Traditionally, Western management approached production from the perspective of internal standards (often quantity produced), a focus on workers, and independent quality inspection. In contrast, the quality management philosophy approaches production from the perspective of external standards driven by customers, a focus on the system, and the belief that quality is integral to the work process.[2] Therefore, quality management becomes customer driven. It is the customer who is the source of standards for defining quality. The quality approach underscores the importance of the system in determining performance. Traditional Western management focuses on employee motivation and ability levels, whereas a quality approach emphasizes characteristics of the production system as the major influence on quality outcomes. Further, quality management emphasizes the empowerment of workers and their responsibility for the quality of the outcomes of work processes. Thus, workers in an organization, guided by a quality philosophy, are often responsible for inspecting the quality of their own work. In contrast, a traditional Western management approach typically keeps quality inspections separate, performed by separate personnel. According to Deming, inspection as a separate function puts fear into workers. He believed the work process was better if workers were responsible for their own work processes and the quality of outputs.

The quality management philosophy resulted in the development of a program called Total Quality Management. **Total quality management (TQM)** is based on the belief that all of an organization's activities should be focused on improving its product. TQM has been described as "a total commitment to quality and attitude expressed by everybody's involvement in the process of continuous improvement of products and services, through the use of innovative scientific methods."[3] One focus of TQM is on the use of SPC tools. Thus, a TQM program often emphasizes training workers in the use of SPC tools and then empowering workers to use the tools to measure the quality of work processes and the effectiveness of attempts to improve quality. While the TQM acronym virtually stands for every quality management perspective, Deming never espoused the use of the term. He believed that quality will be meaningfully improved by managers who understand the quality philosophy, not by applying a stand-alone, set program of steps. Recently TQM has become less visible, but not because quality is less important. To the contrary, quality continues to be critically important to the survival and competitiveness of organizations. Quality is now commonly viewed as simply part of the operation of an organization. That is, quality is often "baked in" to the management process, rather than treated as a separate element of the production recipe.

Four interrelated steps make up the quality approach according to Deming: plan, do, check, and act (also called the *PDCA cycle* or the *Deming wheel*). These processes are ongoing and will result in total quality management. At each step in the cycle, firms must focus on customer needs, emphasize participation and teamwork of all involved in the firm's activities (suppliers, employees, and customers), and establish an organizational climate of continuous improvement by all employees.

The quality management approach can be utilized by any manager. Management Is Everyone's Business 15.1 offers suggestions for you to apply the quality management approach in your role as manager.

MANAGEMENT AND THE QUALITY PHILOSOPHY Deming's 14 points for management, as discussed in Chapter 1, provide the underlying management structure for the quality process. They define the tenets that make up the philosophy. Operations management also draws from Deming's theory of variance. Deming believed that variance causes unpredictability, which increases uncertainty and reduces control. Variations from standard work flows and activities can be seen as a major source of operations management problems. Correcting these variances by using quality principles to find and correct their source is one form of continuous improvement.

total quality management (TQM)
An organization-wide management approach that focuses on quality as an overarching goal. The basis of this approach is the understanding that all employees and organizational units should be working harmoniously to satisfy the customer.

MANAGEMENT IS EVERYONE'S BUSINESS 15.1

WORKING AS A MANAGER A manager who *builds quality into the process* that provides products or services to customers can reap substantial benefits from this approach. This entails delegating the responsibility for quality to front-line employees who make the product or interact directly with customers. Instead of inspecting quality after the fact and then inform subordinates of their mistakes, a manager can empower subordinates by establishing a feedback loop that delivers information to them with an ongoing measure of quality of the operation. This way employees can make corrections to quality on the spot. By empowering employees to manage quality themselves, substantial cost savings in time and labor can be realized. This approach also frees up a manager to do other important tasks that may require his or her attention.

Common causes of ongoing variances that operations management should correct include weak designs, scheduling errors, chronic equipment problems, and inaccurate documentation. Individual employees can correct specific problems as part of their responsibilities, such as alerting their supervisor to late deliveries and suggesting ways to improve scheduling.

EMPLOYEES AND QUALITY Operations managers must be certain employees understand that the quality approach means each worker is responsible for improving quality. They must also be willing to act on any suggestions or problems that employees identify. **Quality circles**—groups of employees who meet regularly to discuss ways to increase quality—were a useful means of finding sources of and solutions to poor quality. As with TQM, there are now fewer references to quality circles since quality is integrated into the responsibilities of employees and teams of employees.

Goals should be set for each employee so that management can evaluate how well each has achieved these goals. When individual quality goals are met, employees should be recognized and rewarded.

CUSTOMERS AND TQM Customers ultimately decide what constitutes quality through purchasing decisions. Other departments may identify what customers want as well as what the firm actually is providing to them. Operations management can focus on improving the **quality gap**—the difference between what customers want and what they actually get from the company. By consistently monitoring the production process, as discussed earlier in this chapter, managers can determine if improvements are taking place.

SUPPLIERS AND QUALITY From a quality perspective, suppliers are regarded as partners with the firm. Poor quality in a product is often caused by poor quality in its inputs. The problem may be traced to the quality of the supplier's materials. On the other hand, it may be a function of the design and the materials the supplier was requested to provide. Involving suppliers during the design and production process takes advantage of their expertise in the materials that are available and any qualifications for using them.

Suppliers who are perceived (and perceive themselves) as partners with the firm will be proactive in solving problems. Operations managers should work to develop cooperative, long-term relationships with suppliers.

In addition to partnerships, many organizations are employing established standards and asking their suppliers to also adhere to those same standards. The International Organization for Standardization (ISO) is the world's largest developer of standards. It is a network of national standards institutes from 146 countries. ISO develops technical standards that guide, for example, production and distribution. The purpose of these standards is to make the development, manufacture, and supply of products and services safer, more efficient, and cleaner. In addition, the standardization is meant to make international trade easier and fairer. There are numerous ISO guidelines and standards. The ISO 9000 family of standards focuses on quality management in organizations. The ISO 1400 family of standards focuses on environmental management so that organizations minimize harmful impacts on the environment. While exploring the details of these standards is beyond the scope of this discussion, you can find more information about ISO standards at the ISO Web site (www.iso.ch/iso/en/ISOOnline.frontpage).

QUALITY AND THE PRODUCTION PROCESS Operations management uses quality techniques to focus on the production process. Products that can be manufactured with fewer components, for example, can be assembled more quickly and with fewer steps and typically have fewer defects. The quality of the product improves, the wasted labor spent in making and dealing with defective products decreases, and the firm's profitability is improved. While quality management is often associated with producing goods, the approach can also be applied to providing services.

One way to combat defects is by adhering to the six-sigma philosophy. Sigma is a statistical measurement of defects in parts per million. Four sigma, where most firms operate, equals 6,210 defects per million. Five sigma equals 233 defects per million, which is considerably improved over four sigma. Six sigma, however, is the ultimate goal, where defects occur at the rate of 1 per 3.4 million—a product or process that is 99.999666 percent defect-free.

---

quality circles
Groups of employees who meet regularly to discuss ways to increase quality.

quality gap
The difference between what customers want and what they actually get from the company.

LOC-In 4 Learning Objective Check-In

Becca is a member of an employee group that meets every three weeks to discuss ways to increase quality in all aspects of production. Recently, the group identified some differences between what the customers say they want and what the company has actually been producing. Becca is assembling a report to give to her operations manager that should help them monitor the production process better in order to build quality into the products.

1. What is the name given to the type of group Becca belongs to at work?
   a. Work group
   b. SDWT
   c. Quality circle
   d. Task force

2. The difference between what customers want and what they actually get from the company is called a(n) _____.
   a. avoidable cost
   b. kaizen
   c. production gap
   d. quality gap

Kaizen (Continuous Improvement) and Efficiency

Kaizen is the Japanese term for the need for continuous improvement in the organization's production system from numerous small, incremental improvements in production processes. The principles of kaizen were introduced in 1985 by Masaaki Imai.[4] According to these principles, process should be dealt with in three steps: maintenance, kaizen, innovation.

The maintenance step is the status quo of the process—how it is done. Kaizen is the interim step of identifying small ways to improve maintenance. Innovation is the resulting changes to the process. After the process is modified, the innovated process then becomes the new status quo and the kaizen process begins again. Table 15.2 lists suggestions from the Kaizen Institute for implementing kaizen in an organization. The kaizen principle of continuous improvement is now incorporated into the ISO 9000 standards and is a part of most quality improvement efforts. Thus, as with TQM, kaizen may not be readily visible in organizations, because it is integrated into organizational operations, rather than standing out as a separate program.

kaizen
The Japanese process of continuous improvement in the organization's production system from numerous small, incremental improvements in production processes.

LOC-In 5 Learning Objective Check-In

Dance Strong Inc. manufactures all types of dance apparel equipment, and training tools. The industry is very dynamic and while there are some traditional styles that remain largely unchanged, there are also many new and innovative styles that require products tailored to the trends. In order to remain as efficient as possible while still meeting customer demands, Dance Strong makes small, incremental improvements to its production lines. One advantage that Dance Strong has achieved is the fact that it uses the same types of fabrics and materials in the production of its most popular products as well as the custom products. This allows the company to forecast its own demand for resources and to minimize inventory. It also allows the company to create the product in the shortest possible amount of time.

1. What principle is being applied by making incremental, continuous improvements to the production line's efficiency and design?
   a. just-in-time
   b. Kanban
   c. Total quality management
   d. kaizen

2. What principle is demonstrated by Dance Strong's making all of its products in the shortest amount of time possible?
   a. Kaizen
   b. Just-in-time
   c. Kanban
   d. Business process reengineering

TABLE 15.2 Implementing Kaizen

MAINTENANCE
- Question current practices without making excuses or justifying them.
- Question everything five times to identify the root causes of waste and to come up with solutions.

KAIZEN
- Discard conventional ideas and methods in finding causes and devising solutions.
- Remember that kaizen ideas are limitless.
- Think positively of how to accomplish something, not negatively about why it can't be done.
- Focus wisdom on the kaizen process and solutions, not money.
- Understand that undergoing hardship increases wisdom.
- The wisdom of ten people is more valuable than the knowledge of one.

INNOVATION
- Begin implementing solutions right away—don't wait until the solutions have been perfected.
- Correct mistakes immediately, as they occur, before they can cause further problems.

Kaizen is present and affects the lives of workers, particularly in terms of how they work as team members. Management Is Everyone's Business 15.2 addresses some implications of continuous improvement for you as a team member.

One of the main principles of kaizen is reducing waste in materials, inventory, production steps, and activities that don't add value, such as moving parts from one machine to another. According to the Kaizen Institute, every second that is spent in adding value to a product is offset by 1,000 seconds of activities that add no value.[5] Sources of waste include inefficient facilities layouts. Implementing flexible manufacturing systems and facilities layouts is consistent with the kaizen approach. Another waste-reduction technique is using a limited number of suppliers, which enables the organization to control inputs. Just-in-time manufacturing, discussed next, is another method of operations management that firms use as part of their quality efforts.

MANAGEMENT IS EVERYONE'S BUSINESS | 15.2

WORKING AS A TEAM   Encouraging team members to *share knowledge* with each other on a regular basis is a work practice that can intensify the quality principle of continuous improvement. Knowledge sharing lets team members improve their job skills and their ability to satisfy customers on an ongoing basis. Here a few useful team knowledge sharing practices:

- Create a team Web site that allows "best practices" to be posted on the site and informs team members of the posting with an e-mail message. For example, in a sales application one of the top performing sales representatives can share on the Web site some unique ways to close a sale to the customer of a newly released product for other sales staff who may be struggling to meet their sales quotas on the product.

- Establish a monthly seminar series that features well-known industry experts that speak to professionals on a timely topic of interest. Make sure that the invited speaker or panelists complete their talk with enough time at the end to answer questions from team members. After the seminar have refreshments available so that team members can discuss among themselves the implications of the speaker's ideas for how they could impact their own work. Law firms and consulting firms often use this strategy to keep their colleagues current on the latest topics in their field so they can be more valuable to customers.

- Encourage a team member who attends a professional conference to share some of the key teaching points with other team members. This can simply take the form of sending a brief e-mail message to the team summarizing the conference teaching points (i.e., conference notes can be distributed to interested people as electronic files) and letting team members know how they can learn more about the topic or attend the conference if they are interested. For example, a team member who attends a conference on mastering the skill of "servant leadership" (a leadership style used in service firms and non-profits) may share this knowledge with interested team members and offer to coach individuals who want to learn this leadership skill.

Just-In-Time Systems

The concept of creating the firm's product in the least amount of time led to another operations management approach. The goal of a **just-in-time (JIT)** system is improving the firm's profitability. Managers develop a smooth, integrated production process in which steps are performed just as subsequent steps require them, from inputs and the conversion process through disposition of the product.

Like TQM and kaizen, JIT is implemented at the strategic level rather than the operations management level. Product design, employee compensation, accounting, and sales are all affected by JIT. Under JIT, product design can be as up to date as possible, because the production process won't begin until orders are received. Inventory levels can be more easily modified. On the other hand, product design must be finished when it is needed in the JIT production process or the cost of the product will increase.

In a JIT system, the firm's inventory of inputs—the raw materials, components, labor, and energy that the firm has available—are kept at the lowest level possible. Inputs arrive at the organization when, not before, they are needed. Close relationships with suppliers are critical to JIT inventory systems. Wal-Mart generates its inventory reorders with a computer network that receives data as each purchase is scanned at the checkout counter. When inventory levels for the product reach a predetermined level, information about the number of replacement items needed and where to send them is sent to the suppliers' computers. Suppliers agree to use this method of managing inventory and almost become Wal-Mart's warehouses, as the suppliers must maintain enough inventory to fill Wal-Mart's orders on demand.

JIT inventory systems are valuable in several ways. They save on warehouse space and labor, and financial resources are not tied up in inputs waiting to be used. They also play a major role in identifying production errors. Since inputs are received and put into the production process immediately, any defects in them quickly become apparent and replacements are sent by the firm's suppliers. Because orders are processed only after they are received, products are produced in small batches. Consequently, problems in the production process can be remedied before another batch goes through.

KANBAN   A form of JIT systems called *kanban* originated in Japan. **Kanban**, from the Japanese word for "card" or "sign," uses cards to generate inventory. Inputs are shipped to manufacturers in containers with a card in a side pocket. Upon receipt, the card is removed and returned to the supplier. The supplier then sends more inputs based on a predetermined schedule so that they will arrive just when the preceding shipment is used up.

The Kanban system is meant to change an organization's production system from one based on creating batches of a product to one driven by customer demand. In order to be driven by customer demand, the Kanban system uses the return of cards attached to containers to signal that more parts are needed. Conceptually, this is a simple and effective system, but the operational reality leaves room for improvement. For example, cards are sometimes not returned, with an estimate of 1 percent card loss per day among major auto suppliers.[6] Cards are sometimes misplaced, thrown in the garbage, or inadvertently placed in a pocket. While these errors may not occur frequently, when they do the nonreturned cards can cause parts shortages, stop production, and cost a surprising amount of time lost in trying to diagnose the source of the problem. An e-kanban system promises to solve the problem of lost cards and to make the customer demand system even more efficient.

An electronic kanban system uses a scanner to read in a code on a container. Rather than having this information on a physical card, the information is sent electronically to the upstream supplier. The problem of lost cards is eliminated.

Further, the demand information can be immediately sent to the suppliers. The electronic signal can be sent via the Internet and can, therefore, closely link the manufacturer and supplier even though they are geographically remote from each other. The electronic kanban system appears to deliver on its promise to solve problems and increase performance. Danaher Sensors and Control Group, for instance, conducted trial-runs with e-kanban to see if the system would reduce wasted time.[7] The organization found that it spent a lot of time expediting and chasing cards around with the traditional kanban system. The e-kanban

Computerized cash register transactions at Wal-Mart automatically trigger inventory restocking by the firm's suppliers. Wal-Mart's computer database is second only to the Pentagon's in capacity.

just-in-time (JIT)
The concept behind creating the firm's product in the least amount of time.

kanban
A form of JIT systems originated in Japan that uses cards to generate inventory; from the Japanese word for "card" or "sign."

system reduced this wasted time by about half, freeing up people to work on more value-added activities.

DRAWBACK TO JIT Some organizations utilize a modified JIT system because one major drawback of JIT is that having just enough inventory leaves the firm without a buffer. Thus, it becomes difficult to cover problems that sometimes arise, such as unexpected orders or labor disputes involving the firm's suppliers. Warehouse employees are forced to carefully monitor supplies to continue to be able to meet JIT deadlines with quality parts.

Another problem is keeping the labor supply stable. Unexpected demand means a firm must either increase its staff or pay overtime wage scales to meet order deadlines, since no inventory of products is available under a JIT system. The additional labor costs typically must be absorbed by the firm, cutting into profit margins.

A related problem is maintaining production equipment and other factors when demand is higher than expected. The firm's resources typically are focused on filling orders and not on maintenance of machines. Company employees may also not be able to take advantage of training opportunities to keep their skills up to date, another form of maintenance. Delaying maintenance for both equipment and skills puts the firm at a competitive disadvantage later.

Other Quality Management Systems

There are many exciting new ways to enhance quality in organizations. Whereas JIT systems are based on each area supplying materials or services to other areas for them to be built upon, and kaizen and TQM effect change in ongoing small increments over time, process reengineering is a new and different technique. Also, enterprise resource planning, or ERP, is an information technology form of quality management. Both process engineering and ERP are relatively new approaches for improving processes.

process reengineering
A method of changing the entire production process rather than making incremental changes.

PROCESS REENGINEERING A more dramatic approach to quality includes changing the entire production process rather than making incremental adjustments. In **process reengineering**, the firm is viewed as a complete process—a series of activities that produce the products and services necessary to fulfill the firm's mission. Therefore the objective is to change the entire process at one time.

Process reengineering focuses on processes rather than individual activities. Its goal, like that of the other quality management techniques, is to reduce waste and improve the firm's profitability. Process reengineering involves fundamentally rethinking and radically redesigning the entire process, including cutting out steps that aren't needed and reducing paperwork. The result should be improvements in cost, quality, timeliness, and service as a whole.

The management team at Ford reengineered the company procurement process when they discovered that their strategic business partner, Mazda, had five people in its accounts payable department while Ford had 500 people in its U.S. accounts payable department. As a result of the reengineering, a buyer in Ford's purchasing department now enters purchase orders into an online database and, at the same time, they are sent to the supplier. Upon receipt, the goods are verified against the online database. If they are acceptable, the database is updated and payment to the supplier is automatically authorized rather than the authorization being granted by the accounts payable department. If the goods are not acceptable against the online database, they are returned to the supplier.

As a result of this process reengineering, Ford greatly reduced the size of the company's accounts payable department. The unproductive activities of the accounting staff and the operations employees in maintaining records and verifying deliveries manually were also eliminated. This reengineering effort increased the efficiency of the entire organization.[8]

From materials requirements planning to process reengineering, operations management is a vibrant and highly relevant area for any organization. The philosophies, principles, and tools of operations management impact the nature of work and have important implications for all of us. Management Is Everyone's Business 15.3 highlights some key implications of the operations management area for you as an individual worker.

MANAGEMENT IS EVERYONE'S BUSINESS   15.3

WORKING AS AN INDIVIDUAL   The quality management philosophy, just-in-time systems, continuous improvement, and other operations management tools will impact how you do your work. The following are some ways that individual employees can be prepared to deal with a work environment where change is pervasive.

- Important responsibilities and decision making are increasingly being delegated to front-line employees who interact regularly with customers. Be prepared to be given unique problems to solve and expect challenges that you have not been trained to deal with. Those who succeed will be those who take risks and experiment with new ways of working and are able to learn from their mistakes while maintaining a focus on the key goals that must be attained.
- Learning is an ongoing activity that will be expected of all employees. Learning will not only take the form of formal classroom instruction or computerized training modules that an employee will take for credit. It will also consist of experiential learning on the job through trial and error and vicarious learning that builds on other employees' experiences. Vicarious learning can be achieved by observing successful employees at work or by exchanging knowledge with them during social events or scheduled meetings, for example. Other learning will tap into resources available on the Internet by exploiting opportunities to learn from others on social network Web sites such as LinkedIn or from the company's internal computer network or intranet that facilitates sharing information among employees.

■ What Is Management Control?

Control is the measurement of an employee's, division's, or company's performance against established standards or benchmarks and the taking of corrective action as needed. Control is the way in which managers ensure that performance objectives are being measured. These objectives can be nonsubjective measurements such as producing 50 widgets in an hour, or they can be subjective measurements as in the case of providing superior customer service.

control
The process of comparing performance to standards and taking corrective action.

Bureaucratic Control

Bureaucratic control is the top-down-driven formal process of control that consists of four steps: (1) establishing standards, (2) measuring performance against standards, (3) identifying shortcomings, and (4) taking corrective action. Managers often use written guidelines and standards to establish internal performance expectations. Written guidelines ensure that everyone understands their expectations and roles and reduce the number of discrepancies between the standards and performance. Once discrepancies between the company's standards and the employee's performance are identified, corrective action is taken to ensure the gap between the standards and performance does not widen.

bureaucratic control
A formal control approach involving a cycle of (1) establishing standards, (2) performance measurement, (3) identifying gaps, and (4) corrective action.

THE CONTROL PROCESS   The control process, as previously mentioned, consists of four steps: (1) establishing standards, (2) measuring performance against standards, (3) identifying shortcomings, and (4) taking corrective action. Each step is considered next.

Establishing Standards   Consider the following standards set by businesses:

- Make 10 outgoing sales calls per hour.
- Accept returns without arguing with the customer.
- Sell two cars per month.
- Be helpful and available to customers at all times.
- Produce 20 widgets per hour.

The point of the list above is to demonstrate that standards take all forms; some are easily measured in terms of quantity or time, and some are not easily measured and are open to interpretation (such as being helpful and available to customers). Regardless of the form they take, all standards are benchmarks that managers use as a ruler in measuring employee performance. If an employee comes up short, corrective action is likely to be taken.

How are standards developed? That depends on the company's culture. Standards can be developed by managers in a top-down way and disseminated to employees through training sessions, informal meetings, or written guidelines. Alternatively, standards may be developed in a more participatory fashion with employees giving their input to managers and working with them to refine the standards as necessary. While it is often easier for a company if as few people as possible develop the standards, this top-down approach can lead to resistance by employees who may feel that their performance is being measured against standards created by people who do not understand how difficult their job is.

Measuring Performance   As stated earlier, quantitative standards are easier to measure than qualitative standards. Let's take a leather coat factory, for example. It would be easy for a manager to determine how many coats were produced in a day, but it would be harder for a manager to determine that each coat matches the exact hue of brown that the factory is striving for. Beyond passing inspection, there will be some coats that appear to be a darker brown than others or some coats that appear to have flaws in the leather. The manager cannot personally examine every single coat. The manager may, instead, perform a random sampling check, but that could give the manager a skewed perspective. Perhaps the manager might randomly choose the two coats out of 20 that are perfect. Furthermore, what might be considered a flaw by the manager may not be considered a flaw by the employee or even the customer. Or, conversely, what the manager may see as a perfect shade of brown the customer may think is too dark.

Quantitative standards and data, therefore, can be measured objectively. Qualitative standards and data, on the other hand, can only be measured subjectively. Subjective data are open to human interpretation, error, and bias. The manager at the coat factory, for example, may not like the particular machine operator that made the 20 coats, so she may judge his work more harshly. Human judgment and the work environment contribute to the interpretation of subjective data.

While there are pitfalls in using subjective data, they often complement objective data. Let's take the BP example at the beginning of this chapter. BP has a standard to have zero accidents, and they did not have one until the drilling rig in the Gulf of Mexico exploded in April 2010. Quantitatively, before April 2010, this standard had been met. However, BP employees had been speaking out prior to the accident sounding alarm bells that an accident could and likely would occur. Qualitatively, then, the drilling rig was an accident waiting to happen. If managers had taken these subjective data, the concerns of the employees, seriously, perhaps the accident could have been prevented.

Regardless of whether the data are quantitative or qualitative, they still must be measured and collected in order for a company to maintain and improve its performance. An old adage states, "If you don't measure it, you can't manage it."

Identifying Shortcomings   The next step in the control process is to compare actual performance with set standards and determine where the variation is. A manager may even find that the actual performance exceeds standards, and if this happens on a regular basis, that manager may need to revise the standards. More commonly, however, a manager will find that performance meets or is below standards. Deviations may be insignificant or significant. A challenge in identifying the shortcomings, and addressing them, is in determining how significant a deviation may be. Figure 15.5, a control chart, is a tool managers can use in determining whether deviations from the standards are meaningful.

As presented in Figure 15.5, the control chart includes upper and lower control limits. A common method for using the control process is to set standards at two standard deviations above or below the average performance level. Looking at the chart, you will see that Team 2 performs the best and Team 3 is the slowest. However, none of these deviations significantly strays from the preferred performance level. These deviations instead fall within the limits and are considered normal variations. If the performance of the teams was to fall outside the variations, however, those meaningful gaps would need to be addressed.

Taking Corrective Action   In the previous example, even though Team 3 was slower than Team 2, the performance of the team was still within the normal deviations. Therefore, the manager would not take any action. And if a vigilant manager did take punitive action, it would likely

FIGURE 15.5

The Control Chart: Determining if Deviations Are Meaningful Gaps

decrease morale and make Team 3's performance decline to the point that it would fall outside the normal deviation.

However, let's suppose that Team 3's performance is much worse than what is depicted in Figure 15.5 and that it does fall outside the normal range of deviation. What should a manager do? The first step would be to look at the standards. Are the standards reasonable and achievable? Are they too harsh or arbitrary? In the case of Team 3, Team 2 is well outperforming them, so it is reasonable to assume that the standards are fair, especially if other teams have a similar performance to that of Team 2. However, aside from this particular example, standards can be set too high or be unreasonable and the manager must address these cases.

Once the manager has come to the conclusion that the standards are achievable and should be met, the manager must look at the performance of the individual or team and address it. The manager must determine at what point or step in the process the individual or team falters. What is the cause for this? Then the manager must directly address the cause. For example, an individual in a call center may be spending too much time talking to her coworkers, which leaves her less time to make the 20 outgoing calls per day she is expected to make. In this case, the manager would directly address the employee's nonnecessary conversations with her coworkers. Or she may be a slow typist and spend too much time typing the details of every call into the computer, leaving her unable to make 20 calls per day. In this case, the manager might look into further training opportunities so the employee can improve her data entry speed. Regardless of why the employee is falling below expectations, the situation must be addressed by the manager as the manager's ultimate responsibility is to the company and ensuring that it is successful.

TYPES OF BUREAUCRATIC CONTROL The three basic control types that a manager can exercise are feedforward control, concurrent control, and feedback control. To examine each of these, we will look at how the Glove Corporation would implement the different types of controls. The Glove Corporation makes fire-resistant gloves for firefighters. One of its clients, for example, is the New York Fire Department. The company has corporate headquarters in Alexandria, Indiana, and a manufacturing plant in Heber Springs, Arkansas.

Feedforward Control   The Glove Corporation uses feedfoward controls to ensure that problems are prevented before they occur. For example, maintenance on all its sewing equipment is

LOC-In 6   Learning Objective Check-In

Dan has been on a work team that is developing limits that act as performance standards on the number of accidents incurred by linemen electrical field workers, on the job. This is the first in a series of steps that Dan's company will be taking in order to actually achieve an acceptable minimum number of accidents per year.

1. The above example illustrates which of the following steps in the control process?
   a. Performance measurement
   b. Establishing standards
   c. Taking corrective action
   d. Identifying gaps

2. The team receives data that was collected by linemen about the number of accidents reported over the last two years. The data includes causes and frequency of types of accidents. What is the next step once this data is collected?
   a. Monitor
   b. Identify gaps
   c. Allocate resources
   d. Take corrective action

completed on a regular basis. The leather and other materials used go through a quality control process in which they are vigorously tested before they are cut for the gloves. Rules and procedures are written and enforced to ensure that safety accidents do not happen. All the staff are trained and retrained to ensure that they are using the equipment in the safest possible way. The Glove Corporation can use feedforward control because it knows, based on recent sales and past experience, the market demand for its gloves and how many gloves it should produce per day. In addition, the Glove Corporation has years of experience in making gloves, and the managers can implement feedforward controls based on past performance.

Concurrent Control   Unlike feedforward control, concurrent control takes place as the work is being carried out. The Glove Corporation, for example, has plant managers that monitor production and randomly check the quality of the gloves as they are being produced. If one pair of gloves is sewn incorrectly, the managers can stop production to correct the problem and ensure that other gloves will not be sewn incorrectly (as that would waste time and inventory of leather and other raw materials). Information technology provides real-time access to data for many companies and enables concurrent control to be more effectively implemented.

Feedback Control   Feedback control is used on occasion in every company, but it is the least useful type of control. Feedback control is information from past performance and occurs after a process has been completed. The plant manager at the Glove Corporation may be reviewing production output from the past two months and notice that during one week, six weeks ago, the machine operator had a dramatically low output. The manager might go to him and try to understand what the problem was. He may not remember what happened six weeks ago, and the problem cannot be adequately addressed. Furthermore, the operator now has his mind on other projects and may not be interested in hearing that he did not do a good job several weeks ago for unknown reasons. Feedback is only motivational and helpful if it is provided in a timely fashion. Customer complaints about quality or timeliness are a common type of feedback control as the customer experiences the product weeks, months, or years after it was produced.

CONCLUDING THOUGHTS

After the introductory vignette that described BP's broken undersea oil pipeline in the Gulf of Mexico that discharged several million barrels of oil into the Gulf, some critical thinking questions were asked. Now that you have read about the basics of operations management and management control, it is time to revisit these questions. The stage of operations management that is most closely related to the BP oil spill into the Gulf of Mexico is the stage that deals with acquiring inputs. The input of concern in this situation is the oil that is acquired below the surface of the ocean by the oil drilling rig and piped to the drilling platform where it can be loaded onto ships that can transport the crude oil to a refinery where the oil can be converted into useful products, such as fuels, plastics, or carbon-based materials. Once the oil reaches the refinery, the second stage—the conversion process—of operations management occurs that converts the crude oil into products or materials that can be used commercially.

Of the three types of control that managers can exercise, the feedforward control is the one that would have been most beneficial to BP in averting the damaging oil spill into the Gulf of Mexico. Feedforward control is designed to prevent problems before they occur. Once the undersea oil pipeline is ruptured and oil gushes into the ocean, it is very difficult and dangerous to repair the broken pipeline since it is located below 5,000 feet (almost one mile) of water where pressures are enormous. During the three months that the undersea oil pipeline discharged oil into the ocean, several unsuccessful attempts were made to cap the hole in the pipeline before it was finally repaired. The best management control tactic is to use feedforward control that minimizes the likelihood of a pipeline breaking by applying preventer systems designed to shut off the flow of oil. If BP had put additional resources into enriching its feedforward control system to inform petroleum engineers of potential risks to the integrity of the pipeline, the economic and ecological disaster attributed to the oil spill described in the opening vignette probably would have been avoided.

FOCUSING ON THE FUTURE: Using Management Theory in Daily Life

Operations Management

Mark Hasting, a Group Vice President for Target Corp., deals with operations issues on a daily basis, so he knows how critical acquiring inputs, controlling the conversion processes, and delivering the output are. Mark uses his knowledge of the operations process to make changes that improve Target's profitability and customer service.

Several years ago, Mark was tasked with the job of streamlining operations for Target. His first action was to convene a task force of experienced store managers. Without their input, he knew that he wouldn't be able to see the issues involved clearly or to create the ideas that were critical for reducing costs to an acceptable level. The task force agreed that the pricing process was an ideal target for streamlining, since it included both material and personnel costs.

Once the task force was assembled, they turned their attention to analyzing the conversion process—that is, looking at the major steps in the pricing process, the amount of time each takes, their order, and their flow. Each Target store uses a plan-o-gram prepared by Target's corporate offices to determine how and where products are displayed throughout the store. Since plan-o-grams change from week to week, pricing labels have to change as well. At Target, all pricing appears on the shelving holding the product, and all pricing is left justified to appear exactly under the first item on the shelf, reading from left to right. The task force knew that stores were responsible for using the plan-o-gram to print out a price label for each product. Price labels were printed on adhesive paper that cost approximately 25 cents for one 8.5 x 11 inch sheet. The adhesive labels were good because they were unlikely to fall off a shelf during the course of a week, but every time the plan-o-gram changed, Target store managers would have to print new labels and hire people to remove the label and the old adhesive and reapply new labels throughout the store. The process was time-consuming and costly.

The first idea for changing the process was proposed by a vendor who had met with one of the members of the task force. The vendor wanted to sell Target a new product—channel strips. These plastic strips can be put on the front of shelving, and they hold plain paper labels. The idea was a good one, and the group discussed how it would affect conversion processes—reducing both the cost of the paper used to create labels (plain paper was much less expensive than adhesive label paper) and the costs associated with employees who were hired to remove the adhesive left behind by old labels. Implementing the change is fairly straightforward and involves only purchasing the channel strips, setting them up, printing the new labels, and putting them in the strips.

As the group talked, however, it occurred to Mark that rather than putting one label up at a time, the process could be even more cost effective if the paper labels came in long strips, each strip the length of a four-foot shelving unit. Implementing this idea was complex, because it required finding a printer that could create four-foot labels at a reasonable price and convincing corporate management to make the change. Mark worked with numerous vendors, finally finding one who could supply the necessary hardware. Now, plan-o-gram packages are delivered from Target's corporate office complete with preprinted pricing strips, which are easily inserted into channel strips. The output of the process is that pricing is standardized, customers are satisfied because they know what different items cost, and Target saves money on both materials and personnel.

Another operations project for Mark involved reorganizing backroom operations. When Mark was a store manager, he realized that his employees were spending a considerable amount of time searching for items in the company back rooms. After talking with his employees and analyzing scanning data routinely provided by Target, he realized that employees had to scan location tags up to eight times to find an individual item. The reason for this was that items were stored in "sections"—lengths of four-foot shelving that were identified with scannable labels. The problem was that within each section, items were further organized into one-foot "waco" boxes, which were not labeled. Mark's solution to the problem was to put location scanning labels on each of the waco boxes, as well as on the shelving sections. Interestingly enough, this logical choice was difficult to implement. Operations at Target are highly centralized, and Mark's idea was not the commonly accepted practice at the time. In order to finally get the change put in place, Mark had to do his own research on the conversion process—measuring the number of scans it took to identify a given item in the back room. Fortunately, Mark was able to show that his new system reduced the average number of scans from over 8 to under 2, saving the organization time and money, while increasing customer satisfaction. As a result, Mark's idea was implemented companywide.

Mark describes another operations innovation that influences how Target handles inventory. Using the idea that the optimum inventory level is the amount of product that fits in the shelving space allocated to that product on the sales floor, Mark helped to create a program called "Make It Fit." This program encourages vendors to supply their product to Target in lots that exactly match the space available for the product on the sales floor. For example, if 12 bottles of shampoo fit into the shelving unit allocated to them, the vendors are asked to send cases that contain only 12 bottles of their product. Vendors that produce larger products, for example, liquid household cleansers, might be asked to ship cases of their product that contain only 6 bottles. This system works well, but not all vendors can comply with Target's request. To deal with the problem, Mark helped to create a system where excess items were reboxed once they got to the Target distribution center. This process change, combined with Target's sophisticated computerized reordering system, ensures that each store gets the exact amount of product they need from centralized distribution centers every day.

Summary of Learning Objectives

Operations management is at the very heart of the competitiveness of an organization. This chapter has described the process of operations management and presented the major tools used in operations management. Effective operations management requires understanding of the stages of operation management and the tools used to manage these processes. The material presented in the chapter to meet each of the learning objectives set out of the start of the chapter is summarized below.

1 Define operations management and its three stages: inputs, conversion, and disposition.

- Operations management is the process of obtaining materials or ideas, transforming them into the product, and providing the final product to a user.
- Stages of operations management are acquiring inputs, controlling the conversion process, and delivering the output.

2 Describe **materials requirements planning (MRP)** and understand its use in operations management.

- **MRP** is an essential part of the input stage.
- It is the process of analyzing a design to determine the required materials and parts.

3 Be familiar with the conversion process tools of operations management, including Gantt charts, PERT networks, and statistical process control.

- Several tools can be used to determine an efficient sequence and to monitor the conversion process.
- **Gantt charts** provide a visual sequence of the process steps.
- **PERT networks** are a technique used to coordinate efforts on a project.

- **Statistical process control** is a group of quantitative techniques used to detect and eliminate deviations in the conversion process. Statistical process control techniques include: check sheets, Pareto analysis, process flow analysis, cause-and-effect diagrams, process capability measure, and control charts.

4 Explain the role quality management plays in the operations management process.

- Quality management approach focuses on the system; uses customer driven standards; approaches quality as integral to the work process; and empowers workers and uses *PDCA* cycle.

5 Understand and apply the principles of kaizen, just-in-time manufacturing, and kanban,

- **Kaizen** is the quality management technique of continuous improvement, identifying small improvement steps and focusing on waste reduction/efficiency.
- In **just-in-time manufacturing** steps are performed just as subsequent steps require them to keep inventory levels low. This requires close relationships with suppliers.
- **Kanban** uses cards to generate inventory.

6 Describe *management control* and understand the importance of control systems.

- Control is the process of comparing performance to standards and taking any needed corrective actions.
- Control is the means by which management assures that desired objectives are being achieved.

7 Identify the major types of bureaucratic control.

- Feedforward control is designed to anticipate any problems before they occur.
- Concurrent control takes place as the work process is going on.
- Feedback control uses past data to improve future performance.

Discussion Questions

1. Why do you think Deming's work was more widely accepted by Japanese firms than by U.S. firms?
2. Why is the supplier relationship so important in operations management? What problems do you think might occur for the firm if it used too many suppliers? Too few? Do you think being an exclusive supplier for a firm is advantageous for the supplier?
3. How do you think an Internet provider might structure its operations management for its product, which is a service rather than a good? Describe what you think would be the inputs, transformation process, and disposition of its service.
4. Why is the concept of reducing waste so important to quality management systems?
5. Why do you think statistical tools are important in a total quality management organization?
6. Can a service industry use just-in-time principles? Explain your answer.
7. In what circumstances do you think a firm would choose process reengineering to improve its operations management? When might it choose the kaizen process?
8. Standards are critical to control efforts. How do you think they should be developed?

Management Minicase 15.1
Customers Report Problems with Apple's Latest Smart Phone

Since Apple launched the latest version of its popular smart phone, iPhone 4 in 2010, bloggers that report on new consumer technology have been sending reports over the Internet that the phone loses signal strength and may even drop calls when held in a certain way. Shortly after these reports circulated, *Consumer Reports*, a respected product-testing magazine, said it would not recommend the iPhone 4 to potential buyers because of a faulty antenna.

When criticisms of the smart phone first became known, Steve Jobs, Apple's CEO purportedly told one irate customer to not hold it in a certain way or to buy a case for it. Apparently, the criticism has not dented consumers' enthusiasm for the iPhone because it is estimated

that over two million of the phones were sold within a few months of being released to the market.

In defense of phone's product design, Apple has argued that faulty software lies at the heart of the iPhone 4's connectivity problem. However, a growing body of evidence, including a *Consumer Reports* finding suggests that Apple's decision to wrap the phone's two antennas around the device rather than place them inside may be to blame. The phone's signal strength drops when a user grips the phone by the metal antenna band. This in turn suggests that testing of the iPhone 4 may not have been sufficiently rigorous.

Apple is well known for the skill with which it manages manufacturing. Yet some analysts have speculated that a glitch in the production process for the iPhone 4 may be to blame. Whatever the root cause, Apple's executives need to bring it to light as soon as possible and move fast to correct it.

DISCUSSION QUESTIONS

1. Do you agree with how Steve Jobs handled the criticism of the performance of the iPhone 4 when it first became known that customers were having problems with the device? How should he have handled this situation?

2. Which stage of the operations management process is the most likely source of the problem?

3. Which type of control—feedforward, concurrent or feedback control—would be most beneficial to fix the problem with the iPhone 4?

Sources: Based on *The Economist*, "Antennaegate: A Minor Glitch in Apple's Latest Phone Hints at Bigger Problems," July 17, 2010, p. 68; J. Yarrow, "Uh Oh, Is Apple's iPhone 4 a Lemon?," *Business Insider*, June 24, 2010, www.businessinsider.com; L. Latif, "Jobs Encases Apple's iPhone 4 Problem," *The Inquirer*, July 17, 2010, www.theinquirer.net.

Management Minicase 15.2

Facebook Users Want to Control More of Their Personal Information

While in 2010 Facebook reported having 500 million global users of their social networking site, at the same time some people are leaving Facebook because the site changed its rules such that a lot of personal information—like where you went to school, where you work, and what music you like—now gets made public by default. Some information is even shared with companies that are special partners of Facebook, such as Yelp, Pandora, and Microsoft. While there are ways to protect some of this information by tinkering with the privacy settings on Facebook, it is tricky to figure out the settings.

At the end of 2009 Facebook changed the default settings on its privacy controls so that individual's personal information would be shared with everyone on the network rather than selected friends. Facebook argued that this reflected a shift in society toward greater openness and noted that users could still adjust privacy settings back again. Privacy activists have lobbied for it to be reversed.

Activists fear that people are being lured into Facebook with the promise of a fun, free service, and do not realize that they are paying for it by giving up a lot of their personal information. Facebook then attempts to monetize the data entered by users by selling it to advertisers that want to send targeted messages.

The switch should not have come as a surprise. Initially, many social networks impose fairly tough privacy policies in order to attract and reassure users. However, when more users join, controls are gradually loosened to encourage more sharing. As people share more information, Facebook can increase the traffic against which it sells advertising. The more Facebook learns about users' likes and dislikes, the better it can target ads that generate hundreds of millions of dollars.

DISCUSSION QUESTIONS

1. Why did Facebook decide to make it more difficult for users to control who has access to the personal information they post on the Web site?

2. Which type of control is of concern to the Facebook users and privacy activists—feedforward, concurrent, or feedback control?

3. Should Facebook use more control in managing how the information is used among the users of the social networking Web site? What is the basis of your answer?

Sources: Based on D. Lyons, "The High Price of Facebook," *Newsweek*, June 7, 2010, p. 12; *The Economist*, "Lives of Others: Facebook and Google Face a Backlash from Users and Regulators Alike Over the Way They Have Handled Sensitive Data, " May 22, 2010, pp. 667–68; J. Hempel, "How Facebook Is Taking Over Our Lives," *Fortune*, March 2, 2009, pp. 49–56.

Internet Exercise 15.1

Andersen Windows

www.andersenwindows.com

Visit the Web site of Andersen Windows and read Andersens's timeline in the corporation history portion of the "About Andersen" section of the side. Then answer the following questions:

1. How did Andersen use effective operations management in its first 10 years?

2. Although Andersen may not have instituted a kaizen program, identify some examples of quality management techniques the company has used over the years.

3. What quality management principles can you see at work in the timeline?

Endnotes

1. M. Gupta, A. Adams, and L. Raho, "Traditional Management, Quality Management, and Constraints Management: Perceptions of ASQ Members". *The Quality Management Journal 10* (2003): 25–37.
2. A. Kumar, "Software Takes the Sting out of Horseradish Production: System Automatically Ages Ingredient and End-Item Lots Ensuring Stock Won't Be Wasted," *Food Engineering 75* (2003): 781.
3. N. Logothetis, *Managing for Total Quality* (Hertfordshire, UK: Prentice Hall International, 1992), p. 5.
4. M. Imai, *Kaizen: The Key to Japan's Competitive Success* (New York: Random House, 1986).
5. R. Gourlay, "Back to Basics on the Factory Floor," *Financial Times*, January 4, 1994, p. 12.
6. D. Drickhamer, "The Kanban E-volution," *Material Handling Management* 60 (2005): 24–26.
7. Ibid.
8. M. Hammer and J. Champy, *Reengineering the Corporation* (New York: Harper Business, 1993), p. 35.

References

Chapter 1

Ante, S. E. (2006, February 13). Giving the boss the big picture. *BusinessWeek*, 48–50.

Back, A., & L. Chao (2010, March 24). Google braces for fallout in China. *The Wall Street Journal*, A-1.

Barboza, D. (2006, February 25). Google cuts 2 features for China. *The New York Times*, C-l.

Barboza, D. (2006, February 9). Some assembly needed: China as Asia factory. *The New York Times*, C-l.

Barnard, C. I. (1938). *The functions of the executive.* Cambridge, MA: Harvard University Press.

Barnes, B. (2003, January 3). The new face of air rage. *The Wall Street Journal*, W-l.

Bartol, K. M., & Martin, D. C. (1998). *Management* (3rd ed.). New York: McGraw-Hill/Irwin.

Bateman, T. S., & Snell, S. A. (1999). *Management* (3rd ed.). New York: McGraw-Hill/Irwin.

Bloomberg BusinessWeek Research Service (2010, March 29). Poor Math and Science education in the U.S. will lead to higher unemployment, 15.

Boulding, K. E. (1956). General systems theory: The skeleton of science. *Management Science, 2,* 197–208.

Burns, T., & Stalker, B. M. (1961). *The management of innovation.* London, UK: Tavistock Publications.

Business Performance Management software dashboard web (2011). www.business.com.

Business Schools receive only a C+ in ethics (2010, March 30). *Ethics World.* http://www.ethicsworld.org.

Can't afford employees? Then outsource/subcontract (2011). www.prlog.org.

Chappell, L. (2006, February 7). Toyota to spurn Michigan. www.autoweek.com.

Cohen, W. M., & Levinthal, D. A. (1990). Absorptive capacity: A new perspective on learning and innovation. *Administrative Science Quarterly, 35,* 128–152.

Conlin, M., & M. Herbst (2010, January 18). The disposable worker. *BusinessWeek*, 19–21.

Crovitz, L. (2010, January 11). China's web crackdown continues. *The Wall Street Journal*, A-17.

Daft, R. L. (2000). *Management* (4th ed.). Fort Worth: Dryden Press.

Daft, R. L. (2005). *Management.* Thompson: Southwestern Press.

Dean, J. W., & Bowen, D. E. (1994). Management theory and total quality: Improving research and practice through theory development. *Academy of Management Review, 19,* 392–418.

Deming, W. E. (1986). *Out of the crisis.* Cambridge, MA: MIT Center for Advanced Engineering Study.

Denning, L. (2010, January 11). Detroit's life after death is no paradise. *BusinessWeek*, 39–40.

Dolan, M. (2010, January 26). Ford to begin hiring at new lower wages. *The Wall Street Journal.*

Donaldson, L. (1996). The normal science of structural contingency theory. In S. Clegg & C. Hardy (Eds.), *Handbook of organization studies* 57–76. Thousand Oaks, CA: Sage Publishing.

Duncan, W. J. (1989). *Great ideas in management.* San Francisco: Jossey-Bass.

Einhorn, B. (2010, January 25). Google and China: A Win for liberty and strategy. *BusinessWeek*, 35.

Elgin, B. (2006, February 20). Outrunning China's web cops. *BusinessWeek,* 38–40.

Engardio, P. (2006, January 30). The future of outsourcing. *BusinessWeek,* 50–56.

Ethics education at top 50 business schools (2010, March 30). *Ethics World.* http://www.ethicsworld.org.

Farnham, A. (1997, July 21). The man who changed work forever. *Fortune,* 114.

Fast, N. (1982). The Lincoln Electric Company. In F. K. Foulkes (Ed.), *Human resources management.* Englewood Cliffs, NJ: Prentice Hall.

Feder, B. J. (1995, September 5). Rethinking a model incentive plan. *The New York Times,* 1, 33.

Federico, S. (2010, February). Outsourcing versus integration at home or abroad and firm heterogeneity. *Empirica, 37(1),* 15–28.

Foust, D. (2003, January 27). What worked at GE isn't working at Home Depot. *BusinessWeek,* 40.

Gerdes, L. (2010, September 15). The best places to launch a career. *BusinessWeek*, 22–23.

Gloeckler, G. (2010, March 15). With jobs scarce, business schools get creative. *BusinessWeek*, 18–19.

Goldberg, J. (2007, April 19). Compliance officers take their own path. *New York Law Journal*, 15–25.

Gomez-Mejia, L. R., Balkin, D. B., & Cardy, R. (2004). *Managing human resources.* Englewood Cliffs, NJ: Prentice Hall.

Gomez-Mejia, L. R., Balkin, D. B., & Cardy, R. L. (2001). *Managing human resources* (2nd ed.). Upper Saddle River, NJ: Prentice Hall.

Grossman, L., & Beech, H. (2006, February 13). Google under the gun. *Time,* 53–54.

Hamel, G., & Prahalad, C. K. (1994). *Competing for the future.* Boston: Harvard Business School Press.

Hammer, M., & Champy, J. (1993). *Reengineering the corporation.* New York: Harper Business.

Heizer, J., & Render, B. (1996). *Production and operations management.* Englewood Cliffs, NJ: Prentice Hall.

Huber, G. P. (1991). Organizational learning: The contributing processes and the literatures. *Organization Science, 2,* 88–115.

Hyde, P. (2003, January 22). Timesizing: Less work and more pay – What a crazy idea! www.timesizing.com.

Ignatius, A. (2006, February 20). In search of the real Google. *Time,* 36–50.

Ihiwan, M. (2010, January 18). While Sony bets on outsourcing TV's, the Korean giant is building an edge by making its own. *BusinessWeek*, 11–12.

Jackson, J. H., Morgan, C. P., & Paolillo, J. G. (1986). *Organization theory* (3rd ed.). Englewood Cliffs, NJ: Prentice Hall.

Jay, A. (1970). *Management and Machiavelli.* New York: Harper & Row.

Jones, G. R., George, J. M., & Hill, C. W. (2000). *Contemporary management.* New York: McGraw-Hill/Irwin.

Jones, G. R., George, J. M., & Hill, C. W. (2001). *Contemporary management.* New York: McGraw-Hill/Irwin.

Kast, F. E., & Rosenweig, J. E. (1972). General systems theory: Applications for organization and management. *Academy of Management Journal, 15,* 447–465.

Kranthammer, C. (2006, February 13). Don't believe the hype. We are still no. 1. *Time,* 41.

Lawrence, P. R., & Lorsch, J. W. (1967). *Organization and environment.* Boston: Graduate School of Business Administration, Harvard University.

Linebaugh, K. (2010, January 28). Toyota heir faces crisis at the wheel. *The Wall Street Journal.*

Linebaugh, K., & N. Shirouzu (2010, February 8). Toyota's U.S. chief is on the hot seat. *The Wall Street Journal,* C-1.

Lohr, S. (2006, February 16). Outsourcing is climbing skills ladder. *The New York Times,* C-1.

MacMillan, D. (2010, February 22). Google's new billion dollar baby. *BusinessWeek,* 22.

Management dashboards (2011). www.LogiXML.com.

Mandel, M. (2009, November 9). By overlooking cuts in research and development, product design, and worker training, GDP is greatly overstating the economy's strength. *BusinessWeek,* 35.

Maslow, A. H. (1954). *Motivation and personality.* New York: Harper & Row.

McCracken, J. (2006, March 1). Detroit's symbol of dysfunction: Paying employees not to work. *The Wall Street Journal,* A-1.

McGregor, D. (1960). *The Human Side of Enterprise.* New York: McGraw-Hill. 33–48.

McKinnon, R. (2010, January 14). Google gets on the right side of history. *The Wall Street Journal,* C-1.

Needleman, S. (2010, January 28). Study asks: Who has easy path to top? *The Wall Street Journal,* A-1.

O'Connor, M. (2010). Federal Procurement Ethics: The complete legal guide. http://books.google.com.

Oh, H. (2006, February 6). Upfront. *BusinessWeek,* 14.

Ohnsman, J. Green, & K. Inoue (2010, March 22). The humbling of Toyota. *BusinessWeek,* 17–19.

Onifade, A. (2010). The indispensable secretary. *Journal of Social Science, 22(1),* 47–51.

Peters, J. W. (2006, March 1). Both Ford and GM scale back. *The New York Times,* C-1.

Prasad, E. R., Prasad, V. S., & Satyanarayana, P. *Administrative thinkers.* New Delhi, India: Sterling Publishers.

Quinn, R. E., Faerman, S. R., Thompson, M. P., & M. R. McGrath (1996). *Becoming a master manager* (2nd ed.). New York: John Wiley.

Reh, J. (2011). "Key performance indicators." About.com Management. http://management.about.com.

Ripley, A., & Sieger, M. (2003, January 6). The special agent. *Time,* 34–40.

Roethlisberger, F., & Dickson, W. (1939). *Management and the worker: An account of a research program conducted by the Western Electric Company, Hawthorne Works, Chicago.* New York: John Wiley & Sons.

Saporito, B. (2010, February 22). Toyota got tangled. *BusinessWeek,* 29–32.

Saporito, B. (2010, February 25). Toyota's recall. *BusinessWeek,* 32–34.

Schiller, Z. (1996, January 22). A model incentive plan gets caught in a vise. *BusinessWeek,* 89.

Schlosser, J. (2003, February 3) Uphill battle. *Fortune,* 64.

Sharplin, A., & Seeger, J. (1998). The Lincoln Electric Company, 1996. In A. A. Thompson, & A. J. Strickland (Eds.), *Strategic management* (10th ed). New York: McGraw-Hill/Irwin.

Sheldrake, J. (1996). *Management theory.* London, UK: International Thompson Business Press.

Shellenberger, S. (2006, February 16). Avoiding the next Enron: Today's crop of soon to be grads seeks job security. *The Wall Street Journal,* D-1.

Smith, A. (1937). *The wealth of nations.* New York: Modern Library.

Spencer, B. A. (1994). Models of organization and total quality management: A comparison and critical evaluation. *Academy of Management Review, 19,* 446–471.

Steveman, B. (2010, January 4). The action stays offshore. *BusinessWeek,* 34–36.

Tzu, S. (1963). *The art of war.* Oxford, UK: Oxford University Press.

Vascellaro, J. (2010, March 25). Brim drove Google's pullback. *The Wall Street Journal,* B-1.

Vascellaro, J. (2010, January 13). Google warns China exit over hacking. *The Wall Street Journal,* A-1.

Vascellaro, J., & A. Back (2010, January 20). Google prepares for its next step in China. *The Wall Street Journal,* B-5.

Vergano, D. (2006, February 9). U.S. could fall behind in global brain race. *USA Today,* D-1.

Visual calc-management dashboards and online calculators (2011). www.visualcalc.com.

Weber, J. (2006, February 13). The new ethics enforcers. *BusinessWeek,* 75–77.

Welch, D., N. Naughton, & B. Helm (2010, February 22). Detroit's big chance. *BusinessWeek,* 22–23.

Welch, D. (2010, March 1). The man with the toughest job at GM. *BusinessWeek.*

Welch, D. (2010, January 25). Why VW is the car giant to watch. *BusinessWeek,* 16–18.

Wessel, D. (2010, January 27). U.S. Keeps foreign Ph.D's. *The Wall Street Journal,* A-3.

Womack, J. P. (2006, February 13). Why Toyota won. *The Wall Street Journal,* C-3.

Wratley, G. R. (2011). Are you serious about ethics: For companies that can't guarantee confidentiality the answer is no. *The Conference Board.* www.conference-board.org.

Zeller, T. (2006, February 1). Microsoft amends its policy for shutting down blogs. *The New York Times.*

Zeller, T. (2006, February 15). Internet firms face questions about censoring online searches in China. *The New York Times,* C-3.

Zeller, T. (2006, February 16). Web firms are grilled on dealings in China. *The New York Times,* C-1.

Chapter 2

Balfour, F., & Roberts, D. (2005, September 26). Stealing managers from the big boys. *BusinessWeek,* 54.

Ball, D. A., McCullouch, W. H., Frantz, P. L., Geringer, J. M., & Minor, M. S. (2002). *International Business: The challenge of global competition.* New York: McGraw-Hill.

Belforti, R. K., Wall, M. S., Lindenauer, P., Pekow, P., & Rothberg, M. (2010). International outsourcing of medical research by high income countries. *Journal of Investigative Medicine, 58(2),* 287–294.

Bellman, E., & Koppel, N. (2005, September 28). More U.S. legal work moves to India's low-cost lawyers. *The Wall Street Journal*, B-l.

Bernstein, A. (2005, October 10). Sweatshop Swipe. *BusinessWeek*, 14.

Blow the whistle – No, wait: Ethics hotlines may be illegal in Europe (2005, Fall). *Business Ethics*, 10.

Bremner, B., Schiller, Z., Smart, T, & Holstein, W. (1996, July 22). Keiretsu connections. *BusinessWeek*, 52–53.

Brunk, K. H. (2010). Exploring origins of ethical company/ brand perceptions – A Consumer perspective of corporate ethics. *Journal of Business Research, 63(3)*, 255–262.

Buckman, R. (2005, August 18). "Cellphone game rings in new niche: Ultracheap." *The Wall Street Journal*, B-4.

Burt, S. (2010). *Retailing in Europe: The International Review of Retail Distribution and Consumer Research, 20(1)*, 9–27.

Can't afford employees? Then outsource, subcontract (2011). http://www.prlog.org.

Castells, M. (2010). *End of millennium: The information age: Economy, society, and culture*. New York, NY: Wiley-Blackwell.

Chandler, C. (2005, October 31). "India's bumpy ride." *Fortune*, 134.

Cohen, R. (1991, November 21). For Coke, world is its oyster. *The New York Times*, Dl, D5.

Darling, J., & Nauss, D. (1995, February 19). Stall in the fast lane. *Los Angeles Times*, 1.

De Jonquieres, G. (1998, November 11). Foreign direct investment worldwide figures to reach $430 billion. *Financial Times*, 6.

Donnelly, J. H., Gibson, J., & Ivancevich, J. M. (1995). *Fundamentals of management*. Burr Ridge, IL: McGraw-Hill/Irwin.

Dvorak, P. (2005, September 19), Stringer faces first big test as Sony's chief. *The Wall Street Journal*, B-l.

Dvorak, P. (2005, September 24). Culture clash crimps Sony CEO. *The Wall Street Journal*, A-6.

Edmondson, G., & C. Faivre de' Arcier (2005, July 4). Got 5,000 euros? Need a new car? *BusinessWeek*, 49.

El-Rashidi, Y. (2005). D'oh! Arabized Simpsons aren't getting many laughs. *The Wall Street Journal*.

Fackler, M. (2005, October 29). Wal-Mart doubles down on its investment in Japan. *The New York Times*, B-4.

Ganesan, S., George, M., Jap, S., Palmatier, R. W., & B. Weitz (2009). Supply chain manager and retailer performance. *Journal of Retailing, 85(1)*, 84–94.

Gewaltig, Natascha (2006, February 13). Can Germany escape the doldrums? *BusinessWeek Online*. www.businessweek.com.

The global 500. (1995, August 7). *Fortune*, 130–131.

Graff, J. (2005, November 14). Why France is burning. *Time*, 36.

Grant, L. (1997, April 14). That overseas job could derail your career. *Fortune*, 166.

Greenberger, R. S., & Smith, C. S. (1997, April 28). CD piracy flourishes in China. *The Wall Street Journal*, Al.

Gunther, M. (2005, Fall). Can factory monitoring ever really work? *Fortune*, 12.

Gunther, M. (2005, June 27). Cops of the global village. *Fortune*, 158.

Hardwig, J. (2010). The stockholders – A lesson for business ethics from bioethics. *Journal of Business Ethics, 91(3)*, 329–341.

Hill, C. (2003). *International business*. New York: McGraw-Hill/Irwin.

Hill, C. W., & Jones, G. R. (1995). *Strategic management theory*. Boston: Houghton Mifflin.

Hofstede, G. (1984). *Culture consequences: International differences in work related values*. Beverly Hills, CA: Sage.

http://en.wikipedia.org/wiki/Dacia-Logan. 2011.

http://indiacar.com. 2011.

http://Java.sun.com/features/. 2011.

http://Java.sys-con.com. 2011.

http://www.IBM.com.developerworks.Java. 2011.

http://www.renault-dacia-Logan.com. 2011.

Hudson, R. L. (2003, January 24). Europe's great expectations. *The Wall Street Journal*, A-10.

Hymowitz, C. (2005, October 17). More American chiefs are taking top posts at overseas concerns. *The Wall Street Journal*, B-l.

Ihlwan, M., & Roberts, D. (2005, August 1). Made in Korea, assembled in China. *BusinessWeek*, 48.

Koretz, G. (1999, September 13). A woman's place is. . . *BusinessWeek*, 28.

Kripalani, M. (2005, October 10). A quiet shopping spree overseas. *BusinessWeek*, 54.

Landler, Mark (2006, February 3). Selling well everywhere but home. *The New York Times*, C-1, C-4.

Latta, G. W. (2005). High mobility international employees. *WorldatWork Journal*, 48.

Lustgarten, A. (2005, August 8). Drug testing goes offshore. *Fortune*, 67–72.

Matlack, C., & Burrows, P. (2005, October 10). HP's French twist. *BusinessWeek*, 53.

Mehta, S. N. (1994, July 7). Enterprise: Small companies look to cultivate foreign businesses. *The Wall Street Journal*, B2.

Naik, G. V., Karp, J., Millman, J., Fassiti, F., & Slater, J. (2003, January 24). Global baby bust. *The Wall Street Journal*, B-l.

Oster, P. (1993, November). Why Japan's execs travel better. *BusinessWeek*, 68.

Premiums and allowances for expatriates (2005, August 5). *Workspan*, 13.

Reilly, D. (2005, November 21). France Ends Impasse with SEC. *The Wall Street Journal*, A-8.

Rhoads, C. (2005, June 23). Motorola's modernizer. *The Wall Street Journal*, B-l.

Rosenzwaig, R. (2005, July 5). How much did we spend this year? *Workspan*, 25.

Runnion, T. T. (2005, July 5). Expatriate programs. *Workspan*, 19.

Sains, A., Palmer, A. J., Bush, J., Roberts, D., & K. Hall (2005, November 14). Ikea: How the Swedish retailer became a global cult brand. *BusinessWeek*, 95–106.

Shellenberger, S. (2005, October 27). Separation anxiety: Short job transfers create problems for families left behind. *The Wall Street Journal*, D-l.

Sims, G. T. (2005, November 1). Corn Flakes clash shows the glitches in European Union. *The Wall Street Journal*, A-l.

Special issue of *BusinessWeek* on globalization (2003, February 2).

Steverman, B. (2010, January 4). The action stays offshore. *BusinessWeek*, 60–64.

Taylor, A. (2003, January 20). Got 300,000? *Fortune*, 118–125.

Trent, R. J. (2010). Pathology practice and pharmacogenomics. *Pharmacogenomics, 11(1)*, 105–111.

Trolman, S. (2005, August 5). Rationalizing global incentive pay plans look at the big picture. *Workspan,* 17.

Wild, J. J., Wild K. L., & Han, J. C. Y. (2000). *International Business,* Upper Saddle River, NJ: Prentice Hall.

World Trade Organization (1998). *International Trade Trends and Statistics.* Geneva: WTO.

Wrighton, J., & Sapsford, J. (2005, April 26). For Nissan's rescuer, Ghosn new road rules await at Renault. *The Wall Street Journal,* A-1.

www.best-german-gifts.com/playmobil-toys.html. 2011.

www.collectorbil.com. 2011.

www.en.wikipedia.org/wiki/playmobil. 2011.

www.Ikea.com. 2011.

www.markosweb.com. 2011.

www.millionaireplay.com. 2011.

www.playmobil.com. Accessed April 2010.

Chapter 3

Argenti, P. (2004, Fall). Collaborating with activists: How Starbucks works with NGOs. *California Management Review,* 91–116.

Barrett, A. (2004, November 22). Merck: How much misery after Vioxx? *BusinessWeek,* 48–50.

Ben & Jerry's social and environmental assessment (2004). www.benjerry.com/our_company/about_us/.

Big trouble for Merck (2004, November 6). *The Economist,* 61–62.

Boeing v. Airbus (1997, July 26). *The Economist,* 59–61.

Brull, S. V. (1999, May 10). For all that tobacco money, don't stint on the smoking war. *BusinessWeek,* 40.

Byrne, J. (1988, February 15). Businesses are signing up for ethics 101. *BusinessWeek,* 56–57.

Carroll, A. B. (1996). *Business and society* (3rd ed.). Cincinnati: OH: South-Western Publishing.

Chez Panisse Foundation. www.chezpanisse.com. Accessed April 11, 2010.

Cochran, P. L., & Wood, R. A. (1984). Corporate social responsibility and financial performance. *Academy of Management Journal, 31,* 854–872.

Consumer group to boycott Unilever products (2000, December 6). *Reuters.* http://dailynews.yahoo.com/h/nm/20001206/bs/unilever_benjerrys_dc_2.html.

Corporate Citizenship at Matsushita (2010). www.panasonic.net/citizenship/index.html.

Daft, R. L. (2005). *The Leadership Experience* (3rd ed.). Mason, OH: Thompson. 576.

Donaldson, T., & Preston, L. E. (1995). The stakeholder theory of the corporation: Concepts, evidence, and implications. *Academy of Management Review, 20,* 65–91.

Driscoll, D. (1998, March). Business ethics and compliance: What management is doing and why. *Business and Society Review, 99,* 33–51.

Dworkin, T. M., & Near, J. P. (1997). A better statutory approach to whistle blowing. *Business Ethics Quarterly, 7(1),* 1–16.

Dwyer, P., & Carney, D. (2002, December 16). Year of the whistleblower. *BusinessWeek,* 107–110.

Eli Lilly and Company, (1990). Guidelines of company policy.

Field, D. (1997, August 5). UPS strike stifles shippers. *USA Today,* 1A.

Freeman, R. E. (1984). *Strategic management: A stakeholder approach.* Boston: Pitman Publishing.

Frooman, J. (1999). Stakeholder influence strategies. *Academy of Management Review, 24,* 191–205.

Gard, L. (2004, November 22). We're good guys, buy from us. *BusinessWeek,* 72–74.

Gelman, E. (1985, February 11). A giant under fire: General Dynamics faces numerous charges of fraud. *Newsweek,* 24–25.

General Dynamics (1988). Standards of business ethics and conduct.

Global corruption report 2003. www.globalcorruptionreport.org.

Greenberg, J. (1990). Organizational justice: Yesterday, today and tomorrow. *Journal of Management, 16,* 399–432.

Greenwald, J. (1989, March 22). Let's make a deal. *Time,* 84–86.

Grow, B. (2005, August 15). The debate over doing good. *BusinessWeek,* 76–78.

Gundlach, M., Douglas, S., & Martinko, M. (2003). The decision to blow the whistle. A social information processing framework. *Academy of Management Review, 28,* 107–123.

Gunther, M. (2004, May 31). A pesky environmental group called the Rainforest Action Network is getting under the skin of corporate America. *Fortune,* 158–164.

Hanson, A. (1990, July). What employees say about drug testing. *Personnel,* 32–36.

Harrington, S. J. (1991). What corporate America is teaching about ethics. *Academy of Management Executive, 5(1),* 21–30.

Harrison, J. S., & St. John, C. H. (1996). Managing and partnering with external stakeholders. *Academy of Management Executive, 10(2),* 46–59.

Hemphill, T. A. (1994, Summer). Strange bedfellows cozy up for a clean environment. *Business and Society Review,* 38–44.

Henderson, V. E. (1982). The ethical side of enterprise. *Sloan Management Review, 23,* 37–47.

Hoffman, W. M., & Moore, J. M. (1990). *Business ethics* (2nd ed.) New York: McGraw-Hill.

Hymowitz, C. (2005, February 22). Asked to be charitable, more CEOs seek to aid their businesses as well. *The Wall Street Journal,* B-1.

Jackson, J. H., Miller, R. L., & Miller, S. G. (1997). *Business and society today,* St. Paul: West Publishing.

Jackson, M. (1997, May 12). 50% of workers commit unethical acts, survey says. *Boulder Daily Camera,* 1B.

JD Edwards & Company (1993). Corporate ideals and values.

Kotter, J. P. (1997, March 31). Matsushita: The World's Greatest Entrepreneur. *Fortune,* 105–110.

Likierman, A. (2009). The five traps of performance management. *Harvard Business Review, 87(10),* 96–101.

McGuire, J. B., Sundgren, A., & Schneeweis, T. (1988). Corporate social responsibility and firm financial performance. *Academy of Management Journal, 27,* 42–56.

McLean, B. (2001, December 24). Why Enron went bust. *Fortune,* 58–68.

Moore, T. (1982, November 29). The fight to save Tylenol. *Fortune,* 48–49.

Munk, N. (1999, April 12). How Levi's trashed a great American brand. *Fortune,* 82–90.

Murphy, P. E. (1989). Creating ethical corporate structures. *Sloan Management Review, 30,* 81–89.

Narvan, F. (2005). Ethical dilemmas in the everyday workplace. www.ethics.org/resources.

Near, J. P., & Miceli, M. P. (1985). Organizational dissidence: The case of whistleblowing. *Journal of Business Ethics, 4,* 1–16.

New Belgium Brewery: Four principles of sustainable business (2008, June 7). www.triplepundit.com.

New Belgium Brewing Web site (2010). www.newbelgium.com/sustainability.

Ordonez, L., Schweitzer, M., Galinsky, A., & Bazerman, M. (2009). *Academy of Management Perspectives, 4(1),* 6–16.

Park, A. (2003, February 10). Family feuds don't get nastier than this. *BusinessWeek,* 62–63.

Pharmaceuticals: Pushing pills (2003, February 15). *The Economist,* 61.

Robbins, S. P., & Coulter, M. (1996). *Management* (5th ed.). Upper Saddle River, NJ: Prentice Hall.

Roberts, N. C, & King, P. J. (1989, Winter). The stakeholder audit goes public. *Organizational Dynamics,* 63–79.

Saekel, Karola (2005, September 7). Culinary Pioneers Pioneering Garden Marks a Decade. *San Francisco Chronicle,* F-2.

Sager, I. (2003, February 10). Tech's kickback culture, *BusinessWeek,* 74–77.

Sashkin, M., & Kiser, K. J. (1993). *Putting total quality management to work.* San Francisco: Berrett-Koehler.

Savage, G. T., Nix, T. W., Whitehead, C. J., & Blair, J. D. (1991). Strategies for assessing and managing organizational stakeholders. *Academy of Management Executive,* 5(2), 61–75.

Schrage, E. (2004, June). Supply and Brand. *Harvard Business Review,* 20–21.

Schwartz, B. (2009, November 23). The Dark Side of Incentives. *BusinessWeek,* 84.

Server, A. (2004, January 26). Hot Starbucks to Go. *Fortune,* 60–74.

Severson, Kim (2004, August 29). Food joins academic menu in Berkeley school district. *San Francisco Chronicle,* A-1.

Sherman, S. (1997, May 12). Levi's: As ye sew, so shall ye reap, *Fortune,* pp. 104–116.

Slater, D. (2010, April 1). At law firms, reconsidering the model for associates' pay. *The New York Times,* F-10.

Spors, K. (2008, October 13). Top workplaces, 2008. *The Wall Street Journal,* R-8.

Starbucks Company Web site (2000). www.starbucks.com/responsibility/...coffee/.

Steinberg, M., & Kaufman, S. (2005, August). Minimizing corporate liability exposure when the whistle blows in the post-Sarbanes-Oxley era. *Journal of Corporation Law,* 445–463.

Sturdivant, F. D., & Vernon-Wortzel, H. (1990). *Business and society* (4th ed.). Homewood, IL: Irwin.

Taylor, A. (1997, April 28). Yo, Ben! Yo, Jerry! It's just ice cream! *Fortune,* 374.

Tozzi, J. (2010, April 26). The Ben & Jerry's law: Principles before profit. *Bloomberg BusinessWeek,* 65–66.

Trevino, L. K., & Nelson, K. A. (2004). *Managing business ethics* (3rd ed.). New York: John Wiley & Sons.

Turban, D. B., & Greening, D. W. (1997). Corporate social performance and organizational attractiveness to prospective employees. *Academy of Management Journal, 40,* 658–672.

Waters, Alice (2006, February 24). Eating for credit. *The New York Times,* A-23.

Weaver, G. R., Trevino, L. K., & Cochran, P. L. (1999). Corporate ethics programs as control systems: Influence of executive commitment and environmental factors. *Academy of Management Journal, 42,* 41–57.

Will, R. (1995, Spring). Corporations with a conscience. *Business and Society Review,* 17–20.

www.benjerry.com.

Zellner, W. (2002, January 28). The whistleblower: A hero—and a smoking-gun letter. *BusinessWeek,* 34–35.

Zellner, W., & Forest, S. (2001, December 17). The fall of Enron, *BusinessWeek,* 30–36.

Chapter 4

Arndt, M., & Berstein, A. (2000, March 20). From milestone to millstone. *BusinessWeek,* 120–122.

Baker, S. (2000, April 10). Telefonica: Takeover escape artist? *BusinessWeek,* 58–60.

Barlow, W., Hatch, D., & Murphy, B. (1996, April). Employer denies jobs to smoker applicants. *Personnel Journal,* 142.

Bateman, T., & Snell, S. (1999). *Management: Building competitive advantage.* New York: McGraw-Hill/Irwin.

Bernstein, A. (1997, August 25). This package is a heavy one for the Teamsters. *BusinessWeek,* 40–41.

Bird, Shelley (2006, January; 2005, December). Communicating through changes in leadership at NCR. *Strategic Communication Management, 10(1),* 30–34.

Briefing: Reshaping Cisco (2009, August 29). *The Economist,* 59–62.

Change management: An inside job (2000, July 15). *The Economist,* 61.

Cisco Systems Web site (2010). www.cisco.com/en/US/products/...index.html.

Conlin, M. (2000, June 12). Workers, surf at your own risk. *BusinessWeek,* 105–106.

Crockett, R. O. (2000, April 17). A new company called Motorola. *BusinessWeek,* 86–91.

Crockett, R., & Rosenbush, S. (2000, February 7). Doug Daft isn't sugarcoating things. *BusinessWeek,* 36–38.

Currie, A. (2000, February). Merrill's Internet conversion. *Euromoney,* 10.

Daft, R. L. (1997). *Management* (4th ed.). Fort Worth: Dryden Press.

Daft, R. L. (2000). *Management* (5th ed.). Fort Worth: Dryden Press.

Daft, R. L. (1999). *Leadership.* Fort Worth: Dryden Press. 444–445.

Daly, J. P., Pouder, R. W., & Kabanoff, B. (2004). The effects of initial differences in firm's espoused values on their post-merger performance. *Journal of Applied Behavioral Science, 40,* 323–343.

Davidson, J. (2002). Overcoming resistance to change. *Public Management, 84,* 20–23.

Deal, T. E., & Kennedy, A. A. (1982). *Corporate cultures: The rites and rituals of corporate life.* Reading, MA: Addison-Wesley.

Deresky, H. L. (2000). *International management: Managing across borders and cultures.* Englewood Cliffs, NJ: Prentice Hall.

Doyle, J. P. (2010, May 3–9). Hard choices. *Bloomberg BusinessWeek,* 84.

The e.biz: Masters of the Web world (2000, May 15). *BusinessWeek,* 25.

Gale, S. F. (2002). For ERP success, create a culture change. *Workforce,* September, 88–94.

General Motors Corp.: Saturn unit of General Motors is laying off about 490 workers (2000, May 26). *The Wall Street Journal,* B10.

George, J., & Jones, G. (1999). *Understanding and managing organizational behavior.* Reading, MA: Addison-Wesley.

Gomez-Mejia, L. R., Balkin, D. B., & Cardy, R. (2001). *Managing human resources.* Englewood Cliffs, NJ: Prentice Hall.

Gomez-Mejia, L. R., & Welbourne, T. (1991). Compensation strategies in a global context. *Hitman Resource Planning, 14(1),* 38.

Good scores or else (1999, October 23). *The Economist,* 28.

Greenwald, J. (2000, February 28). Lloyd's of London falling down. *Time,* 54–58.

Griffin, R. W., & Pustay, M. W. (1998). *International business: A managerial perspective.* Reading, MA: Addison-Wesley.

Hamilton, J. (2000, April 3). The panic over hiring. *BusinessWeek,* 130–131.

Hamm, S., & Kripalani, M. (2000, March 6). Software's tough guy. *BusinessWeek,* 131–136.

Hellriegel, D., Jackson, S., & Slocum, J. (2005). *Management: A competency-based approach* (10th ed.). Mason, OH: Thompson. 328–329.

Hof, R. D., Green, H., & Brady, D. (2000, February 21). An eagle eye on customers. *BusinessWeek,* 67–81.

Horovitz, B. (2009, December 16). Domino's Pizza delivers change in its core pizza recipe. www.usatoday.com/.../2009-12-16-dominosl...

Hymowitz, C. (1989, July 13). Which culture fits you? *The Wall Street Journal,* B-l.

Jones, G. R., George, J. M., & Hill, C. W. L. (2001). *Contemporary management* (2nd ed.). New York: McGraw-Hill/Irwin.

Karachanns, E., Evaristo, J.R., & Srite, M. (2005). Levels of culture and individual behavior: An integrated perspective. *Journal of Global Information Management, 13,* 1–20.

Kerwin, K. (2000, September 4). Fighting to stay on the road: Firestone's woes have dragged in Ford too. *BusinessWeek,* 44.

Kerwin, K., Burrows, P., & Foust, D. (2000, February 21). Workers of the world, logon. *BusinessWeek,* 52–53.

Kiger, P. J. (2002). Acxiom rebuilds from scratch. *Workforce, 81,* 52–55.

Kotter, J. P., & Heskett, J. L. (1992). *Corporate culture and performance.* New York: Free Press.

Kotter, J. P., & Schlesinger, L. A. (1979, March–April). Choosing strategies for change. *Harvard Business Review,* 106–114.

Lee, C., Tan, B., & J. Chiu (2008). The impact of organizational culture and learning on innovation performance. *International Journal of Innovation and Learning, 5,* 413–428.

Lelyveld, N. (2000, August 4). Pike Place fishmongers showing up as examples of fun at work. *The Philadelphia Inquirer.*

Lewin, K. (1951). *Field theory in social science: Selected theoretical papers.* New York: Harper & Brothers.

Lewis, L. K., & Seibold, D. R. (1993). Innovation modification during intra-organizational adoption. *Academy of Management Review, 10(2),* 322–354.

Makri, M., Lane, P., & Gomez-Mejia, L. R. (2000). *Patent quality, firm performance, and CEO pay in high and tow technology firms.* Unpublished manuscript, Management Department, Arizona State University.

Mandel, M. J. (2000, January 3). The new economy. It works in America. Will it go global? *BusinessWeek,* 24–28.

Mandel, R. (2000, April 3). Up front. *BusinessWeek,* 8–9.

Milo, M. (2009, December 31). Not the Cisco you think you know. www.portfolio.com.

Mitchell, M. A., & Yates, D. (2002). How to use your organizational culture as a competitive tool. *Nonprofit World, 20,* 33–34.

Moorhead, G., & Griffin, R. W. (2001). *Organizational behavior.* New York: Houghton Mifflin.

Mornell, P. (2000, July). Nothing endures but change. *Inc,* 131–132.

Morris, B., & Sellers, P. (2000, January 10). What really happened at Coke. *Fortune,* 114–117.

Nahavandi, A., & Malekzadeh, A. R. (1999). *Organizational behavior: The person-organization fit.* Englewood Cliffs, NJ: Prentice Hall.

O'Reilly, C. A., & Chatman, J. A. (1996). Culture as social control: Corporations, cults, and commitment. In B. Staw & L. L. Cummings (Eds.), *Research in Organizational Behavior, 18,* 157–200.

Peek, R. (2000, March). Jump-starting electronic books. *Information Today,* 46–48.

Pettigrew, A. M. (1979). On studying organizational cultures. *Administrative Science Quarterly, 24,* 570–582.

Pfeffer, J., & Veiga, J. F. (1999). Putting people first for organizational success. *Academy of Management Executive, 13(2),* 38.

Pike Place Fish Market Web site (2010). www.pikeplacefish.com/philosophy.html.

Quinn, J. (1994, November). What a work-out! *Performance,* 58–63.

Quinn, R., Faerman, S., Thompson, M., & McGrath, M. (1996). *Becoming a master manager* (2nd ed.). New York: John Wiley & Sons.

Reingold, J., Stepanek, M., & Brady, D. (2000, February 14). The boom. *BusinessWeek,* 100–118.

Reinhardt, A. (2000, January 31). I have left a few dead bodies. *BusinessWeek,* 69–70.

Robbins, S. (2001). *Organizational behavior.* Englewood Cliffs, NJ: Prentice Hall.

Rossant, J. (2000, January 31). Old world, new mandate. *BusinessWeek,* 92–93.

Sarros, J. C., Gray, J., Demsten, I. L., & Cooper, B. (2005). The organizational culture profile revisited and revised: An Australian perspective. *Australian Journal of Management, 30,* 159–182.

Schein, E. H. (1983). The role of the founder in creating organizational culture. *Organizational Dynamics, 12,* 13–28.

Speer, P. (2005). Managing change requires diligence, homework and a systematic approach to the CEO's office. *Insurance Networking News: Executive Strategies for Technology Management, 8,* 12.

Terpstra, V., & David, K. (1991). *The cultural environment of international business.* Cincinnati: South-Western Publishing.

Trice, H. M., & Beyer, J. M. (1993). *The cultures work organizations.* Englewood Cliffs, NJ: Prentice Hall.

Van Maanen, J. V. (1975). Police socialization: A longitudinal examination of job attitudes in an urban police department. *Administrative Science Quarterly, 20,* 207–228.

Walt Disney Company Web site (2010). www.corporate. disney.go.com/.../learning.html.

Watson, B. (2010, March 3). Domino's Pizza reborn? Risky campaign, new recipe helps boost sales. www. dailyfinance.com/story/.../19383979/.

Watson, T. (2002). Goodnight, sweet prince. *Canadian Business, 75,* 77–78.

Welch, D. (2000, February 21). Running rings around Saturn. *BusinessWeek,* 114–117.

Wilkins, A., & Ouchi, W. G. (1983, September). Efficient cultures: Exploring the relationship between cultures and organizational performance. *Administrative Science Quarterly,* 468–481.

Wiscombe, J. (2002). CEO takes HR to prime time. *Workforce, 81,* 10.

Wright, P. M., & Noe, R. A. (1996). *Management of organizations.* Burr Ridge, IL: Irwin.

Yokoyama, J., & J. Michelli (2004). *When fish fly: lessons for creating a vital and energized workplace – From the world famous Pike Place Fish Market.* New York: Hyperion. www.accessmylibarary.com/...pike-place-fish...

www.ge.com/news/leadership.html. Accessed July 25, 2001.

Chapter 5

The 100 top brands (2005, August 1). *BusinessWeek,* 90–92.

Ahmed, N. V., Montagno, R. V., & Frienze, R. J. (1998). Organizational performance and environmental consciousness: An empirical study. *Management Decision, 36(2),* 57–63.

Ang, J. S., & Chua, J. H. (1979, April). Long range planning in large United States corporations: A survey. *Long Range Planning, 12(2),* 99–102.

Applebaum, S. H., & Hughes, B. (1998). Ingratiation as a political tactic. *Management Planning, 36(2),* 85–96.

Audit Bureau of Circulations (2011). Certified circulation figures. http://accessaba.com.

Barkdoll, G., & Bosin M. R. (1997, August). Targeted planning: A paradigm for public service. *Management Planning,* 529–540.

Barrett, A., Carey, J., & Brull, S. (1999, May 3). Bitter medicine ahead for drug companies. *BusinessWeek,* 50.

Barrett, P. (1998, June 8). Hot war over herbal remedies. *BusinessWeek,* 42.

Berner, R. (2005, October 31). At Sears, a great communicator. *BusinessWeek,* 50.

Bonamici, K. (2005, June 27). Ford decides to let the Pinto explode. *Fortune,* 77.

Brinckmann, J., Grichnik, D., & Kapsa, D. (2010). Should entrepreneurs plan or just storm the castle? A meta analysis on contextual factors impacting the business planning—performance relationship in small firms. *Journal of Business Venturing, 25(1),* 22–40.

Brown, E. (1999, March 1). America's most admired companies. *Fortune,* 68–76.

Brown, E. (1999, May 24). 9 ways to win on the web. *Fortune,* 112–118.

Bulkeley W. M. (2005, December 21). Kodak swings to $1.03 billion loss. *The Wall Street Journal,* A-1.

Burack, E. H., (1988). *Creative human resource planning and applications.* Englewood Cliffs, NJ: Prentice Hall.

Burack, E. H., Hochwarter, W., & Mathys, N. J. (1997). The new management development paradigm. *Human Resource Planning, 20(1),* 14–22.

Burdeau, C., & A. Mohr (2010, May 1). BP didn't plan for accident, data says. *The Eagle,* 1.

Burrows, P. (1999, September 20). The big squeeze in the PC market. *BusinessWeek,* 40.

Bylinsky, G. (1999, July 5). Hot new technologies, *Fortune,* 168–176.

Byrne, J. A. (1998, June 8). How Jack Welch runs GE. *BusinessWeek,* 90–110.

Byrne, J. A. (2003, February 17). Leaders are made, not born. *BusinessWeek,* 16.

Byrne, J. (1999, October 4). The search for the young and gifted. *BusinessWeek,* 108–112.

Byrnes, N., & Judge, P. L. (1999, June 28). Internet anxiety. *BusinessWeek,* 79–88.

Byrnes, N. (2005, October 10). Cover story. *BusinessWeek,* 69.

Chozick, A. (2005, September 19). Appearances are deceiving. *The Wall Street Journal,* R-7.

Churchill, N. (1984, July-August). Budgeting choice: Planning vs. control. *Harvard Business Review,* 150–164.

Cilmi, A. P. (2005, November). In a successful rewards and recognition program. *Workspan,* 19.

Cilmi, A.P. (2005, September 19).

Cisco webex: Extend your reach with web collaboration from webex. http://www.webex.com. Accessed April 2010.

Cohen, A. J., & Hall, M. E. (2005). Automating your performance and competency evaluation process. *WorldatWork Journal,* 64.

Colvin, G. (2005, October 3). An executive risk handbook. *Fortune,* 69–70.

Cox, A., & Thompson, I. (1998). On the appropriateness of benchmarking. *Journal of General Management, 23(3),* 1–21.

Cravens, D. W., Greenley, G., Piercy, N. F., & Slater, S. (1997, August). Integrating contemporary strategic management perspectives. *Management Planning,* 493–507.

Crockett, R. O. (1999, June 21). Motorola is ringing again. *BusinessWeek,* 40.

Crockett, R. O. (1999, August 30). Why Motorola should hang up on iridium. *BusinessWeek,* 46.

Denizer-Guillet, B., & Tasci, A. D. A. (2010). An exploratory study of multicultural view on the Disney-McDonald's alliance. *Journal of Travel and Tourism Marketing, 27(1),* 82–95.

Disaster planning reports (2011). http://www.bitpipe.com.

Do More, Travel Less, Enjoy the freedom of online meetings (2011). http://www.GoToMeeting.com. Accessed April 2010.

Donnelly, J. H., Gibson, J. L., & Ivancevich, J. M. (1998). *Fundamentals of management.* New York: McGraw-Hill/Irwin.

Easterbrook, C. (2003, February 10). The space shuttle must be stopped. *Time,* 46–47.

Einhorn, B. (1999, October 4). Big brother and the e-revolution. *BusinessWeek,* 132–136.

Einhorn, B. (2005, November 14). Listen: The sound of hope. *BusinessWeek,* 68.

Ernst, R., & Ross, D. N. (1993). The Delta force approach to balancing long run performance. *Business Horizons,* 4–9.

Faust, D., Smith, G., & Rocks, D. (1999, May 3). Man on the spot. *BusinessWeek,* 142–147.

Genentech Inc. Web site. www.gene.com.

Giancola, F. (2005). A total rewards design fool that measures up. *WorldatWork Journal,* 6.

Godzilla rampage slows (2005, June 1). *USA Today,* D-1.

Gomez-Mejia, L. R., & Balkin, D. B. (1992). *Compensation, organizational strategy, and firm performance.* Cincinnati, OH: South-Western Publishing.

Gomez-Mejia, L. R., Balkin, D. B., & Cardy, R. (2005). *Managing human resources.* Englewood Cliffs, NJ: Prentice Hall.

Gorman, P., & Thomas, H. (1997, August). Strategy at the leading edge: The theory and practice of competence-based competition. *Management Planning,* 615–628.

Grant, L. (1998, May 11). Why Kodak still isn't fixed. *Fortune,* 179–181.

Green, G. T. (2005, November). Recognition and the generational divide. *Workspan,* 10.

Greising, D. (1998, April 13). I would like the world to buy a Coke: The life and leadership of Robert Goizueta. *BusinessWeek,* 70–76.

Grundy, T. (1997). Human resource management: A strategic approach. *Management Planning,* 507–518.

Grundy, T. (1998). How are corporate strategy and human resources strategy linked? *Journal of General Management, 23(3),* 49–73.

Gurley, W. J. (1999, March 15). How the net is changing competition. *Fortune,* 168.

Hagan, J. (2005, November 8). Circulation continues to decline at most major newspapers. *The Wall Street Journal,* B-7, B-8.

Hanm, S. (1999, April 5). Netscapes storm the valley. *BusinessWeek,* 104.

Hax, A., & Majluf, N. S. (1996). *The strategy concept and process.* Upper Saddle River, NJ: Prentice Hall.

Hay, M., & Williamson, P. (1997, October). Good strategy: The view from below. *Management Planning,* 661–665.

Hitt, M. A., Ireland, D. R., & Hoskisson, R. E. (1998). *Strategic management: Competitiveness and globalization.* St. Paul, MN: West Publishing.

Ho, Doris. Hong Kong Disneyland (2006, February 15). *BusinessWeek Online.* www.businessweek.com.

Hof, R. D. (1999, October 4). A new era of bright hopes and terrible fears. *BusinessWeek,* 84–98.

Hof, R. D. (2005, July 20). The power of us: Mass collaboration on the Internet is shaking up business. *BusinessWeek,* 78–81.

Holland, K.(1998, May 4). China slams a door in Amway's face. *BusinessWeek,* 54.

Holmes, S. (2003, January 20). GE little engines that could. *BusinessWeek,* 62–64, www.ge.com.

Hong Kong Disneyland expansion – 2010–2014. http://www.youtube.com.

Hong Kong's Tsang hits out at Disneyland woes (2006, February 5). *Forbes.com.* www.forbes.com.

Hoskisson, R. E., Hitt, M. A., Wan, W. P., & Yui, D. (1999). Theory and research in strategic management. *Journal of Management,* 417–456.

Festive Hong Kong 2010–2011 (2011). http://www.discoverhongkong.com.

http://nasa.gov. Accessed April 2011.

Hymowitz, C. (2005, September 19). Middle managers are unsung heroes on corporate stage. *The Wall Street Journal,* A-l.

Hymowitz, C. (2005, August 16). Balancing security and trust. *The Wall Street Journal,* B-l.

Jarrell, D. W. (1993). *Human resource planning.* Englewood Cliffs, NJ: Prentice Hall.

Kaplan, R. S., & Norton, D. P. (1993, September-October). Putting the balanced scorecard to work. *Harvard Business Review,* 134–147.

Kluger, J. (2005, August 8). Why NASA can't get it right. *Time,* 25.

Kochanski, J., & Sorensen, A. (2005, September). Managing performance. *Workspan,* 21.

Kovac, J. (2005, November). Smart goal setting. *Workspan,* 63.

Kress, N. (2005, May). Engaging your employees through the power of communication. *Workspan,* 27.

Kripalani, M., & Clifford, M. L. (2003, February 10). Finally, Coke gets it right. *BusinessWeek,* 47.

Kudia, R. J. (1979). The components of strategic planning. *Long Range Planning, 11(6),* 48–52.

Kumar, P. (1978). Long range planning practices by U.S. companies. *Managerial Planning, 26(4),* 31–33.

Kunii, I. M. Thorton, E., & Rae-Dupree, J. (1999, March 22). Sony's shake. *BusinessWeek,* 52.

Labich, K. (1999, March 1). Boeing finally hatches a plan. *Fortune,* 101–106.

Landro, L. (2005, September 28). Compassion 101: Teaching M.D.s to be nicer. *The Wall Street Journal,* D-3.

Leonard, D. (2005, October 3). The only lifeline was the Wal-Mart. *Fortune,* 74–80.

Light, L. (1998, May 25). Litigation: The choice of a generation. *BusinessWeek,* 42.

Makridakis, S., Wheelwright, S., & McGee, V. (1982). *Forecasting methods and applications.* New York: John Wiley & Sons.

Malakis, S., Kontogiannis, T., & B. Kirwan (2010). Managing emergencies and abnormal situations in air traffic control. *Applied Ergonomics, 41(4),* 620–627.

Mandel, M. J. (1999, October 4). The Internet economy. *BusinessWeek,* 72–77.

Mandel, M. J. (2005, May 23). Sure, the trade deficit is scary – but we can handle it. *BusinessWeek,* 41.

Marren, P. B. (2010). Scenario planning for economic recovery. *Strategy & Leadership, 38(1),* 15–26.

Mass collaboration (2011). http://en.wikipedia.org.

McCracken, J. (2005, October 11). Delphi presses for cuts as Ford plans shake-up. *The Wall Street Journal.*

McCracken, J. (2005, October 28). Delphi seeks far-reaching givebacks. *The Wall Street Journal.*

McKay, B., & Vranica, S. (2003, January 9). Cracking the China market. *The Wall Street Journal,* B-1–B-2.

Mullaney, T. J. (2005, September 5). Making it easy to size up a hospital. *BusinessWeek,* 102.

A multitude of medical miracles (2005, June 6). *BusinessWeek,* 138.

Munk, N. (1999, June 21). Title flight. *Fortune,* 84–86.

Narisetti, R. (1998, March 12). How IBM turned around its ailing PC division. *The Wall Street Journal,* B-1.

Narpovich, A. (2010). Theoretical approaches to film-motivated tourism. *Tourism and hospitality planning and development, 7(1),* 7–20.

NASA (2011). http://en.wikipedia.org.

Newspaper for sale? (2011). http://www.forbes.com.

Newspaper sales fall record $3B in 6 months (2011). http://newsosaur.blogspot.com.

Nussbaum, B. (2005, August 1). How to build innovative companies. *BusinessWeek,* 61.

O'Connell, V. (2005, October 7). Rx from Marlboro man: Device that delivers drugs, not smoke. *The Wall Street Journal,* A-2.

O'Connor, R.V. (1986). *Corporate guides to long range planning* (Conference Board Report No. 687). New York: Conference Board.

Odiorne, G,S. (1987, July/August). Measuring the unmeasurable: Setting standards for management performance. *Business Horizons,* 69–75.

O'Neill, J. (2010). NASA is making preliminary plans to extend shuttle launches beyond 2010. http://www.universe today.com.

Overholt, M.H. (1997). Flexible organizations: Using organizational design as a competitive advantage. *Human Resource Planning, 20(1),* 22–23.

Pearson, G. (1986). Business strategy should not be bureaucratic. *Accountancy, 97(1112),* 109–112.

Port, O. (1999, October 4). Customers move into the driver's seat. *BusinessWeek.* 103–110.

Preble, J. F. (1992). Environmental scanning for strategic control, *Journal of Managerial Issues, 4,* 254–268.

Prestowitz, C. (1998, May 11). Asia's flawed fundamentals. *Fortune,* 52.

Reingold, J., & Brody, D. (1999, September 20). Brain drain. *BusinessWeek,* 113–122.

Revell, J. (2003, February 3). Can Home Depot get its groove back? *Fortune,* 110–112.

Sager, I. (1999, June 21). Big Blue at your service. *BusinessWeek,* 130–131.

Sager, I., Burrow, P., & Reinhardt, A. (1998, May 25). Back to the future at Apple. *BusinessWeek,* 56–58.

Sandberg, J. (2005, August 17). Sometimes colleagues are just too bad not to get promoted. *The Wall Street Journal,* B-1.

Sandersen, S. M. (1998). New approaches to strategy: New ways of thinking for the millennium. *Management Decision, 36(1),* 9–14.

Schlange, L. E., & Juttner, V. (1997, October). Helping managers to identify the key strategic issues, *Management Planning,* 777–787.

Singer, J., & Piluso, J. (2010). Five tools to prepare for future discontinuities. *Strategy & Leadership, 38(1),* 27–39.

Special issue on planning (1985, September 17). *BusinessWeek.*

Stepanek, M. (1999, June 7). Closed, gone to the net. *BusinessWeek,* 113–116.

Stipp, D. (1988, May 11). Why Pfizer is so hot. *Fortune,* 88.

Sullivan, L. (2011). Wal-Mart: Lessons of the storm. *InformationWeek* Global CIO. http://www. informationweek.com.

Symonds, W.C. (2005, May 23). A digital warrior for Kodak. *BusinessWeek,* 42.

Taylor, A., III. (2005, October 17). Ford: the hamlet of Dearborn. *Fortune,* 36.

Tenet's bills to Calpers 50% more than other hospitals. (2003, February 3). *Sacramento BEE.*

Thurlby, B. (1998). Competitive forces are also subject to change. *Managerial Decisions, 36(1),* 19–25.

Tosi, H. L., Katz, J. R, & Gomez-Mejia, L. R. (1997). Disaggregating the agency contract: The effects of monitoring, incentive alignment, and term in office on agent decision making. *Academy of Management Journal, 40,* 584–602.

Tsao, P. (1998, June 8). Reports of cancer's imminent death were an exaggeration. *BusinessWeek,* 13.

Tushman, M. L., & O'Reily, C. A., III (1997). *Winning through innovation.* Boston: Harvard Business School Press.

Useem, J. (2005, June 27). Ford offers $5 a day. *Fortune,* 65.

Wallace, D., & Pekel, J. Twin Cities based consultants in the Fulcrum Group.

Wal-Mart stores Inc. (2011). http://www.en.wikipedia.org.

Weir, D., & Smallman, C. (1998). *Management Decision, 36(1),* 43–50.

Welch, J. (2005, April 18). It's all in the sauce. *Fortune,* 138.

Wright, P. M., & Noe, R. A. (1998). *Management of organizations.* New York: McGraw-Hill/Irwin.

Xratz, E. F. (2005, October 3). For FedEx, it was time to deliver. *Fortune,* 83–84.

Chapter 6

Bateman, T. S., & Snell, S. A. (1996). *Management* (3rd ed.). Burr Ridge, IL: Irwin.

Bazerman, M. (2005). *Judgment in Managerial Decision Making* (6th ed.). New York: Wiley.

Bazerman, M., & Chugh, D. (2006, January). Decisions without blinders. *Harvard Business Review,* 88–97.

Benartzi, S., & Thaler, R. H. (1999). Risk aversion or myopia? Choices in repeated gambles and retirement investments. *Management Science, 45,* 364–381.

Bowen, J., & Qui, Q. (1992). Satisficing when buying information. *Organizational Behavior and Human Decision Process, 51,* 471–481.

Bram, J., Orr, J., & Rappaport, C. (2002, November). Measuring the September 11 attack on New York City. *Economic Policy Review,* 5–20.

Carter, B. (1997, December 26). Seinfeld says it's over, and it's no joke for NBC, *The New York Times,* A-1, A-15.

Cohen, M. D., March, J. G., & Olsen, J. P. (1972). The garbage can model of organizational choice. *Administration Science Quarterly, 17,* 1–25.

Conlon, D. E., & Garland, H. (1993). The role of project completion information in resource allocation decisions. *Academy of Management Journal, 36,* 401–413.

Covey, S. R. (1989). *The 7 habits of highly effective people.* New York: Simon & Schuster.

Daft, R. L. (1997). *Management* (4th ed.). Fort Worth: Dryden Press.

Daft, R. L. (1999). *Leadership: Theory and practice.* Fort Worth: Dryden Press. 467–468.

Dean, J. W., & Evans, J. R. (1994). *Total quality.* St. Paul, MN: West Publishing.

Delbecq, A. L., Van de Ven, A. H., & Gustafson, D. H. (1975). *Group techniques for program planning.* Glenview, IL: Scott Foresman.

Eisenhardt, K. M. (1988). Agency and institutional theory explanations: The case of retail sales compensation. *Academy of Management Journal, 31,* 488–511.

Elgin, Ben (2005, January 25). Google's dicey dance in China. *BusinessWeek Online.* www.businessweek.com.

Gerstner, L. (2002). *Who says elephants can't dance? Leading a great enterprise through dramatic change.* New York: HarperBusiness.

Gladwell, M. (2005). *Blink: The power of thinking without thinking.* New York: Little, Brown.

Grove, A. (1996). *Only the paranoid survive.* New York: Currency Doubleday, 11–16.

Haddad, C. (2001, October 1). How UPS delivered through the disaster. *BusinessWeek*, 66.

Hall, R. H. (1999). *Organizations*. Upper Saddle River, NJ: Prentice Hall.

Hammond, et al. (2006, January). The hidden traps of decision making. *Harvard Business Review*, 118–126.

Horn, P. W., & Griffeth, R. W. (1995). *Employee turnover*. Cincinnati, OH: South-Western Publishing.

Howard, R. (1988). Decision analysis: Practice and promise. *Management Science, 34*, 679–695.

Huey, J. (1997, December 29). In search of Roberto's secret formula. *Fortune*, 230–234.

Jackson, J. A., Kloeber, J. M., Ralson, B. E., & Deckro, R. F. (1999). Selecting a portfolio of technologies: An application of decision analysis. *Decision Sciences, 30*, 217–238.

Jones, G. R., George, J. M., & Hill, C. W. (1998). *Contemporary management*. New York: McGraw-Hill/Irwin.

Kavilanz, P. (2009, January 16). Circuit City to shut down. *CNNMoney*. www.cnn.com.

Kiley, T. (1993, January). The idea makers. *Technology Review*, 33–40.

Kreitner, R., & Kinicki, A. (1995). *Organizational behavior* (3rd ed.). Burr Ridge, IL: Irwin.

Kristoff, Nicholas (2006, February 19). China's cyberdissidents and the yahoos at Yahoo. *The New York Times*, WK-13.

Leana, R. R. (1986). Predictors and consequences of delegation. *Academy of Management Journal, 29*, 754–774.

Leonard, E. (2005, October 3). The only lifeline was the Wal-Mart. *Fortune*, 74–80.

Leonhardt, D. (2007, April 4). 3,400 Layoffs send a message to millions. *The New York Times Online*. www.nytimes.com.

Levy, Stephen (2006, February 13). Google and the China syndrome. *Newsweek*. Accessed at http://msnbc.msn.com.

Mackenzie, R. A. (1972). *The time trap*. New York: McGraw-Hill.

Maier, N. R. (1973). *Psychology in industrial organizations* (4th ed.). Boston: Houghton Mifflin.

Mankins, M. (2004, September). Stop wasting valuable time. *Harvard Business Review*, 58–65.

March, J. G., & Simon, H. A. (1958). *Organizations*. New York: John Wiley & Sons.

Markoff, J. (1994, December 6). Chip Error continuing to dog officials at Intel. *The New York Times Online*. www.nytimes.com.

Mathews, C. (2009, January 17). Lessons from Circuit City's bankruptcy. www.teleread.com.

McNamara, G., & Bromily, P. (1999). Risk and return in organizational decision making. *Academy of Management Journal, 42*, 330–339.

Mealiea, L. W., & Latham, G. P. (1996). *Skills for managerial success*. Burr Ridge, IL: Irwin.

The panda has two faces (2010, April 3). *The Economist*, 70.

Pearson, C. M., & Clair, J. A. (1998). Reframing organizational crisis. *Academy of Management Review, 23*, 59–76.

Quinn, R. E., Faerman, S. R., Thompson, M. P., & McGrath, M. R. (2003). *Becoming a master manager* (3rd ed.). New York: John Wiley & Sons.

Rifkin, F. (1999). Mach 3: Anatomy of Gillette's latest global launch. *Journal of Strategy and Business*, 2nd quarter. www.strategy-business.com.

Rimer, S. (1996, March 6). A hometown feels less like home. *The New York Times*, A-1, A-8–A-9.

Robbins, S. P., & Coulter, M. (1996). *Management* (5th ed.). Upper Saddle River, NJ: Prentice Hall.

Rosenbloom, S. (2009, January 16). Circuit City to shut down. *The New York Times Online*. www.nytimes.com.

Rowe, A., & Mason, R. (1987). *Managing with style: A guide to understanding, assessing, and improving your decision making*. San Francisco: Jossey-Bass.

Simon, H. A. (1957). *Models of man*. New York: Wiley.

Sitkin, S. B., & Pablo, A. L. (1992). Reconceptualizing the determinants of risk behavior. *Academy of Management Review, 17*, 9–38.

Sitkin, S. B., & Weingart, L. R. (1995). Determinants of risky decision making behavior: A test of the mediating role of risk perceptions and risk propensity. *Academy of Management Journal, 38*, 1573–1592.

Stoner, J. (1968). Risk and cautious shifts in group decisions. *Journal of Experimental and Social Psychology, 4*, 442–459.

Thompson, A. A., & Strickland, A. J. (1998). *Strategic management: Concepts and cases* (10th ed.). New York: McGraw-Hill/Irwin.

Thompson, R. (1993, July). An employee's view of empowerment. *HR Focus*, 14–15.

Time management: Tips to reduce stress and improve productivity (2008, September 4). www.mayoclinic.com/health/.../w10004.

Vroom, V. H., & Jago, A. G. (1988). *The new leadership: Managing participation in organizations*. Englewood Cliffs, NJ: Prentice Hall.

Waller, M. J. (1999). The timing of adaptive group responses to nonroutine events. *Academy of Management Journal, 42*, 127–137.

Watkins, M., & Bazerman, M. (2003, March). Predictable surprises: The disasters you should have seen coming. *Harvard Business Review*, 72–80.

Whetton, D. A., & Cameron, K. S. (2010). *Developing Management Skills* (8th ed.). Upper Saddle River, NJ: Prentice Hall.

Whyte, G. (1989). Groupthink reconsidered. *Academy of Management Review, 14*, 40–56.

Wolfe, A. (1994, November 7). Intel fixes a Pentium Fpu glitch. *Electronic Engineering Times*. www.davefag.com/opinions/.../pentium.html.

Wright, P. M., & Noe, R. A. (1996). *The management of organizations*. Burr Ridge, IL: Irwin.

Wu, G. (1999). Nonlinear decision weights in choice under uncertainty. *Management Science, 45*, 74–85.

Zeller, Tom, Jr. (2006, February 16). Web firms questioned on dealings in China. *The New York Times Online*. www.nytimes.com.

Chapter 7

2010 Fall Ratings (2011). http://www.healthgrades.com.

The 25 top managers of the year (1998, January 12). *BusinessWeek*, 54–60.

Acohido, B., & Baig, E. G. (2006, January 5). Gates shares spotlight with new windows. *USA Today*, B-1.

Adams, M. (2006, January 5). Independence CEO says he doesn't regret gamble. *USA Today*, B-5.

Afuah, A. (1998). *Innovation management*. New York: Oxford University Press.

Amato, I. (1999, June 7). Industrializing the search for new drugs. *Fortune*, 110–118.

Armstrong, L. (1999, March 22). Amgen nurses itself back to health. *Fortune*, 76–78.

Associated Press. (1996, February 7). Southwest Airlines earns triple crown award again. *Arizona Republic,* A-15.

Aveni, R. A. D. (2010). *Beating the Commodity trap: How to maximize your competitive position.* Boston: Harvard Business Press.

Awa, H. O., & Kalu, S. E. (2010). Repositioning the non-incremental changes and business strategic windows correlates. *International Journal of Business and Management, 5(2),* 15–26.

Barboso, M. (2006, January 13). State mandate for Wal-Mart on health care. *The New York Times,* A-1.

Barboza, D., & Zeller, Jr., T. (2006, January 6). Microsoft shuts blog's site after complaints by Beijing. *The New York Times,* C-3.

Barnes, K. (2006, January 5). Alburn sales slump as downloads rise. *USA Today,* D-1.

Barney, J. B. (1995). Looking inside for competitive advantage. *Academy of Management Executive, 9(4),* 59–60.

Barney, J. B., & Hoskisson, R. (1990). Strategic groups: Untested assertions and research proposals. *Managerial and Decision Economics, 11,* 198–208.

Barret, P. (1999, May 3). Bitter medicine ahead for drug companies. *BusinessWeek,* 50.

Bergh, D. (1995). Size and relatedness of units sold: An agency theory and resource based perspective. *Strategic Management Journal, 16,* 221–229.

Berner, R. (2005, November 21). Watch out, Best Buy and Circuit City. *BusinessWeek,* 46.

Berstein, R. (2006, January 12). Men chafe as Norway ushers women into boardroom. *The New York Times,* A-3.

Bettis, R., & Hitt, M. A. (1995, Summer). The new competitive landscape [Special Issue]. *Strategic Management Journal, 16,* 7–19.

Borrus, A. (2005, November 21). Learning to love Sarbanes-Oxley. *BusinessWeek,* 126.

Boyle, M. (2005, June 13). Drug wars. *Fortune,* 25–36.

Brody, D. (1999, April 2). Xerox. *BusinessWeek,* 93–94.

Brown, E. (1999, March 1). America's most admired companies. *Fortune,* 68–75.

Brown, E. (1999, May 24). 9 ways to win on the Web. *Fortune,* 112–120.

Brush, T. A. (1996). Predicted change in operational synergy and post acquisition performance of acquired businesses. *Strategic Management Journal, 17,* 1–24.

Bulkeley, W. M. (2005, December 21). Kodak swings to $1.03 billion loss. *The Wall Street Journal,* A-I.

Burns, J. (2006, January 12). Board members find independence. *The Wall Street Journal,* C-ll.

Burrows, P. (1999, September 20). The big squeeze in the PC market. *BusinessWeek,* 40–41.

Bylinsky, G. (2000, June 26). Hot new technologies for American factories. *Fortune,* 288.

Byrnes, N. (1999, June 28). Internet anxiety. *BusinessWeek,* 79–86.

Campbell, A., Goold, M., & Alexander, M. (1995). Corporate strategy: The question for parenting advantage. *Harvard Business Review, 73(2),* 120–132.

Campbell, A., & Luchs, K. (1998). *Core competency-based strategy.* London, UK: International Thompson Business Press.

Carey, S. (2006, January 13). As airlines pull out of dive, Limited charts its own course. *The Wall Street Journal,* A-l.

Charkham, J. (1994). *Keeping good company: A study of corporate governance in five countries.* New York: Oxford University Press.

Chon, G. (2006, January 5). GM and Ford lose more market share. *The Wall Street Journal,* A-13.

Clarkson, M. B. E. (1995). A stakeholder framework for analyzing and evaluating corporate social performance. *Academy of Management Review, 20,* 92–117.

Coates, T. P. (2005, September 5). Wal-Mart's urban room. *Time,* 44.

Colvin, G. (1998, November 23). How Rubbermaid managed to fail. *Fortune,* 32–36.

Crockett, R. O. (1999, August 30). Why Motorola should hang up on iridium. *BusinessWeek,* 46–47.

Crockett, R. O. (1999, June 21). Motorola is ringing again. *BusinessWeek,* 40–42.

Darlin, Damon (2006, February 3). The iPod econsystem: Add-ons have become a billion-dollar bonanza. *The New York Times Online.* www.nytimes.com.

D'Aveni, R. A. (1995). Coping with hypercompetition: Utilizing the new 75's framework. *Academy of Management Executive, 9(3),* 54.

Davis, J. B. (2003, February). Sorting out Sarbanes-Oxley. *ABA Journal,* 44–50.

Desmond, E. W. (1998, February 2). Can Canon keep clicking? *Fortune,* 98–107.

Dessler, G. (2000). *Hitman resource management.* Englewood Cliffs, NJ: Prentice Hall.

DeWit, R., & Meyer, R. (1998). *Strategy: Process, content, context.* London, UK: International Thompson Business Press.

Donaldson, T., & Preston, L. E. (1995). The stakeholder theory of the corporation: Concepts, evidence, and implications. *Academy of Management Review, 20,* 65–91.

Durham, K., & Smith, R. A. (2005, August 18). Behind zooming condo prices. *The Wall Street Journal,* A-l.

Dvorak, P., & Ramstad, E. (2006, January 3). TV marriage: Behind Sony-Samsung rivalry, an unlikely alliance develops. *The Wall Street Journal,* A-l.

Echikson, W. (1999, October 11). Designers climb onto the virtual catwalk. *BusinessWeek,* 164–166.

Einhorn, B. (1999, February 15). Foreign rivals vs. the Chinese: If you can't beat them. *BusinessWeek,* 78.

Einhorn, B. (2005, November 14). Listen: The sound of hope. *BusinessWeek,* 68.

Eisenhardt, K., & Zbaracki, M. (1992, Winter). Strategic decision making [Special Issue]. *Strategic Management Journal, 13,* 17–37.

Fahey, L., & Narayanan, V. K. (1986). *Macroenvironmental analysis for strategic management.* St. Paul, MN: West Publishing Co.

Farzad, R., & Elgin, B. (2005, December 5). Googling. *BusinessWeek,* 61.

Fine, C. H. (1999, March 29). The ultimate core competency. *Fortune,* 144–149.

Fineman, P. L., & Lipper, T. (2003, January 27). Spinning race. *BusinessWeek,* 25–30.

Finkelstein, S., & Hambrick, D. C. (1996). *Strategic leadership: Top executives and their effects on organizations.* St. Paul, MN: West Publishing Co.

Fisher, A. B. (1996, March 6). Corporate reputations. *Fortune,* 90–93.

Flynn, J., Carey, J., & Crockett, R. (1998, January 26). A fierce downdraft at Boeing. *BusinessWeek,* 34–35.

Flynn, Laurie J. (2006, March 1). Apple offers hi-fi system to use iPod in the home. *The New York Times Online.* www.nytimes.com.

Fortt, J. (2010, March 22). Software that saves money and lives. *Fortune,* 28.

Foust, D. (2002, September 9). The changing heartland. *BusinessWeek,* 80–83.

Fry, S. (2010, April 12). On the mothership: A confessed Apple fanblog gets finger time with the iPad – and facetime with Steve Jobs. *Time,* 111.

Galbraith, J. R. (1995). *Designing organizations.* San Francisco: Jossey-Bass.

Genus, A. (1998). *Managing change: Perspective and practice.* London, UK: International Thompson Business Press.

Gibney, F. (1999, March 1). Nissan calls a low. *Time,* 48.

Godfrey, P. C, & Hill, C. W. L. (1995). The problem of unobservables in strategic management research. *Strategic Management Journal, 16,* 519–533.

Gomez, P. (1998). *Value management.* London, UK: International Thompson Business Press.

Gomez-Mejia, L. R., Balkin, D. B., & Cardy, R. (2001). *Managing human resources.* Englewood Cliffs, NJ: Prentice Hall.

Goold, M., & Luchs, K. (1993). Why diversify? Four decades of management thinking. *Academy of Management Executive, 7(3),* 7–25.

Gorman, M. F. (2010). Management insights. *Management Science, 56(1),* iv–vii.

Grant, D., & Latour, A. (2005, November 21). Changing channels. *The Wall Street Journal,* A-l.

Greene, J. (2003, March 3). The Lenux uprising. *BusinessWeek,* 78–86.

Grossman, L. (2010, April 12). Launch iPad. It is here, it is hot. But what on earth is the iPad for? *Time,* 36–40.

Grow, B. (2005, December 5). The great rebate runaround. *BusinessWeek,* 34.

Gullapalli, D. (2005, October 17). Living with Sarbanes-Oxley. *The Wall Street Journal,* R-l.

Guth, R. A. (2005, November 18). Microsoft, Palm unite to fight Blackberry. *The Wall Street Journal,* B-l.

Guth, R. A. (2005, September 27). Getting Xbox 360 to market. *The Wall Street Journal,* B-l.

Hall, R. H. (1996). *Organizations: Structures, processes, outcomes.* Englewood Cliffs, NJ: Prentice Hall.

Hamel, G., & Prahalad, C. K. (1993). Strategy as stretch and leverage. *Harvard Business Review, 72(2),* 75–84.

Hamel, G., & Prahalad, C. K. (1994). *Competing for the future.* Boston: Harvard Business School Press.

Hamm, S. (1999, April 5). Netscapees storm the valley. *BusinessWeek,* 104–105.

Hancock, C. (2010). You are connected, now, what are you going to do about it? *Design Management Review, 21(1),* 62–67.

Heinzl, M. (2005, November 2). A new crop of gadgets challenge the BlackBerry. *The Wall Street Journal,* D-l.

Helyar, J. (2003, August 12). Will Harley-Davidson Hit the Wall? *Fortune,* 120–124.

Hesseldahl, A. (2005, December 5). For every Xbox, a big fat loss. *BusinessWeek,* 13.

Hill, C. H. (2000). *International business.* New York: McGraw-Hill/Irwin.

Hill, C. W. L. (1994). Diversification and economic performance: Bringing structure and corporate management back into the picture. In R. P. Rumelt et al. (Eds.), *Fundamental issues in strategy* (297–321). Boston: Harvard Business School Press.

Hitt, M. A., Ireland, R. D., & Hoskisson, R. E. (2001). *Strategic management.* New York: McGraw-Hill/Irwin.

Hitt, M. A., Park, D., Hardee, C., & Tyler, B. B. (1995). Understanding strategic intent in the global market place. *Academy of Management Executive, 9(2),* 12–19.

Holstein, W. J. (2002, October 14). Canon takes aim at Xerox. *Fortune,* 215–220.

Hoskisson, R. E., Hitt, M. A., Wan, W. P., & Yui, D. (1999). Theory and research in strategic management. *Journal of Management,* 417–456.

http://gizmodo.com. 2011.

http://investor.walgreens.com. 2011.

http://myhealthcareadviser.com. 2011.

http://www.cinemablend.com/games. 2011.

http://www.consumerhealthratings.com. 2011.

http://www.videogamesblogger.com. 2011.

Hughes, J., Ralf, M., & Michels, W. (1998). *Transform your supply chain.* London, UK: International Thompson Business Press.

Hughes, K., & Oughton, C. (1993). Diversification, multimarket contact, and profitability. *Economics, 60,* 203–224.

Hunt, M. S. (1972). *Competition in the major home appliance industry,* Cambridge, MA: Harvard University Press.

Ireland, D., & Hitt, M. A. (1999). Achieving and maintaining strategic competitiveness in the 21st century: The role of strategic leadership. *Academy of Management Executive, 13(1),* 43–58.

Jacoby, M. (2005, October 17). The global agenda. *The Wall Street Journal,* R-7.

Jenison, D. B., & Sitkin, S. B. (1986). Corporate acquisitions: A process perspective. *Academy of Management Review, 11,* 145–163.

Jones, T. M. (1995). Instrumental stakeholder theory: A synthesis of ethics and economics. *Academy of Management Review, 20,* 404–437.

Kahn, J. (1999, June 7). Wal-Mart goes shopping in Europe. *Fortune,* 105–110.

Kelm, K. M., Narayanan, V. K., & Pinches, G. E. (1995). Shareholder value creation during R&D innovation and commercialization stages. *Academy of Management Journal, 3S,* 770–780.

Kerwin, K., & Ewing, J. (1999, September 27). Nasser: Ford be nimble. *BusinessWeek,* 42–43.

Kolko, J. (2010). Abductive thinking and sensemaking: The drivers of design synthesis. *Design Issues, 26(1),* 15–27.

Kosnik, R., & Chatterjee, S. (1997). *Corporate governance.* St. Paul, MN: West Publishing Co.

Kotha, S., & Nair, A. P. (1995). Strategy and environment as determinants of performance: Evidence from the Japanese machine tool industry. *Strategic Management Journal, 16,* 497–518.

Kumii, I. M. (1999, March 22). Sony's shake up. *BusinessWeek,* 52–54.

Labich, K. (1999, March 1). Boeing finally hatches a plan. *Fortune,* 101–106.

Lado, A. A., Boyd, N. G., & Wright, P. (1992). A competency based model of sustainable advantage: Toward a conceptual integration. *Journal of Management, 18,* 77–91.

Levine, J. (2010). Invisible Branding. *Design Management Review, 20(4),* 32–37.

Lohr, S. (2005, November 6). Just Googling it is striking fear into companies. *The New York Times.*

Lundegaard, K. (2006, January 10). Ford, GM make big push to promote 'flex-fuel' vehicles. *The Wall Street Journal,* B-l.

Lundwall, B. A. (2010). *National Systems of Innovation.* Anthem Press.

Martin, R. L. (2006, January 16). What innovation advantage? *BusinessWeek,* 102.

Martin-Herran, G. (2010). The dilemma of pull and push-price promotions. *Journal of Retailing, 86(1),* 51–58.

Maynard, M. (2006, January 3). Toyota shows big three how it is done. *The New York Times,* C-l.

Maynard, M. (2006, January 8). Is there a future in Ford's future? *The New York Times,* 3.

McCracken, J. (2006, February 17). Ford focuses on market-share slide. *The Wall Street Journal,* A-l.

McDonald, I., & Adamy, J. (2006, January 13). Whole Foods fare's pricey? *The Wall Street Journal,* C-l.

McGahan, A. M. (1994). Industry structure and competitive advantage. *Harvard Business Review, 72(5),* 115–124.

McGrath, R. G., MacMillan, I. C., & Venkataraman, S. (1995). Defining and developing competence: A strategic process paradigm. *Strategic Management Journal, 16,* 251–275.

Meznar, M. B., & Nigh, D. (1995). Buffer or bridge? Environmental and organizational determinants of public affairs activities in American firms. *Academy of Management Journal, 38,* 975–996.

Milestones (2003, February 24). *Time Magazine,* 16.

Monks, R. A. G., & Minow, N. (1995). *Corporate governance.* Cambridge, MA: Blackwell Business.

Montgomery, C. A. (1994). Corporate diversification. *Journal of Economic Perspectives, 8,* 163–178.

Mullaney, T. J. (2005, September 5). Making it easy to size up a hospital. *BusinessWeek,* 102.

Munk, N. (1999, June 21), Title fight. *Fortune,* 84–94.

Naughton, K. (1999, January 25). The global six. *BusinessWeek,* 68–76.

Nerf, R. (1991, December 9). Guess who is selling Barbies in Japan now? *BusinessWeek,* 72–76.

Neuman, C., & Srinivasan, J. (2010). *Managing innovation for the land of ideas and talent.* Springer Publishing Co.

Nocera, J. (2006, February 4). Good luck with that broken iPod. *The New York Times,* C-1.

Nuttavuthisit, K. (2010, April 15). If you can't beat them, let them join: The development of strategies to foster consumers' co-creative priorities. *Business Horizons,* 19–26.

Oosterwal, D. (2010). *The lean machine: How Harley-Davidson drove top line growth.* New York, NY: Amacon.

Peteraf, M. A. (1993). The cornerstone of competitive strategy: A resource based view. *Strategic Management Journal, 14,* 179–191.

Petrick, J. A., Scherer, R. F., Brodzinski, J. D., Quinn, J. F., & Ainina, M. F. (1999). Global leadership skills and reputational capital: Intangible resources for sustainable competitive advantage. *Academy of Management Executive, 13(1),* 58–70.

Pfeffer, J. (1994). *Competitive advantage through people: Unleashing the power of the workforce.* Boston: Harvard Business School Press.

Porter, M. E. (1990). *Competitive advantage.* New York: Free Press.

Porter, M. E. (1994). Toward a dynamic theory of strategy. In R. P. Rumelt, D. E. Schendel, & D. J. Teece (Eds.), *Fundamental issues in strategy.* Cambridge: Harvard University Press.

Pound, J. (1995). The promise of the governed corporation. *Harvard Business Review, 73(2),* 90.

Prahalad, C. K., & Hamel, G. (1990). The core competence of the organization. *Harvard Business Review, 68(3),* 79–91.

Preble, J. F. (1992). Environmental scanning for strategic control. *Journal of Managerial Issues, 4,* 254–268.

Price, R. (1996). Technology and strategic advantage. *California Management Review, 38(3),* 38–56.

Reed, S. (1999, February 22). Busting up Sweden Inc. *BusinessWeek,* 52–53.

Reger, R. K., & Huffs, A. S. (1993). Strategic groups: A cognitive perspective. *Strategic Management Journal, 14,* 103–123.

Richardson, K. (2006, January 5). Blockbuster's backbreaker: No-late-fee policy. *The Wall Street Journal,* B-l.

Rogers, B. (1998). *Seize the future for your business.* London, UK: International Thompson Business Press.

Rowley, I., Tashiro, H., & Lee, L. (2005, September 5). Canon: Combat-ready. *BusinessWeek,* 48.

Sager, I. (1999, June 21). Big Blue at your service. *BusinessWeek,* 131–136.

San Jose Mercury News (1998, May 2). Gates too busy to define government, [story appearing in *Arizona Republic,* El].

Schendler, B. (1999, April 12). Sony's new game. *Fortune,* 30–31.

Schrivastava, P. (1995). Ecocentric management for a risk society. *Academy of Management Review, 20,* 119.

Serwer, A. (2005, April 18). Bruised in Bentonville. *Fortune,* 84.

Sherman, S. (1995, November 13). Stretch goals: The dark side of asking for miracles. *Fortune,* 231–232.

Siekman, P. (1999, April 26). Where build-to-order works best. *Fortune,* 160.

Silke, S. (2006, January 5). Most automakers see their sales fall in December. *USA Today,* B-l.

Sirois, C. (1995, August 25). Unifi, Inc. *Value Pine,* 1640.

Sorkin, R. (2006, January 6). To Battle, armed with shares: Big holders wield their stakes to push for corporate change. *The New York Times,* C1.

Sparks, D. (1999, October 25). Partners. *BusinessWeek,* 106–107.

Stiles, T. (1995). Collaboration for competitive advantage. *Long Range Planning, 28,* 109–112.

Symonds, W. C. (1999, April 5). Looking to lose just a few more pounds. *BusinessWeek,* 64–70.

Symonds, W. C., & Burrows, D. (2005, May 23). A digital warrior for Kodak. *BusinessWeek,* 42.

Taylor A., III. (1999, January 11). The Germans take charge. *Fortune,* 92–96.

Taylor, A., III. (1995, September 18). Ford's really B16 leap at the future: It's risky, it's worthy, and it may work. *Fortune,* 134–144.

Taylor, A., III. (2005, October *17).* Ford: the hamlet of Dearborn. *Fortune,* 36.

Taylor, A., III. (1999, April 26). Why DuPont is trading oil for corn. *Fortune,* 154–160.

UpFront. (2005, December 5). The big picture. *BusinessWeek,* 16.

Veale, J. (1999, August 30). How Daewoo ran itself off the road. *BusinessWeek,* 48–49.

Vlasic, B., & Naughton, K. (1997, September 22). The small car wars are back. *BusinessWeek,* 40–42.

Walgreen Co., News and photos (2011). *The Chicago Tribune online*. http://www.chicagotribune.com.

The Walgreen Company (2011). http://en.wikipedia.org.

Weber, J. (1999, June 14). As the world restructures. *BusinessWeek,* 150–152.

Weber, J., Holmes, S., & Palmeri, C. (2005, November 7). Mosh pits of creativity. *BusinessWeek,* 98–101.

Weber, J., Holmes, S., & Palmeri, C. (2005, November 7). Older workers may have a hard time giving up private offices. *BusinessWeek,* 100.

Welsul, K. (2005, December 5). A shine on their shoes. *BusinessWeek,* 84.

White, J., & Power, S. (2006, January 9). VW's Bernhard says labor costs dent profit. *The Wall Street Journal,* A-10.

White, J. B., & McCracken, J. (2006, January 7). Troubled legacy: Auto industry, at a crossroads, finds itself stalled by history. *The Wall Street Journal,* B-l.

Wiles, R. (2003, February 18). Manage your money, control your future. *The Arizona Republic,* D-l.

Wineman, J. D., Kabo, F. W., & Davis, G. F. (2009). Spatial and social networks in organizational innovation. *Environment and Behavior, 41(3),* 427–442.

www.fisher-price.com. 2011.

www.harley-davidson.com.

www.Mattel.com. 2011.

Zappos Web page. www.zappos.com.

Zellner, W. (1999, February 8). Southwest's new direction. *BusinessWeek,* 58–59.

Zhang, H. (1995). Wealth effects of U.S. bank takeovers. *Applied Financial Economics, 5,* 329–336.

Zomerdijk, L. G., & Voss, C. A. (2010). Service design for experience—centric services. *Journal of Service Research, 13(1),* 67–82.

Zuckerman, G., McDonald, I., & Hawkins, L. (2006, January 12). If GM's big yield vanishes, investors may do the same. *The Wall Street Journal,* C-l.

Chapter 8

Armstrong, L. (1997, May 26). Powerwave technologies: Pump up the volume. *BusinessWeek,* 102.

Auntie Anne's Web site. Fact Sheet. www.auntieannes.com. Accessed July 3, 2010.

Auntie Anne's. www.wikipedia.org/wiki/Auntie_Anne's. Accessed July 3, 2010.

Barefoot into PARC (1993, July 10). *The Economist,* 68.

Barker, E. (1999, June). Maker of rugged PCs crumbles in IPO bid. *Inc,* 25.

Baron, R. A. (1998). Cognitive mechanisms in entrepreneurship: Why and when entrepreneurs think differently than other people. *Journal of Business Venturing, 13,* 275–294.

Barrett, C. (2003, January 27). Good times and bad: Innovation is key. *Information Week,* 20.

Batelle, J. (2005). The 70 percent solution. Business 2.0, 6, 134.

Berringer, B. R., & Bluedorn, A. C. (1999). The relationship between corporate entrepreneurship and strategic management. *Strategic Management Journal, 20,* 421–444.

Bildner, J. (1995, July). Hitting the wall. *Inc,* 21–22.

Borland, V. S. (2005). New directions for apparel and home fabrics. *Textile World, 155,* 53–55.

Brody, W. R. (2005). What happened to American innovation? *Chief Executive, 214,* 22–24.

Bruno, A. V., Leidecker, J. K., & Harder, J. W. (1987, March-April). Why firms fail. *Business Horizons,* 50–58.

Bruno, A. V., & Tyebjee, T. (1985). The entrepreneur's search for capital. *Journal of Business Venturing, 1,* 61–74.

Burgelman, R. A, (1983). Corporate entrepreneurship and strategic management: Insights from a process study. *Management Science, 29,* 1349–1364.

Burgelman, R. A., Maidique, M. A., & Wheelwright, S. G. (1996). *Strategic management of technology and innovation* (2nd ed.). Burr Ridge, IL: Irwin.

Busenitz, L. A., & Barney, J. B. (1997). Differences between entrepreneurs and managers in large organizations: Biases and heuristics in strategic decision-making. *Journal of Business Venturing, 12,* 9–30.

Buttner, E. H., & Moore, D. P. (1997). Women's organizational exodus to entrepreneurship: Self-reported motivations and correlated with success. *Journal of Small Business Management, 34(4),* 1–13.

Byrt, F. (2005, Novermber 17). Clothes get wired at digital-edge design shops: Textronics foresees t-shirts that monitor heart rates, but market not yet certain. *The Wall Street Journal,* B-4.

Callan, C., & Warshaw, M. (1995, September). The 25 best business schools for entrepreneurs. *Success,* 37–54.

Carland, J., Hoy, F., Boulton, W., & Carland, J. (1984). Differentiating entrepreneurs from small business owners: A conceptualization. *Academy of Management Review, 9,* 354–359.

Cassidy, M. (2003, December 5). Creative marketing: The mouse tap. *Detroit Free Press,* www.freep.com/money tech/mice5.,20021205.htm, accessed February 19, 2003.

Cherwitz, R. A., & Sullivan, C. A. (2002). Intellectual entrepreneurship: A vision for graduate education. *Change, 34,* 23–28.

Covin, J. G., Slevin, D. P., & Covin, T. J. (1990). Content and performance of growth-seeking strategies: A comparison of small firms in high- and low-technology industries. *Journal of Business Venturing, 5,* 391–412.

Daly, J. (2010, June 14). Sam Adams beer pleads to keep craft status. *Huffington Post.* www.huffingtonpost.com.

DeCastro, J. D. (1997, March). When firms disappear have they really failed? *Colorado Business Review,* 3.

Dell Inc. Web site. Facts about Dell. www.dell.com. Accessed July 3, 2010.

Dollinger, M. J. (1995). *Entrepreneurship.* New York: McGraw-Hill/Irwin.

Dubini, P., & Aldrich, H. (1991). Personal and extended networks are central to the entrepreneurial process. *Journal of Business Venturing, 6,* 305–313.

Eckberg, J, (2002, October 14). Innovation spells success. *Cincinnati Enquirer,* B-6.

Engardio, P., Einhorn, B., Kripalini, M., Reinhardt, A., Nussbaum, B., & Burrows, P. (2005, March 21). Outsourcing innovation. *BusinessWeek Online.*

Fisher, R., & Ury, W. (1983). *Getting to yes.* New York: Penguin Books.

Gartner, W. B. (1985). A conceptual framework for describing the phenomena of new venture creation. *Academy of Management Review, 10,* 696–706.

Gartner, W. B. (1989). Who is an entrepreneur? Is the wrong question. *Entrepreneurship Theory and Practice, 13,* 47–64.

Gersick, C. J. (1994). Pacing strategic change: The case of a new venture. *Academy of Management Journal, 37,* 9–45.

Gomez-Mejia, L. R., Balkin, D. B., & Welbourne, T. (1990). Influence of venture capitalists on high tech management. *Journal of High Technology Management Research, 1,* 90–106.

Hambrick, D. C, & Crazier, L. M. (1985). Stumblers and stars in the management of rapid growth. *Journal of Business Venturing, 1,* 31–45.

Hamel, G., Doz, Y., & Prahalad, C. K. (1989, January-February). Collaborate with your competitors—and win. *Harvard Business Review,* 133–139.

Heun, C. T. (2002, February 11). New "ink" veers display toward the good old look. *InformationWeek,* 18.

Himelstein, L. (1998, September 7). Yahoo! The company, the strategy, the stock. *BusinessWeek,* 66–76.

Hisrich, R. D., & Peters, M. P. (1998). *Entrepreneurship* (4th ed.). New York: McGraw-Hill/Irwin.

Hof, R. D. (1998, December 14). Amazon.com: The wild world of e-commerce. *BusinessWeek,* 106–119.

Hofman, M. (1997, August). Desperation capital. *Inc,* 54–57.

Hopkins, J. (2003, February 24). Start-up succeeding study says. *The Arizona Republic,* Dl.

Hyatt, J. (2010, May 24 & 31). Beer baron. *Newsweek,* 54.

InnoCentive Web site (2010). About InnoCentive. www.innocentive.com.

Jones, G. R., & Butler, J. E. (1992). Managing internal corporate entrepreneurship: An agency theory perspective. *Journal of Management, 18,* 733–749.

Kazanjian, R. K. (1988). Relation of dominant problems to stages of growth in technology-based new ventures. *Academy of Management Journal, 31,* 257–279.

Kirkpatrick, D. (2005). Throw it at the wall and see if it sticks. *Fortune, 152,* 142.

Klein, ICE. (2005, August 25). Minority startups: A measure of progress. *BusinessWeek Online.*

Kotter, J., & Sathe, V. (1978). Problems of human resource management in rapidly growing companies. *California Management Review, 21(2),* 29–36.

Kunze, R. J. (2001). The dark side of multilevel marketing: Appeals to the symbolically incomplete. Dissertation at Arizona State University.

Kuratko, D. F., & Hodgetts, R. M. (1992). *Entrepreneurship* (2nd ed.). Fort Worth: Dryden Press.

Larson, J. (2003). Musician beams with joy. *The Arizona Republic,* pp. Dl, D2.

Lehn, D. I., Neely, C. W., Schoonover, K., Martin, T. L., Jones, M. T. (2004, January). E-TAGs: e-Textile attached gadgets. Paper presented at the Communication Networks and Distributed Systems Modeling and Simulation Conference.

Lesley, E., & Mallory, M. (1993, November 29). Inside the black business network. *BusinessWeek,* 70.

Lindsay, N., & Craig, J. (2002). A Framework for Understanding Opportunity Recognition: Entrepreneurs versus Private Equity Financiers. *Journal of Private Equity, 6,* 13–24.

Lumpkin, G. T. (1996). Clarifying the entrepreneurial orientation construct and linking it to performance. *Academy of Management Review, 21,* 135–172.

A Market for Ideas (2009, September 19). *The Economist,* 75–76.

Marsh, R. (2005, January/February). Ready, willing, & able. *BizAZ,* 37–43.

Martin, R. L. (2005, December 13). India and China: Not just cheap. *BusinessWeek Online.*

McNamee, M. (1997, September 1). Good news from small biz. *BusinessWeek,* 24.

Megginson, W. L., Boyd, M. J., Scott, C. R., & Megginson, L. C. (1997). *Small business management* (2nd ed.). Burr Ridge, IL: Irwin.

Meyer, G. D., & Dean, T. J. (1995, July). Why entrepreneurs fail. *Colorado Business Review,* 3–4.

Mottram, B., Rigby, S., & Webster, A. (2003, January). The freedom to call your own shots. *Transmission & Distribution World,* 55.

Nadel, B. (2005). Unraveling the mysteries of innovation. *Fortune, 152,* 554–556.

National Commission on Entrepreneurship (2001). Five myths about entrepreneurs: Understanding how businesses start and grow. www.ncoe.org, accessed February 19, 2003.

Nussbaum, B., Berner, R., & Brady, D. (2005, August 1). Get creative! How to build innovative companies. *BusinessWeek Online.*

O'Reilly, B. (1999, June 7). What it takes to start a startup. *Fortune,* 135–140.

Patnaik, D. (2005, December 21) The true measure of a good idea. *BusinessWeek Online.*

Pellet, J. (2002). Leading creative charge. *Chief Executive, 1,* 6–11.

Pinchot, G. (1985). *Intrapreneuring.* New York: Harper & Row.

Raz, T. (2003, January). The 10 secrets of a master networker, *Inc. Magazine,* 90–99.

Riddle, D. (2000). Training staff to innovate. *International Trade Forum, 2,* 28–30.

Rodgers, M. (2004). Networks, Firm size and innovation. *Small Business Economics, 22,* 141–153.

Roha, R. R. (1997, May). Home alone. *Kiplinger's Personal Finance Magazine,* 85–89.

Russo, J. E., & Schoemaker, P. J. (1992). Managing overconfidence. *Sloan Management Review, 33(2),* 7–17.

Schlender, B. (1997, July 7). Cool companies. *Fortune,* 84–110.

Schmitt, B. (2002, February). Growth signs for new "ink." *Chemical Week, 164,* 46.

Schubert, S. (2005). The ultimate silver lining: How Bill McNally turned his idea for an antibacterial fabric into $50 million sensation. *Business 2.0, 6,* 78.

Serwer, A. (1998, May 11). Michael Dell rocks. *Fortune,* 59–70.

Serwer, A. (1997, September 8). Michael Dell turns the PC world inside out. *Fortune,* 76–86.

Shane, S. (2000). Prior knowledge and discovery of entrepreneurial opportunities. *Organization Science, 11,* 448–469.

Small Business Administration (2002). Small business by the numbers, www.sba.gov/advo/stats/, accessed April 6, 2003 (see "Small Business Frequently Asked Questions").

Statistical Abstracts of the United States. (1994). Washington, DC: U.S. Government Printing Office.

Stewart, W. H., Watson, W. E., Carland, J. C, & Carland, J. W. (1999). A proclivity for entrepreneurship: A comparison of entrepreneurs, small business owners, and corporate managers. *Journal of Business Venturing, 14,* 189–214.

Threads that think (2005, December 10). *The Economist.*

Timmons, J. A. (1994). *New venture creation* (4th ed.). New York: McGraw-Hill/Irwin.

Usdansky, M. L. (1991, August 2). Asian businesses big winners in '80s. *USA Today,* 1A.

Useem, J. (1998, August). Partners on the edge. *Inc,* 52–64.

Vincent, V. C. (1996). Decision-making policies among Mexican-American small business entrepreneurs. *Journal of Small Business Management, 34(4),* 1–13.

Williams, D. L. (1999). Why do entrepreneurs become franchisees? An empirical analysis of organizational choice. *Journal of Business Venturing, 14,* 103–124.

www.bostonbeer.com. Accessed July 1, 2010.

The White House (2003). Taking action to strengthen small business, www.whitehouse.gov/infocus/smallbusiness, accessed April 6, 2003.

Zahorsky, D. (2010). Sole Proprietorship: The Right Business Structure? www.sbinformation.about.com.

Chapter 9

Barrett, P. (2010, May 10–16). The departed: A merger of United and Continental makes sense, but can it bring back the business of flying? *Bloomberg BusinessWeek,* 7–8.

Bartol, K. M., & Martin, D. C. (1998), *Management* (3rd ed.). New York: McGraw-Hill.

Brown, S., & Blackmon, K. (2005). *Journal of Management Studies, 42,* 793–815.

Budros, A. (1999). A conceptual framework for analyzing why organizations downsize. *Organization Science, 10,* 69–82.

Burns, T., & Stalker, G. (1961). *The management of innovation.* London, UK: Tavistock Institute.

Burrows, P. (1999, August 12). The boss: Carly Fiorina's challenge will be to propel staid Hewlett-Packard into the Internet age without sacrificing the very things that have made it great. *BusinessWeek,* 76–84.

Byrne, J. A. (1998, June 8). Jack: A close-up look at how America's #1 manager views GE. *BusinessWeek,* 40–51.

Caroll, P. (1993). *Big blues: The unmaking of IBM.* New York: Crown Publishers.

Clark, K., & Wheelwright, S. (1992). Organizing and leading "heavyweight" development teams. *California Management Review, 34(2),* 9–28.

Cobb, A. T. (1980). Informal influence in the formal organization: Perceived sources of power among work unit peers, *Academy of Management Journal, 23,* 55–61.

Colvin, G., and J. Shambora (2009, May 4). J&J: Secrets of Success. *Fortune,* 117–121.

Conglomorates on trial (1997, April 5). *The Economist,* 59.

Covery, S., & R. Merrill (1998, February 6). New ways to get organized at work. *USA Weekend,* 18.

Crockett, R. O. (1998, May 4). How Motorola lost its way, *BusinessWeek,* 140–148.

Crockett, R. O. (1999, June 21). Motorola is ringing again. *BusinessWeek,* 40.

Daft, R. L. (1983). *Organization theory and design,* St. Paul, MN: West Publishing Company.

Daft, R. L. (1997). *Management* (4th ed.). Fort Worth: Dryden Press.

Daft, R. L. (1999). *Leadership: Theory and practice.* Fort Worth: Dryden Press.

Das, S. (2006). Designing service processes: A design factor based process model. *International Journal of Services Technology and Management, 7(1),* 85.

Deal, T. E., & Kennedy, A. A. (1982). *Corporate cultures.* Reading, MA: Addison-Wesley.

Duncan, R. (1979, Winter). What is the right organization structure? Decision tree analysis provides the answer. *Organizational Dynamics,* 59–80.

Evans, B. (2005, December 19–26). Google becomes an irresistible force. *InformationWeek,* 76.

Fama, E. F. (1980). Agency problems and the theory of the firm. *Journal of Political Economy, 88,* 288–307.

Fama, E. F., & Jensen, M. L. (1983). Separation of ownership and control. *Journal of Law and Economics, 26,* 301–325.

Ford, R. C, & Randolph, W. A. (1992). Cross-functional structures: A review and integration of matrix organization and project management. *Journal of Management, 18,* 267–294.

Frank, K. A., & Fahrbach, K. (1999). Organization culture as a complex system: Balance and information models of influence and selection. *Organization Science, 10,* 253–277.

Freedman, A. M. (1988, October 20). Phillip Morris's bid for Kraft could limit product innovation. *The Wall Street Journal,* A-l.

Galuszka, P. (2008, July 2). Johnson & Johnson CEO: Decentralization works. www.blogs.bnet.com/ceo/?p=1199.

Garten, J. (1998, July 20). Daimler has to steer the Chrysler merger. *BusinessWeek,* 20.

Glasgall, W. (1998, April 20). Citigroup: Just the start? *BusinessWeek,* 34–40.

Gomez-Mejia, L. R., Balkin, D. B., & Cardy, R. L. (2012). *Managing human resources* (2nd ed.). Upper Saddle River, NJ: Prentice Hall.

Gooding, R., & Wagner, J. (1985). A meta-analytic review of the relationship between size and performance: The productivity and efficiency of organizations and their subunits. *Administrative Science Quarterly, 30,* 462–481.

Goold, M. & Campbell, A. (2002, March). Do you have a well-designed organization? *Harvard Business Review,* 117–124.

Hatch, M. J. (1997). *Organization theory.* Oxford, UK: Oxford University Press.

Hodge, B. J., & Anthony, W. P. (1979). *Organization theory.* Boston: Allyn and Bacon.

Hoskisson, R. E., & Hitt, M. A. (1994). *Downscoping: How to tame the diversified firm.* New York: Oxford University Press.

How to manage a dream factory (2003, January 18). *The Economist,* 73–75.

How to merge: After the deal (1999, January 9). *The Economist,* 21–23.

Johnson & Johnson Web site (2010). Company Overview. www.jnj.com/company-overview.cfm.

Jones, G. R. (1998). *Organizational theory* (2nd ed.). Reading, MA: Addison-Wesley.

Kirkpatrick, D. (1996, November 25). They're all copying Compaq. *Fortune,* 28–32.

Kochan, T. A., & Osterman, P. (1994). *The mutual gains enterprise.* Boston: Harvard Business School Press.

Kraatz, M. S., & Zajac, E. J. (2001). How organizational resources affect strategic change and performance in turbulent environments: Theory and evidence. *Organization Science, 12,* 632–657.

Kruse, D. L. (1993). *Profit sharing.* Kalamazoo, MI: W. E. Upjohn Institute for Employment Research.

Lacy, S. (2006, January 23). The hardest job in Silicon Valley. *BusinessWeek,* 65–66.

Larson, E. W., & Gobeli, D. H. (1987, Summer). Matrix management: Contradictions and insights. *California Management Review,* 126–138.

Larsson, R., & Finkelstein, S. (1999). Integrating strategic, organizational, and human resource perspectives on mergers and acquisitions: A case survey of synergy realization. *Organization Science, 10,* 1–26.

Lawler, E. E. (1992). *The ultimate advantage.* San Francisco: Jossey-Bass.

Lei, D., Hitt, M., & Goldhar, J. (1996). Advanced manufacturing technoloogy: Organization design and strategic flexibility. *Organization Studies, 17(3),* 501–523.

Love is in the air: UAL and Continental agree to merge (2010, May 8). *The Economist,* 64.

McWilliams, G. (1998, February 9). Power play: How the Compaq-Digital deal will reshape the entire world of computers. *BusinessWeek,* 90–97.

Meyer, M. (1998, July 6). The call of the wired. *Newsweek,* 44–47.

Miller, A. (1998). *Strategic management* (3rd ed.). New York: Mc-Graw-Hill/Irwin.

Miller, C., Glick, W., Wang, Y., & Huber, G. (1991). Understanding technology-structural relationships: Theory development and meta-analytic theory testing. *Academy of Management Journal, 34,* 370–399.

Mintzberg, H. (1979). *Structuring organizations.* Englewood Cliffs, NJ: Prentice Hall.

Montealegre, R., Nelson, J., Knoop, C., & Applegate, L. (1996). *BAE Automated Systems(A): Denver International Airport baggage-handling system.* Boston: Harvard Business School Publishing.

Moore, M. T. (1992, April 10). Hourly workers apply training in problem solving, *USA Today,* C1.

Mouawad, J., & de la Merced, M. (2010, May 2). United and Continental said to merge. *The New York Times Online.* www.nytimes.com/2010/05/.../03merger.html.

Murphy, K. R., & Cleveland, J. N. (1995), *Understanding performance appraisal.* Thousand Oaks, CA: Sage Publications.

A new kind of car company (1998, May 9). *The Economist,* 61–62.

Quinn, R. E., Faerman, S. R., Thompson, M. P., & McGrath, M. R. (1996). *Becoming a manager* (2nd ed.). New York: John Wiley & Sons.

Rebello, K. (1994, March 7). A juicy apple? *BusinessWeek,* 88–90.

Robbins, S. P., & Coulter, M. (1996.). *Management* (5th ed.). Upper Saddle River, NJ: Prentice Hall.

Robey, D., & Sayles, C. A. (1994). *Designing organizations.* Burr Ridge, IL: Irwin.

Sanchez, R., & Mahoney, J. (1996, Winter). Modularity, flexibility and knowledge management in product and organization design. *Strategic Management Journal, 17,* 63–76

Sara Lee: chock full o' Brands (2005, November 12). *The Economist.*

Schlangenstein, M., Credeur, M., Hughes, J., & Bliss, J. (2010, May 10-16). United and Continental reach for the sky. *Bloomberg BusinessWeek,* 19–20.

Segal, J., Horowitz, L., Jaffe-Gill, E., Smith, M., & Segal, R. (2008, November). How to Reduce and Manage Workplace Stress. www.helpguide.org/mental/work_stress_management.htm.

Separate and Life (1997, September 20). *The Economist,* 69.

Silverman, G. (1999, August 16). Citigroup: So much for 50–50. *BusinessWeek,* 80.

Smart, T. (1996, October 28), Jack Welch's encore. *Business-Week,* 155–160.

Smircich, L. (1983). Concepts of culture and organizational analysis. *Administrative Science Quarterly, 28,* 339–358.

Smith, S. (2005, September 12). A date with digital. *Mediaweek,* 38–39.

Special report: Yum! Brands: Fast food's yummy secret (2005, August 27) *The Economist,* 60–62.

Taking the hill less climbed (2009, October 31). *The Economist,* 76.

Tatge, M. (2003, February 17). Prescription for growth. *Fortune,* 64–66.

Van Fleet, D., & Bedeian, A. (1977). A history of the span of management. *Academy of Management Review, 2,* 356–372.

Welch, J. (2005). *Winning.* New York, NY: Harper Business.

Whetton, D. A., & Cameron, K.S. (1995). *Developing management skills* (3rd ed.). New York, NY: HarperCollins.

Woodward, J. (1965). *Industrial organizations: Theory and practice.* London: Oxford University Press.

Wright, P. M., & Noe, R. A. (1996). *Management of organizations.* Burr Ridge, IL: McGraw-Hill Irwin.

Yum! Brands Web site (2010). Yum! FAQs. www.yum.com/investors/faqs.asp

Chapter 10

The 100 best companies to work for (2006, January 23). *Fortune.* 89–108.

Abelson, R. (2005, November 1). Dr. Saves-a-Lot. *The New York Times,* C-1, C-5.

Alpern, D. M. (1995, July). Why women are divided on affirmative action. *Working Woman,* 18.

Applebee's International (2011). Trabon. www.trabonsolutions.com.

Applebee's turnover recipe. http://www.workforce.com.

Averill, R., Goldfield, N., Vertrees, J. C., McCullough, E. C., Fuller, R. L., & Eisenhandler, J. (2010). Achieving cost control, care coordination, and quality improvement through incremental payment system reform. *Journal of Ambulatory Care Management, 33(1),* 2–23.

Balancing job and personal responsibilities (2011). *Work & Family Life.* http://www.workandfamilylife.com.

Bernardin, H. J., & Cooke, D. K. (1993). Validity of an honesty test in predicting theft among convenience store employees. *Academy of Management Journal, 36,* 1097–1108.

Bloomberg News. (2006, January 13). Starbucks to add movie products. *The New York Times,* C-5.

Blumenthal, R. (2006, January 13). In Houston, Teachers Get Merit Pay. *The New York Times,* A-12.

Branch, S. (1999, January 11). The 100 best companies to work for in America. *Fortune,* 118.

Burack, E. H. (1988). *Creative human resource planning and applications.* Englewood Cliffs, NJ: Prentice Hall.

Bureau of Labor Statistics. (1999). *Employment and earnings* (Tables 44 and 45). Washington, D.C.: Government Printing Office.

Caillier, J. (2010). Paying teachers according to student achievement: Questions regarding pay-for-performance models in public education. *The Clearing House, 83(2),* 58–61.

Carrell, M. R., & Heavrin, C. (1998). *Labor relations and collective bargaining.* Upper Saddle River, NJ: Prentice Hall.

Cerrito, J. C., & McLean, G. N. (2010). Developing content validity selection procedures. *Performance Improvement, 49(2),* 29–35.

Cowan, T. R. (1989). Drugs and the workplace. *Public Personnel Management, 16,* 313–322.

Damodt, M. G., Bryan, D. A., & Whitcomb, A. J. (1993). Predicting performance with letters of recommendation. *Public Personnel Management, 22,* 81–90.

Dessler, G. (2007). *Human resource management.* Upper Saddle River, NJ: Prentice Hall.

Diener, E., Helliwell, J. F., & Kahneman, D. (2010). International differences in well being. In: A. E. Clark (ed) (2010). *Work, Jobs and Well Being Across the Millennium.* London, U.K.: Oxford University Press.

EEOC meets new, higher burden of proof in race bias case in California court (1993, September 13). *BNA's Employee Relations Weekly,* 11, 991.

Eisenberg, D. (1999, August 16). We are for hire, just click. *Time,* 46–50.

Filipzak, B. (1993, October). Training budgets boom. *Training,* 37–44.

Fitzgerald, W. (1992). Training versus development. *Training and Development,* 46–81.

Foust, D., Grow, B., & Pascual, M. M. (2002, September 9). The changing heartland. *BusinessWeek,* 80–82.

Goldstein, I. C. (1986). Training in organizations: Needs assessment, development, and evaluation (2nd ed.). Monterey, CA: Brooks/Cole.

Gomez-Mejia, L. R., & Blakin, D. B. (1992). *Compensation, organizational strategy, and firm performance.* Cincinnati, OH: South-Western Publishing.

Gomez-Mejia, L. R., Balkin, D. B., & Cardy, R. (2007). *Managing human resources.* Upper Saddle River, NJ: Prentice Hall.

Gratz, D. B. (2010). *The peril and promise of performance pay: Making education compensation work.* New York, NY: Rowman & Littlefield.

Gray, S. (2006, January 2). Fill'er up—with latte. *The Wall Street Journal,* A-l.

Griggs v. Duke Power Co., 401 U.S. 424 (1971).

Gryphon, M. (2011). Better teachers: A lesson plan. http://www.cato.org.

Gunsch, D. (1993, September). Comprehensive college entry strengthens NCR's recruitment. *Personnel Journal,* 58–62.

Henderson, R. I. (1997). *Compensation management* (7th ed.). Upper Saddle River, NJ: Prentice Hall.

Hill, C. W. C. (2007). *International business.* New York: McGraw-Hill/Irwin.

Hogan, R. (1991). Personality and personality measurement. In M. D. Dunnette, & L. M. Hough (Eds.), *Handbook of industrial and organization psychology* (2nd ed., vol. 1). Palo Alto, CA: Consulting Psychologists.

Holmes, S., Bennett, D., Carlisle, K., & Dawson, C. (2002, September 9). To keep up the growth, it must go global quickly. *BusinessWeek,* 126–138.

HR Management (2011). http://www.workforce.com.

HR News. (1994, February). No beard rule found to have disparate impact, 17.

Hunter, J. E. (1986). Cognitive ability, cognitive aptitudes, job knowledge, and job performance. *Journal of Vocational Behavior, 29,* 340–362.

Kasindorf, M. (1999, September 10). Hispanics and blacks find their futures entangled. *USA Today,* 21A.

Kiger, P. J. (2010). Throwing out the rules of work. http://www.workforce.com.

Kjerulf, A. (2010). Chief happiness officer. http://positivesharing.com.

Konig, C. J., Klehe, U. Christine, & Berchtold, M. (2010). Reasons for being selective when choosing personnel selection procedures. *International Journal of Selection and Assessment, 18(1),* 17–27.

Koretz, G. (1996, December 2). College majors that really pay. *BusinessWeek,* 34.

Langbein, L. (2010). Economics, public service motivation and pay for performance. *International Public Management Journal, 13(1),* 9–23.

Levering, R., & Moskowitz, M. (2003, January 20). 100 best companies to work for. *Fortune,* 127–150.

Longnecker, B. M., Petersen, B., & Hitt, R. (1999). Long-term incentives: How private companies can complete with public companies. *Compensation and Benefits Review, 31(1),* 44–53.

Lopez, J. A. (1993, October 6). Firms force job seekers to jump through hoops. *The Wall Street Journal,* B-l, B-6.

Mandel, M. J. (1996, October 28). The high risk society: Coping with uncertainty, *BusinessWeek,* 86–94.

McDonough, D. C. (1999, April 26). A fair workplace? Not everywhere. *BusinessWeek,* 6.

McEvoy, G. M., & Beatty, R. W. (1989). Assessment centers and subordinate appraisal of managers. *Personnel Psychology, 42,* 37–52.

Milkovich, G. T., & Newman, J. M. (2005). *Compensation* (8th ed.). New York: McGraw-Hill/Irwin.

Mongiol, F. T., Jr. (2010). The human element of supply chain security. http://www.books.google.com.

Morris, B. (2006, January 23). No. 1 Genentech. *Fortune,* 80–86.

Muchinsky, P. M. (1979). The use of reference reports in personnel selection. *Journal of Occupational Psychology, 52,* 287–297.

Mullaney, C. A., & Trask, L. D. (1992, October). Show them the ropes. *Technical & Skills Training,* 8–11.

Murphy, K. R. (1993). *Honesty in the workplace.* Belmont, CA: Brooks/Cole.

Murphy, N. J. (1993). Performance measurement and appraisal. *Employment Relations Today,* 47–62.

Newman, B. (2003, January 9). For ill immigrants, doctors' orders get lost in translation. *The Wall Street Journal,* A-l.

O'Keefe, E. (2010, February 23). Hiring to expand veteran's services. *The Washington Post,* A-1.

Overview: What is work life (2011). WFC Resources. *Work-Life and Human Capital Solutions.* http://www.workfamily.com/aboutworklife/aboutworklife.htm.

Prasso, S. (2003, February 18). The UAW answers a cry for help. *BusinessWeek,* 8.

Ray, H. H., & Altmansberger, H. N. (1999). Introducing goal sharing in a public sector organization. *Compensation and Benefits Review, 31(3),* 40–45.

Reese, J. (1996, December 9). Starbucks: Inside the coffee cult. *Fortune,* 191–200.

Reinhardt, A., & Holf, R. D. (1999, October 4). The search for the young and gifted. *BusinessWeek,* 108–112.

Russell, C. J., Mattson, J., Devlin, S. E., & Atwater, D. (1990). Predictive validity of biodata items generated from retrospective life experience essays. *Journal of Applied Psychology, 75,* 569–580.

Rynes, S. L. (1991). Recruitment, job choice, and post hire consequences. *Handbook of industrial and organizational psychology* (2nd ed., Vol. 2). 399–344.

Schwartz, N. D. (1999, May 24). Still perking after all these years. *Fortune,* 203–210.

Scott, C. (2010). Never again. *Nature Biotechnology, 28,* 131–142.

Shellenberger, S. (2005, October 20). Work and Family. *The Wall Street Journal,* D-l.

Steckler, D. E., Epstein, F., & Riner, R. N. (September, 2009). Physician-Hospital alignment; Finding the sweetspot. http://www.invasivecardiology.com.

Stein, N. (2003, March 3). America's most admired companies. *Fortune,* 81–94.

Supermarket chain settles sex bias suit (1997, January 25). *Arizona Republic,* E-l.

Symons, J. L. (1995, May-June). Is affirmative action in America's interest? *Executive Female,* 52.

Trend Watch (2010, February). American Hospital Association, 5.

Toyota counting on veterans at Congress hearing (2010). http://newsday.com.

Toyota on a military mission (2011). http://www.workforce.com.

Toyota's hire a hero program debuts at Richmond (2004, September 8). www.theautochannel.com.

Toyota's 'hire a hero' to aid veterans' return to civilian workforce (2006, March 16). Toyota press release. www.glassbytes.com. Accessed March 16, 2006.

Thottam, J. (2005, July 5). Reworking work. *Time,* 50–55.

Useem, J. (1999, May 24). Read this before you put your resume on line. *Fortune,* 290.

Useem, J. (1999, July 5). Getting job on line. *Fortune,* 69.

Walker, J. (1992). *Human resource management strategy.* New York: McGraw-Hill.

Wanous, J. P. (1992). *Organizational entry* (2nd ed.). Reading, MA: Addison-Wesley.

Wessel, D. (1989, September 7). Evidence is skimpy that drug testing works, but employers embrace the practice. *The Wall Street Journal,* B-l.

What makes a successful Applebee's manager? (2011). http://www.amrestapplebees.com.

White, E. (2005, November 28). How to reduce turnover. *The Wall Street Journal,* C-3.

Williams, R. (2006, February 27). Toyota helps guards, reservists find jobs. www.americasupportsyou.mil.

Wright, P., Licthenfels, P., & Prusell, E. D. (1989). The structure interview: Additional studies and a meta-analysis. *Journal of Occupational Psychology, 6,* 191–199.

www.etoyota.com/joblink/main.asp. Accessed March 16, 2006.

Uris, Auren (1988). *88 mistakes interviewers make and how to avoid them.* AMACON Books.

Chapter 11

Aging workforce presents new opportunities, challenges for employers (2005, November 2). *Workspan,* 16.

Aji, A. (2006, February 5). Syrians burn embassies over cartoons. *Arizona Republic,* A-ll.

Alonso-Zaldivar, R. (2003, February 1). Immigrants at 7 million, revised INS report says. *Arizona Republic,* A-5.

Alster, N. (2005, January 3). When grey heads roll. *The New York Times,* B-3.

Anands and Recognition (2011). http://www-03.ibm.com.

Anderson, J. (2006, January 10). Six women at Dresdner file bias suit. *The New York Times,* C-l.

Antilla, S. (2010). In the companies of men: A rash of gender-discrimination suits suggests the Morgan Stanley payout may be only the beginning. *The New York Magazine.* http://www.nymag.com.

Armendariz, Y. (2003, February 10). Disabled workers can telecommute. *Arizona Republic,* D-3.

Ashton, A. (2002, February). Around-the-clock child care. *Working Women,* 14.

Banach, E. (1990, September). Today's supply of entry level workers reflect diversity. *Savings Institution,* 74–75.

Banking Latino immigrants (2011). *Hispanic Bank Markets.* http://nubank.cust.digitalwest.net.

Bateman, T. S., & Snell, S. A. (1999). *Management: Building competitive advantage* (4th ed.). New York: McGraw-Hill/Irwin.

Berstein, R. (2006, February 13). The undoing of a done deal. *BusinessWeek,* 54.

Best Buy Considers layoffs (2010). http://www.promomagazine.com.

Bilefsky, D. (2006, January 8). Denmark is unlikely front in Islam-West culture war. *The New York Times,* 3.

Briefs (2003, February 22). *Workforce strategies, 4(2),* WS-12.

Bryson, B. P., & Davis, A. K. (2010). Conquering stereotypes in research on race and gender. *Sociological Forum, 25 (1),* 161–166.

Champion, M. (2006, February 3). Muslim outrage mounts over cartoons in EU. *The Wall Street Journal,* B-2.

Chao addresses challenges of aging workforces at conference (2005, April 27). *Newsline.* http://resourcespro.worldatwork.org/.

Childs, T. (2005, Spring). Managing workforce diversity at IBM. *Human Resources Management, 114(1),* 73–77. www.ibm.com (2006).

Chu, J., & Mustafa, N. (2006, January 16). Between two worlds. *Time,* 67.

Colvin, G. (1999, July 19). 50 best companies for Asians, Blacks, and Hispanics. *Fortune,* 52–59.

Cowell, A. (2006, February 2). More European papers print cartoons of Muhammad, fueling dispute among Muslims. *The New York Times,* A-3.

Cowell, A. (2006, February 4). Cartoons force Danish Muslims to examine loyalties, *The New York Times,* B-l.

Cox, T. H., & Blake, S. (1991). Managing cultural diversity: Implications for organizational competiveness. *Academy of Management Executive, 5(3),* 45–46.

Coy, P. (2005, June 27). Surprise! The graying of the workforce is better news than you think. *BusinessWeek,* 78.

Crockett, R. O. (1999, May 24). African-Americans get the investing bug. *BusinessWeek,* 39.

Crossen, C. (2006, January 9). How U.S. immigration evolved as the nation grew and changed. *The Wall Street Journal,* B-3.

Demographic Change and Local Government: Overview of Issues (2011). http://www.mrsc.org.

Denissen, A. M. (2010, March). The right tools for the job: constructing gender meanings and identities in the male-dominated building trades. *Human Relations*, 1–19.

Diversity 3.0, Leveraging our differences for innovation, collaboration, and client success (2011). http://www-03.ibm.com,

Diversity Management (2011). http://www.diversityinc.com.

Diversity Programs. Hilton Hotels Corporation. http://cvmsolutions.com/hilton. Accessed April, 2010.

Doyle, R. (2002, February). Assembling the future. *Scientific American*, 30.

Egan, T. (2005, April 1). Wanted: Border hoppers. *Arizona Republic*, A-12.

Engardio, P., Matlack, C., Edmondson, G., Rowley, I., Barraclough, C., Smith, G. (2005, January 31). Global aging: Now, the geezer glut. *BusinessWeek*, 44–47.

Fahrenthold, D. A. (2005, January 16). Cap on migrant workers hurting seafood processors. *Arizona Republic*, A-16.

Fellows, D. S. (2001). Striking gold in a silver mine: Leveraging senior workers as knowledge champions. *Worldatwork Journal*, 10(4), 1–12.

Ferraro, G. (2010). *The cultural dimension of international business*. Upper Saddle River, NJ: Pearson Education.

Fine, M. C., Johnson, P. L., & Ryan, S. M. (1990). Cultural diversity in the workplace. *Public Personnel Management*, 19(3), 305–319.

Fineman, H., & Lipper, T. (2003, January 23). Spinning race. *Newsweek*, 27–38.

Fisher, A. (2005, March 31). How to battle the coming brain drain. *Fortune*, 21–28.

Former Manhattan Madam Kristin Davis dishes insider information on flip side of Wall Street boysclub (2011). http://www.image.examiner.com.

Freudenheim, M. (2005, March 23). Help wanted: Older workers please apply. *The New York Times*, A-1.

Global demographic changes (2011). http://www.w3.org.

Gomez-Mejia, L. R., Balkin, D. B., & Cardy, R. (2007). *Managing human resources*. Englewood Cliffs, NJ: Prentice Hall.

Gomez-Mejia, L. R., Balkin, D. B., & Cardy, R. (2012). *Managing human resources*. New York: Prentice Hall.

Green, H. (2006, January 16). Chocolate mess. *BusinessWeek*, 14.

Greene, K. (2005, September 20). Bye-bye boomers? *The Wall Street Journal*, B-1.

Greenhouse, L. (2006, January 22). Broad survey of day laborers finds high level of injuries and pay violations. *The New York Times*, A-17.

Grow, B. (2005, January 17). Tapping a market that is hot, hot, hot. *BusinessWeek*, 36.

Grow, B. (2005, July 18). Embracing illegals. *BusinessWeek*, 55.

Hastings, C. (2003, April). Engaging in a growing workforce. *Workspan*, 35–39.

Helyar, J. (2006, May 10). 50 and fired. *Fortune*, 78–86.

Hennens, J. (2011). Online communities are getting old. http://blog.vovici.com.

Hispanic banking; "The race is on" (2011). http://www.hispanicbusiness.com.

Hispanic Press Kit (2011). Bank of America. http://newsroom.bankofamerica.com.

Hispanic products and services (2011). Bank of America. http://www.bankofamerica.com.

Huge Best Buy Layoffs coming tomorrow (2010). http://www.gizmodo.com.

IBM workforce diversity policy (2011). http://www-03.ibm.com.

Jacobs, K. (2010). Two Best Buy plans layoffs at headquarters. *Forbes*. http://www.forbes.com.

Jones, D. (1997, February 26). U.S. managers earn global credentials. *USA Today*, A1.

Jordan, M. (2006, January 24). Blacks vs. Latinos at work. *The Wall Street Journal*, B-1.

Kanmamm, J., & Rozenberg, H. (2002, February 7). Survey looks at residents with recent foreign roots. *Arizona Review*, A-8.

Kershaw, S. (2006, January 23). On Engine 22, it is women who answer the bell. *The New York Times*, A-14.

Kiviat, B. (2005, August). Dessi dollars. Inside business issue, A21–A23.

Koss-Feder, L. (1999, January 25). Spurred by the Americans with Disabilities Act, more firms take on those ready, willing and able to work. *Time*, 82.

Lang, S. (2011). Women firefighters can take the heat, but too few firehouses give them the chance, study finds. *Chronicle Online*. http://www.news.cornell.edu.

Leduff, C., & Flores, E. (2005, February 9). The everymigrant's guide to crossing the border illegally. *The New York Times*, A-16.

Levy, C. J. (2006, January 29). The new corporate outsourcing. *The New York Times*, D-1.

Magnusson, P. (2005, October 10). Wipsaved on the border. *BusinessWeek*, 64–66.

McKinley, J. C. (2005, March 22). Mexican pride and death in U.S. service. *The New York Times*, A-6.

McKinley, J. C. (2005, March 23). At Mexican border, tunnels, vile river, rusty fence. *The New York Times*, A-8.

Mendoza, A., Gollwitzer, P. M., & Amodio, D. M. (2010). Reducing the expression of implicit stereotypes: Reflexive control through implementation discussions. *Personality and Social Psychology Bulletin*, 36(4), 512–523.

Mendosa, R. (1996, October). The $152 billion engine. *Hispanic Business*, 28–29.

Millman, J. (2005, January 24). Changing face of immigrants. *The Wall Street Journal*, A-4.

More bad news for KC: 8,000 Sprint layoffs (2010). http://www.economy.kansascity.com.

NAFE 2010 Top 50 companies for executive women (2011). http://www.nafe.com.

Nassauer, S. (2006, January 9). France's new race relations. *The Wall Street Journal*, A-11.

Newman, A. M. (2002, February). Fair shares. *Working Women*, 64–71.

Pear, R. (2006, February 4). Bush to propose vast cost savings in Medicare plan. *The New York Times*, B-1.

Population profile of the United States (2010). http://www.census.gov.

Prystay, C., & Ellison, S. (2003, February 27). Time for marketers to grow up? *The Wall Street Journal*, B-1.

Racanelli, V. J. (2011). The World's Most Respected Companies. http://www.online.barrons.com.

Research National Phone Poll (1994, March 4). *Chattanooga Times*, 1.

Roberts, S. (2006, January 13). Come October, body count will make 300 million or so. *The New York Times*, A-1.

Sessa, V. I., Jackson, S. E., & Rapini, D. T. (1995). Workforce diversity: The good, the bad, and the reality. In G, Ferris, S. D. Rosen, & D. T. Barnum (Eds.), *Handbook of human resource management* (263–282). Cambridge, MA: Blackwell Publishers.

Shellenberger, S. (2005, October 20). You can work from home—Can you coach little league from the office? *The Wall Street Journal,* D-1.

Society for Human Resource Management. (2006). *HR resources.* http://www.shim.org/diversity.

Spencer, S., Logel, C., & Davies, P. G. (2011, January). Stereotype threat. *Annual Review of Psychology,* 26–48.

Swarns, R. L. (2006, January 19). Chamber and two unions forge alliance on immigration bill. *The Wall Street Journal,* A-15.

Talking to diversity experts. (2003). http://www.fortune.com/sections.

Thornburgh, N. (2006, February 6). Inside the lives of the migrants next door. *BusinessWeek,* 36–46.

Valdez, L. (2006, February 5). Migration a 2-nation concern. *Arizona Republic,* D-1.

Van Der Vegt, G. S., Ulert, E. V. & Huang, X. (2005). Location level links between diversity and innovative climate depend on national power distance. *Academy of Management Journal, 48(6),* 1171–1182.

Varadarajan, T. (2003, February 21). At least it is ok to back away with stereotypes. *The Wall Street Journal,* W-15.

Walsh, M. W. (2006, January 22). When your pension is frozen. *The New York Times,* A-1.

Welch, J., & Welch, S. (2006, February 13). What is holding women back. *BusinessWeek,* 100.

Wheeler, M. L. (1996, December 9). Diversity: Making the business case. *BusinessWeek,* special advertising section.

Wheeler, M. L. (1996, December 14). Capitalizing on diversity. *BusinessWeek,* special advertising section.

Women and Wall Street (2006, August 13). *The New York Times,* A-1.

Women in Fire and emergency services (2011). http://www.i-women.org.

Wrongful termination (2011). http://www.fairmeasures.com.

Zebrowitz, L. A., Kikuchi, M., and J. M. Fellows (2010). Facial resemblance to emotions; group differences, impression effects, and race stereotypes. *Journal of Personality and Social Psychology, 98(2),* 175–189.

Chapter 12

About Photon dynamics (2011). http://www.newsblaze.com.

Adams, J. S. (1965). Inequity in social exchanges. In L. Berkowitz (Ed.), *Advances in experimental social psychology,* pp. 267–300. New York: Academic Press.

Adler, N. (1997). *International dimensions of organizational behavior* (3rd ed.). Cincinnati, OH: South-Western Publishing.

AES Corporation: The Global Power company (2010). www.aes.com.

Alderfer, C. (1972). *Existence, relatedness, and growth: Human needs in organizational settings.* Glencoe, IL: Free Press.

All a matter of priorities. (2003, February 10). *Editor and Publisher.*

Anders, G. (2003, January 13). Carly Fiorina, up close—How shrewd strategic moves in grueling proxy battle let H-P chief take control. *The Wall Street Journal,* Eastern Edition, B-1.

Arnold, H. J. (1981, April) A test of the multiplicative hypothesis of expectancy-valence theories of work motivation. *Academy of Management Journal,* 128–141.

Bass, B., Avolio, B., & Goodheim, L. (1987). Biography in the assessment of transformational leadership at the world class level. *Journal of Management, 13,* 7–20.

Bass, B. M. (1985). *Leadership and performance beyond expectations.* New York: Free Press.

Bass, B. M. (1990). *Bass and Stogdill's handbook of leadership: Theory, research and managerial application* (3rd ed.). New York: Free Press.

Bass, B. M., & Avolio, B. J. (1990, January). Developing transformational leadership: 1992 and beyond. *Journal of European Industrial Training,* 23.

Becker, C. (2005, December 19–26). Fast Start for Hospitals. *Modern Healthcare,* 8–9.

Bennis, W., & Nanus, B. (1985). *Leaders: The strategies for taking charge.* New York: Harper & Row.

Biskupic, J. (2002), July 24). Why it's tough to indict CEOs. *USA Today,* Al, A2.

Blake, R. R., & Mouton, J. S. (1964). *The managerial grid.* Houston: Gulf.

Blank, D. (2003). A matter of ethics: In organizations where honesty and integrity rule, it is easy for employees to resist the many temptations today's business world offers. *Internal Auditor, 60,* 26, 31.

Bloomberg Survey (2010, April 19). Indicators now point in the right direction: The stock and bond markets have returned to health and the consensus outlook is far brighter. *BusinessWeek,* chart on stock values, 30.

Boyatzis, R. E. (1984). The need for close relationships and the manager's job. In D. A. Kolls, I. M. Rubin, & J. M. McIntyre (Eds.), *Organizational psychology: Readings on human behavior in organizations* (4th ed.). Englewood Cliffs, NJ: Prentice Hall.

Brillian President and CEO, Vincent Sollito, to speak at upcoming USDC investment conference (2011). http://www.news.ecoustics.com.

Brooker, K. (1999, April 26). Can Procter and Gamble change its culture, protect its market share, and find the next Tide? *Fortune,* 146–153.

Buhler, P. M. (2003). Managing in the new millennium. *SuperVision, 64,* 20–22.

Burns, J. M. (1978). *Leadership.* New York: Harper & Row.

Burrows, P. (2010, April 26). Apple's endlessly expanding universe. *BusinessWeek,* 93–98.

Byrne, J. A. (1998, July 6). How Al Dunlap self-destructed. *BusinessWeek,* 58–64.

Can Texan Marjorie Scardino transform Britain's Pearson into a global media colossus? (2001, January 22). *BusinessWeek,* 78–88.

Cannella, C. (2004, August). Kill the Commissions. *Inc,* 38.

Carpenter, L. (2002). Inspirational leadership. *Management Services, 46,* 34–36.

Carvell, T. (1998, September 28). By the way...your staff. *Fortune,* 200–206.

Chandler, S. (1999, October 17). Stumbling Sears seeks to launch 2nd revolution. *Arizona Republic,* D-1.

Chang, J. (2003). Cracking the whip: In a perfect world, sales managers would use only positive incentives to get the best performance from their teams. But in less-than-ideal situations, is there a time and place for negative motivation? *Sales & Marketing Management, 155,* 241.

Charan, R., & Colvin, G. (1999, June 21). Why CEOs fail. *Fortune,* 69–78.

Colvin, G. (1999, May 24). How to be a great CEO. *Fortune,* 104–110.

Compaq Management (2011). http://www. thinkingmanagers.com.

Conger, J. A., & Kanungo, R. A. (1987). Toward a behavioral theory of charismatic leadership in organizational settings. *Academy of Management Review, 12,* 637–647.

Crockett, R. O. (2001, January 22). Motorola can't seem to get out of its own way. *BusinessWeek,* 72.

Daft, R. L. (2005). *The leadership experience* (3rd ed.). South-Western/Thomson Learning.

Darlington, H. (2002). People—your most important asset. *Supply House Times, 45,*113–114.

Dickson, G. W., & DeSanctis, G. (Eds). (2001). *Information technology and the future enterprise: New models for managers.* Upper Saddle River, NJ: Prentice Hall.

Digital Hollywood (2011). http://www.digitalhollywood.com.

Dorning, M. (2010, April 19) Why the Obama plan is working. *BusinessWeek,* 29–36.

Early, P. C., Connolly, T., & Ekegren, G. (1989). Goals, strategy development, and task performance: Some limits on the efficacy of goal setting. *Journal of Applied Psychology, 74,* 24–33.

Edwards, C., Burrows, P., & Greene, J. (2001, January 15). Microsoft and Intel: Moving in on PC makers' turf. *BusinessWeek,* 41.

Eichenberg, J. (2010). Investigating sales team performance problems—Diagnose the root problem to tackle the issues. *Corp Magazine,*www.corpmagazine.com.

Fiedler, F. E. (1967). *A theory of leadership effectiveness.* New York: McGraw-Hill.

Fiedler, F. E. (1971). Validation and extension of the contingency model of leadership effectiveness. *Psychological Bulletin, 76,* 128–148.

Fisher, A. (1998, October 26). Success secret: A high emotional IQ. *Fortune,* 295–298.

Fortune 500: Largest U.S. corporations (2010, May 3). *Fortune,* F1–F26.

Foss, B. (2002, December 30). Corporate image: Greed, deceit, handcuffs, *The Arizona Republic,* D-4.

Foster, S. (2001). *Managing Quality.* (Upper Saddle River, NJ: Prentice Hall, 333–334, 346–347.

Foust, D., Smith, G., & Rocks, D. (1999, May 3). Man on the spot. *BusinessWeek,* 142–152.

Fox, J. (1997, July 7) The next best thing to free money. *Fortune,* 52–62.

French, J. & Raven, B. (1959). The bases of social power. In D. Cartwright (Ed.), *Studies in social power.* Ann Arbor, MI: Institute for Social Research.

Fry, S. (2010, April 12). On the Mothership. A confessed Apple Famboy gets finger time with the iPad and face time with Steve Jobs. *Time,* 40–41.

Gale, S. F. (2002). Building leaders at all levels. *Workforce, 81,* 82–85.

Garten, J. E. (2001). *The mind of the CEO.* New York: Basic Books/Perseus Publishing.

Gitomer, J. (2005, April 18). Define leadership: Now redefine it in terms of you. *Business Record (Des Moines),* 23, 31.

Gomez-Mejia, L. R., & Balkin, D. B. (1992). *Compensation, organizational strategy and firm performance.* Cincinnati, OH: South-Western Publishing.

Gomez-Mejia, L. R., Welbourne, T., & Wiseman, R. (2000). The role of risk sharing and risk taking under gainsharing. *Academy of Management Review, 25(3),* 492–509.

Grimaldi, L. (2005). Study proves recognition pays off. *Meetings & Conventions, 40,* 32.

Grosman, L. (2010, April 12). Launch iPad. It is here, it is hot; But what on earth is the iPad for? *Time,* 36–42.

Guyon, J. (1999, March 29). Getting the bugs out at VW. *Fortune,* 96–99.

Hackman, J. R., Oldham, G., Janson, R., & Purdy, K. (1975). A new strategy for job enrichment. *California Management Review, 16,* 57–71.

Hamm, S., Sager, I., & Burrowns, P. (1999, July 26). The lion in winter. *BusinessWeek,* 108–120.

Harper, C. (2010). Goldman Sachs clients—just pledge undercut by SEC. *BusinessWeek.* http://www.business week.com.

Hofstede, G. (1980). *Culture's consequences: International differences in work related values.* Beverly Hills, CA: Sage.

House, R. J. (1971). A path goal theory of leader effectiveness. *Administrative Science Quarterly, 16,* 321–338.

House, R. J., & Aditya, R. (1997). The social scientific study of leadership: Quo vadis? *Journal of Management, 23(3),* 409–475.

House, R. J., & Michell, T. R. (1974). Path goal theory of leadership. *Journal of Contemporary Business, 3,* 81–97.

House, R. J., Shane, S., & Herold, D. (1996). Rumors of the death of dispositional theory and research in organizational behavior are greatly exaggerated. *Academy of Management Review, 21(1),* 203–224.

http://www.interimmanagers.com. 2011.

http://www.molsoncoors.com. Accessed April 2010.

http://www.sas.com.

Huey, J. (1994, February 21). The new post-heroic leadership. *Fortune,* 42–50.

Hunsberger, B. (2011). Motivating low wage workers. http://blog.oregonlive.com.

Hyer, N. L., & Wemmerlow, U. (2002). The office that lean built: Applying cellular thinking to administrative work. *IIE Solutions, 34,* 36–43.

Hymowitz, C. (2010).Crises Test a CEO's Leadership Ability. *The Wall Street Journal Online.* www.career journal.com.

Ivancevich, J. M., Lorenzi, P., Skinner, S. J., & Crosby, P. B. (1997). *Management: Quality and competitiveness.* Burr Ridge, IL: Irwin.

Jones, A. (2011). A crash course on the financial meltdown. http://motherjones.com.

Jones, G. R., George, J. M., & Hill, C W. (2001). *Contemporary management* New York: McGraw-Hill/Irwin.

Kahn, R., & Katz, D. (1960). Leadership practices in relation to productivity and morale. In D. Cartwright & A. Sander (Eds.), *Group dynamics: Research and theory.* Elmsford, NY: Row, Peterson.

Kanetsar, R., & Stern, J. (1999, September 27). Get rich.com. *Time,* 65–78.

Kaplan, D. A. (2010, February 8). #1 SAS: How do you build a tech powerhouse without offering any stock options? *Fortune,* 57–64.

Kaufman, B. (2003). Stories that sell, stories that tell: Effective storytelling can strengthen an organization's bonds with all of its stakeholders. *Journal of Business Strategy, 24,* 11.

Kenny, D. A., & Hallmark, B. W. (1992). Rotation designs in leadership research. *Leadership Quarterly, 3(1),* 25–41.

Kenny, D. A., & Zaccaro, S. J. (1983). An estimate of the variance due to traits in leadership. *Journal of Applied Psychology, 68(4),* 678–685.

Kerr, S., Schriesheim, C. A., Murphy, C. J., & Stogdill, R. M. (1974, August). Toward a contingency theory of leadership based upon the consideration and initiating structure literature. *Organizational Behavior and Human Performance,* 62–82.

Khurallah, D. R. (2001, January 15). Where having fun really pays. *Information Week,* 87.

King, W. A., & Zeithaml, C. P. (2001). Competencies and firm performance. *Strategic Management Journal, 22(1),* 75–87.

Kirkpatrick, D. (1999, May 24). Eckhard's fall, but the PC rocks on. *Fortune,* 153–161.

Kraemer, H. M. J. (2003). Do the right thing: Practice values-based leadership. *Executive Excellence, 20,* 5–6.

Kulik, C. T., & Ambrose, M. L. (1992). Personal and situational determinants of referent choice. *Academy of Management Review, 17,* 212–237.

Kupfer, A. (1999, April 26). Mike Armstrong's AT&T. *Fortune,* 82–86.

Labich, K., & Davies, E. (1996, February 19). Elite teams get the job done. *Fortune,* 90–98.

Lavelle, L. (2001, January 15). Undermining pay for performance. *BusinessWeek,* 70–71.

Le Pine, J. A., & Dyne, L. V. (2001). Peer responses to low performers: An attributional model of helping in the context of groups. *Academy of Management Review,* 67–85.

Lewis, M. (2010, May 2). A message to Wall Street's fabulous fabs. *BusinessWeek,* 15.

Little carrots, big results (2003). *Sales & Marketing Management, 155,* 36.

Locke, E. (1968). Toward a theory of task motivation and incentives. *Organizational Behavior and Human Performance, 3,* 157–189.

Lord, R. G., DeVader, C. C., & Alleger, G. M. (1986). A metaanalysis of the relation between personality traits and leadership perceptions. *Journal of Applied Psychology, 71(3),* 402–410.

Mandel, M. (2001, February 5). The new economy's cruel math. *BusinessWeek,* 42–43.

Manz, C., & Sims, H. P. (1990). *Superleadership.* New York: Berkeley.

Maslow, A. H. (1943, July). A theory of human motivation. *Psychological Review,* 370–396.

Maynard, R. (1997, May). How to motivate low wage workers. *Nation's Business,* 35–40.

McClelland, D. (1961). *The achieving society.* New York: Van Nostrand Reinhold.

McClelland, D. C, & Boyatzis, R. (1982). Leadership motive pattern and long-term success in management. *Journal of Applied Psychology, 67,* 737–743.

McClelland, D. C, & Winter, D. C. (1969). *Motivating economic achievement.* New York: Free Press.

McGinnn, D. (2005, March 21). The green machine. *Newsweek,* E-8–E-12.

McGregor, D. (1960). *The human side of enterprise.* New York: McGraw-Hill.

McGregor, J. (2010, March 22). How to become an exec-for rent. *Fortune,* 41–44.

Mehta, S. M. (2009, November 23). Why him? *Fortune,* 89–92.

Mischel, W. (1973). Toward a cognitive social learning reconceptualization of personality. *Psychological Review, 80,* 252–283.

Molson Coors is Icecold with less froth. www.ethicalcorp. com. Accessed April, 2010.

Molyneux, J. (2009, March). Do rapid response teams save lives? *American Journal of Nursing,* 19.

Morse, J., Bennett, B., Donnelley, S., & Hequet, M. (2003, April 14). Saving Private Jessica, *Time,* 66–67.

Moskowitz, M., Levering, R., & Tkaczyk, C. (2010, February 8). 100 best companies. *Fortune,* 75–92.

Muller, J. (2001, January 15). Thinking out of the cereal box. *BusinessWeek,* 54–70.

Munk, N. (1999, April 12). How Levi's trashed a great American brand. *Fortune,* 83–88.

O'Reilly, B. (1999, June 7). What it takes to start a startup. *Fortune,* 135–139.

Osterloh, M., & Frey, B. S. (2000). Motivation, knowledge transfer, and organizational forms. *Organization Science, 11(5),* 538–551.

Palmer, B. (1999, June 21). Hasbro's new action figure. *Fortune,* 189–192.

The pay is in the bank (2001, January 29). *BusinessWeek,* 10.

Peter Swinburn's profile. *Forbes Online.* http://www.forbes. com. Accessed April 2010.

Pieffer, J. (1998). The human equation: Building profits by putting people first. Boston, MA: Harvard Business School Press, 77.

Piturro, M. (2011). The temporary executive. http://www. journalofaccountancy.com.

Randolph, D.S. (2005). Predicting the effect of extrinsic and intrinsic job satisfaction factors on recruitment and retention of rehabilitation professionals. *Journal of Healthcare Management, 50,* 49.

Rapid response teams: The case for early intervention (2007). *Institute for Healthcare Improvement.* www.ihi.org.

Reason, T. (2003). Incentive confrontation: A bitter dispute over bonuses highlights the hazards of incentive pay. CEO: *The Magazine for Senior Financial Executives, 19,* 46–51.

Robbins, S. P. (1999). *Organizational behavior* (7th ed.). Englewood Cliffs, NJ: Prentice Hall.

Ronan, J. (2003). A boot to the system: How does a training company shake up its leadership style? It marches its managers off to boot camp. *T&D, 57,* 38.

Ronen, S. (1986, April). Equity perception in multiple comparisons: A field study. *Human Relations,* 333–346.

Rosenbush, S. (2001, February 5). Armstrong's last stand. *BusinessWeek,* 88–91.

Rynes, S. L., Gerhart, B., & Minette, K. A. (2004). The importance of pay in employee motivation: Discrepancies between what people say and what they do. *Human Resource Management, 43,* 381–394.

Saposnick, K. (2001). Achieving breakthrough business results through personal change: An interview with Rick Fox. Pegasus Communications, accessed February 26, 2003 at http://www.pegasuscom.com/levpoints/foxint.html.

Schlender, B. (1999, April 12). e-Business According to Gates. *Fortune,* 75–80.

Schurenberg, E. (1999, May 24). The fly boys. *Fortune,* 236–240.

Schwab, D. P., & Cummings, L. L. (1970, October). Theories of performance and satisfaction: A review. *Industrial Relations*, 403–430.

Shalley, C. E. (1991). Effects of productivity goals, creativity goals, and personal discretion on individual creativity. *Journal of Applied Psychology, 76*, 179–185.

Sharpe, F. (2011). Guide to Manage Minimum Wage Workers. http://www.business.com.

Shellenberger, S. (1997, March 19). Investors seem attracted to firms with happy employees. *The Wall Street Journal*, B-l.

Shipper, F., & Manz, C. C. (1992, Winter). Employee self-management without formally designated teams: An alternative road to empowerment. *Organizational Dynamics*, 48–61.

Simonton, D. K. (1987). Presidential inflexibility and veto behavior: Two individual situational interactions. *Journal of Personality, 55(1)*, 1–18.

Sinclair, A. (1992). The tyranny of team ideology. *Organization Studies, 13*, 611–626.

Smith, G. (2001, February 5). Are high-tech stocks headed for more turmoil? *BusinessWeek*, 50.

Sparks, D. (2001, January 15). Options put grants in a jam. *BusinessWeek*, 68–69.

Spragins, E. (2002). Unmasking your motivations. *Fortune Small Business, 12*, 861.

Steve Paul Jobs. http://www.ei.cs.vc.edu. Accessed April 2010.

Stogdill, R. M. (1948). Personal factors associated with leadership: A survey of the literature. *Journal of Psychology, 25*, 35–71.

Stogdill, R. M. (1974). *Handbook of leadership: A survey of theory and research*. New York, NY: Free Press.

Stogdill, R. M., & Coons, A. E. (1957). *Leader behavior: Its description and measurement*. Columbus, OH; Ohio State University Press.

Summers, T. P., & DeNisi, A. S. (1990, June). In search of Adam's other: Reexamination of referents used in the evaluation of pay. *Human Relations*, 495–511.

Symonds, W., Smith, G., & Judge, P. (1999, June 21). Fisher's photo finish. *BusinessWeek*, 34–36.

The top 25 managers (2001, January 8). *BusinessWeek*, 60–81.

Thrive Networks Web site (2010). www.thrivenetworks.com/about.us/careers.html.

Tips for motivating low wage workers (2011). http://www.workforce.com.

Tyler, K. (2003). Sink-or-swim attitude strands new managers. *HRMagazine, 48*, 78–83.

Vasilash, G. S., Sawyer, C. A., & Kelly, K. M. (2005). Nissan: The extraordinary happens every day. *Automotive Design & Production, 117*, 48.

Vroom, V. H. (1964). *Work and motivation*, New York: John Wiley & Sons.

Wahba, M., & Birdwell, L. (1975) Maslow reconsidered: A review of the need hierarchy theory. *Organizational Behavior and Human Performance, 15(2)*, 212–240.

Weiss, H. (1977) Subordinate imitation of supervisor behavior: The role of modeling in organizational socialization. *Organizational Behavior and Human Performance, 19*, 89–105.

Weiss, J., & Hughes, J. (2005, March). Want collaboration? Accept—and actively manage—conflict. *Harvard Business Review*, 93–101.

Weld, J. (2010, May 2). Goldman slapped. *BusinessWeek*, 13.

White, R., & Lippit, R. (1960). *Autocracy and democracy: An experimental inquiry*. New York, NY: Harper & Brothers.

Whole Foods Market (2010). www.wholefoodsmarket.com/company/.

Yammering is good (2010, March 1). *BusinessWeek*, 37–38.

Zellner, W. (1999, August 16). Earth to herb: Pick a co-pilot. *BusinessWeek*, 70–73.

Zuckerman, G., et al (2010). Goldman Sachs charged with fraud. *The Wall Street Journal*. http://online.WSJ.com.

Chapter 13

Albanese, R. E., & Van Fleet, D. D. (1985). Rational behavior in groups: The free-riding tendency. *Academy of Management Review, 20*, 244–255.

Armour, S. (2006, March 13). Cost-effective 'homesourcing' grows. *USA Today*.

Balkin, D. B., Dolan, S., & Forgues, K. (1997). Rewards for team contributions to quality. *Journal of Compensation and Benefits, 13(1)*, 41–46.

Banker, R. A., Field, J. M., Schroeder, R. G., & Sinha, K. K. (1996). Impact of work teams on manufacturing performance: A longitudinal field study. *Academy of Management Journal, 42*, 58–74.

Bantel, K., & Jackson, S. (1989). Top management and innovations in banking: Does the demography of the top team make a difference? Strategic *Management Journal, 10*, 107–124.

Blogging: Outreach and outrage (2006, March 11). *The Economist*, 77.

Bovée, C., & Thill, J. (2000). *Business Communication Today* (6th ed.). Upper Saddle River, NJ: Prentice Hall, 38.

Boyd, S. (2004, October 20). Tips to improve your listening ability. *School for Champions*, www.school-forchampions.com.

Brake, D. (2003). *Dealing with e-mail*. London, U.K.: DK.

Brodie, D. (2010). 10 tips for giving effective feedback. *Ezine Articles*. www.ezinearticles.com.

Bunderson, J., & Sutcliffe, K. (2002). Comparing alternative conceptualizations of functional diversity in management teams: Process and performance effects. *Academy of Management Journal, 45*, 875–893.

Carbonara, P. (1997, March). Fire me. I dare you! *Inc*, 58–64.

Caudron, S. (1993, December). Are self-directed teams right for your company? *Personnel Journal*, 76–84.

Chang, A., Bordia, P., & Dune, J. (2003). Punctuated equilibrium and linear progression: Toward a new understanding of group development. *Academy of Management Journal, 4*, 106–117.

Clancy, H. (November 2008). Cyber agents: New travel planners aren't your everyday Orbitz. *Entrepreneur Magazine*. www.entprereur.com.

Cohen, A., & Fink, S. (2001). *Effective behavior in organizations* (7th ed.). Boston: McGraw-Hill/Irwin.

Cohen, S. G., & Bailey, D. E. (1997). What makes teams work: Group effectiveness research from the shop floor to the executive suite. *Journal of Management, 23*, 239–290.

Conlin, M. (2006, January 23). Call centers in the rec room. *BusinessWeek*, 76–77.

Covey, S. (2009). How the best leaders build trust. *Leadership Now*. www.leadershipnow.com.

Crittenden, V., & Klepper, K. (2010, May-June). Social media and the B-school. *BizEd*, 72–73.

Daft, R. L, (2002). *The leadership experience* (2nd ed.). Cincinnati, OH: South-Western.

Daly, R. E., & Nicoll, D. (1997). Accelerating a team's developmental process. *OD Practitioner, 24(1),* 20–28.

Deming, W. E. (1986). *Out of the crisis.* Cambridge, MA: MIT Press.

Denning, S. (2005). *The leader's guide to storytelling.* San Francisco: Jossey-Bass. 12–18.

Denton, D. K. (1992). Multi-skilled teams replace old work systems. *HR Magazine, 37,* 48–56.

Dumaine, B. (1990, May 7). Who needs a boss? *Fortune,* 52–60.

Dumaine, B. (1994, September 5). The trouble with teams. *Fortune,* 86–92.

Fan, E., & Grueneld, D. (1998). When needs outweight desires: The effects of resource interdependence and reward interdependence on group problem solving. *Basic and Applied Social Psychology, 20,* 45–56.

Fisher, B., & Boynton, A. (2005, July-August). Virtuoso teams. *Harvard Business Review,* 117–123.

Fisher, R., & Ury, W. (1981). *Getting to yes: Negotiating agreement without giving in.* New York, NY: Penguin Books.

Forest, H. (2000). Effective story telling performance skills. *Story Arts.* www.storyarts.org.

Freedman, T. (2010, May 21). Five minute tip: Managing your team meetings. *ICT in Education.* www.ictineducation.org.

Geber, B. (1992, June). Saturn's grand experiment. *Training,* 27–35.

Gersick, C. J. (1988). Time and transition in work teams: Toward a new model of group development. *Academy of Management Journal,* 31, 9–41.

Greene, J. (2005, September 26). Mystery blogger: A rendezvous with Microsoft's deep throat. *BusinessWeek,* 104.

Gross, S. E. (1995), *Compensation for teams.* New York, NY: American Management Association.

Hammer, M., & Champy, J. (1993). *Reengineering the corporation.* New York, NY: HarperCollins.

Hammer, M., & Champy, J. (1994, April). Avoiding the hottest new management cure. *Inc,* 25–26.

Hempel, J. (2010, April 12). How LinkedIn will fire up your career. *Fortune,* 74–82.

Hertel, G., Geister, S., & Kouradt, U. (2005). Managing virtual teams: A review of current empirical research. *Human Resource Management Review, 15,* 69–95.

Hosmer, L. T. (1995). Trust: The connecting link between organizational theory and philosophical ethics. *Academy of Management Review, 20,* 379–403.

Jones, G. R., & George, J. M. (1998). The experience and evolution of trust: Implications for cooperation and teamwork. *Academy of Management Review, 23,* 531–546.

Katzenbach, J. R., & Smith, D. K. (1993, March-April). The discipline of teams. *Harvard Business Review,* 111–120.

Kets De Vries, M. F. (1999, Winter). High performance teams: Lessons from the pygmies. *Organizational Dynamics,* 66–77.

Kidwell, R. E., & Bennett, N. (1993). Employee propensity to withhold effort: A conceptual model to intersect three avenues of research. *Academy of Management Review, 18,* 429–456.

Kirkman, B. L., & Rosen, B. (1999). Beyond self-management: Antecedents and consequences of team empowerment. *Academy of Management Journal, 42,* 58–74.

Kranz, G. (2007). *Communicating Effectively.* New York: HarperCollins.

Kreitner, R., & Kinicki, A. (1995). *Organizational behavior* (3rd ed.). Burr Ridge, IL: Irwin.

Labich, K. (1996, February 16). Elite teams get the job done. *Fortune,* 90–99.

Lawler, E. E. (1992). *The ultimate advantage.* San Francisco: Jossey-Bass.

Le Baron, M. (2003, July). Crass-cultural communication. *Beyond Intractability.* www.beyondintractability.org.

Lewicki, R., & Litterer, J. (1985). *Negotiation.* Burr Ridge, IL: Irwin.

Maidique, M. A., & Hayes, R. H. (1984). The art of high-technology management. *Sloan Management Review, 25,* 18–31.

Mayer, R. C., Davis, J. H., & Schoorman, F. D. (1995). An integrative model of organizational trust. *Academy of Management Review, 20,* 709–734.

McConnon, A. (2007, September). Social networking is graduating – and hitting the job market. How do online rolodexes stack up? *IN,* 4–6.

McCune, J. C. (1998, July-August). That elusive thing called trust. *Management Review,* 10–16.

Montemayor, E. F. (1995, Summer). A model for aligning teamwork and pay. *ACA Journal,* 18–25.

Nelson, B. (1994). *1001 ways to reward employees.* New York, NY: Workman Publishing.

O'Lone, R. (1991, June 3). *777 revolutionizes Boeing aircraft development process. Aviation Week and Space Technology,* 34–36.

Osborne, C. (2001). *Dealing with difficult people.* London: DK.

Pachter, B. (1996, November) Tips for technological correctness. *HR Focus,* 21.

Phillips, J. M. (1999). Antecedents of leader utilization of staff input in decision-making teams. *Organizational Behavior and Human Decision Processes, 77,* 215–242.

Rahim, M. A. (1983). A measure of styles of handling interpersonal conflict. *Academy of Management Journal, 26,* 368–376.

Raisanen, M. (2010). How brands can build trust among consumers. *iMedia Connection.* www.imediaconnection.com.

Raz, T. (2003, May). Taming the savage genius: The delicate art of managing employees who are way, way smarter than you. *Inc,* 33–35.

Robbins, S. P., & Hunsaker, P. L. (1996). *Training in interpersonal skills* (2nd ed.). Upper Saddle River, NJ: Prentice Hall, 73–75.

Sashkin, M., & Kiser, K. J. (1993). *Putting total quality management to work.* San Francisco: Barrett-Koehler.

Sashkin & Morris (1984). *Organizational behavior.* Upper Saddle River, NJ: Pearson Education, Inc.

Sauer, P. (2004, May). Quick show of hands: Who hates meetings? *Inc,* 73–78, 112.

Shaiken, H., Lopez, S., & Mankita, I. (1997). Two routes to team production: Saturn and Chrysler compared. *Industrial Relations, 36,* 17–45.

Shaw, M. (1981). *Group dynamics: The psychology of small group behavior.* New York: Harper.

Simmons, A. (2010). Business story telling. *Mind Tools.* www.mindtools.com.

Steers, R. M. (1984). *Introduction to organizational behavior.* Glenview, IL: Scott, Foresman.

Stone, F. M. (1989, January). *Supervisory management.* New York, NY: American Management Association.

Swearingen, J. (2010). How to get started with LinkedIn. *BNET,* www.bnet.com.

Swinton, L. (2005, August 17). 7 Tips for Giving Positive Feedback. *Management for the Rest of Us.* www.mftrou.com.

Thompson, L. (2004). *Making the team: A guide for managers* (2nd ed.). Upper Saddle River, NJ: Pearson.

Tjosvold, D. (1993). *Learning to manage conflict: Getting people to work together cooperatively.* New York, NY: Lexington Books.

Townsend, A. M., DeMarie, S. M., & Hendrickson, A. R. (1996, September). Are you ready for virtual teams? *HR Magazine, 123–126.*

Varela, J., Fernandez, P., & Del Rio, M. (2005, December). Cross-functional conflict, conflict handling behaviors, and new product performance in Spanish firms. *Creativity and Innovation Management, 14,* 355.

Voice mail vs. email (2007, September 10). *Broken Perfection.* www.brokenperfection.com.

Volkema, R., & Niederman, F. (1996, July). Planning and managing organizational meetings: An empirical analysis of written and oral communication. *Journal of Business Communication, 33,* 275–293.

Vonk, N. (2006, February 17). A blogger's guide to blogging. *Campaign,* 28–29.

Wageman, R. (1995). Interdependence and group effectiveness. *Administrative Science Quarterly, 40,* 145–180.

Wall, J. A. (1985). *Negotiation: Theory and practice.* Glenview, IL: Scott, Foresman.

Wecker, J. (1998, October 12). Powers of Persuasion. *Fortune,* 161–164.

Weiss, W. H. (1999). Teams and teamwork. *Supervision, 59(7),* 9–11.

Whetton, D. A., & Cameron, K. S. (1995). *Developing management skills* (3rd ed.). New York, NY: HarperCollins.

Wilson, C. (2006, March). The blogger at work. *T+D,* 15.

Wu, C. (2000). Cultural gestures. *Tripod.* www.soc302.tripod.com.

Zand, D. E. (1972). Trust and managerial problem solving. *Administrative Science Quarterly, 17,* 229–239.

Chapter 14

After the leak: The gusher in the gulf may soon be sealed. BP's woes will be harder to cap (2010, July 24). *The Economist,* 62–64.

Alert! Enbrel supply shortage (2003). http://arthritiscentral.com/enbrel/. Accessed May 20, 2003.

Antennaegate: A minor glitch in Apple's latest phone hints at bigger problems (2010, July 17). *The Economist,* 68.

Black storm rising: The deepwater horizon disaster will affect everyone from pelicans to politicians (2010, May 8). *The Economist,* 69–71.

Brake, D. (2003). *Dealing with e-mail.* London, U.K.: DK.

Conlin, M. (2002, September 30). Watch what you put in that office e-mail. *BusinessWeek,* 114–115.

Creighton, J. L. (1998, January). The cybermeeting's about to begin. *Management Review,* 29–31.

Daft, R. L. & Lengel, R. H. (1986). Organizational information requirements, media richness, and structural design. *Managerial Science, 32,* 554–572.

Delays for Enbrel continue. www.psoriasis.org/news/news/2002/20020524enbrel.php. Accessed May 20, 2003.

Falcone, P. (1998, October). Communication breakdown. *HR Focus,* 8.

Fried, J. (2005, October). Everything you ever wanted to know about e-mail. *Inc.,* 113–128.

Gillis, J., & Kaufman, L. (2010, August 5). Oil spill calculations stir debate on damage. *The New York Times,* A-16.

Greengrad, S. (1998, September). 10 ways to protect intranet data. *Workforce,* 78–81.

Hempel, J. (2009, March 2). How Facebook is taking over our lives. *Fortune,* 49–56.

Knapp, M. (1980). *Essentials of nonverbal communication.* New York: Holt, Rinehart and Winston.

Labinch, K. (1999, March 1). Boeing finally hatches a plan. *Fortune,* 100–106.

Latif, L. (2010, July 17). Jobs encases Apple's iPhone 4 problem. *The Inquirer.* www.theinquirer.net.

Lives of others: Facebook and Google face a backlash from users and regulators alike over the way they have handled sensitive data (2010, May 22). *The Economist,* 667–668.

Loyd, L. (2006, January 9). Wyeth signs three Biotech product deals—The agreements were an indicator of the direction that major pharmaceutical companies are heading. *The Philadelphia Inquirer,* section C, 1.

Lyons, D. (2010, June 7). The high price of Facebook. *Newsweek,* 12.

McCune, J. C. (1998, July/August). That elusive thing called trust. *Management Review,* 10–16.

McDermott, M. (1996, September). Boeing's modern approach. *Profiles,* 41–44.

Melnyk, S. & Denzler, D. (1996). *Operations Management.* New York: McGraw-Hill/Irwin.

Mouawad, J. (2010, May 6). Fast-growing BP also has a mounting list of spills and safety lapses. *The New York Times,* A-18.

Munter, M. (1993, May-June). Cross-cultural communication for managers. *Business Horizons,* 69–78.

The oil well and the damage done: BP counts the political and financial cost of Deepwater Horizon (2010, June 19). *The Economist,* 65–67.

Osborn, C. (2001). *Dealing with difficult people.* London, U.K.: DK.

Pearl, J. (1993, July). The e-mail quandry. *Management Review,* 3.

Price, C. (1994). *Assertive Communication.* Boulder, CO: Career Track.

Rice, R. E. (1991). Task analyzability, use of new media, and effectiveness: A multi-site exploration of media richness. *Organization Science, 2,* 475–500.

Robbins, S. P., & Hunsaker, P. L. (1996). *Training in interpersonal skills* (2nd ed). Upper Saddle River, NJ: Prentice Hall.

Rogers, E., & Albritton, M. (1995, April). Interactive communications technologies in business organizations. *Journal of Business Communication, 32,* 177–195.

Shook, D. (2001, February 8). Immunex' supply-side cliffhanger. *BusinessWeek.*

Sullivan, C. (1995, January). Preferences for electronic mail in organizational communication tasks. *Journal of Business Communication, 32,* 49–64.

Thumma, S. A. (1998, July). E-mail zaps the workplace. *HR Focus,* 9.

Townsend, A., DeMarie, S., & Hendrickson, A. (1996, September). Are you ready for virtual teams? *HR Magazine,* 123–126.

Volkema, R., & Niederman, F. (1996, July). Planning and managing organizational meetings: An empirical analysis of written and oral communication. *Journal of Business Communication,* 275–293.

Weeks, D. (1995, February). Voice mail: Blessing or curse? *World Traveler,* 51–54.

Weilner, A. (2005, September). Lost in translation. *Inc,* 37–38.

Wellner, A. (2005, January). Playing well with others: Office cliques sap morale and kill productivity. Does your firm have them? *Inc,* 29–31.

Yarrow, J. (2010, June 24). Uh oh, is Apple's iPhone 4 a lemon? *Business Insider.* www.businessinsider.com.

Chapter 15

Aston, A., & Arndt, M. (2003, May 5). The flexible factory: Leaning heavily on technology, some U.S. plants stay competitive with offshore rivals. *BusinessWeek,* 90–91.

Bickens, J., & Elliott, B. B. (1997). *Operations management: An active learning approach.* Cambridge, MA: Blackwell.

Braganza, A., & Myers, A. (1998). *Business process redesign: A view from the inside.* Boston, MA: Thompson.

Bremner, B. (2000, May 23). Nissan's Ghosn: Can he bring back Japan's samurai spirit? *BusinessWeek.*

Connor, G. (2003). Benefiting from six sigma. *Manufacturing Engineering, 130,* 53–59.

D'Aveni, R. (1994). *Hypercompetition.* New York, NY: Free Press.

Deming, W. E. (1981–1982, Winter). Improvement of quality and production through action by management. *National Productivity Review, 1,* 12–22.

Deming, W. E. (1986). *Out of the crisis.* Cambridge, MA: MIT Press.

Deming, W. E. (1986). *Out of the crisis.* Cambridge, MA: Center for Advanced Engineering Study.

Drickhamer, D. (2005). The kanban E-volution. *Material Handling Management, 60,* 24–26.

Faltin, D. M., & Faltin, F. W. (2003). Toe the line: No more Worldcoms. *Quality Progress, 36,* 29–35.

Gabor, A. (1990). *The man who discovered quality.* New York, NY: Times Books.

Galuszka, P. (1999, November 8). Just-in-time manufacturing is working overtime. *BusinessWeek.*

Garvin, D. (1988). *Managing quality: The strategic and competitive edge.* New York, NY: Free Press.

Garvin, D. (1984, Fall). What does product quality really mean? *Sloan Management Review, 26,* 24–25.

Gourlay, R. (1994, January 4). Back to basics on the factory floor. *Financial Times,* 12.

Hammer, M., & Champy, J. (1993). *Reengineering the corporation.* New York, NY: Harper Business.

How to spot counterfeit parts: Caveat emptor, or buyer beware, is appropriate advice for buyers sourcing in China. (2002). *Purchasing, 131,* 31.

Imai, M. (1986). *Kaizen: The key to Japan's competitive success.* New York, NY: Random House.

JIT just won't be the same: Security rules could affect cross border trade, (2003, May). *World Trade, 16,* 28.

Jones, G. R., George, J. M., & Hill, C. W. L. (2000). *Contemporary management* (2nd ed.). New York: McGraw-Hill/Irwin.

The Kaizen Institute, www.kaizen-institute.com.

Kontoghiorghes, C. (2003). Examining the association between quality and productivity performance in a service organization. *The Quality Management Journal, 10,* 32–42.

Krajewski, L. L., & Ritzman, L. R. (2001). *Operations management: Strategy and analysis* (6th ed.). Upper Saddle River, NJ: Prentice Hall.

Kren, L. (2005). Decline of U.S. manufacturing threatens national security. *Machine Design, 77,* 173.

Logothetis, N. (1992). *Managing for total quality.* Hertfordshire, UK: Prentice Hall International.

Loyd, L. (January 9, 2006). Wyeth signs three biotech product deals—The agreements were an indicator of the direction that major pharmaceutical companies are heading. *The Philadelphia Inquirer,* C-1.

Markland, R. E., Vickery, S. K., & Davis, R. A. (1998). *Operations management: Concepts in manufacturing and service* (2nd ed.). Cincinnati, OH: South-Western Publishing.

Melnyk, S., & Denzler, D. (1996). *Operations management.* New York: McGraw-Hill/Irwin.

Noon, C E., Hankings, C. T., & Cote, M. J. (2003). Understanding the impact of variation in the delivery of healthcare services. *Journal of Healthcare Management, 48,* 82–98,

Porter, M. E. (1985). *Competitive advantage.* New York, NY: Free Press.

Powell, T. C. (1995, January). Total quality management as competitive advantage: A review and empirical study. *Strategic Management Journal,* 15–37.

Russell, R. S., & Taylor, B. W. (2000). *Operations management.* Upper Saddle River, NJ: Prentice Hall.

Skinner, W. (1969, May/June). Manufacturing—Missing link in corporate strategy. *Harvard Business Review,* 136–145.

Slack, N. (1997). *The Blackwell encyclopedia of operations management.* Cambridge, MA: Blackwell.

Stevenson, W. (2001). *Operations management* (7th ed.). New York, NY: McGraw-Hill.

Stocker, G. (2003). Use symbols instead of words. *Quality Progress, 35,* 68–72.

Taiichi, O. (1990). *Toyota production system.* Cambridge, MA: Productivity Press.

Young, S. M. (1992, October). A framework for successful adoption and performance of Japanese manufacturing practices in the United States. *Academy of Management Review, 17,* 677–701.

Glossary

360-degree feedback. Multirater feedback from peers, suppliers, other levels of management, and internal and external customers.

absolute judgments. A performance appraisal approach in which the performance of employees is evaluated against performance standards, and not in comparison to each other.

academy culture. A type of organization culture that seeks to hire people with specialties and technical mastery who will be confined to a set of jobs within a particular function and be rewarded by long-term association and a slow, steady climb up the organization ladder.

acceptance sampling. An operations management monitoring tool in which a sample of materials or products is measured against a benchmark.

accommodation strategy. A means of dealing with stakeholder groups when a firm decides to accept social responsibility for its business decisions after pressure has been exerted by stakeholder groups.

accountability. The expectation that the manager must be able to justify results to a manager at a higher level.

acquisition. The process of purchasing other firms.

actions. The specific steps the firm intends to take to achieve the desired objectives.

adjourning stage. A stage of team development in which teams complete their work and disband, if designed to do so.

administrative management. The management approach that examines an organization from the perspective of the managers and executives responsible for coordinating the activities of diverse groups and units across the entire organization.

adversarial relations. U.S. labor laws view management and labor as natural adversaries who want to have a larger share of the firm's profits and who must reach a compromise through collective bargaining.

adverse impact. A form of discrimination, also called disparate impact, that occurs when one standard that is applied to all applicants or employees negatively affects a protected class.

affirmative action. A federal government-mandated program that requires corporations to provide opportunities to women and members of minority groups who traditionally had been excluded from good jobs; it aims to accomplish the goal of fair employment by urging employers to make a conscious effort to hire members of protected classes.

aggressive communication. A forceful style of communication with others that expresses dominance and even anger. The needs and wants of others are ignored.

assessing. Evaluating the environmental data received to study the implications for the firm.

assessment phase. A career development step in which employees are helped to choose personally fitting career paths that are realistically attainable and to determine any obstacles they need to overcome to succeed.

attribution theory. The idea that the major function of the leader is to be blamed or given credit for a bad or a good situation, even if the leader has little or no control over the factors that led to the results.

authority. The formal right of a manager to make decisions, give orders, and expect the orders to be carried out.

avoiding style. Conflict resolution used when the individual decides it is better to avoid the conflict rather than to deal with it.

bankruptcy. A legal procedure that distributes company assets to creditors and protects the debtor from unfair demands of creditors when the debtor fails to make scheduled loan repayments.

base compensation. The fixed amount of money the employee expects to receive in a paycheck weekly or monthly or as an hourly wage.

baseball team culture. The fast-paced, competitive, high-risk form of corporate culture typically found in organizations in rapidly changing environments, with short product life cycles, with high-risk decision making, and dependent on continuous innovation for survival.

behavioral anchored rating scales. Performance appraisal tools that assess the effectiveness of the employee's performance using specific examples of good or bad behaviors at work.

behavioral appraisal instruments. Performance appraisal tools that assess certain-employee behaviors, such as coming to work on time.

behavioral perspective. The management view that knowledge of the psychological and social processes of human behavior can result in improvements in productivity and work satisfaction.

benchmarking. A strategic management approach that assesses capabilities by comparing the firm's activities or functions with those of other firms.

benefits. A compensation component that accounts for almost 40 percent of the typical total compensation package and includes health insurance, pension plans, unemployment insurance, vacations, sick leave, and the like.

bona fide occupational qualification (BFOQ). A defense against discrimination in which a firm must show that a personal characteristic must be present to do the job.

bottom-up change. Organizational change that originates with employees.

boundaryless organization design. A management design that eliminates internal and external structural boundaries that inhibit employees from collaborating with each other or that inhibit firms from collaborating with customers, suppliers, or competitors.

brainstorming. A technique to generate creative ideas for solving problems by reducing critical and judgmental reactions to ideas from group members.

brand managers. A management role that coordinates the ongoing activities of branded consumer products.

budgeting. Controlling and allocating the firm's funds; *variable budgeting* allows for deviations between planned output and actual output by considering the fact that variable costs depend on the level of output, whereas fixed costs do not; *moving budgeting* creates a tentative budget for a fixed period of time and then revises and updates it on a periodic basis to take changes into account.

bureaucratic control. A formal control approach involving a cycle of (1) establishing standards, (2) performance measurement, (3) identifying gaps, and (4) corrective action.

bureaucratic management. The management approach that examines the entire organization as a rational entity, using impersonal rules and procedures for decision making.

business ethics. Standards or guidelines for the conduct and decision making of employees and managers.

business network. A firm's alliances formed with other businesses to achieve mutually beneficial goals.

business plan. The business's blueprint that maps out its business strategy for entering markets and that explains the business to potential investors.

business process. A value-adding, value-creating activity such as product development or order fulfillment.

business unionism. Unions that focus on "bread and butter" issues such as wages, benefits, and job security.

capacity. The firm's ability to produce the product during a given period.

career path. The steps for advancement to a career goal and a plausible time frame for accomplishing them.

centralization. The location of decision authority at the top of the organization hierarchy.

certainty. The condition when all the information needed to make a decision is available.

chain of command. The superior-subordinate authority relationship.

change agents. People who act as catalysts and assume responsibility for managing change.

charismatic leader. A leader who can engender a strong emotional attachment from followers; charisma is associated with admiration, trust, and a willingness to believe what the leader says.

civil law. The legal system that relies on a comprehensive set of rules that form part of a highly structured code; enforcement and interpretation of laws are made in reference to this code.

club culture. A type of organizational culture that seeks people who are loyal, committed to one organization, and need to fit into a group, and rewards them with job security, promotion from within, and slow progress.

coaching. Ongoing, mostly spontaneous, meetings between managers and their employees to discuss career goals, roadblocks, and available opportunities.

coalitions. Political alliances between managers who agree on goals and priorities.

code of ethics. A formal statement of ethics and values that is designed to guide employee conduct in a variety of business situations.

coercive power. Power based on the fear that the leader may cause people harm unless they support him or her.

cohesiveness. The emotional closeness group members feel toward each other and how supportive they are of each other.

collective bargaining. Negotiations between union and management with little, if any, government involvement.

common law. The legal system in which precedents based on past court decisions play a key role in interpreting the meaning and intent of legal statutes.

communication. The process of transmitting meaningful information from one party to another through the use of shared symbols.

communication channel. Influences the quantity and quality of information that is conveyed to the receiver. Channels of communication include face-to-face conversations, group meetings, memos, policy manuals, e-mail, voice mail.

compensable factors. A set of evaluation criteria used in job evaluation.

competitive behavior. Team behavior that views other people as rivals for a limited pool of resources and focuses on individual goals, noncollaboration, and the withholding of information.

compromising style. Conflict resolution used when the manager or team member makes some concessions to the other party and the other party is willing to reciprocate.

concentration strategy. A form of diversification strategy that focuses on a single business operating in a single industry segment.

concentric diversification strategy. A form of diversification strategy in which the firm expands by creating or acquiring new businesses that are related to the firm's core business.

confrontation strategy. One means a firm may use to deal with a stakeholder group whose goals are perceived to threaten company performance; the firm may use the courts, engage in public relations, or lobby against legislation.

conglomerate diversification. A form of diversification strategy that involves managing a portfolio of businesses that are unrelated to each other.

consideration. The behavioral dimensions of leadership involving the concern that the leader has for the feelings, needs, personal interest, problems, and well-being of followers; also called employee-oriented behaviors.

content validity. The measurement that the selection process represents the actual activities or knowledge required to successfully perform the job.

contingency theory. The management theory that there is no "one best way" to manage and organize an organization because situational characteristics, called contingencies, differ; also, the view that no HR strategy is "good" or "bad" in and of itself but rather depends on the situation or context in which it is used.

control. The process of comparing performance to standards and taking corrective action.

controlling. The management function that measures performance, compares it to objectives, implements necessary changes, and monitors progress.

conversion process. The operations management stage in which the product's inputs are converted to the final product.

cooperation. Team behavior that is manifested in members' willingness to share information and help others.

cooperative strategies. Establishing partnerships or strategic alliances with other firms.

coordination. Linking activities so that diverse departments or divisions work in harmony and learn from each other.

core competencies. The unique skills and/or knowledge an organization possesses that give it an edge over competitors.

core values. A firm's principles that are widely shared, that operate unconsciously, and that are considered nonnegotiable.

corporate credo. A formal statement focusing on principles and beliefs, indicating the company's responsibility to its stakeholders.

corporate-level strategy. The corporation's overall plan concerning the number of businesses the corporation holds, the variety of markets or industries it serves, and the distribution of resources among those businesses.

corporation. A form of business that is a legal entity separate from the individuals who own it.

cost-leadership strategy. Providing products and services that are less expensive than those of competitors.

cultural symbols. The icons and objects that communicate organizational values, used by management to convey and sustain shared meaning among employees.

culture shock. The reaction when exposed to other cultures with different norms, customs, and expectations.

damage control strategy. A means a firm may use to deal with a stakeholder group when it decides that it may have made mistakes and wants to improve its relationship with the stakeholders and to elevate its public image.

debt financing. A means of obtaining financial resources that involves obtaining a commercial loan and setting up a plan to repay the principal and interest.

decentralization. The location of decision authority at lower levels in the organization.

decision acceptance. The aspect of decision making that is based on people's feelings; decision acceptance happens when people who are affected by a decision agree with what is to be done.

decision making. The process of identifying problems and opportunities and resolving them.

decision quality. The aspect of decision making that is based on such facts as costs, revenues, and product design specifications.

decision scope. The effect and time horizon of the decision.

decoding. Translating the symbolic verbal, written, or visual symbols into an undistorted, clear message.

delegation. The transfer of decision making authority from a manager to a subordinate or a team at a lower level in the organization.

Delphi technique. A decision-making technique in which group members are presented with a problem and complete an anonymous questionnaire soliciting solutions; the results are tabulated, summarized, and returned to the group members, and each is asked again for solutions; the process continues until a consensus decision is reached.

departmentalization. The horizontal basis for organizing jobs into units in an organization.

development and conduct of training phase. A stage in the training process that ensures training will solve an organizational problem or need; this step is critical to ensuring that training will be beneficial to the organization.

development phase. A career development step in which actions are designed to help the employee grow and learn the necessary skills to move along the desired career path.

devil's advocate. The role of criticizing and challenging decision alternatives that are agreed on by other members of the group, to induce creative conflict and possible alternative better solutions.

differentiation strategy. Delivering products and services that customers perceive as unique.

direction phase. The step in career development that involves determining the steps employees must take to reach their career goals.

discrimination. The unfair treatment of employees because of personal characteristics that are not job-related.

disparate treatment. A form of discrimination that occurs when an employer treats an employee differently because of his or her protected class status.

diversity. The wide spectrum of individual and group differences.

divestiture. The corporate process of selling a business in order to generate cash, which the corporation can better deploy elsewhere, or to refocus on a core business which is better understood by management.

division of labor. The production process in which each worker repeats one step over and over, achieving greater efficiencies in the use of time and knowledge.

divisional approach. A departmentalization approach, sometimes called the product approach, that organizes employees into units based on common products, services, or markets.

diversification strategy. A firm's strategic plan to create and manage a mix of businesses owned by the firm.

dominating style. Conflict resolution used when the manager or team member acts assertively and forcefully and persuades the other party to abandon his or her objectives.

Drug-Free Workplace Act. Federal legislation that requires employers to implement policies that restrict drug use.

downsizing. A management strategy used to reduce the scale and scope of a business to improve its financial performance.

downward communication. Sending a message from a high position in the organization to an individual or group lower in the hierarchy.

dysfunctional conflict. Conflict that has a negative effect on team and organizational performance.

e-mail. Electronic mail via computers.

emotional intelligence. The attributes of self-awareness, impulse control, persistence, confidence, self-motivation, empathy, social deftness, trustworthiness, adaptability, and a talent for collaboration.

empirical validity. Statistical evidence that the selection method distinguishes between higher and lower performing employees.

employment at will. A very old legal doctrine stating that unless there is an employment contract (such as a union contract or an implied contract), both employer and employee are free to end the employment relationship whenever and for whatever reasons they choose.

empowerment. The process of transferring control of individual work behavior from the supervisor to the employee.

encounter stage. The stage of socialization at which the individual begins to compare expectations about the firm's culture with reality.

entrepreneur. An individual who creates an enterprise that becomes a new entry to a market.

entrepreneurship. The process of creating a business enterprise capable of entering new or established markets by deploying resources and people in a unique way to develop a new organization.

equity financing. A means of obtaining financial resources that involves the sale of part of the ownership of the business to investors.

equity theory. The view that people develop beliefs about the fairness of the rewards they receive relative to their contributions.

ERG theory. A theory of needs based on three core groups: existence, relationships, and growth (ERG).

escalation of commitment. The refusal to abandon an earlier decision even when it is no longer appropriate, which happens because the decision maker is highly committed to a course of action and wants to stay the course.

espoused values. The aspects of corporate culture that are not readily observed, but instead can be perceived from the way managers and employees explain and justify their actions and decisions.

ethical policy statements. A firm's formal guidelines that provide specific formulas for employees' ethical conduct.

ethical structure. The procedures and the division or department within a company that promotes and advocates ethical behavior.

ethics. Principles that explain what is good and right and what is bad and wrong and that prescribe a code of behavior based on these definitions.

ethics training. A means of providing employees and managers practice in handling ethical dilemmas that they are likely to experience.

ethnocentric approach. An approach to managing an international subsidiary that involves filling top management and other key positions with people from the home country (expatriates).

ethnocentrism. A belief that may become prevalent among majority-group employees, meaning that they believe that their way of doing things, their values, and their norms are inherently superior to those of other groups and cultures.

evaluation. The organization's reexamination of whether training is providing the expected benefits and meeting the identified needs.

expectancy theory. The view that having the strength to act in a particular way depends on people' beliefs that their actions will produce outcomes they find valuable and attractive.

expert power. Power deriving from the leader's valued knowledge or skills, which other people recognize as worthy of respect.

exporting. A means of entering new markets by sending products to other countries and retaining production facilities within domestic borders.

extinction. The removal of positive consequences when undesired behavior is performed.

external equity. The perceived fairness of the compensation employees receive relative to what other companies pay for similar work.

external locus of control. A strong belief that luck, fate, or factors beyond one's control determine one's progress, causing feelings of helplessness and decreasing intensity of goal-seeking efforts in the face of failure.

facilities. The design and location of an operation.

facilities layout. The grouping and organization of equipment and employees.

facilities layout design. The physical arrangement for the facility that will allow for efficient production.

facts. Bits of information that can be objectively measured or described, such as the retail price of a new product, the cost of raw materials, the defect rate of a manufacturing process, or the number of employees who quit during a year.

Family and Medical Leave Act. Federal legislation that requires employers to provide unpaid leave for childbirth, adoption, and illness.

feedback. Information received back from the receiver, which allows the sender to clarify the message if its true meaning is not received.

feelings. An individual's emotional responses to decisions made or actions taken by other people.

flexible manufacturing. Operations management techniques that help reduce the setup costs associated with the production system.

force-field analysis. A model of organizational change that states that two sets of opposing forces are at equilibrium before a change takes place and put at disequilibrium to make change come about: the driving forces, which are pushing for change, and the restraining forces, which are opposed to change.

forecasting. Predicting what is likely to happen in the future, the intensity of the anticipated event, its importance to the firm, and the pace or time frame in which it may occur.

formal planning. A system designed to identify objectives and to structure the major tasks of the organization to accomplish them.

formalization. The degree of written documentation that is used to direct and control employees.

forming stage. The first stage of team development, which brings the team members together so they can get acquainted and discuss their expectations.

fortress culture. An organizational culture with the primary goal of surviving and reversing business problems, including economic decline and hostile competitors.

franchising. A means of entering new markets similar to licensing, mainly used by service companies, in which the franchisee pays a fee for using the brand name and agrees to strictly follow the standards and abide by the rules set by the franchise.

free riders. Individuals who find it rational to withhold effort and provide minimum input to the team in exchange for a full share of the rewards.

functional analysis. A strategic management approach that establishes organizational capabilities for each of the major functional areas of the business.

functional conflict. Conflict that stimulates team and organizational performance.

functional structure. A departmentalization approach that places similar jobs into departments.

Gantt charts. A visual sequence of the process steps used in planning, scheduling, and monitoring production.

General Agreement on Tariffs and Trade (GATT). A treaty signed by 120 nations to lower trade barriers for manufactured goods and services.

geocentric approach. An approach to managing an international subsidiary in which nationality is deliberately downplayed, and the firm actively searches on a worldwide or regional basis for the best people to fill key positions.

geographic-based divisions. A variation of the product-based departmentalization structure in which divisions are organized by geographic region.

glass ceiling. The intangible barrier that prevents women and minorities from rising to the upper levels in business.

global shift. A term used to characterize the effects of changes in the competitive landscape prompted by world-wide competition.

grapevine. Informal communication that takes place at the workplace.

groupthink. Team behavior that occurs when members prefer to avoid conflict rather than tolerate a healthy diversity of opinions.

Hawthorne effect. The finding that paying special attention to employees motivates them to put greater effort into their jobs (from the Hawthorne management studies, performed from 1924 through 1932 at Western Electric Company's plant near Chicago).

horizontal communication. Communication between a sender and a receiver at a similar level in the organization.

horizontal dimension. The element of dividing work into specific jobs and tasks and assigning jobs into units.

HR tactics. The implementation of human resource programs to achieve the firm's vision.

human relations approach. A management approach that views the relationships between employees and supervisors as the most salient aspect of management.

illusion of control. The tendency for decision makers to be overconfident of their ability to control activities and events.

implementation guidelines. The planning step that shows how the intended actions will be carried out.

individualism. The degree to which a society values personal goals, autonomy, and privacy over group loyalty, commitment to group norms, involvement in collective activities, social cohesiveness, and intense socialization; ethical decisions based on individualism promote individual self-interest as long as it does not harm others.

information richness. The potential information-carrying capacity of data.

initiating structure. The behavioral dimension of leadership that refers to activities designed to accomplish group goals, including organizing tasks, assigning responsibilities, and establishing performance standards; also called production-oriented behaviors.

inputs. The supplies needed to create a product, which can include materials, energy, information, management, technology, facilities, and labor.

intangible resources. Resources that are difficult to quantify and include on a balance sheet, which often provide the firm with the strongest competitive advantage.

integrating manager. A management position designed to coordinate the work of several different departments: the integrating manager is not a member of any of the departments whose activities are being coordinated.

integrating style. Conflict resolution demonstrated by framing the issue as a problem and encouraging the interested parties to identify the problem, examine alternatives, and agree on a solution.

interdependence. The extent that team members depend on each other for resources, information, assistance, or mutual support to accomplish their tasks.

internal equity. The perceived fairness of the pay structure within a firm.

internal locus of control. A strong belief in one's own ability to succeed, so that one accepts responsibility for outcomes and tries harder after making mistakes.

Internet. A computer network with multimedia communication capabilities, allowing a combination of text, voice, graphics, and video to be sent to a receiver; a network of networks, connecting hundreds of thousands of corporate, educational, and research computer networks around the world.

intrapreneurship. A form of business organization in which new business units are developed within a larger corporate structure in order to deploy the firm's resources to market a new product or service; also called corporate entrepreneurship.

intrinsic reward design theory. The perspective that a potent motivator for work is the intangible reward people derive from performing well in a job they find interesting, challenging, and intriguing and that provides an opportunity for continued learning.

intuition. When a decision maker depends on gut feelings or innate beliefs as a basis for making a decision.

inventory. The stock of raw materials, inputs, and component parts that the firm keeps on hand.

job analysis. The systematic gathering and organizing of information about the tasks, duties, and responsibilities of various jobs.

job-based unionism. Unions that are organized by type of job.

job description. A formal document that identifies, defines, and describes the duties, responsibilities, and working conditions.

job evaluation. A rational, orderly, and systematic judgment of how important each job is to the firm and how each job should be compensated.

job preview. Information about the positive and negative aspects of the job that is provided to potential applicants.

job relatedness. A defense against discrimination claims in which the firm must show that the decision was made for job-related reasons.

job rotation. A formal program in which employees are assigned to different jobs to expand their skills base and to learn more about various parts of the organization.

job specification. The knowledge, skills, and abilities needed to successfully perform the job.

joint venture. A means of entering new markets where two or more independent firms agree to establish a separate firm; the firms normally own equivalent shares of the joint venture and contribute a corresponding proportion of the management team.

just-in-time (JIT). The concept behind creating the firm's product in the least amount of time.

justice approach. An approach to decision making based on treating all people fairly and consistently when making business decisions.

kaizen. The Japanese process of continuous improvement in the organization's production system from numerous small, incremental improvements in production processes.

kanban. A form of JIT systems originated in Japan that uses cards to generate inventory; from the Japanese word for "card" or "sign."

knowledge workers. Employees who manage information and make it available to decision makers in the organization.

labor contract. A written agreement negotiated between union and management.

labor demand. The forecast of how many and what type of workers the organization will need in the future.

labor supply. The availability of workers with the required skills to meet the firm's labor demand.

liaison role. A management role used to facilitate communications between two or more departments.

licensing. A means of entering new markets, primarily used by manufacturing firms, by transferring the rights to produce and sell products overseas to a foreign firm. In return, the licensing company receives a negotiated fee, normally in the form of a royalty.

line authority. The manager's control of subordinates by hiring, discharging, evaluating, and rewarding.

line managers. The management level that contributes directly to the strategic goals of the organization.

leadership substitute view. The leadership theory that contends that people overestimate the effect of leaders even when leader behaviors are irrelevant, so organizations need to develop mechanisms to replace or substitute the influence role assigned to leaders.

leading. The management function that energizes people to contribute their best individually and in cooperation with other people.

learning organization. The management approach based on an organization anticipating change faster than its counterparts to have an advantage in the market over its competitors.

legitimate power. The legal or formal authority to make decisions subject to certain constraints.

load chart. A type of Gantt chart that is based on departments or specific resources that are used in the process.

long-term/short-term orientation. The extent to which values are oriented toward the future as opposed to the past or present.

make-buy analysis. An operations management tool used to help make the decision as to whether to produce an item or to purchase it.

management by objectives (MBO). A goal-setting program for managers and subordinates.

management by wandering around (MBWA). Dropping in unannounced at a work site and engaging employees in spontaneous conversations.

managerial grid. A system of classifying managers based on leadership behaviors.

masculinity/femininity. The degree to which a society views assertive or "masculine" behavior as important to success and encourages rigidly stereotyped gender roles.

Maslow's hierarchy of needs. The theory that people tend to satisfy their needs in a specified order, from the most to the least basic.

materials requirements planning (MRP). The process of analyzing a design to determine the materials and parts that it requires in the production process.

matrix approach. A departmentalization approach that superimposes a divisional structure over a functional structure in order to combine the efficiency of the functional approach with the flexibility and responsiveness to change of the divisional approach.

mechanistic organization design. A management design based on the classical perspective of management, emphasizing vertical control with rigid hierarchical relationships, top-down "command and control" communication channels, centralized decision authority, highly formalized work rules and policies, and specialized, narrowly defined jobs; sometimes called a *bureaucratic design.*

mentoring. Developmental activities carried out by more seasoned employees to help those who are learning the ropes.

merger. The process of integrating two firms.

metamorphosis stage. The stage of socialization at which the employee is induced to bring his or her values and ways of doing things closer to those of the organization.

monitoring. Observing environmental changes on a continuous basis to determine whether a clear trend is emerging.

monoculture. The homogeneous organizational culture that results from turnover of dissimilar employees.

Muslim law. The legal system based on religious Muslim beliefs that regulates behavior; strict interpretation and enforcement varies significantly from country to country.

NAFTA. The major economic alliance in the Americas.

need for achievement. The drive to accomplish things, in which the individual receives great satisfaction from personal attainment and goal completion.

need for affiliation. The desire to be liked by others, to receive social approval, and to establish close interpersonal relationships.

need for power. The desire to influence or control other people.

needs assessment. A training tool that is used to determine whether training is needed.

negative reinforcement. The removal of unpleasant consequences associated with a desired behavior, resulting in an increase in the frequency of that behavior.

noise. Anything that can interfere with sending or receiving a message.

nominal group technique (NGT). A decision-making technique that helps a group generate and select solutions while letting group members think independently; group members are given the problem and each presents one solution without discussion; then all solutions are discussed, evaluated, and ranked to determine the best alternative.

nonconforming high performer. A team member who is individualistic and whose presence is disruptive to the team.

nonprogrammed decision. The process of identifying and solving a problem when a situation is unique and there are not previously established routines or procedures that can be used as guides.

nonverbal communication. The sending and decoding of messages with emotional content. Important dimensions include body movements and gestures, eye contact, touch, facial expressions, physical closeness, and tone of voice.

norming stage. A stage in team development that is characterized by resolution of conflict and agreement over team goals and values.

objectives. The goals or targets that the firm wishes to accomplish within a stated amount of time.

obliging style. Conflict resolution demonstrated when the party managing the conflict is willing to neglect his or her own needs in order to accommodate the needs of the other party.

off-the-job training. Training that takes place away from the employment site.

on-the-job training (OJT). Training that takes place in the actual work setting under the guidance of an experienced worker, supervisor, or trainer.

one-way communications. Communication channels that provide no opportunity for feedback.

operational action plan. A management plan normally created by line managers and employees directly responsible for carrying out certain tasks or activities.

operational decisions. Decisions with a short time perspective, generally less than a year, and that often are measured on a daily or weekly basis.

operational managers. The firm's lower-level managers who supervise the operations of the organization.

operational perspective. The management perspective formed during the 19th and early 20th centuries when the factory system and modern corporations evolved to meet the challenges of managing large, complex organizations.

operations management. The process an organization uses to obtain the materials or ideas, the process of transforming them into the product, and the process of providing the final product to a user.

opportunistic planning. A type of planning that involves programmatic actions triggered by unforeseen circumstances; it can coexist with formal planning and can help the formal plan function more smoothly.

optimizing. Selecting the best alternative from among multiple criteria.

order review/release (ORR) activity. An operations management tool that is used to evaluate and track the order through the process, including creating order documentation, material checking, capacity evaluation, and load leveling (releasing orders so that the work load is evenly distributed).

organic organization design. A management design that is focused on change and flexibility, emphasizing horizontal relationships that involve teams, departments, or divisions, and provisions to coordinate these lateral units.

organization chart. A graphic depiction that summarizes the lines of authority in an organization.

organization design. The selection of an organization structure that best fits the strategic goals of the business.

organization politics. The exercise of power in an organization to control resources and influence policy.

organization structure. The formal system of relationships that determines lines of authority and the tasks assigned to individuals and units.

organizational culture. A system of shared values, assumptions, beliefs, and norms that unite the members of an organization.

organizing. The management function that determines how the firm's human, financial, physical, informational, and technical resources are arranged and coordinated to perform tasks to achieve desired goals; the deployment of resources to achieve strategic goals.

outcome appraisal instruments. Performance appraisal tools that measure workers' results, such as sales volume, number of units produced, and meeting deadlines.

parallel teams. Sometimes called *problem-solving teams* or *special purpose teams,* groups that focus on a problem or issue that requires only part-time commitment from team members.

partial productivity. The measurement of the contribution of a single input, such as labor or materials, to the final product.

partnership. A form of business that is an association of two or more persons acting as co-owners of a business.

passive communication. Style of communication whereby individual does not let others know directly what he or she wants or needs.

passive-aggressive communication. Style of communication whereby individual avoids giving direct responses to other's requests or feedback.

path-goal theory. A contingency model of leadership that focuses on how leaders influence subordinates' perceptions of work goals and the path to achieve those goals.

pay incentives. Compensation that rewards employees for good performance, including variable pay and merit pay.

performing stage. A stage of team development that is characterized by a focus on the performance of the tasks delegated to the team.

personal network. The relationships between an entrepreneur and other parties, including other entrepreneurs, suppliers, creditors, investors, friends, former colleagues, and others.

planning. The management function that assesses the management environment to set future objectives and map out activities necessary to achieve those objectives.

policy. A general guide for managers and employees to follow.

polycentric approach. An approach to managing an international subsidiary in which subsidiaries are managed and staffed by personnel from the host country (local nationals).

pooled interdependence. Team behavior where team members share common resources such as fax and copy machines, supplies, and secretarial support, but most of the work is performed independently.

portfolio analysis. An approach to classify the processes of a diversified company within a single framework or taxonomy.

positive reinforcement. A pleasurable stimulus or reward following a desired behavior that induces people to continue the behavior.

postheroic leadership perspective. The view that most top executives, no matter how good they are, are limited in what they can do to solve problems, so that leadership responsibilities are spread throughout the firm.

power distance. The extent to which individuals expect a hierarchical structure that emphasizes status differences between subordinates and superiors.

prearrival. The first stage of socialization, consisting of the values, attitudes, biases, and expectations the employee brings to the organization when first hired.

prejudgment. Type of perceptual barrier that involves making incorrect assumptions about a person due to membership in a group or about a thing based on earlier positive or negative experiences.

proactive management. A management style in which problems are anticipated before they become pervasive and time is set aside on both a daily and weekly basis to plan goals and priorities.

proactive strategy. A means of dealing with stakeholders when a firm determines that it wants to go beyond stakeholder expectations.

problem-solving team. A group representing different departments that solves problems; sometimes called a *parallel team.*

process. How a product or service will be produced.

process reengineering. A method of changing the entire production process rather than making incremental changes.

product managers. A management role that coordinates the development of new products.

profit sharing. Providing a share of a company's profits to the employees in the form of a bonus.

program evaluation and review technique (PERT) network. A tool for analyzing the conversion process.

programmed decision. Identifying a problem and matching the problem with established routines and procedures for resolving it.

project manager. A management role that coordinates work on a scientific, aerospace, or construction project.

project team. A group that works on a specific project that has a beginning and an end.

proprietorship. A form of business that is owned by one person.

protected class. The legal definition of specified groups of people who suffered widespread discrimination in the past and who are given special protection by the judicial system.

public offerings. A means of raising capital by the sale of securities in public markets such as the New York Stock Exchange and NASDAQ.

punishment. An aversive or unpleasant consequence following undesired behavior.

quality circles. Groups of employees who meet regularly to discuss ways to increase quality.

quality gap. The difference between what customers want and what they actually get from the company.

reactive management. The management style of responding to the most urgent problem first when not enough time is available.

receiver. Individual or party that receives message from sender.

reciprocal interdependence. The greatest amount of interdependence that occurs when team members interact intensively back and forth with each other until their work is judged to meet performance standards.

recruitment. The process of generating a pool of qualified candidates for a particular job.

referent power. Power derived from the satisfaction people receive from identifying themselves with the leader.

relationship-building role. The team-member role that focuses on sustaining harmony between team members.

relationship-oriented leadership. A leadership style that focuses on maintaining good interpersonal relationships.

relative judgments. A performance appraisal approach in which employees are compared to one another.

reliability. The consistency of results from the selection method.

reordering systems. The process used to help keep inventory levels more or less constant.

resource allocation. The planning step that determines where the resources will come from (for instance, borrowing versus internally generated funds) and how the resources will be deployed to achieve the agreed-on objectives.

resource-based view. A strategic management viewpoint that basing business strategy on what the firm is capable of doing provides a more sustainable competitive advantage than basing it on external opportunities.

responsibility. The manager's duty to perform assigned tasks.

reward power. Power derived from the belief that the leader can provide something that other people value so that they trade their support for the rewards.

rights approach. A means of making decisions based on the belief that each person has fundamental human rights that should be respected and protected.

risk. The level of uncertainty as to the outcome of a management decision.

role modeling. The leadership mechanism in which managers serve as examples of the behaviors they would like employees to emulate.

roles. Expectations regarding how team members should act in given situations.

rule. Written statement of the general permissible bounds for the application of particular policies.

satisficing. Selecting the first alternative solution that meets a minimum criterion.

scanning. The analysis of general environmental factors that may directly or indirectly be relevant to the firm's future.

scientific management. A management method that applies the principles of the scientific method to the management process: determining the one best way to do a job and sharing the rewards with the workers.

segmented communication. Flows of information within the firm that are far greater within groups than between groups.

selection. The screening process used to decide which job applicant to hire.

selective perception. Type of perception barrier whereby the receiver focuses on the parts of the message that are most salient to his or her interests and ignores other parts that are not relevant.

self-leadership. Leadership that stresses the individual responsibility of employees to develop their own work priorities aligned with organizational goals; the manager is a facilitator who enhances the self-leadership capabilities of subordinates, encouraging them to develop self-control skills.

self-managed team (SMT). Sometimes called a *process team*, a group that is responsible for producing an entire product, component, or service.

sender. Individual or party that initiates communication with another individual or party.

seniority. A defense against discrimination in which companies with a well-established seniority system can give more senior workers priority, even if this has an adverse impact on protected class members.

sequential interdependence. A series of hand-offs of work flow between team members in which output of one team member becomes the input of the next team member, and so forth.

sexual harassment. A form of discrimination that is broadly interpreted to include sexually suggestive remarks, unwanted touching, any physical or verbal act that indicates sexual advances or requests sexual favors, a promise of rewards or hidden threats by a supervisor to induce emotional attachment by a subordinate, and a "hostile environment" based on sex.

single-use plans. Plans implemented for unusual or one-of-a kind situations.

situational context. The factors that are outside the control of the subordinate such as the tasks defining the job, the formal authority system of the organization, and the work group.

skills inventory. A human resource inventory that keeps track of the firm's internal supply of talent by listing employees' education, training, experience, and language abilities; the firm can use this information to identify those eligible for promotion or transfer before trying to fill the position from the external market.

small business. Any business that is independently owned and operated, that is small in size, and that is not dominant in its markets.

social responsibility. The belief that corporations have a responsibility to conduct their affairs ethically to benefit both employees and the larger society.

socialization. The process of internalizing or taking organizational values as one's own.

span of control. The feature of the vertical structure of an organization that outlines the number of subordinates who report to a manager, the number of managers, and the layers of management within the organization.

spin-off. An independent entrepreneurship that produces a product or service that originated in a large company.

staff authority. Management function of advising, recommending, and counseling line managers.

staff managers. Managers who assist line managers to achieve bottom-line results.

standing plans. Plans created to help the organization deal with issues that come up on a regular basis.

stakeholders. The groups or individuals who have an interest in the performance of the enterprise and how it uses its resources, including employees, customers, and shareholders.

statistical process control. An operations management monitoring tool that uses quantitative methods and procedures to evaluate transformation operations and to detect and eliminate deviations.

storming stage. A stage in team development in which team members voice differences about team goals and procedures.

storyboarding. A variation of brainstorming in which group members jot down ideas on cards and then can shuffle, rewrite, or even eliminate cards to examine complex processes.

strategic action plans. Management plans based on macro approaches for analyzing organizational features, resources, and the environment and establishing long-term corporatewide action programs to accomplish the stated objectives in light of that analysis.

strategic alliances. Cooperative arrangements between competitors or potential competitors from different countries, possibly to establish a formal joint venture or collaboration between firms on specific projects.

strategic compensation. Compensation practices that best support the firm's business strategy.

strategic decision. Decisions that have long-term perspective of two to five years and affect the entire organization.

strategy formulation. The design of an approach to achieve the firm's mission.

strategic HR planning (SHRP). The development of a vision about where the company wants to be and how it can use human resources to get there.

strategic intent. The firm's internally focused definition of how the firm intends to use its resources, capabilities, and core competencies to win competitive battles.

strategic managers. The firm's senior executives who are responsible for overall management.

strategic meeting. Bringing people from different departments or divisions together to synchronize plans and objectives and to coordinate activities.

strategic mission. The firm's externally focused definition of what it plans to produce and market, utilizing its internally based core competence.

SWOT analysis. A strategic management tool to evaluate the firm, which is accomplished by identifying its strengths and weaknesses and identifying its opportunities and threats.

synergy. When individuals blend complementary skills and talents to produce a product that is more valuable than the sum of the individual contributions.

systems theory. A modern management theory that views the organization as a system of interrelated parts that function in a holistic way to achieve a common purpose.

tactical action plans. Management action plans at the division or department level that indicate what activities must be performed, when they must be completed, and what resources will be needed at the division or departmental level to complete the portions of the strategic action plan that fall under the purview of that particular organizational subunit.

tactical decisions. Decisions that have a short-term perspective of one year or less and focus on subunits of the organization, such as departments or project teams.

tactical managers. The firm's management staff who are responsible for translating the general goals and plan developed by strategic managers into specific objectives and activities.

tangible resources. Assets that can be quantified and observed, including financial resources, physical assets, and manpower.

task-facilitating role. The team-member role with the priority of helping the team accomplish its task goals.

task force. A temporary interdepartmental group formed to study an issue and make recommendations.

task-oriented leadership. A leadership style that emphasizes work accomplishments and performance results.

team. A small number of people with complementary skills who are committed to a common purpose, a set of performance goals, and an approach for which they hold themselves mutually accountable.

team cohesiveness. The extent to which team members feel a high degree of camaraderie, team spirit, and sense of unity.

team norms. Shared beliefs that regulate the behavior of team members.

Theory X. A negative perspective on human behavior.

Theory Y. A positive perspective on human behavior.

third-country nationals. Citizens of countries other than the host nation or the firm's home country.

three-step model. A model of organizational change that features the three steps of unfreezing, change, and refreezing.

top-down change. Organizational change that is initiated by managers.

total factor productivity. The measurement of how well an organization utilizes all of its resources, such as capital, labor, materials, or energy, to produce its outputs.

total quality management (TQM). An organization-wide approach that focuses on quality as an overarching goal. The basis of this approach is the understanding that all employees and organizational units should be working harmoniously to satisfy the customer.

trait appraisal instruments. Performance appraisal tools that evaluate employees based on consistent and enduring worker characteristics.

transactional leaders. Leaders who use legitimate, coercive, or reward powers to elicit obedience and attempt to instill in followed the ability to question standard modes of operation.

transformational leaders. Leaders who revitalize organizations by instilling in followers the ability to question standard modes of operation.

trust. The willingness of one team member to increase his or her vulnerability to the actions of another person whose behavior he or she cannot control.

tuition assistance programs. Support by the firm for employees' education and development by covering the cost of tuition and other fees for seminars, workshops, and continuing education programs.

turnkey projects. A specialized type of exporting in which the firm handles the design, construction, start-up operations, and workforce training of a foreign plant, and a local client is handed the key to a plant that is fully operational.

two-way communications. Communication channels that provide for feedback.

uncertainty. The condition when the information available to make a management decision is incomplete.

uncertainty avoidance. The extent to which a society places a high value on reducing risk and instability.

unity of command. The management concept that a subordinate should have only one direct supervisor.

upward communication. Sending a message from a position lower in the hierarchy to a receiver higher in the hierarchy.

utilitarianism. A means of making decisions based on what is good for the greatest number of people.

validity. The measurement of how well a technique used to assess candidates is related to performance in the job.

value-chain analysis. Strategic management analysis that breaks the firm down into a sequential series of activities and attempts to identify the value-added of each activity.

venture capitalists. Financial investors who specialize in making loans to entrepreneurships that have the potential for rapid growth but are in high-risk situations with few assets and would therefore not qualify for commercial bank loans.

vertical dimension. The element of who has the authority to make decisions and who supervises which subordinates.

vertical integration strategy. A form of diversification strategy in which a firm integrates vertically by acquiring businesses that are supply channels or distributors to the primary business; producing its own inputs is backward integration, and distributing its own outputs is forward integration.

virtual teams. Groups that use interactive computer technologies such as the Internet, groupware (software that permits people at different computer workstations to collaborate on a project simultaneously), and computer-based videoconferencing to work together regardless of distance.

visible culture. The aspects of culture that an observer can hear, feel, or see.

voluntary contracts. Because both parties enter the labor contract freely, one party can use the legal system to enforce the terms of the contract if the other party does not fulfill its responsibilities.

whistleblower policies. A method by which employees who disclose their employer's illegal, immoral, or illegitimate practices can be protected; companies with whistle-blower policies rely on whistleblowers to report unethical activities to the ethics officer or committee, which will then gather facts and investigate the situation in a fair and impartial way.

wholly owned subsidiary. A means of entering new markets in which a firm fully owns its subsidiary in foreign countries.

win–lose style. Negotiating style used when there is a single issue that consists of a fixed amount of resources in which one party attempts to gain at the expense of the other.

win–win style. Negotiating style requiring all interested parties to convert a potential conflict into a problem-solving process in which each party seeks to identify common, shared, or joint goals.

work group. A group whose members are held accountable for individual work, but are not responsible for the output of the entire group.

World Trade Organization (WTO). Organization created in 1993 to ensure compliance with GATT.

Photo Credits

Index